子連れ狼

LONE WOLF & CUB

OMNIBUS

1

STORY
KAZUO KOIKE

ART
GOSEKI KOJIMA

TRANSLATION
DANA LEWIS

LETTERING
DIGITAL CHAMELEON

COVER ART
FRANK MILLER WITH
LYNN VARLEY

DARK HORSE MANGA

PRESIDENT and PUBLISHER
MIKE RICHARDSON

SERIES EDITORS
MIKE HANSEN AND **DAN HARRIS**

COLLECTION EDITOR
CHRIS WARNER

ASSISTANT EDITOR
SHANTEL LAROCQUE

DESIGNER
TINA ALESSI

LONE WOLF AND CUB OMNIBUS VOLUME 1

This volume collects material previously published in the Dark Horse graphic novels *Lone Wolf and Cub Volume 1: The Assassin's Road, Lone Wolf and Cub Volume 2: The Gateless Barrier,* and *Lone Wolf and Cub Volume 3: The Flute of the Fallen Tiger.*

Dark Horse Manga
A division of Dark Horse Comics LLC
10956 SE Main Street
Milwaukie, OR 97222

DarkHorse.com

To find a comics shop in your area, go to comicshoplocator.com

First edition: May 2013
ISBN 978-1-61655-134-6
20 19 18 17 16 15 14 13
Printed in Italy

A NOTE TO READERS

L ONE WOLF AND CUB is renowned
for its carefully researched re-creation
of Edo-period Japan. To preserve the
flavor of the work, we have chosen to
retain terms of the period that have no
direct equivalents in English. Japanese is
written in a mix of Chinese ideograms
and a syllabic writing system, resulting in
numerous words with multiple meanings.
In the glossary, you may encounter these
words. A Japanese reader seeing the
different ideograms would know instantly
which meaning is intended, but these
synonyms can cause confusion when
Japanese is spelled out in our alphabet.
O-yurushi o (please forgive us)!

CONTENTS

SON FOR HIRE,
SWORD FOR HIRE

1

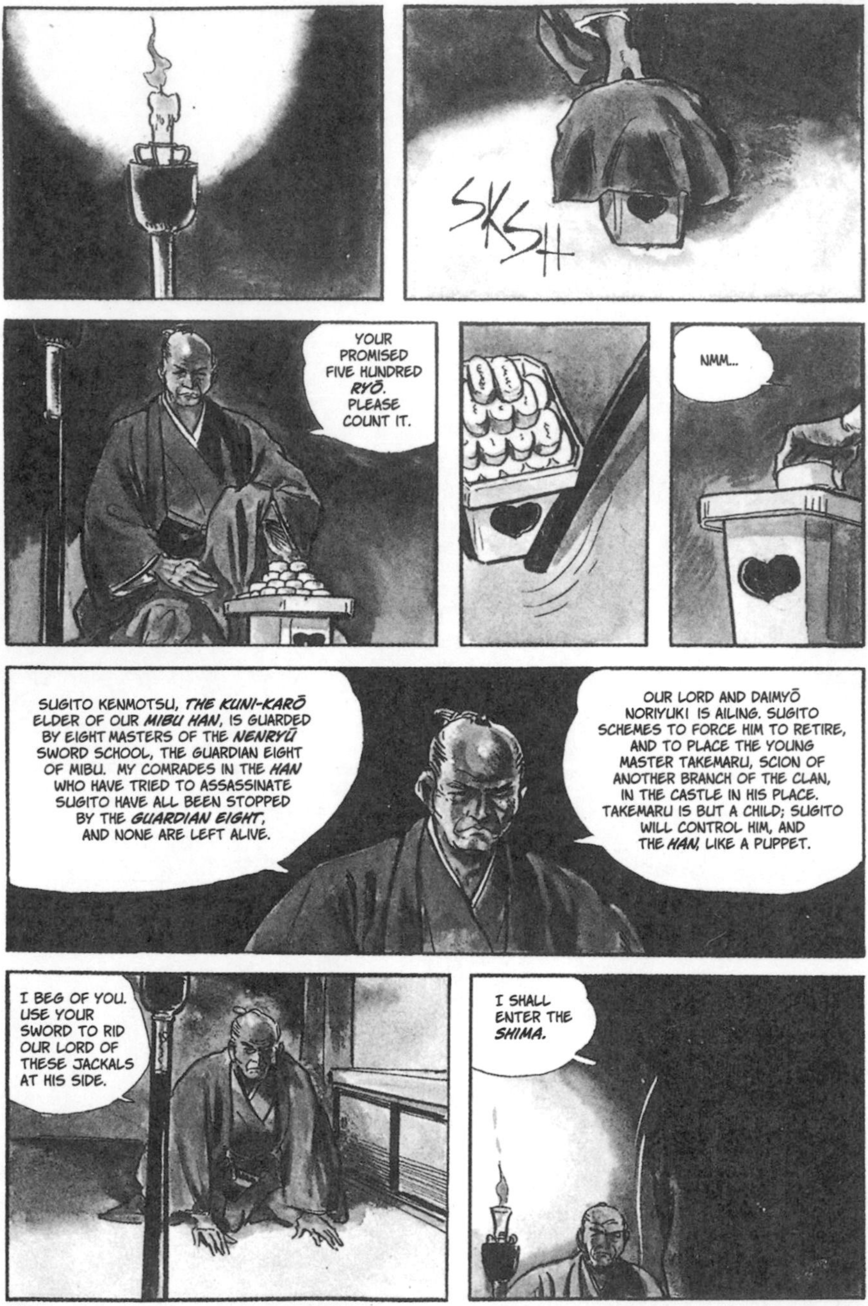
SKSH
YOUR PROMISED FIVE HUNDRED *RYŌ*. PLEASE COUNT IT.
NMM...
SUGITO KENMOTSU, *THE KUNI-KARŌ* ELDER OF OUR *MIBU HAN*, IS GUARDED BY EIGHT MASTERS OF THE *NENRYŪ* SWORD SCHOOL, THE GUARDIAN EIGHT OF MIBU. MY COMRADES IN THE *HAN* WHO HAVE TRIED TO ASSASSINATE SUGITO HAVE ALL BEEN STOPPED BY THE *GUARDIAN EIGHT*, AND NONE ARE LEFT ALIVE.
OUR LORD AND DAIMYŌ NORIYUKI IS AILING. SUGITO SCHEMES TO FORCE HIM TO RETIRE, AND TO PLACE THE YOUNG MASTER TAKEMARU, SCION OF ANOTHER BRANCH OF THE CLAN, IN THE CASTLE IN HIS PLACE. TAKEMARU IS BUT A CHILD; SUGITO WILL CONTROL HIM, AND THE *HAN*, LIKE A PUPPET.
I BEG OF YOU. USE YOUR SWORD TO RID OUR LORD OF THESE JACKALS AT HIS SIDE.
I SHALL ENTER THE *SHIMA*.

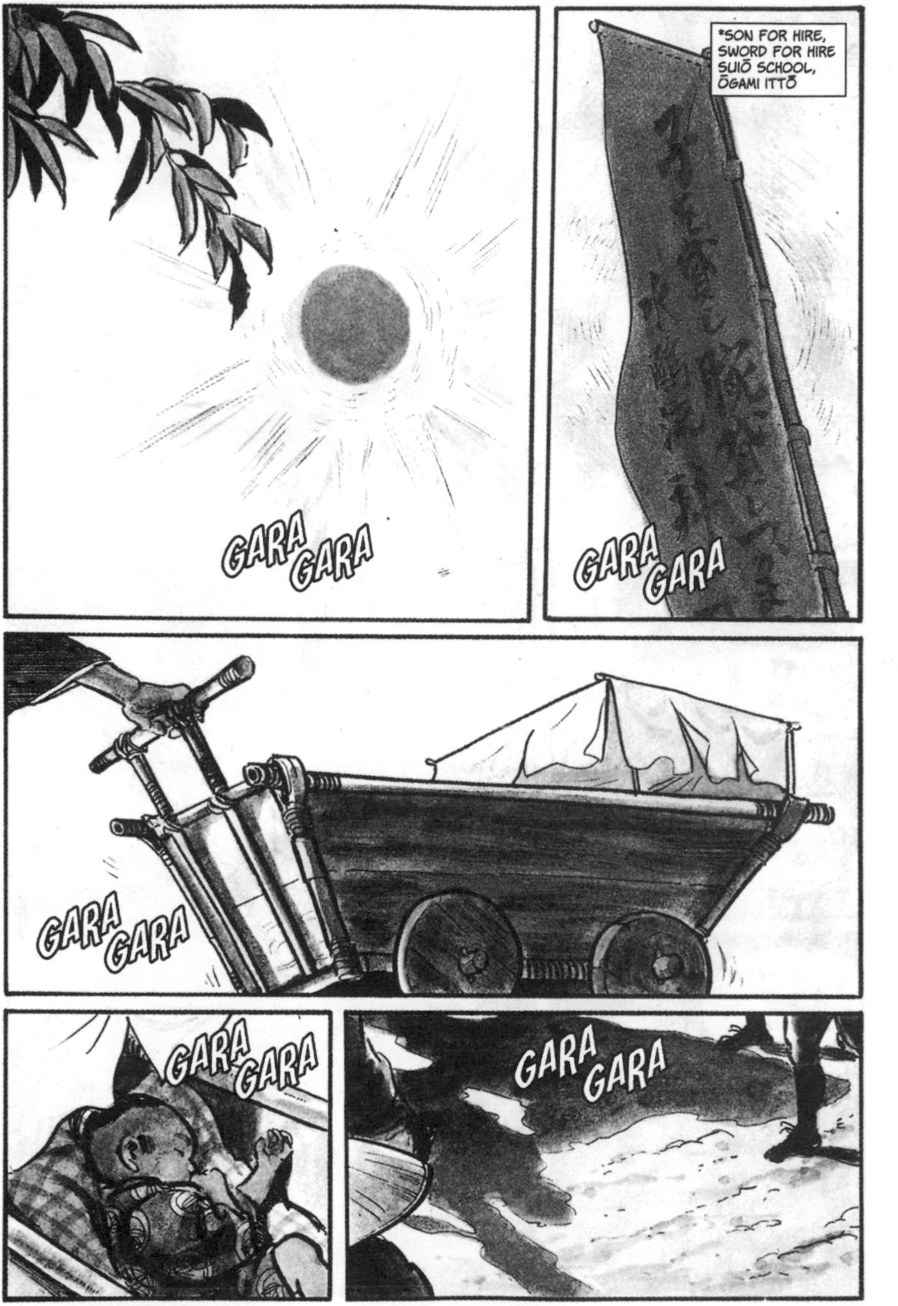
*SON FOR HIRE, SWORD FOR HIRE SUIŌ SCHOOL, ŌGAMI ITTŌ
GARA GARA
GARA GARA
GARA GARA
GARA GARA
GARA GARA

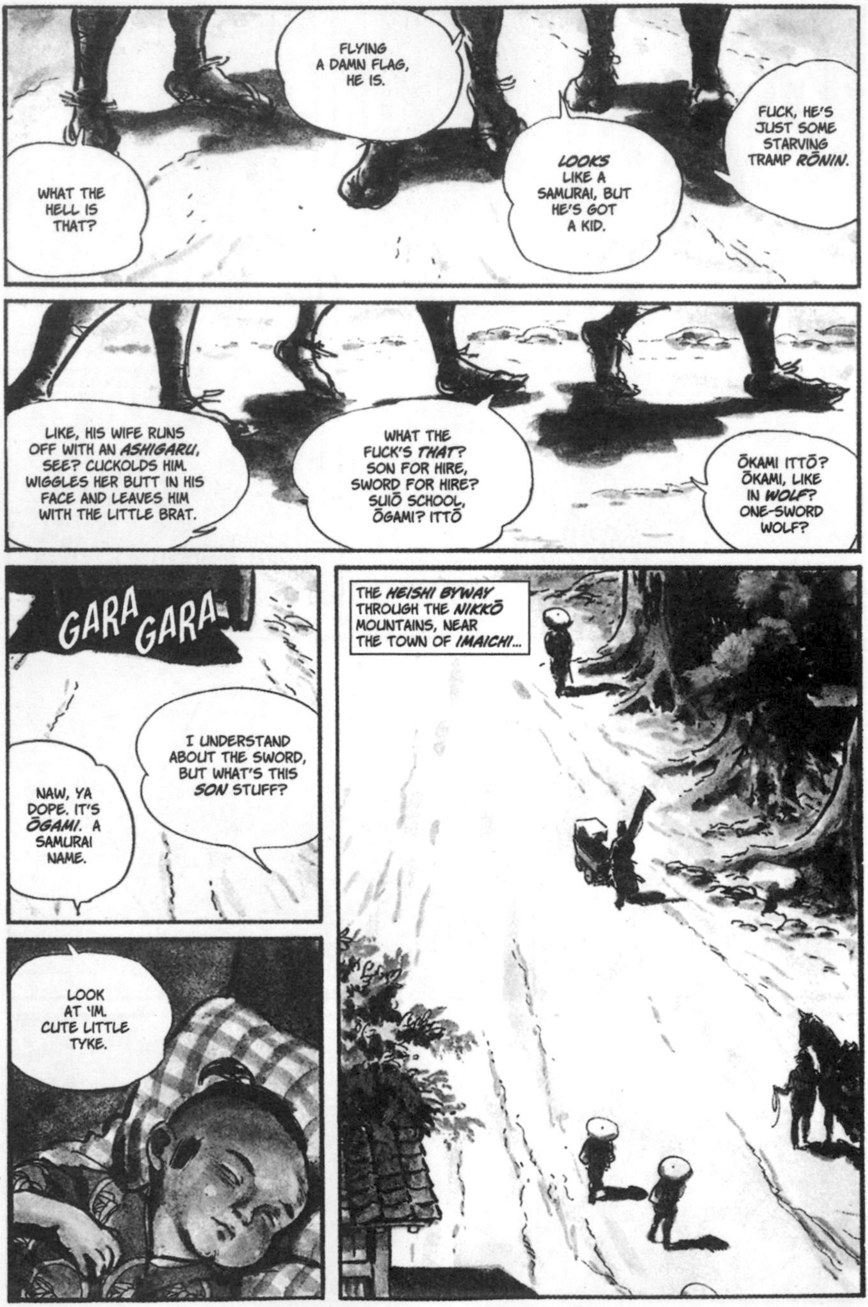
WHAT THE HELL IS THAT?
FLYING A DAMN FLAG, HE IS.
LOOKS LIKE A SAMURAI, BUT HE'S GOT A KID.
FUCK, HE'S JUST SOME STARVING TRAMP RŌNIN.
LIKE, HIS WIFE RUNS OFF WITH AN ASHIGARU, SEE? CUCKOLDS HIM. WIGGLES HER BUTT IN HIS FACE AND LEAVES HIM WITH THE LITTLE BRAT.
WHAT THE FUCK'S THAT? SON FOR HIRE, SWORD FOR HIRE? SUIŌ SCHOOL, ŌGAMI? ITTŌ
ŌKAMI ITTŌ? ŌKAMI, LIKE IN WOLF? ONE-SWORD WOLF?
GARA GARA
NAW, YA DOPE. IT'S ŌGAMI. A SAMURAI NAME.
I UNDERSTAND ABOUT THE SWORD, BUT WHAT'S THIS SON STUFF?
LOOK AT 'IM. CUTE LITTLE TYKE.
THE HEISHI BYWAY THROUGH THE NIKKŌ MOUNTAINS, NEAR THE TOWN OF IMAICHI...

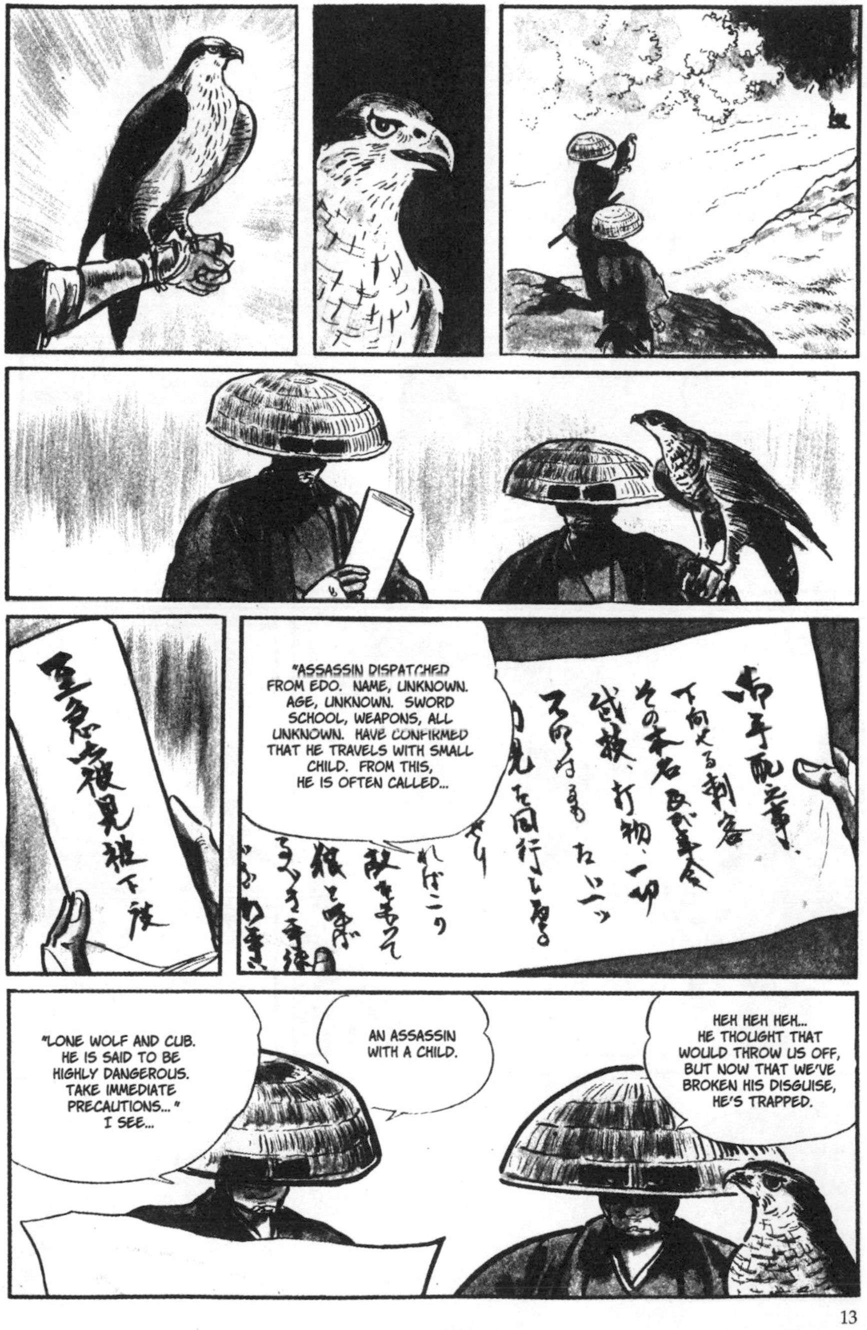
"ASSASSIN DISPATCHED FROM EDO. NAME, UNKNOWN. AGE, UNKNOWN. SWORD SCHOOL, WEAPONS, ALL UNKNOWN. HAVE CONFIRMED THAT HE TRAVELS WITH SMALL CHILD. FROM THIS, HE IS OFTEN CALLED...
"LONE WOLF AND CUB. HE IS SAID TO BE HIGHLY DANGEROUS. TAKE IMMEDIATE PRECAUTIONS..." I SEE...
AN ASSASSIN WITH A CHILD.
HEH HEH HEH... HE THOUGHT THAT WOULD THROW US OFF, BUT NOW THAT WE'VE BROKEN HIS DISGUISE, HE'S TRAPPED.

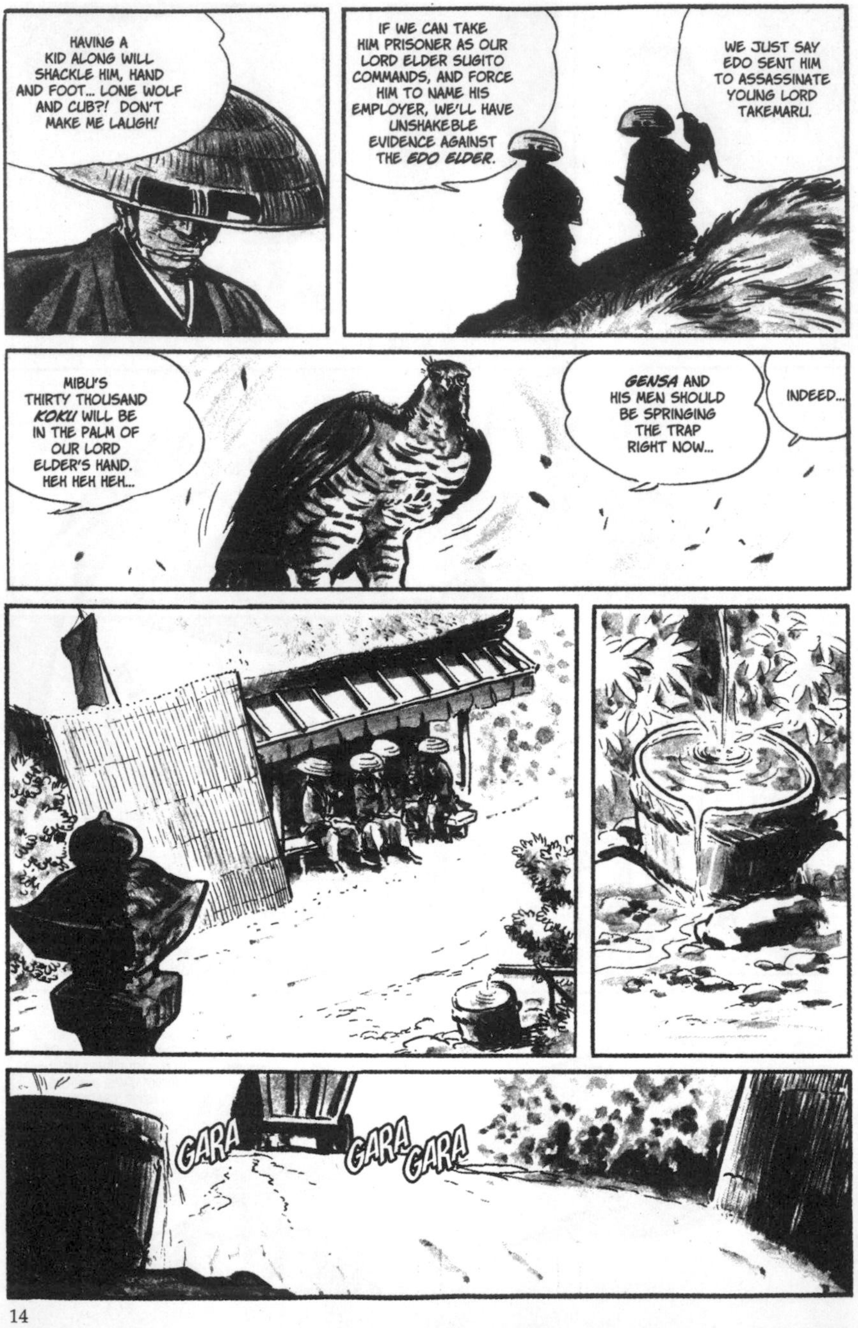
HAVING A KID ALONG WILL SHACKLE HIM, HAND AND FOOT... LONE WOLF AND CUB?! DON'T MAKE ME LAUGH!
IF WE CAN TAKE HIM PRISONER AS OUR LORD ELDER SUGITO COMMANDS, AND FORCE HIM TO NAME HIS EMPLOYER, WE'LL HAVE UNSHAKEBLE EVIDENCE AGAINST THE *EDO ELDER*.
WE JUST SAY EDO SENT HIM TO ASSASSINATE YOUNG LORD TAKEMARU.
MIBU'S THIRTY THOUSAND *KOKU* WILL BE IN THE PALM OF OUR LORD ELDER'S HAND. HEH HEH HEH...
GENSA AND HIS MEN SHOULD BE SPRINGING THE TRAP RIGHT NOW...
INDEED...
GARA
GARA GARA

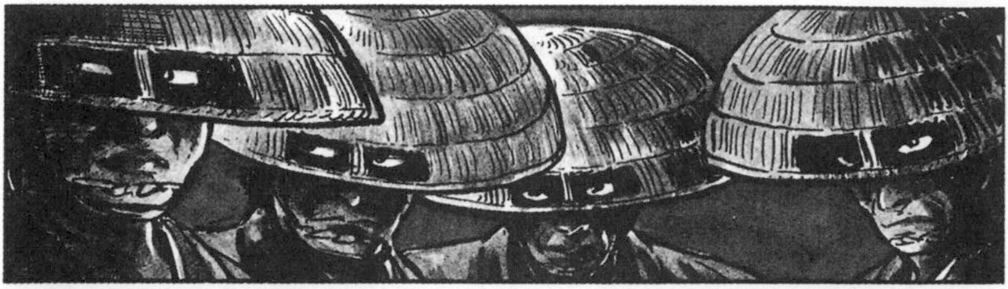
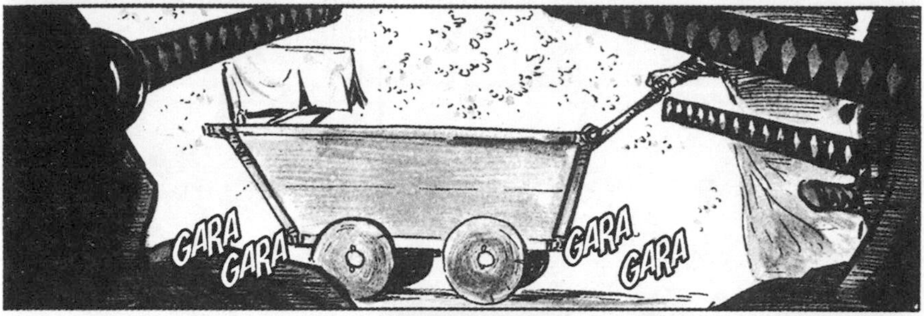
GARA GARA
GARA GARA
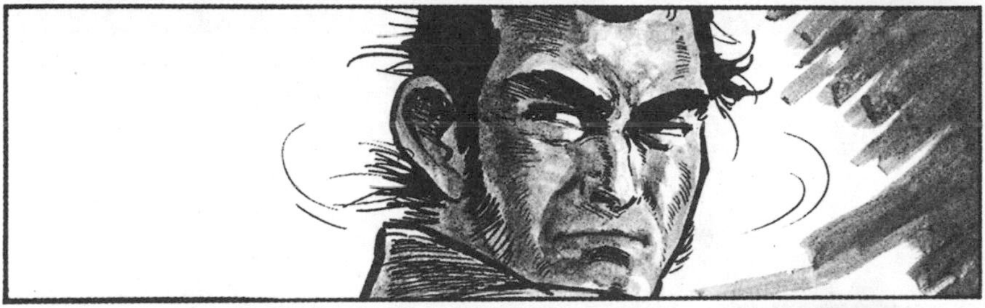
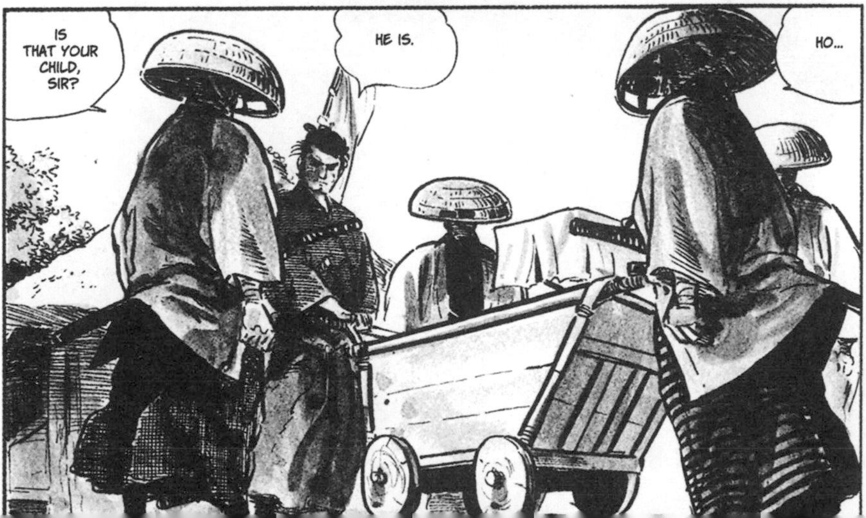
IS THAT YOUR CHILD, SIR?
HE IS.
HO...

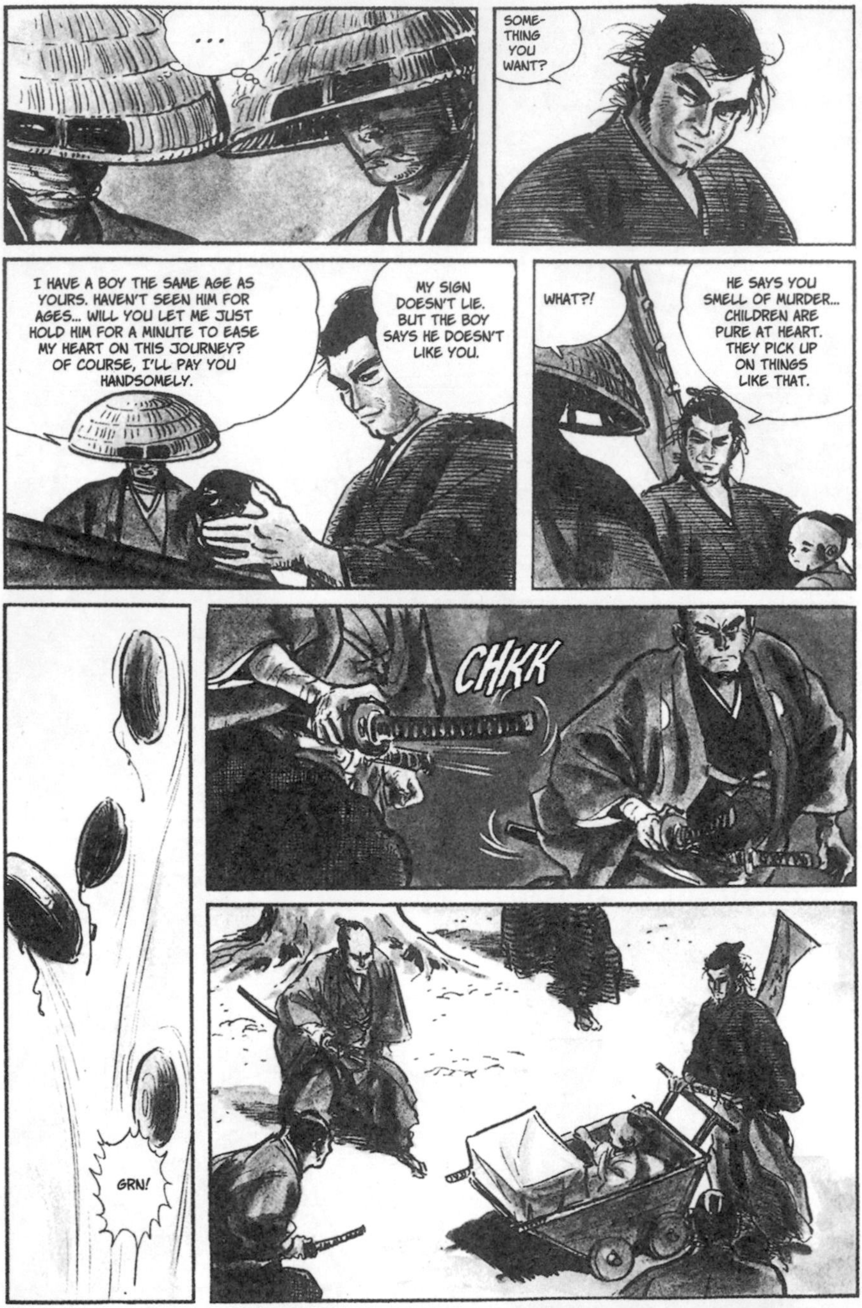
...
SOME-
THING
YOU
WANT?
I HAVE A BOY THE SAME AGE AS YOURS. HAVEN'T SEEN HIM FOR AGES... WILL YOU LET ME JUST HOLD HIM FOR A MINUTE TO EASE MY HEART ON THIS JOURNEY? OF COURSE, I'LL PAY YOU HANDSOMELY.
MY SIGN DOESN'T LIE. BUT THE BOY SAYS HE DOESN'T LIKE YOU.
WHAT?!
HE SAYS YOU SMELL OF MURDER... CHILDREN ARE PURE AT HEART. THEY PICK UP ON THINGS LIKE THAT.
GRN!
CHKK

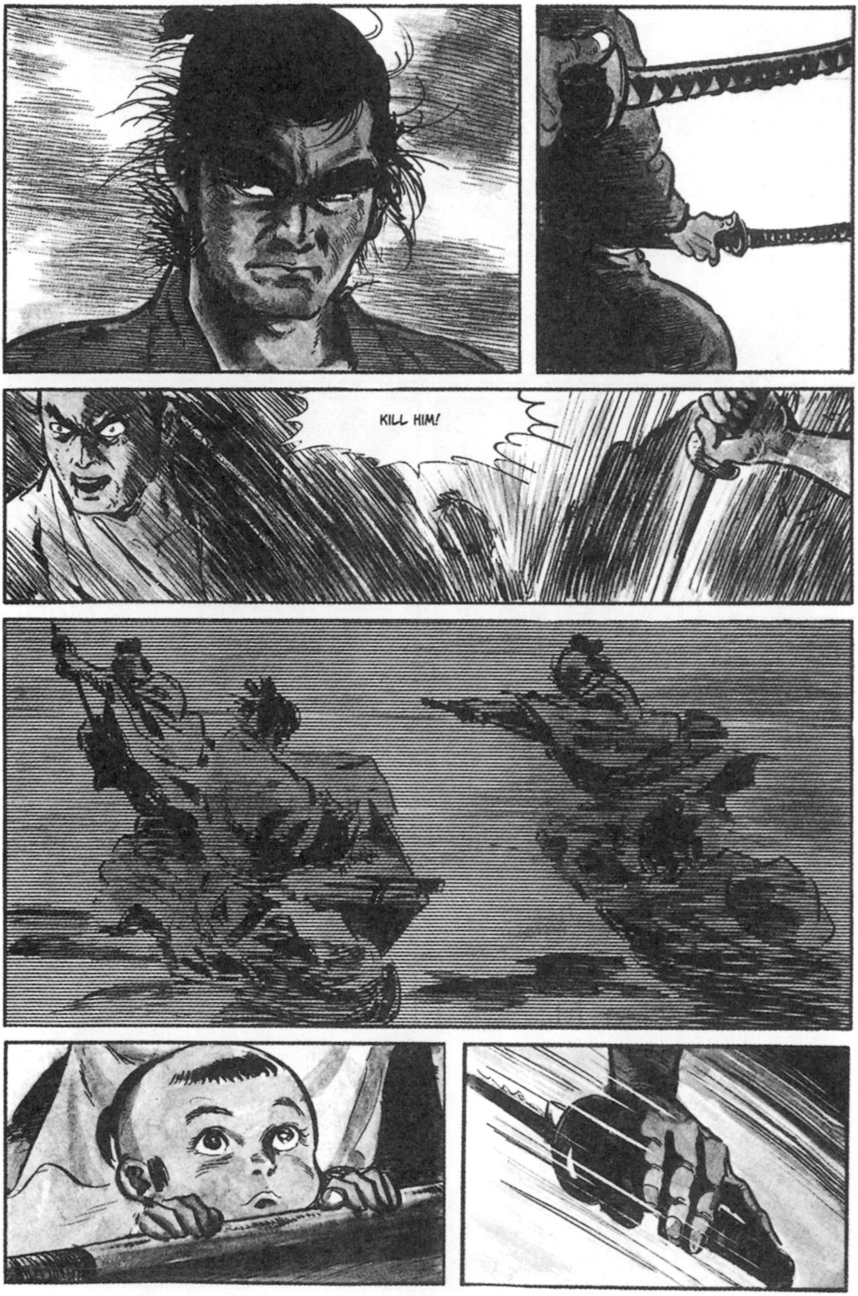
KILL HIM!

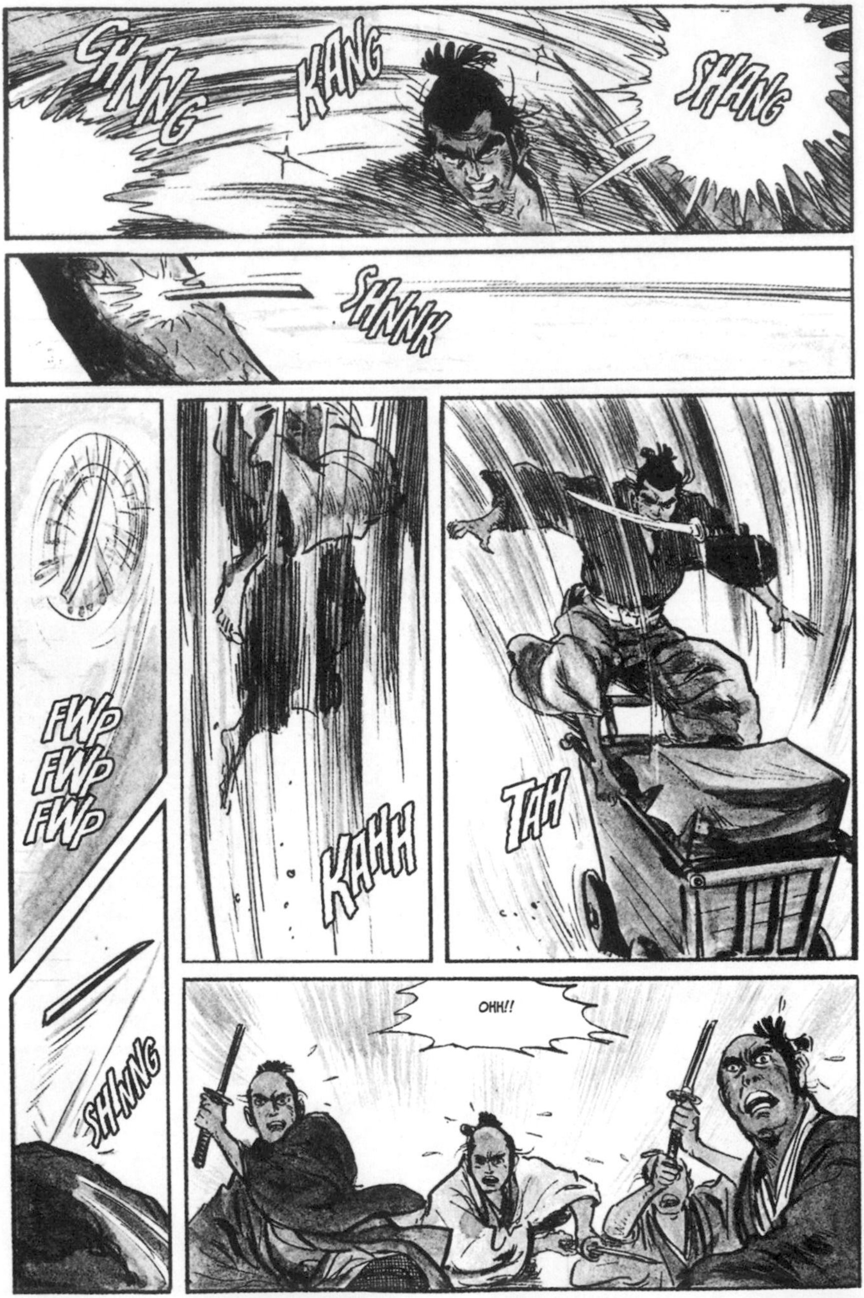
SHANG
KANG
CHNNG
SHNNK
TAH
KAHH
FWP
FWP
FWP
OHH!!
SHWNG

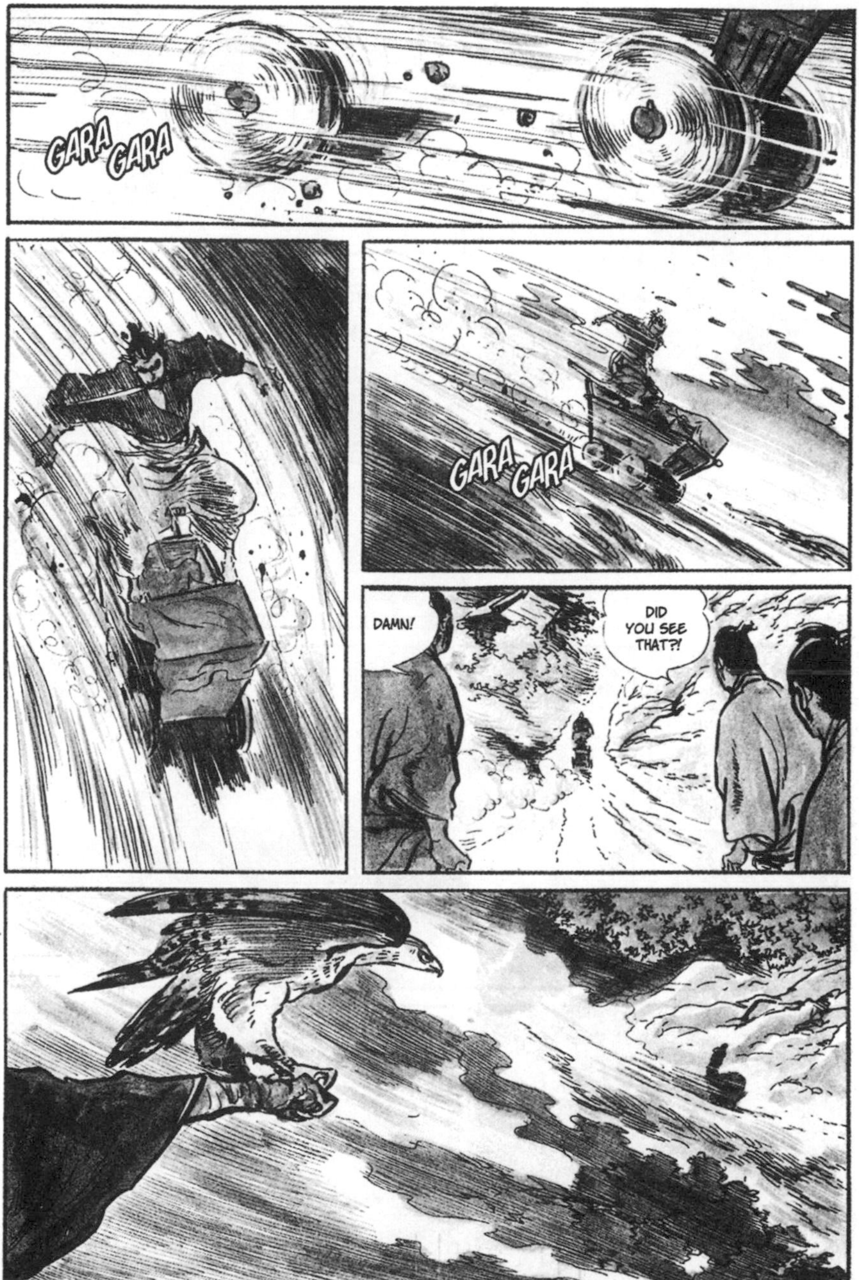
GARA GARA
GARA GARA
DID YOU SEE THAT?!
DAMN!

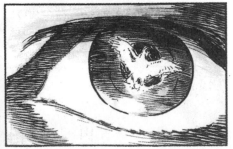

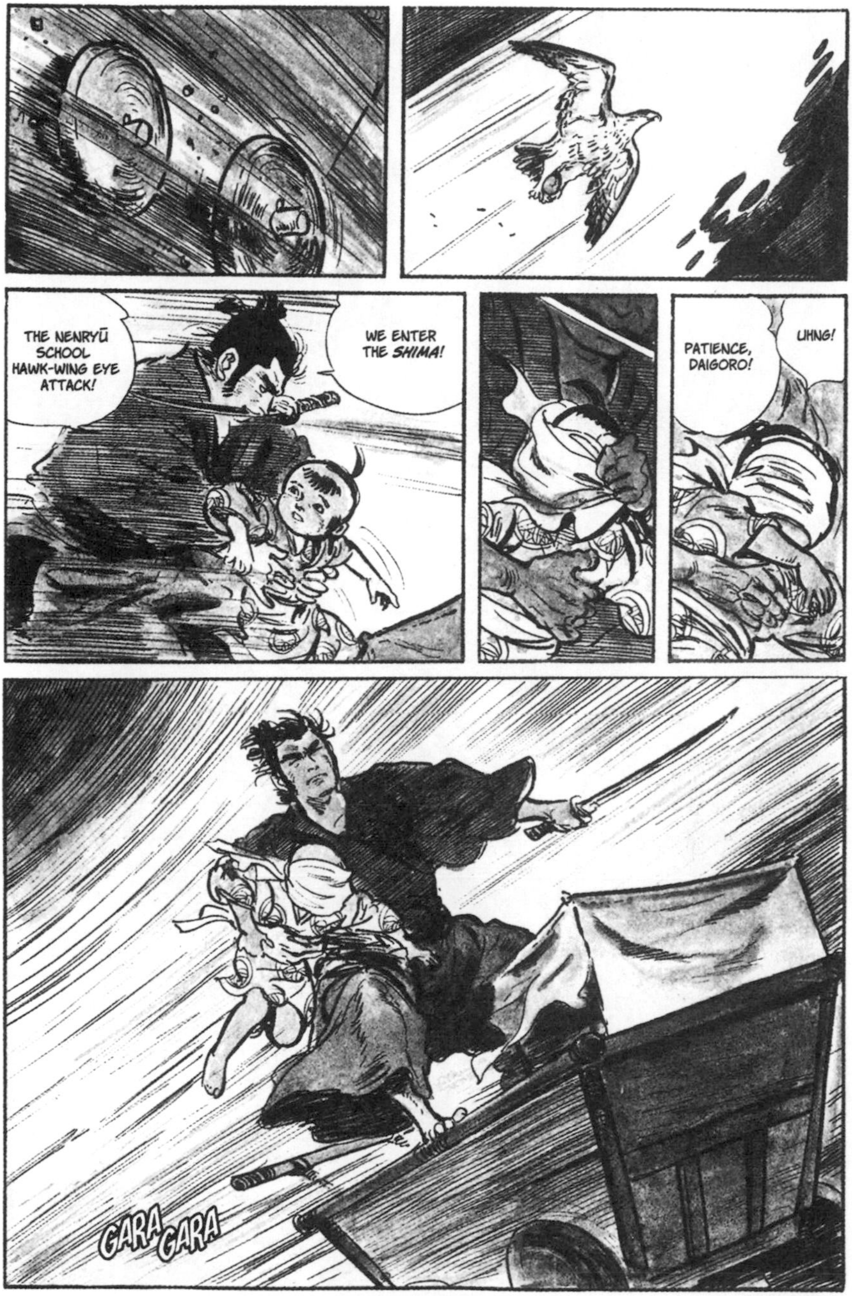
THE NENRYŪ SCHOOL HAWK-WING EYE ATTACK!
WE ENTER THE *SHIMA*!
PATIENCE, DAIGORO!
UHNG!
GARA GARA

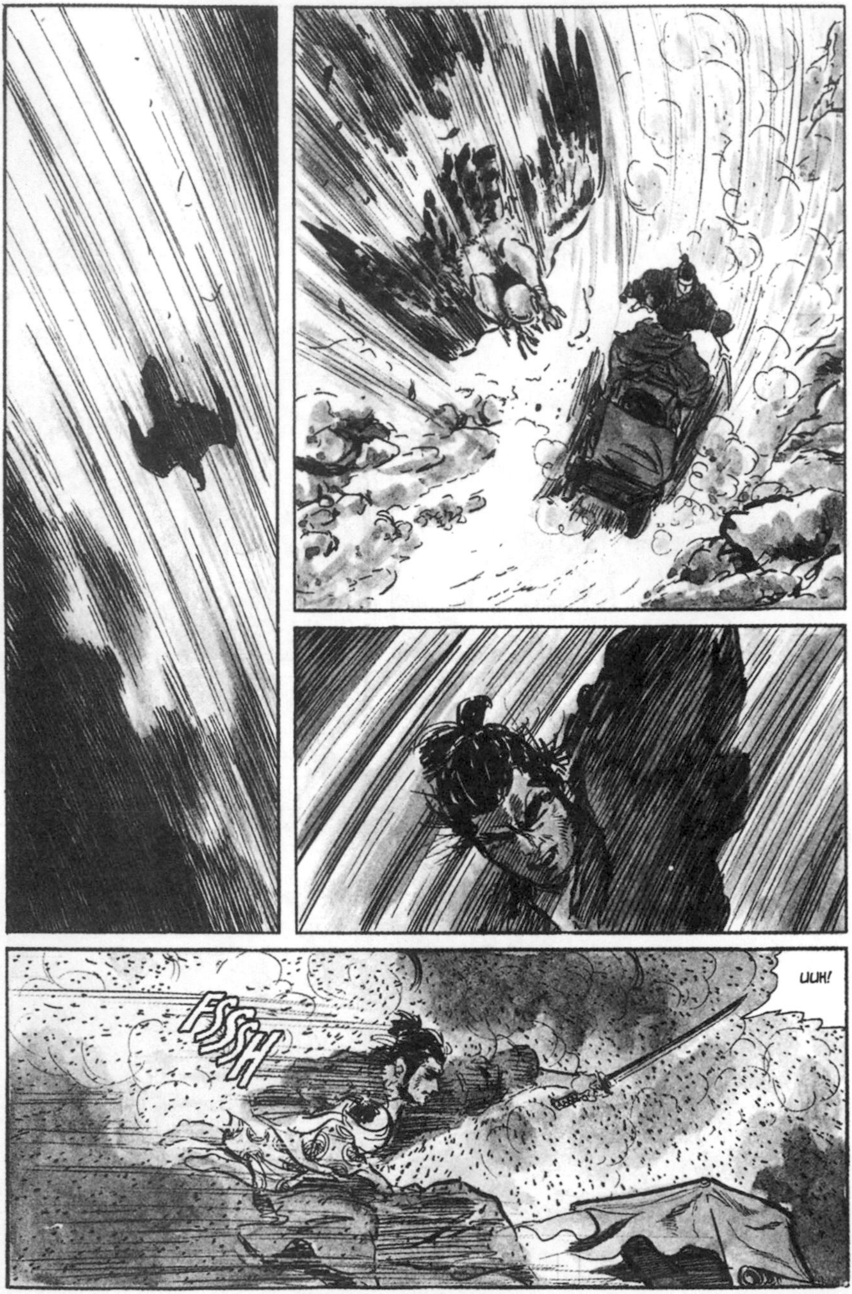
UUH!
FSSSH

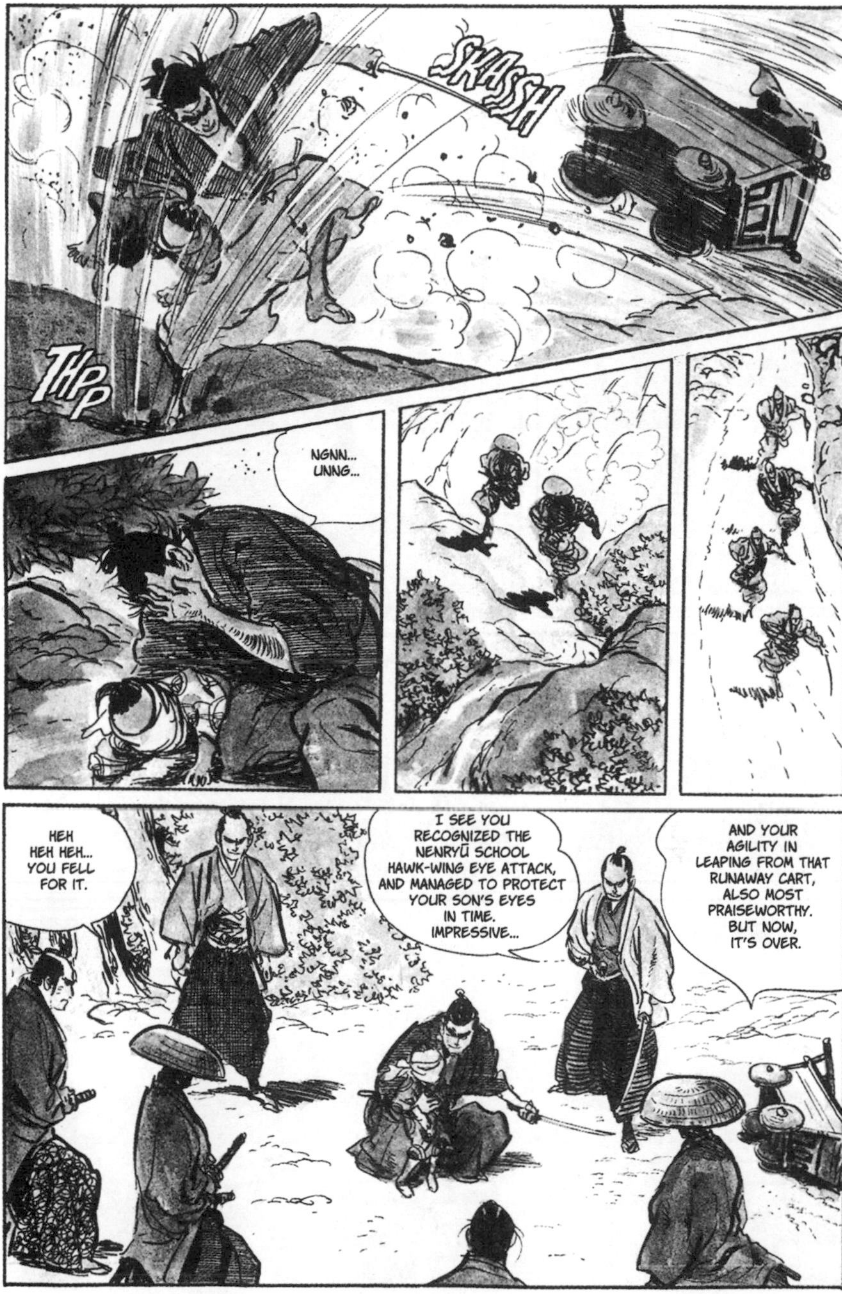
SKASSH
THPP
NGNN... UNNG...
HEH HEH HEH... YOU FELL FOR IT.
I SEE YOU RECOGNIZED THE NENRYŪ SCHOOL HAWK-WING EYE ATTACK, AND MANAGED TO PROTECT YOUR SON'S EYES IN TIME. IMPRESSIVE...
AND YOUR AGILITY IN LEAPING FROM THAT RUNAWAY CART, ALSO MOST PRAISEWORTHY. BUT NOW, IT'S OVER.

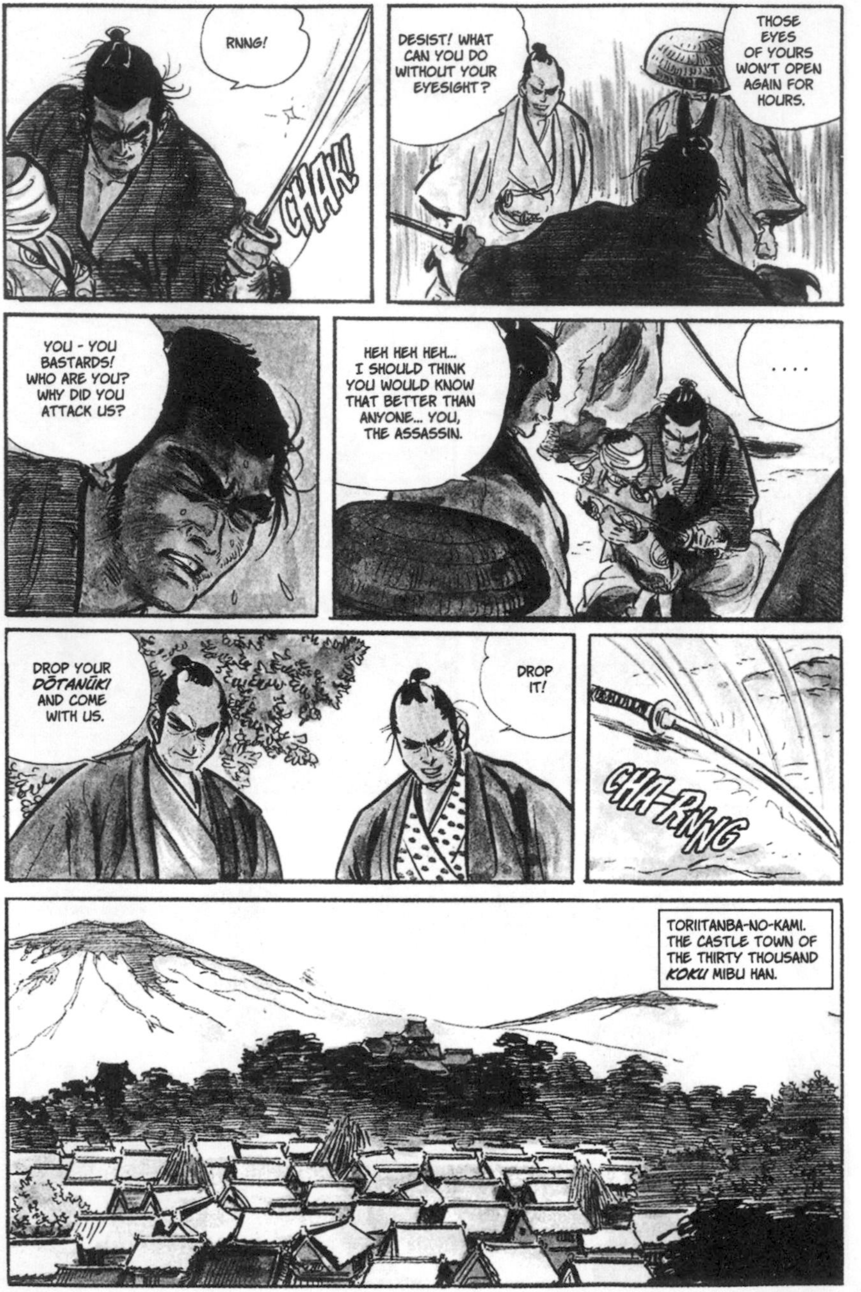
RNNG!
CHAK!
DESIST! WHAT CAN YOU DO WITHOUT YOUR EYESIGHT?
THOSE EYES OF YOURS WON'T OPEN AGAIN FOR HOURS.
YOU - YOU BASTARDS! WHO ARE YOU? WHY DID YOU ATTACK US?
HEH HEH HEH... I SHOULD THINK YOU WOULD KNOW THAT BETTER THAN ANYONE... YOU, THE ASSASSIN.
. . . .
DROP YOUR *DŌTANŪKI* AND COME WITH US.
DROP IT!
CHA-RNNG
TORIITANBA-NO-KAMI. THE CASTLE TOWN OF THE THIRTY THOUSAND *KOKU* MIBU HAN.

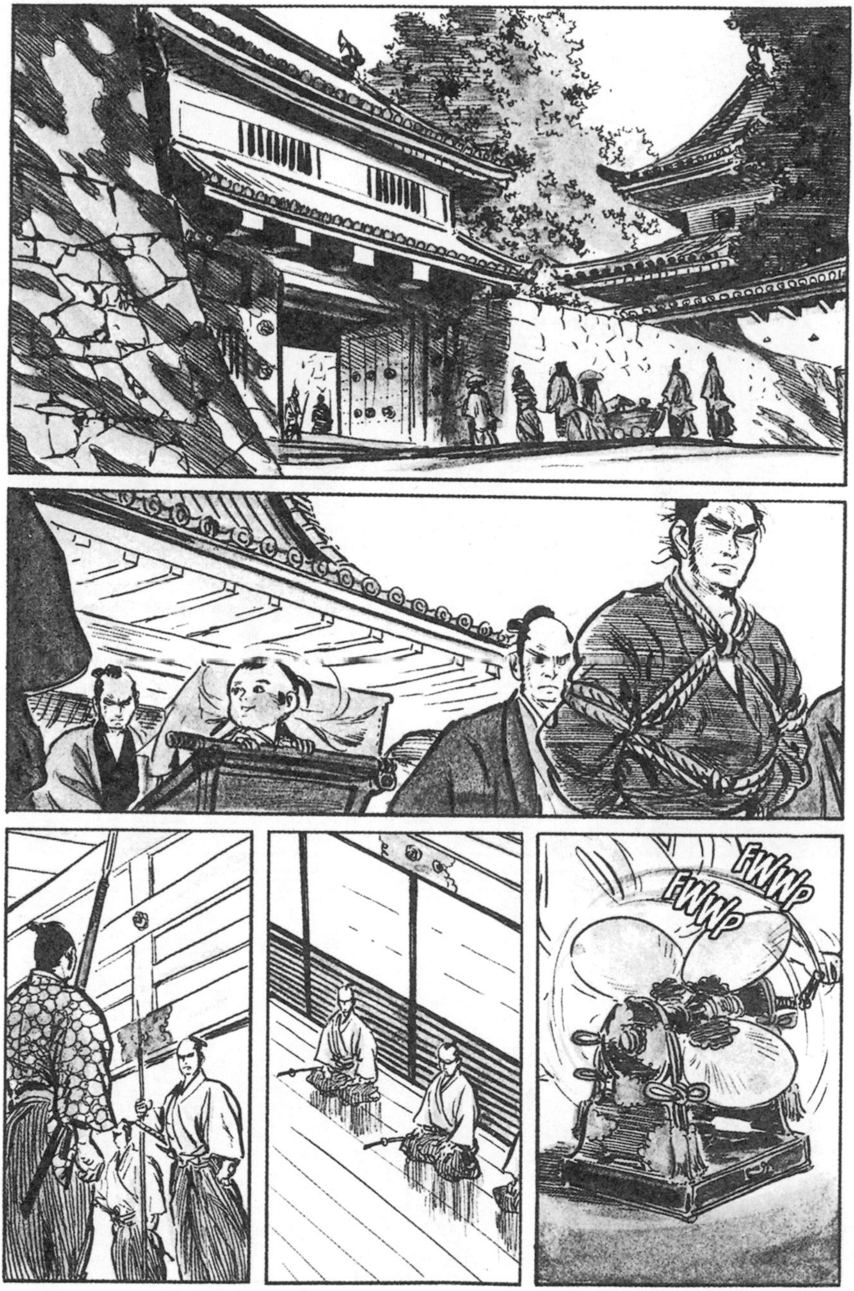
FWWP
FWWP

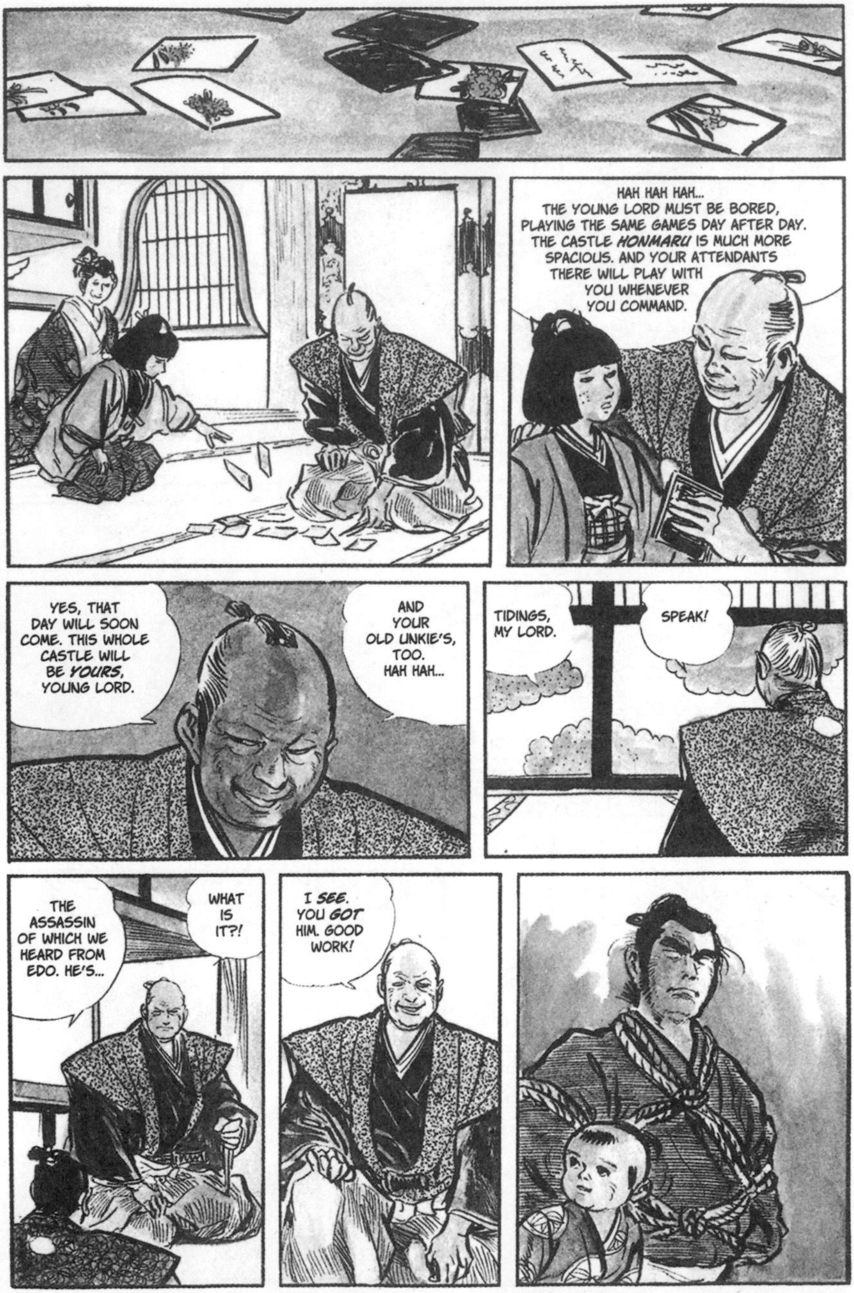
HAH HAH HAH...
THE YOUNG LORD MUST BE BORED, PLAYING THE SAME GAMES DAY AFTER DAY. THE CASTLE *HONMARU* IS MUCH MORE SPACIOUS. AND YOUR ATTENDANTS THERE WILL PLAY WITH YOU WHENEVER YOU COMMAND.
YES, THAT DAY WILL SOON COME. THIS WHOLE CASTLE WILL BE *YOURS*, YOUNG LORD.
AND YOUR OLD UNKIE'S, TOO. HAH HAH...
TIDINGS, MY LORD.
SPEAK!
THE ASSASSIN OF WHICH WE HEARD FROM EDO. HE'S...
WHAT IS IT?!
I *SEE*. YOU *GOT* HIM. GOOD WORK!

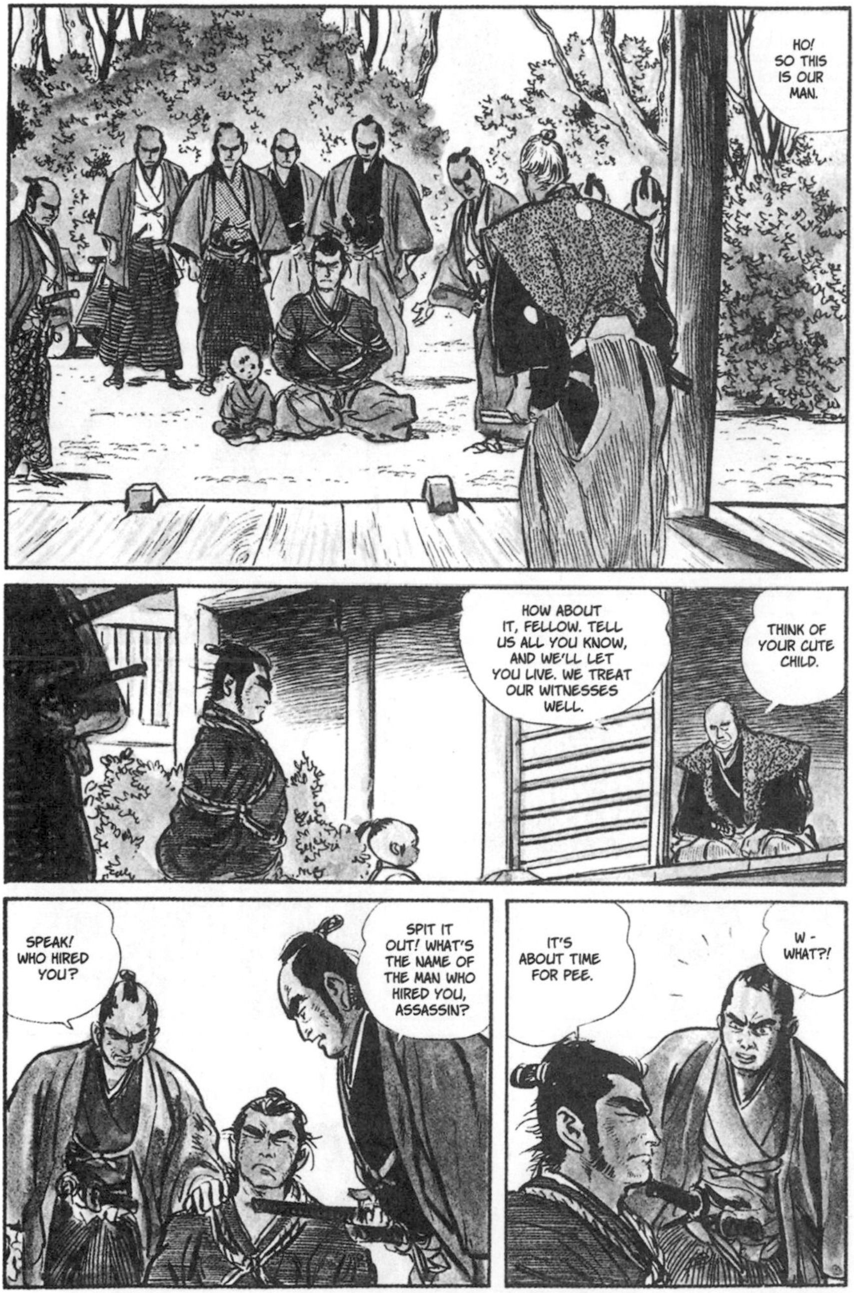
HO! SO THIS IS OUR MAN.
HOW ABOUT IT, FELLOW. TELL US ALL YOU KNOW, AND WE'LL LET YOU LIVE. WE TREAT OUR WITNESSES WELL.
THINK OF YOUR CUTE CHILD.
SPEAK! WHO HIRED YOU?
SPIT IT OUT! WHAT'S THE NAME OF THE MAN WHO HIRED YOU, ASSASSIN?
IT'S ABOUT TIME FOR PEE.
W - WHAT?!

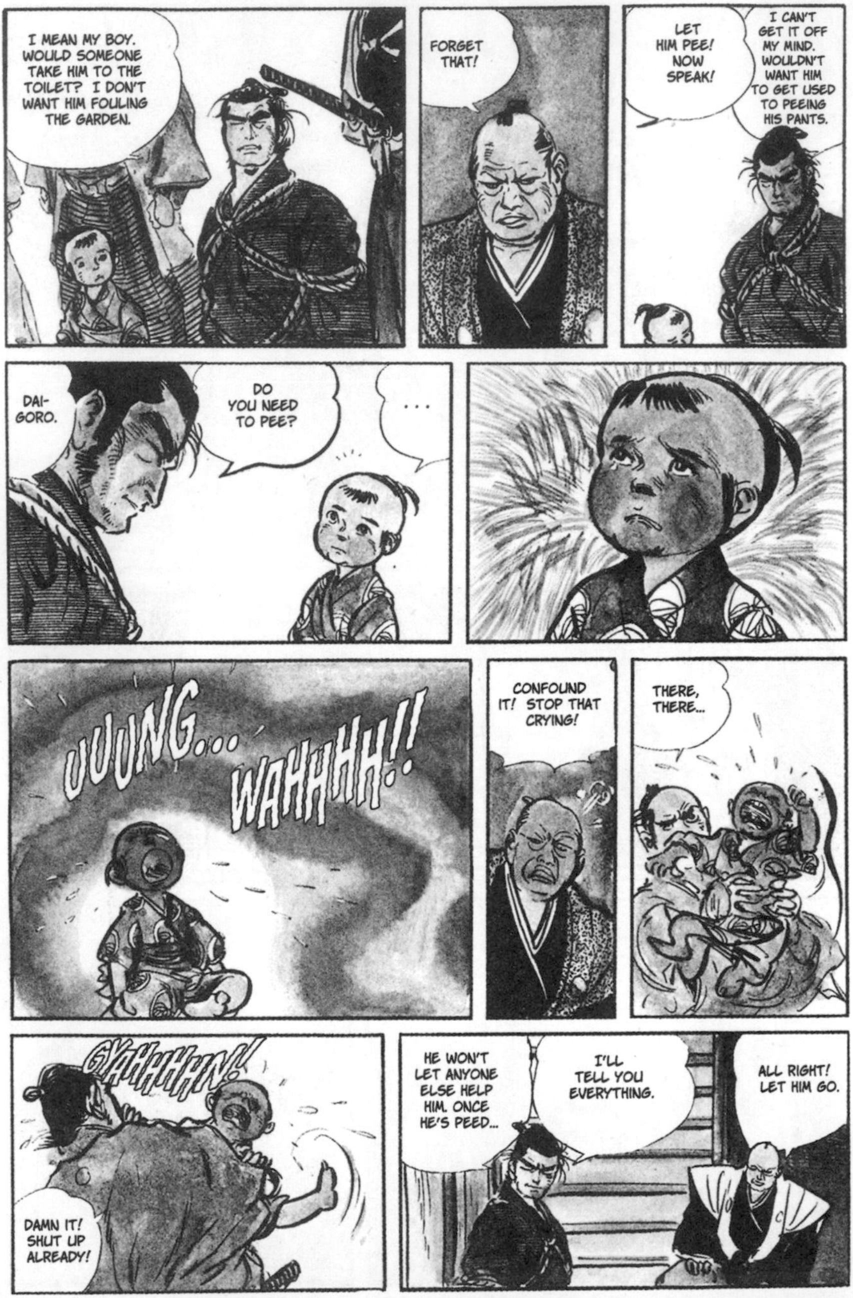
I MEAN MY BOY. WOULD SOMEONE TAKE HIM TO THE TOILET? I DON'T WANT HIM FOULING THE GARDEN.
FORGET THAT!
LET HIM PEE! NOW SPEAK!
I CAN'T GET IT OFF MY MIND. WOULDN'T WANT HIM TO GET USED TO PEEING HIS PANTS.
DAI-GORO.
DO YOU NEED TO PEE?
. . .
UUUNG... WAHHHH!!
CONFOUND IT! STOP THAT CRYING!
THERE, THERE...
GYAHHHHN!
DAMN IT! SHUT UP ALREADY!
HE WON'T LET ANYONE ELSE HELP HIM. ONCE HE'S PEED...
I'LL TELL YOU EVERYTHING.
ALL RIGHT! LET HIM GO.

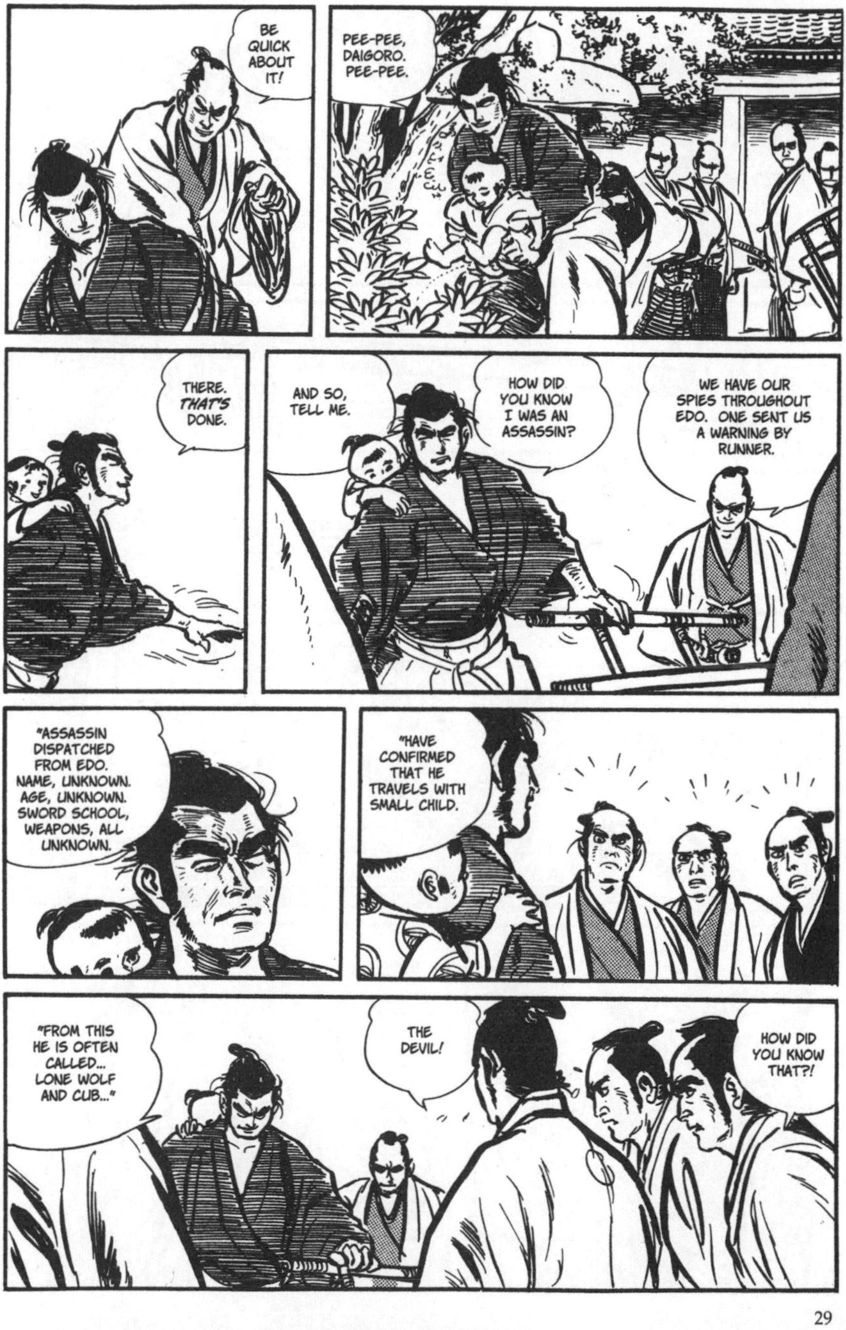
BE QUICK ABOUT IT!
PEE-PEE, DAIGORO. PEE-PEE.
THERE. *THAT'S* DONE.
AND SO, TELL ME.
HOW DID YOU KNOW I WAS AN ASSASSIN?
WE HAVE OUR SPIES THROUGHOUT EDO. ONE SENT US A WARNING BY RUNNER.
"ASSASSIN DISPATCHED FROM EDO. NAME, UNKNOWN. AGE, UNKNOWN. SWORD SCHOOL, WEAPONS, ALL UNKNOWN.
"HAVE CONFIRMED THAT HE TRAVELS WITH SMALL CHILD.
"FROM THIS HE IS OFTEN CALLED... LONE WOLF AND CUB..."
THE DEVIL!
HOW DID YOU KNOW THAT?!

BECAUSE I **WROTE** IT!

AFTER I KILLED YOUR SPY IN EDO!

KRAK

SPRNNG

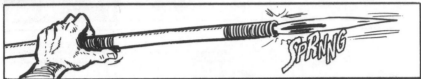

HSSSH

GHKKK!

CHOK

AHH?!

MY LORD!!

30

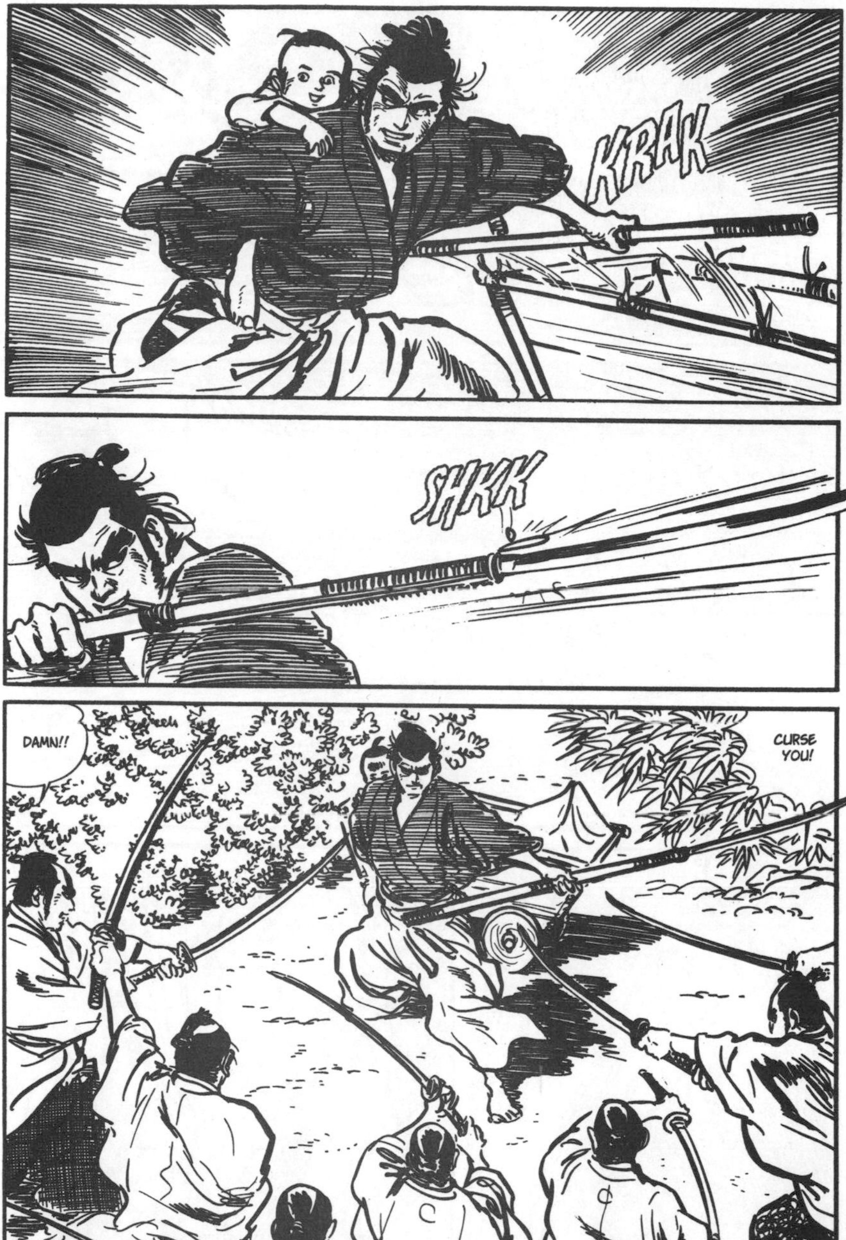
KRAK
SHKK
CURSE YOU!
DAMN!!

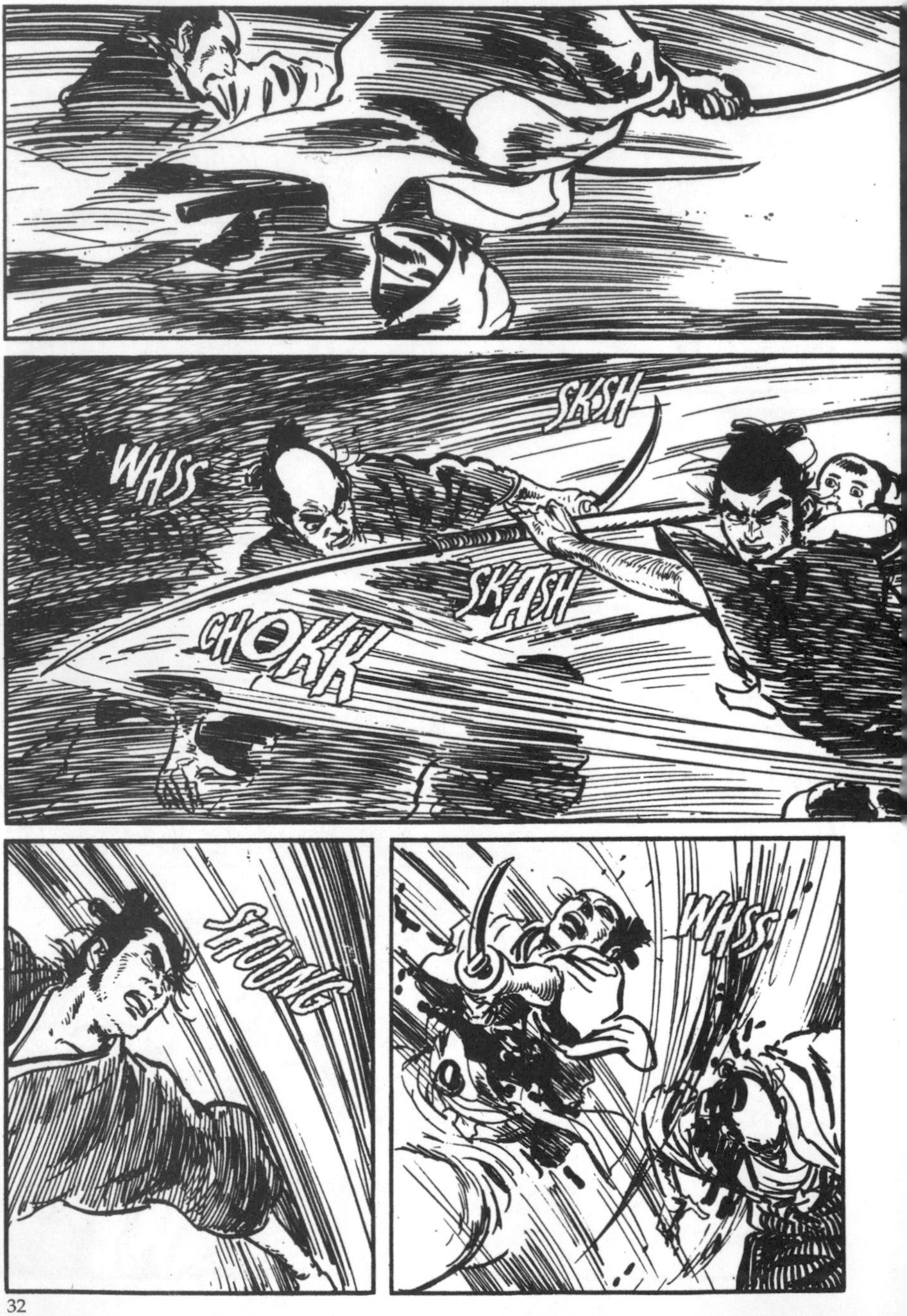
SKSH
WHSS
SKASH
CHOKK
WHSS
SHUNG

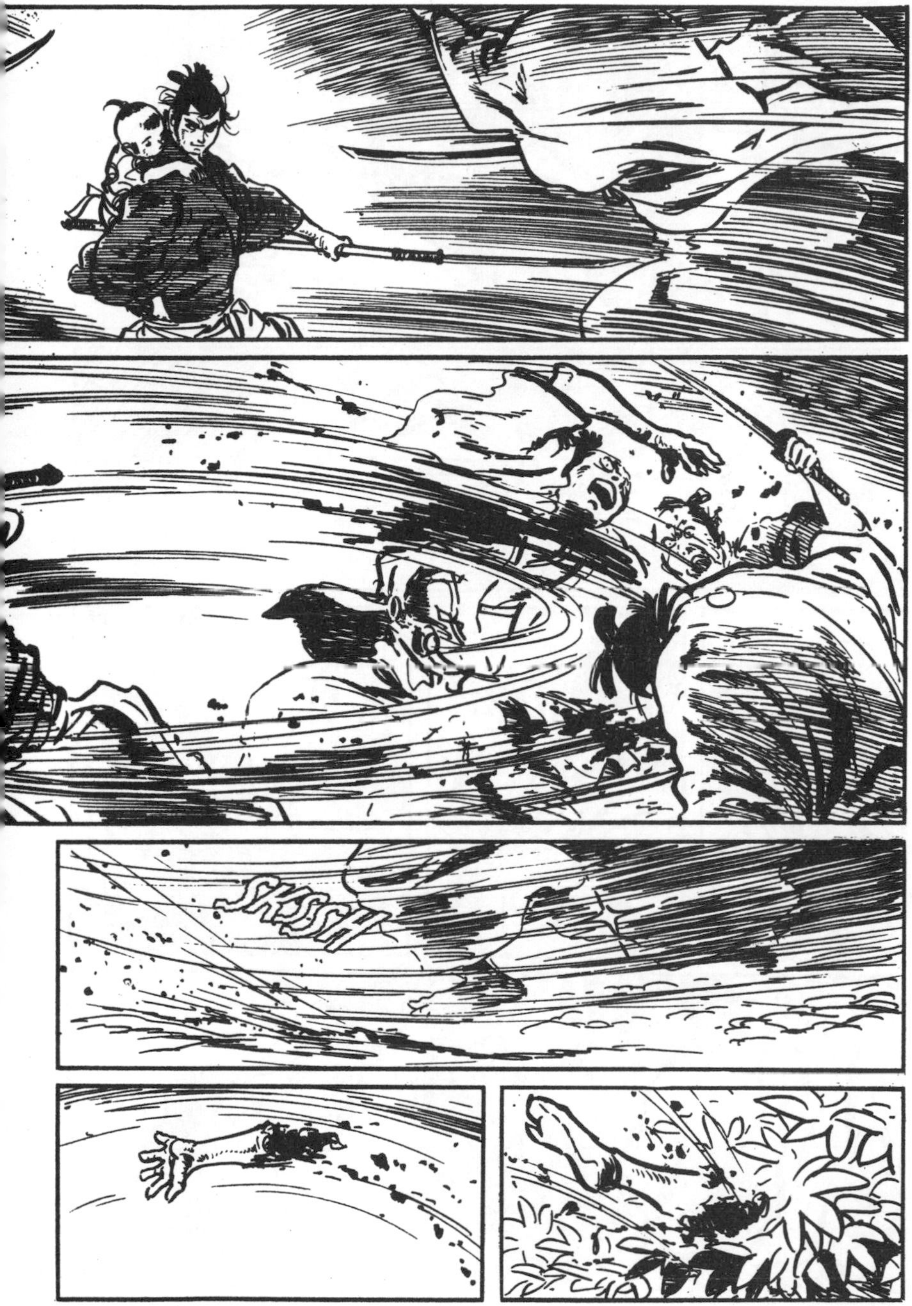
SKSSH

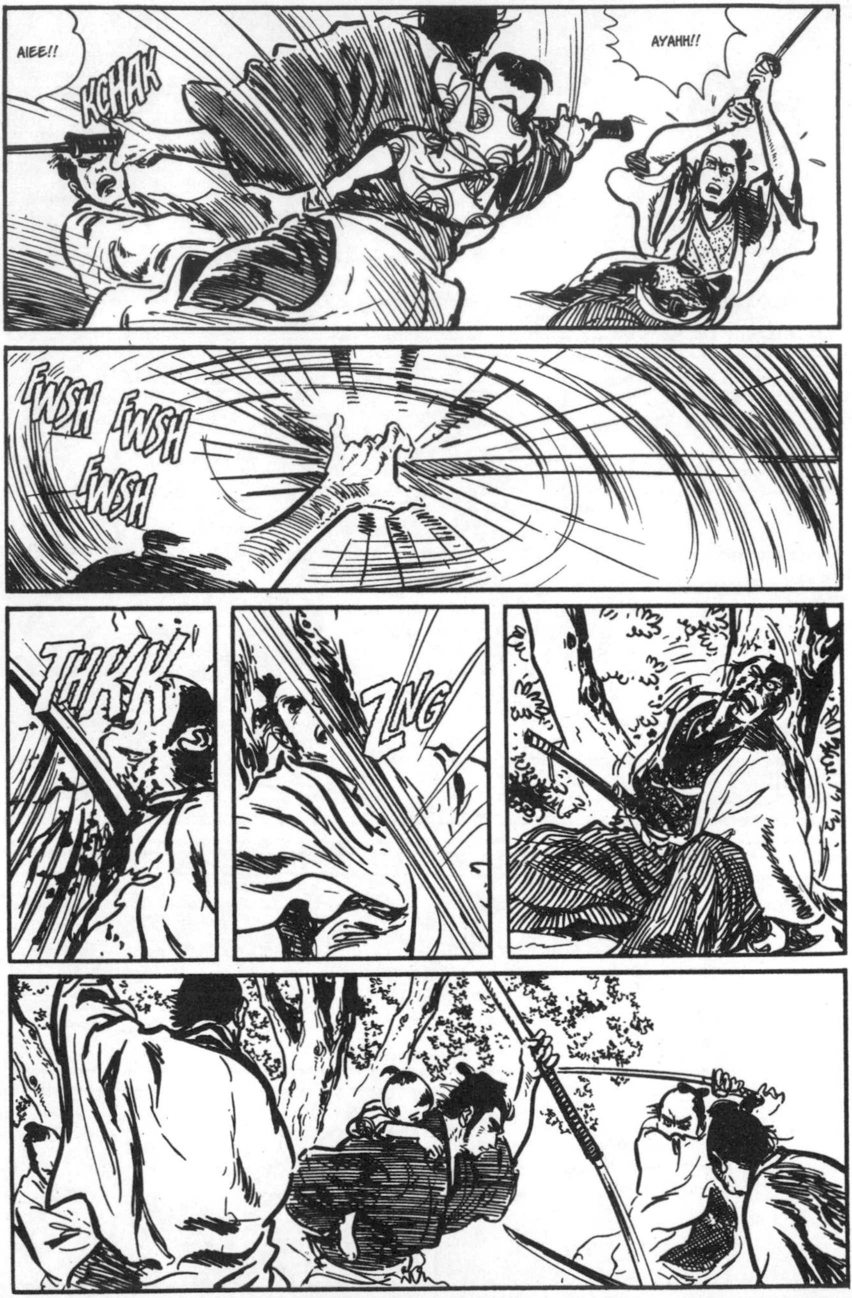
AYAHH!!
AIEE!!
KCHAK
FWSH
FWSH
FWSH
ZNG
THKK

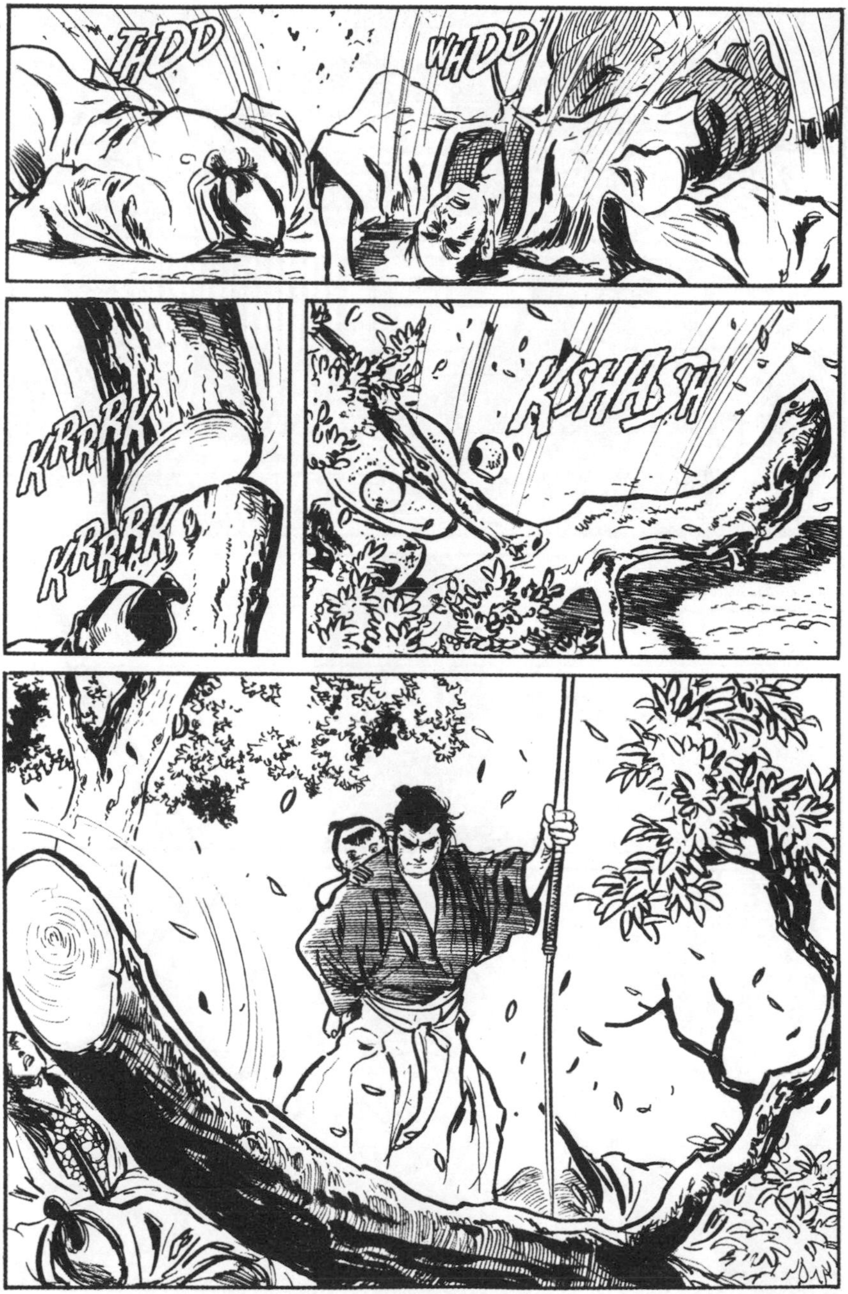
WHDD
THDD
KSHASH
KRRRK
KRRRK

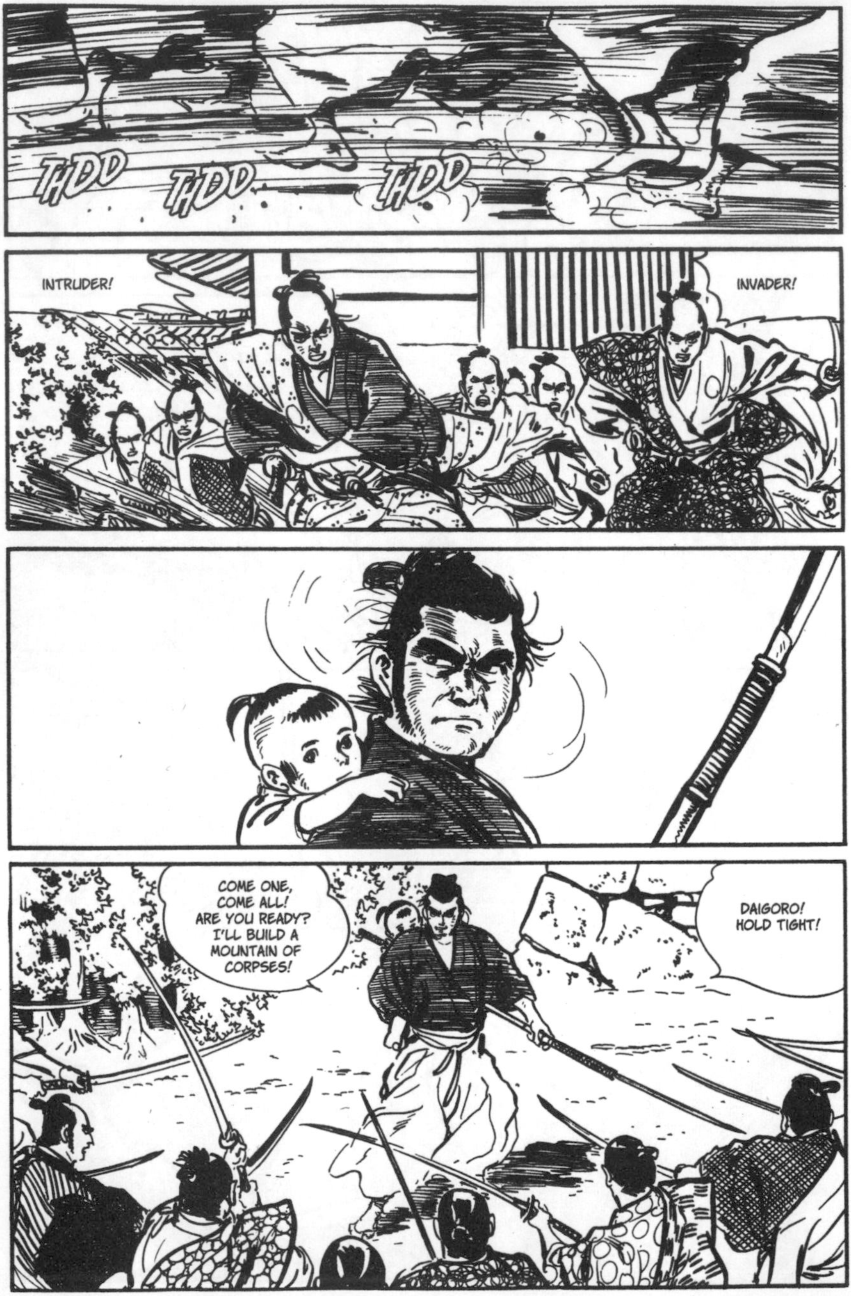
THDD
THDD
THDD
INVADER!
INTRUDER!
DAIGORO! HOLD TIGHT!
COME ONE, COME ALL! ARE YOU READY? I'LL BUILD A MOUNTAIN OF CORPSES!

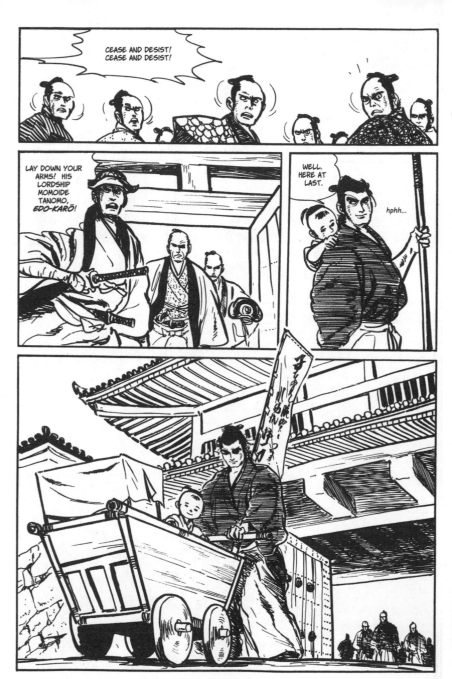

CEASE AND DESIST!
CEASE AND DESIST!

LAY DOWN YOUR ARMS! HIS LORDSHIP MOMOIDE TANOMO, *EDO-KARŌ!*

WELL. HERE AT LAST.

hphh...

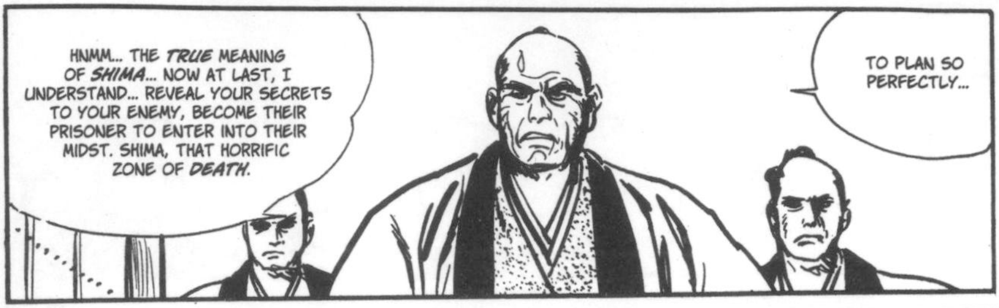
HNMM... THE *TRUE* MEANING OF *SHIMA*... NOW AT LAST, I UNDERSTAND... REVEAL YOUR SECRETS TO YOUR ENEMY, BECOME THEIR PRISONER TO ENTER INTO THEIR MIDST. SHIMA, THAT HORRIFIC ZONE OF *DEATH*.
TO PLAN SO PERFECTLY...

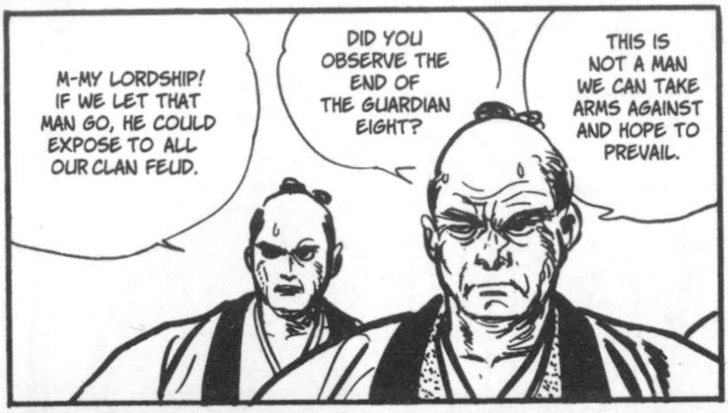
M-MY LORDSHIP! IF WE LET THAT MAN GO, HE COULD EXPOSE TO ALL OUR CLAN FEUD.
DID YOU OBSERVE THE END OF THE GUARDIAN EIGHT?
THIS IS NOT A MAN WE CAN TAKE ARMS AGAINST AND HOPE TO PREVAIL.

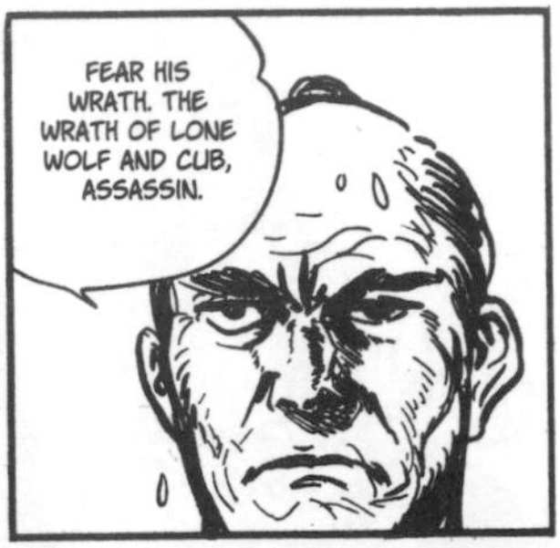
FEAR HIS WRATH. THE WRATH OF LONE WOLF AND CUB, ASSASSIN.

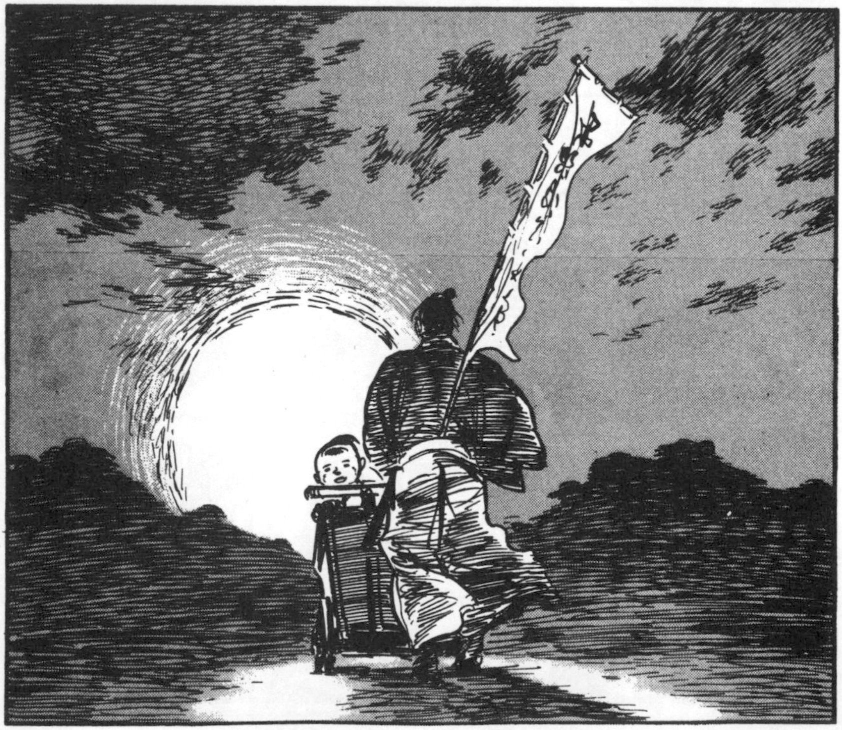

A FATHER KNOWS HIS CHILD'S HEART,
AS ONLY A CHILD CAN KNOW HIS FATHER'S

2

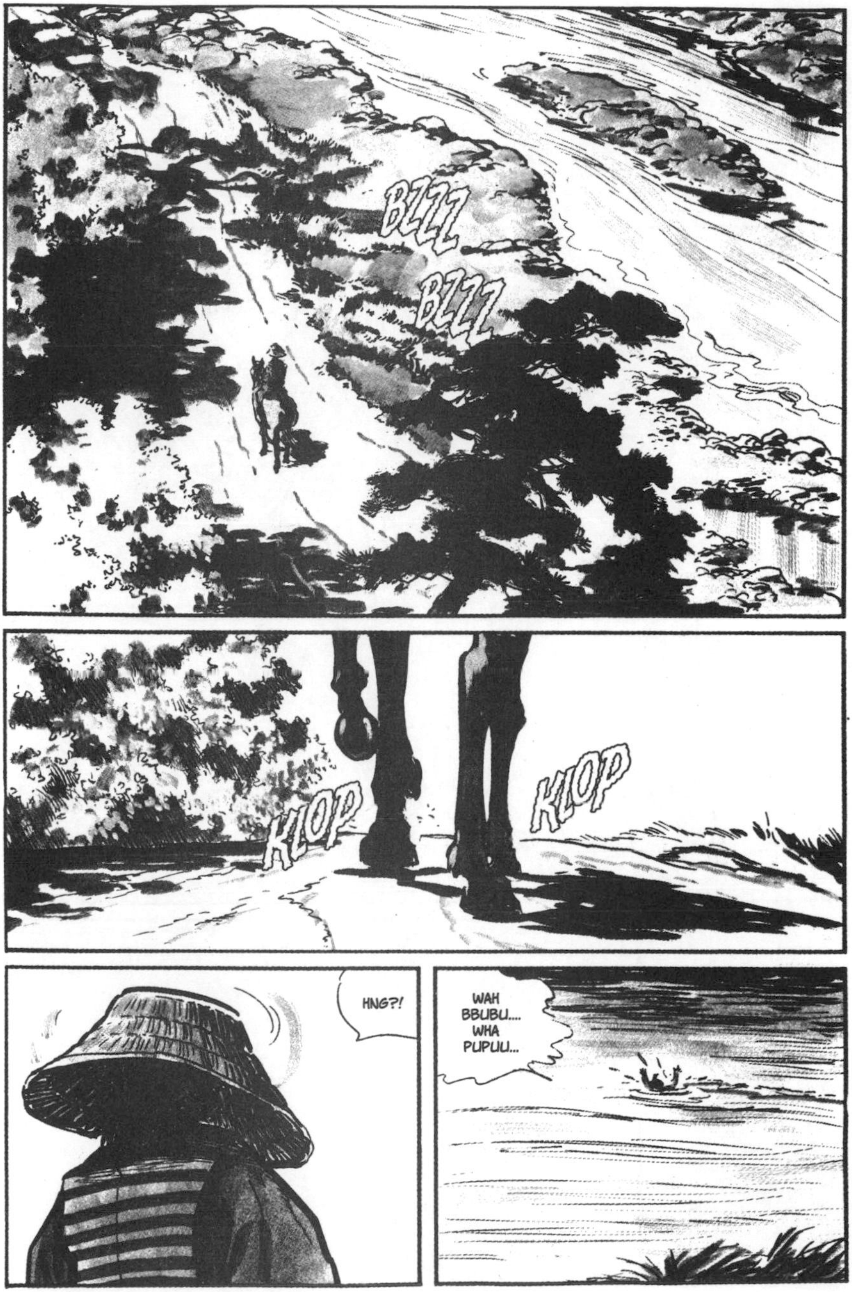
BZZZ
BZZZ
KLOP
KLOP
WAH BBUBU.... WHA PUPUU...
HNG?!

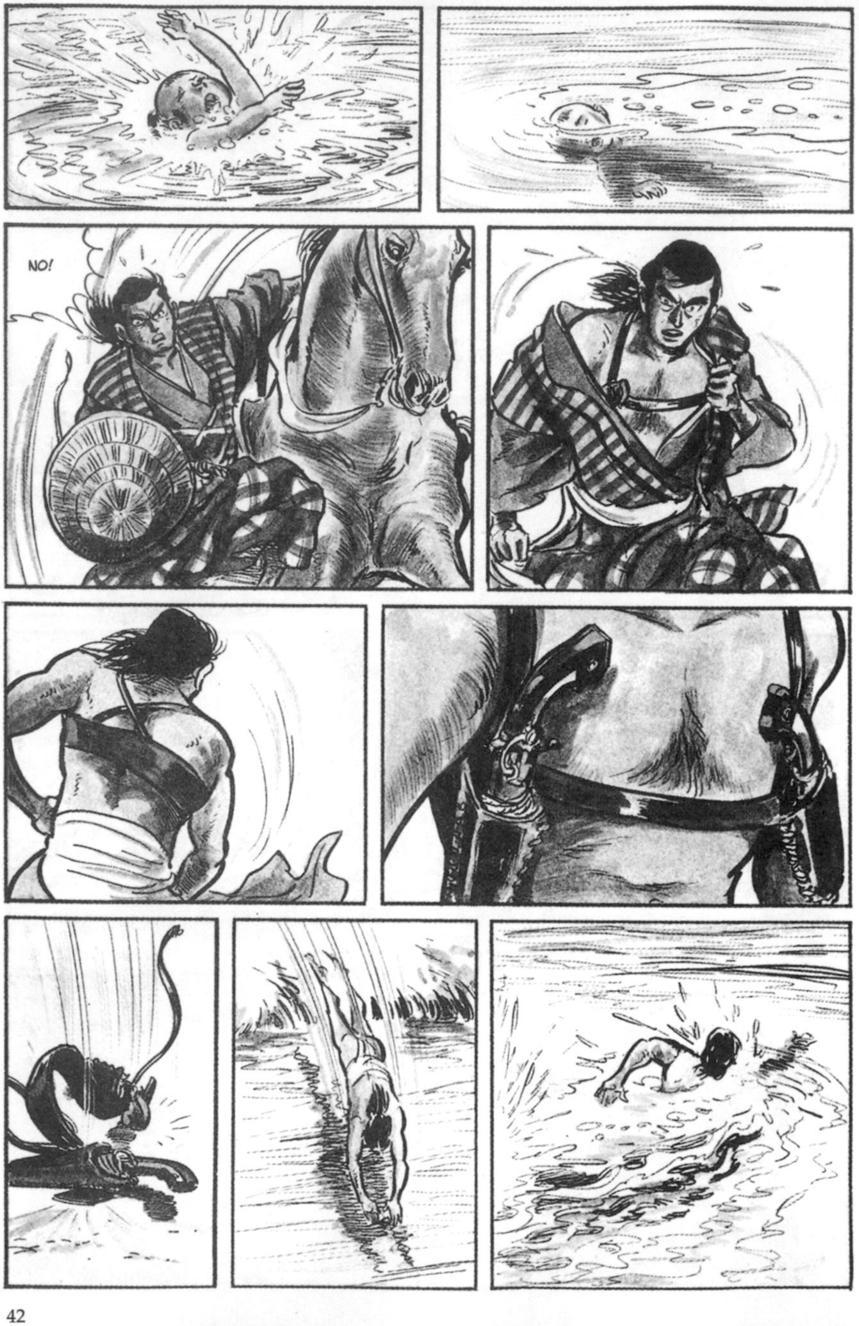
NO!

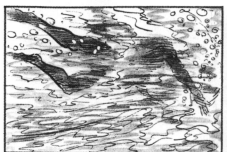

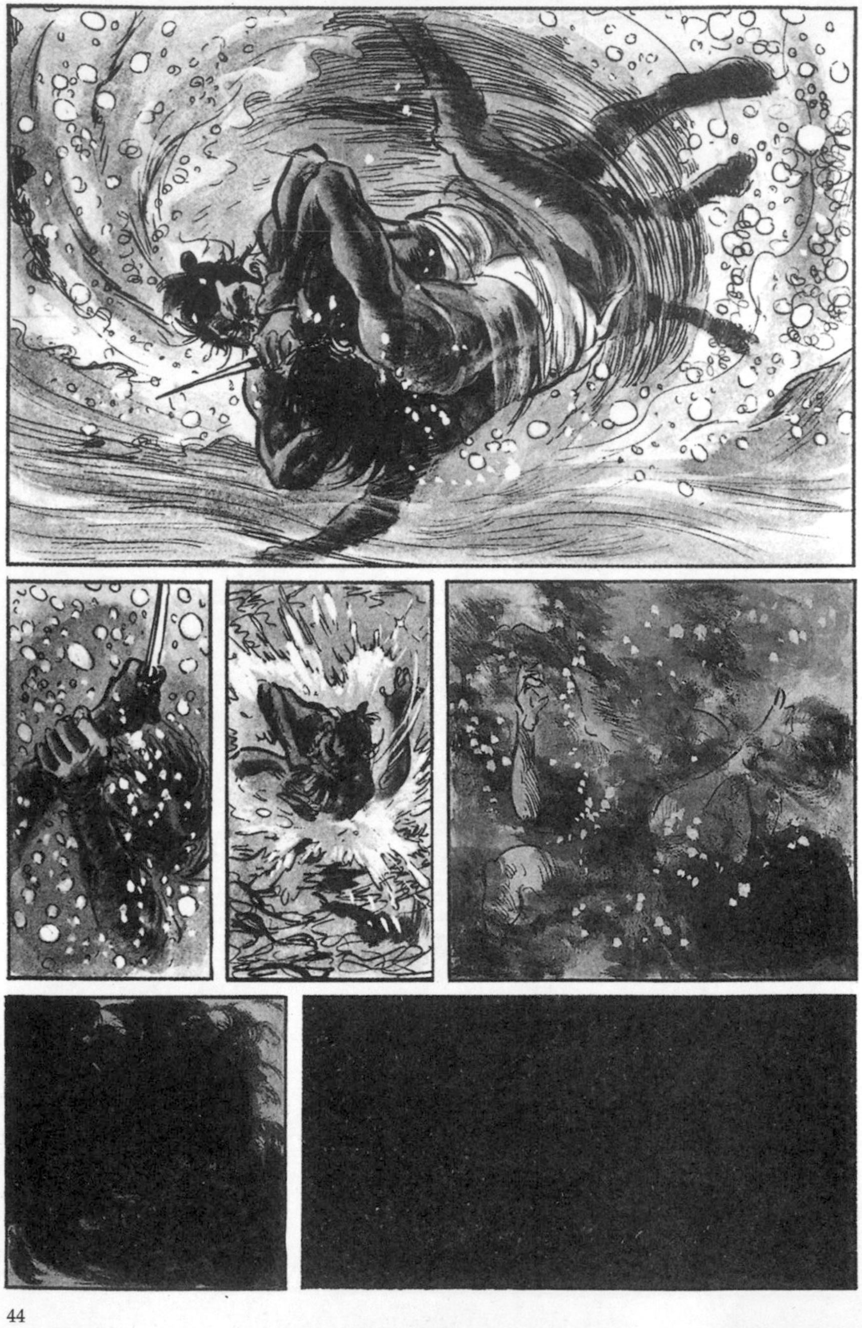

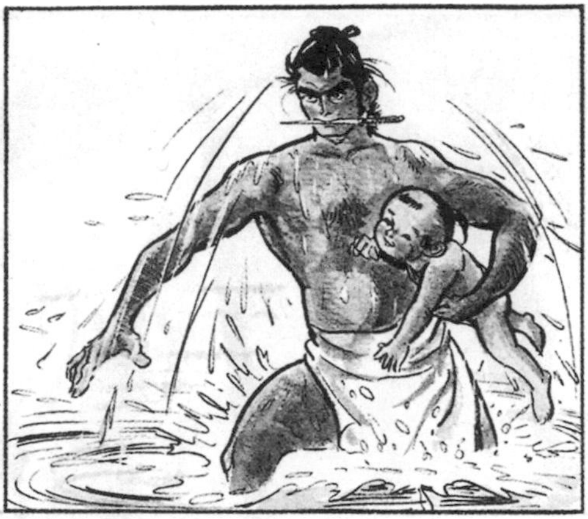
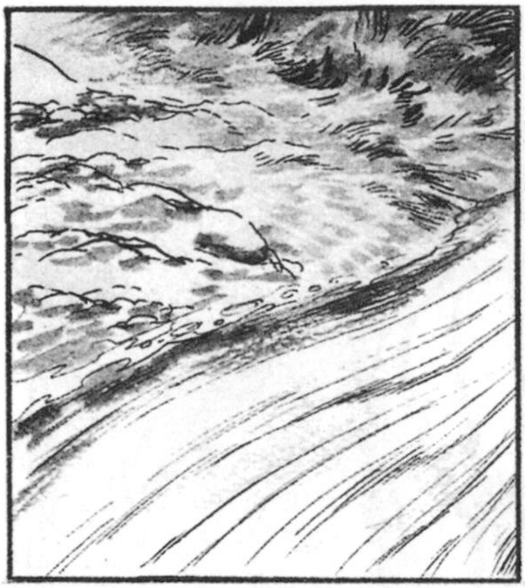
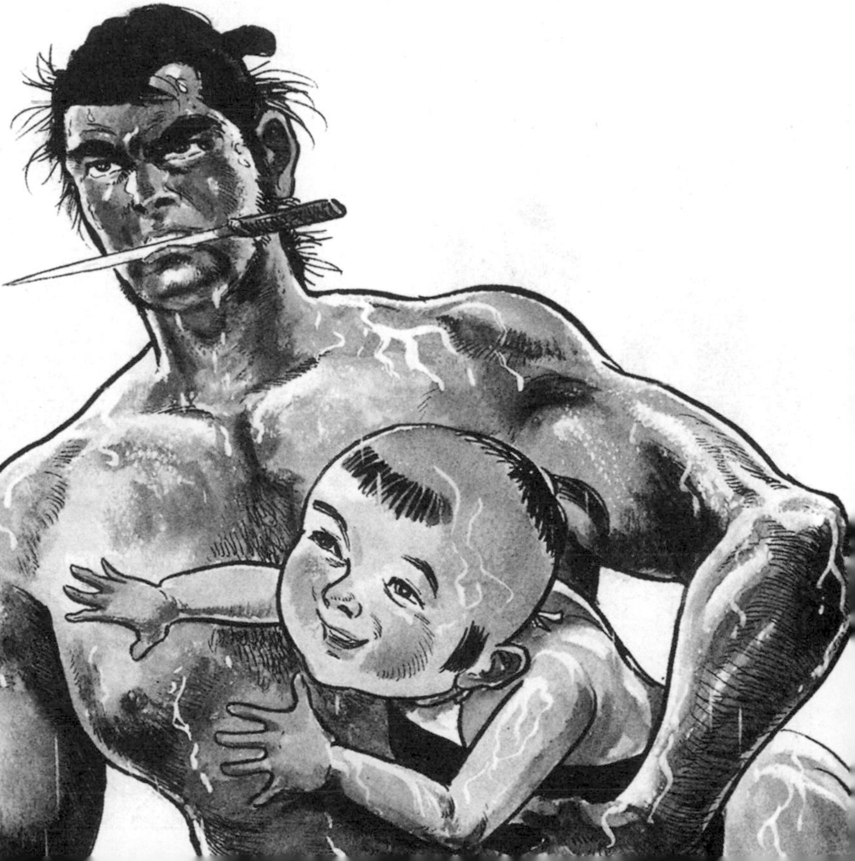

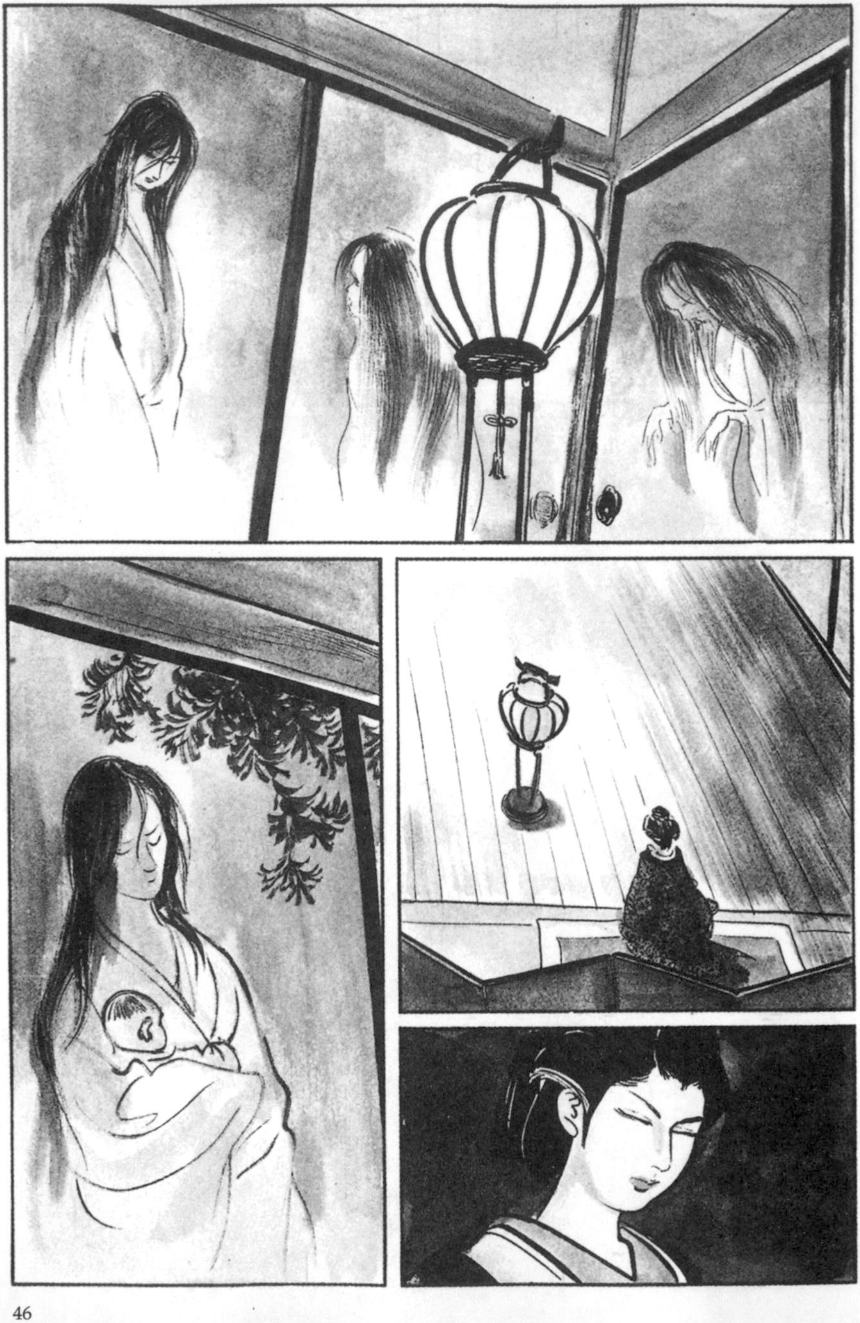

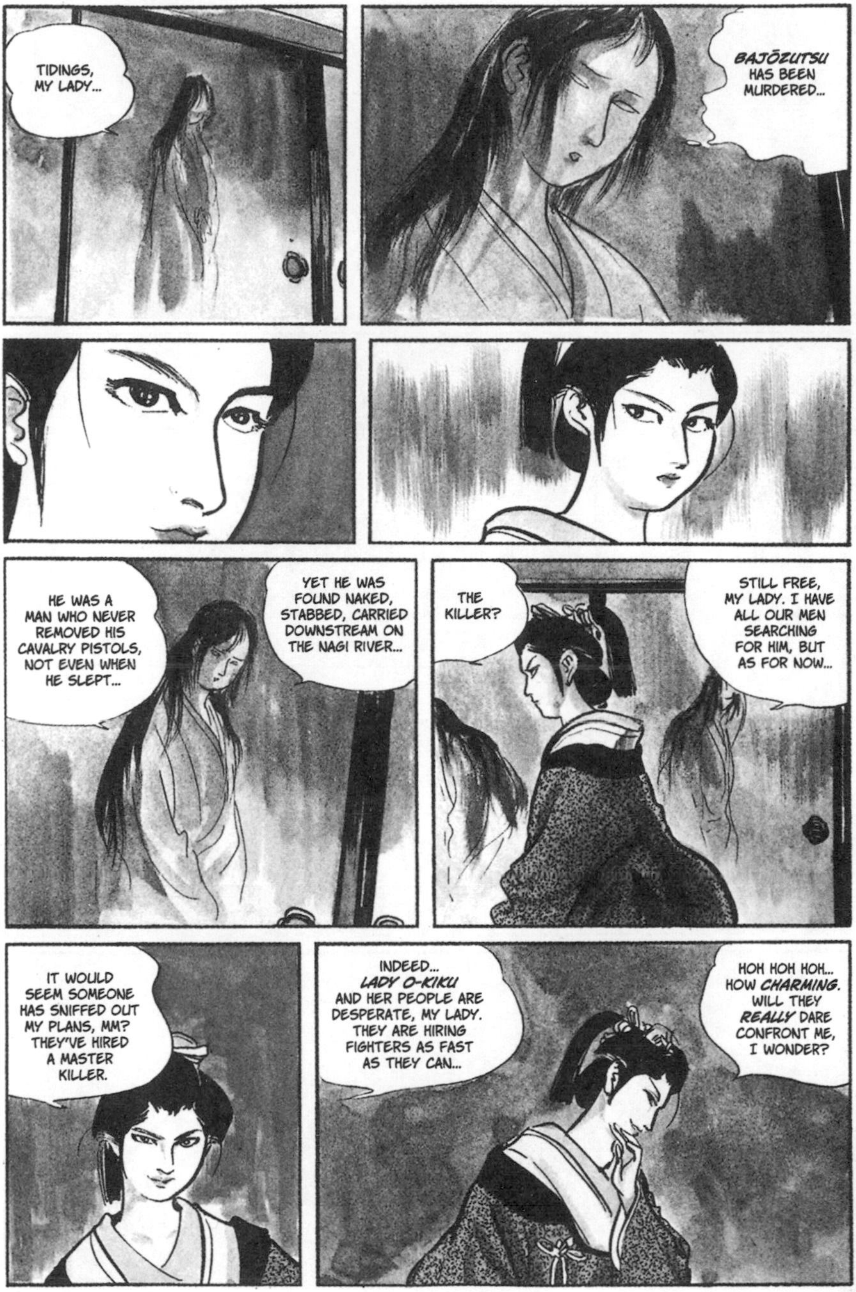
TIDINGS, MY LADY...
BAJŌZUTSU HAS BEEN MURDERED...
HE WAS A MAN WHO NEVER REMOVED HIS CAVALRY PISTOLS, NOT EVEN WHEN HE SLEPT...
YET HE WAS FOUND NAKED, STABBED, CARRIED DOWNSTREAM ON THE NAGI RIVER...
THE KILLER?
STILL FREE, MY LADY. I HAVE ALL OUR MEN SEARCHING FOR HIM, BUT AS FOR NOW...
IT WOULD SEEM SOMEONE HAS SNIFFED OUT MY PLANS, MM? THEY'VE HIRED A MASTER KILLER.
INDEED... *LADY O-KIKU* AND HER PEOPLE ARE DESPERATE, MY LADY. THEY ARE HIRING FIGHTERS AS FAST AS THEY CAN...
HOH HOH HOH... HOW *CHARMING*. WILL THEY *REALLY* DARE CONFRONT ME, I WONDER?

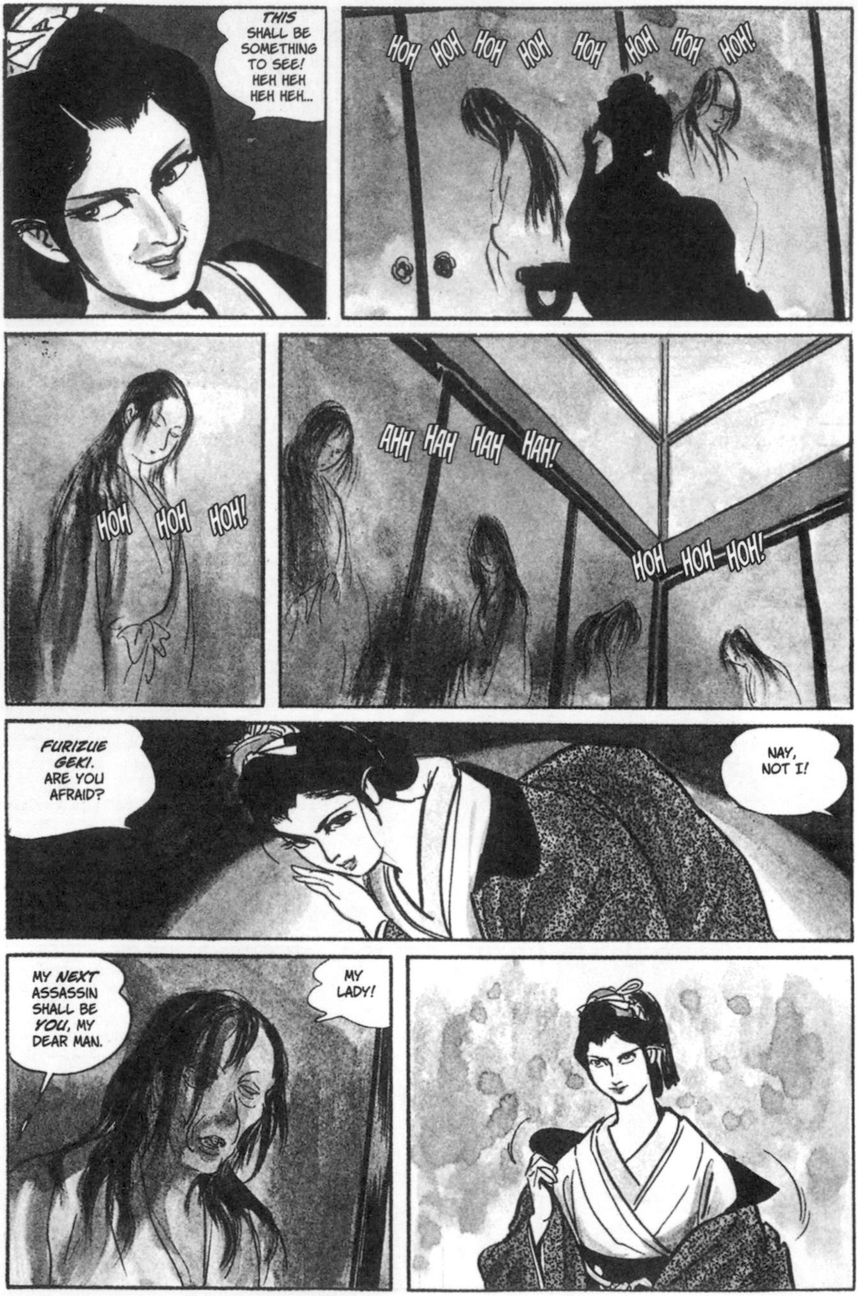
HOH HOH HOH HOH HOH HOH HOH HOH!
THIS SHALL BE SOMETHING TO SEE! HEH HEH HEH HEH...
AHH HAH HAH HAH!
HOH HOH-HOH!
HOH HOH HOH!
FURIZUE GEKI. ARE YOU AFRAID?
NAY, NOT I!
MY LADY!
MY NEXT ASSASSIN SHALL BE YOU, MY DEAR MAN.

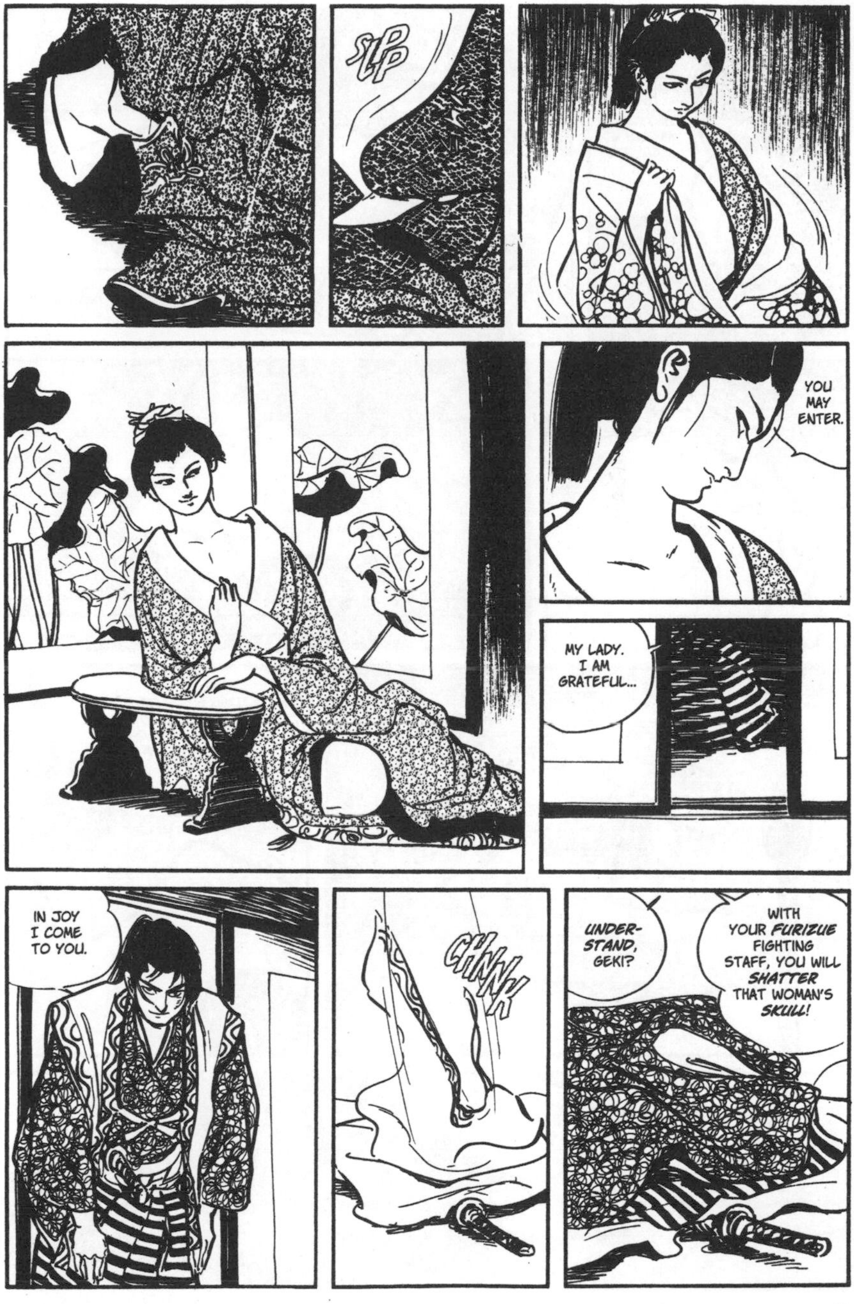
SLIP
YOU MAY ENTER.
MY LADY. I AM GRATEFUL...
WITH YOUR *FURIZUE* FIGHTING STAFF, YOU WILL ***SHATTER*** THAT WOMAN'S ***SKULL!***
UNDER-STAND, GEKI?
CHNNK
IN JOY I COME TO YOU.

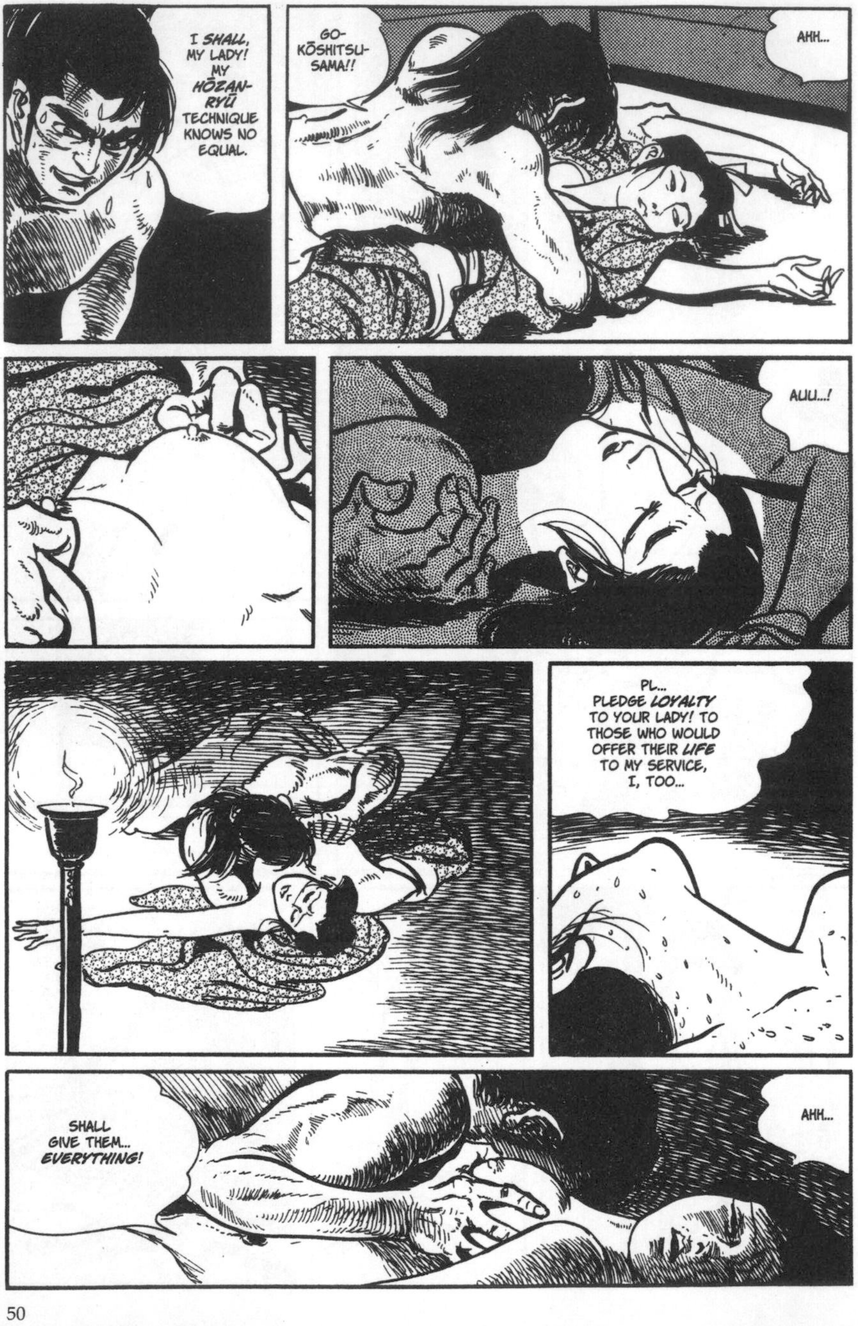
I SHALL, MY LADY! MY HŌZAN-RYŪ TECHNIQUE KNOWS NO EQUAL.
GO-KŌSHITSU-SAMA!!
AHH...
AUU...!
PL... PLEDGE LOYALTY TO YOUR LADY! TO THOSE WHO WOULD OFFER THEIR LIFE TO MY SERVICE, I, TOO...
SHALL GIVE THEM... EVERYTHING!
AHH...

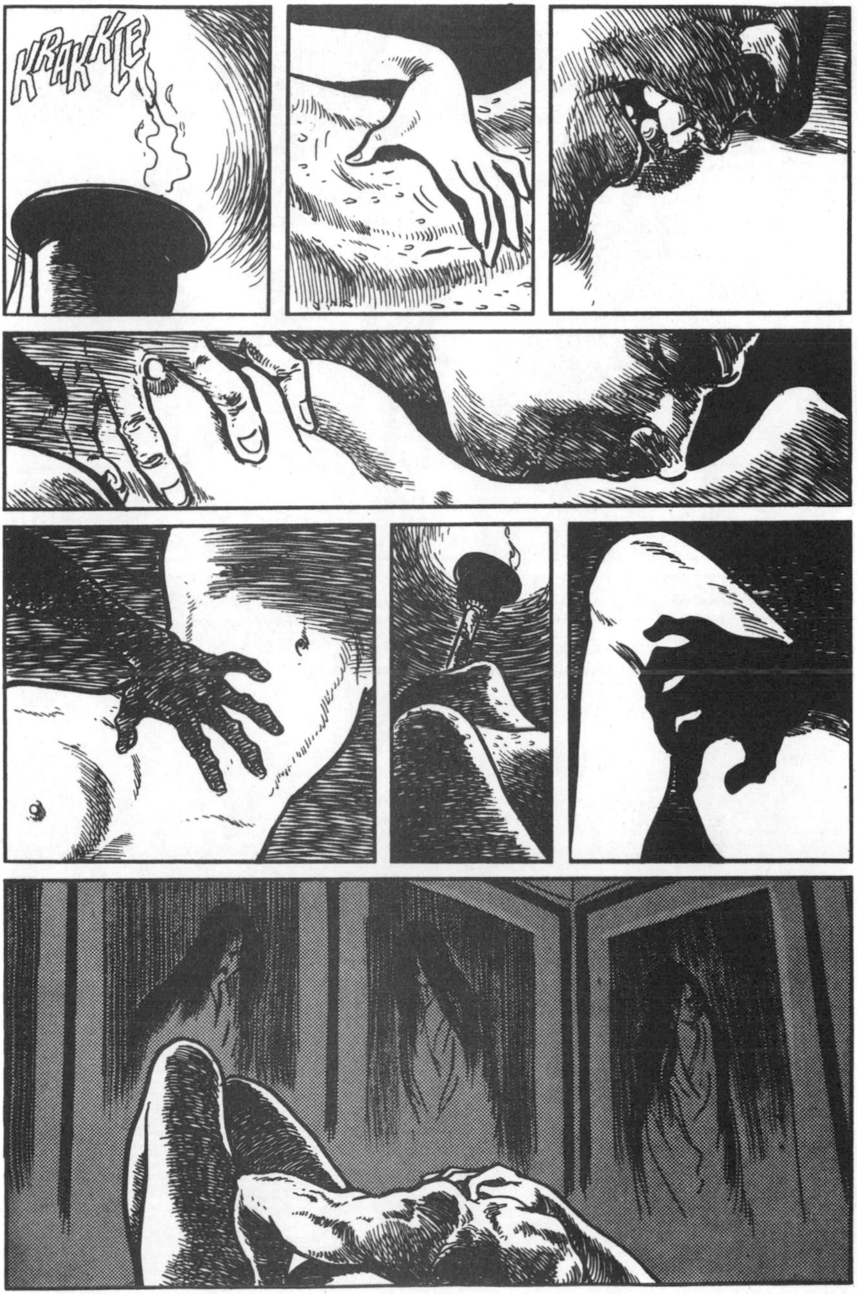
KRAKKLE

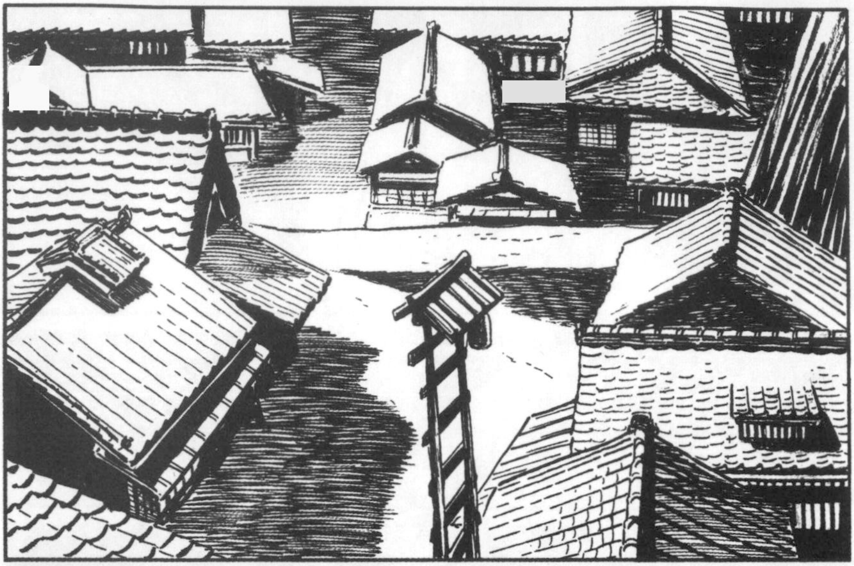

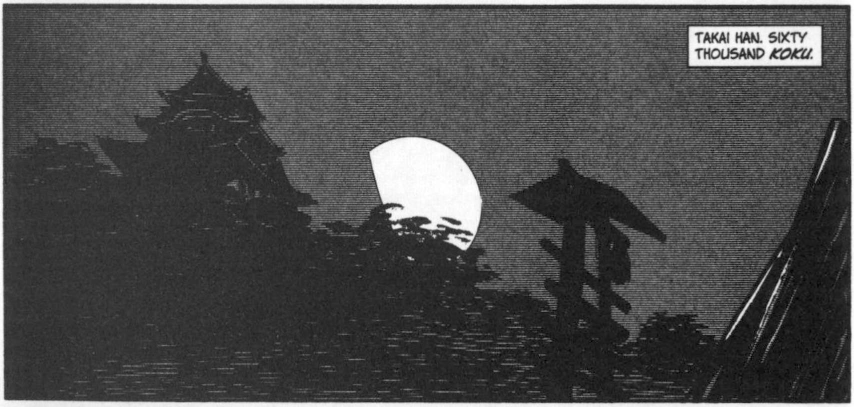
TAKAI HAN. SIXTY THOUSAND *KOKU.*

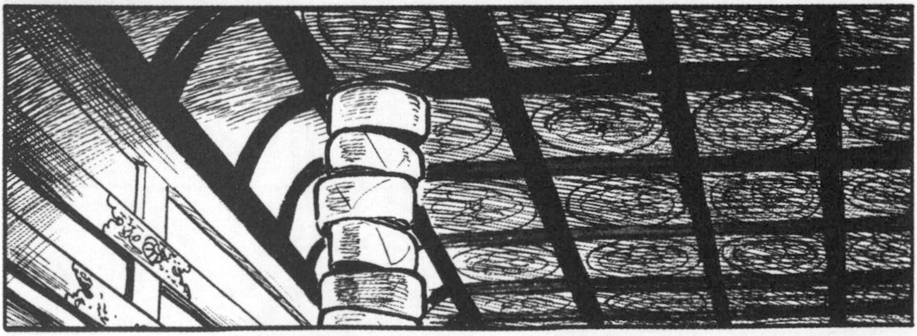

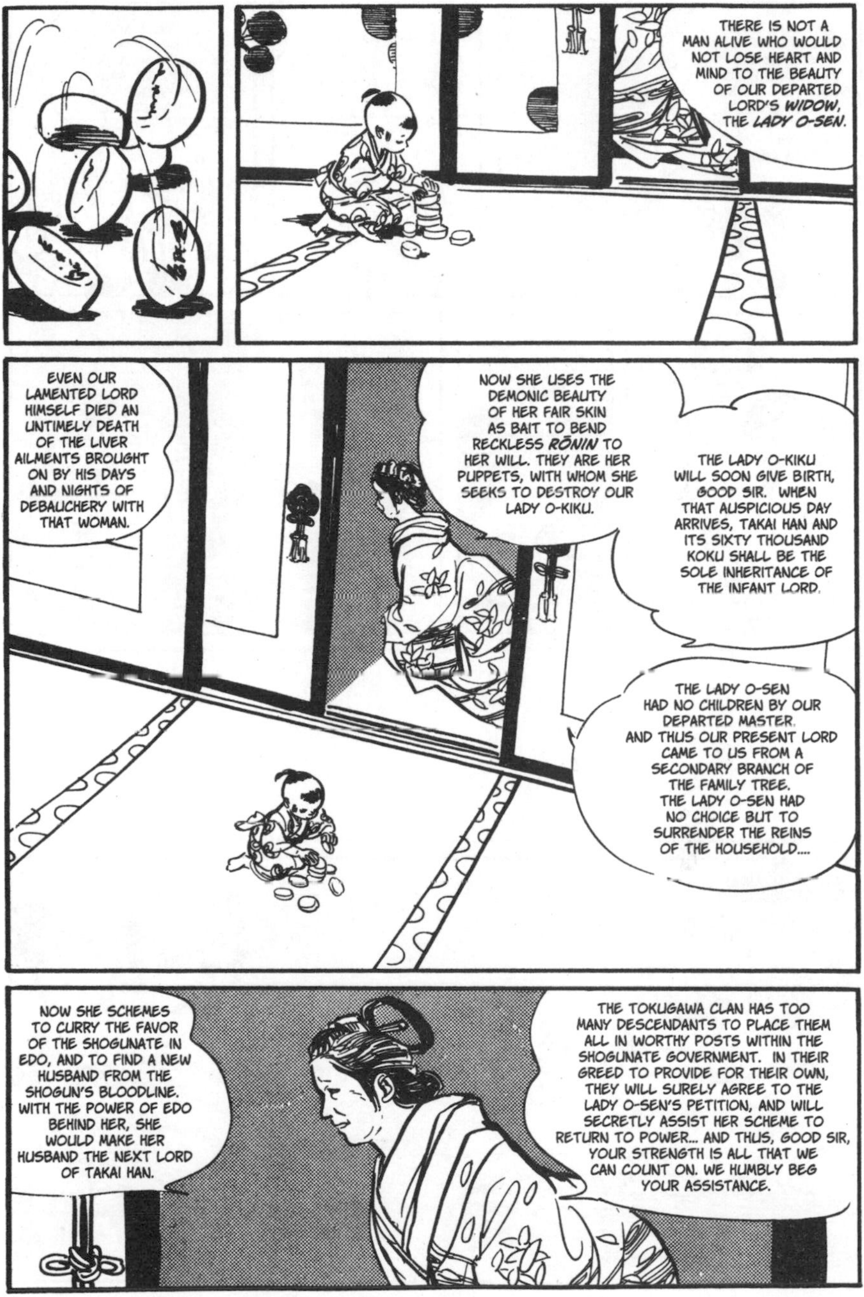
THERE IS NOT A MAN ALIVE WHO WOULD NOT LOSE HEART AND MIND TO THE BEAUTY OF OUR DEPARTED LORD'S *WIDOW*, THE *LADY O-SEN*.
EVEN OUR LAMENTED LORD HIMSELF DIED AN UNTIMELY DEATH OF THE LIVER AILMENTS BROUGHT ON BY HIS DAYS AND NIGHTS OF DEBAUCHERY WITH THAT WOMAN.
NOW SHE USES THE DEMONIC BEAUTY OF HER FAIR SKIN AS BAIT TO BEND RECKLESS *RŌNIN* TO HER WILL. THEY ARE HER PUPPETS, WITH WHOM SHE SEEKS TO DESTROY OUR LADY O-KIKU.
THE LADY O-KIKU WILL SOON GIVE BIRTH, GOOD SIR. WHEN THAT AUSPICIOUS DAY ARRIVES, TAKAI HAN AND ITS SIXTY THOUSAND KOKU SHALL BE THE SOLE INHERITANCE OF THE INFANT LORD.
THE LADY O-SEN HAD NO CHILDREN BY OUR DEPARTED MASTER. AND THUS OUR PRESENT LORD CAME TO US FROM A SECONDARY BRANCH OF THE FAMILY TREE. THE LADY O-SEN HAD NO CHOICE BUT TO SURRENDER THE REINS OF THE HOUSEHOLD....
NOW SHE SCHEMES TO CURRY THE FAVOR OF THE SHOGUNATE IN EDO, AND TO FIND A NEW HUSBAND FROM THE SHOGUN'S BLOODLINE. WITH THE POWER OF EDO BEHIND HER, SHE WOULD MAKE HER HUSBAND THE NEXT LORD OF TAKAI HAN.
THE TOKUGAWA CLAN HAS TOO MANY DESCENDANTS TO PLACE THEM ALL IN WORTHY POSTS WITHIN THE SHOGUNATE GOVERNMENT. IN THEIR GREED TO PROVIDE FOR THEIR OWN, THEY WILL SURELY AGREE TO THE LADY O-SEN'S PETITION, AND WILL SECRETLY ASSIST HER SCHEME TO RETURN TO POWER... AND THUS, GOOD SIR, YOUR STRENGTH IS ALL THAT WE CAN COUNT ON. WE HUMBLY BEG YOUR ASSISTANCE.

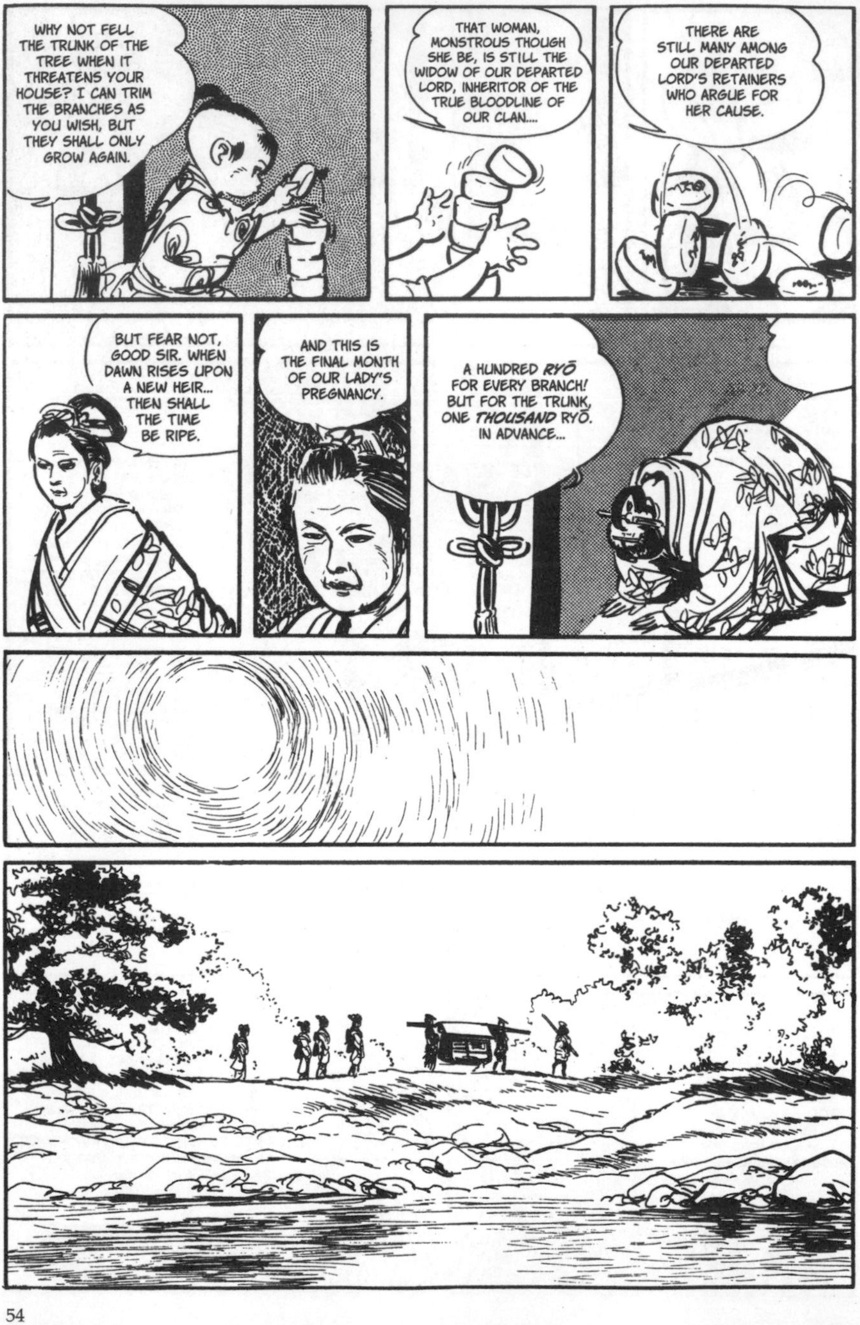
WHY NOT FELL THE TRUNK OF THE TREE WHEN IT THREATENS YOUR HOUSE? I CAN TRIM THE BRANCHES AS YOU WISH, BUT THEY SHALL ONLY GROW AGAIN.
THAT WOMAN, MONSTROUS THOUGH SHE BE, IS STILL THE WIDOW OF OUR DEPARTED LORD, INHERITOR OF THE TRUE BLOODLINE OF OUR CLAN....
THERE ARE STILL MANY AMONG OUR DEPARTED LORD'S RETAINERS WHO ARGUE FOR HER CAUSE.
BUT FEAR NOT, GOOD SIR. WHEN DAWN RISES UPON A NEW HEIR... THEN SHALL THE TIME BE RIPE.
AND THIS IS THE FINAL MONTH OF OUR LADY'S PREGNANCY.
A HUNDRED *RYŌ* FOR EVERY BRANCH! BUT FOR THE TRUNK, ONE *THOUSAND* RYŌ. IN ADVANCE...

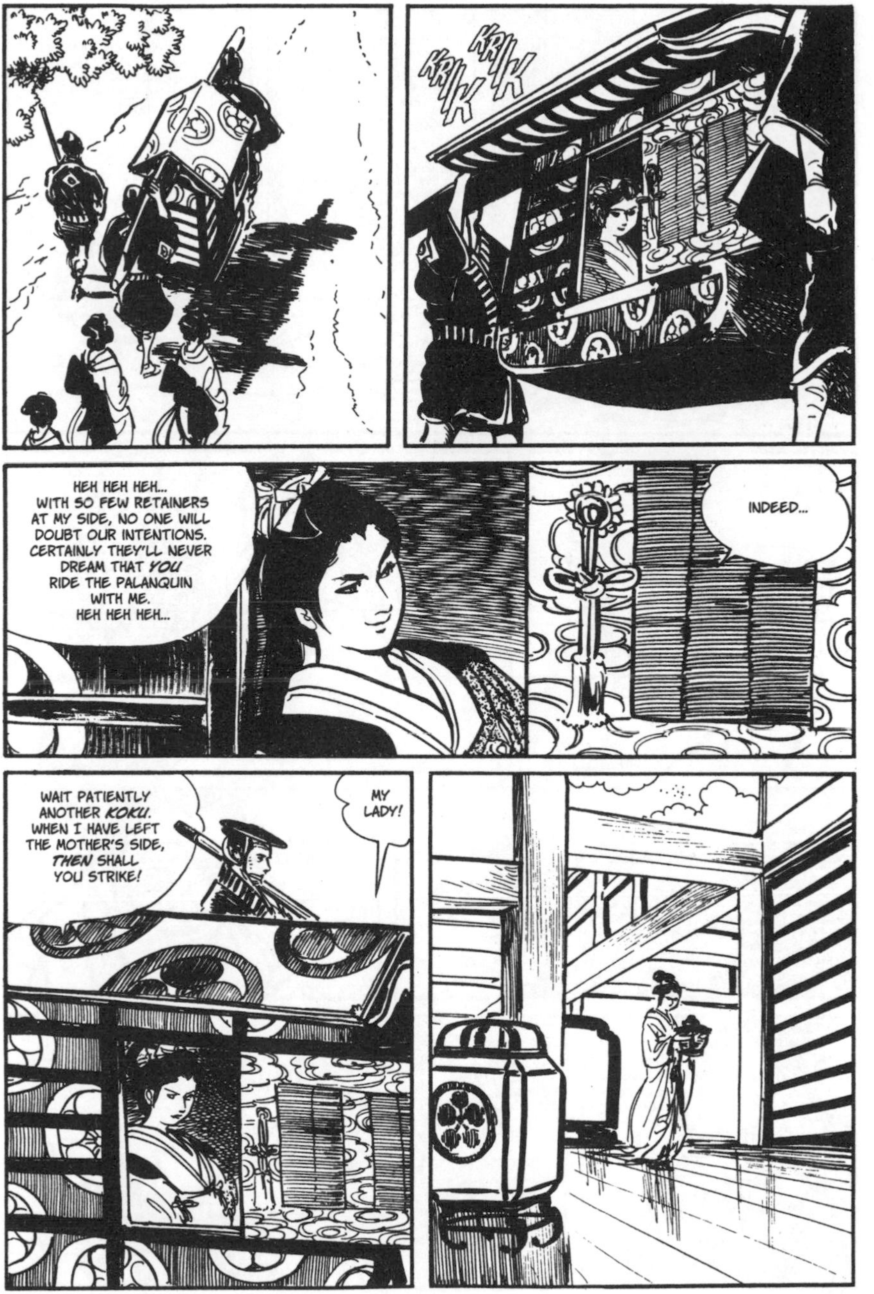
KRIK
KRIK
HEH HEH HEH... WITH SO FEW RETAINERS AT MY SIDE, NO ONE WILL DOUBT OUR INTENTIONS. CERTAINLY THEY'LL NEVER DREAM THAT *YOU* RIDE THE PALANQUIN WITH ME. HEH HEH HEH...
INDEED...
WAIT PATIENTLY ANOTHER *KOKU*. WHEN I HAVE LEFT THE MOTHER'S SIDE, *THEN* SHALL YOU STRIKE!
MY LADY!

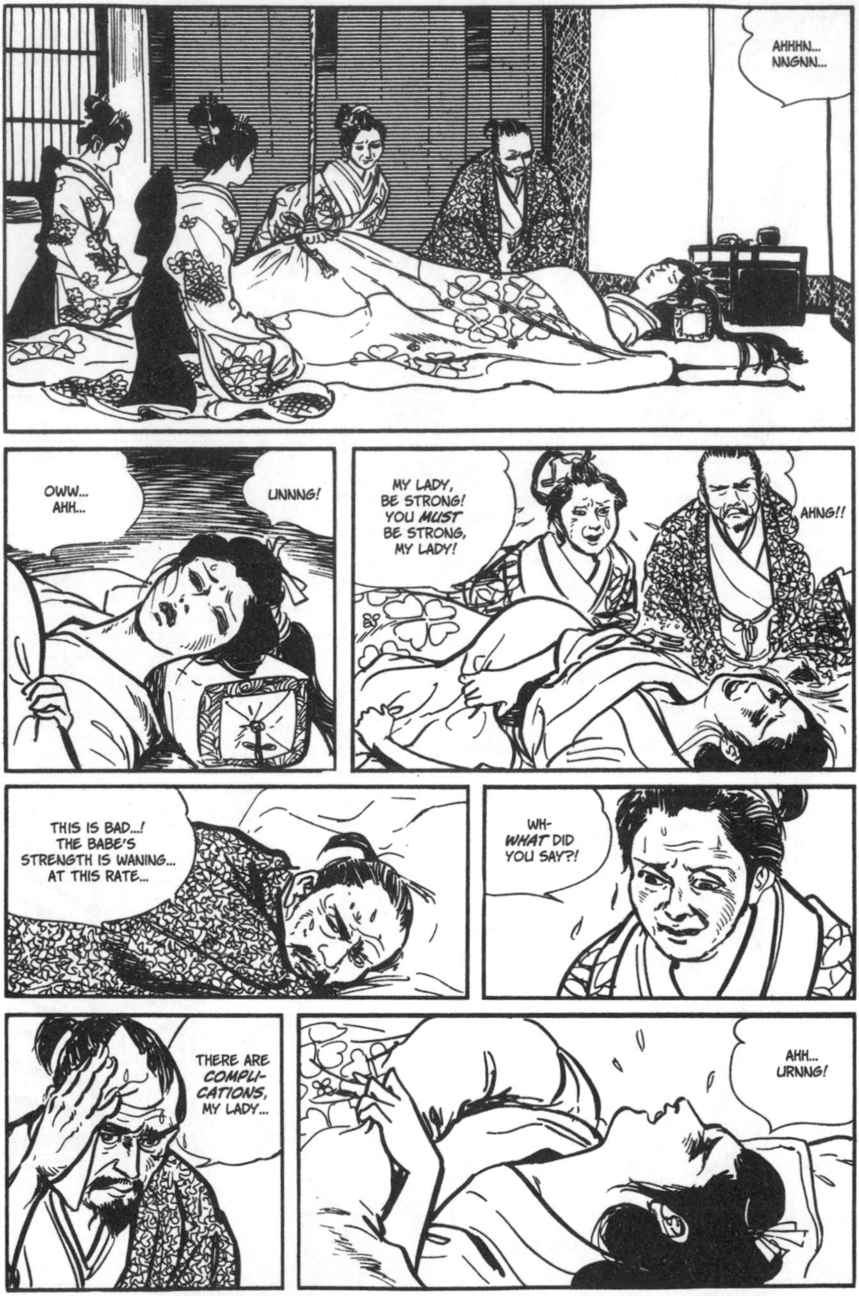
AHHHN... NNGNN...
OWW... AHH...
UNNNG!
MY LADY, BE STRONG! YOU *MUST* BE STRONG, MY LADY!
AHNG!!
THIS IS BAD...! THE BABE'S STRENGTH IS WANING... AT THIS RATE...
WH- *WHAT* DID YOU SAY?!
THERE ARE *COMPLI-CATIONS*, MY LADY...
AHH... URNNG!

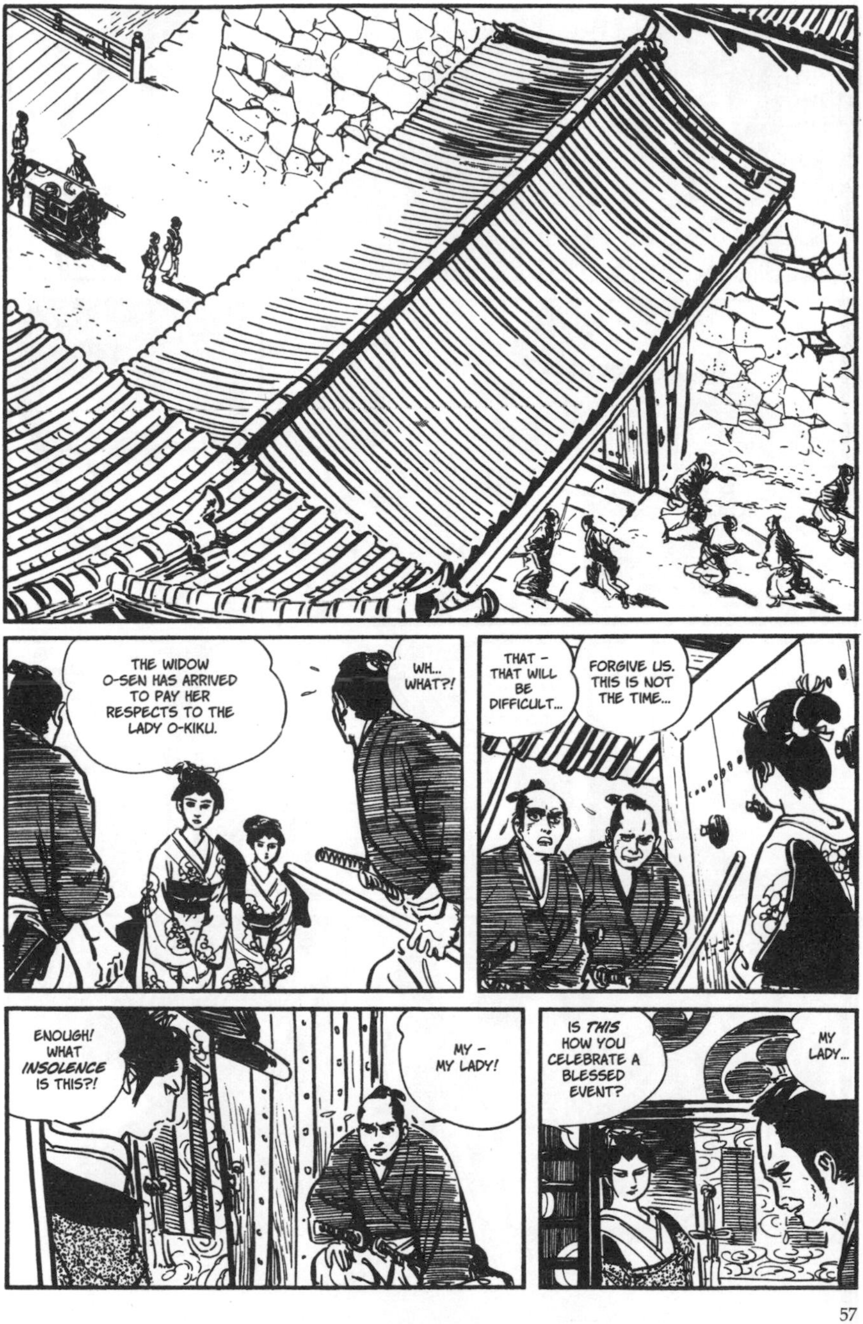
THE WIDOW O-SEN HAS ARRIVED TO PAY HER RESPECTS TO THE LADY O-KIKU.
WH... WHAT?!
THAT - THAT WILL BE DIFFICULT...
FORGIVE US. THIS IS NOT THE TIME...
ENOUGH! WHAT *INSOLENCE* IS THIS?!
MY - MY LADY!
IS *THIS* HOW YOU CELEBRATE A BLESSED EVENT?
MY LADY...

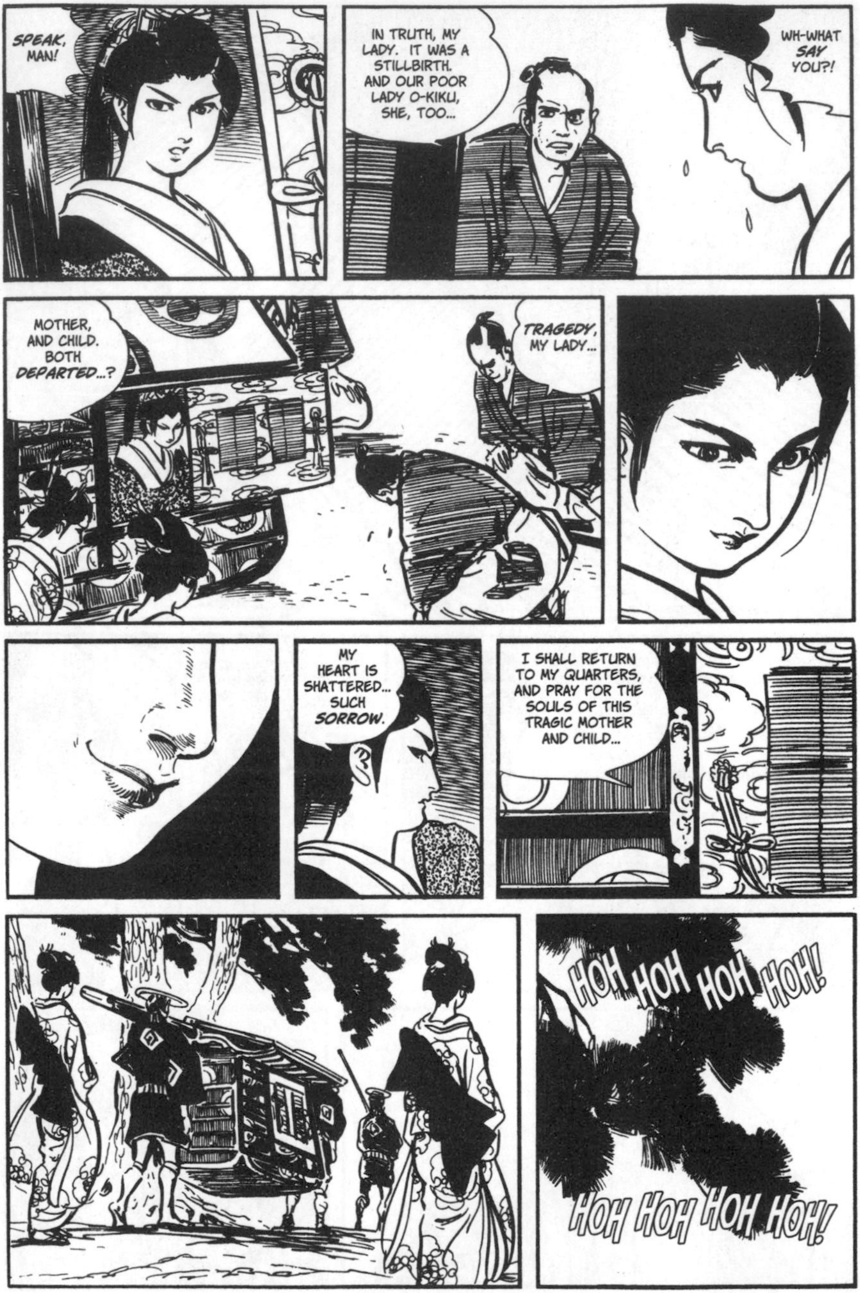
SPEAK, MAN!
IN TRUTH, MY LADY. IT WAS A STILLBIRTH. AND OUR POOR LADY O-KIKU, SHE, TOO...
WH-WHAT SAY YOU?!
MOTHER, AND CHILD. BOTH DEPARTED...?
TRAGEDY, MY LADY...
MY HEART IS SHATTERED... SUCH SORROW.
I SHALL RETURN TO MY QUARTERS, AND PRAY FOR THE SOULS OF THIS TRAGIC MOTHER AND CHILD...
HOH HOH HOH HOH!
HOH HOH HOH HOH!

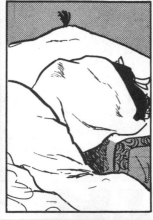

NAMU AMIDA BITSU...

ARE THERE NO *GODS*? IS THERE NO *BUDDHA*...

YOUNG LORD... NONE BUT *YOU* SHALL HAVE IT! NONE BUT *YOU* SHALL INHERIT TAKAI HAN'S SIXTY THOUSAND KOKU, DARLING CHILD!

THOUGH YOU COME INTO THIS WORLD STILLBORN, IT IS *YOURS*, MY LORD! *YOU* ARE STILL MY LORD!

THAT *RŌNIN* SHALL SEE TO IT, MY LORD! THAT *RŌNIN* AND HIS LITTLE BOY!

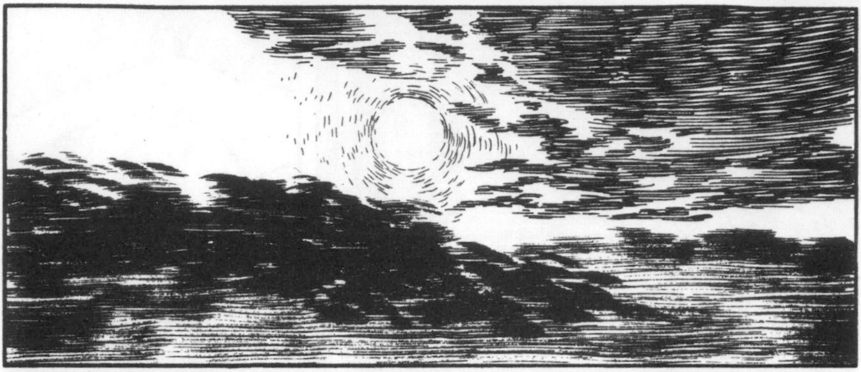

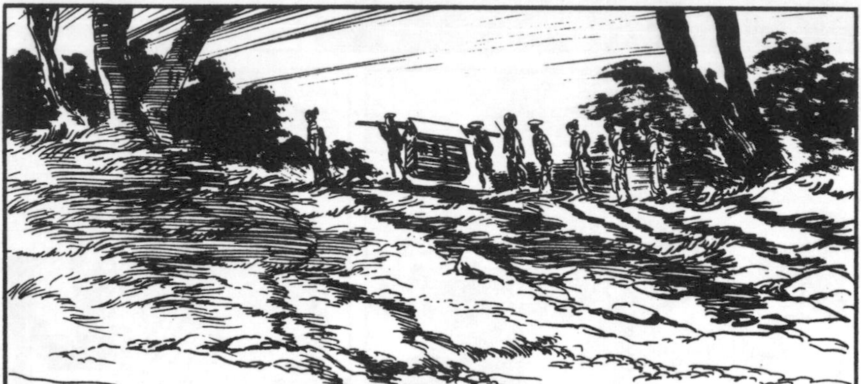

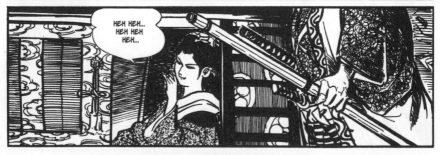

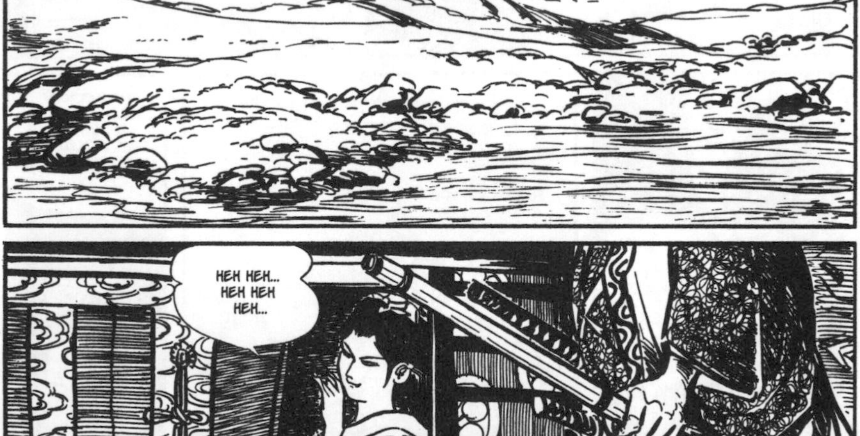
HEH HEH... HEH HEH HEH...

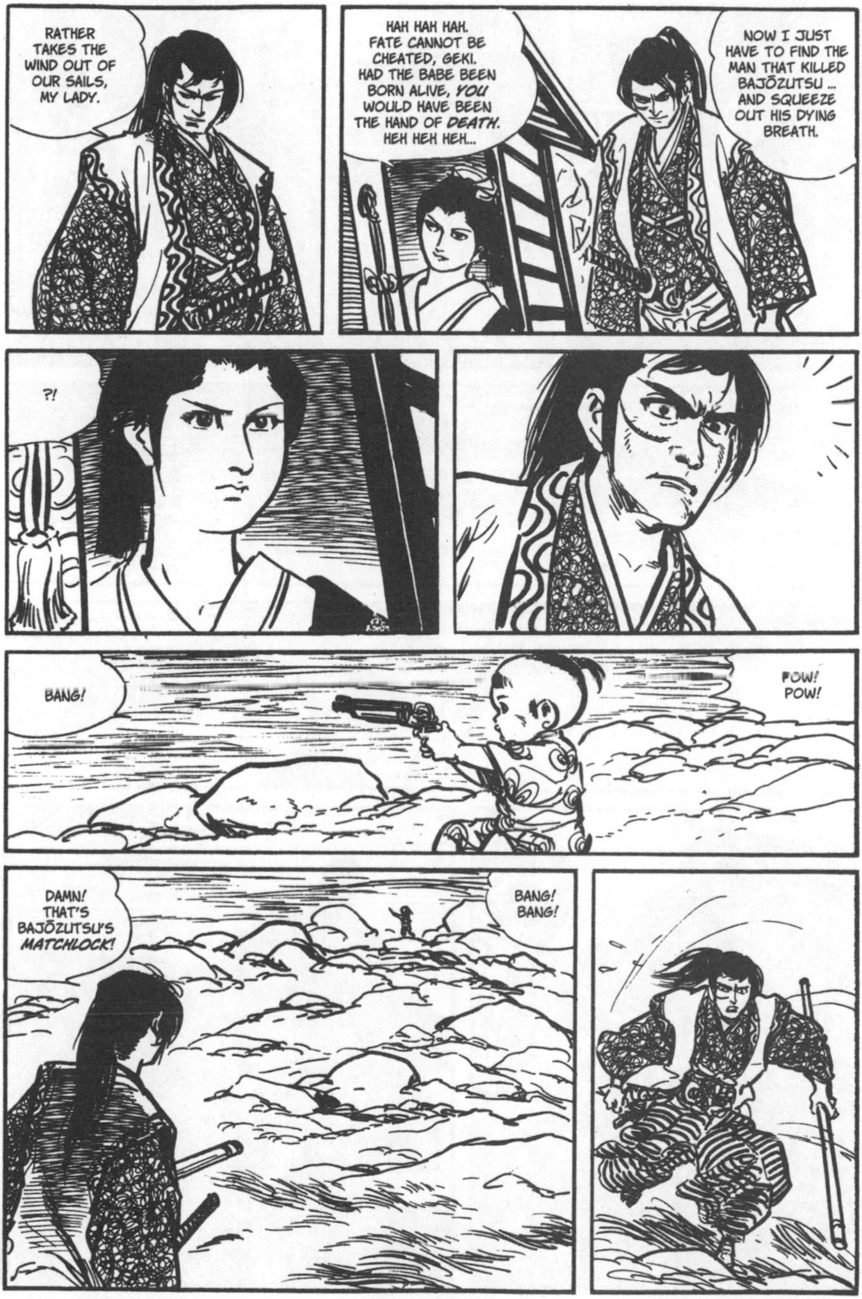
RATHER TAKES THE WIND OUT OF OUR SAILS, MY LADY.
HAH HAH HAH. FATE CANNOT BE CHEATED, GEKI. HAD THE BABE BEEN BORN ALIVE, *YOU* WOULD HAVE BEEN THE HAND OF *DEATH*. HEH HEH HEH...
NOW I JUST HAVE TO FIND THE MAN THAT KILLED BAJŌZUTSU ... AND SQUEEZE OUT HIS DYING BREATH.
?!
BANG!
POW! POW!
DAMN! THAT'S BAJŌZUTSU'S *MATCHLOCK!*
BANG! BANG!

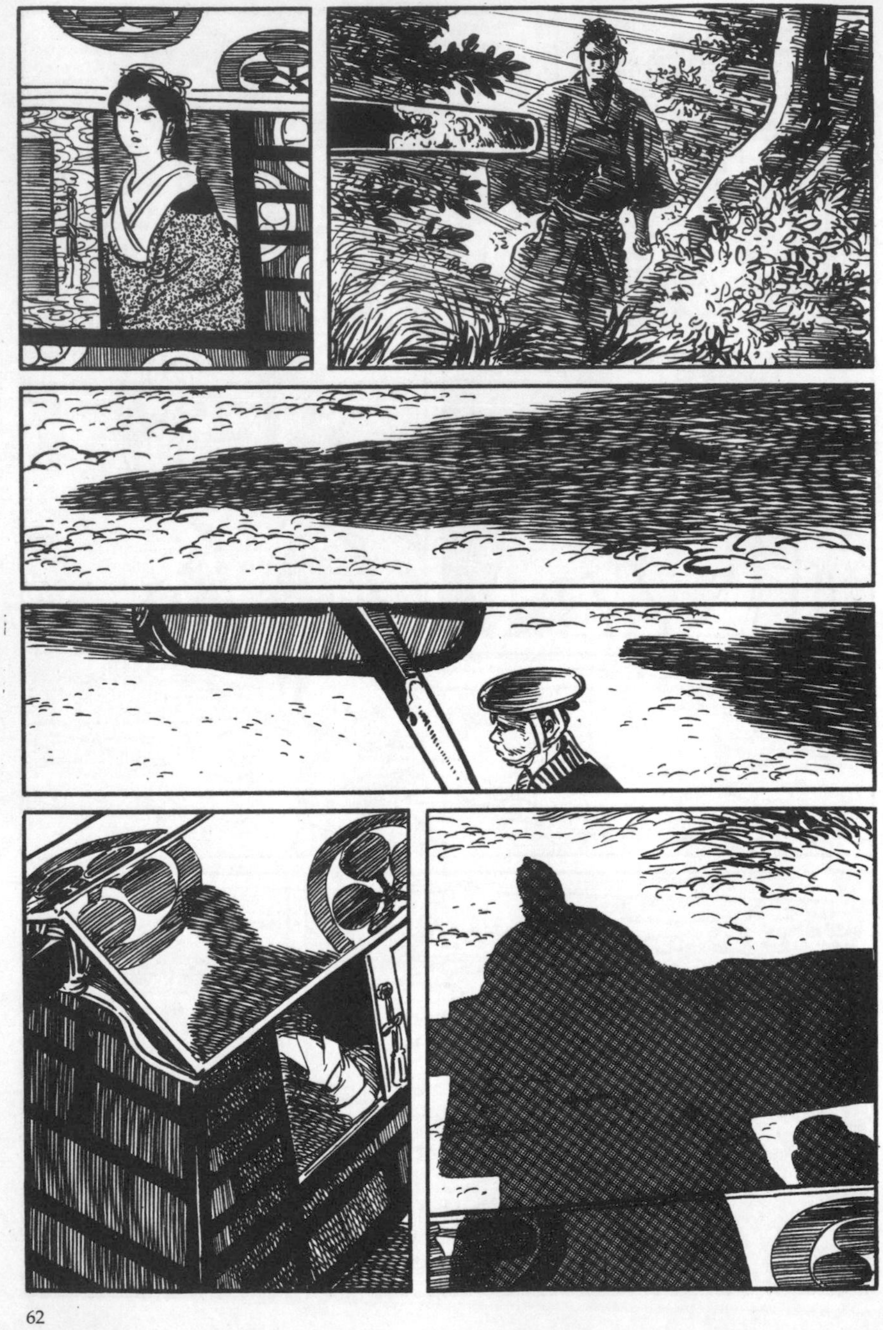

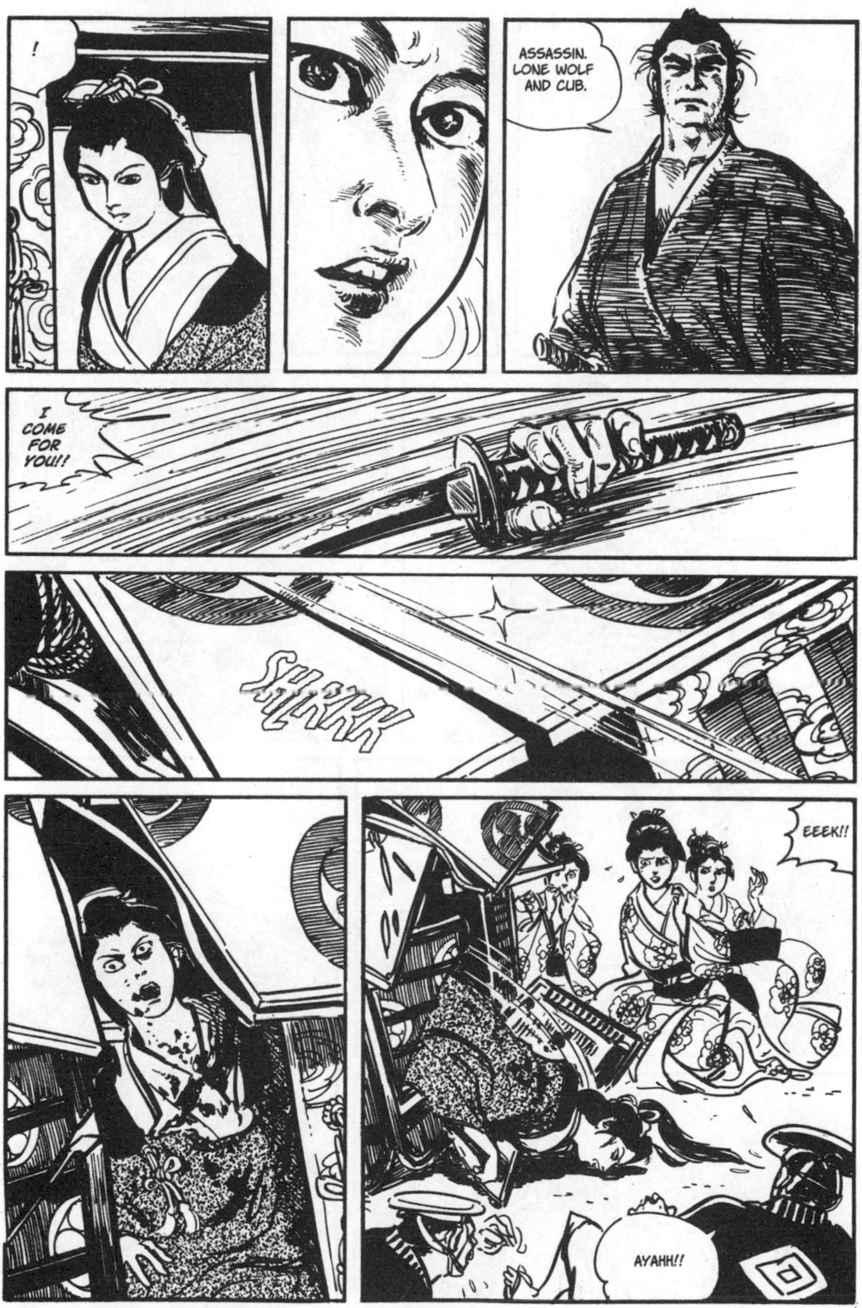
!
ASSASSIN. LONE WOLF AND CUB.
I COME FOR YOU!!
SHRKK
EEEK!!
AYAHH!!

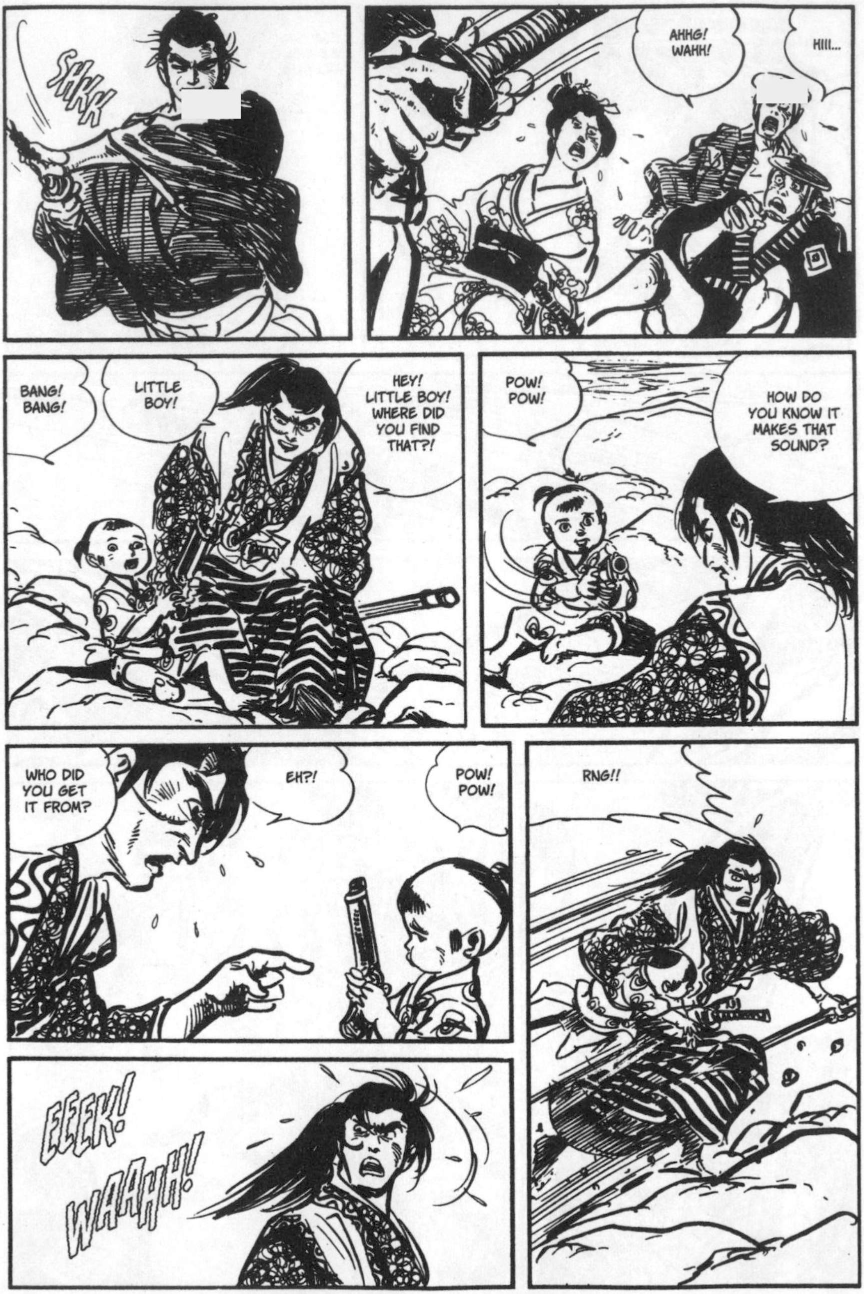
SHKK
AHHG! WAHH!
HIII...
BANG! BANG!
LITTLE BOY!
HEY! LITTLE BOY! WHERE DID YOU FIND THAT?!
POW! POW!
HOW DO YOU KNOW IT MAKES THAT SOUND?
WHO DID YOU GET IT FROM?
EH?!
POW! POW!
EEEK!
WAAHH!
RNG!!

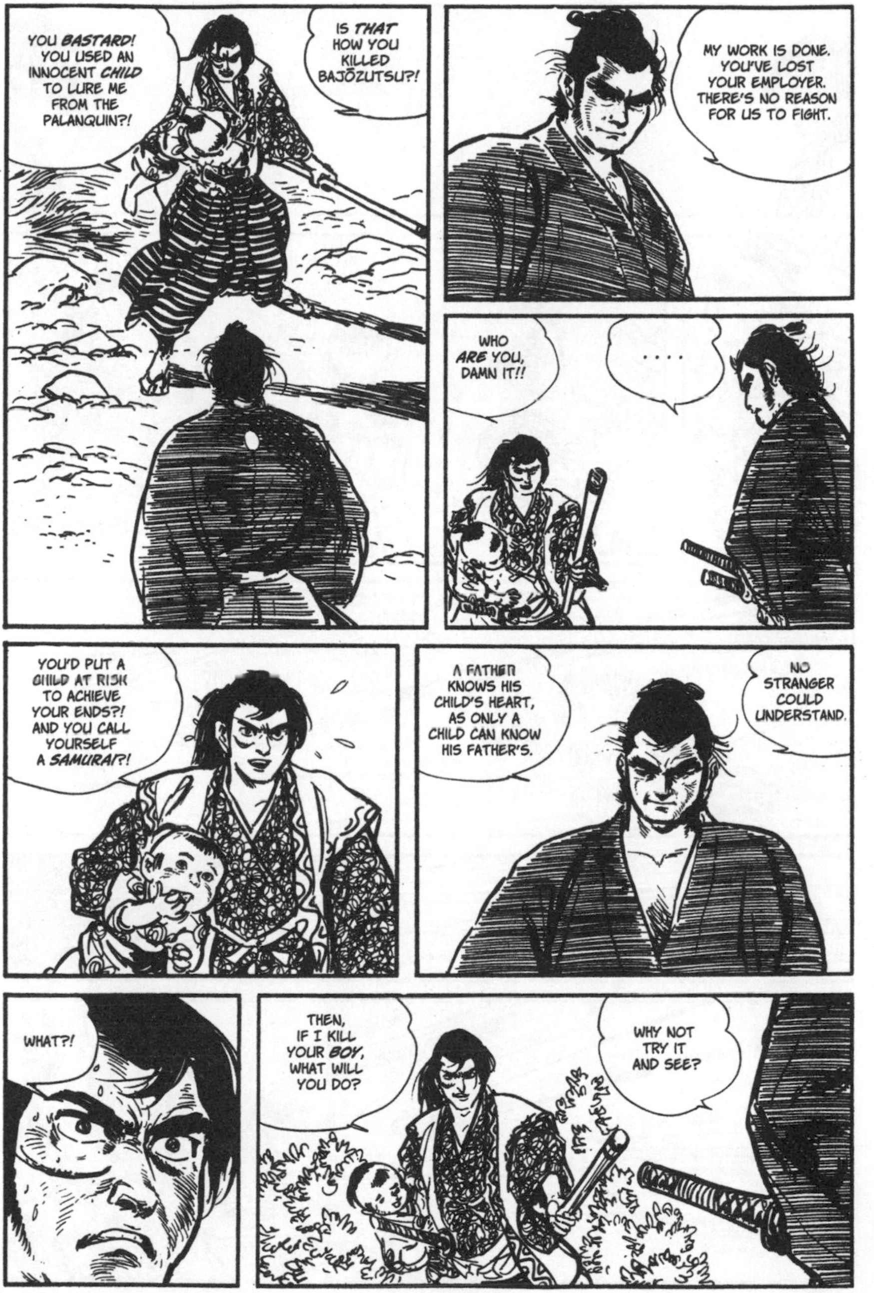
YOU BASTARD! YOU USED AN INNOCENT CHILD TO LURE ME FROM THE PALANQUIN?!
IS THAT HOW YOU KILLED BAJŌZUTSU?!
MY WORK IS DONE. YOU'VE LOST YOUR EMPLOYER. THERE'S NO REASON FOR US TO FIGHT.
WHO ARE YOU, DAMN IT!!
. . . .
YOU'D PUT A CHILD AT RISK TO ACHIEVE YOUR ENDS?! AND YOU CALL YOURSELF A SAMURAI?!
A FATHER KNOWS HIS CHILD'S HEART, AS ONLY A CHILD CAN KNOW HIS FATHER'S.
NO STRANGER COULD UNDERSTAND.
WHAT?!
THEN, IF I KILL YOUR BOY, WHAT WILL YOU DO?
WHY NOT TRY IT AND SEE?

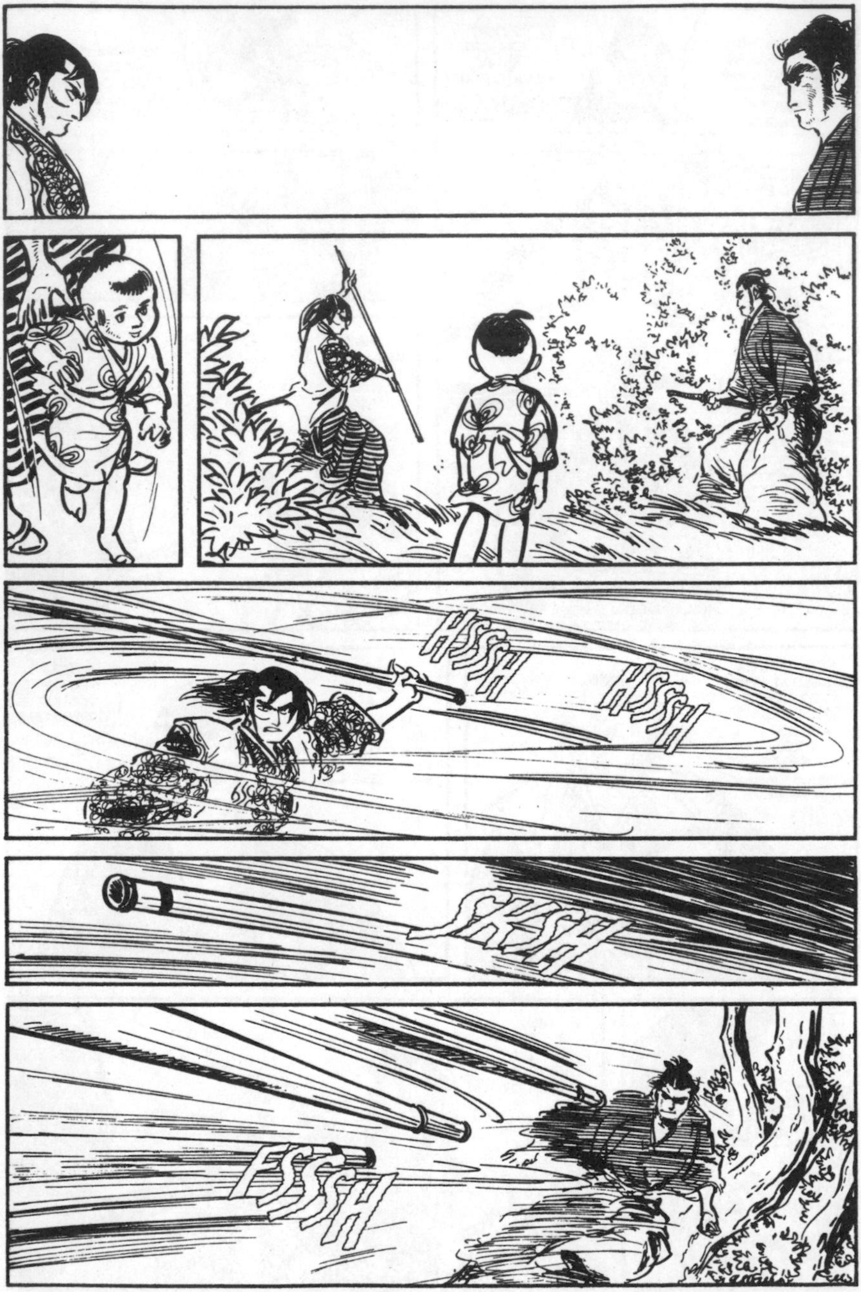
HSSH
HSSH
SKSH
FSSH

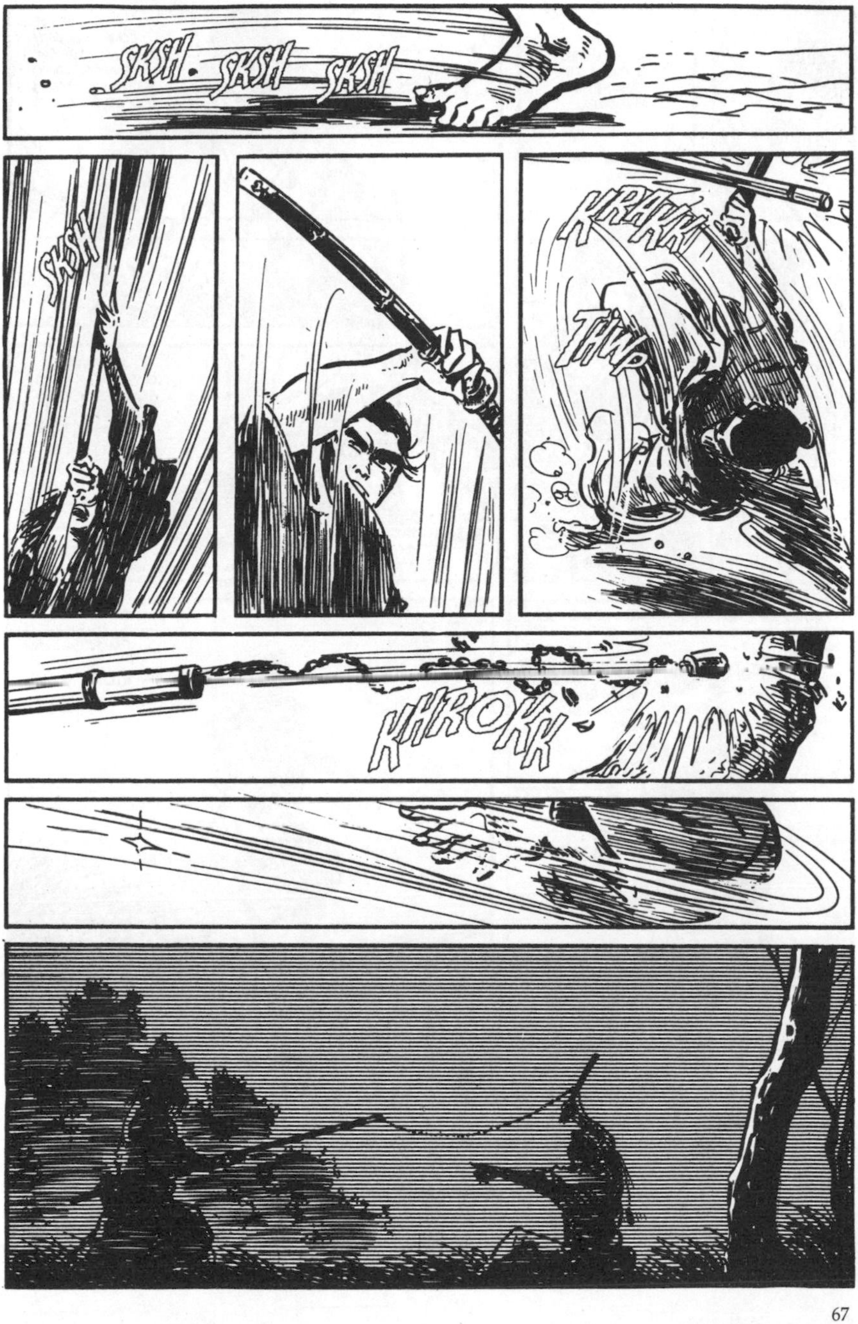
SKSH SKSH SKSH
KRAKK
THWP
SKSH
KHROKK

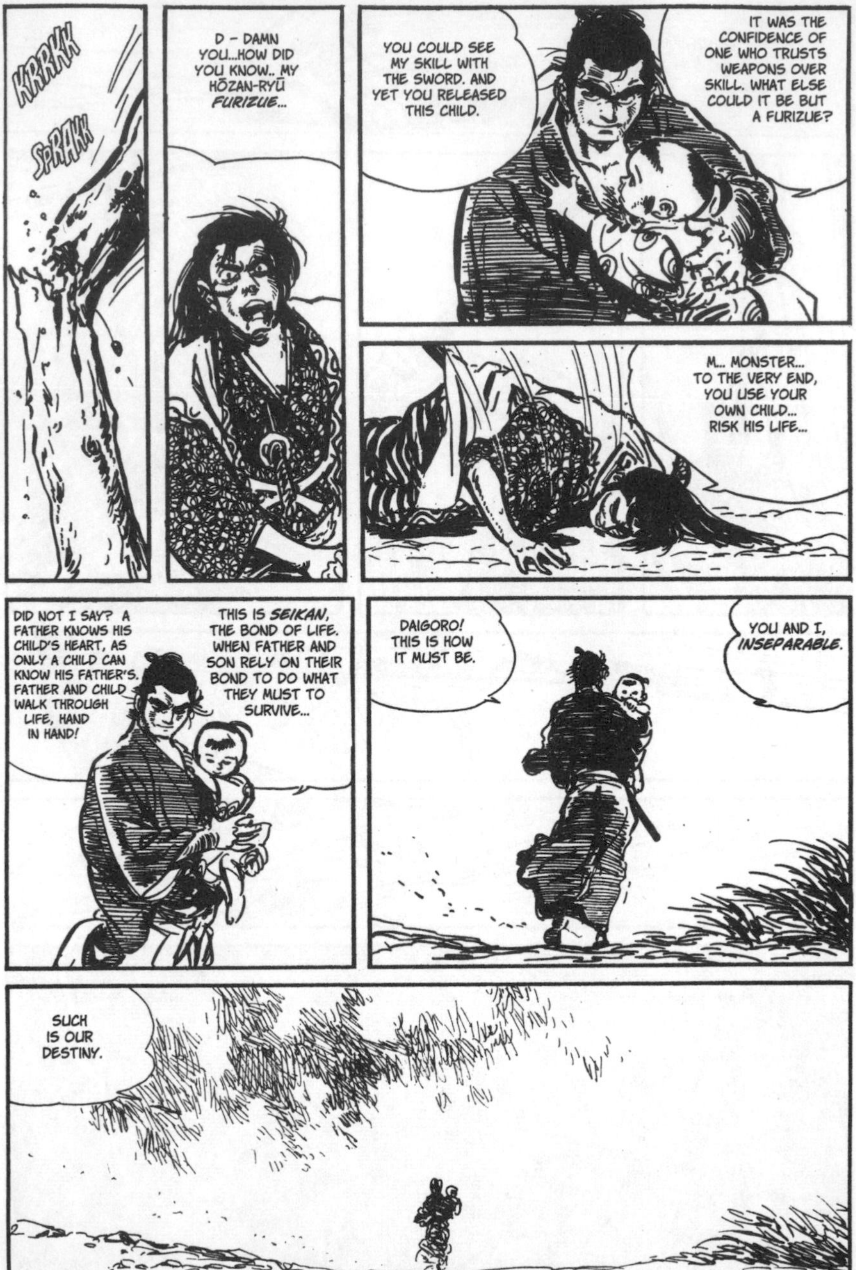
KRRKK
SPRAKK
D – DAMN YOU...HOW DID YOU KNOW.. MY HŌZAN-RYŪ *FURIZUE*...
YOU COULD SEE MY SKILL WITH THE SWORD. AND YET YOU RELEASED THIS CHILD.
IT WAS THE CONFIDENCE OF ONE WHO TRUSTS WEAPONS OVER SKILL. WHAT ELSE COULD IT BE BUT A FURIZUE?
M... MONSTER... TO THE VERY END, YOU USE YOUR OWN CHILD... RISK HIS LIFE...
DID NOT I SAY? A FATHER KNOWS HIS CHILD'S HEART, AS ONLY A CHILD CAN KNOW HIS FATHER'S. FATHER AND CHILD WALK THROUGH LIFE, HAND IN HAND!
THIS IS *SEIKAN*, THE BOND OF LIFE. WHEN FATHER AND SON RELY ON THEIR BOND TO DO WHAT THEY MUST TO SURVIVE...
DAIGORO! THIS IS HOW IT MUST BE.
YOU AND I, *INSEPARABLE*.
SUCH IS OUR DESTINY.

FROM NORTH TO SOUTH, FROM WEST TO EAST

3

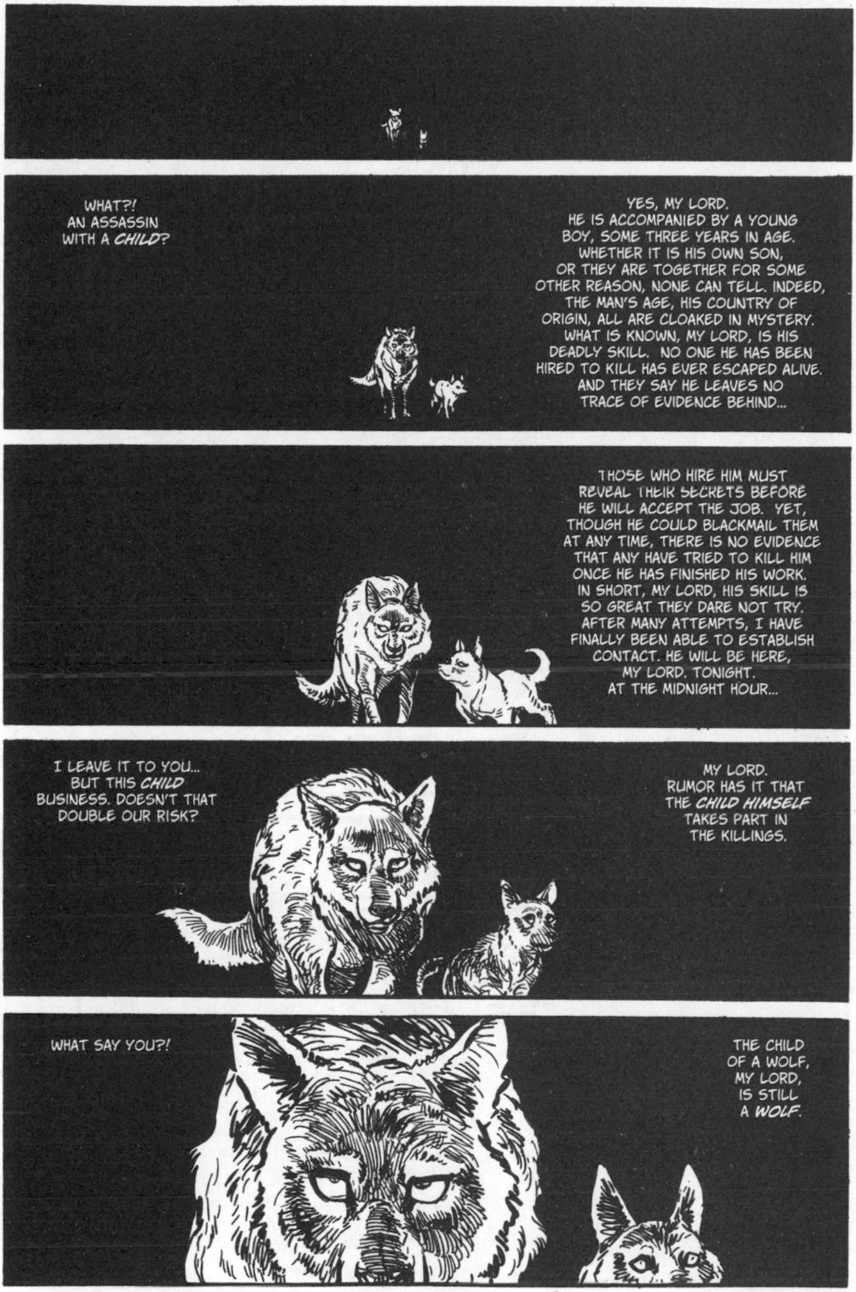
WHAT?! AN ASSASSIN WITH A *CHILD*?
YES, MY LORD. HE IS ACCOMPANIED BY A YOUNG BOY, SOME THREE YEARS IN AGE. WHETHER IT IS HIS OWN SON, OR THEY ARE TOGETHER FOR SOME OTHER REASON, NONE CAN TELL. INDEED, THE MAN'S AGE, HIS COUNTRY OF ORIGIN, ALL ARE CLOAKED IN MYSTERY. WHAT IS KNOWN, MY LORD, IS HIS DEADLY SKILL. NO ONE HE HAS BEEN HIRED TO KILL HAS EVER ESCAPED ALIVE. AND THEY SAY HE LEAVES NO TRACE OF EVIDENCE BEHIND...
THOSE WHO HIRE HIM MUST REVEAL THEIR SECRETS BEFORE HE WILL ACCEPT THE JOB. YET, THOUGH HE COULD BLACKMAIL THEM AT ANY TIME, THERE IS NO EVIDENCE THAT ANY HAVE TRIED TO KILL HIM ONCE HE HAS FINISHED HIS WORK. IN SHORT, MY LORD, HIS SKILL IS SO GREAT THEY DARE NOT TRY. AFTER MANY ATTEMPTS, I HAVE FINALLY BEEN ABLE TO ESTABLISH CONTACT. HE WILL BE HERE, MY LORD. TONIGHT. AT THE MIDNIGHT HOUR...
I LEAVE IT TO YOU... BUT THIS *CHILD* BUSINESS. DOESN'T THAT DOUBLE OUR RISK?
MY LORD. RUMOR HAS IT THAT THE *CHILD HIMSELF* TAKES PART IN THE KILLINGS.
WHAT SAY YOU?!
THE CHILD OF A WOLF, MY LORD, IS STILL A *WOLF*.

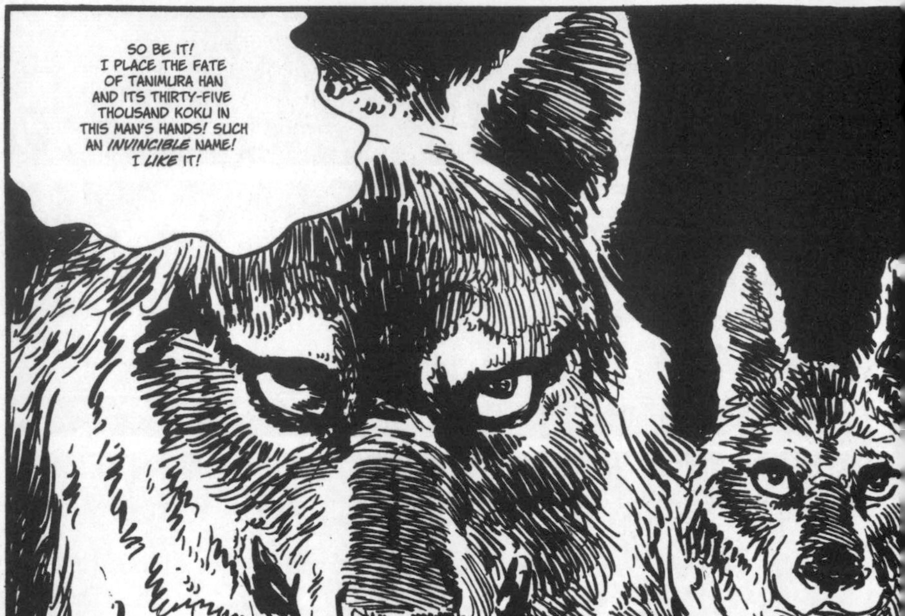
SO BE IT! I PLACE THE FATE OF TANIMURA HAN AND ITS THIRTY-FIVE THOUSAND KOKU IN THIS MAN'S HANDS! SUCH AN *INVINCIBLE* NAME! I *LIKE* IT!
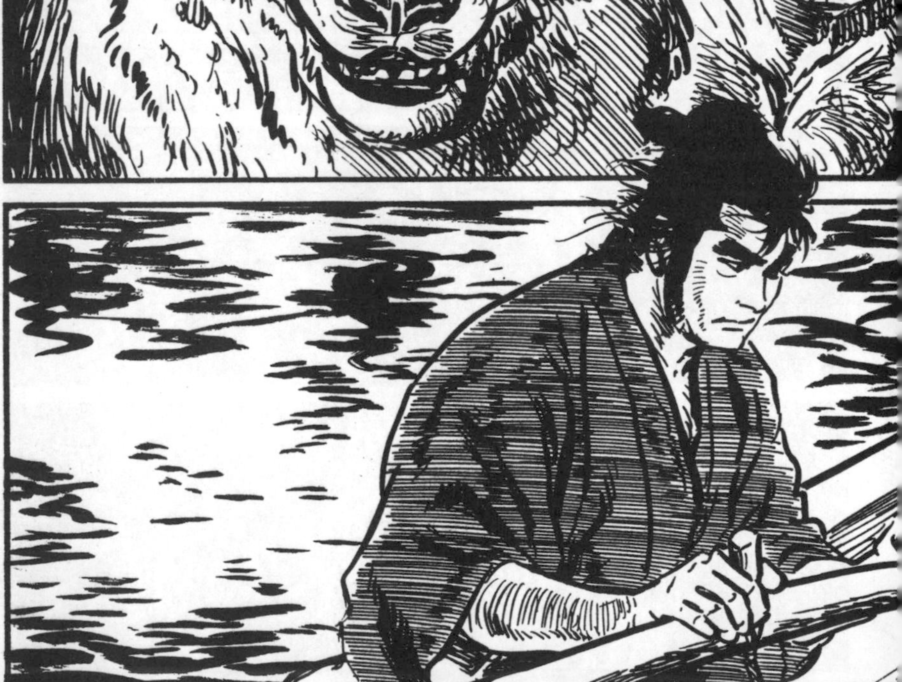

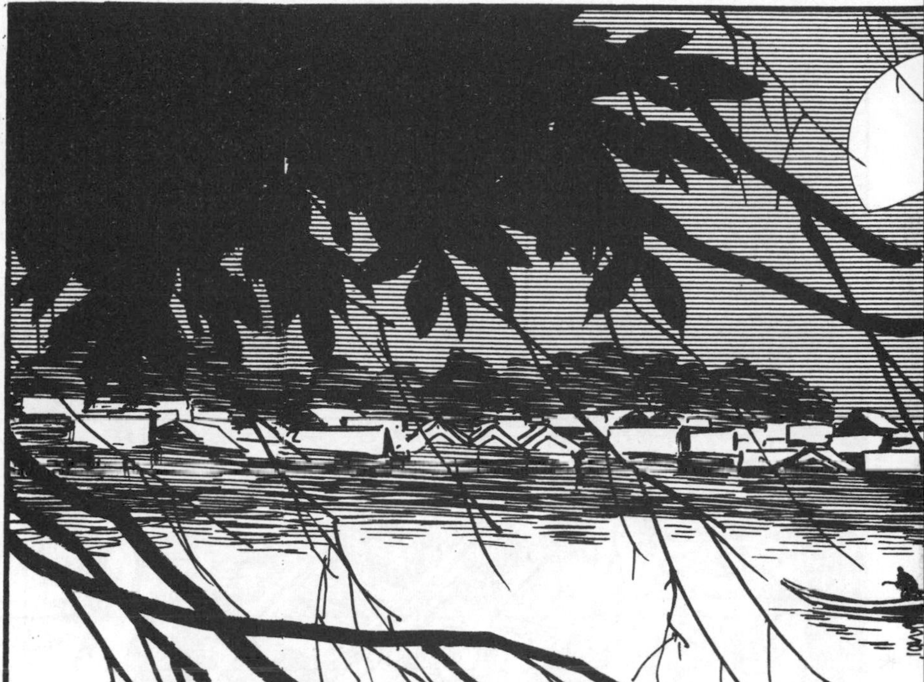
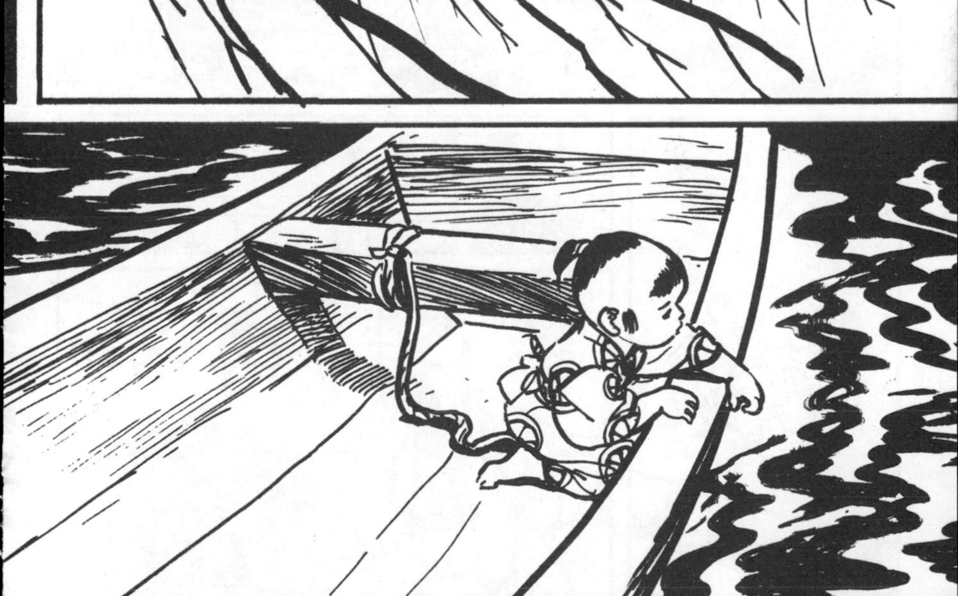

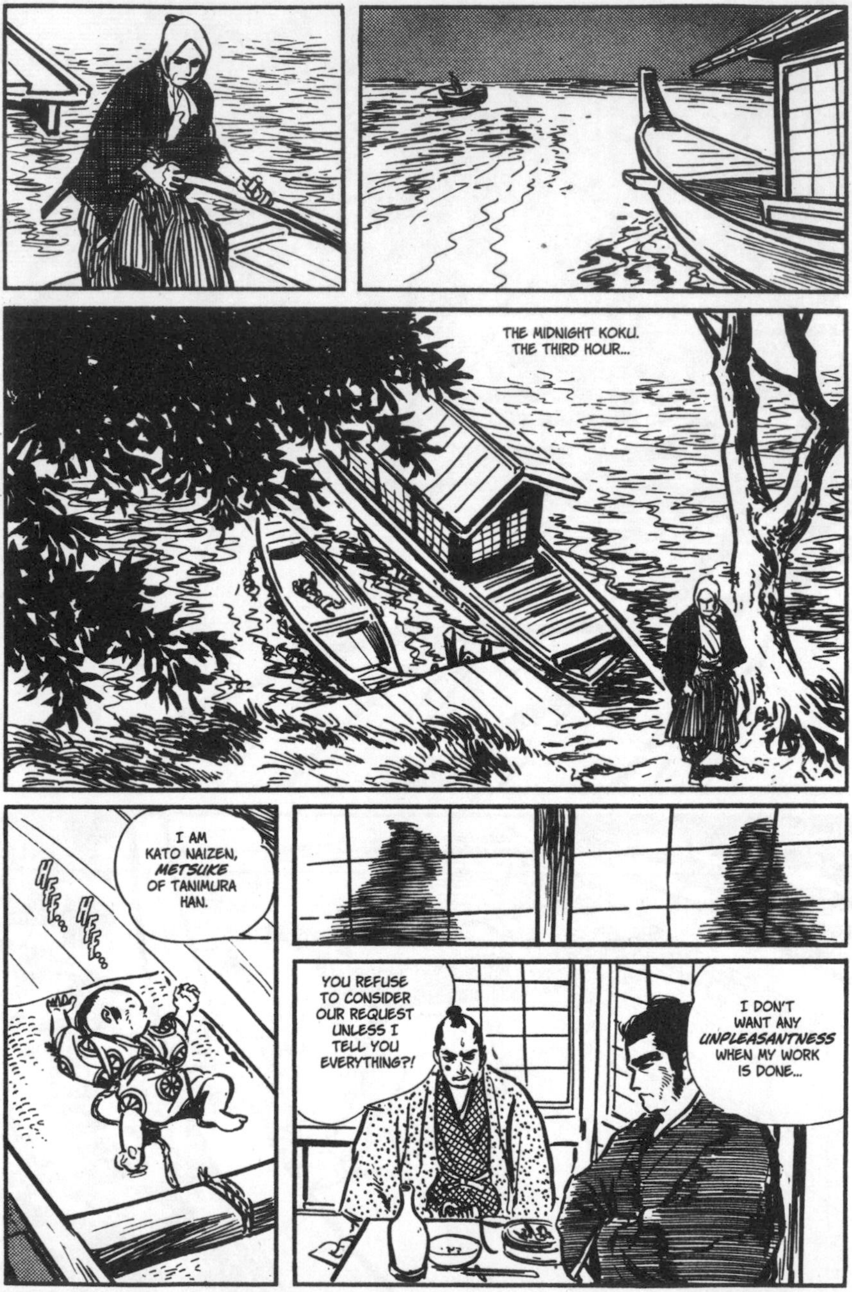
THE MIDNIGHT KOKU. THE THIRD HOUR...
I AM KATO NAIZEN, *METSUKE* OF TANIMURA HAN.
HFF... HFF...
YOU REFUSE TO CONSIDER OUR REQUEST UNLESS I TELL YOU EVERYTHING?!
I DON'T WANT ANY *UNPLEASANTNESS* WHEN MY WORK IS DONE...

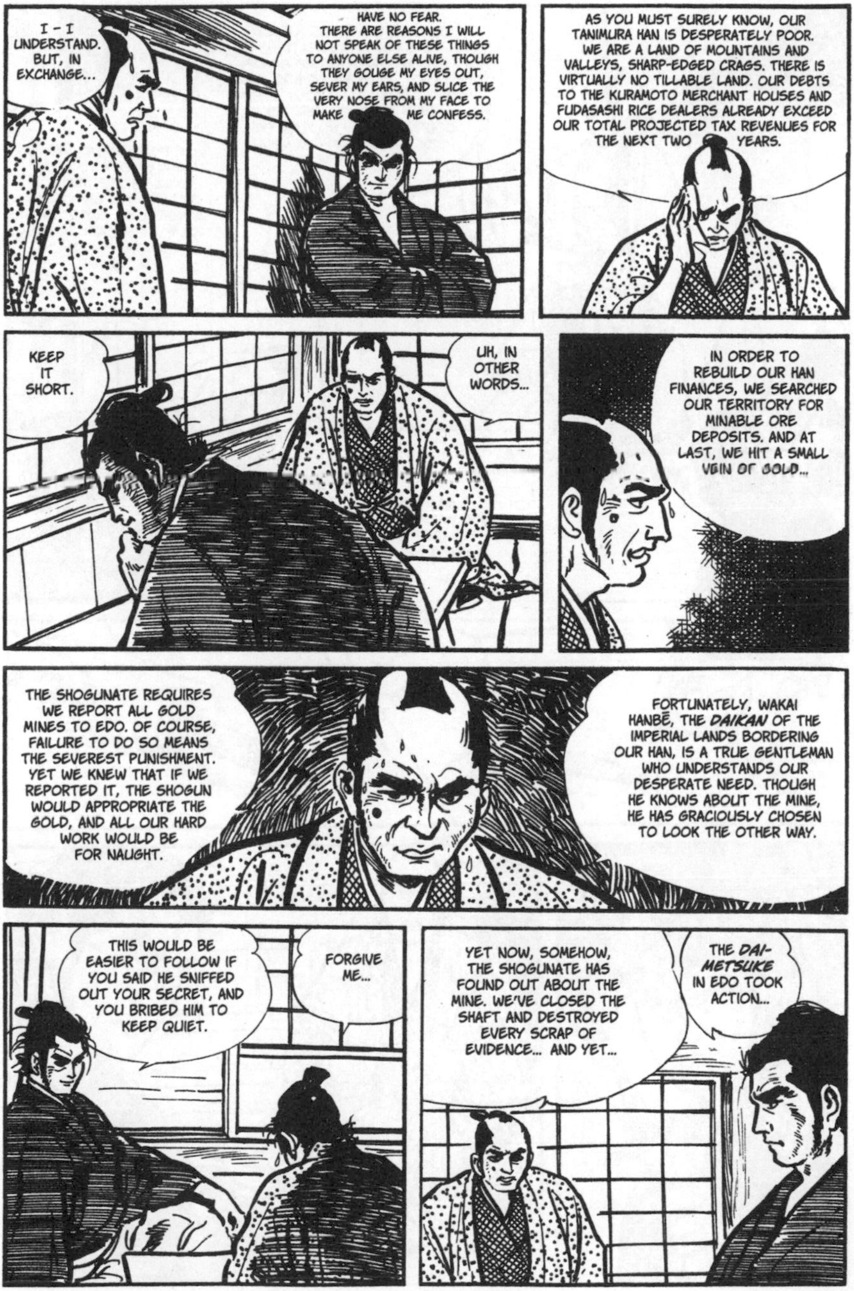
I - I UNDERSTAND. BUT, IN EXCHANGE...
HAVE NO FEAR. THERE ARE REASONS I WILL NOT SPEAK OF THESE THINGS TO ANYONE ELSE ALIVE, THOUGH THEY GOUGE MY EYES OUT, SEVER MY EARS, AND SLICE THE VERY NOSE FROM MY FACE TO MAKE ME CONFESS.
AS YOU MUST SURELY KNOW, OUR TANIMURA HAN IS DESPERATELY POOR. WE ARE A LAND OF MOUNTAINS AND VALLEYS, SHARP-EDGED CRAGS. THERE IS VIRTUALLY NO TILLABLE LAND. OUR DEBTS TO THE KURAMOTO MERCHANT HOUSES AND FUDASASHI RICE DEALERS ALREADY EXCEED OUR TOTAL PROJECTED TAX REVENUES FOR THE NEXT TWO YEARS.
KEEP IT SHORT.
UH, IN OTHER WORDS...
IN ORDER TO REBUILD OUR HAN FINANCES, WE SEARCHED OUR TERRITORY FOR MINABLE ORE DEPOSITS. AND AT LAST, WE HIT A SMALL VEIN OF GOLD...
THE SHOGUNATE REQUIRES WE REPORT ALL GOLD MINES TO EDO. OF COURSE, FAILURE TO DO SO MEANS THE SEVEREST PUNISHMENT. YET WE KNEW THAT IF WE REPORTED IT, THE SHOGUN WOULD APPROPRIATE THE GOLD, AND ALL OUR HARD WORK WOULD BE FOR NAUGHT.
FORTUNATELY, WAKAI HANBĒ, THE *DAIKAN* OF THE IMPERIAL LANDS BORDERING OUR HAN, IS A TRUE GENTLEMAN WHO UNDERSTANDS OUR DESPERATE NEED. THOUGH HE KNOWS ABOUT THE MINE, HE HAS GRACIOUSLY CHOSEN TO LOOK THE OTHER WAY.
THIS WOULD BE EASIER TO FOLLOW IF YOU SAID HE SNIFFED OUT YOUR SECRET, AND YOU BRIBED HIM TO KEEP QUIET.
FORGIVE ME...
YET NOW, SOMEHOW, THE SHOGUNATE HAS FOUND OUT ABOUT THE MINE. WE'VE CLOSED THE SHAFT AND DESTROYED EVERY SCRAP OF EVIDENCE... AND YET...
THE *DAI-METSUKE* IN EDO TOOK ACTION...

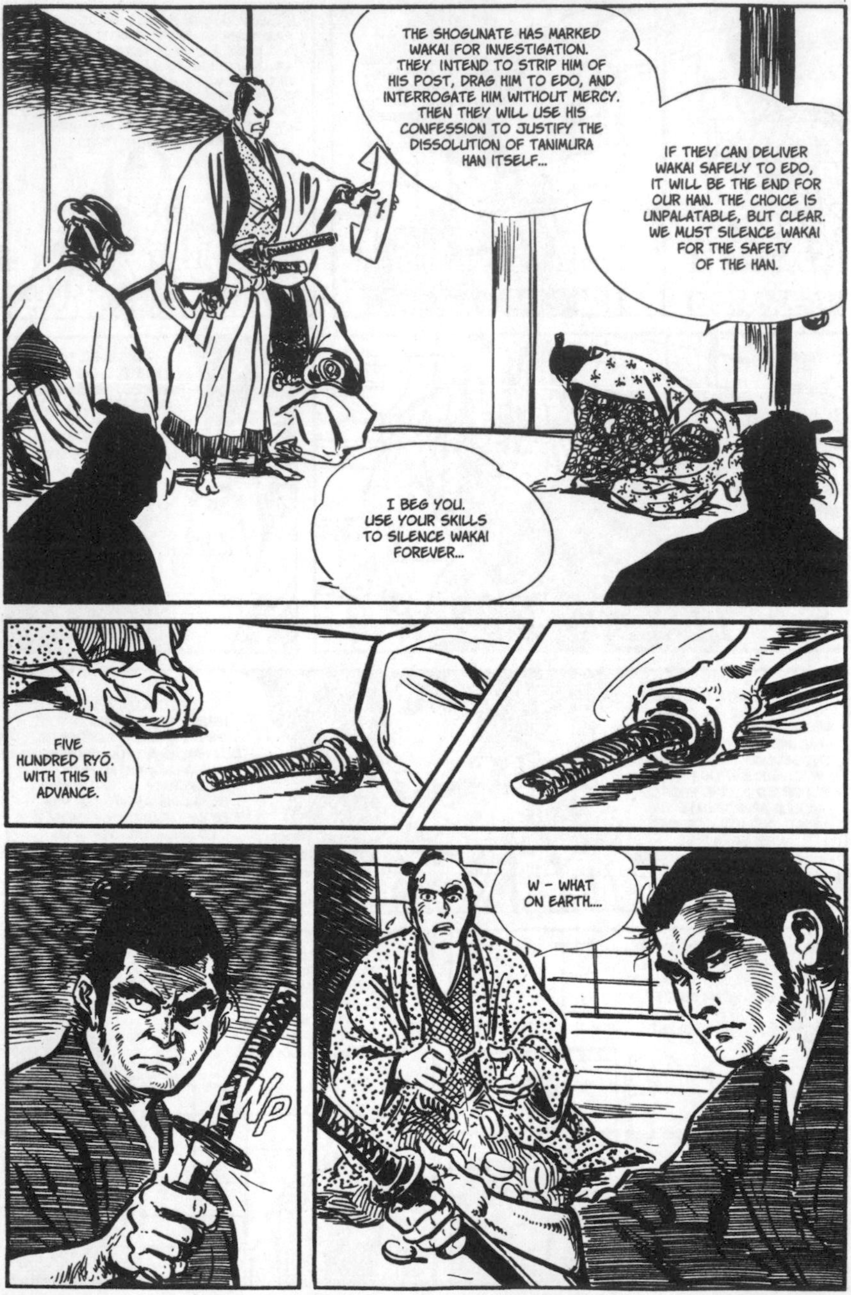
THE SHOGUNATE HAS MARKED WAKAI FOR INVESTIGATION. THEY INTEND TO STRIP HIM OF HIS POST, DRAG HIM TO EDO, AND INTERROGATE HIM WITHOUT MERCY. THEN THEY WILL USE HIS CONFESSION TO JUSTIFY THE DISSOLUTION OF TANIMURA HAN ITSELF...
IF THEY CAN DELIVER WAKAI SAFELY TO EDO, IT WILL BE THE END FOR OUR HAN. THE CHOICE IS UNPALATABLE, BUT CLEAR. WE MUST SILENCE WAKAI FOR THE SAFETY OF THE HAN.
I BEG YOU. USE YOUR SKILLS TO SILENCE WAKAI FOREVER...
FIVE HUNDRED RYŌ. WITH THIS IN ADVANCE.
FWP
W - WHAT ON EARTH....

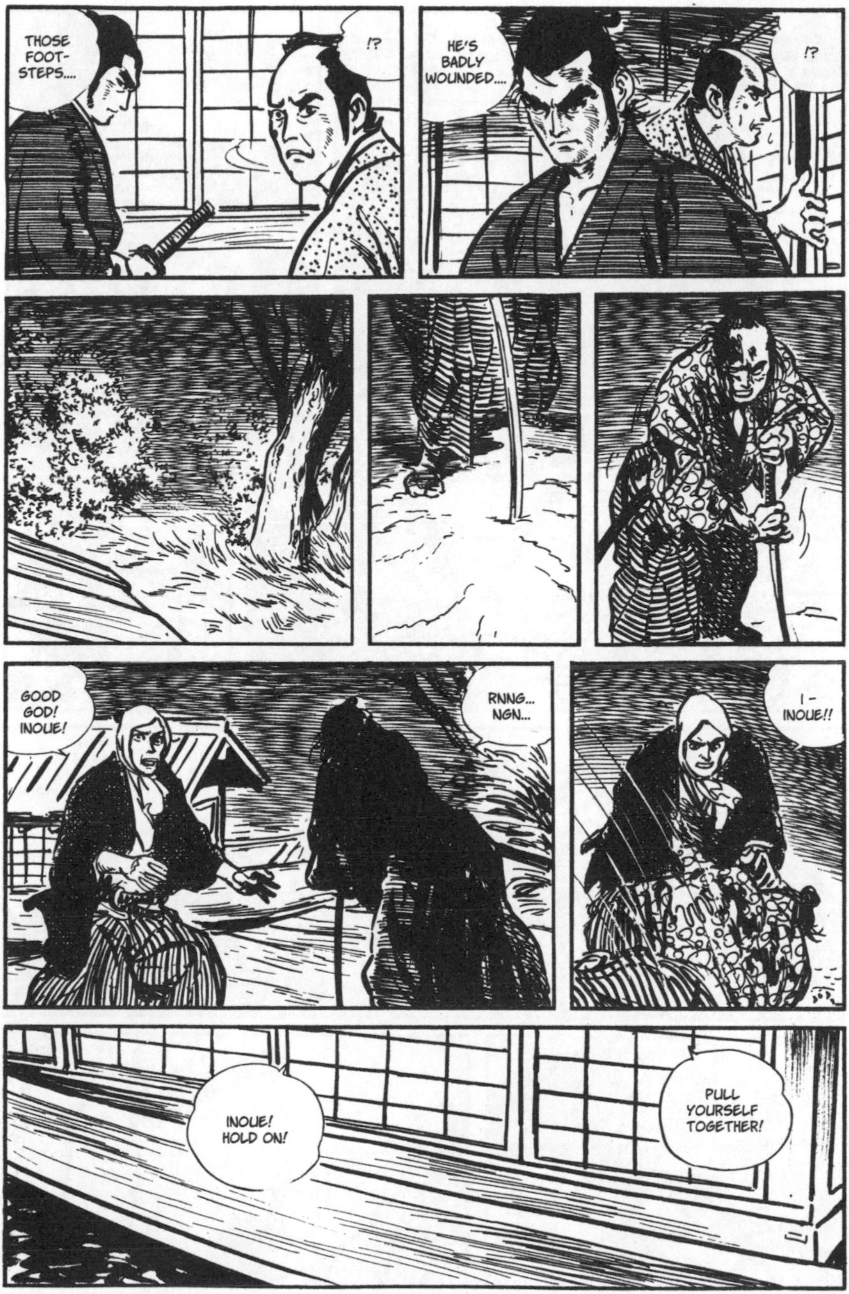
THOSE FOOT-STEPS....
!?
HE'S BADLY WOUNDED....
!?
GOOD GOD! INOUE!
RNNG... NGN...
I- INOUE!!
INOUE! HOLD ON!
PULL YOURSELF TOGETHER!

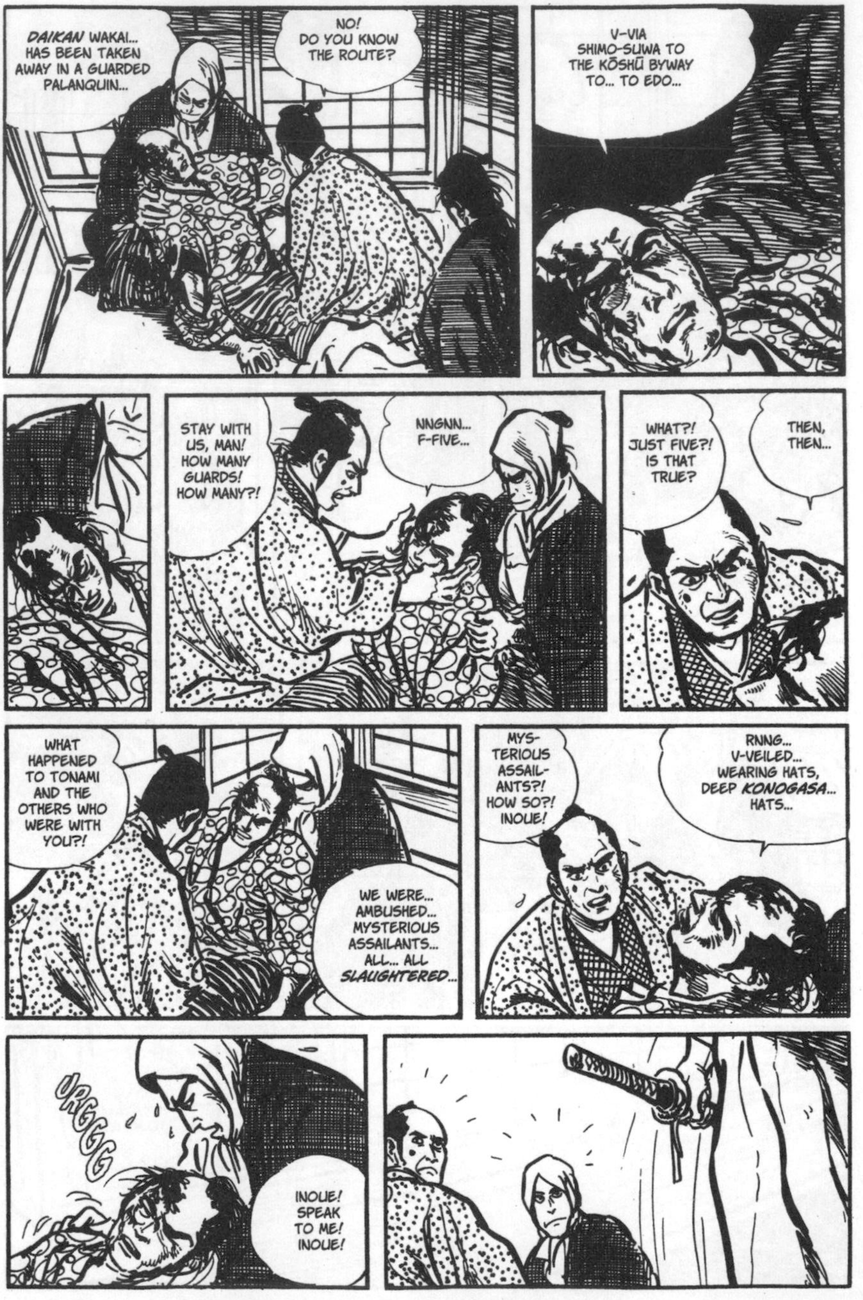
DAIKAN WAKAI... HAS BEEN TAKEN AWAY IN A GUARDED PALANQUIN...
NO! DO YOU KNOW THE ROUTE?
V-VIA SHIMO-SUWA TO THE KŌSHŪ BYWAY TO... TO EDO...
STAY WITH US, MAN! HOW MANY GUARDS! HOW MANY?!
NNGNN... F-FIVE...
WHAT?! JUST FIVE?! IS THAT TRUE?
THEN, THEN...
WHAT HAPPENED TO TONAMI AND THE OTHERS WHO WERE WITH YOU?!
WE WERE... AMBUSHED... MYSTERIOUS ASSAILANTS... ALL... ALL SLAUGHTERED...
MYS-TERIOUS ASSAIL-ANTS?! HOW SO?! INOUE!
RNNG... V-VEILED... WEARING HATS, DEEP KONOGASA... HATS...
URGGG
INOUE! SPEAK TO ME! INOUE!

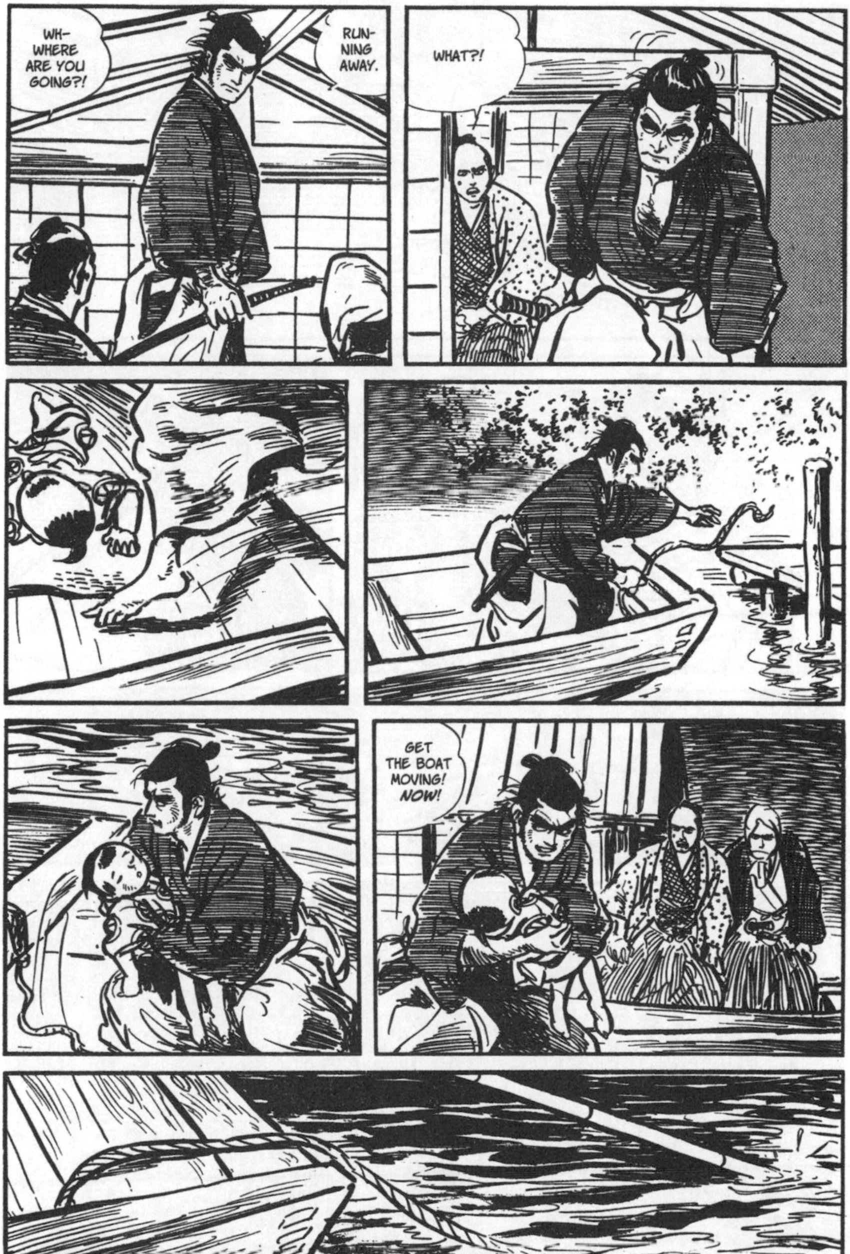
WH-WHERE ARE YOU GOING?!
RUN-NING AWAY.
WHAT?!
GET THE BOAT MOVING! *NOW!*

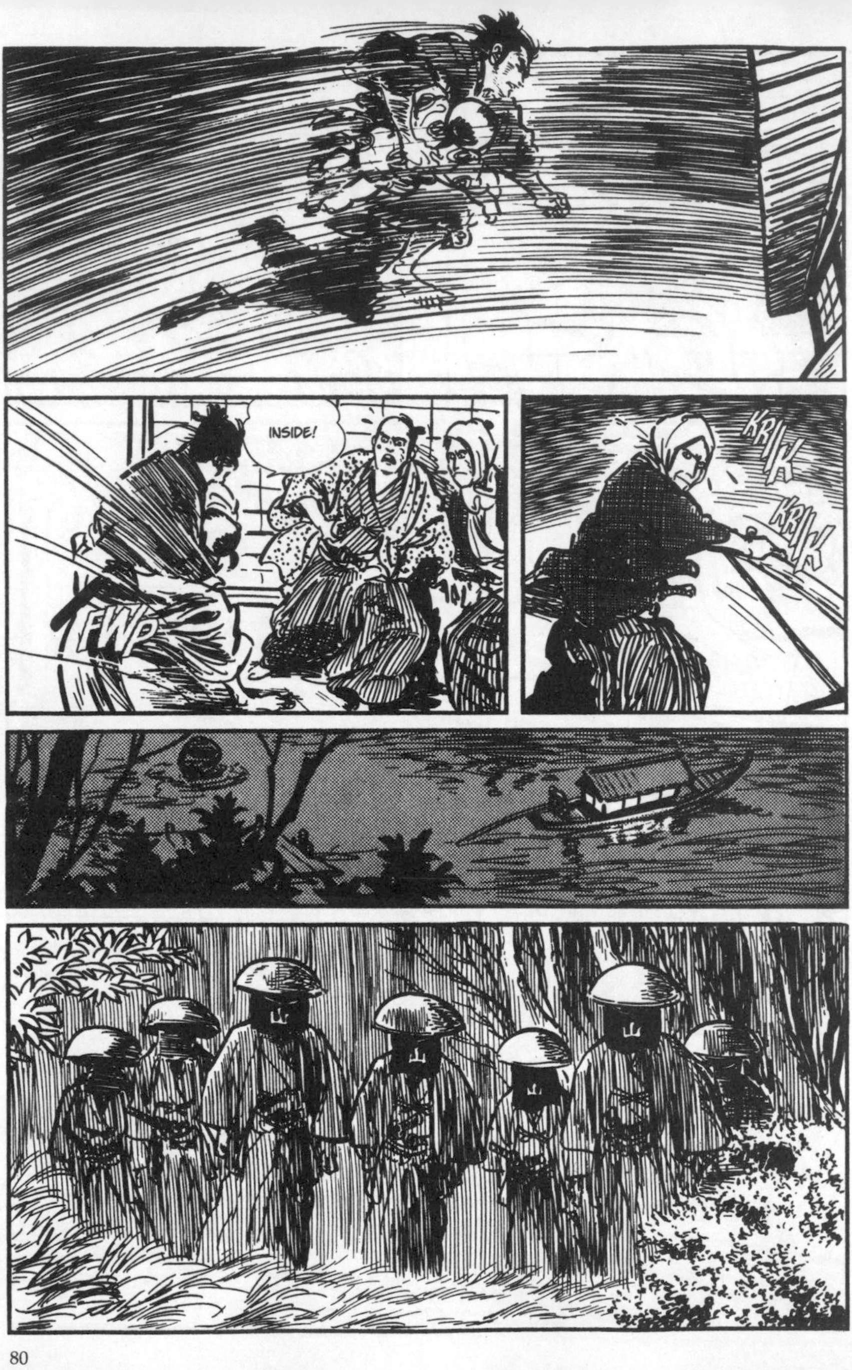
INSIDE!
FWP
KRIK
KRIK

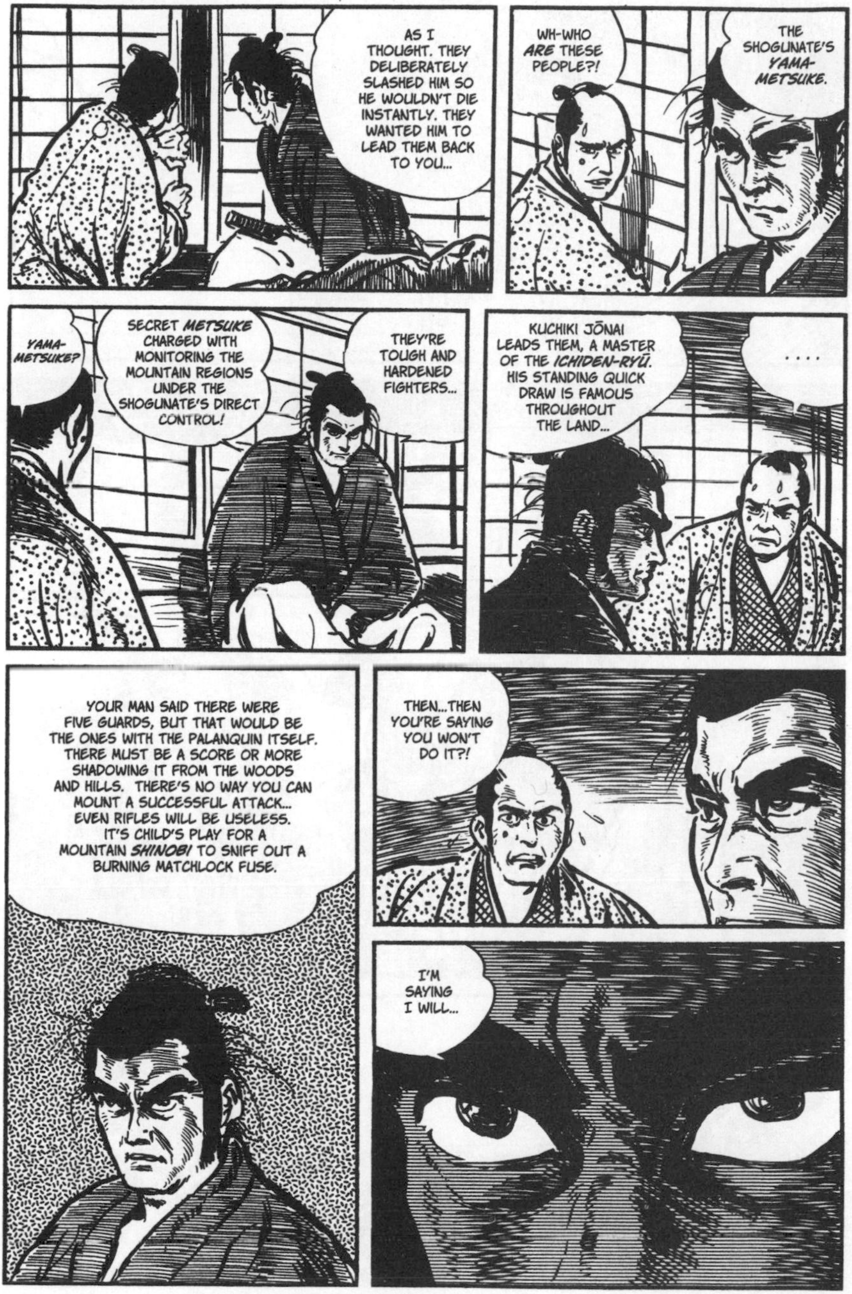
AS I THOUGHT. THEY DELIBERATELY SLASHED HIM SO HE WOULDN'T DIE INSTANTLY. THEY WANTED HIM TO LEAD THEM BACK TO YOU...
WH-WHO *ARE* THESE PEOPLE?!
THE SHOGUNATE'S *YAMA-METSUKE*.
YAMA-METSUKE?
SECRET *METSUKE* CHARGED WITH MONITORING THE MOUNTAIN REGIONS UNDER THE SHOGUNATE'S DIRECT CONTROL!
THEY'RE TOUGH AND HARDENED FIGHTERS...
KUCHIKI JŌNAI LEADS THEM, A MASTER OF THE *ICHIDEN-RYŪ*. HIS STANDING QUICK DRAW IS FAMOUS THROUGHOUT THE LAND...
....
YOUR MAN SAID THERE WERE FIVE GUARDS, BUT THAT WOULD BE THE ONES WITH THE PALANQUIN ITSELF. THERE MUST BE A SCORE OR MORE SHADOWING IT FROM THE WOODS AND HILLS. THERE'S NO WAY YOU CAN MOUNT A SUCCESSFUL ATTACK... EVEN RIFLES WILL BE USELESS. IT'S CHILD'S PLAY FOR A MOUNTAIN *SHINOBI* TO SNIFF OUT A BURNING MATCHLOCK FUSE.
THEN...THEN YOU'RE SAYING YOU WON'T DO IT?!
I'M SAYING I WILL...

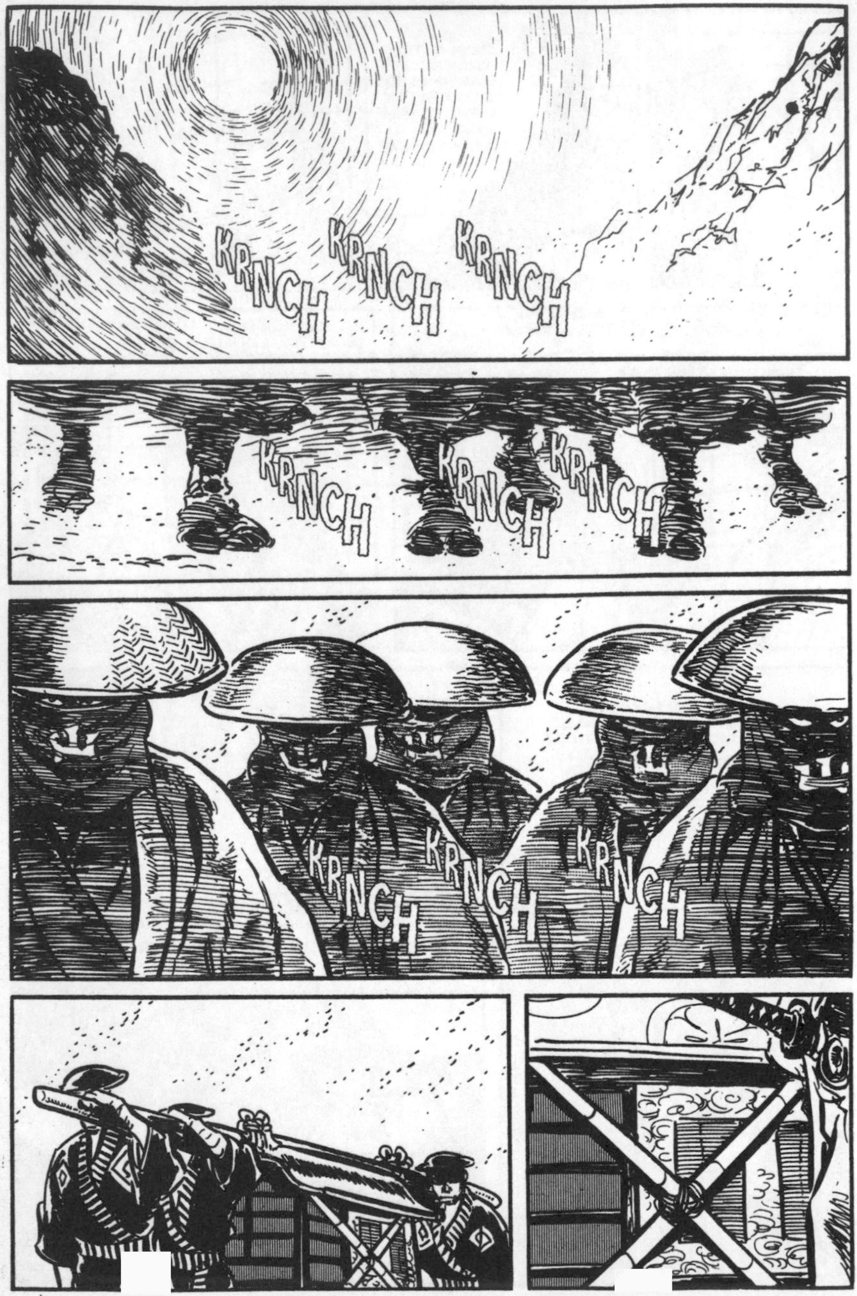
KRNCH
KRNCH
KRNCH
KRNCH
KRNCH
KRNCH
KRNCH
KRNCH
KRNCH

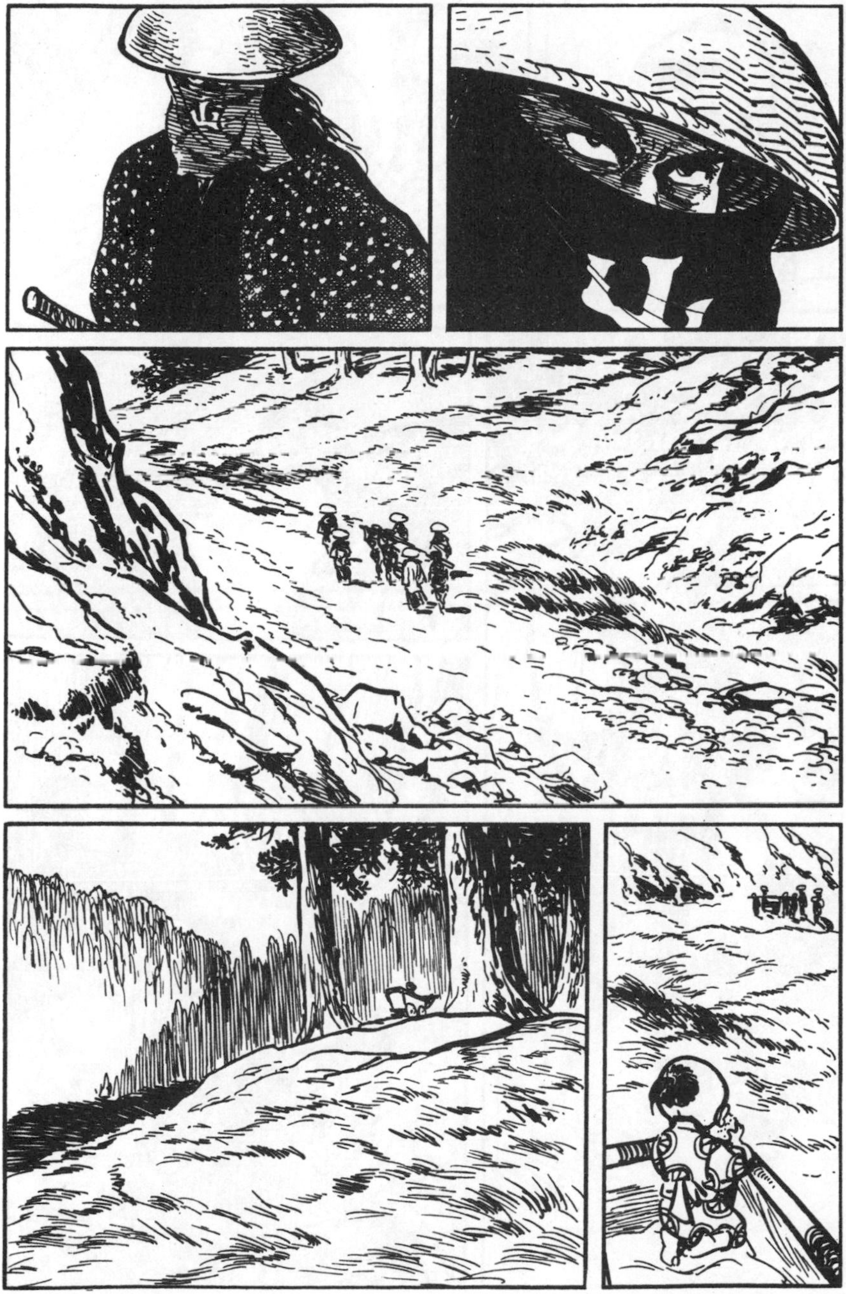

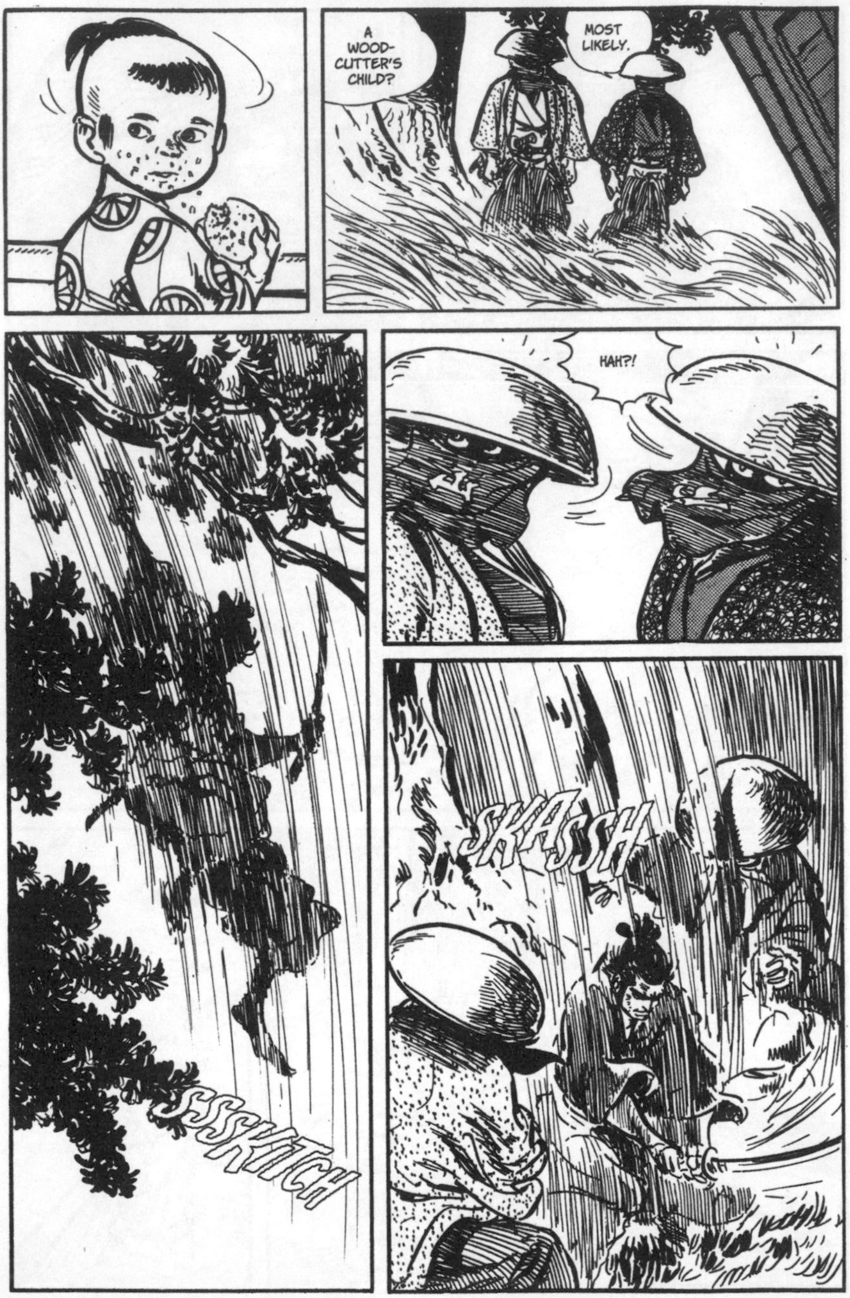
A WOOD-CUTTER'S CHILD?
MOST LIKELY.
SSSKITCH
HAH?!
SKASSH

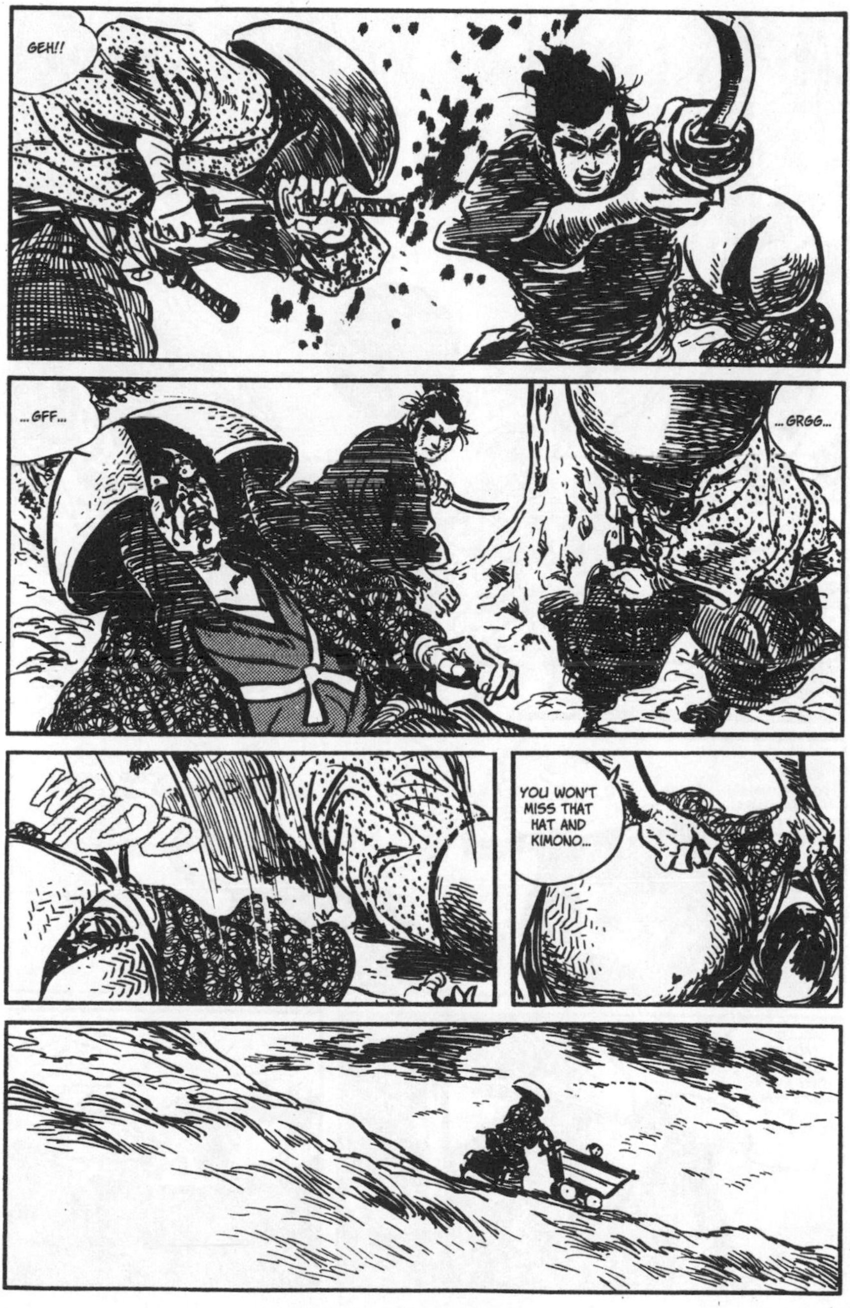
GEH!!
...GFF...
...GRGG...
WHDD
YOU WON'T MISS THAT HAT AND KIMONO...

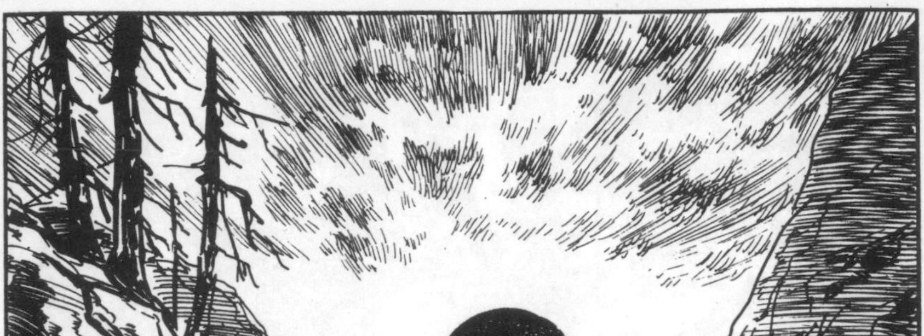

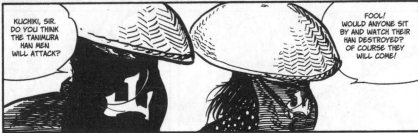

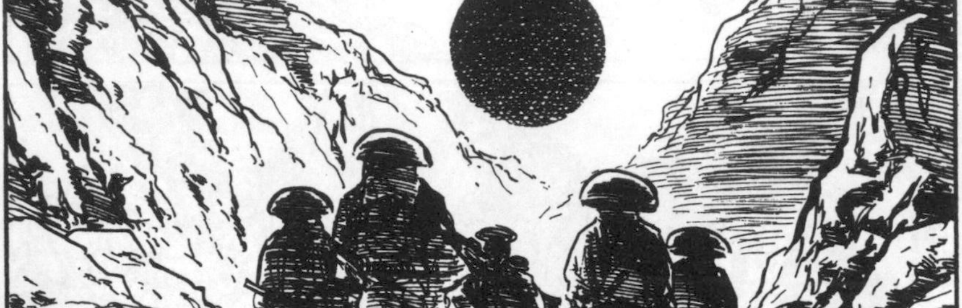
KUCHIKI, SIR. DO YOU THINK THE TANIMURA HAN MEN WILL ATTACK?
FOOL! WOULD ANYONE SIT BY AND WATCH THEIR HAN DESTROYED? OF COURSE THEY WILL COME!

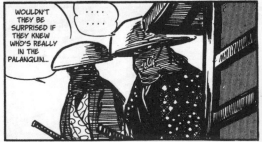

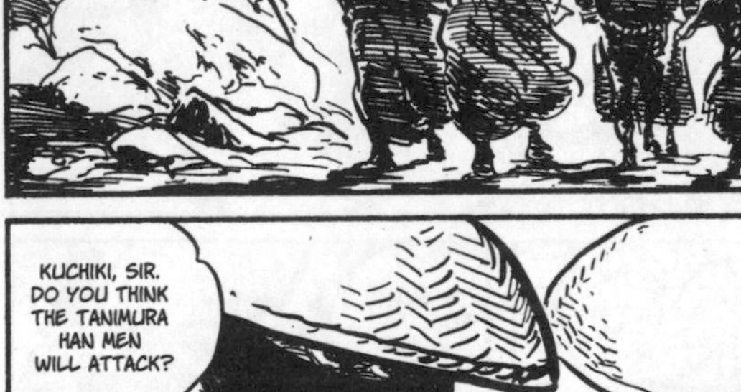
WOULDN'T THEY BE SURPRISED IF THEY KNEW WHO'S REALLY IN THE PALANQUIN...
....

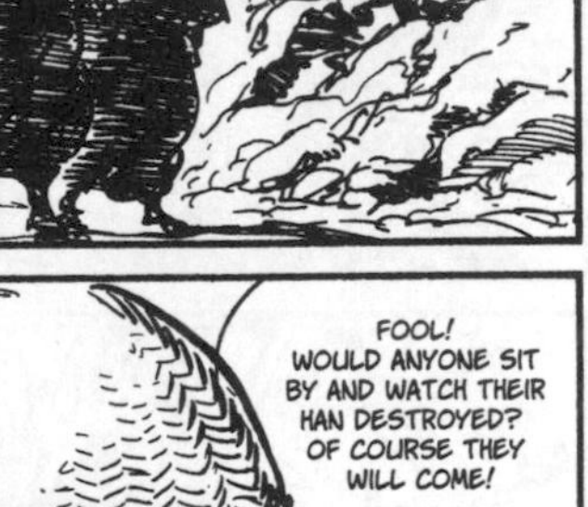

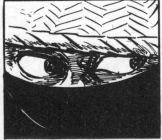

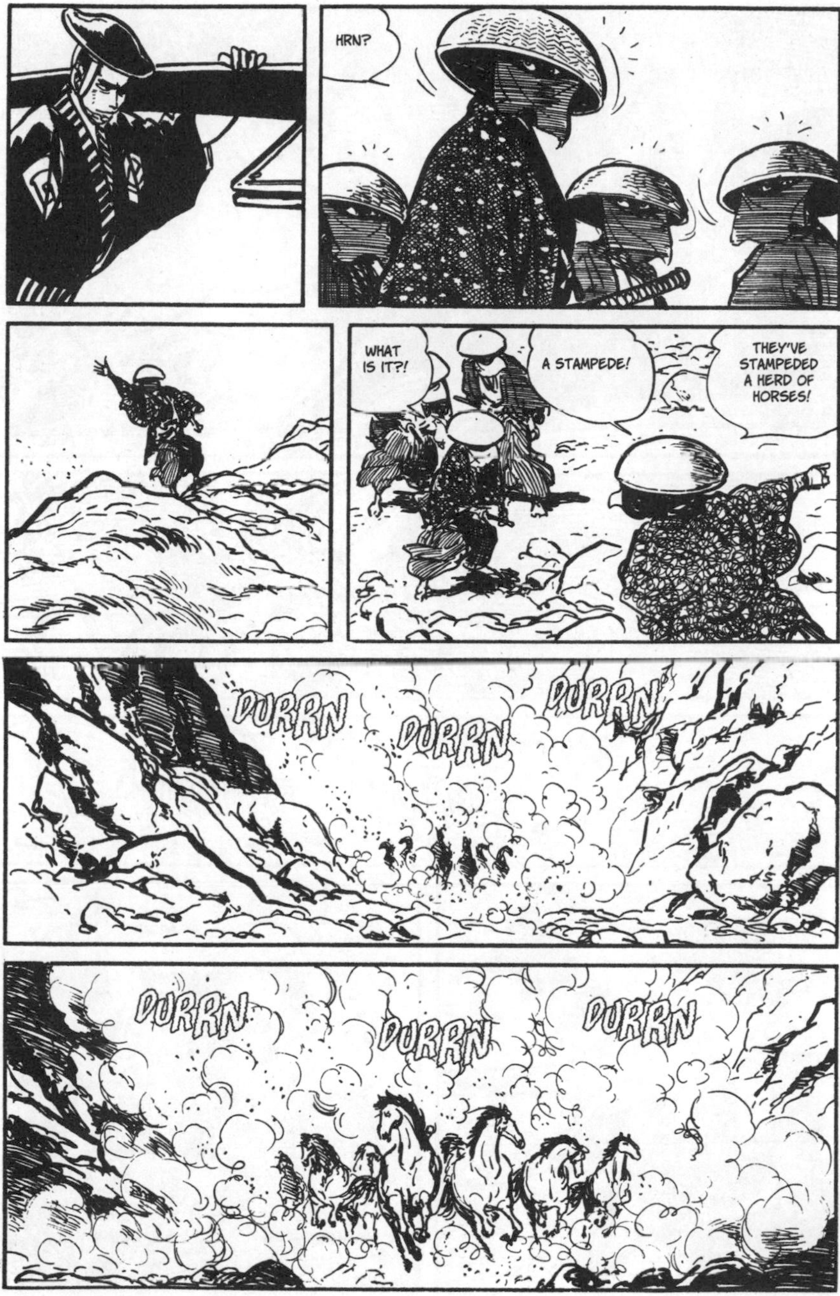
HRN?
WHAT IS IT?!
A STAMPEDE!
THEY'VE STAMPEDED A HERD OF HORSES!
DURRN
DURRN
DURRN
DURRN
DURRN
DURRN

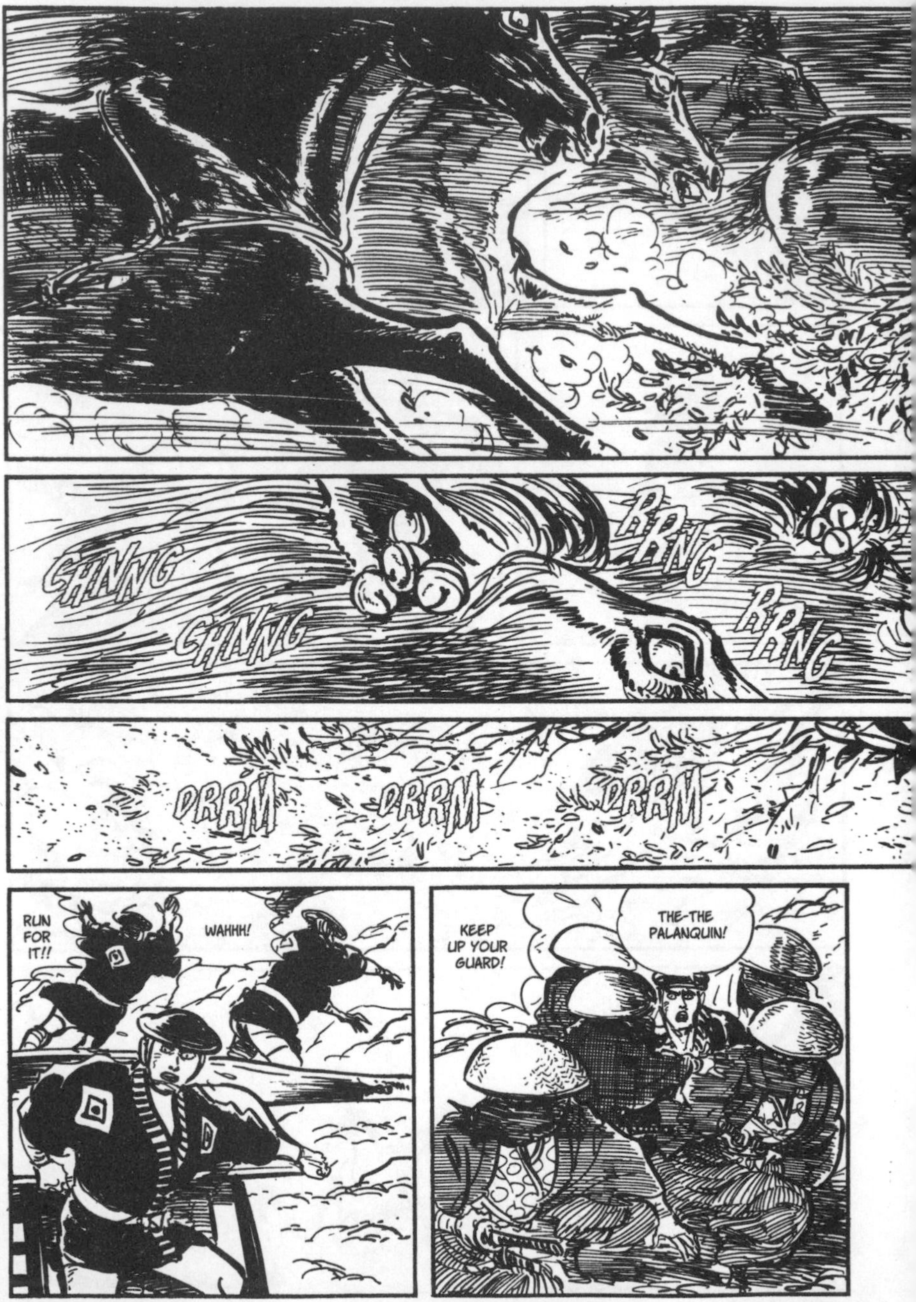
BRRNG
BRRNG
CHNNG
CHNNG
DRRM
DRRM
DRRM
THE-THE PALANQUIN!
KEEP UP YOUR GUARD!
WAHHH!
RUN FOR IT!!

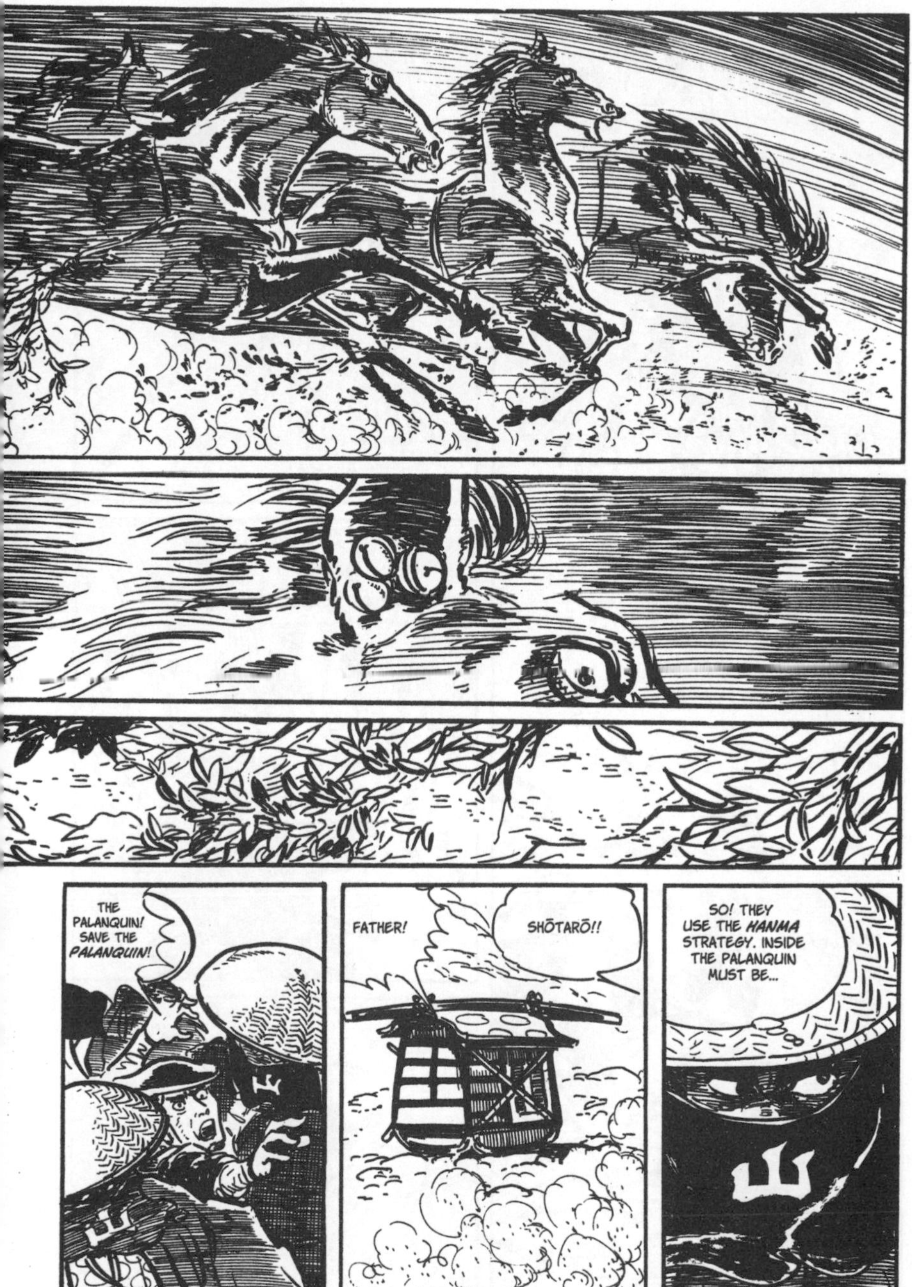
THE PALANQUIN! SAVE THE PALANQUIN!
FATHER!
SHŌTARŌ!!
SO! THEY USE THE HANMA STRATEGY. INSIDE THE PALANQUIN MUST BE...

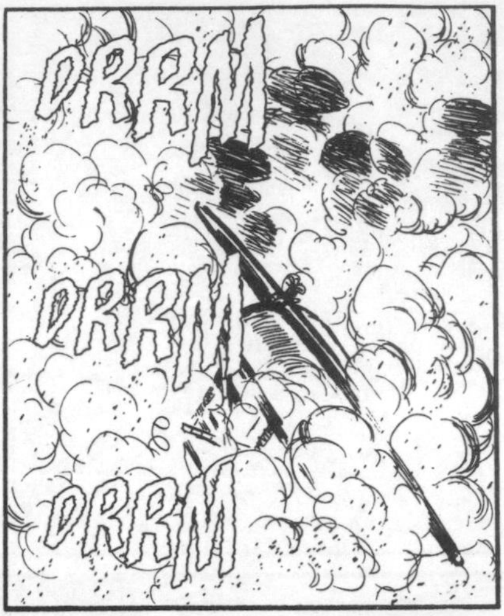
DRRM
DRRM
DRRM
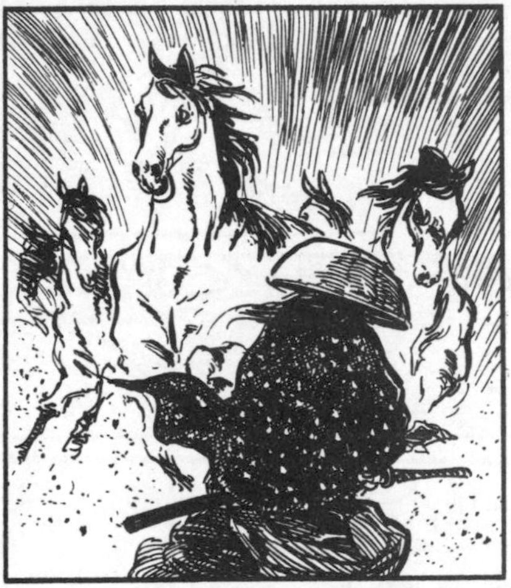
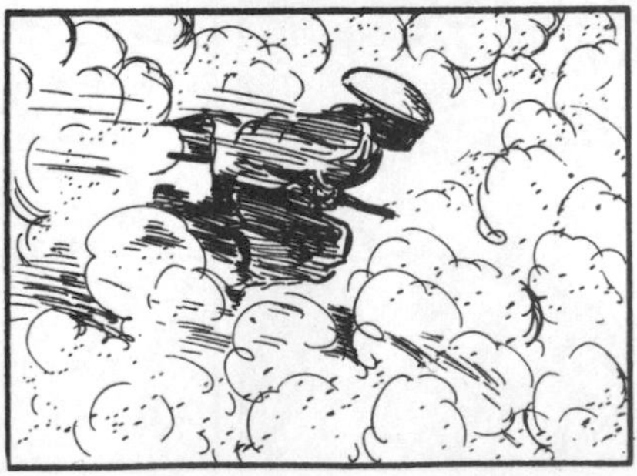
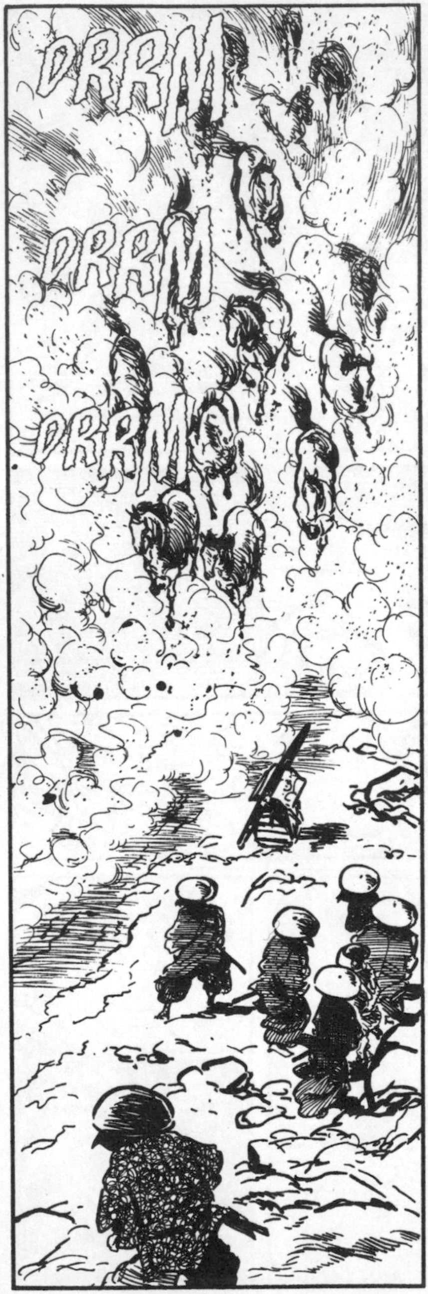
DRRM
DRRM
DRRM

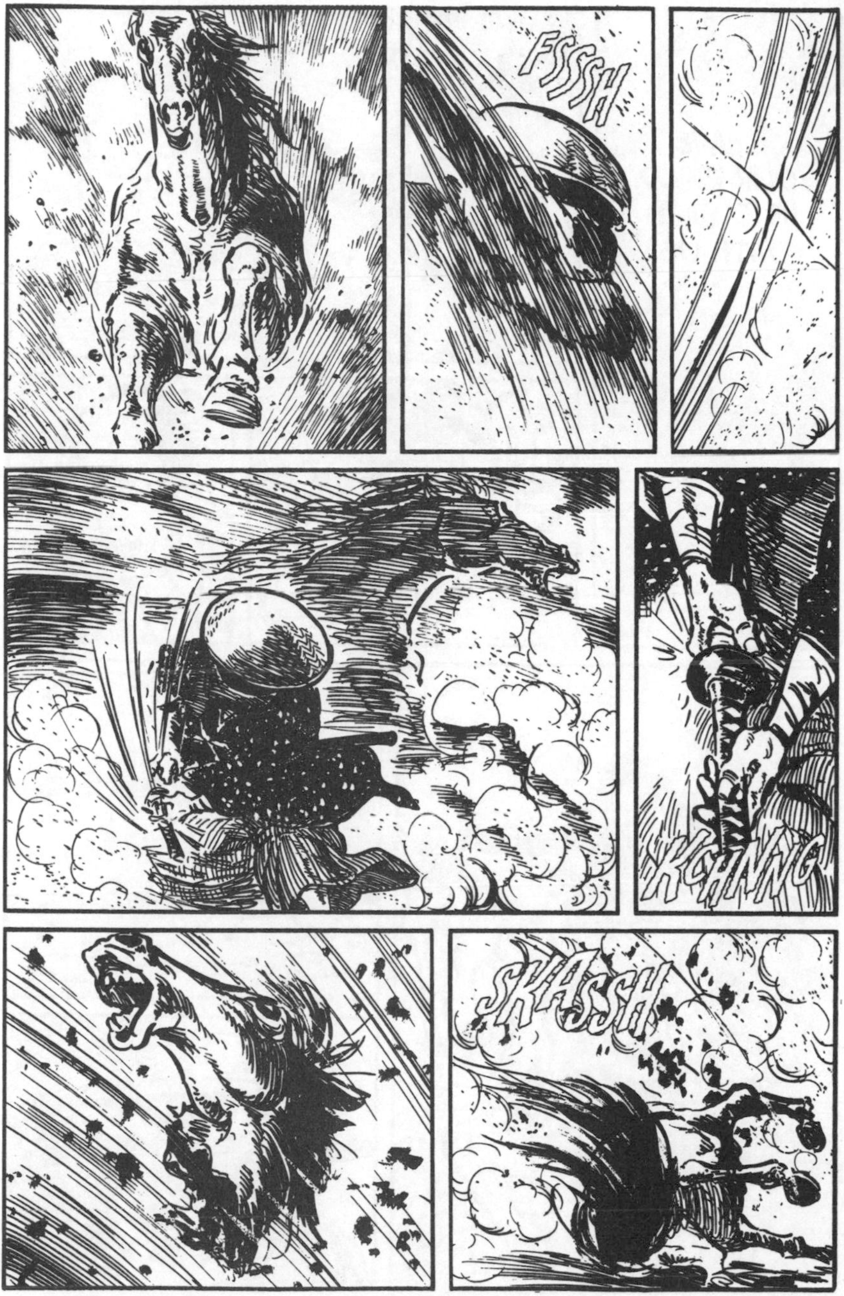
FSSSH
KCHNNG
SKASSH

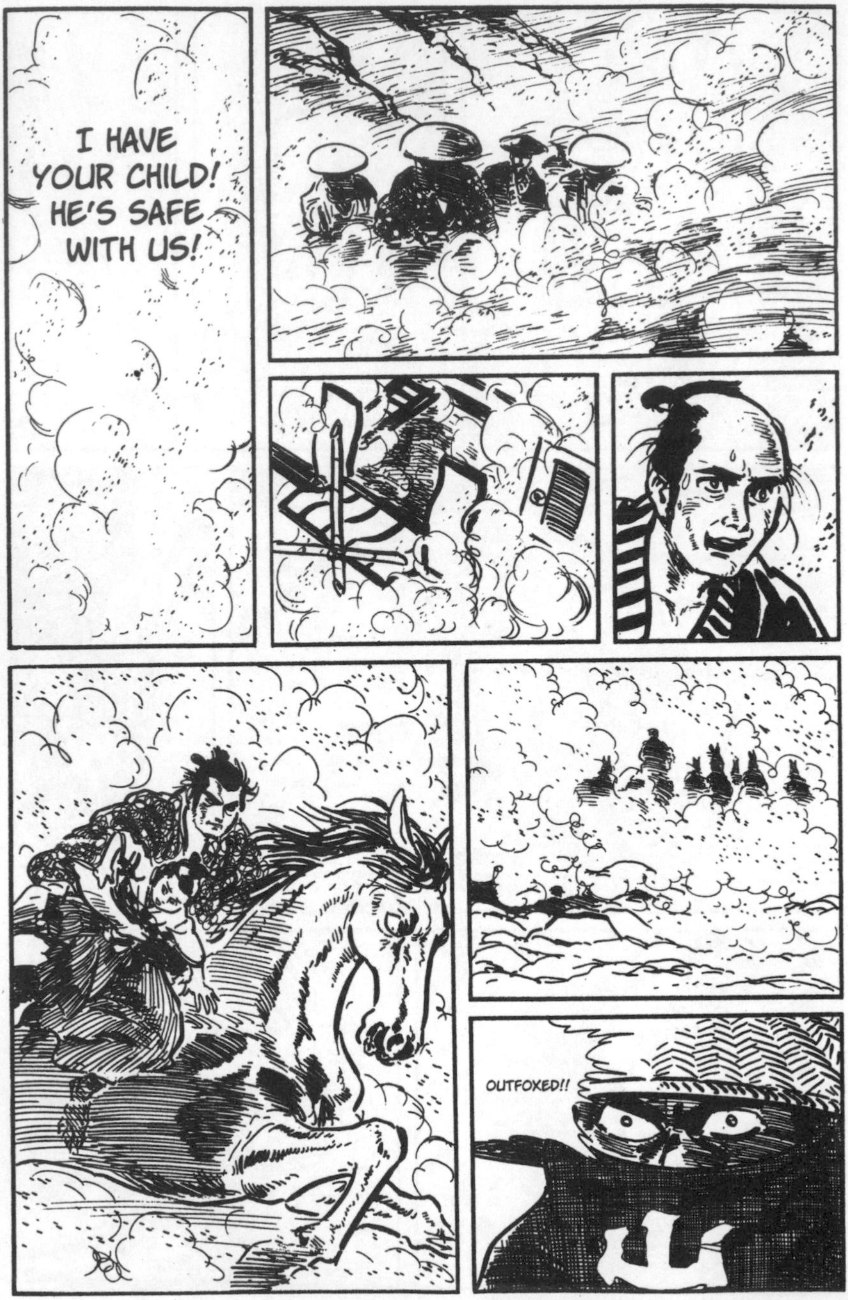
I HAVE YOUR CHILD! HE'S SAFE WITH US!
OUTFOXED!!

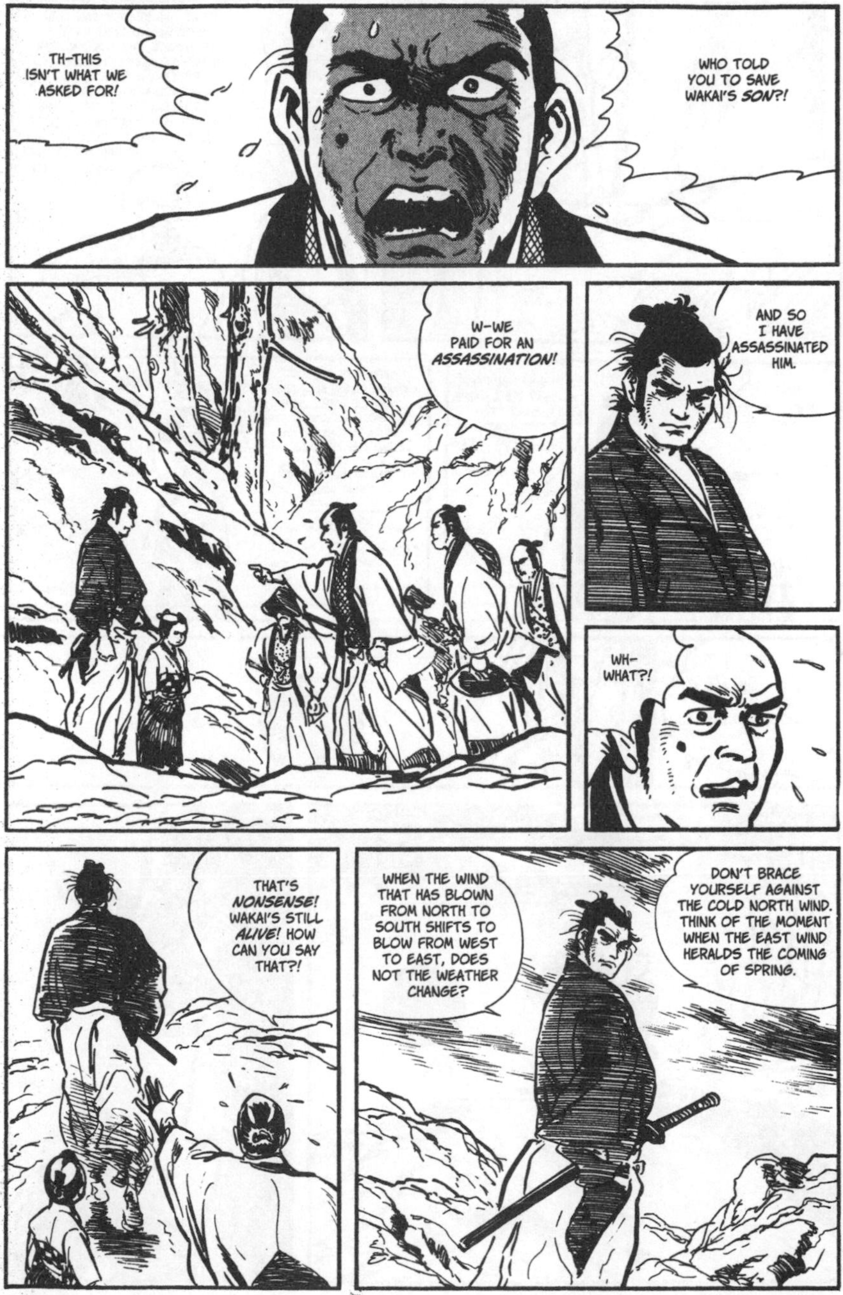
TH-THIS ISN'T WHAT WE ASKED FOR!
WHO TOLD YOU TO SAVE WAKAI'S *SON*?!
W-WE PAID FOR AN *ASSASSINATION*!
AND SO I HAVE ASSASSINATED HIM.
WH-WHAT?!
THAT'S *NONSENSE*! WAKAI'S STILL *ALIVE*! HOW CAN YOU SAY THAT?!
WHEN THE WIND THAT HAS BLOWN FROM NORTH TO SOUTH SHIFTS TO BLOW FROM WEST TO EAST, DOES NOT THE WEATHER CHANGE?
DON'T BRACE YOURSELF AGAINST THE COLD NORTH WIND. THINK OF THE MOMENT WHEN THE EAST WIND HERALDS THE COMING OF SPRING.

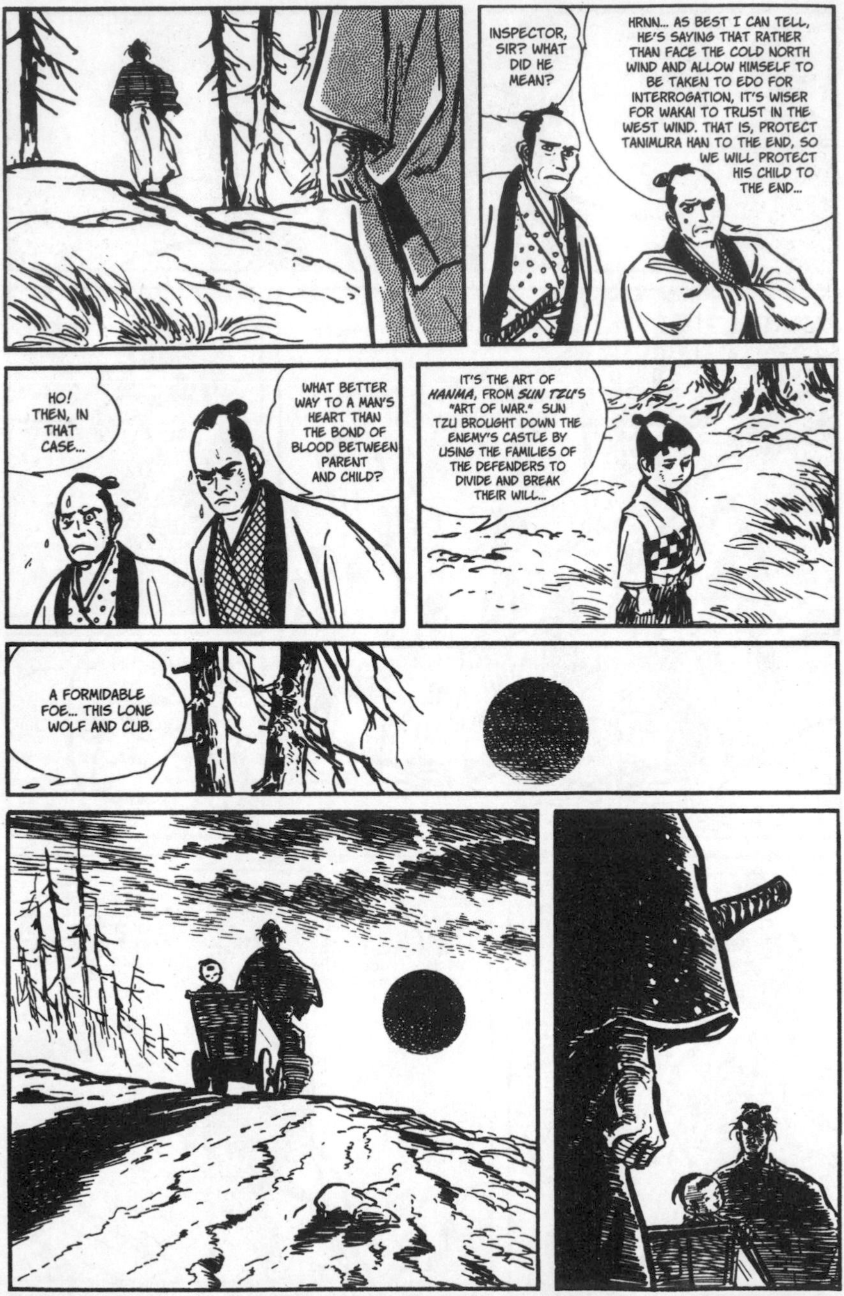
INSPECTOR, SIR? WHAT DID HE MEAN?
HRNN... AS BEST I CAN TELL, HE'S SAYING THAT RATHER THAN FACE THE COLD NORTH WIND AND ALLOW HIMSELF TO BE TAKEN TO EDO FOR INTERROGATION, IT'S WISER FOR WAKAI TO TRUST IN THE WEST WIND. THAT IS, PROTECT TANIMURA HAN TO THE END, SO WE WILL PROTECT HIS CHILD TO THE END...
HO! THEN, IN THAT CASE...
WHAT BETTER WAY TO A MAN'S HEART THAN THE BOND OF BLOOD BETWEEN PARENT AND CHILD?
IT'S THE ART OF HANMA, FROM SUN TZU'S "ART OF WAR." SUN TZU BROUGHT DOWN THE ENEMY'S CASTLE BY USING THE FAMILIES OF THE DEFENDERS TO DIVIDE AND BREAK THEIR WILL...
A FORMIDABLE FOE... THIS LONE WOLF AND CUB.

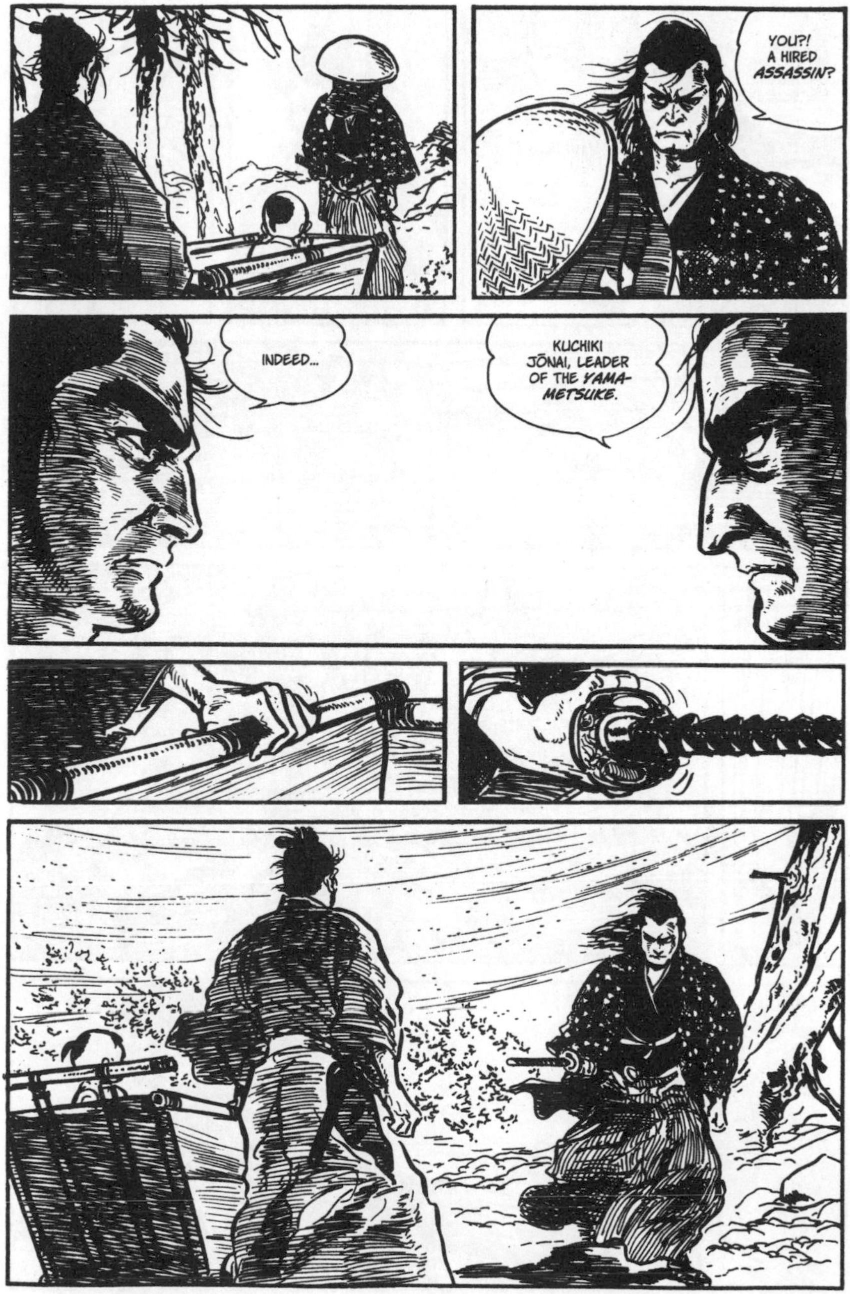
YOU?! A HIRED ASSASSIN?
KUCHIKI JŌNAI, LEADER OF THE YAMA-METSUKE.
INDEED...

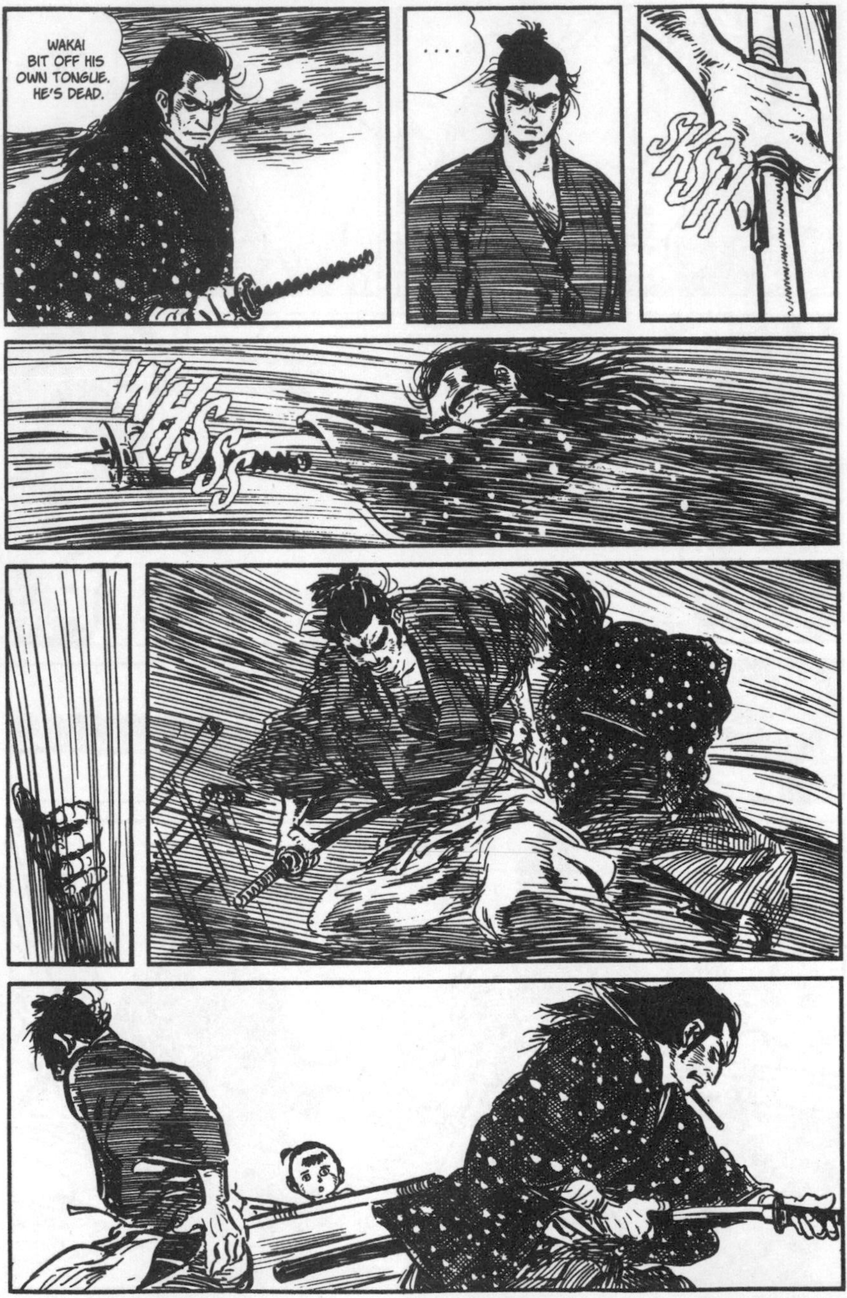
WAKAI BIT OFF HIS OWN TONGUE. HE'S DEAD.
....
SKSH
WHSSS

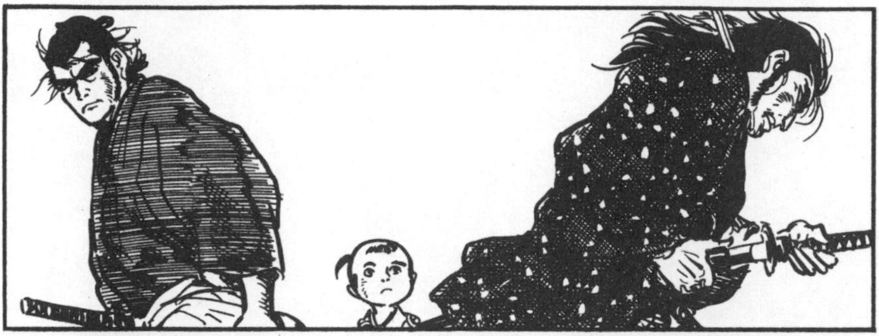
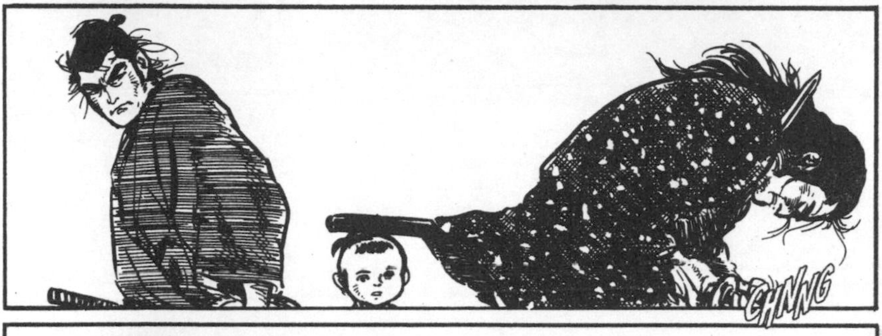
CHNNG
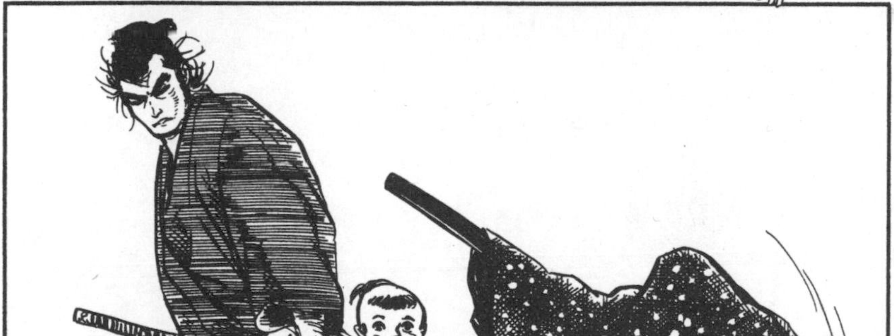
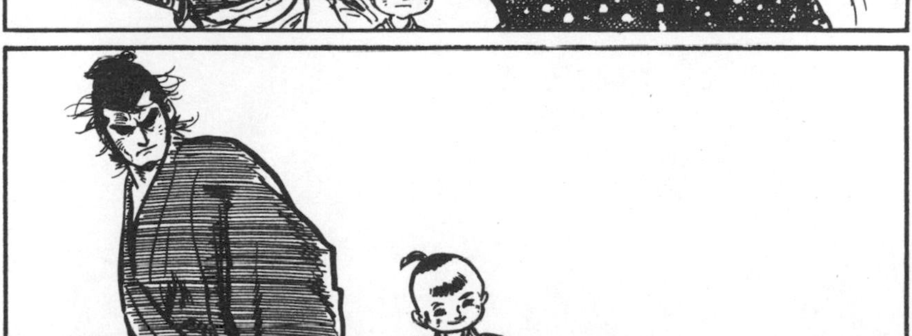

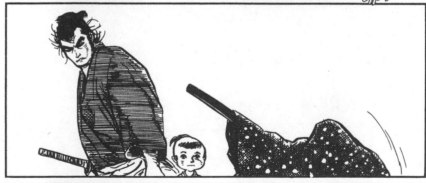

BABY CART ON
THE RIVER STYX

4

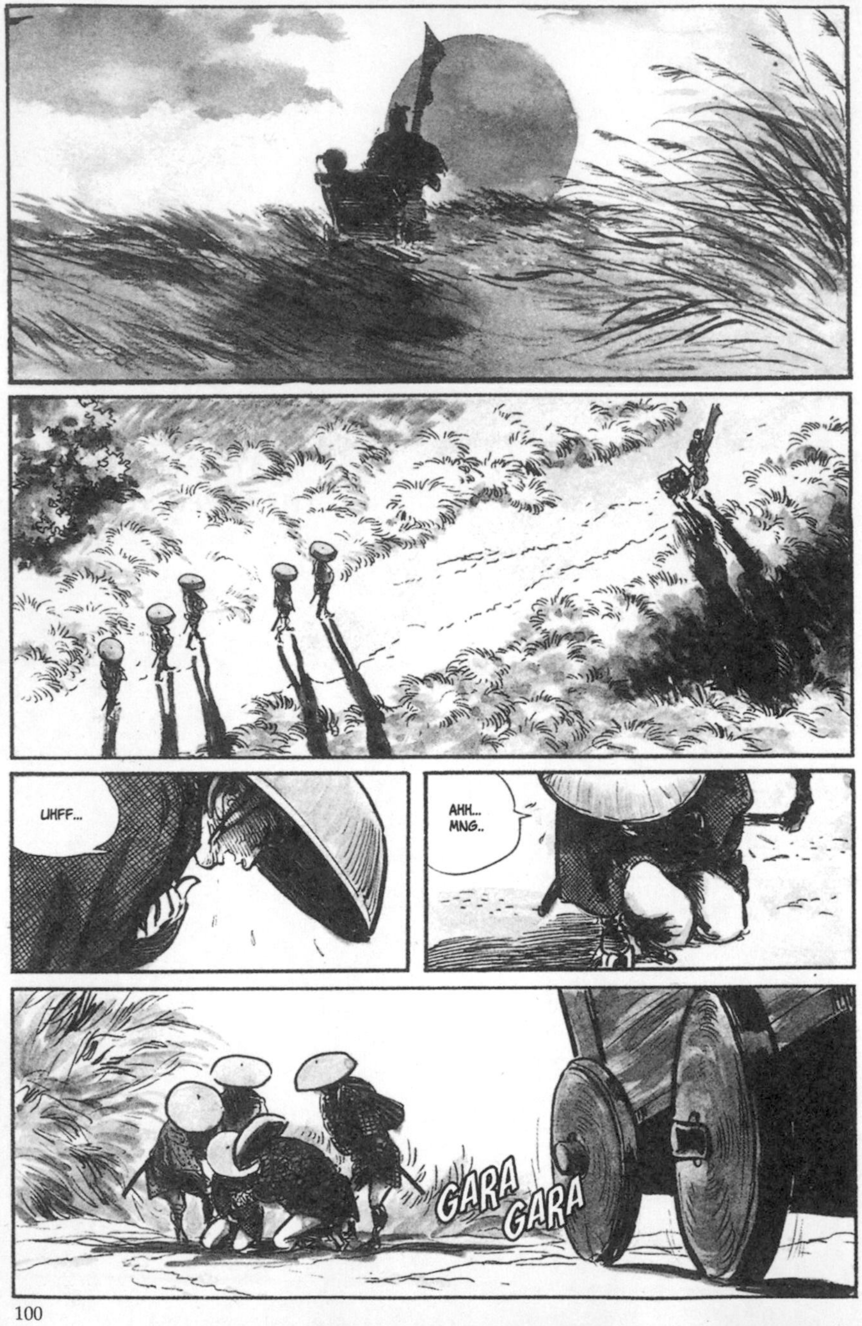
AHH... MNG..
UHFF...
GARA GARA

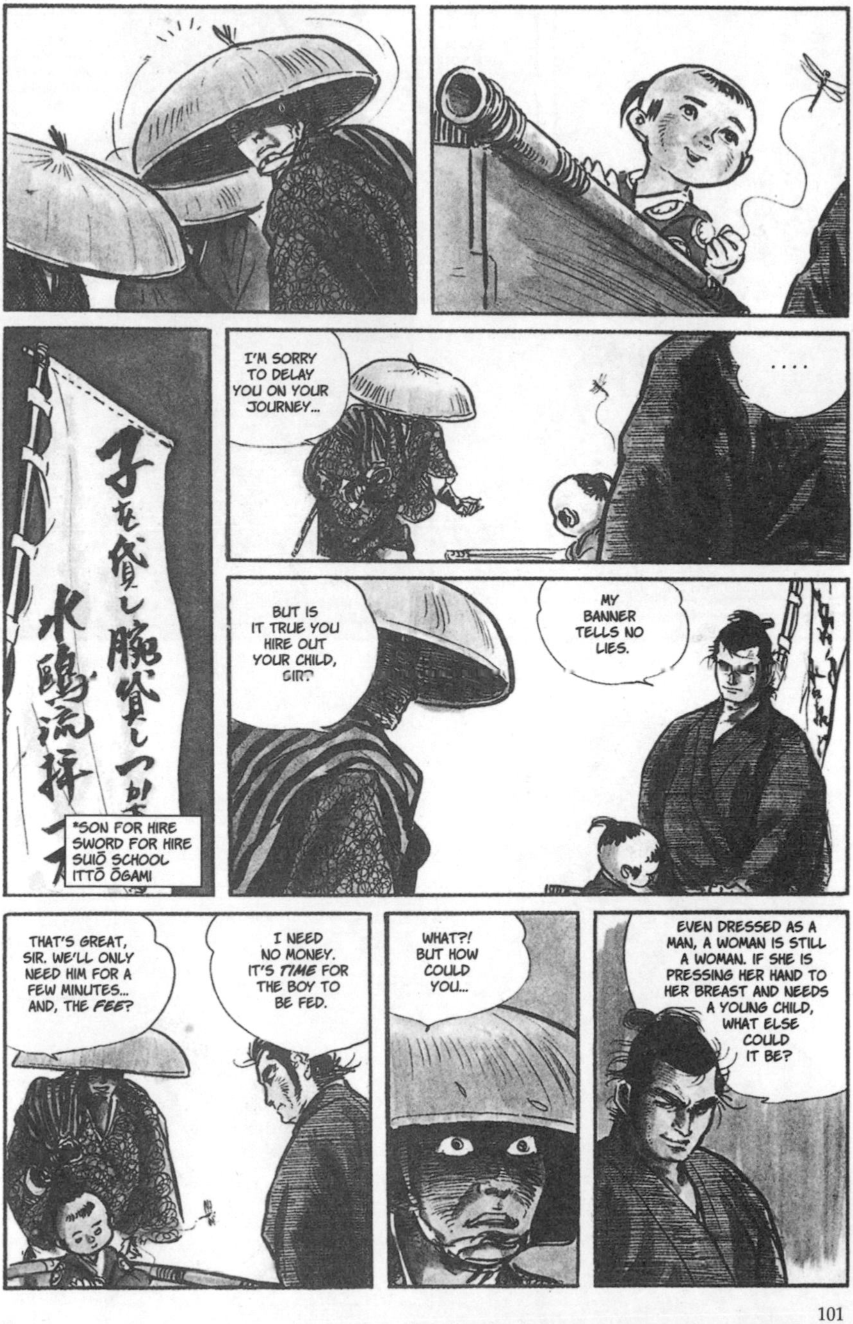
子を貸し腕貸しつか
水鴎流拝
*SON FOR HIRE SWORD FOR HIRE SUIŌ SCHOOL ITTŌ ŌGAMI
I'M SORRY TO DELAY YOU ON YOUR JOURNEY...
....
BUT IS IT TRUE YOU HIRE OUT YOUR CHILD, SIR?
MY BANNER TELLS NO LIES.
THAT'S GREAT, SIR. WE'LL ONLY NEED HIM FOR A FEW MINUTES... AND, THE *FEE*?
I NEED NO MONEY. IT'S *TIME* FOR THE BOY TO BE FED.
WHAT?! BUT HOW COULD YOU...
EVEN DRESSED AS A MAN, A WOMAN IS STILL A WOMAN. IF SHE IS PRESSING HER HAND TO HER BREAST AND NEEDS A YOUNG CHILD, WHAT ELSE COULD IT BE?

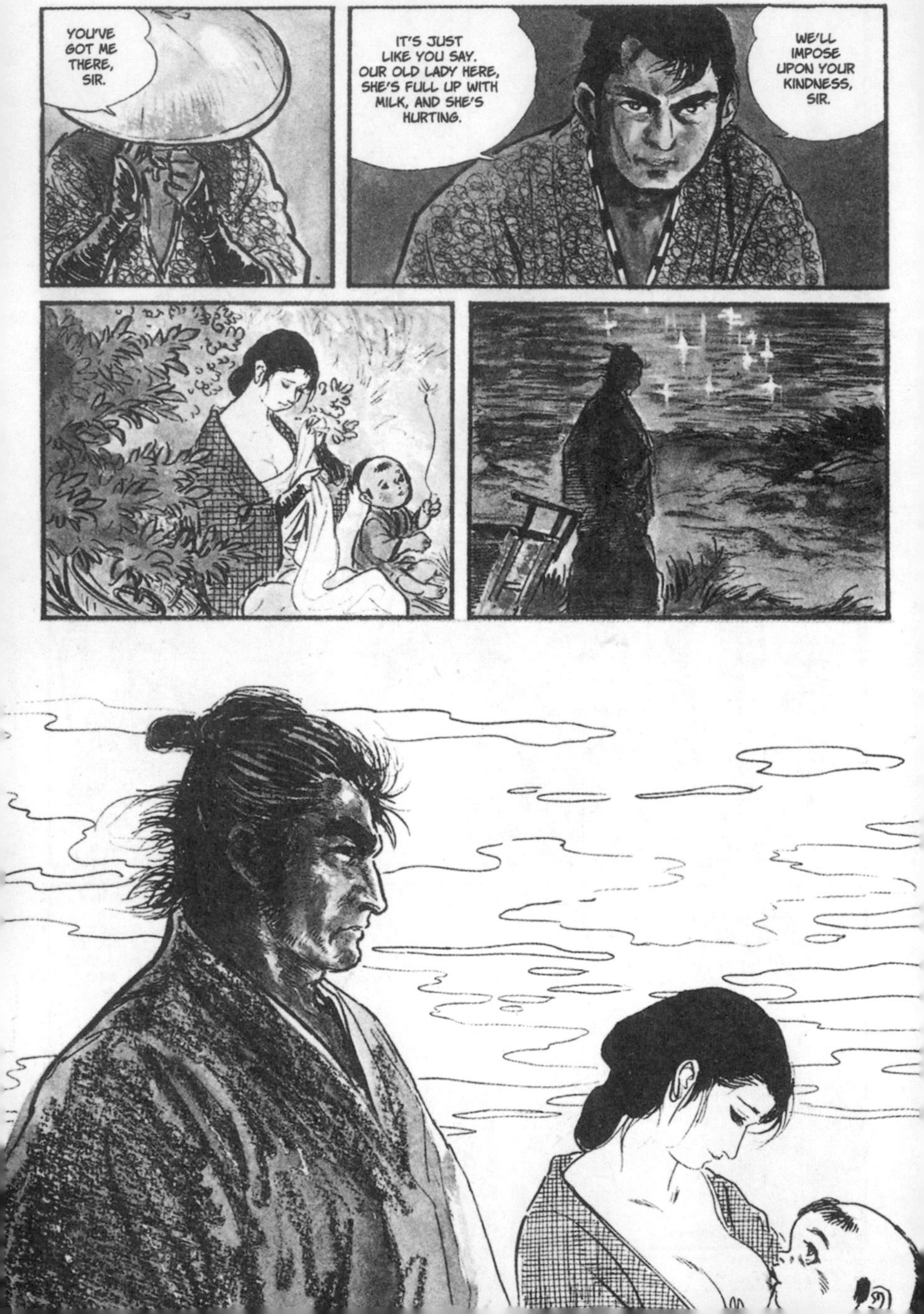
YOU'VE GOT ME THERE, SIR.
IT'S JUST LIKE YOU SAY. OUR OLD LADY HERE, SHE'S FULL UP WITH MILK, AND SHE'S HURTING.
WE'LL IMPOSE UPON YOUR KINDNESS, SIR.

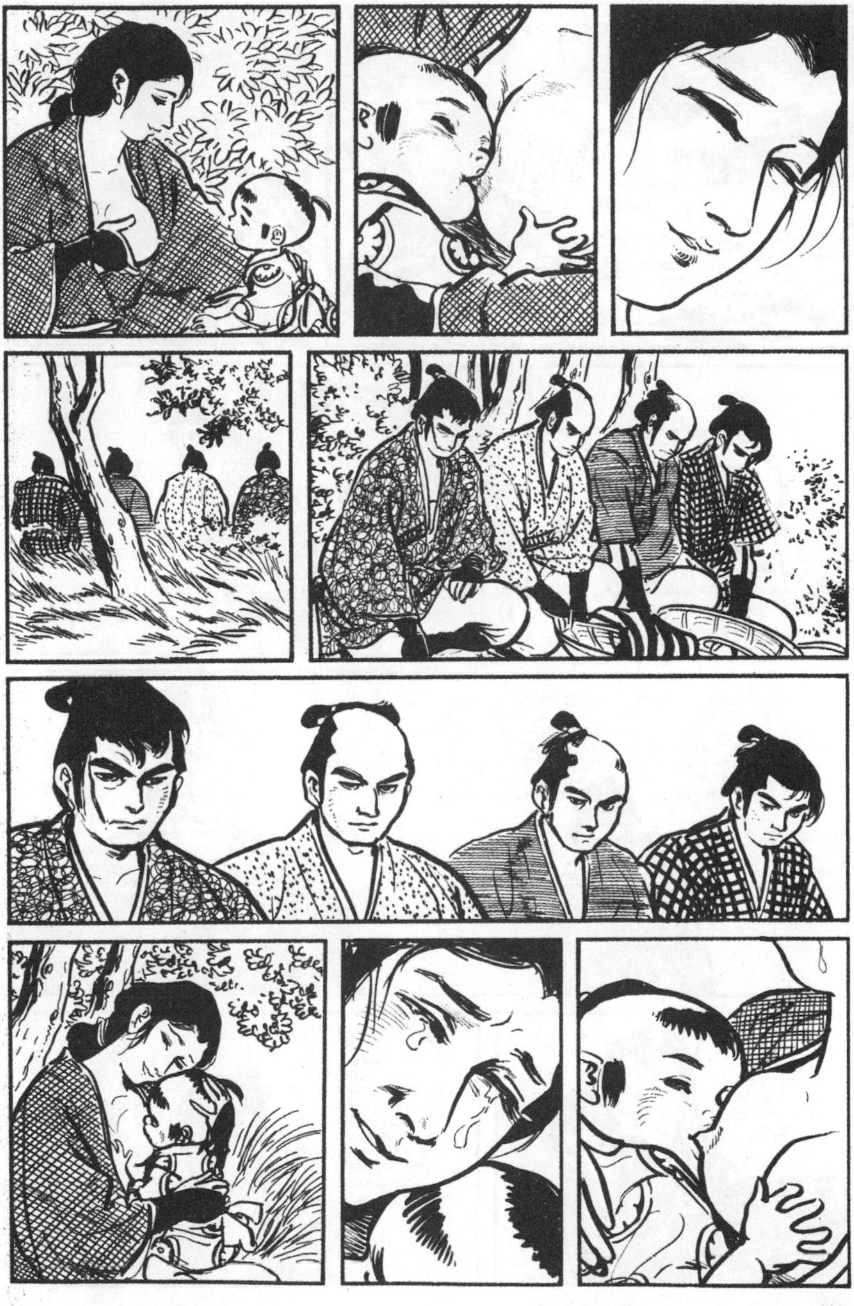

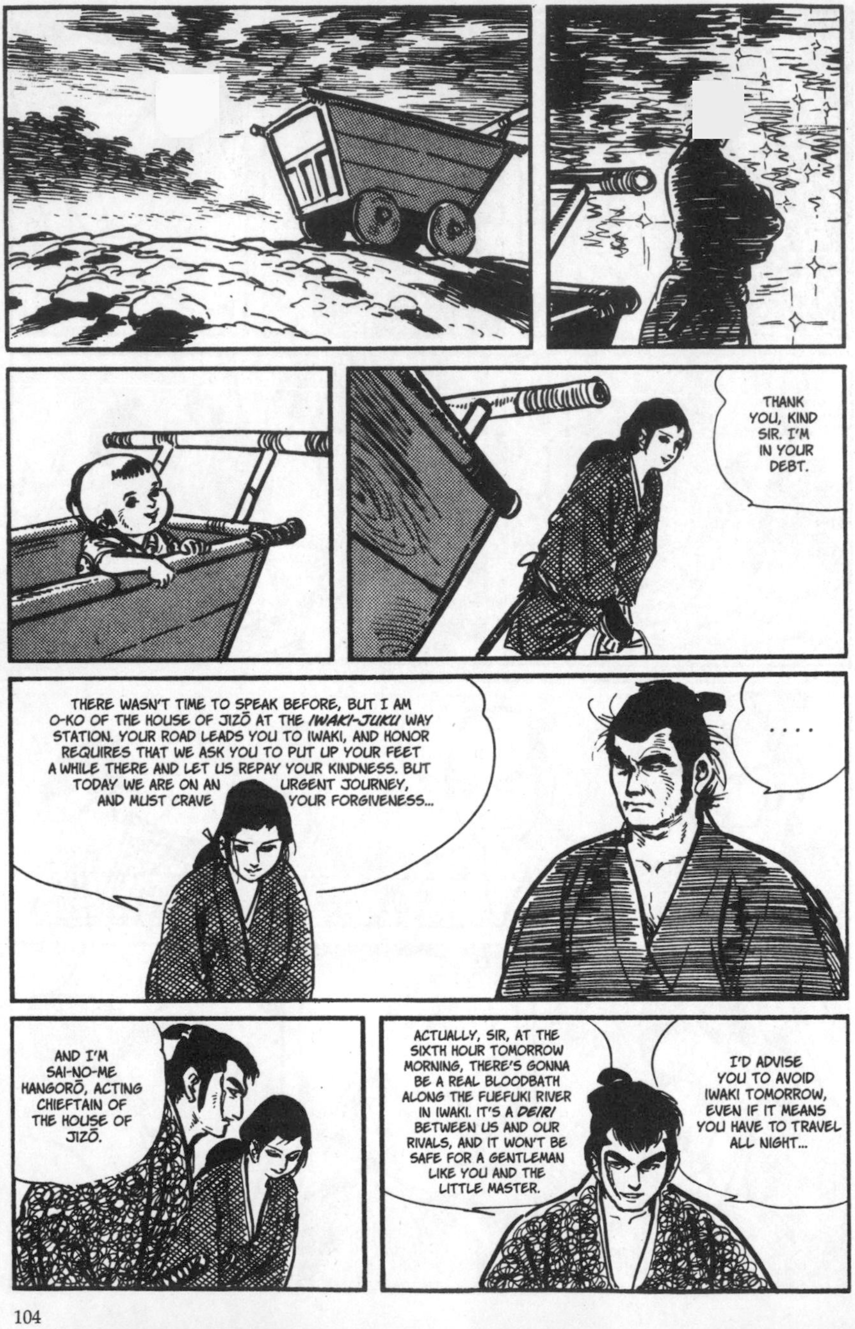
THANK YOU, KIND SIR. I'M IN YOUR DEBT.
THERE WASN'T TIME TO SPEAK BEFORE, BUT I AM O-KO OF THE HOUSE OF JIZŌ AT THE *IWAKI-JUKU* WAY STATION. YOUR ROAD LEADS YOU TO IWAKI, AND HONOR REQUIRES THAT WE ASK YOU TO PUT UP YOUR FEET A WHILE THERE AND LET US REPAY YOUR KINDNESS. BUT TODAY WE ARE ON AN URGENT JOURNEY, AND MUST CRAVE YOUR FORGIVENESS...
. . . .
AND I'M SAI-NO-ME HANGORŌ, ACTING CHIEFTAIN OF THE HOUSE OF JIZŌ.
ACTUALLY, SIR, AT THE SIXTH HOUR TOMORROW MORNING, THERE'S GONNA BE A REAL BLOODBATH ALONG THE FUEFUKI RIVER IN IWAKI. IT'S A *DEIRI* BETWEEN US AND OUR RIVALS, AND IT WON'T BE SAFE FOR A GENTLEMAN LIKE YOU AND THE LITTLE MASTER.
I'D ADVISE YOU TO AVOID IWAKI TOMORROW, EVEN IF IT MEANS YOU HAVE TO TRAVEL ALL NIGHT...

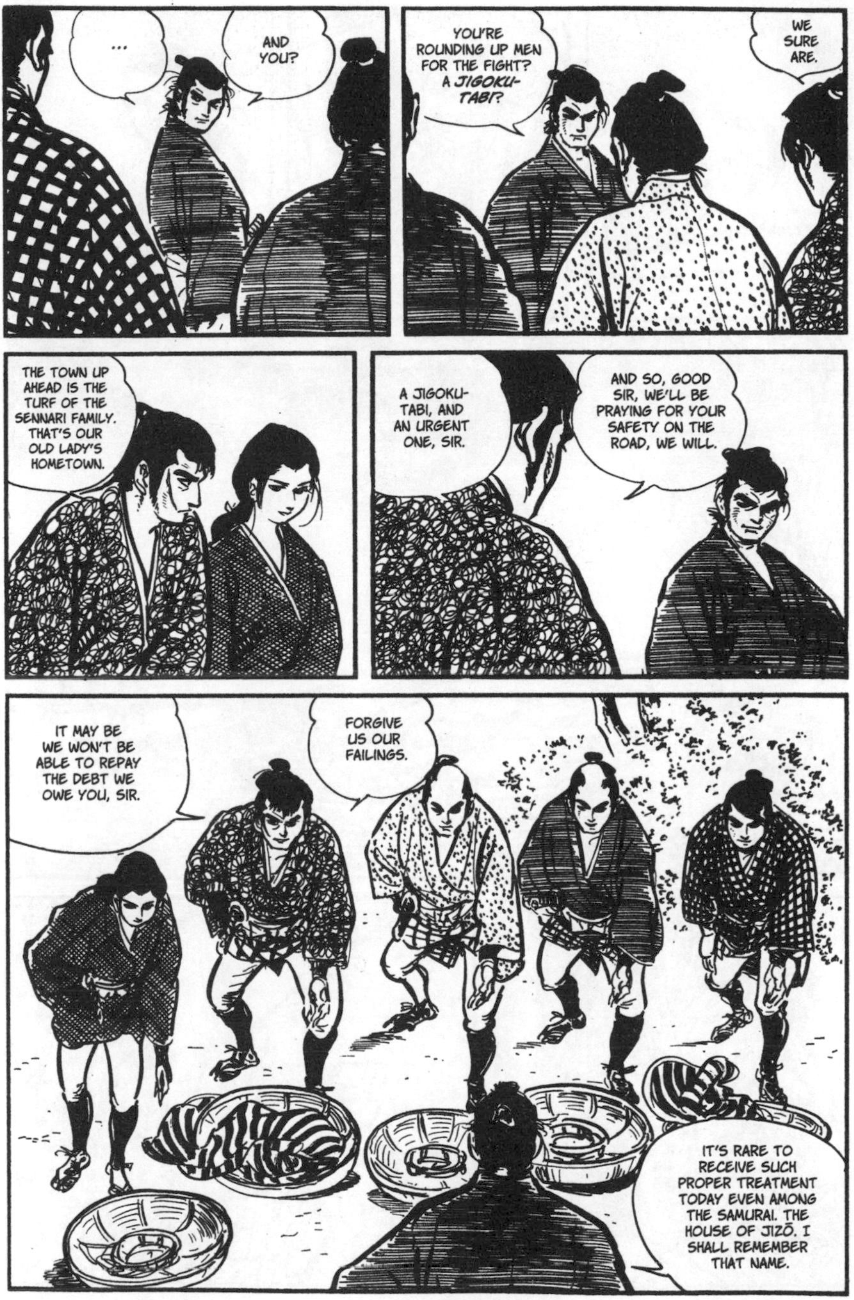
...
AND YOU?
YOU'RE ROUNDING UP MEN FOR THE FIGHT? A *JIGOKU-TABI*?
WE SURE ARE.
THE TOWN UP AHEAD IS THE TURF OF THE SENNARI FAMILY. THAT'S OUR OLD LADY'S HOMETOWN.
A JIGOKU-TABI, AND AN URGENT ONE, SIR.
AND SO, GOOD SIR, WE'LL BE PRAYING FOR YOUR SAFETY ON THE ROAD, WE WILL.
IT MAY BE WE WON'T BE ABLE TO REPAY THE DEBT WE OWE YOU, SIR.
FORGIVE US OUR FAILINGS.
IT'S RARE TO RECEIVE SUCH PROPER TREATMENT TODAY EVEN AMONG THE SAMURAI. THE HOUSE OF JIZŌ. I SHALL REMEMBER THAT NAME.

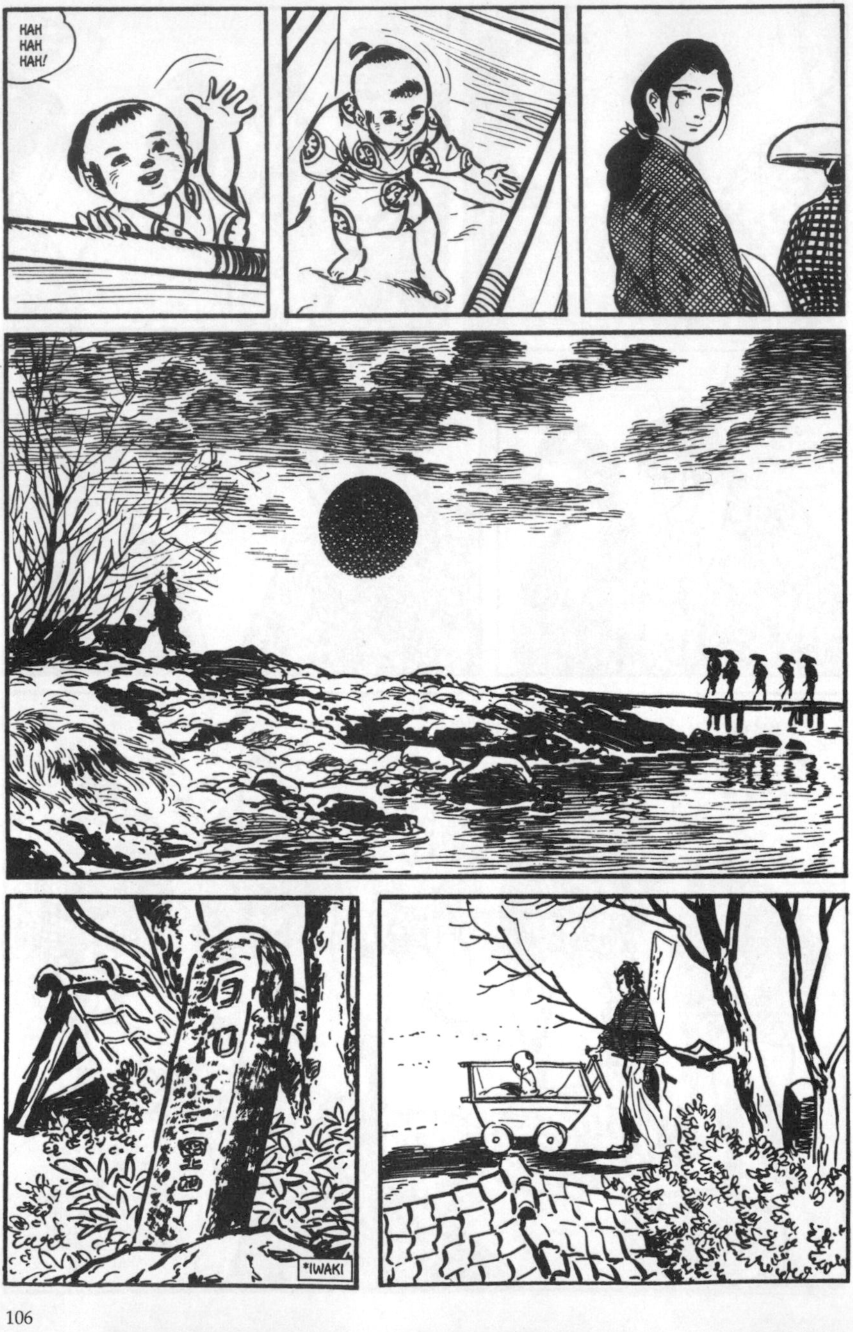
HAH HAH HAH!
*IWAKI

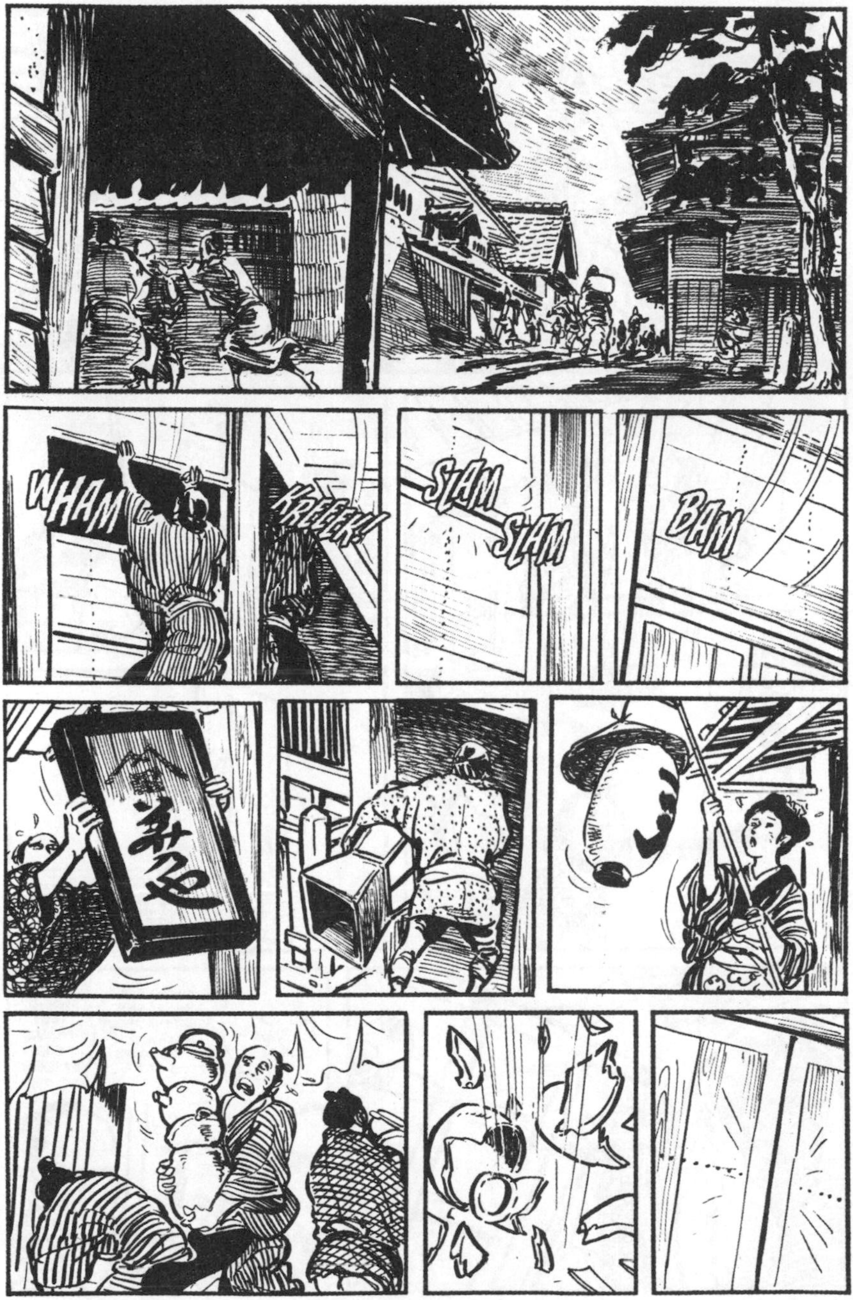
BAM
SLAM
SLAM
KREEEK!
WHAM

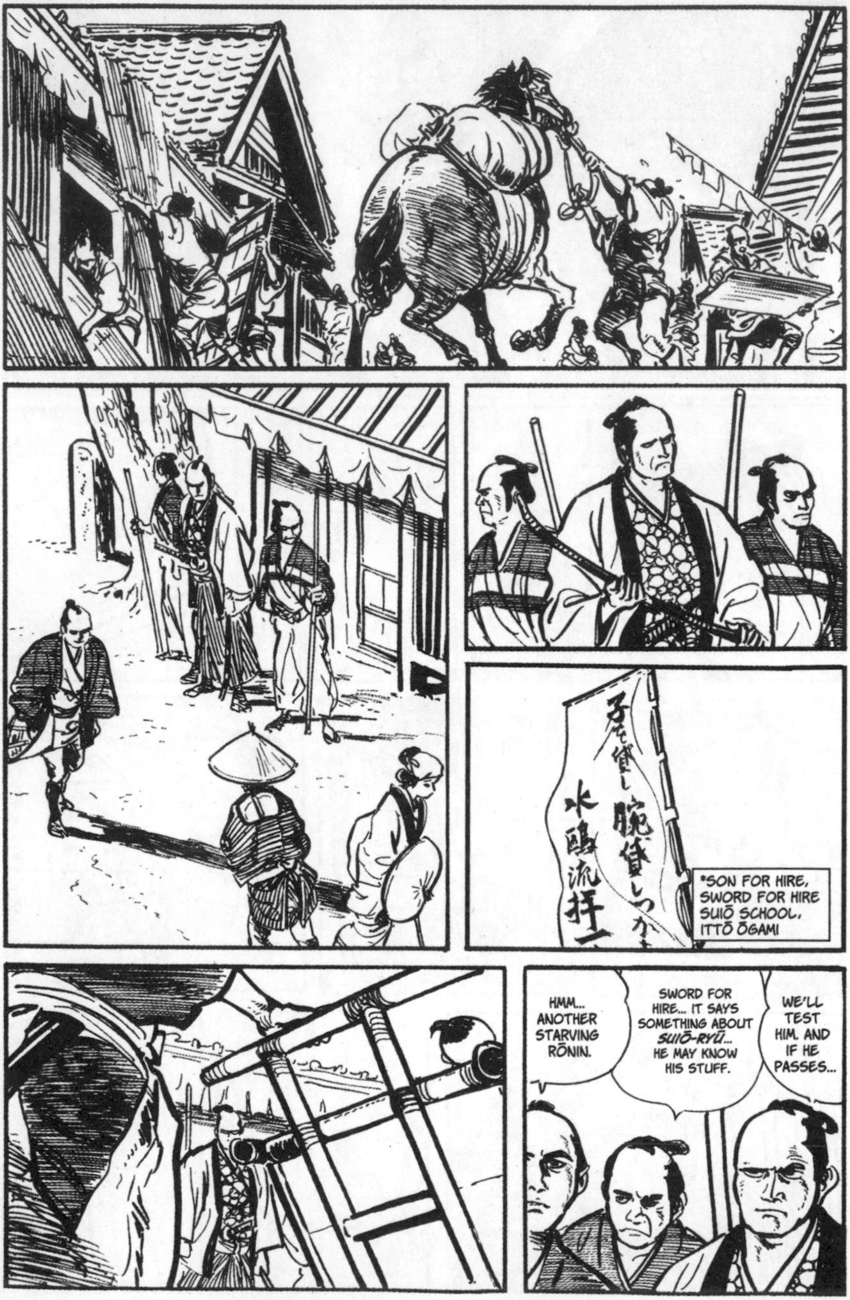
子を貸し 腕貸しつか
水鴎流拝一
*SON FOR HIRE, SWORD FOR HIRE SUIŌ SCHOOL, ITTŌ ŌGAMI
WE'LL TEST HIM. AND IF HE PASSES...
SWORD FOR HIRE... IT SAYS SOMETHING ABOUT *SUIŌ-RYŪ*... HE MAY KNOW HIS STUFF.
HMM... ANOTHER STARVING RŌNIN.

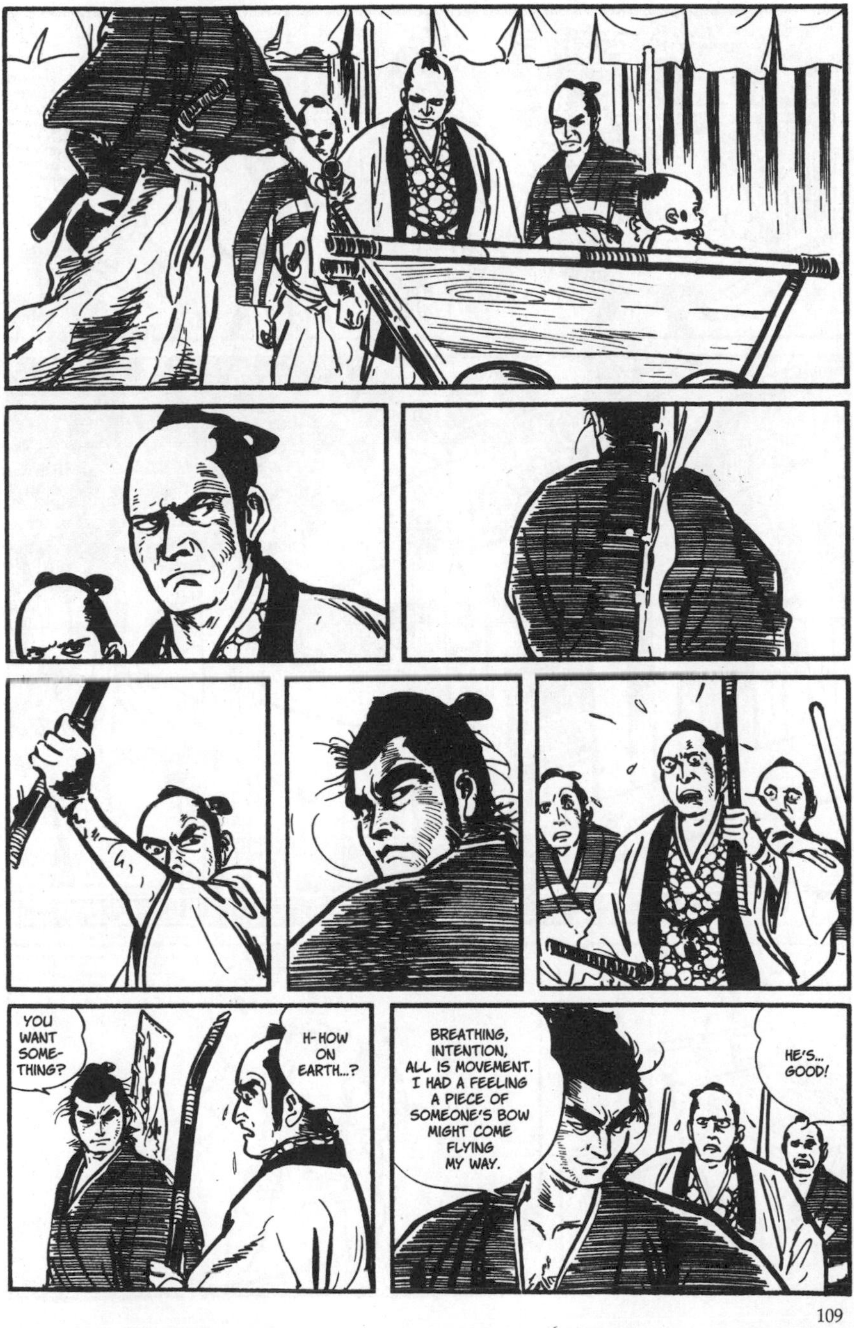
YOU WANT SOME-THING?
H-HOW ON EARTH...?
BREATHING, INTENTION, ALL IS MOVEMENT. I HAD A FEELING A PIECE OF SOMEONE'S BOW MIGHT COME FLYING MY WAY.
HE'S... GOOD!

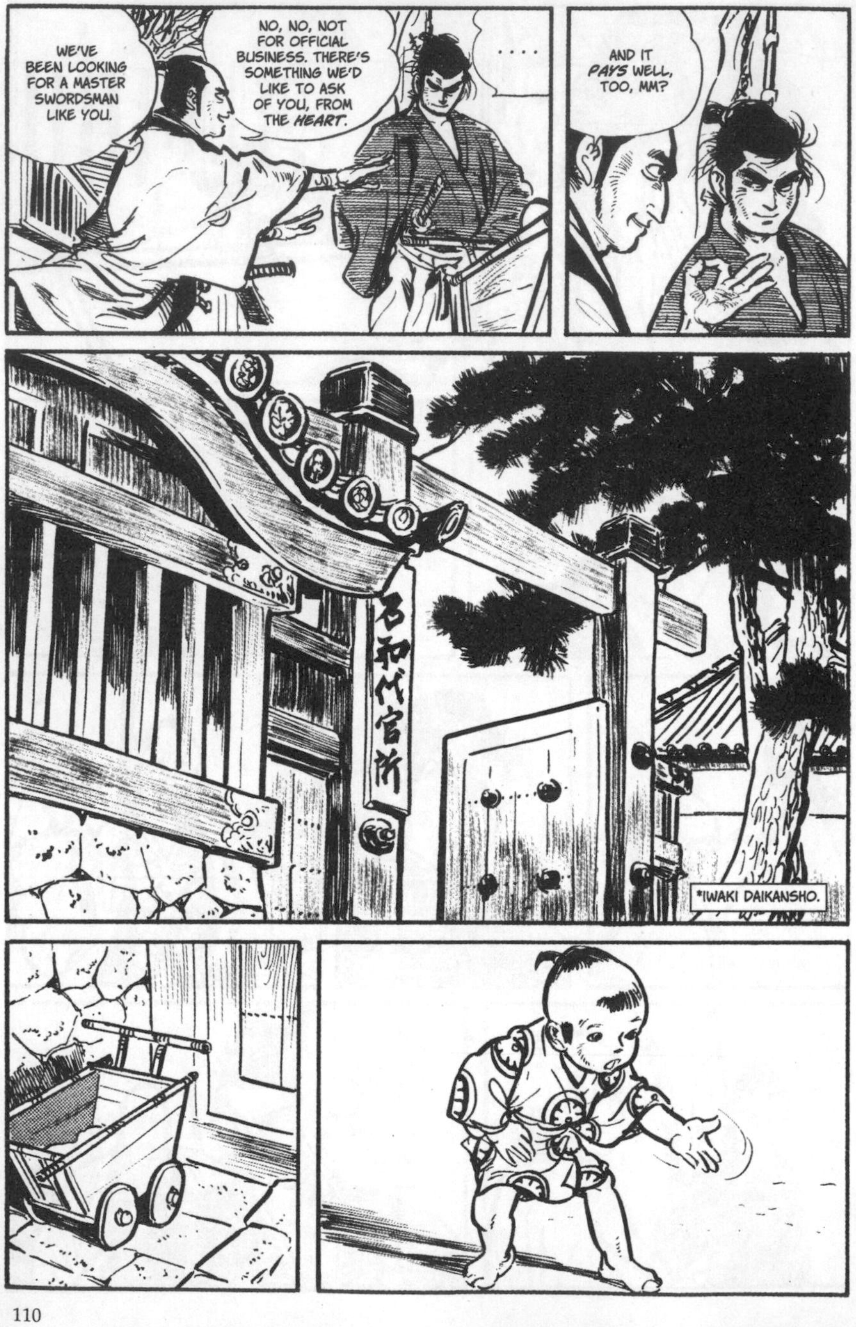
WE'VE BEEN LOOKING FOR A MASTER SWORDSMAN LIKE YOU.
NO, NO, NOT FOR OFFICIAL BUSINESS. THERE'S SOMETHING WE'D LIKE TO ASK OF YOU, FROM THE *HEART*.
....
AND IT *PAYS* WELL, TOO, MM?
石和代官所
*IWAKI DAIKANSHO.

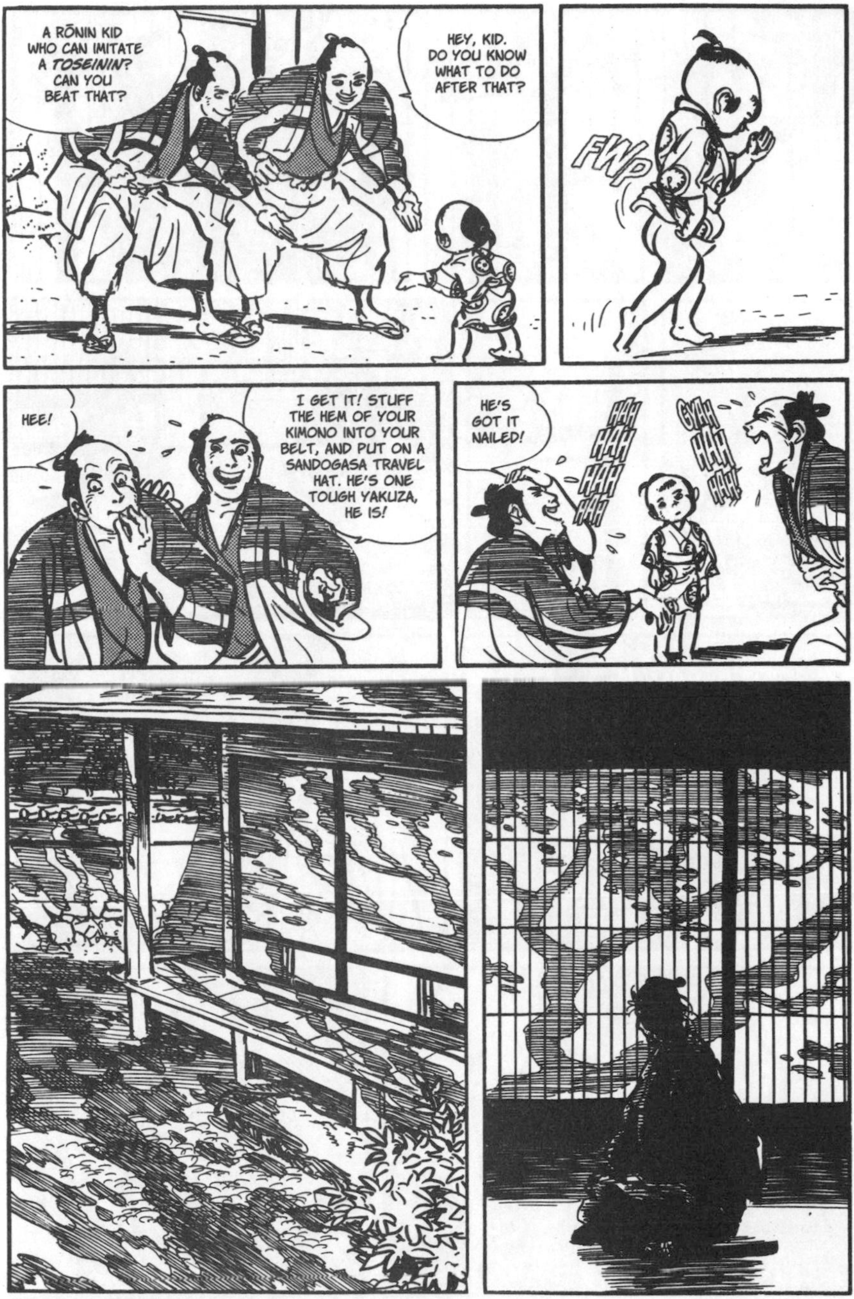
A RŌNIN KID WHO CAN IMITATE A *TOSEININ*? CAN YOU BEAT THAT?
HEY, KID. DO YOU KNOW WHAT TO DO AFTER THAT?
FWP
HEE!
I GET IT! STUFF THE HEM OF YOUR KIMONO INTO YOUR BELT, AND PUT ON A SANDOGASA TRAVEL HAT. HE'S ONE TOUGH YAKUZA, HE IS!
HE'S GOT IT NAILED!
HAH HAH HAH HAH
GYAH HAH HAH!

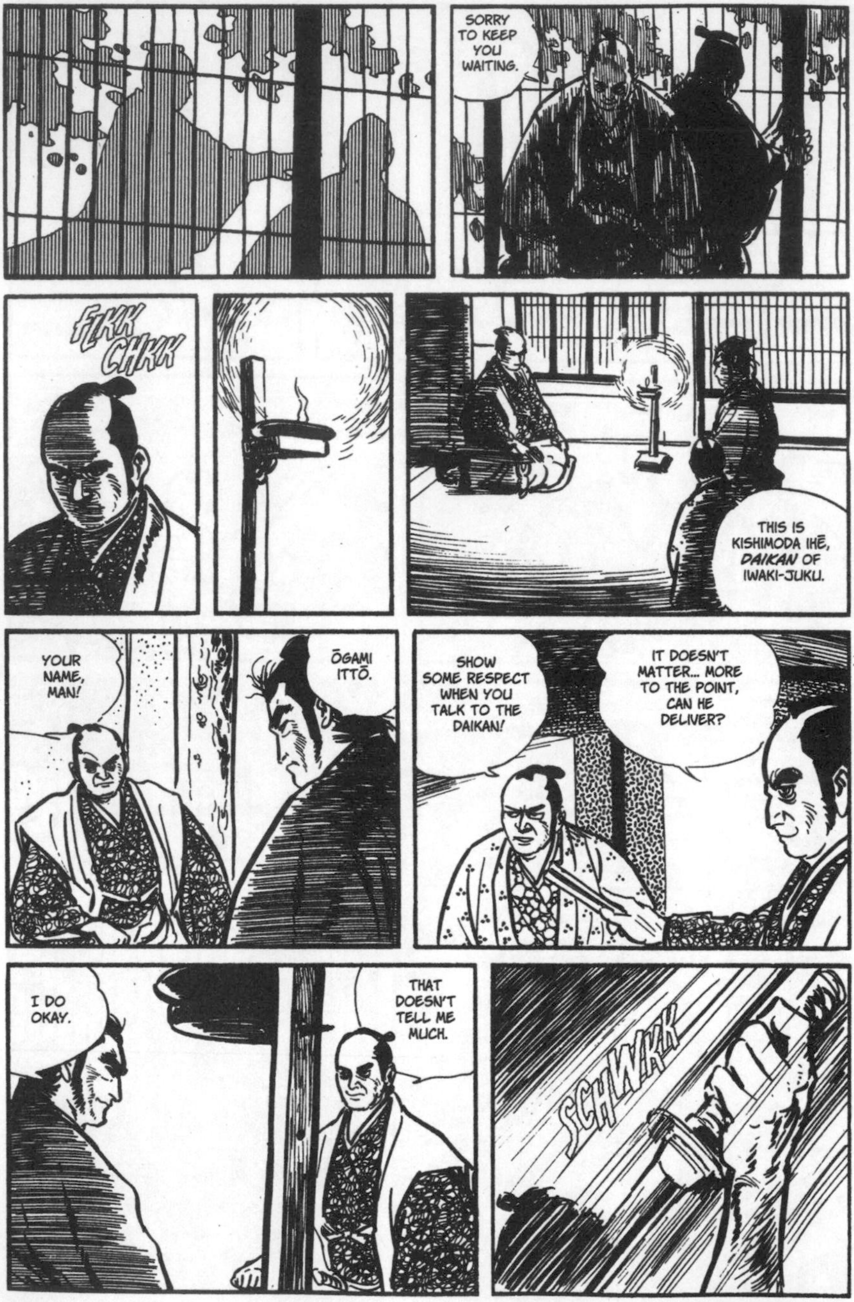
SORRY TO KEEP YOU WAITING.
FLKK CHKK
THIS IS KISHIMODA IHĒ, *DAIKAN* OF IWAKI-JUKU.
YOUR NAME, MAN!
ŌGAMI ITTŌ.
SHOW SOME RESPECT WHEN YOU TALK TO THE DAIKAN!
IT DOESN'T MATTER... MORE TO THE POINT, CAN HE DELIVER?
I DO OKAY.
THAT DOESN'T TELL ME MUCH.
SCHWKK

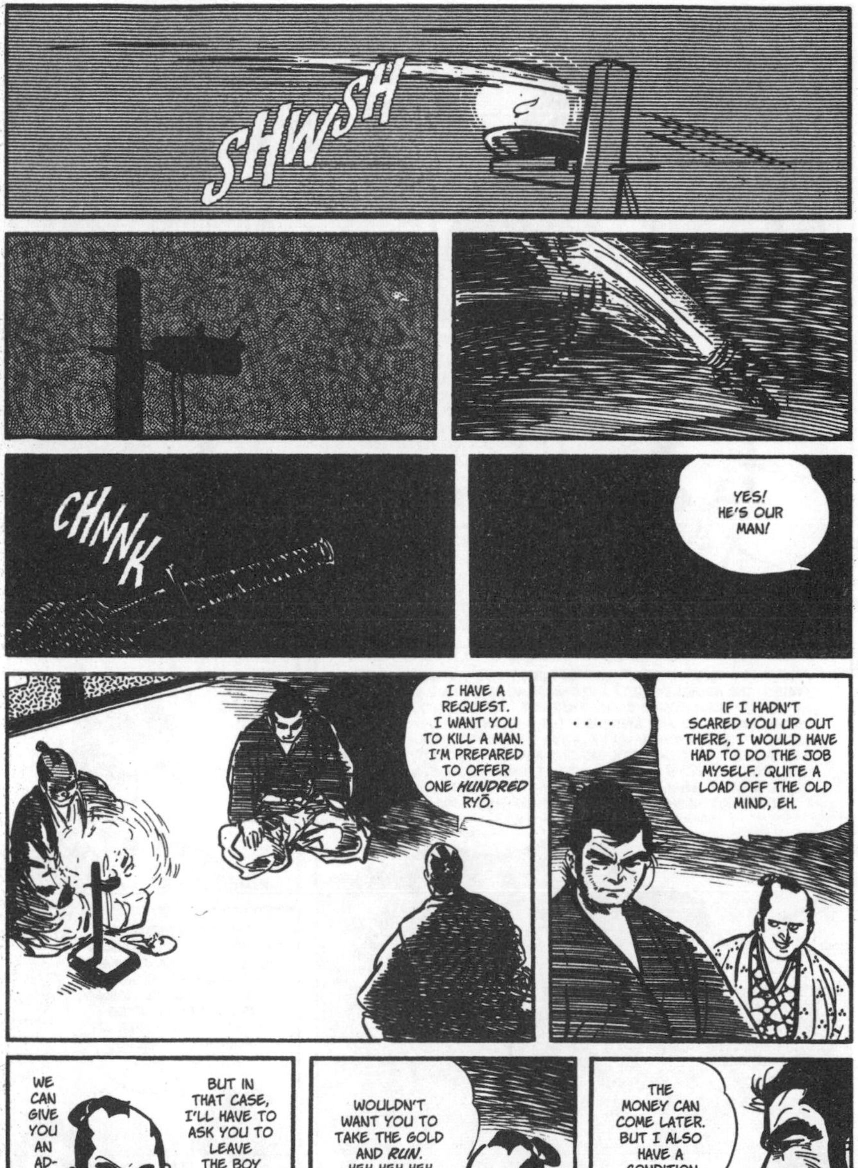
SHWSH
CHNNK
YES! HE'S OUR MAN!
I HAVE A REQUEST. I WANT YOU TO KILL A MAN. I'M PREPARED TO OFFER ONE *HUNDRED* RYŌ.
....
IF I HADN'T SCARED YOU UP OUT THERE, I WOULD HAVE HAD TO DO THE JOB MYSELF. QUITE A LOAD OFF THE OLD MIND, EH.
WE CAN GIVE YOU AN ADVANCE.
BUT IN THAT CASE, I'LL HAVE TO ASK YOU TO LEAVE THE BOY WITH US.
WOULDN'T WANT YOU TO TAKE THE GOLD AND *RUN*. HEH HEH HEH.
THE MONEY CAN COME LATER. BUT I ALSO HAVE A CONDITION.

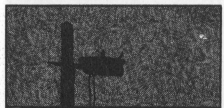

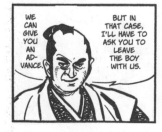

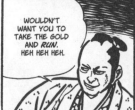

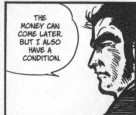

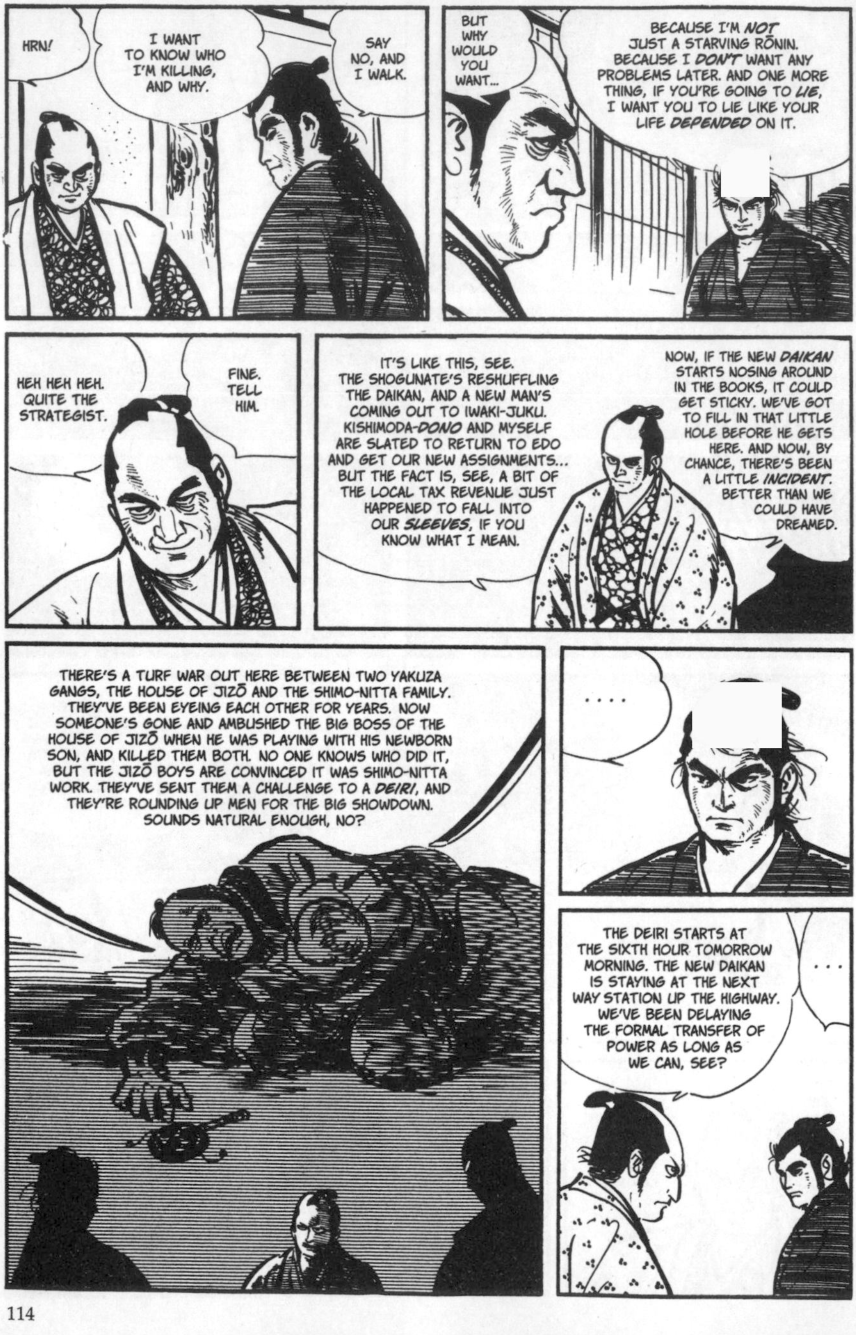
HRN!
I WANT TO KNOW WHO I'M KILLING, AND WHY.
SAY NO, AND I WALK.
BUT WHY WOULD YOU WANT...
BECAUSE I'M *NOT* JUST A STARVING RŌNIN. BECAUSE I *DON'T* WANT ANY PROBLEMS LATER. AND ONE MORE THING, IF YOU'RE GOING TO *LIE*, I WANT YOU TO LIE LIKE YOUR LIFE *DEPENDED* ON IT.
HEH HEH HEH. QUITE THE STRATEGIST.
FINE. TELL HIM.
IT'S LIKE THIS, SEE. THE SHOGUNATE'S RESHUFFLING THE DAIKAN, AND A NEW MAN'S COMING OUT TO IWAKI-JUKU. KISHIMODA-*DONO* AND MYSELF ARE SLATED TO RETURN TO EDO AND GET OUR NEW ASSIGNMENTS... BUT THE FACT IS, SEE, A BIT OF THE LOCAL TAX REVENUE JUST HAPPENED TO FALL INTO OUR *SLEEVES*, IF YOU KNOW WHAT I MEAN.
NOW, IF THE NEW *DAIKAN* STARTS NOSING AROUND IN THE BOOKS, IT COULD GET STICKY. WE'VE GOT TO FILL IN THAT LITTLE HOLE BEFORE HE GETS HERE. AND NOW, BY CHANCE, THERE'S BEEN A LITTLE *INCIDENT*. BETTER THAN WE COULD HAVE DREAMED.
THERE'S A TURF WAR OUT HERE BETWEEN TWO YAKUZA GANGS, THE HOUSE OF JIZŌ AND THE SHIMO-NITTA FAMILY. THEY'VE BEEN EYEING EACH OTHER FOR YEARS. NOW SOMEONE'S GONE AND AMBUSHED THE BIG BOSS OF THE HOUSE OF JIZŌ WHEN HE WAS PLAYING WITH HIS NEWBORN SON, AND KILLED THEM BOTH. NO ONE KNOWS WHO DID IT, BUT THE JIZŌ BOYS ARE CONVINCED IT WAS SHIMO-NITTA WORK. THEY'VE SENT THEM A CHALLENGE TO A *DEIRI*, AND THEY'RE ROUNDING UP MEN FOR THE BIG SHOWDOWN. SOUNDS NATURAL ENOUGH, NO?
....
THE DEIRI STARTS AT THE SIXTH HOUR TOMORROW MORNING. THE NEW DAIKAN IS STAYING AT THE NEXT WAY STATION UP THE HIGHWAY. WE'VE BEEN DELAYING THE FORMAL TRANSFER OF POWER AS LONG AS WE CAN, SEE?
...

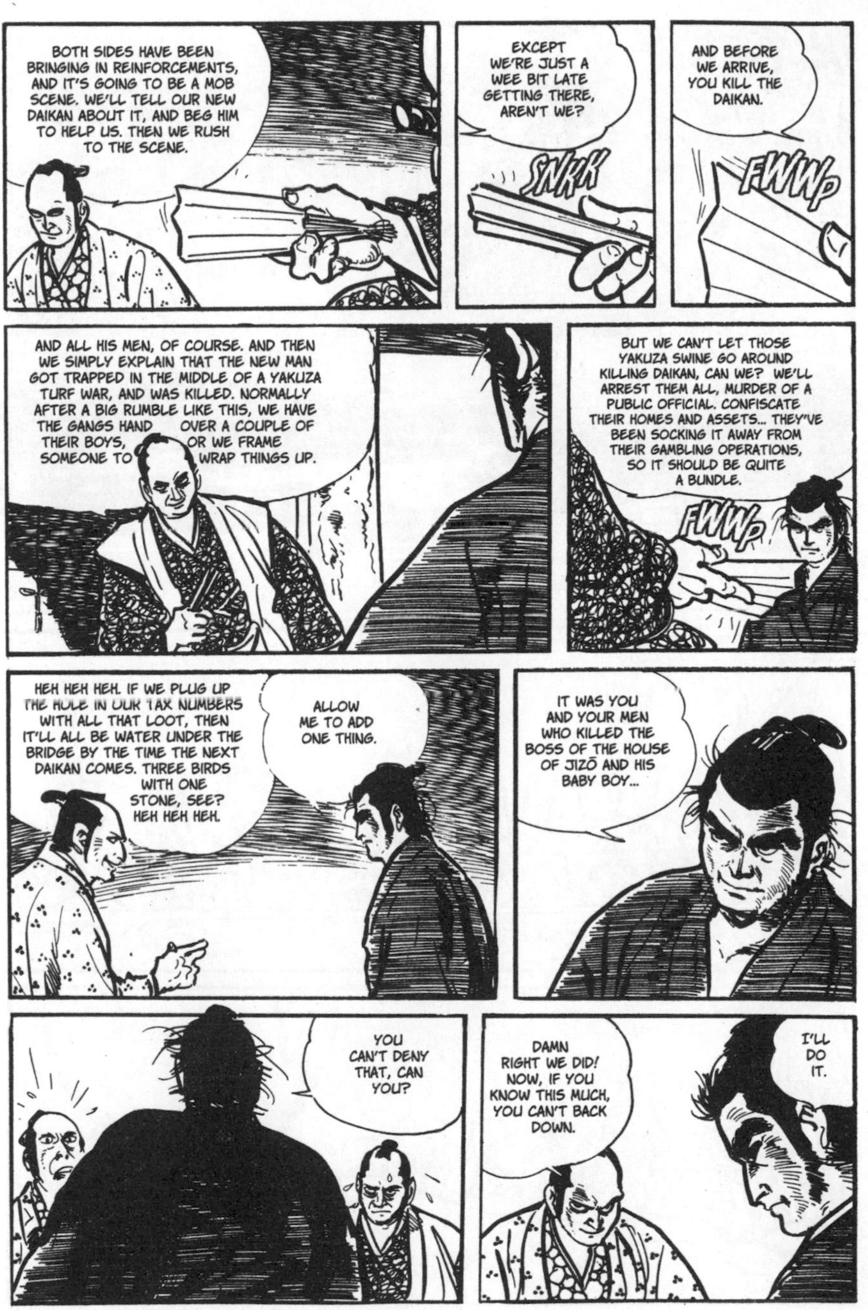
BOTH SIDES HAVE BEEN BRINGING IN REINFORCEMENTS, AND IT'S GOING TO BE A MOB SCENE. WE'LL TELL OUR NEW DAIKAN ABOUT IT, AND BEG HIM TO HELP US. THEN WE RUSH TO THE SCENE.
EXCEPT WE'RE JUST A WEE BIT LATE GETTING THERE, AREN'T WE?
SNKK
AND BEFORE WE ARRIVE, YOU KILL THE DAIKAN.
FWWP
AND ALL HIS MEN, OF COURSE. AND THEN WE SIMPLY EXPLAIN THAT THE NEW MAN GOT TRAPPED IN THE MIDDLE OF A YAKUZA TURF WAR, AND WAS KILLED. NORMALLY AFTER A BIG RUMBLE LIKE THIS, WE HAVE THE GANGS HAND OVER A COUPLE OF THEIR BOYS, OR WE FRAME SOMEONE TO WRAP THINGS UP.
BUT WE CAN'T LET THOSE YAKUZA SWINE GO AROUND KILLING DAIKAN, CAN WE? WE'LL ARREST THEM ALL, MURDER OF A PUBLIC OFFICIAL. CONFISCATE THEIR HOMES AND ASSETS... THEY'VE BEEN SOCKING IT AWAY FROM THEIR GAMBLING OPERATIONS, SO IT SHOULD BE QUITE A BUNDLE.
FWWP
HEH HEH HEH. IF WE PLUG UP THE HOLE IN OUR TAX NUMBERS WITH ALL THAT LOOT, THEN IT'LL ALL BE WATER UNDER THE BRIDGE BY THE TIME THE NEXT DAIKAN COMES. THREE BIRDS WITH ONE STONE, SEE? HEH HEH HEH.
ALLOW ME TO ADD ONE THING.
IT WAS YOU AND YOUR MEN WHO KILLED THE BOSS OF THE HOUSE OF JIZŌ AND HIS BABY BOY...
YOU CAN'T DENY THAT, CAN YOU?
DAMN RIGHT WE DID! NOW, IF YOU KNOW THIS MUCH, YOU CAN'T BACK DOWN.
I'LL DO IT.

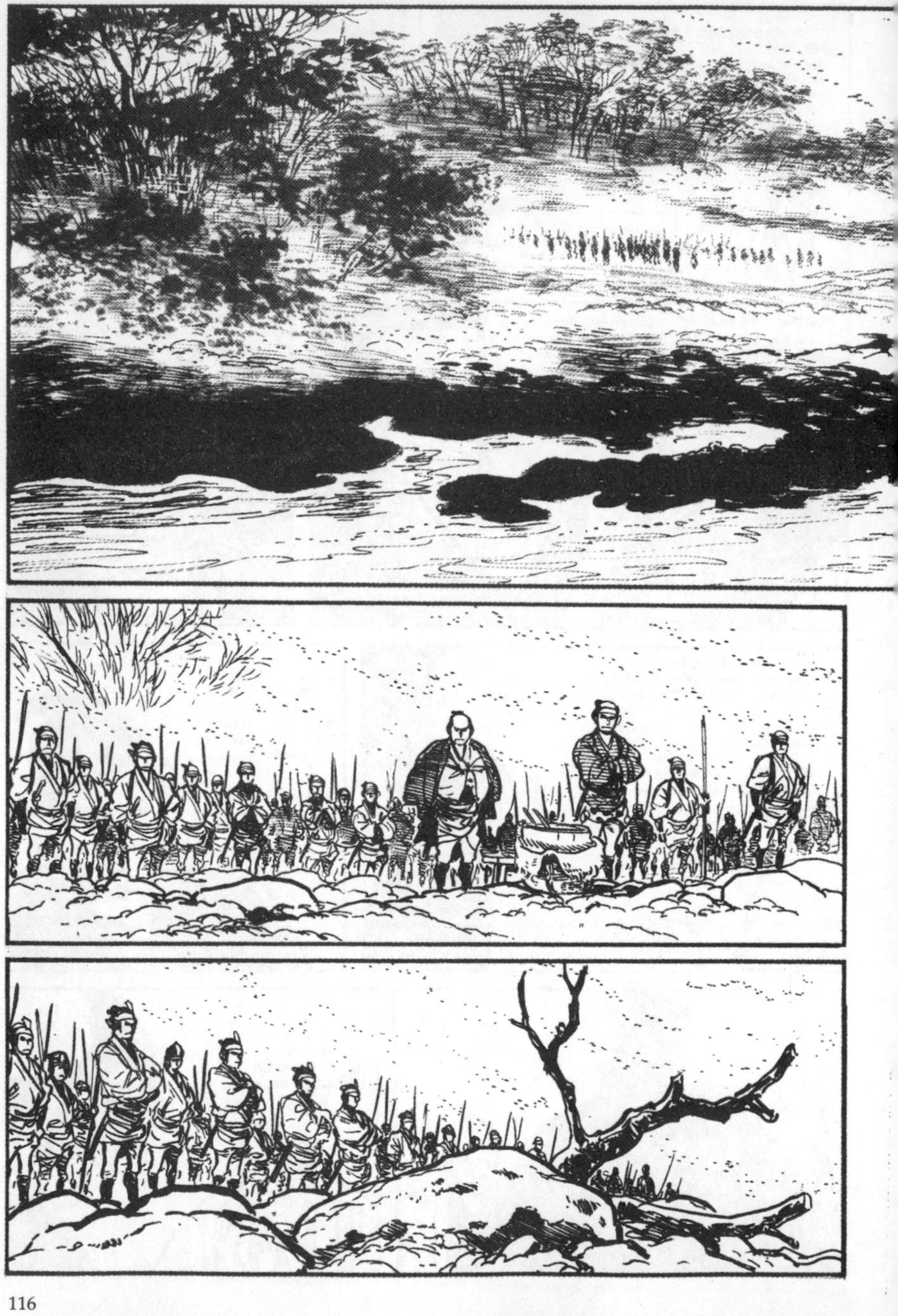

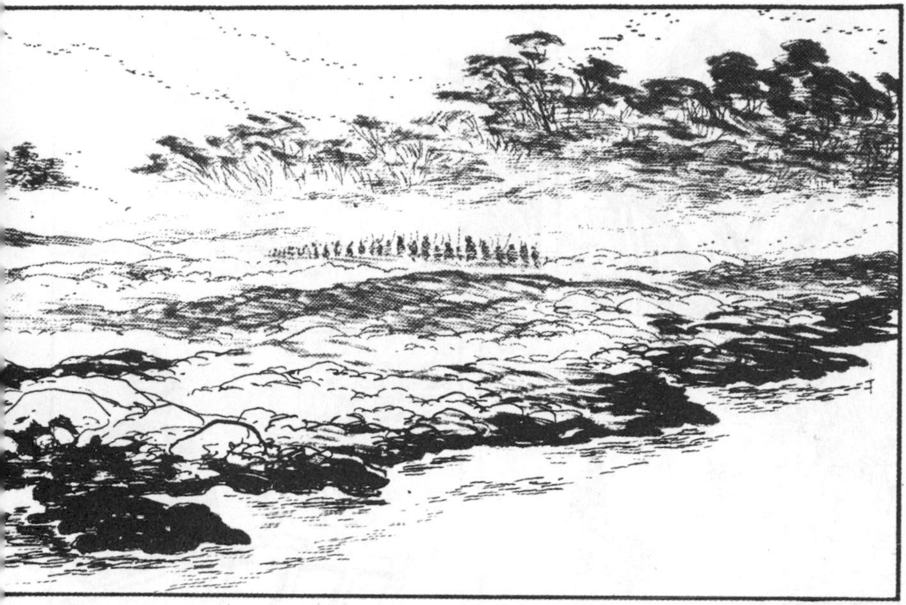
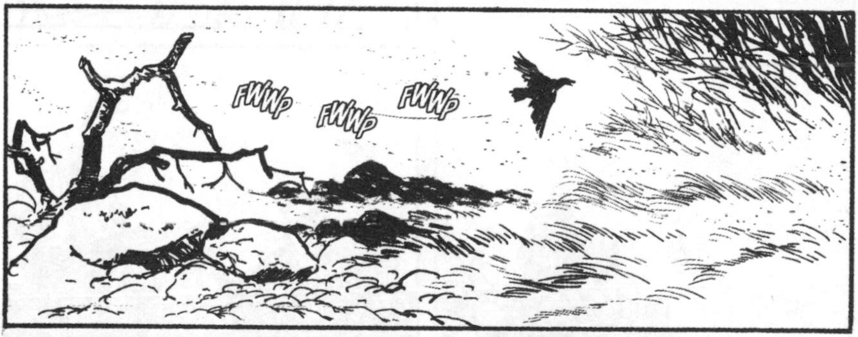
FWWP
FWWP
FWWP
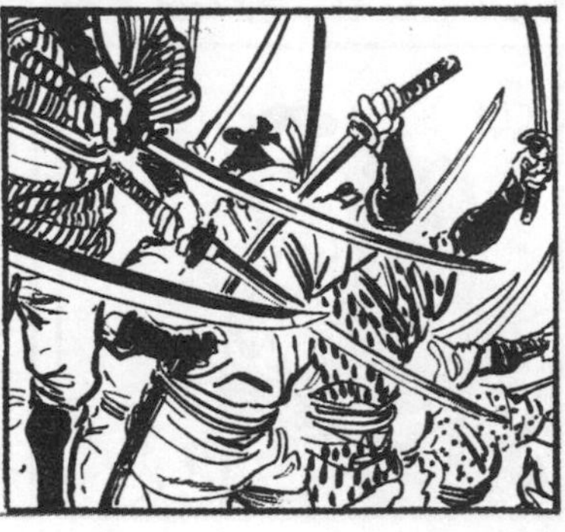
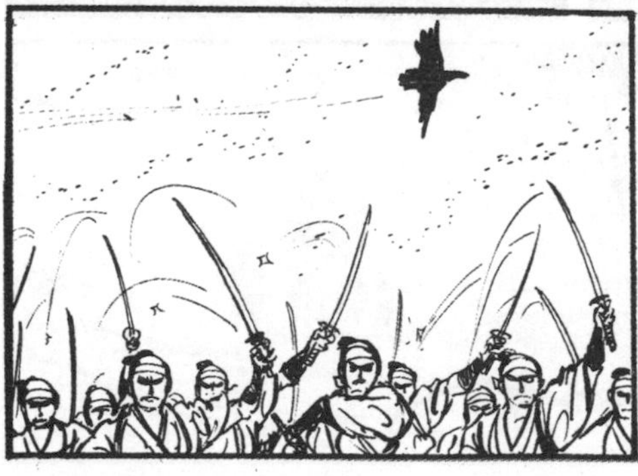

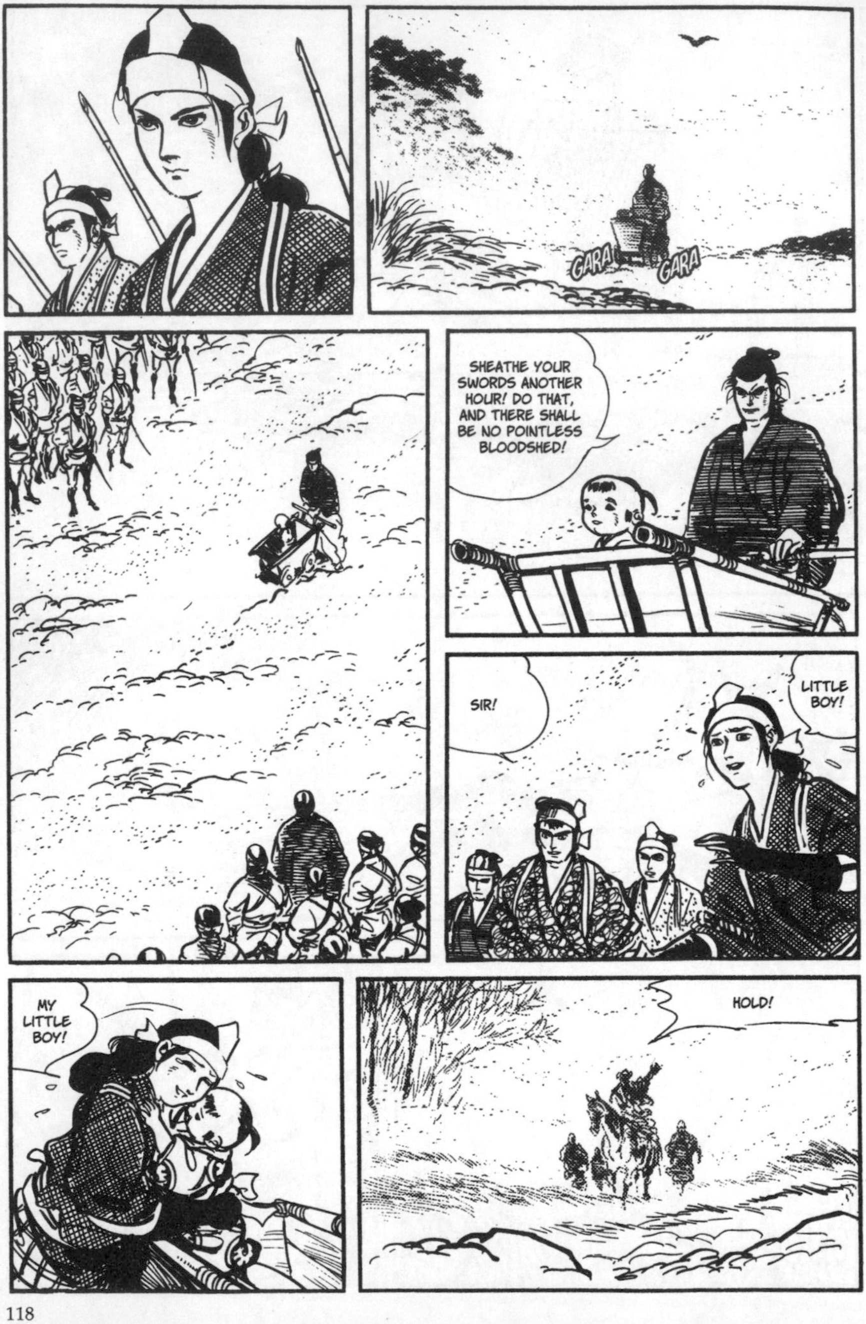
GARA GARA
SHEATHE YOUR SWORDS ANOTHER HOUR! DO THAT, AND THERE SHALL BE NO POINTLESS BLOODSHED!
SIR!
LITTLE BOY!
MY LITTLE BOY!
HOLD!

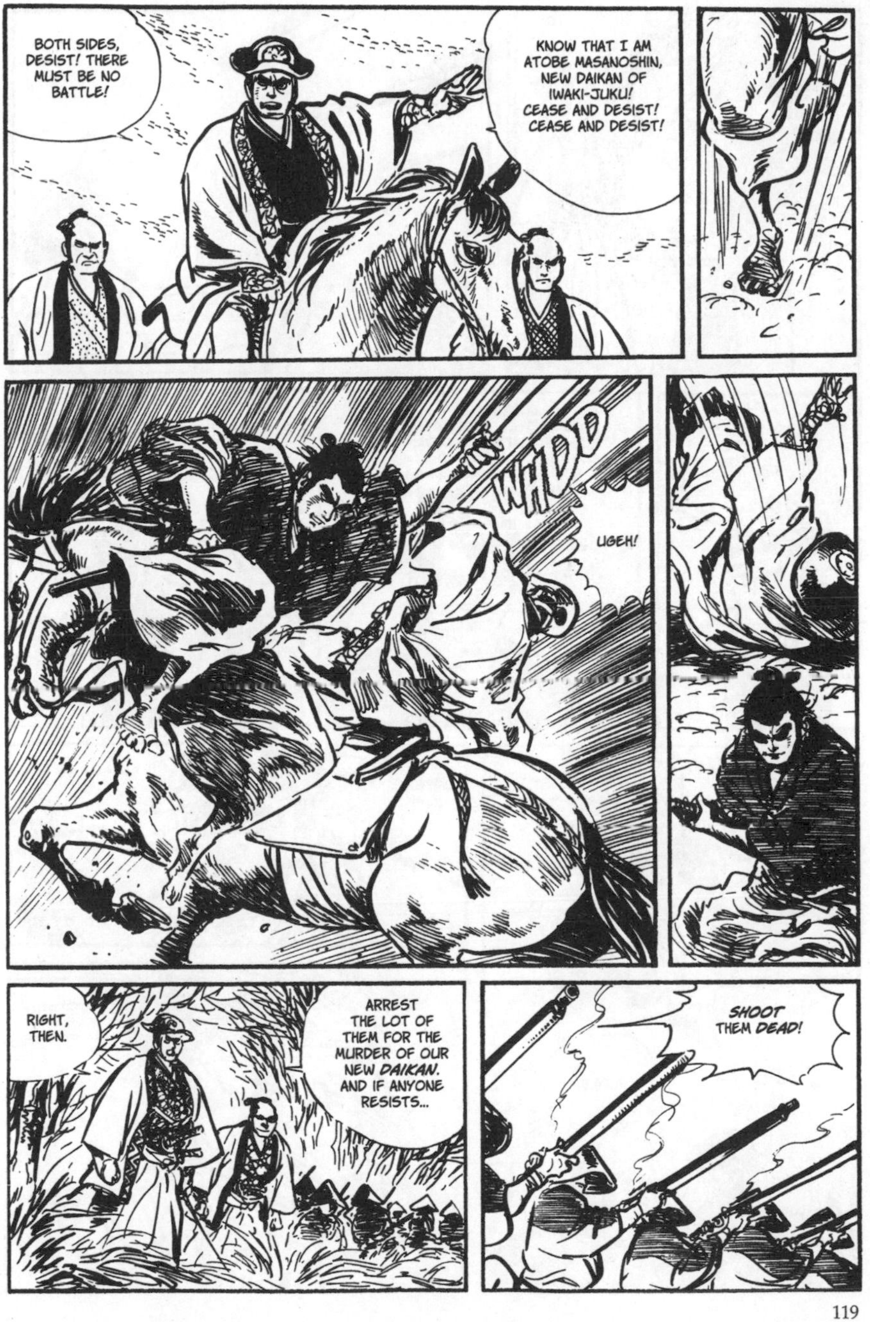
BOTH SIDES, DESIST! THERE MUST BE NO BATTLE!
KNOW THAT I AM ATOBE MASANOSHIN, NEW DAIKAN OF IWAKI-JUKU! CEASE AND DESIST! CEASE AND DESIST!
WHDD
UGEH!
RIGHT, THEN.
ARREST THE LOT OF THEM FOR THE MURDER OF OUR NEW *DAIKAN*. AND IF ANYONE RESISTS...
SHOOT THEM *DEAD!*

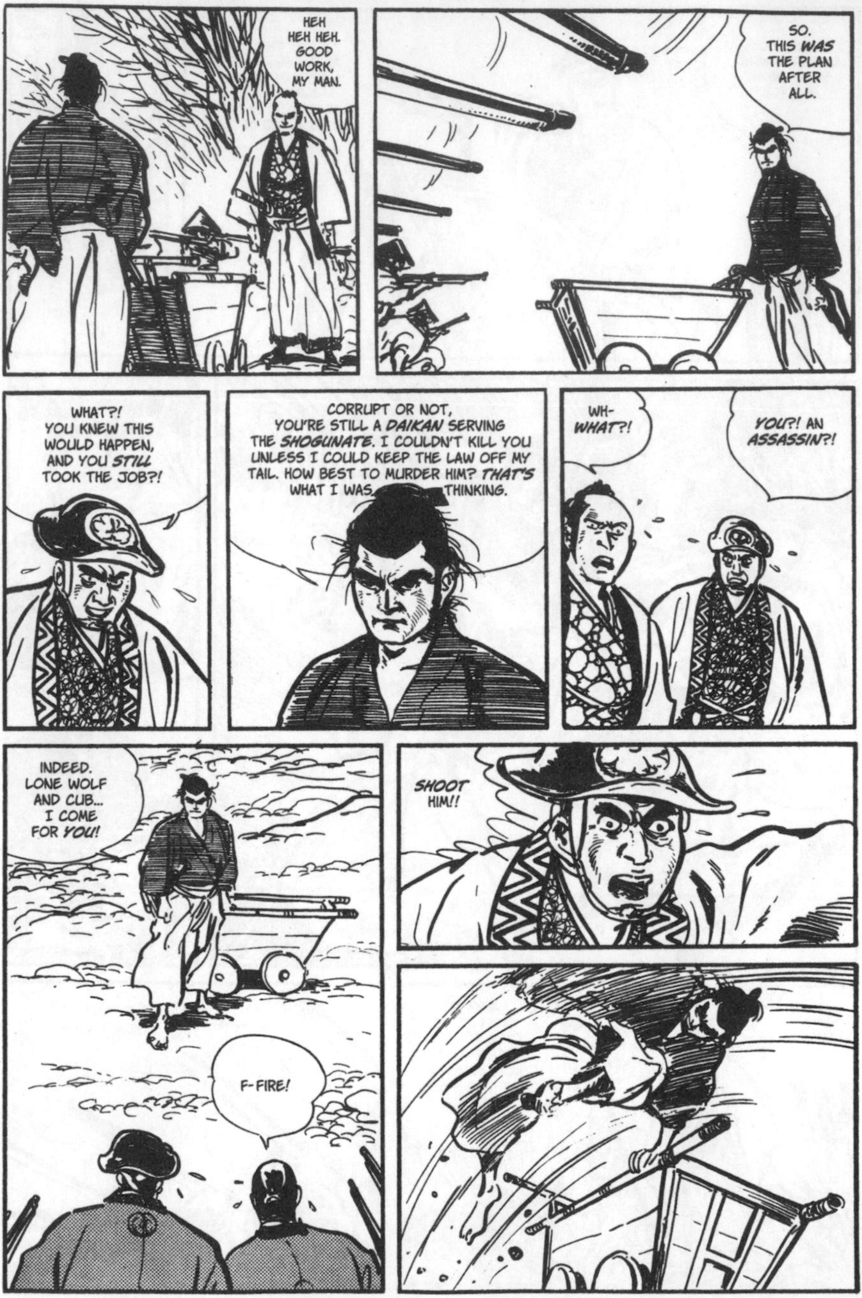
HEH HEH HEH. GOOD WORK, MY MAN.
SO. THIS *WAS* THE PLAN AFTER ALL.
WHAT?! YOU KNEW THIS WOULD HAPPEN, AND YOU *STILL* TOOK THE JOB?!
CORRUPT OR NOT, YOU'RE STILL A *DAIKAN* SERVING THE *SHOGUNATE*. I COULDN'T KILL YOU UNLESS I COULD KEEP THE LAW OFF MY TAIL. HOW BEST TO MURDER HIM? *THAT'S* WHAT I WAS THINKING.
WH- *WHAT?!*
YOU?! AN *ASSASSIN?!*
INDEED. LONE WOLF AND CUB... I COME FOR *YOU!*
F-FIRE!
SHOOT HIM!!

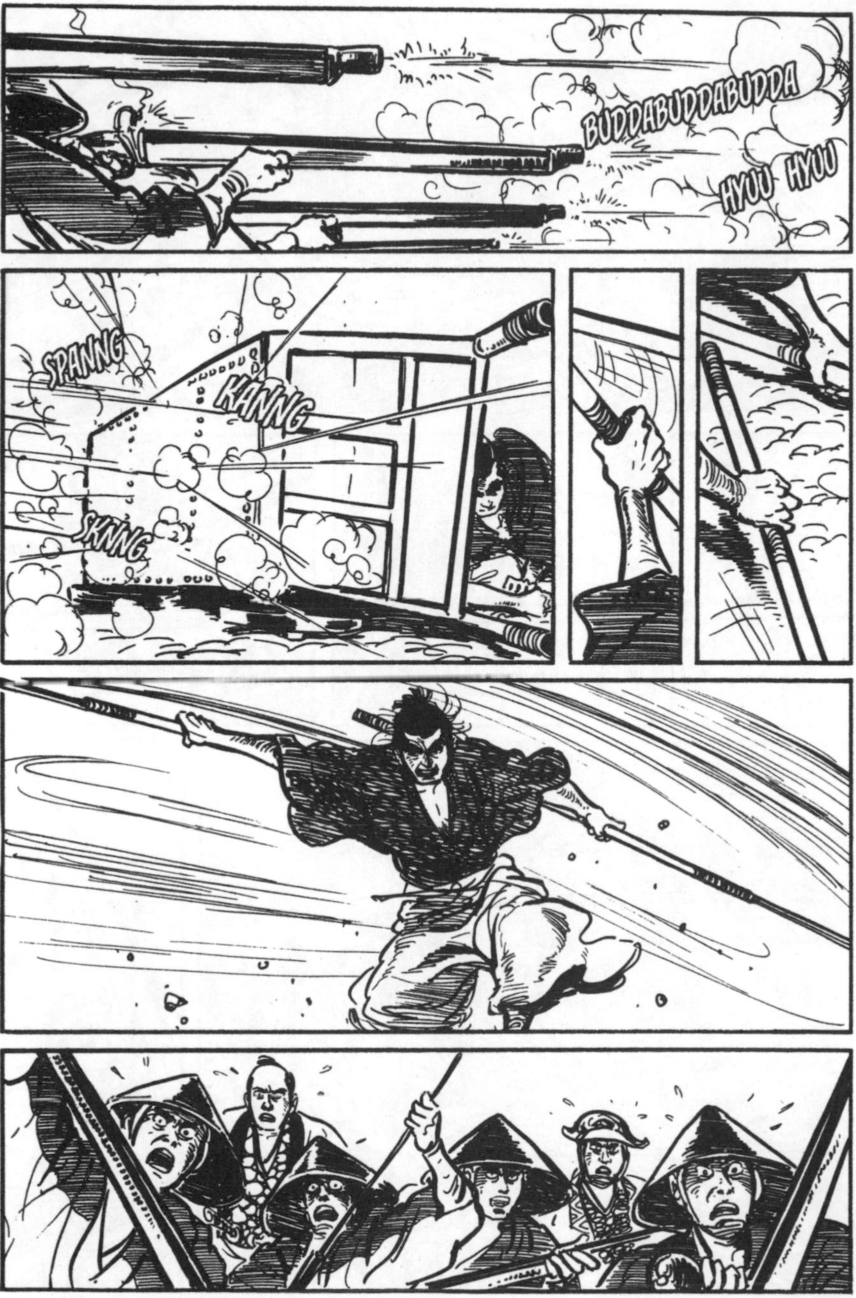
BUDDABUDDABUDDA
HYUU HYUU
KANNG
SPANNG
SKNNG

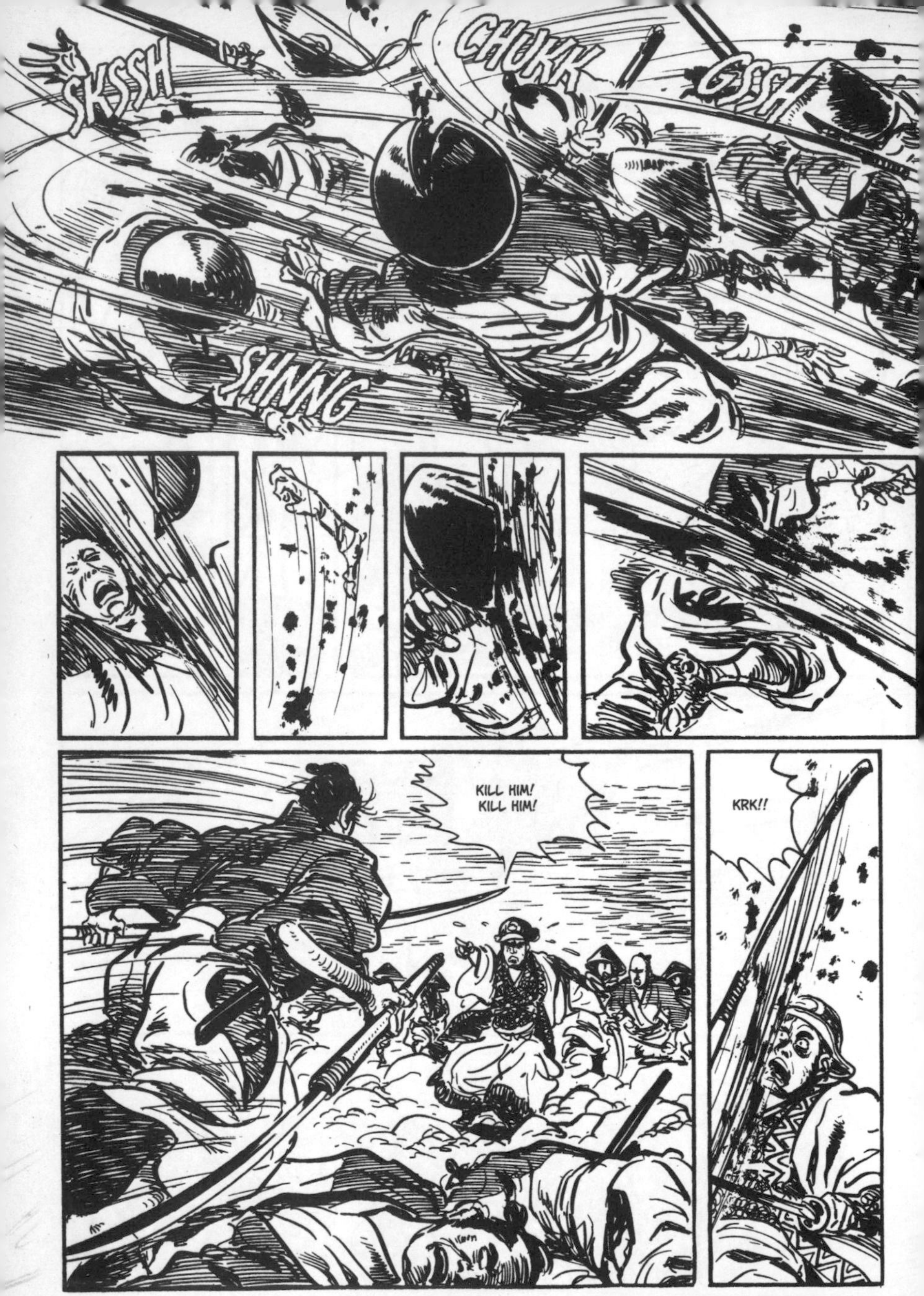
SKSSH
CHUKK
GSSH
SHNNG
KILL HIM!
KILL HIM!
KRK!!

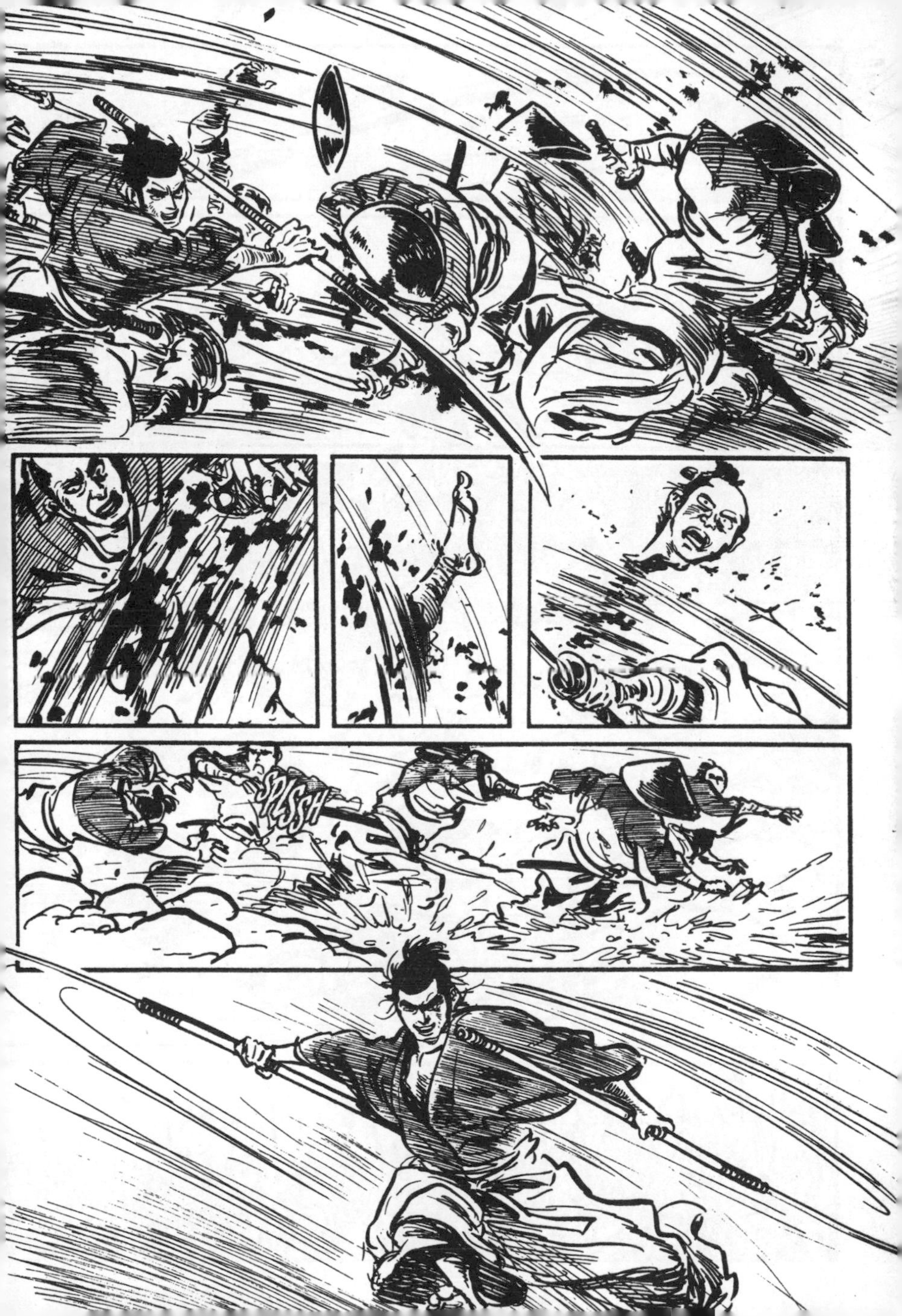
SPLSSH

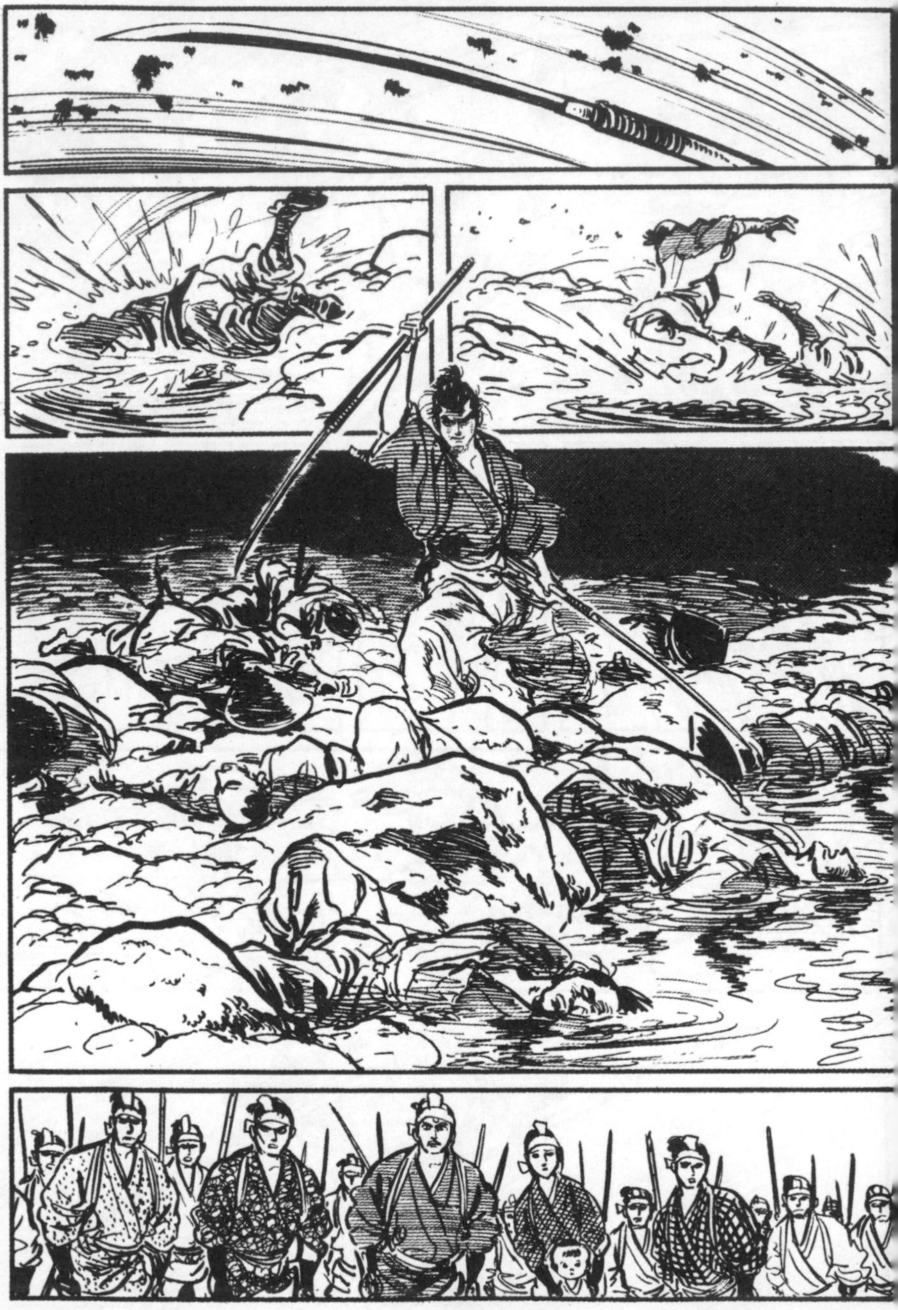

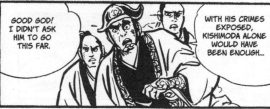

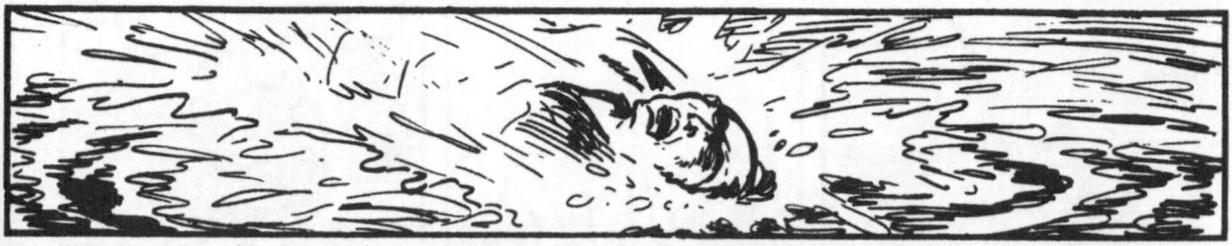
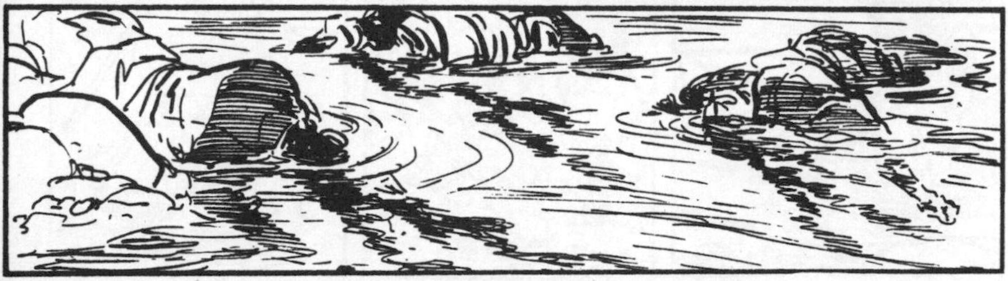
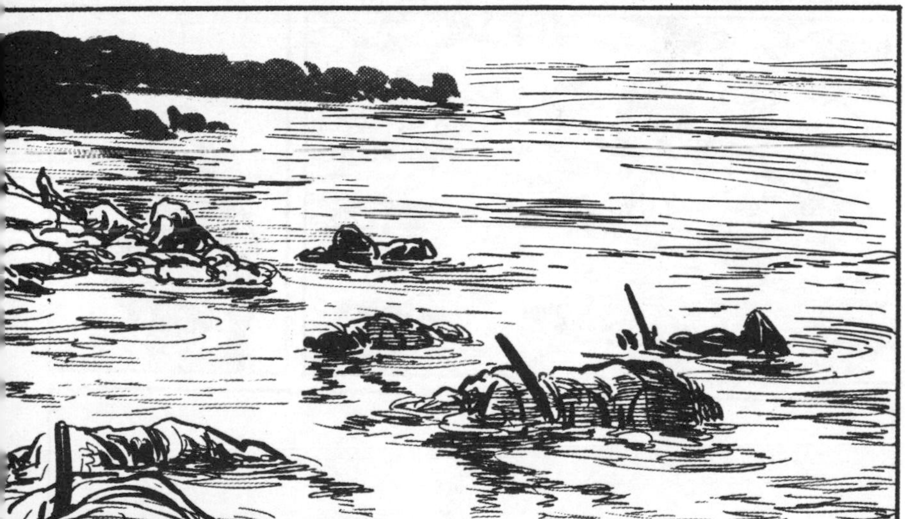
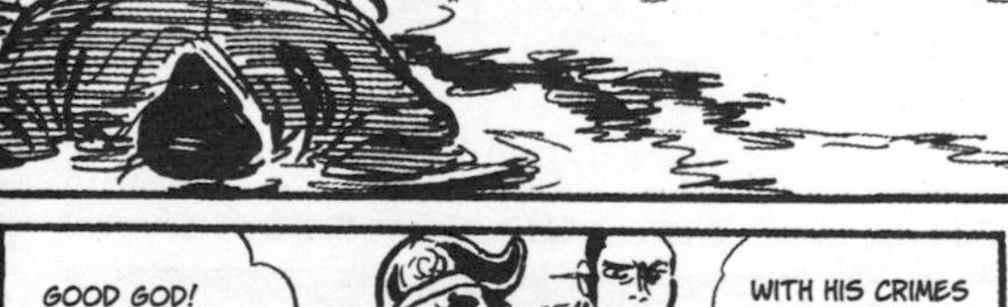
GOOD GOD! I DIDN'T ASK HIM TO GO THIS FAR.
WITH HIS CRIMES EXPOSED, KISHIMODA ALONE WOULD HAVE BEEN ENOUGH...
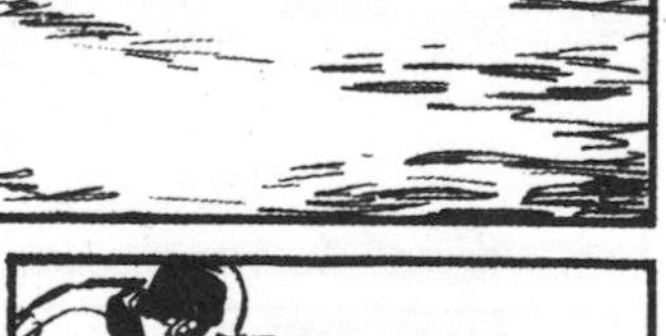
gff!
uhff!!

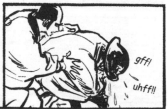

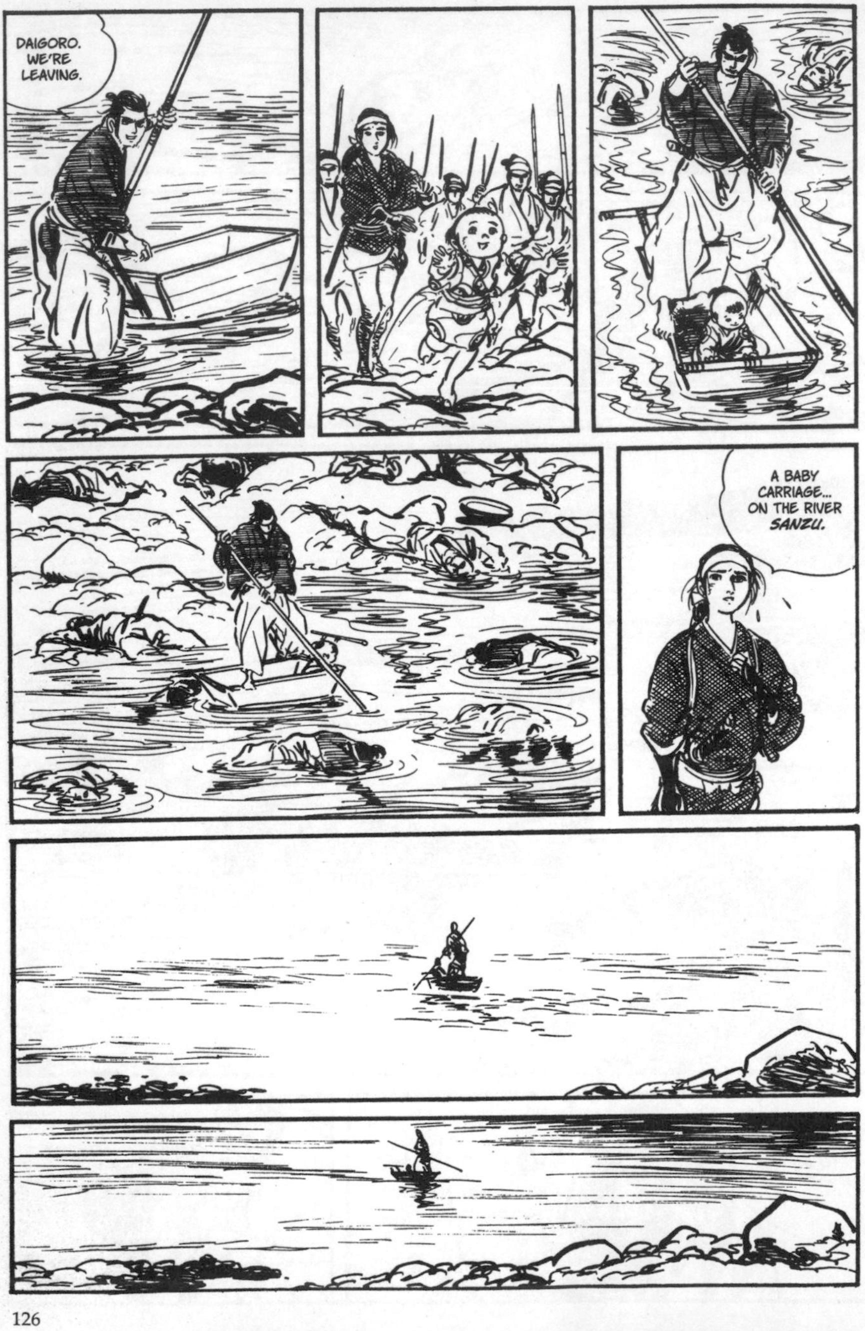
DAIGORO. WE'RE LEAVING.
A BABY CARRIAGE... ON THE RIVER *SANZU*.

子連れ狼

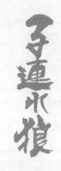

Suiō School Zanbatō

5

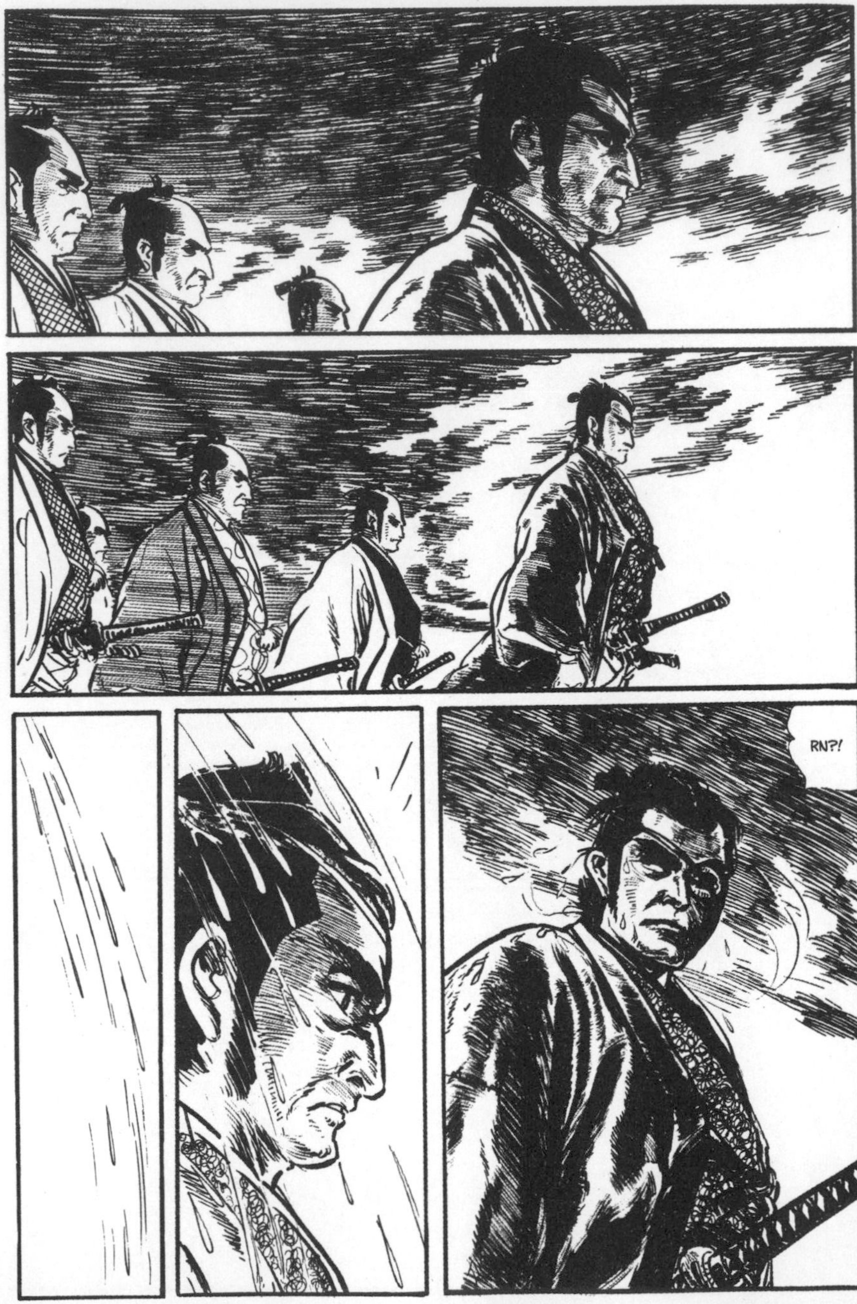
RN?!

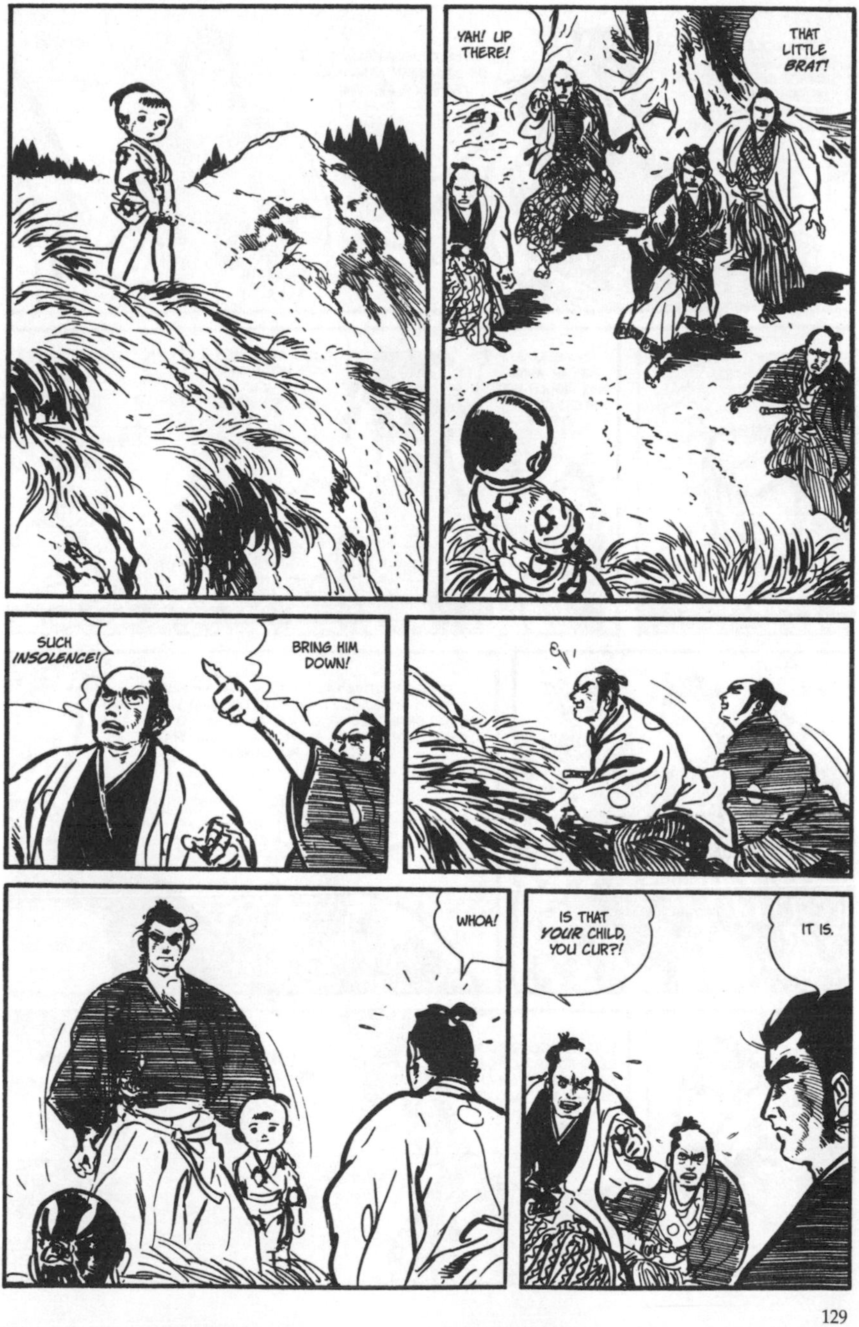
YAH! UP THERE!
THAT LITTLE BRAT!
SUCH INSOLENCE!
BRING HIM DOWN!
WHOA!
IS THAT YOUR CHILD, YOU CUR?!
IT IS.

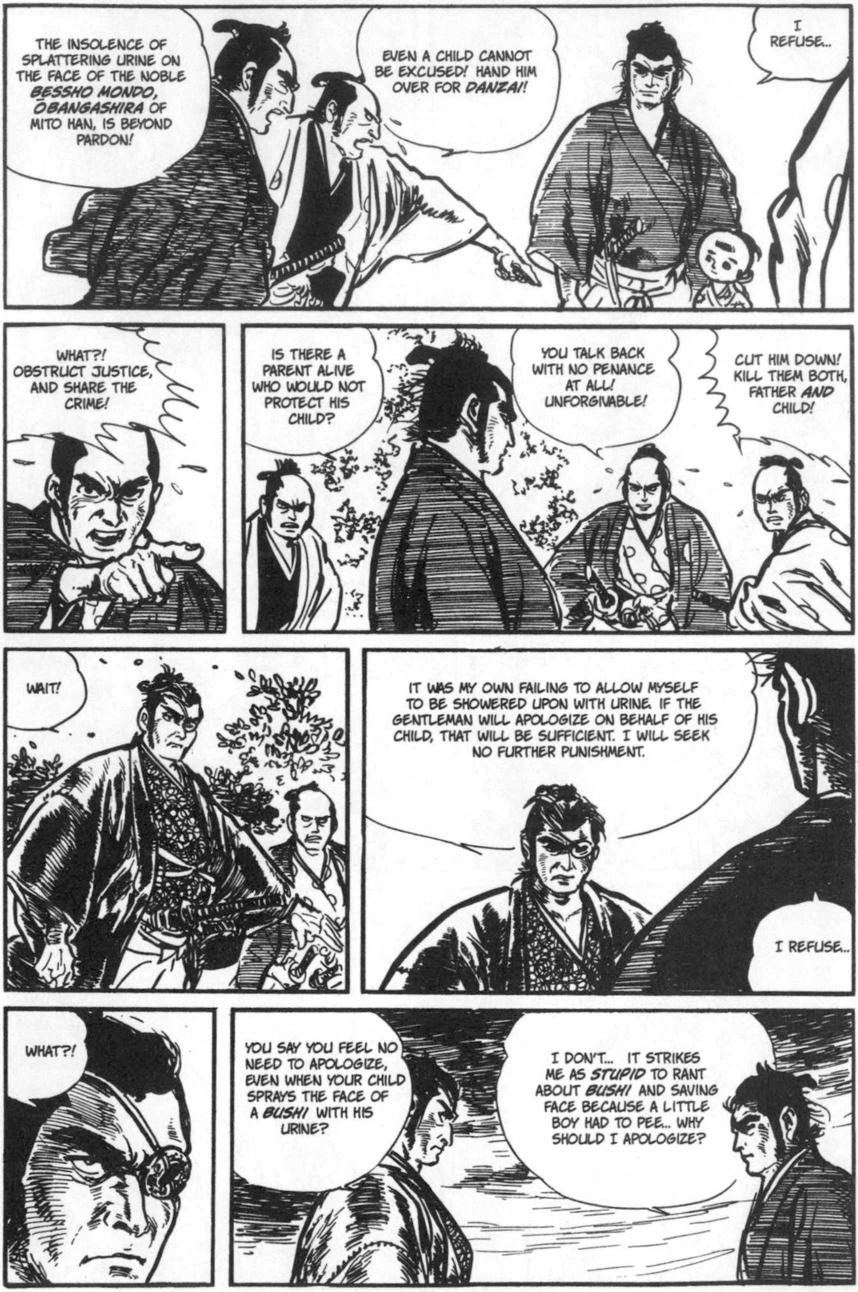
THE INSOLENCE OF SPLATTERING URINE ON THE FACE OF THE NOBLE *BESSHO MONDO*, *ŌBANGASHIRA* OF MITO HAN, IS BEYOND PARDON!
EVEN A CHILD CANNOT BE EXCUSED! HAND HIM OVER FOR *DANZAI*!
I REFUSE...
WHAT?! OBSTRUCT JUSTICE, AND SHARE THE CRIME!
IS THERE A PARENT ALIVE WHO WOULD NOT PROTECT HIS CHILD?
YOU TALK BACK WITH NO PENANCE AT ALL! UNFORGIVABLE!
CUT HIM DOWN! KILL THEM BOTH, FATHER *AND* CHILD!
WAIT!
IT WAS MY OWN FAILING TO ALLOW MYSELF TO BE SHOWERED UPON WITH URINE. IF THE GENTLEMAN WILL APOLOGIZE ON BEHALF OF HIS CHILD, THAT WILL BE SUFFICIENT. I WILL SEEK NO FURTHER PUNISHMENT.
I REFUSE...
WHAT?!
YOU SAY YOU FEEL NO NEED TO APOLOGIZE, EVEN WHEN YOUR CHILD SPRAYS THE FACE OF A *BUSHI* WITH HIS URINE?
I DON'T... IT STRIKES ME AS *STUPID* TO RANT ABOUT *BUSHI* AND SAVING FACE BECAUSE A LITTLE BOY HAD TO PEE... WHY SHOULD I APOLOGIZE?

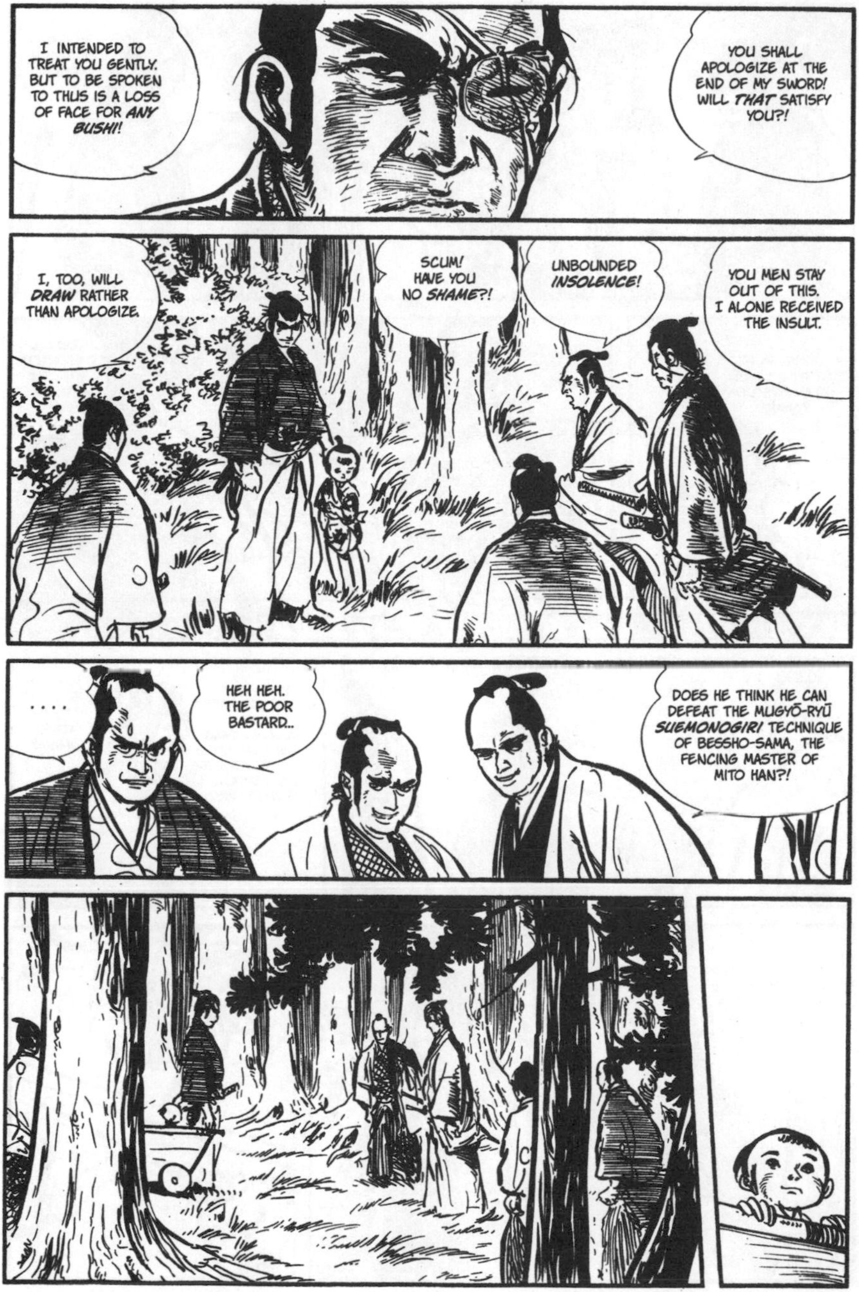
I INTENDED TO TREAT YOU GENTLY. BUT TO BE SPOKEN TO THUS IS A LOSS OF FACE FOR *ANY BUSHI*!
YOU SHALL APOLOGIZE AT THE END OF MY SWORD! WILL *THAT* SATISFY YOU?!
I, TOO, WILL *DRAW* RATHER THAN APOLOGIZE.
SCUM! HAVE YOU NO *SHAME*?!
UNBOUNDED *INSOLENCE*!
YOU MEN STAY OUT OF THIS. I ALONE RECEIVED THE INSULT.
. . . .
HEH HEH. THE POOR BASTARD..
DOES HE THINK HE CAN DEFEAT THE MUGYŌ-RYŪ *SUEMONOGIRI* TECHNIQUE OF BESSHO-SAMA, THE FENCING MASTER OF MITO HAN?!

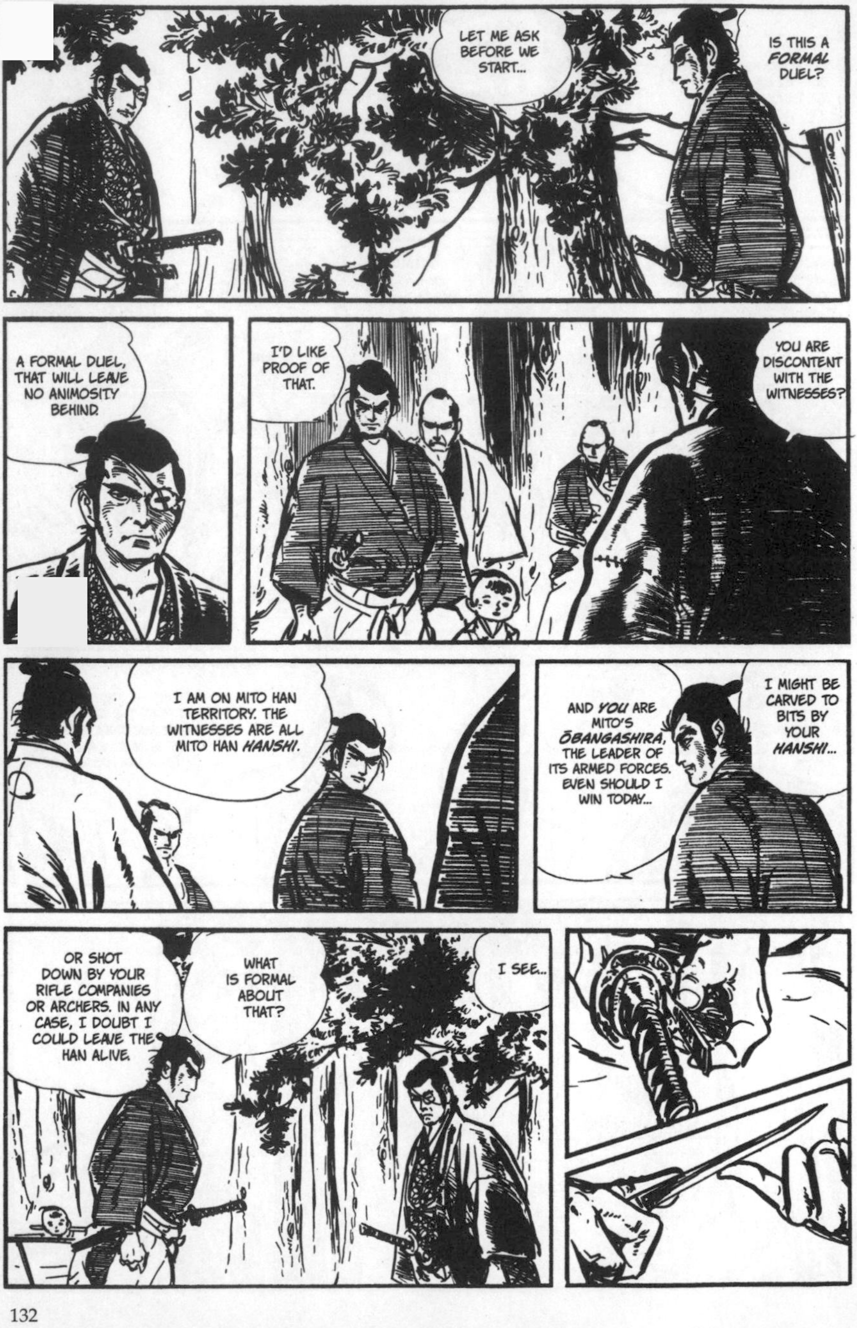

LET ME ASK BEFORE WE START...
IS THIS A *FORMAL* DUEL?
A FORMAL DUEL, THAT WILL LEAVE NO ANIMOSITY BEHIND.
I'D LIKE PROOF OF THAT.
YOU ARE DISCONTENT WITH THE WITNESSES?
I AM ON MITO HAN TERRITORY. THE WITNESSES ARE ALL MITO HAN *HANSHI*.
AND *YOU* ARE MITO'S *ŌBANGASHIRA*, THE LEADER OF ITS ARMED FORCES. EVEN SHOULD I WIN TODAY...
I MIGHT BE CARVED TO BITS BY YOUR *HANSHI*...
OR SHOT DOWN BY YOUR RIFLE COMPANIES OR ARCHERS. IN ANY CASE, I DOUBT I COULD LEAVE THE HAN ALIVE.
WHAT IS FORMAL ABOUT THAT?
I SEE...

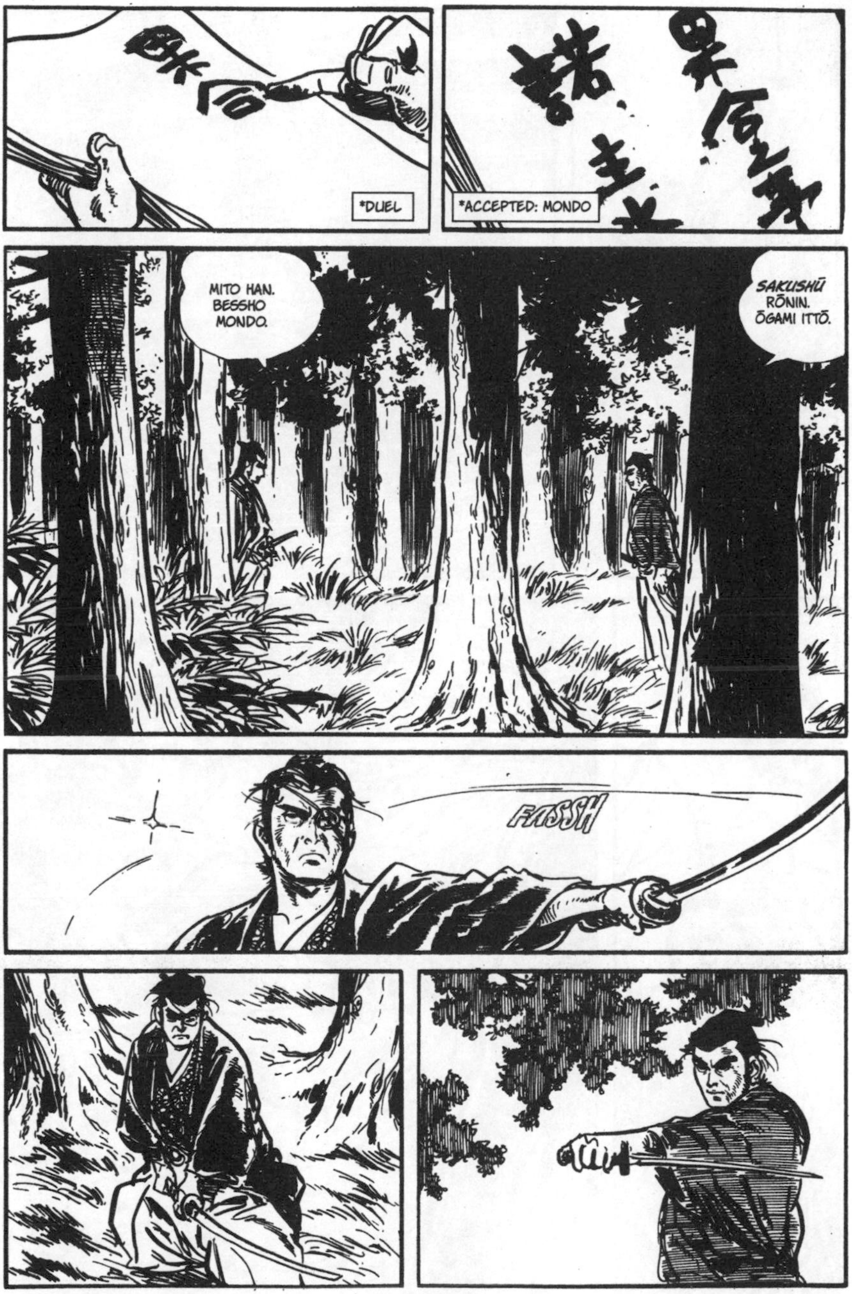
*ACCEPTED: MONDO
*DUEL
SAKUSHŪ RŌNIN. ŌGAMI ITTŌ.
MITO HAN. BESSHO MONDO.
FASSH

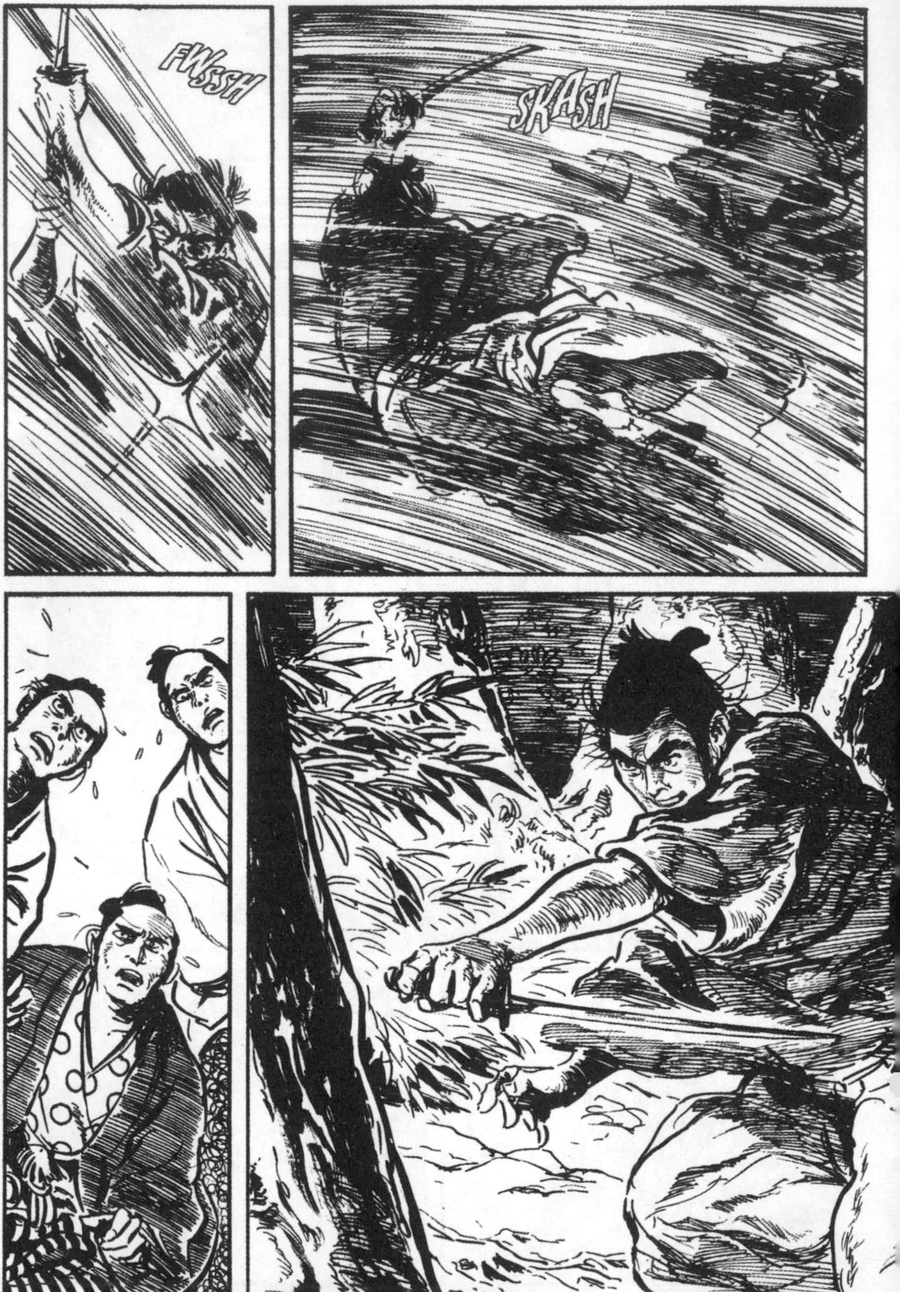
SKASH
FWSSH

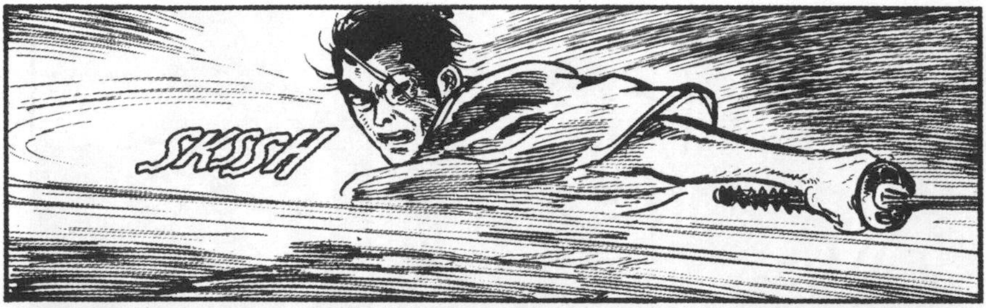
SKSSH
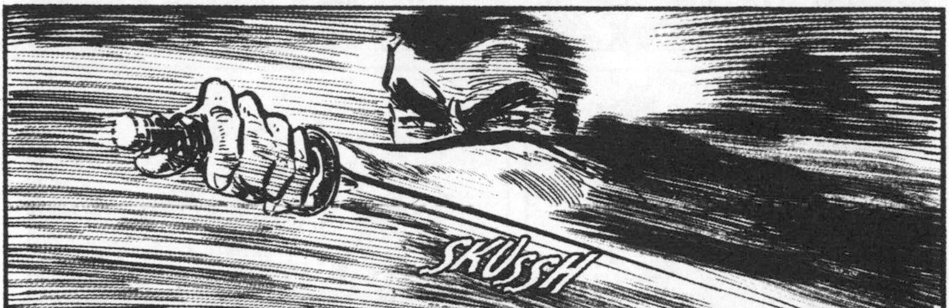
SKUSSH
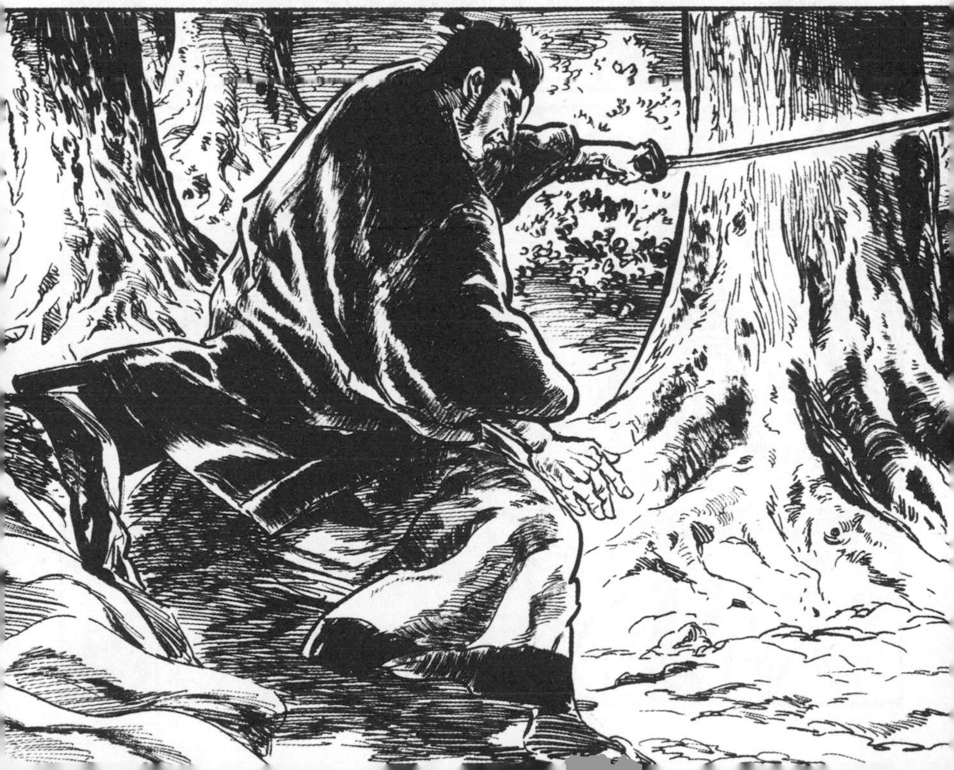

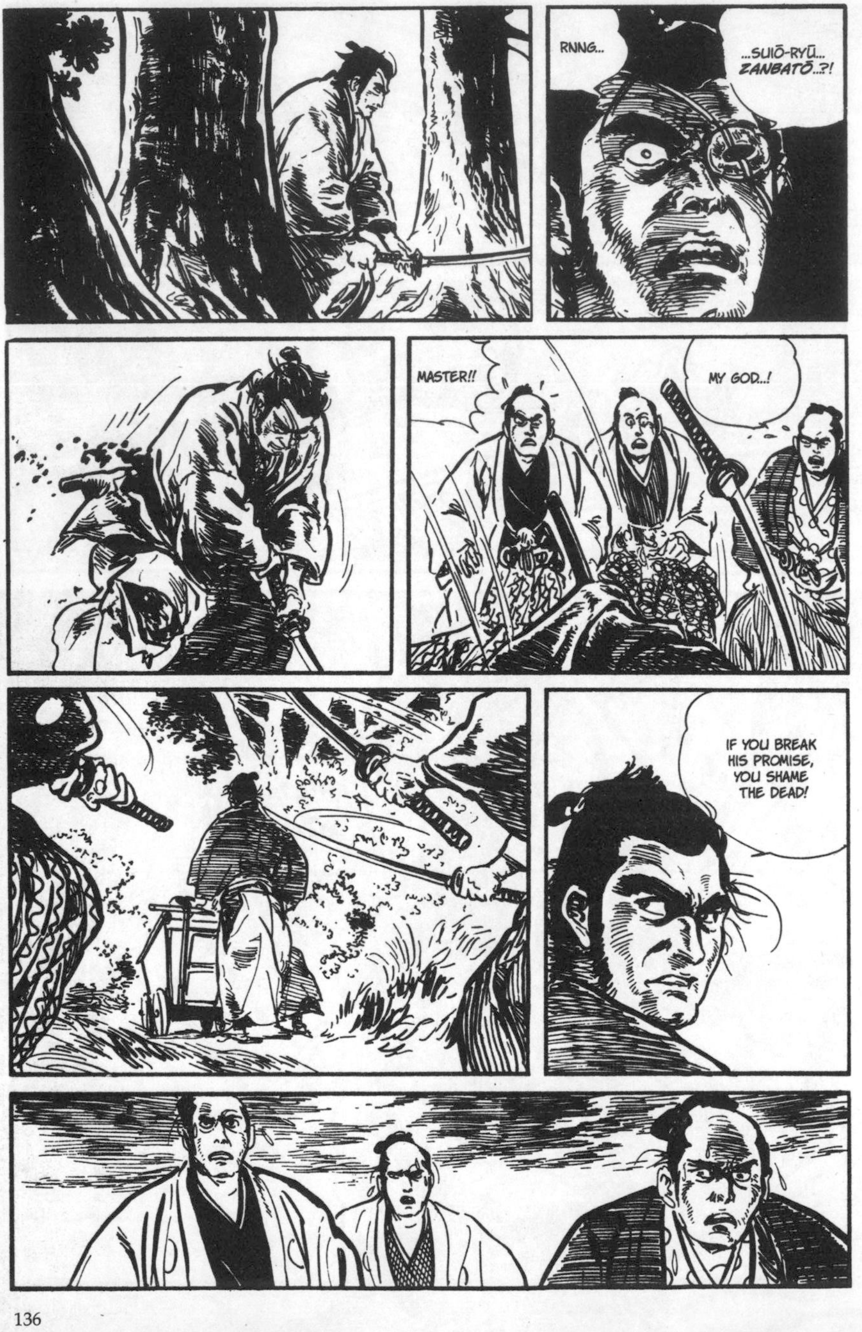
RNNG...
...SUIŌ-RYŪ... ZANBATŌ...?!
MY GOD...!
MASTER!!
IF YOU BREAK HIS PROMISE, YOU SHAME THE DEAD!

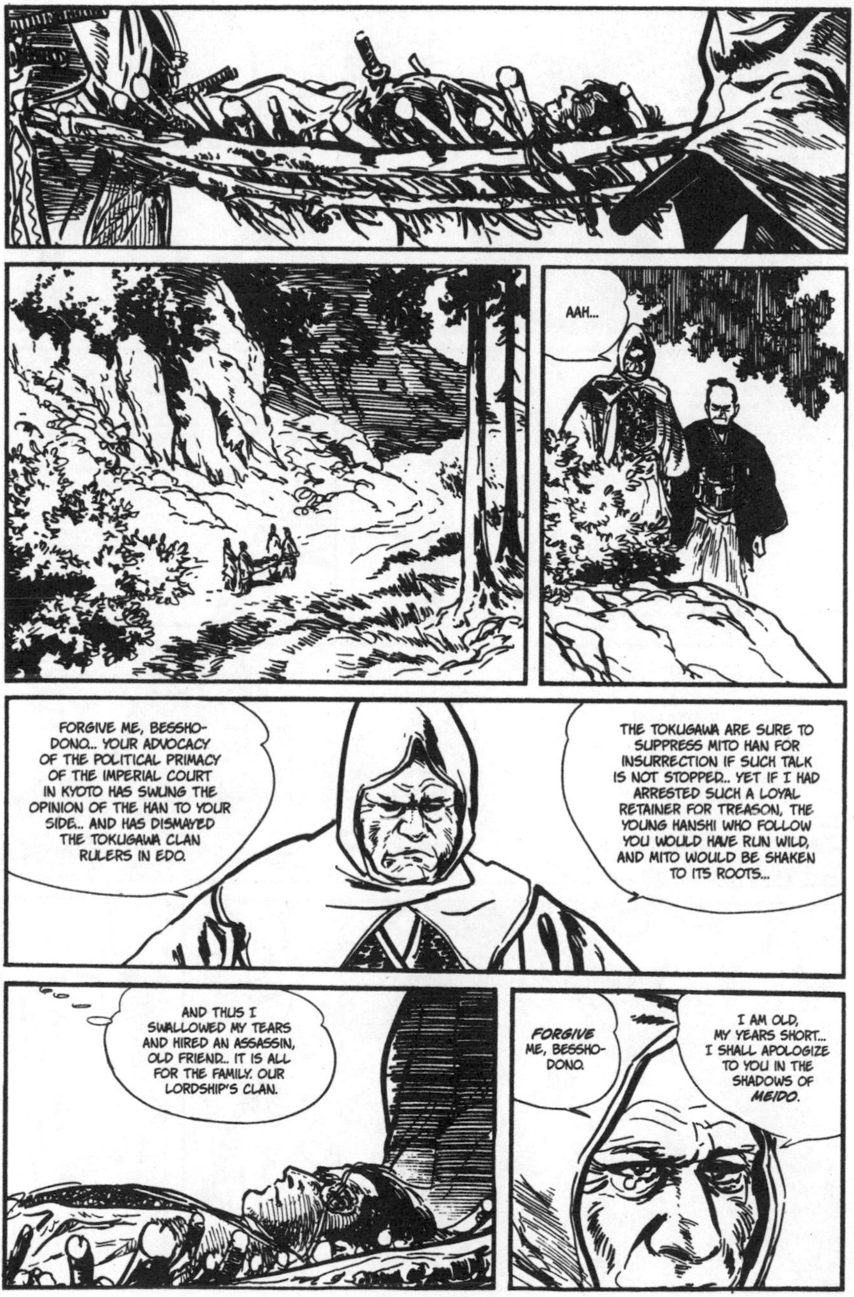
AAH...
FORGIVE ME, BESSHO-DONO... YOUR ADVOCACY OF THE POLITICAL PRIMACY OF THE IMPERIAL COURT IN KYOTO HAS SWUNG THE OPINION OF THE HAN TO YOUR SIDE.. AND HAS DISMAYED THE TOKUGAWA CLAN RULERS IN EDO.
THE TOKUGAWA ARE SURE TO SUPPRESS MITO HAN FOR INSURRECTION IF SUCH TALK IS NOT STOPPED... YET IF I HAD ARRESTED SUCH A LOYAL RETAINER FOR TREASON, THE YOUNG HANSHI WHO FOLLOW YOU WOULD HAVE RUN WILD, AND MITO WOULD BE SHAKEN TO ITS ROOTS...
AND THUS I SWALLOWED MY TEARS AND HIRED AN ASSASSIN, OLD FRIEND... IT IS ALL FOR THE FAMILY. OUR LORDSHIP'S CLAN.
FORGIVE ME, BESSHO-DONO.
I AM OLD, MY YEARS SHORT... I SHALL APOLOGIZE TO YOU IN THE SHADOWS OF *MEIDO*.

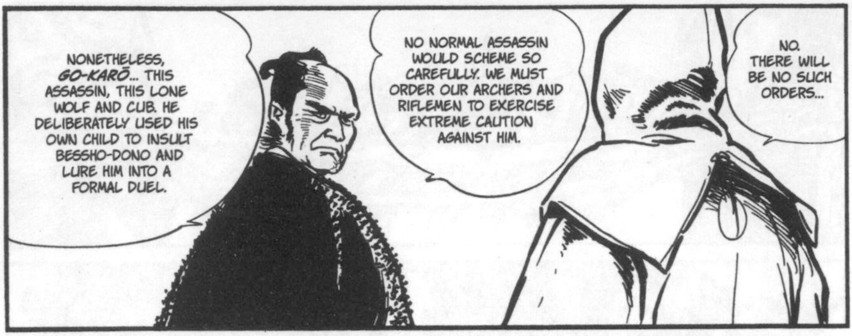
NONETHELESS, *GO-KARŌ*... THIS ASSASSIN, THIS LONE WOLF AND CUB. HE DELIBERATELY USED HIS OWN CHILD TO INSULT BESSHO-DONO AND LURE HIM INTO A FORMAL DUEL.
NO NORMAL ASSASSIN WOULD SCHEME SO CAREFULLY. WE MUST ORDER OUR ARCHERS AND RIFLEMEN TO EXERCISE EXTREME CAUTION AGAINST HIM.
NO. THERE WILL BE NO SUCH ORDERS...

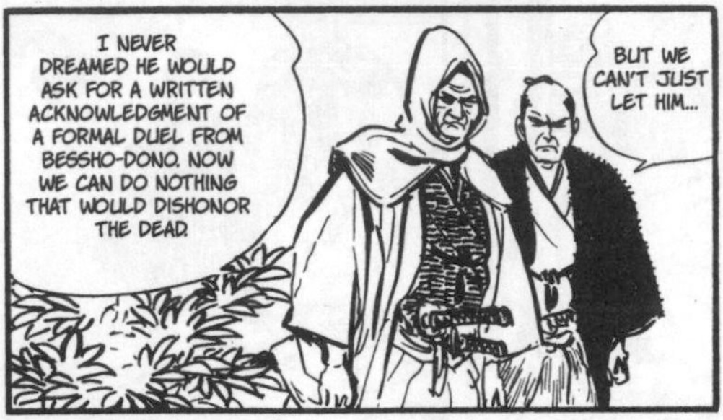
I NEVER DREAMED HE WOULD ASK FOR A WRITTEN ACKNOWLEDGMENT OF A FORMAL DUEL FROM BESSHO-DONO. NOW WE CAN DO NOTHING THAT WOULD DISHONOR THE DEAD.
BUT WE CAN'T JUST LET HIM...

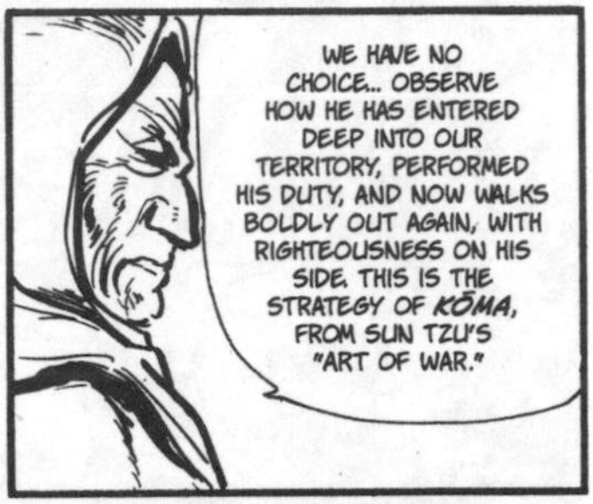
WE HAVE NO CHOICE... OBSERVE HOW HE HAS ENTERED DEEP INTO OUR TERRITORY, PERFORMED HIS DUTY, AND NOW WALKS BOLDLY OUT AGAIN, WITH RIGHTEOUSNESS ON HIS SIDE. THIS IS THE STRATEGY OF *KŌMA*, FROM SUN TZU'S "ART OF WAR."

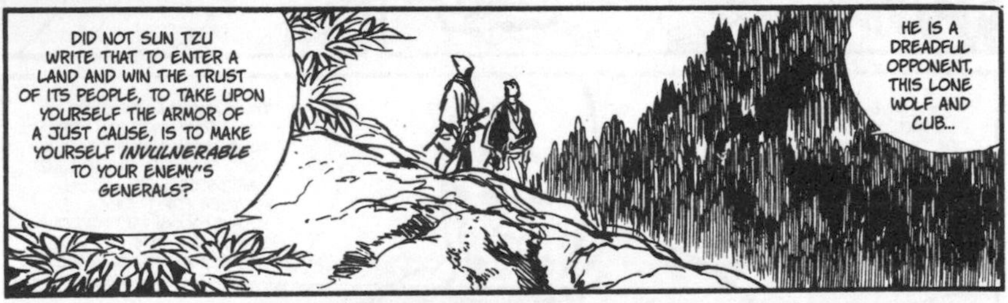
DID NOT SUN TZU WRITE THAT TO ENTER A LAND AND WIN THE TRUST OF ITS PEOPLE, TO TAKE UPON YOURSELF THE ARMOR OF A JUST CAUSE, IS TO MAKE YOURSELF *INVULNERABLE* TO YOUR ENEMY'S GENERALS?
HE IS A DREADFUL OPPONENT, THIS LONE WOLF AND CUB...

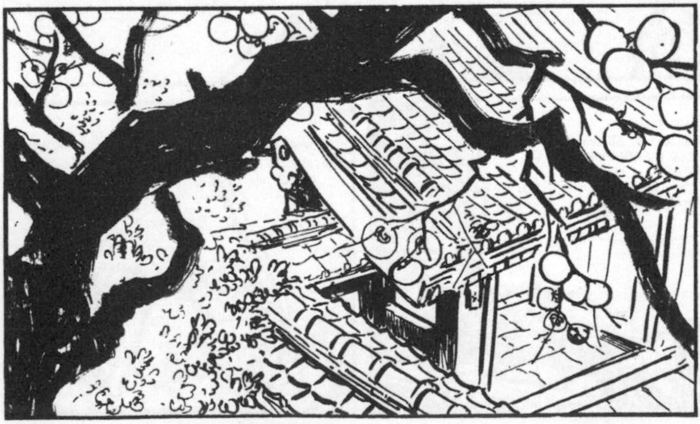

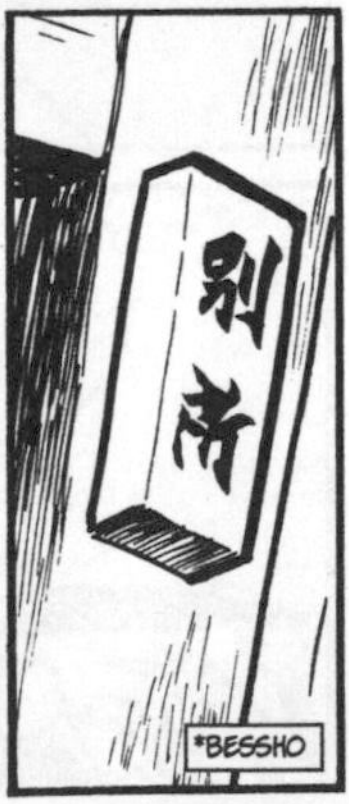
別所
*BESSHO

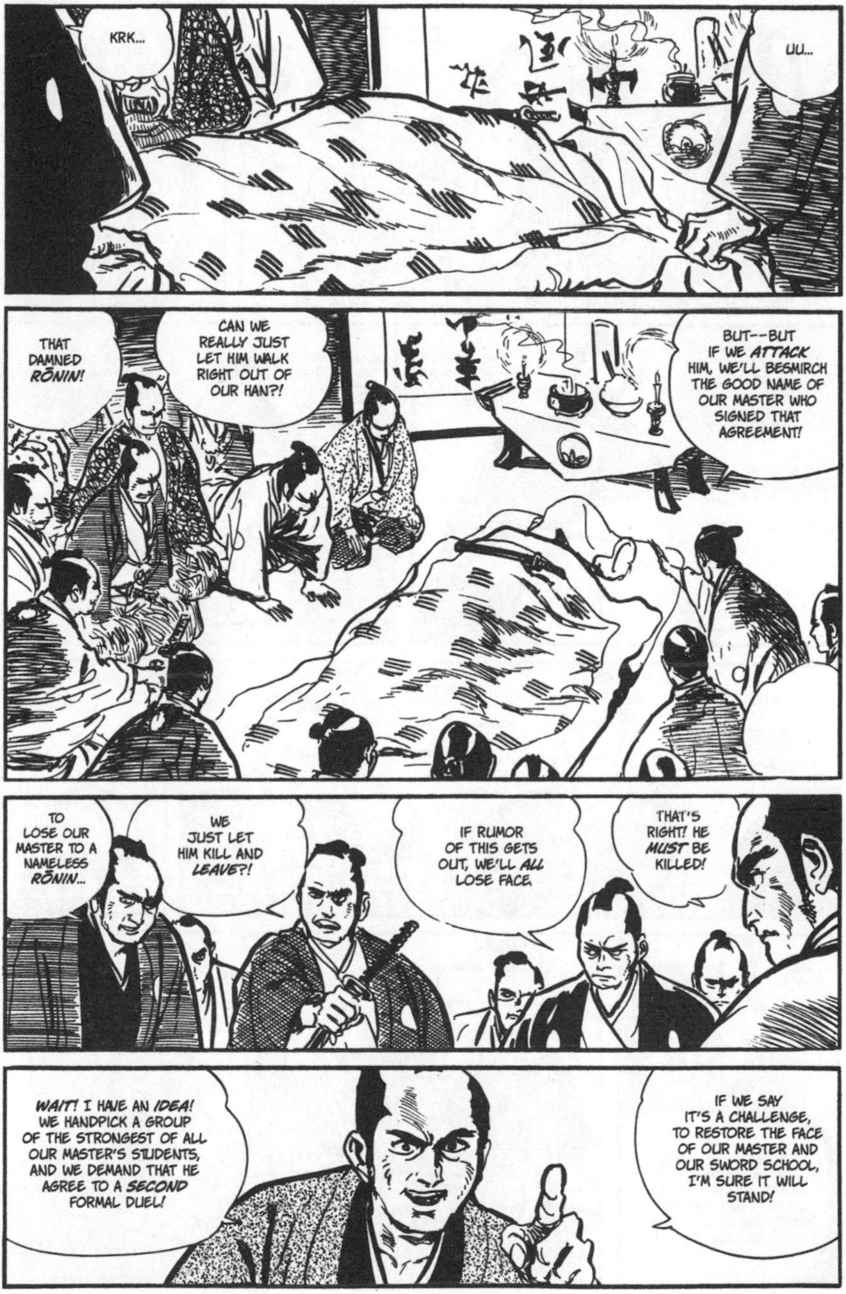
KRK...
UU...
THAT DAMNED RŌNIN!
CAN WE REALLY JUST LET HIM WALK RIGHT OUT OF OUR HAN?!
BUT--BUT IF WE ATTACK HIM, WE'LL BESMIRCH THE GOOD NAME OF OUR MASTER WHO SIGNED THAT AGREEMENT!
TO LOSE OUR MASTER TO A NAMELESS RŌNIN...
WE JUST LET HIM KILL AND LEAVE?!
IF RUMOR OF THIS GETS OUT, WE'LL ALL LOSE FACE.
THAT'S RIGHT! HE MUST BE KILLED!
WAIT! I HAVE AN IDEA! WE HANDPICK A GROUP OF THE STRONGEST OF ALL OUR MASTER'S STUDENTS, AND WE DEMAND THAT HE AGREE TO A SECOND FORMAL DUEL!
IF WE SAY IT'S A CHALLENGE, TO RESTORE THE FACE OF OUR MASTER AND OUR SWORD SCHOOL, I'M SURE IT WILL STAND!

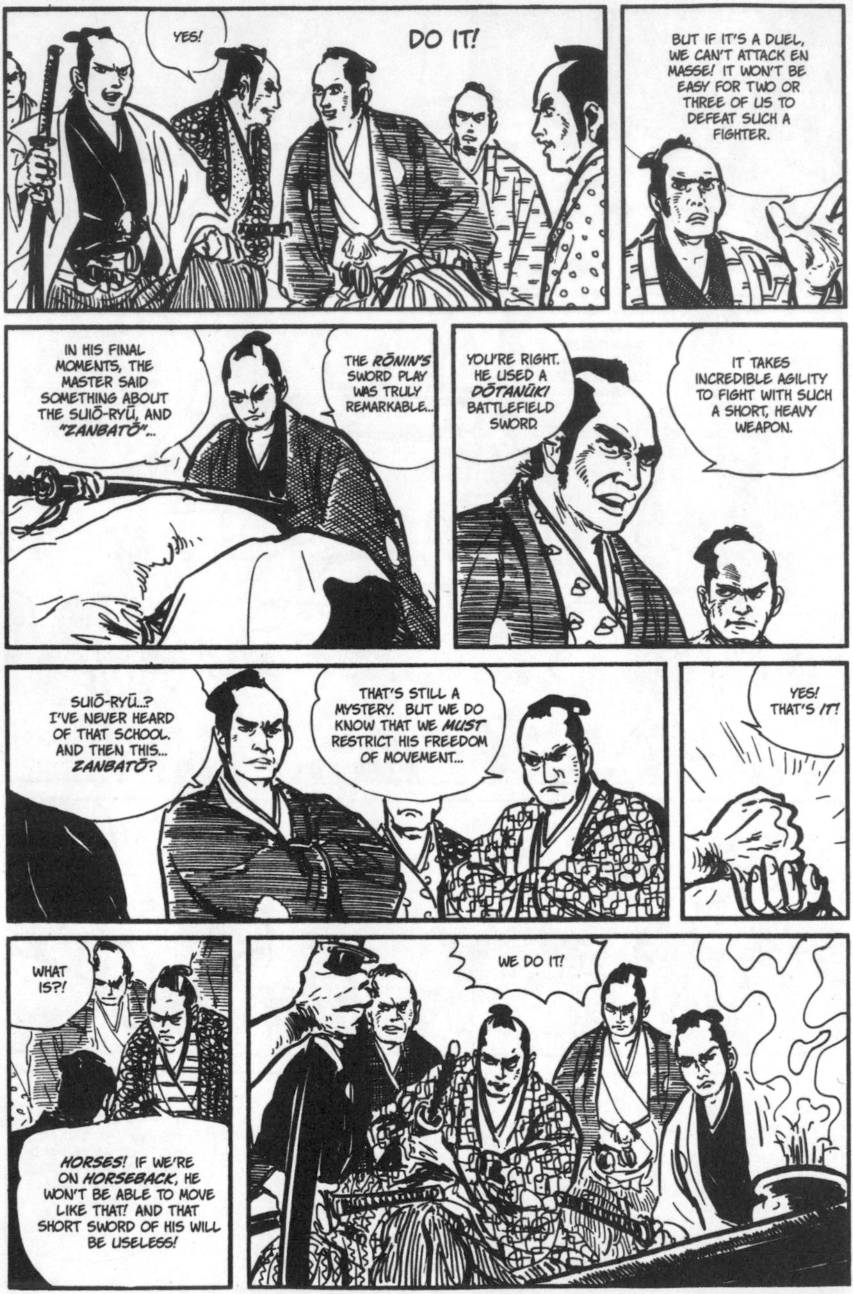
YES!
DO IT!
BUT IF IT'S A DUEL, WE CAN'T ATTACK EN MASSE! IT WON'T BE EASY FOR TWO OR THREE OF US TO DEFEAT SUCH A FIGHTER.
IN HIS FINAL MOMENTS, THE MASTER SAID SOMETHING ABOUT THE SUIŌ-RYŪ, AND *"ZANBATŌ"*...
THE *RŌNIN'S* SWORD PLAY WAS TRULY REMARKABLE...
YOU'RE RIGHT. HE USED A *DŌTANUKI* BATTLEFIELD SWORD.
IT TAKES INCREDIBLE AGILITY TO FIGHT WITH SUCH A SHORT, HEAVY WEAPON.
SUIŌ-RYŪ...? I'VE NEVER HEARD OF THAT SCHOOL. AND THEN THIS... *ZANBATŌ*?
THAT'S STILL A MYSTERY. BUT WE DO KNOW THAT WE *MUST* RESTRICT HIS FREEDOM OF MOVEMENT...
YES! THAT'S *IT*!
WHAT IS?!
HORSES! IF WE'RE ON *HORSEBACK*, HE WON'T BE ABLE TO MOVE LIKE THAT! AND THAT SHORT SWORD OF HIS WILL BE USELESS!
WE DO IT!

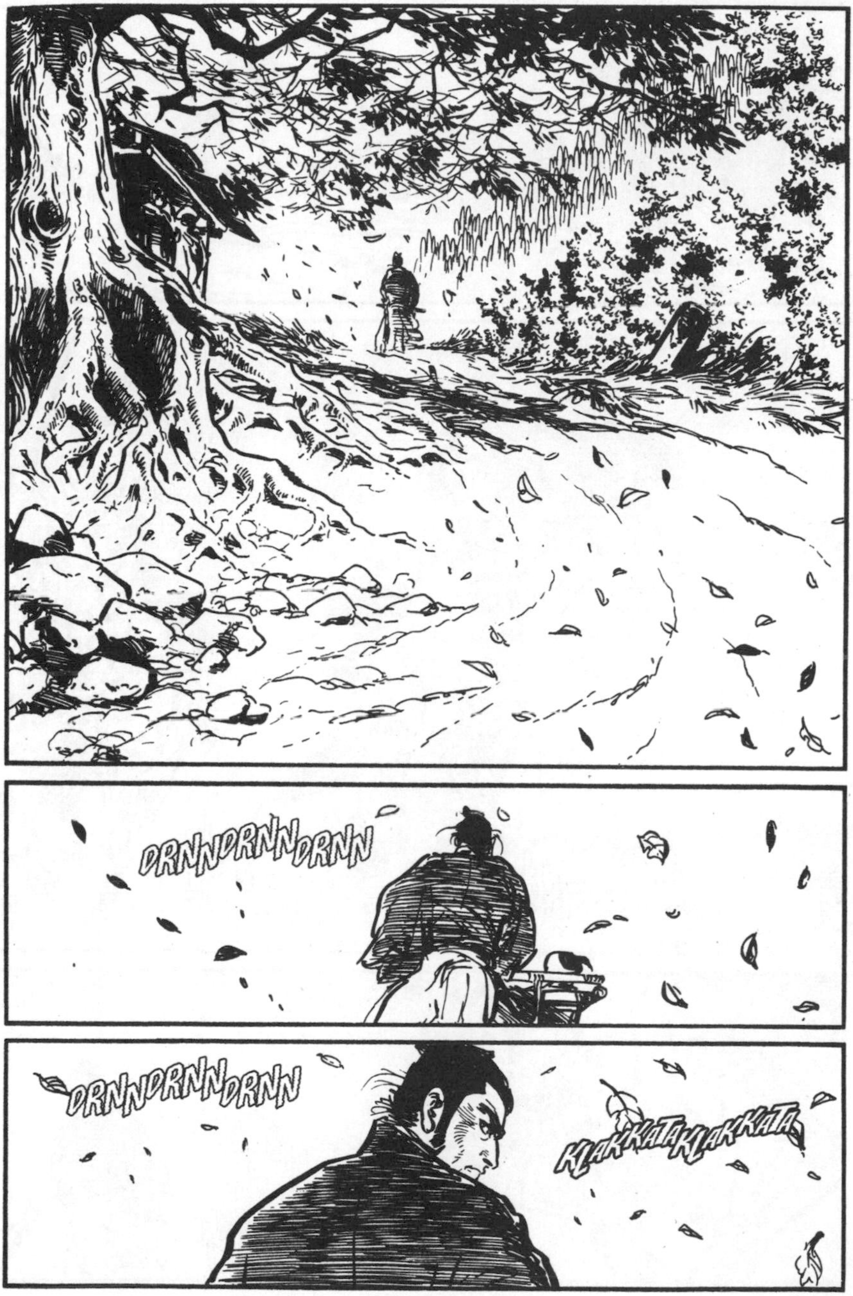
DRNNDRNNDRNN
DRNNDRNNDRNN
KLAKKATAKLAKKATA

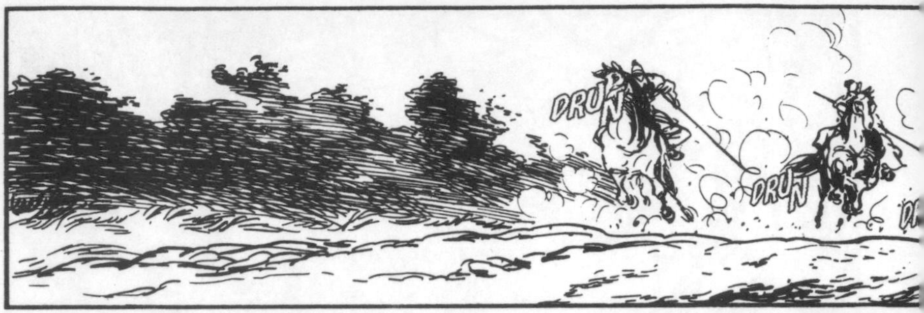
DRUN
DRUN
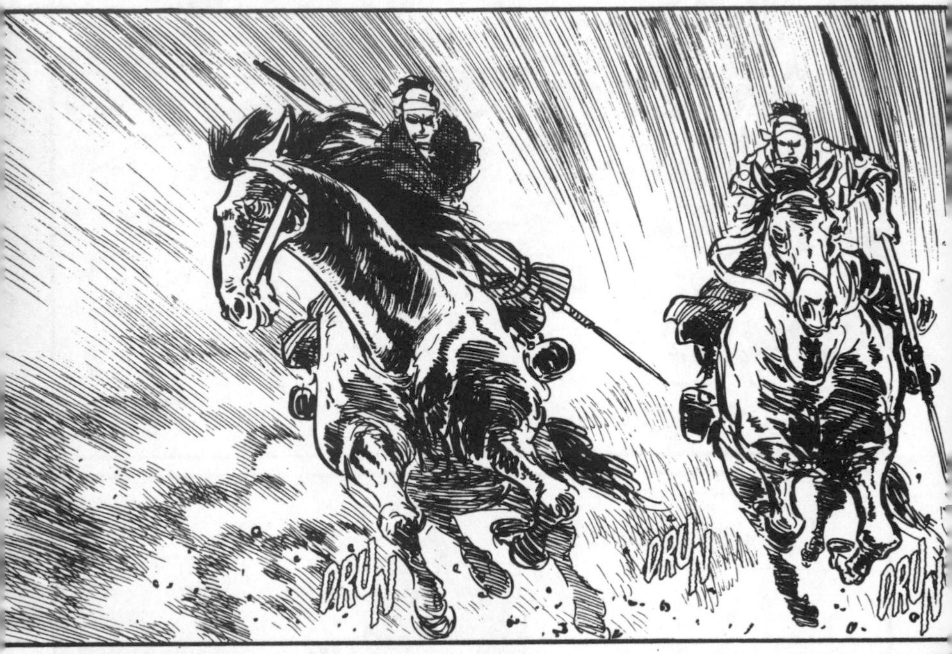
DRUN
DRUN
DRUN
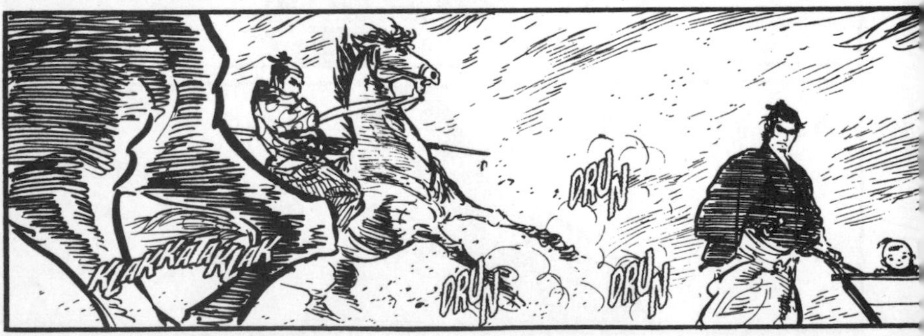
DRUN
DRUN
DRUN
KLAKKATAKLAK

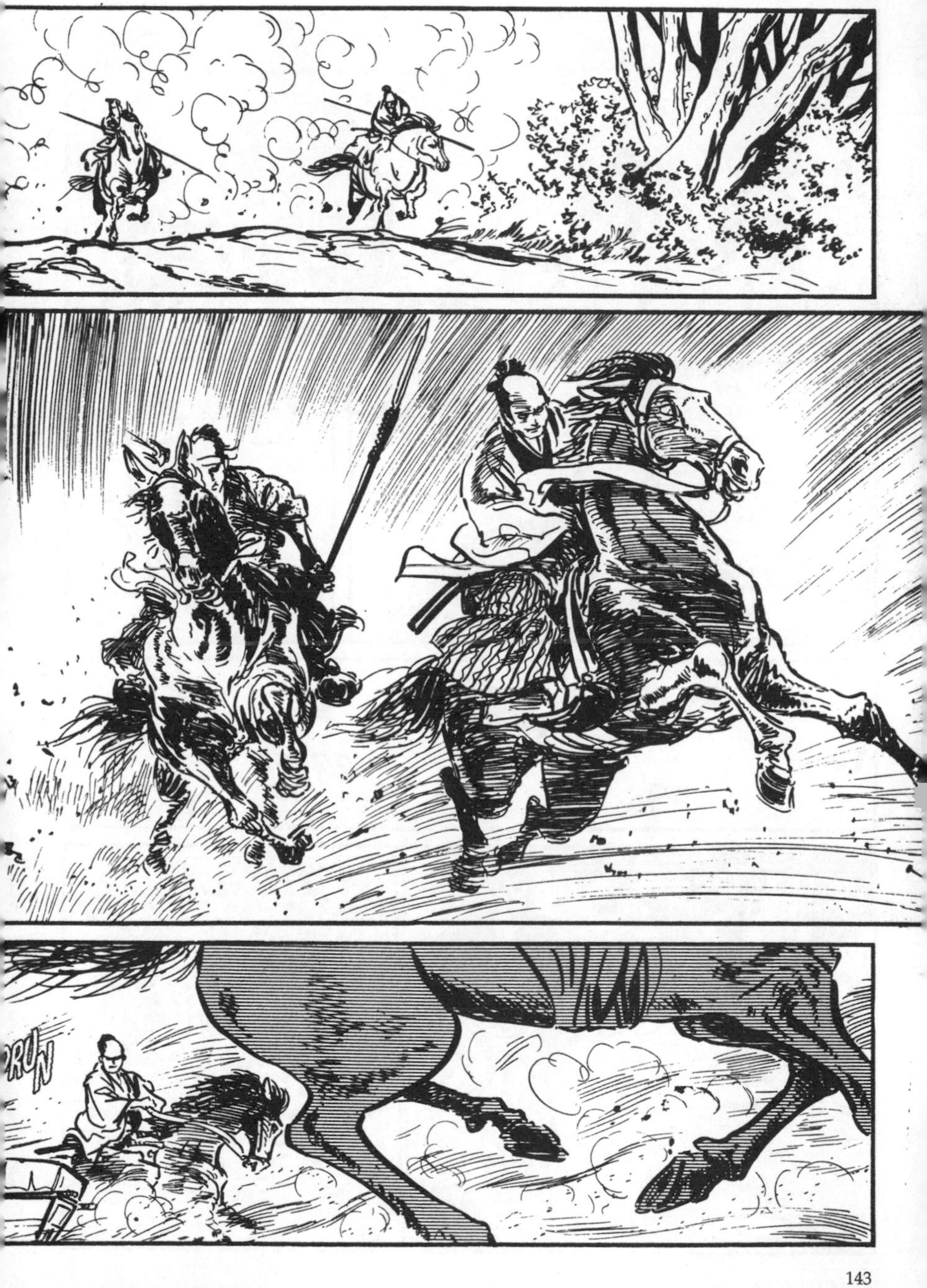
RUN

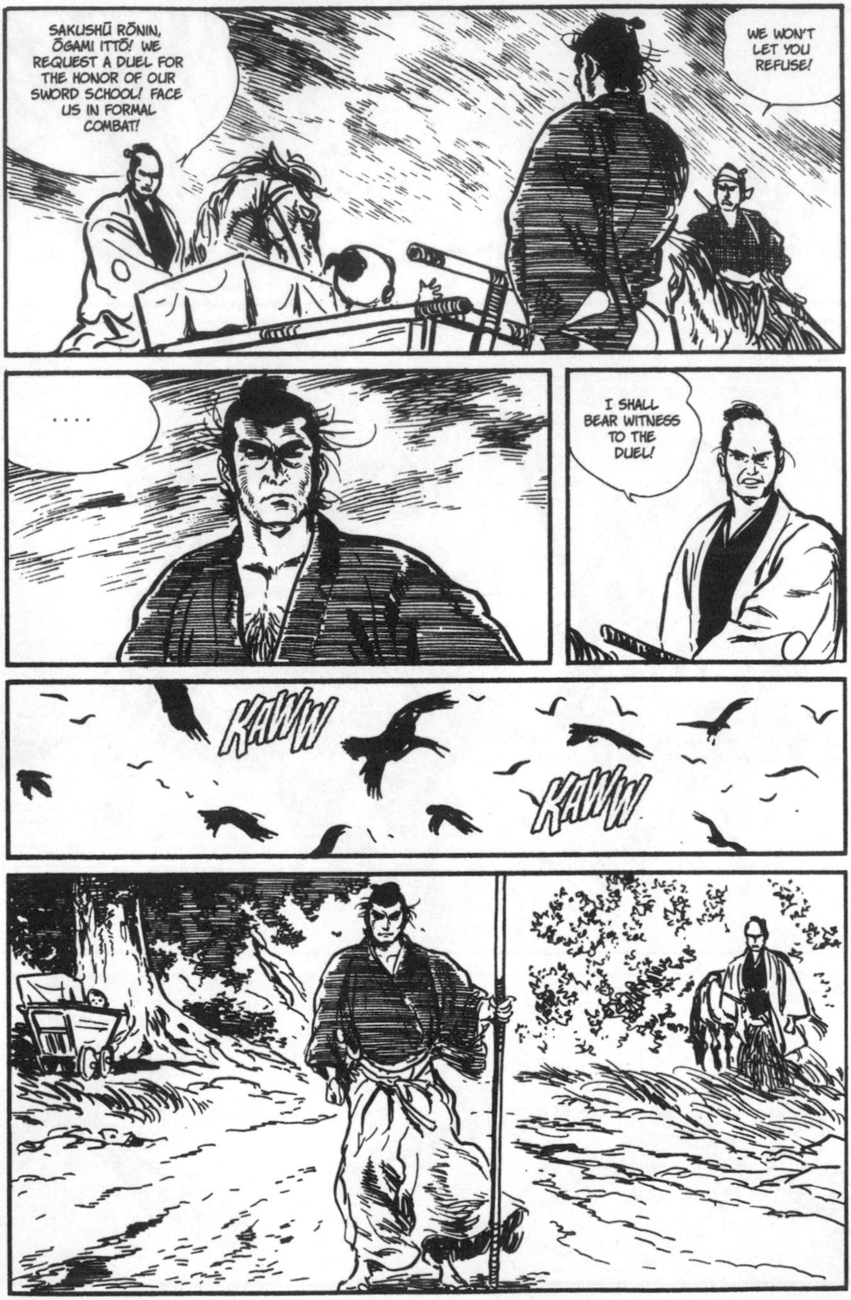
SAKUSHŪ RŌNIN, ŌGAMI ITTŌ! WE REQUEST A DUEL FOR THE HONOR OF OUR SWORD SCHOOL! FACE US IN FORMAL COMBAT!
WE WON'T LET YOU REFUSE!
....
I SHALL BEAR WITNESS TO THE DUEL!
KAWW
KAWW

WHAT DOES HE MEAN TO DO WITH THAT POLE..?

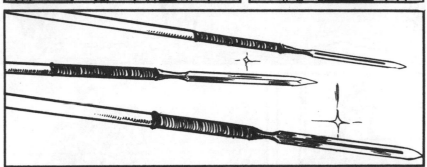

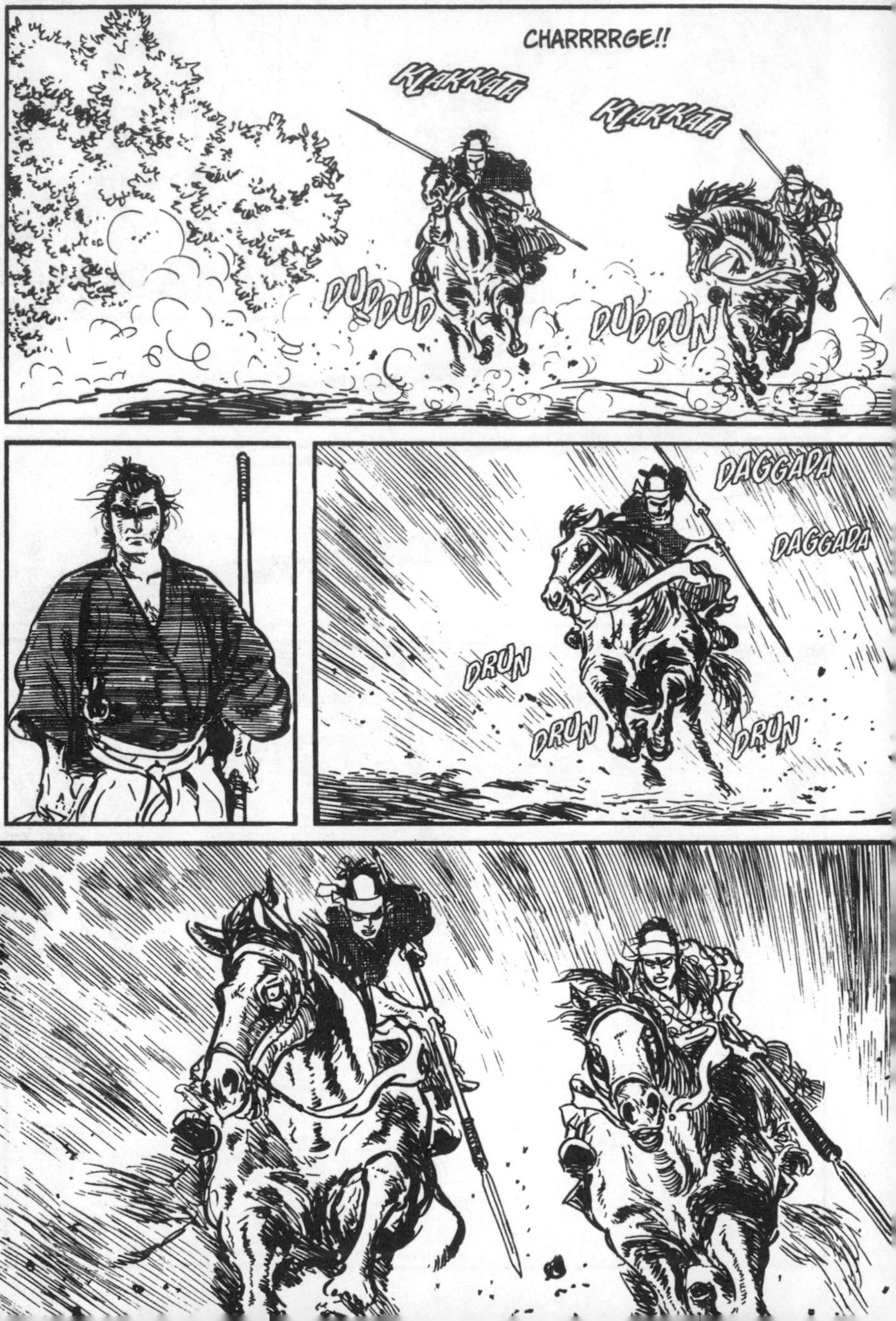
CHARRRRGE!!
KLAKKATA
KLAKKATA
DUDDUN
DUDDUD
DAGGADA
DAGGADA
DRUN
DRUN
DRUN

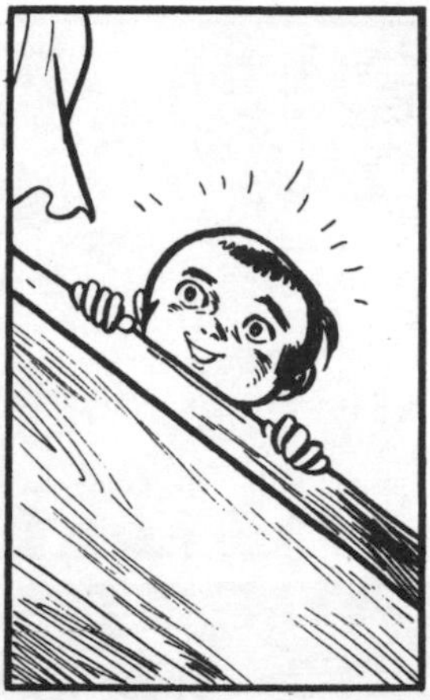

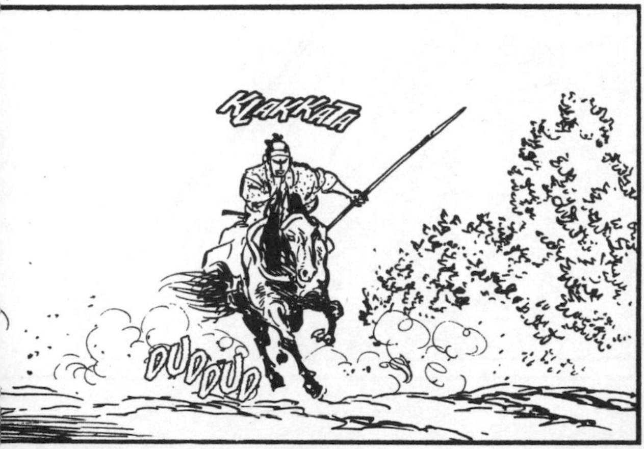
KLAKKATA
DUDDUD

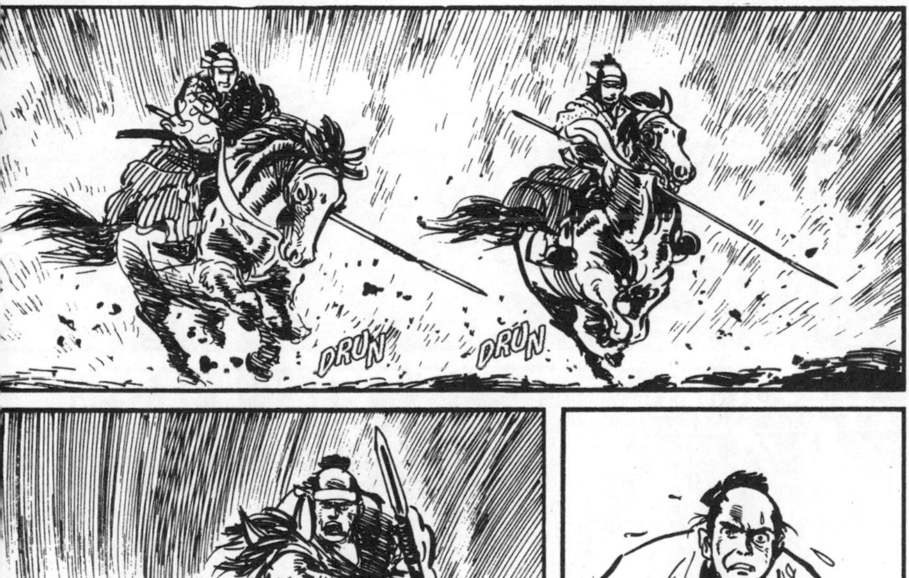
DRUN
DRUN

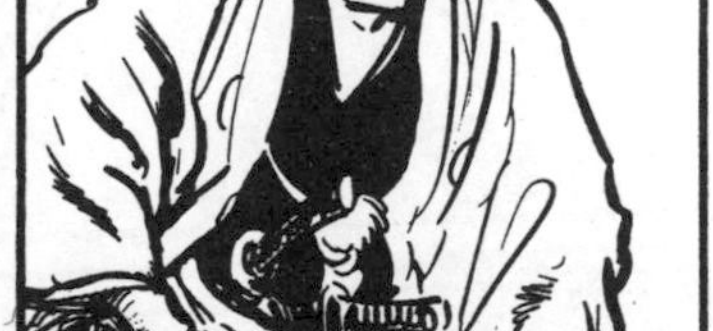

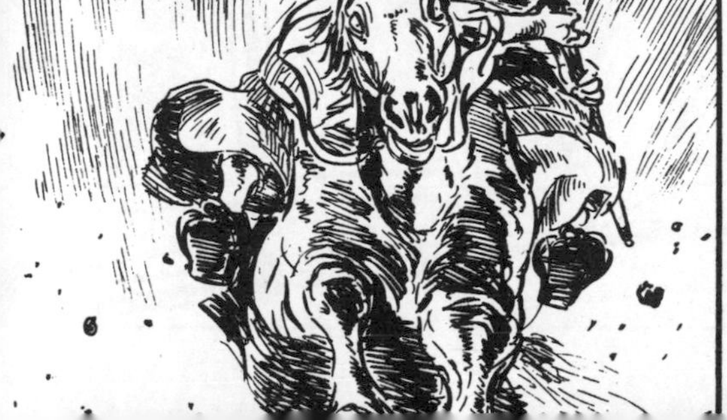

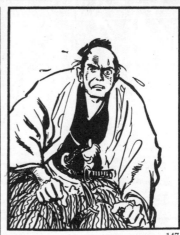

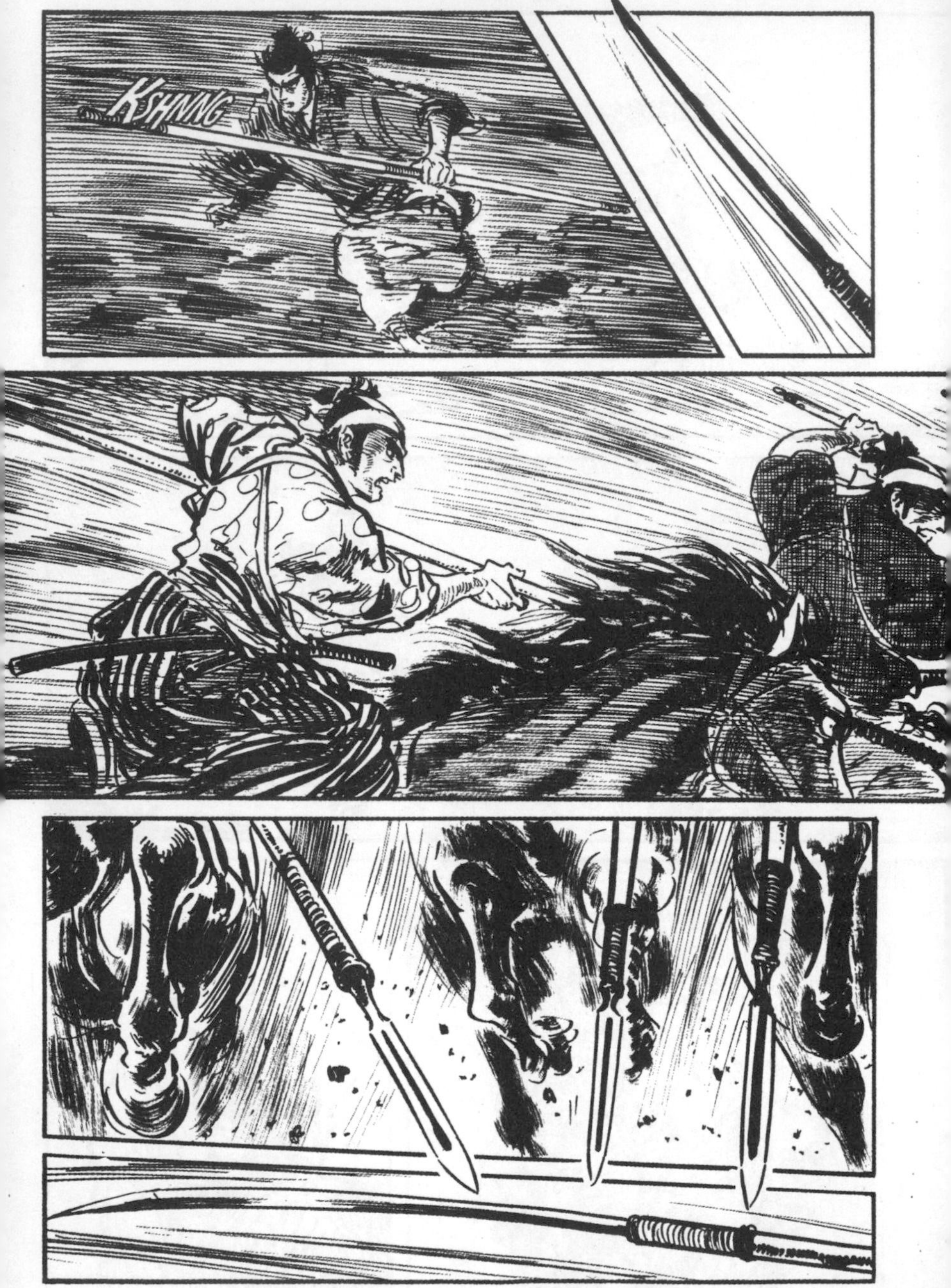
KSHNNG

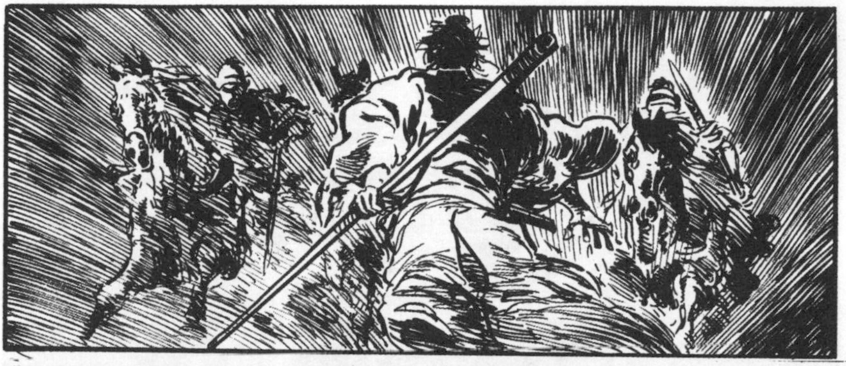

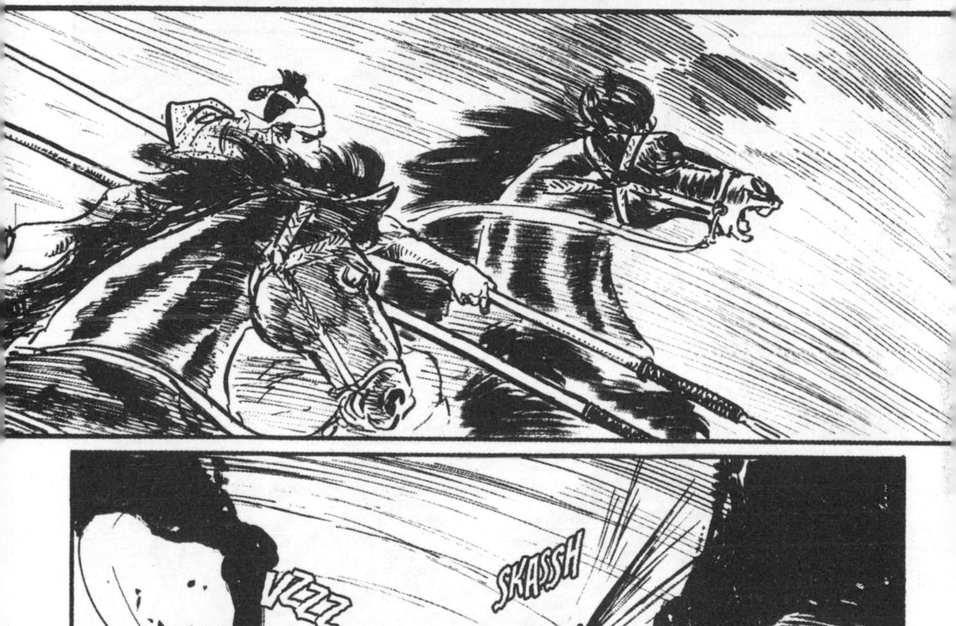

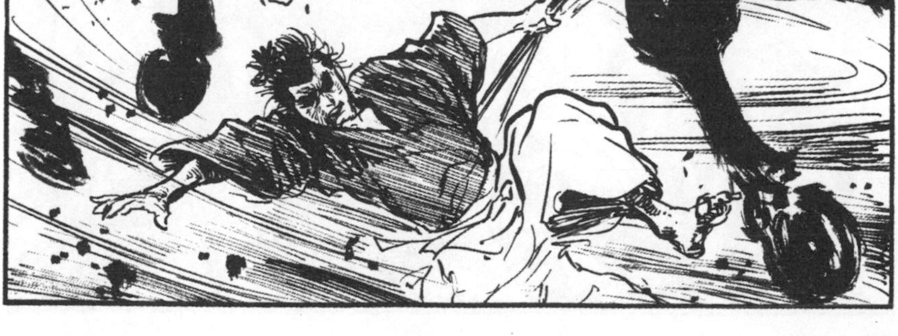
SKASSSH
VZZZ

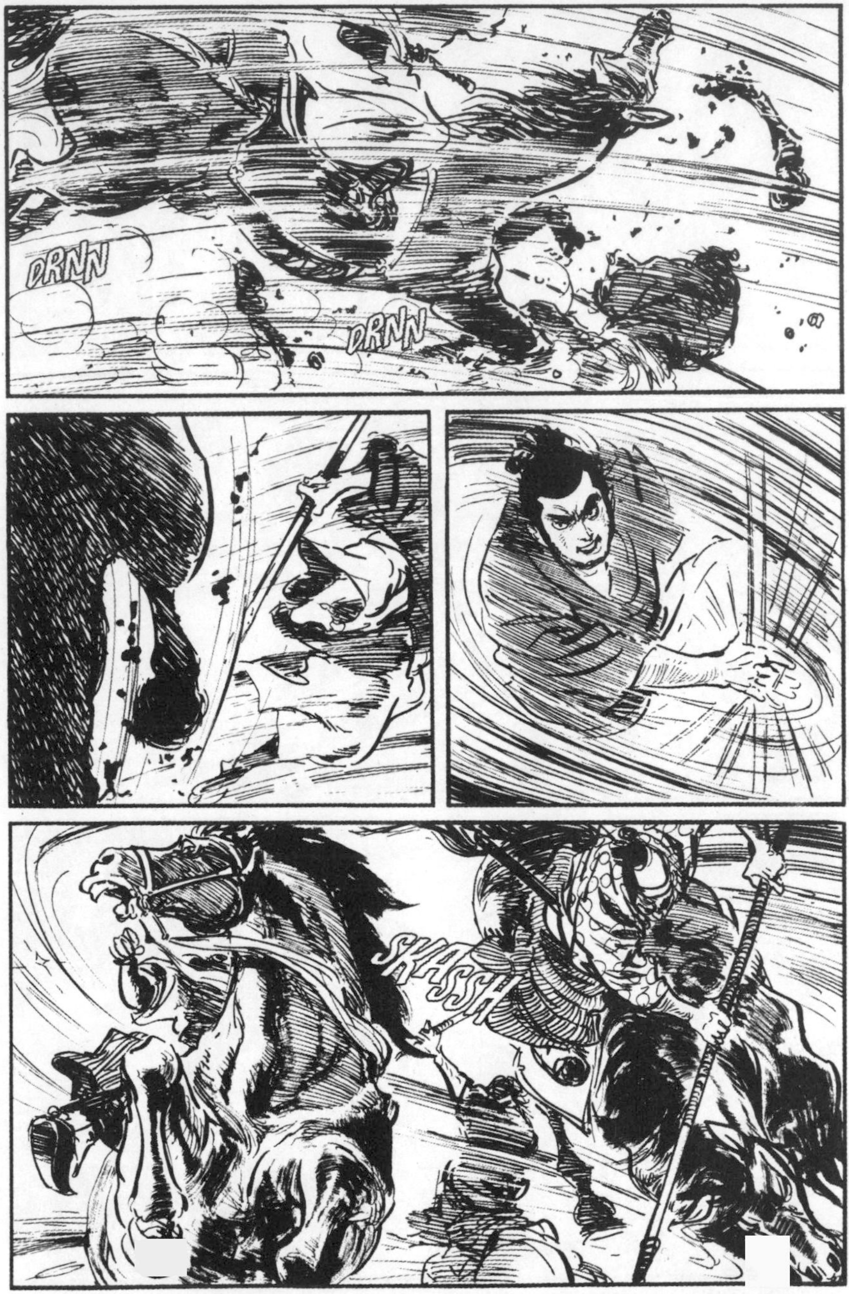
DRNN
DRNN
SKASSH

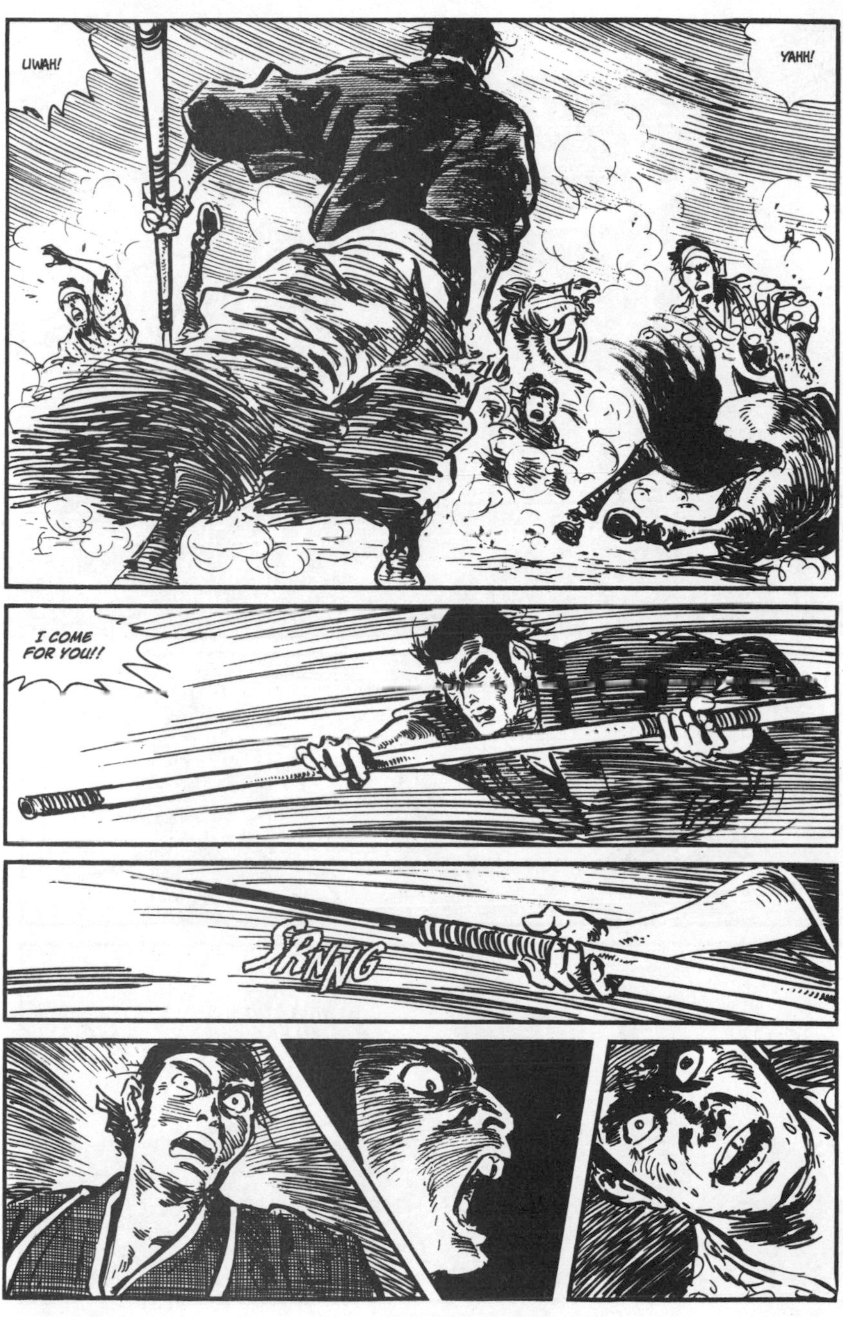
YAHH!
UWAH!
I COME FOR YOU!!
SRNNG

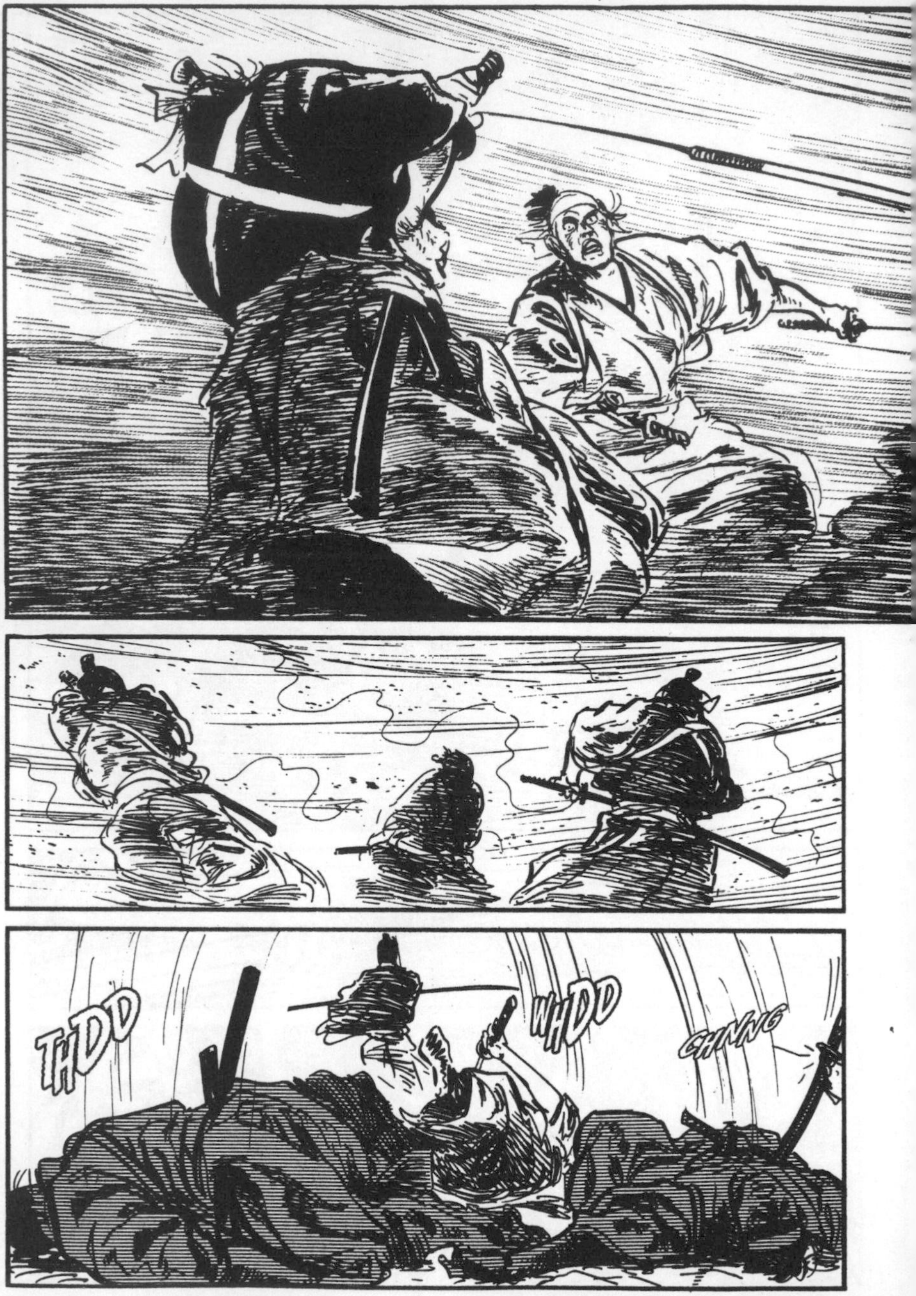
CHNNG
WHDD
THDD

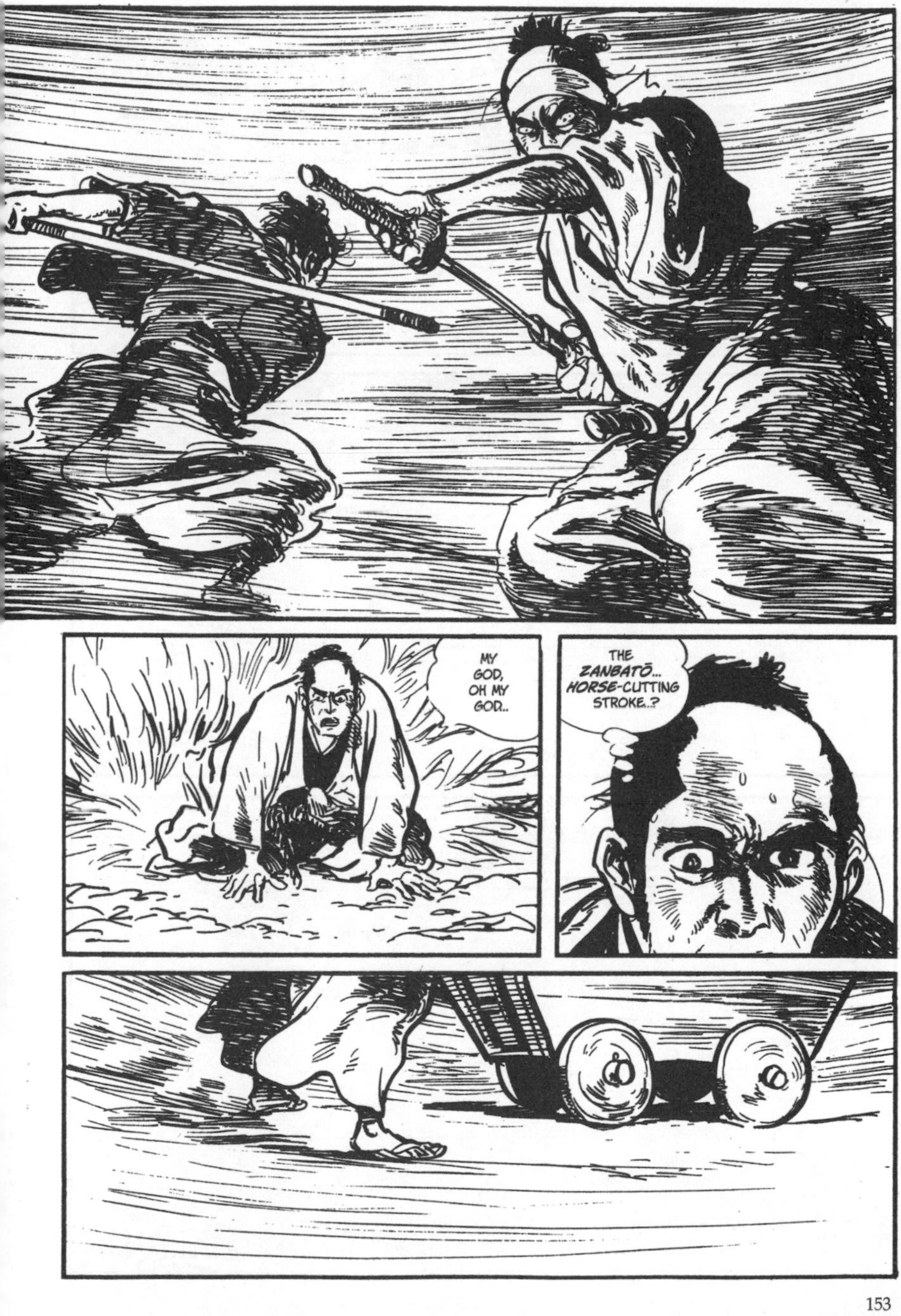
THE *ZANBATŌ*... *HORSE*-CUTTING STROKE..?
MY GOD, OH MY GOD..

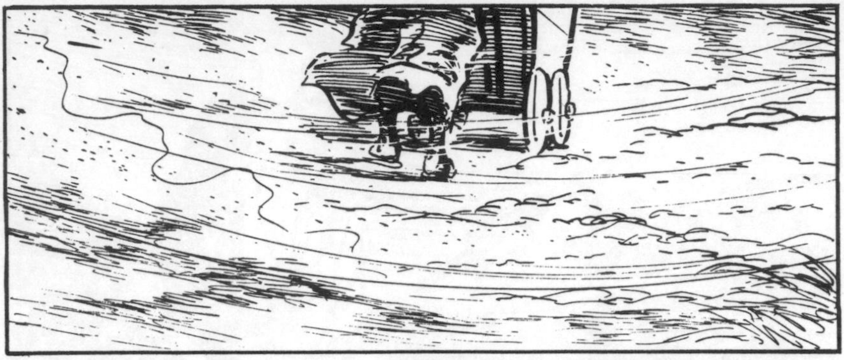
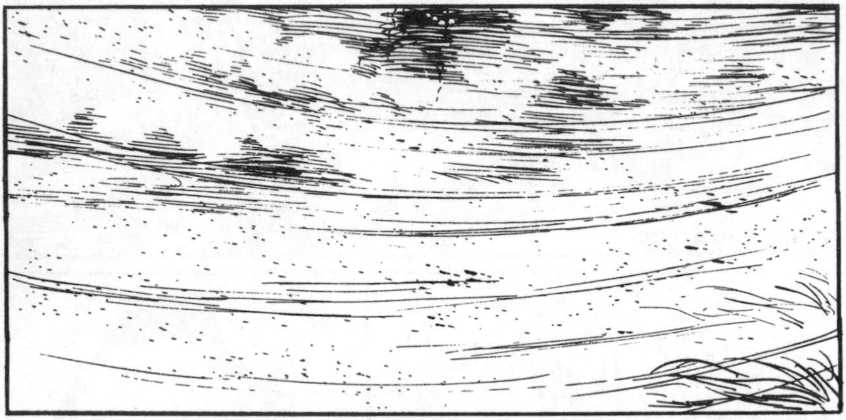
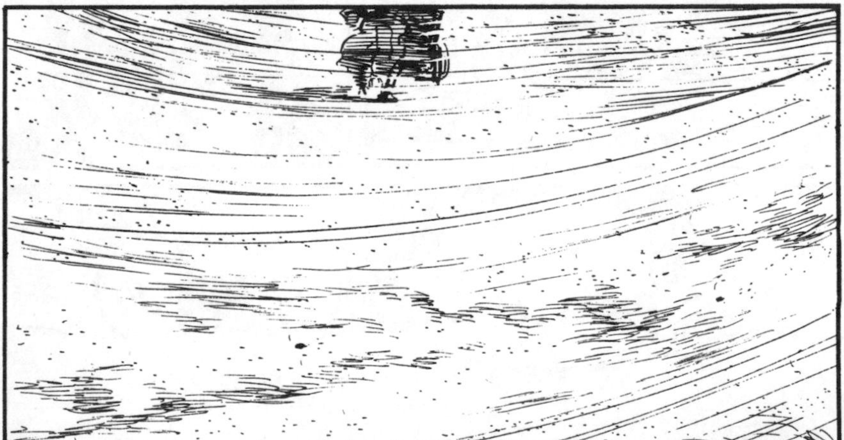

子連れ狼

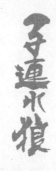

Waiting for the Rains

6

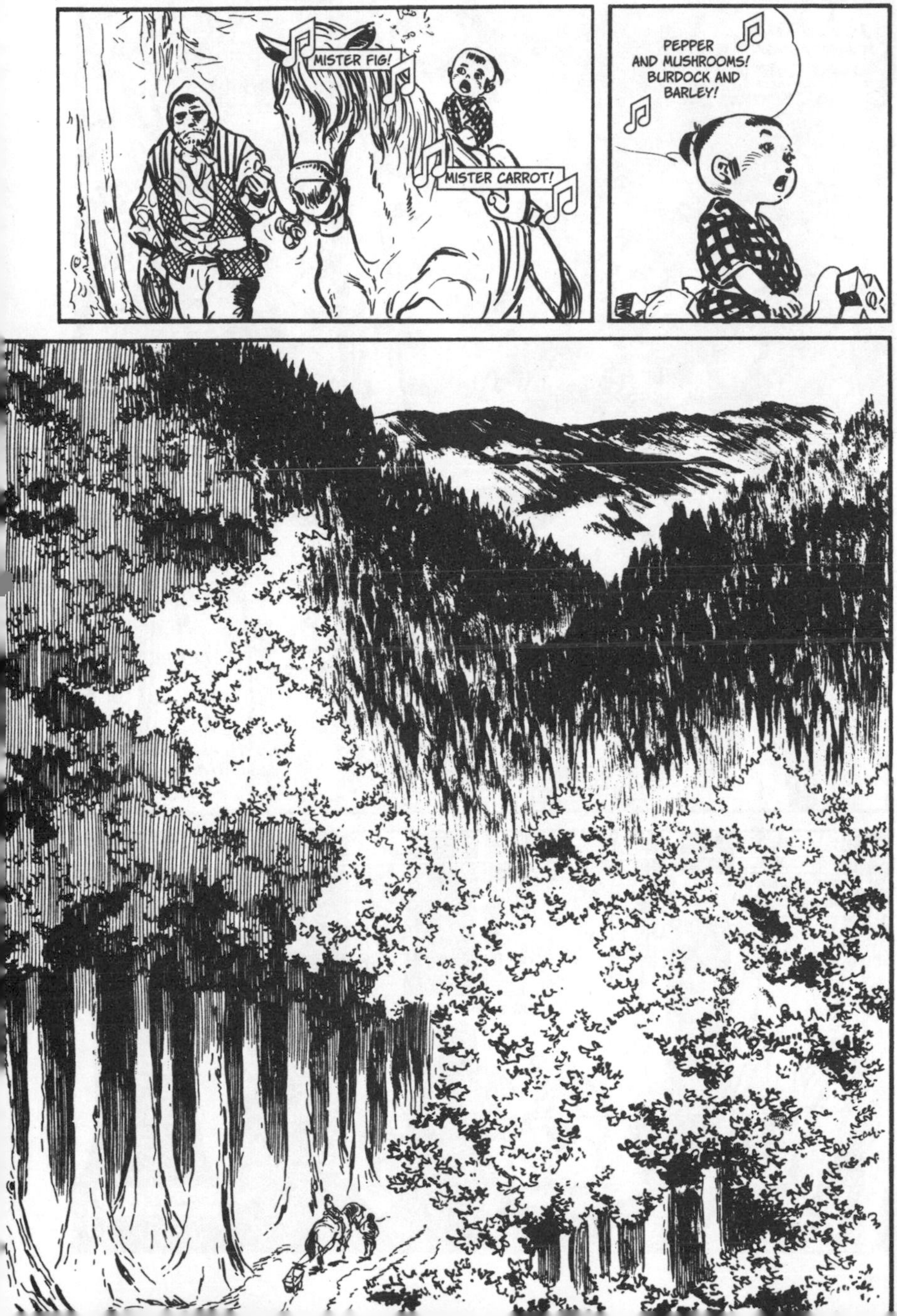
MISTER FIG!
MISTER CARROT!
PEPPER AND MUSHROOMS! BURDOCK AND BARLEY!

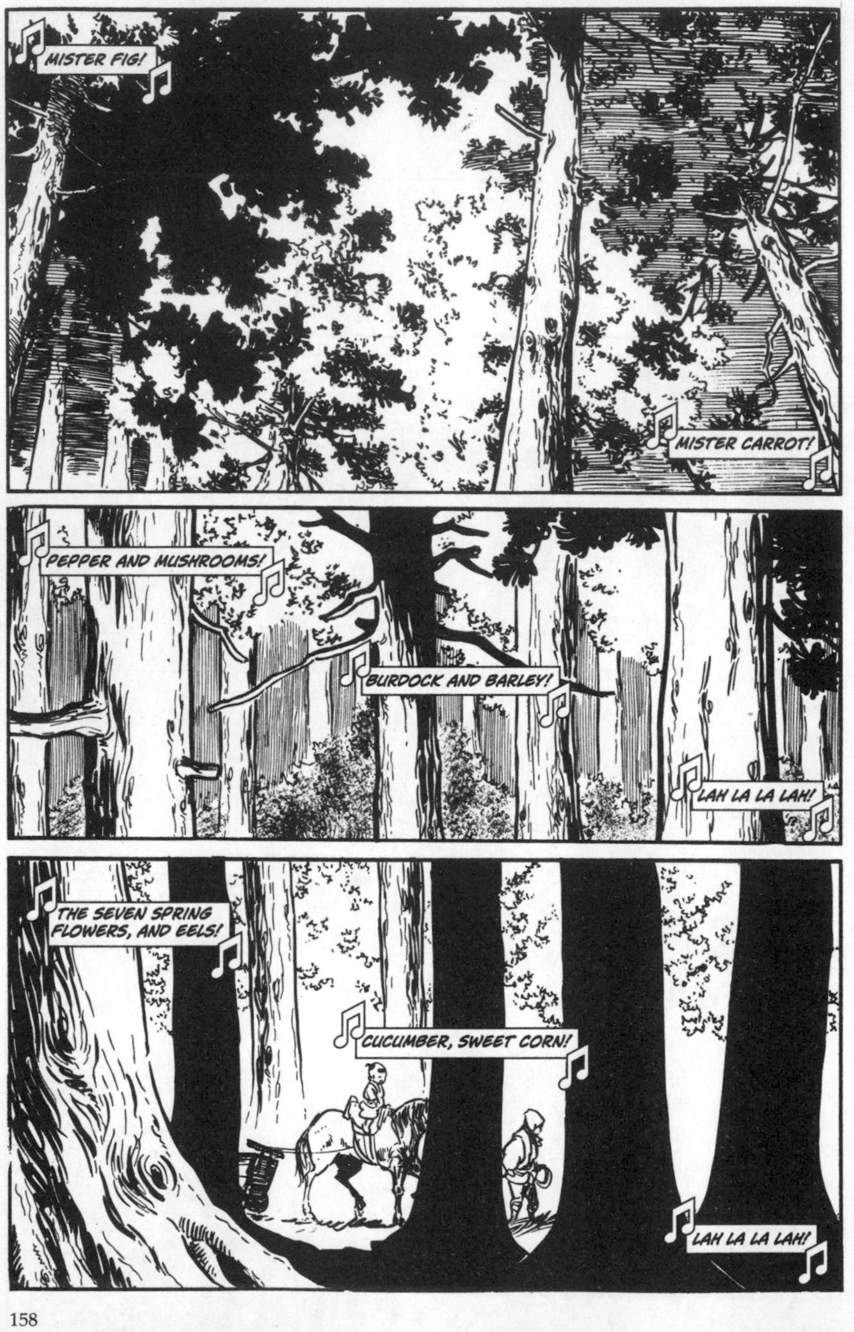
MISTER FIG!
MISTER CARROT!
PEPPER AND MUSHROOMS!
BURDOCK AND BARLEY!
LAH LA LA LAH!
THE SEVEN SPRING FLOWERS, AND EELS!
CUCUMBER, SWEET CORN!
LAH LA LA LAH!

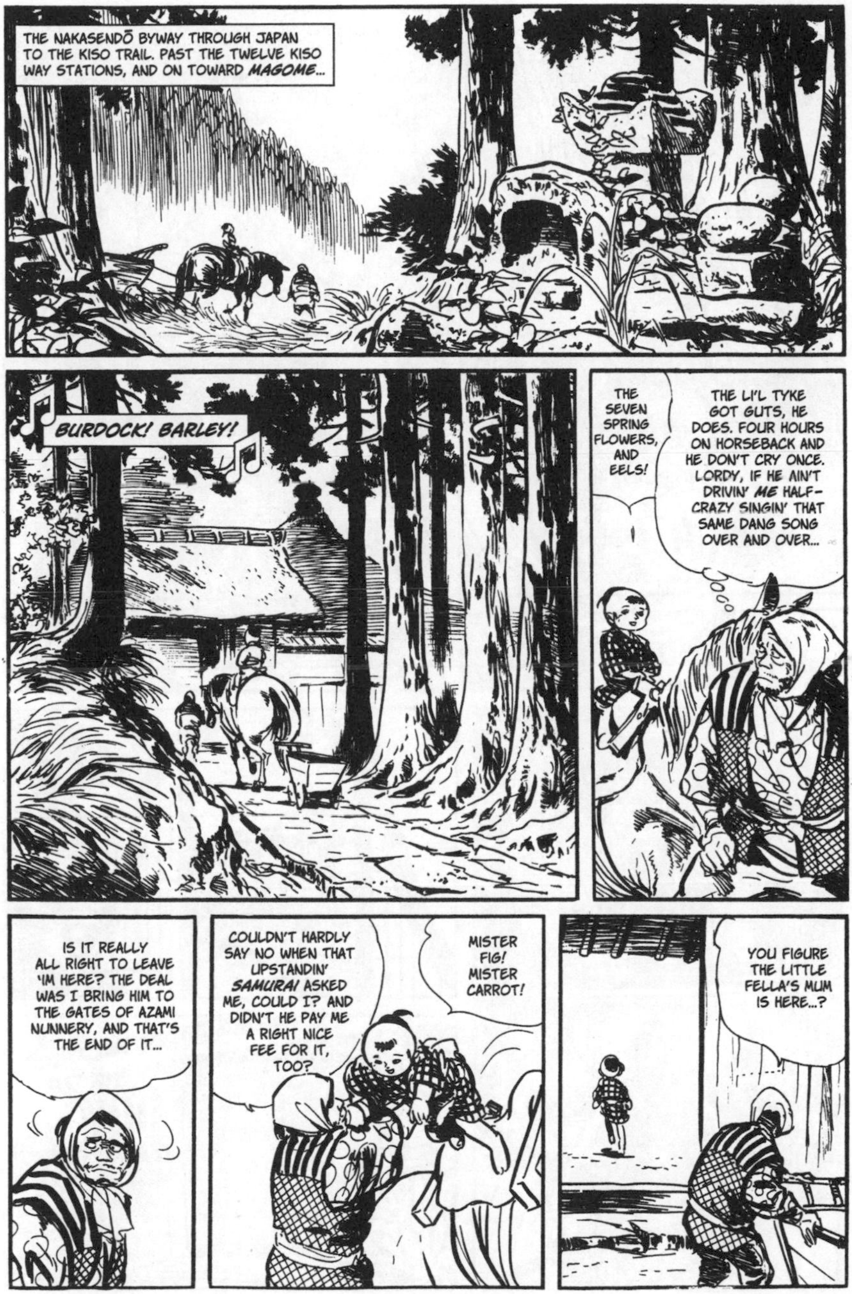
THE NAKASENDŌ BYWAY THROUGH JAPAN TO THE KISO TRAIL. PAST THE TWELVE KISO WAY STATIONS, AND ON TOWARD *MAGOME*...
BURDOCK! BARLEY!
THE SEVEN SPRING FLOWERS, AND EELS!
THE LI'L TYKE GOT GUTS, HE DOES. FOUR HOURS ON HORSEBACK AND HE DON'T CRY ONCE. LORDY, IF HE AIN'T DRIVIN' *ME* HALF-CRAZY SINGIN' THAT SAME DANG SONG OVER AND OVER...
IS IT REALLY ALL RIGHT TO LEAVE 'IM HERE? THE DEAL WAS I BRING HIM TO THE GATES OF AZAMI NUNNERY, AND THAT'S THE END OF IT...
COULDN'T HARDLY SAY NO WHEN THAT UPSTANDIN' *SAMURAI* ASKED ME, COULD I? AND DIDN'T HE PAY ME A RIGHT NICE FEE FOR IT, TOO?
MISTER FIG! MISTER CARROT!
YOU FIGURE THE LITTLE FELLA'S MUM IS HERE...?

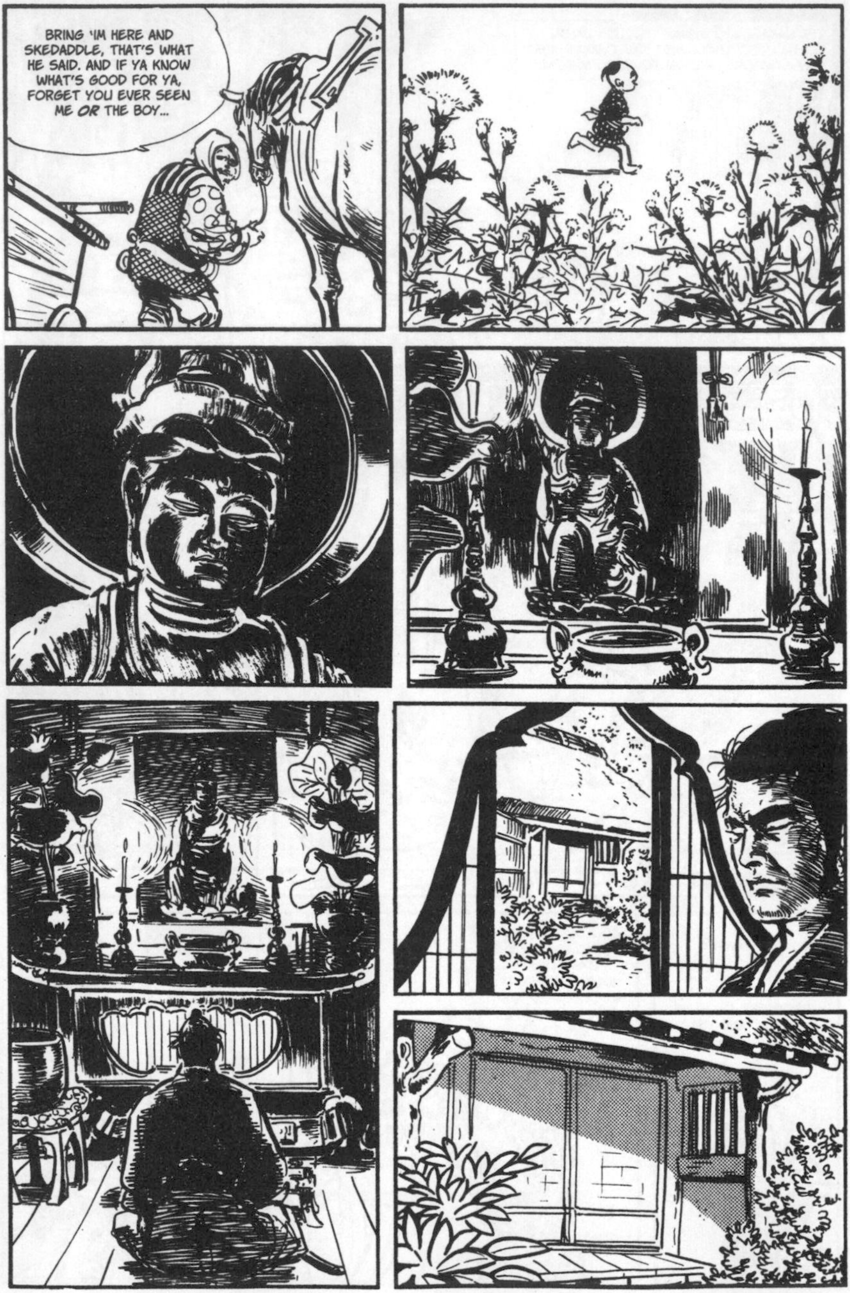
BRING 'IM HERE AND SKEDADDLE, THAT'S WHAT HE SAID. AND IF YA KNOW WHAT'S GOOD FOR YA, FORGET YOU EVER SEEN ME *OR* THE BOY...

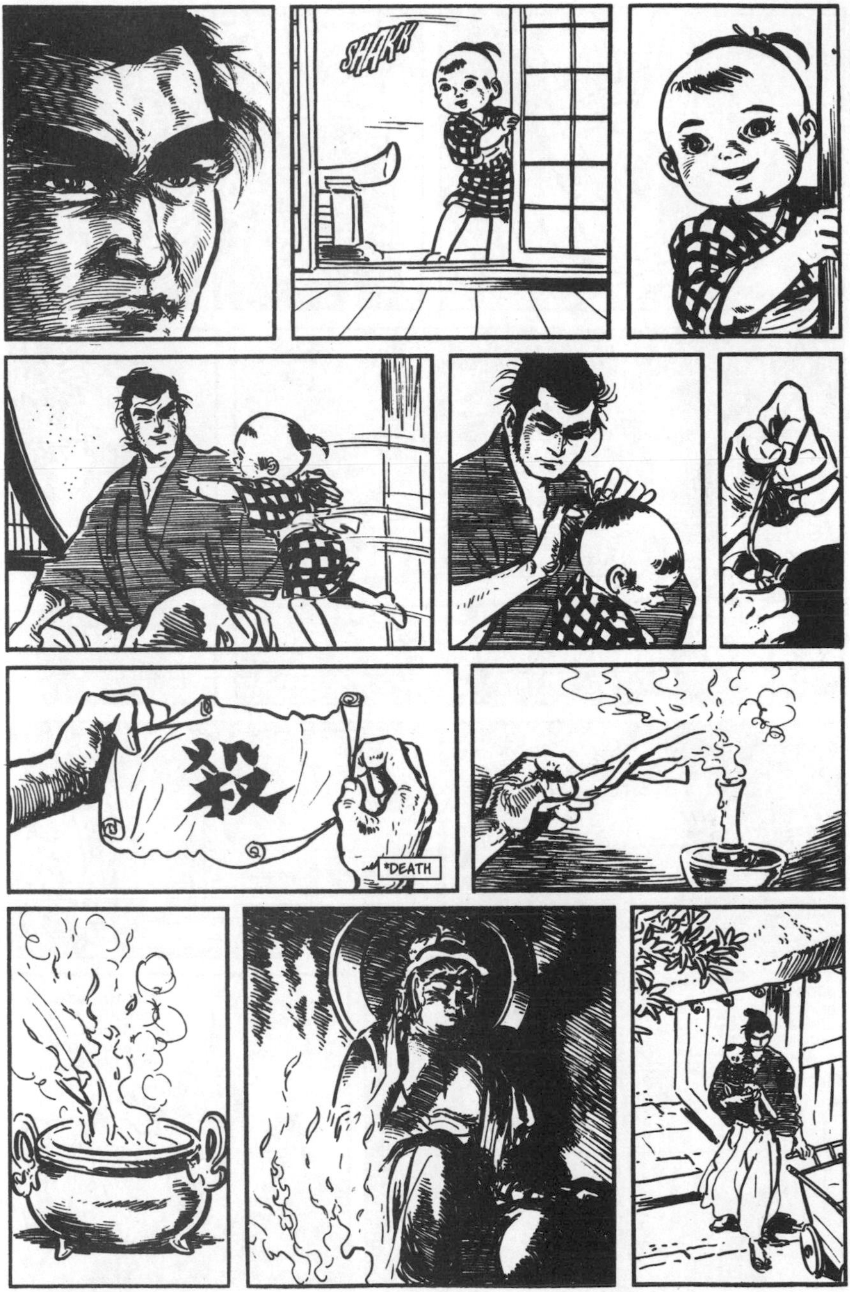
SHAKK
殺
*DEATH

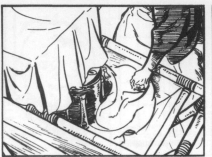

GOODNESS ME, WHAT A DARLING YOUNG MAN.

FORGIVE US FOR IMPOSING ON YOUR HOSPITALITY.

TUT TUT, NONE OF THAT. IT'S MY *DUTY* TO LOOK AFTER THOSE WHO COME FOR RETREATS.

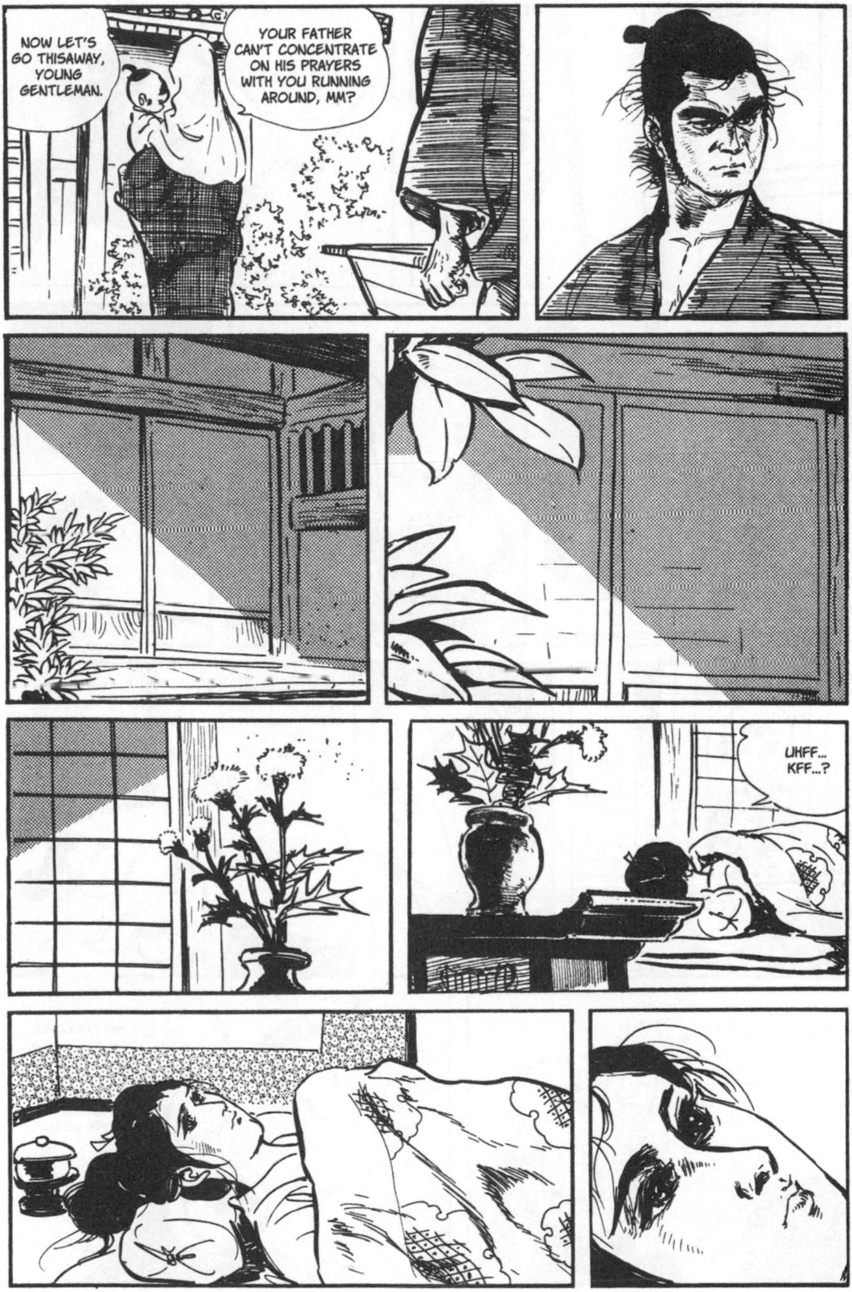
YOUR FATHER CAN'T CONCENTRATE ON HIS PRAYERS WITH YOU RUNNING AROUND, MM?
NOW LET'S GO THISAWAY, YOUNG GENTLEMAN.
UHFF... KFF...?

TUT TUT!

WE MUSTN'T DO THAT AGAIN, MM?

YOU'VE BEEN HERE TWO LONG YEARS, AND THIS IS THE FIRST TIME I'VE SEEN YOU SMILE, MY DEAR.

SO CUTE... WHO'S...?

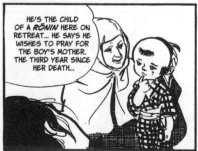

HE'S THE CHILD OF A *RŌNIN* HERE ON RETREAT... HE SAYS HE WISHES TO PRAY FOR THE BOY'S MOTHER. THE THIRD YEAR SINCE HER DEATH...

THEN... THIS LITTLE BOY?

SO CHEERFUL FOR A CHILD WHO LOST HIS MOTHER SO YOUNG. HIS FATHER MUST HAVE RAISED HIM WELL.

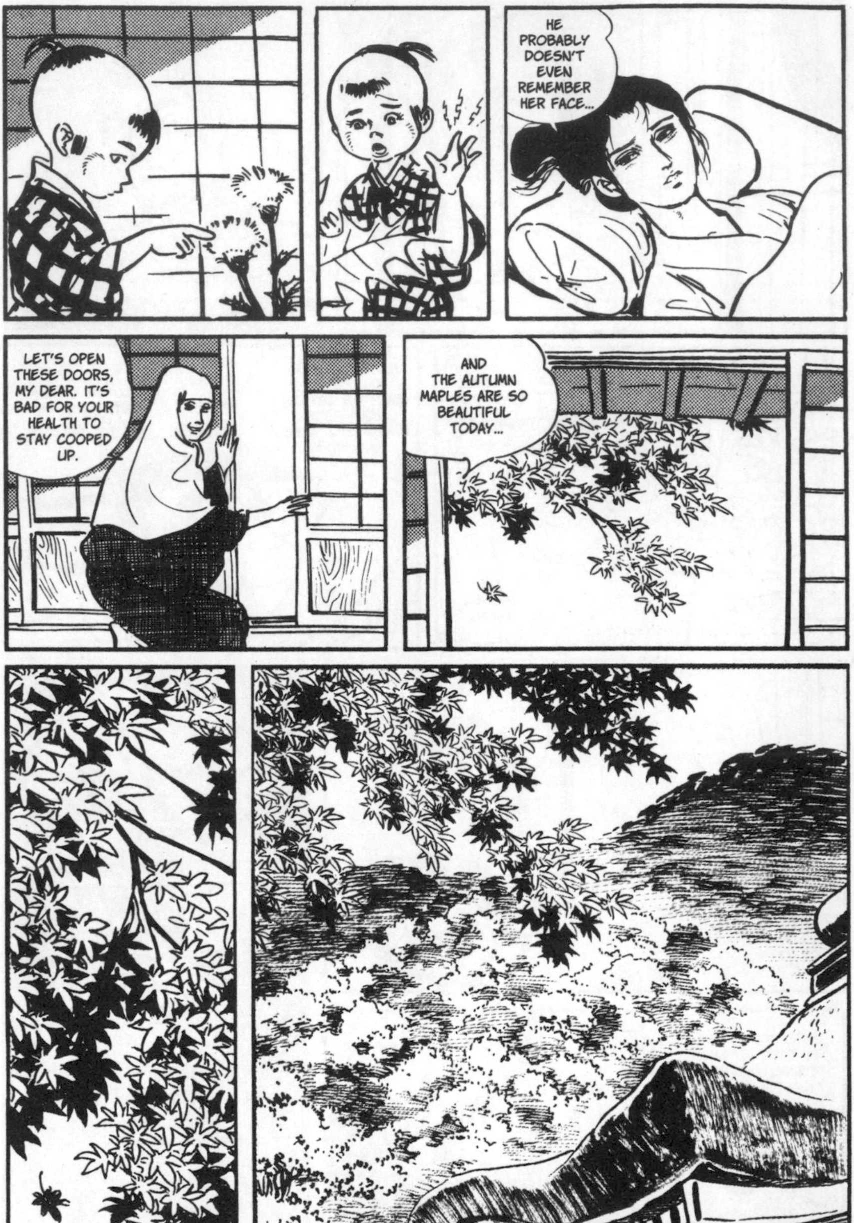
HE PROBABLY DOESN'T EVEN REMEMBER HER FACE...
LET'S OPEN THESE DOORS, MY DEAR. IT'S BAD FOR YOUR HEALTH TO STAY COOPED UP.
AND THE AUTUMN MAPLES ARE SO BEAUTIFUL TODAY...

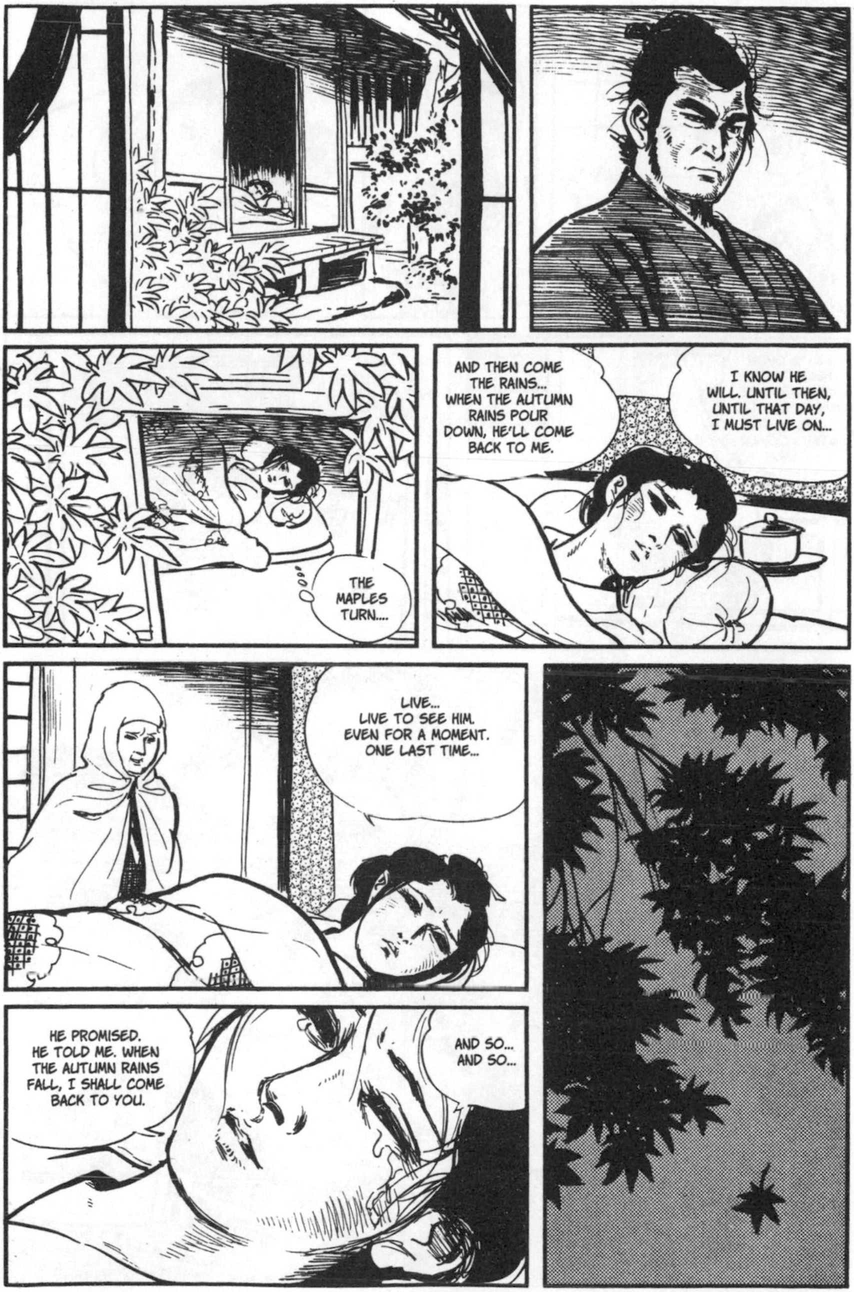
THE MAPLES TURN....
AND THEN COME THE RAINS... WHEN THE AUTUMN RAINS POUR DOWN, HE'LL COME BACK TO ME.
I KNOW HE WILL. UNTIL THEN, UNTIL THAT DAY, I MUST LIVE ON...
LIVE... LIVE TO SEE HIM. EVEN FOR A MOMENT. ONE LAST TIME...
HE PROMISED. HE TOLD ME. WHEN THE AUTUMN RAINS FALL, I SHALL COME BACK TO YOU.
AND SO... AND SO...

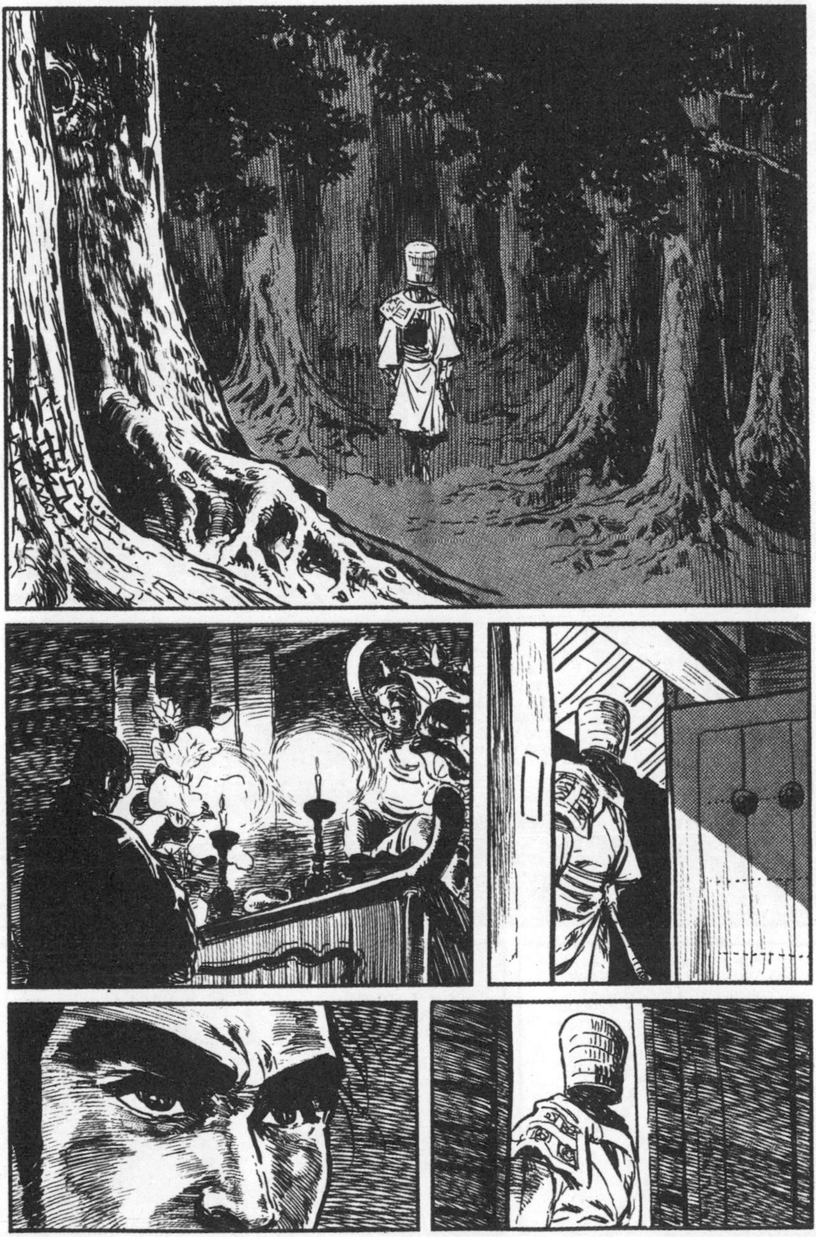

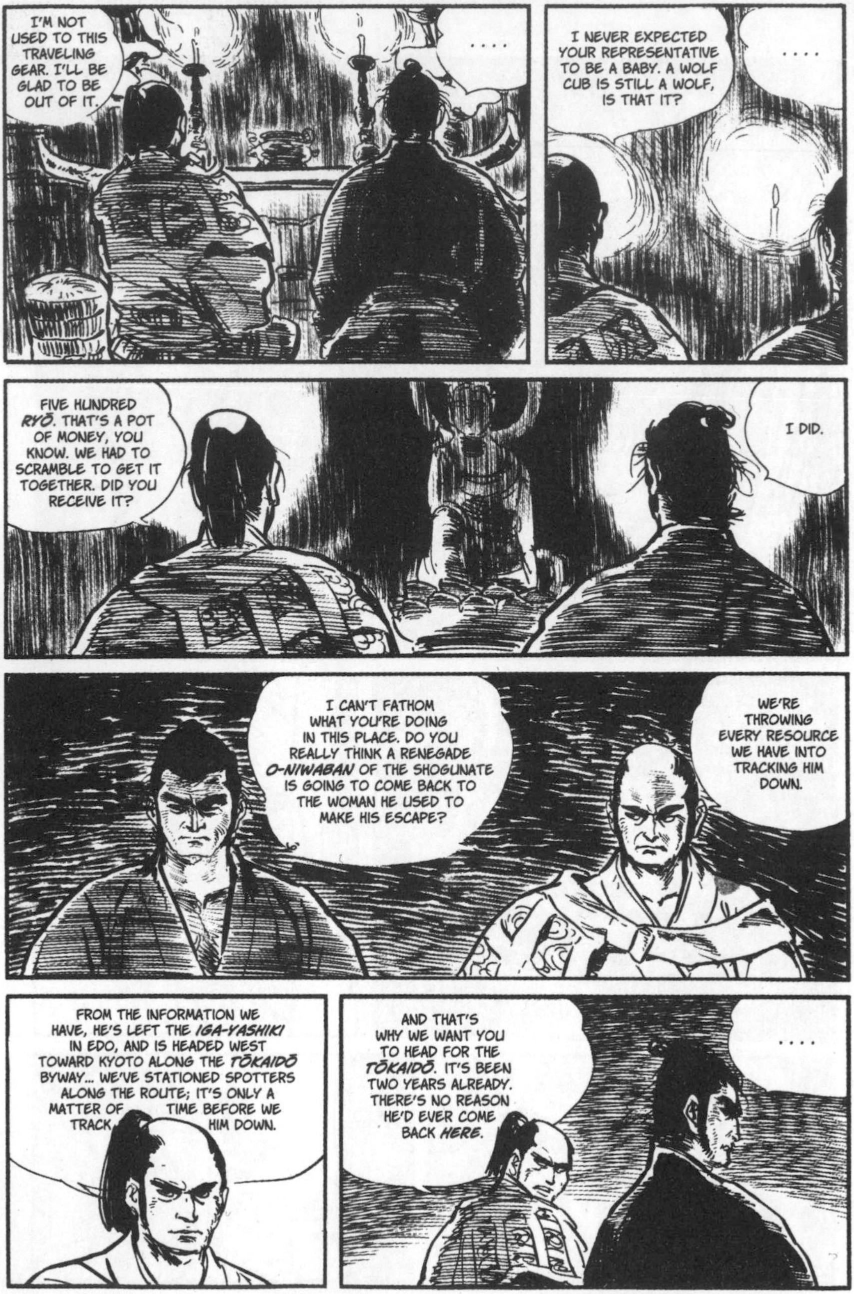
I'M NOT USED TO THIS TRAVELING GEAR. I'LL BE GLAD TO BE OUT OF IT.
. . . .
I NEVER EXPECTED YOUR REPRESENTATIVE TO BE A BABY. A WOLF CUB IS STILL A WOLF, IS THAT IT?
. . . .
FIVE HUNDRED *RYŌ*. THAT'S A POT OF MONEY, YOU KNOW. WE HAD TO SCRAMBLE TO GET IT TOGETHER. DID YOU RECEIVE IT?
I DID.
I CAN'T FATHOM WHAT YOU'RE DOING IN THIS PLACE. DO YOU REALLY THINK A RENEGADE *O-NIWABAN* OF THE SHOGUNATE IS GOING TO COME BACK TO THE WOMAN HE USED TO MAKE HIS ESCAPE?
WE'RE THROWING EVERY RESOURCE WE HAVE INTO TRACKING HIM DOWN.
FROM THE INFORMATION WE HAVE, HE'S LEFT THE *IGA-YASHIKI* IN EDO, AND IS HEADED WEST TOWARD KYOTO ALONG THE *TŌKAIDŌ* BYWAY... WE'VE STATIONED SPOTTERS ALONG THE ROUTE; IT'S ONLY A MATTER OF TIME BEFORE WE TRACK HIM DOWN.
AND THAT'S WHY WE WANT YOU TO HEAD FOR THE *TŌKAIDŌ*. IT'S BEEN TWO YEARS ALREADY. THERE'S NO REASON HE'D EVER COME BACK *HERE*.
. . . .

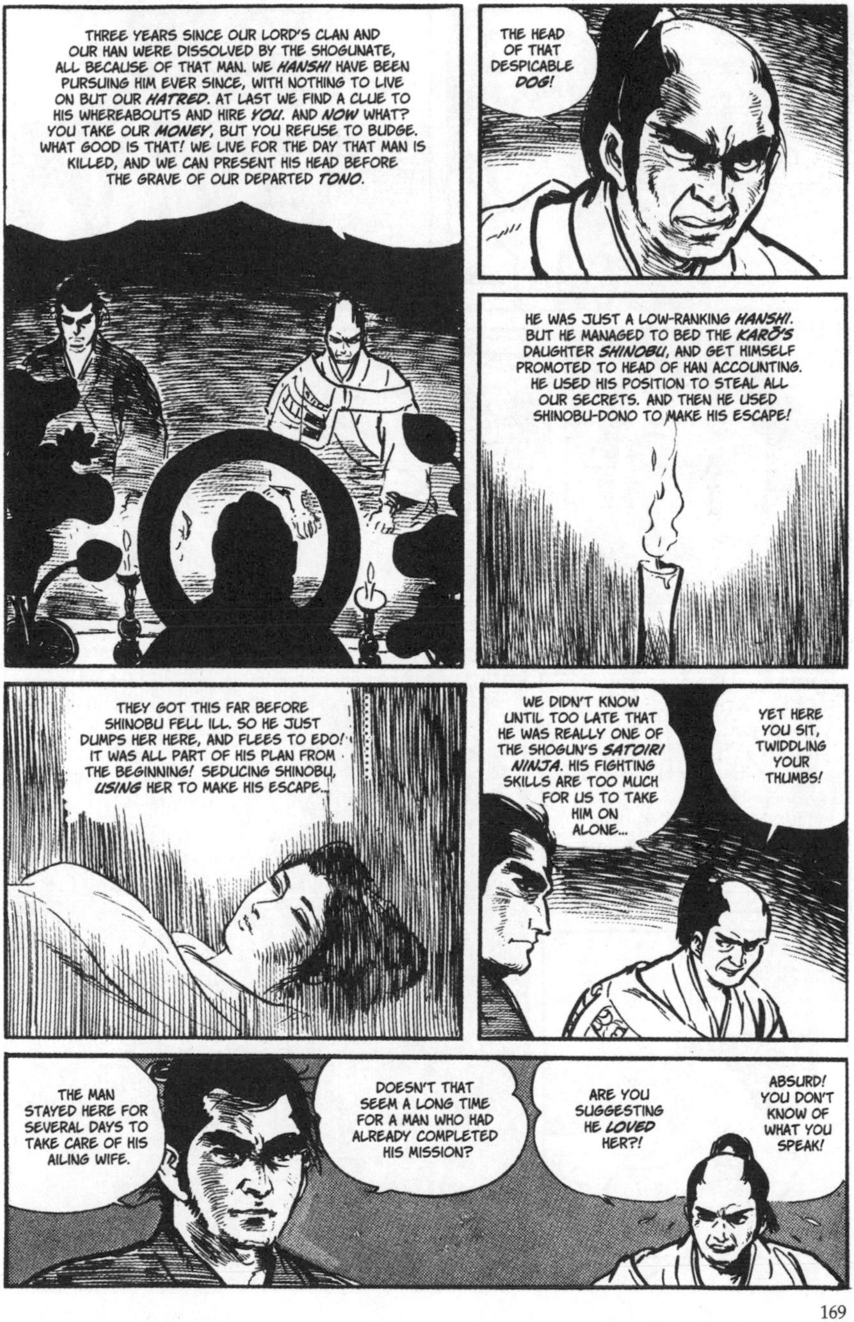
THREE YEARS SINCE OUR LORD'S CLAN AND OUR HAN WERE DISSOLVED BY THE SHOGUNATE, ALL BECAUSE OF THAT MAN. WE *HANSHI* HAVE BEEN PURSUING HIM EVER SINCE, WITH NOTHING TO LIVE ON BUT OUR *HATRED*. AT LAST WE FIND A CLUE TO HIS WHEREABOUTS AND HIRE *YOU*. AND *NOW* WHAT? YOU TAKE OUR *MONEY*, BUT YOU REFUSE TO BUDGE. WHAT GOOD IS THAT! WE LIVE FOR THE DAY THAT MAN IS KILLED, AND WE CAN PRESENT HIS HEAD BEFORE THE GRAVE OF OUR DEPARTED *TONO*.
THE HEAD OF THAT DESPICABLE *DOG*!
HE WAS JUST A LOW-RANKING *HANSHI*. BUT HE MANAGED TO BED THE *KARŌ'S* DAUGHTER *SHINOBU*, AND GET HIMSELF PROMOTED TO HEAD OF HAN ACCOUNTING. HE USED HIS POSITION TO STEAL ALL OUR SECRETS. AND THEN HE USED SHINOBU-DONO TO MAKE HIS ESCAPE!
THEY GOT THIS FAR BEFORE SHINOBU FELL ILL. SO HE JUST DUMPS HER HERE, AND FLEES TO EDO! IT WAS ALL PART OF HIS PLAN FROM THE BEGINNING! SEDUCING SHINOBU, *USING* HER TO MAKE HIS ESCAPE...
WE DIDN'T KNOW UNTIL TOO LATE THAT HE WAS REALLY ONE OF THE SHOGUN'S *SATOIRI NINJA*. HIS FIGHTING SKILLS ARE TOO MUCH FOR US TO TAKE HIM ON ALONE...
YET HERE YOU SIT, TWIDDLING YOUR THUMBS!
THE MAN STAYED HERE FOR SEVERAL DAYS TO TAKE CARE OF HIS AILING WIFE.
DOESN'T THAT SEEM A LONG TIME FOR A MAN WHO HAD ALREADY COMPLETED HIS MISSION?
ARE YOU SUGGESTING HE *LOVED* HER?!
ABSURD! YOU DON'T KNOW OF WHAT YOU SPEAK!

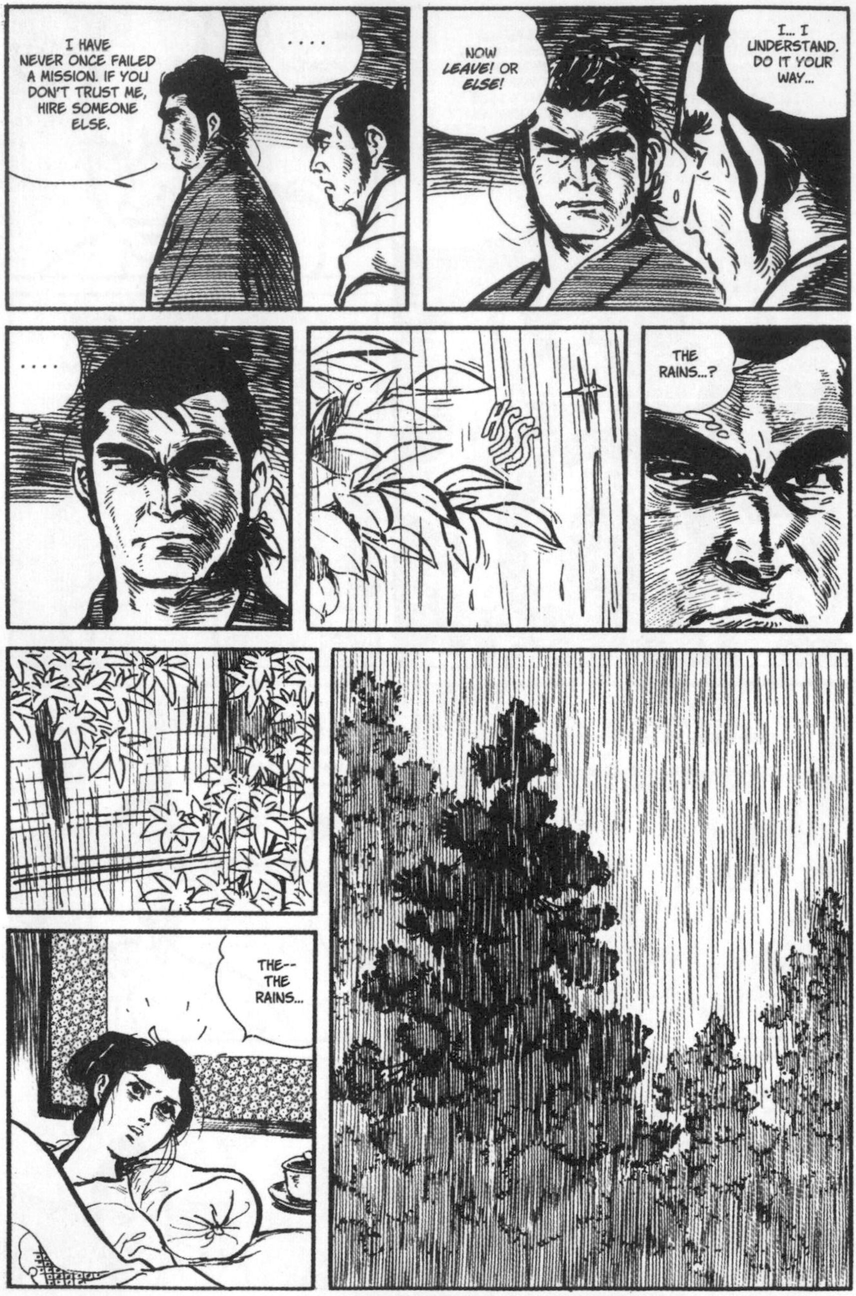
I HAVE NEVER ONCE FAILED A MISSION. IF YOU DON'T TRUST ME, HIRE SOMEONE ELSE.
....
NOW *LEAVE!* OR *ELSE!*
I... I UNDERSTAND. DO IT YOUR WAY...
....
HSS
THE RAINS...?
THE-- THE RAINS...

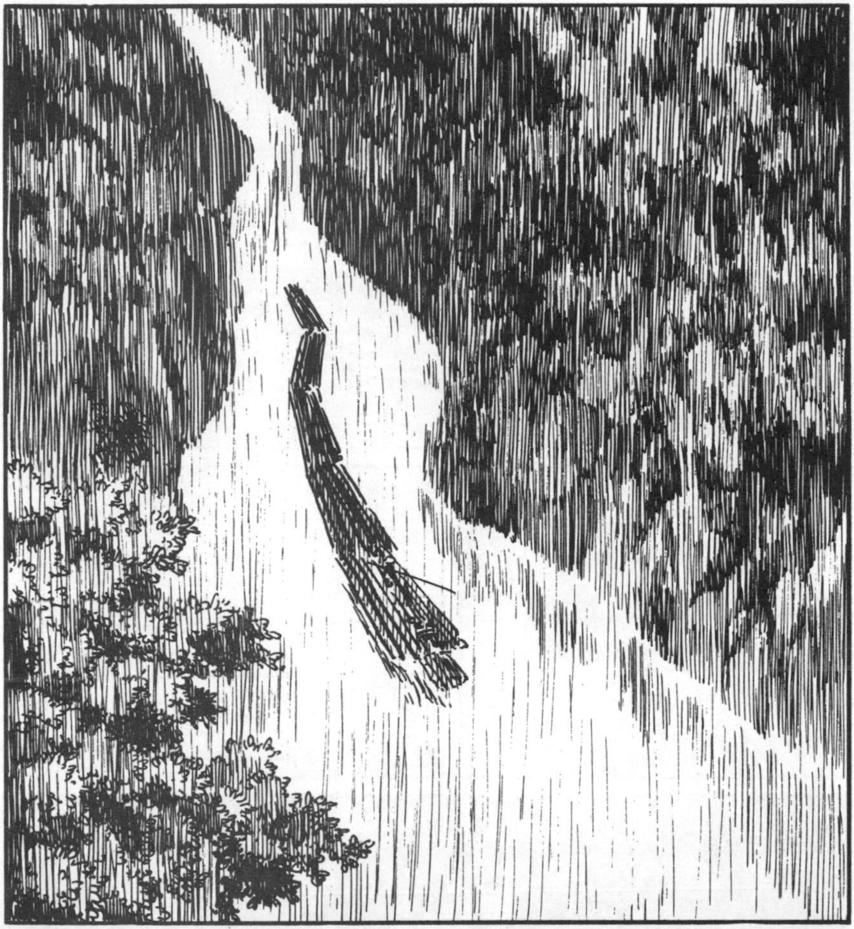
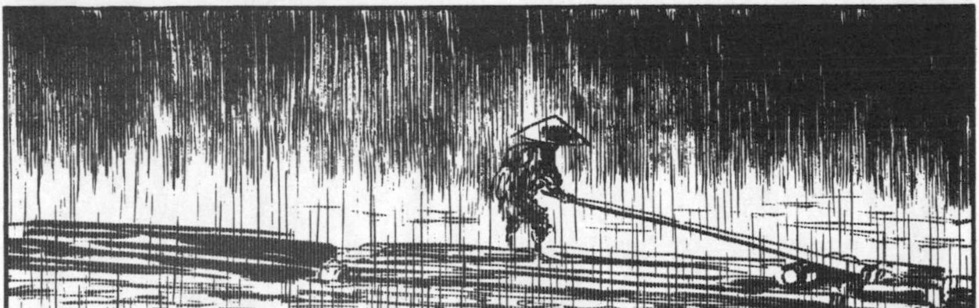

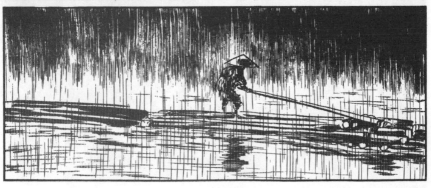

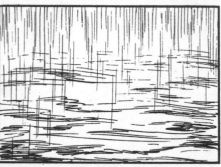

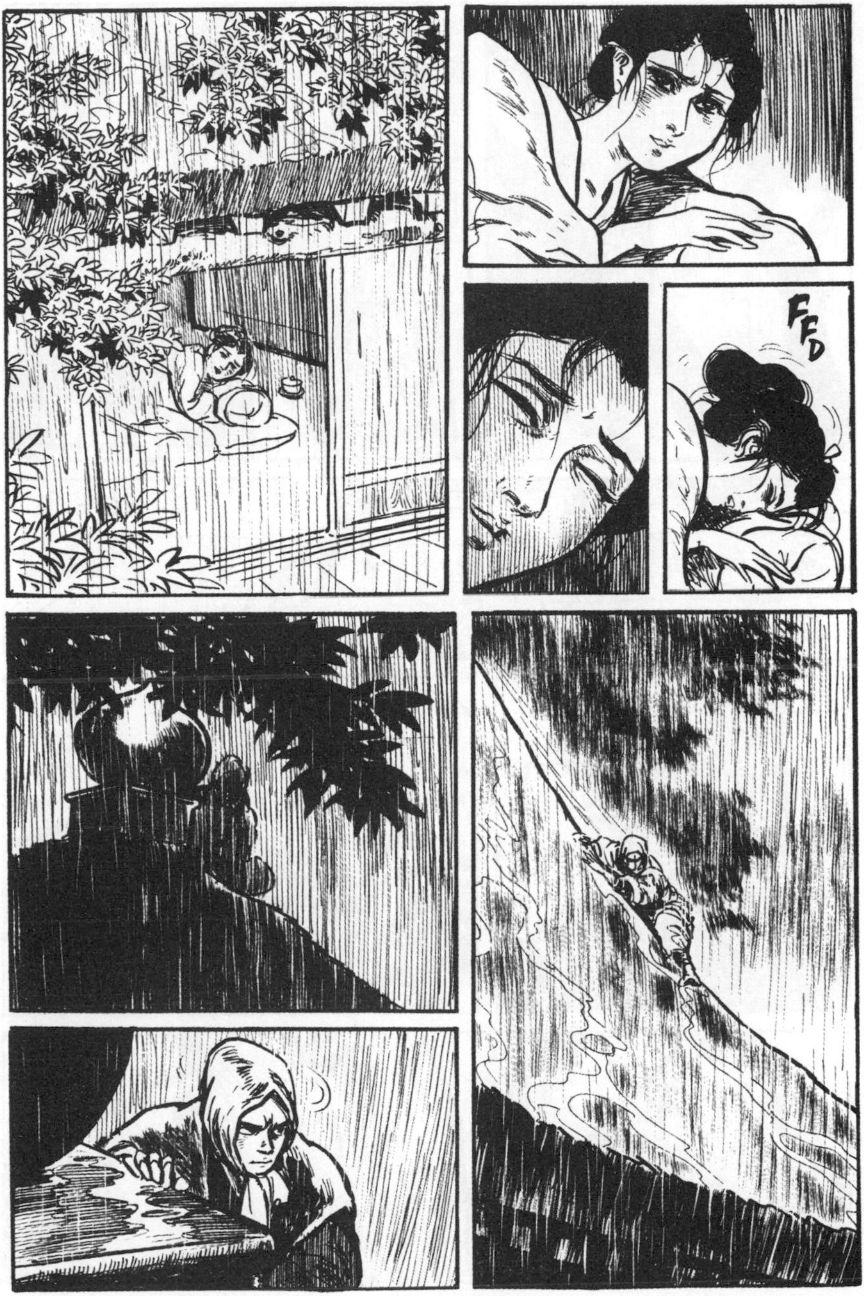
FFD

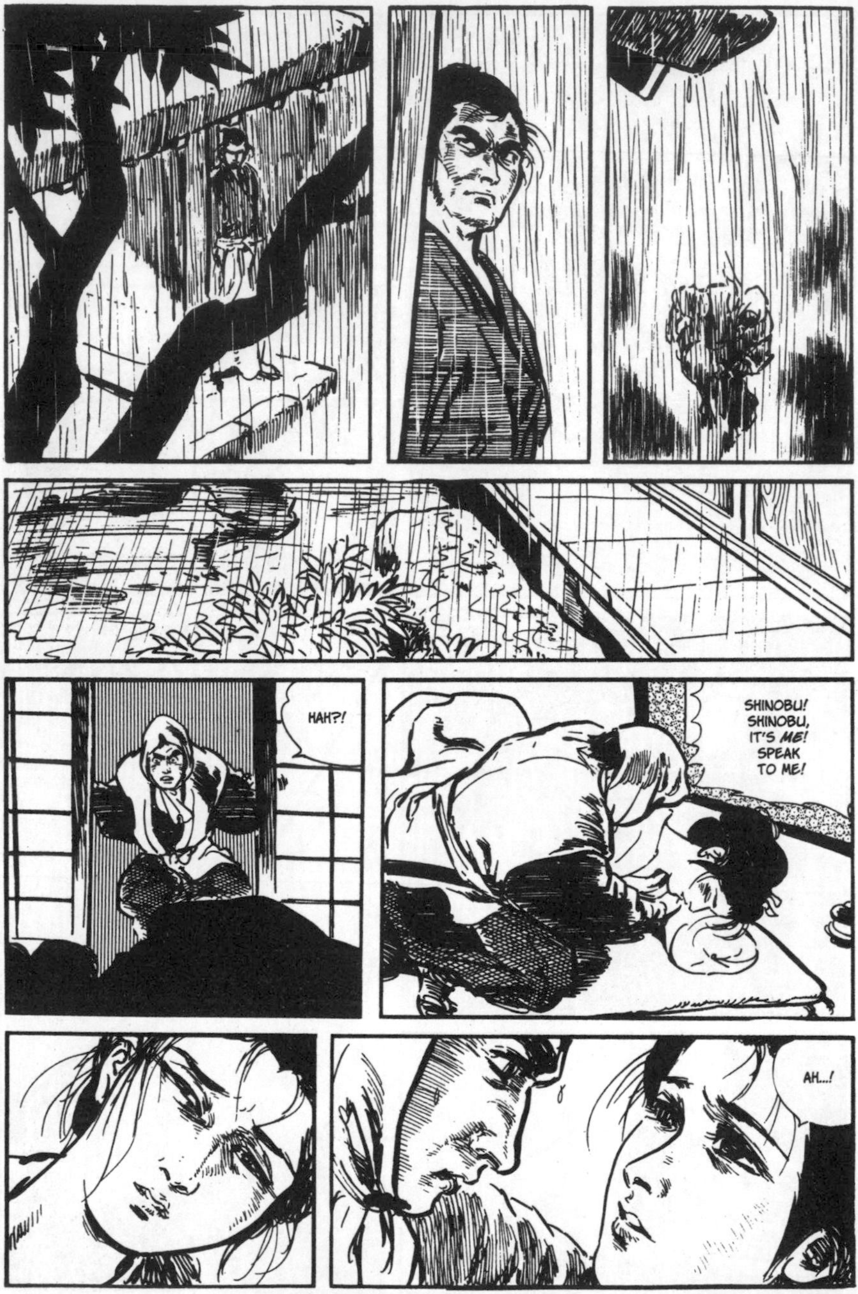
SHINOBU! SHINOBU, IT'S *ME*! SPEAK TO ME!
HAH?!
AH...!

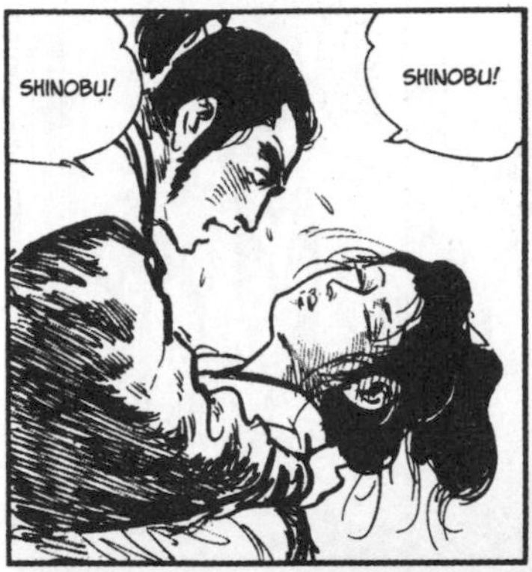
SHINOBU!
SHINOBU!
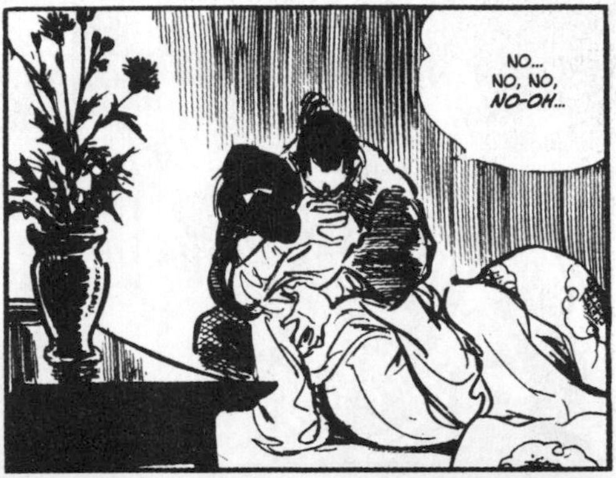
NO...
NO, NO,
NO-OH...
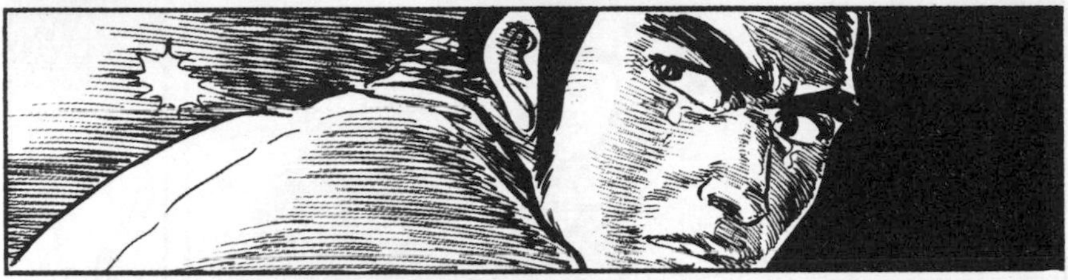
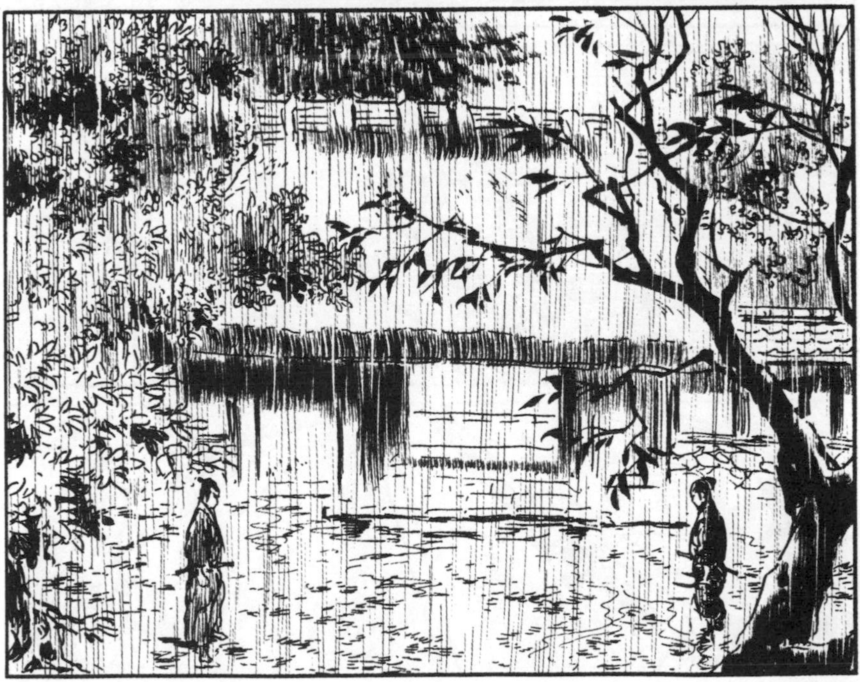

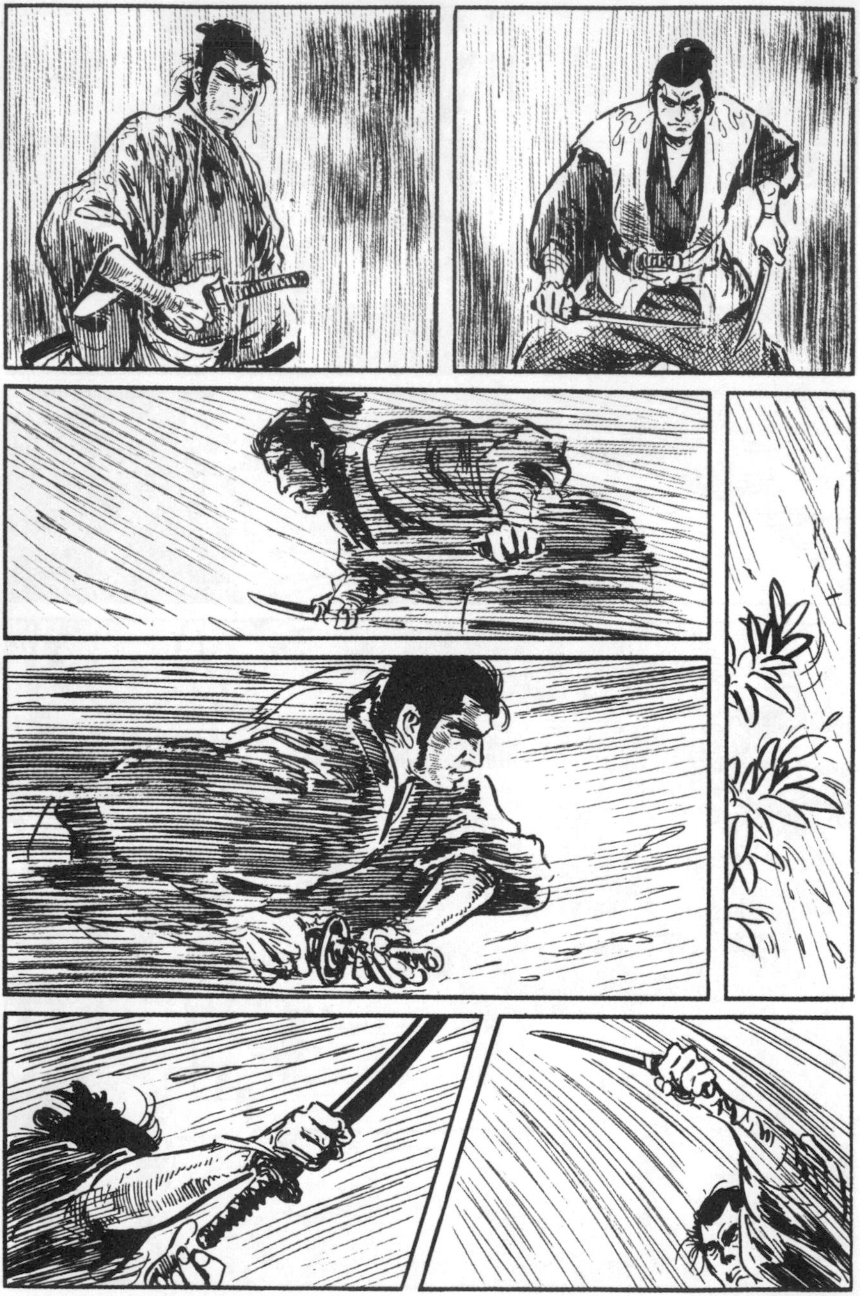

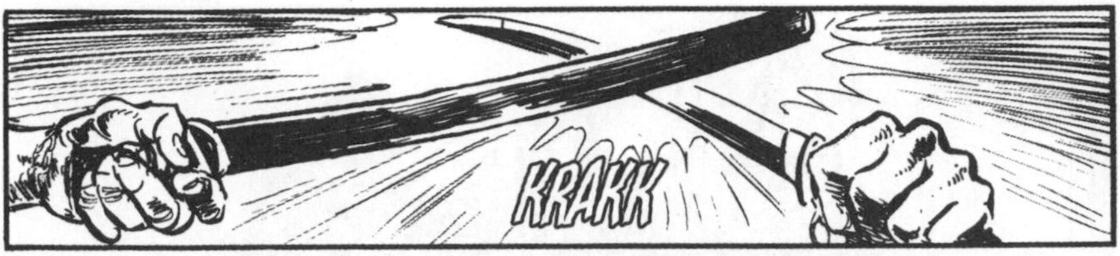
KRAKK
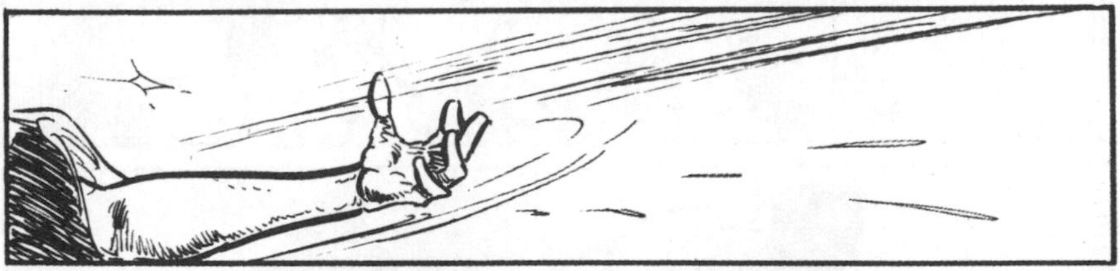
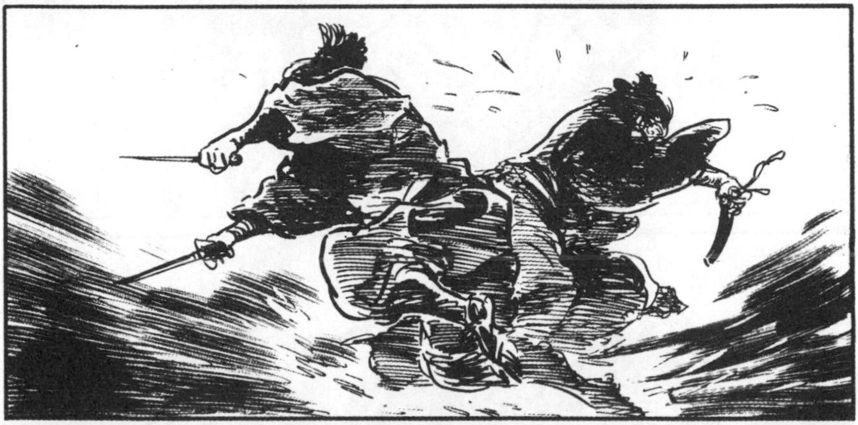
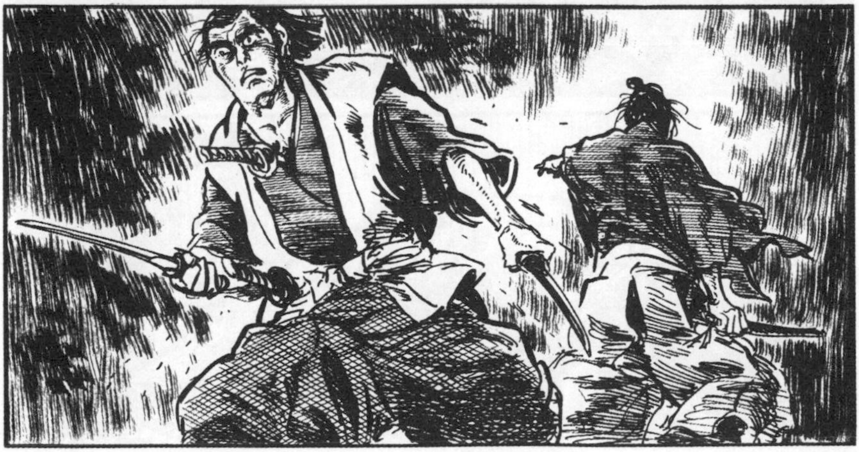

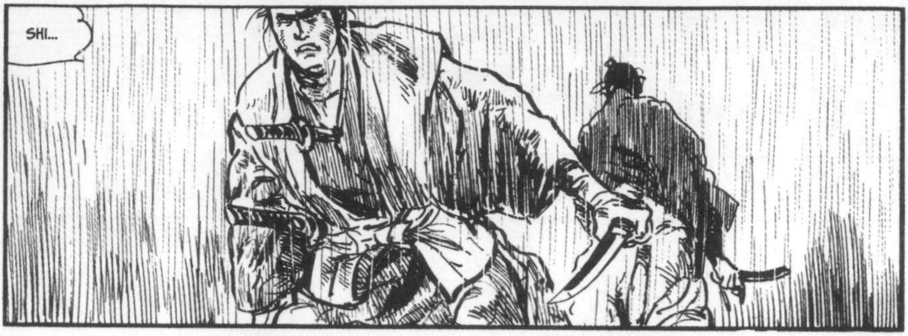
SHI...
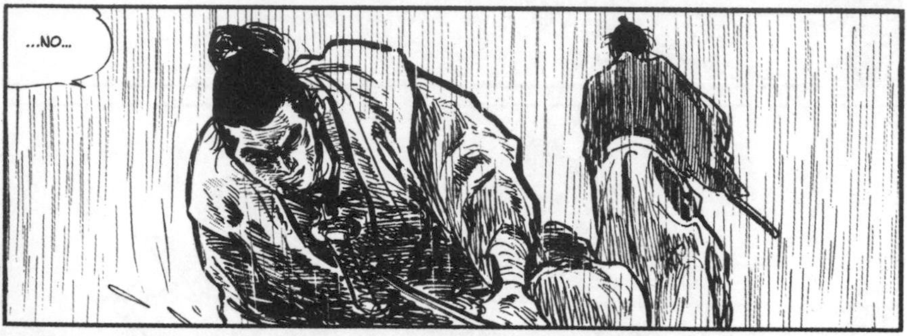
...NO...
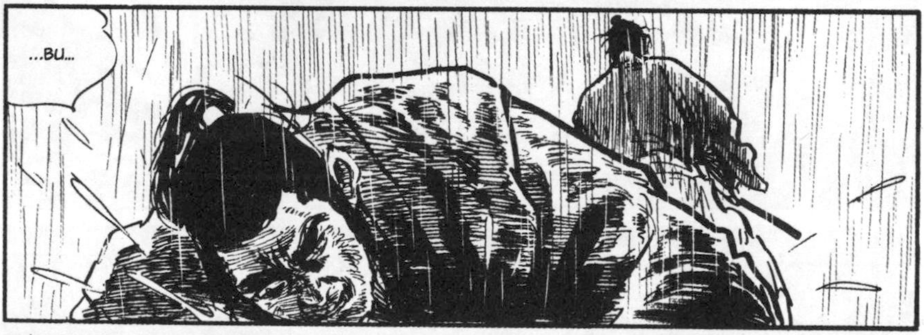
...BU...
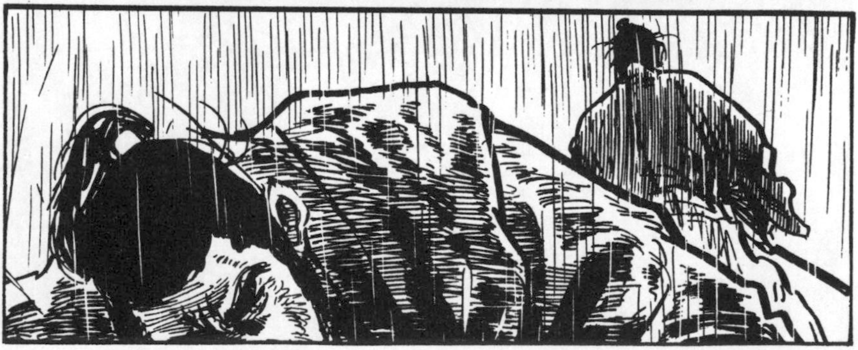

子連れ狼

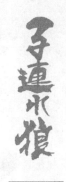

Eight Gates of Deceit

7

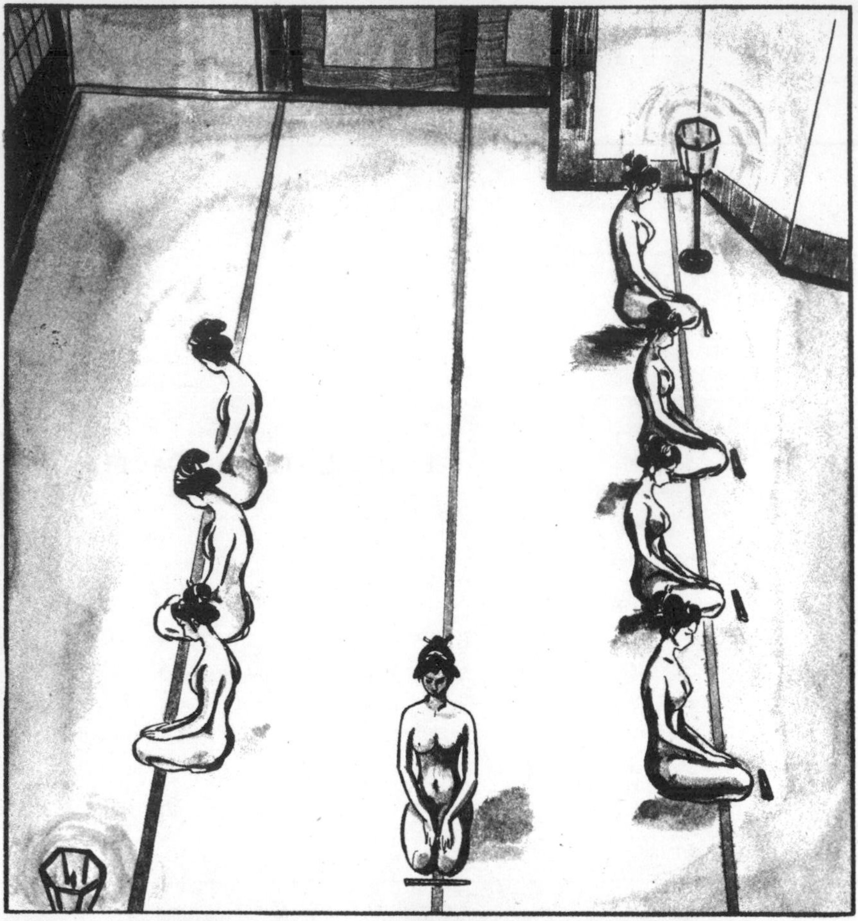
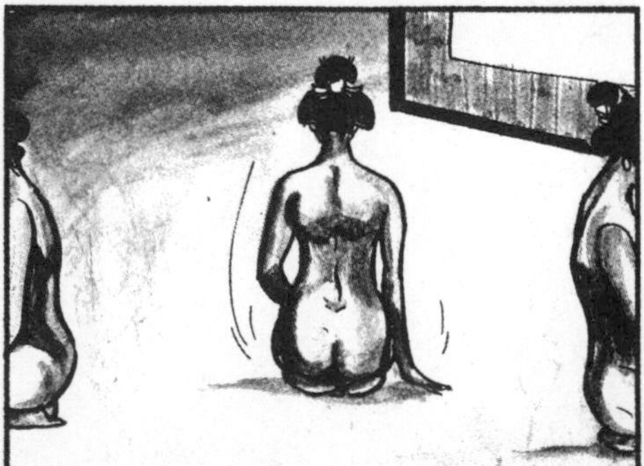
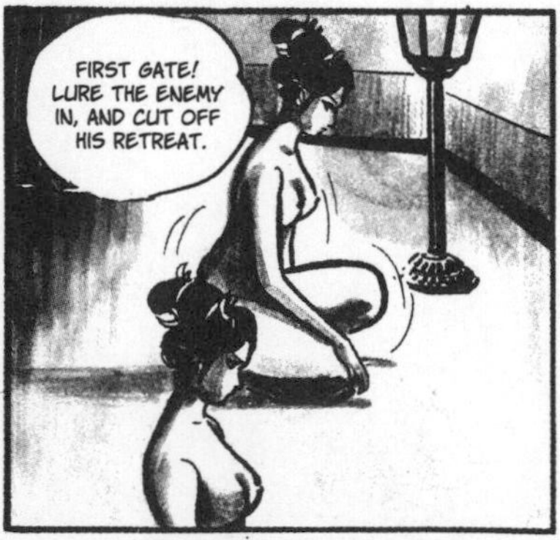
FIRST GATE! LURE THE ENEMY IN, AND CUT OFF HIS RETREAT.

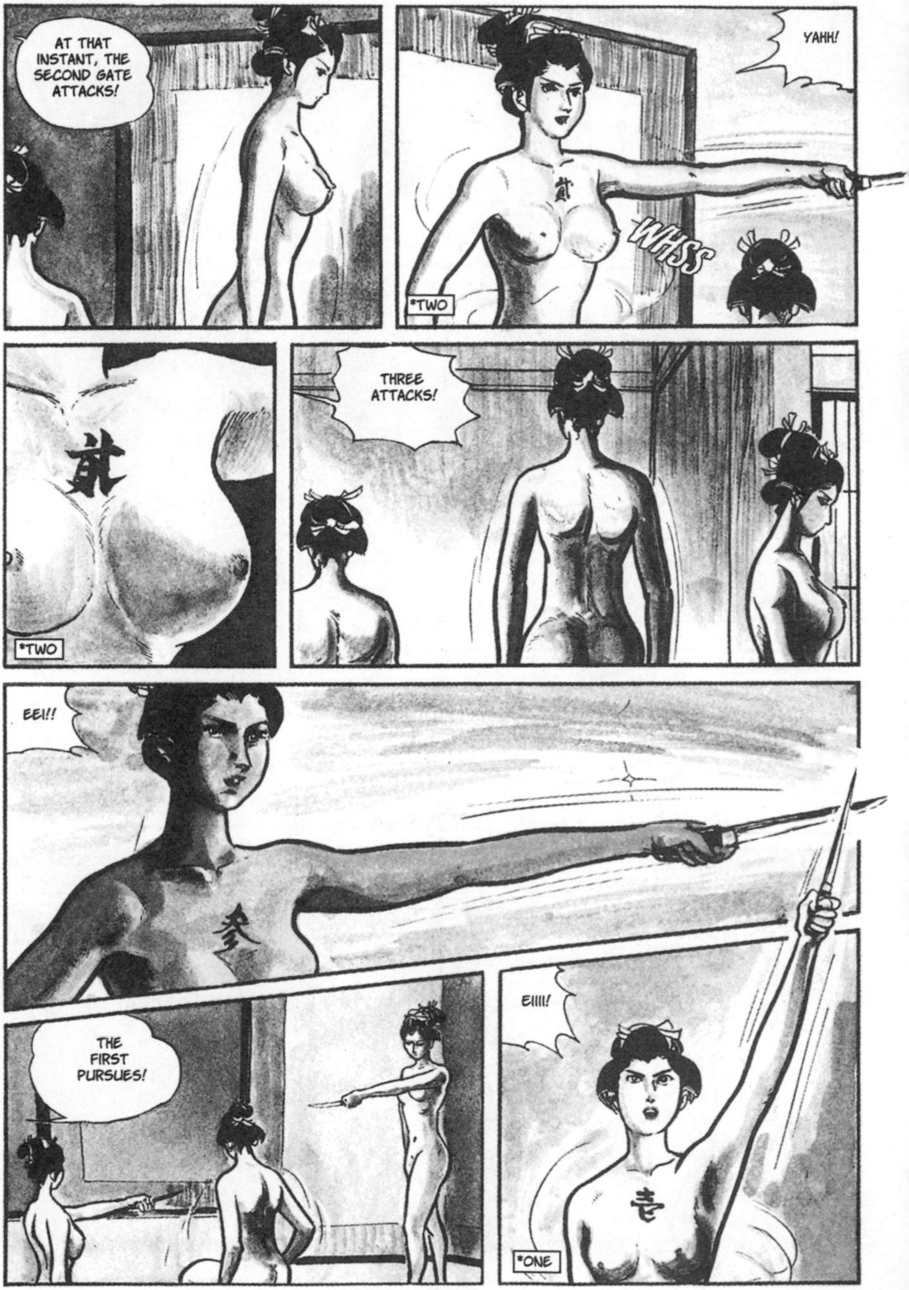
AT THAT INSTANT, THE SECOND GATE ATTACKS!
YAHH!
WHSS
*TWO
*TWO
THREE ATTACKS!
EEI!!
THE FIRST PURSUES!
EIIII!
*ONE

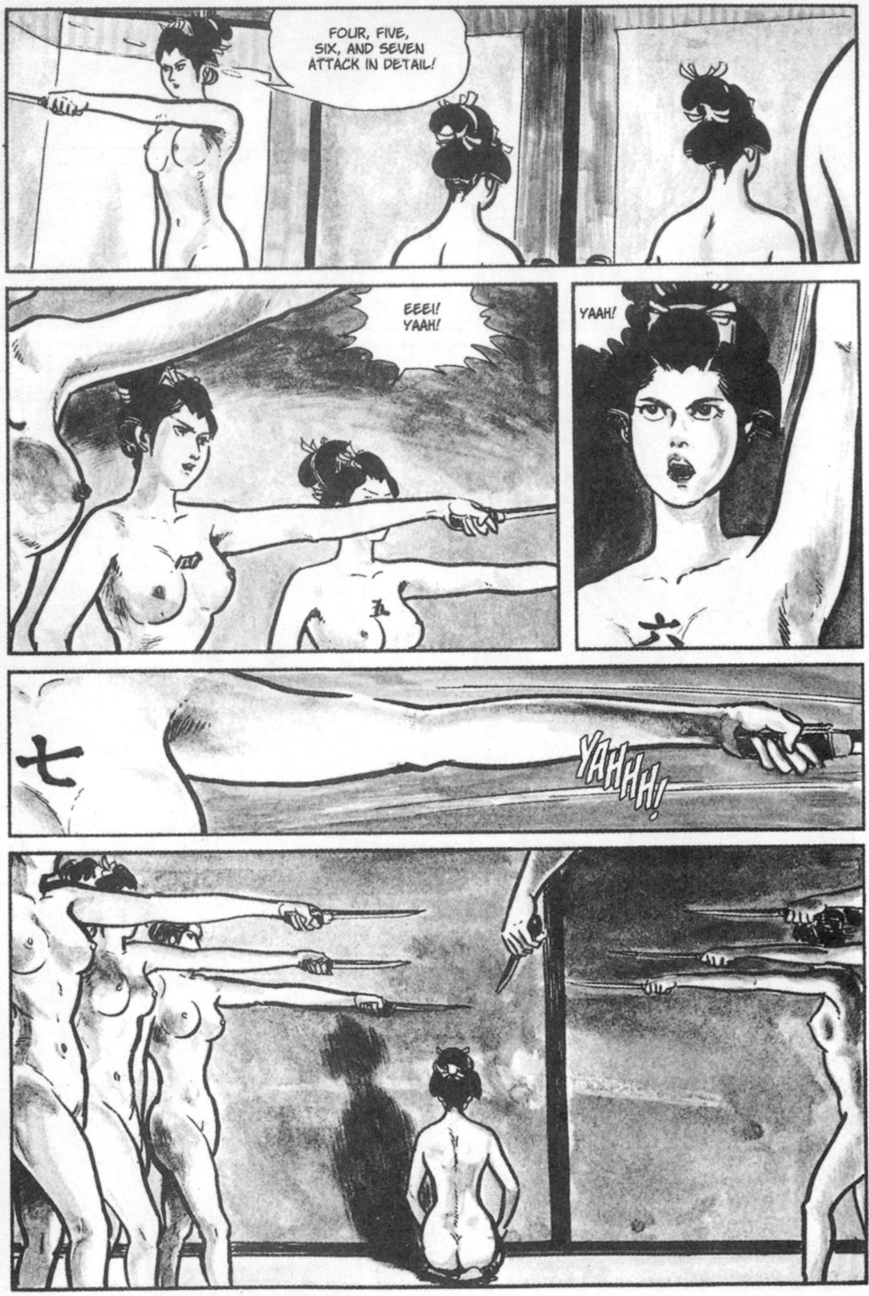
FOUR, FIVE, SIX, AND SEVEN ATTACK IN DETAIL!
YAAH!
六
EEEI! YAAH!
YAHHHH!
七

THE ENEMY'S ONLY PATH OF ESCAPE IS THE EIGHTH GATE.

DRIVEN AND FATIGUED, HE REACHES THIS EIGHTH GATE...

THE PERFECT MOMENT TO END HIS LIFE!

EI!!

THIS IS THE ONLY WAY TO DEFEAT YOUR STRONGEST ENEMIES!

DO YOU UNDERSTAND? YOU ARE THE HUNTERS! DRIVE YOUR PREY BEFORE YOU!

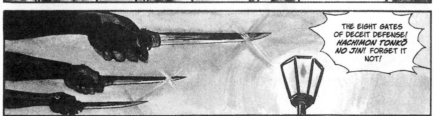

THE EIGHT GATES OF DECEIT DEFENSE! HACHIMON TONKŌ NO JIN! FORGET IT NOT!

183

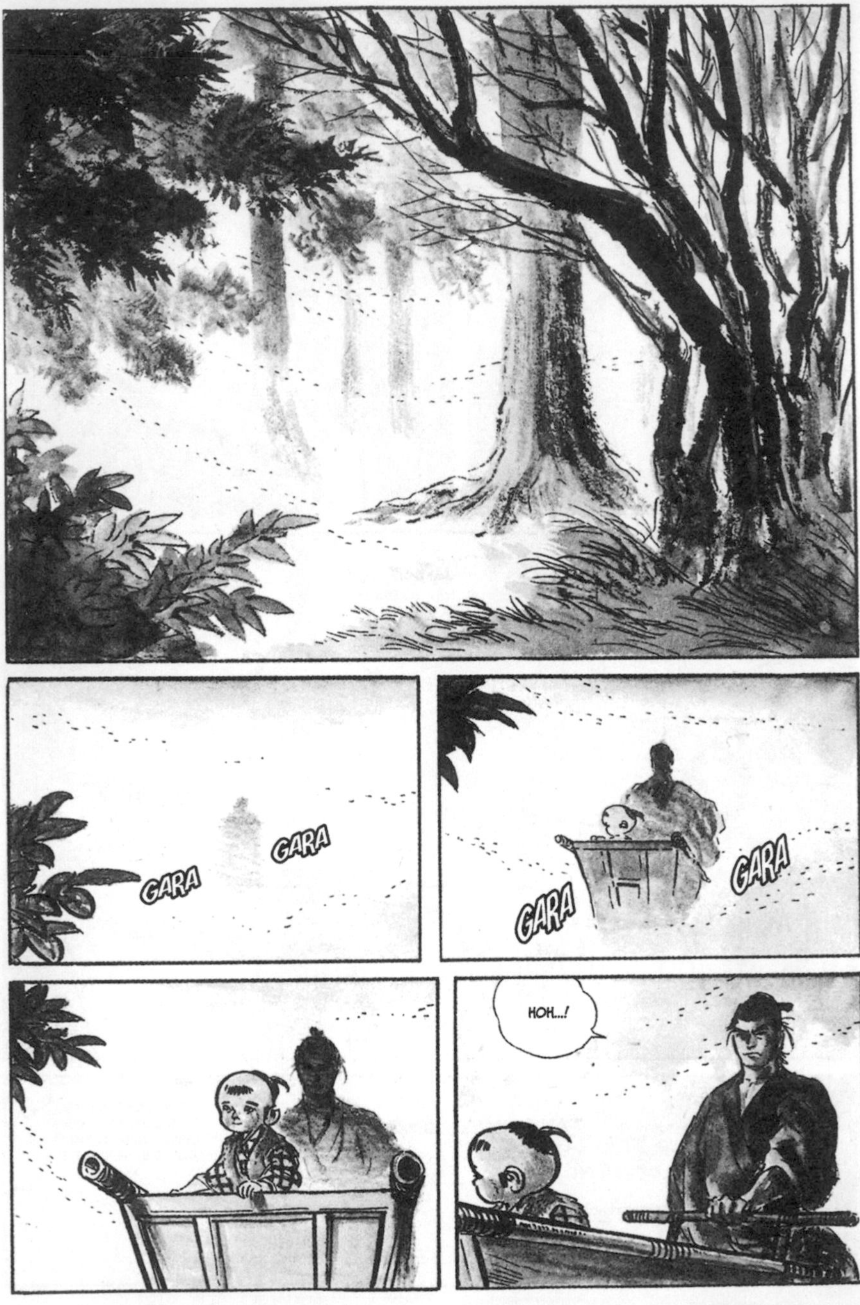
GARA
GARA
GARA
GARA
HOH...!

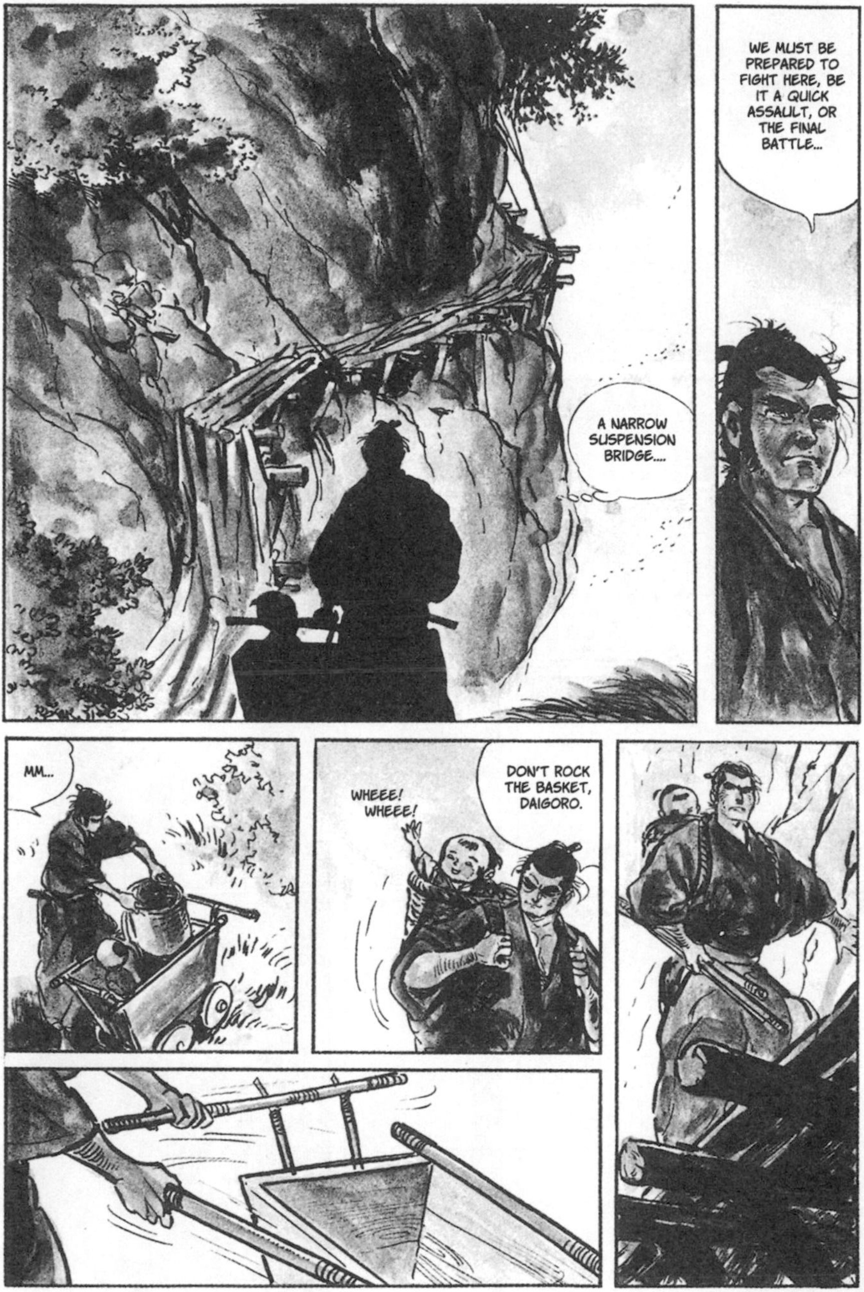
A NARROW SUSPENSION BRIDGE....
WE MUST BE PREPARED TO FIGHT HERE, BE IT A QUICK ASSAULT, OR THE FINAL BATTLE...
MM...
WHEEE! WHEEE!
DON'T ROCK THE BASKET, DAIGORO.

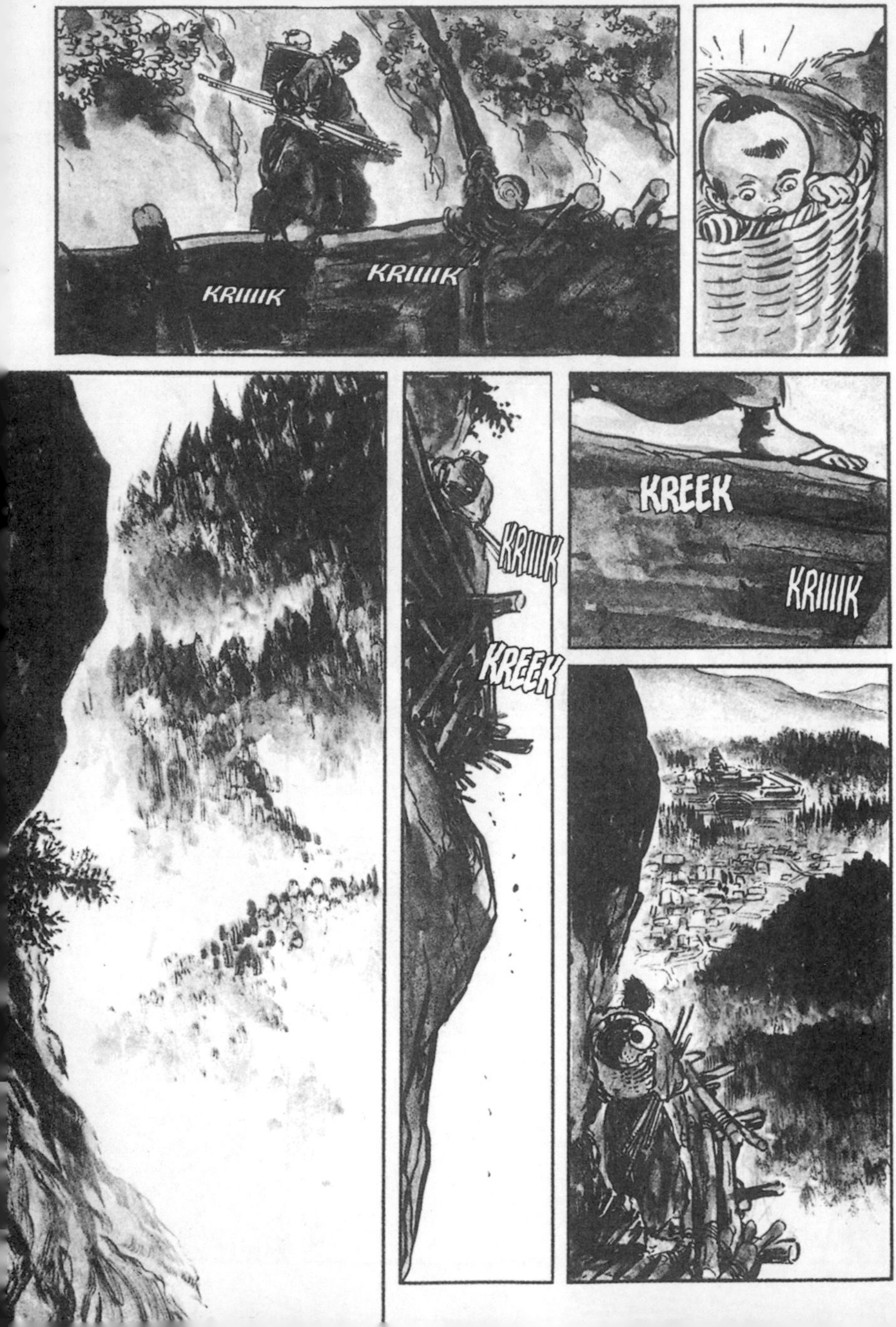
KRIIIIK
KRIIIIK
KREEK
KRIIIIK
KRIIIIK
KREEK

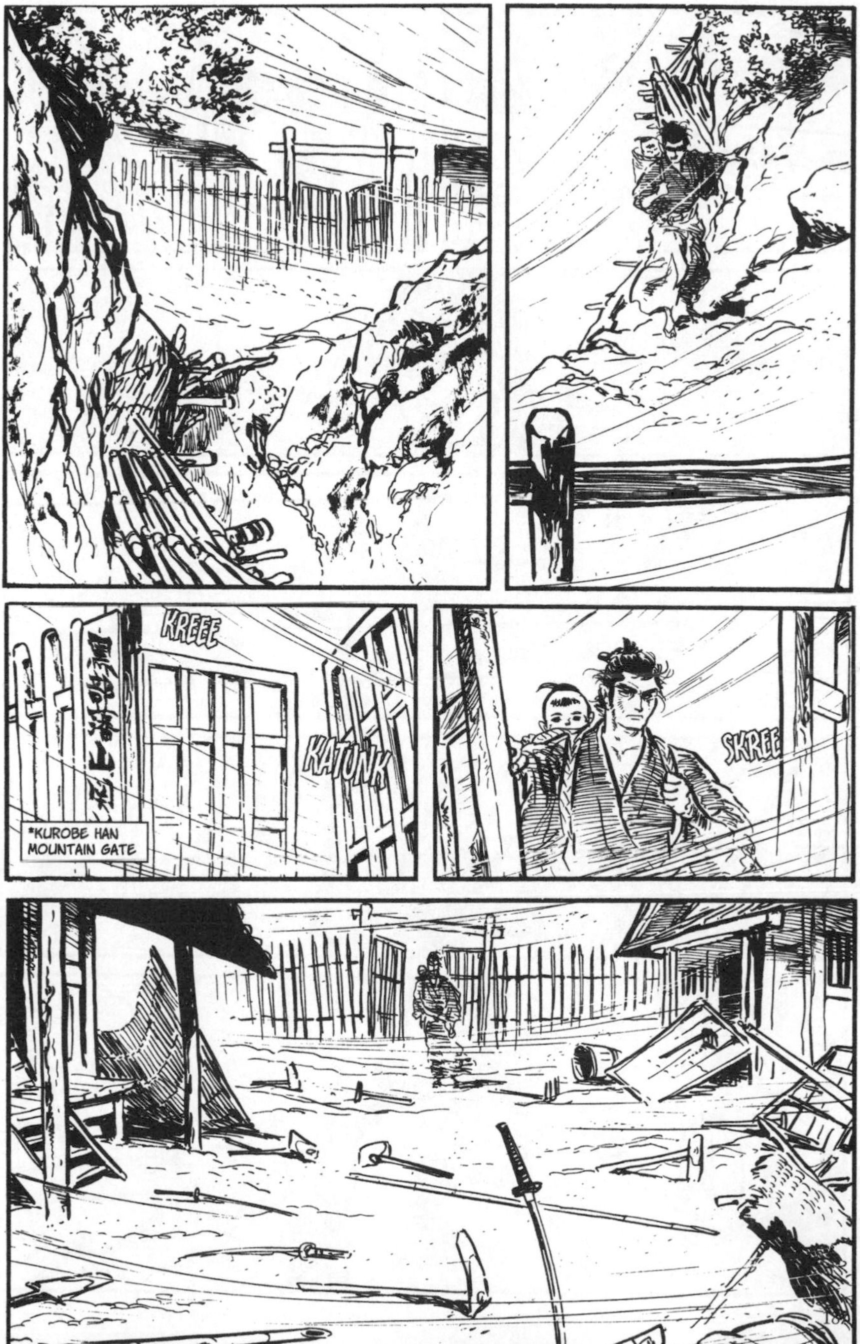
SKREE
KREEE
KATUNK
*KUROBE HAN
MOUNTAIN GATE

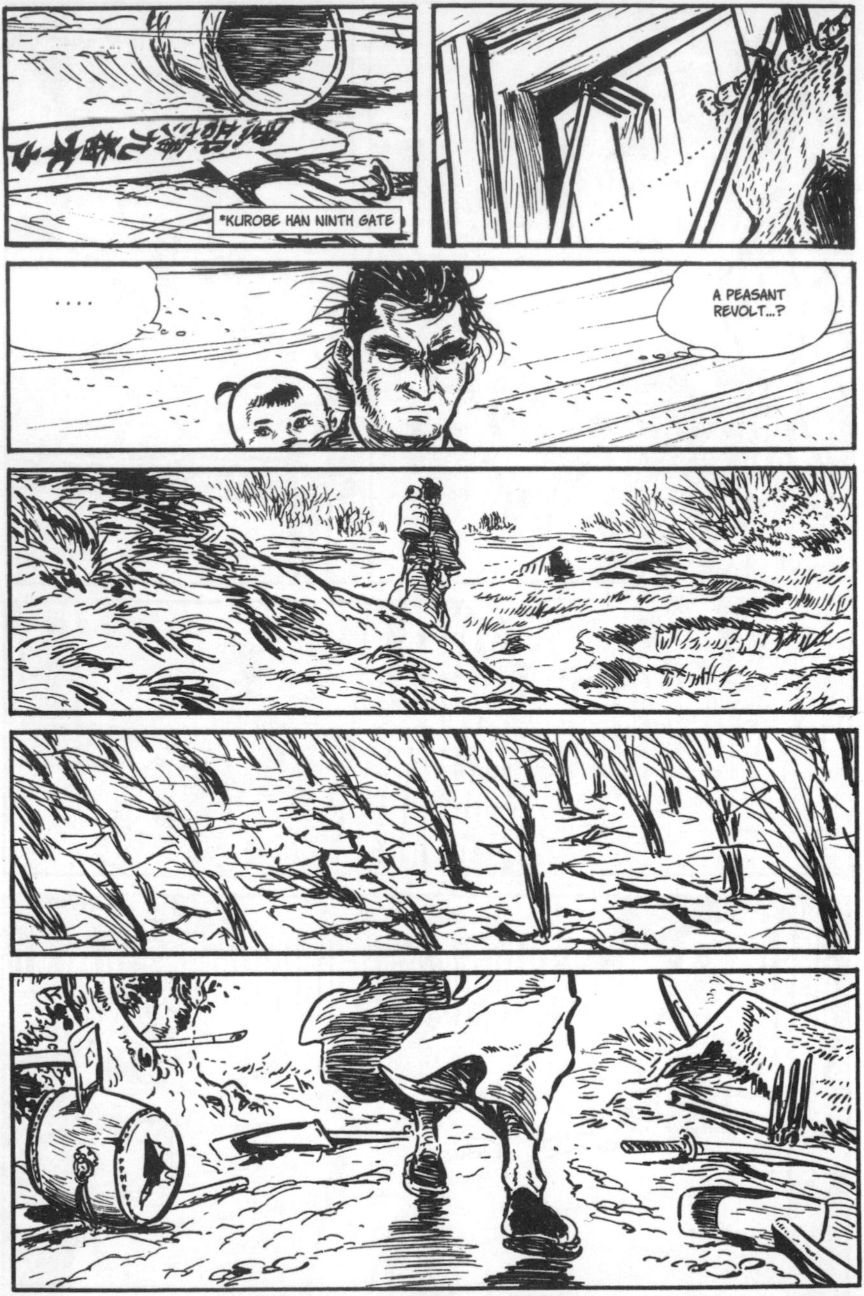
*KUROBE HAN NINTH GATE
A PEASANT REVOLT...?
. . . .

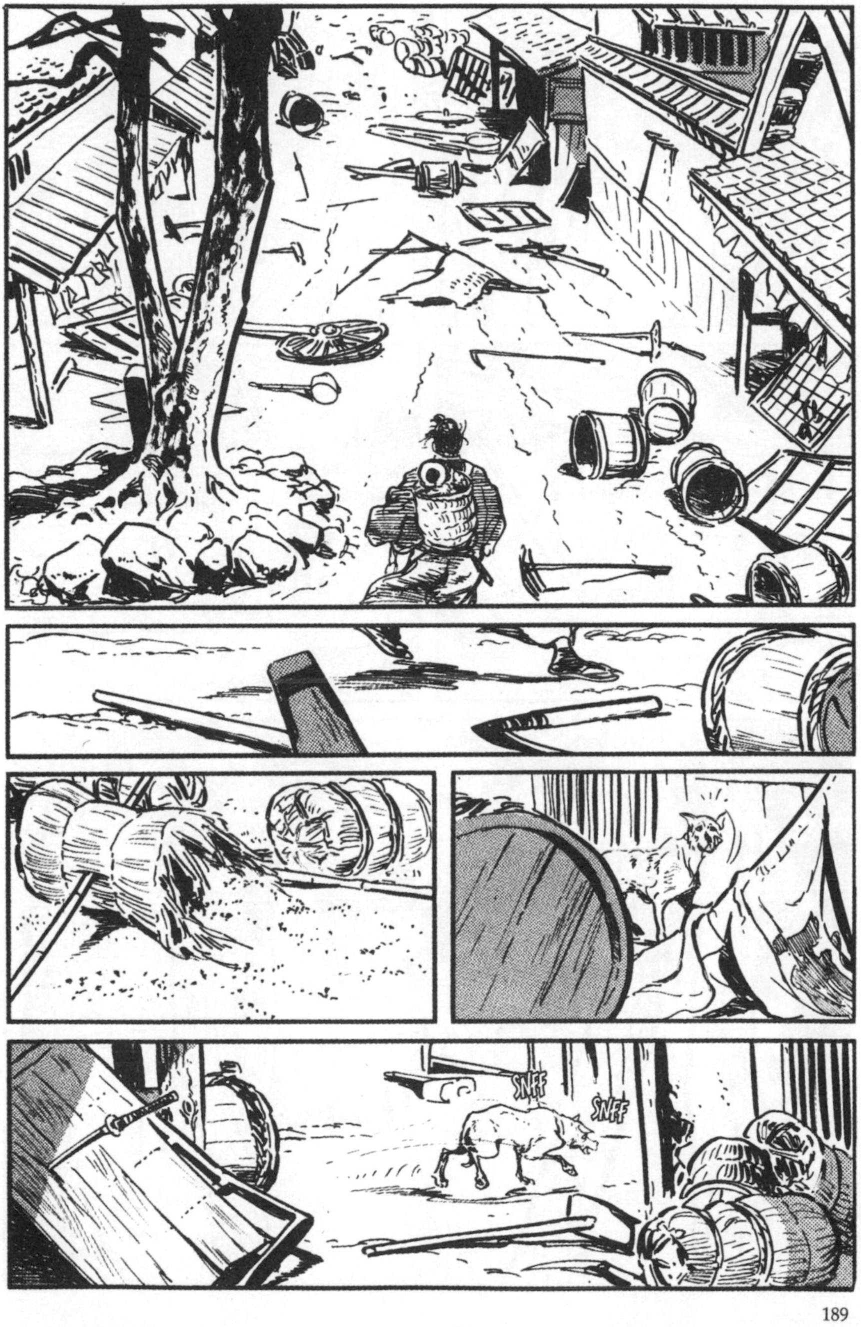
SNFF
SNFF

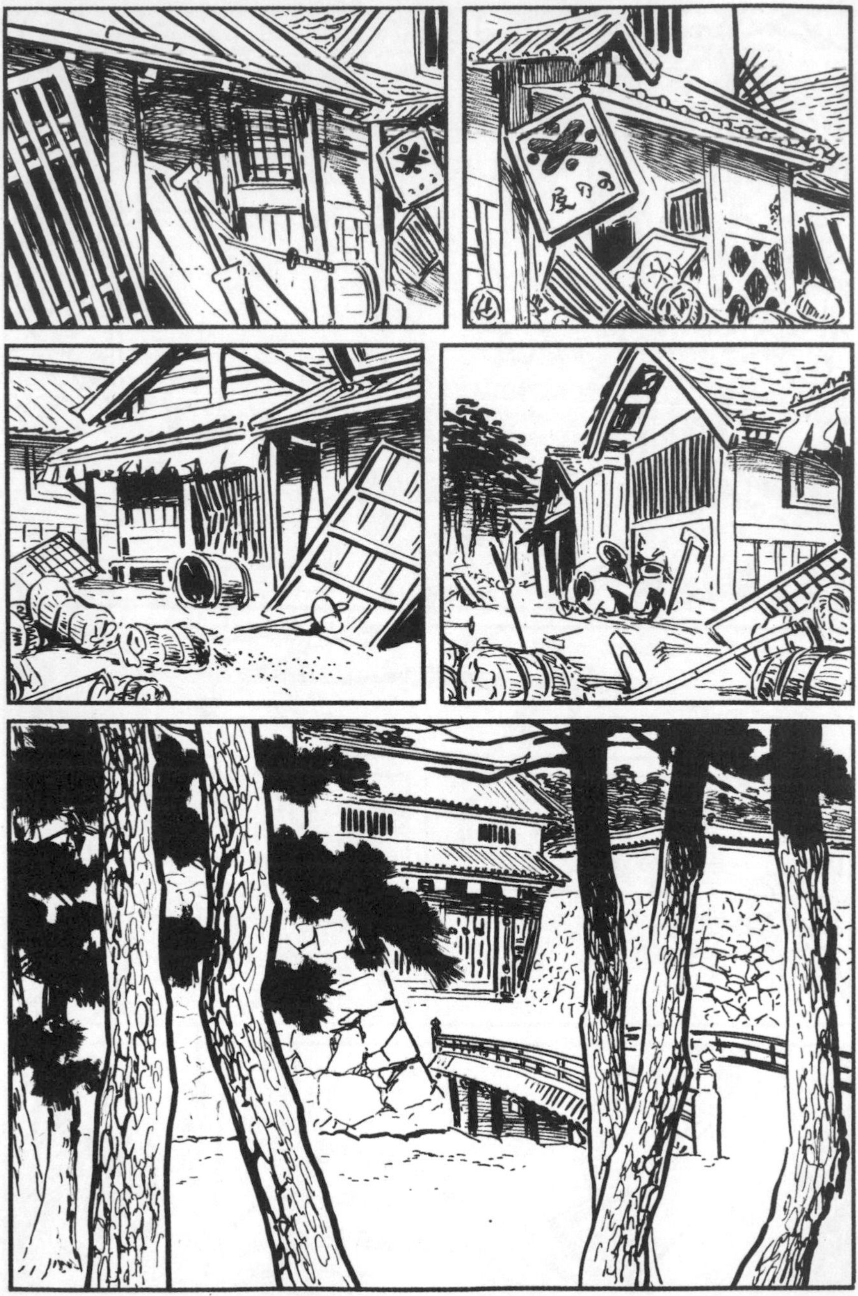

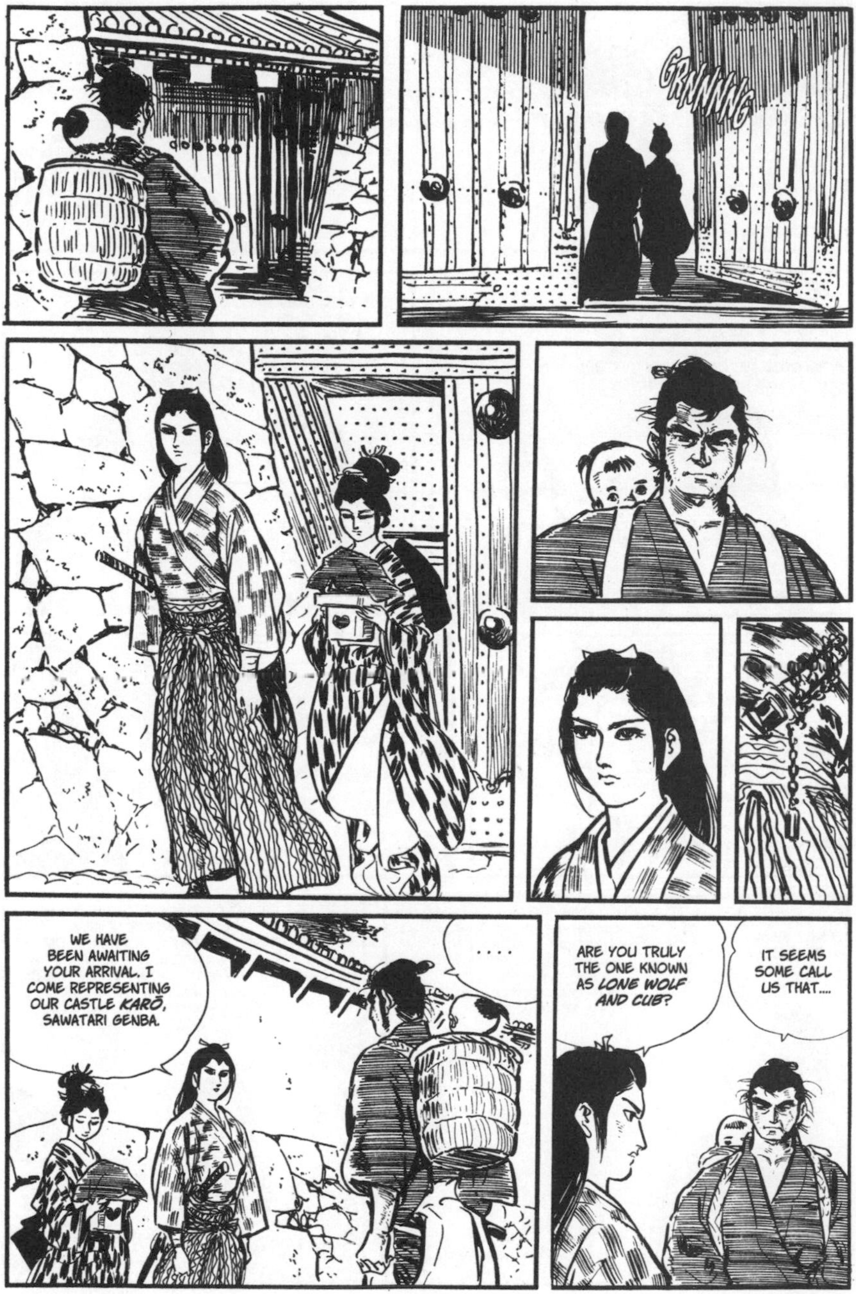
GRNNNG
WE HAVE BEEN AWAITING YOUR ARRIVAL. I COME REPRESENTING OUR CASTLE *KARŌ*, SAWATARI GENBA.
....
ARE YOU TRULY THE ONE KNOWN AS *LONE WOLF AND CUB*?
IT SEEMS SOME CALL US THAT....

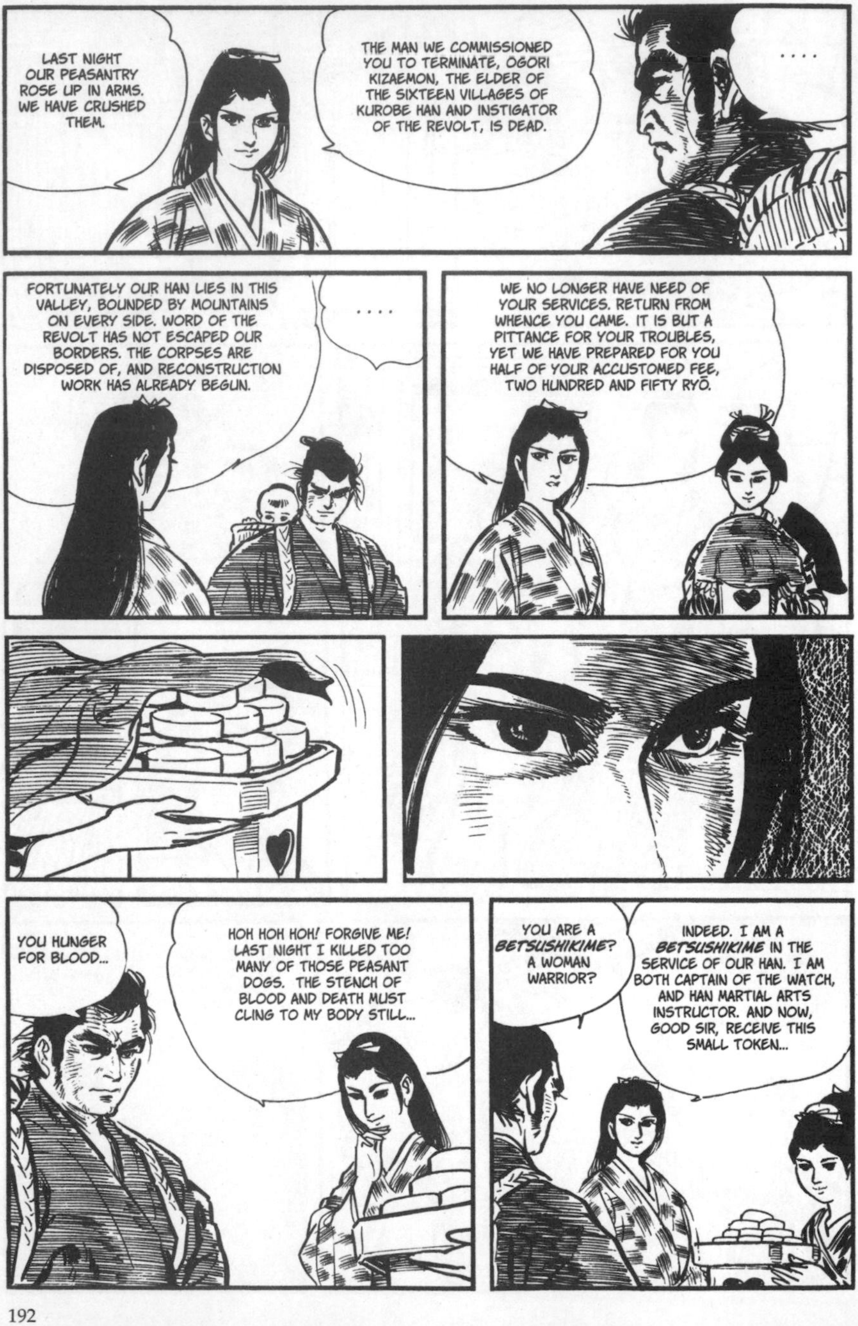

LAST NIGHT OUR PEASANTRY ROSE UP IN ARMS. WE HAVE CRUSHED THEM.
THE MAN WE COMMISSIONED YOU TO TERMINATE, OGORI KIZAEMON, THE ELDER OF THE SIXTEEN VILLAGES OF KUROBE HAN AND INSTIGATOR OF THE REVOLT, IS DEAD.
....
FORTUNATELY OUR HAN LIES IN THIS VALLEY, BOUNDED BY MOUNTAINS ON EVERY SIDE. WORD OF THE REVOLT HAS NOT ESCAPED OUR BORDERS. THE CORPSES ARE DISPOSED OF, AND RECONSTRUCTION WORK HAS ALREADY BEGUN.
....
WE NO LONGER HAVE NEED OF YOUR SERVICES. RETURN FROM WHENCE YOU CAME. IT IS BUT A PITTANCE FOR YOUR TROUBLES, YET WE HAVE PREPARED FOR YOU HALF OF YOUR ACCUSTOMED FEE, TWO HUNDRED AND FIFTY RYŌ.
YOU HUNGER FOR BLOOD...
HOH HOH HOH! FORGIVE ME! LAST NIGHT I KILLED TOO MANY OF THOSE PEASANT DOGS. THE STENCH OF BLOOD AND DEATH MUST CLING TO MY BODY STILL...
YOU ARE A *BETSUSHIKIME*? A WOMAN WARRIOR?
INDEED. I AM A *BETSUSHIKIME* IN THE SERVICE OF OUR HAN. I AM BOTH CAPTAIN OF THE WATCH, AND HAN MARTIAL ARTS INSTRUCTOR. AND NOW, GOOD SIR, RECEIVE THIS SMALL TOKEN...

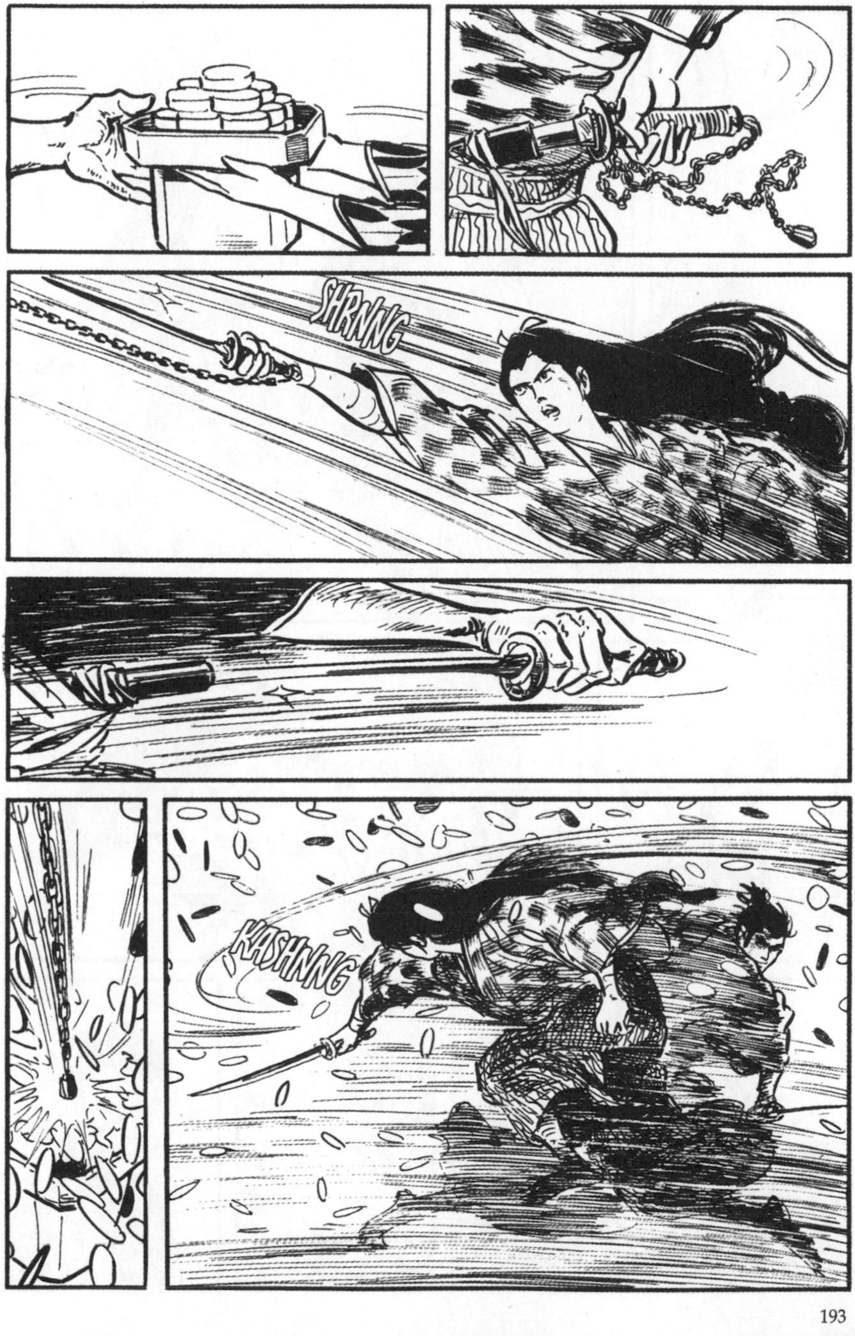
SHRNNG
KASHNNG

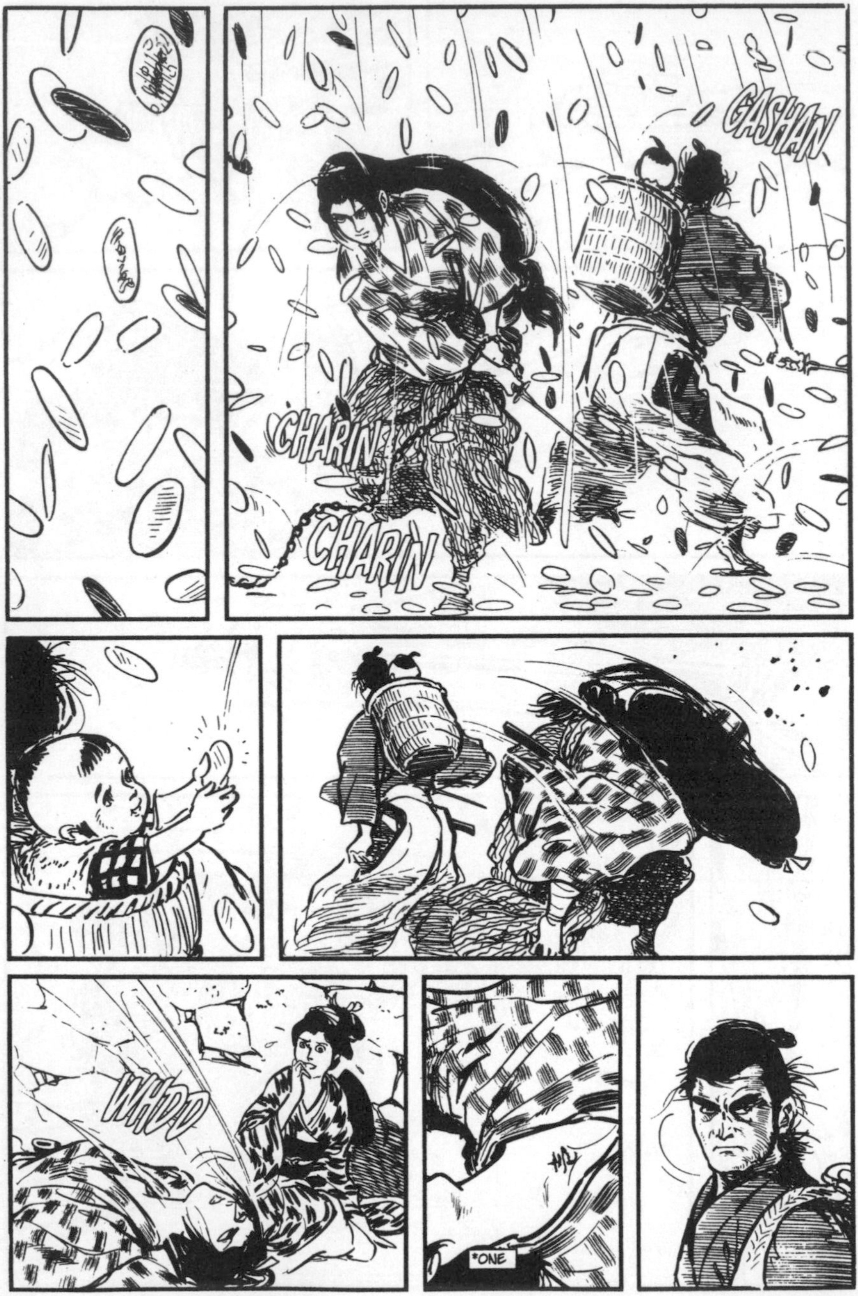
GASHAN
CHARIN
CHARIN
*ONE
WHOO

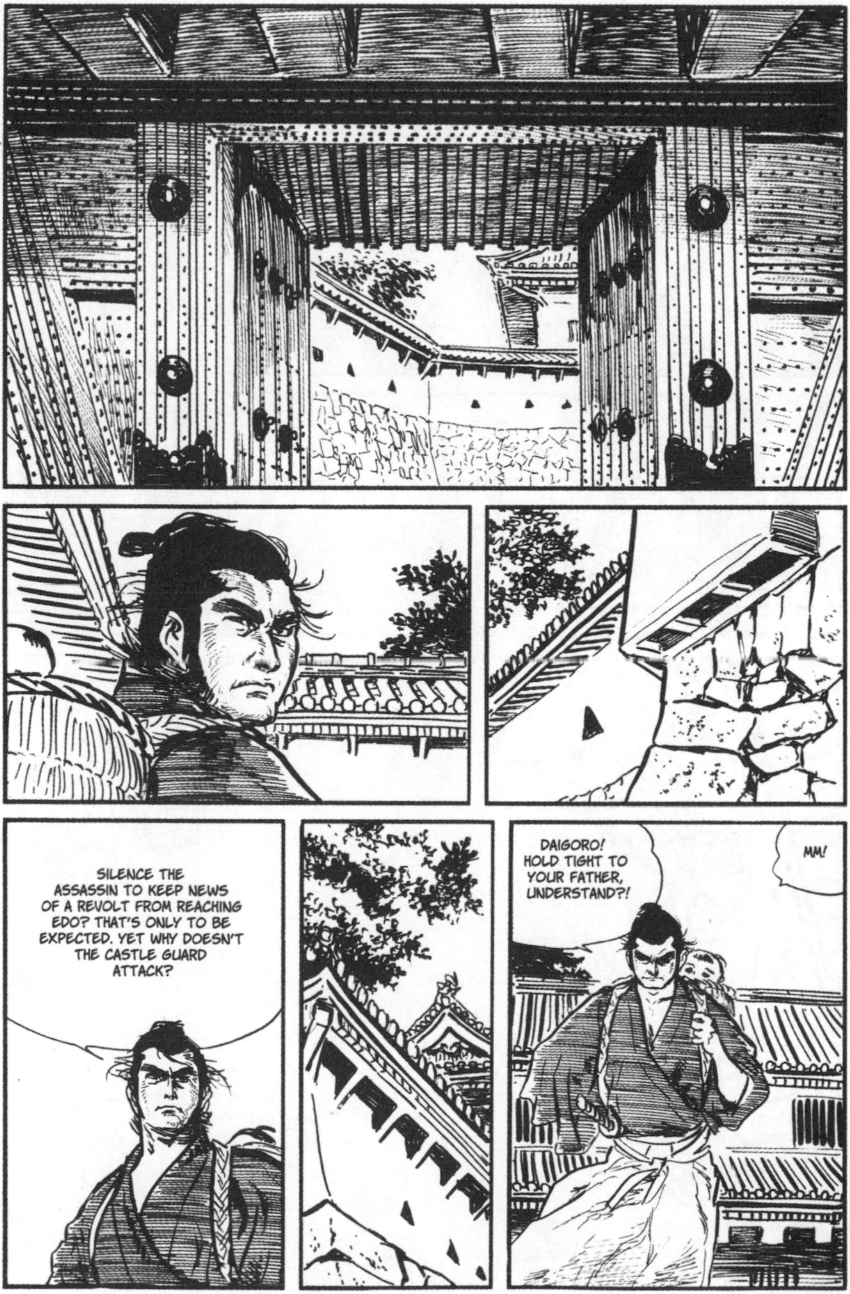
SILENCE THE ASSASSIN TO KEEP NEWS OF A REVOLT FROM REACHING EDO? THAT'S ONLY TO BE EXPECTED. YET WHY DOESN'T THE CASTLE GUARD ATTACK?
DAIGORO! HOLD TIGHT TO YOUR FATHER, UNDERSTAND?!
MM!

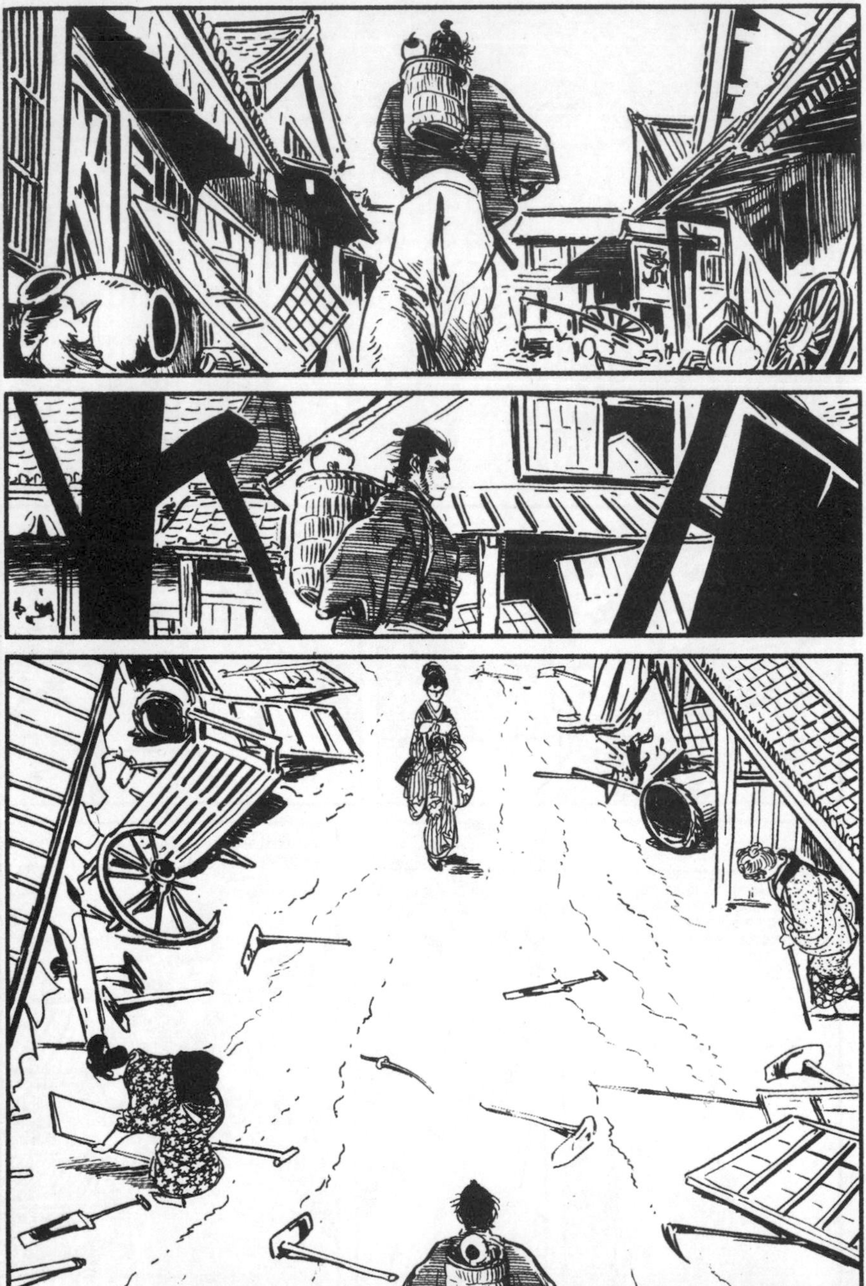

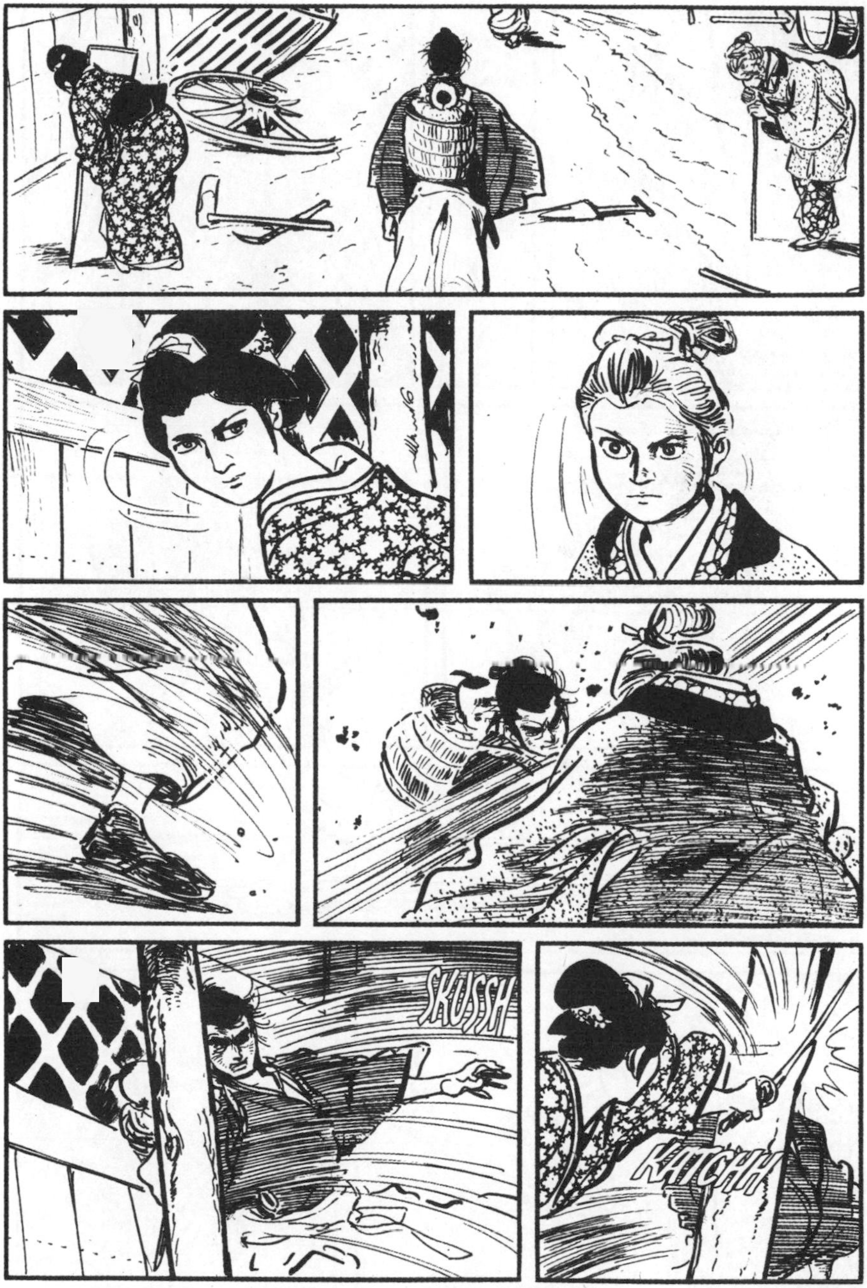
KATCHH
SKUSSH

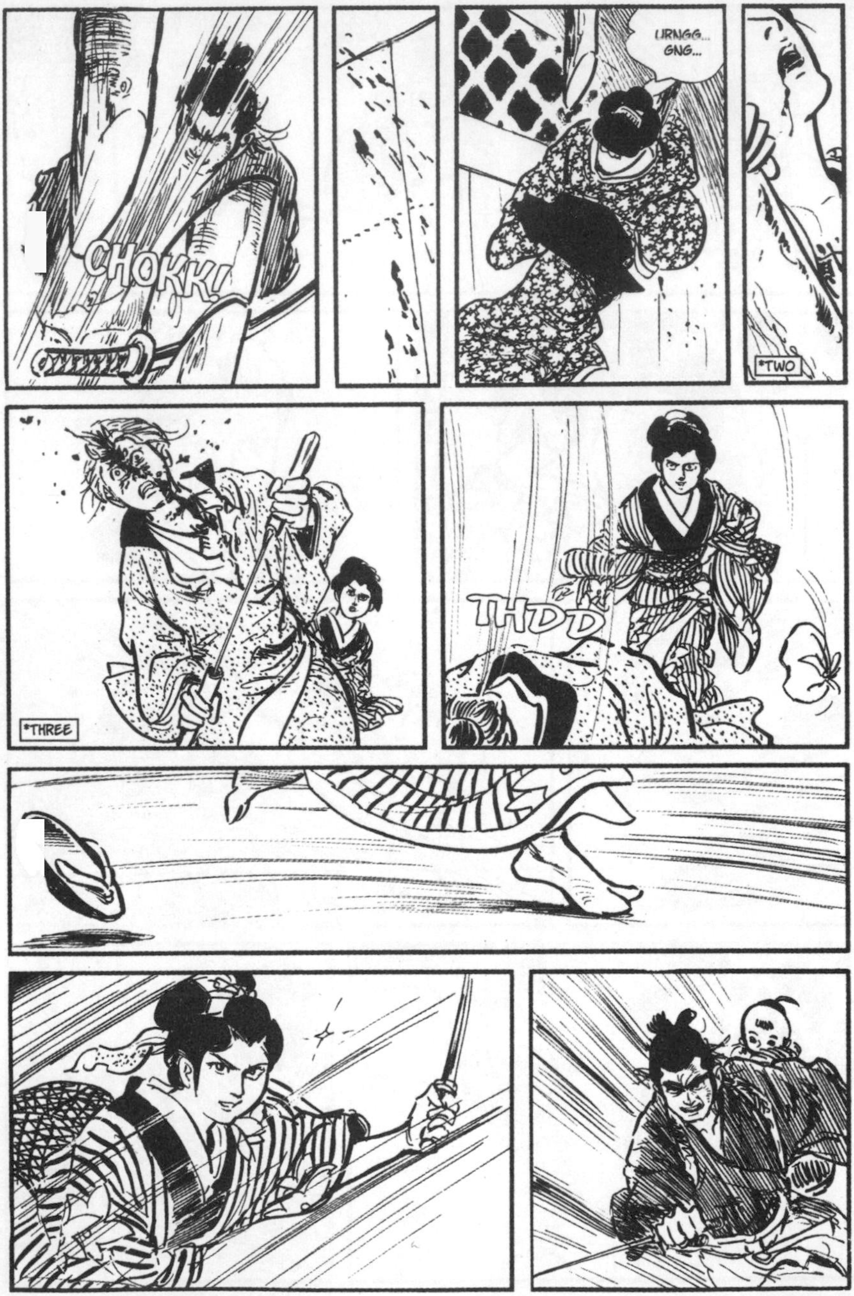
*TWO
URNGG... GNG...
CHOKK!
THDD
*THREE

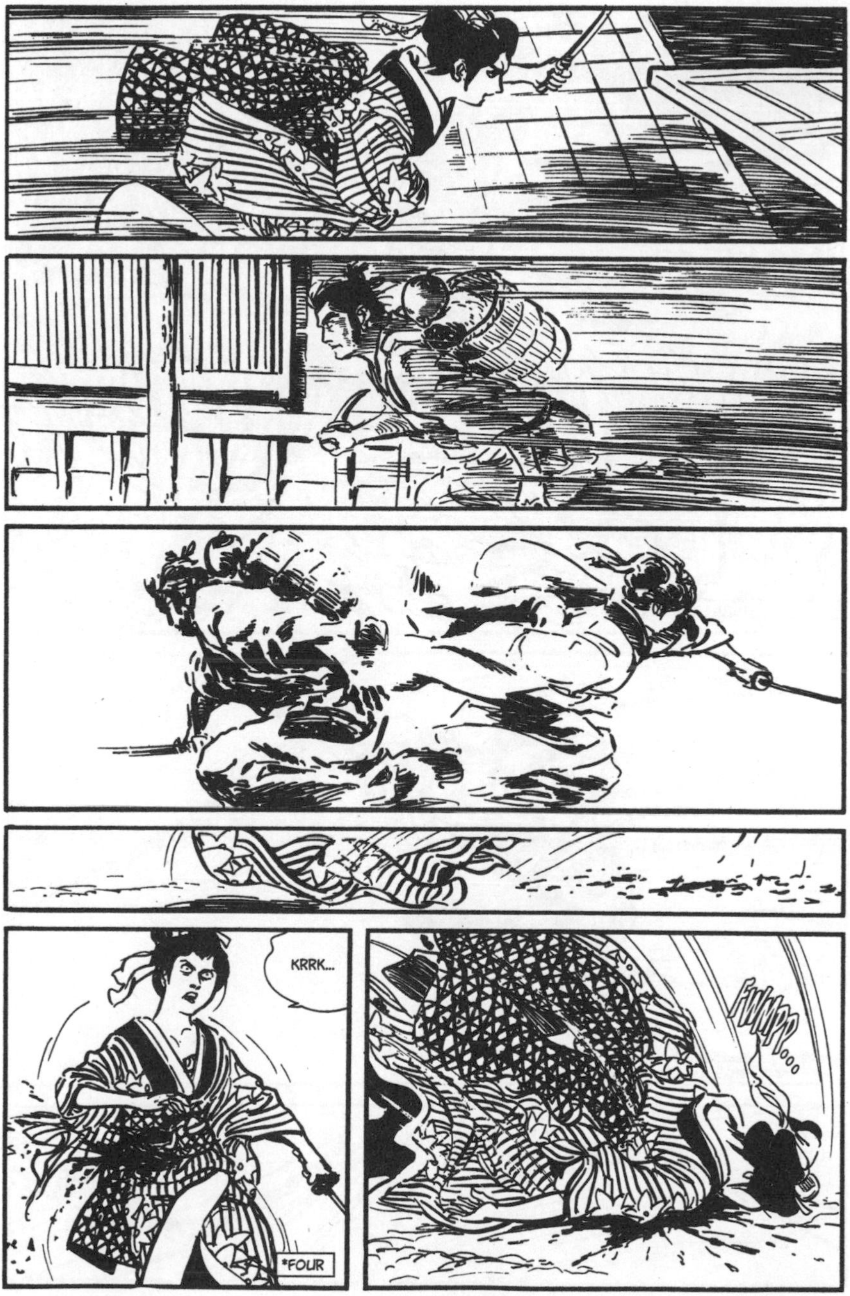
FWUPPoooo
KRRK...
*FOUR

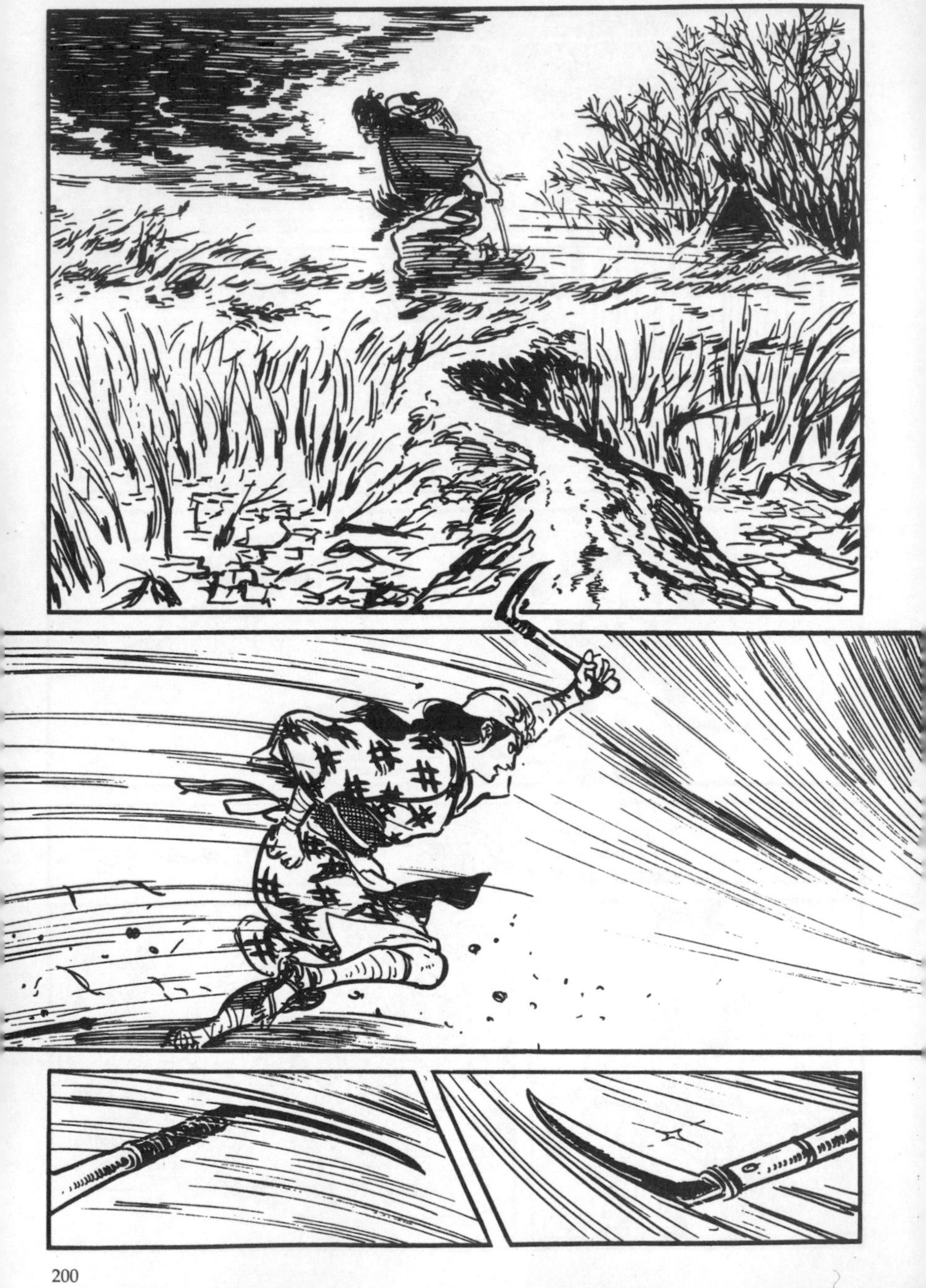

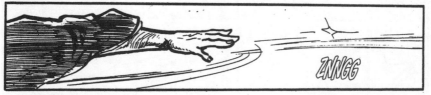

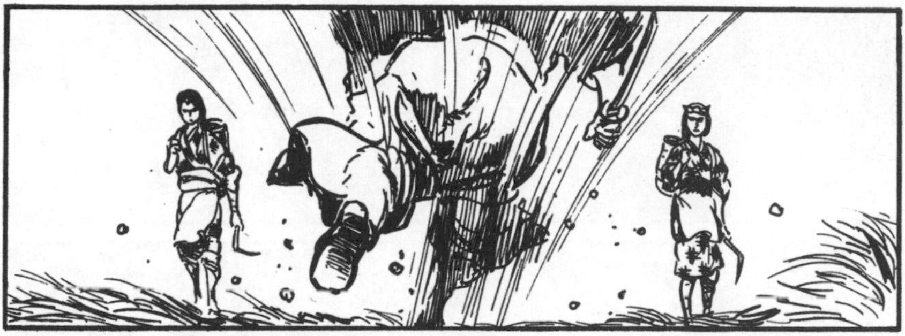
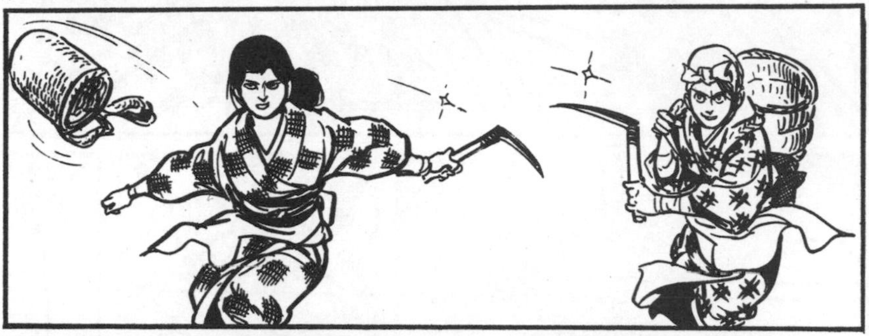
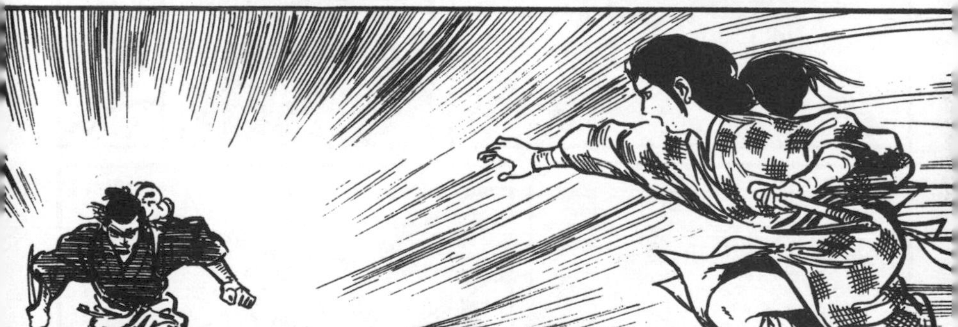
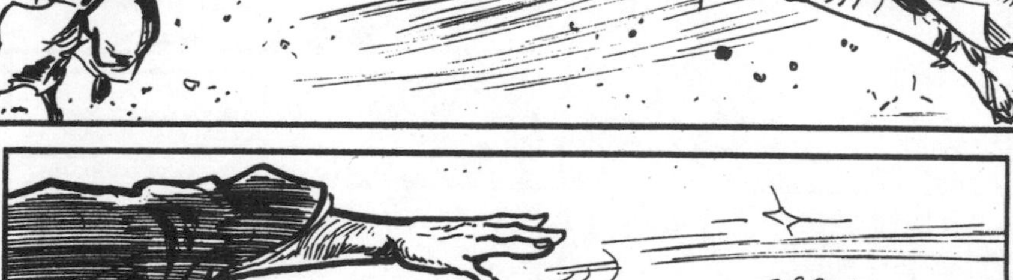
ZNNGG

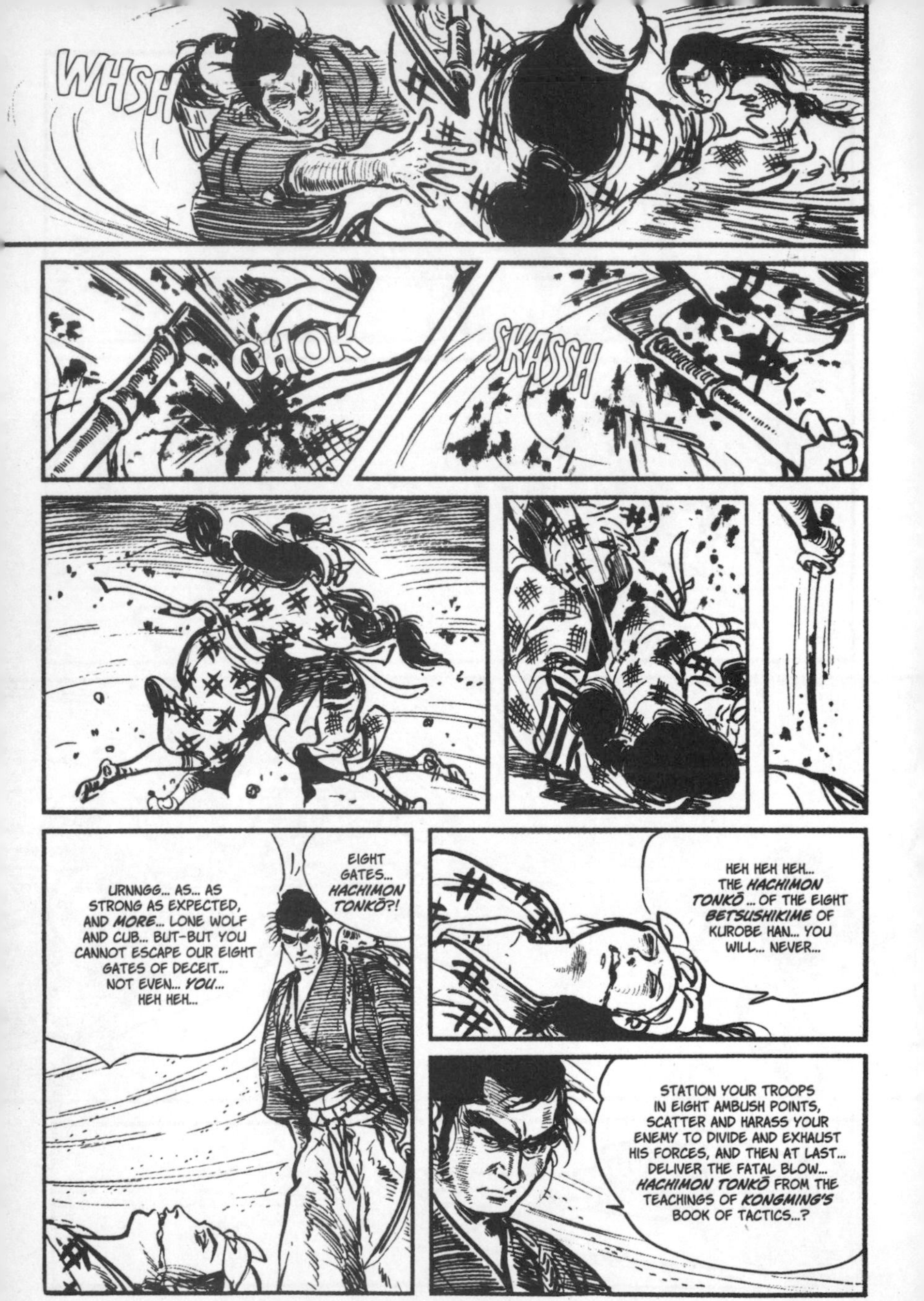
WHSH
CHOK
SKASSH
URNNGG... AS... AS STRONG AS EXPECTED, AND *MORE*... LONE WOLF AND CUB... BUT-BUT YOU CANNOT ESCAPE OUR EIGHT GATES OF DECEIT... NOT EVEN... *YOU*... HEH HEH...
EIGHT GATES... *HACHIMON TONKŌ*?!
HEH HEH HEH... THE *HACHIMON TONKŌ*... OF THE EIGHT *BETSUSHIKIME* OF KUROBE HAN... YOU WILL... NEVER...
STATION YOUR TROOPS IN EIGHT AMBUSH POINTS, SCATTER AND HARASS YOUR ENEMY TO DIVIDE AND EXHAUST HIS FORCES, AND THEN AT LAST... DELIVER THE FATAL BLOW... *HACHIMON TONKŌ* FROM THE TEACHINGS OF *KONGMING'S* BOOK OF TACTICS...?

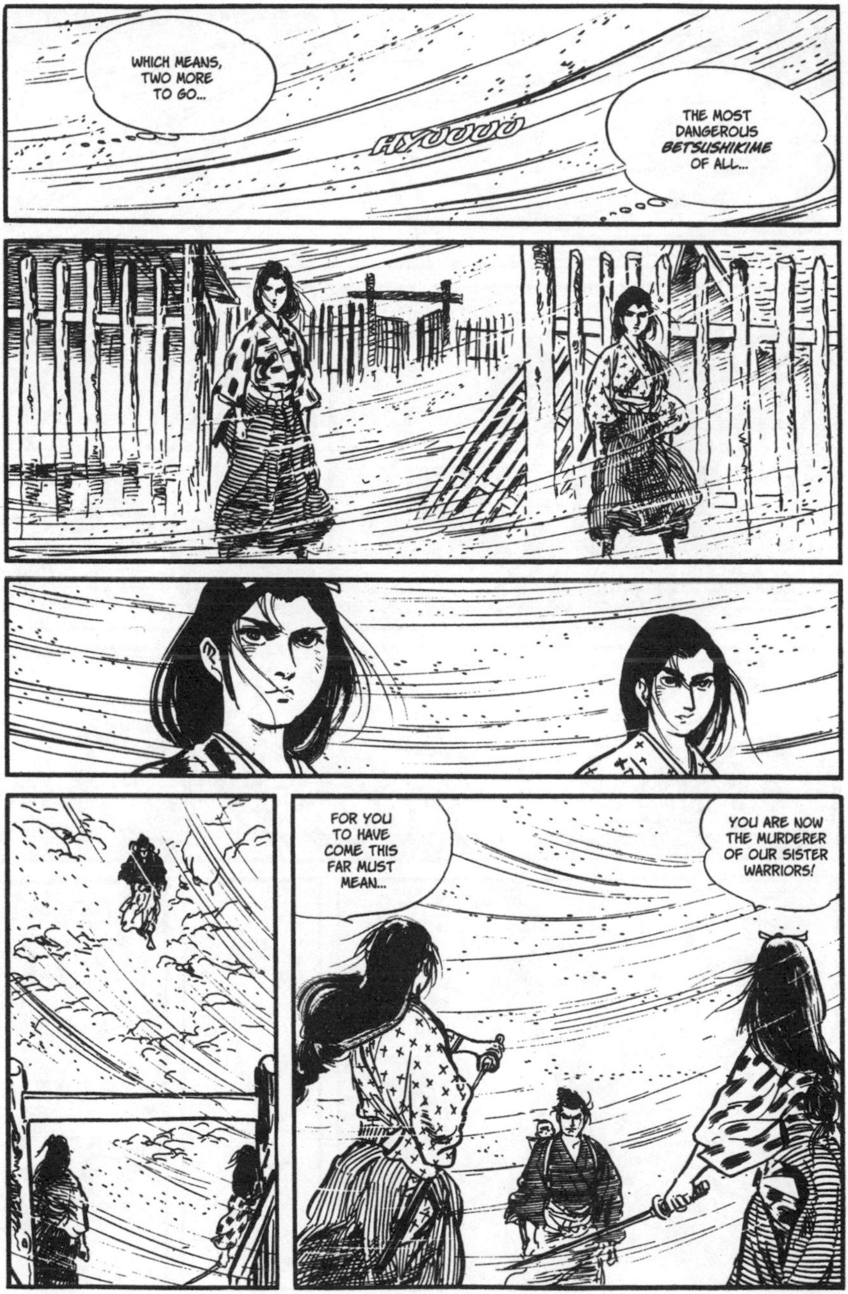
WHICH MEANS, TWO MORE TO GO...
HYUUUU
THE MOST DANGEROUS *BETSUSHIKIME* OF ALL...
FOR YOU TO HAVE COME THIS FAR MUST MEAN...
YOU ARE NOW THE MURDERER OF OUR SISTER WARRIORS!

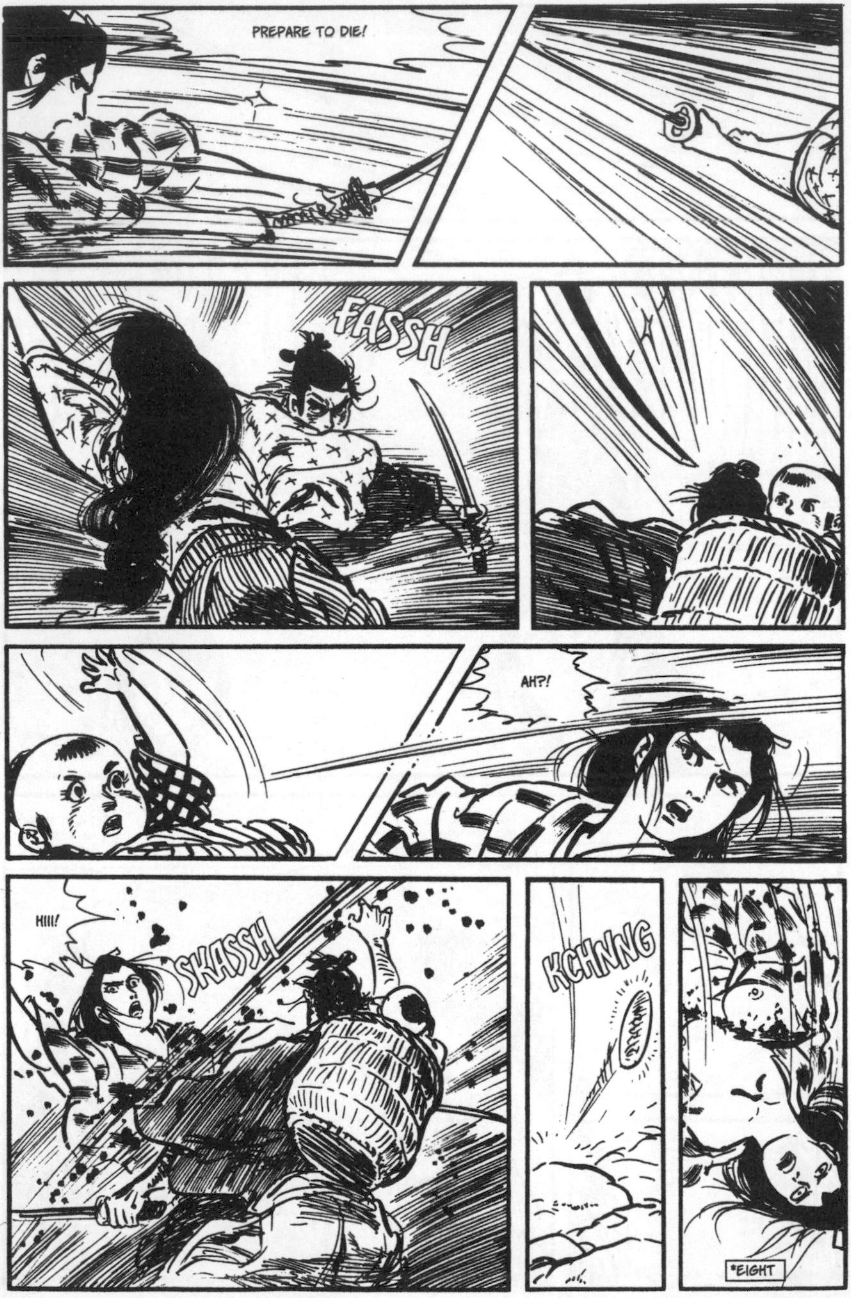
PREPARE TO DIE!
FASSH
AH?!
*EIGHT
KCHNNG
HIII!
SKASSH

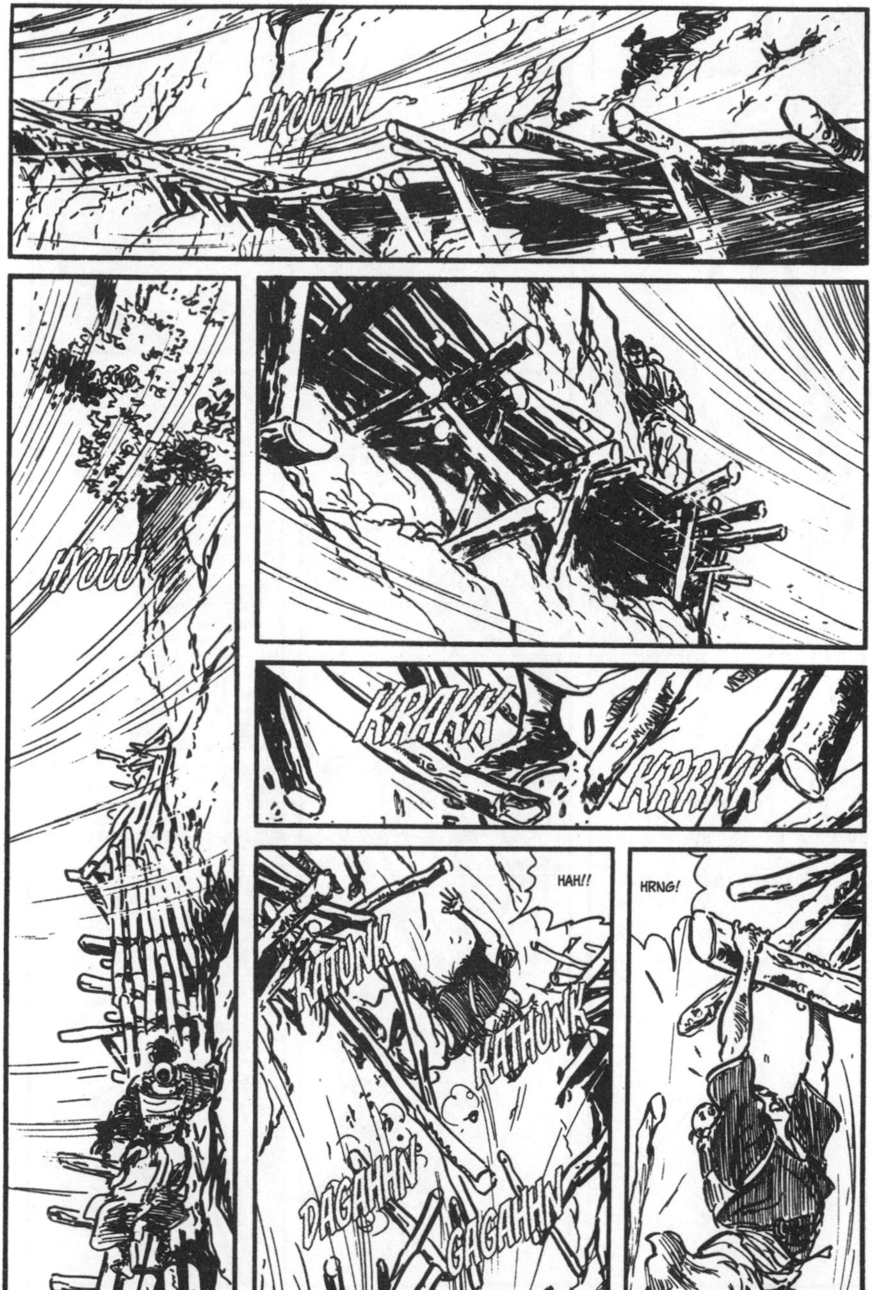
HYUUUN
KRAKK
KRRRKK
HRNG!
HAH!!
KATUNK
KATHUNK
DAGAHHN
GAGAHHN
HYUUU

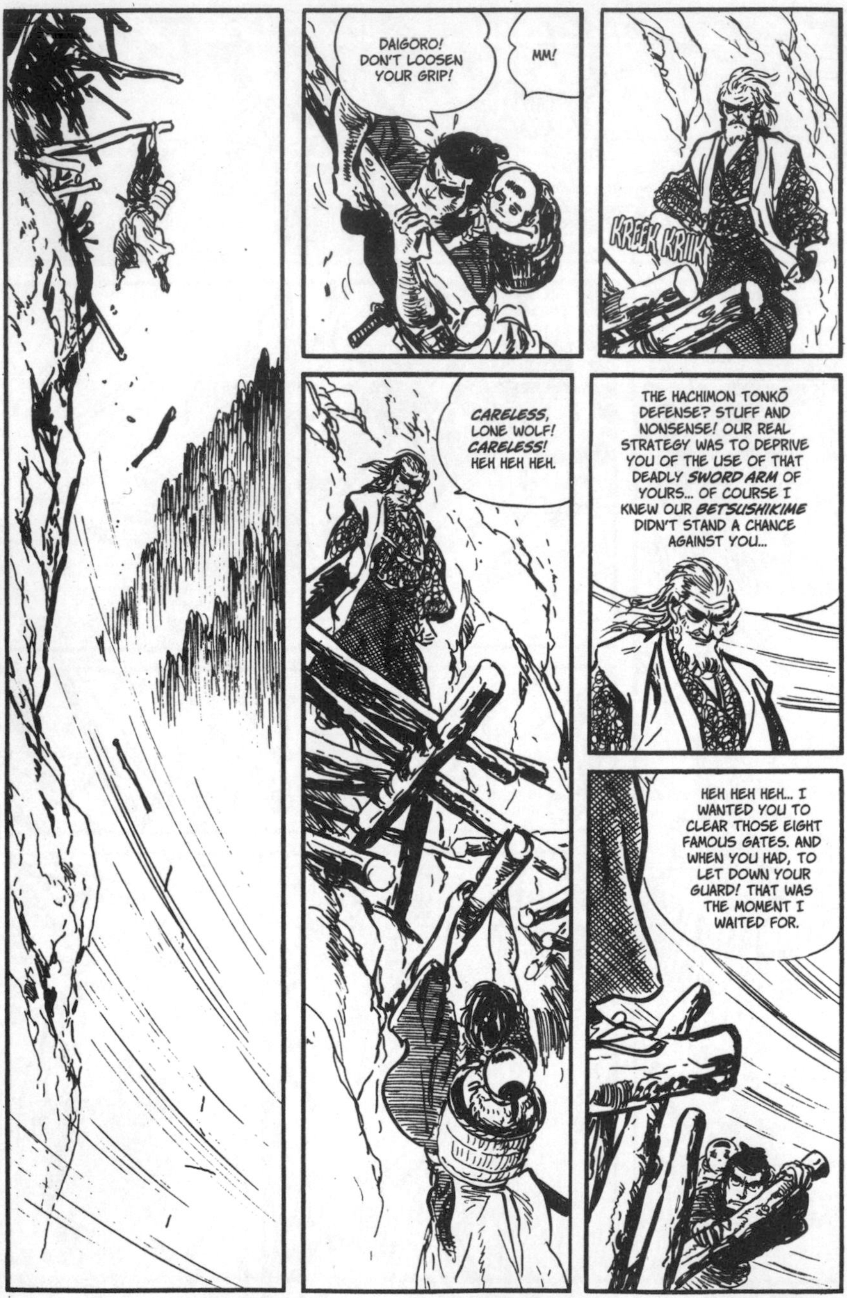
DAIGORO! DON'T LOOSEN YOUR GRIP!
MM!
KREEK KRIK
CARELESS, LONE WOLF! *CARELESS*! HEH HEH HEH.
THE HACHIMON TONKŌ DEFENSE? STUFF AND NONSENSE! OUR REAL STRATEGY WAS TO DEPRIVE YOU OF THE USE OF THAT DEADLY *SWORD ARM* OF YOURS... OF COURSE I KNEW OUR *BETSUSHIKIME* DIDN'T STAND A CHANCE AGAINST YOU...
HEH HEH HEH... I WANTED YOU TO CLEAR THOSE EIGHT FAMOUS GATES. AND WHEN YOU HAD, TO LET DOWN YOUR GUARD! THAT WAS THE MOMENT I WAITED FOR.

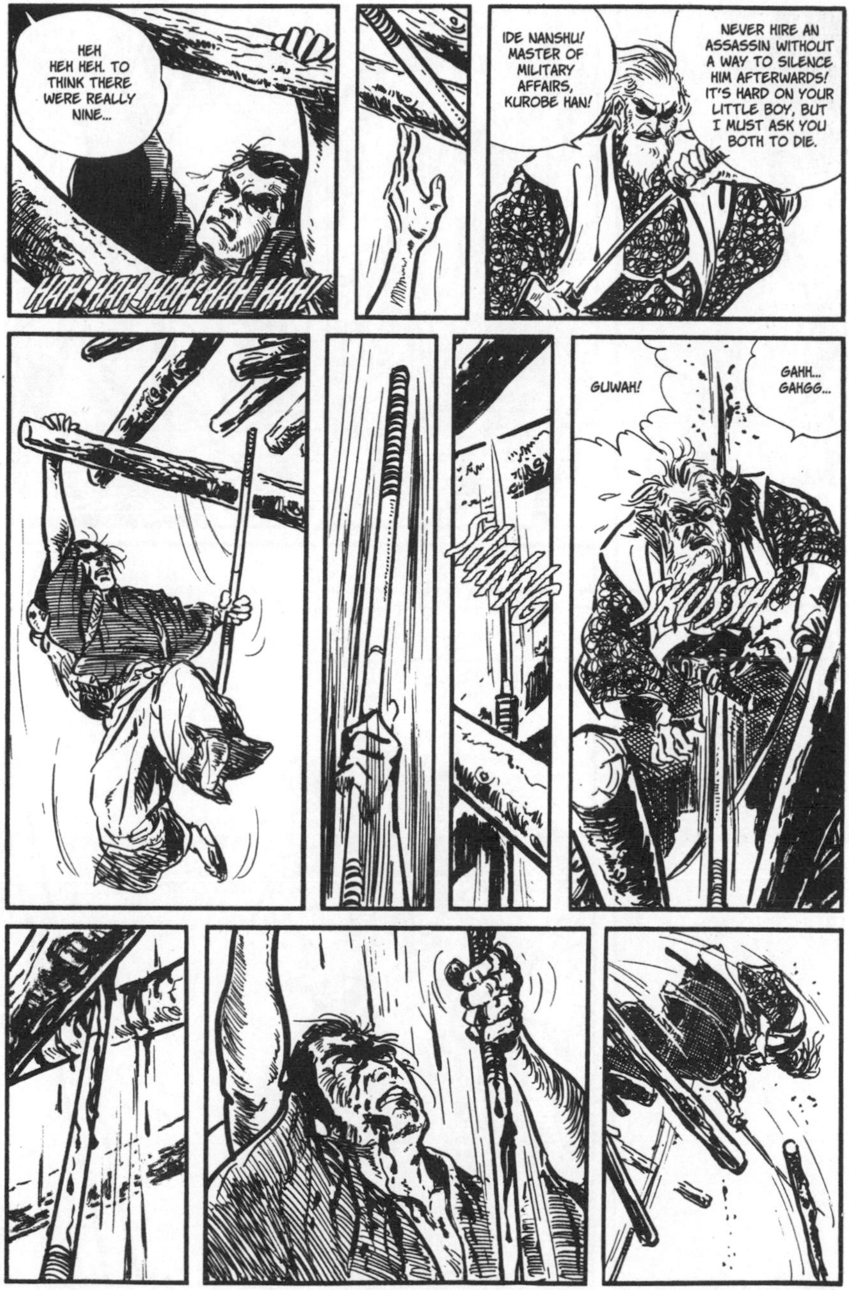
HEH HEH HEH. TO THINK THERE WERE REALLY NINE...
HAH HAH HAH HAH HAH!
IDE NANSHU! MASTER OF MILITARY AFFAIRS, KUROBE HAN!
NEVER HIRE AN ASSASSIN WITHOUT A WAY TO SILENCE HIM AFTERWARDS! IT'S HARD ON YOUR LITTLE BOY, BUT I MUST ASK YOU BOTH TO DIE.
SHING
GUWAH!
GAHH... GAHGG...
SKUSH

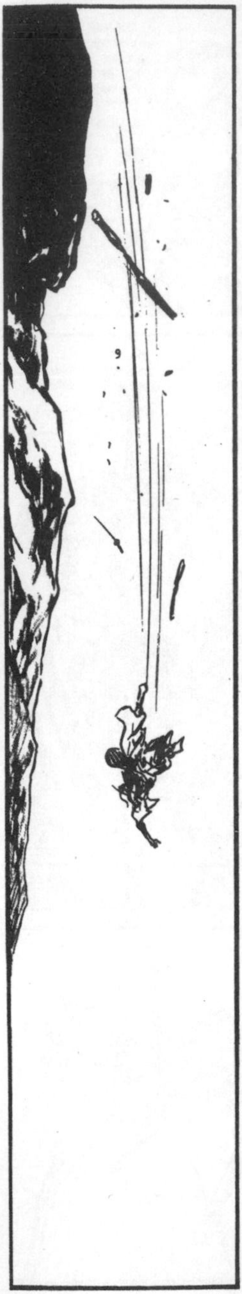

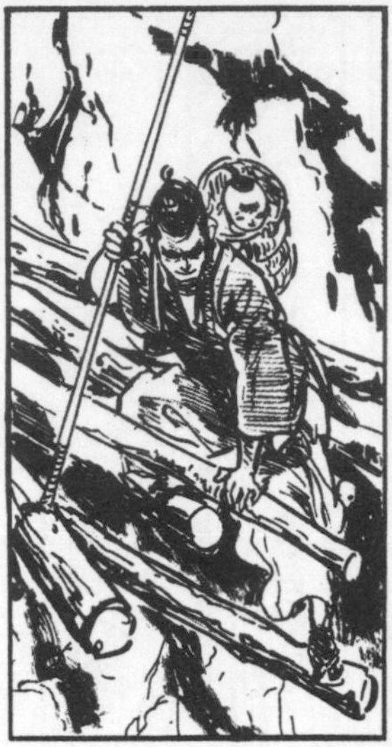

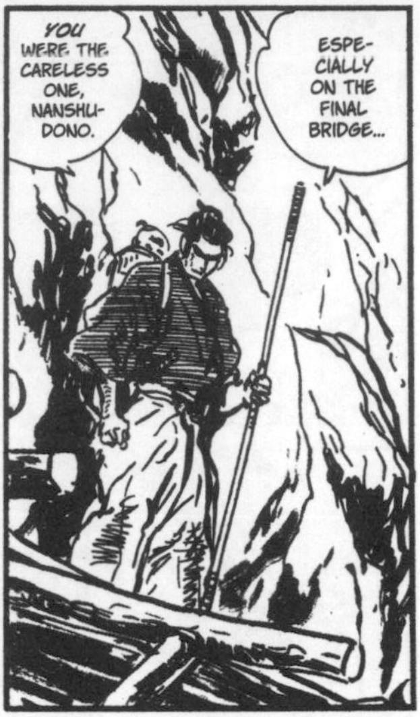
YOU WERE THE CARELESS ONE, NANSHU-DONO.
ESPE-CIALLY ON THE FINAL BRIDGE...

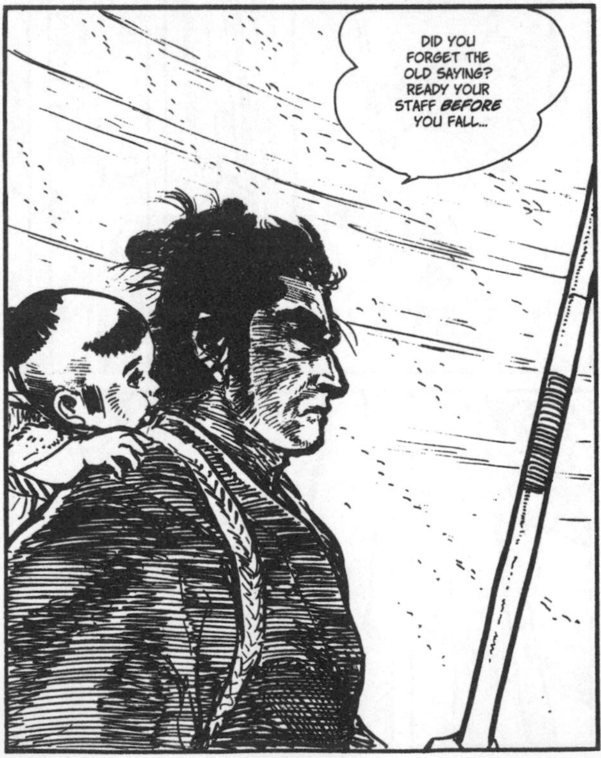
DID YOU FORGET THE OLD SAYING? READY YOUR STAFF BEFORE YOU FALL...

WINGS TO THE BIRDS,
FANGS TO THE BEAST

8

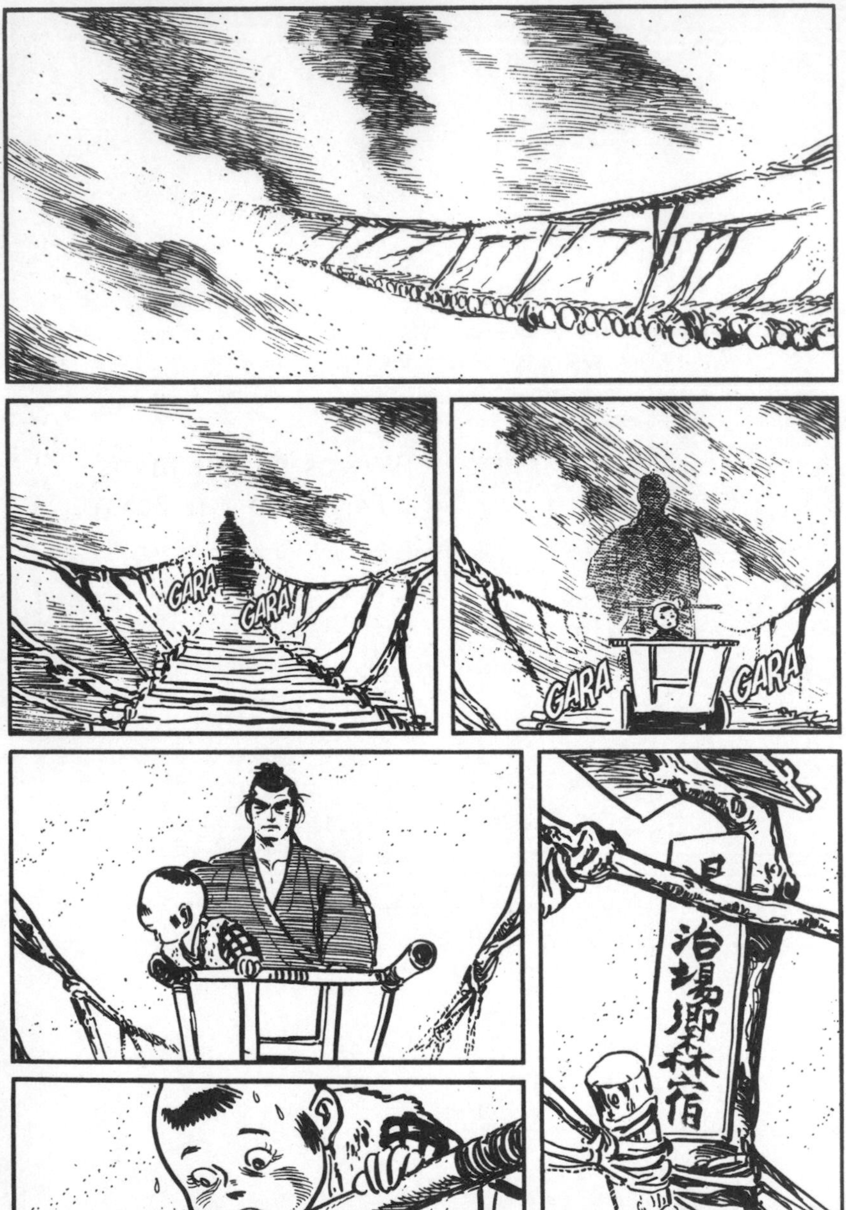
GARA
GARA
GARA
GARA
治場郷森宿
*GŌMORI-JUKU HOT SPRINGS SPA

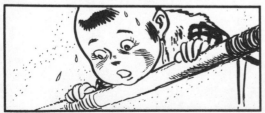

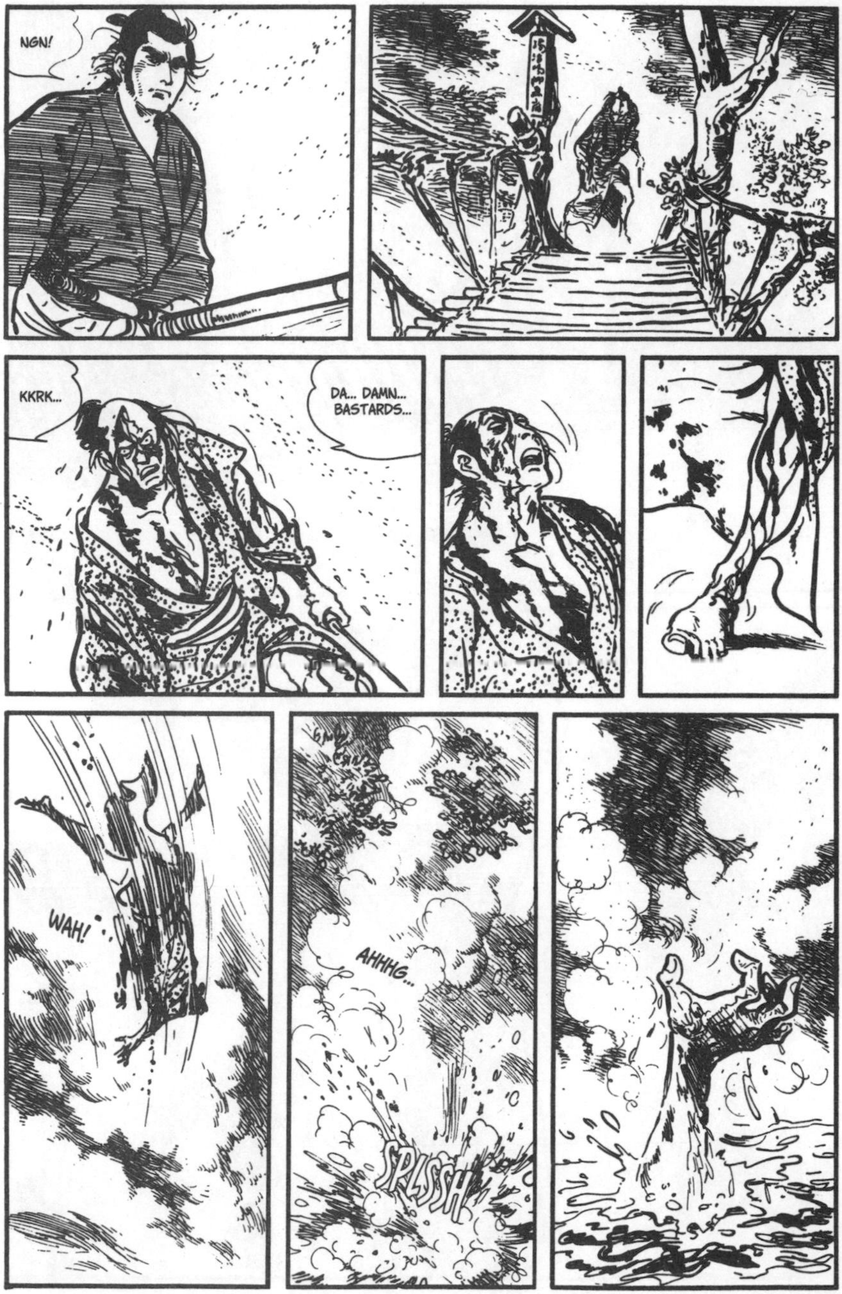
NGN!
DA... DAMN... BASTARDS...
KKRK...
AHHHG...
SPLSSH
WAH!

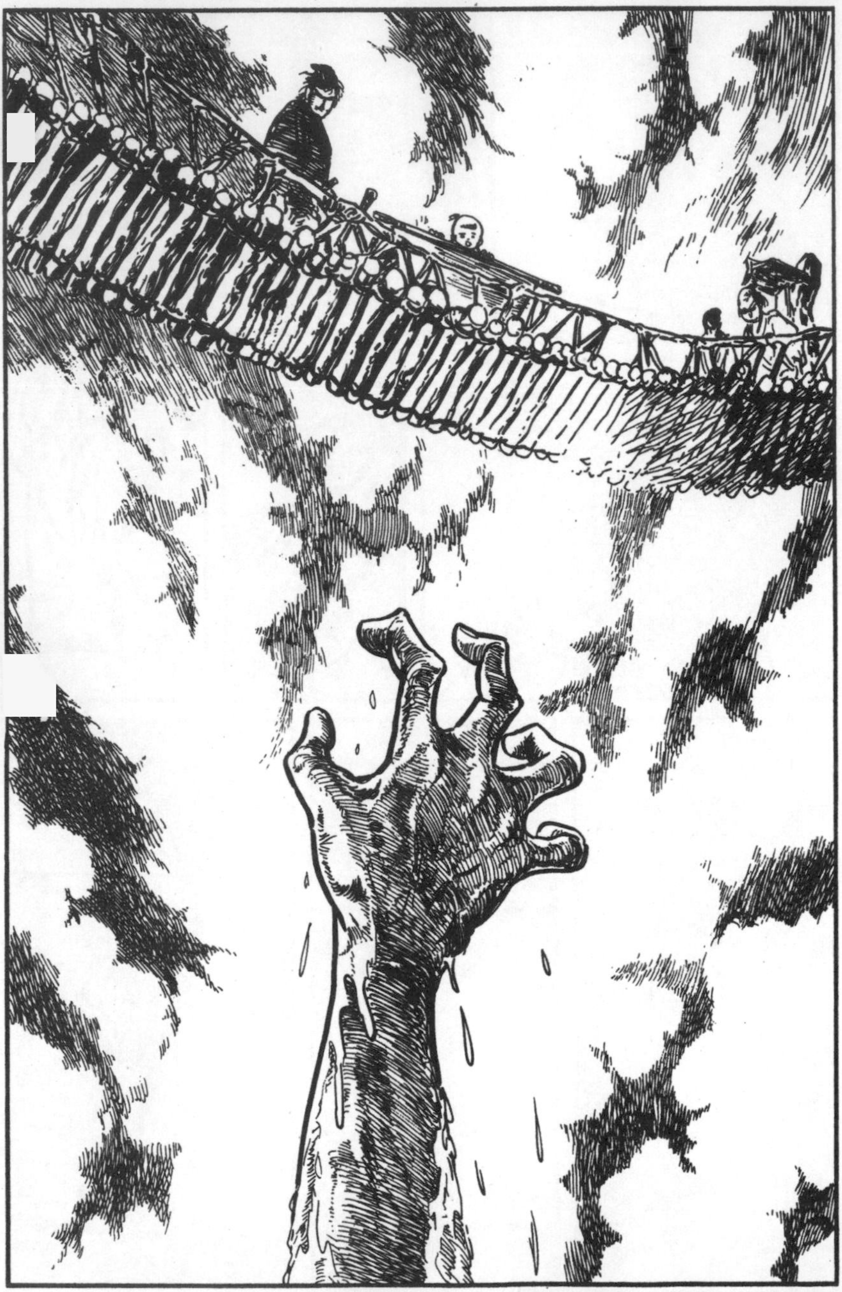

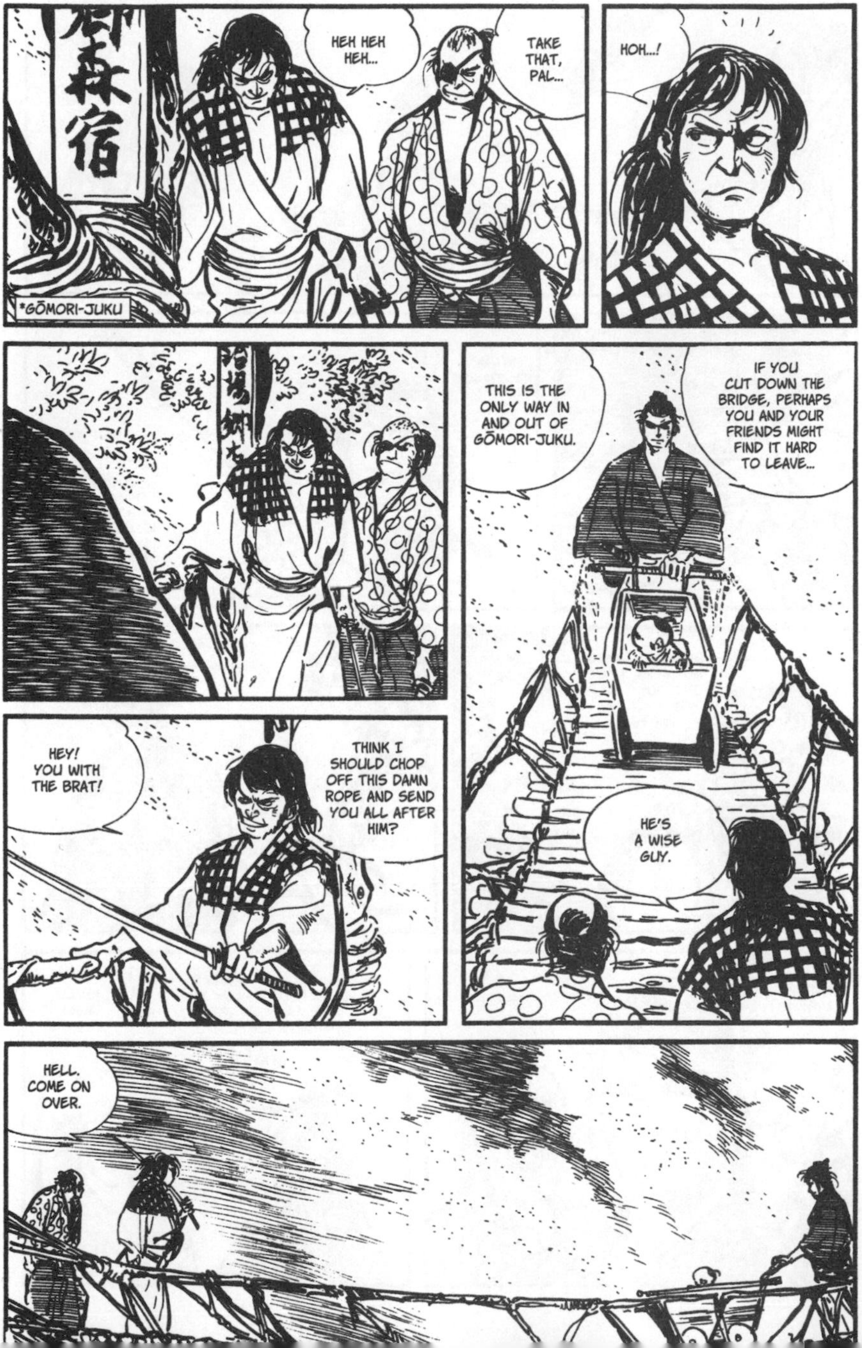
*GŌMORI-JUKU
HEH HEH HEH...
TAKE THAT, PAL...
HOH...!
HEY! YOU WITH THE BRAT!
THINK I SHOULD CHOP OFF THIS DAMN ROPE AND SEND YOU ALL AFTER HIM?
THIS IS THE ONLY WAY IN AND OUT OF GŌMORI-JUKU.
IF YOU CUT DOWN THE BRIDGE, PERHAPS YOU AND YOUR FRIENDS MIGHT FIND IT HARD TO LEAVE...
HE'S A WISE GUY.
HELL. COME ON OVER.

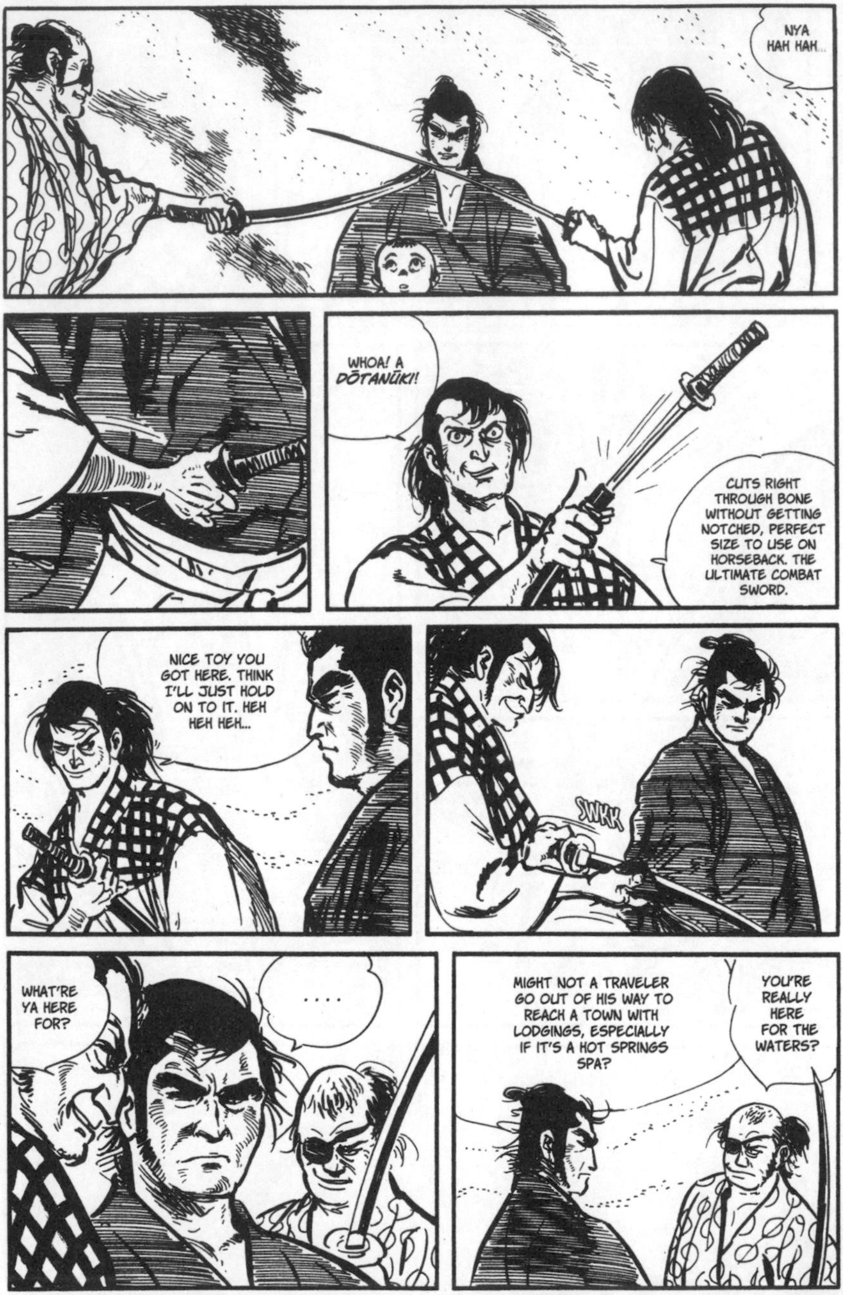
NYA HAH HAH...
WHOA! A DŌTANŪKI!
CUTS RIGHT THROUGH BONE WITHOUT GETTING NOTCHED, PERFECT SIZE TO USE ON HORSEBACK. THE ULTIMATE COMBAT SWORD.
NICE TOY YOU GOT HERE. THINK I'LL JUST HOLD ON TO IT. HEH HEH HEH...
SWKK
WHAT'RE YA HERE FOR?
....
MIGHT NOT A TRAVELER GO OUT OF HIS WAY TO REACH A TOWN WITH LODGINGS, ESPECIALLY IF IT'S A HOT SPRINGS SPA?
YOU'RE REALLY HERE FOR THE WATERS?

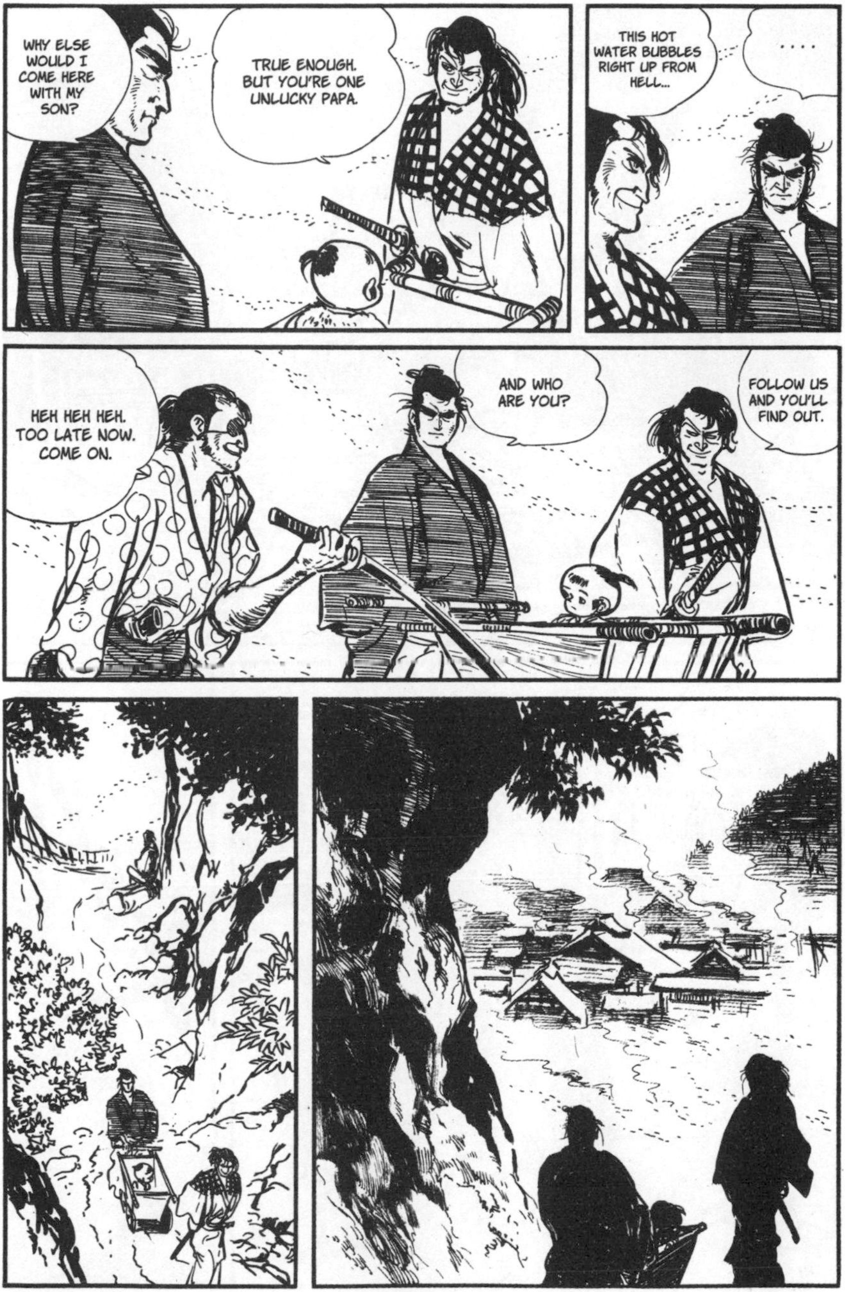
WHY ELSE WOULD I COME HERE WITH MY SON?
TRUE ENOUGH. BUT YOU'RE ONE UNLUCKY PAPA.
THIS HOT WATER BUBBLES RIGHT UP FROM HELL...
. . . .
HEH HEH HEH. TOO LATE NOW. COME ON.
AND WHO ARE YOU?
FOLLOW US AND YOU'LL FIND OUT.

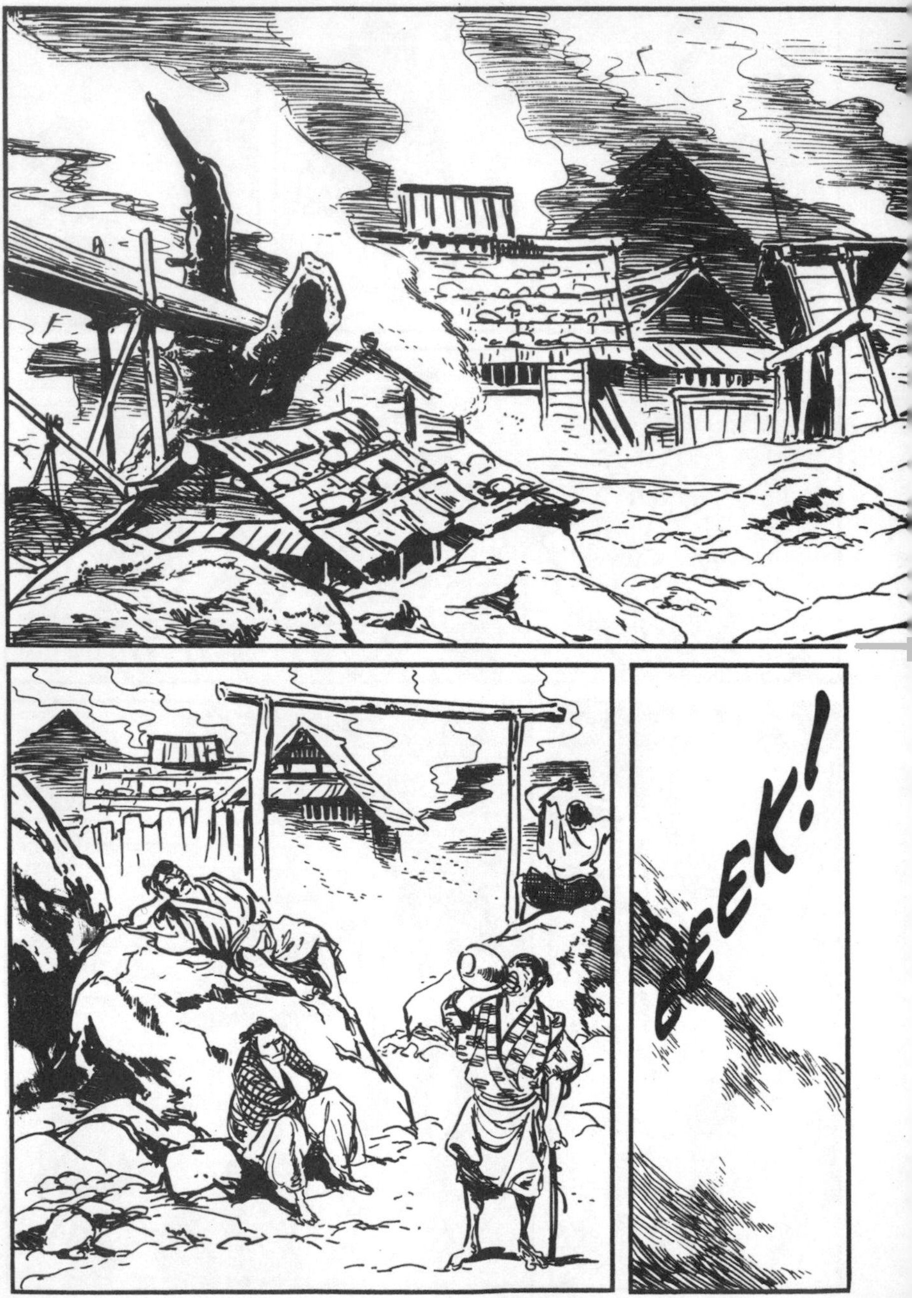
EEEK!

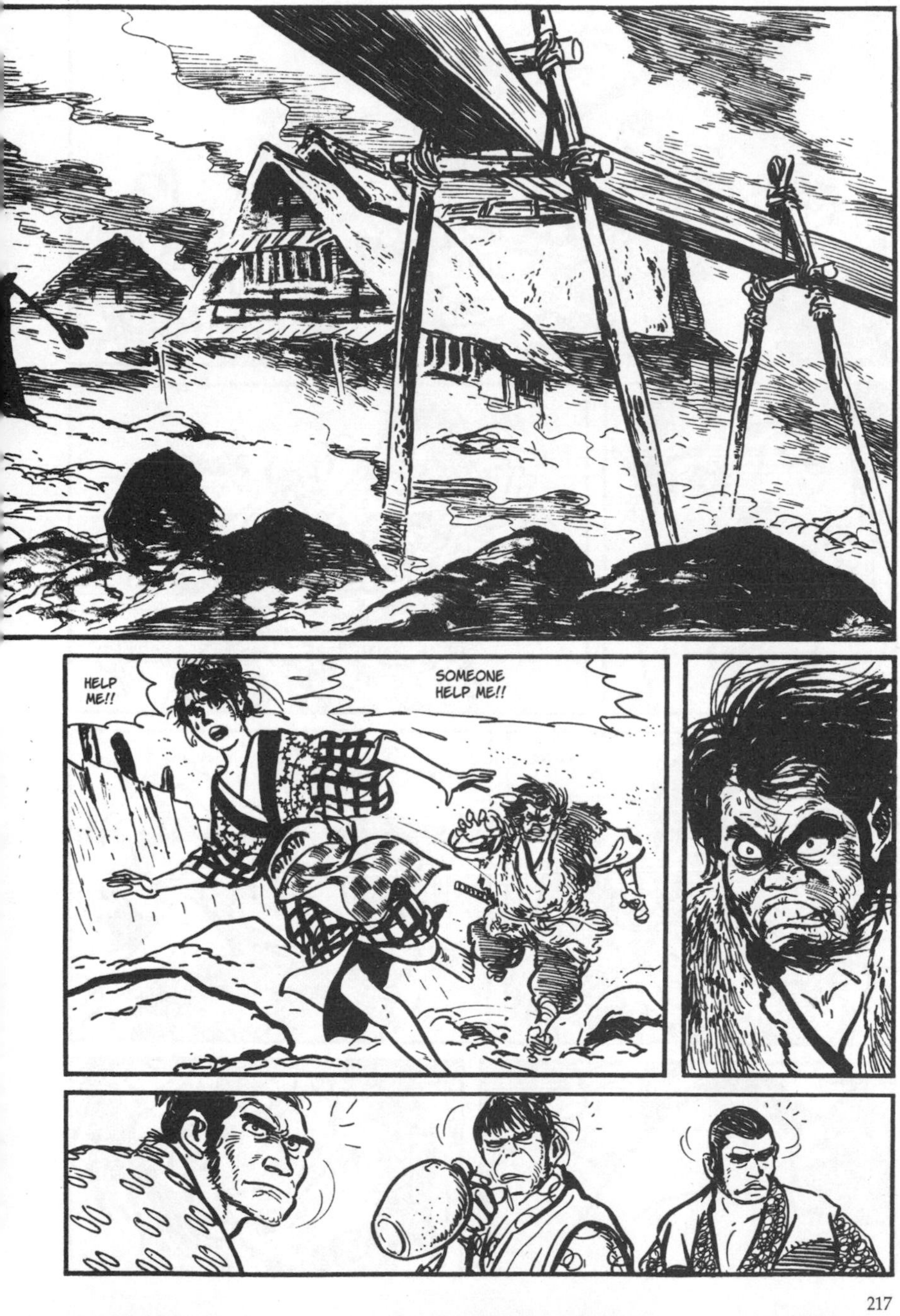
SOMEONE HELP ME!!
HELP ME!!

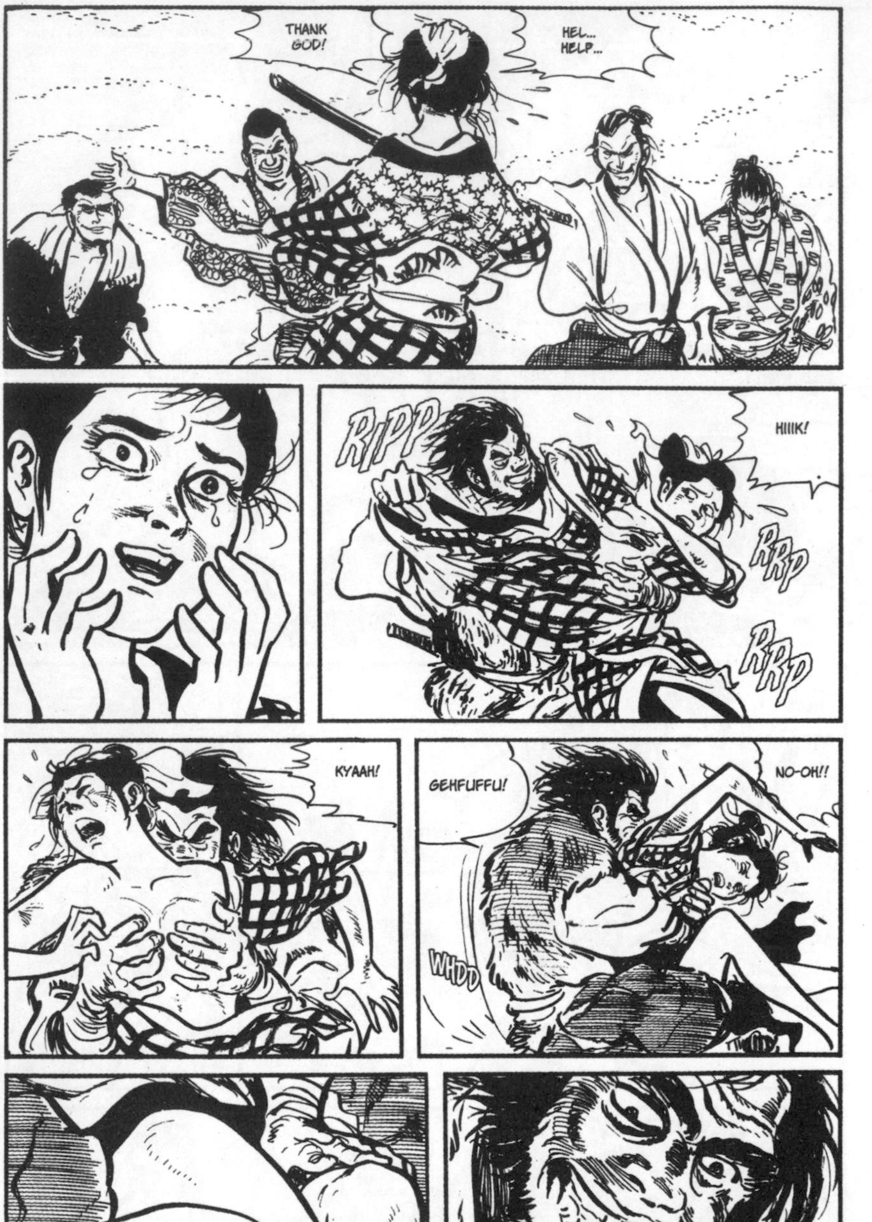
HEL... HELP...
THANK GOD!
HIIIK!
RIPP
RRP
RRP
NO-OH!!
GEHFUFFU!
WHDD
KYAAH!

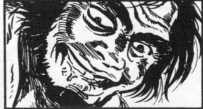

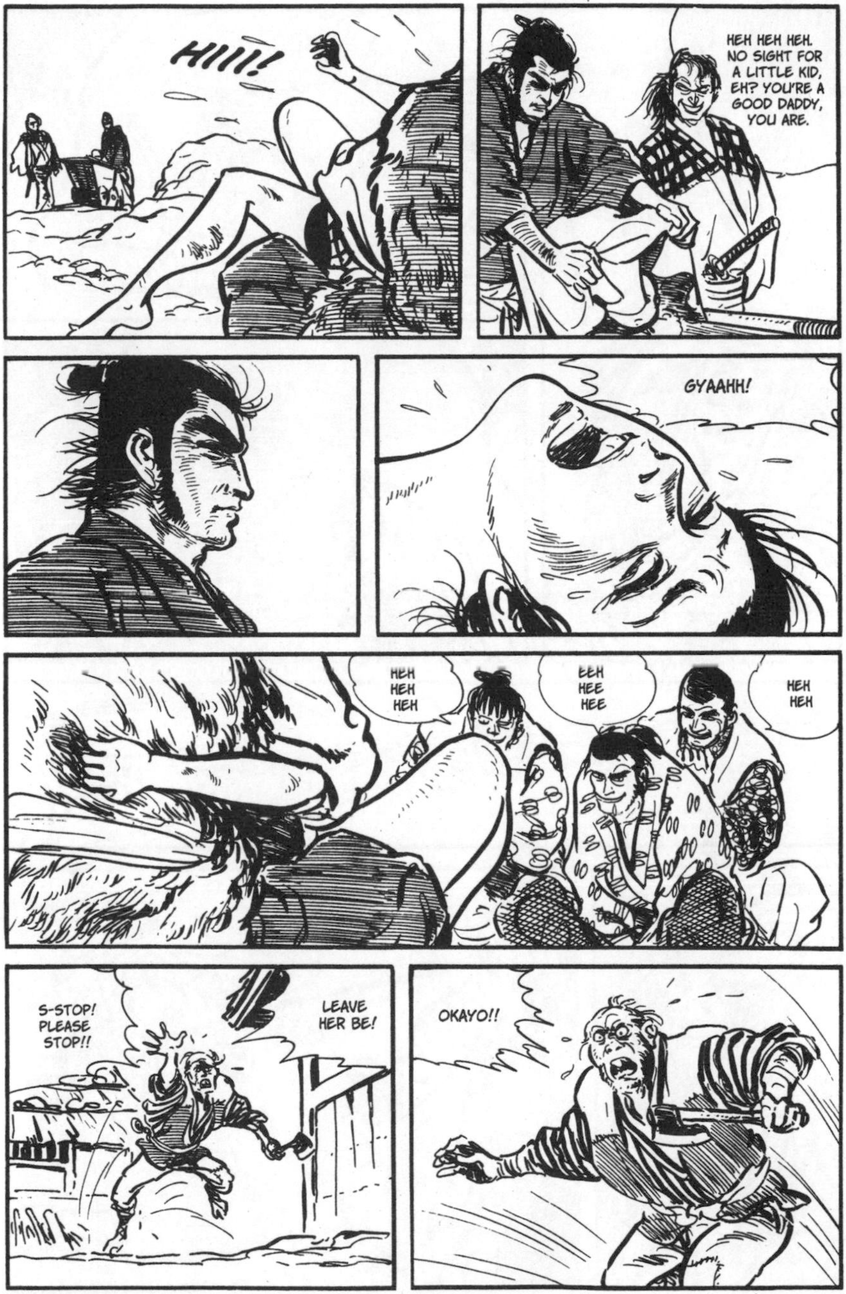
HIIII!
HEH HEH HEH. NO SIGHT FOR A LITTLE KID, EH? YOU'RE A GOOD DADDY, YOU ARE.
GYAAHH!
HEH HEH HEH
EEH HEE HEE
HEH HEH
S-STOP! PLEASE STOP!!
LEAVE HER BE!
OKAYO!!

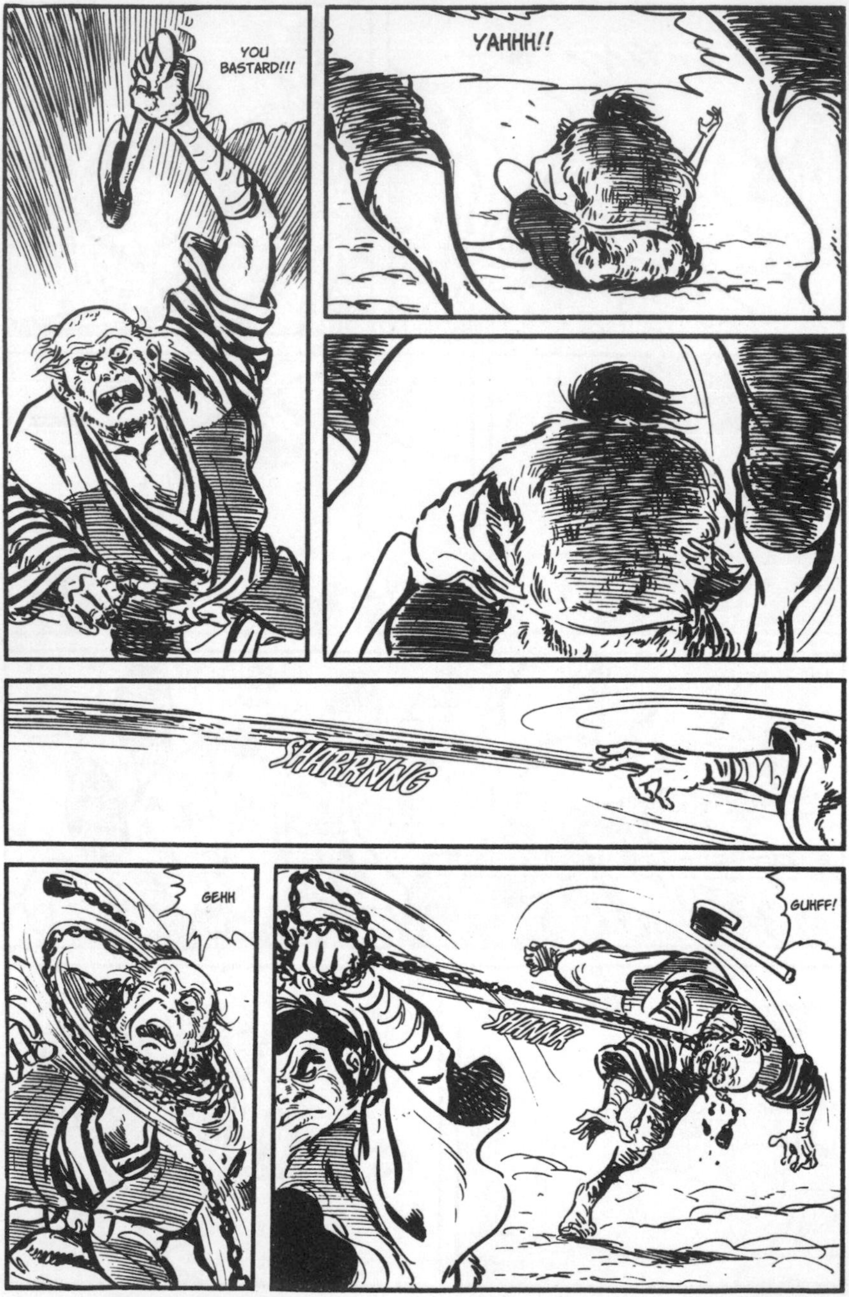
YAHHH!!
YOU BASTARD!!!
SHARRNNG
GUHFF!
SHANK
GEHH

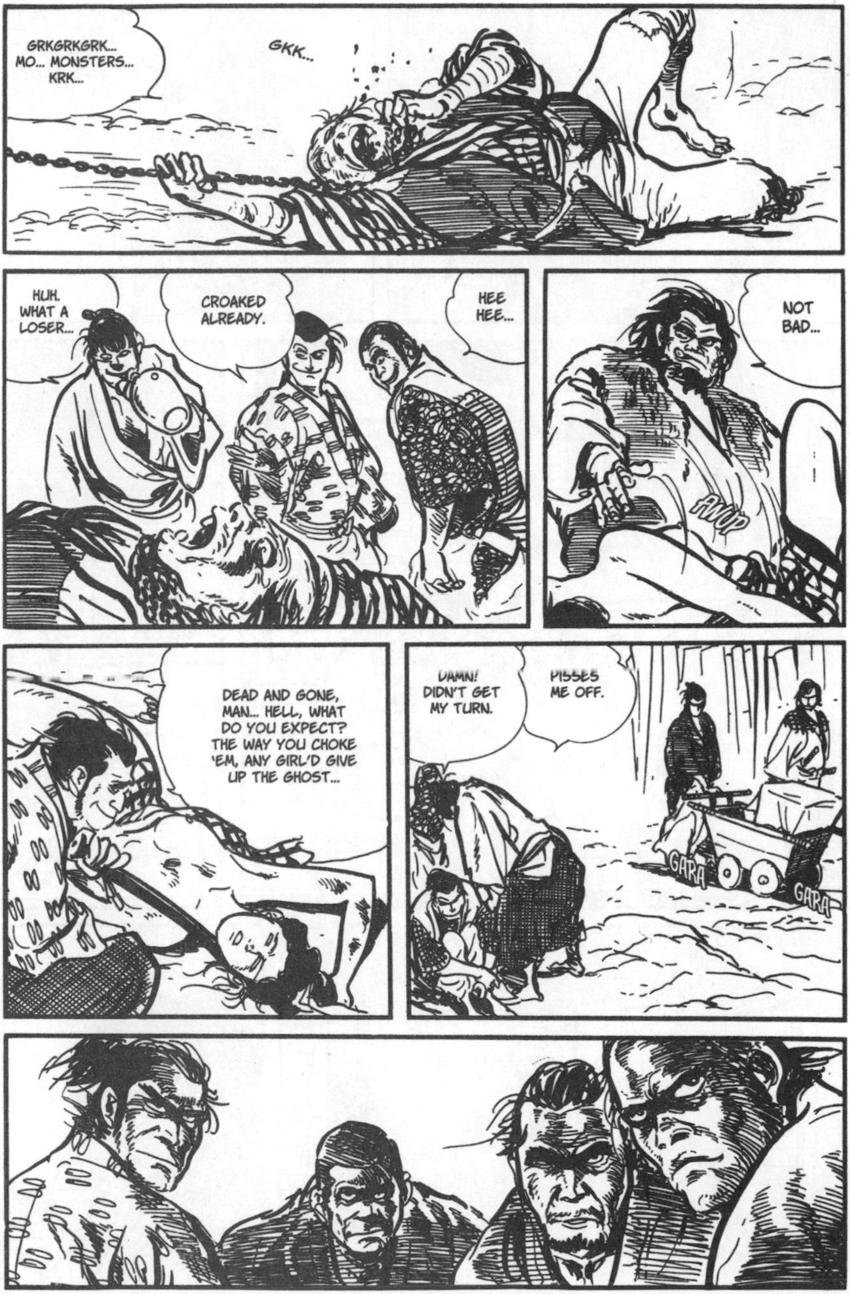
GKK...
GRKGRKGRK... MO... MONSTERS... KRK...
NOT BAD...
HEE HEE...
CROAKED ALREADY.
HUH. WHAT A LOSER...
PISSES ME OFF.
DAMN! DIDN'T GET MY TURN.
GARA
GARA
DEAD AND GONE, MAN... HELL, WHAT DO YOU EXPECT? THE WAY YOU CHOKE 'EM, ANY GIRL'D GIVE UP THE GHOST...

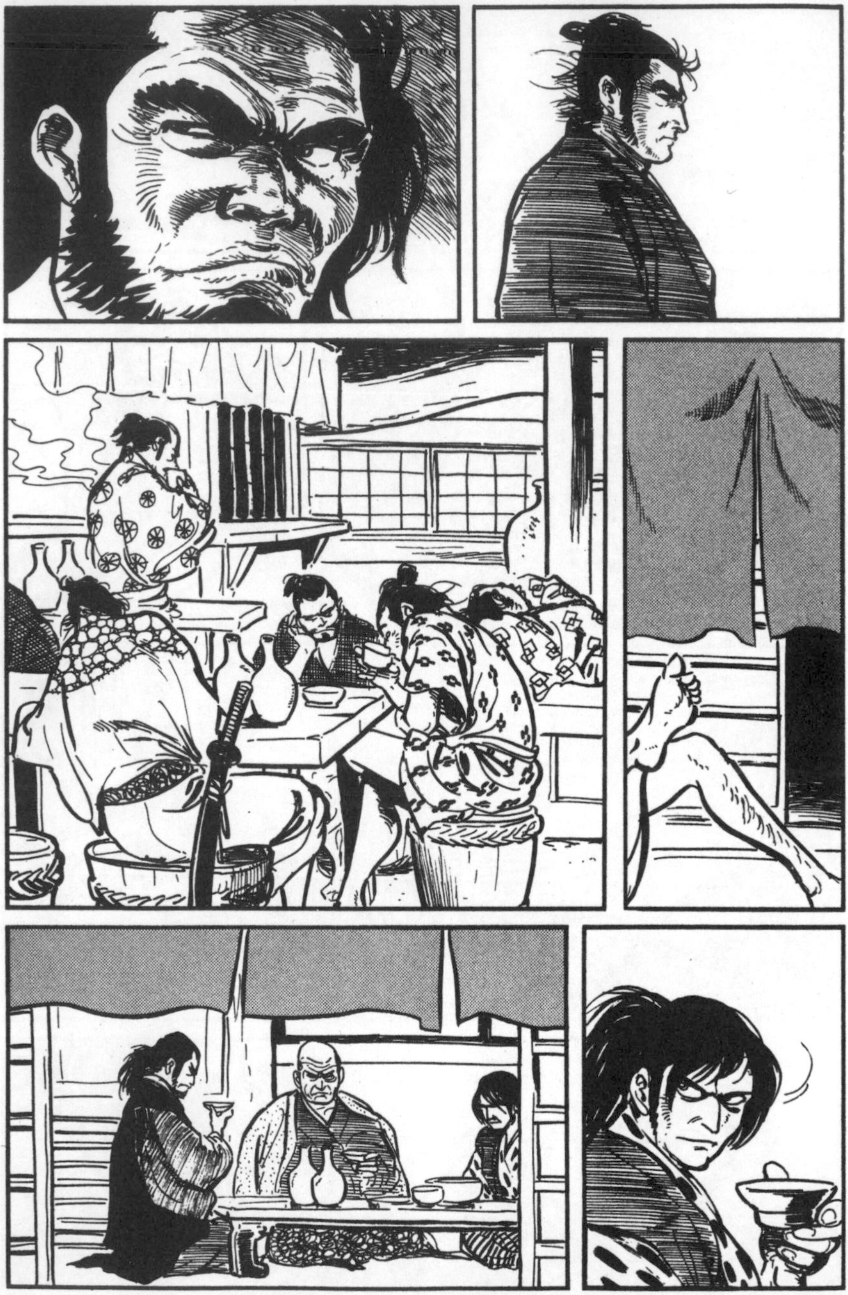

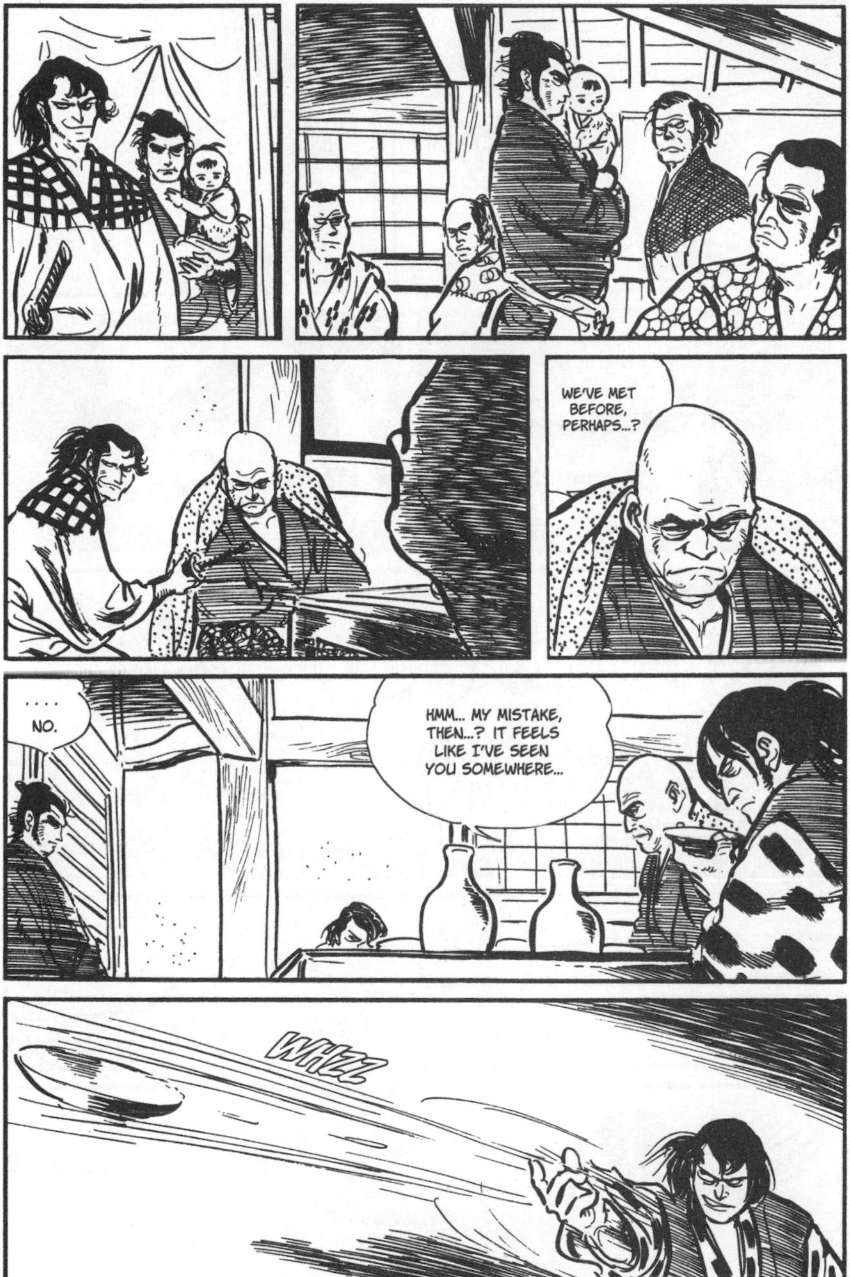
WE'VE MET BEFORE, PERHAPS...?
.... NO.
HMM... MY MISTAKE, THEN...? IT FEELS LIKE I'VE SEEN YOU SOMEWHERE...
WHIZZ

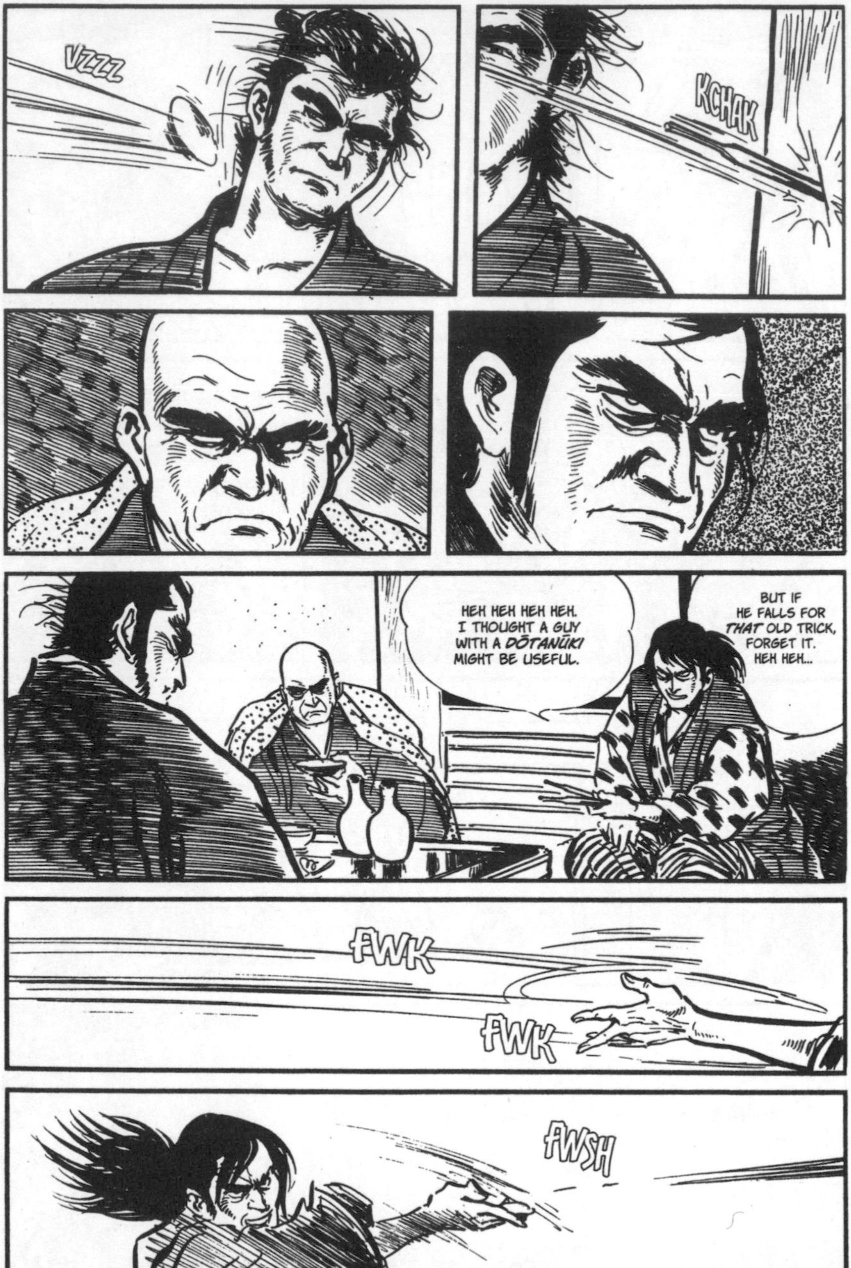
VZZZ
KCHAK
HEH HEH HEH HEH. I THOUGHT A GUY WITH A *DŌTANŪKI* MIGHT BE USEFUL.
BUT IF HE FALLS FOR *THAT* OLD TRICK, FORGET IT. HEH HEH...
FWK
FWK
FWSH

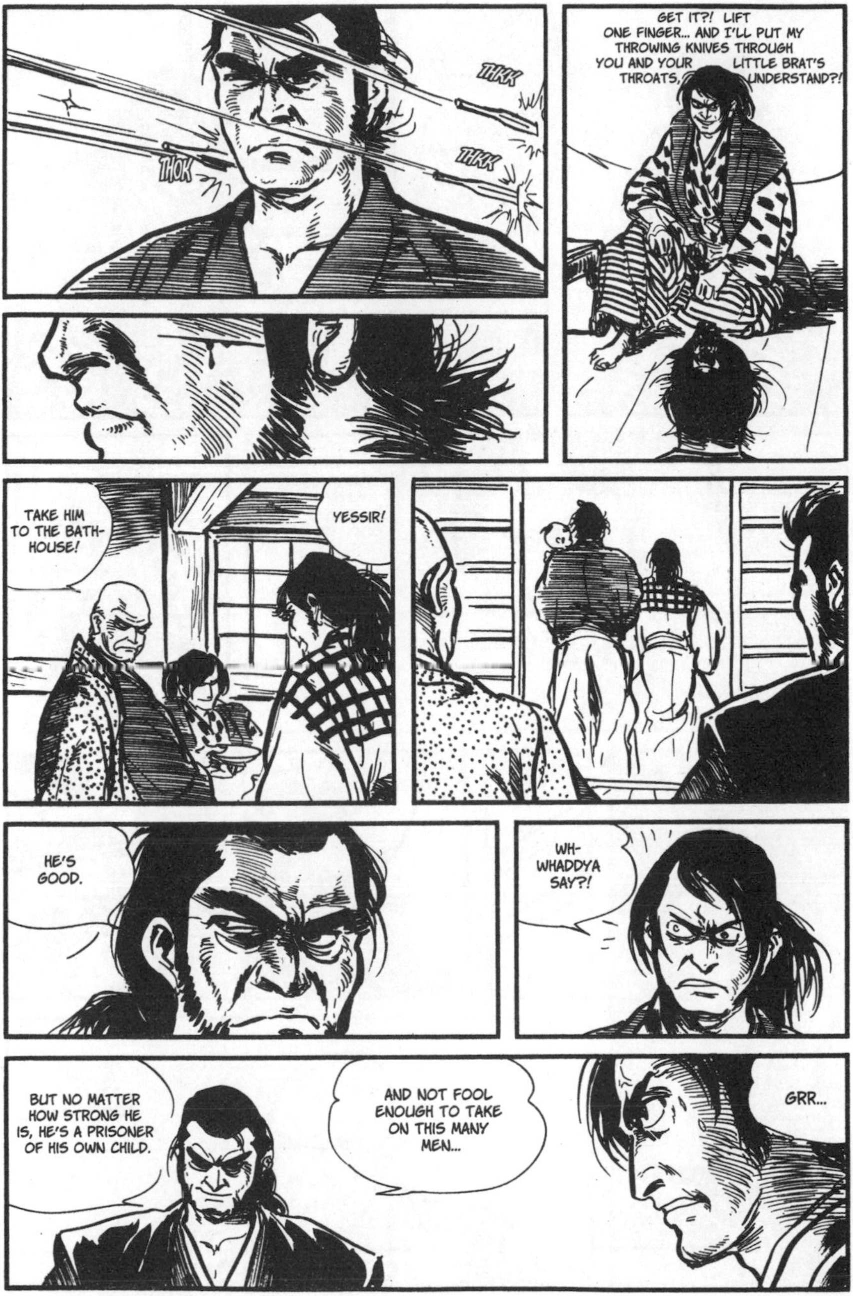
THKK
THOK
THKK
GET IT?! LIFT ONE FINGER... AND I'LL PUT MY THROWING KNIVES THROUGH YOU AND YOUR LITTLE BRAT'S THROATS, UNDERSTAND?!
TAKE HIM TO THE BATH-HOUSE!
YESSIR!
HE'S GOOD.
WH-WHADDYA SAY?!
BUT NO MATTER HOW STRONG HE IS, HE'S A PRISONER OF HIS OWN CHILD.
AND NOT FOOL ENOUGH TO TAKE ON THIS MANY MEN...
GRR...

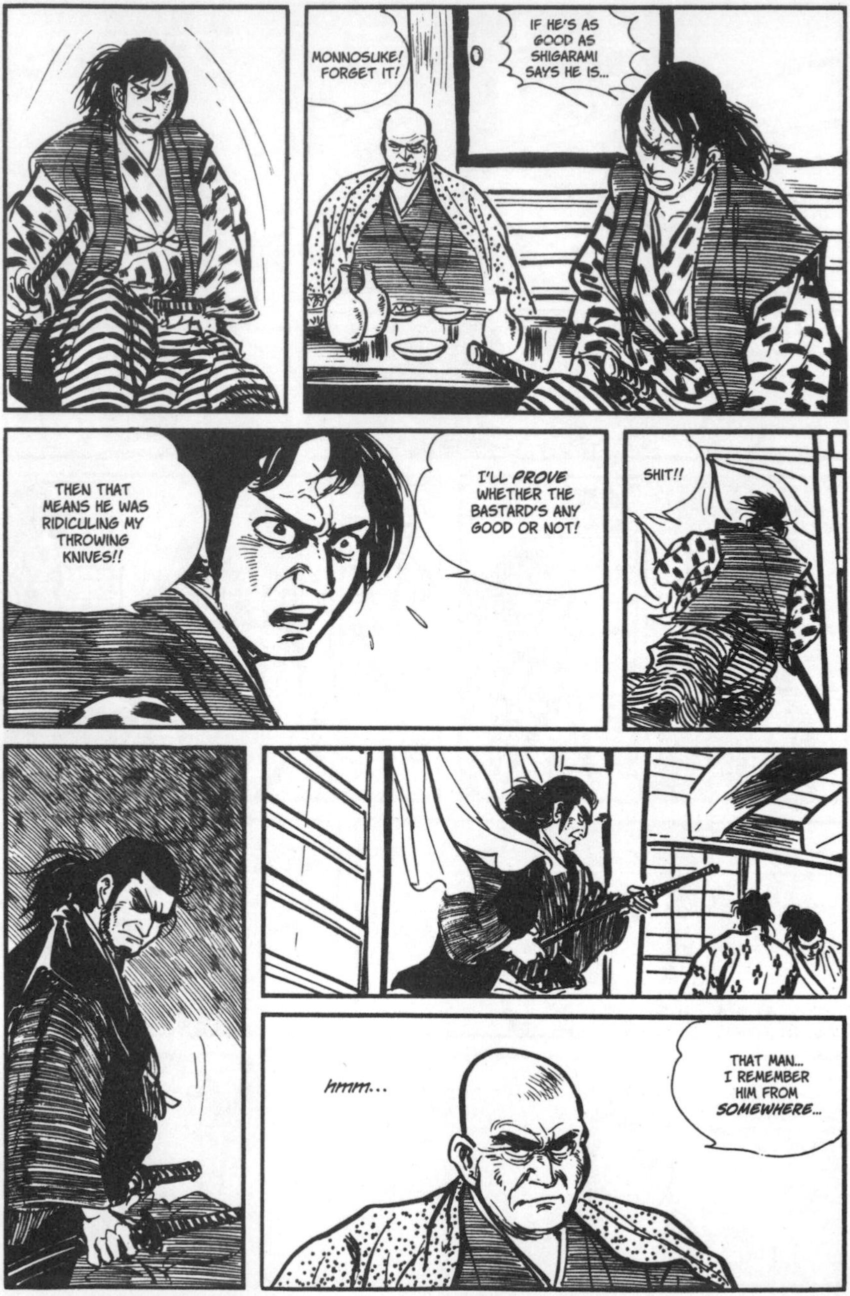
MONNOSUKE! FORGET IT!
IF HE'S AS GOOD AS SHIGARAMI SAYS HE IS...
THEN THAT MEANS HE WAS RIDICULING MY THROWING KNIVES!!
I'LL *PROVE* WHETHER THE BASTARD'S ANY GOOD OR NOT!
SHIT!!
hmm...
THAT MAN... I REMEMBER HIM FROM *SOMEWHERE*...

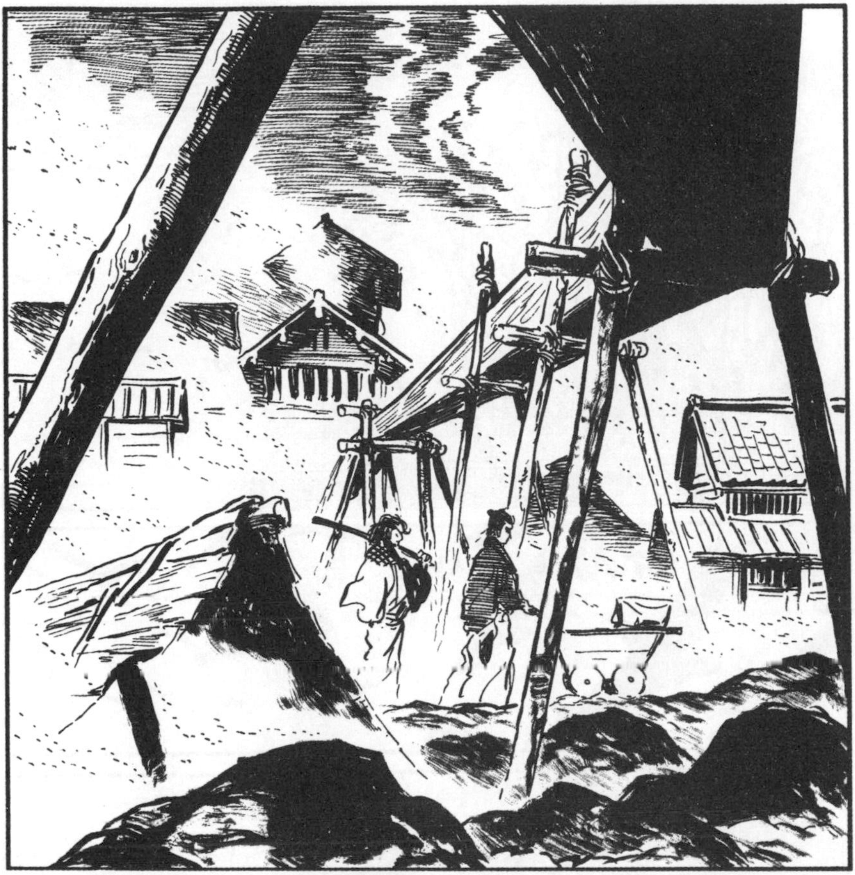

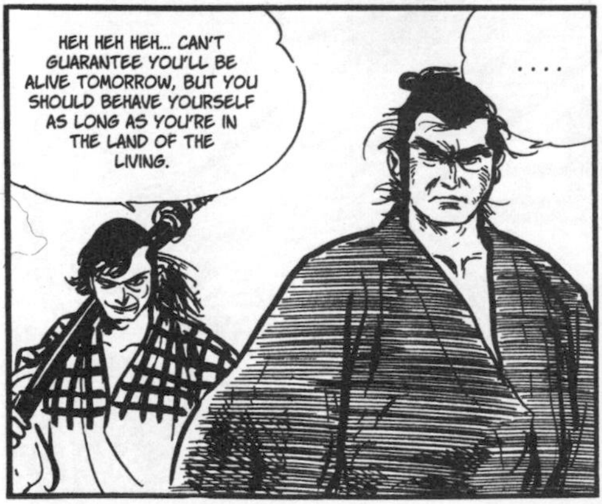
HEH HEH HEH... CAN'T GUARANTEE YOU'LL BE ALIVE TOMORROW, BUT YOU SHOULD BEHAVE YOURSELF AS LONG AS YOU'RE IN THE LAND OF THE LIVING.
....

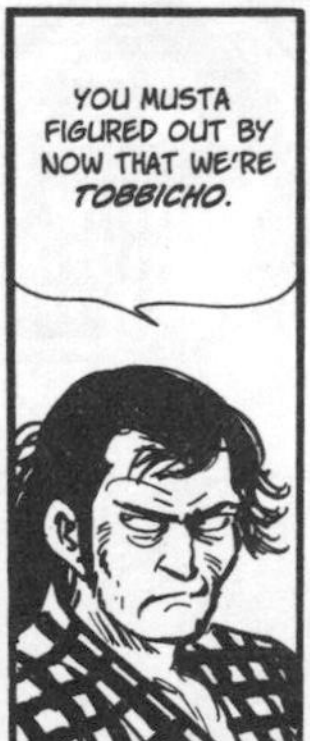
YOU MUSTA FIGURED OUT BY NOW THAT WE'RE *TOBBICHO*.

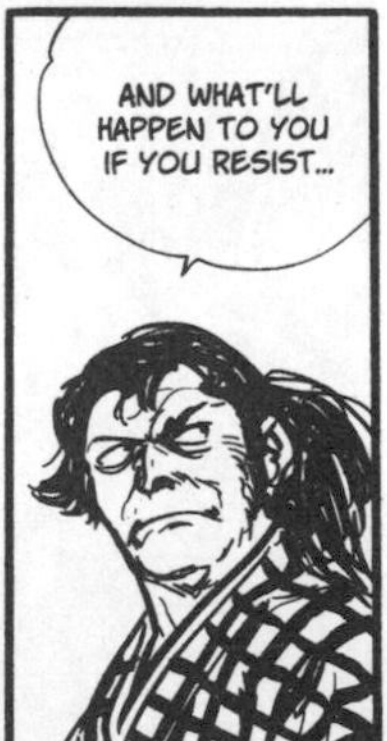
AND WHAT'LL HAPPEN TO YOU IF YOU RESIST...

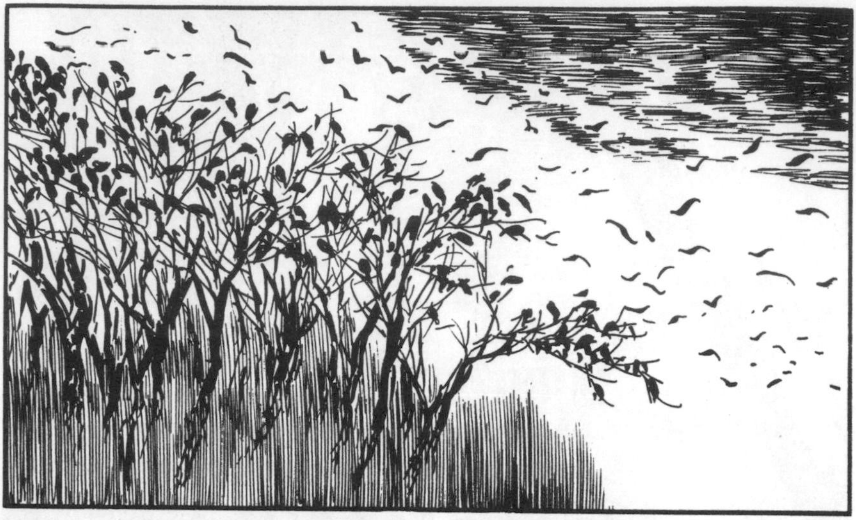

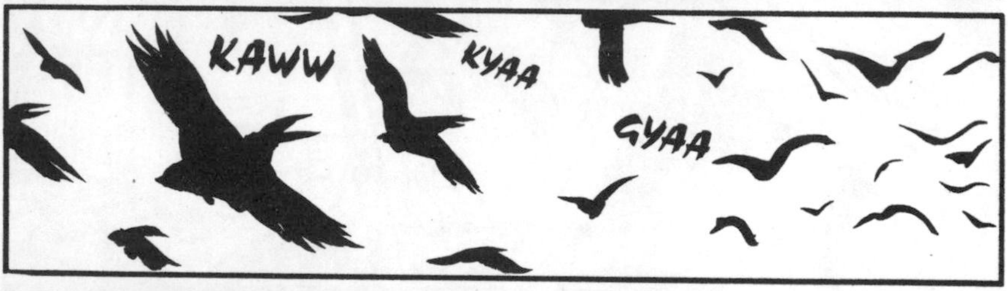

KYAA
GYAA
KAWW

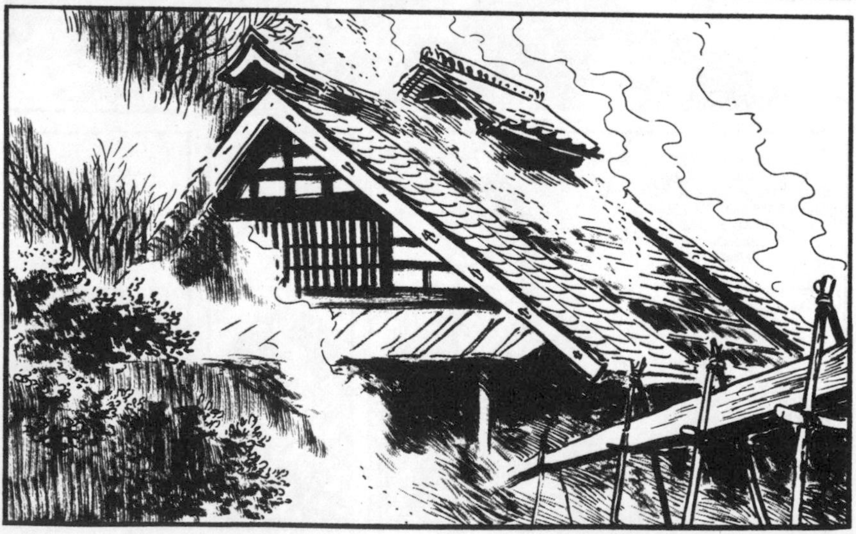

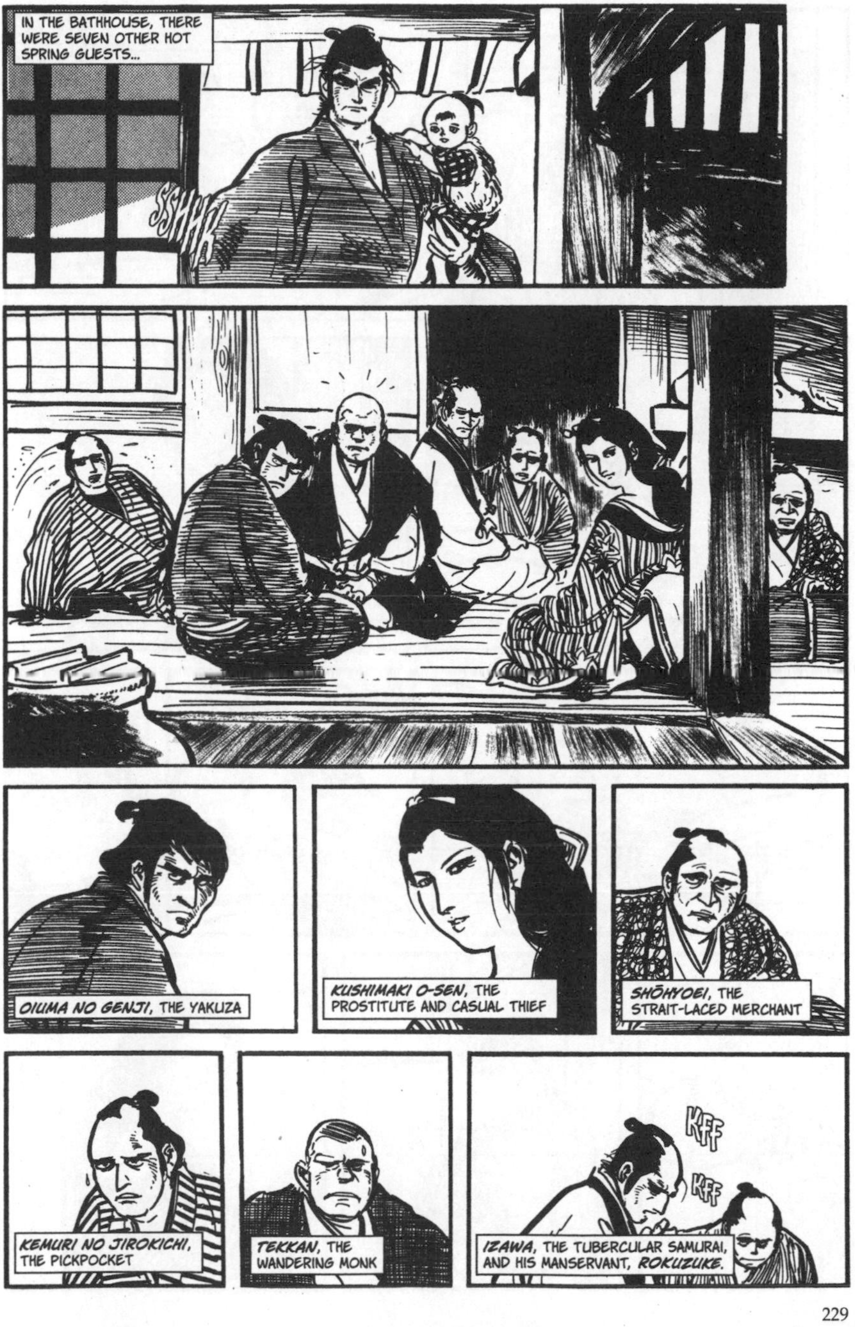
IN THE BATHHOUSE, THERE WERE SEVEN OTHER HOT SPRING GUESTS...
SSHK
OIUMA NO GENJI, THE YAKUZA
KUSHIMAKI O-SEN, THE PROSTITUTE AND CASUAL THIEF
SHŌHYOEI, THE STRAIT-LACED MERCHANT
KEMURI NO JIROKICHI, THE PICKPOCKET
TEKKAN, THE WANDERING MONK
KFF
KFF
IZAWA, THE TUBERCULAR SAMURAI, AND HIS MANSERVANT, ROKUZUKE.

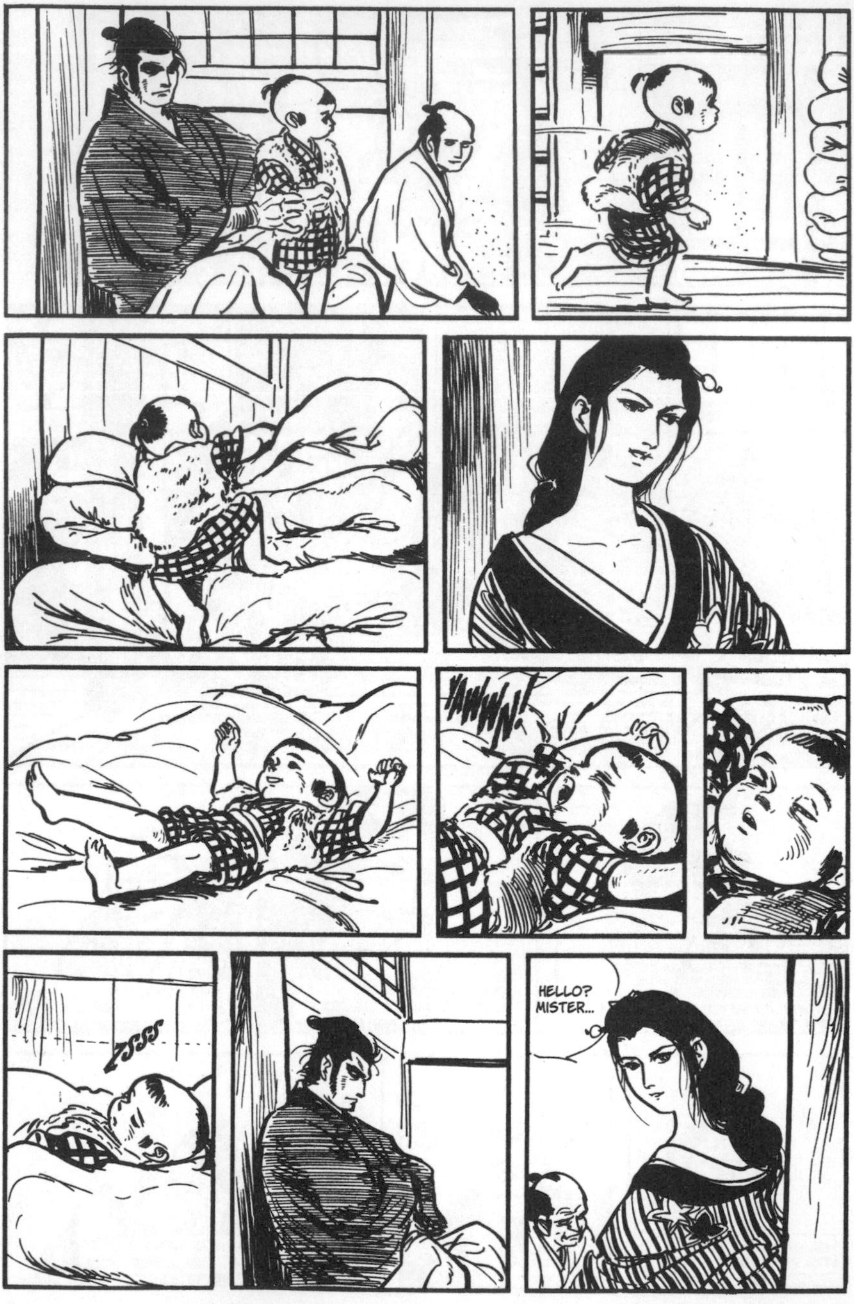
YAWWN!
ZSSS
HELLO? MISTER...

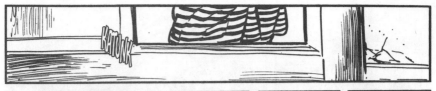

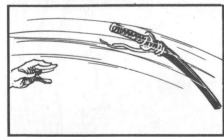

STEP OUTSIDE!

WE'LL SEE WHO'S BEST WITH THE SWORD!

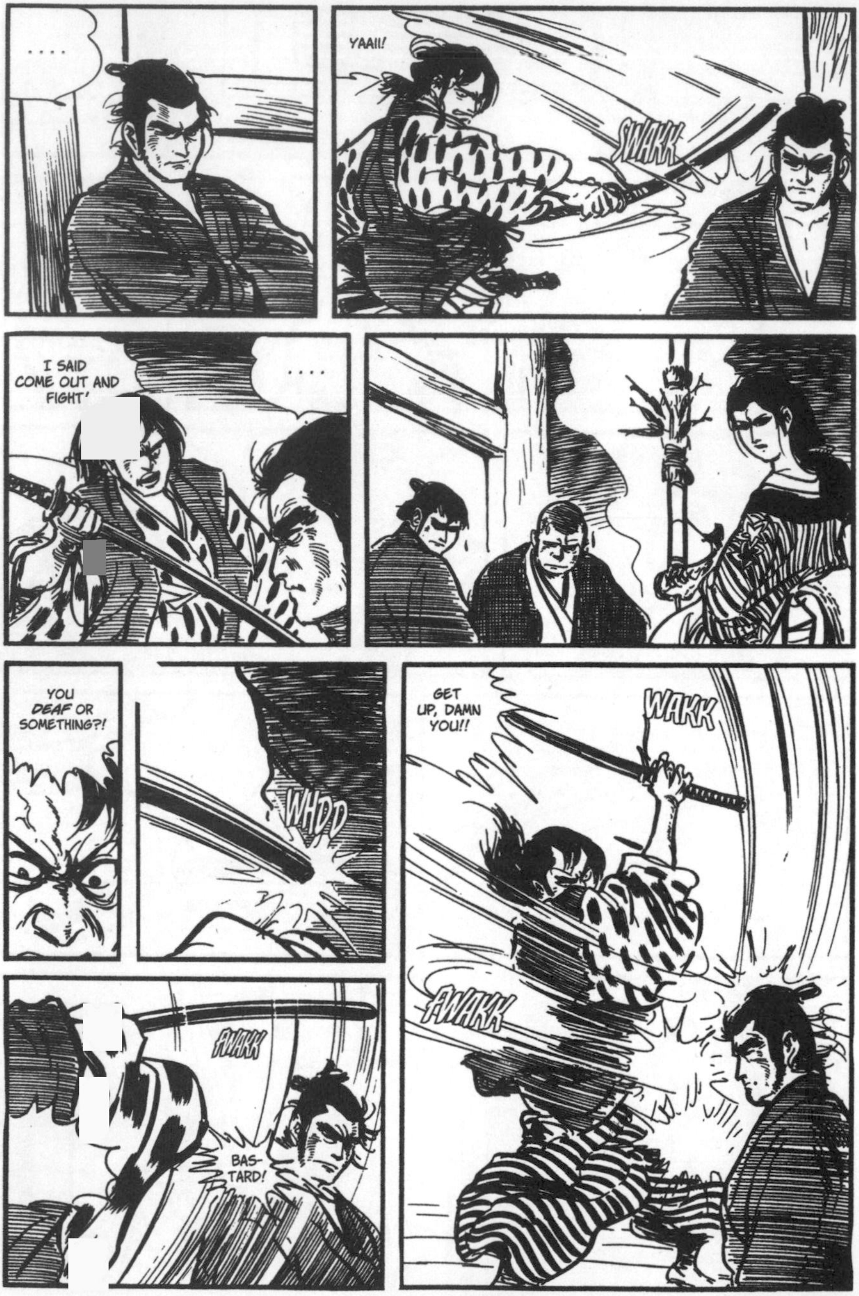
....
YAAII!
SWAKK
I SAID COME OUT AND FIGHT!
....
YOU DEAF OR SOMETHING?!
WHDD
FWAKK
BAS-TARD!
GET UP, DAMN YOU!!
WAKK
FWAKK

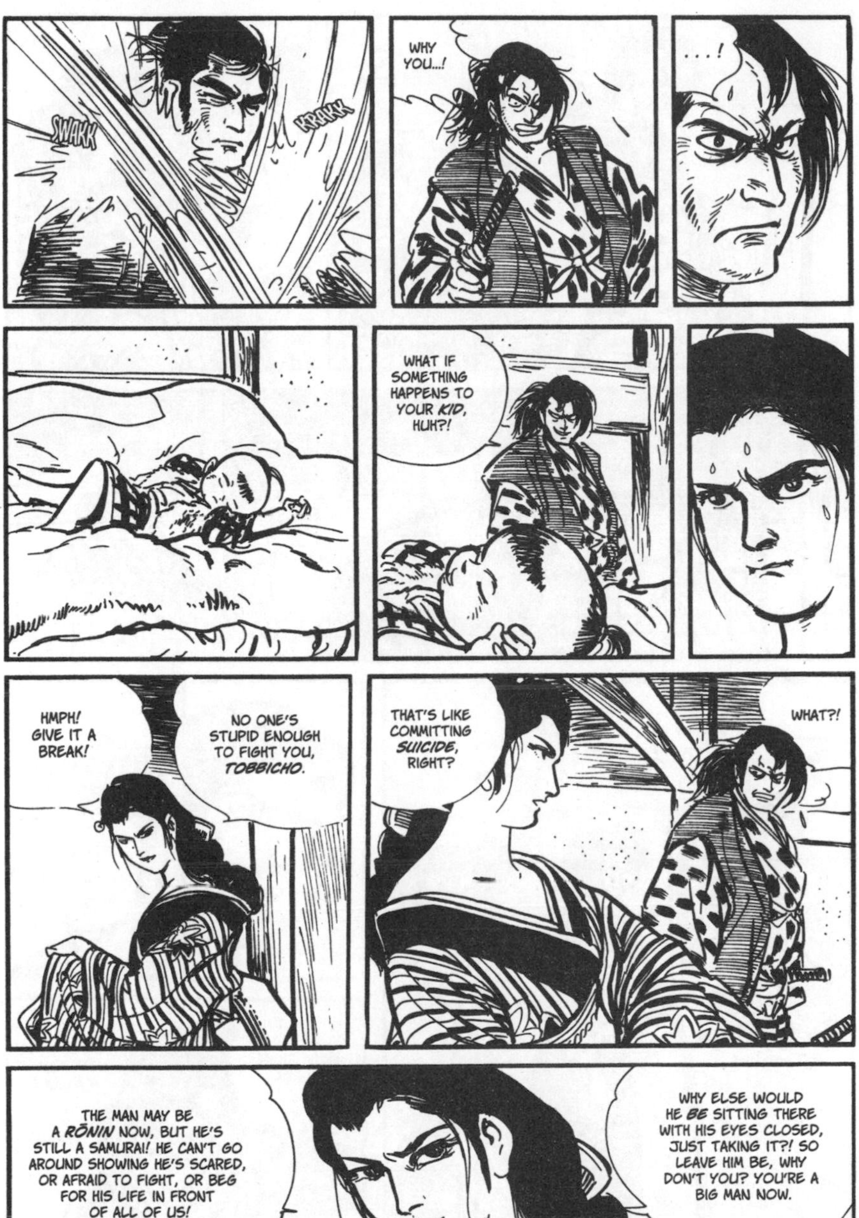

SWAKK
KRAKK
WHY YOU...!
. . . !
WHAT IF SOMETHING HAPPENS TO YOUR *KID*, HUH?!
HMPH! GIVE IT A BREAK!
NO ONE'S STUPID ENOUGH TO FIGHT YOU, *TOBBICHO*.
THAT'S LIKE COMMITTING *SUICIDE*, RIGHT?
WHAT?!
THE MAN MAY BE A *RŌNIN* NOW, BUT HE'S STILL A SAMURAI! HE CAN'T GO AROUND SHOWING HE'S SCARED, OR AFRAID TO FIGHT, OR BEG FOR HIS LIFE IN FRONT OF ALL OF US!
WHY ELSE WOULD HE *BE* SITTING THERE WITH HIS EYES CLOSED, JUST TAKING IT?! SO LEAVE HIM BE, WHY DON'T YOU? YOU'RE A BIG MAN NOW.

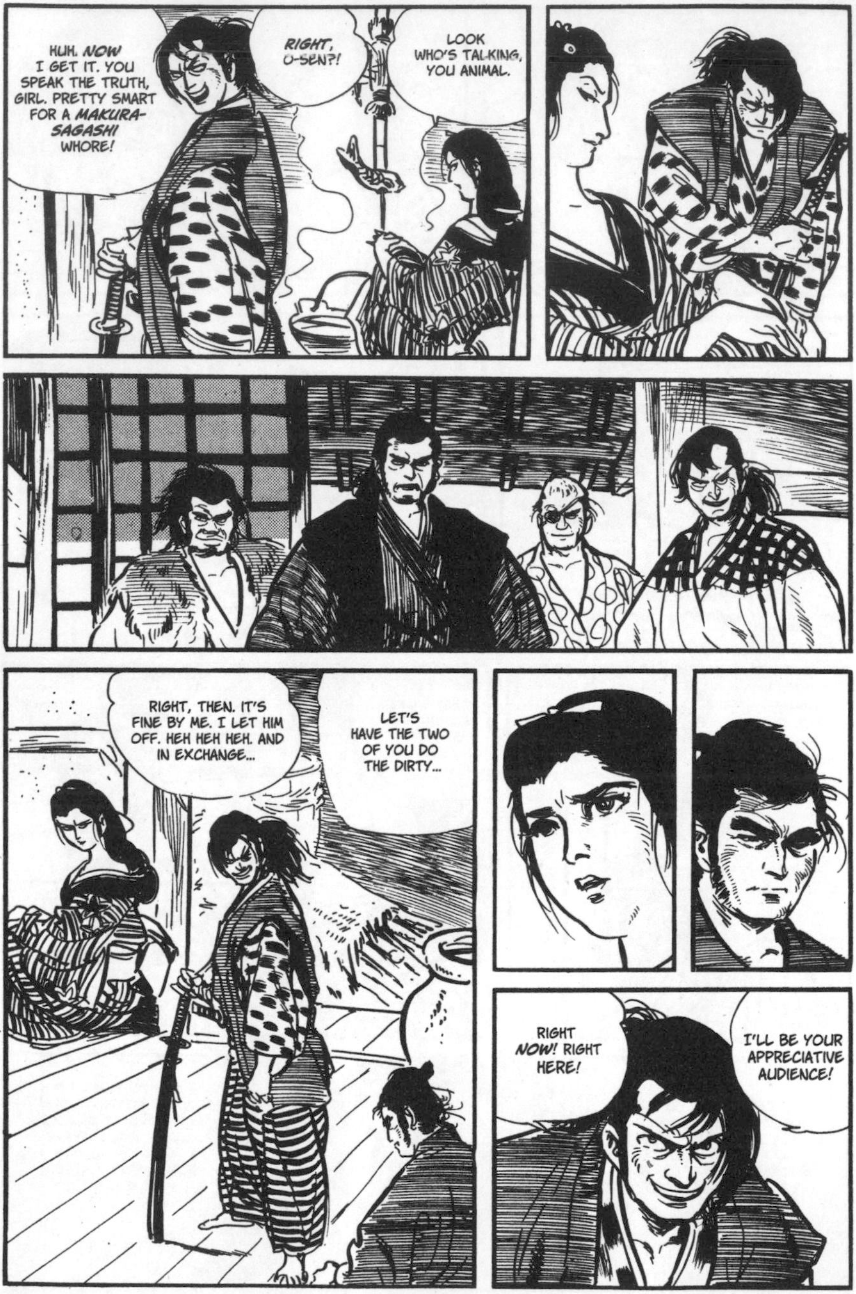
HUH. *NOW* I GET IT. YOU SPEAK THE TRUTH, GIRL. PRETTY SMART FOR A *MAKURA-SAGASHI* WHORE!
RIGHT, O-SEN?!
LOOK WHO'S TALKING, YOU ANIMAL.
RIGHT, THEN. IT'S FINE BY ME. I LET HIM OFF. HEH HEH HEH. AND IN EXCHANGE...
LET'S HAVE THE TWO OF YOU DO THE DIRTY...
RIGHT *NOW!* RIGHT HERE!
I'LL BE YOUR APPRECIATIVE AUDIENCE!

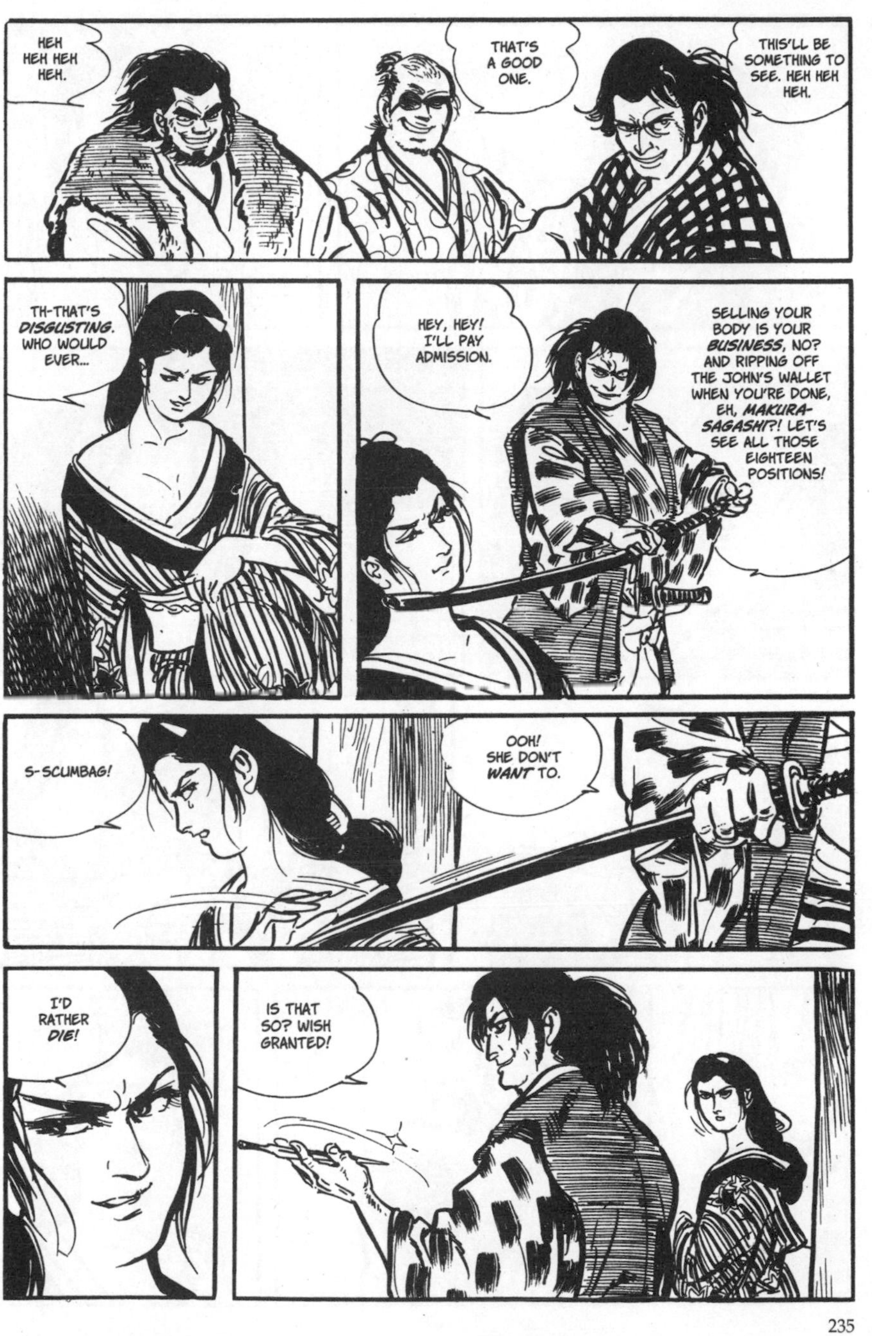
HEH HEH HEH HEH.
THAT'S A GOOD ONE.
THIS'LL BE SOMETHING TO SEE. HEH HEH HEH.
TH-THAT'S *DISGUSTING*. WHO WOULD EVER...
HEY, HEY! I'LL PAY ADMISSION.
SELLING YOUR BODY IS YOUR *BUSINESS*, NO? AND RIPPING OFF THE JOHN'S WALLET WHEN YOU'RE DONE, EH, *MAKURA-SAGASHI*?! LET'S SEE ALL THOSE EIGHTEEN POSITIONS!
S-SCUMBAG!
OOH! SHE DON'T *WANT* TO.
I'D RATHER *DIE*!
IS THAT SO? WISH GRANTED!

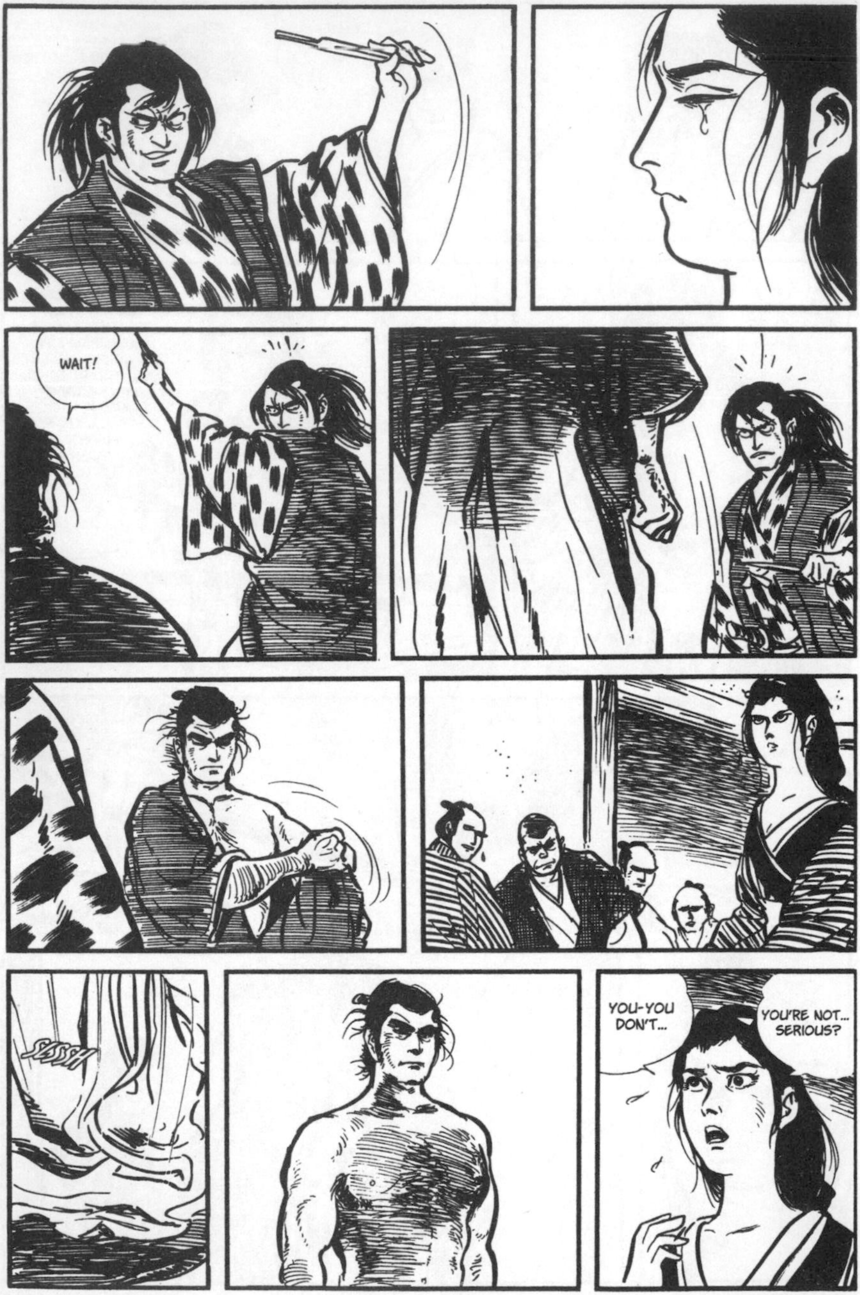
WAIT!
SSSSH
YOU-YOU DON'T...
YOU'RE NOT... SERIOUS?

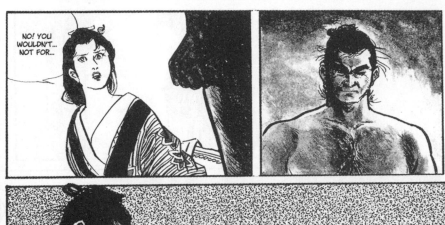

NO! YOU WOULDN'T... NOT FOR...

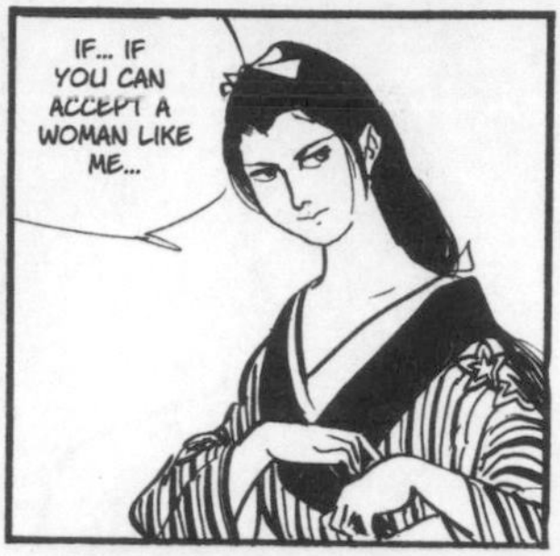
IF... IF YOU CAN ACCEPT A WOMAN LIKE ME...

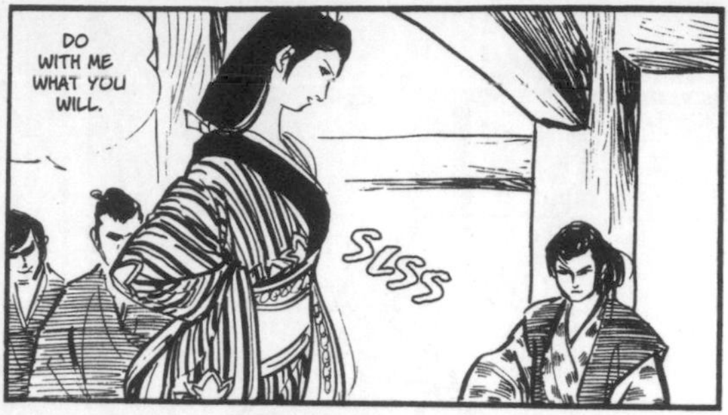
DO WITH ME WHAT YOU WILL.
SLSS

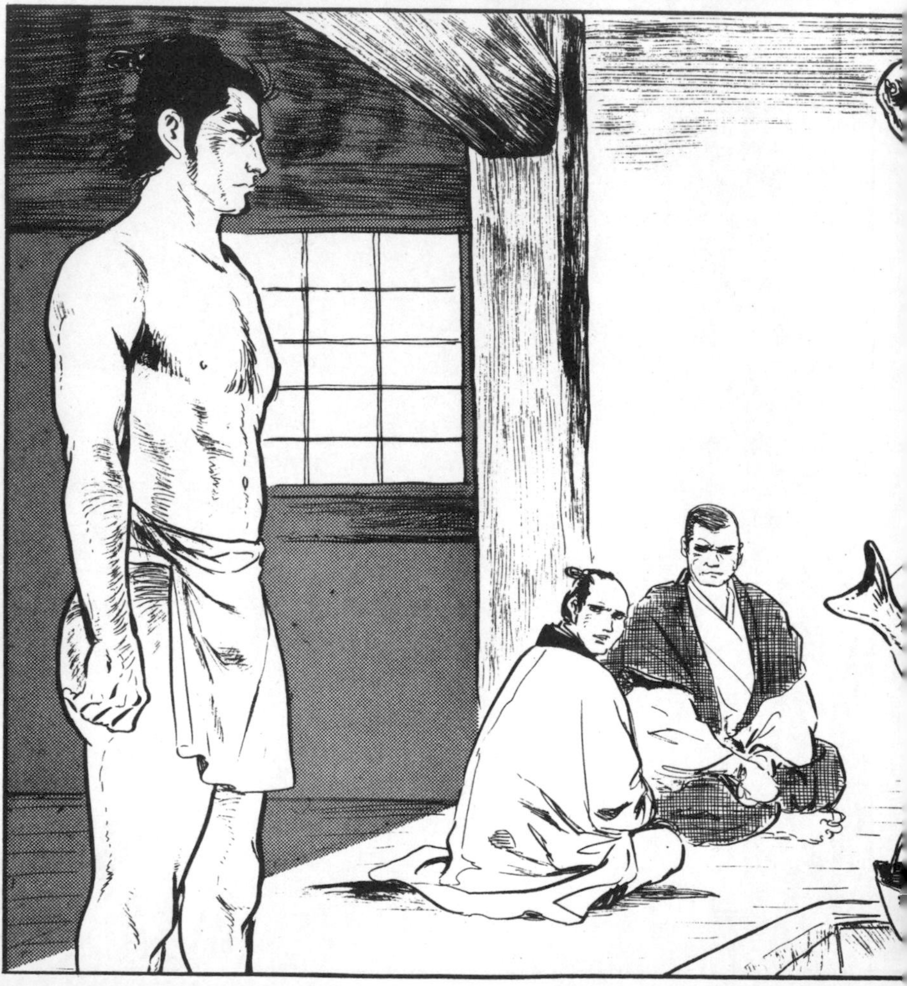

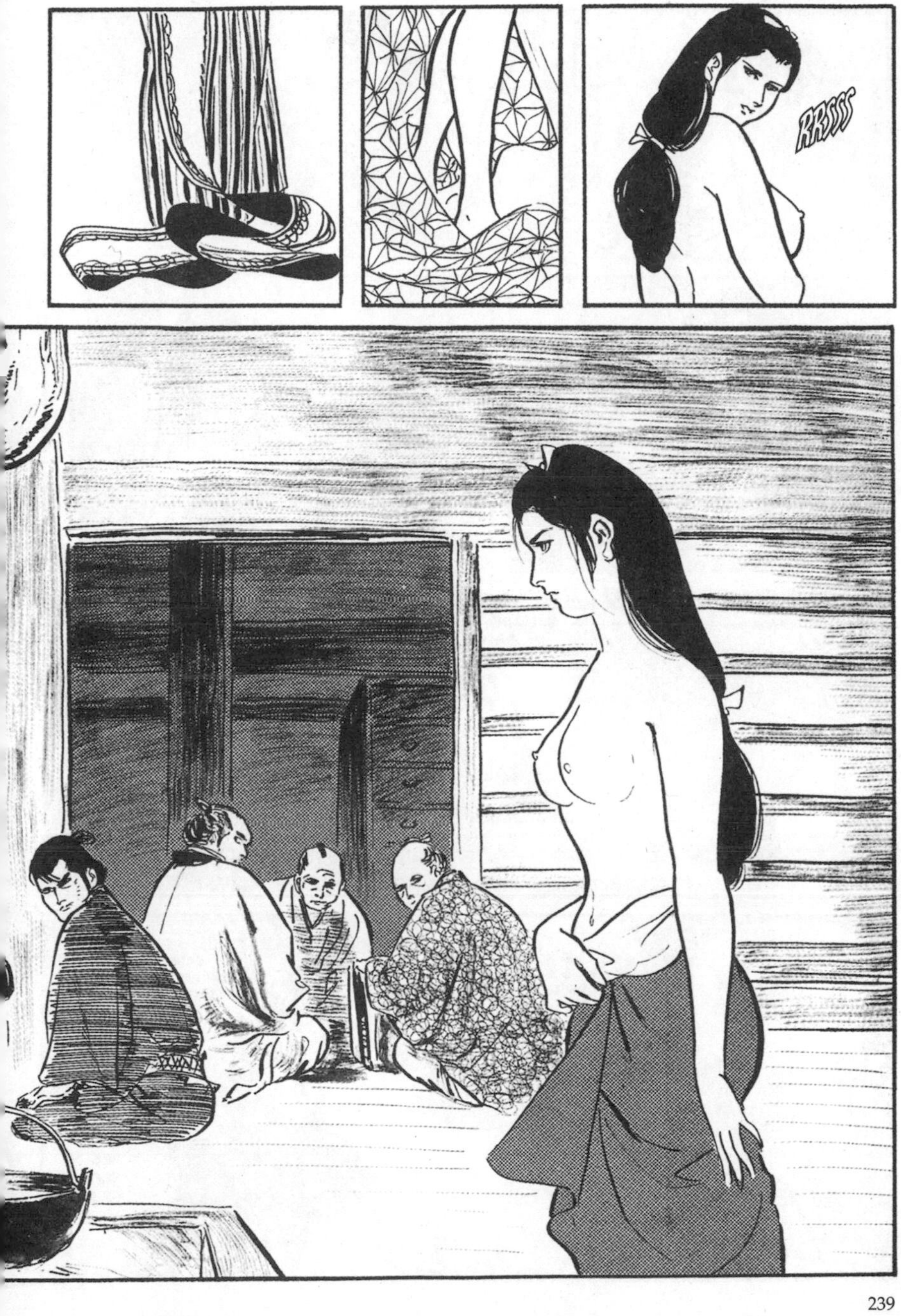
RRSSS

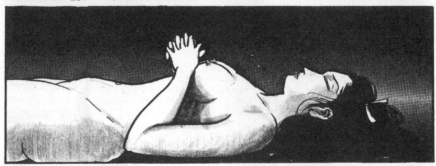

HEH HEH HEH. LOOK AT HER FACE. SHE THINKS SHE'S STILL A *VIRGIN*...

SHE MUST FIGURE SHE'S *KANNON-SAMA* HERSELF TO BE SAVING THAT COWARD. HEE HEE HEE...

OUR GODDESS OF WHOREDOM, MORE LIKE! BWA HAH HAH.

HEE HEE HEE.

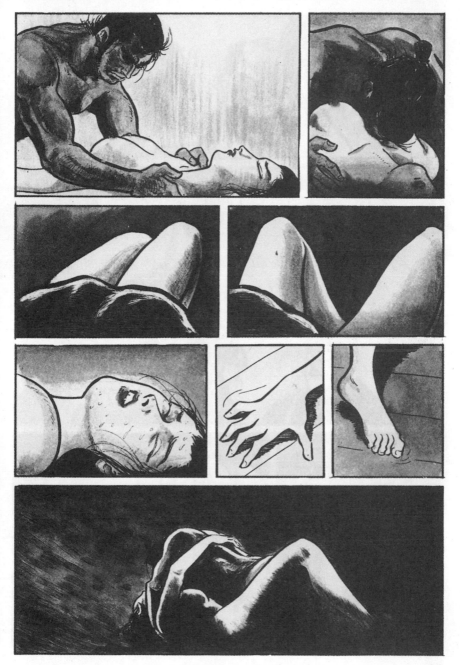

241

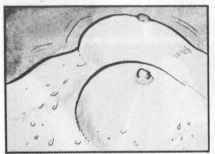
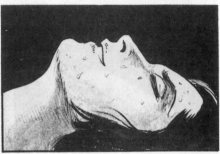

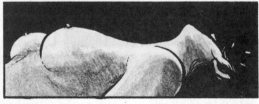

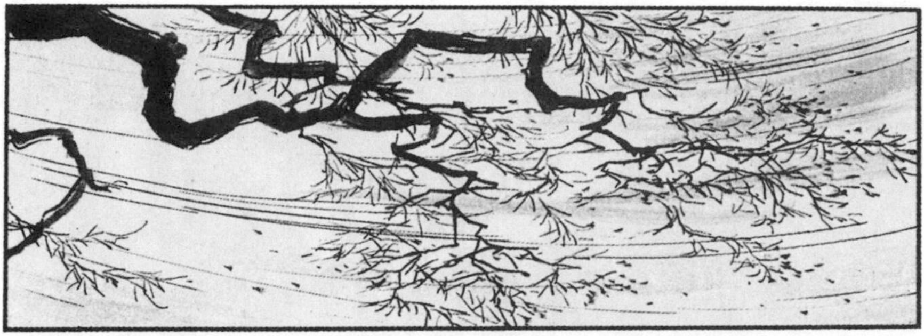
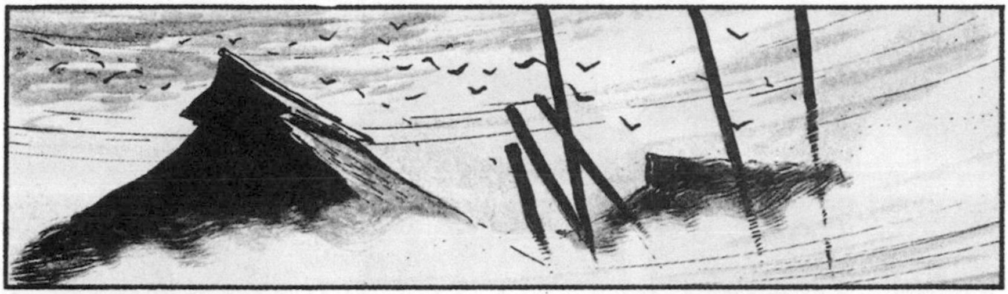
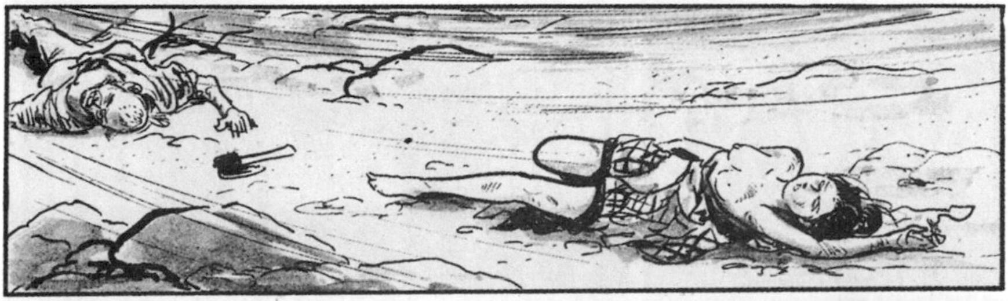
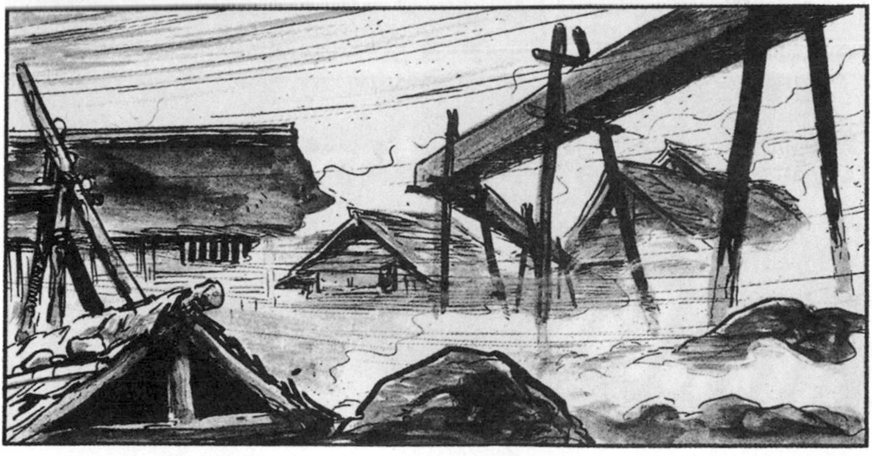

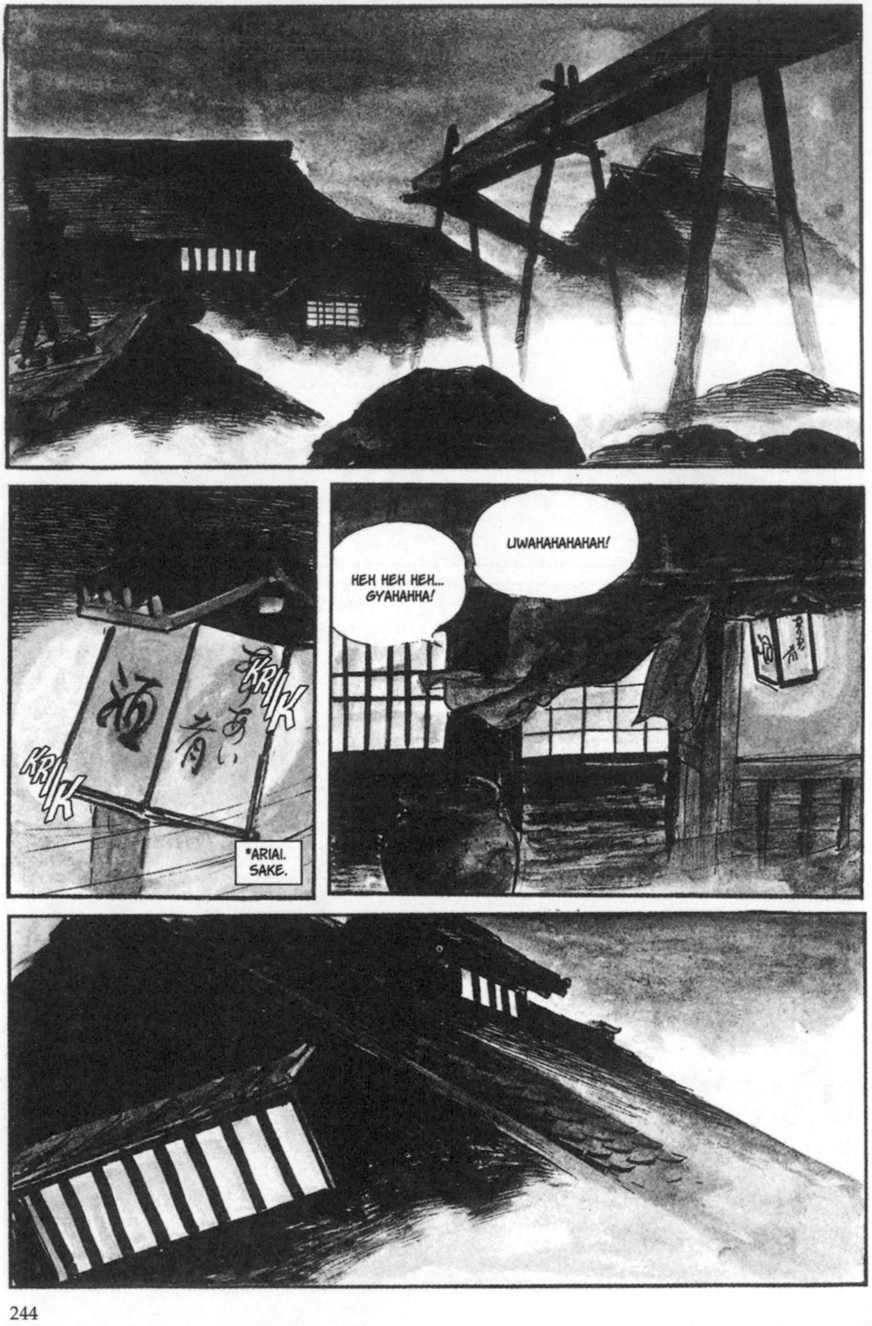
UWAHAHAHAHAH!
HEH HEH HEH... GYAHAHHA!
KRIK
KRIK
*ARIAI. SAKE.

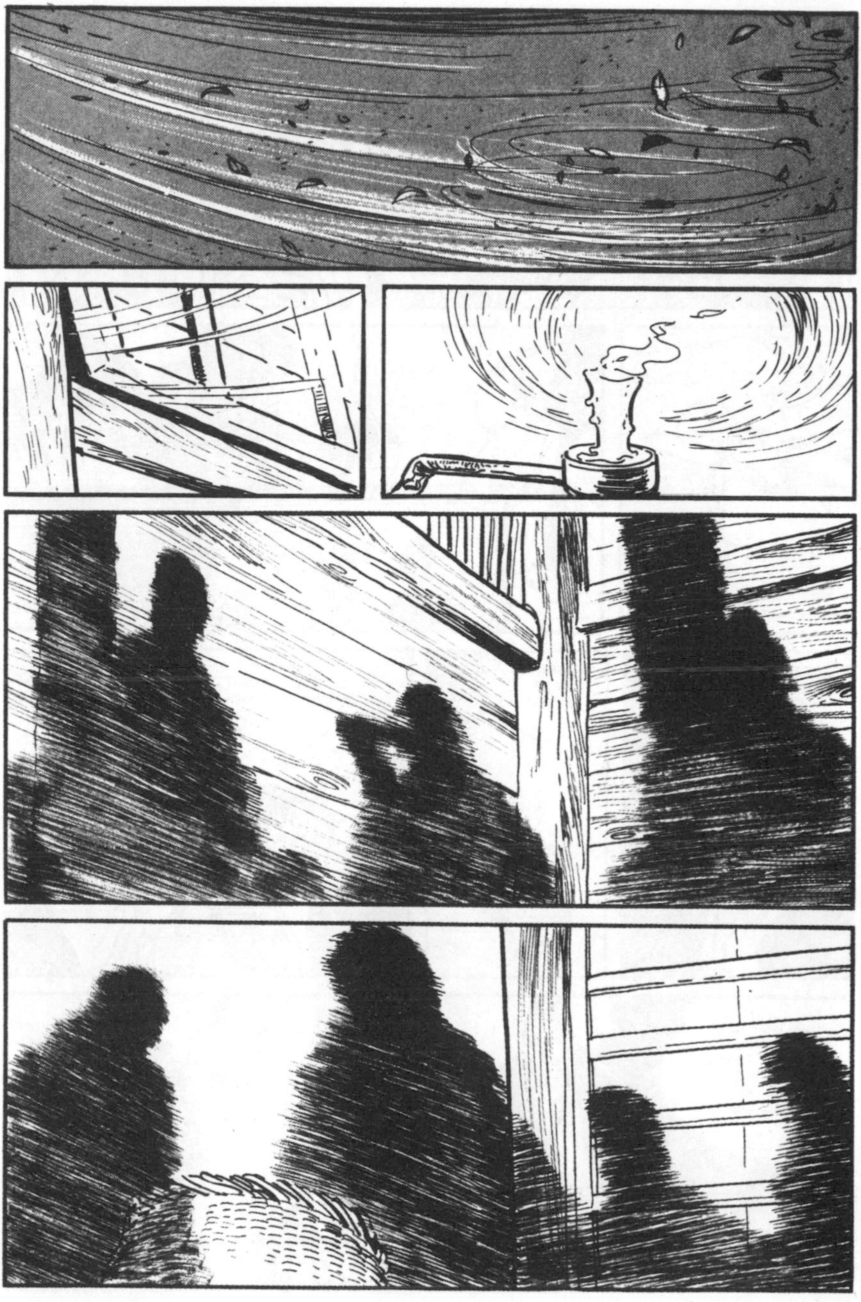

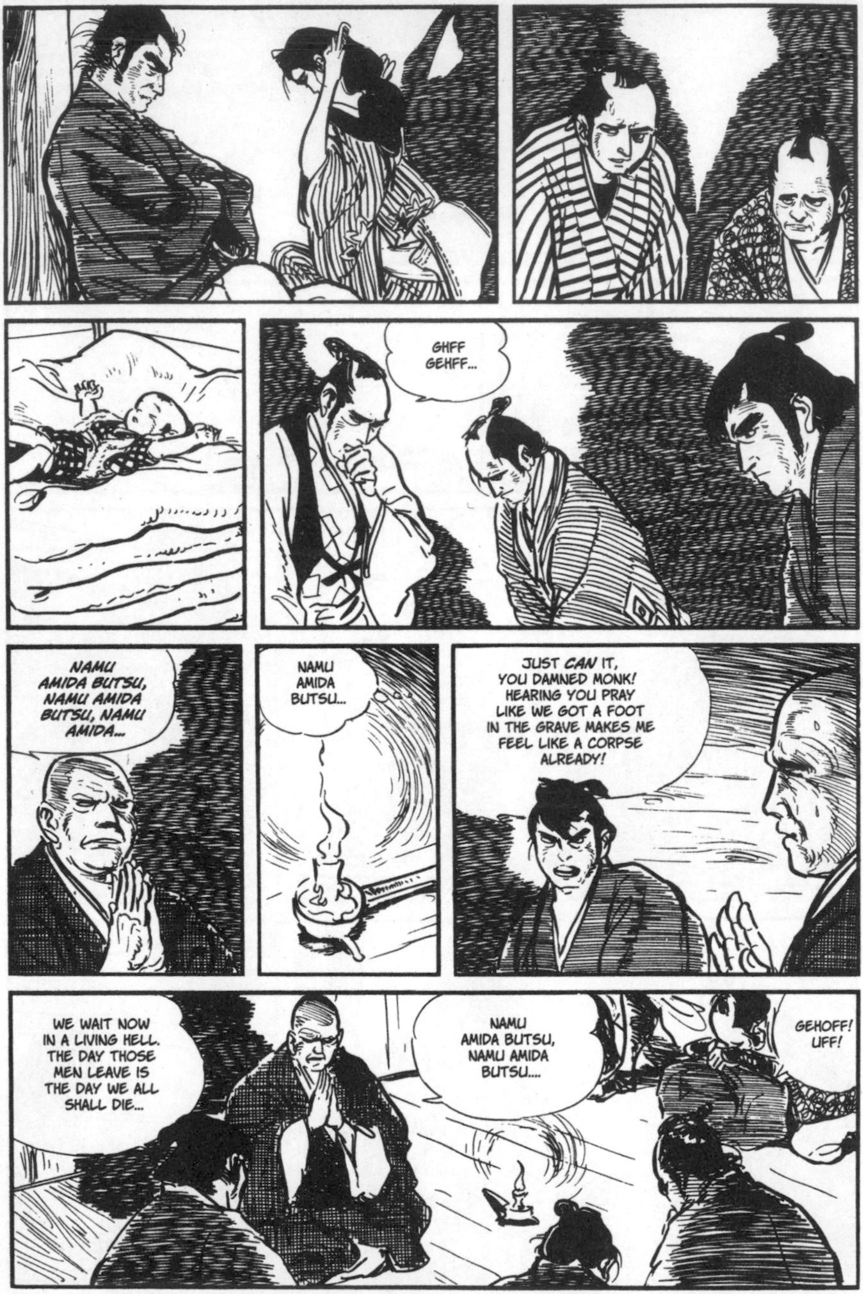
GHFF GEHFF...
NAMU AMIDA BUTSU, NAMU AMIDA BUTSU, NAMU AMIDA...
NAMU AMIDA BUTSU...
JUST CAN IT, YOU DAMNED MONK! HEARING YOU PRAY LIKE WE GOT A FOOT IN THE GRAVE MAKES ME FEEL LIKE A CORPSE ALREADY!
WE WAIT NOW IN A LIVING HELL. THE DAY THOSE MEN LEAVE IS THE DAY WE ALL SHALL DIE...
NAMU AMIDA BUTSU, NAMU AMIDA BUTSU....
GEHOFF! UFF!

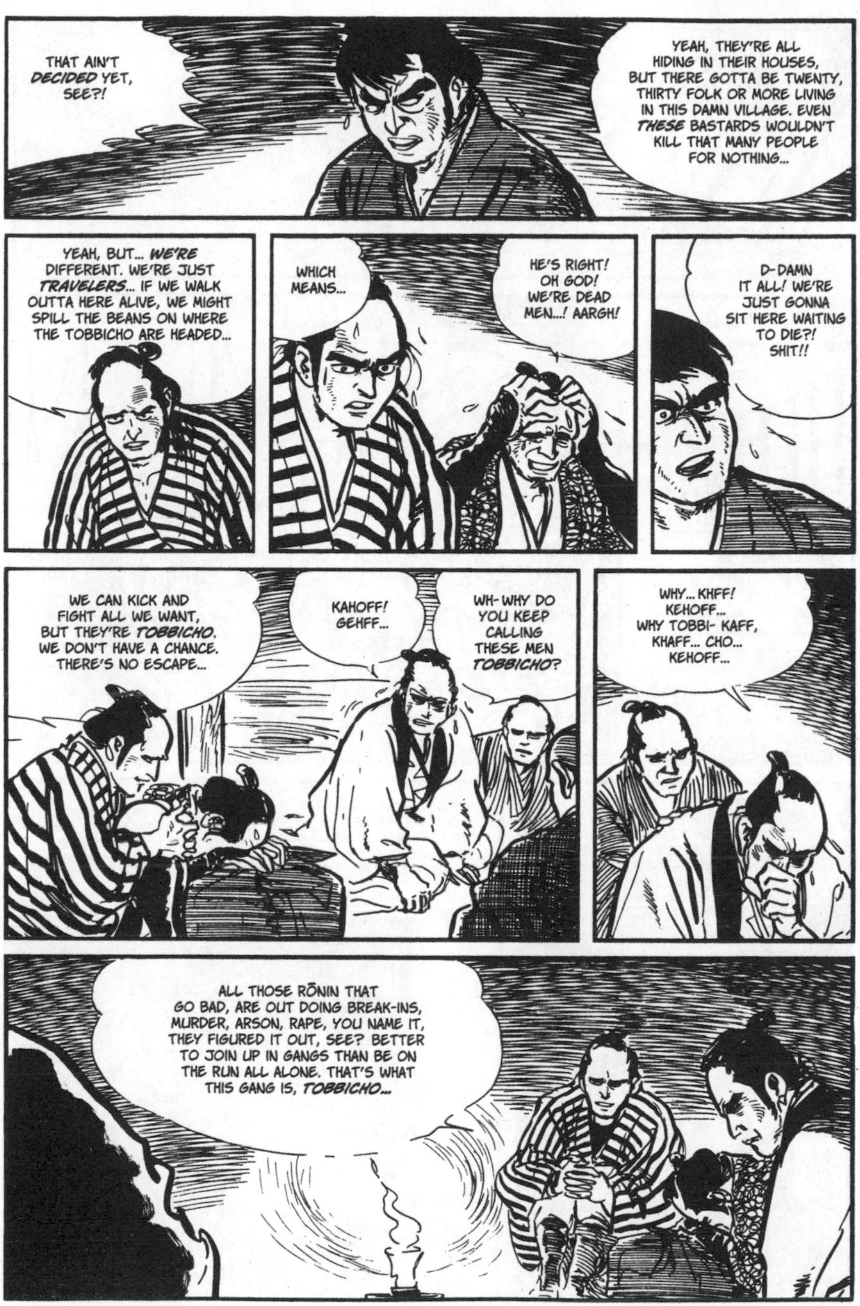
THAT AIN'T *DECIDED* YET, SEE?!
YEAH, THEY'RE ALL HIDING IN THEIR HOUSES, BUT THERE GOTTA BE TWENTY, THIRTY FOLK OR MORE LIVING IN THIS DAMN VILLAGE. EVEN *THESE* BASTARDS WOULDN'T KILL THAT MANY PEOPLE FOR NOTHING...
YEAH, BUT... *WE'RE* DIFFERENT. WE'RE JUST *TRAVELERS*... IF WE WALK OUTTA HERE ALIVE, WE MIGHT SPILL THE BEANS ON WHERE THE TOBBICHO ARE HEADED...
WHICH MEANS...
HE'S RIGHT! OH GOD! WE'RE DEAD MEN...! AARGH!
D-DAMN IT ALL! WE'RE JUST GONNA SIT HERE WAITING TO DIE?! SHIT!!
WE CAN KICK AND FIGHT ALL WE WANT, BUT THEY'RE *TOBBICHO*. WE DON'T HAVE A CHANCE. THERE'S NO ESCAPE...
KAHOFF! GEHFF...
WH-WHY DO YOU KEEP CALLING THESE MEN *TOBBICHO*?
WHY... KHFF! KEHOFF... WHY TOBBI- KAFF, KHAFF... CHO... KEHOFF...
ALL THOSE RŌNIN THAT GO BAD, ARE OUT DOING BREAK-INS, MURDER, ARSON, RAPE, YOU NAME IT, THEY FIGURED IT OUT, SEE? BETTER TO JOIN UP IN GANGS THAN BE ON THE RUN ALL ALONE. THAT'S WHAT THIS GANG IS, *TOBBICHO*...

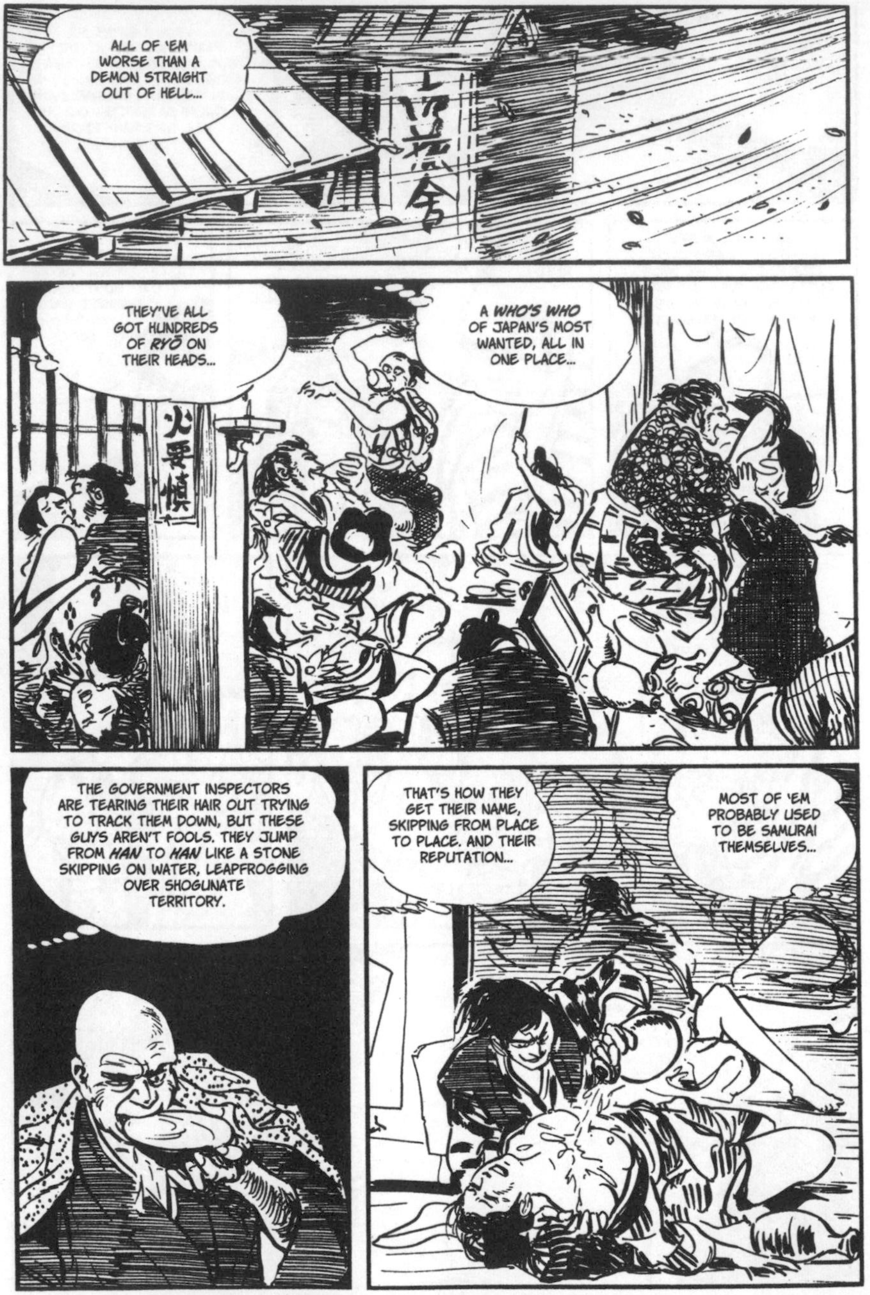

ALL OF 'EM WORSE THAN A DEMON STRAIGHT OUT OF HELL...
THEY'VE ALL GOT HUNDREDS OF *RYŌ* ON THEIR HEADS...
A *WHO'S WHO* OF JAPAN'S MOST WANTED, ALL IN ONE PLACE...
火要慎
THE GOVERNMENT INSPECTORS ARE TEARING THEIR HAIR OUT TRYING TO TRACK THEM DOWN, BUT THESE GUYS AREN'T FOOLS. THEY JUMP FROM *HAN* TO *HAN* LIKE A STONE SKIPPING ON WATER, LEAPFROGGING OVER SHOGUNATE TERRITORY.
THAT'S HOW THEY GET THEIR NAME, SKIPPING FROM PLACE TO PLACE. AND THEIR REPUTATION...
MOST OF 'EM PROBABLY USED TO BE SAMURAI THEMSELVES...

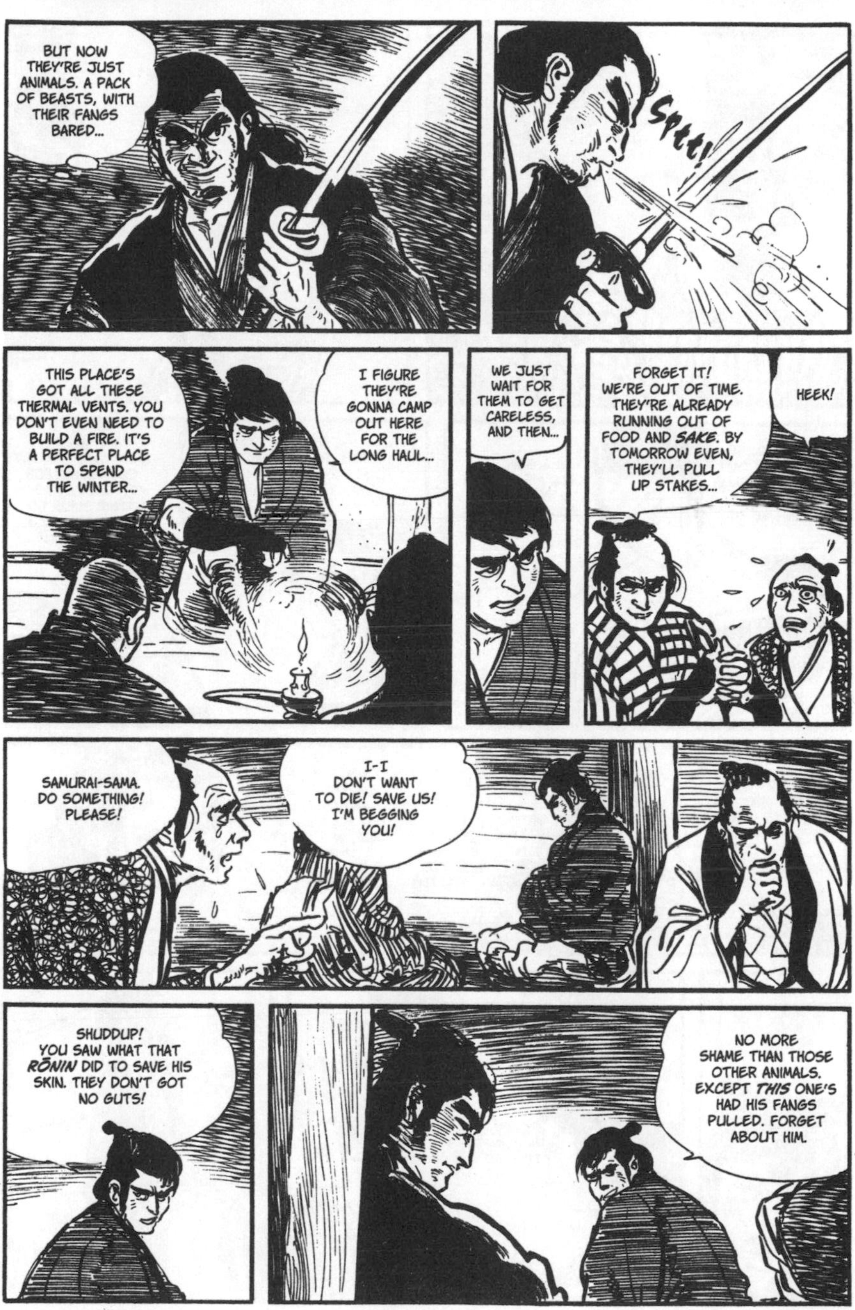
BUT NOW THEY'RE JUST ANIMALS. A PACK OF BEASTS, WITH THEIR FANGS BARED...
Sptt!
THIS PLACE'S GOT ALL THESE THERMAL VENTS. YOU DON'T EVEN NEED TO BUILD A FIRE. IT'S A PERFECT PLACE TO SPEND THE WINTER...
I FIGURE THEY'RE GONNA CAMP OUT HERE FOR THE LONG HAUL...
WE JUST WAIT FOR THEM TO GET CARELESS, AND THEN...
FORGET IT! WE'RE OUT OF TIME. THEY'RE ALREADY RUNNING OUT OF FOOD AND *SAKE*. BY TOMORROW EVEN, THEY'LL PULL UP STAKES...
HEEK!
SAMURAI-SAMA. DO SOMETHING! PLEASE!
I-I DON'T WANT TO DIE! SAVE US! I'M BEGGING YOU!
SHUDDUP! YOU SAW WHAT THAT *RŌNIN* DID TO SAVE HIS SKIN. THEY DON'T GOT NO GUTS!
NO MORE SHAME THAN THOSE OTHER ANIMALS. EXCEPT *THIS* ONE'S HAD HIS FANGS PULLED. FORGET ABOUT HIM.

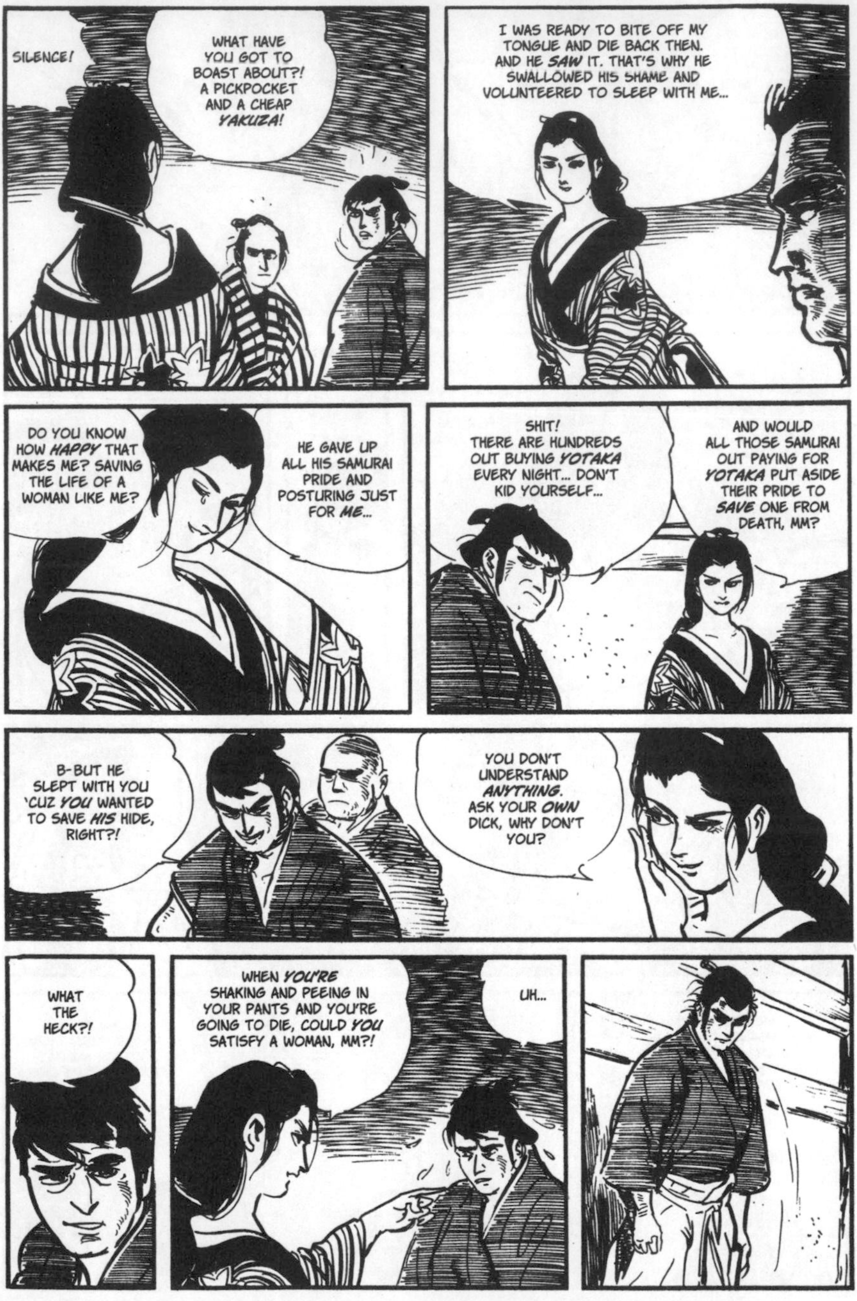
SILENCE!
WHAT HAVE YOU GOT TO BOAST ABOUT?! A PICKPOCKET AND A CHEAP *YAKUZA*!
I WAS READY TO BITE OFF MY TONGUE AND DIE BACK THEN. AND HE *SAW* IT. THAT'S WHY HE SWALLOWED HIS SHAME AND VOLUNTEERED TO SLEEP WITH ME...
DO YOU KNOW HOW *HAPPY* THAT MAKES ME? SAVING THE LIFE OF A WOMAN LIKE ME?
HE GAVE UP ALL HIS SAMURAI PRIDE AND POSTURING JUST FOR *ME*...
SHIT! THERE ARE HUNDREDS OUT BUYING *YOTAKA* EVERY NIGHT... DON'T KID YOURSELF...
AND WOULD ALL THOSE SAMURAI OUT PAYING FOR *YOTAKA* PUT ASIDE THEIR PRIDE TO *SAVE* ONE FROM DEATH, MM?
B-BUT HE SLEPT WITH YOU 'CUZ *YOU* WANTED TO SAVE *HIS* HIDE, RIGHT?!
YOU DON'T UNDERSTAND *ANYTHING*. ASK YOUR *OWN* DICK, WHY DON'T YOU?
WHAT THE HECK?!
WHEN *YOU'RE* SHAKING AND PEEING IN YOUR PANTS AND YOU'RE GOING TO DIE, COULD *YOU* SATISFY A WOMAN, MM?!
UH...

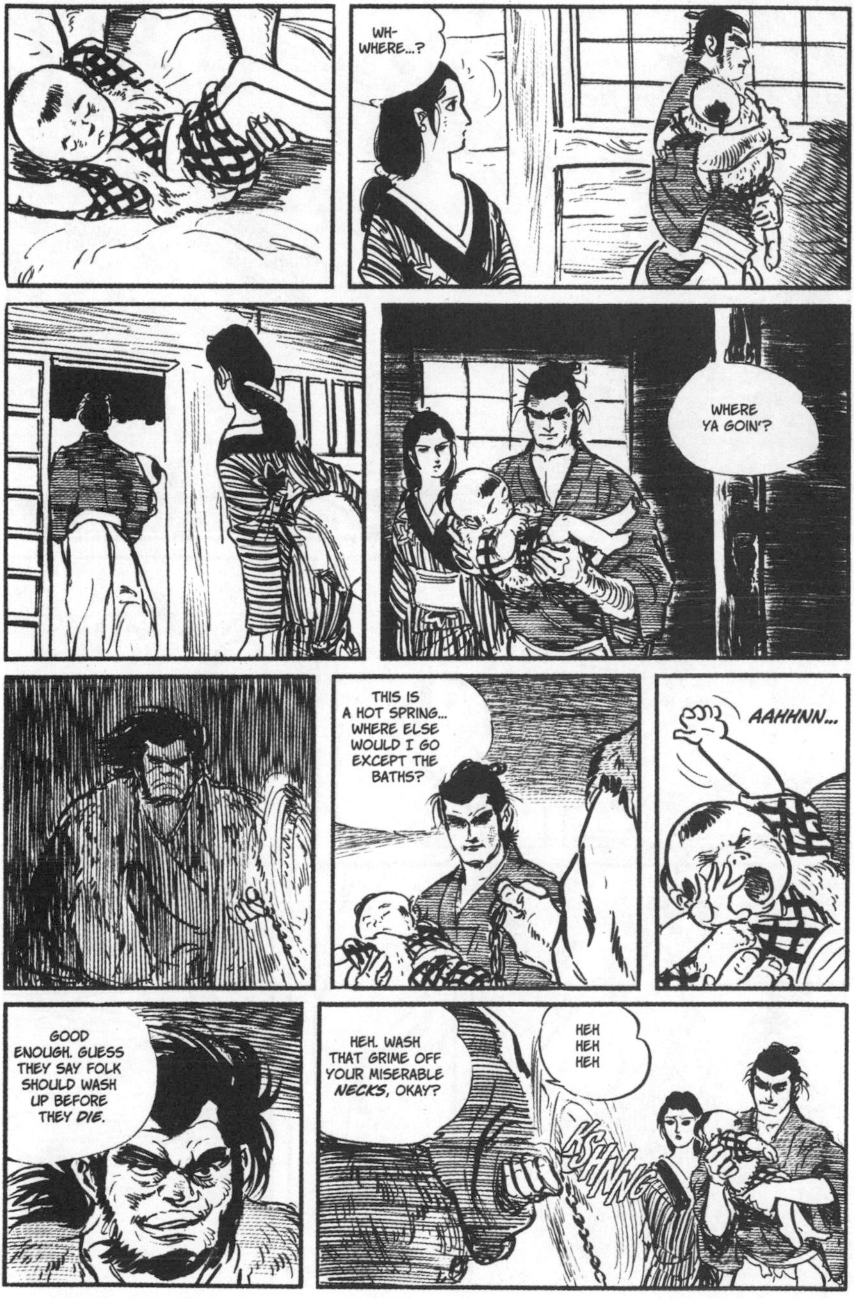
WH- WHERE...?
WHERE YA GOIN'?
THIS IS A HOT SPRING... WHERE ELSE WOULD I GO EXCEPT THE BATHS?
AAHHNN...
GOOD ENOUGH. GUESS THEY SAY FOLK SHOULD WASH UP BEFORE THEY *DIE*.
HEH. WASH THAT GRIME OFF YOUR MISERABLE *NECKS*, OKAY?
HEH HEH HEH
KSHNNG

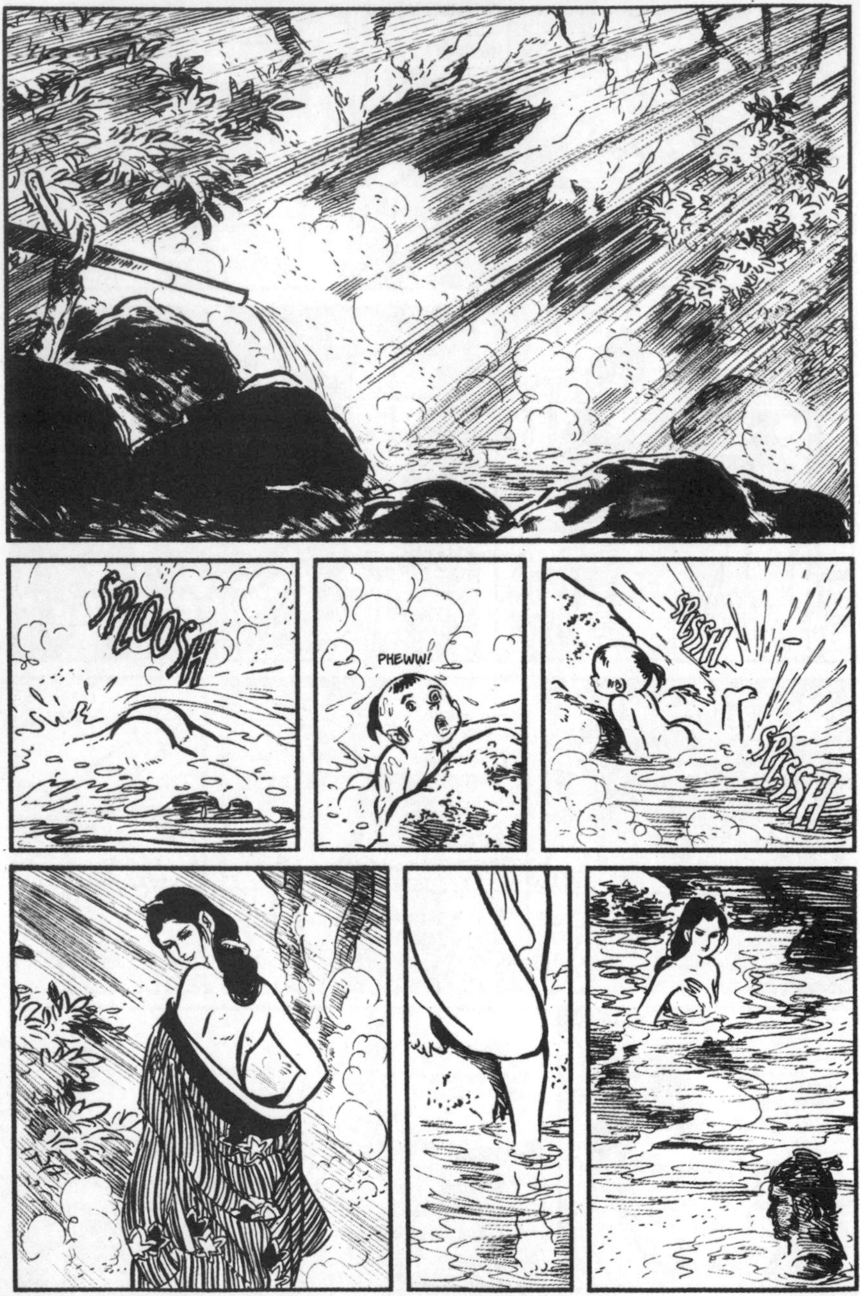
SPLOOSH
PHEWW!
SPISSH
SPISSH

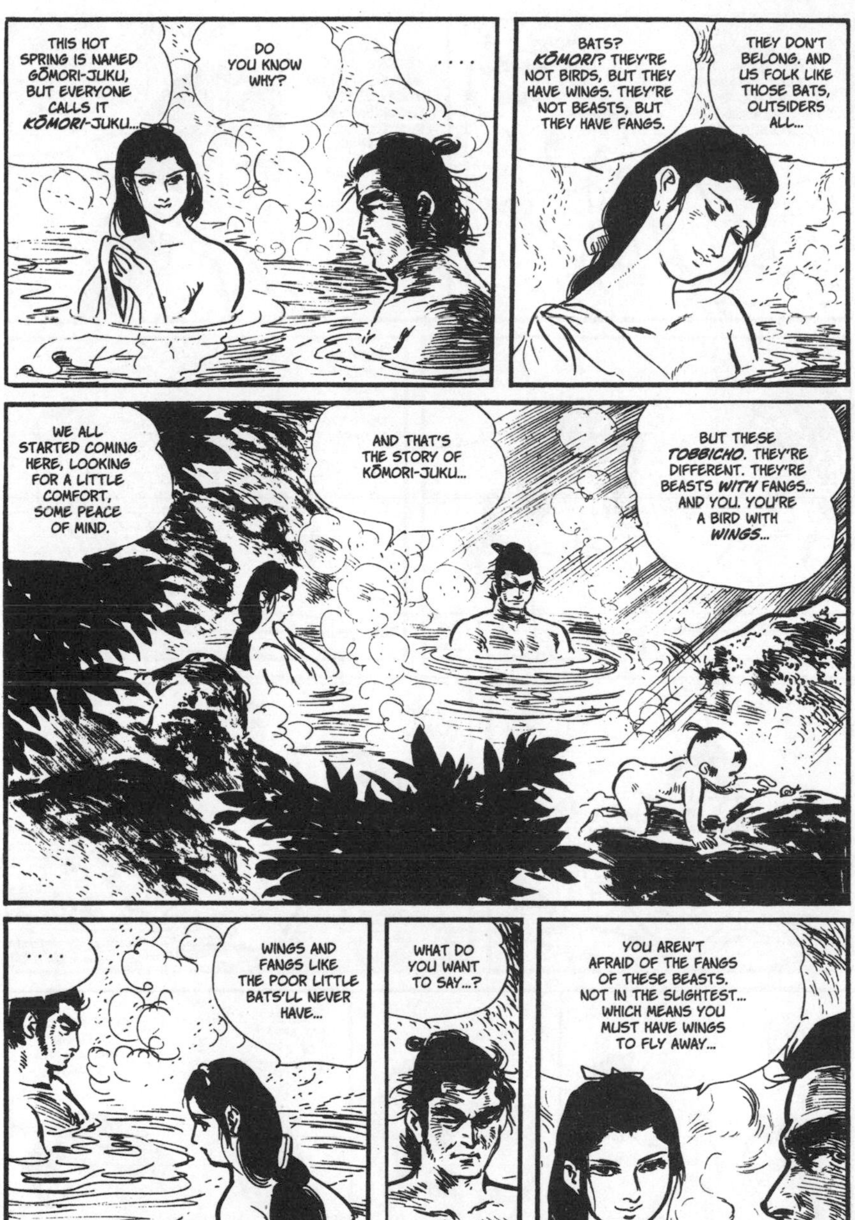
THIS HOT SPRING IS NAMED GŌMORI-JUKU, BUT EVERYONE CALLS IT *KŌMORI*-JUKU...
DO YOU KNOW WHY?
....
BATS? *KŌMORI*? THEY'RE NOT BIRDS, BUT THEY HAVE WINGS. THEY'RE NOT BEASTS, BUT THEY HAVE FANGS.
THEY DON'T BELONG. AND US FOLK LIKE THOSE BATS, OUTSIDERS ALL...
WE ALL STARTED COMING HERE, LOOKING FOR A LITTLE COMFORT, SOME PEACE OF MIND.
AND THAT'S THE STORY OF KŌMORI-JUKU...
BUT THESE *TOBBICHO*. THEY'RE DIFFERENT. THEY'RE BEASTS *WITH* FANGS... AND YOU. YOU'RE A BIRD WITH *WINGS*...
....
WINGS AND FANGS LIKE THE POOR LITTLE BATS'LL NEVER HAVE...
WHAT DO YOU WANT TO SAY...?
YOU AREN'T AFRAID OF THE FANGS OF THESE BEASTS. NOT IN THE SLIGHTEST... WHICH MEANS YOU MUST HAVE WINGS TO FLY AWAY...

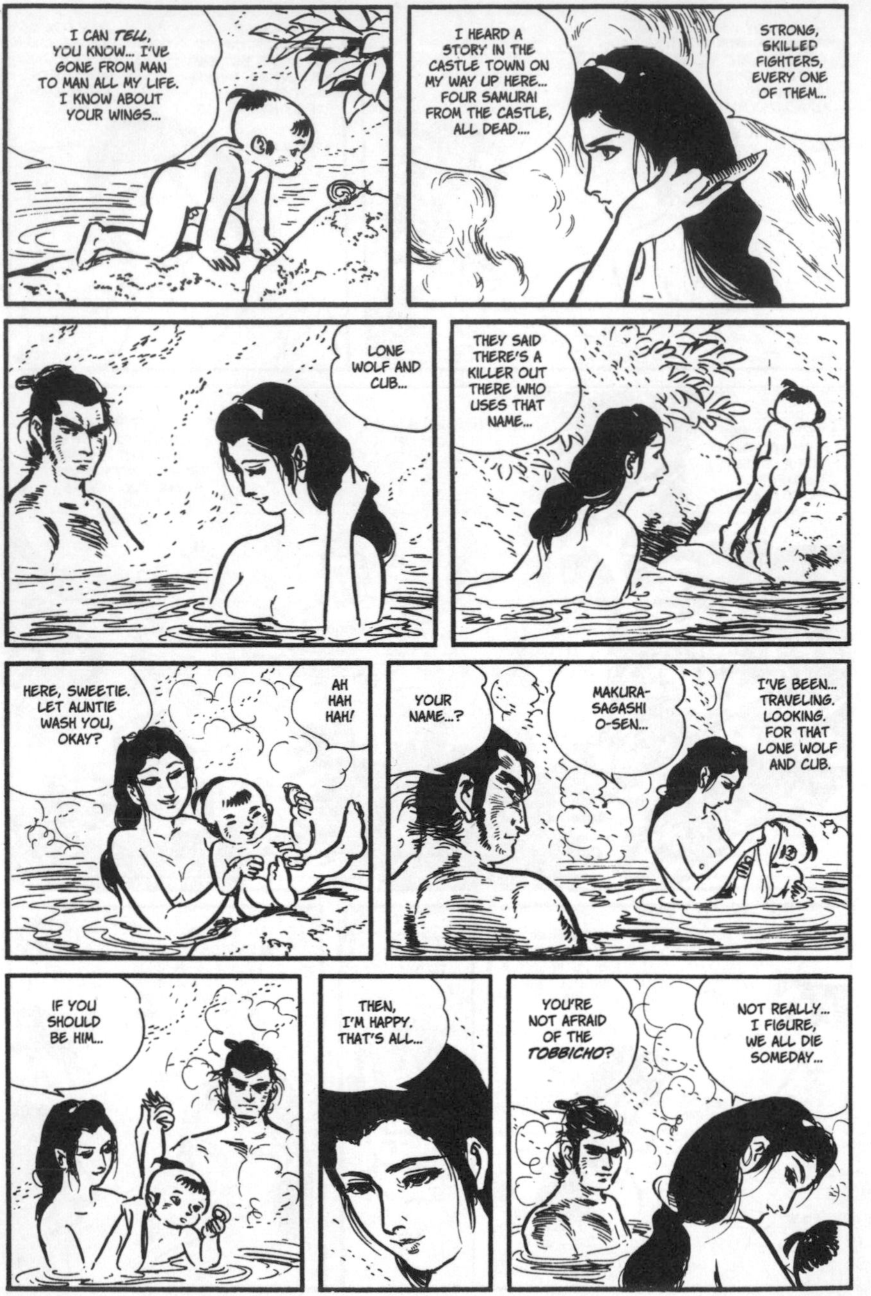
I CAN *TELL*, YOU KNOW... I'VE GONE FROM MAN TO MAN ALL MY LIFE. I KNOW ABOUT YOUR WINGS...
I HEARD A STORY IN THE CASTLE TOWN ON MY WAY UP HERE... FOUR SAMURAI FROM THE CASTLE, ALL DEAD....
STRONG, SKILLED FIGHTERS, EVERY ONE OF THEM...
LONE WOLF AND CUB...
THEY SAID THERE'S A KILLER OUT THERE WHO USES THAT NAME...
HERE, SWEETIE. LET AUNTIE WASH YOU, OKAY?
AH HAH HAH!
YOUR NAME...?
MAKURA-SAGASHI O-SEN...
I'VE BEEN... TRAVELING. LOOKING. FOR THAT LONE WOLF AND CUB.
IF YOU SHOULD BE HIM...
THEN, I'M HAPPY. THAT'S ALL...
YOU'RE NOT AFRAID OF THE *TOBBICHO*?
NOT REALLY... I FIGURE, WE ALL DIE SOMEDAY...

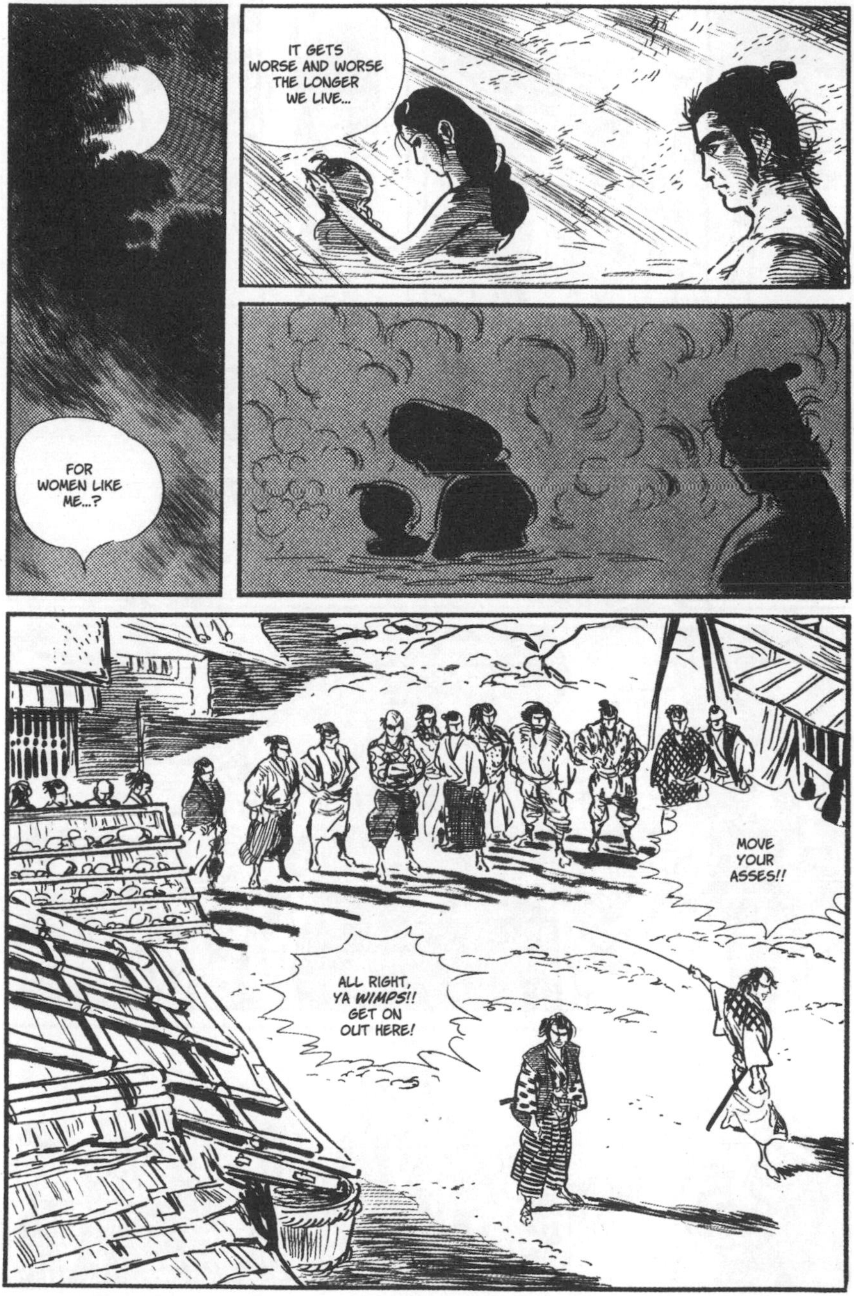
IT GETS WORSE AND WORSE THE LONGER WE LIVE...
FOR WOMEN LIKE ME...?
MOVE YOUR ASSES!!
ALL RIGHT, YA WIMPS!! GET ON OUT HERE!

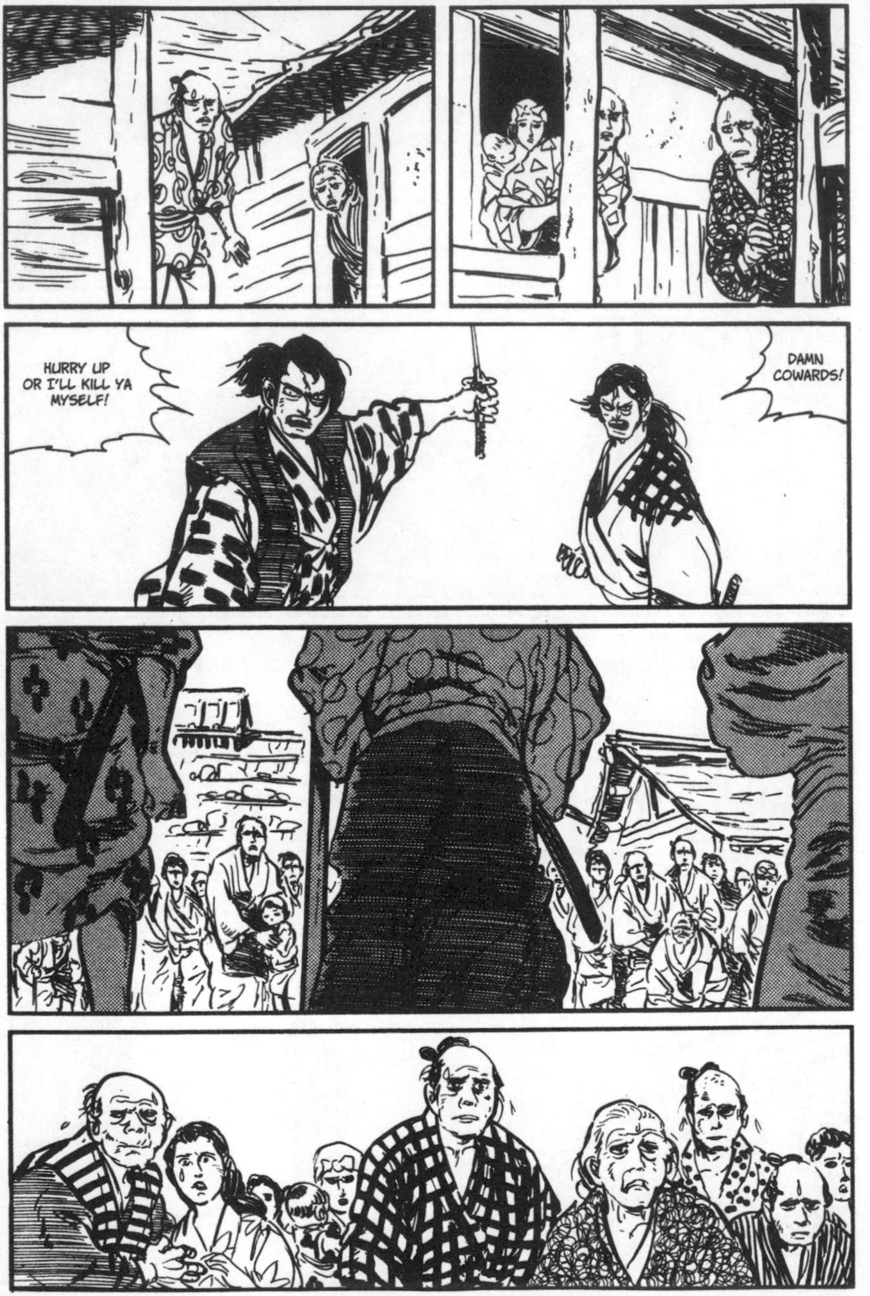
DAMN COWARDS!
HURRY UP OR I'LL KILL YA MYSELF!

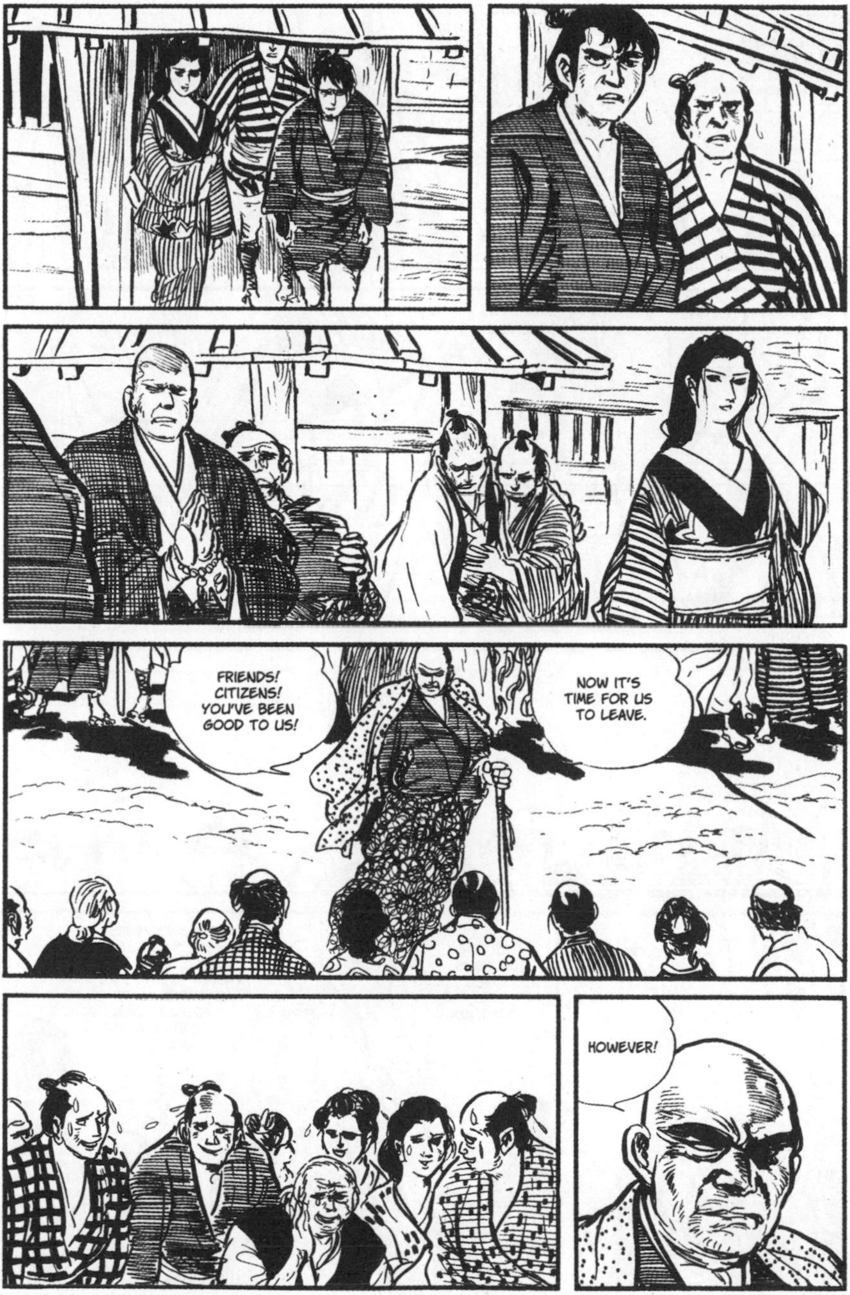
FRIENDS! CITIZENS! YOU'VE BEEN GOOD TO US!
NOW IT'S TIME FOR US TO LEAVE.
HOWEVER!

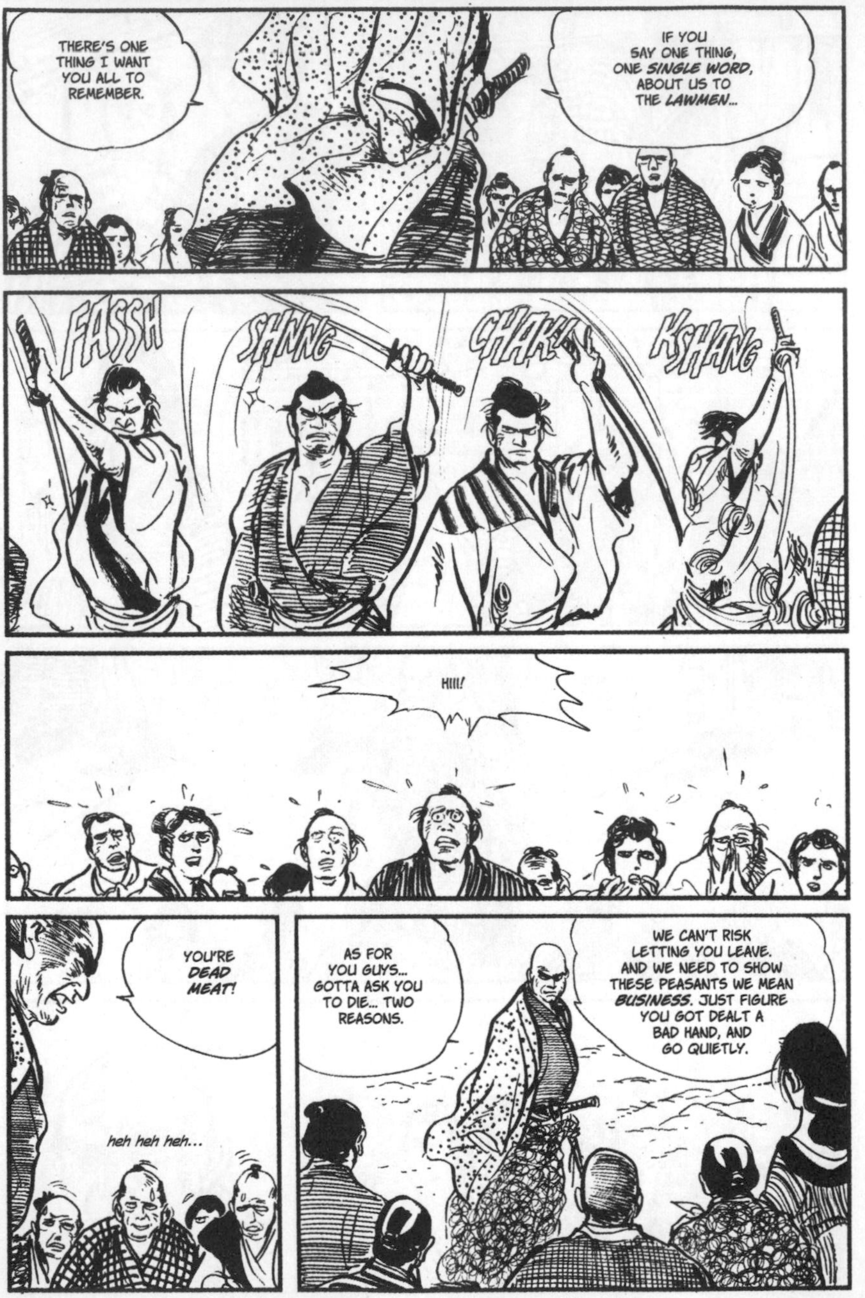
THERE'S ONE THING I WANT YOU ALL TO REMEMBER.
IF YOU SAY ONE THING, ONE *SINGLE WORD*, ABOUT US TO THE *LAWMEN*...
FASSH
SHING
CHAK!
KSHANG
HIII!
YOU'RE *DEAD MEAT!*
heh heh heh...
AS FOR YOU GUYS... GOTTA ASK YOU TO DIE... TWO REASONS.
WE CAN'T RISK LETTING YOU LEAVE. AND WE NEED TO SHOW THESE PEASANTS WE MEAN *BUSINESS*. JUST FIGURE YOU GOT DEALT A BAD HAND, AND GO QUIETLY.

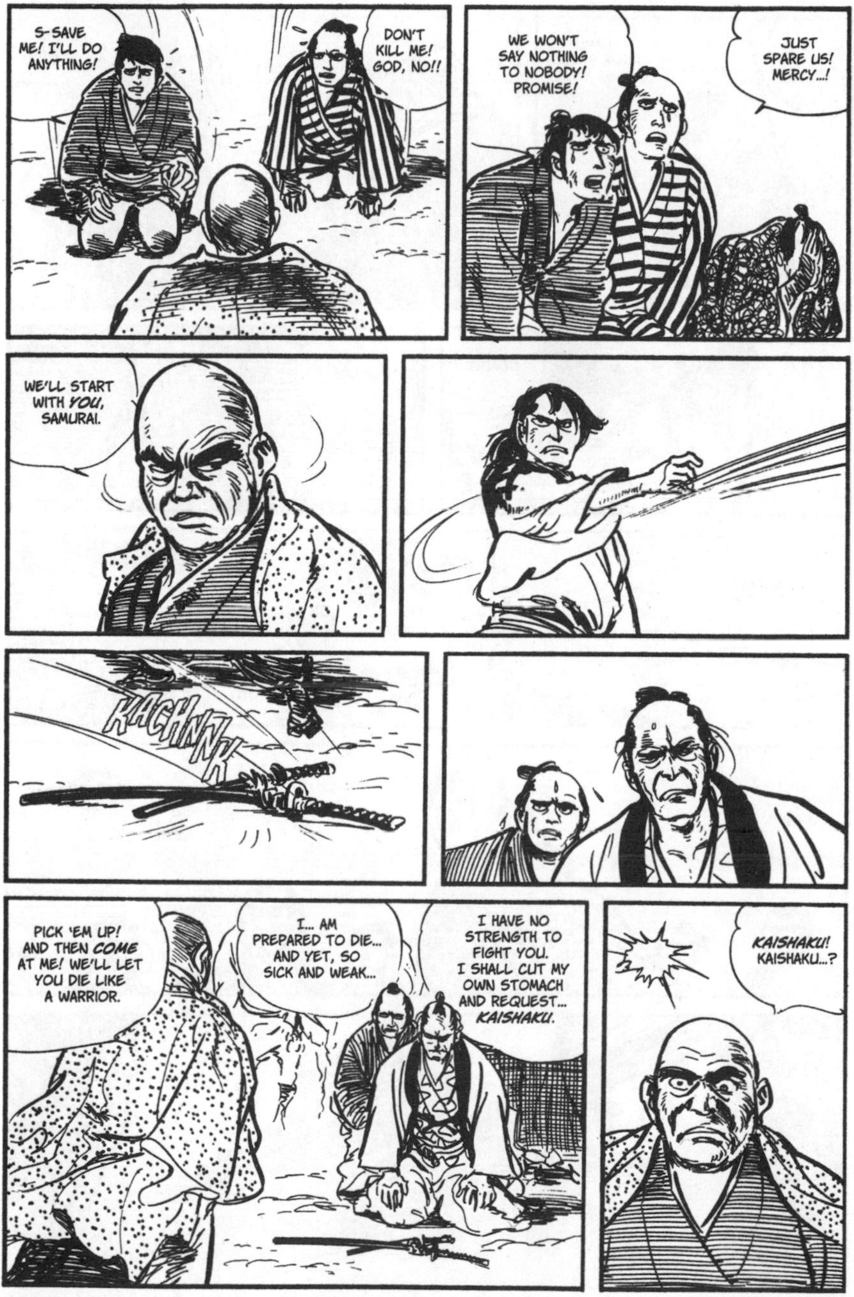
S-SAVE ME! I'LL DO ANYTHING!
DON'T KILL ME! GOD, NO!!
WE WON'T SAY NOTHING TO NOBODY! PROMISE!
JUST SPARE US! MERCY...!
WE'LL START WITH YOU, SAMURAI.
KACHNNNK
PICK 'EM UP! AND THEN COME AT ME! WE'LL LET YOU DIE LIKE A WARRIOR.
I... AM PREPARED TO DIE... AND YET, SO SICK AND WEAK...
I HAVE NO STRENGTH TO FIGHT YOU. I SHALL CUT MY OWN STOMACH AND REQUEST... KAISHAKU.
KAISHAKU! KAISHAKU...?

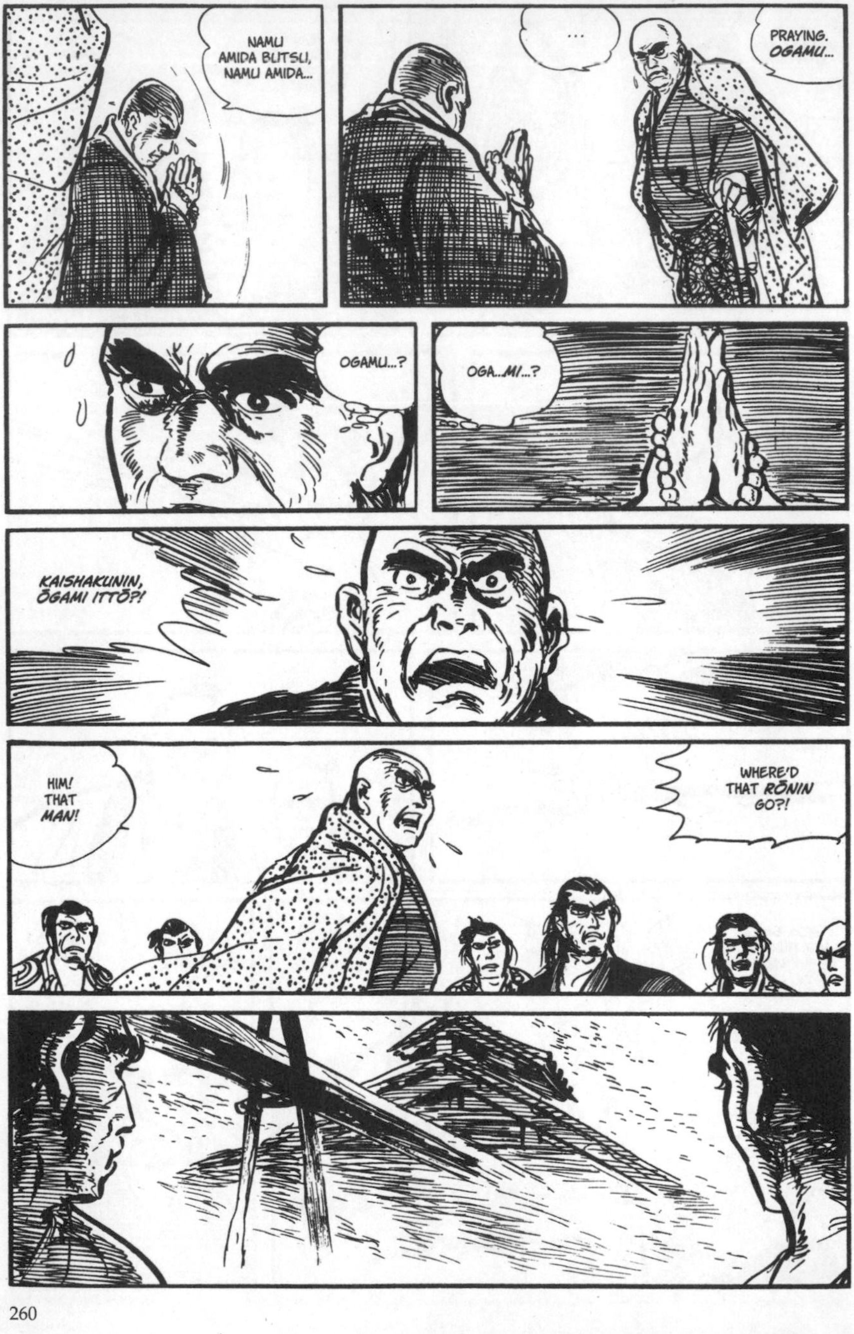
PRAYING. *OGAMU*...
...
NAMU AMIDA BUTSU, NAMU AMIDA...
OGA...*MI*...?
OGAMU...?
KAISHAKUNIN, ŌGAMI ITTŌ?!
WHERE'D THAT *RŌNIN* GO?!
HIM! THAT *MAN!*

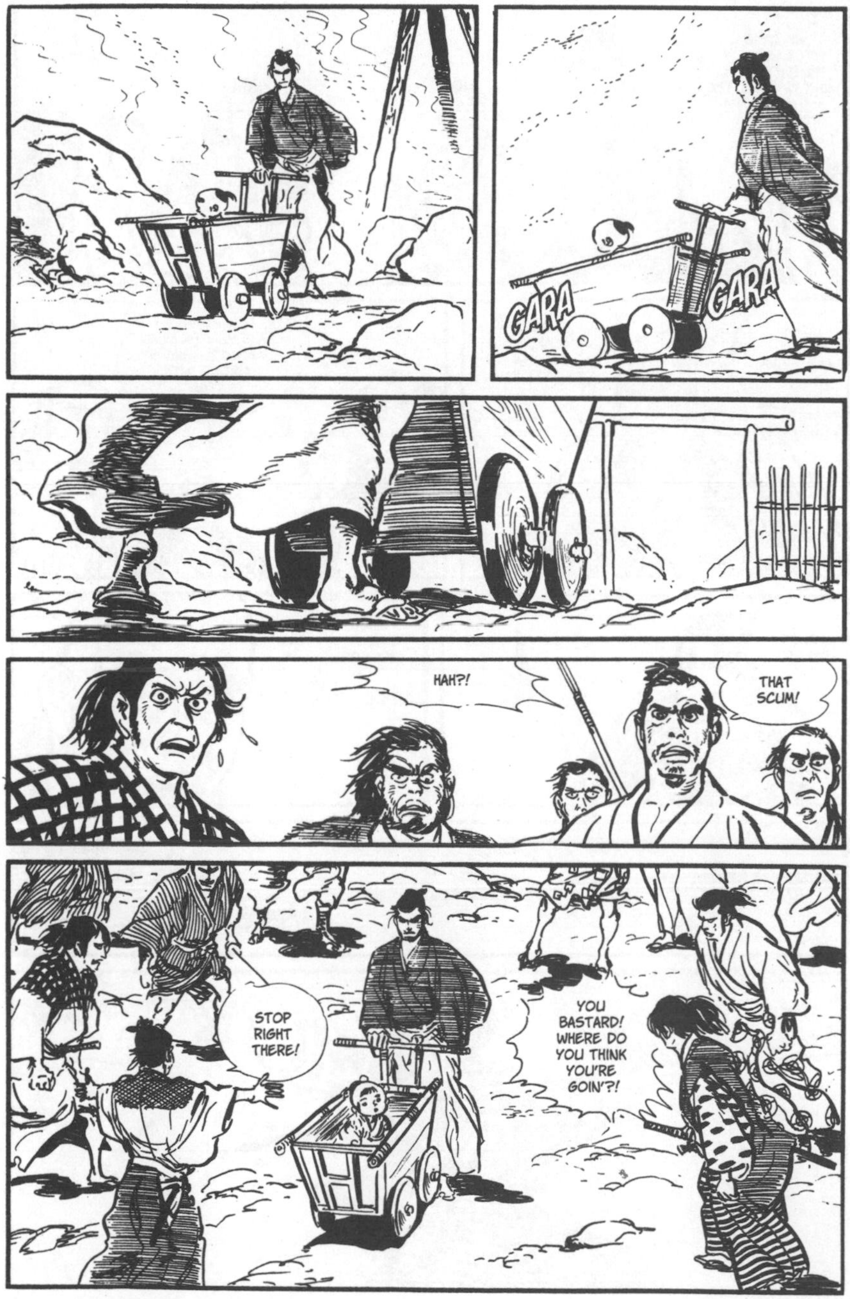
GARA GARA
THAT SCUM!
HAH?!
YOU BASTARD! WHERE DO YOU THINK YOU'RE GOIN'?!
STOP RIGHT THERE!

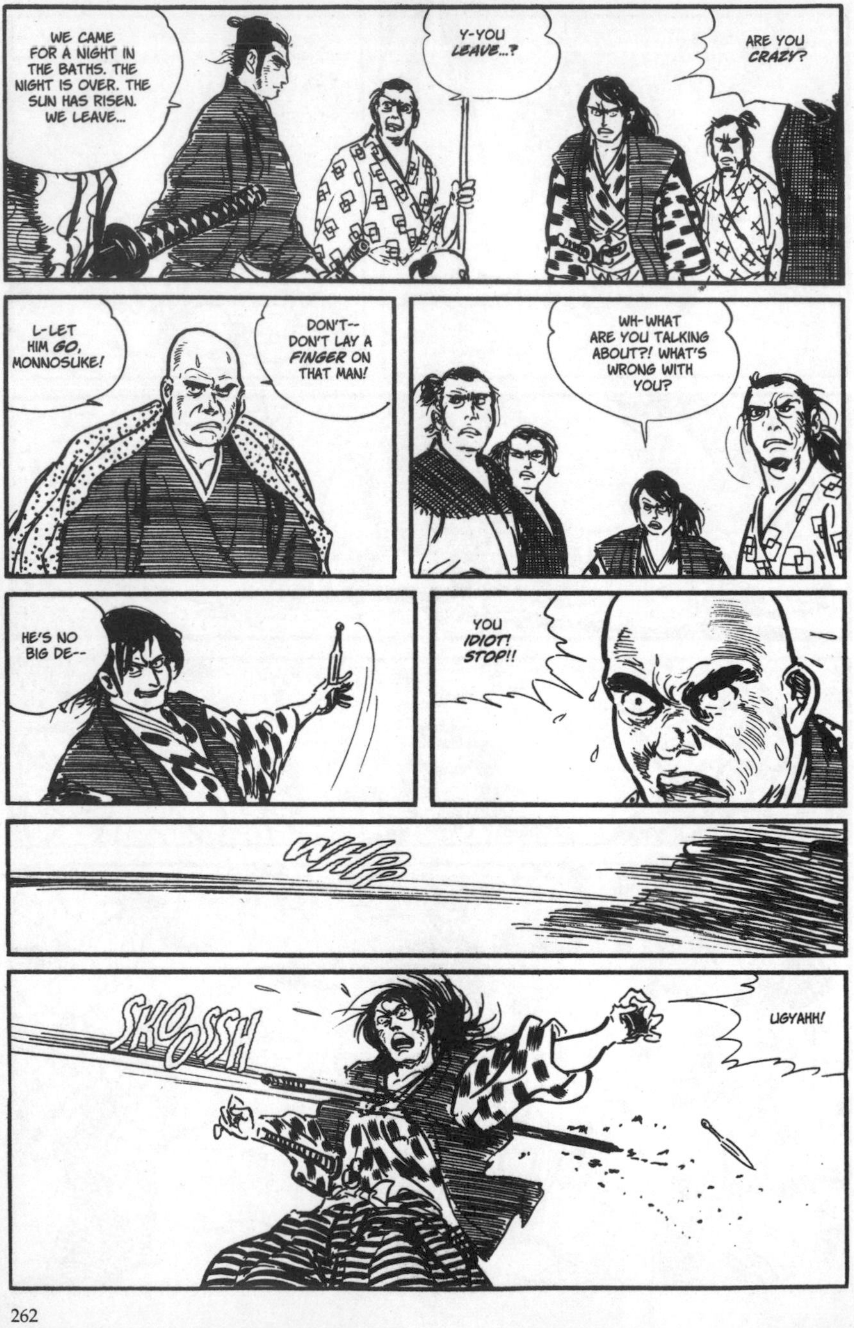
WE CAME FOR A NIGHT IN THE BATHS. THE NIGHT IS OVER. THE SUN HAS RISEN. WE LEAVE...
Y-YOU LEAVE...?
ARE YOU CRAZY?
L-LET HIM GO, MONNOSUKE!
DON'T-- DON'T LAY A FINGER ON THAT MAN!
WH- WHAT ARE YOU TALKING ABOUT?! WHAT'S WRONG WITH YOU?
HE'S NO BIG DE--
YOU IDIOT! STOP!!
WHIP
SKOOSSH
UGYAHH!

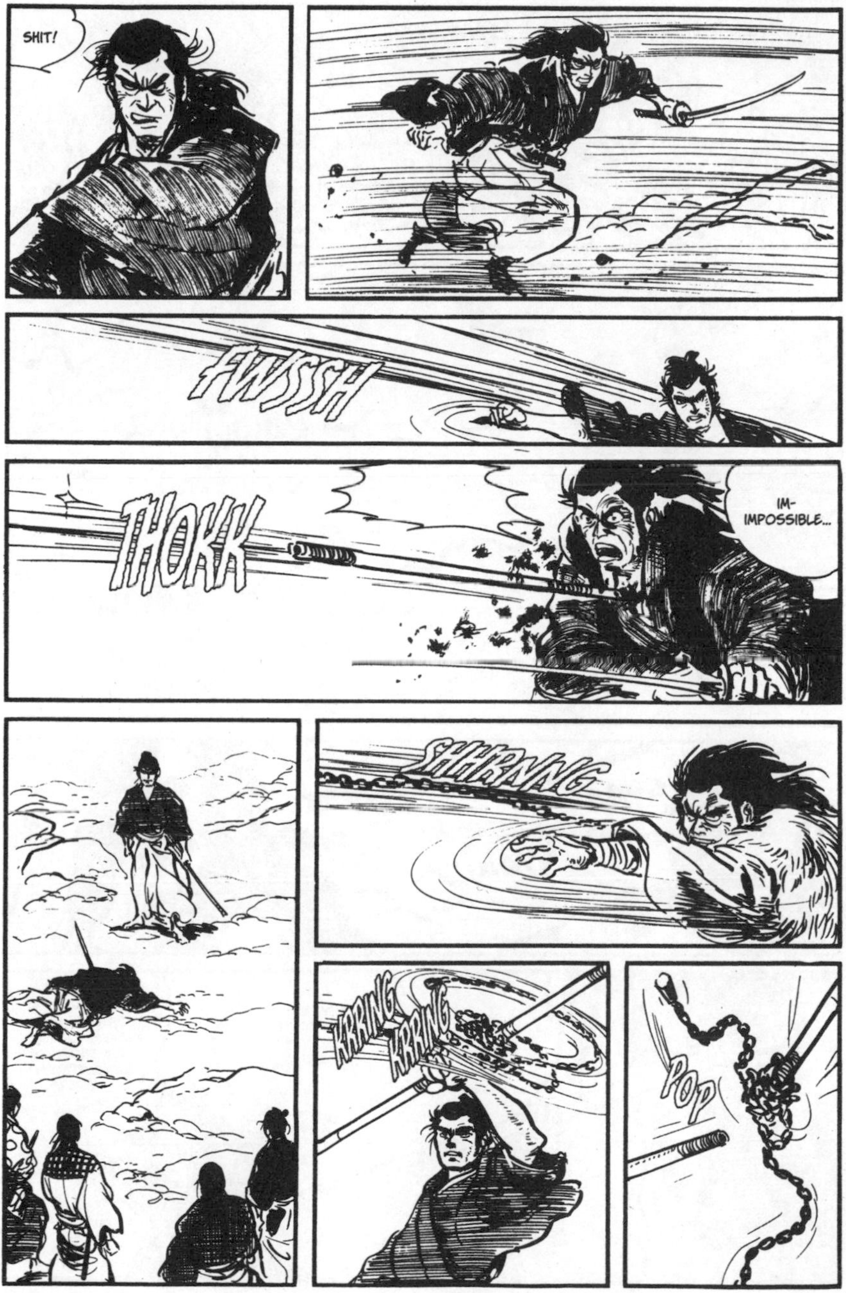
SHIT!
FWSSH
THOKK
IM-
IMPOSSIBLE...
SHHRNNG
POP
KRRING
KRRING

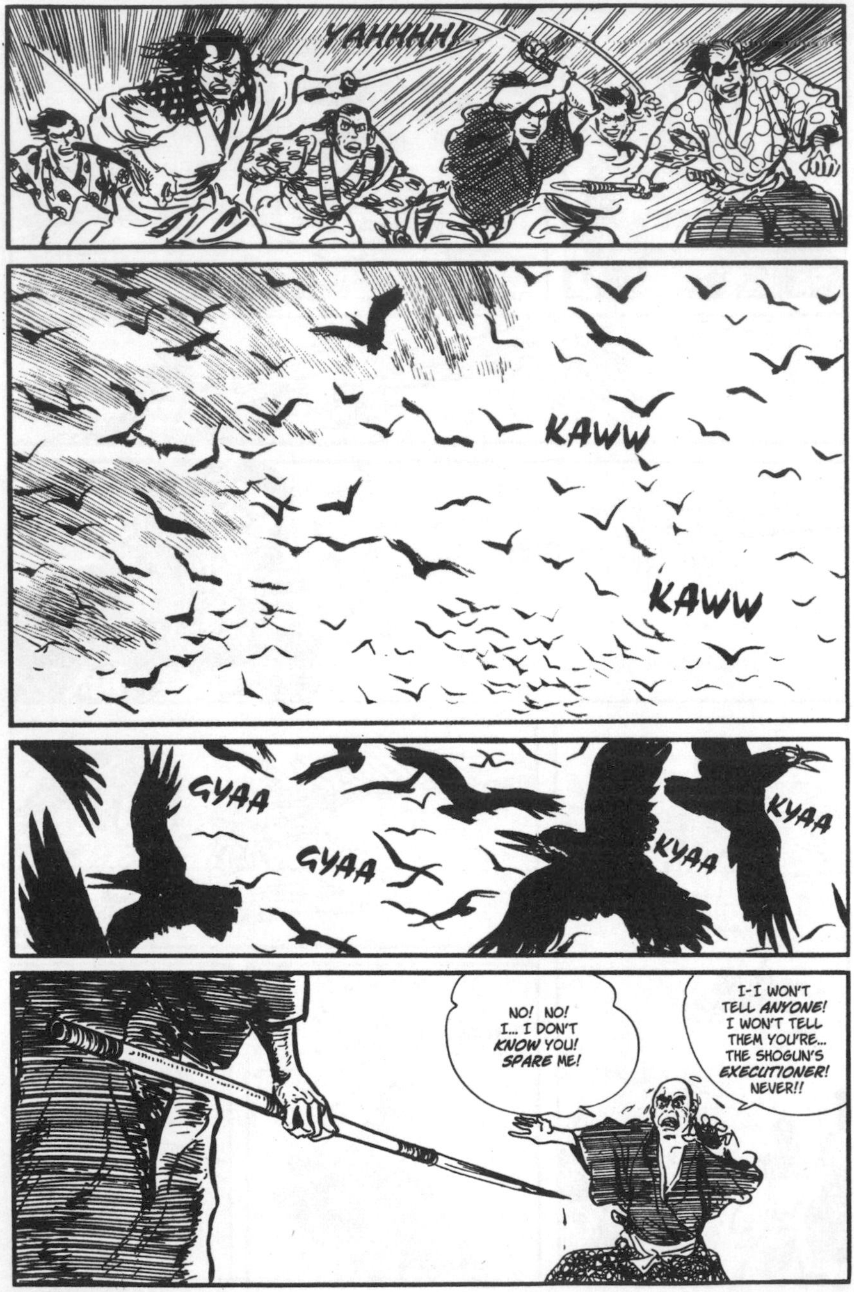

YAHHHH!
KAWW
KAWW
GYAA
GYAA
KYAA
KYAA
NO! NO! I... I DON'T *KNOW* YOU! *SPARE* ME!
I-I WON'T TELL *ANYONE!* I WON'T TELL THEM YOU'RE... THE SHOGUN'S *EXECUTIONER!* NEVER!!

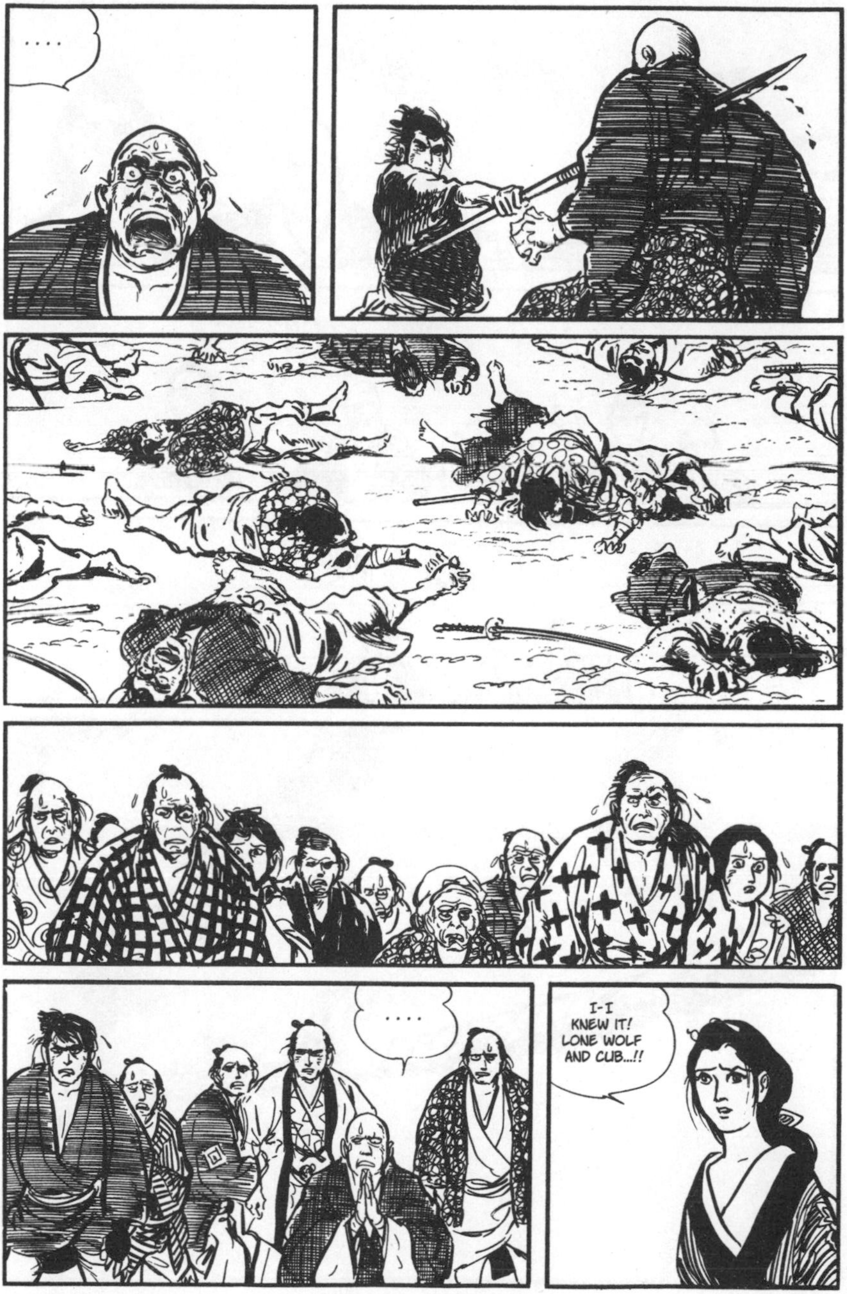
....
I-I KNEW IT! LONE WOLF AND CUB...!!
....

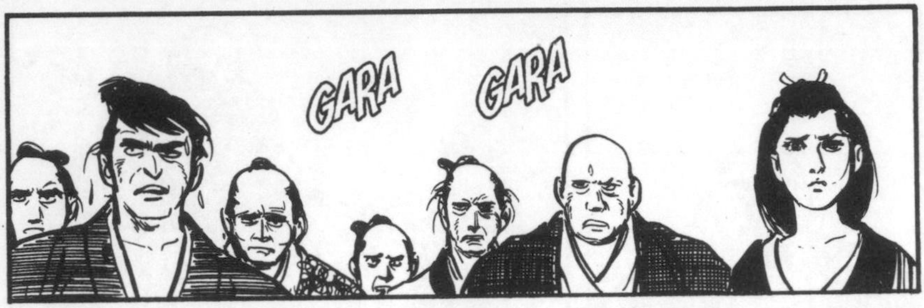
GARA GARA

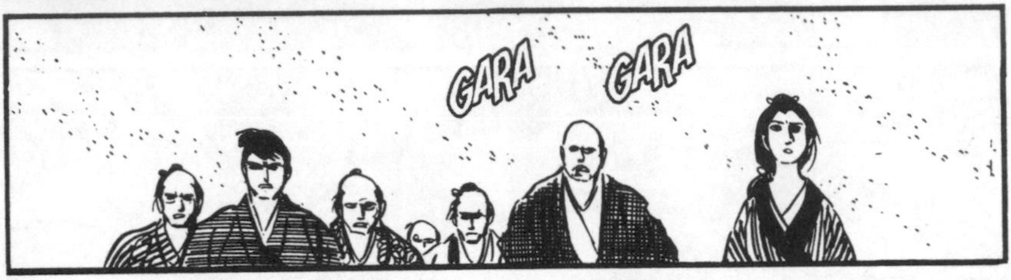
GARA GARA

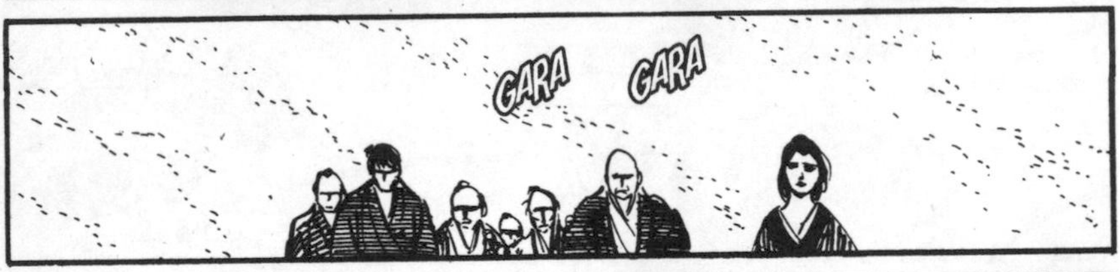
GARA GARA

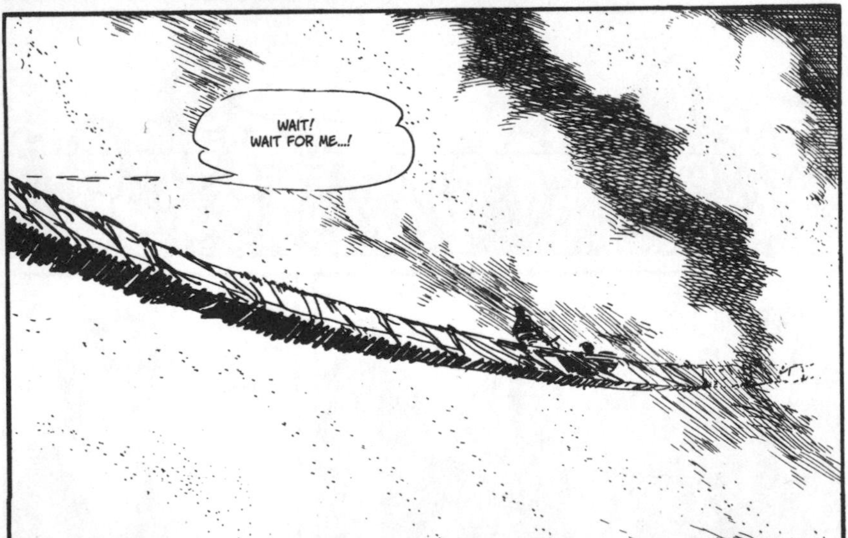
WAIT! WAIT FOR ME...!

子連れ狼

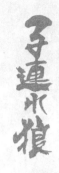

The Assassin's Road

9

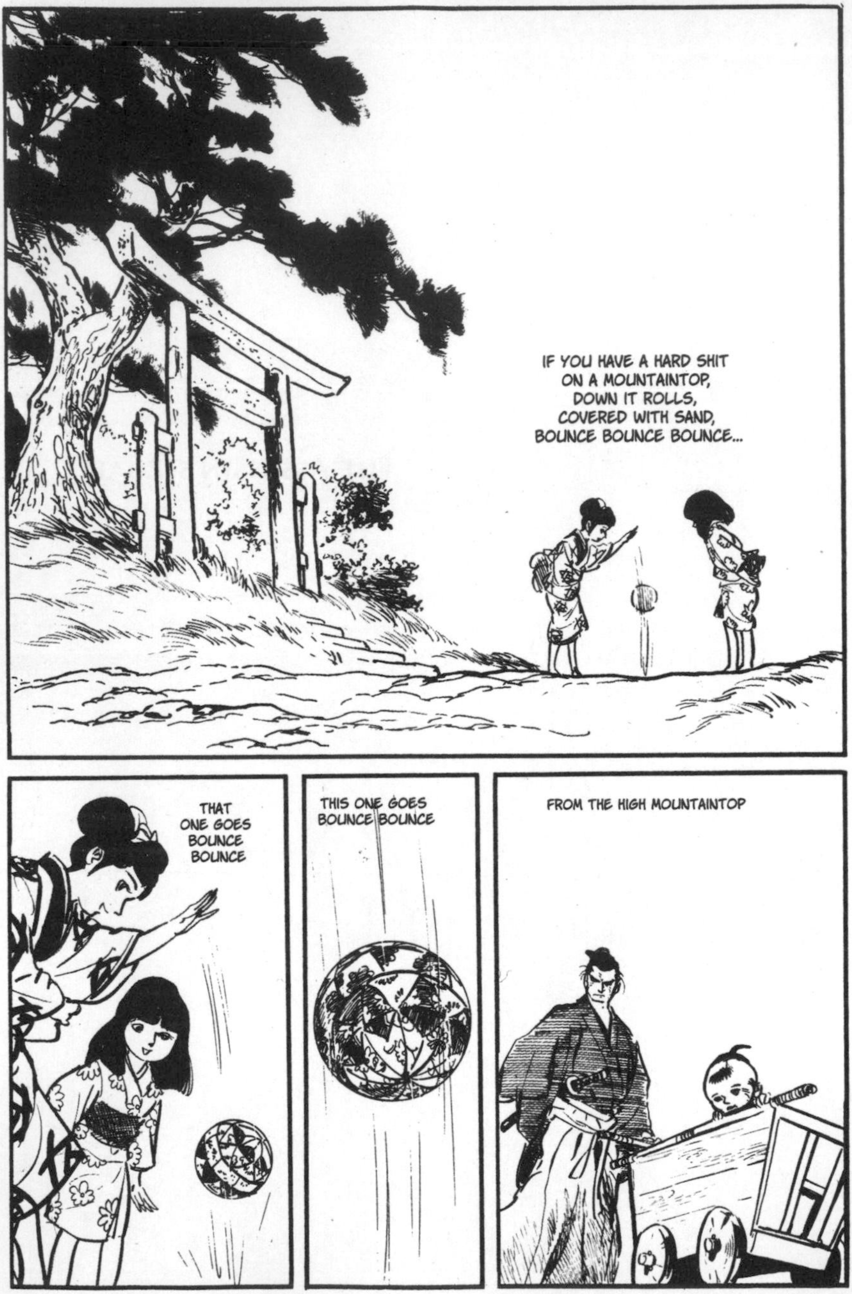
IF YOU HAVE A HARD SHIT ON A MOUNTAINTOP, DOWN IT ROLLS, COVERED WITH SAND, BOUNCE BOUNCE BOUNCE...
FROM THE HIGH MOUNTAINTOP
THIS ONE GOES BOUNCE BOUNCE
THAT ONE GOES BOUNCE BOUNCE

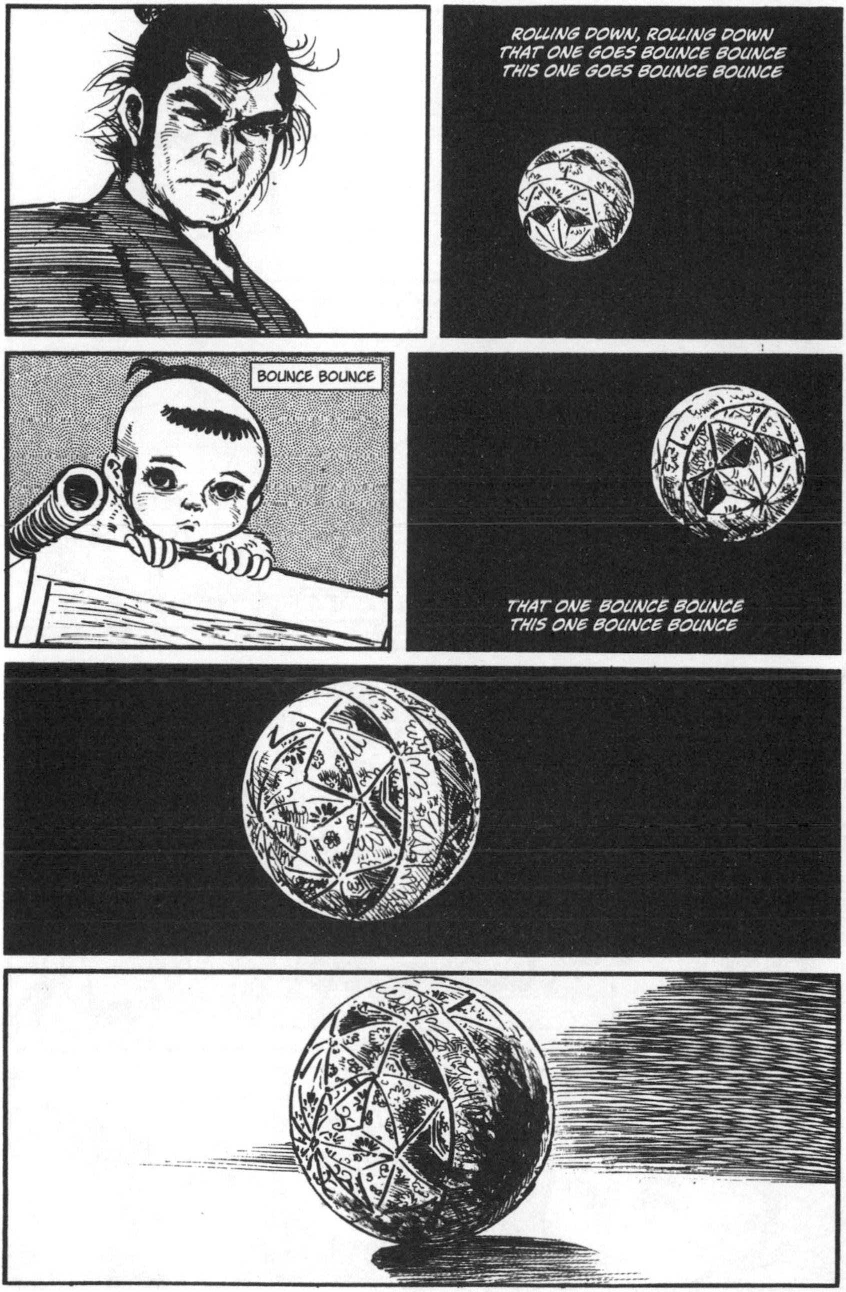
ROLLING DOWN, ROLLING DOWN
THAT ONE GOES BOUNCE BOUNCE
THIS ONE GOES BOUNCE BOUNCE
BOUNCE BOUNCE
THAT ONE BOUNCE BOUNCE
THIS ONE BOUNCE BOUNCE

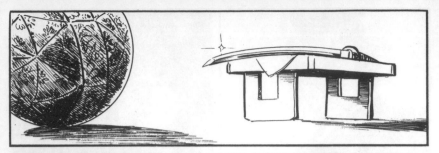

DAIGORO...

THE *KENSHIYAKU* WILL SOON BE HERE... BUT YOUR FATHER IS RESOLVED TO DEFY THE SHOGUN AND *ESCAPE*.

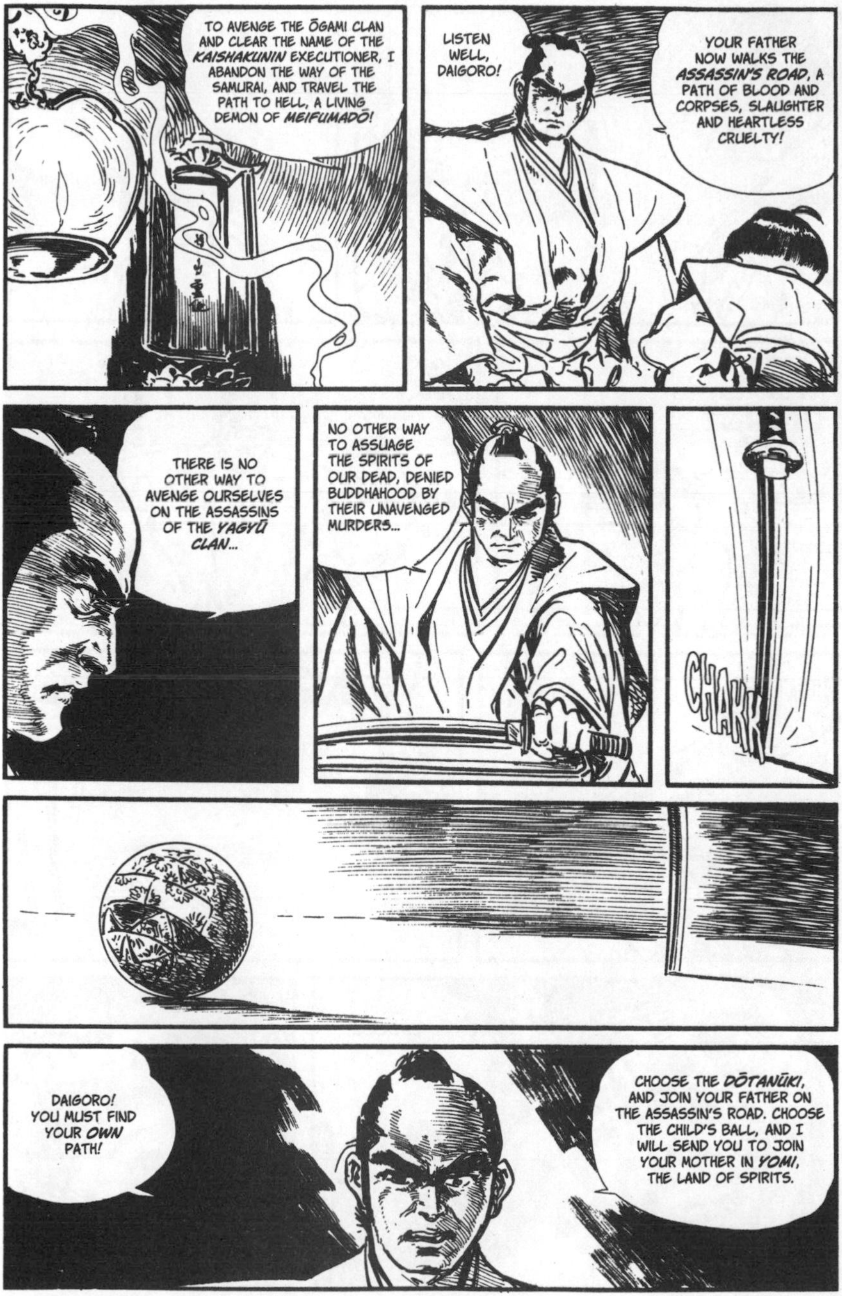
TO AVENGE THE ŌGAMI CLAN AND CLEAR THE NAME OF THE *KAISHAKUNIN* EXECUTIONER, I ABANDON THE WAY OF THE SAMURAI, AND TRAVEL THE PATH TO HELL, A LIVING DEMON OF *MEIFUMADŌ*!
LISTEN WELL, DAIGORO!
YOUR FATHER NOW WALKS THE *ASSASSIN'S ROAD*, A PATH OF BLOOD AND CORPSES, SLAUGHTER AND HEARTLESS CRUELTY!
THERE IS NO OTHER WAY TO AVENGE OURSELVES ON THE ASSASSINS OF THE *YAGYŪ CLAN*...
NO OTHER WAY TO ASSUAGE THE SPIRITS OF OUR DEAD, DENIED BUDDHAHOOD BY THEIR UNAVENGED MURDERS...
CHAKK
DAIGORO! YOU MUST FIND YOUR *OWN* PATH!
CHOOSE THE *DŌTANŪKI*, AND JOIN YOUR FATHER ON THE ASSASSIN'S ROAD. CHOOSE THE CHILD'S BALL, AND I WILL SEND YOU TO JOIN YOUR MOTHER IN *YOMI*, THE LAND OF SPIRITS.

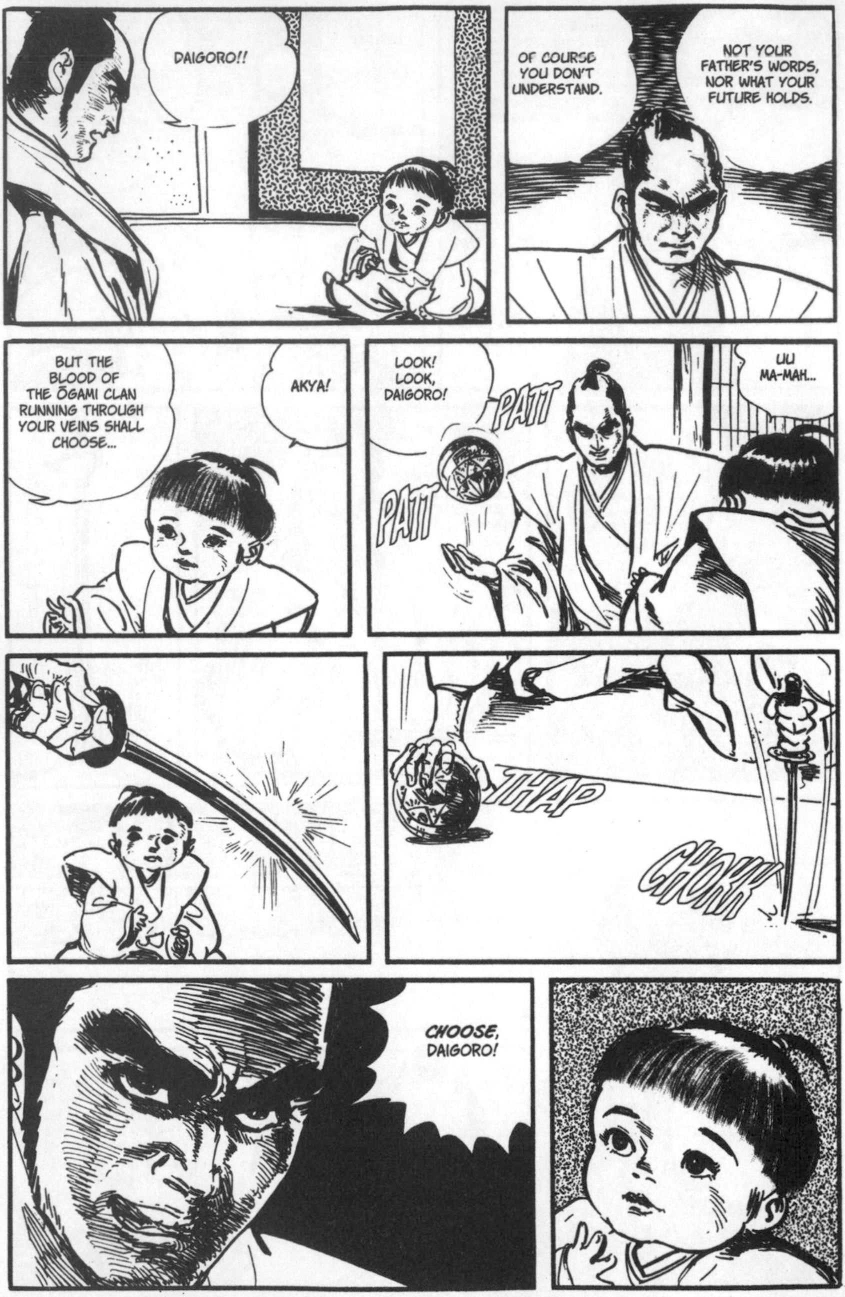
DAIGORO!!
OF COURSE YOU DON'T UNDERSTAND.
NOT YOUR FATHER'S WORDS, NOR WHAT YOUR FUTURE HOLDS.
BUT THE BLOOD OF THE ŌGAMI CLAN RUNNING THROUGH YOUR VEINS SHALL CHOOSE...
AKYA!
LOOK! LOOK, DAIGORO!
PATT
PATT
UU MA-MAH...
THAP
CHOKK
CHOOSE, DAIGORO!

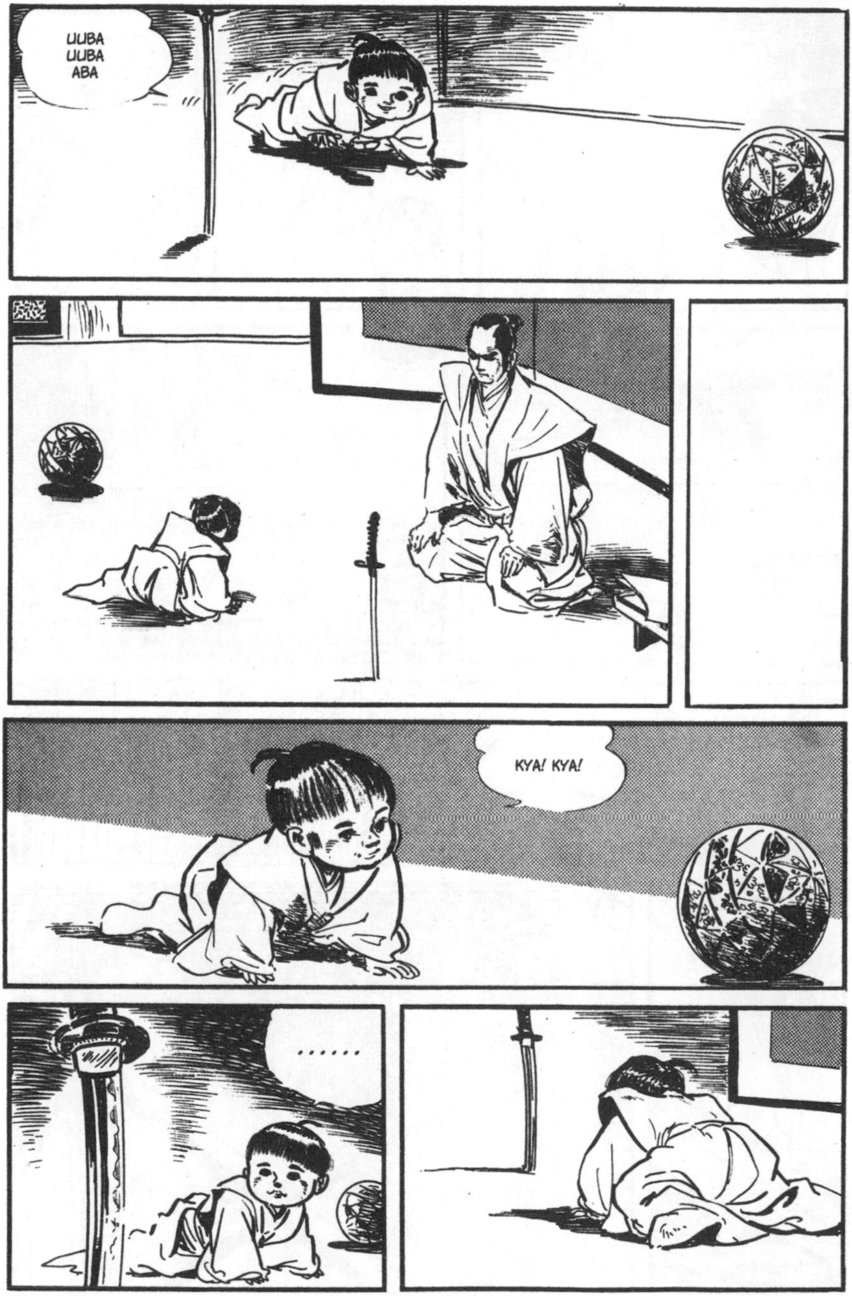
UUBA
UUBA
ABA
KYA! KYA!
......

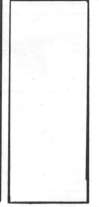

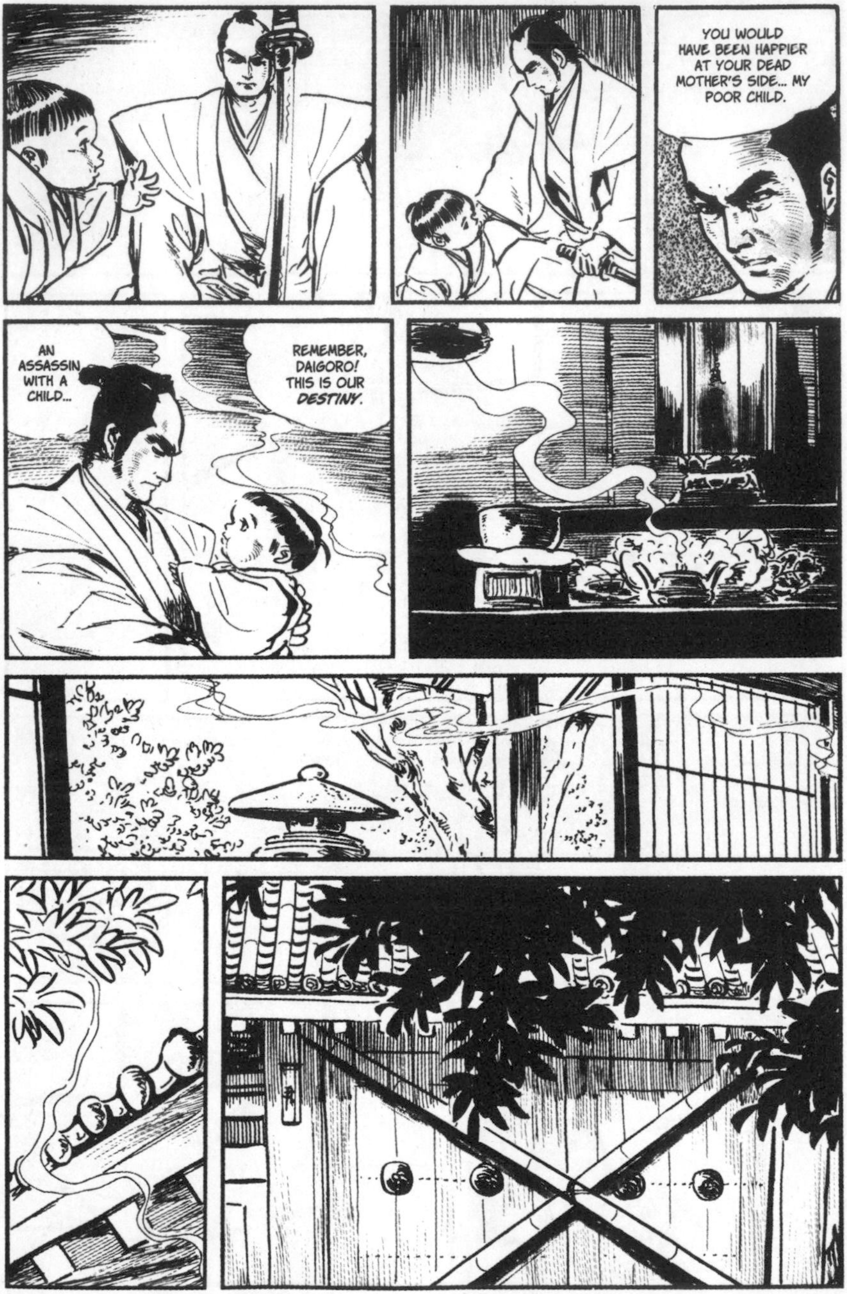
YOU WOULD HAVE BEEN HAPPIER AT YOUR DEAD MOTHER'S SIDE... MY POOR CHILD.
AN ASSASSIN WITH A CHILD...
REMEMBER, DAIGORO! THIS IS OUR *DESTINY*.

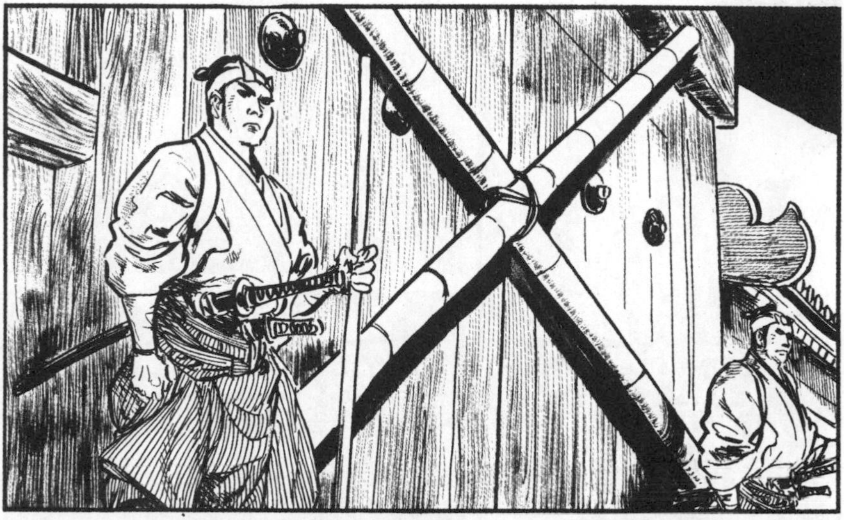

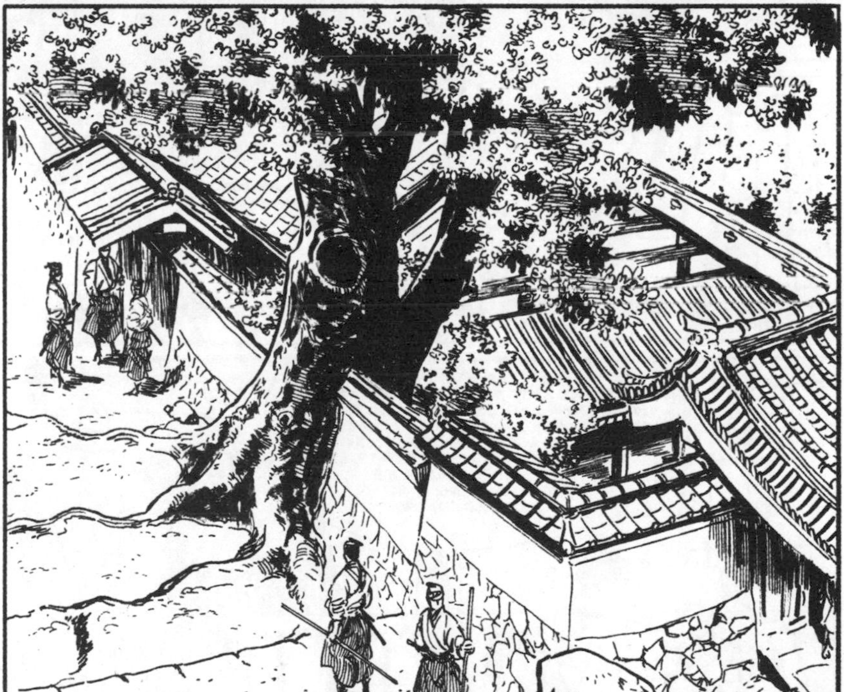

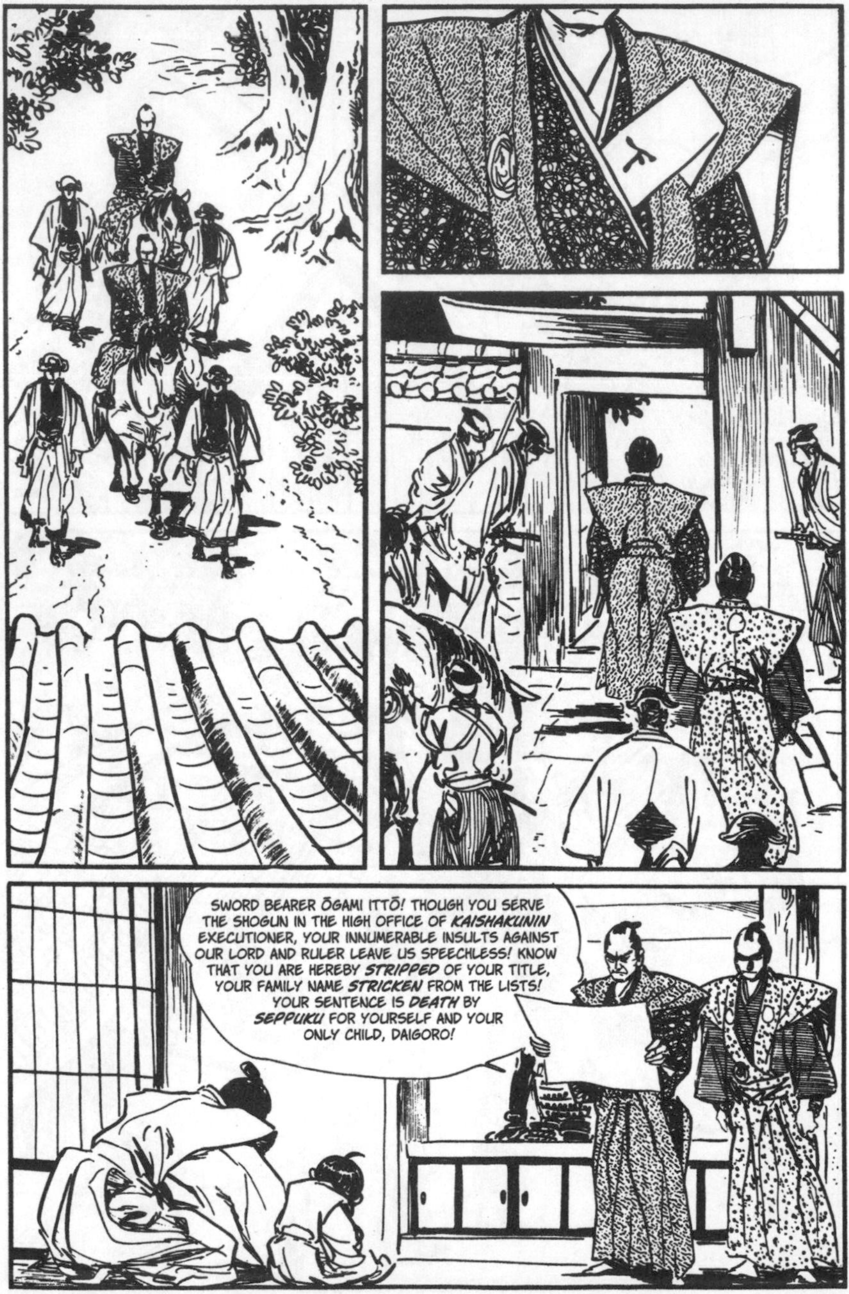
SWORD BEARER ŌGAMI ITTŌ! THOUGH YOU SERVE THE SHOGUN IN THE HIGH OFFICE OF *KAISHAKUNIN* EXECUTIONER, YOUR INNUMERABLE INSULTS AGAINST OUR LORD AND RULER LEAVE US SPEECHLESS! KNOW THAT YOU ARE HEREBY *STRIPPED* OF YOUR TITLE, YOUR FAMILY NAME *STRICKEN* FROM THE LISTS! YOUR SENTENCE IS *DEATH* BY *SEPPUKU* FOR YOURSELF AND YOUR ONLY CHILD, DAIGORO!

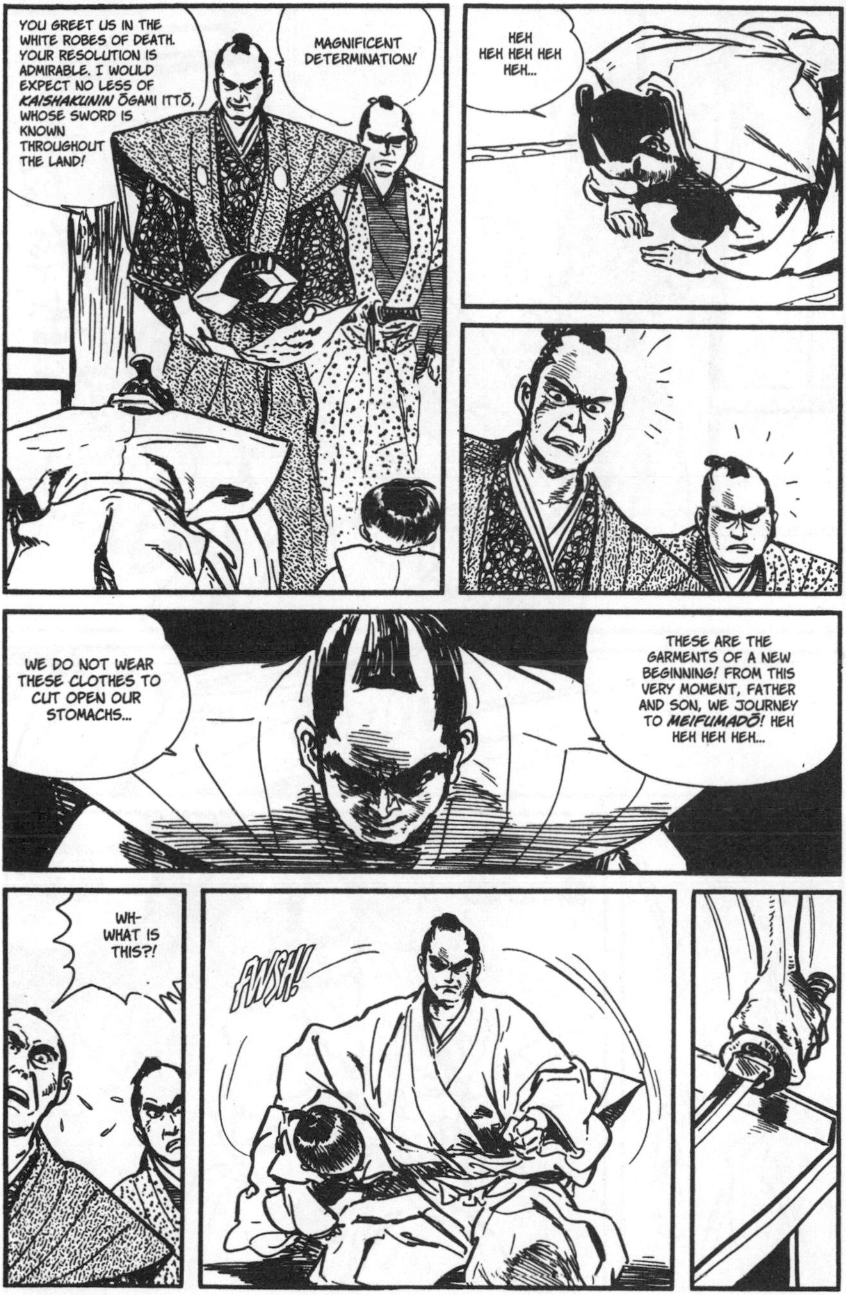
YOU GREET US IN THE WHITE ROBES OF DEATH. YOUR RESOLUTION IS ADMIRABLE. I WOULD EXPECT NO LESS OF *KAISHAKUNIN* ŌGAMI ITTŌ, WHOSE SWORD IS KNOWN THROUGHOUT THE LAND!
MAGNIFICENT DETERMINATION!
HEH HEH HEH HEH HEH...
WE DO NOT WEAR THESE CLOTHES TO CUT OPEN OUR STOMACHS...
THESE ARE THE GARMENTS OF A NEW BEGINNING! FROM THIS VERY MOMENT, FATHER AND SON, WE JOURNEY TO *MEIFUMADŌ*! HEH HEH HEH HEH...
WH- WHAT IS THIS?!
FWSH!

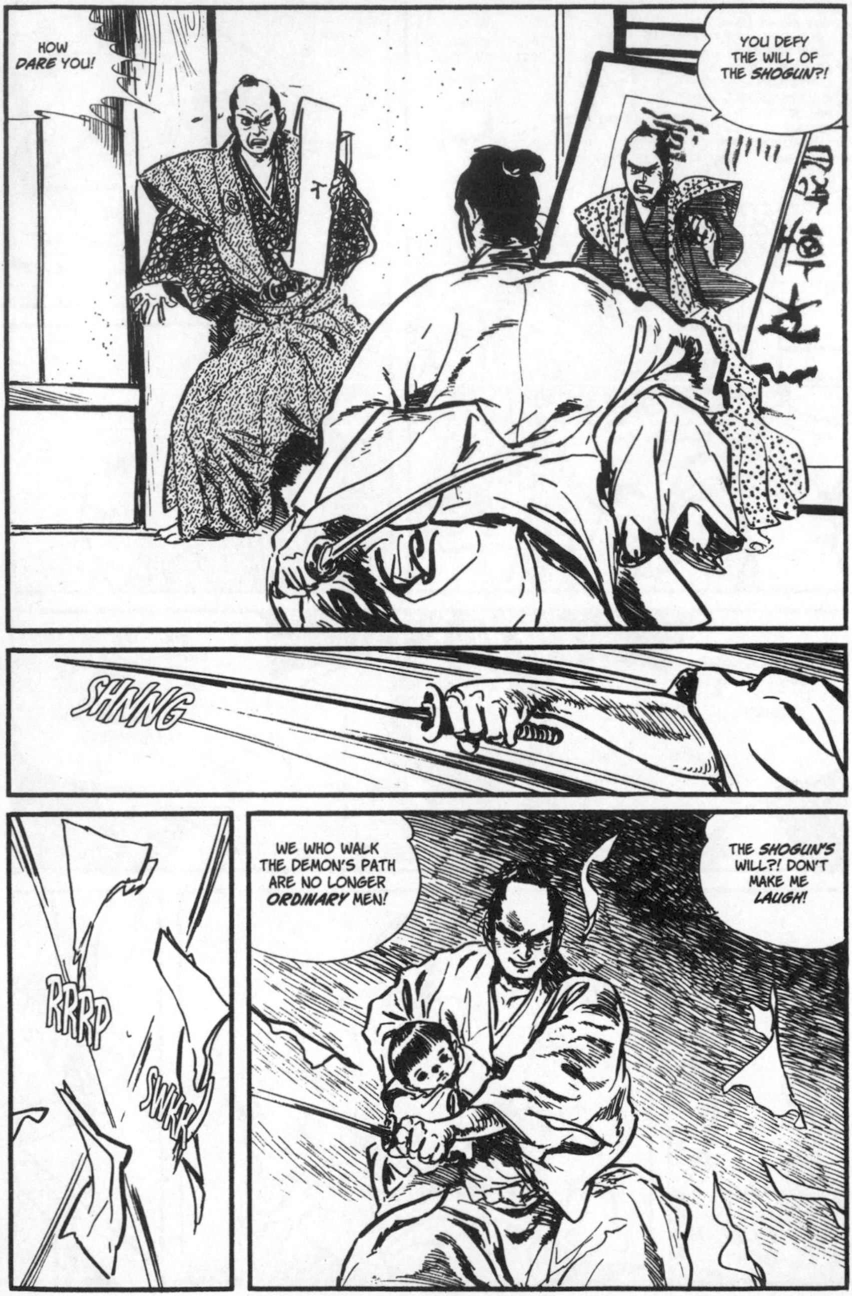
YOU DEFY THE WILL OF THE *SHOGUN*?!
HOW *DARE* YOU!
SHNNG
THE *SHOGUN'S* WILL?! DON'T MAKE ME *LAUGH!*
WE WHO WALK THE DEMON'S PATH ARE NO LONGER *ORDINARY* MEN!
RRRP
SWKK

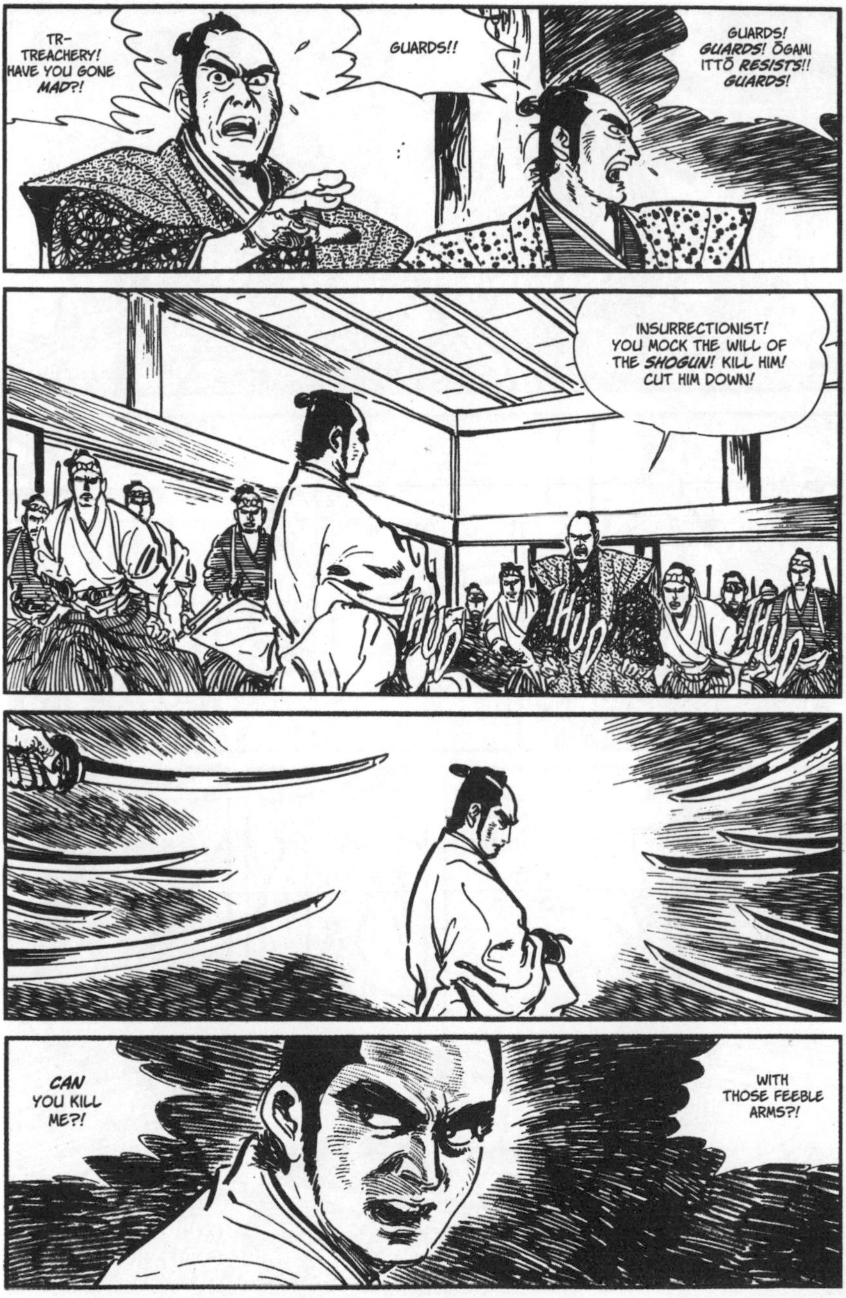
TR-TREACHERY! HAVE YOU GONE MAD?!
GUARDS!!
GUARDS! GUARDS! ŌGAMI ITTŌ RESISTS!! GUARDS!
INSURRECTIONIST! YOU MOCK THE WILL OF THE SHOGUN! KILL HIM! CUT HIM DOWN!
HUP
HUP
HUP
CAN YOU KILL ME?!
WITH THOSE FEEBLE ARMS?!

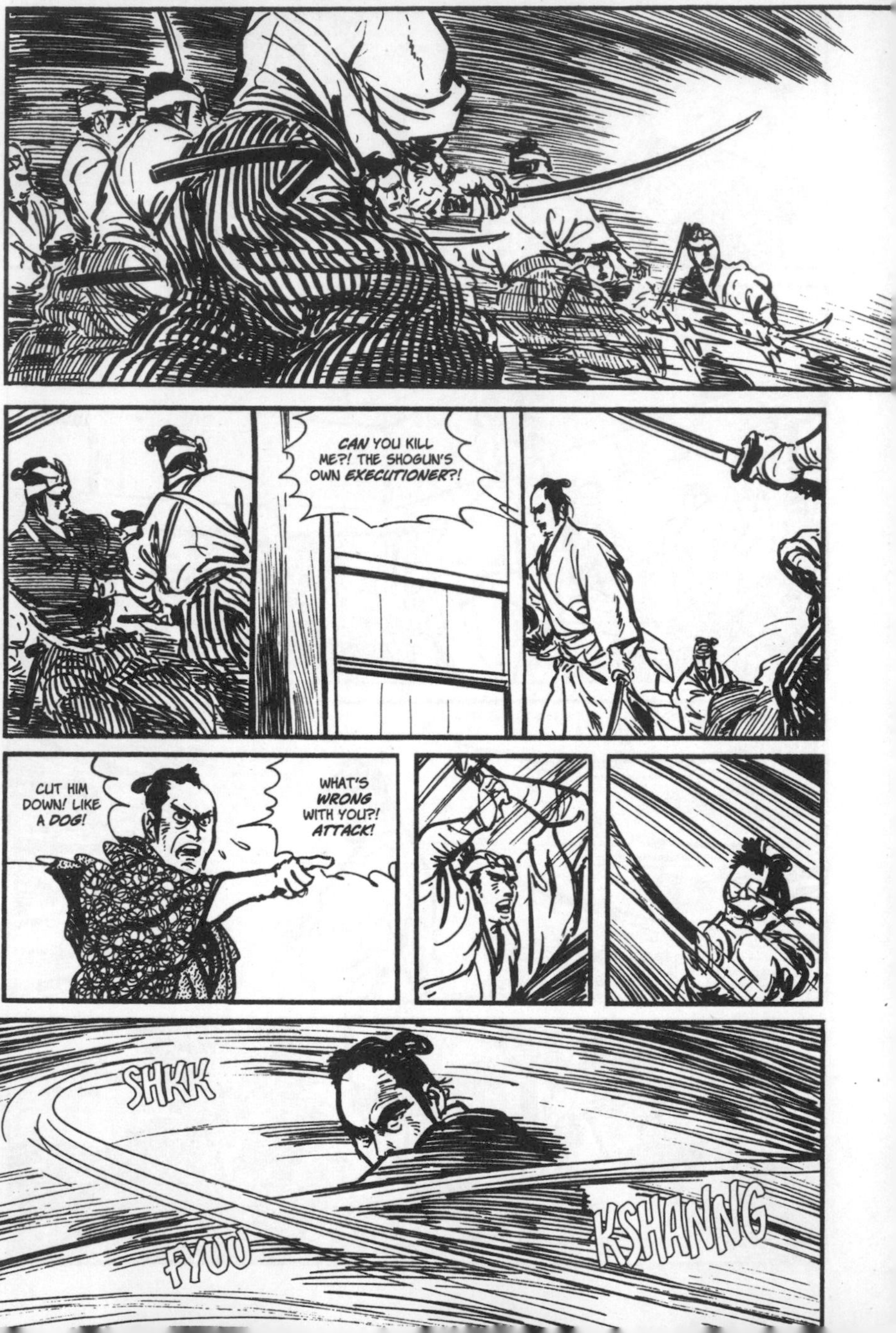
CAN YOU KILL ME?! THE SHOGUN'S OWN EXECUTIONER?!
CUT HIM DOWN! LIKE A DOG!
WHAT'S WRONG WITH YOU?! ATTACK!
SHKK
FYUU
KSHANNG

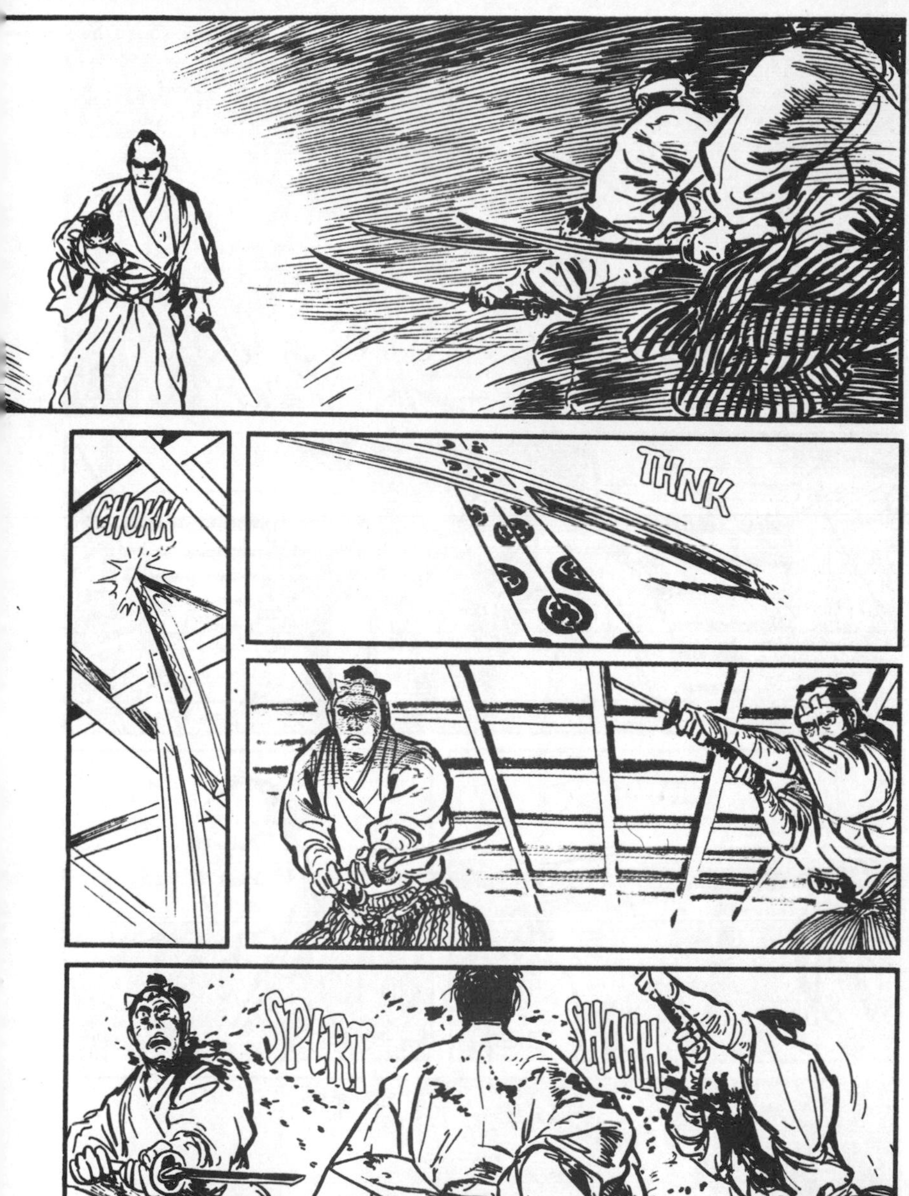
THNK
CHOKK
SHAHH
SPLRT

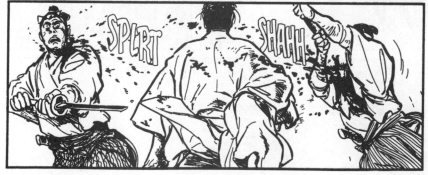

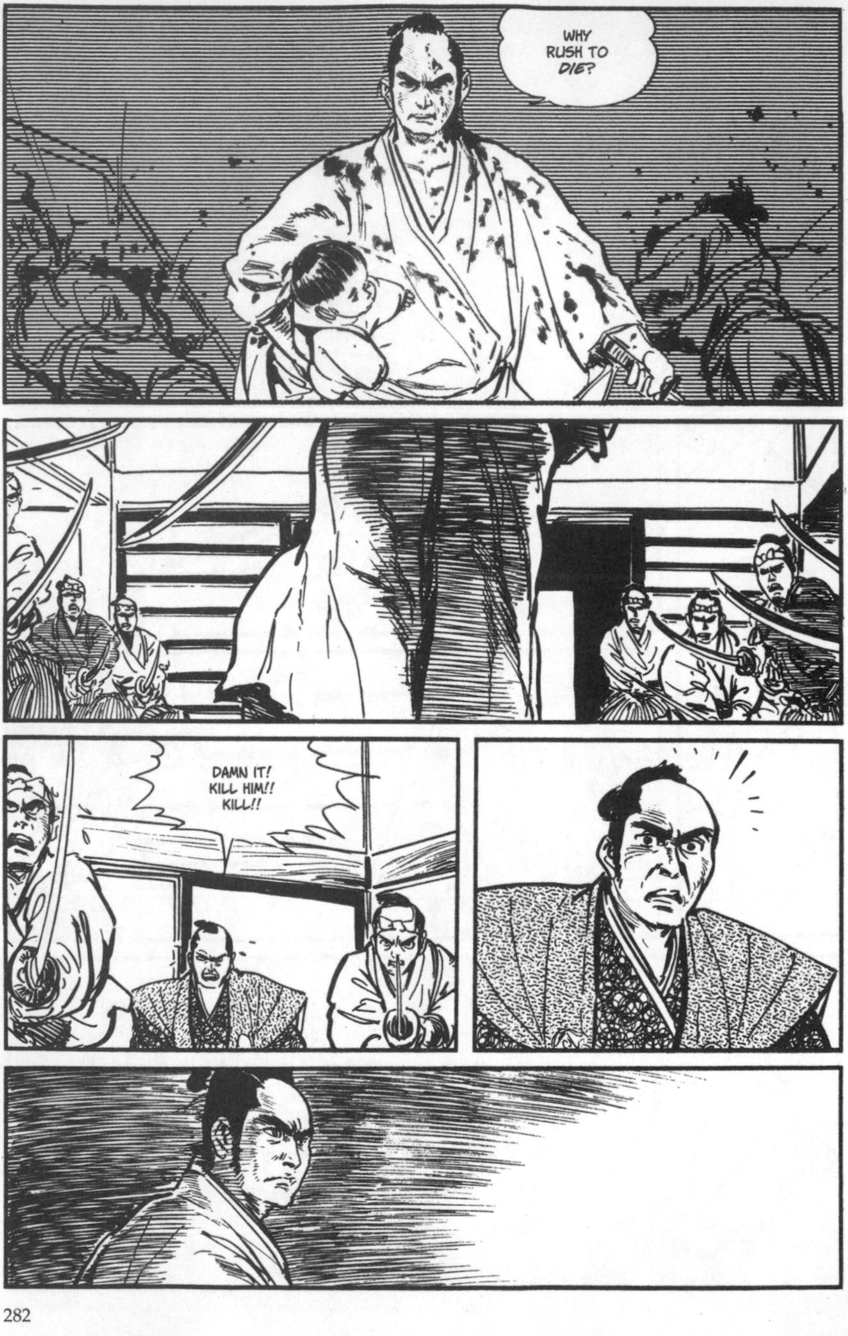
WHY RUSH TO DIE?
DAMN IT! KILL HIM!! KILL!!

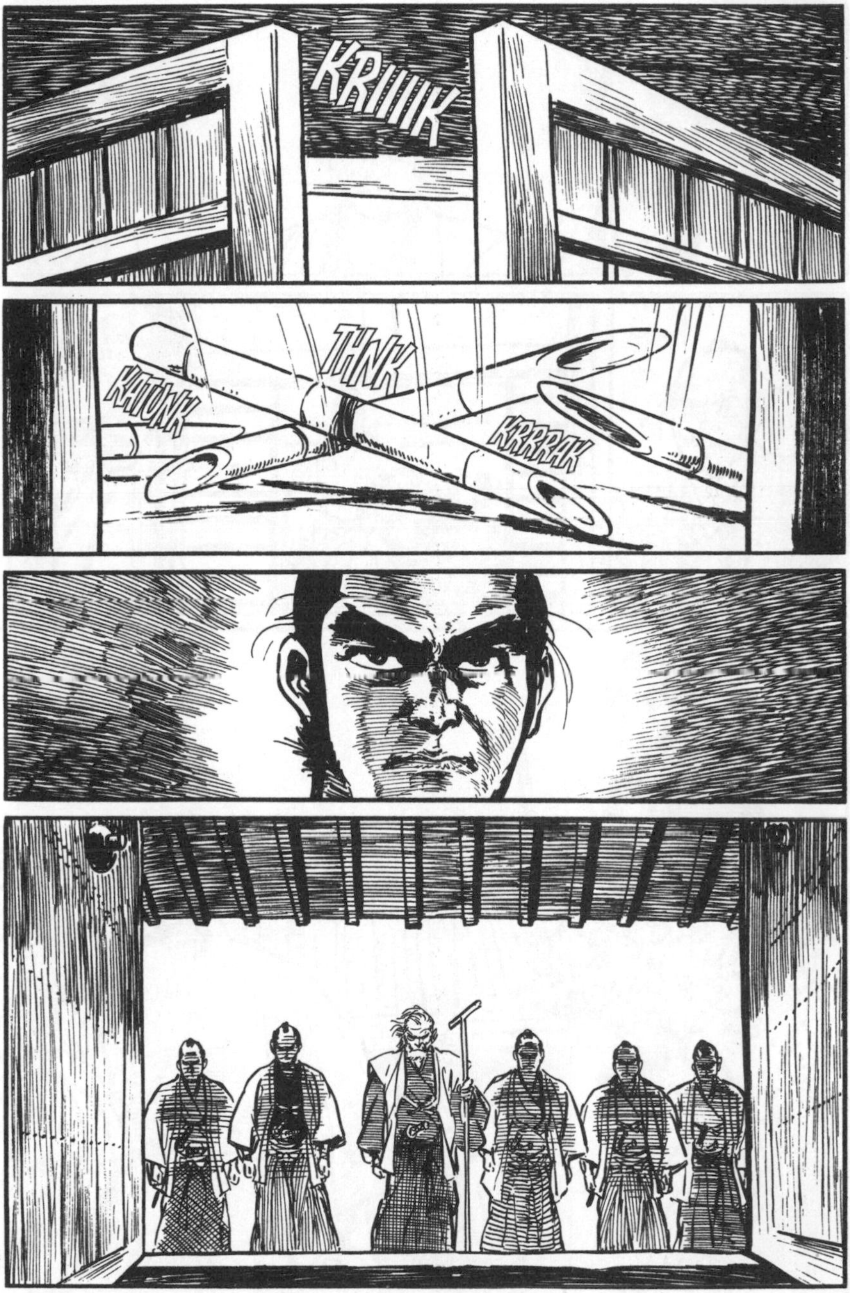
KRIIIK
THNK
KATUNK
KRRRAK

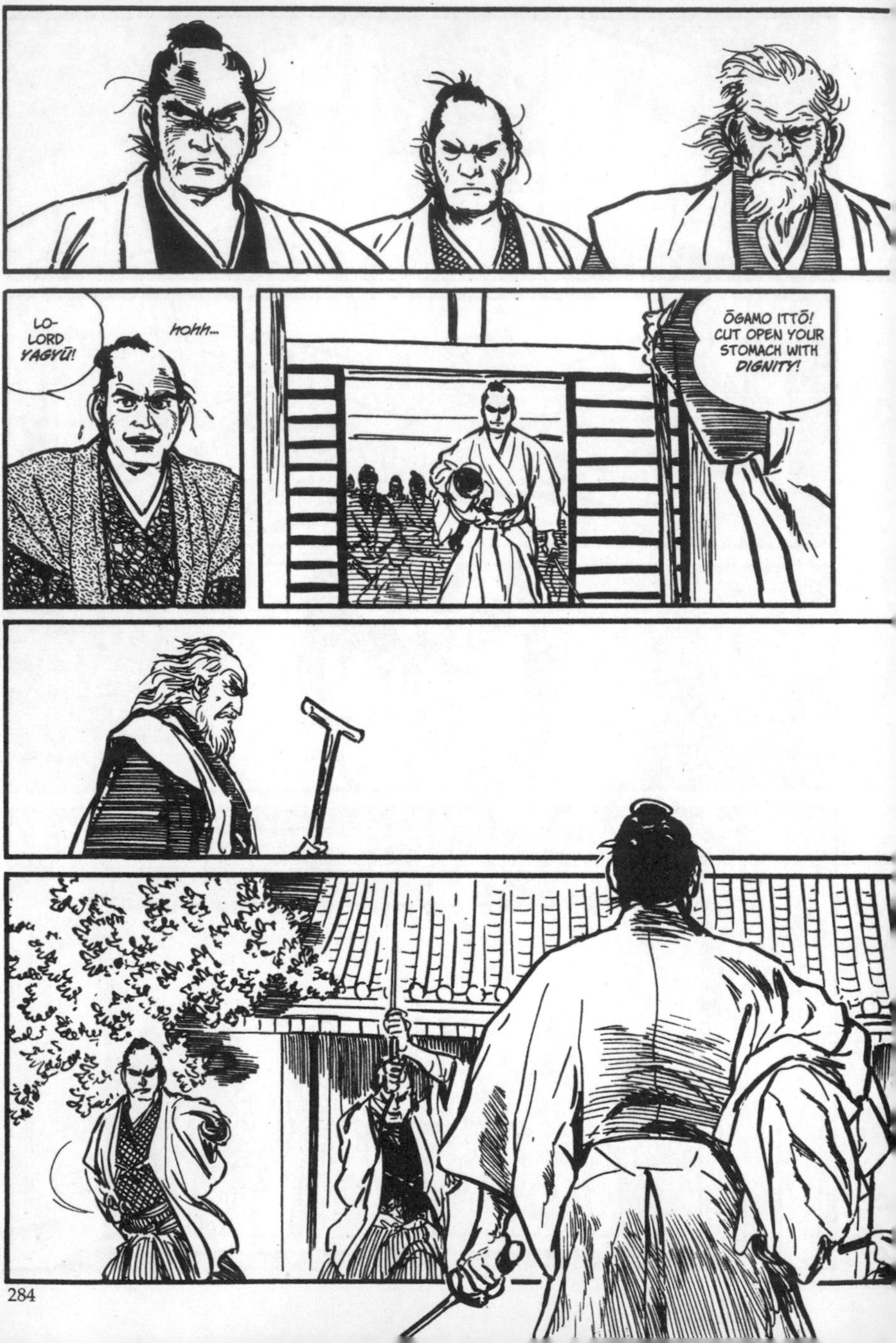
ŌGAMO ITTŌ! CUT OPEN YOUR STOMACH WITH DIGNITY!
hohh...
LO-LORD YAGYŪ!

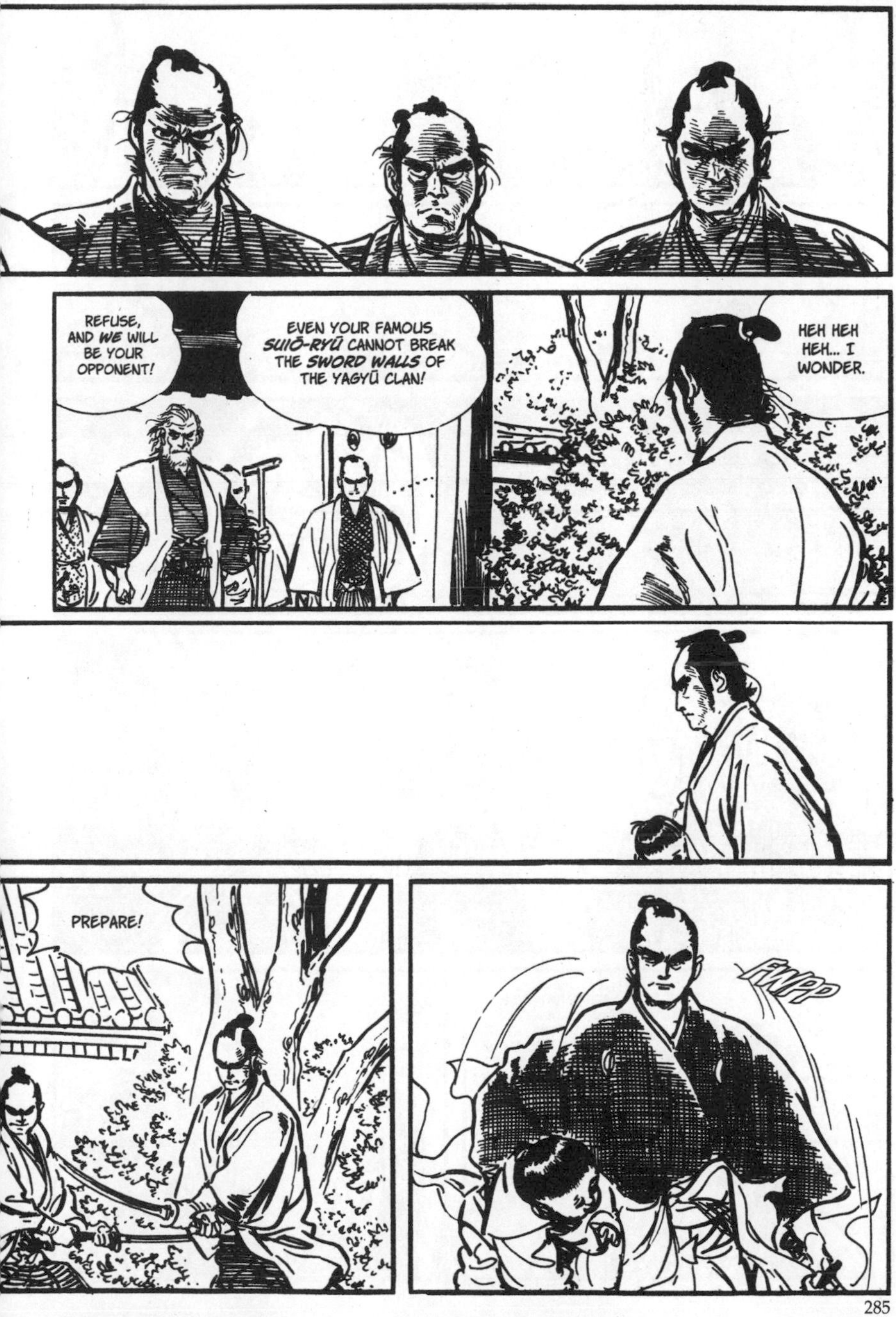

REFUSE, AND *WE* WILL BE YOUR OPPONENT!
EVEN YOUR FAMOUS *SUIŌ-RYŪ* CANNOT BREAK THE *SWORD WALLS* OF THE YAGYŪ CLAN!
HEH HEH HEH... I WONDER.
PREPARE!
FWPP

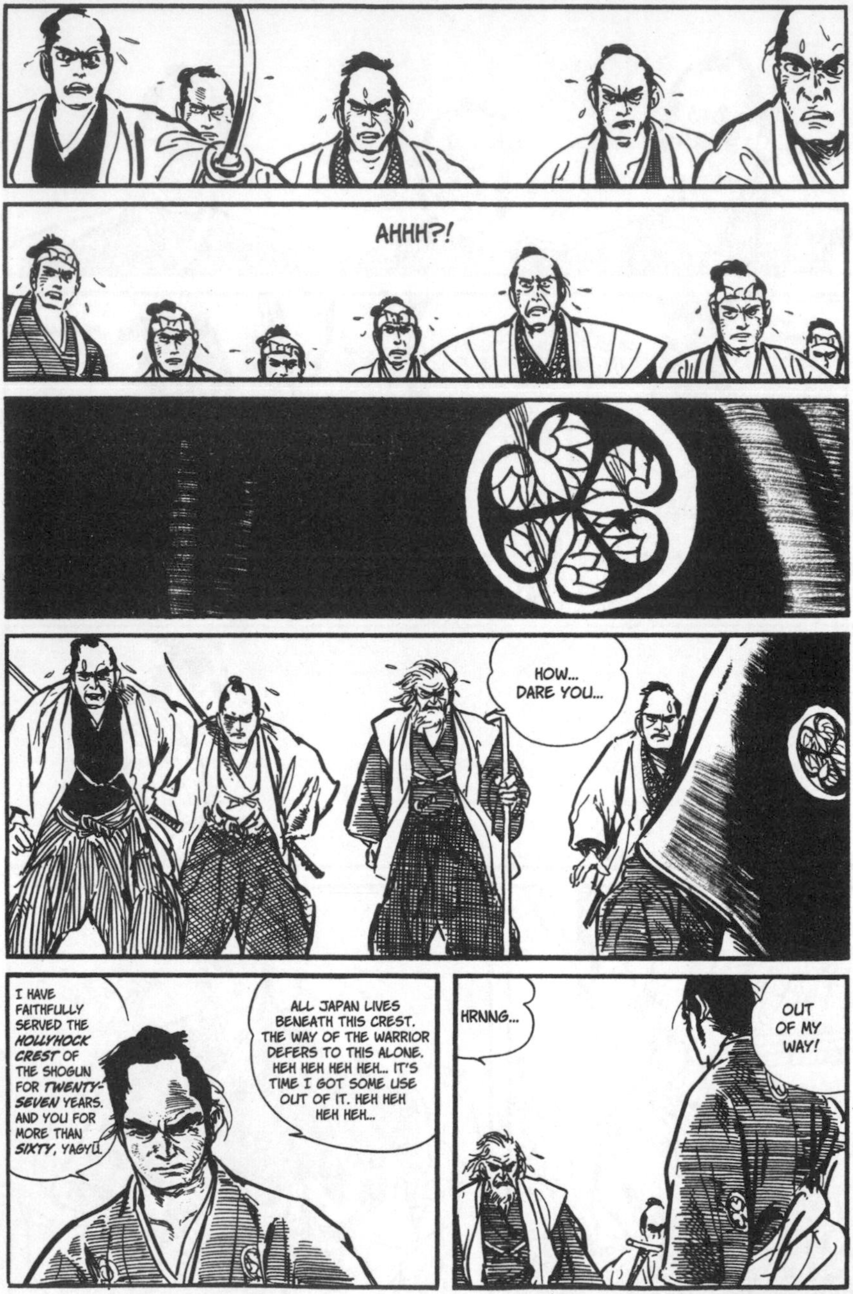
AHHH?!
HOW... DARE YOU...
I HAVE FAITHFULLY SERVED THE HOLLYHOCK CREST OF THE SHOGUN FOR TWENTY-SEVEN YEARS. AND YOU FOR MORE THAN SIXTY, YAGYŪ.
ALL JAPAN LIVES BENEATH THIS CREST. THE WAY OF THE WARRIOR DEFERS TO THIS ALONE. HEH HEH HEH HEH... IT'S TIME I GOT SOME USE OUT OF IT. HEH HEH HEH HEH...
HRNNG...
OUT OF MY WAY!

W-WAIT!

. . . .

SHED YOUR EXECUTIONER'S ROBES! DO THAT, AND THE YAGYŪ CLAN SHALL CHALLENGE YOU AS *KAISHAKUNIN* TO A FORMAL DUEL! IF VICTORY IS YOURS, I WILL LET YOU GO ANYWHERE, DO ANYTHING, SO LONG AS YOU NEVER SET FOOT IN *EDO* AGAIN!

AND IF I SAY... *NO?*

THE ASSASSINS OF THE YAGYŪ CLAN SHALL *PURSUE* YOU TO THE ENDS OF THE *EARTH*...

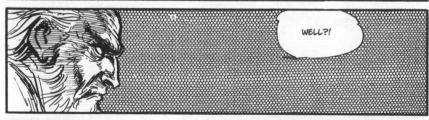

LO-LORD YAGYŪ, YOU *MUSTN'T* PERVERT THE SHOGUN'S WILL! THIS PROMISE *CANNOT* STAND!

SILENCE!! ALL RESPONSIBILITY RESTS WITH ME!

IF HE ABUSES THE *CREST*, IF THIS *SCANDAL* SPREADS, IT WILL SHAKE THE VERY AUTHORITY OF THE *SHOGUNATE* ITSELF!

WELL?!

...I ACCEPT.

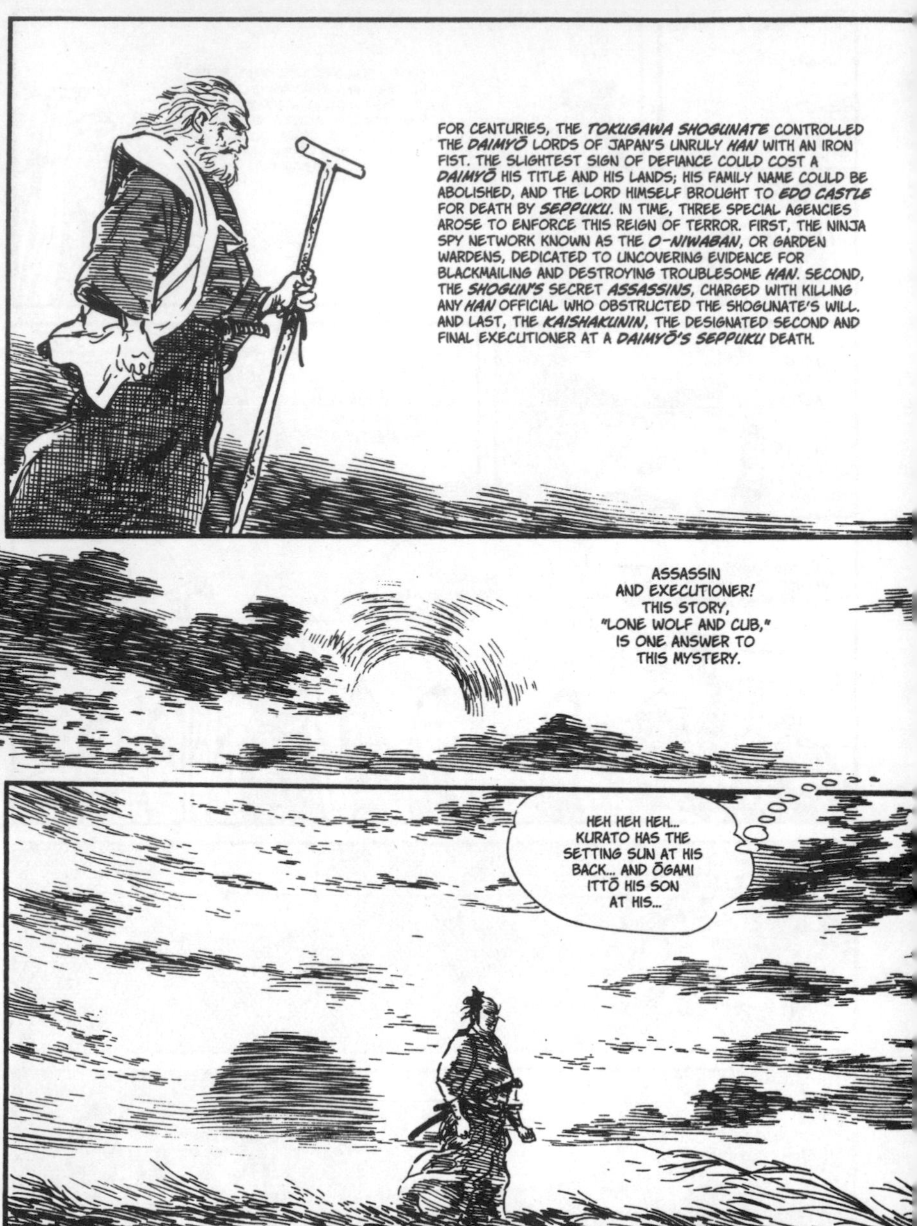
FOR CENTURIES, THE TOKUGAWA SHOGUNATE CONTROLLED THE DAIMYŌ LORDS OF JAPAN'S UNRULY HAN WITH AN IRON FIST. THE SLIGHTEST SIGN OF DEFIANCE COULD COST A DAIMYŌ HIS TITLE AND HIS LANDS; HIS FAMILY NAME COULD BE ABOLISHED, AND THE LORD HIMSELF BROUGHT TO EDO CASTLE FOR DEATH BY SEPPUKU. IN TIME, THREE SPECIAL AGENCIES AROSE TO ENFORCE THIS REIGN OF TERROR. FIRST, THE NINJA SPY NETWORK KNOWN AS THE O-NIWABAN, OR GARDEN WARDENS, DEDICATED TO UNCOVERING EVIDENCE FOR BLACKMAILING AND DESTROYING TROUBLESOME HAN. SECOND, THE SHOGUN'S SECRET ASSASSINS, CHARGED WITH KILLING ANY HAN OFFICIAL WHO OBSTRUCTED THE SHOGUNATE'S WILL. AND LAST, THE KAISHAKUNIN, THE DESIGNATED SECOND AND FINAL EXECUTIONER AT A DAIMYŌ'S SEPPUKU DEATH.
ASSASSIN AND EXECUTIONER! THIS STORY, "LONE WOLF AND CUB," IS ONE ANSWER TO THIS MYSTERY.
HEH HEH HEH... KURATO HAS THE SETTING SUN AT HIS BACK... AND ŌGAMI ITTŌ HIS SON AT HIS...

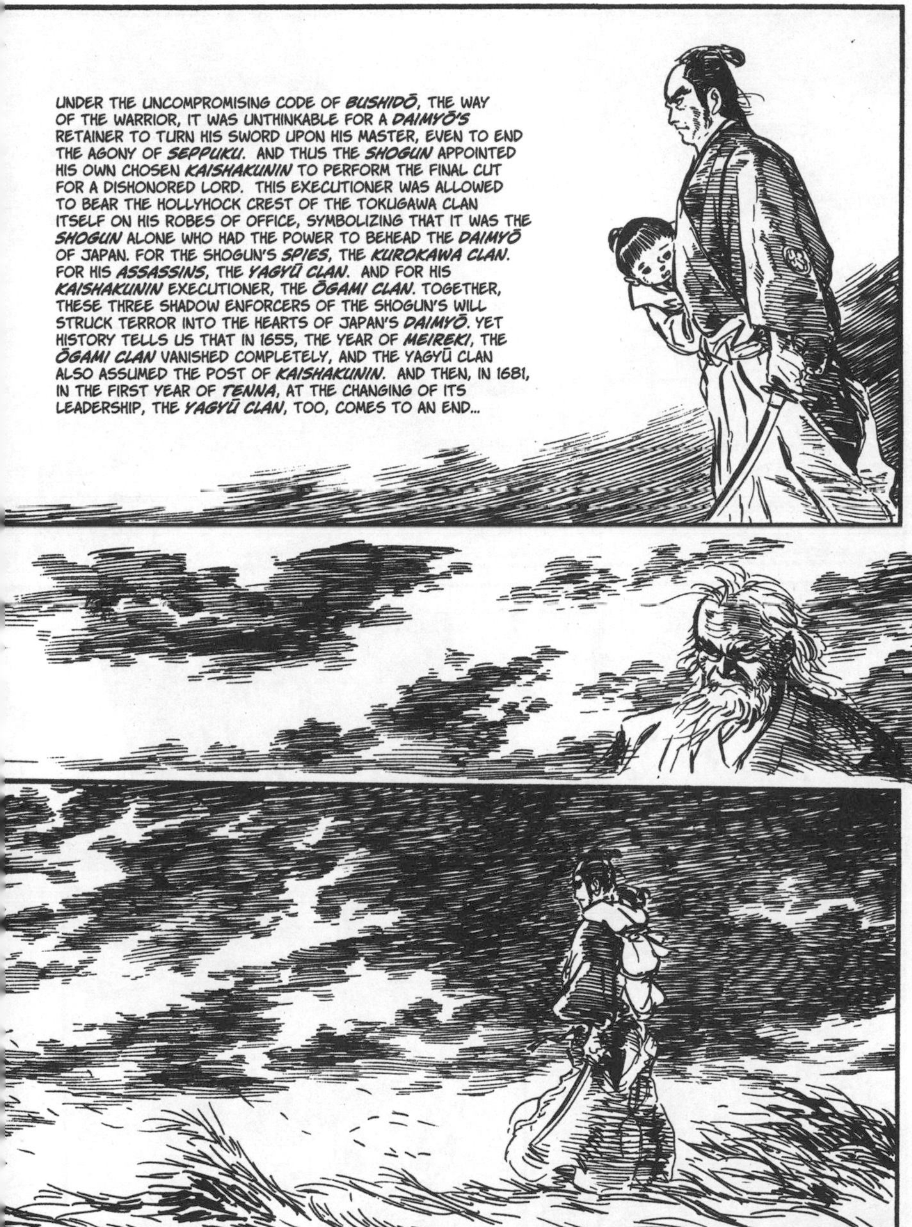
UNDER THE UNCOMPROMISING CODE OF BUSHIDŌ, THE WAY OF THE WARRIOR, IT WAS UNTHINKABLE FOR A DAIMYŌ'S RETAINER TO TURN HIS SWORD UPON HIS MASTER, EVEN TO END THE AGONY OF SEPPUKU. AND THUS THE SHOGUN APPOINTED HIS OWN CHOSEN KAISHAKUNIN TO PERFORM THE FINAL CUT FOR A DISHONORED LORD. THIS EXECUTIONER WAS ALLOWED TO BEAR THE HOLLYHOCK CREST OF THE TOKUGAWA CLAN ITSELF ON HIS ROBES OF OFFICE, SYMBOLIZING THAT IT WAS THE SHOGUN ALONE WHO HAD THE POWER TO BEHEAD THE DAIMYŌ OF JAPAN. FOR THE SHOGUN'S SPIES, THE KUROKAWA CLAN. FOR HIS ASSASSINS, THE YAGYŪ CLAN. AND FOR HIS KAISHAKUNIN EXECUTIONER, THE ŌGAMI CLAN. TOGETHER, THESE THREE SHADOW ENFORCERS OF THE SHOGUN'S WILL STRUCK TERROR INTO THE HEARTS OF JAPAN'S DAIMYŌ. YET HISTORY TELLS US THAT IN 1655, THE YEAR OF MEIREKI, THE ŌGAMI CLAN VANISHED COMPLETELY, AND THE YAGYŪ CLAN ALSO ASSUMED THE POST OF KAISHAKUNIN. AND THEN, IN 1681, IN THE FIRST YEAR OF TENNA, AT THE CHANGING OF ITS LEADERSHIP, THE YAGYŪ CLAN, TOO, COMES TO AN END...

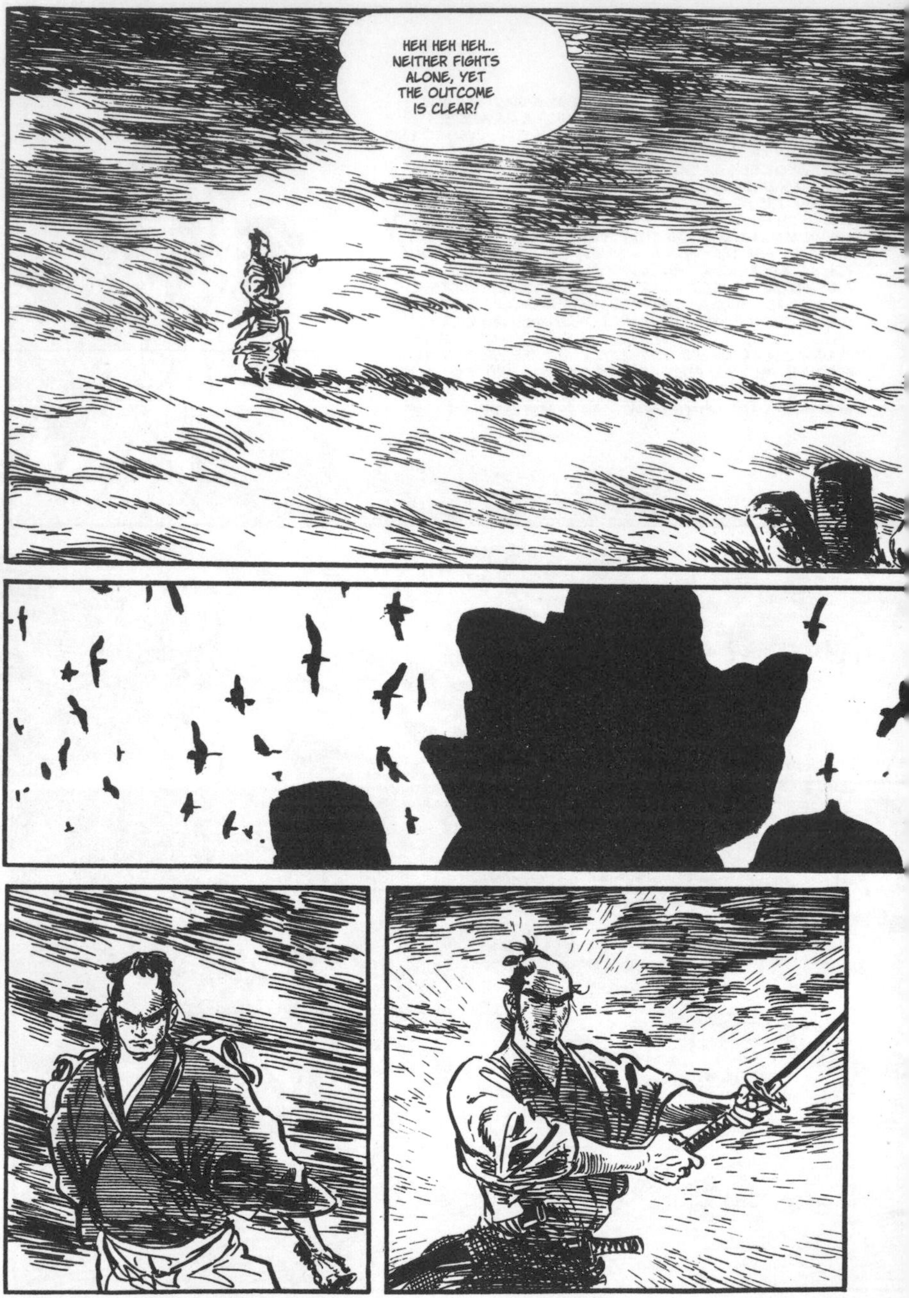
HEH HEH HEH...
NEITHER FIGHTS
ALONE, YET
THE OUTCOME
IS CLEAR!

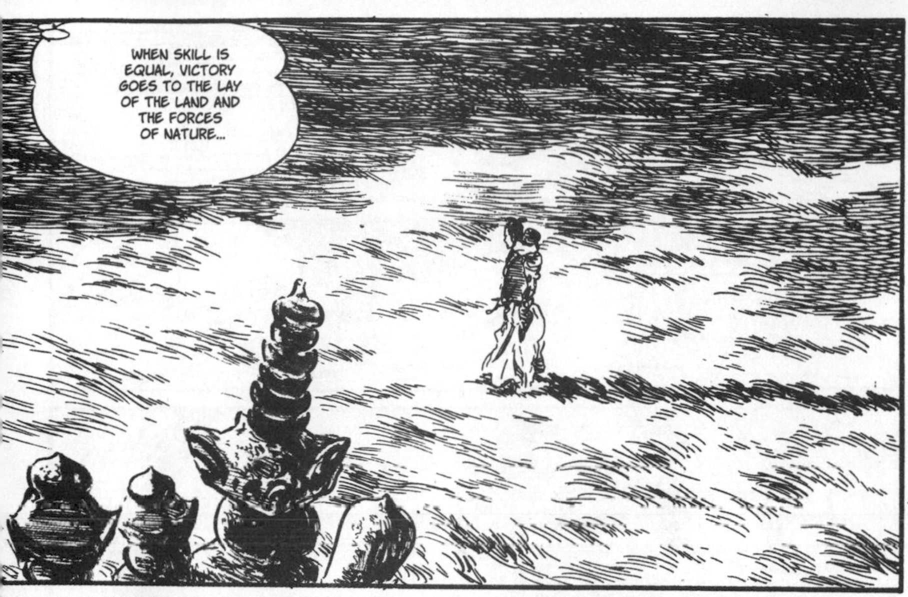
WHEN SKILL IS EQUAL, VICTORY GOES TO THE LAY OF THE LAND AND THE FORCES OF NATURE...

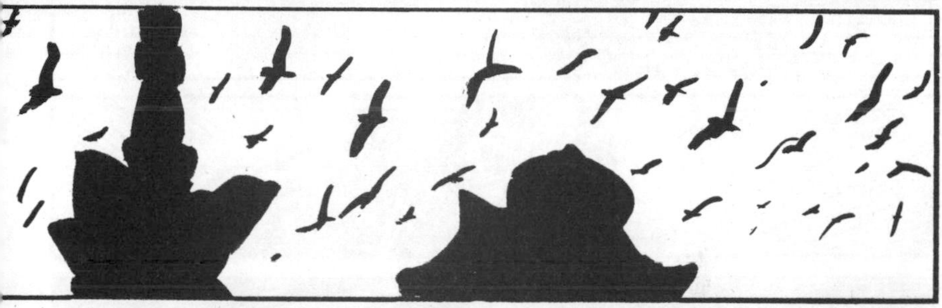

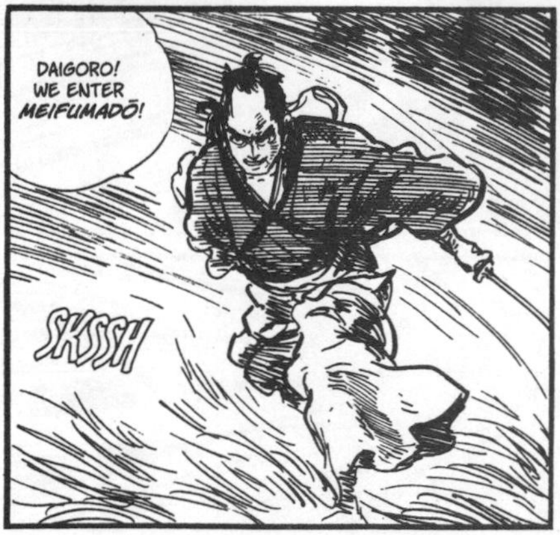
DAIGORO! WE ENTER *MEIFUMADŌ*!
SKSSH

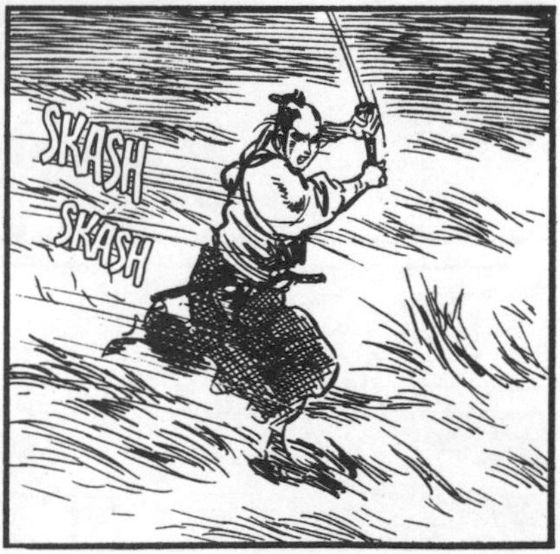
SKASH
SKASH

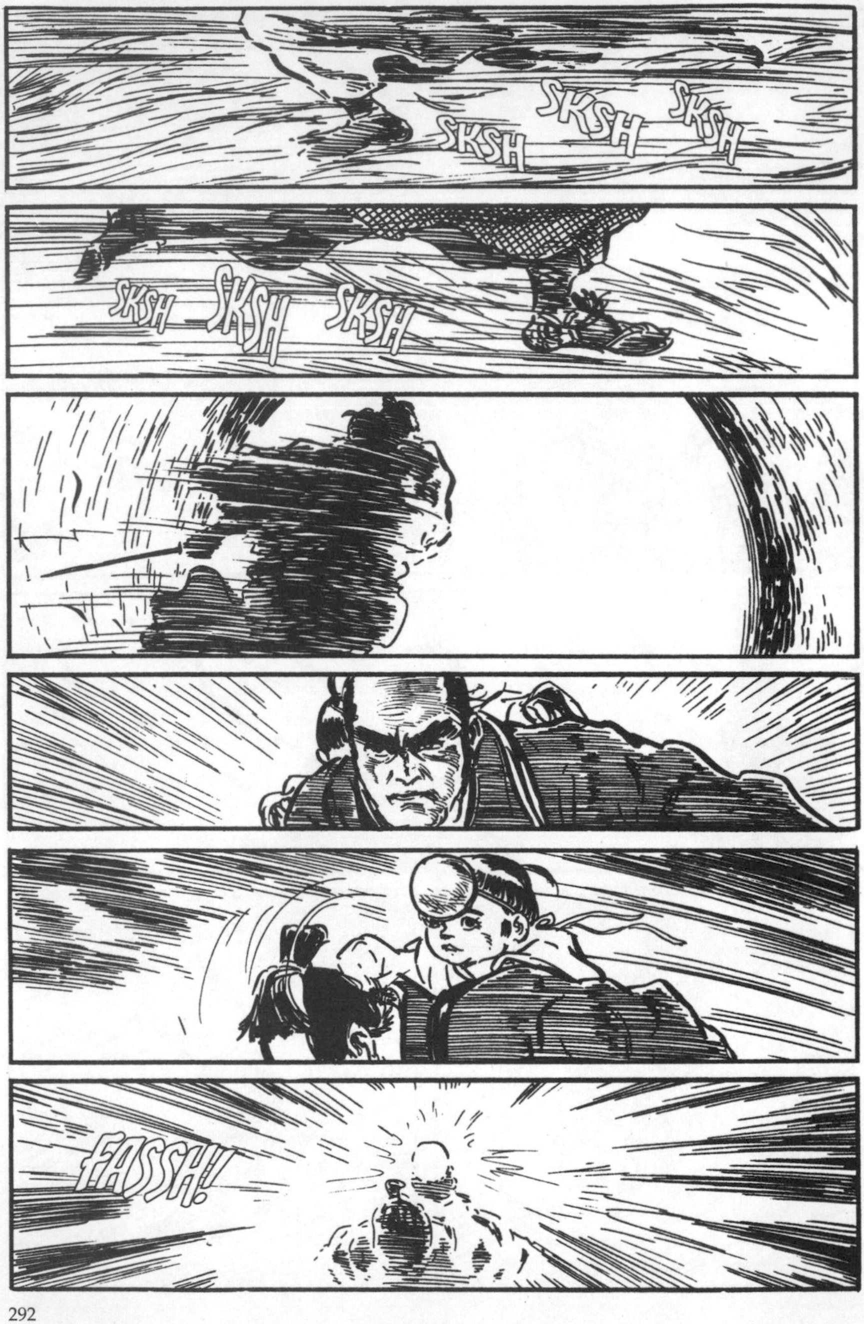
SKSH
SKSH
SKSH
SKSH
SKSH
SKSH
FASSH!

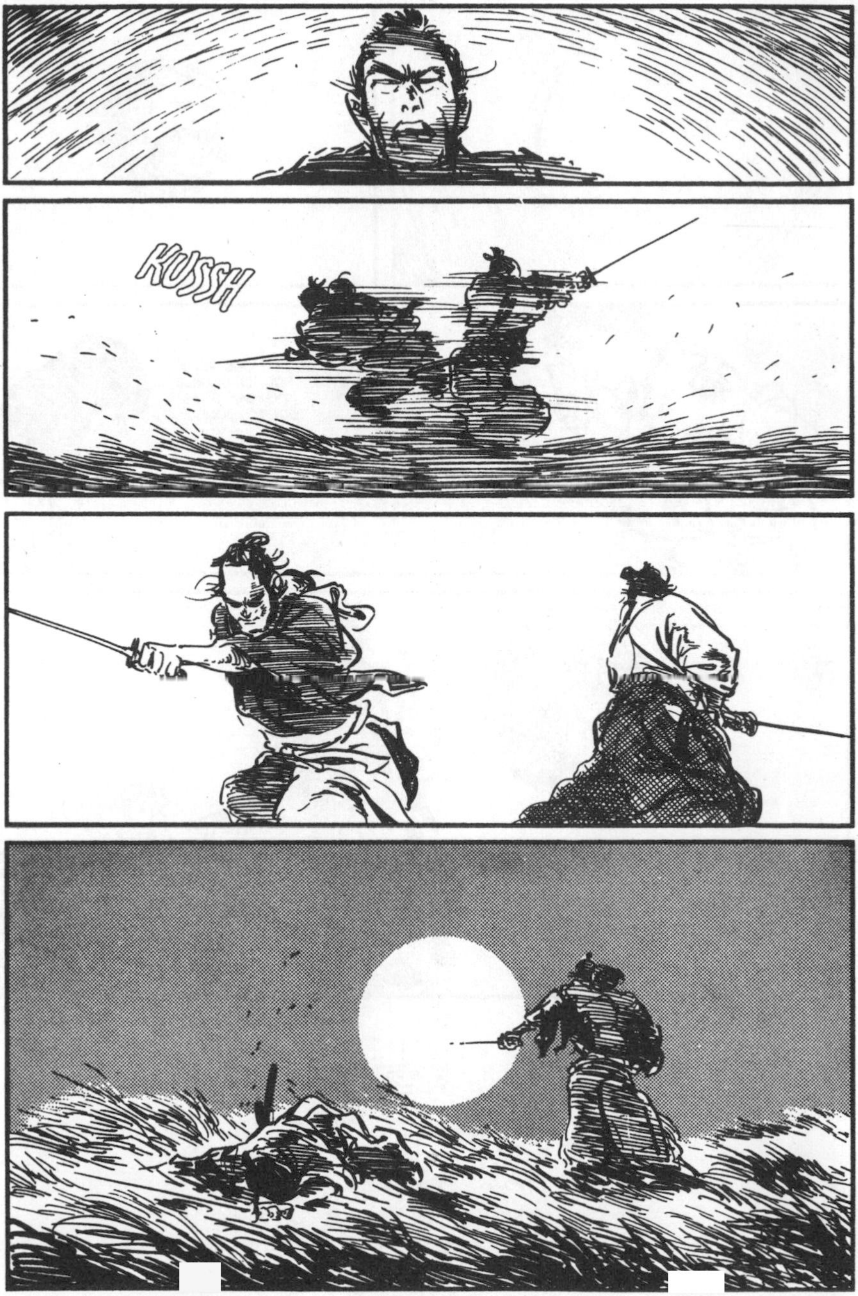
KUSSH

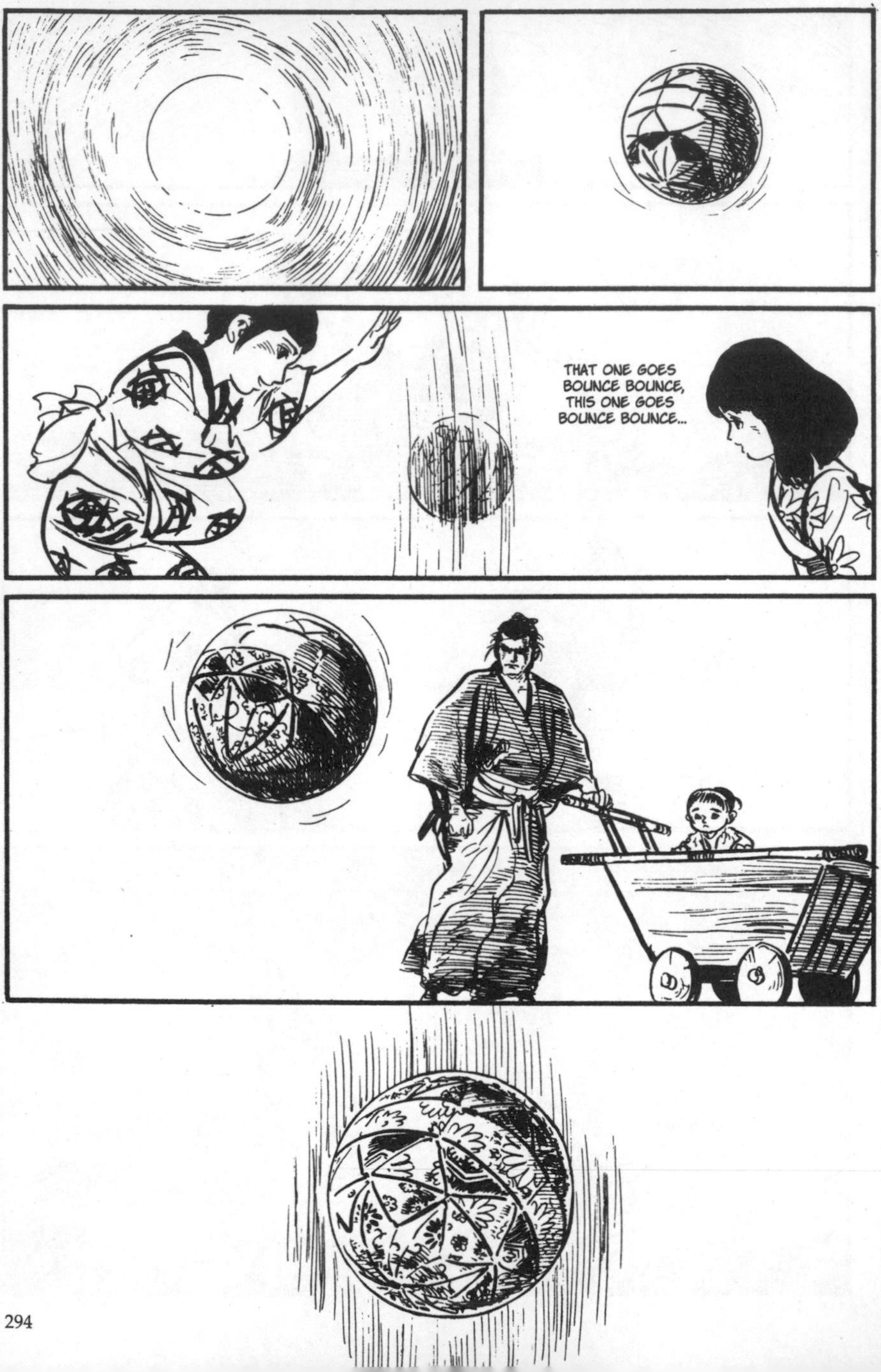
THAT ONE GOES
BOUNCE BOUNCE,
THIS ONE GOES
BOUNCE BOUNCE...

子連れ狼

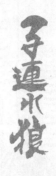

RED CAT

10

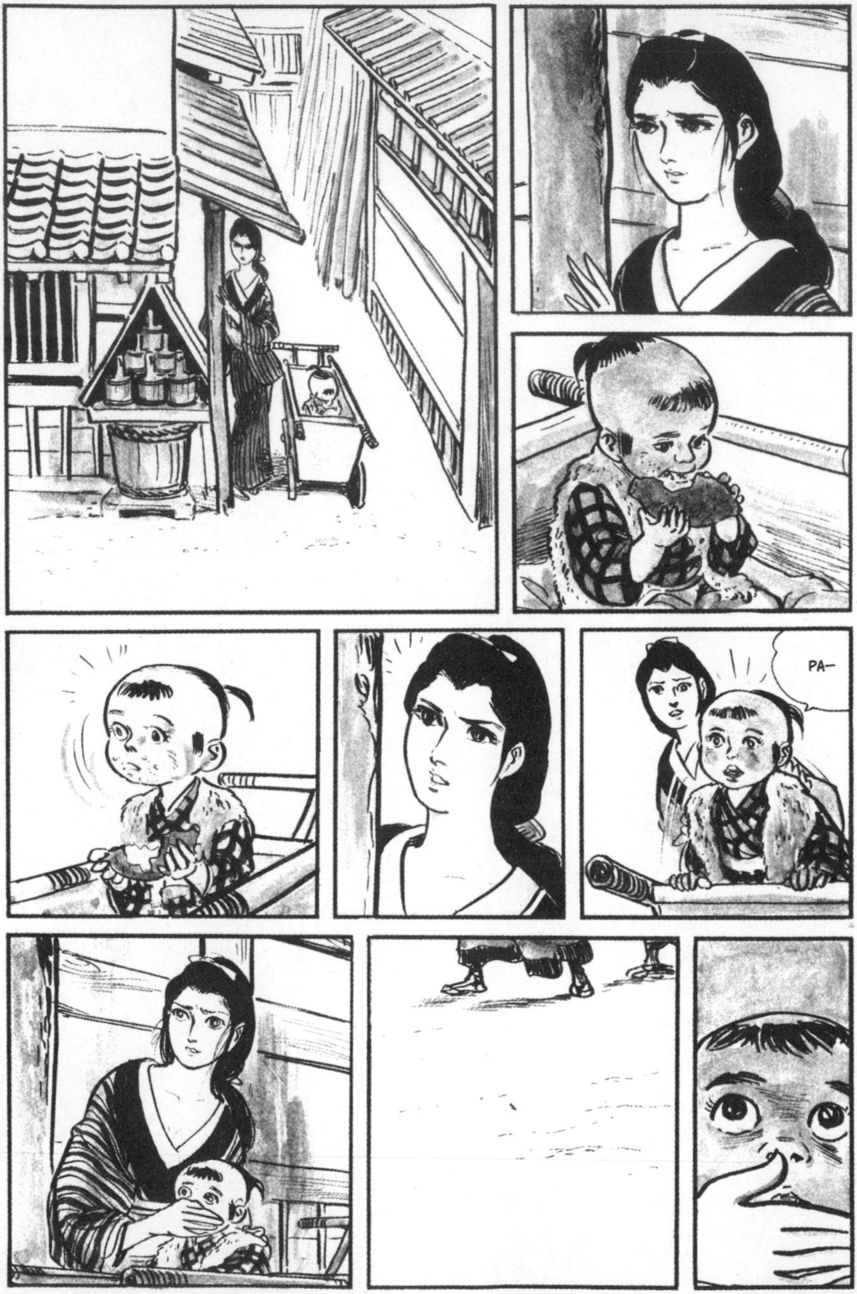
PA—

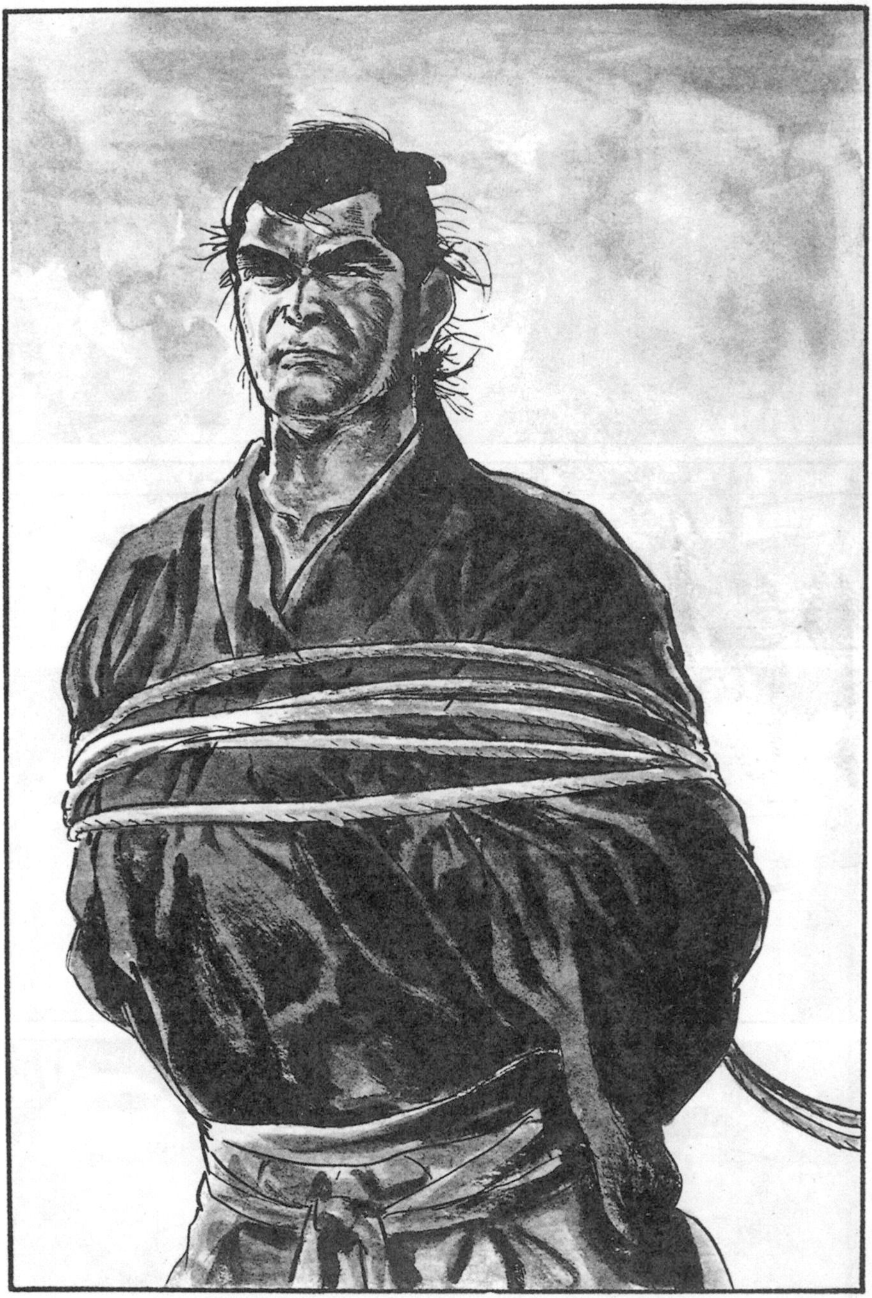

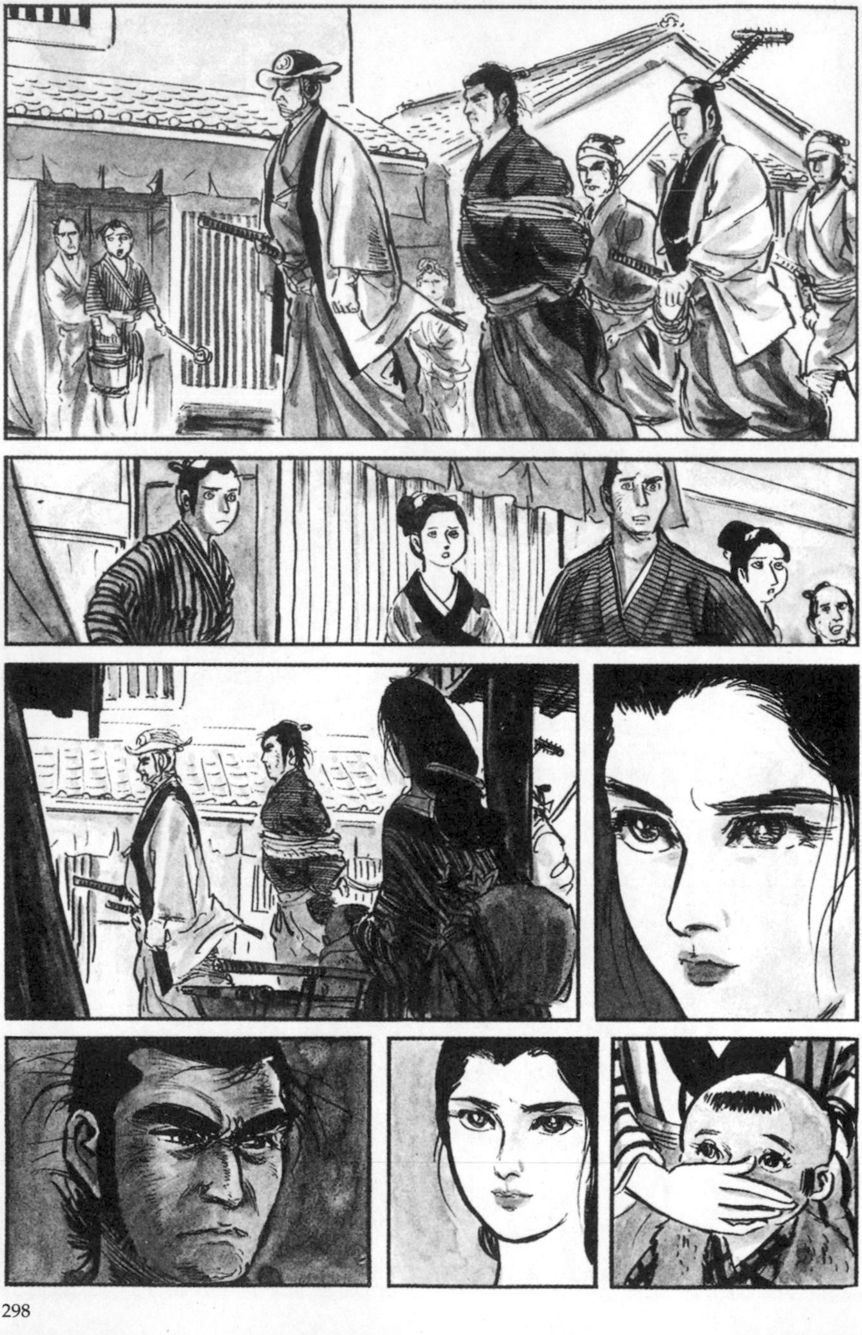

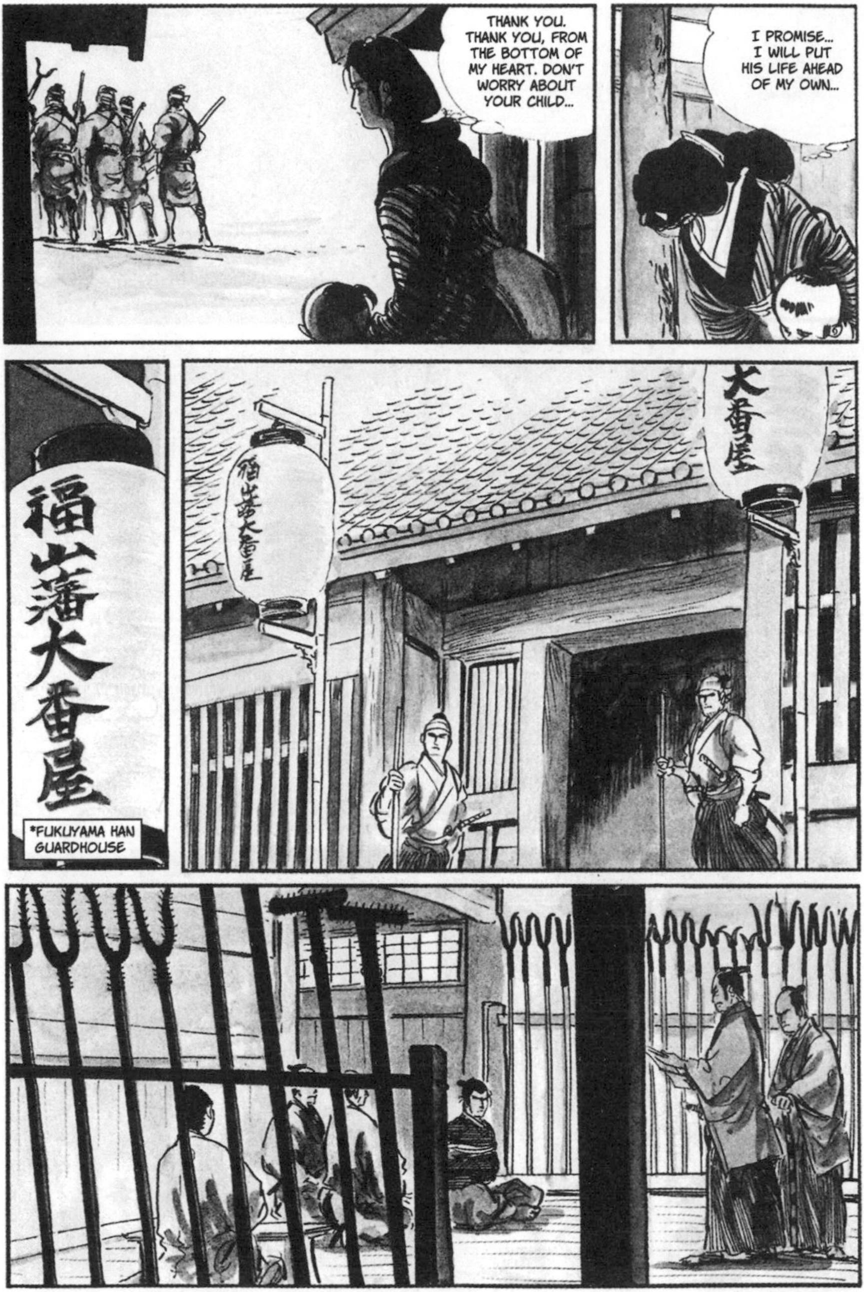
THANK YOU. THANK YOU, FROM THE BOTTOM OF MY HEART. DON'T WORRY ABOUT YOUR CHILD...
I PROMISE... I WILL PUT HIS LIFE AHEAD OF MY OWN...
福山藩大番屋
*FUKUYAMA HAN GUARDHOUSE
大番屋

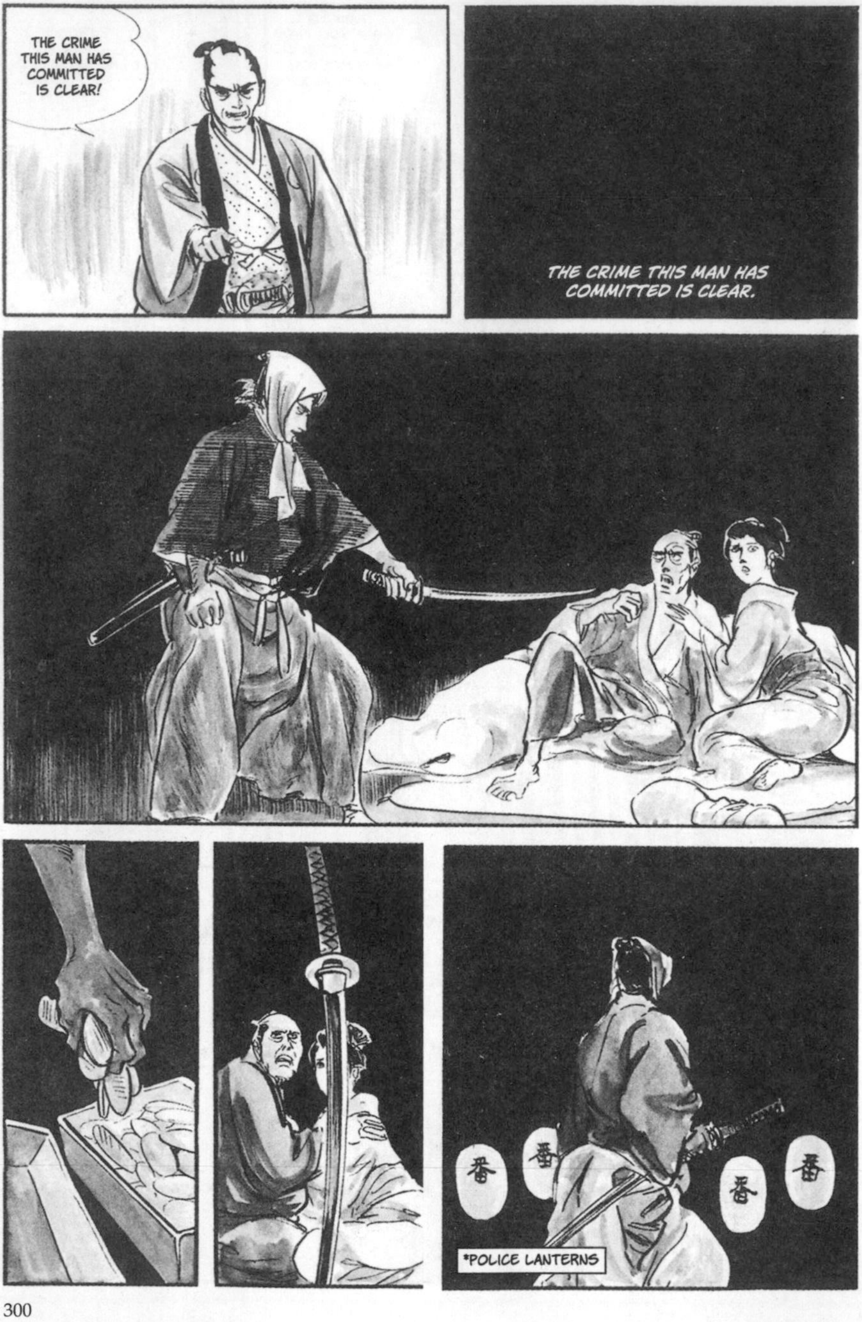
THE CRIME THIS MAN HAS COMMITTED IS CLEAR!
THE CRIME THIS MAN HAS COMMITTED IS CLEAR.
番
番
番
番
*POLICE LANTERNS

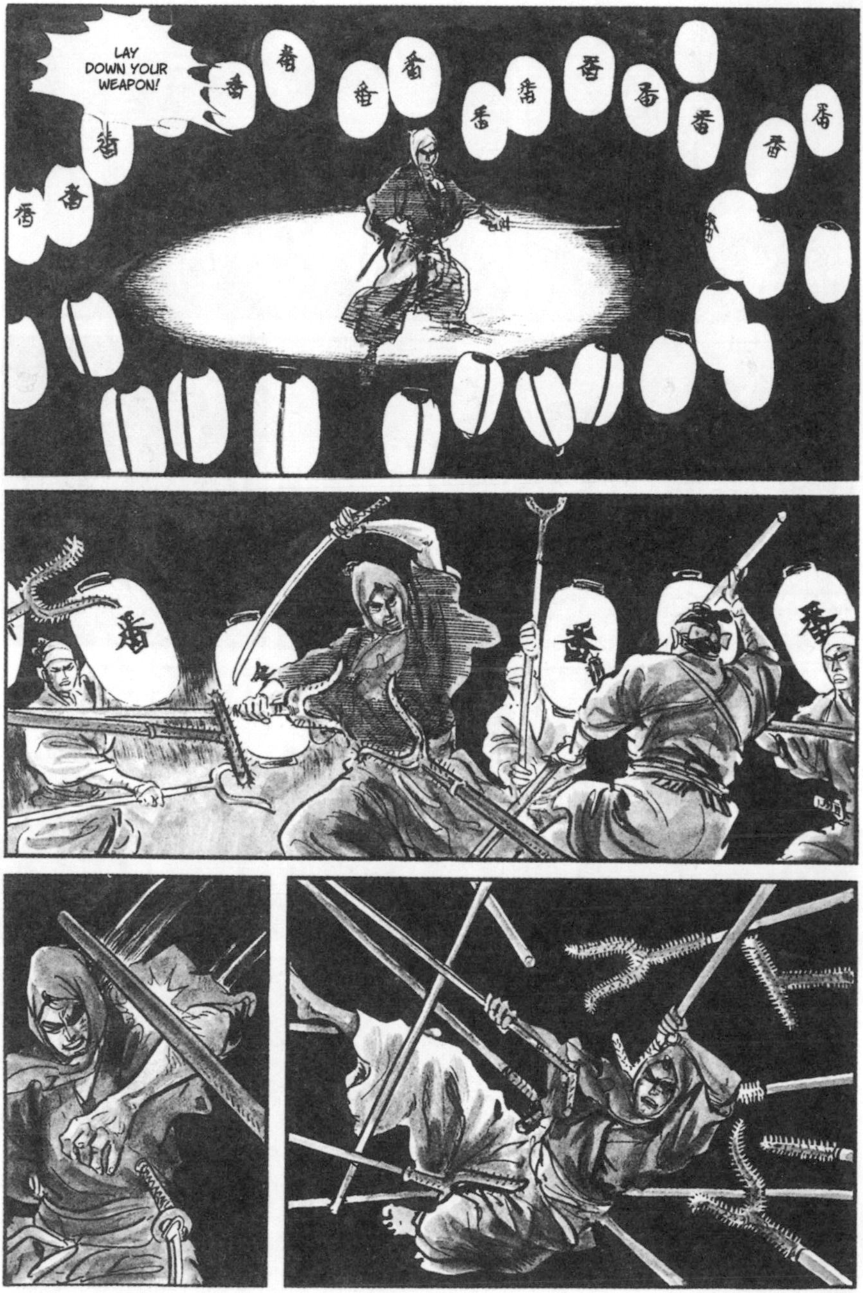
LAY DOWN YOUR WEAPON!

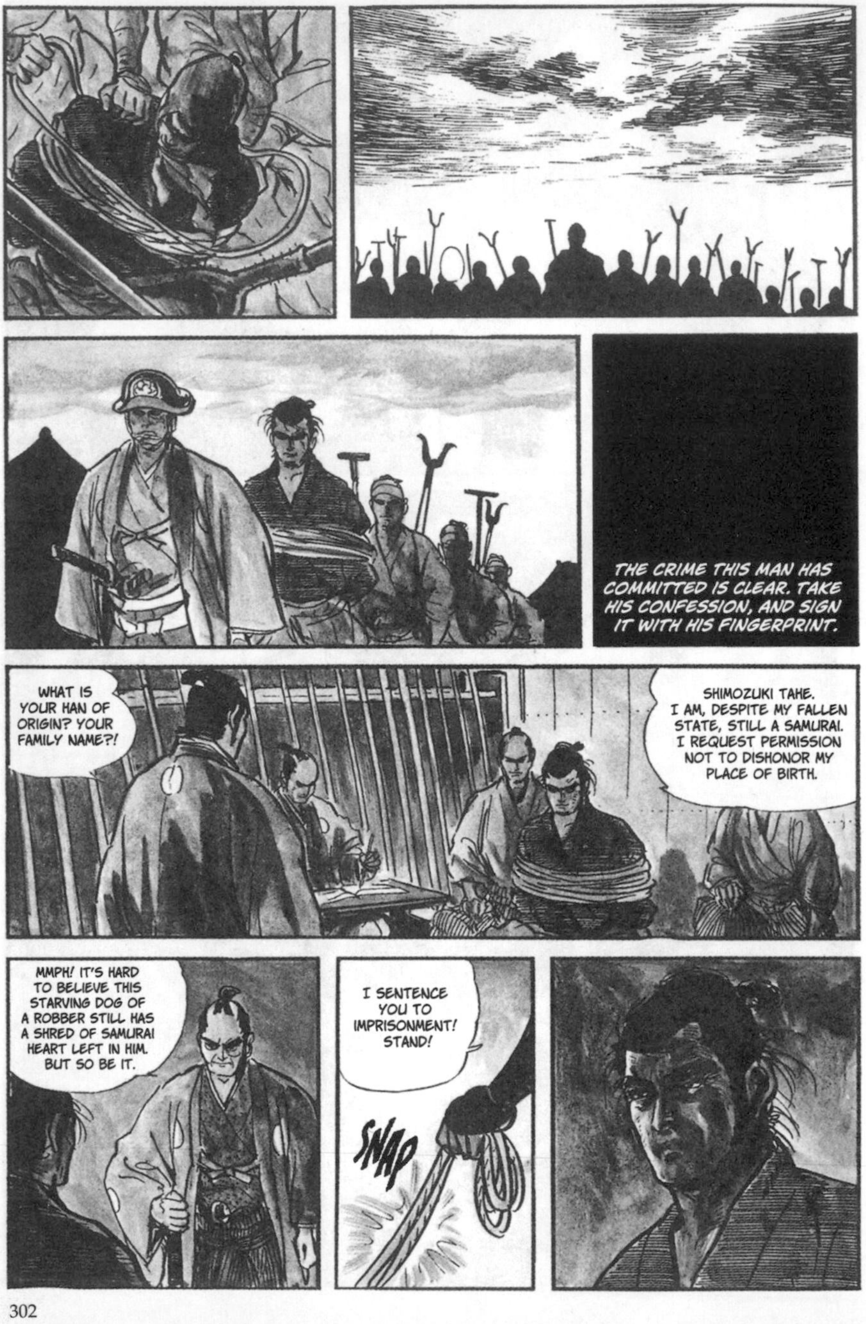
THE CRIME THIS MAN HAS COMMITTED IS CLEAR. TAKE HIS CONFESSION, AND SIGN IT WITH HIS FINGERPRINT.
WHAT IS YOUR HAN OF ORIGIN? YOUR FAMILY NAME?!
SHIMOZUKI TAHE. I AM, DESPITE MY FALLEN STATE, STILL A SAMURAI. I REQUEST PERMISSION NOT TO DISHONOR MY PLACE OF BIRTH.
MMPH! IT'S HARD TO BELIEVE THIS STARVING DOG OF A ROBBER STILL HAS A SHRED OF SAMURAI HEART LEFT IN HIM. BUT SO BE IT.
I SENTENCE YOU TO IMPRISONMENT! STAND!
SNAP

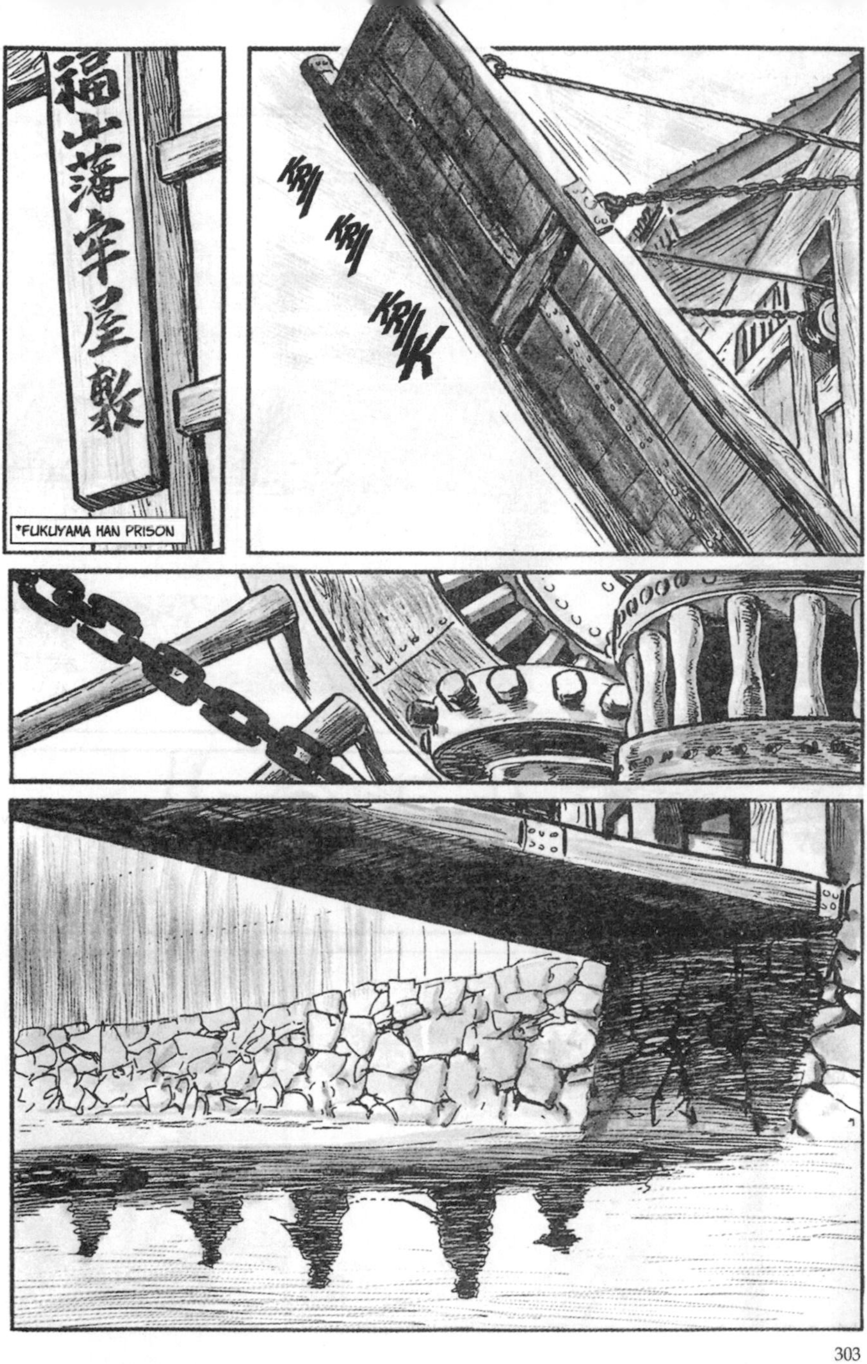
KRII
KRII
KRIIK
福山藩牢屋敷
*FUKUYAMA HAN PRISON

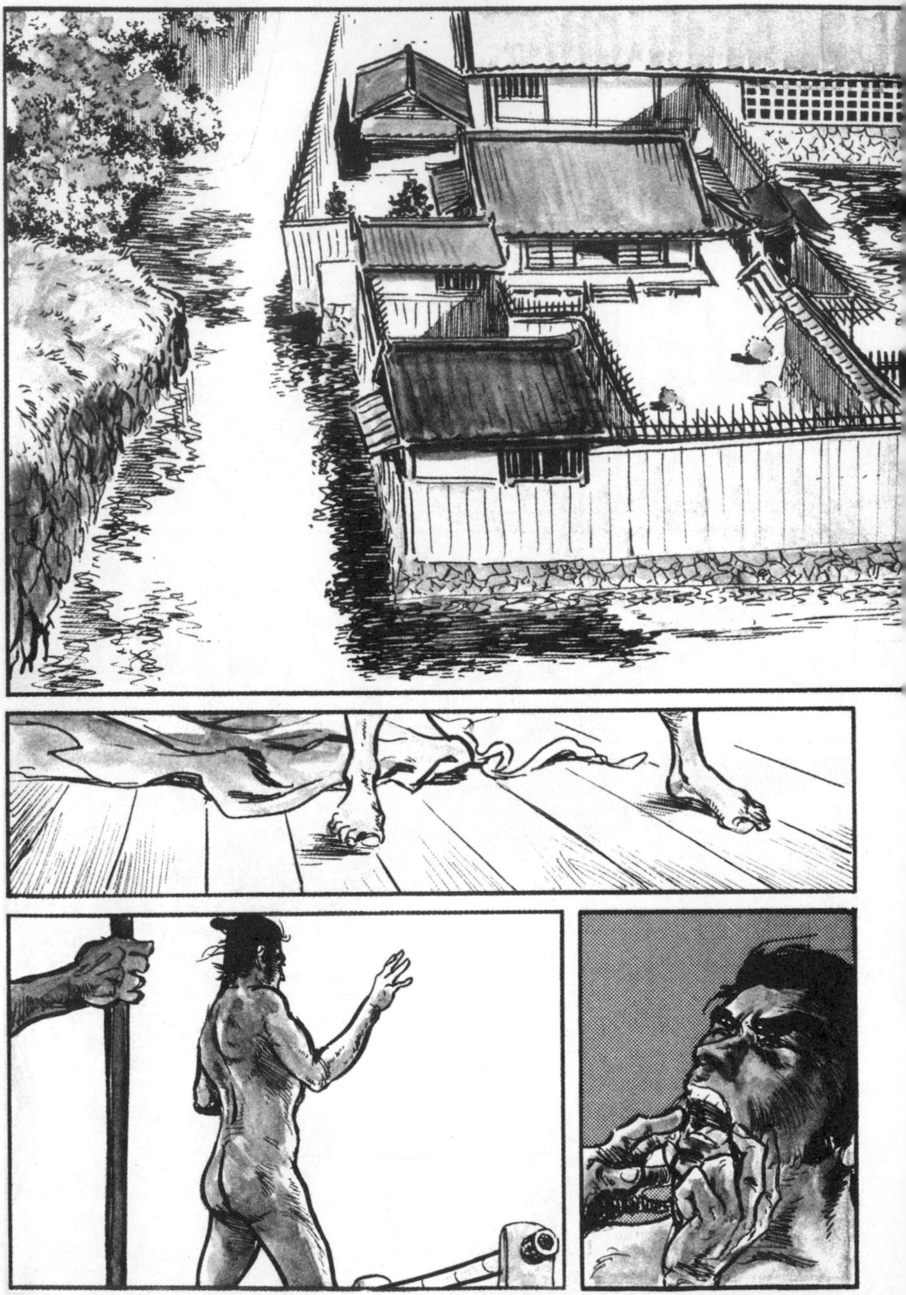

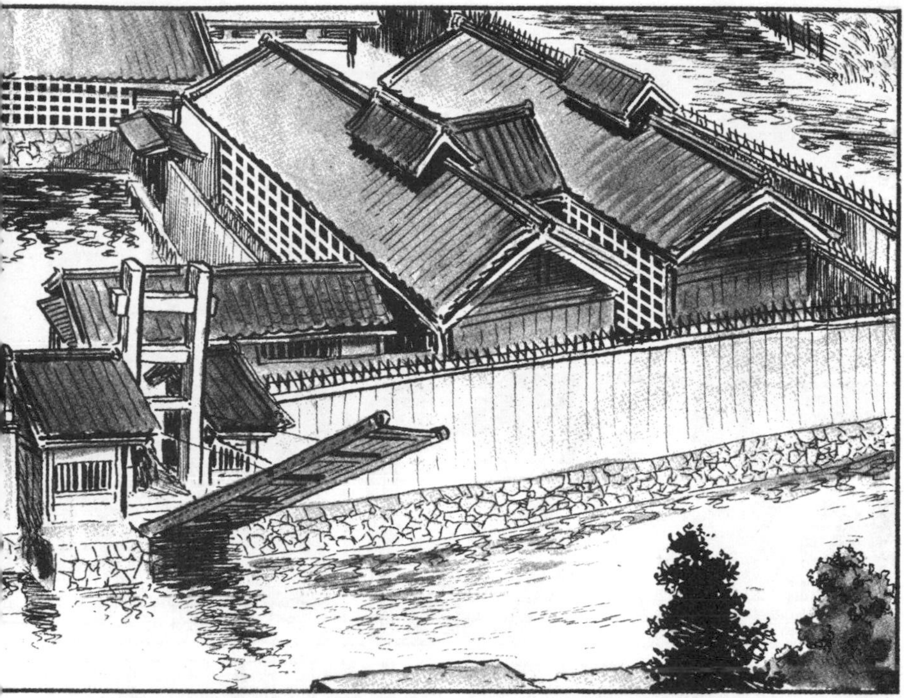

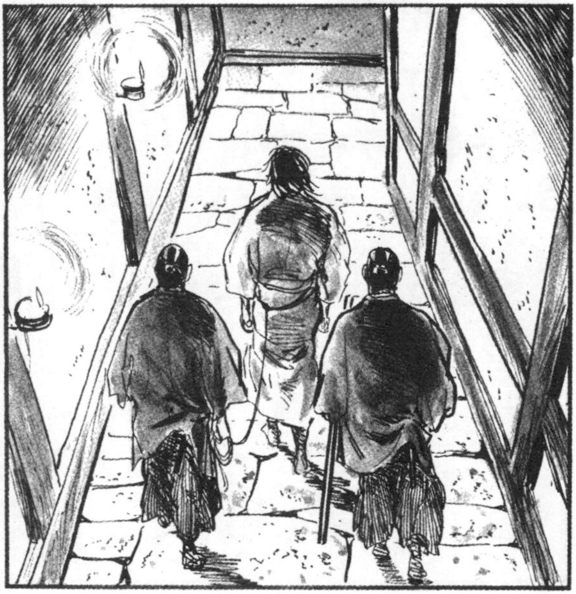

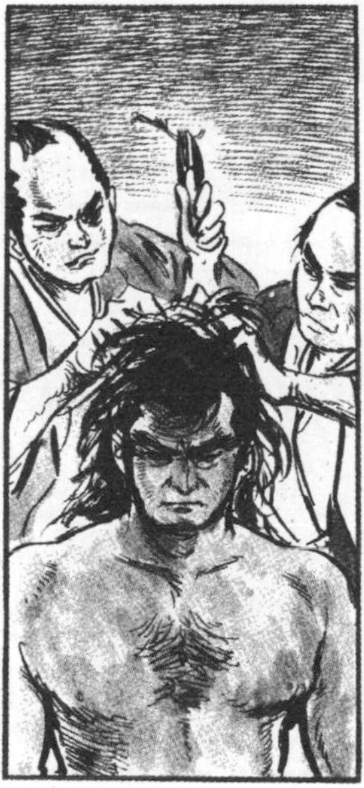

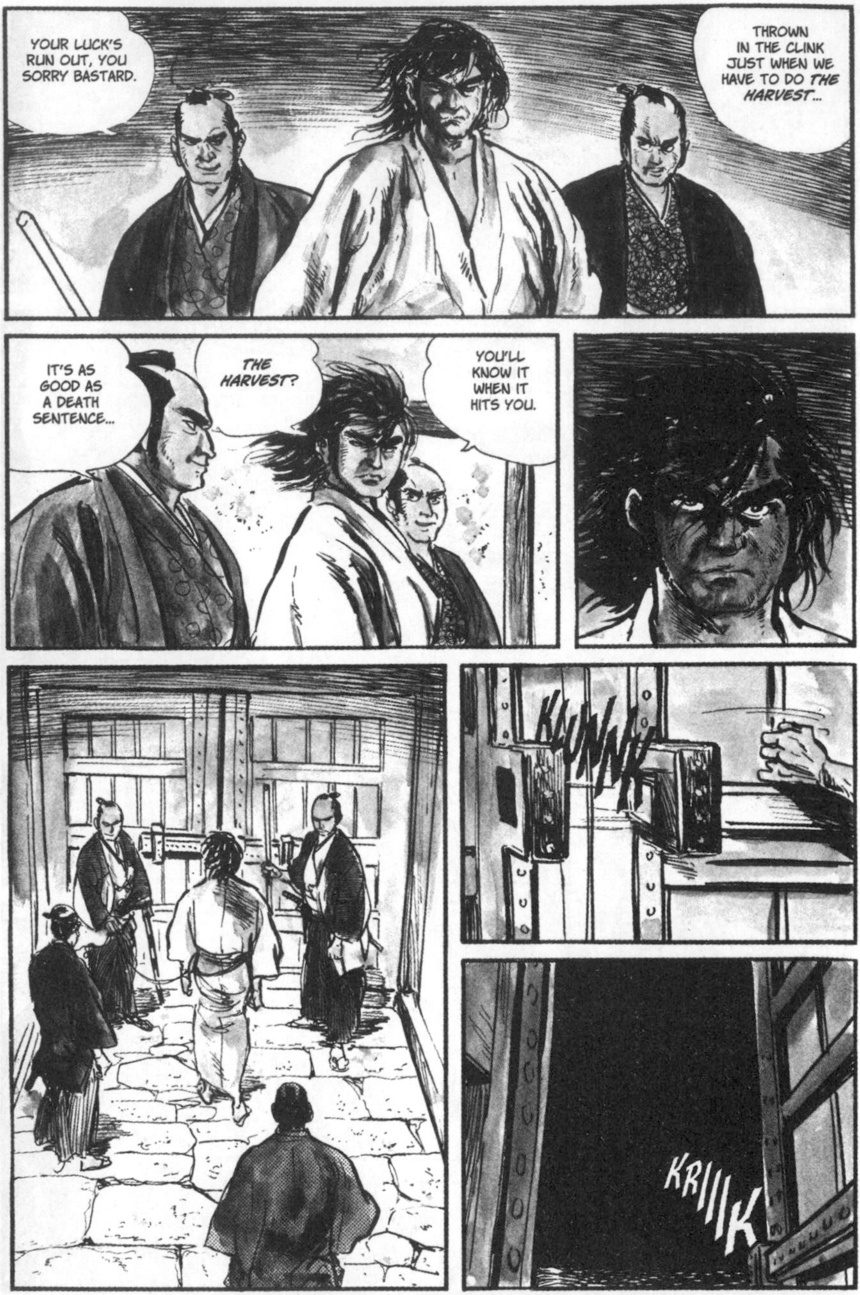
YOUR LUCK'S RUN OUT, YOU SORRY BASTARD.
THROWN IN THE CLINK JUST WHEN WE HAVE TO DO *THE HARVEST*...
IT'S AS GOOD AS A DEATH SENTENCE...
THE HARVEST?
YOU'LL KNOW IT WHEN IT HITS YOU.
KLUNNK
KRIIIK

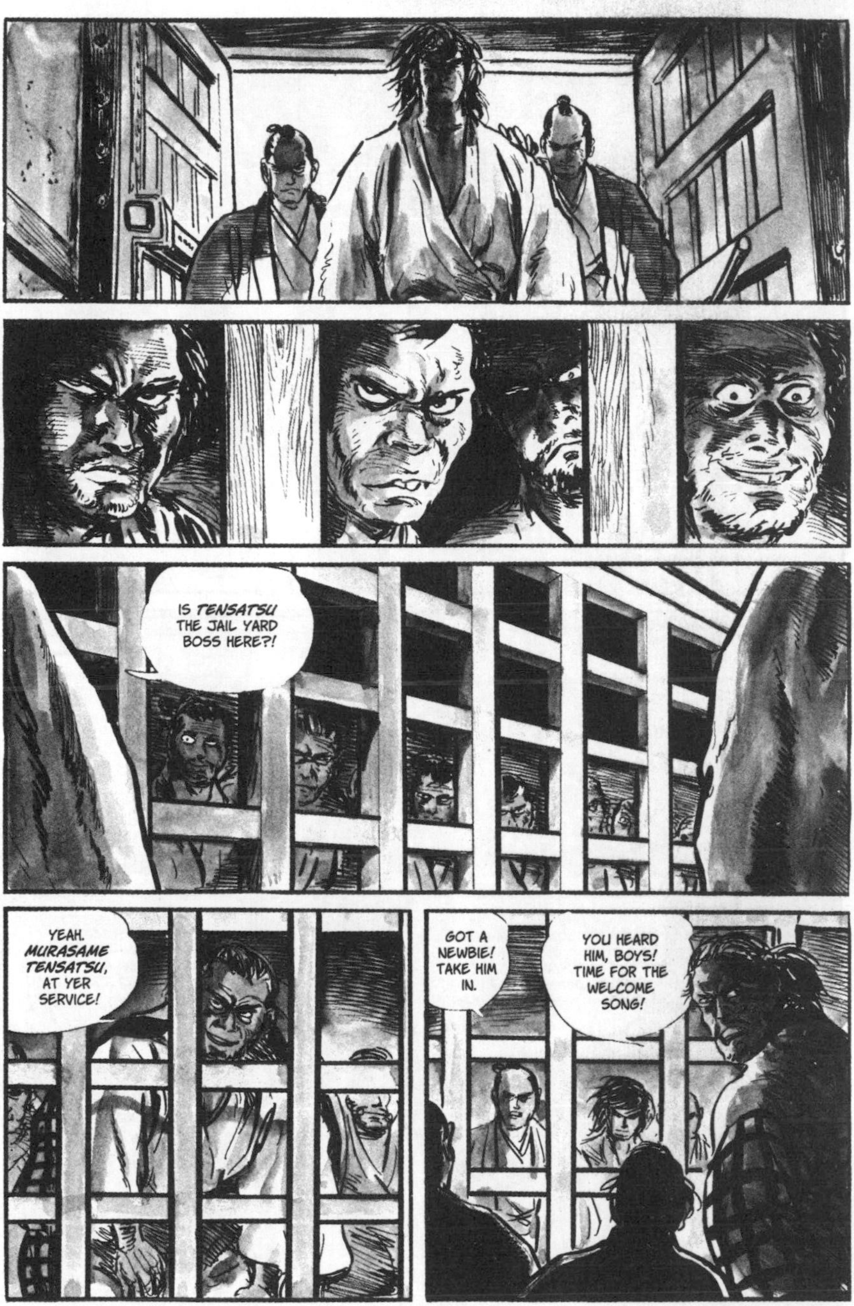
IS *TENSATSU* THE JAIL YARD BOSS HERE?!
YEAH. *MURASAME TENSATSU*, AT YER SERVICE!
GOT A NEWBIE! TAKE HIM IN.
YOU HEARD HIM, BOYS! TIME FOR THE WELCOME SONG!

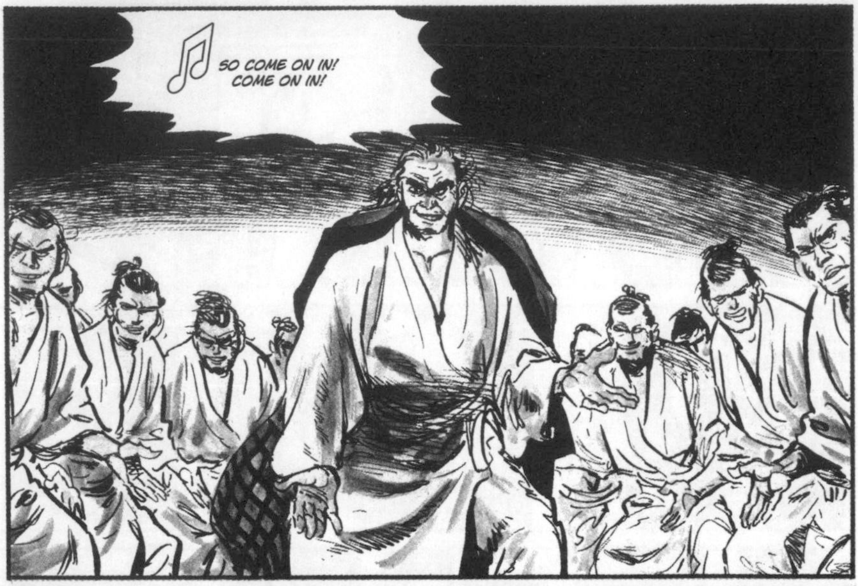
SO COME ON IN! COME ON IN!

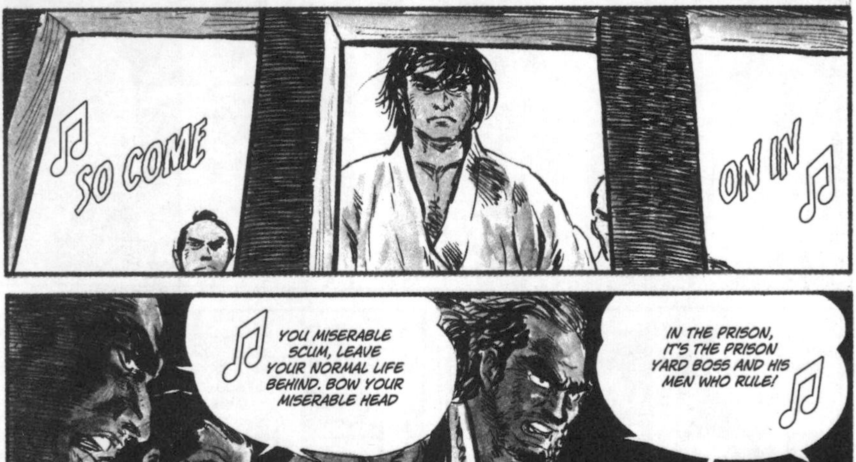
SO COME
ON IN

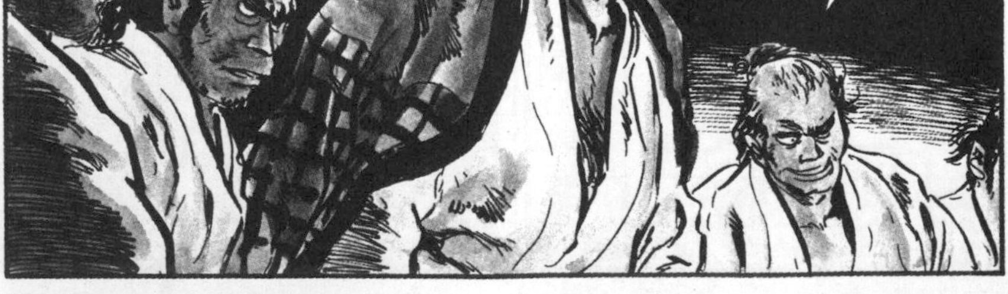
YOU MISERABLE SCUM, LEAVE YOUR NORMAL LIFE BEHIND. BOW YOUR MISERABLE HEAD
IN THE PRISON, IT'S THE PRISON YARD BOSS AND HIS MEN WHO RULE!

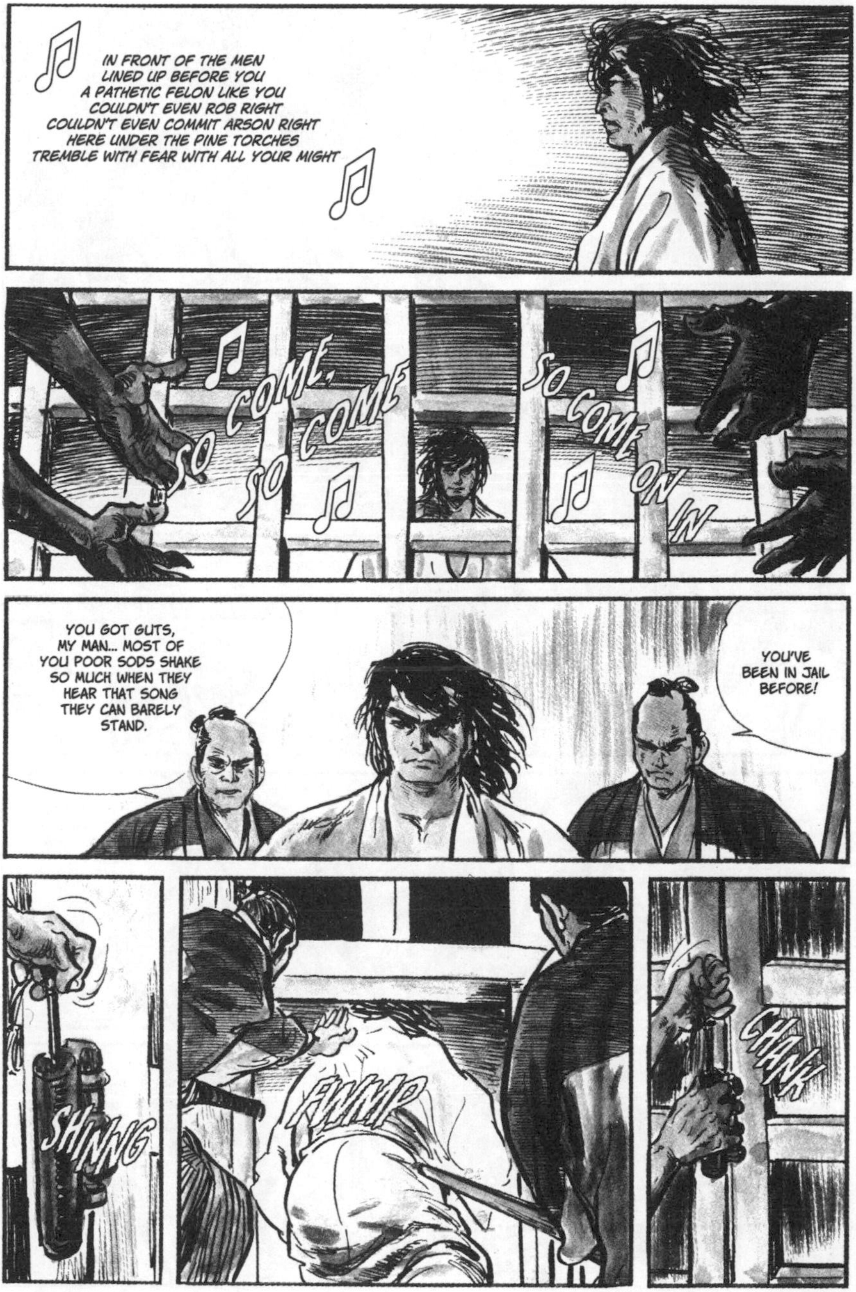
IN FRONT OF THE MEN LINED UP BEFORE YOU A PATHETIC FELON LIKE YOU COULDN'T EVEN ROB RIGHT COULDN'T EVEN COMMIT ARSON RIGHT HERE UNDER THE PINE TORCHES TREMBLE WITH FEAR WITH ALL YOUR MIGHT
SO COME, SO COME
SO COME ON IN
YOU GOT GUTS, MY MAN... MOST OF YOU POOR SODS SHAKE SO MUCH WHEN THEY HEAR THAT SONG THEY CAN BARELY STAND.
YOU'VE BEEN IN JAIL BEFORE!
SHINNG
FUMP
CHINK

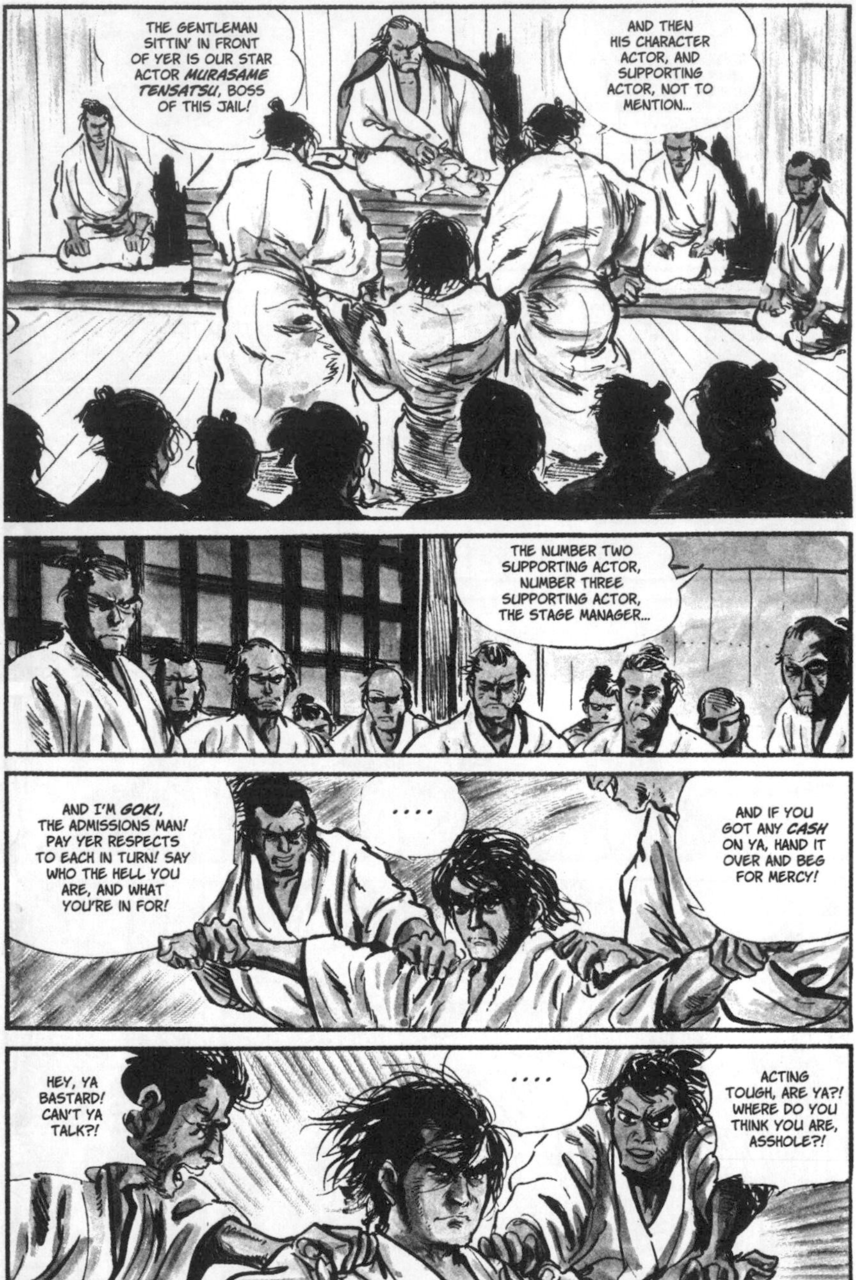
THE GENTLEMAN SITTIN' IN FRONT OF YER IS OUR STAR ACTOR *MURASAME TENSATSU*, BOSS OF THIS JAIL!
AND THEN HIS CHARACTER ACTOR, AND SUPPORTING ACTOR, NOT TO MENTION...
THE NUMBER TWO SUPPORTING ACTOR, NUMBER THREE SUPPORTING ACTOR, THE STAGE MANAGER...
AND I'M *GOKI*, THE ADMISSIONS MAN! PAY YER RESPECTS TO EACH IN TURN! SAY WHO THE HELL YOU ARE, AND WHAT YOU'RE IN FOR!
....
AND IF YOU GOT ANY *CASH* ON YA, HAND IT OVER AND BEG FOR MERCY!
HEY, YA BASTARD! CAN'T YA TALK?!
....
ACTING TOUGH, ARE YA?! WHERE DO YOU THINK YOU ARE, ASSHOLE?!

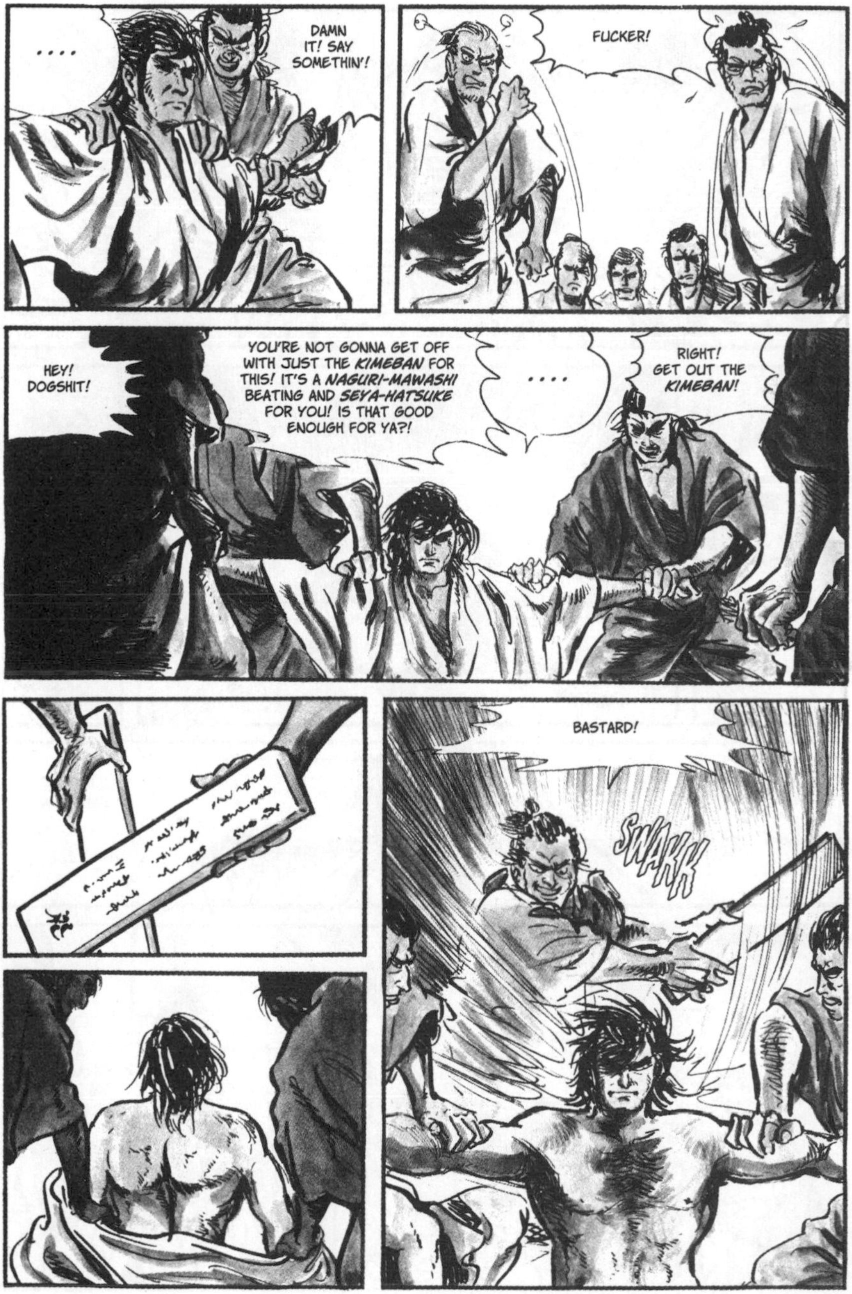
....
DAMN IT! SAY SOMETHIN'!
FUCKER!
HEY! DOGSHIT!
YOU'RE NOT GONNA GET OFF WITH JUST THE *KIMEBAN* FOR THIS! IT'S A *NAGURI-MAWASHI* BEATING AND *SEYA-HATSUKE* FOR YOU! IS THAT GOOD ENOUGH FOR YA?!
....
RIGHT! GET OUT THE *KIMEBAN*!
BASTARD!
SWAKK

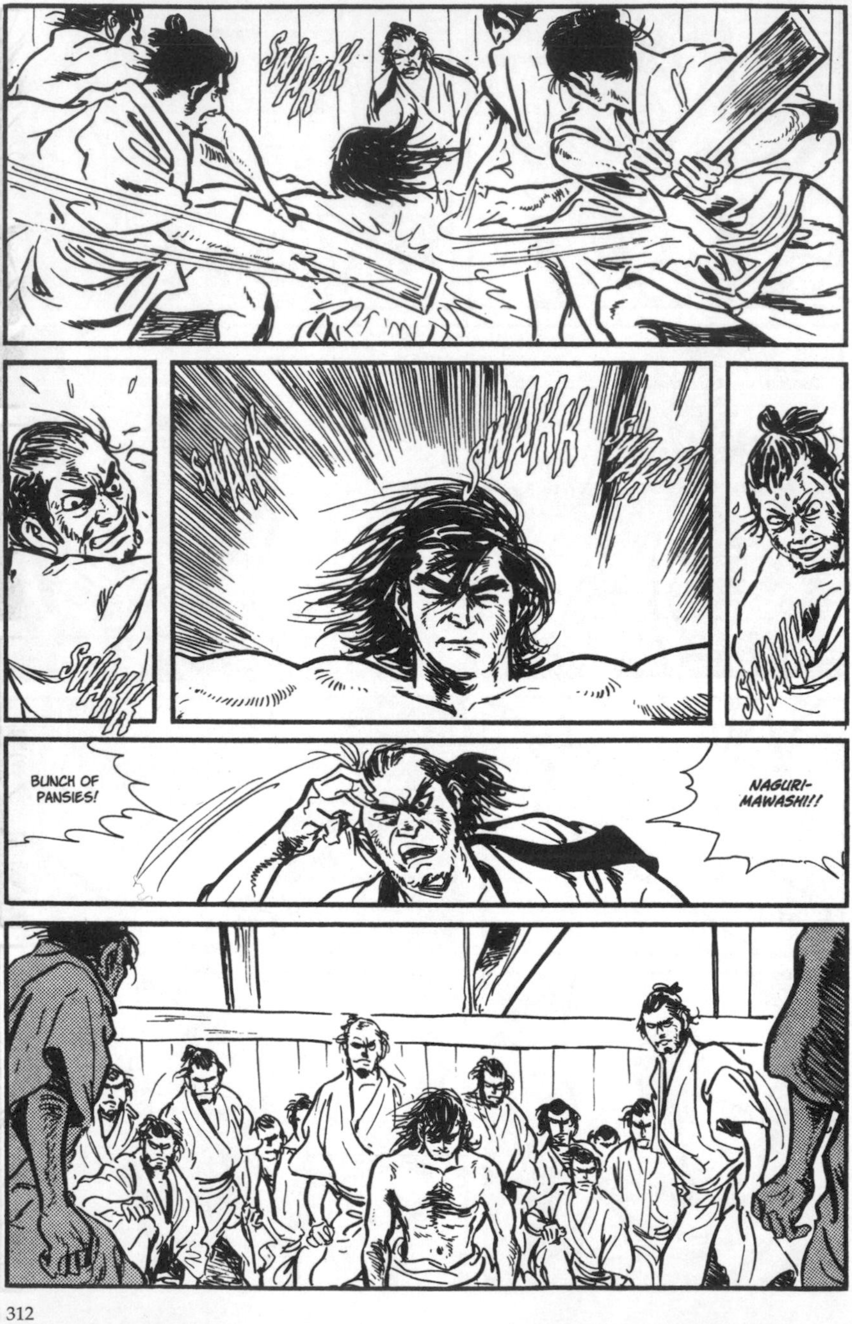
SWAKK
SWAKK
SWAKK
SWAKK
SWAKK
SWAKK
NAGURI-MAWASHI!!
BUNCH OF PANSIES!

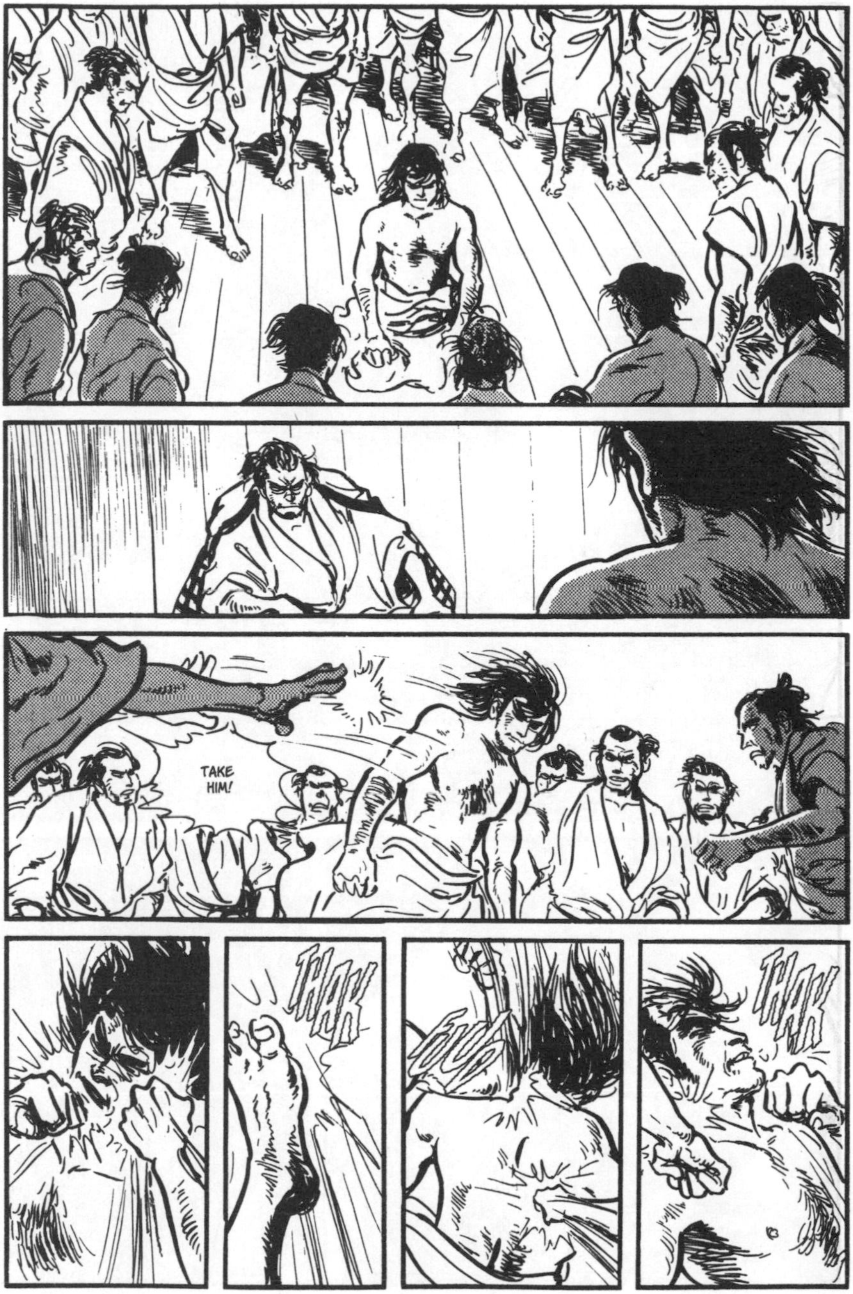
TAKE HIM!
THAK
THAK

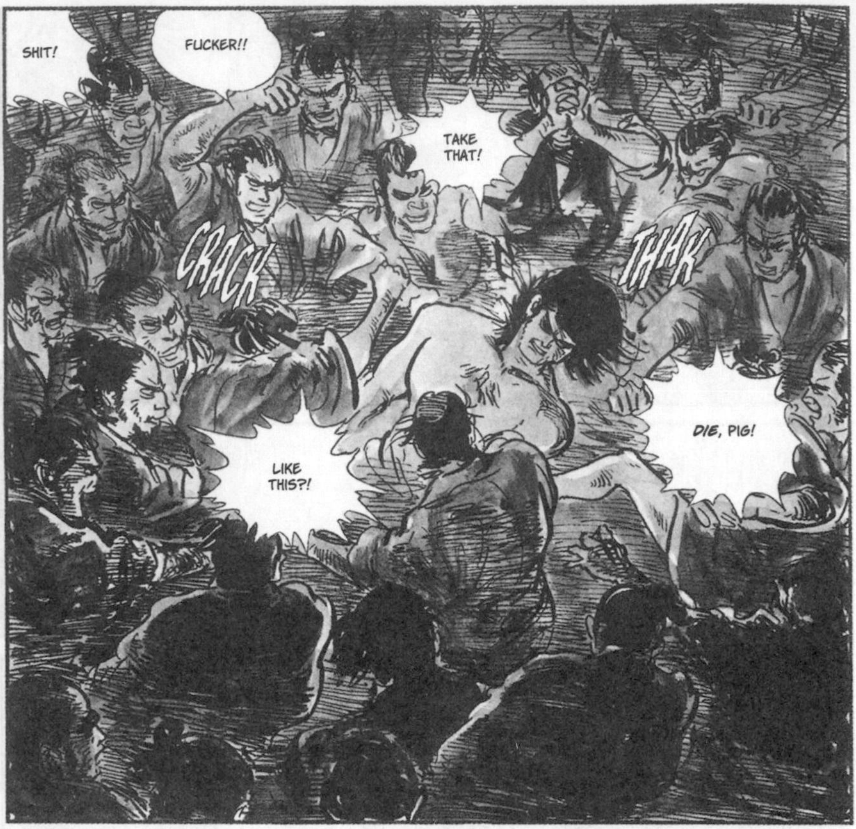
TAKE THAT!
FUCKER!!
SHIT!
THAK
CRACK
DIE, PIG!
LIKE THIS?!
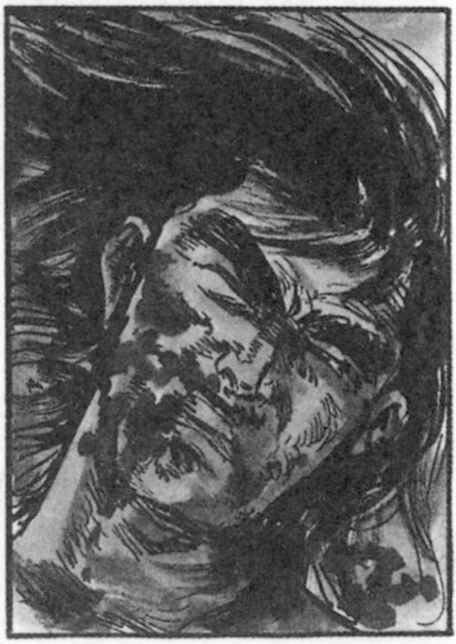
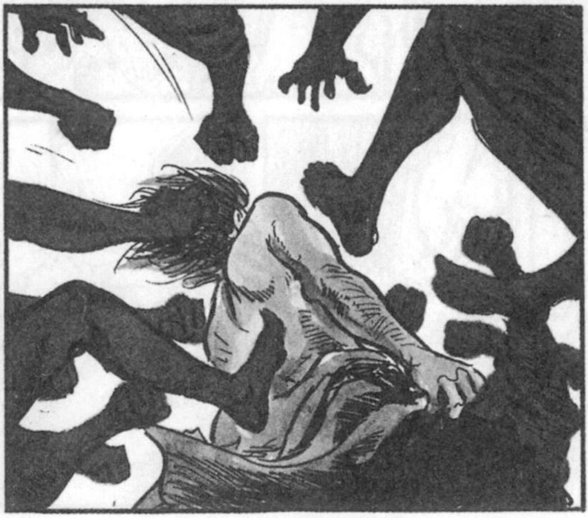

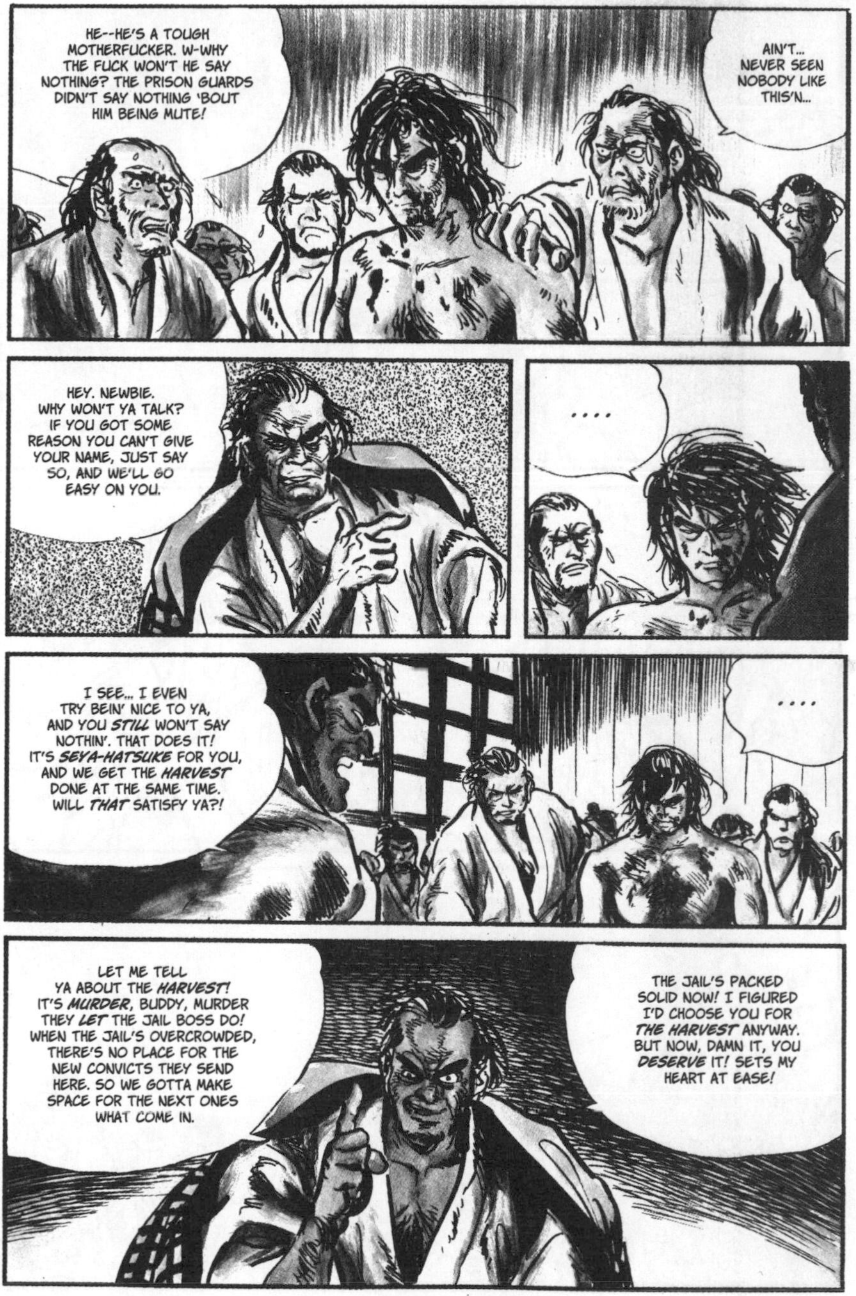
HE--HE'S A TOUGH MOTHERFUCKER. W-WHY THE FUCK WON'T HE SAY NOTHING? THE PRISON GUARDS DIDN'T SAY NOTHING 'BOUT HIM BEING MUTE!
AIN'T... NEVER SEEN NOBODY LIKE THIS'N...
HEY. NEWBIE. WHY WON'T YA TALK? IF YOU GOT SOME REASON YOU CAN'T GIVE YOUR NAME, JUST SAY SO, AND WE'LL GO EASY ON YOU.
....
I SEE... I EVEN TRY BEIN' NICE TO YA, AND YOU STILL WON'T SAY NOTHIN'. THAT DOES IT! IT'S SEYA-HATSUKE FOR YOU, AND WE GET THE HARVEST DONE AT THE SAME TIME. WILL THAT SATISFY YA?!
....
LET ME TELL YA ABOUT THE HARVEST! IT'S MURDER, BUDDY, MURDER THEY LET THE JAIL BOSS DO! WHEN THE JAIL'S OVERCROWDED, THERE'S NO PLACE FOR THE NEW CONVICTS THEY SEND HERE. SO WE GOTTA MAKE SPACE FOR THE NEXT ONES WHAT COME IN.
THE JAIL'S PACKED SOLID NOW! I FIGURED I'D CHOOSE YOU FOR THE HARVEST ANYWAY. BUT NOW, DAMN IT, YOU DESERVE IT! SETS MY HEART AT EASE!

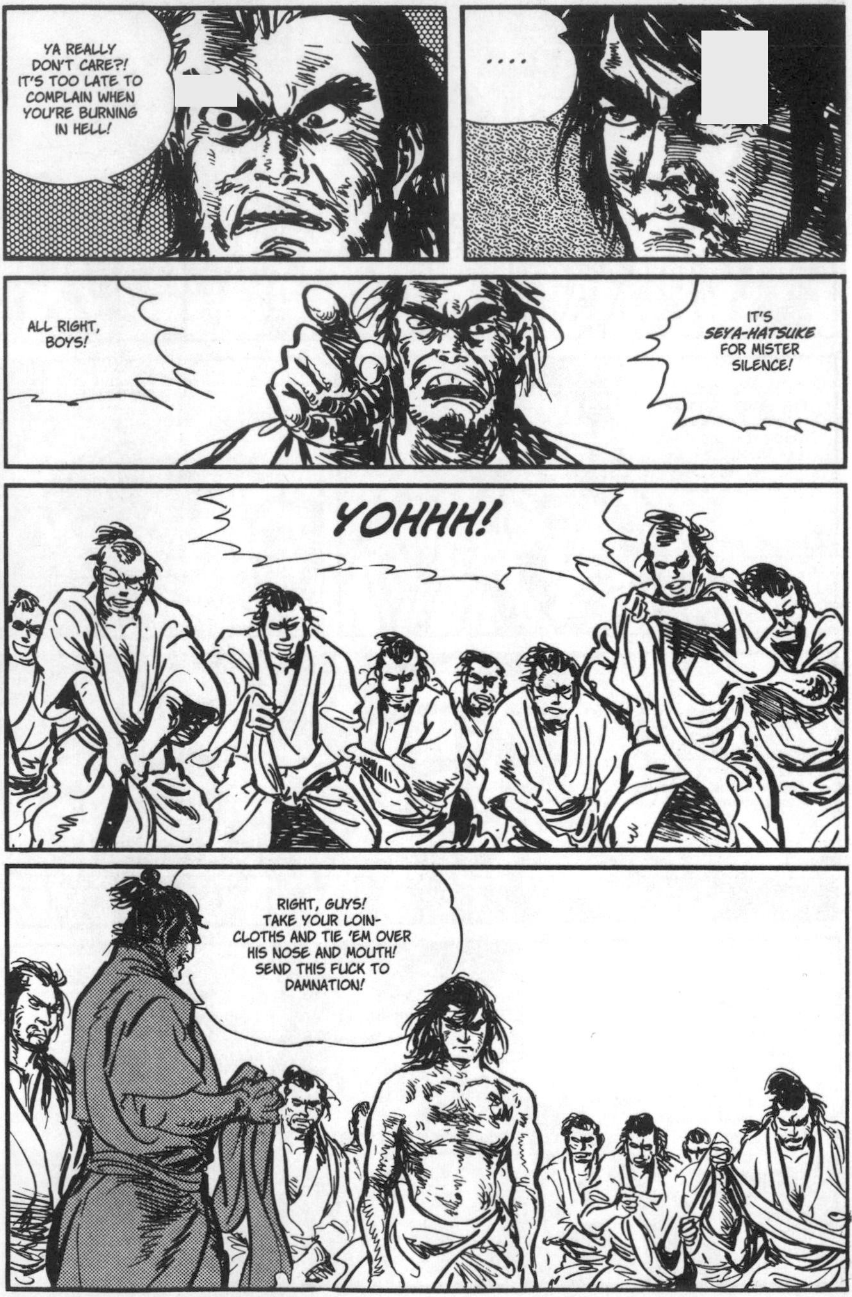
YA REALLY DON'T CARE?! IT'S TOO LATE TO COMPLAIN WHEN YOU'RE BURNING IN HELL!
....
ALL RIGHT, BOYS!
IT'S SEYA-HATSUKE FOR MISTER SILENCE!
YOHHH!
RIGHT, GUYS! TAKE YOUR LOIN-CLOTHS AND TIE 'EM OVER HIS NOSE AND MOUTH! SEND THIS FUCK TO DAMNATION!

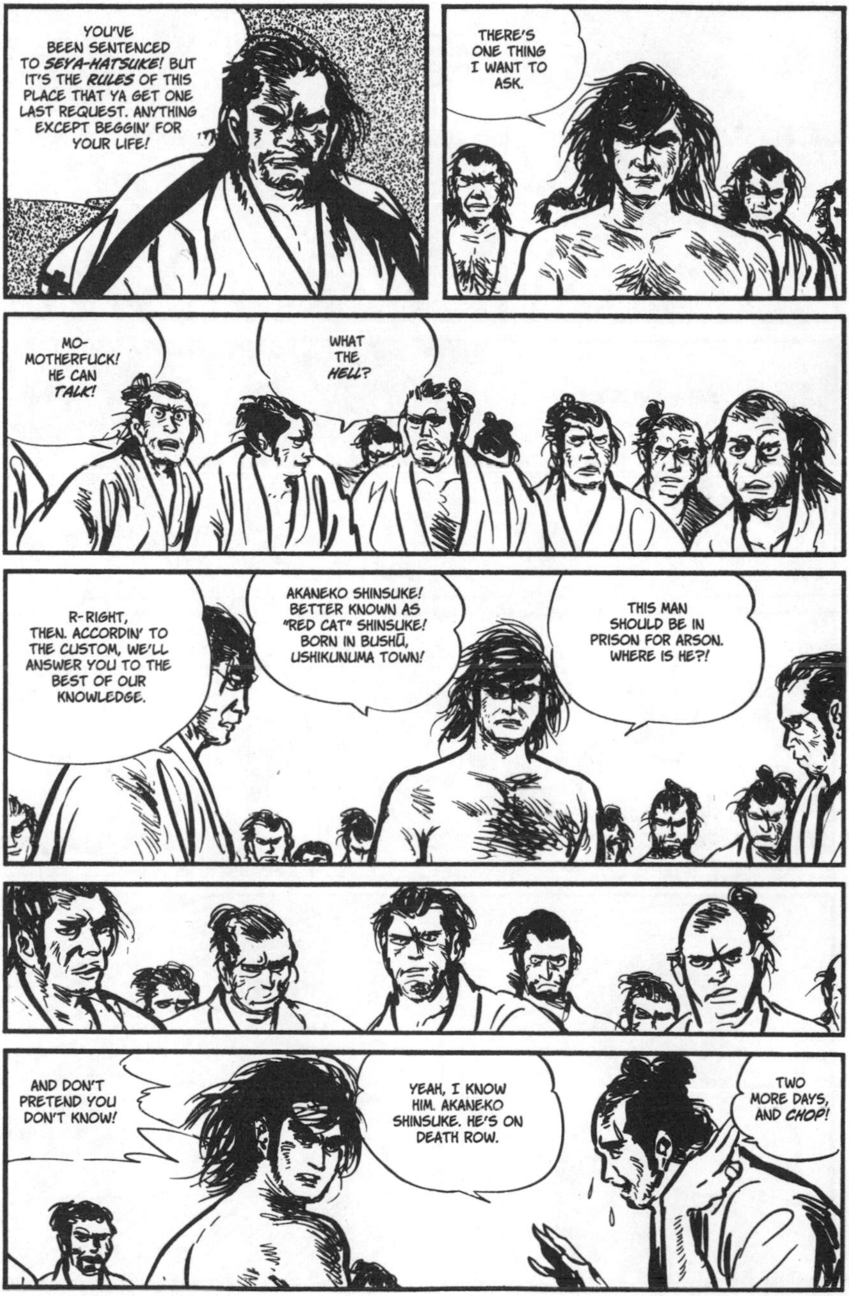
YOU'VE BEEN SENTENCED TO *SEYA-HATSUKE*! BUT IT'S THE *RULES* OF THIS PLACE THAT YA GET ONE LAST REQUEST. ANYTHING EXCEPT BEGGIN' FOR YOUR LIFE!
THERE'S ONE THING I WANT TO ASK.
MO-MOTHERFUCK! HE CAN *TALK*!
WHAT THE *HELL*?
R-RIGHT, THEN. ACCORDIN' TO THE CUSTOM, WE'LL ANSWER YOU TO THE BEST OF OUR KNOWLEDGE.
AKANEKO SHINSUKE! BETTER KNOWN AS "RED CAT" SHINSUKE! BORN IN BUSHŪ, USHIKUNUMA TOWN!
THIS MAN SHOULD BE IN PRISON FOR ARSON. WHERE IS HE?!
AND DON'T PRETEND YOU DON'T KNOW!
YEAH, I KNOW HIM. AKANEKO SHINSUKE. HE'S ON DEATH ROW.
TWO MORE DAYS, AND *CHOP*!

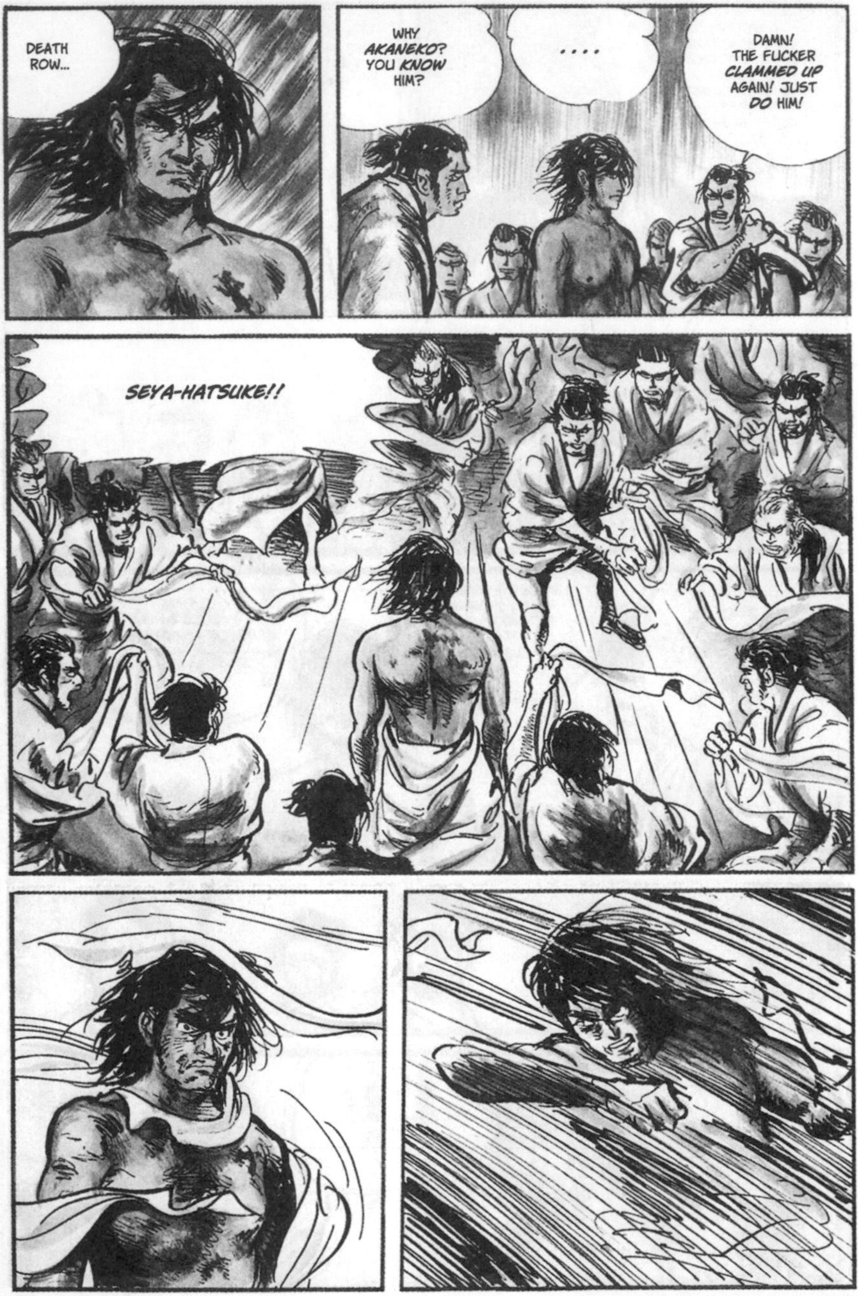
DEATH ROW...
WHY *AKANEKO?* YOU *KNOW* HIM?
....
DAMN! THE FUCKER *CLAMMED UP* AGAIN! JUST *DO* HIM!
SEYA-HATSUKE!!

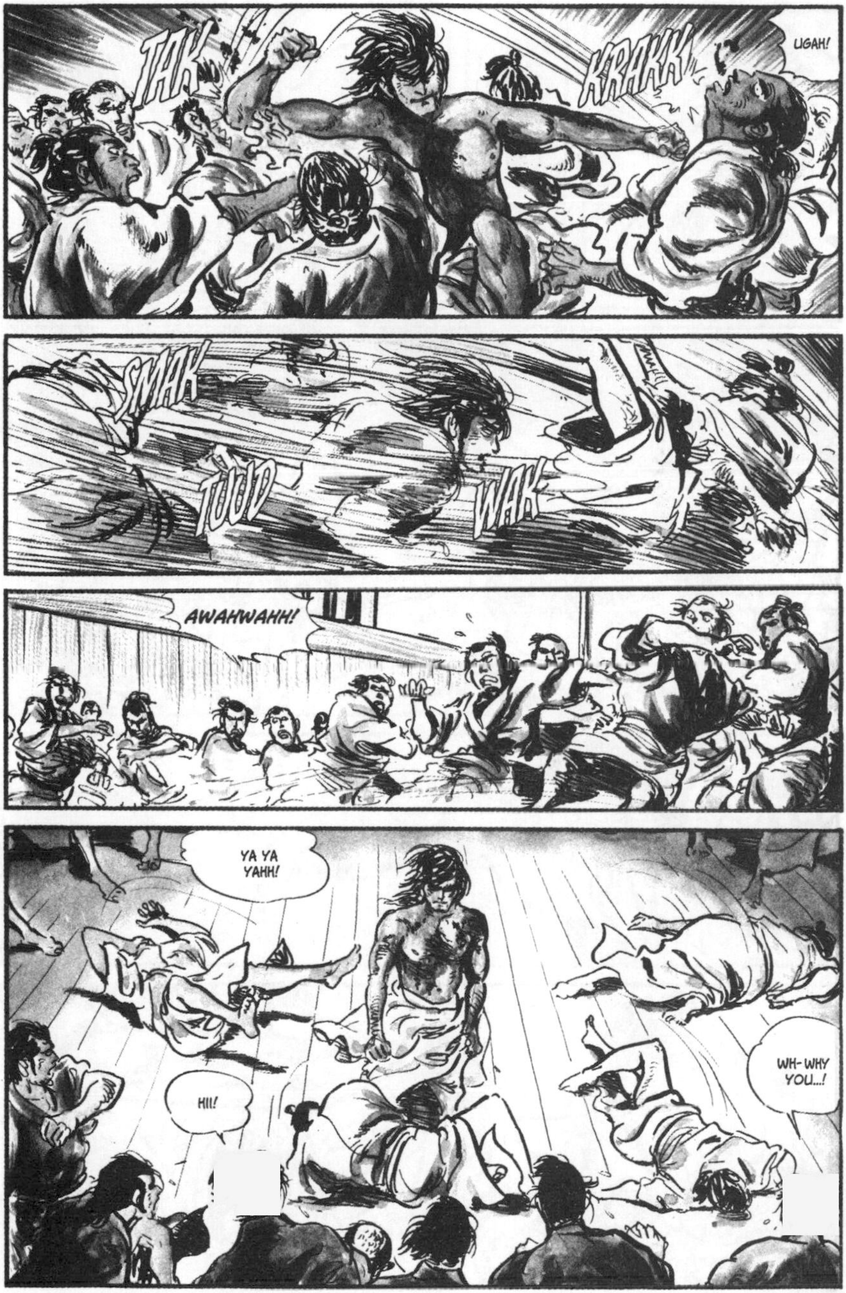
UGAH!
KRAKK
TAK
WAK
TUUD
SMAK
AWAHWAHH!
WH-WHY YOU...!
YA YA YAHH!
HII!

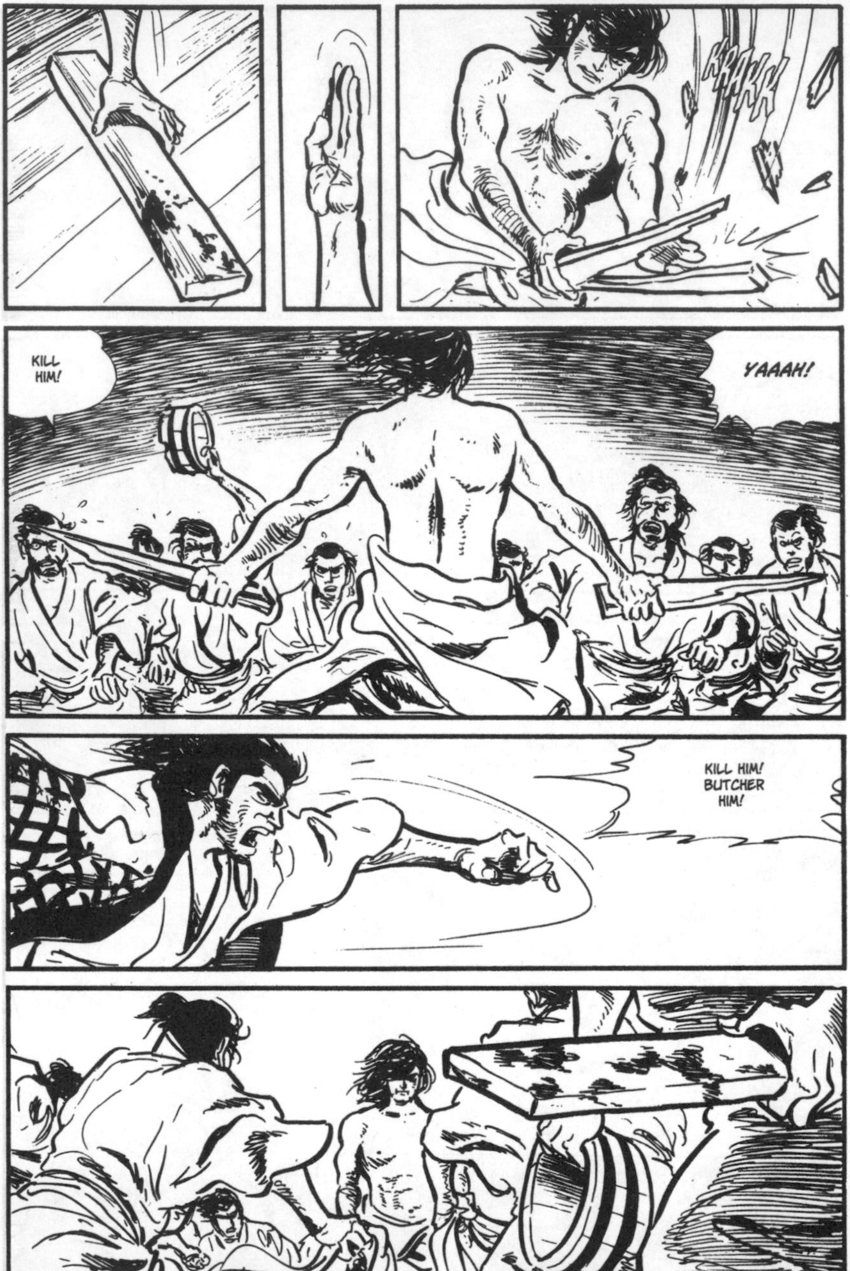
KRAKK
YAAAH!
KILL HIM!
KILL HIM! BUTCHER HIM!

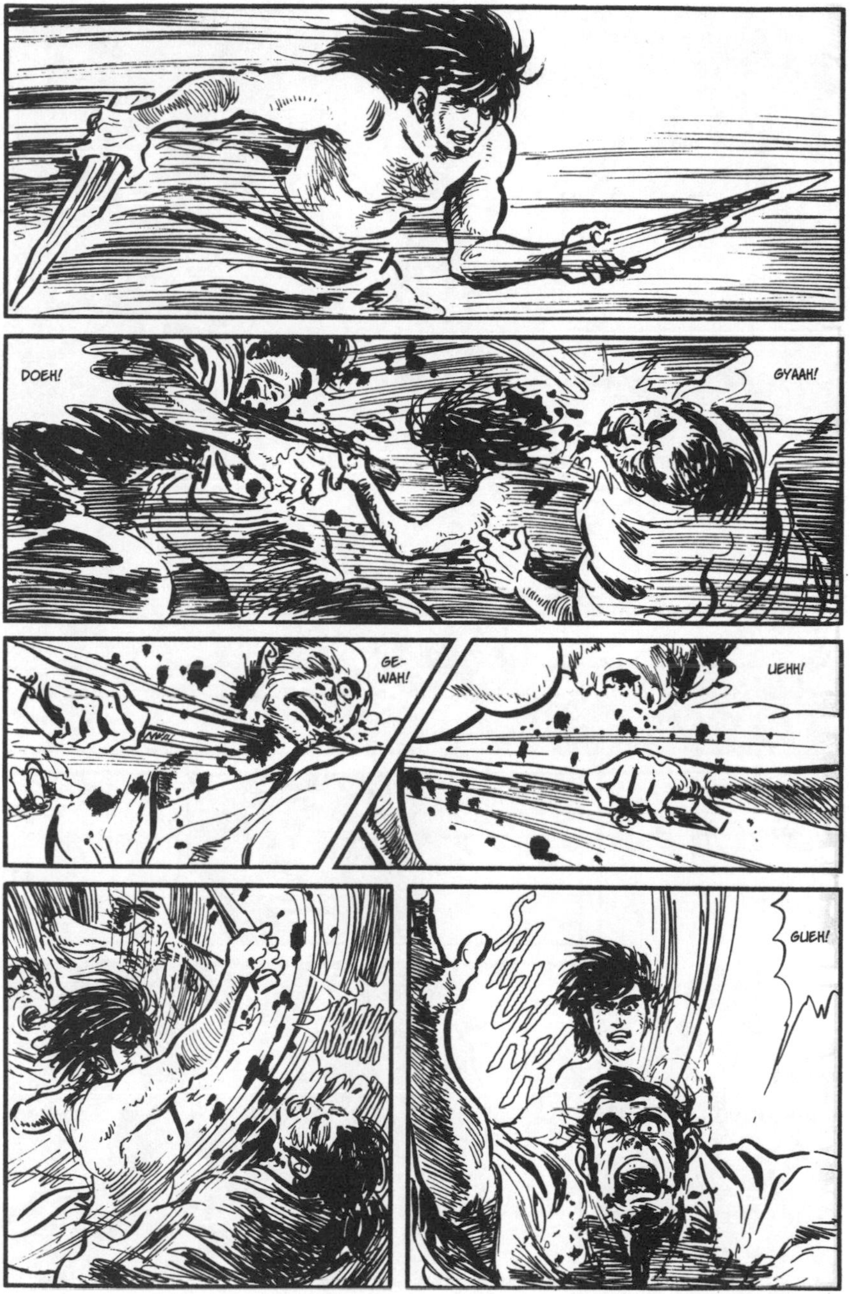
GYAAH!
DOEH!
UEHH!
GE-
WAH!
GUEH!

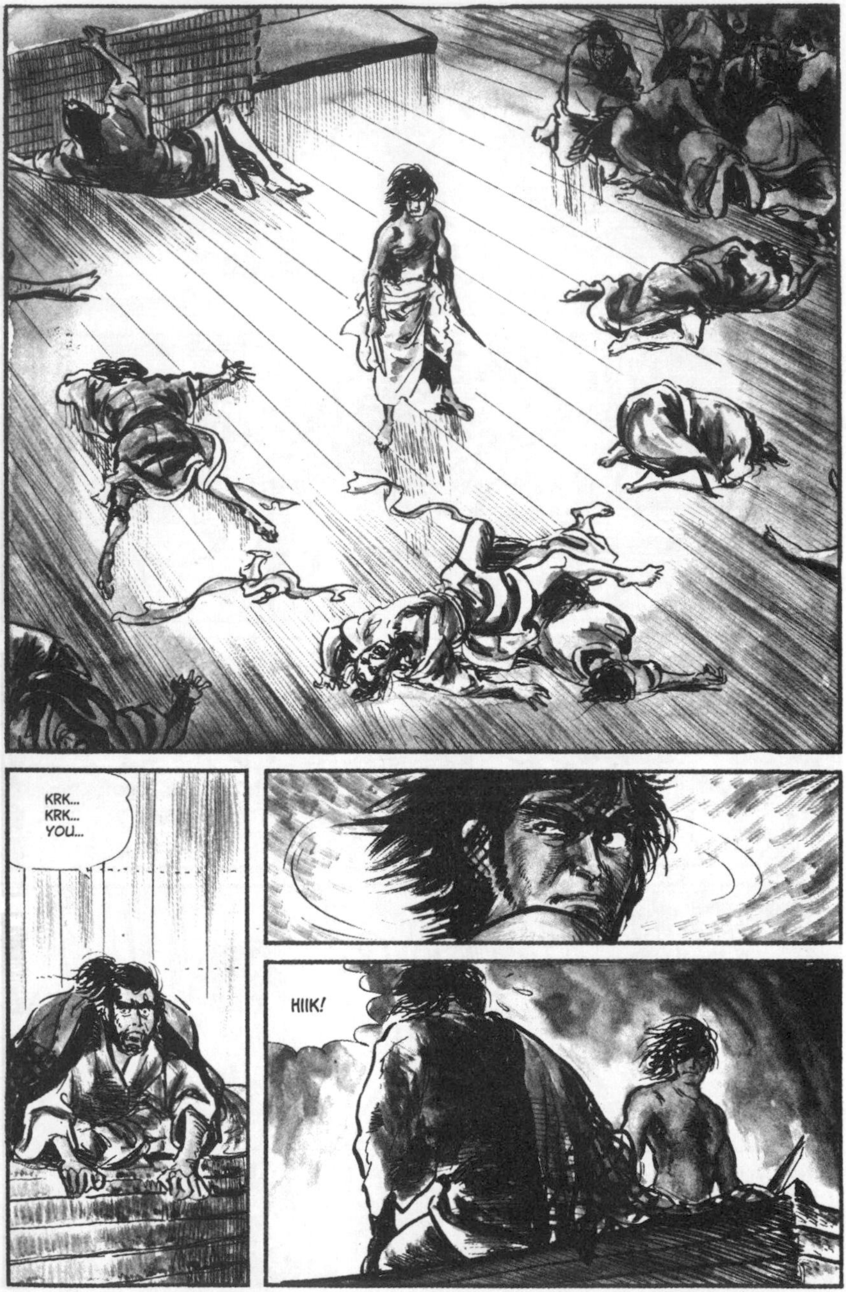
HIIK!
KRK... KRK... YOU...

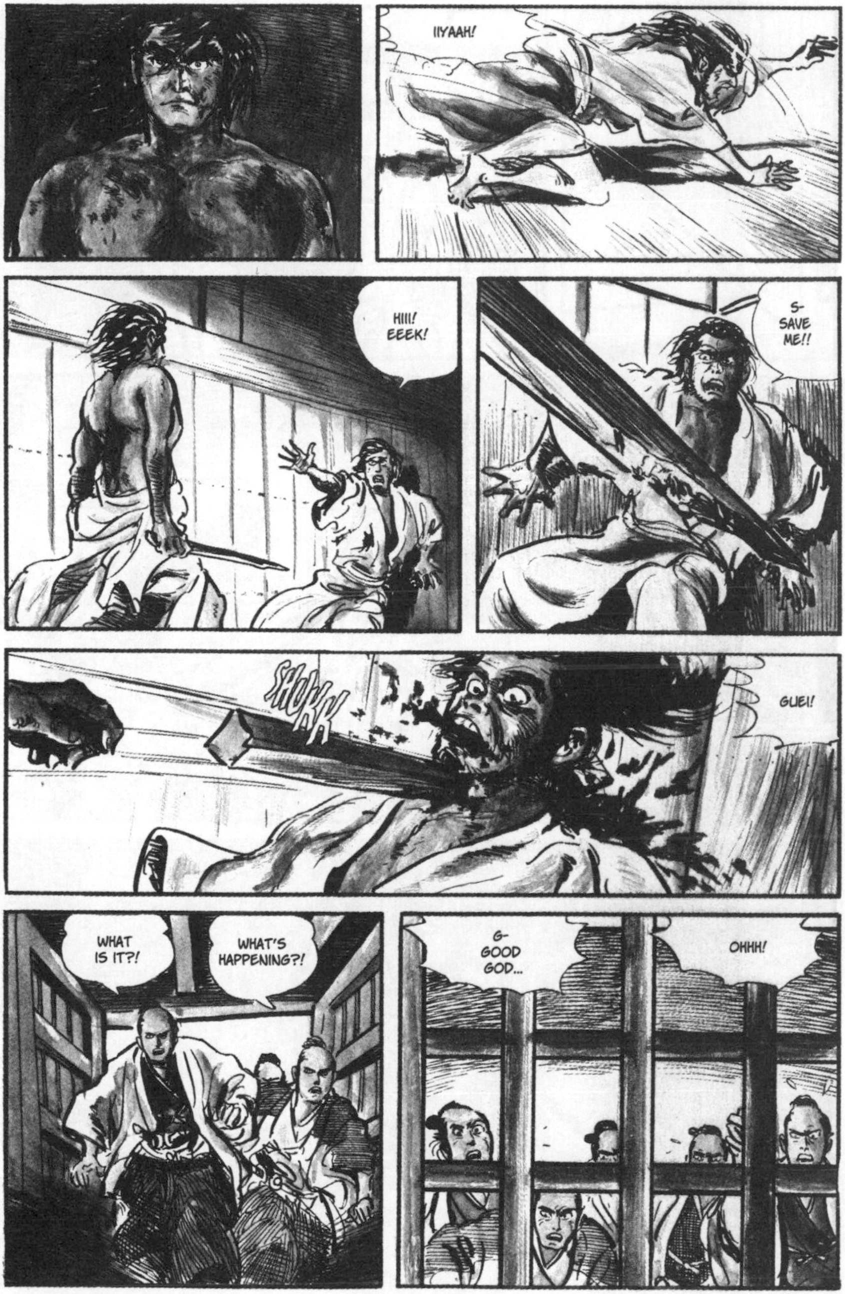
IIYAAH!
HIII! EEEK!
S-SAVE ME!!
SHUKK
GUEI!
WHAT IS IT?!
WHAT'S HAPPENING?!
G-GOOD GOD...
OHHH!

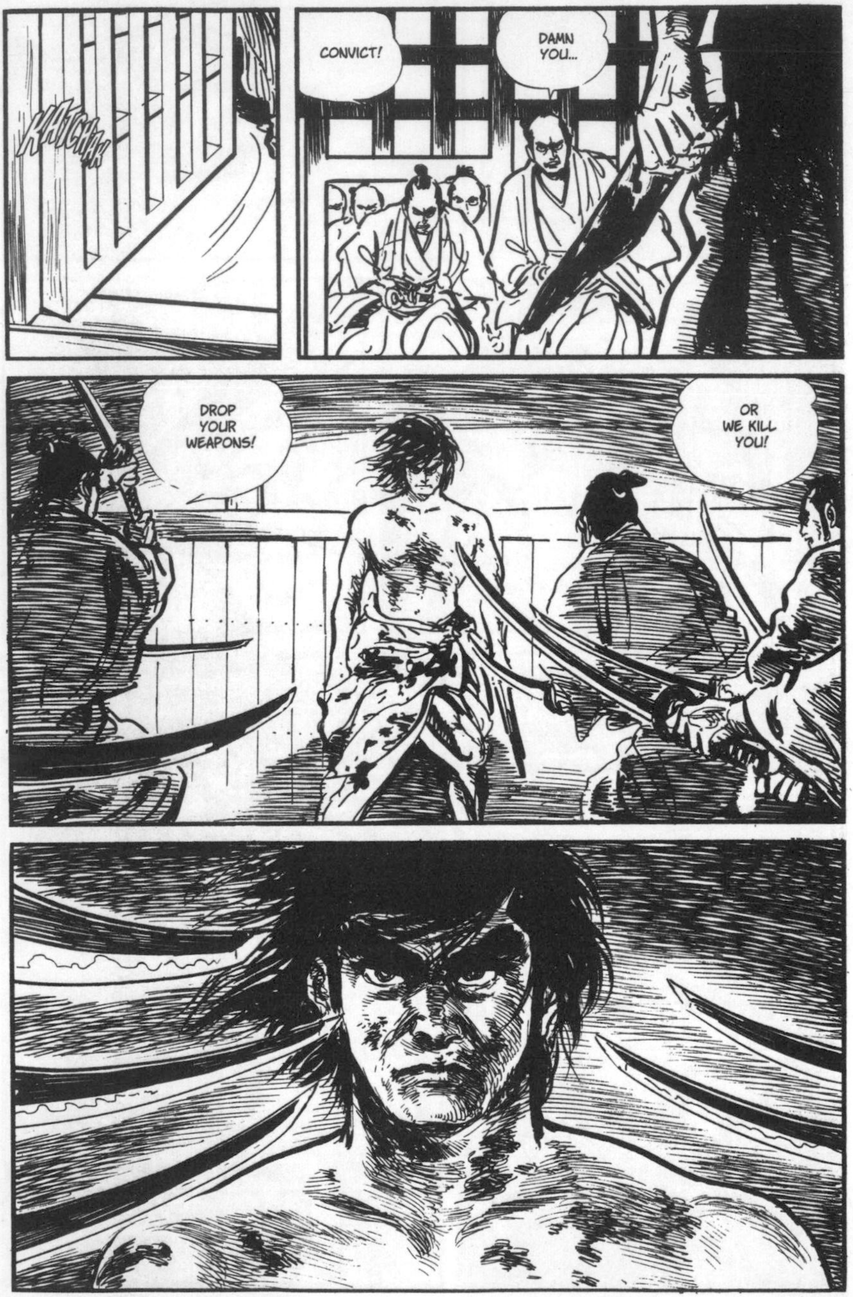
KATCHAK
CONVICT!
DAMN YOU...
DROP YOUR WEAPONS!
OR WE KILL YOU!

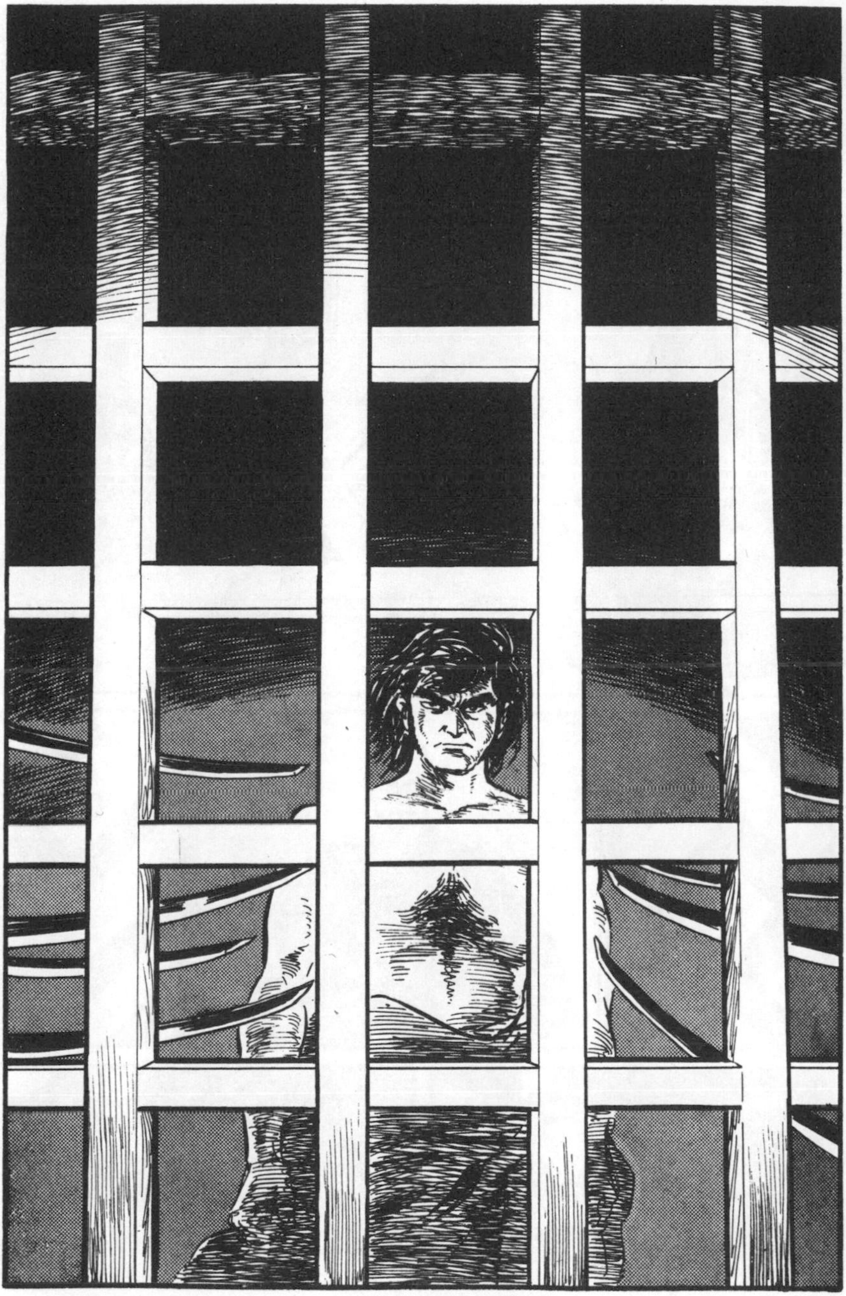

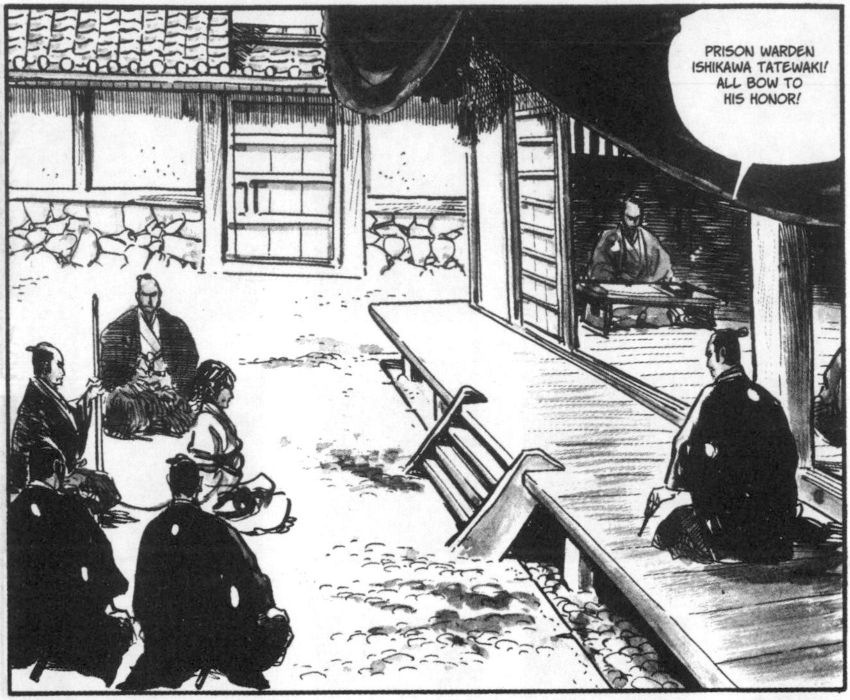
PRISON WARDEN ISHIKAWA TATEWAKI! ALL BOW TO HIS HONOR!
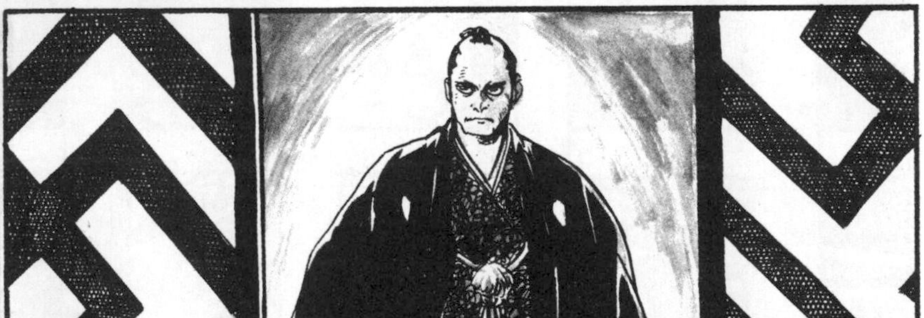
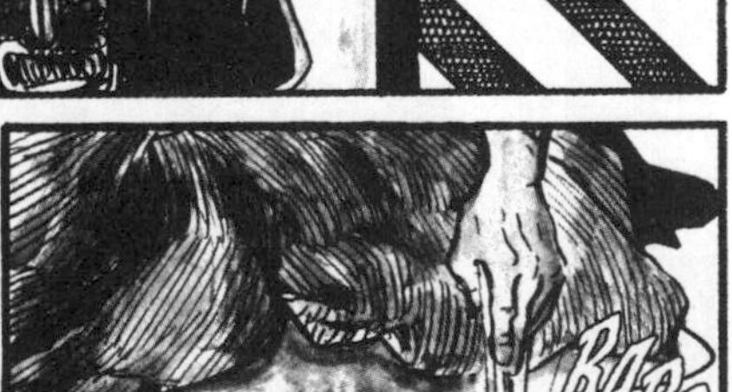
RAPP
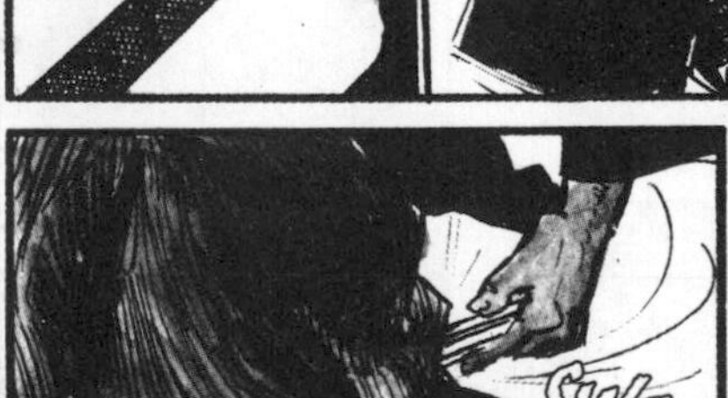
SWIK

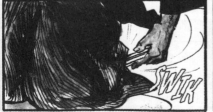

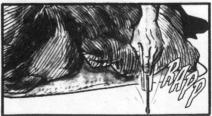

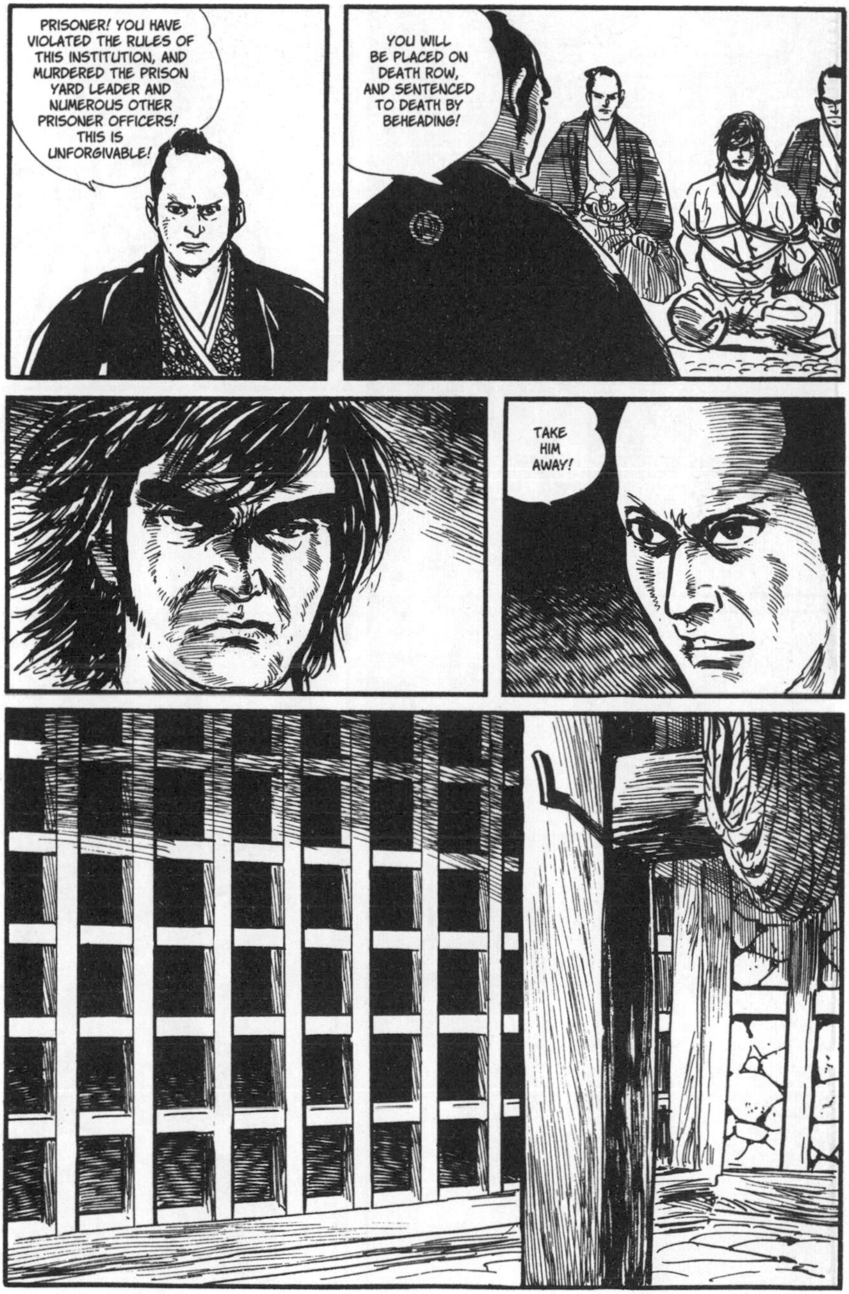
PRISONER! YOU HAVE VIOLATED THE RULES OF THIS INSTITUTION, AND MURDERED THE PRISON YARD LEADER AND NUMEROUS OTHER PRISONER OFFICERS! THIS IS UNFORGIVABLE!
YOU WILL BE PLACED ON DEATH ROW, AND SENTENCED TO DEATH BY BEHEADING!
TAKE HIM AWAY!

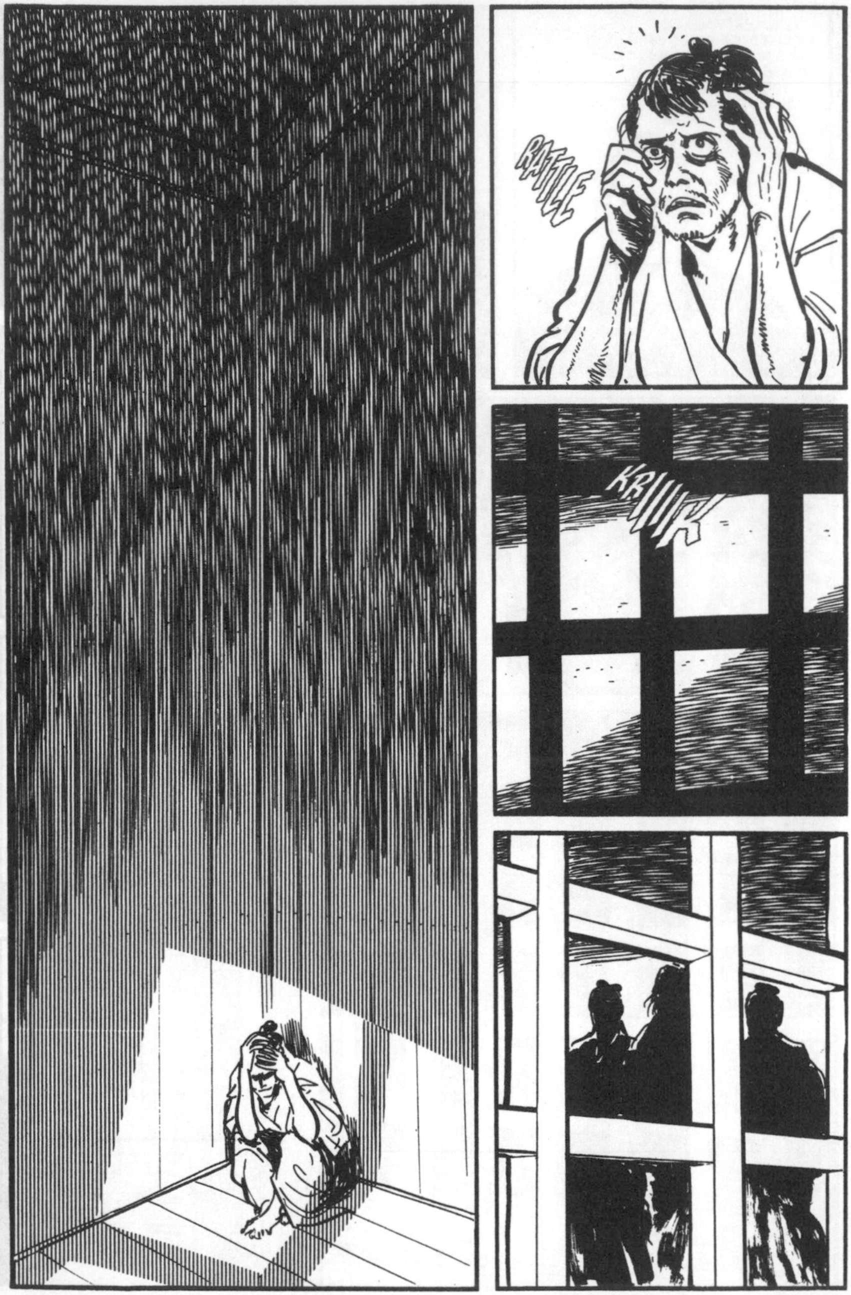
RATTLE
KRIIIK

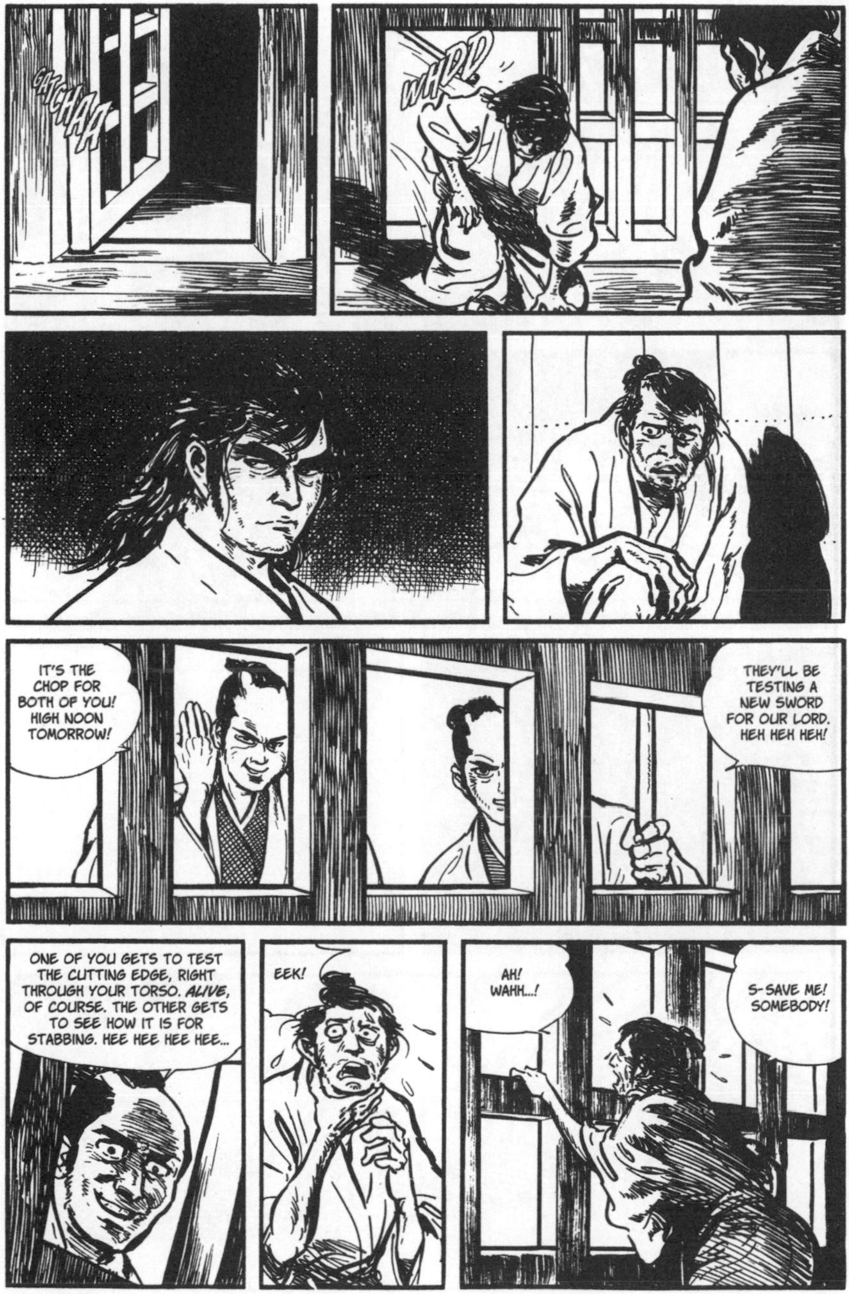
GATCHAA
WHDD
IT'S THE CHOP FOR BOTH OF YOU! HIGH NOON TOMORROW!
THEY'LL BE TESTING A NEW SWORD FOR OUR LORD. HEH HEH HEH!
ONE OF YOU GETS TO TEST THE CUTTING EDGE, RIGHT THROUGH YOUR TORSO. *ALIVE*, OF COURSE. THE OTHER GETS TO SEE HOW IT IS FOR STABBING. HEE HEE HEE HEE...
EEK!
AH! WAHH...!
S-SAVE ME! SOMEBODY!

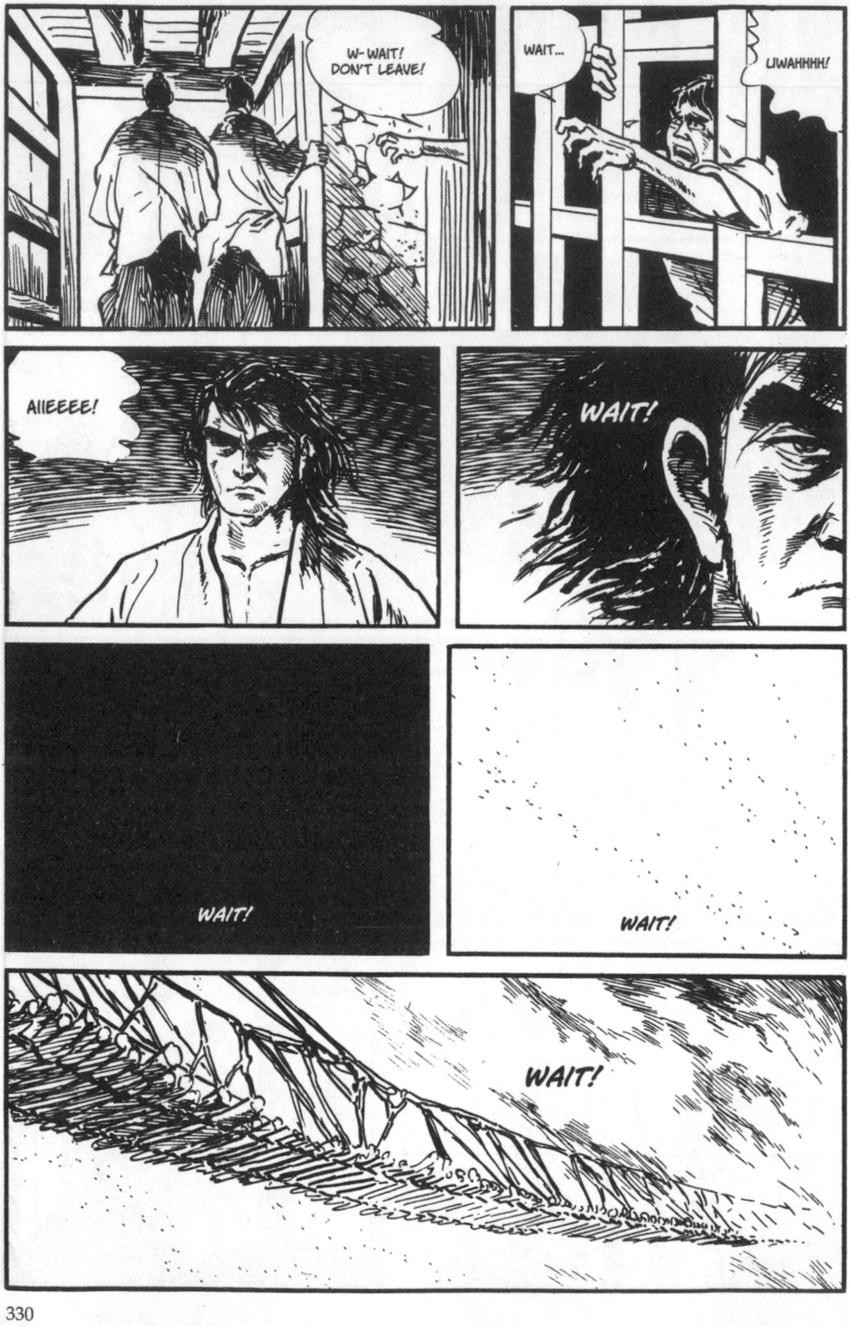
W-WAIT! DON'T LEAVE!
WAIT...
UWAHHHH!
AIIEEEE!
WAIT!
WAIT!
WAIT!
WAIT!

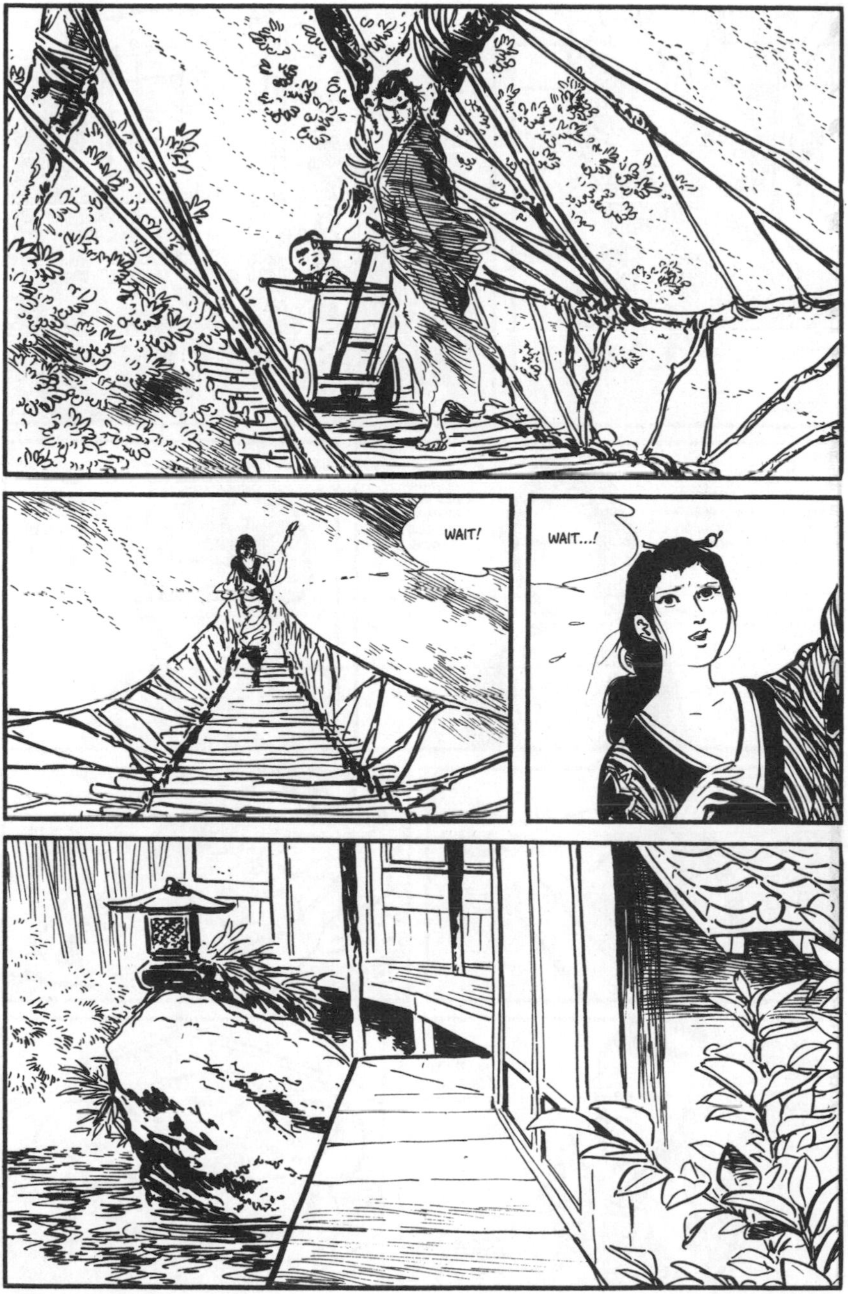
WAIT...!
WAIT!

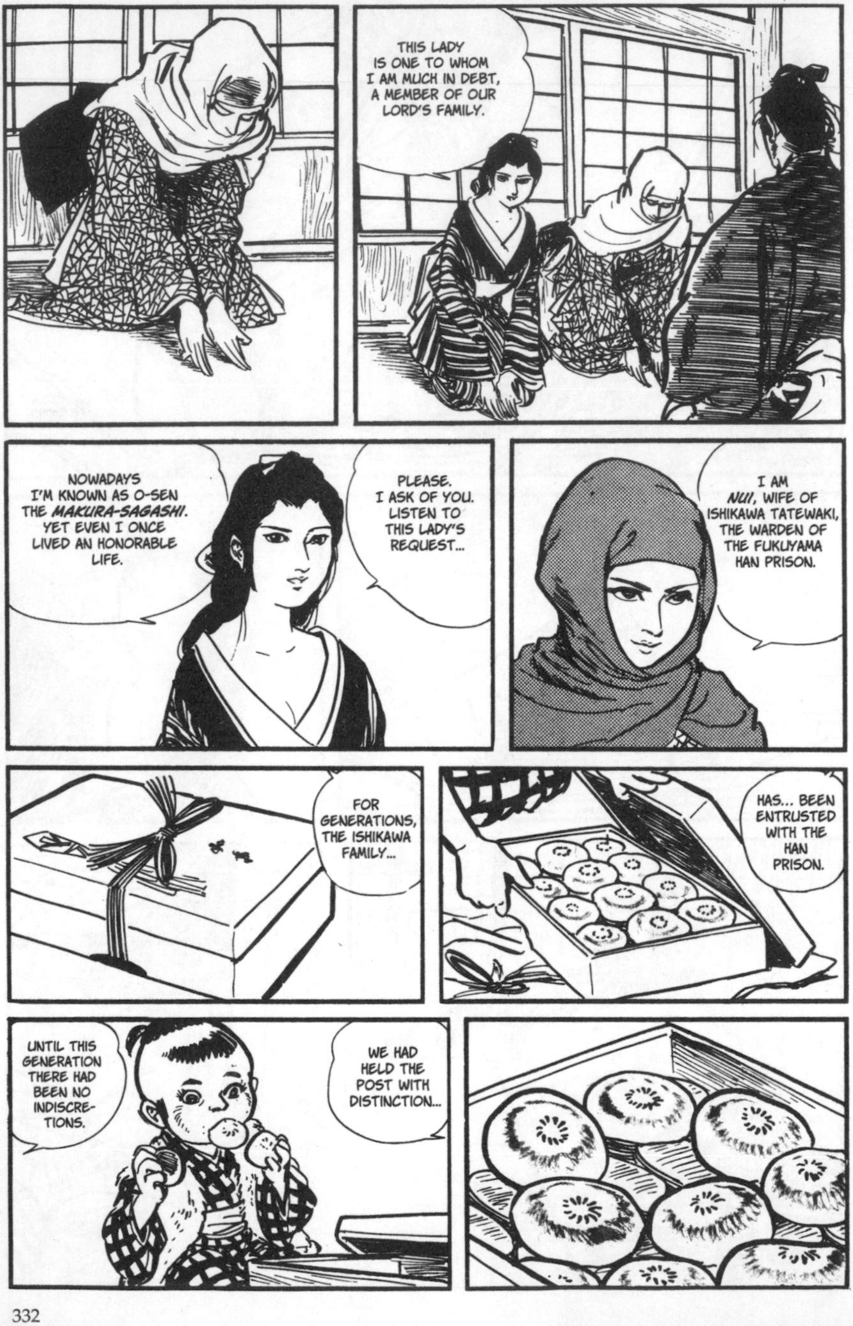
THIS LADY IS ONE TO WHOM I AM MUCH IN DEBT, A MEMBER OF OUR LORD'S FAMILY.
NOWADAYS I'M KNOWN AS O-SEN THE *MAKURA-SAGASHI*. YET EVEN I ONCE LIVED AN HONORABLE LIFE.
PLEASE. I ASK OF YOU. LISTEN TO THIS LADY'S REQUEST...
I AM *NUI*, WIFE OF ISHIKAWA TATEWAKI, THE WARDEN OF THE FUKUYAMA HAN PRISON.
FOR GENERATIONS, THE ISHIKAWA FAMILY...
HAS... BEEN ENTRUSTED WITH THE HAN PRISON.
UNTIL THIS GENERATION THERE HAD BEEN NO INDISCRE-TIONS.
WE HAD HELD THE POST WITH DISTINCTION...

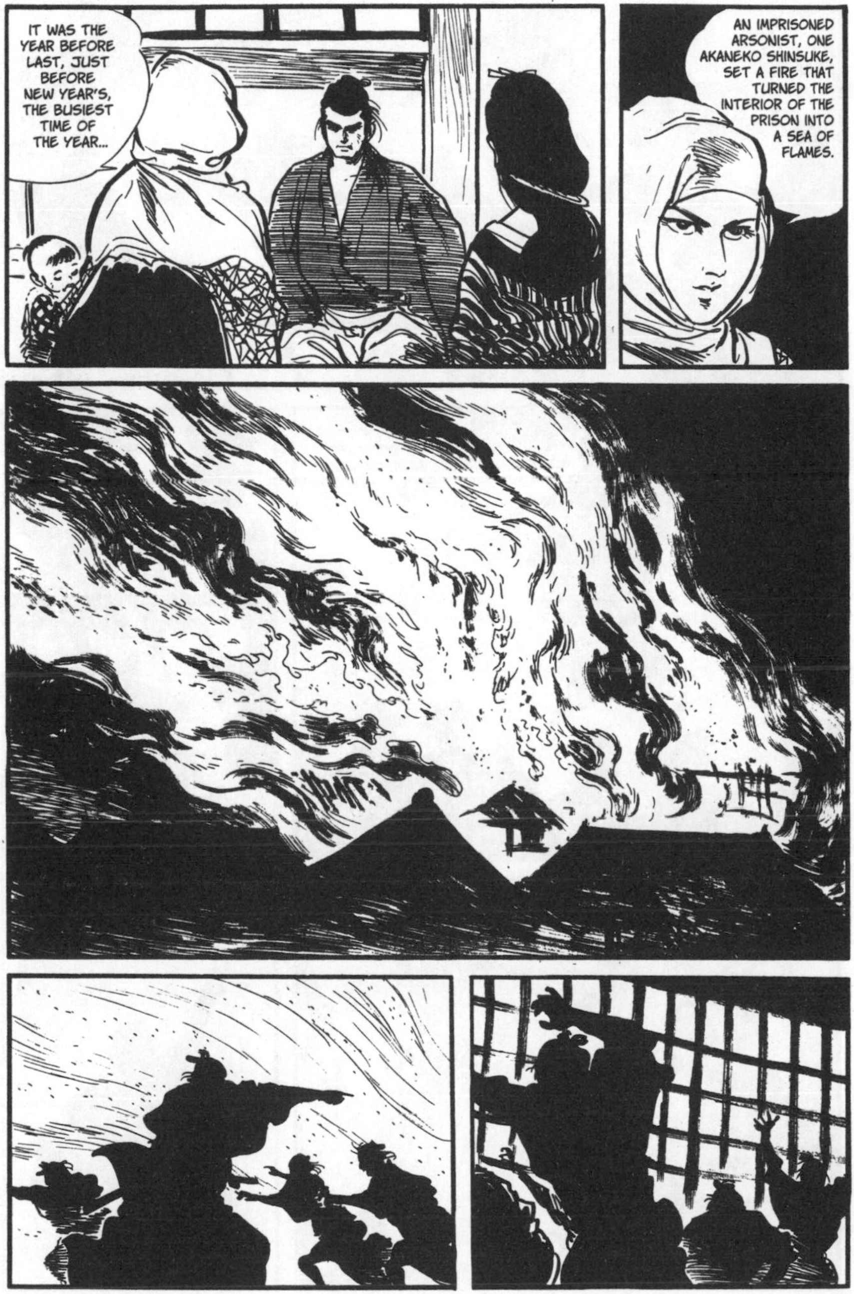
IT WAS THE YEAR BEFORE LAST, JUST BEFORE NEW YEAR'S, THE BUSIEST TIME OF THE YEAR...
AN IMPRISONED ARSONIST, ONE AKANEKO SHINSUKE, SET A FIRE THAT TURNED THE INTERIOR OF THE PRISON INTO A SEA OF FLAMES.

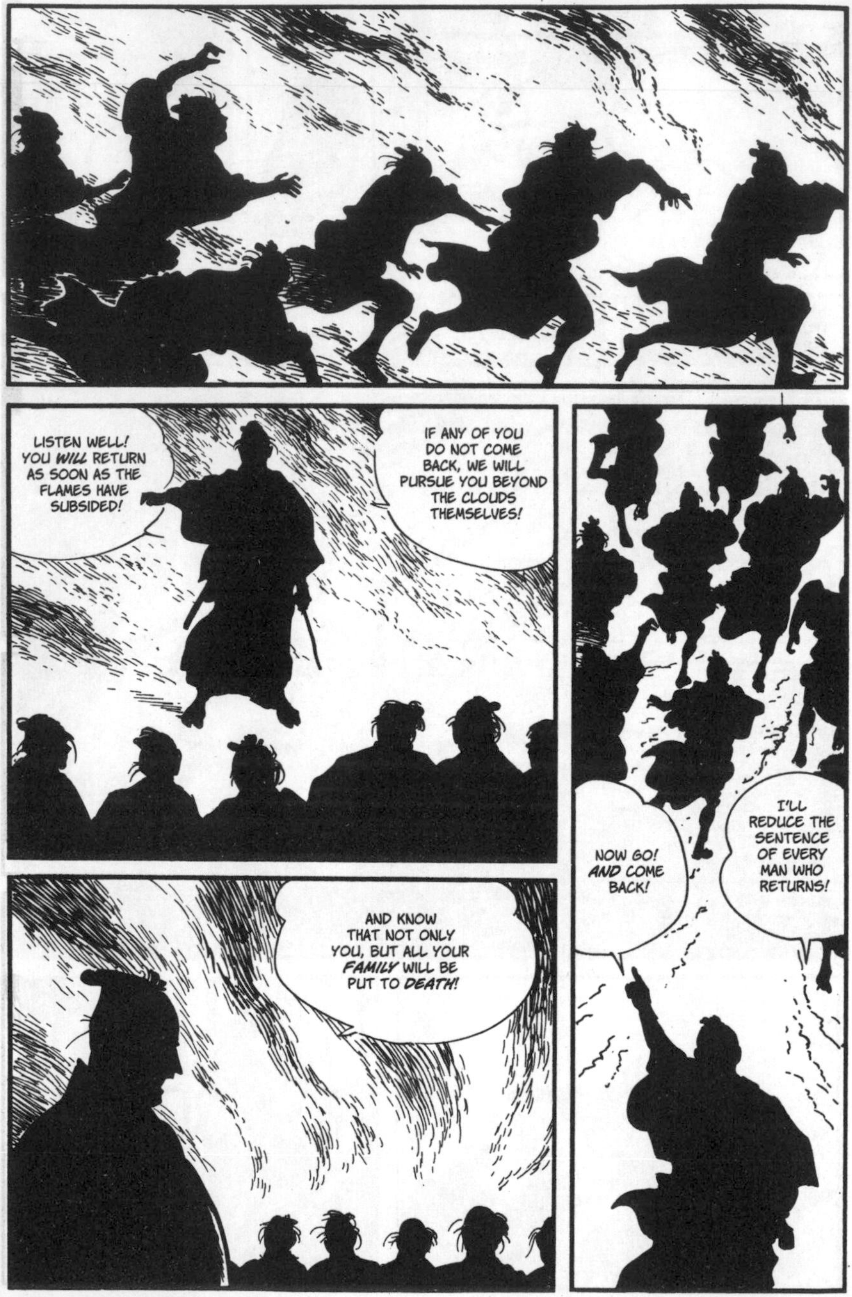
LISTEN WELL! YOU *WILL* RETURN AS SOON AS THE FLAMES HAVE SUBSIDED!
IF ANY OF YOU DO NOT COME BACK, WE WILL PURSUE YOU BEYOND THE CLOUDS THEMSELVES!
AND KNOW THAT NOT ONLY YOU, BUT ALL YOUR *FAMILY* WILL BE PUT TO *DEATH*!
NOW GO! *AND* COME BACK!
I'LL REDUCE THE SENTENCE OF EVERY MAN WHO RETURNS!

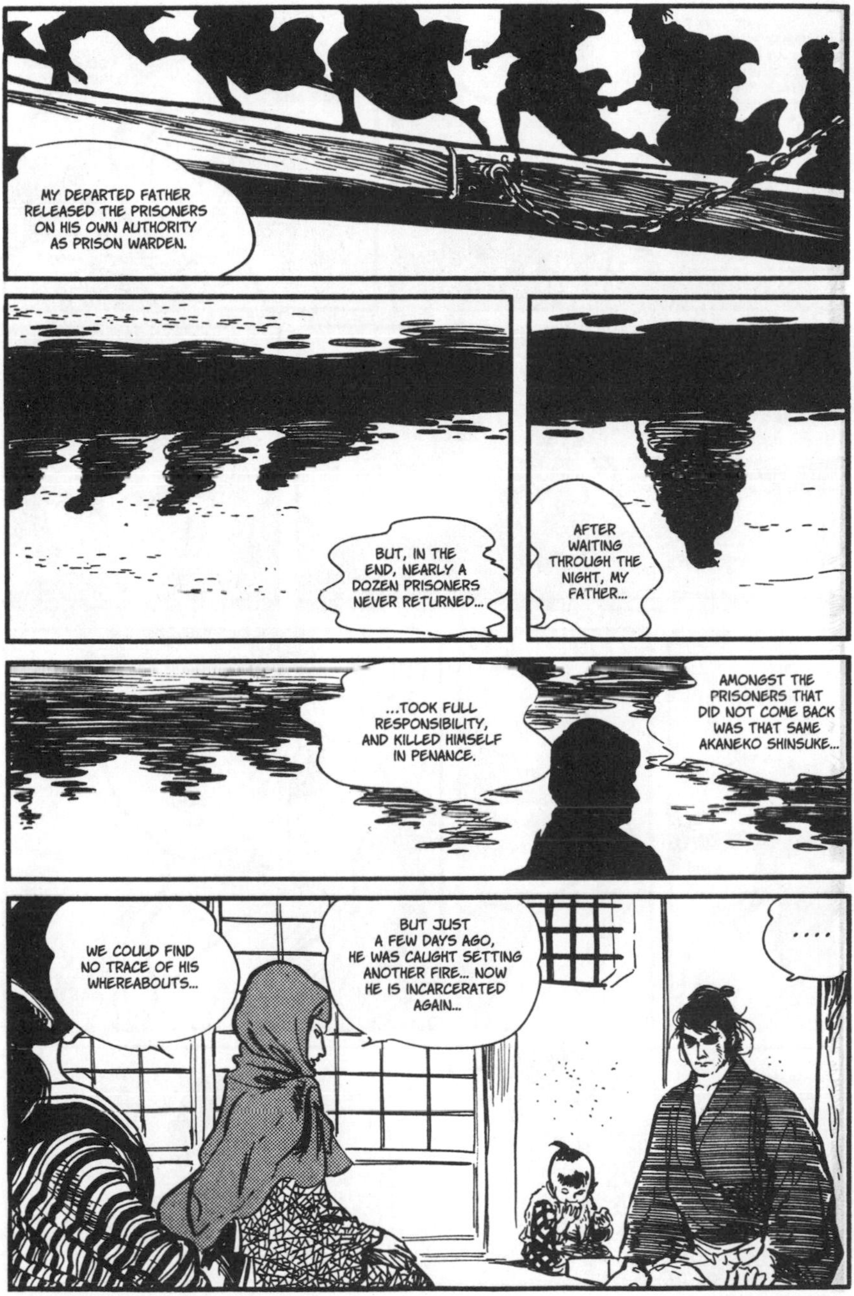
MY DEPARTED FATHER RELEASED THE PRISONERS ON HIS OWN AUTHORITY AS PRISON WARDEN.
BUT, IN THE END, NEARLY A DOZEN PRISONERS NEVER RETURNED...
AFTER WAITING THROUGH THE NIGHT, MY FATHER...
...TOOK FULL RESPONSIBILITY, AND KILLED HIMSELF IN PENANCE.
AMONGST THE PRISONERS THAT DID NOT COME BACK WAS THAT SAME AKANEKO SHINSUKE...
WE COULD FIND NO TRACE OF HIS WHEREABOUTS...
BUT JUST A FEW DAYS AGO, HE WAS CAUGHT SETTING ANOTHER FIRE... NOW HE IS INCARCERATED AGAIN...
....

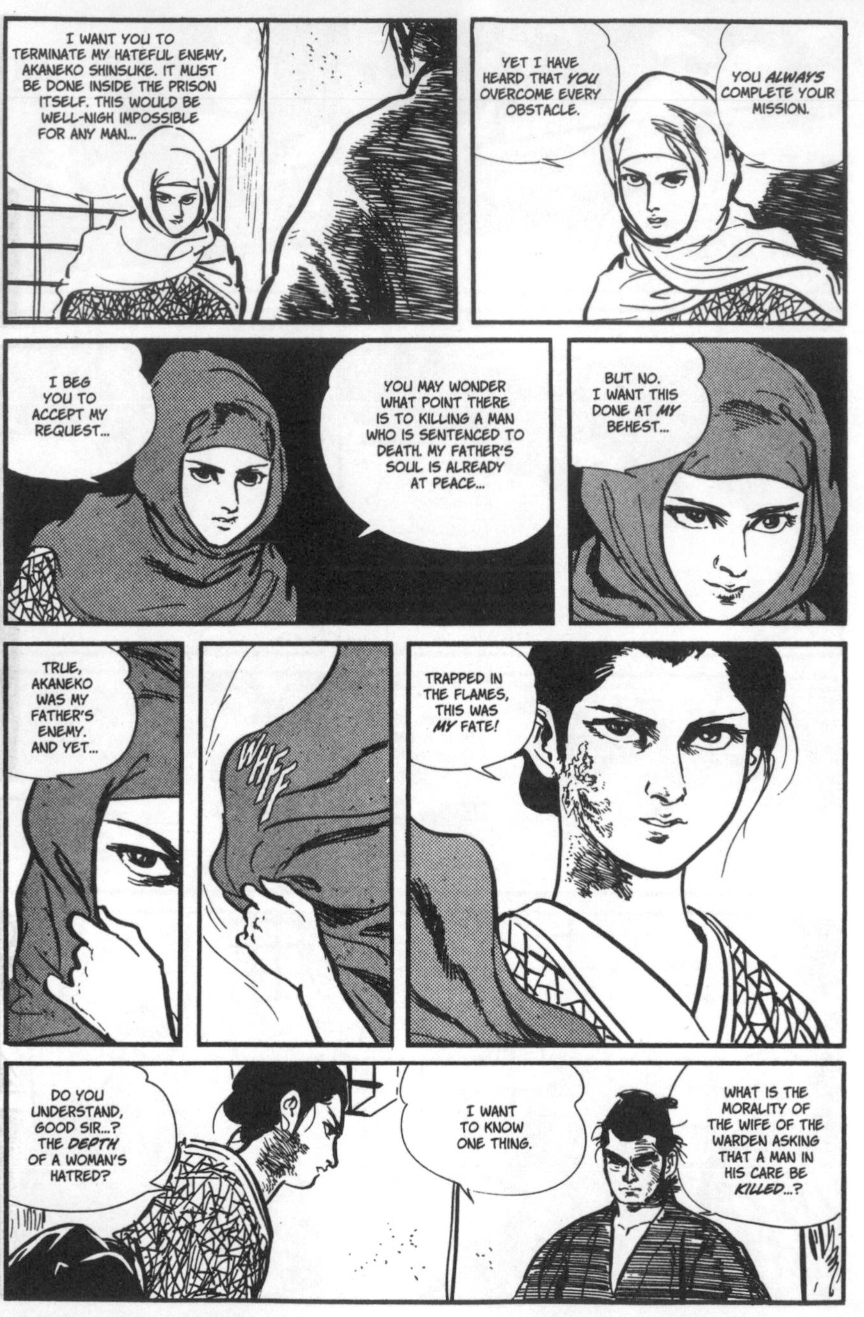
I WANT YOU TO TERMINATE MY HATEFUL ENEMY, AKANEKO SHINSUKE. IT MUST BE DONE INSIDE THE PRISON ITSELF. THIS WOULD BE WELL-NIGH IMPOSSIBLE FOR ANY MAN...
YET I HAVE HEARD THAT *YOU* OVERCOME EVERY OBSTACLE.
YOU *ALWAYS* COMPLETE YOUR MISSION.
I BEG YOU TO ACCEPT MY REQUEST...
YOU MAY WONDER WHAT POINT THERE IS TO KILLING A MAN WHO IS SENTENCED TO DEATH. MY FATHER'S SOUL IS ALREADY AT PEACE...
BUT NO. I WANT THIS DONE AT *MY* BEHEST...
TRUE, AKANEKO WAS MY FATHER'S ENEMY. AND YET...
WHFF
TRAPPED IN THE FLAMES, THIS WAS *MY* FATE!
DO YOU UNDERSTAND, GOOD SIR...? THE *DEPTH* OF A WOMAN'S HATRED?
I WANT TO KNOW ONE THING.
WHAT IS THE MORALITY OF THE WIFE OF THE WARDEN ASKING THAT A MAN IN HIS CARE BE *KILLED*...?

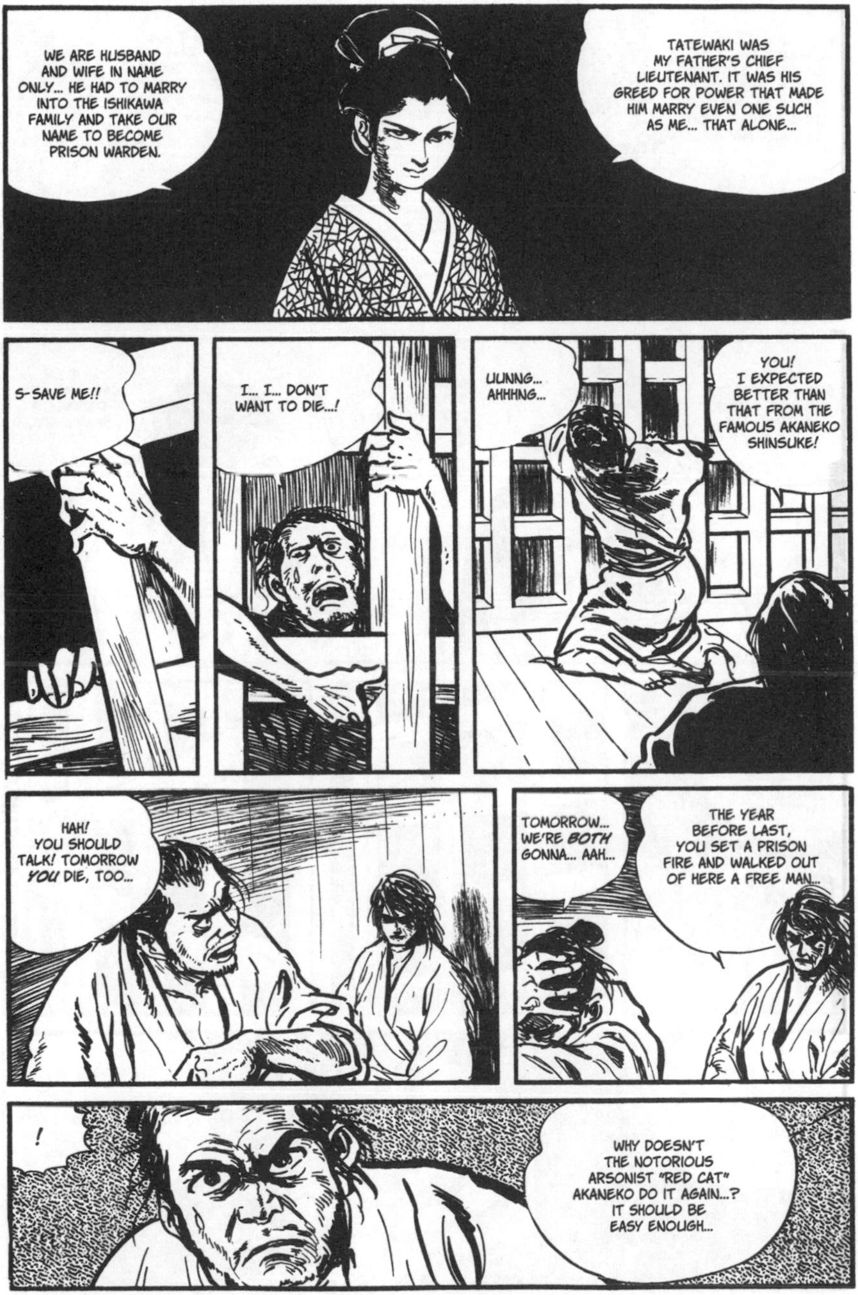

WE ARE HUSBAND AND WIFE IN NAME ONLY... HE HAD TO MARRY INTO THE ISHIKAWA FAMILY AND TAKE OUR NAME TO BECOME PRISON WARDEN.
TATEWAKI WAS MY FATHER'S CHIEF LIEUTENANT. IT WAS HIS GREED FOR POWER THAT MADE HIM MARRY EVEN ONE SUCH AS ME... THAT ALONE...
S-SAVE ME!!
I... I... DON'T WANT TO DIE...!
UUNNG... AHHHNG...
YOU! I EXPECTED BETTER THAN THAT FROM THE FAMOUS AKANEKO SHINSUKE!
HAH! YOU SHOULD TALK! TOMORROW *YOU* DIE, TOO...
TOMORROW... WE'RE ***BOTH*** GONNA... AAH...
THE YEAR BEFORE LAST, YOU SET A PRISON FIRE AND WALKED OUT OF HERE A FREE MAN...
!
WHY DOESN'T THE NOTORIOUS ARSONIST "RED CAT" AKANEKO DO IT AGAIN...? IT SHOULD BE EASY ENOUGH...

WH- WHADDYA THINK?! WHEN IT COMES TO SETTING FIRES, THIS HERE AKANEKO'S RIGHT UP THERE WITH O-SHICHI THE GROCERY GIRL!

BUT—BUT I CAN'T DO *NOTHIN'* WITHOUT SOMETHIN' TO *START* IT BURNING!

DAMN IT ALL! IF I JUST HAD SOME TINDER, I'D TURN THIS HELLHOLE INTO A PILE OF ASHES!

Bam Bam

THAT'S STRANGE. WHY DID YOU HAVE TINDER WITH YOU THE LAST TIME?

NOW, YOU KNOW? THAT'S SOMETHING I CAN'T FIGURE EVEN *NOW*...

IF THEY CATCH ME, IT'S THE *DEATH SENTENCE*, SEE?

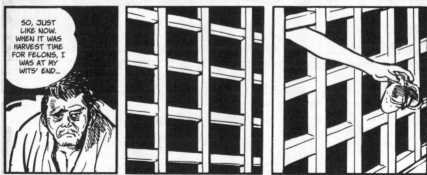

SO, JUST LIKE NOW. WHEN IT WAS HARVEST TIME FOR FELONS, I WAS AT MY WITS' END...

I WAS BARELY HERE, SEE, HALF-CRAZY? BUT I HEARD THIS SOUND, SPRUNG UP...

AND WHAT IF THERE AIN'T SOME OIL-SOAKED RAGS AND A BAMBOO HOLDER WITH A COAL IN IT? EVERYTHING I NEED!

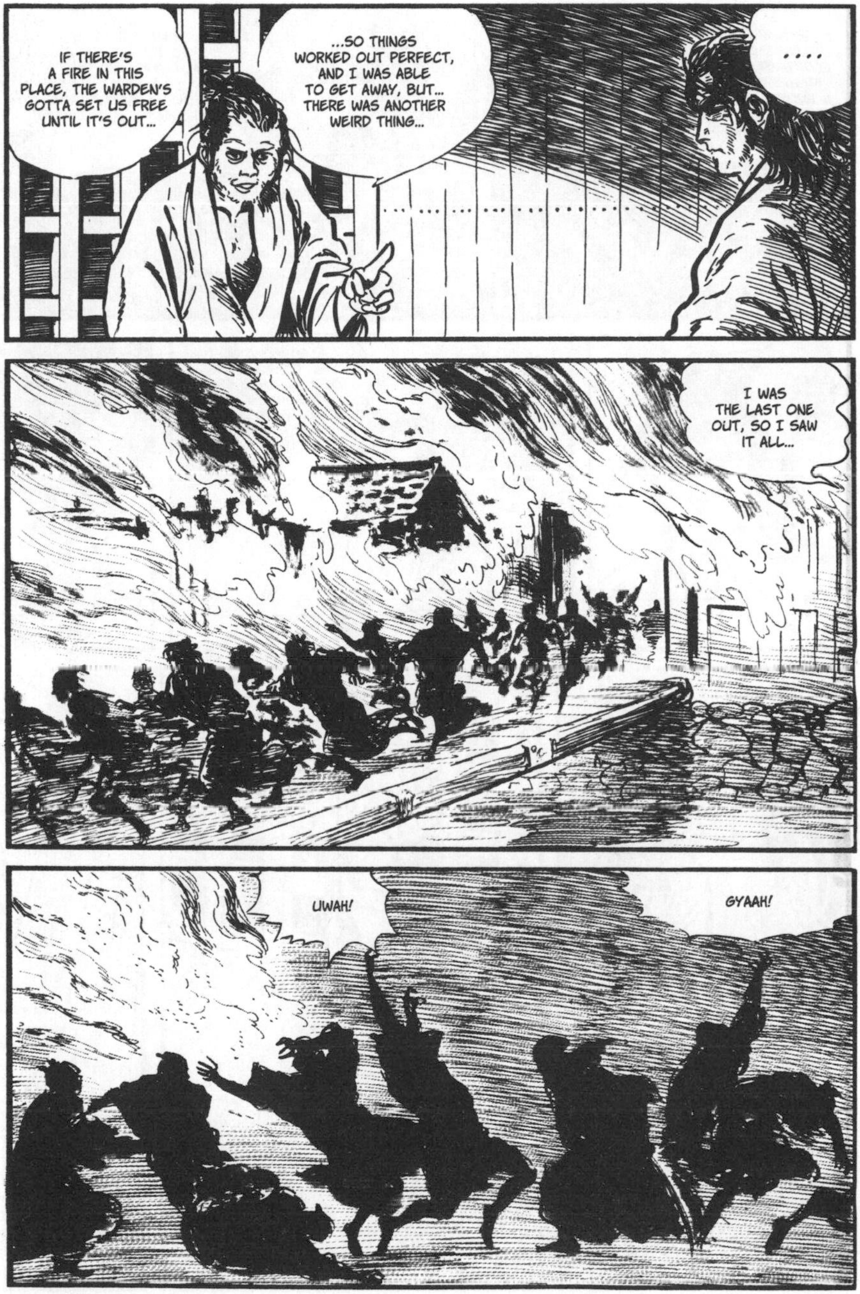
IF THERE'S A FIRE IN THIS PLACE, THE WARDEN'S GOTTA SET US FREE UNTIL IT'S OUT...
...SO THINGS WORKED OUT PERFECT, AND I WAS ABLE TO GET AWAY, BUT... THERE WAS ANOTHER WEIRD THING...
....
I WAS THE LAST ONE OUT, SO I SAW IT ALL...
UWAH!
GYAAH!

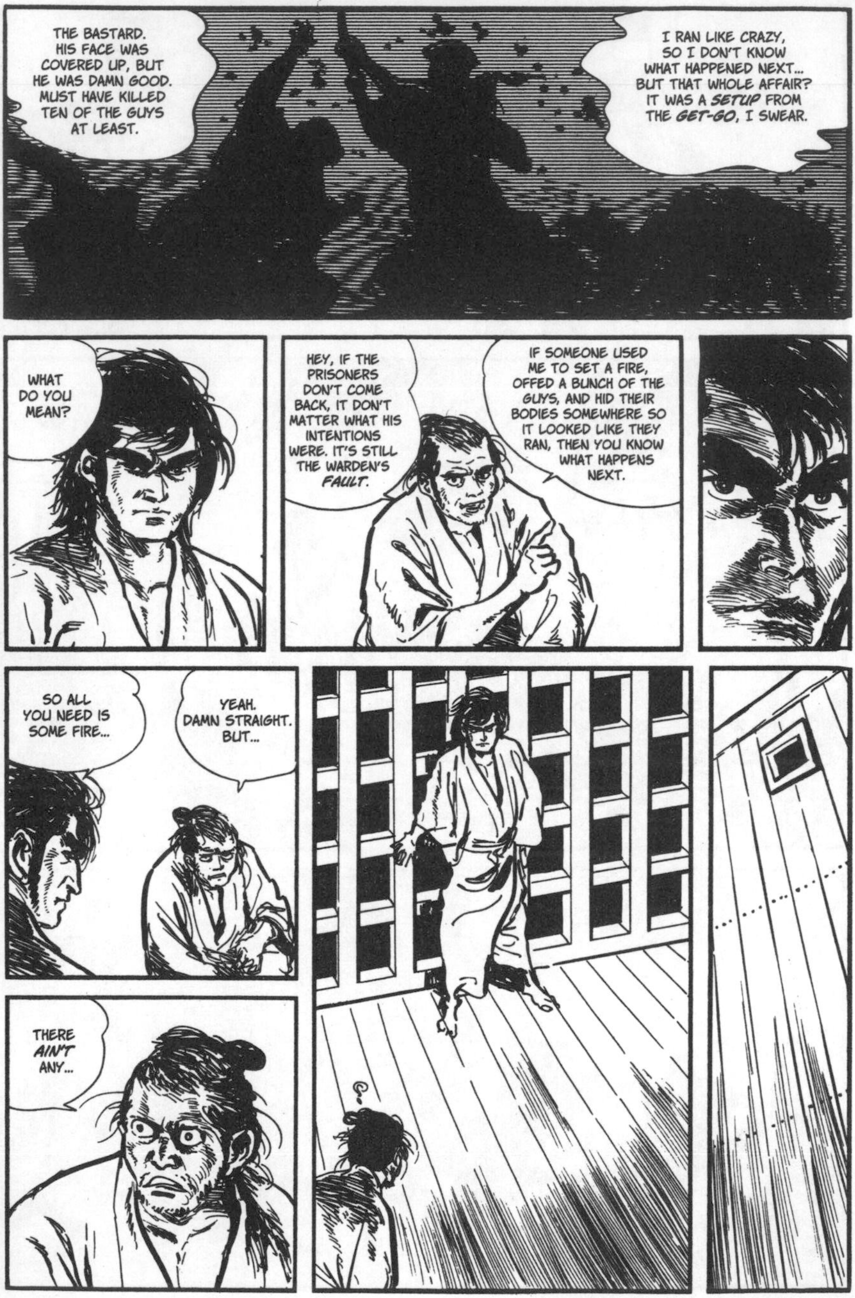
THE BASTARD. HIS FACE WAS COVERED UP, BUT HE WAS DAMN GOOD. MUST HAVE KILLED TEN OF THE GUYS AT LEAST.
I RAN LIKE CRAZY, SO I DON'T KNOW WHAT HAPPENED NEXT... BUT THAT WHOLE AFFAIR? IT WAS A SETUP FROM THE GET-GO, I SWEAR.
WHAT DO YOU MEAN?
HEY, IF THE PRISONERS DON'T COME BACK, IT DON'T MATTER WHAT HIS INTENTIONS WERE. IT'S STILL THE WARDEN'S FAULT.
IF SOMEONE USED ME TO SET A FIRE, OFFED A BUNCH OF THE GUYS, AND HID THEIR BODIES SOMEWHERE SO IT LOOKED LIKE THEY RAN, THEN YOU KNOW WHAT HAPPENS NEXT.
SO ALL YOU NEED IS SOME FIRE...
YEAH. DAMN STRAIGHT. BUT...
THERE AIN'T ANY...

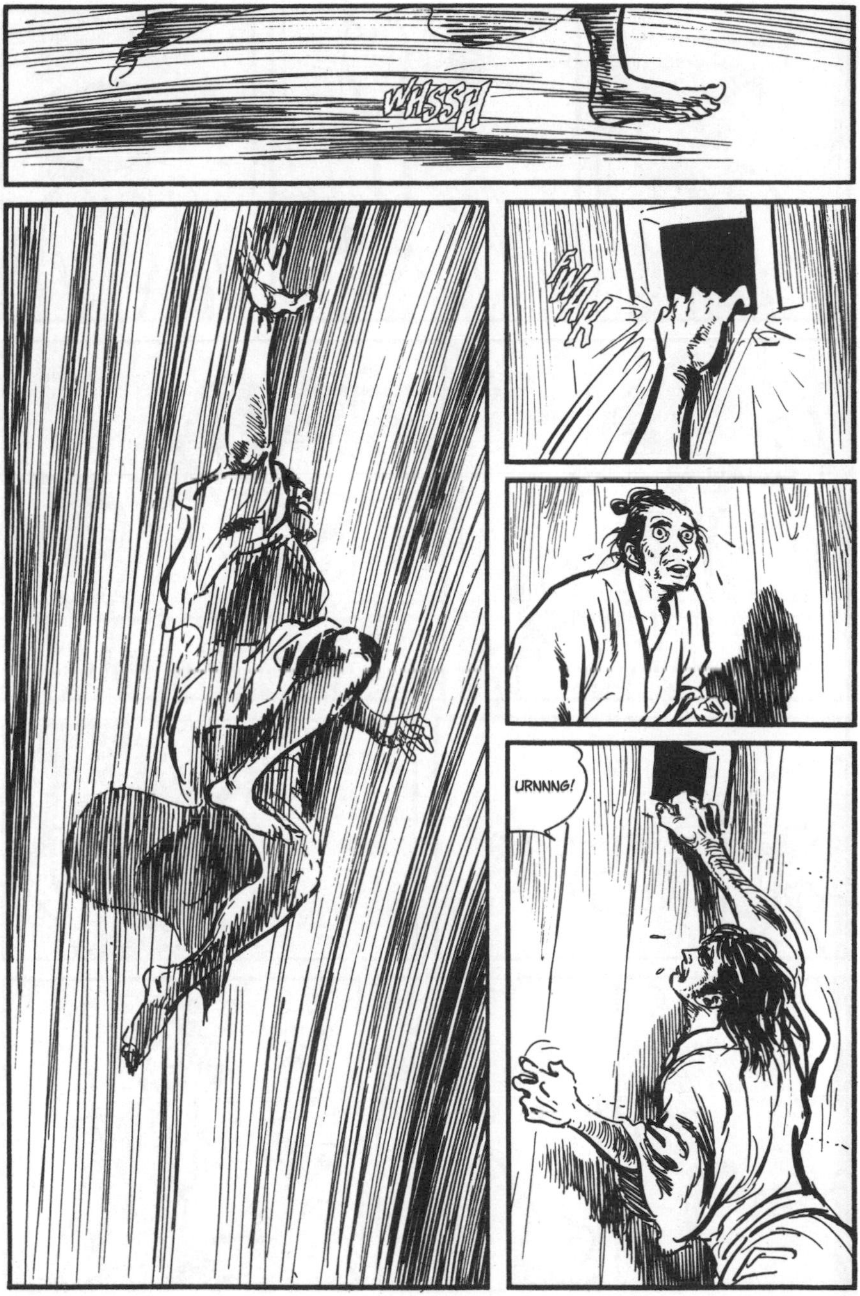
WHSSH
FWAK
URNNNG!

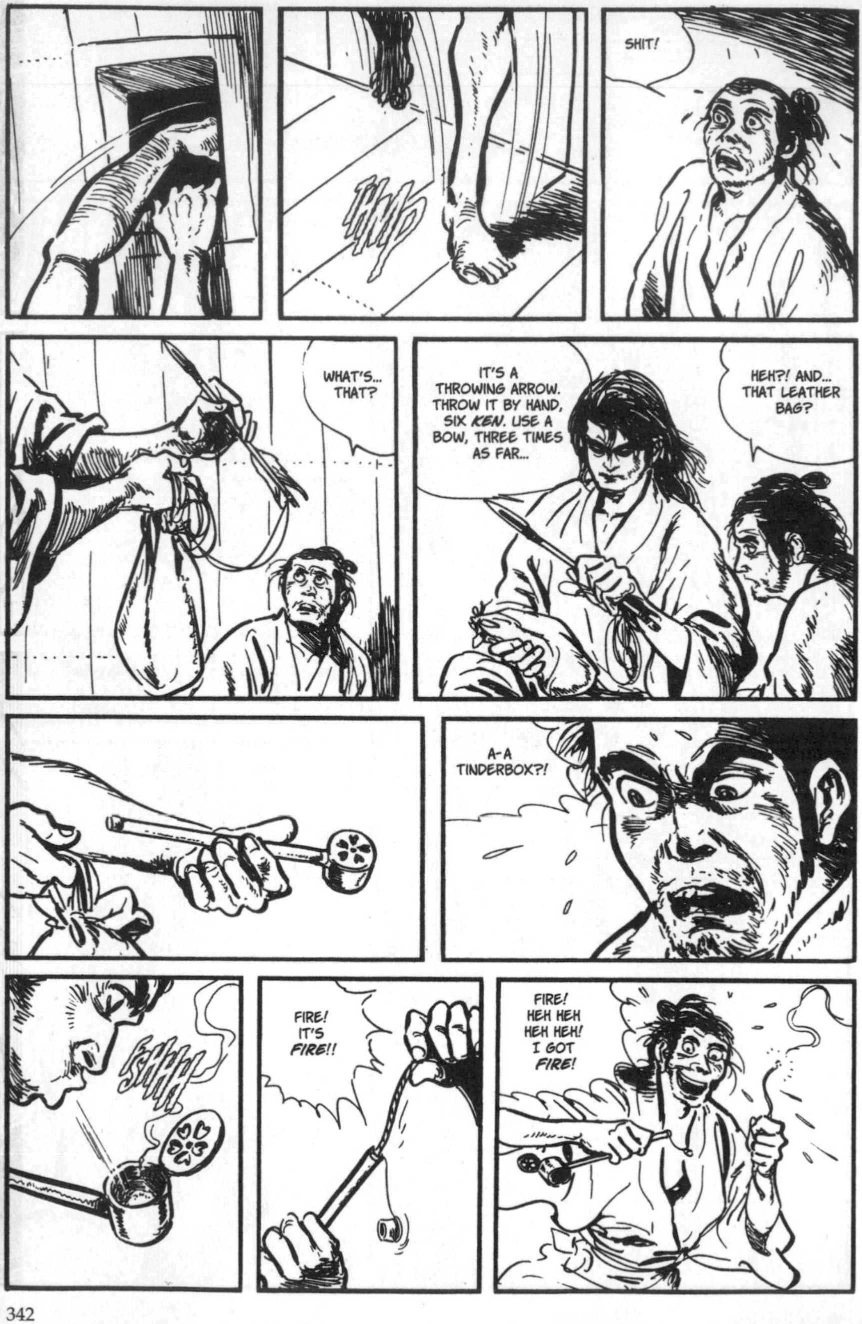

SHIT!
WHAT'S... THAT?
IT'S A THROWING ARROW. THROW IT BY HAND, SIX *KEN*. USE A BOW, THREE TIMES AS FAR...
HEH?! AND... THAT LEATHER BAG?
A-A TINDERBOX?!
FIRE! IT'S *FIRE*!!
FIRE! HEH HEH HEH HEH! I GOT *FIRE*!

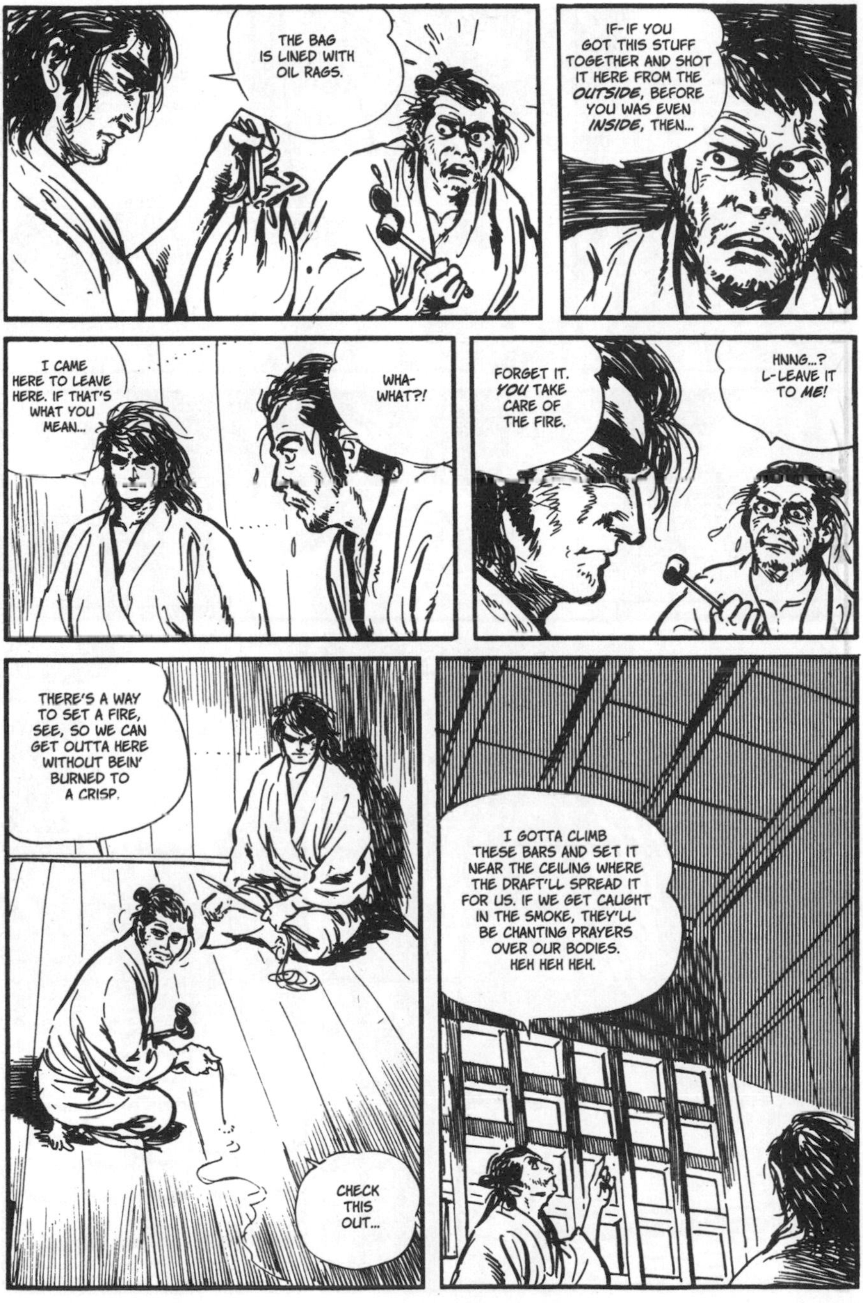
THE BAG IS LINED WITH OIL RAGS.
IF-IF YOU GOT THIS STUFF TOGETHER AND SHOT IT HERE FROM THE *OUTSIDE*, BEFORE YOU WAS EVEN *INSIDE*, THEN...
I CAME HERE TO LEAVE HERE. IF THAT'S WHAT YOU MEAN...
WHA-WHAT?!
FORGET IT. *YOU* TAKE CARE OF THE FIRE.
HNNG...? L-LEAVE IT TO *ME!*
THERE'S A WAY TO SET A FIRE, SEE, SO WE CAN GET OUTTA HERE WITHOUT BEIN' BURNED TO A CRISP.
CHECK THIS OUT...
I GOTTA CLIMB THESE BARS AND SET IT NEAR THE CEILING WHERE THE DRAFT'LL SPREAD IT FOR US. IF WE GET CAUGHT IN THE SMOKE, THEY'LL BE CHANTING PRAYERS OVER OUR BODIES. HEH HEH HEH.

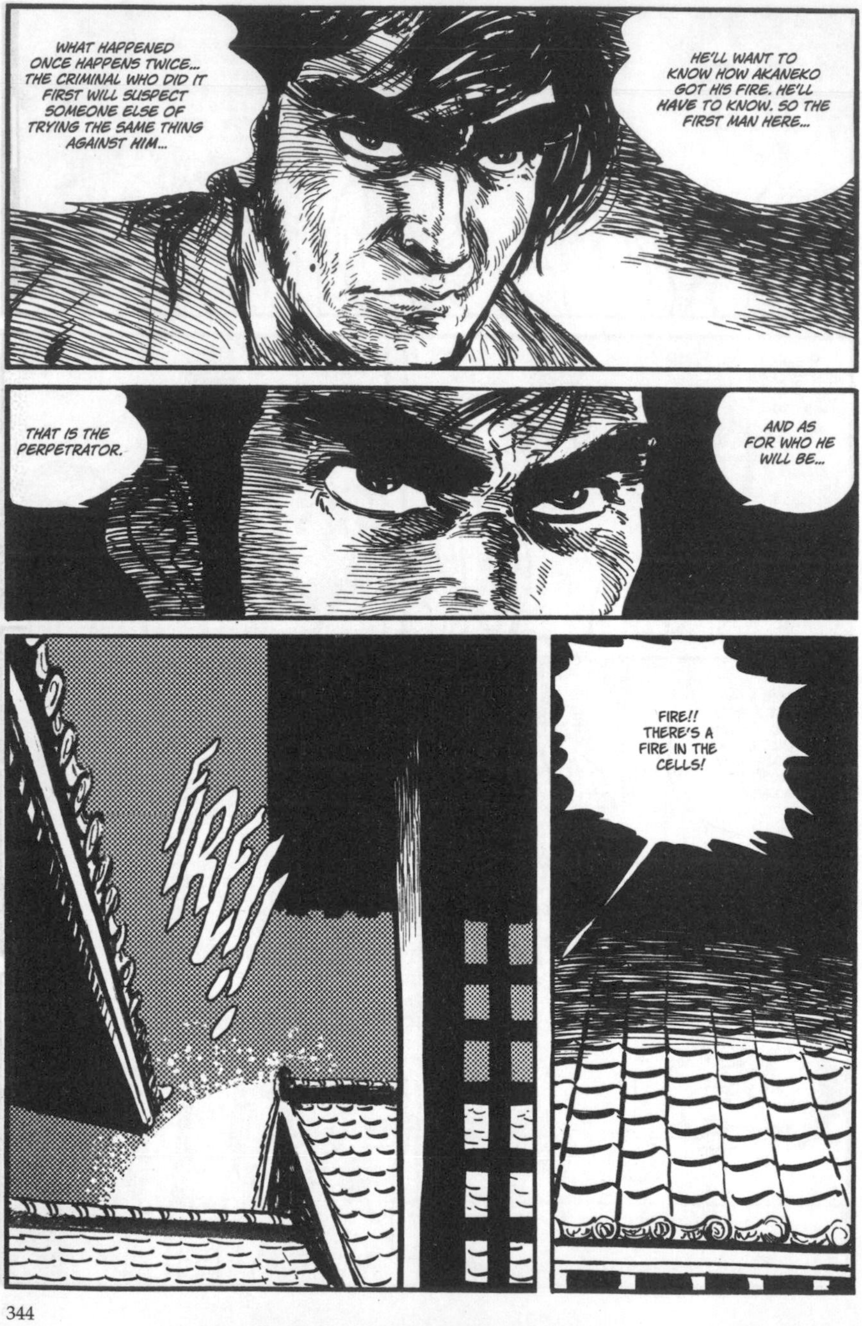
WHAT HAPPENED ONCE HAPPENS TWICE... THE CRIMINAL WHO DID IT FIRST WILL SUSPECT SOMEONE ELSE OF TRYING THE SAME THING AGAINST HIM...
HE'LL WANT TO KNOW HOW AKANEKO GOT HIS FIRE. HE'LL HAVE TO KNOW. SO THE FIRST MAN HERE...
THAT IS THE PERPETRATOR.
AND AS FOR WHO HE WILL BE...
FIRE!!
FIRE!! THERE'S A FIRE IN THE CELLS!

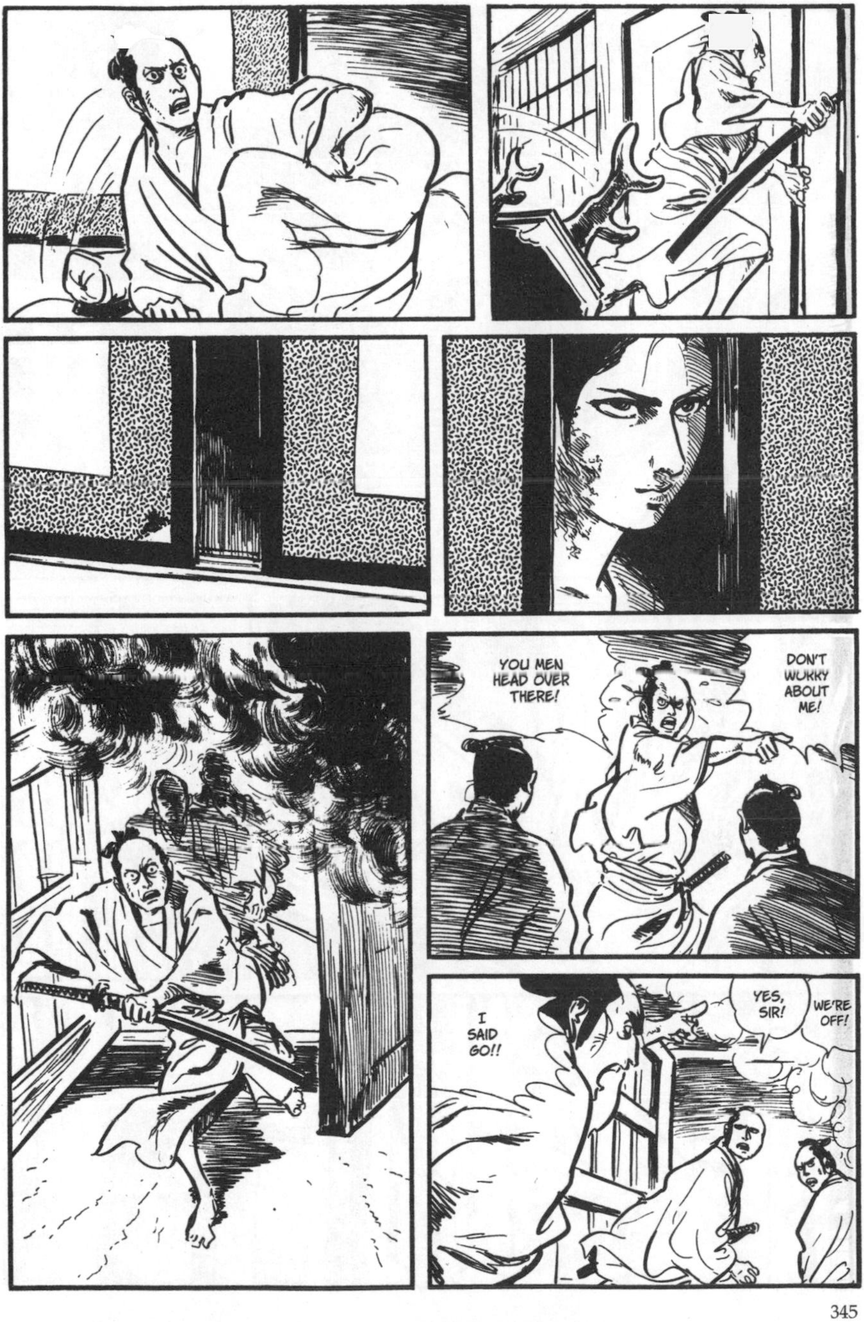
DON'T WORRY ABOUT ME!
YOU MEN HEAD OVER THERE!
WE'RE OFF!
YES, SIR!
I SAID GO!!

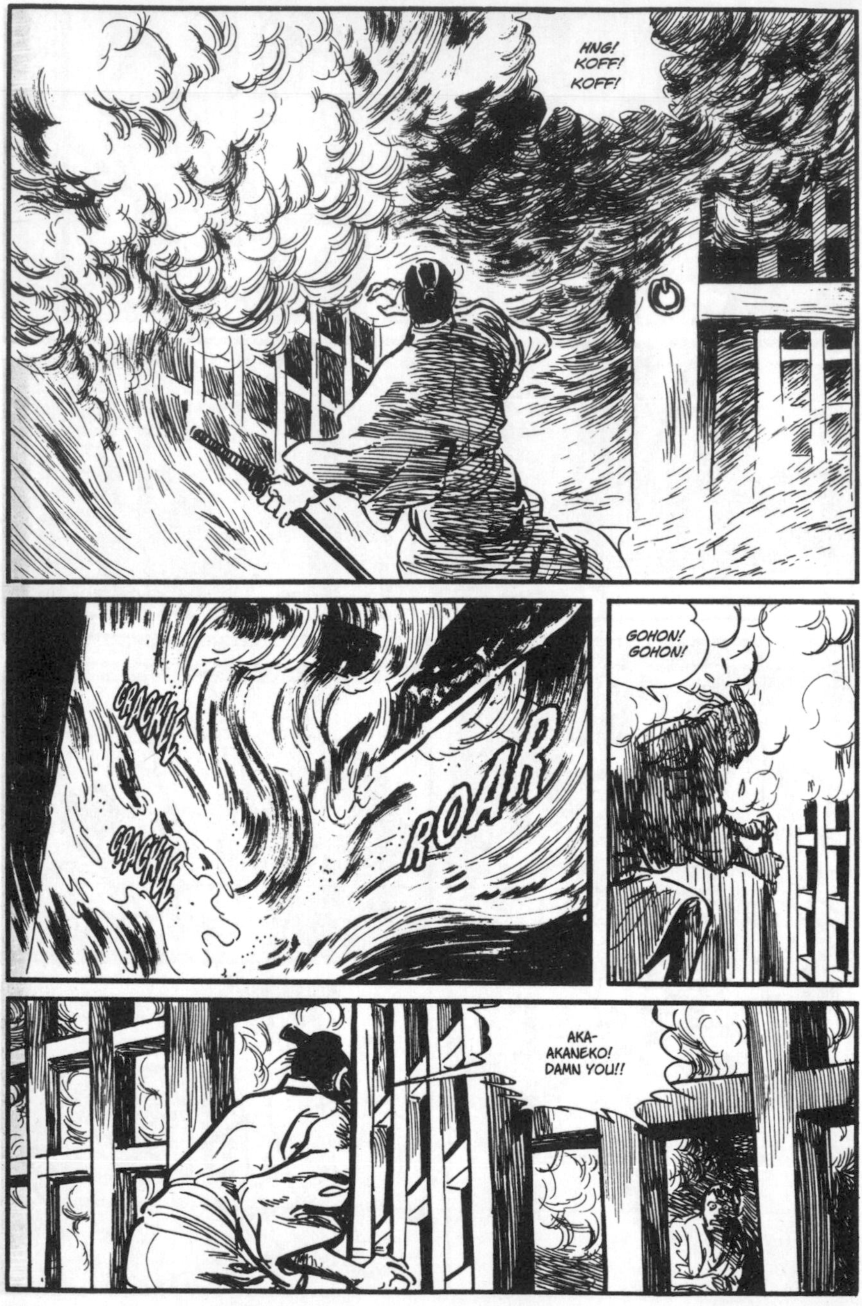
HNG!
KOFF!
KOFF!
GOHON!
GOHON!
ROAR
CRACKLE
CRACKLE
AKA-
AKANEKO!
DAMN YOU!!

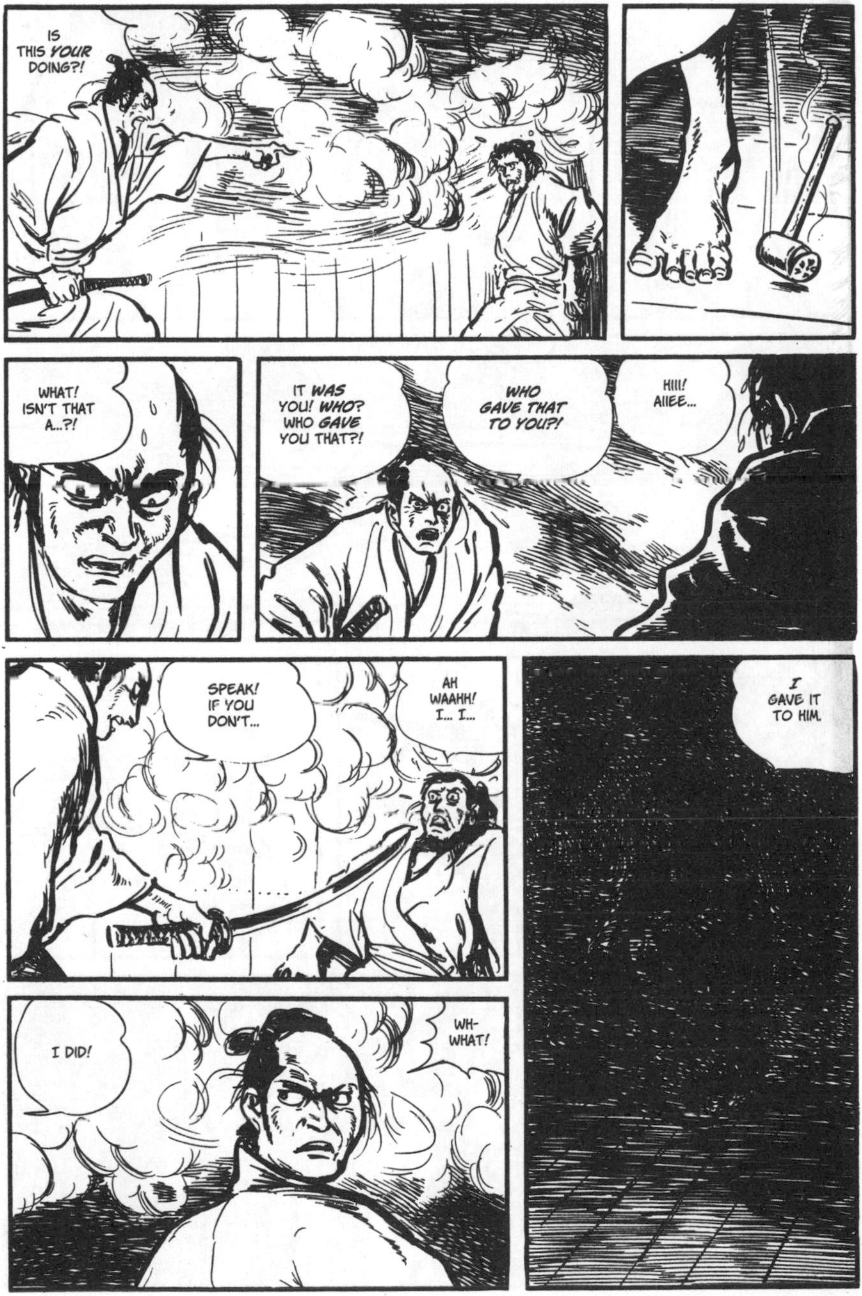
IS THIS YOUR DOING?!
WHAT! ISN'T THAT A...?!
IT WAS YOU! WHO? WHO GAVE YOU THAT?!
WHO GAVE THAT TO YOU?!
HIII! AIIEE...
SPEAK! IF YOU DON'T...
AH WAAHH! I... I...
I DID!
WH-WHAT!
I GAVE IT TO HIM.

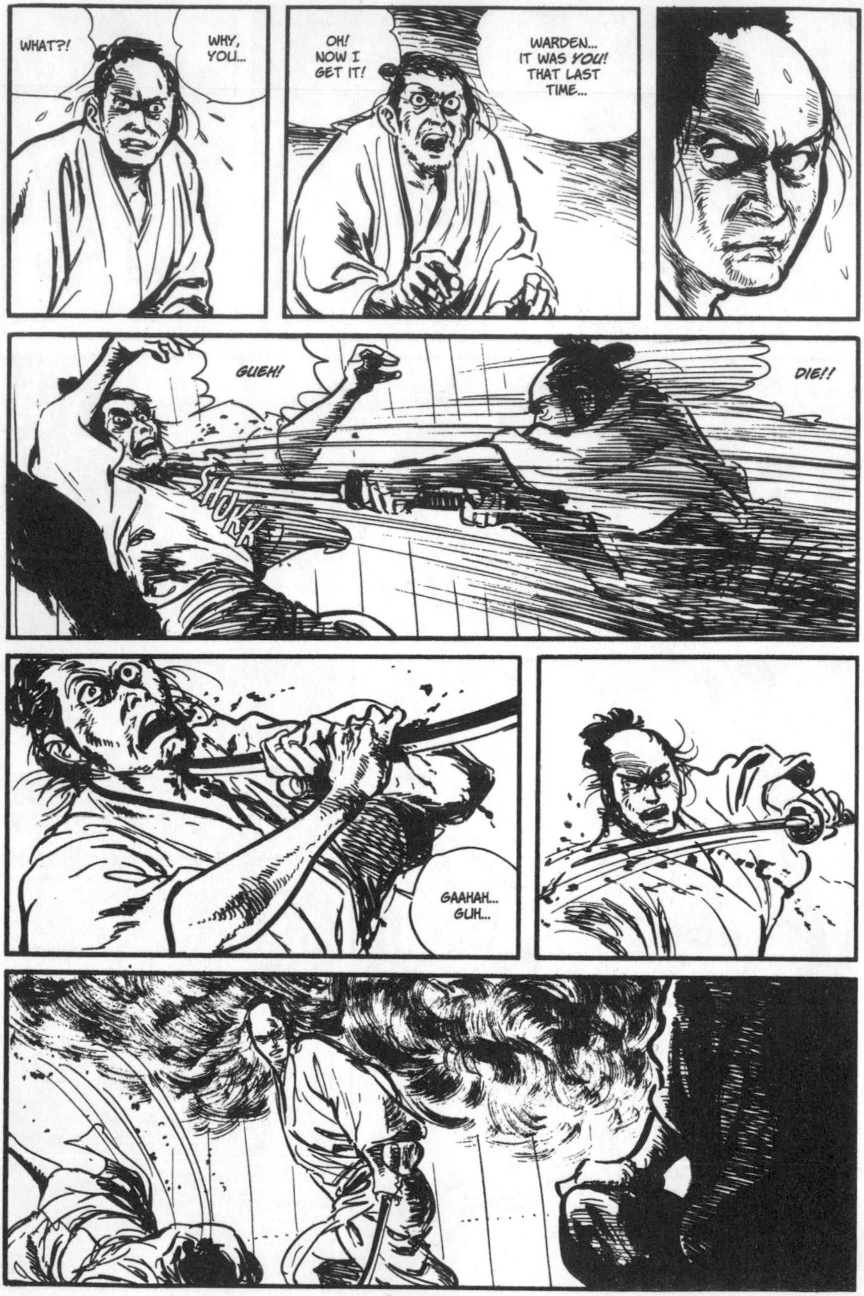
WHAT?!
WHY, YOU...
OH! NOW I GET IT!
WARDEN... IT WAS *YOU!* THAT LAST TIME...
DIE!!
GUEH!
SHUKK
GAAHAH... GUH...

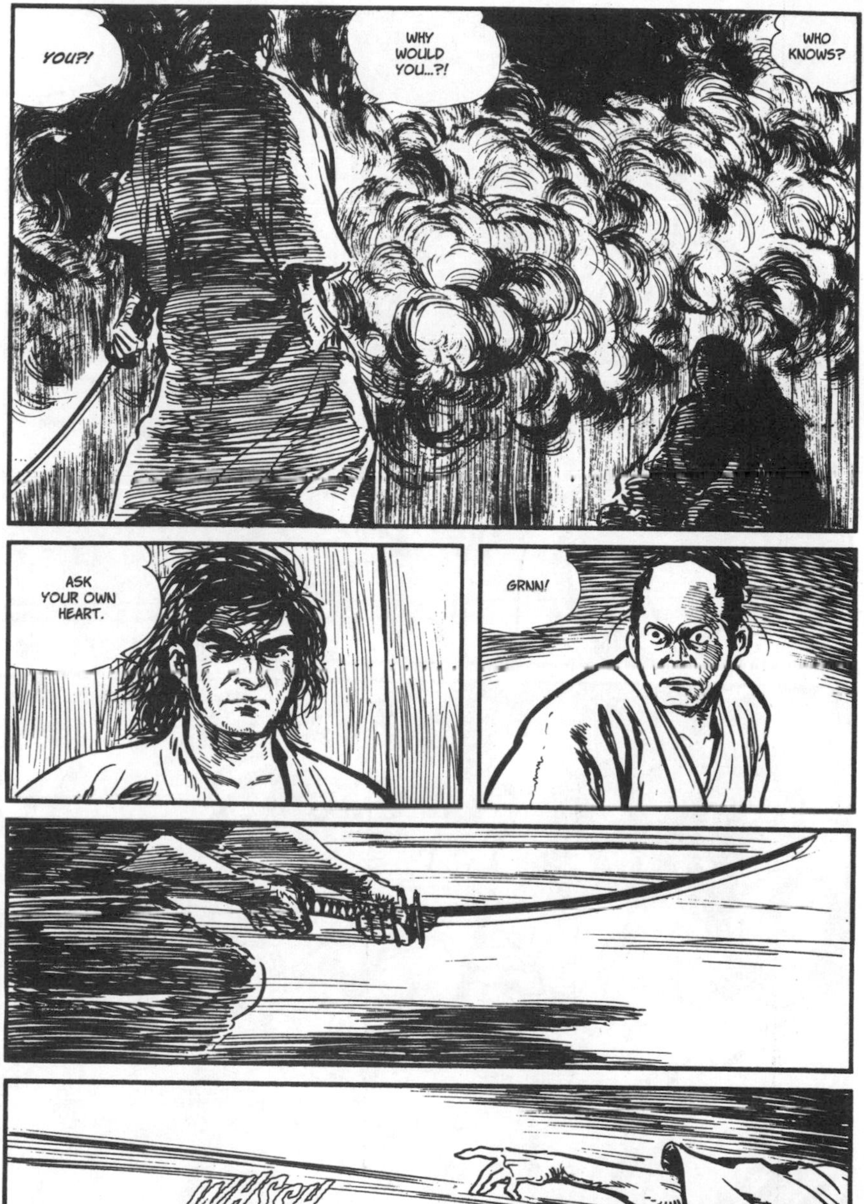
YOU?!
WHY WOULD YOU...?!
WHO KNOWS?
ASK YOUR OWN HEART.
GRNN!
WHSSH

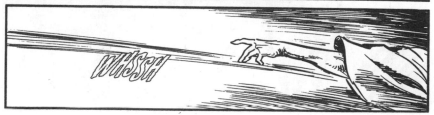

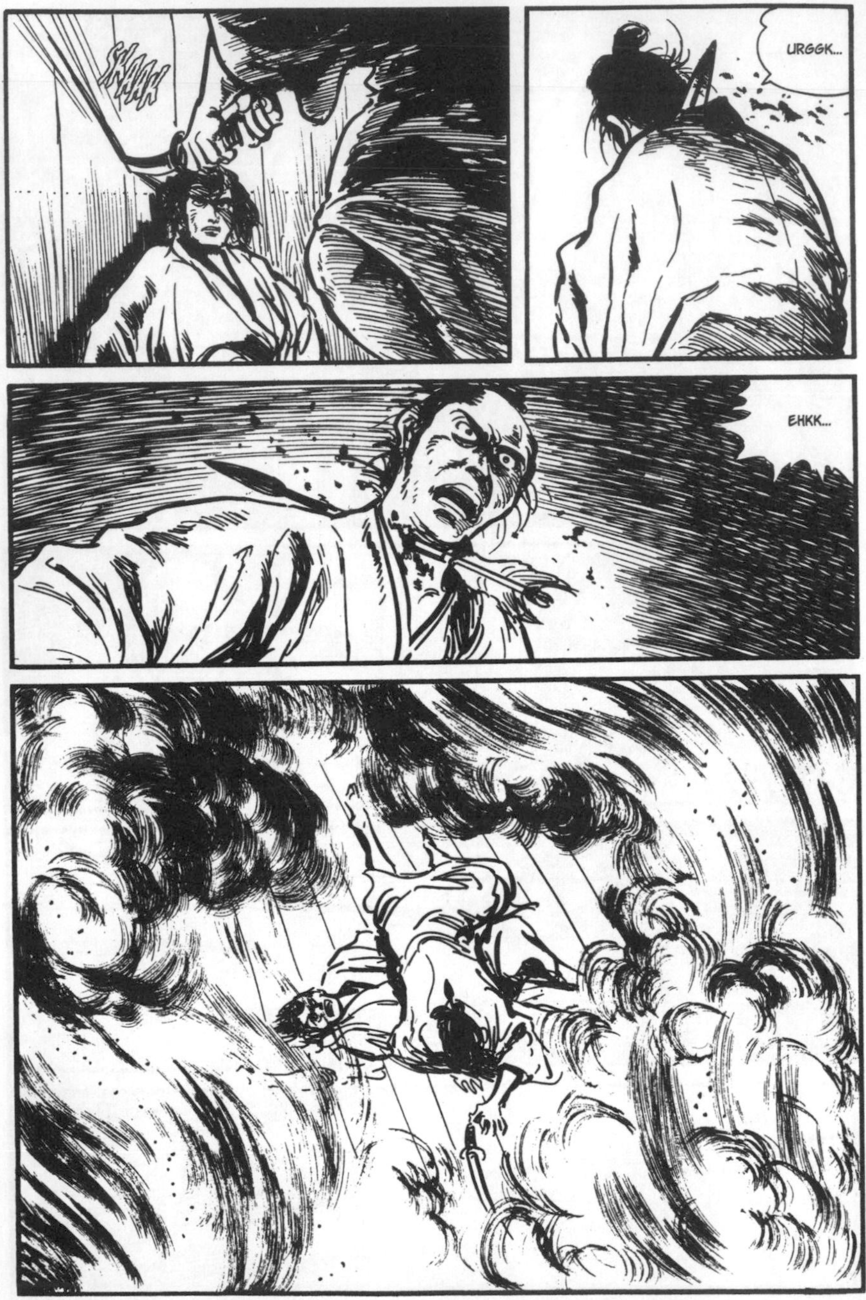
URGGK...
SKAAK
EHKK...

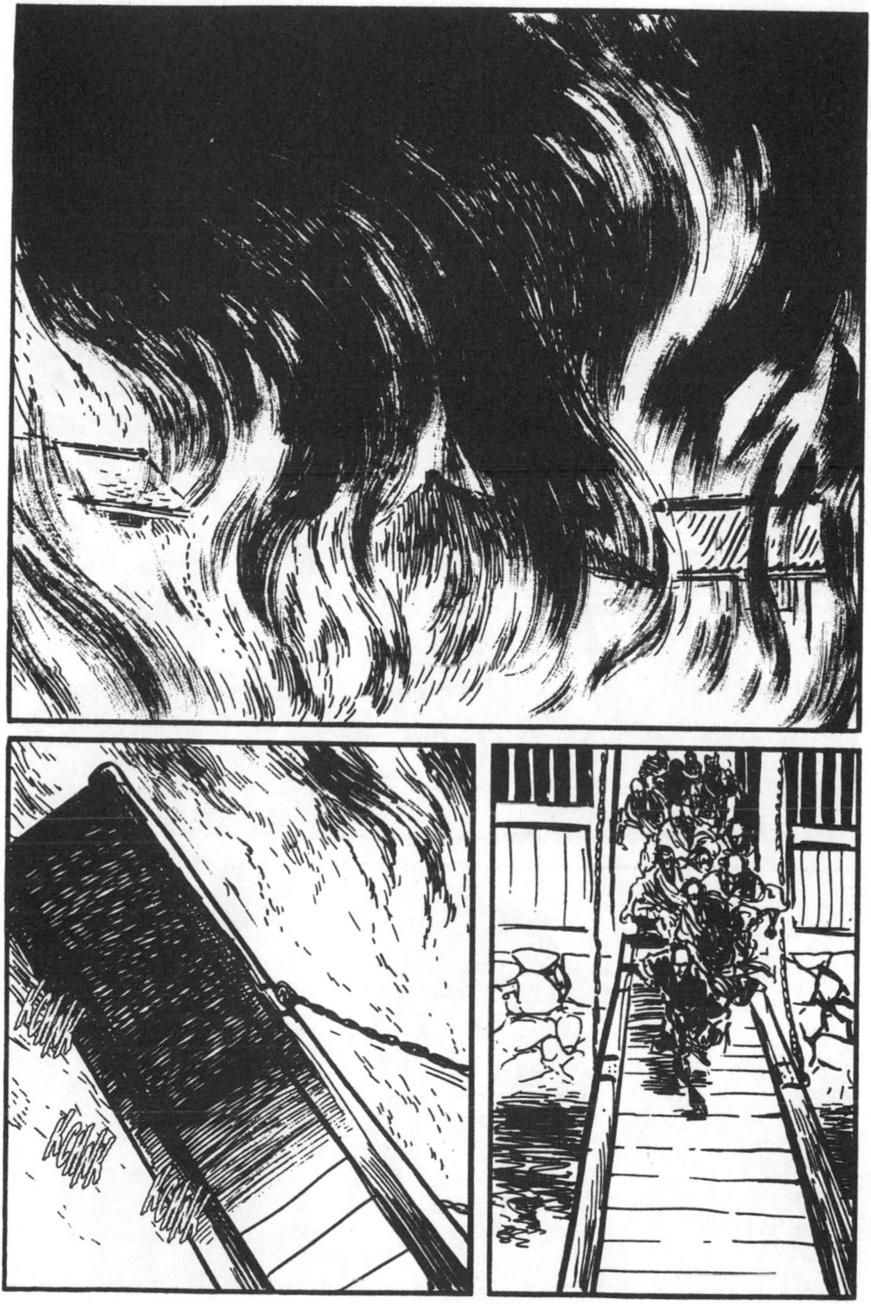
KCHAK
KCHAK
KCHAK

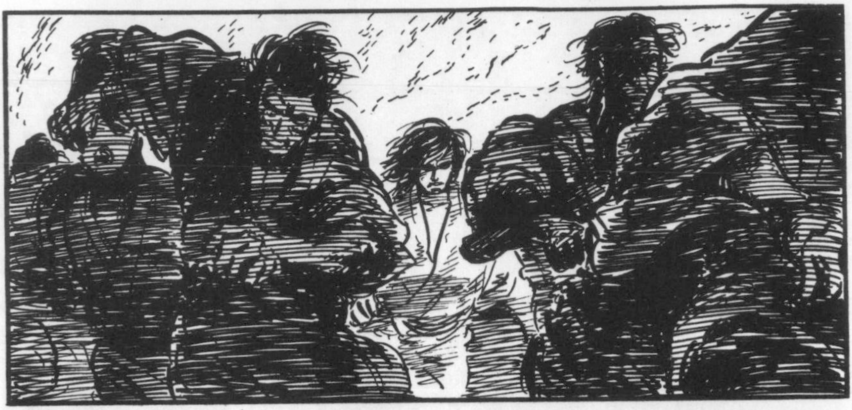
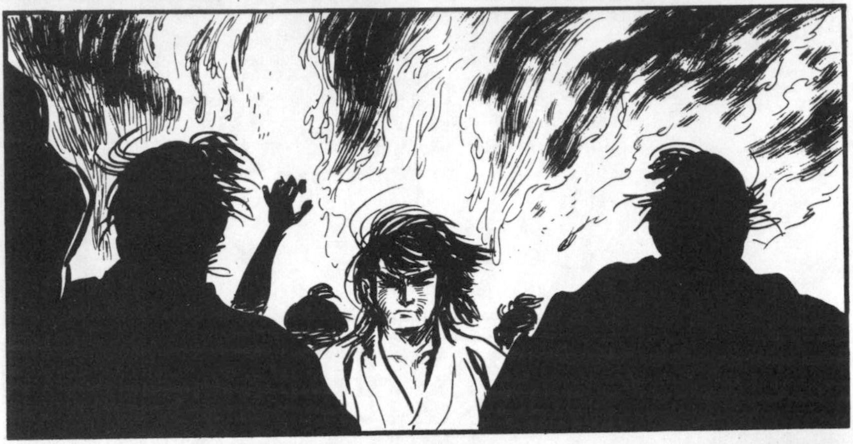
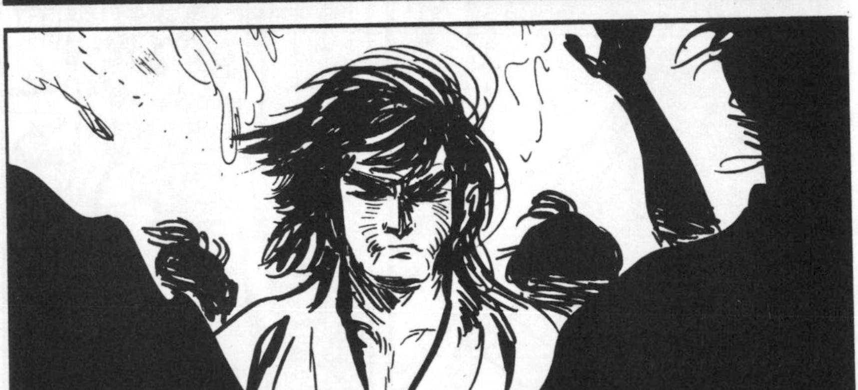

子連れ狼

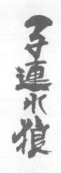

The Coming of the Cold

11

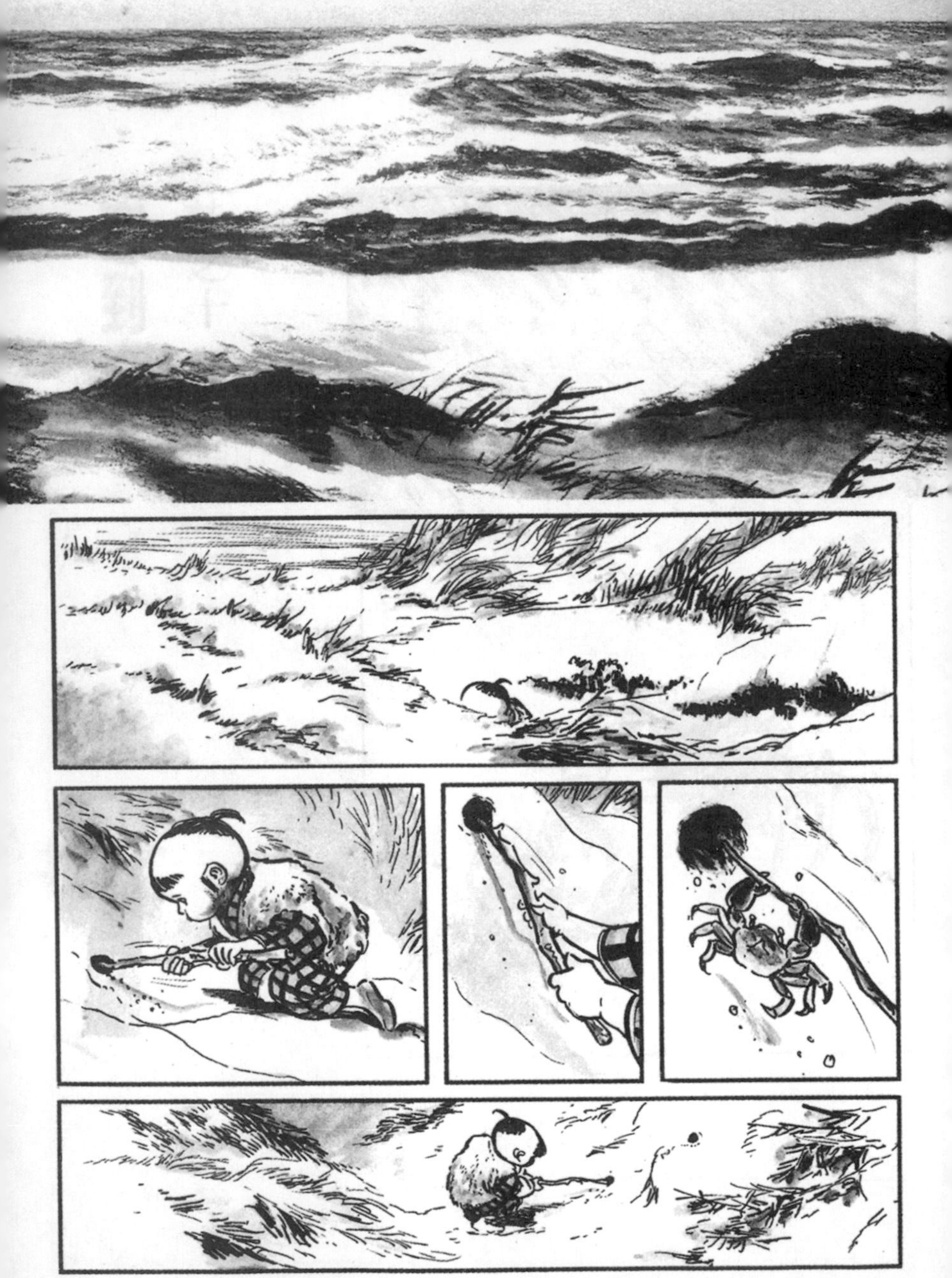

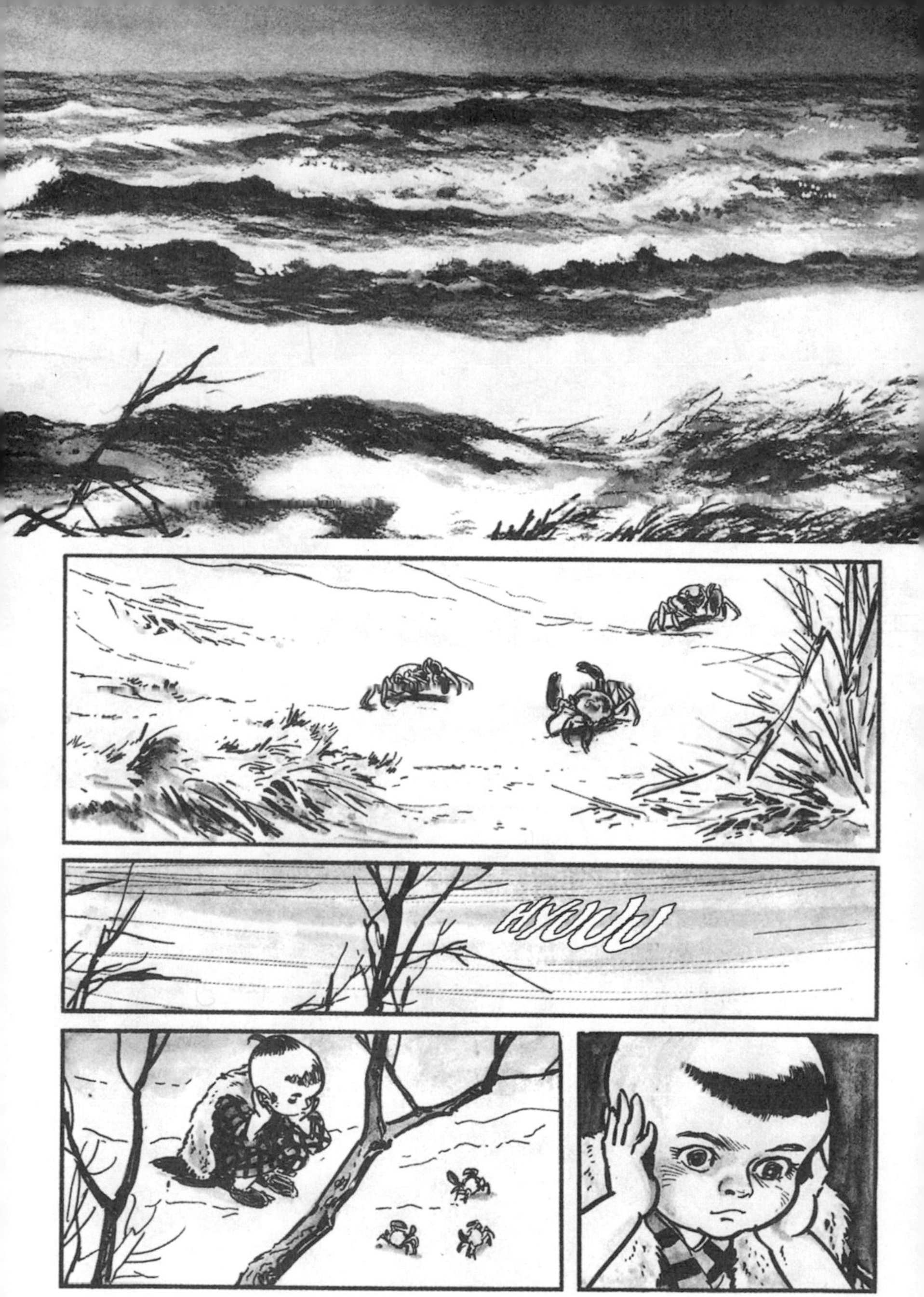
HYUUU

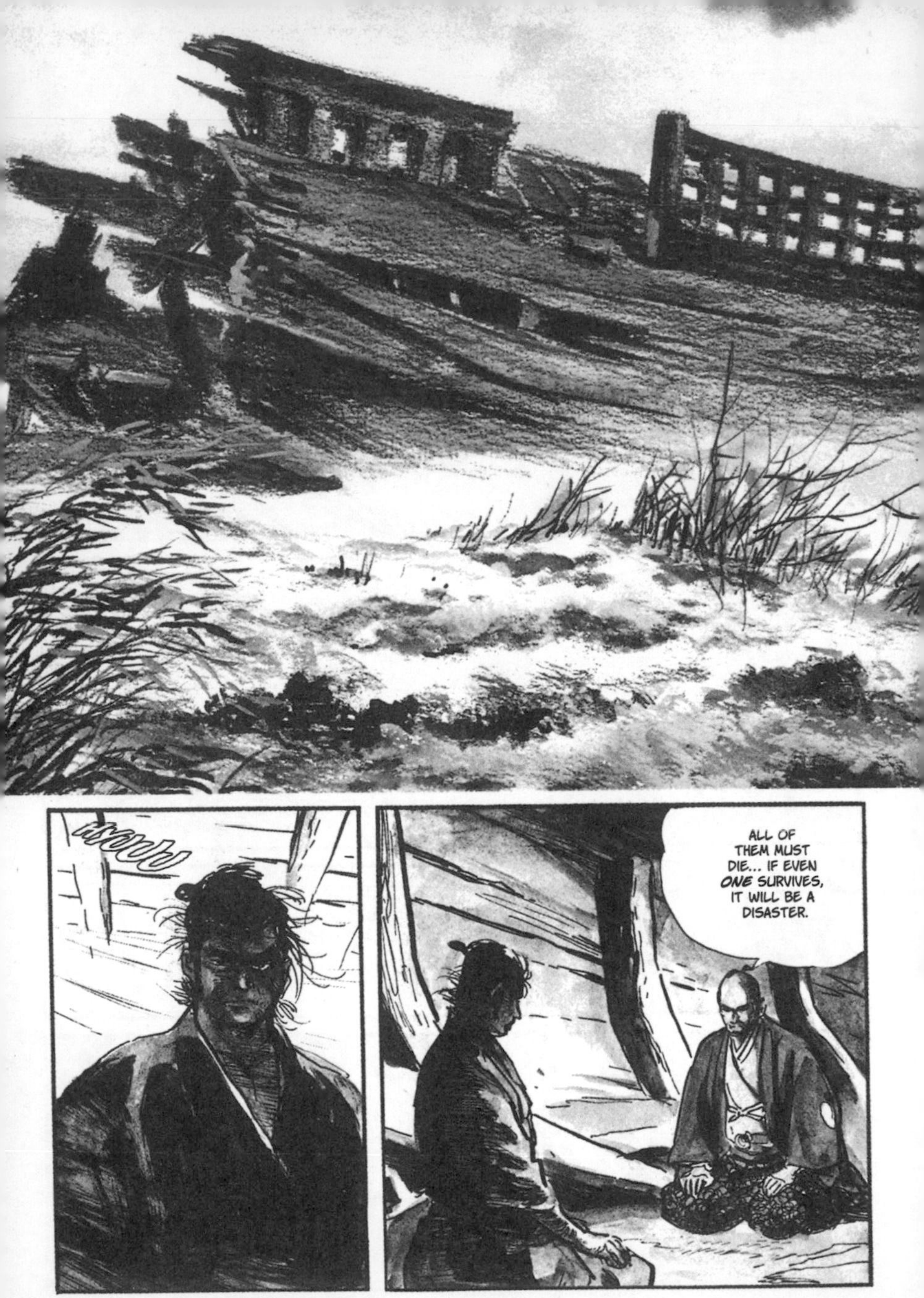
ALL OF THEM MUST DIE... IF EVEN *ONE* SURVIVES, IT WILL BE A DISASTER.
HYUUU

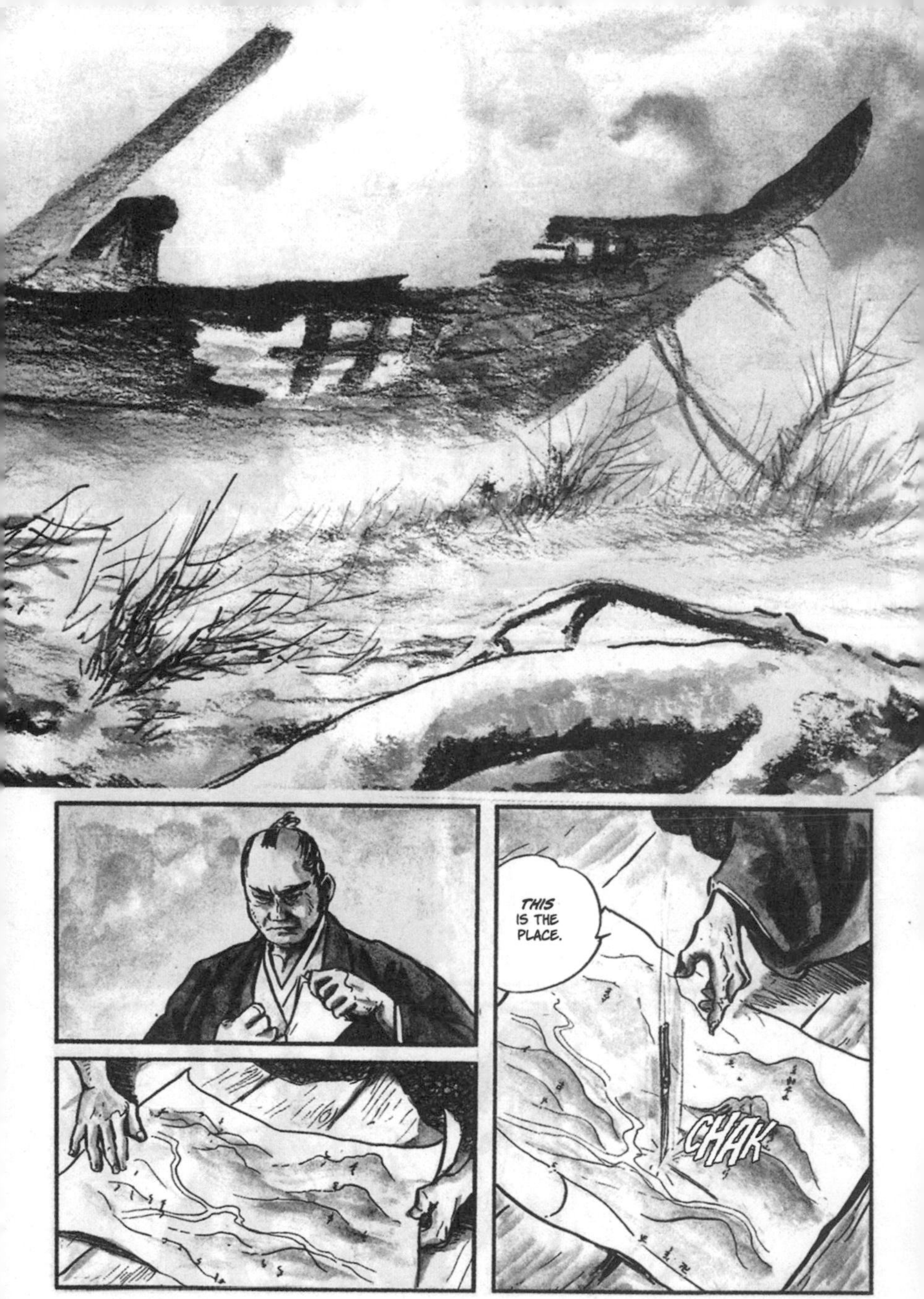
THIS IS THE PLACE.
CHAK

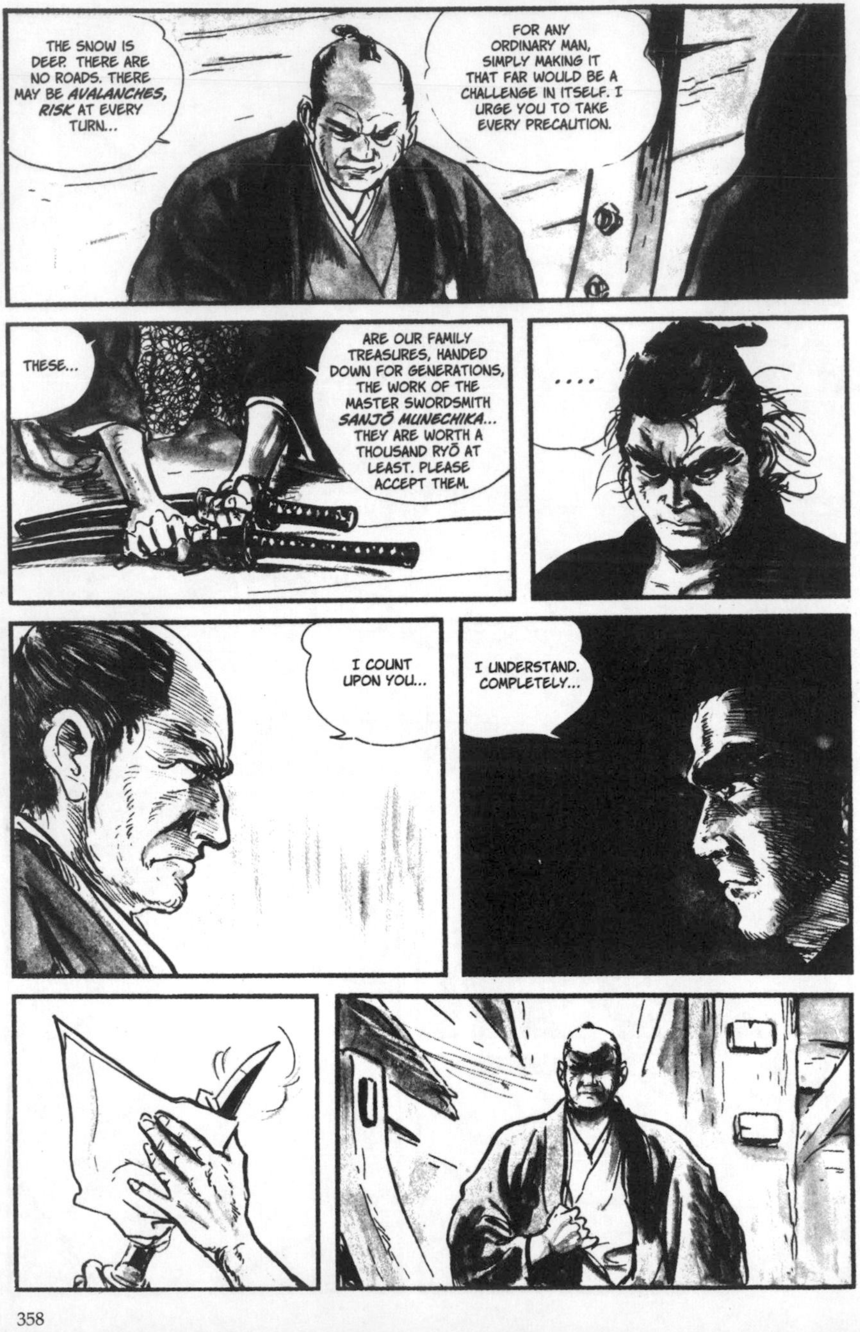
THE SNOW IS DEEP. THERE ARE NO ROADS. THERE MAY BE *AVALANCHES, RISK* AT EVERY TURN...
FOR ANY ORDINARY MAN, SIMPLY MAKING IT THAT FAR WOULD BE A CHALLENGE IN ITSELF. I URGE YOU TO TAKE EVERY PRECAUTION.
THESE...
ARE OUR FAMILY TREASURES, HANDED DOWN FOR GENERATIONS, THE WORK OF THE MASTER SWORDSMITH *SANJŌ MUNECHIKA*... THEY ARE WORTH A THOUSAND RYŌ AT LEAST. PLEASE ACCEPT THEM.
....
I COUNT UPON YOU...
I UNDERSTAND. COMPLETELY...

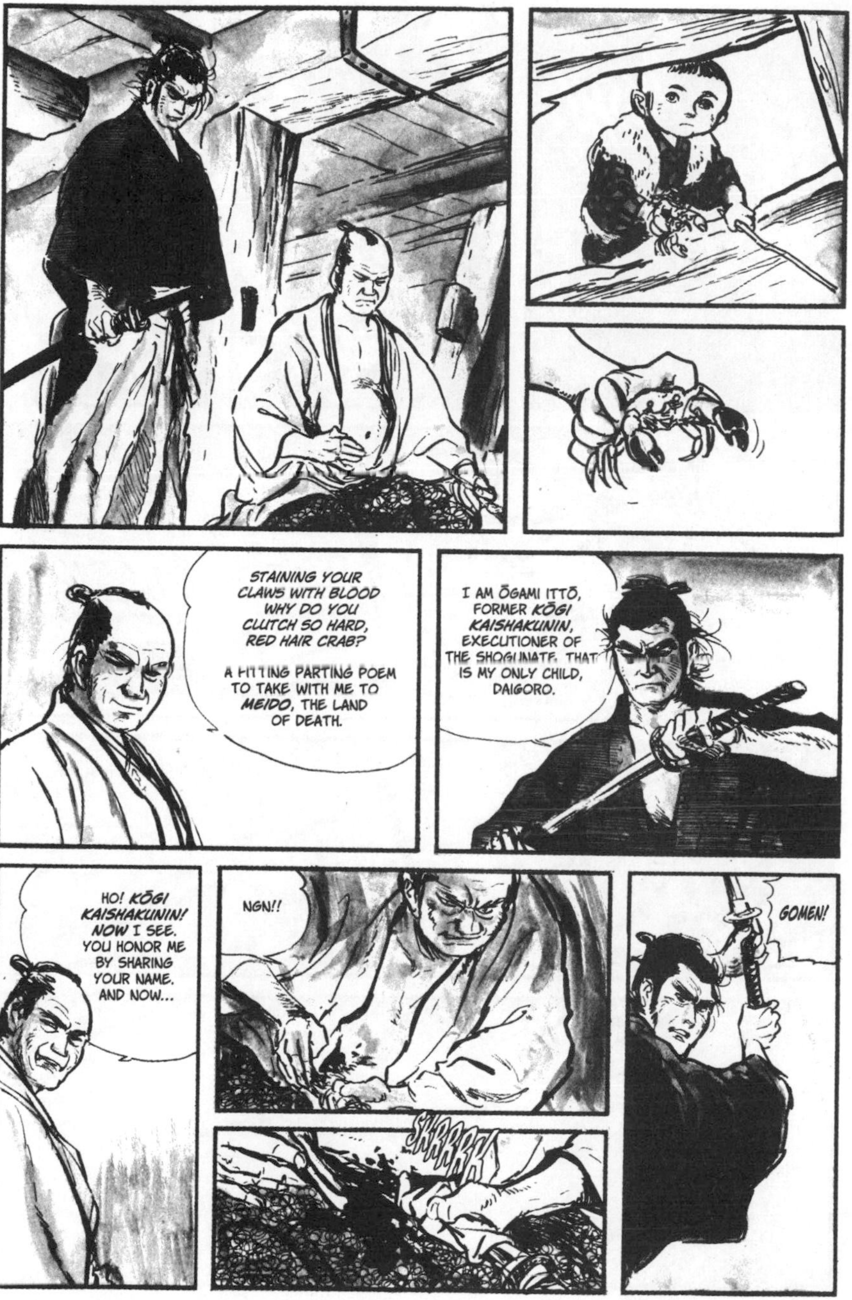
STAINING YOUR CLAWS WITH BLOOD WHY DO YOU CLUTCH SO HARD, RED HAIR CRAB?
A FITTING PARTING POEM TO TAKE WITH ME TO MEIDO, THE LAND OF DEATH.
I AM ŌGAMI ITTŌ, FORMER KŌGI KAISHAKUNIN, EXECUTIONER OF THE SHOGUNATE. THAT IS MY ONLY CHILD, DAIGORO.
HO! KŌGI KAISHAKUNIN! NOW I SEE. YOU HONOR ME BY SHARING YOUR NAME. AND NOW...
NGN!!
GOMEN!
SKRRRK

FSSSH!
FWAP
FWPP
HYUUU

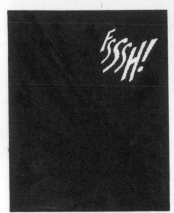

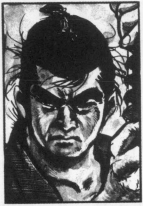

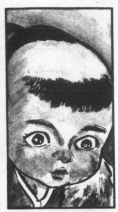

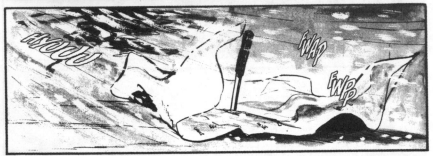

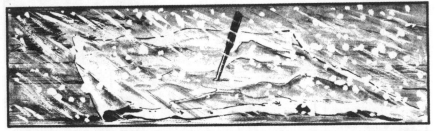

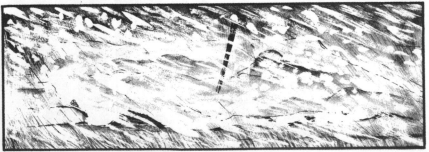

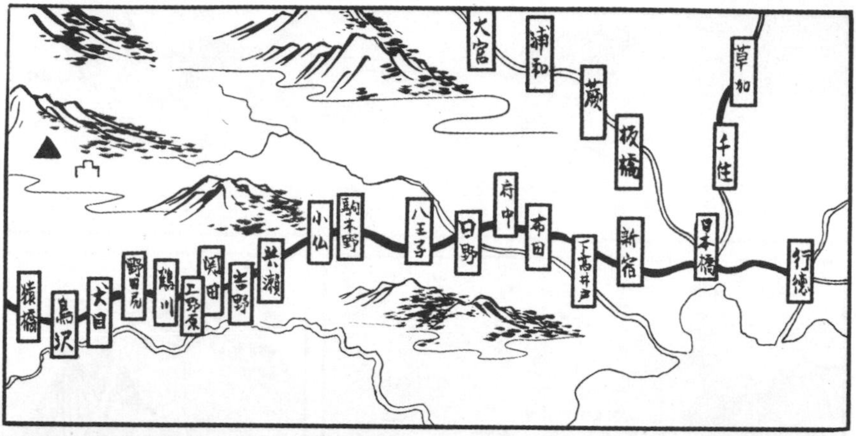
草加
千住
行徳
日本橋
大宮
浦和
蕨
板橋
新宿
下高井戸
布田
府中
日野
八王子
駒木野
小仏
与瀬
吉野
関田
上野原
鶴川
野田尻
犬目
鳥沢
猿橋

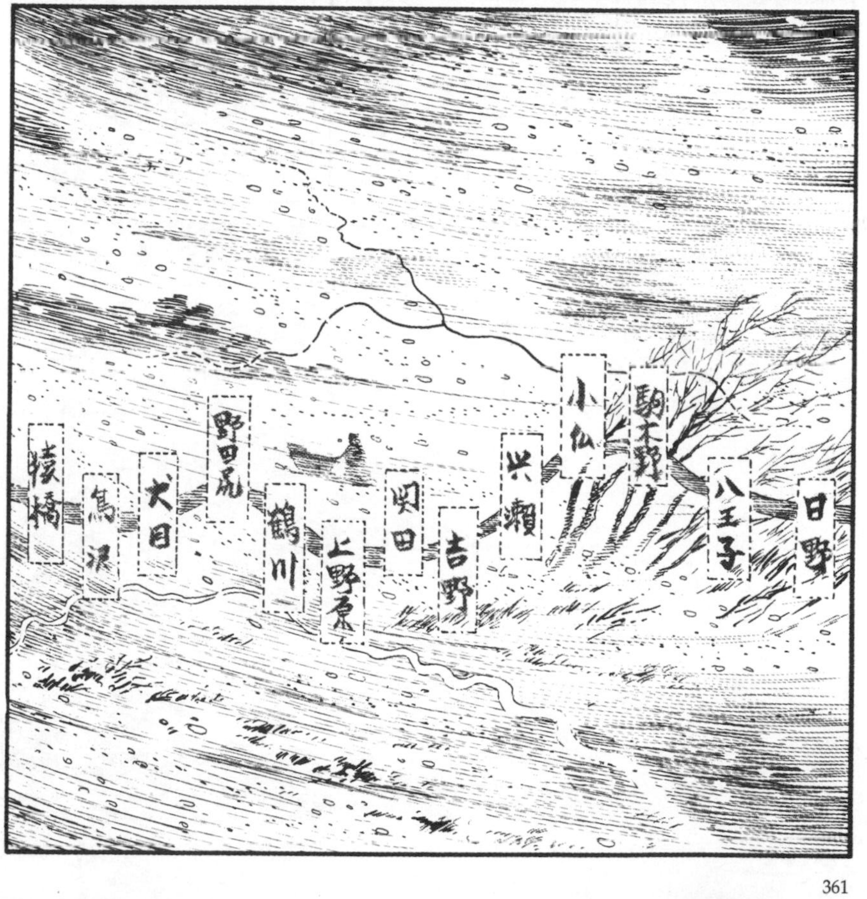
日野
八王子
駒木野
小仏
与瀬
吉野
関田
上野原
鶴川
野田尻
犬目
鳥沢
猿橋

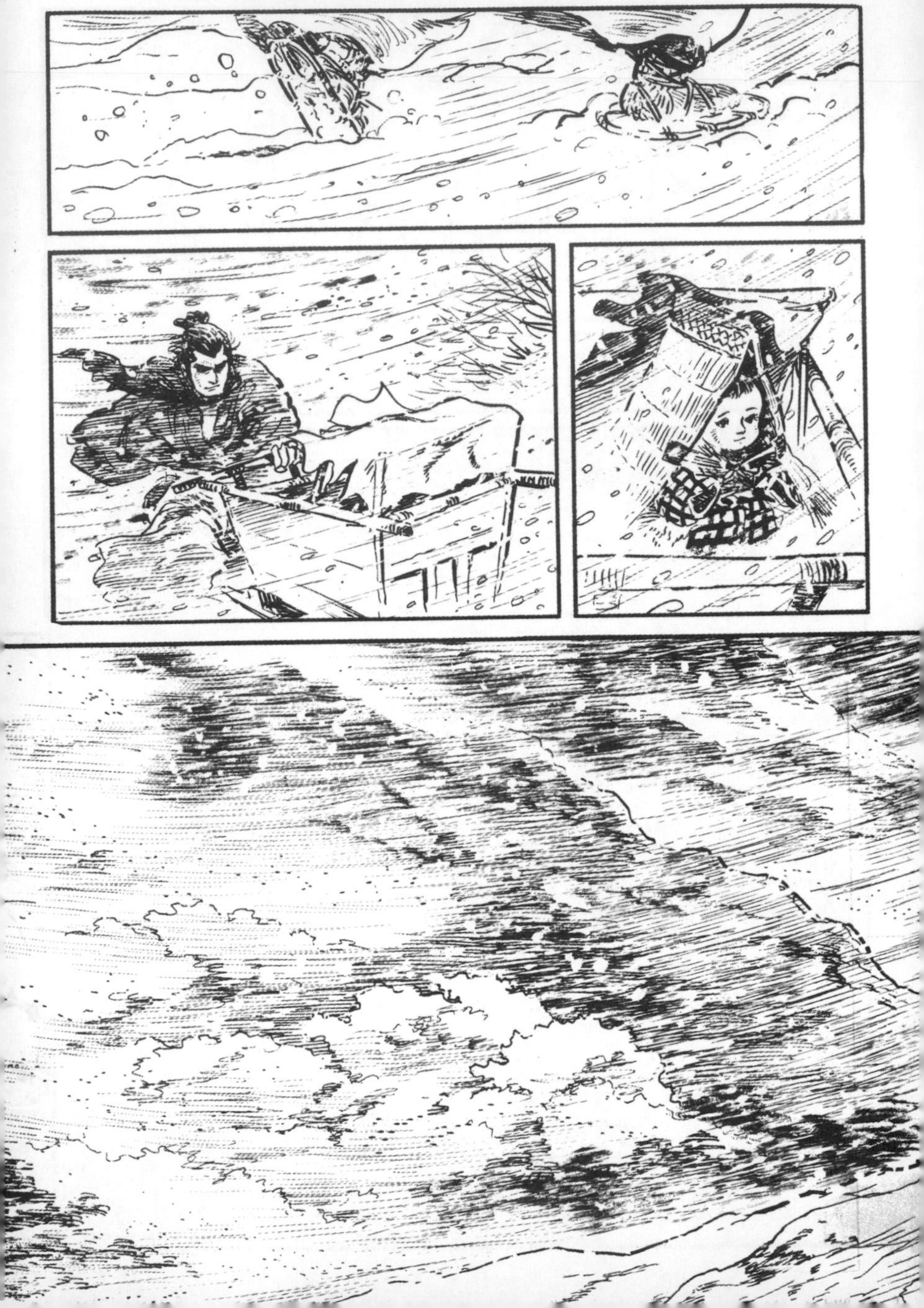

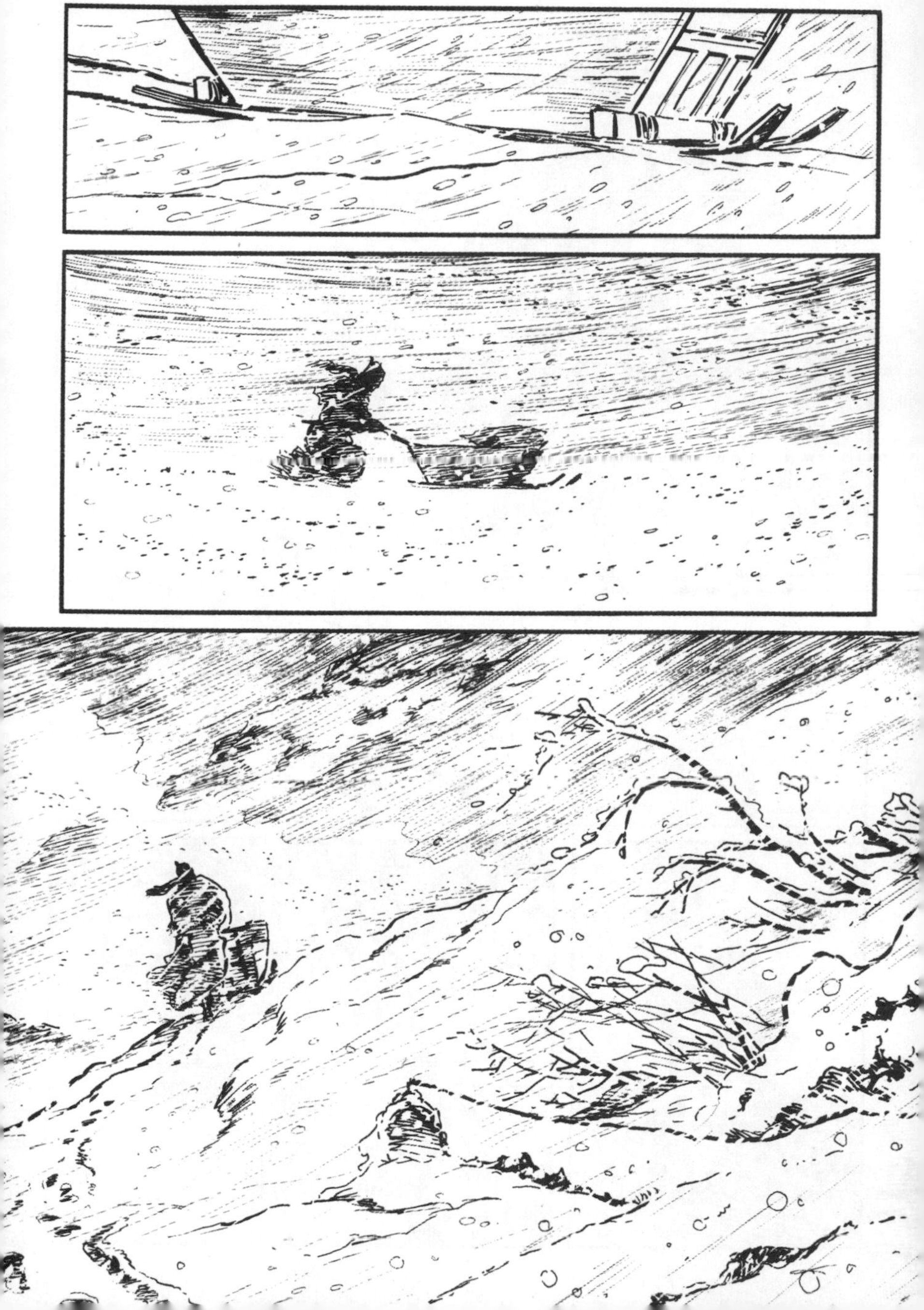

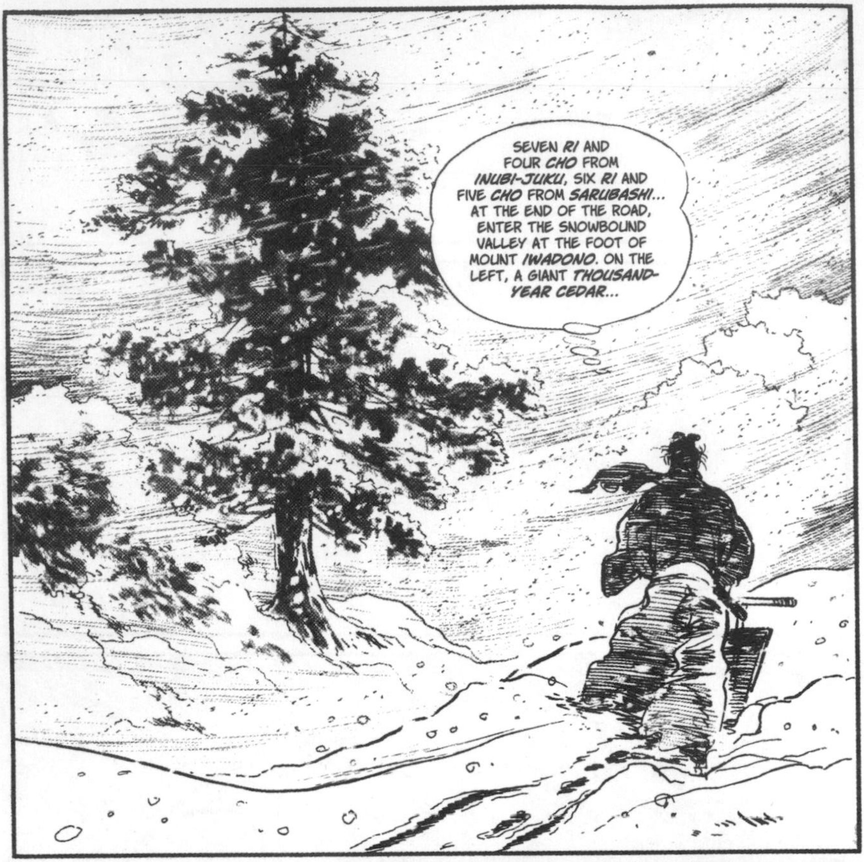
SEVEN *RI* AND FOUR *CHO* FROM *INUBI-JUKU*, SIX *RI* AND FIVE *CHO* FROM *SARUBASHI*... AT THE END OF THE ROAD, ENTER THE SNOWBOUND VALLEY AT THE FOOT OF MOUNT *IWADONO*. ON THE LEFT, A GIANT *THOUSAND-YEAR CEDAR*...

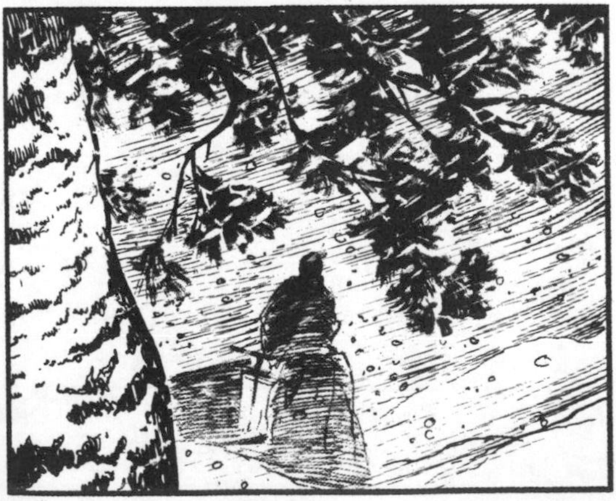

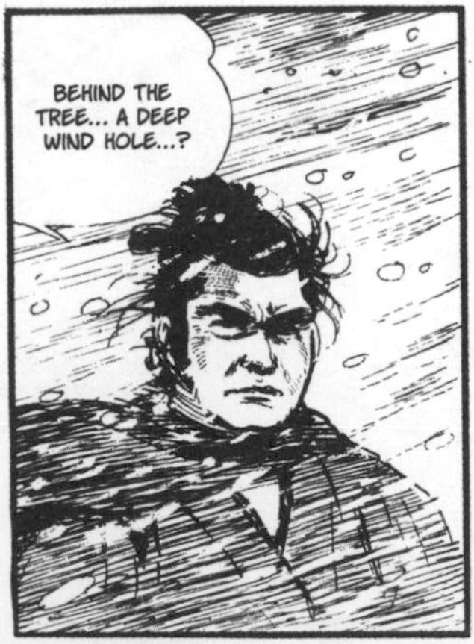
BEHIND THE TREE... A DEEP WIND HOLE...?

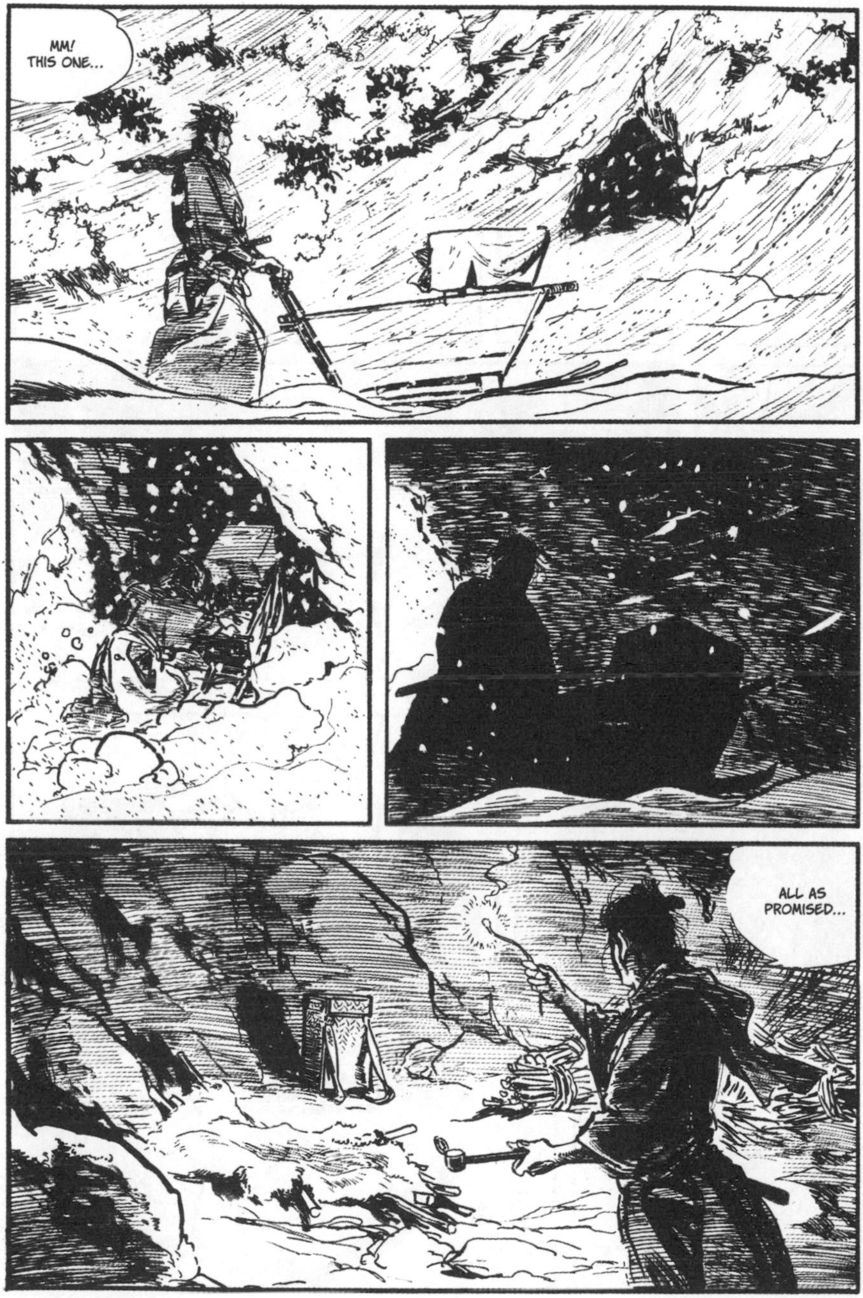
MM! THIS ONE...
ALL AS PROMISED...

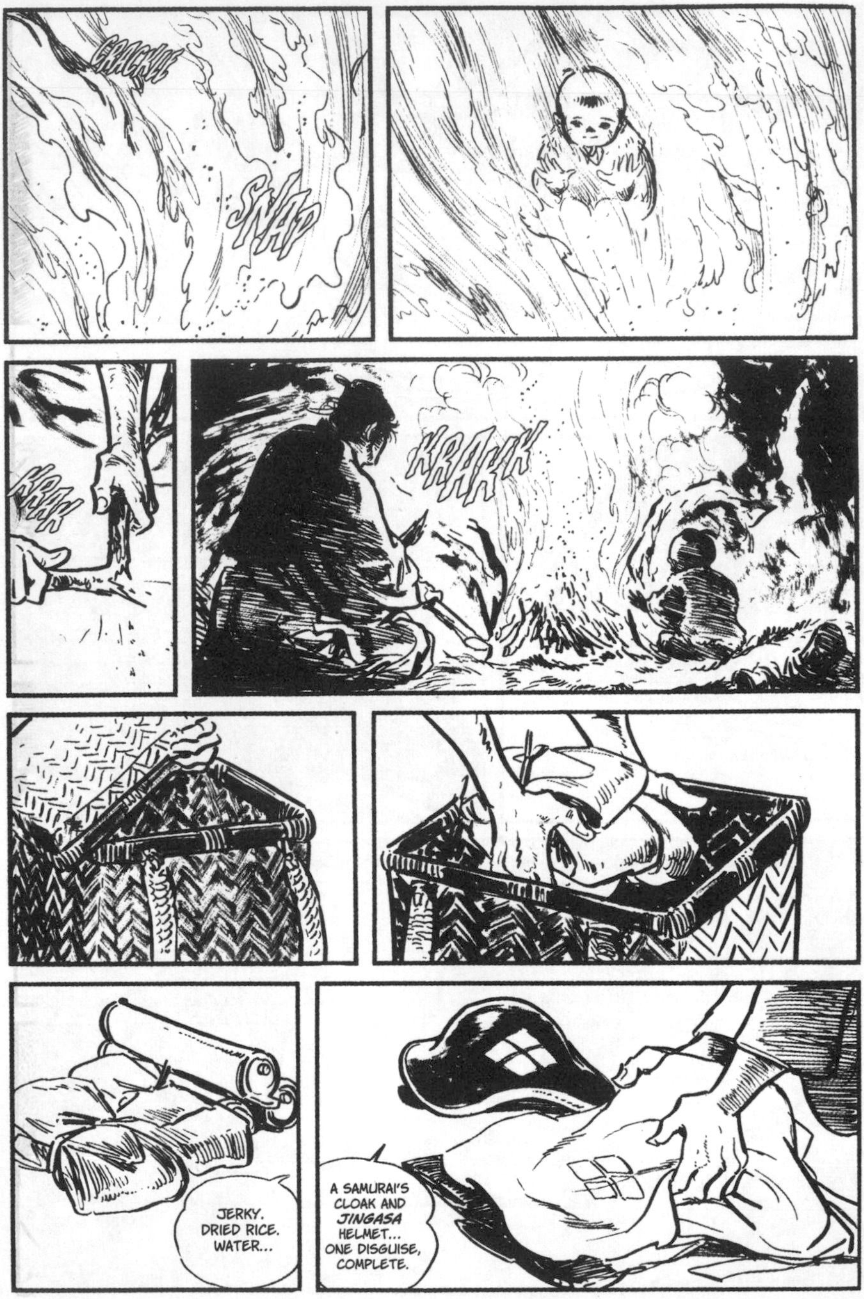
CRACKLE
SNAP
KRAK
KRAKK
JERKY. DRIED RICE. WATER...
A SAMURAI'S CLOAK AND JINGASA HELMET... ONE DISGUISE, COMPLETE.

THIS SHOULD LAST... FIVE DAYS...?

DAIGORO! YOU WILL WAIT FOR FATHER HERE!

UHN!

IF YOU GET HUNGRY, EAT JERKY AND DRY RICE.

IF YOU GET THIRSTY, DRINK WATER FROM THESE BAMBOO PIPES.

UHN.

PEE AND POTTY OVER THERE.

UHN.

NO MATTER WHAT HAPPENS, YOU MUST NOT GO OUTSIDE! IF FATHER DOES NOT RETURN, YOU ALSO DIE!

IF YOU DO NOT CRY EVEN WHEN HUNGRY, IF YOU ENDURE EVEN WHEN COLD, IF YOU WAIT PATIENTLY, YOU, TOO, CAN DIE.

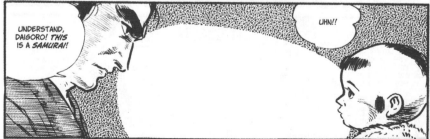

UNDERSTAND, DAIGORO! *THIS* IS A *SAMURAI!*

UHN!!

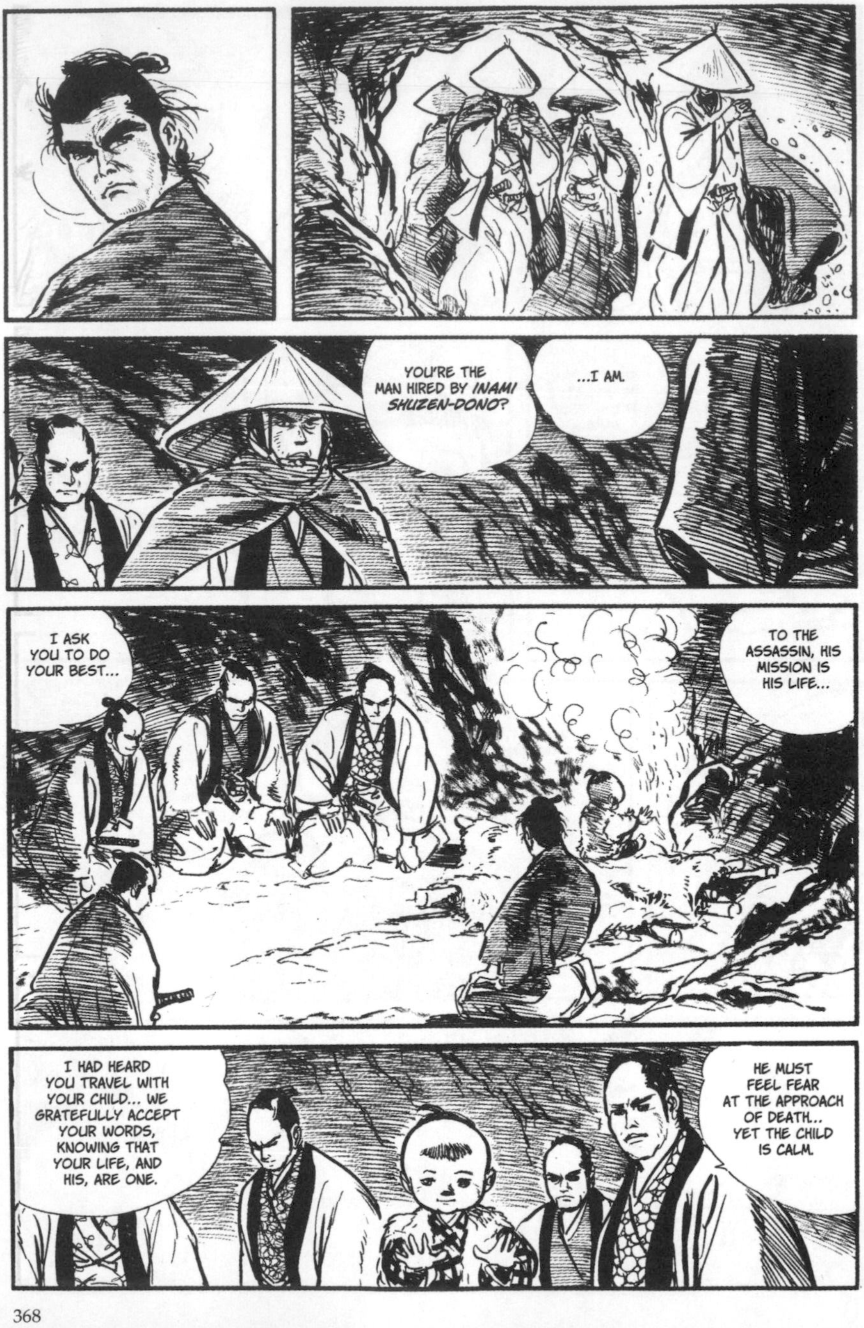
YOU'RE THE MAN HIRED BY *INAMI SHUZEN-DONO?*
...I AM.
TO THE ASSASSIN, HIS MISSION IS HIS LIFE...
I ASK YOU TO DO YOUR BEST...
HE MUST FEEL FEAR AT THE APPROACH OF DEATH... YET THE CHILD IS CALM.
I HAD HEARD YOU TRAVEL WITH YOUR CHILD... WE GRATEFULLY ACCEPT YOUR WORDS, KNOWING THAT YOUR LIFE, AND HIS, ARE ONE.

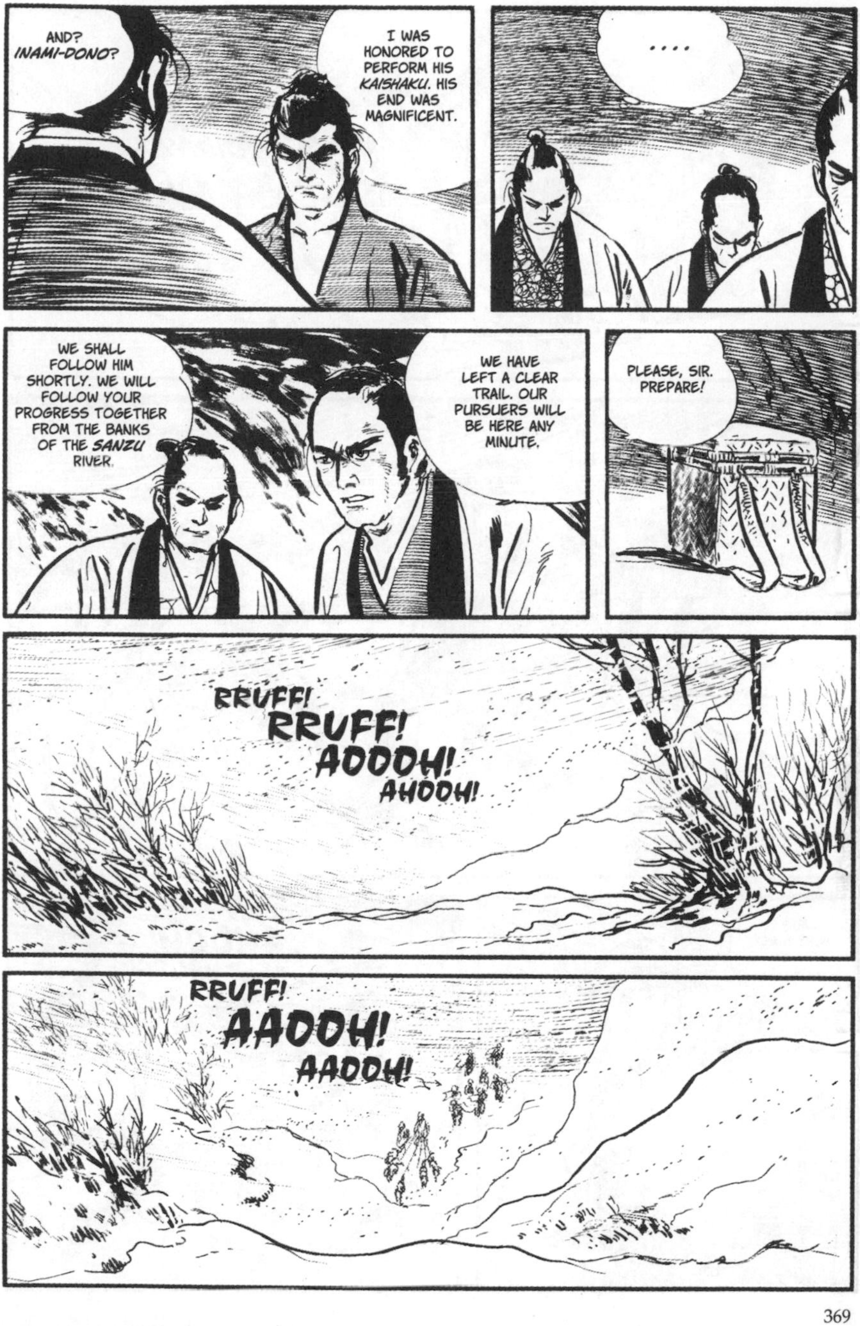
AND? *INAMI-DONO?*
I WAS HONORED TO PERFORM HIS *KAISHAKU.* HIS END WAS MAGNIFICENT.
....
WE SHALL FOLLOW HIM SHORTLY. WE WILL FOLLOW YOUR PROGRESS TOGETHER FROM THE BANKS OF THE *SANZU* RIVER.
WE HAVE LEFT A CLEAR TRAIL. OUR PURSUERS WILL BE HERE ANY MINUTE.
PLEASE, SIR. PREPARE!
RRUFF!
RRUFF!
AOOOH!
AHOOH!
RRUFF!
AAOOH!
AAOOH!

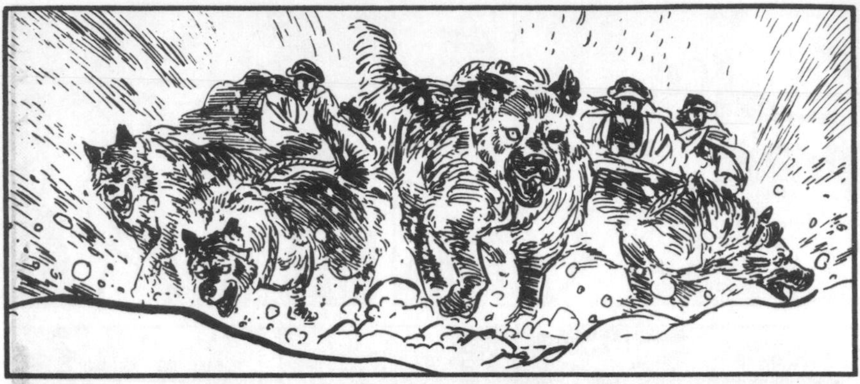

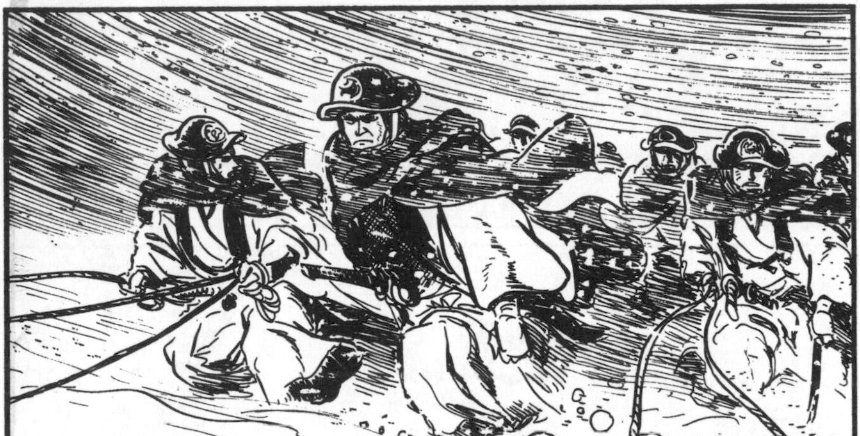

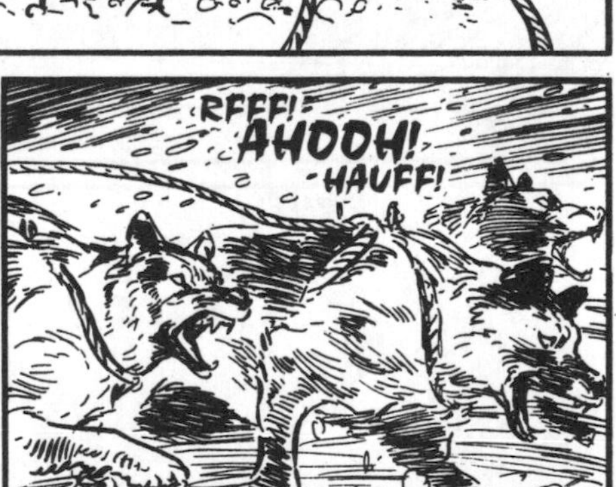
RFFF!
AHOOH!
HAUFF!

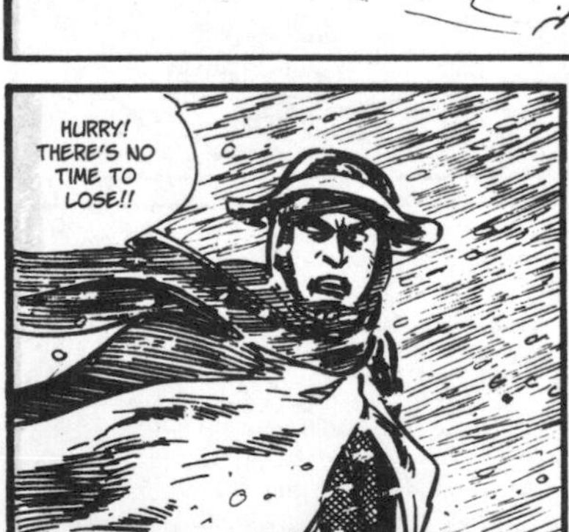
HURRY! THERE'S NO TIME TO LOSE!!

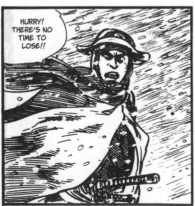

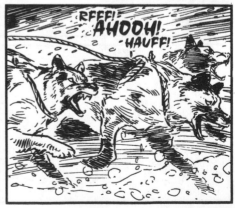

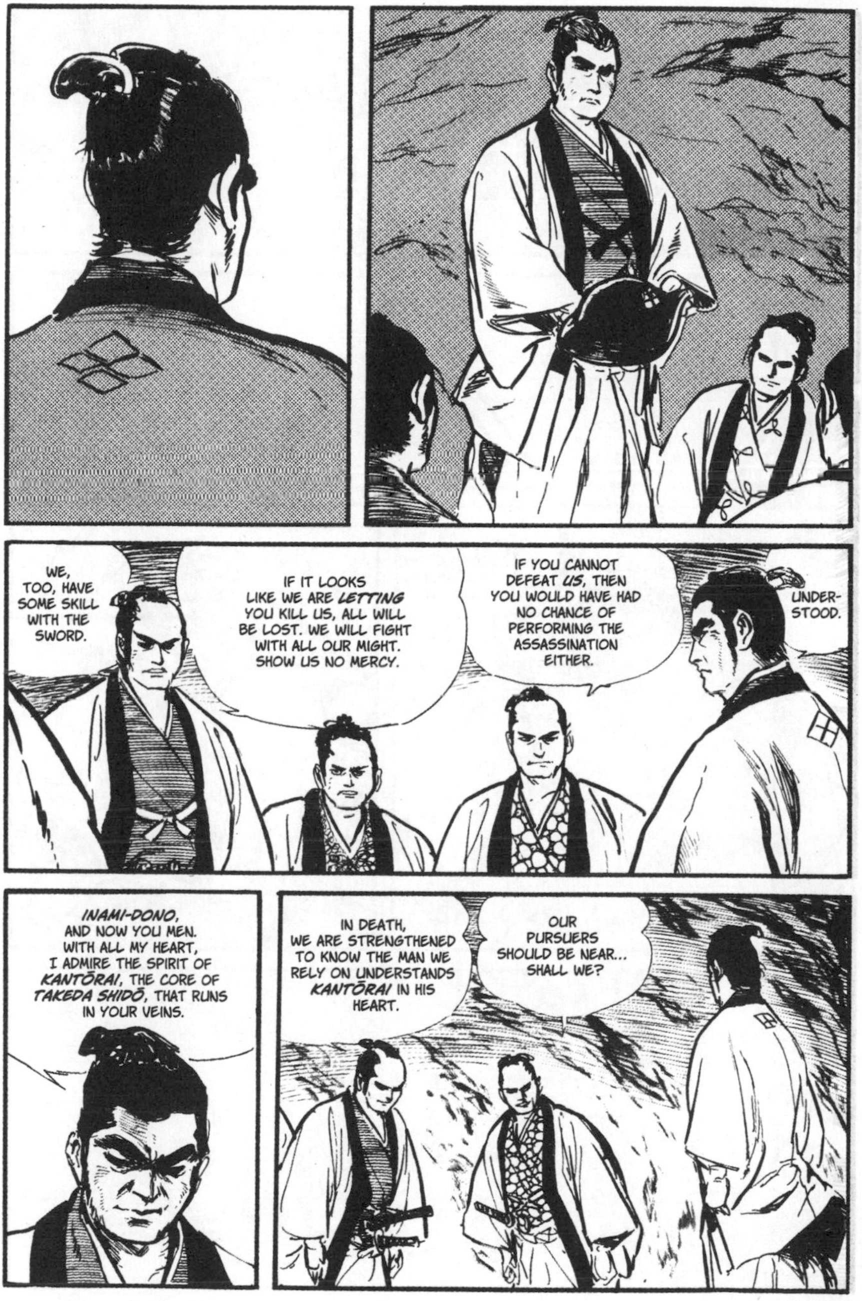
WE, TOO, HAVE SOME SKILL WITH THE SWORD.
IF IT LOOKS LIKE WE ARE *LETTING* YOU KILL US, ALL WILL BE LOST. WE WILL FIGHT WITH ALL OUR MIGHT. SHOW US NO MERCY.
IF YOU CANNOT DEFEAT *US*, THEN YOU WOULD HAVE HAD NO CHANCE OF PERFORMING THE ASSASSINATION EITHER.
UNDER-STOOD.
INAMI-DONO, AND NOW YOU MEN. WITH ALL MY HEART, I ADMIRE THE SPIRIT OF *KANTŌRAI*, THE CORE OF *TAKEDA SHIDŌ*, THAT RUNS IN YOUR VEINS.
IN DEATH, WE ARE STRENGTHENED TO KNOW THE MAN WE RELY ON UNDERSTANDS *KANTŌRAI* IN HIS HEART.
OUR PURSUERS SHOULD BE NEAR... SHALL WE?

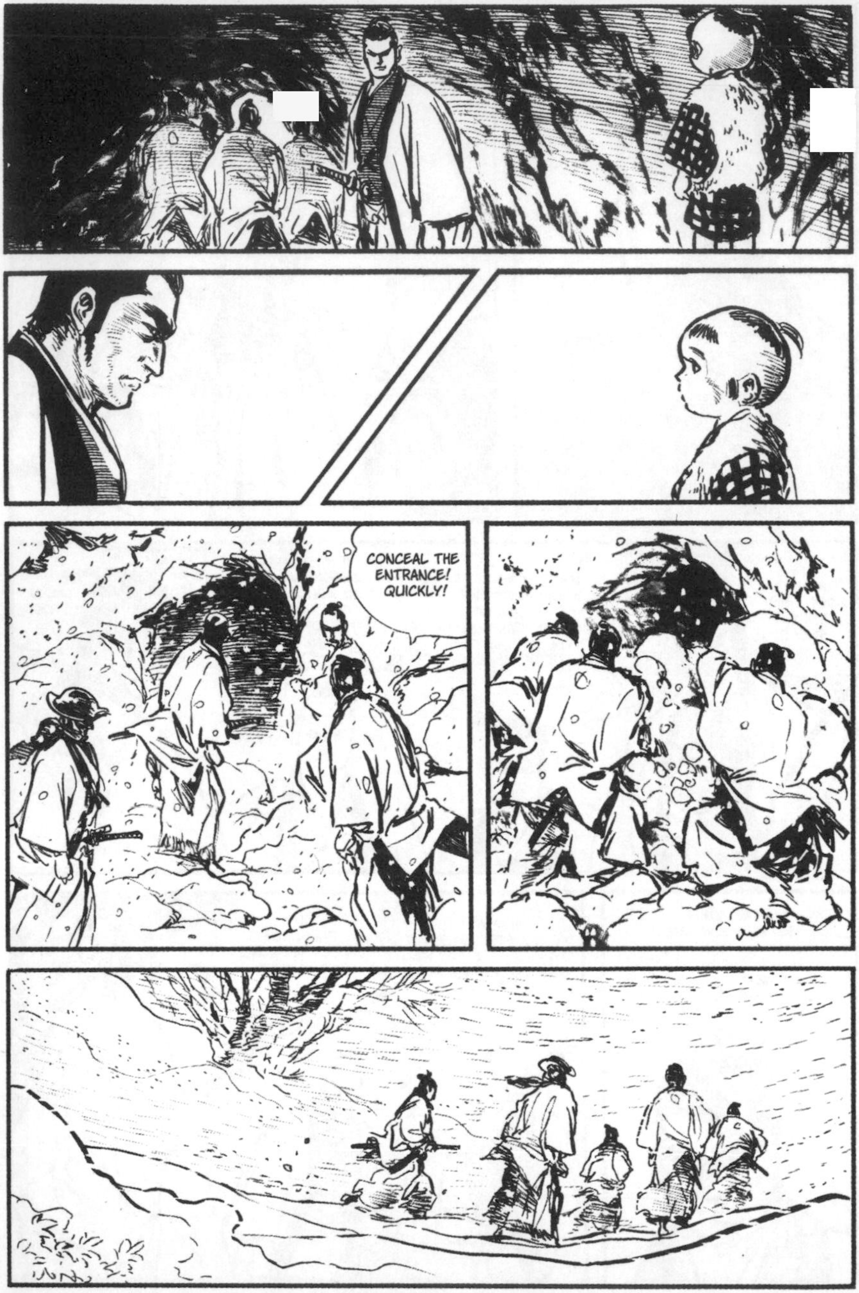
CONCEAL THE ENTRANCE! QUICKLY!

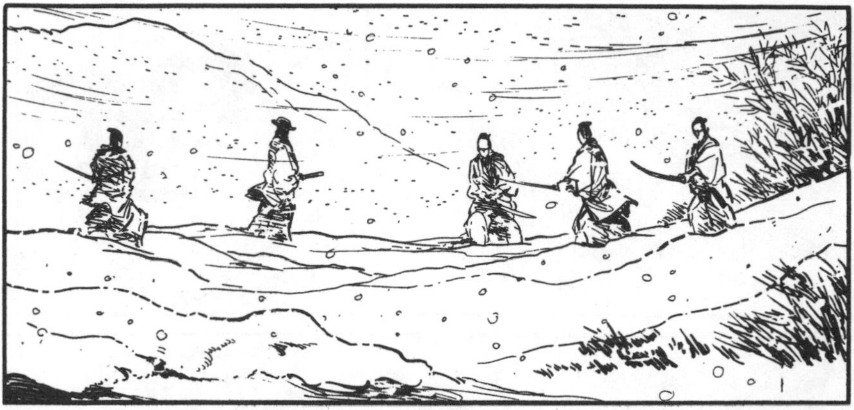

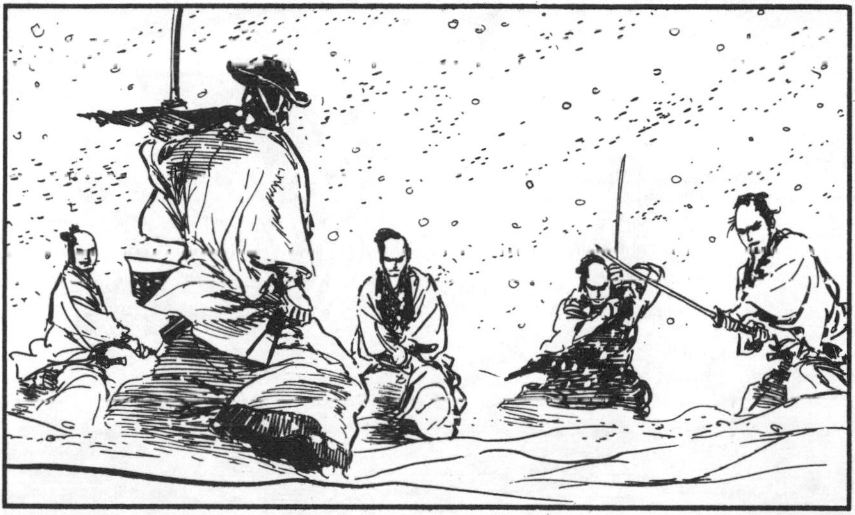

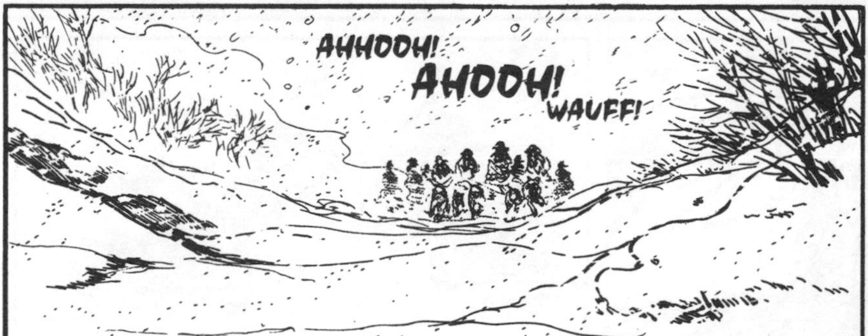
AHHOOH!
AHOOH!
WAUFF!

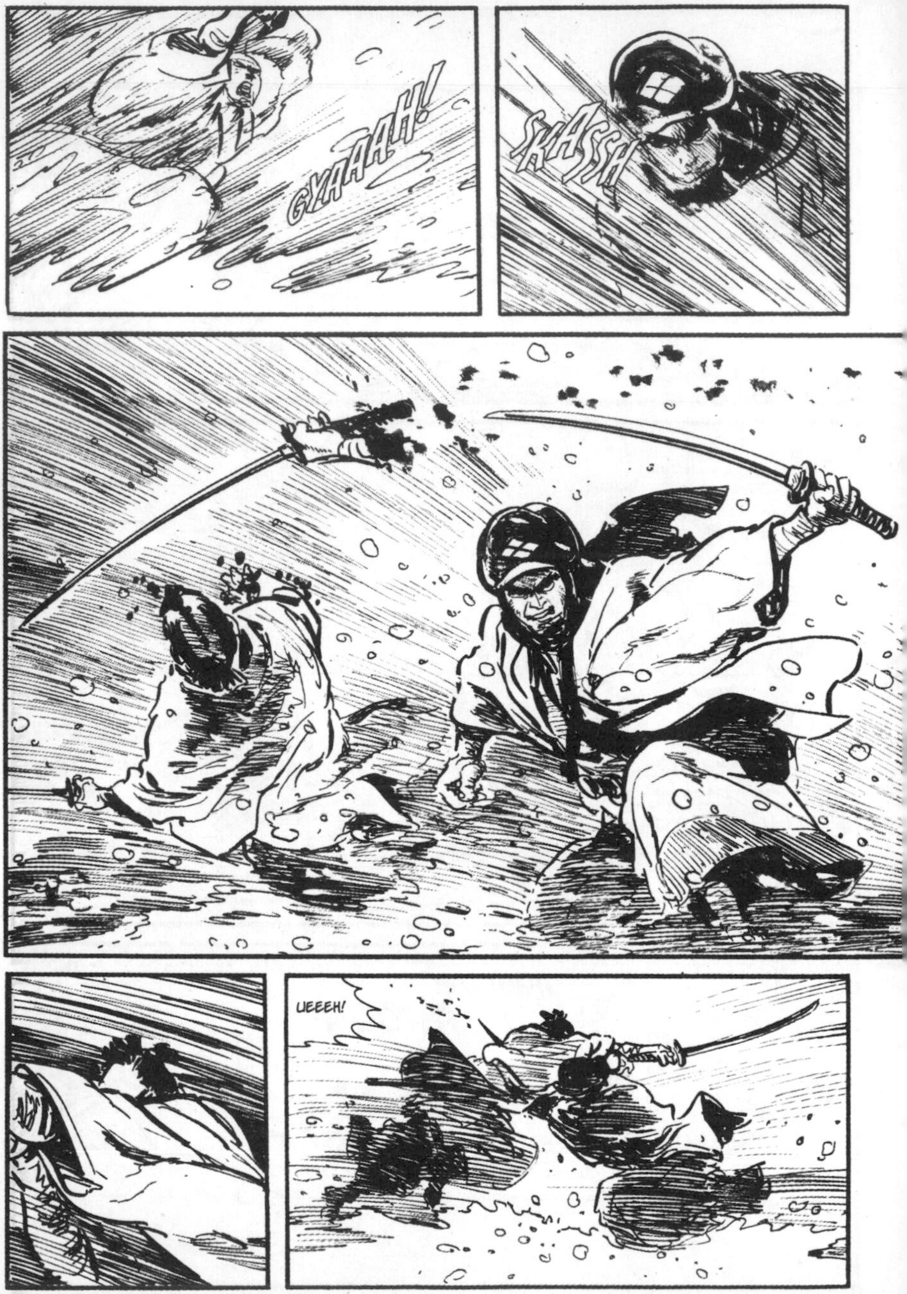
SKASSH
GYAAAH!
UEEEH!

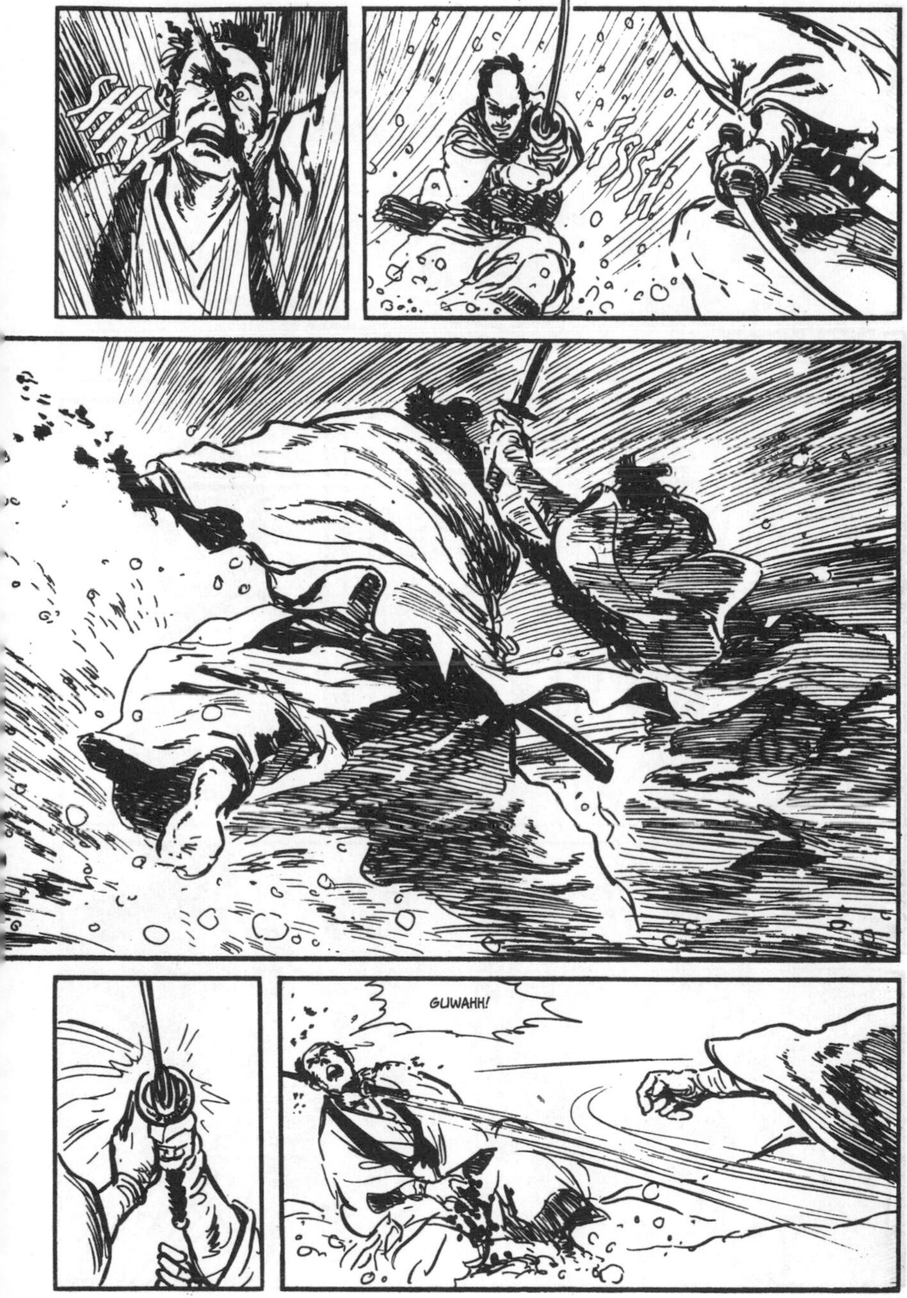
FSH
SHK
GUWAHH!

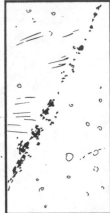

HAUFF
AAOOOH
HAUFF

HAUFF
WFF

HAUU
HAHH

RARRF

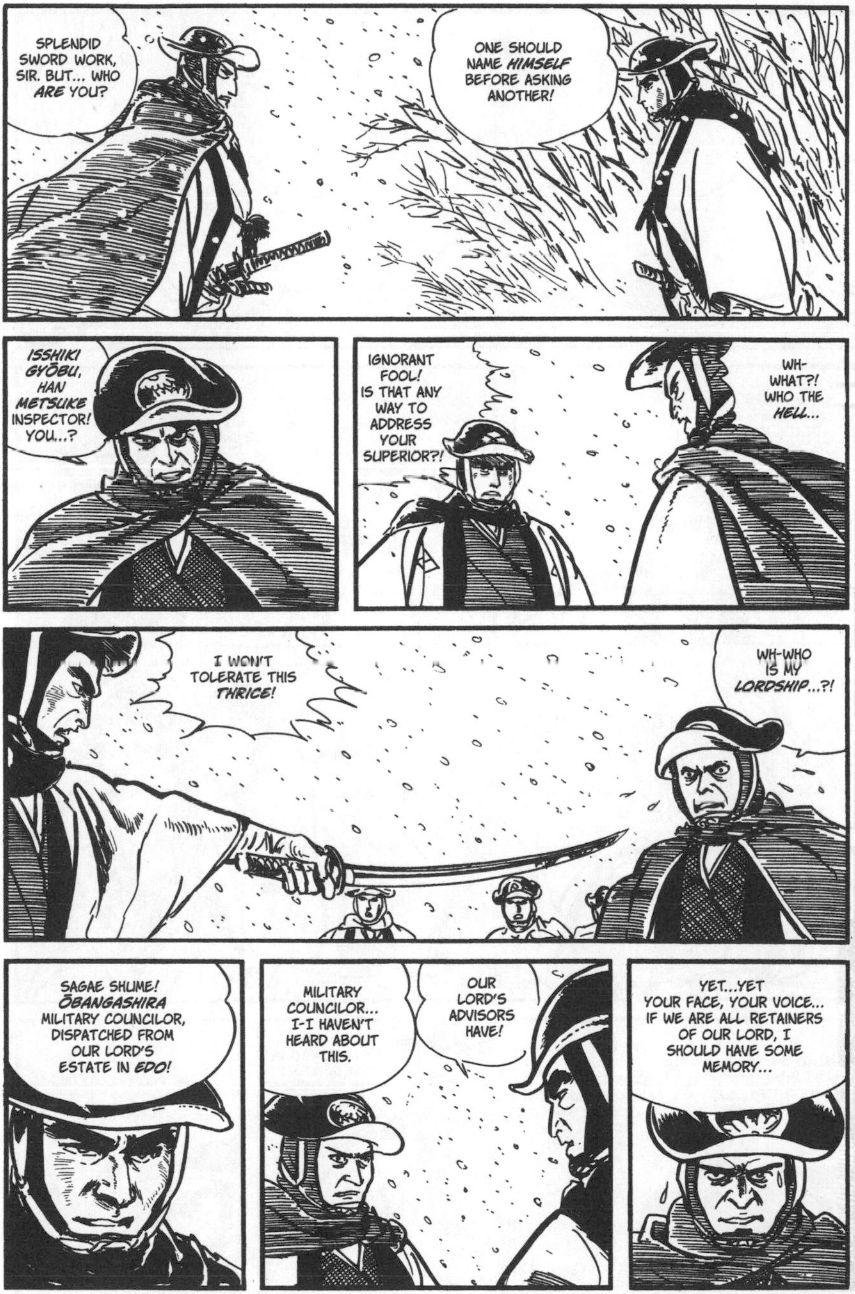
SPLENDID SWORD WORK, SIR. BUT... WHO *ARE* YOU?
ONE SHOULD NAME *HIMSELF* BEFORE ASKING ANOTHER!
ISSHIKI GYŌBU, HAN METSUKE INSPECTOR! YOU...?
IGNORANT FOOL! IS THAT ANY WAY TO ADDRESS YOUR SUPERIOR?!
WH-WHAT?! WHO THE *HELL*...
I WON'T TOLERATE THIS *THRICE*!
WH-WHO IS MY *LORDSHIP*...?!
SAGAE SHUME! *ŌBANGASHIRA* MILITARY COUNCILOR, DISPATCHED FROM OUR LORD'S ESTATE IN *EDO*!
MILITARY COUNCILOR... I-I HAVEN'T HEARD ABOUT THIS.
OUR LORD'S ADVISORS HAVE!
YET...YET YOUR FACE, YOUR VOICE... IF WE ARE ALL RETAINERS OF OUR LORD, I SHOULD HAVE SOME MEMORY...

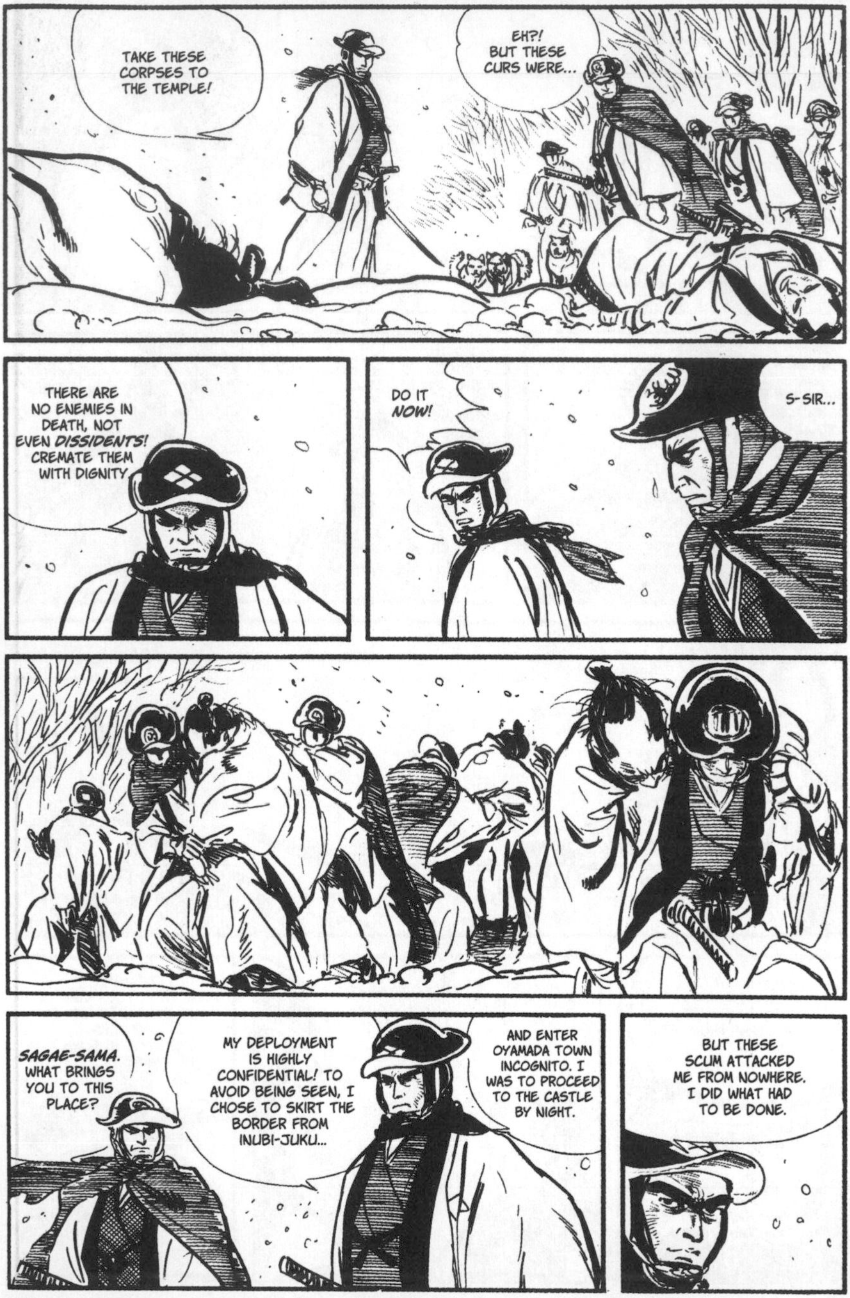
TAKE THESE CORPSES TO THE TEMPLE!
EH?! BUT THESE CURS WERE...
THERE ARE NO ENEMIES IN DEATH, NOT EVEN DISSIDENTS! CREMATE THEM WITH DIGNITY.
DO IT NOW!
S-SIR...
SAGAE-SAMA. WHAT BRINGS YOU TO THIS PLACE?
MY DEPLOYMENT IS HIGHLY CONFIDENTIAL! TO AVOID BEING SEEN, I CHOSE TO SKIRT THE BORDER FROM INUBI-JUKU...
AND ENTER OYAMADA TOWN INCOGNITO. I WAS TO PROCEED TO THE CASTLE BY NIGHT.
BUT THESE SCUM ATTACKED ME FROM NOWHERE. I DID WHAT HAD TO BE DONE.

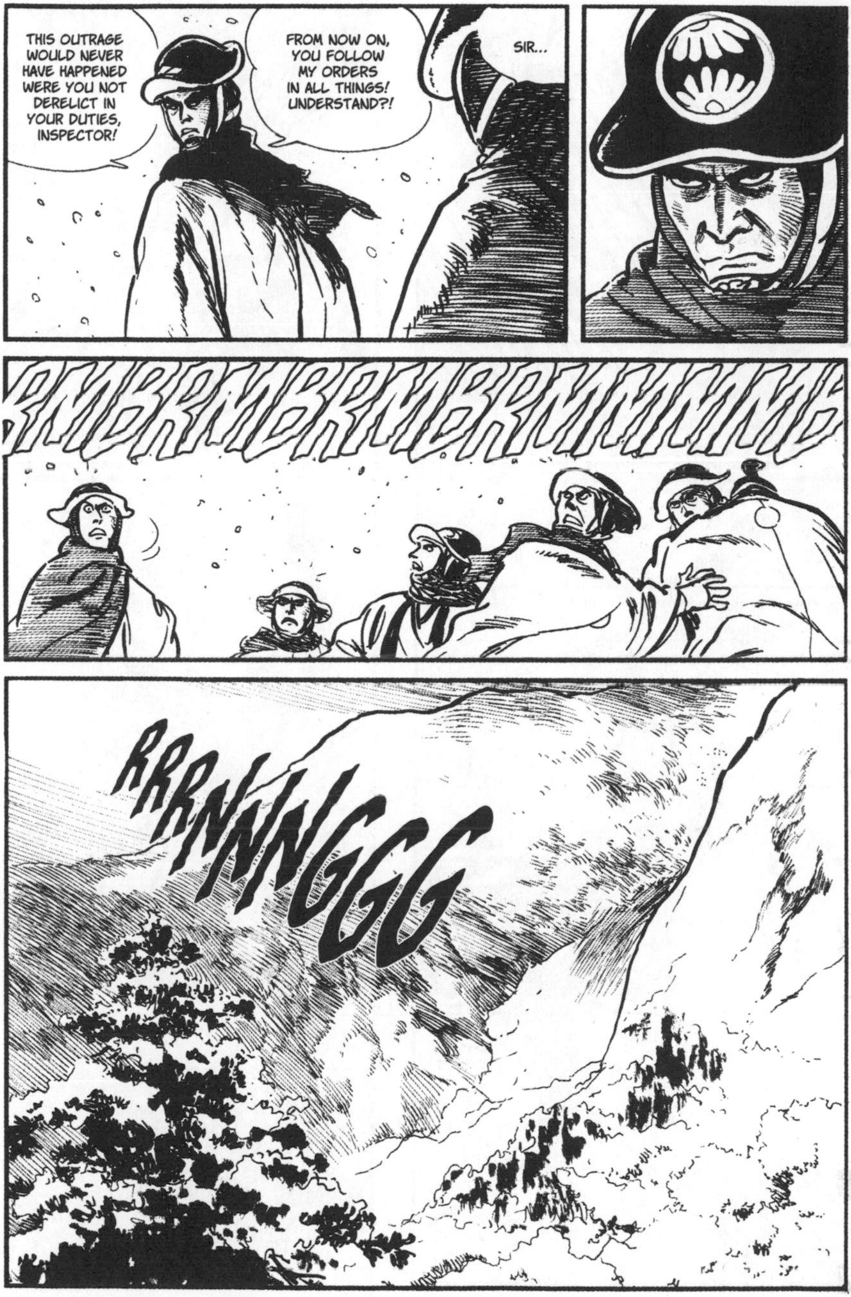
THIS OUTRAGE WOULD NEVER HAVE HAPPENED WERE YOU NOT DERELICT IN YOUR DUTIES, INSPECTOR!
FROM NOW ON, YOU FOLLOW MY ORDERS IN ALL THINGS! UNDERSTAND?!
SIR...
BRMBRMBRMBRMBRMMMMMMG
RRRNNNGGG

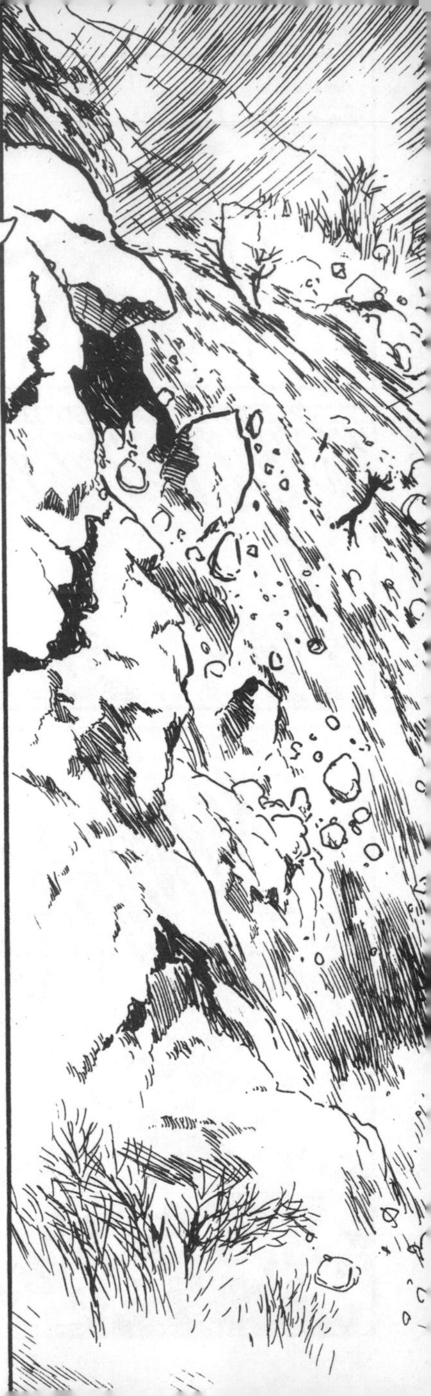

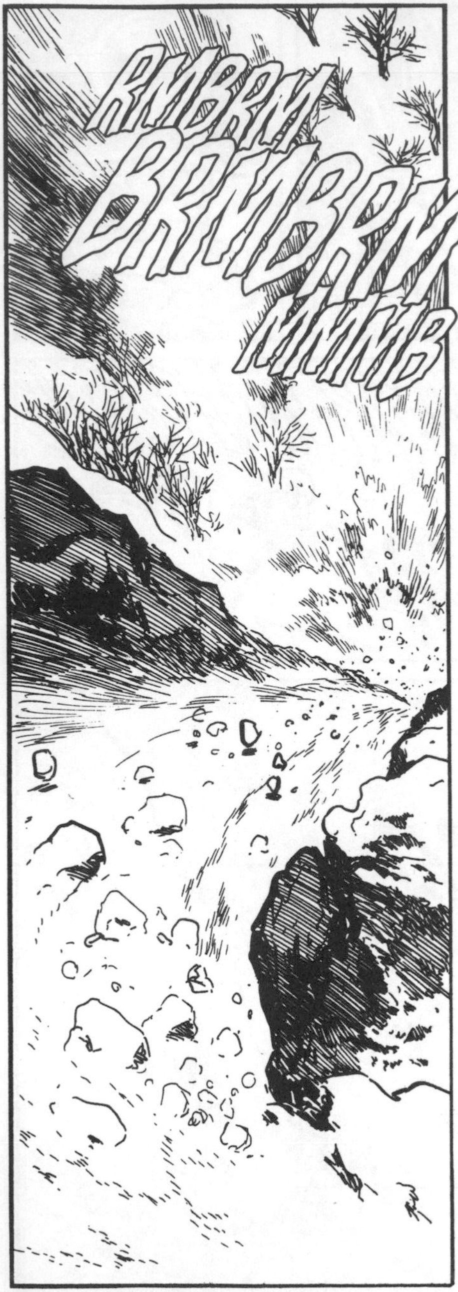
RMBRM
BRMBRM
MMMMB

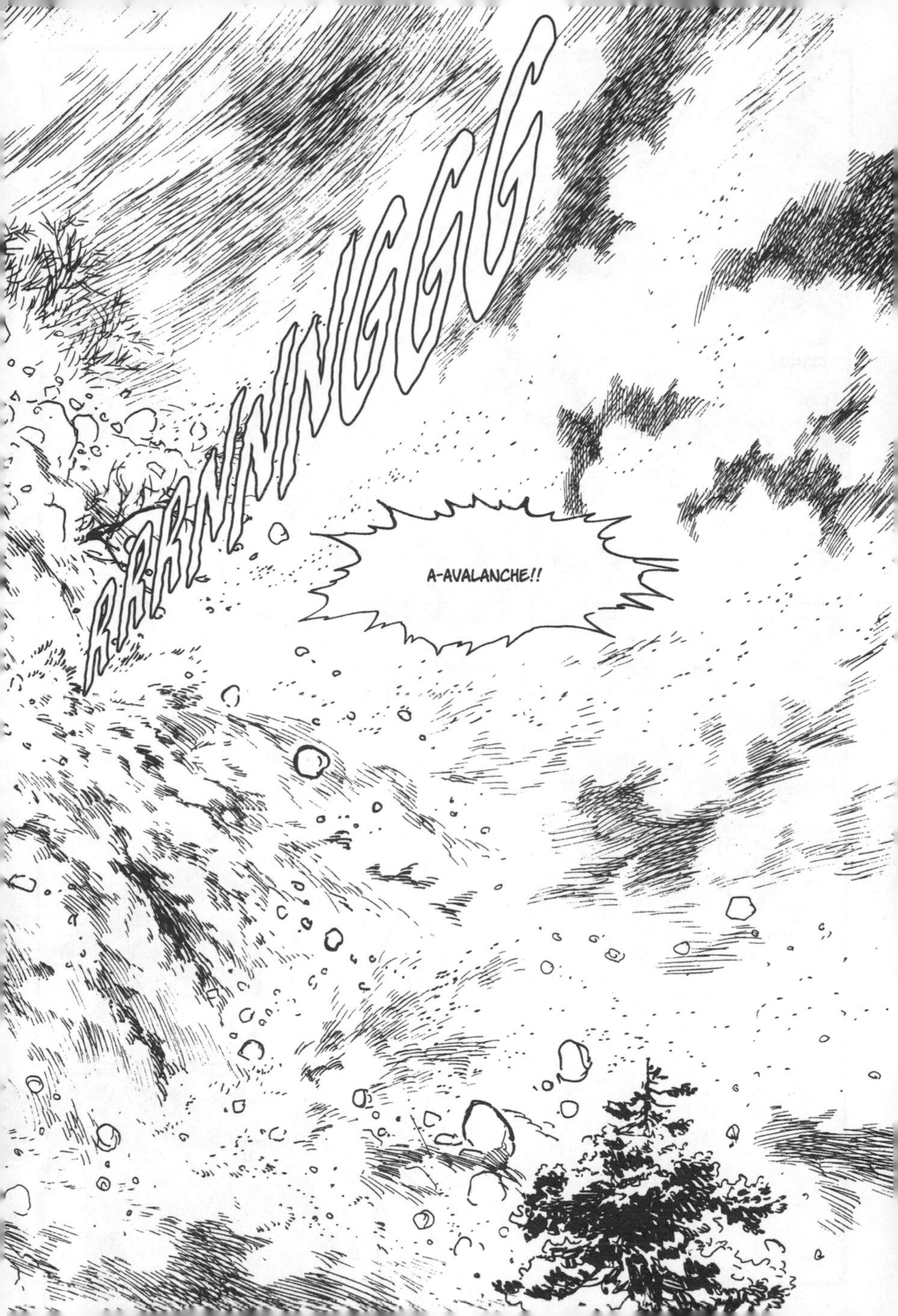
RRRNNNGGG
A-AVALANCHE!!

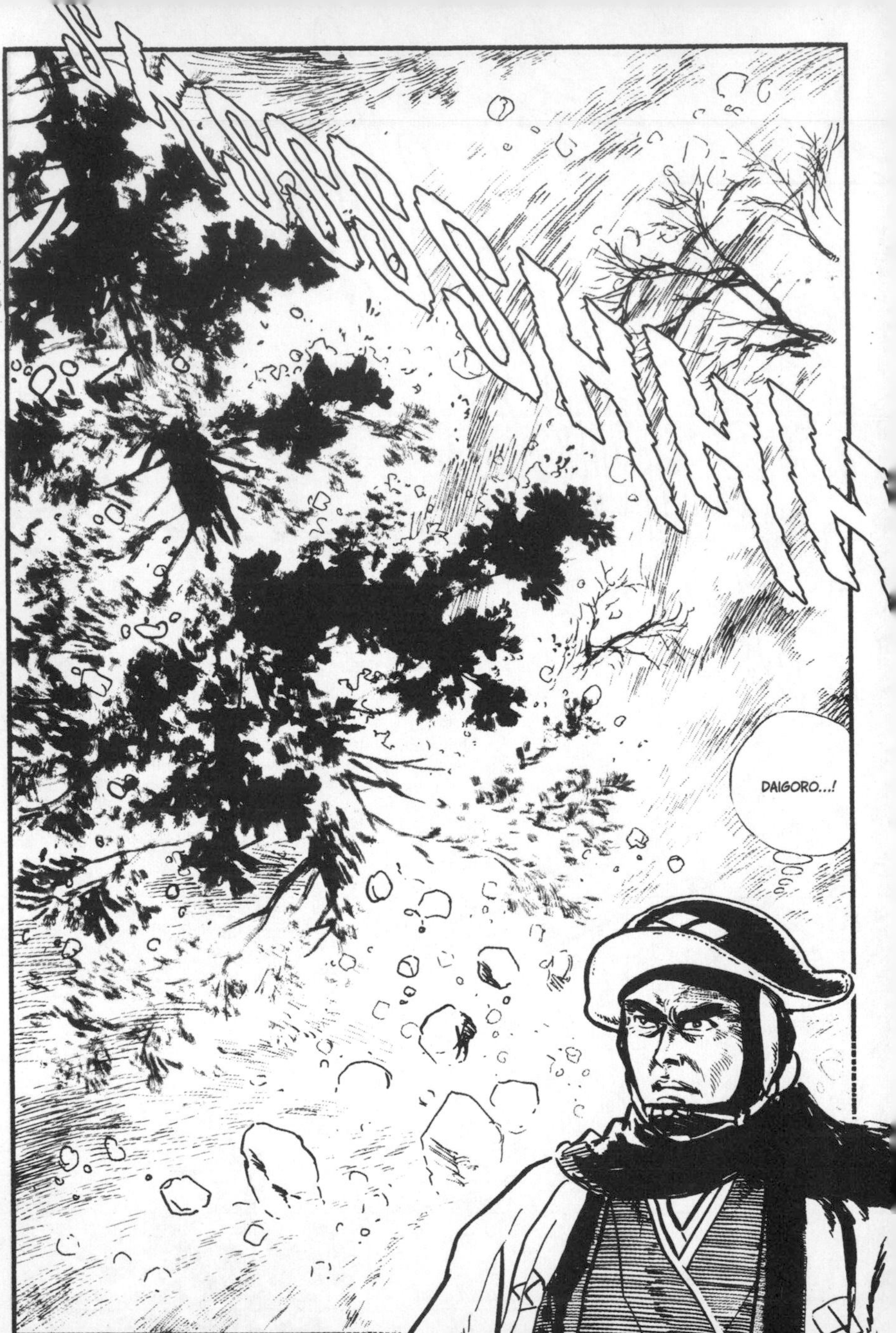
DAIGORO...!

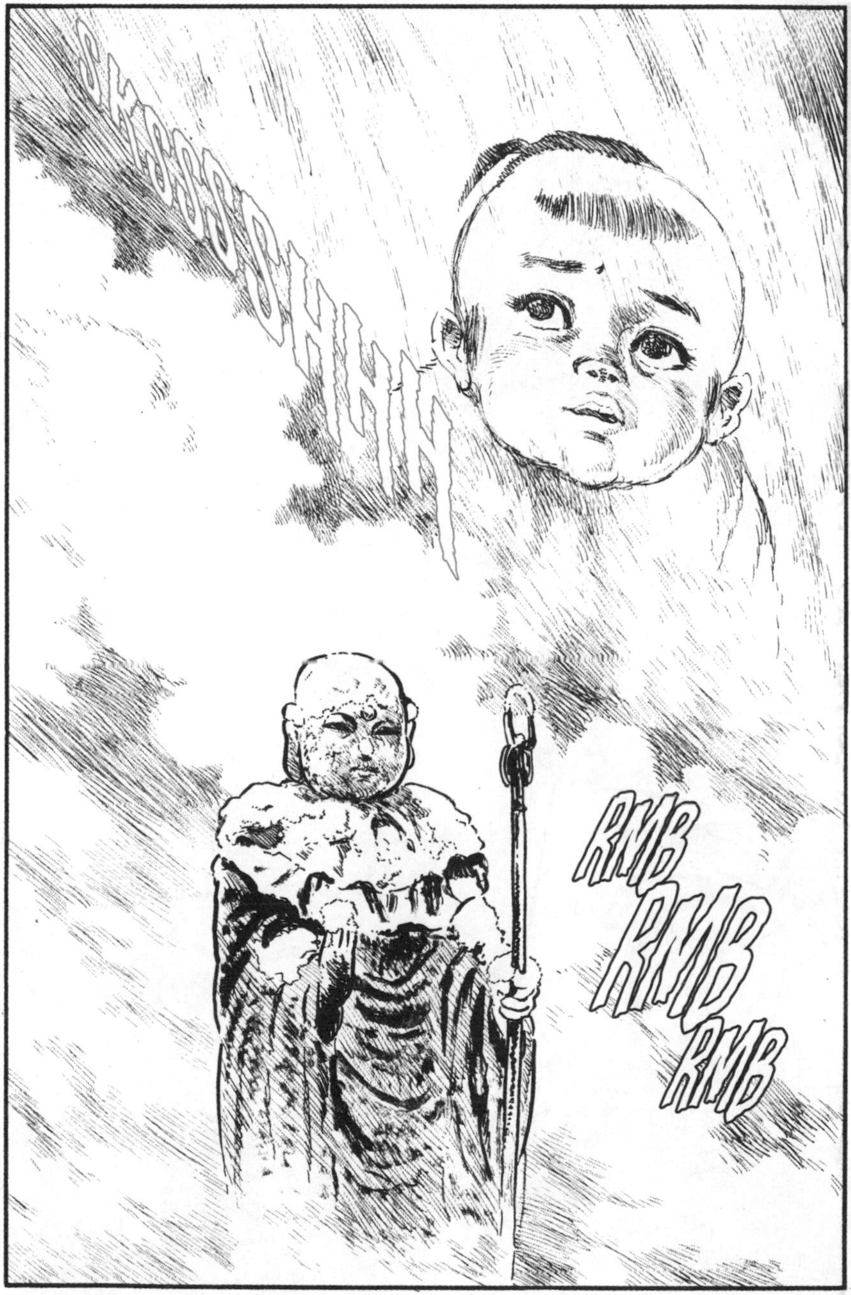
SHOOOOSHHHH
RMB
RMB
RMB
RMB

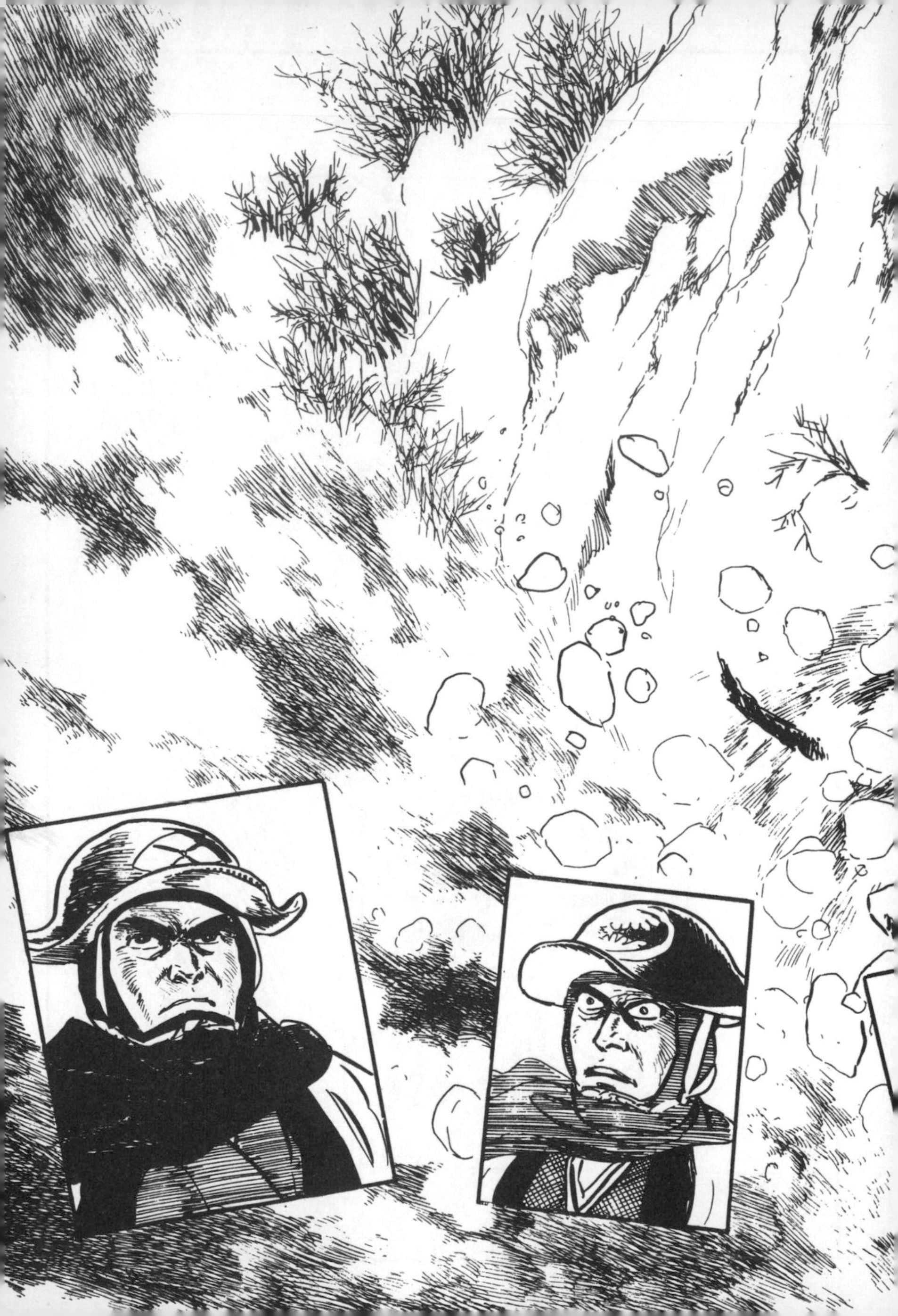

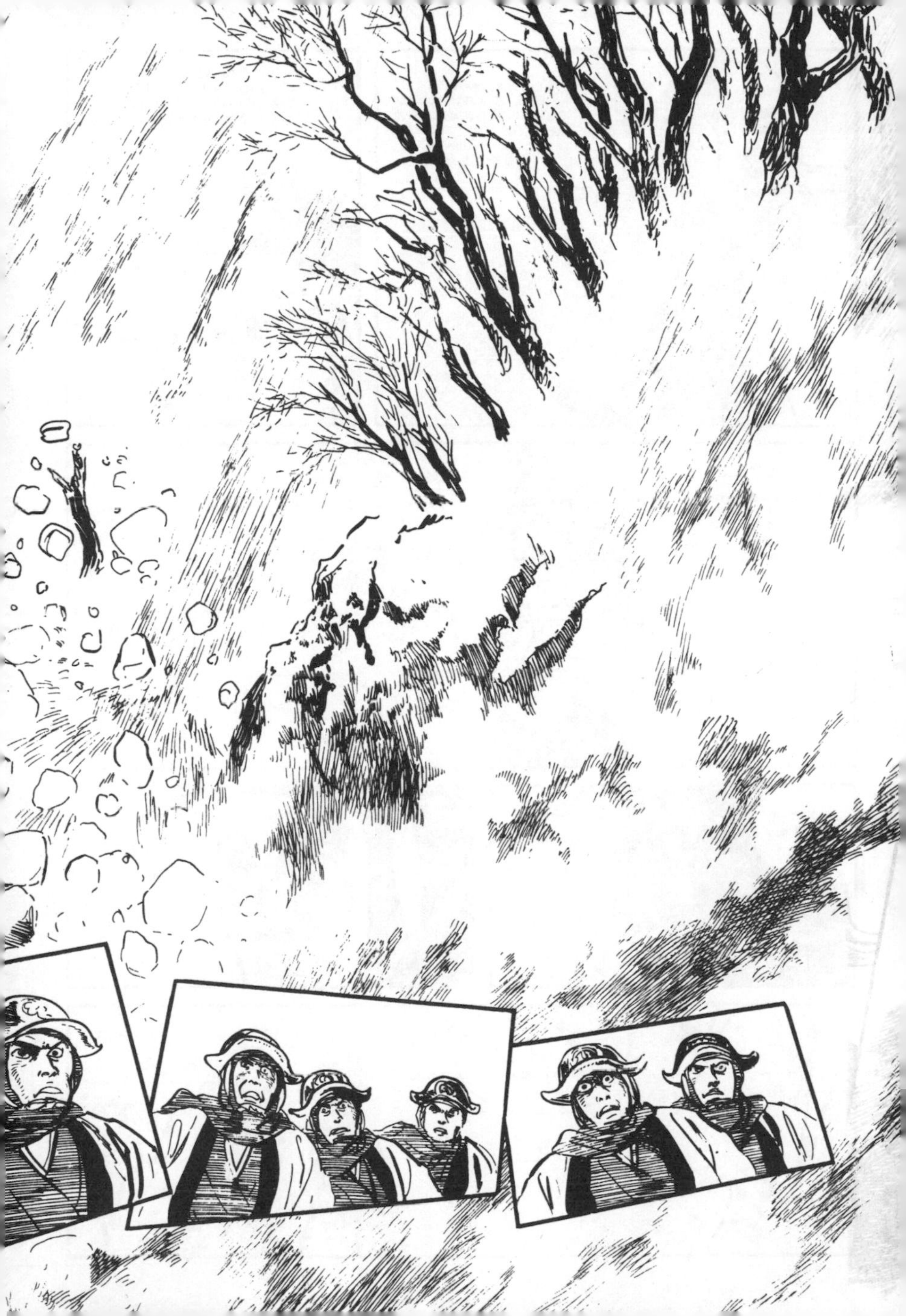

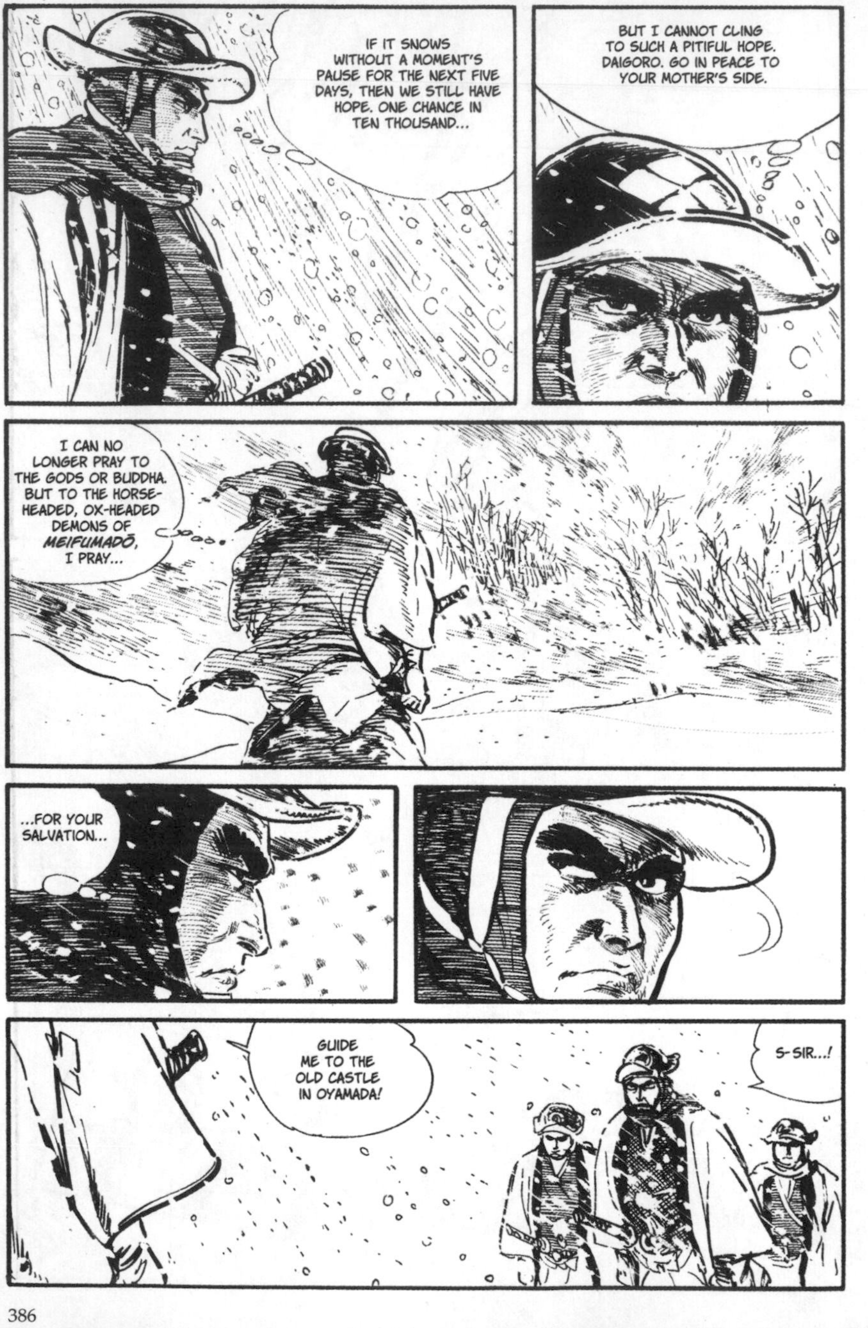
IF IT SNOWS WITHOUT A MOMENT'S PAUSE FOR THE NEXT FIVE DAYS, THEN WE STILL HAVE HOPE. ONE CHANCE IN TEN THOUSAND...
BUT I CANNOT CLING TO SUCH A PITIFUL HOPE. DAIGORO. GO IN PEACE TO YOUR MOTHER'S SIDE.
I CAN NO LONGER PRAY TO THE GODS OR BUDDHA. BUT TO THE HORSE-HEADED, OX-HEADED DEMONS OF *MEIFUMADŌ*, I PRAY...
...FOR YOUR SALVATION...
GUIDE ME TO THE OLD CASTLE IN OYAMADA!
S-SIR...!

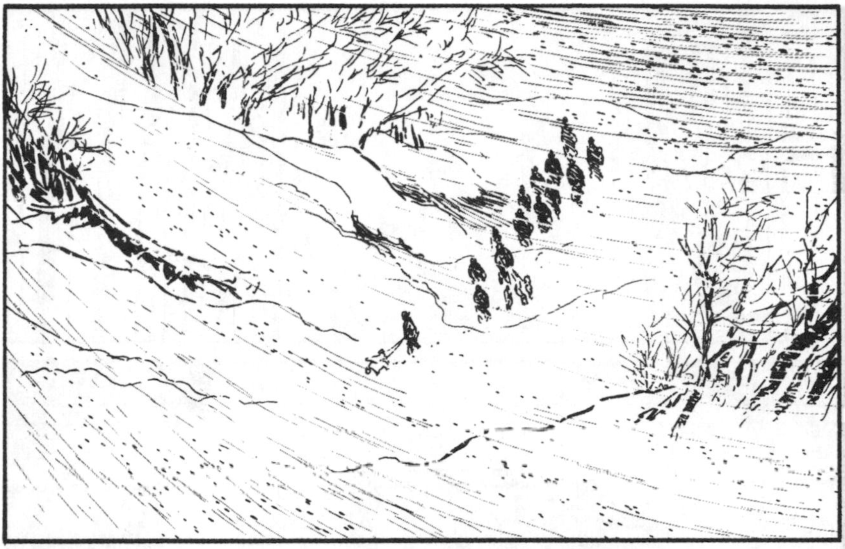

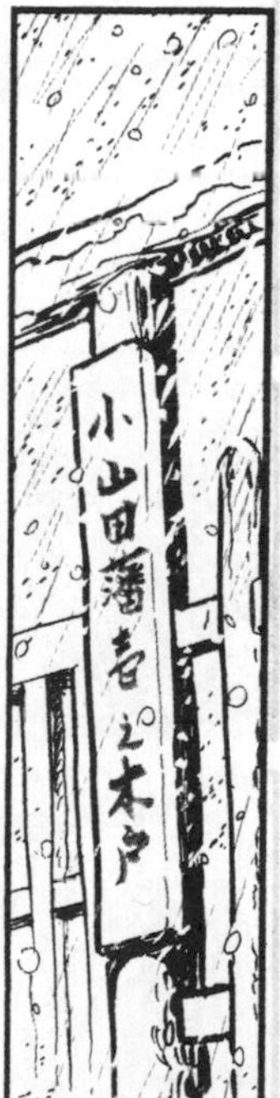
小山田藩壱之木戸
*OYAMADA HAN FIRST GATE

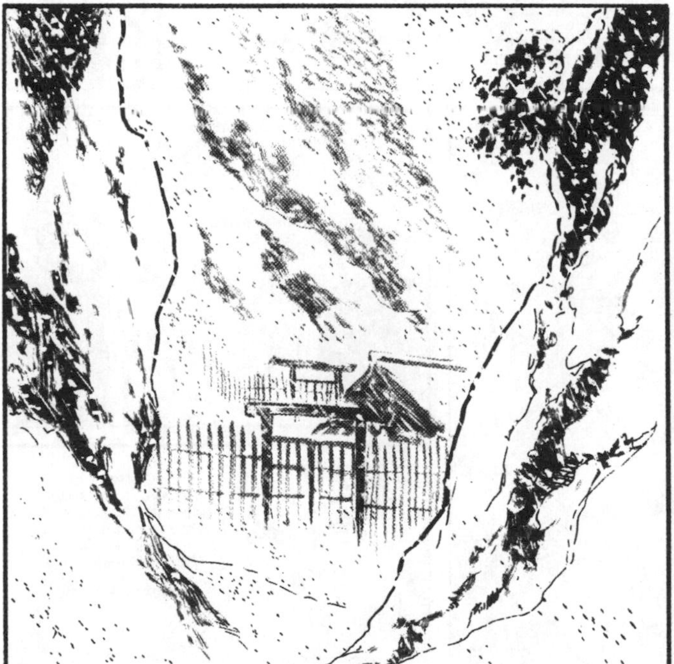

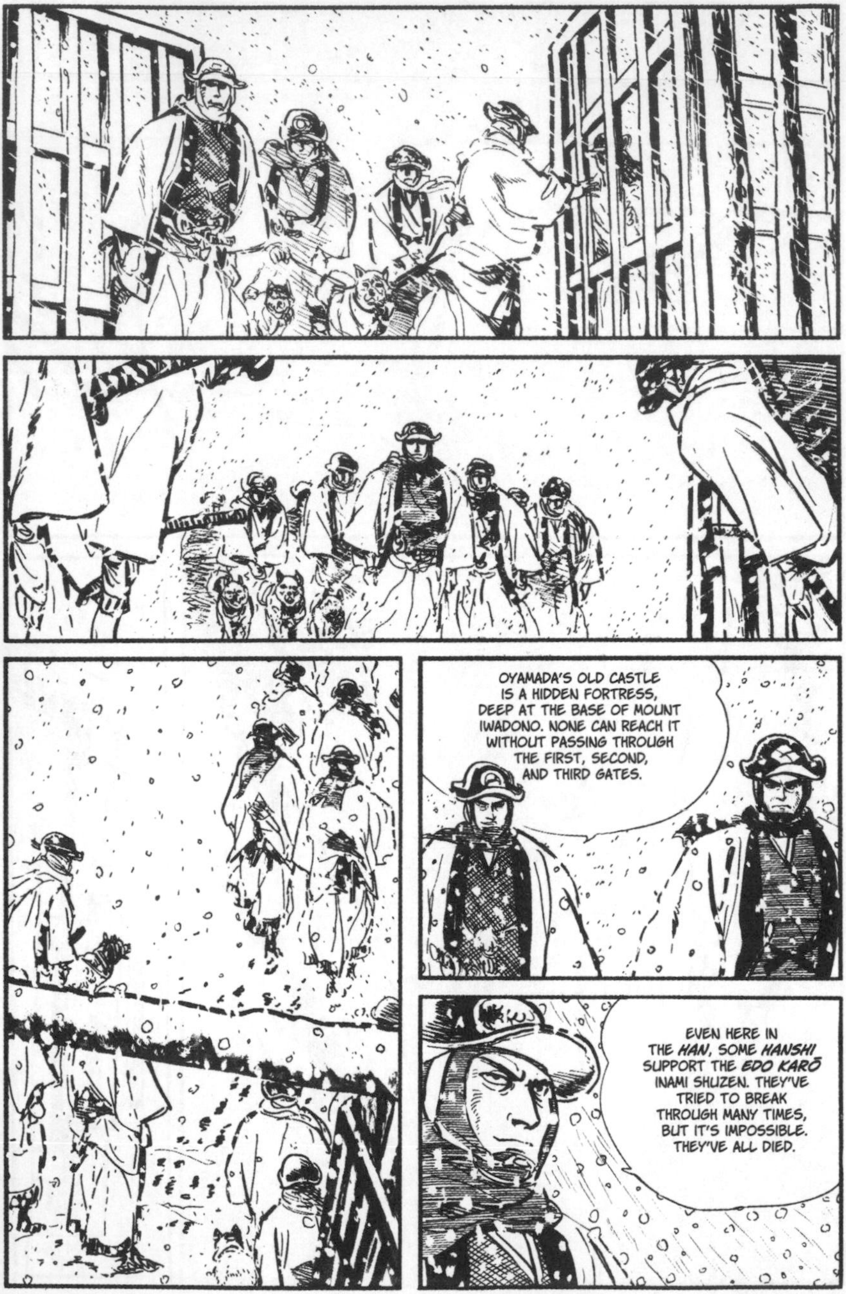
OYAMADA'S OLD CASTLE IS A HIDDEN FORTRESS, DEEP AT THE BASE OF MOUNT IWADONO. NONE CAN REACH IT WITHOUT PASSING THROUGH THE FIRST, SECOND, AND THIRD GATES.
EVEN HERE IN THE *HAN*, SOME *HANSHI* SUPPORT THE *EDO KARŌ* INAMI SHUZEN. THEY'VE TRIED TO BREAK THROUGH MANY TIMES, BUT IT'S IMPOSSIBLE. THEY'VE ALL DIED.

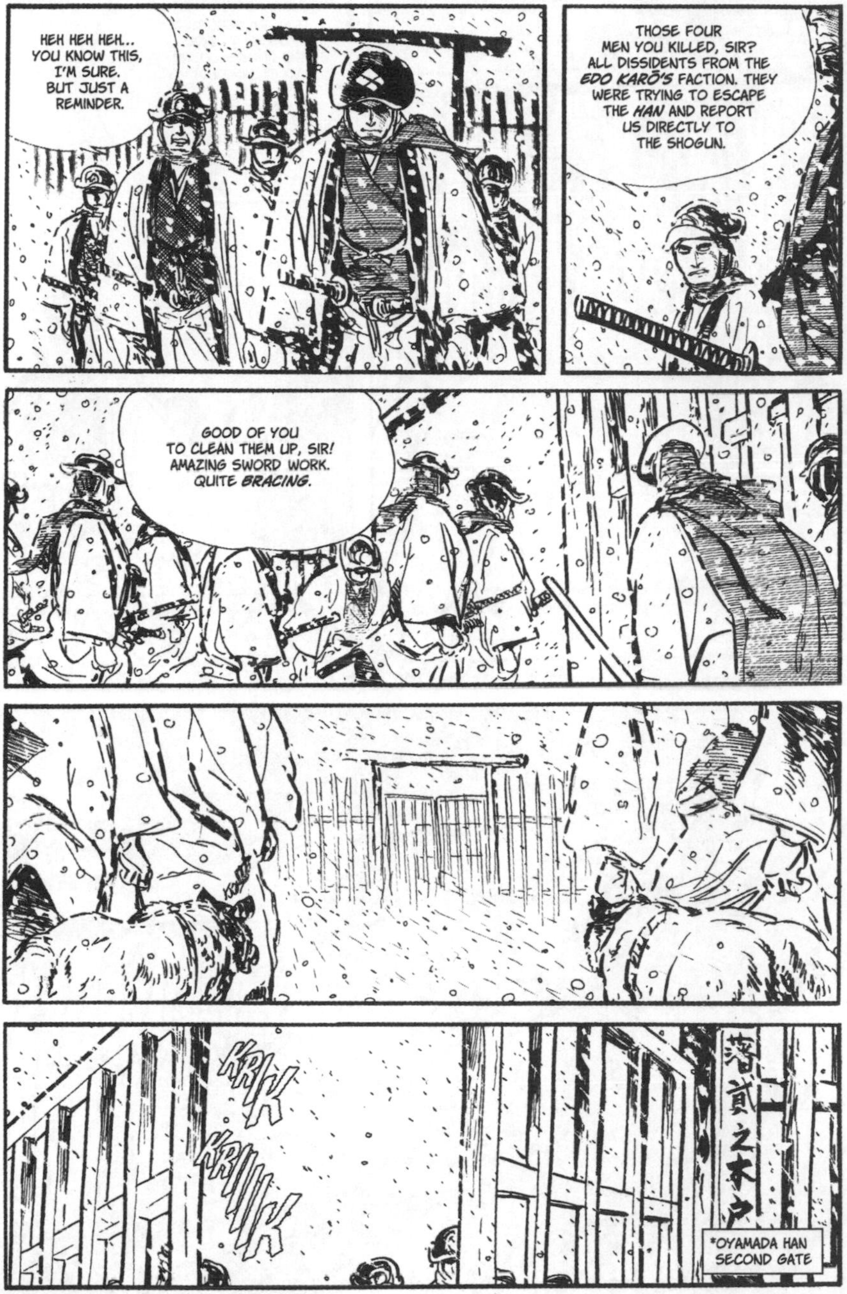
HEH HEH HEH... YOU KNOW THIS, I'M SURE. BUT JUST A REMINDER.
THOSE FOUR MEN YOU KILLED, SIR? ALL DISSIDENTS FROM THE *EDO KARŌ'S* FACTION. THEY WERE TRYING TO ESCAPE THE *HAN* AND REPORT US DIRECTLY TO THE SHOGUN.
GOOD OF YOU TO CLEAN THEM UP, SIR! AMAZING SWORD WORK. QUITE *BRACING*.
KRIK
KRIIIK
*OYAMADA HAN SECOND GATE

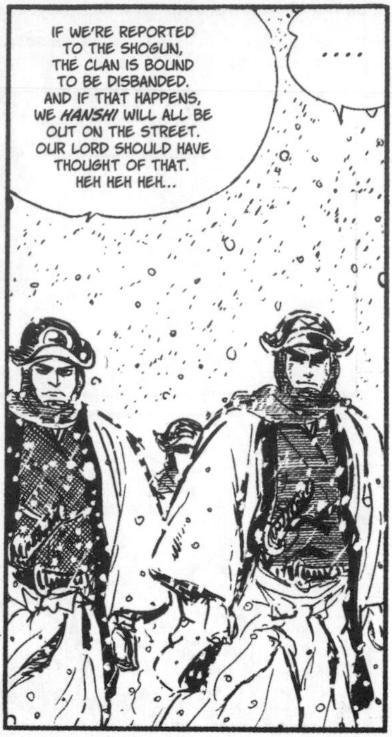
IF WE'RE REPORTED TO THE SHOGUN, THE CLAN IS BOUND TO BE DISBANDED. AND IF THAT HAPPENS, WE *HANSHI* WILL ALL BE OUT ON THE STREET. OUR LORD SHOULD HAVE THOUGHT OF THAT. HEH HEH HEH...
....
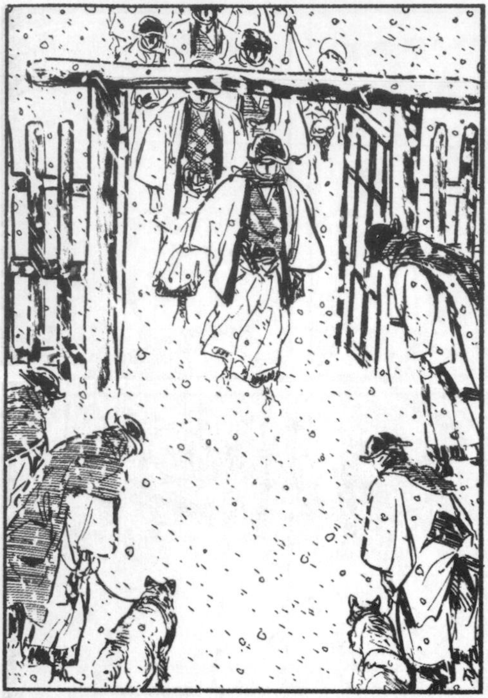
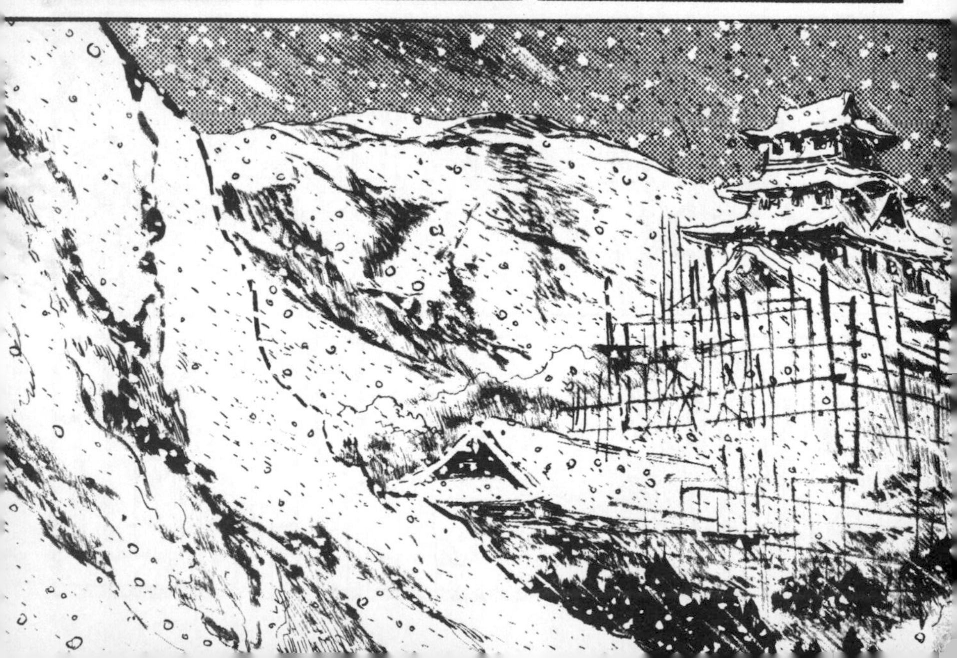

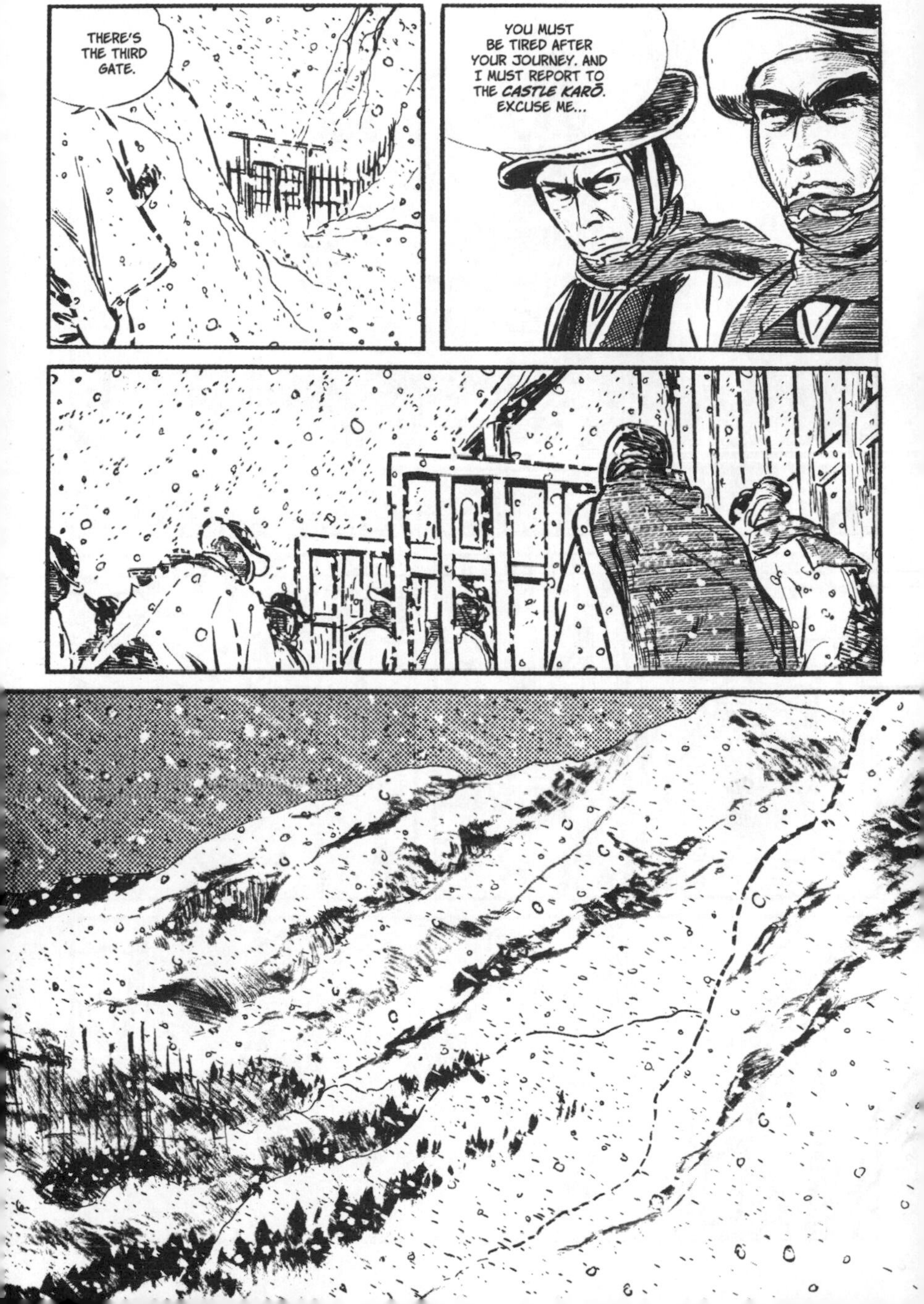
YOU MUST BE TIRED AFTER YOUR JOURNEY. AND I MUST REPORT TO THE *CASTLE KARŌ*. EXCUSE ME...
THERE'S THE THIRD GATE.

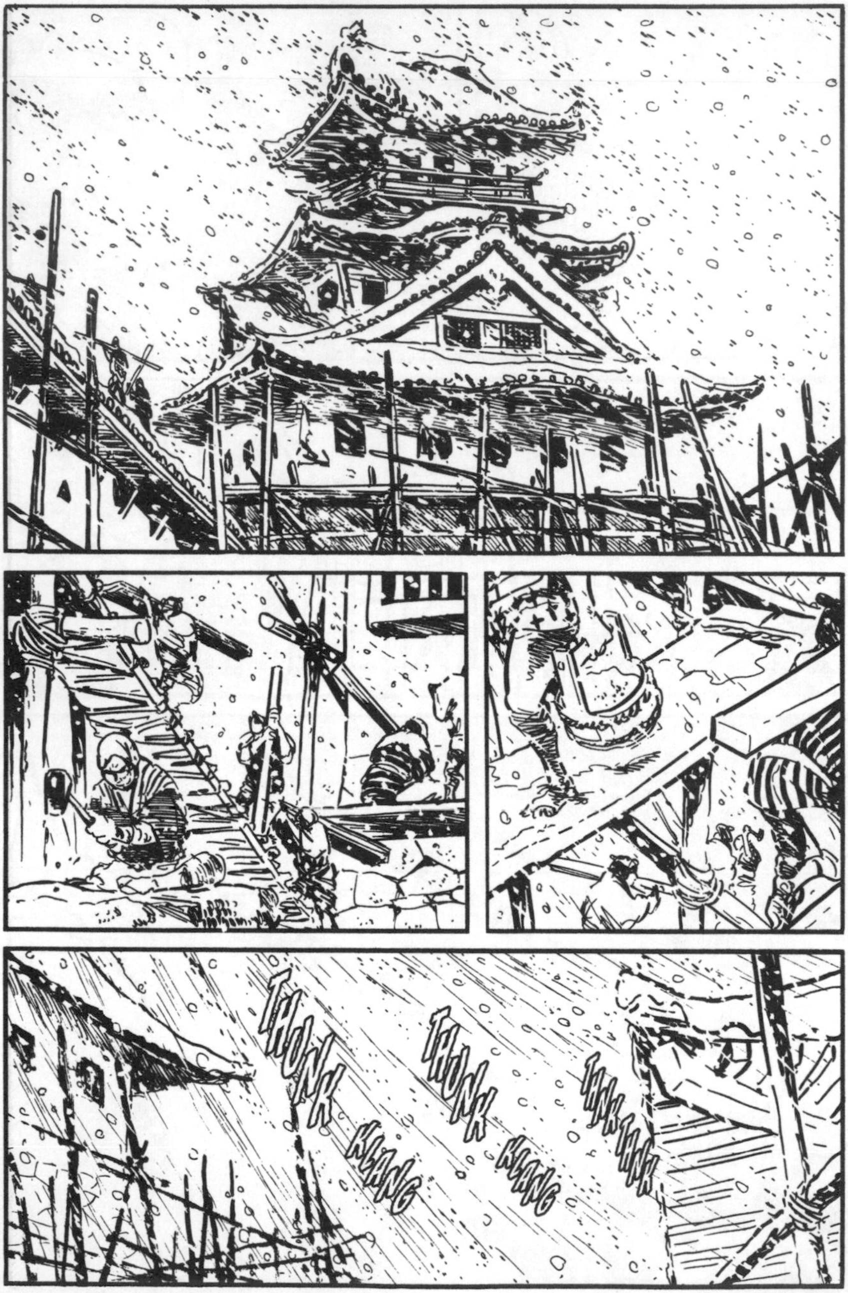
TINK TINK
THUNK
KLANG
THUNK
KLANG

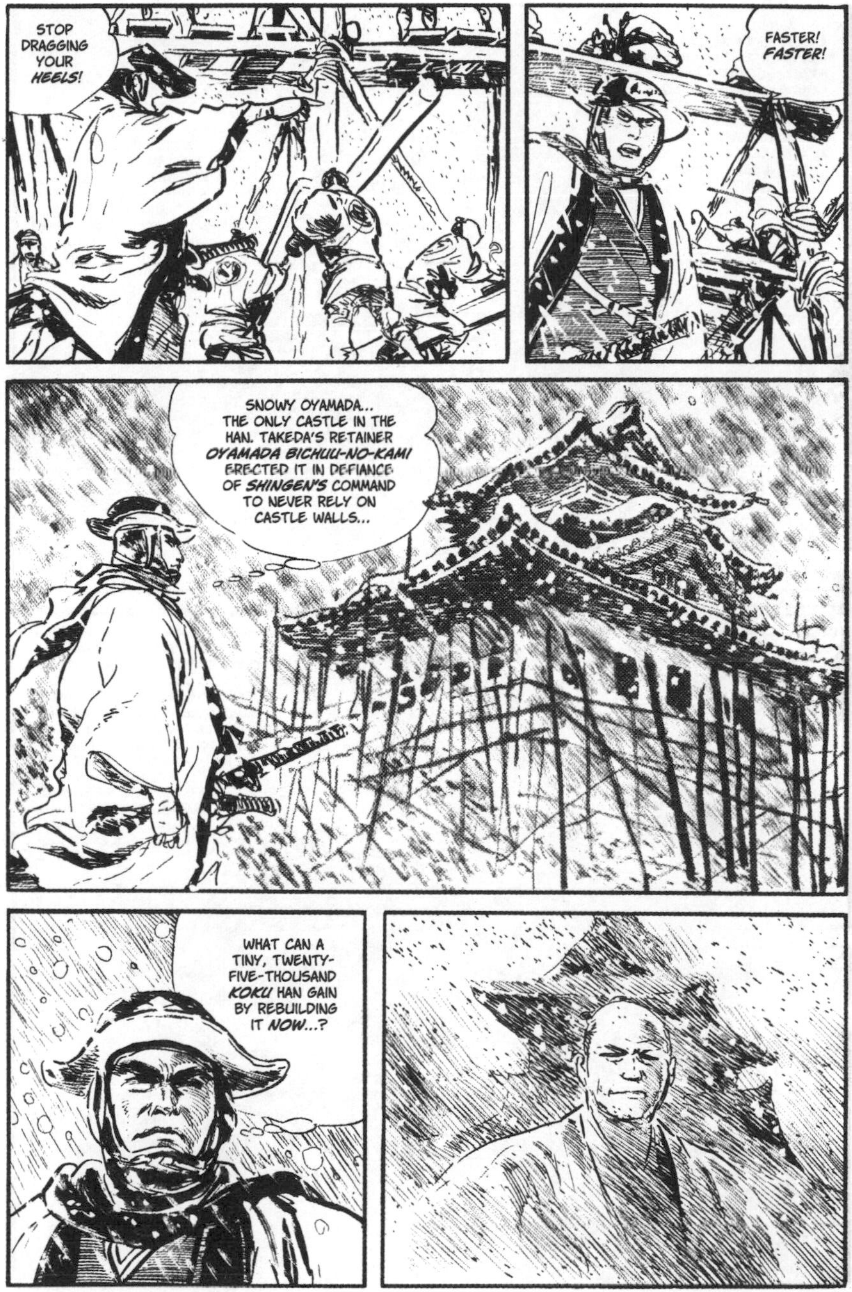
STOP DRAGGING YOUR HEELS!
FASTER! FASTER!
SNOWY OYAMADA... THE ONLY CASTLE IN THE HAN. TAKEDA'S RETAINER OYAMADA BICHUU-NO-KAMI ERECTED IT IN DEFIANCE OF SHINGEN'S COMMAND TO NEVER RELY ON CASTLE WALLS...
WHAT CAN A TINY, TWENTY-FIVE-THOUSAND KOKU HAN GAIN BY REBUILDING IT NOW...?

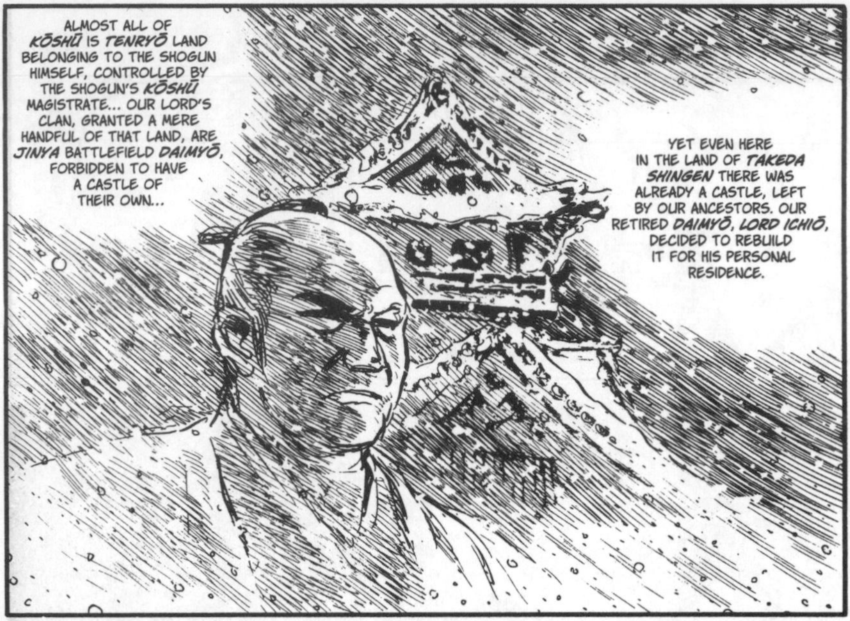
YET EVEN HERE IN THE LAND OF TAKEDA SHINGEN THERE WAS ALREADY A CASTLE, LEFT BY OUR ANCESTORS. OUR RETIRED DAIMYŌ, LORD ICHIŌ, DECIDED TO REBUILD IT FOR HIS PERSONAL RESIDENCE.
ALMOST ALL OF KŌSHŪ IS TENRYŌ LAND BELONGING TO THE SHOGUN HIMSELF, CONTROLLED BY THE SHOGUN'S KŌSHŪ MAGISTRATE... OUR LORD'S CLAN, GRANTED A MERE HANDFUL OF THAT LAND, ARE JINYA BATTLEFIELD DAIMYŌ, FORBIDDEN TO HAVE A CASTLE OF THEIR OWN...
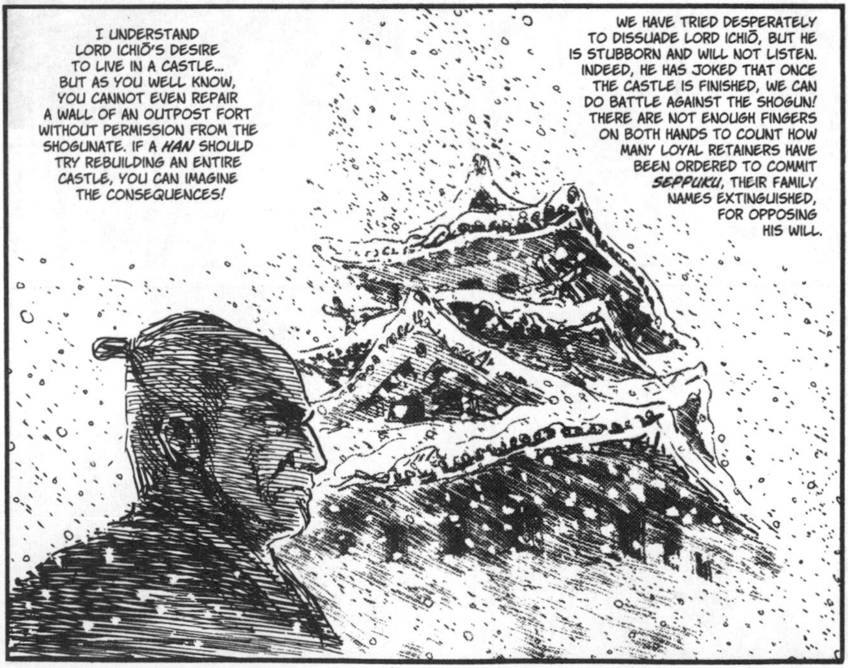
WE HAVE TRIED DESPERATELY TO DISSUADE LORD ICHIŌ, BUT HE IS STUBBORN AND WILL NOT LISTEN. INDEED, HE HAS JOKED THAT ONCE THE CASTLE IS FINISHED, WE CAN DO BATTLE AGAINST THE SHOGUN! THERE ARE NOT ENOUGH FINGERS ON BOTH HANDS TO COUNT HOW MANY LOYAL RETAINERS HAVE BEEN ORDERED TO COMMIT SEPPUKU, THEIR FAMILY NAMES EXTINGUISHED, FOR OPPOSING HIS WILL.
I UNDERSTAND LORD ICHIŌ'S DESIRE TO LIVE IN A CASTLE... BUT AS YOU WELL KNOW, YOU CANNOT EVEN REPAIR A WALL OF AN OUTPOST FORT WITHOUT PERMISSION FROM THE SHOGUNATE. IF A HAN SHOULD TRY REBUILDING AN ENTIRE CASTLE, YOU CAN IMAGINE THE CONSEQUENCES!

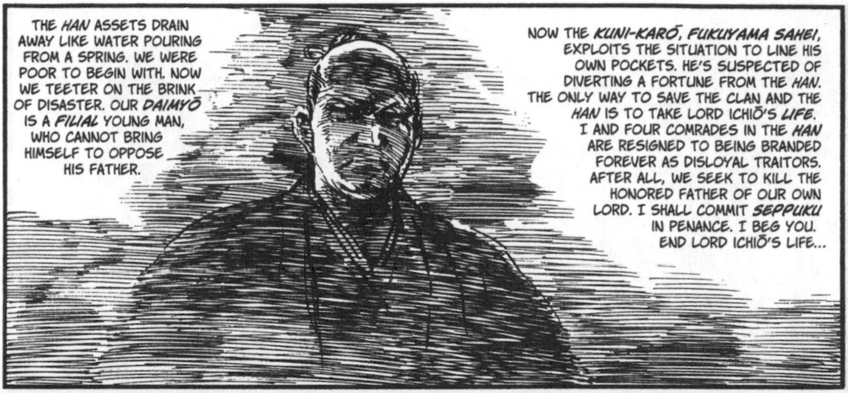
NOW THE KUNI-KARŌ, FUKUYAMA SAHEI, EXPLOITS THE SITUATION TO LINE HIS OWN POCKETS. HE'S SUSPECTED OF DIVERTING A FORTUNE FROM THE HAN. THE ONLY WAY TO SAVE THE CLAN AND THE HAN IS TO TAKE LORD ICHIŌ'S LIFE. I AND FOUR COMRADES IN THE HAN ARE RESIGNED TO BEING BRANDED FOREVER AS DISLOYAL TRAITORS. AFTER ALL, WE SEEK TO KILL THE HONORED FATHER OF OUR OWN LORD. I SHALL COMMIT SEPPUKU IN PENANCE. I BEG YOU. END LORD ICHIŌ'S LIFE...
THE HAN ASSETS DRAIN AWAY LIKE WATER POURING FROM A SPRING. WE WERE POOR TO BEGIN WITH. NOW WE TEETER ON THE BRINK OF DISASTER. OUR DAIMYŌ IS A FILIAL YOUNG MAN, WHO CANNOT BRING HIMSELF TO OPPOSE HIS FATHER.
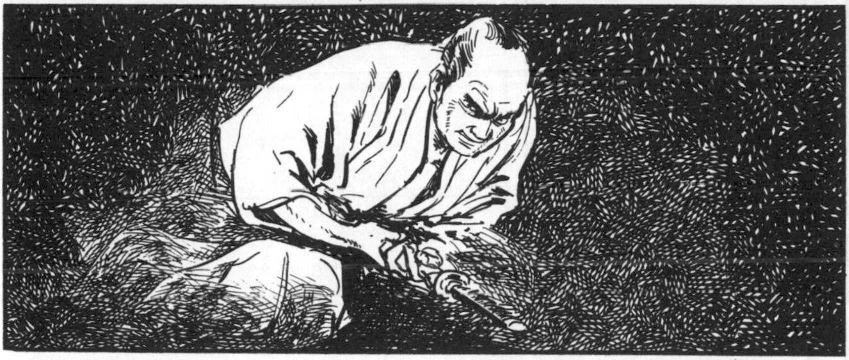
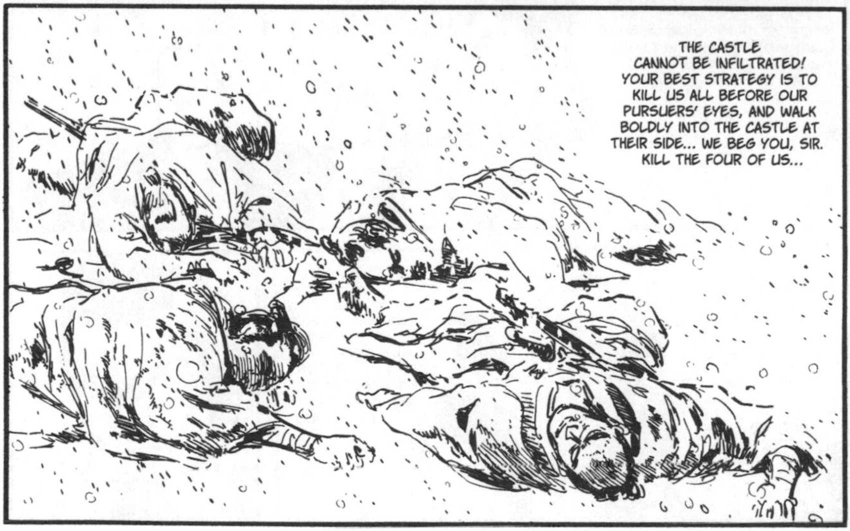
THE CASTLE CANNOT BE INFILTRATED! YOUR BEST STRATEGY IS TO KILL US ALL BEFORE OUR PURSUERS' EYES, AND WALK BOLDLY INTO THE CASTLE AT THEIR SIDE... WE BEG YOU, SIR. KILL THE FOUR OF US...

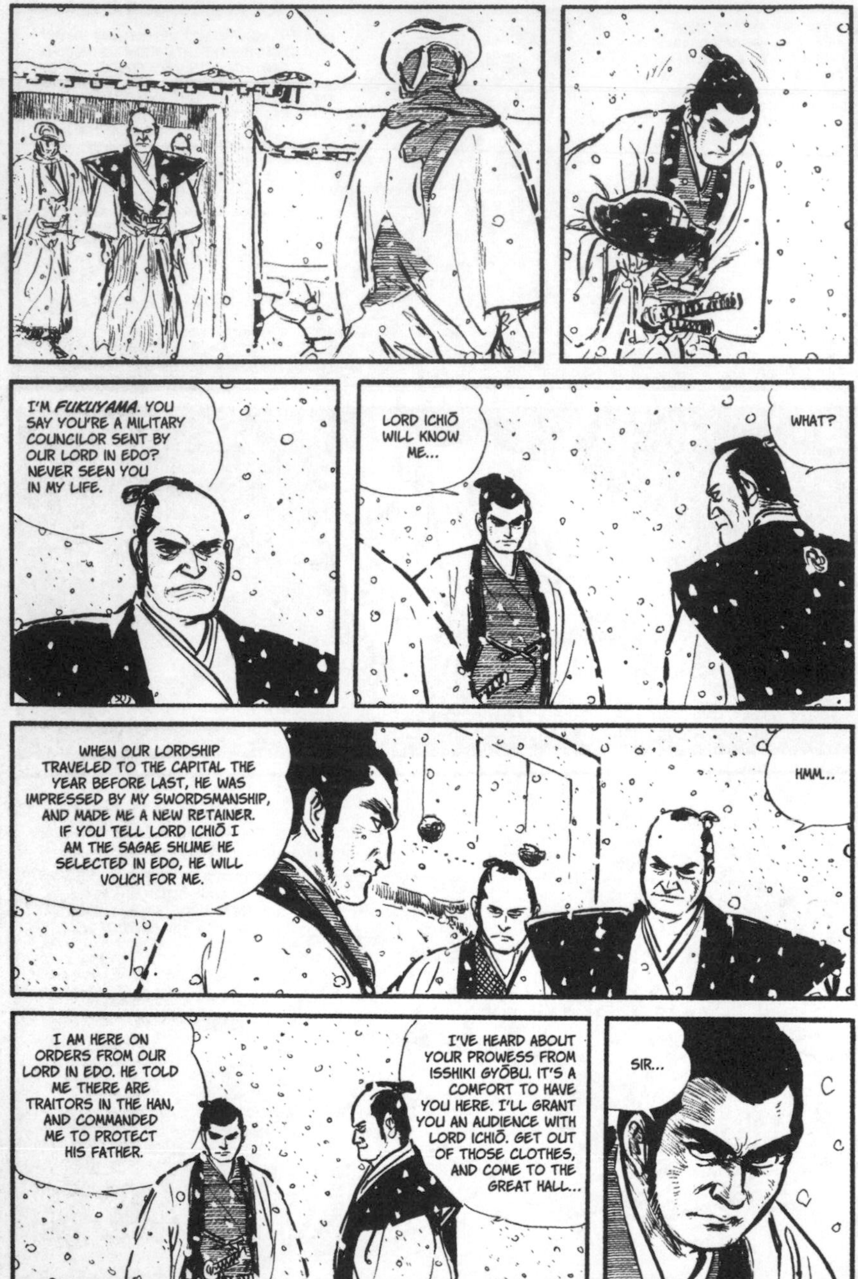
I'M *FUKUYAMA*. YOU SAY YOU'RE A MILITARY COUNCILOR SENT BY OUR LORD IN EDO? NEVER SEEN YOU IN MY LIFE.
LORD ICHIŌ WILL KNOW ME...
WHAT?
WHEN OUR LORDSHIP TRAVELED TO THE CAPITAL THE YEAR BEFORE LAST, HE WAS IMPRESSED BY MY SWORDSMANSHIP, AND MADE ME A NEW RETAINER. IF YOU TELL LORD ICHIŌ I AM THE SAGAE SHUME HE SELECTED IN EDO, HE WILL VOUCH FOR ME.
HMM...
I AM HERE ON ORDERS FROM OUR LORD IN EDO. HE TOLD ME THERE ARE TRAITORS IN THE HAN, AND COMMANDED ME TO PROTECT HIS FATHER.
I'VE HEARD ABOUT YOUR PROWESS FROM ISSHIKI GYŌBU. IT'S A COMFORT TO HAVE YOU HERE. I'LL GRANT YOU AN AUDIENCE WITH LORD ICHIŌ. GET OUT OF THOSE CLOTHES, AND COME TO THE GREAT HALL...
SIR...

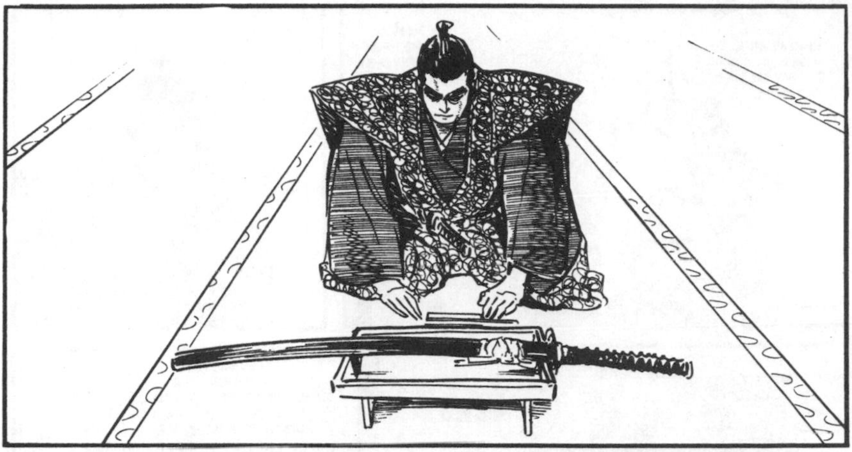
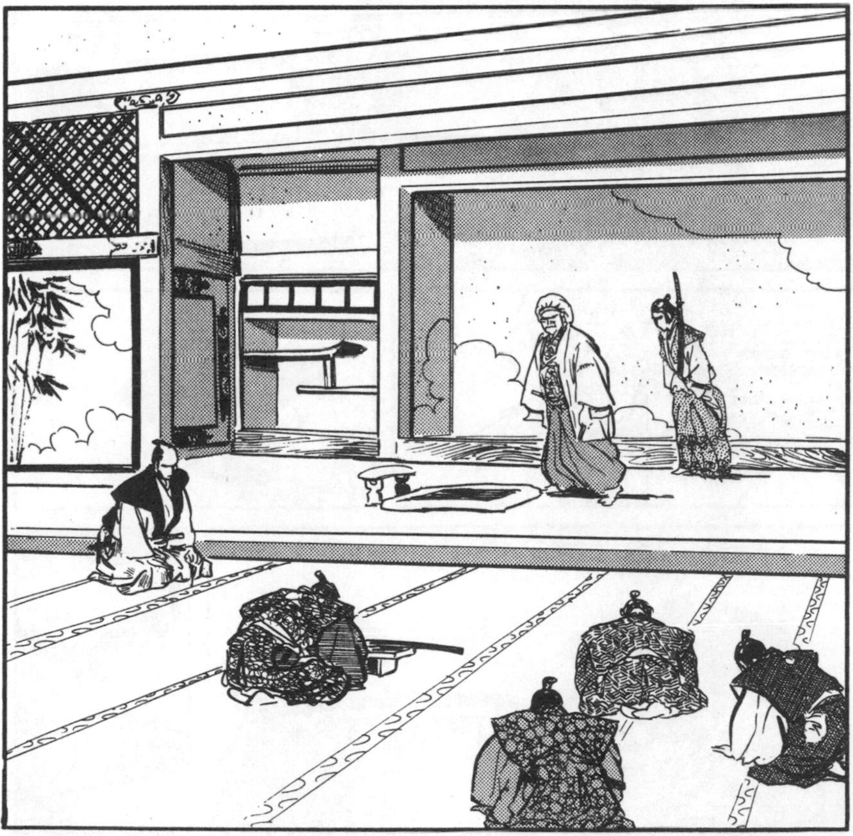

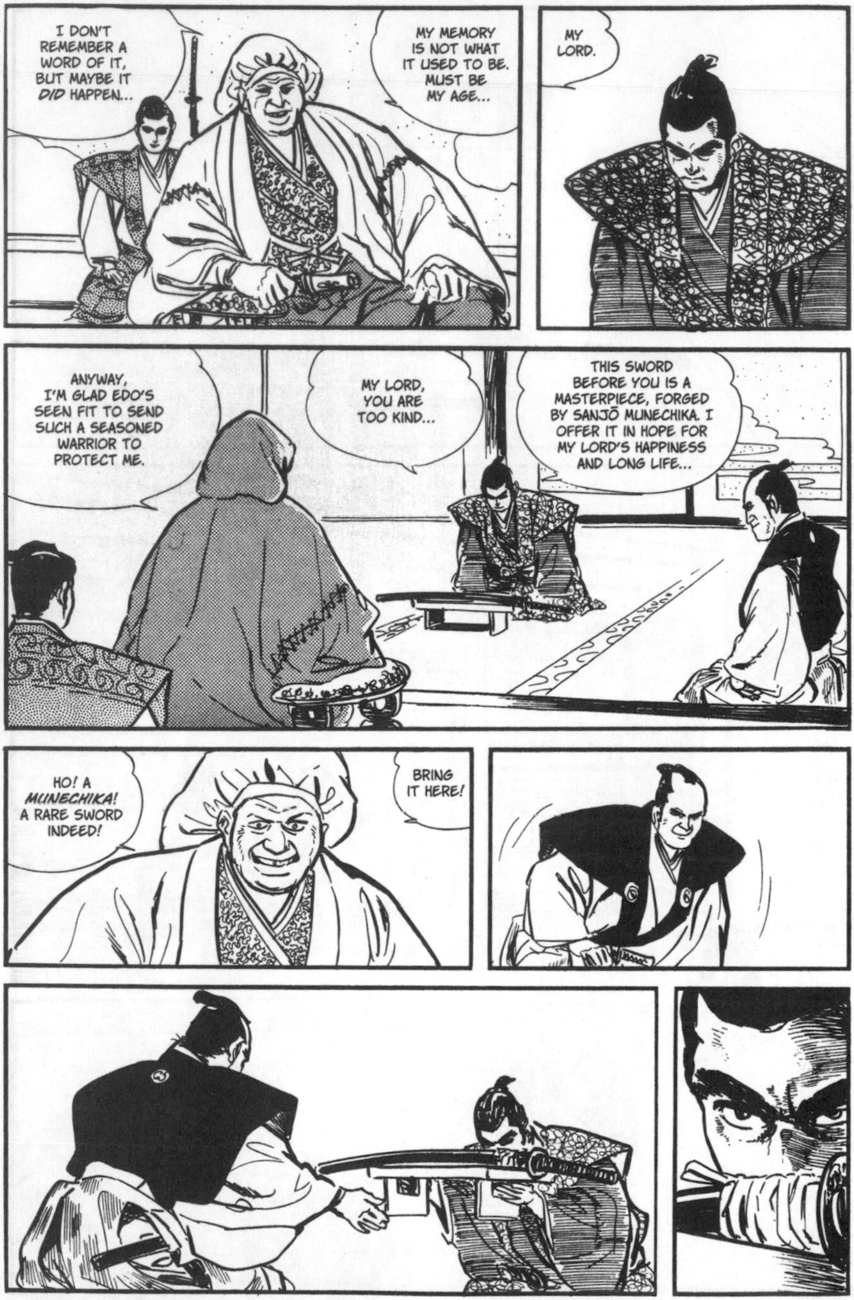
I DON'T REMEMBER A WORD OF IT, BUT MAYBE IT *DID* HAPPEN...
MY MEMORY IS NOT WHAT IT USED TO BE. MUST BE MY AGE...
MY LORD.
ANYWAY, I'M GLAD EDO'S SEEN FIT TO SEND SUCH A SEASONED WARRIOR TO PROTECT ME.
MY LORD, YOU ARE TOO KIND...
THIS SWORD BEFORE YOU IS A MASTERPIECE, FORGED BY SANJŌ MUNECHIKA. I OFFER IT IN HOPE FOR MY LORD'S HAPPINESS AND LONG LIFE...
HO! A ***MUNECHIKA***! A RARE SWORD INDEED!
BRING IT HERE!

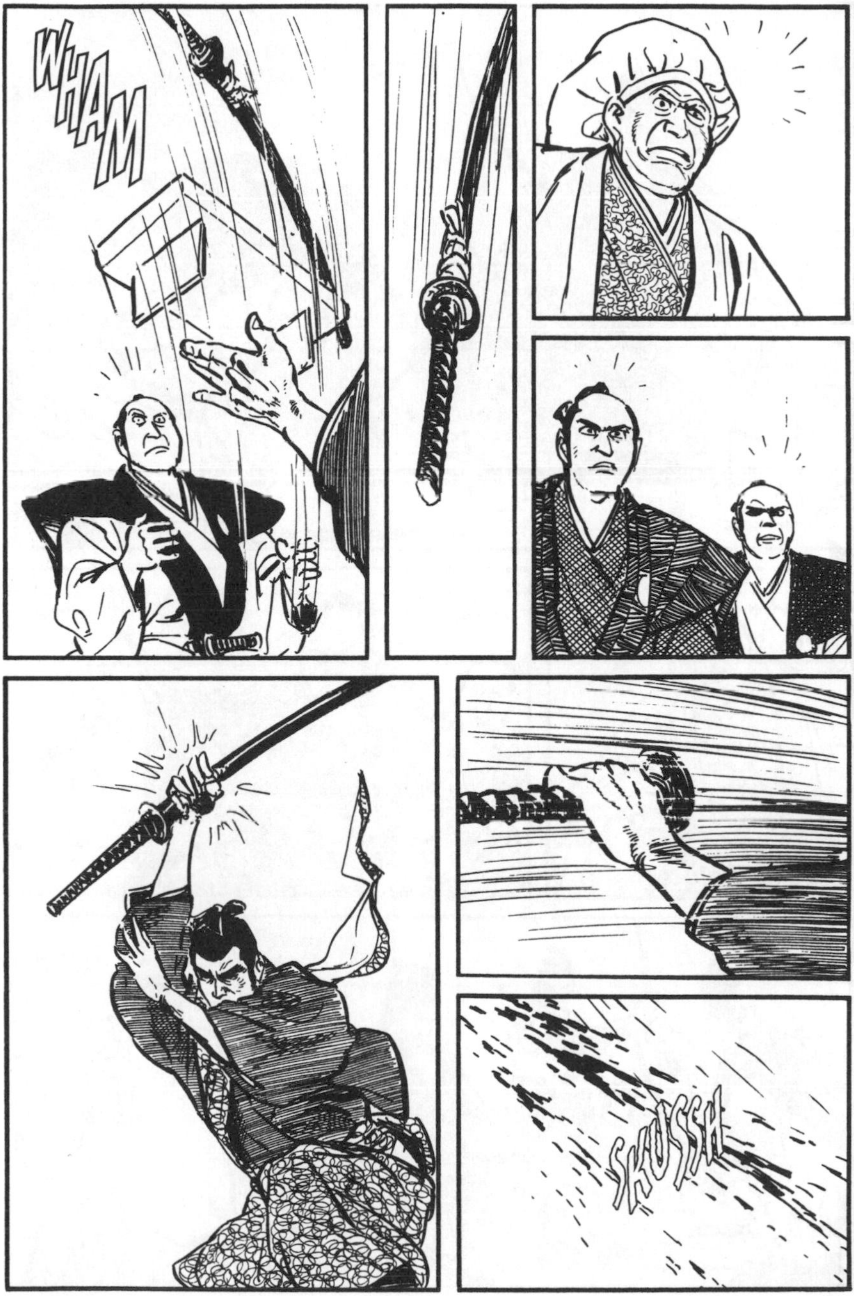
WHAM
SKUSSH

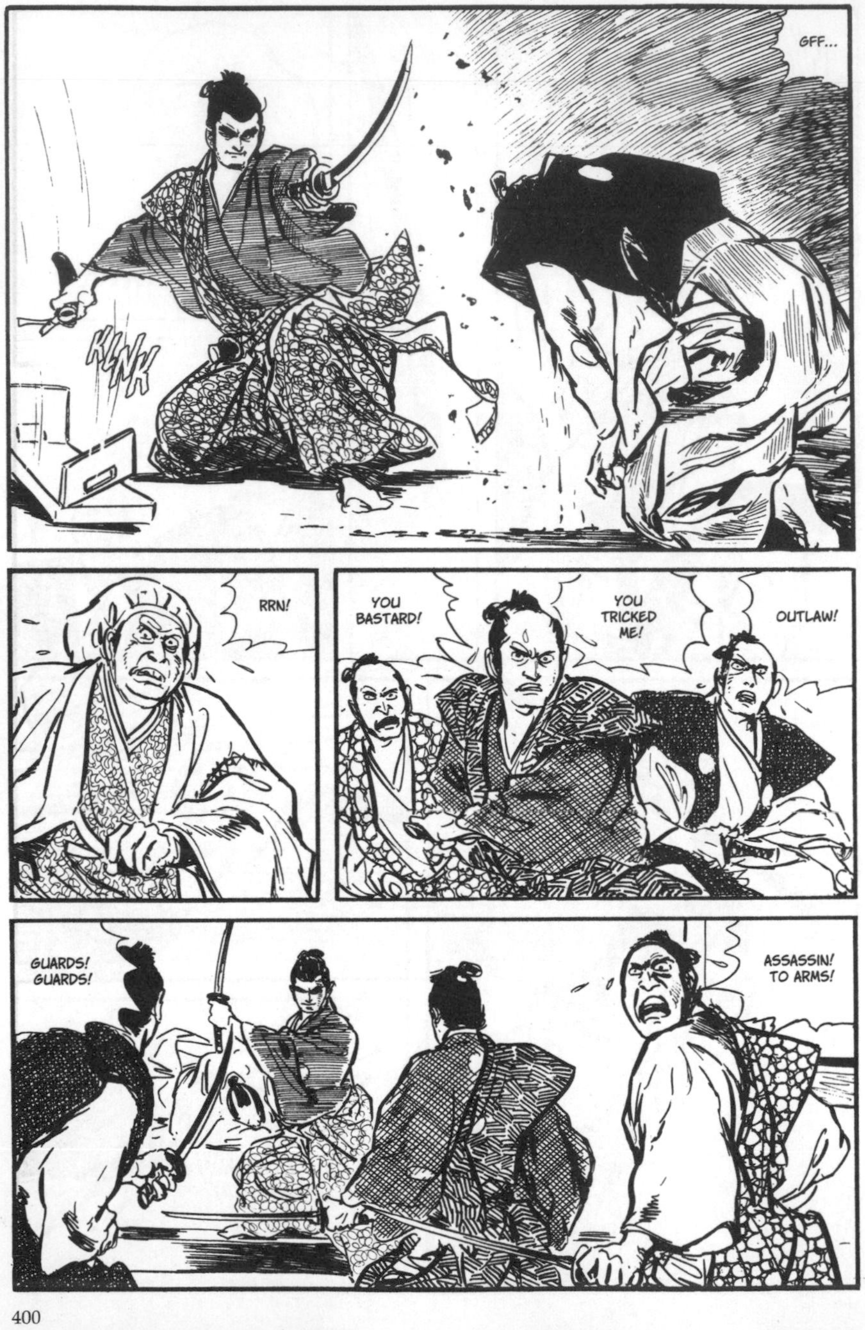
GFF...
KLINK
OUTLAW!
YOU TRICKED ME!
YOU BASTARD!
RRN!
ASSASSIN! TO ARMS!
GUARDS! GUARDS!

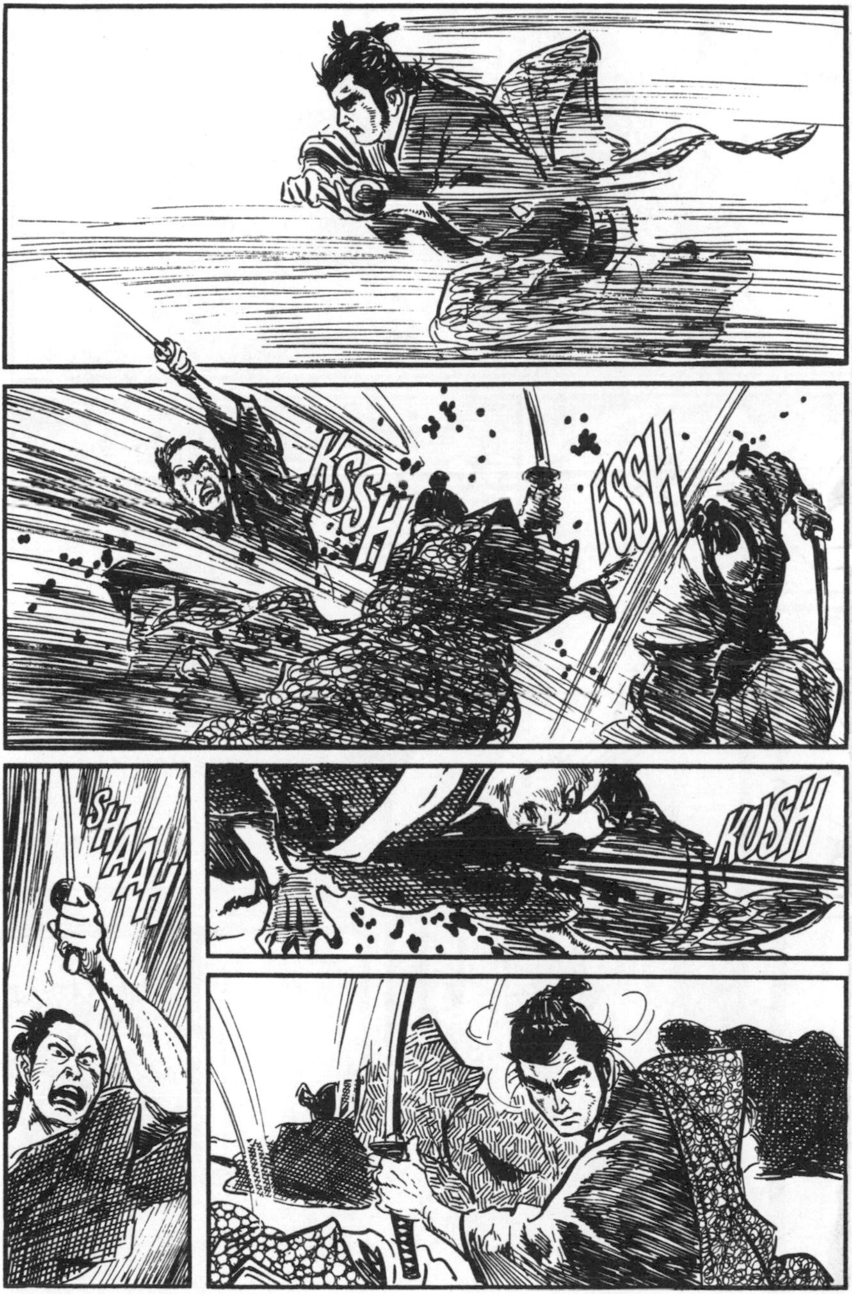
FSSH
KSSH
KUSH
SHAAH

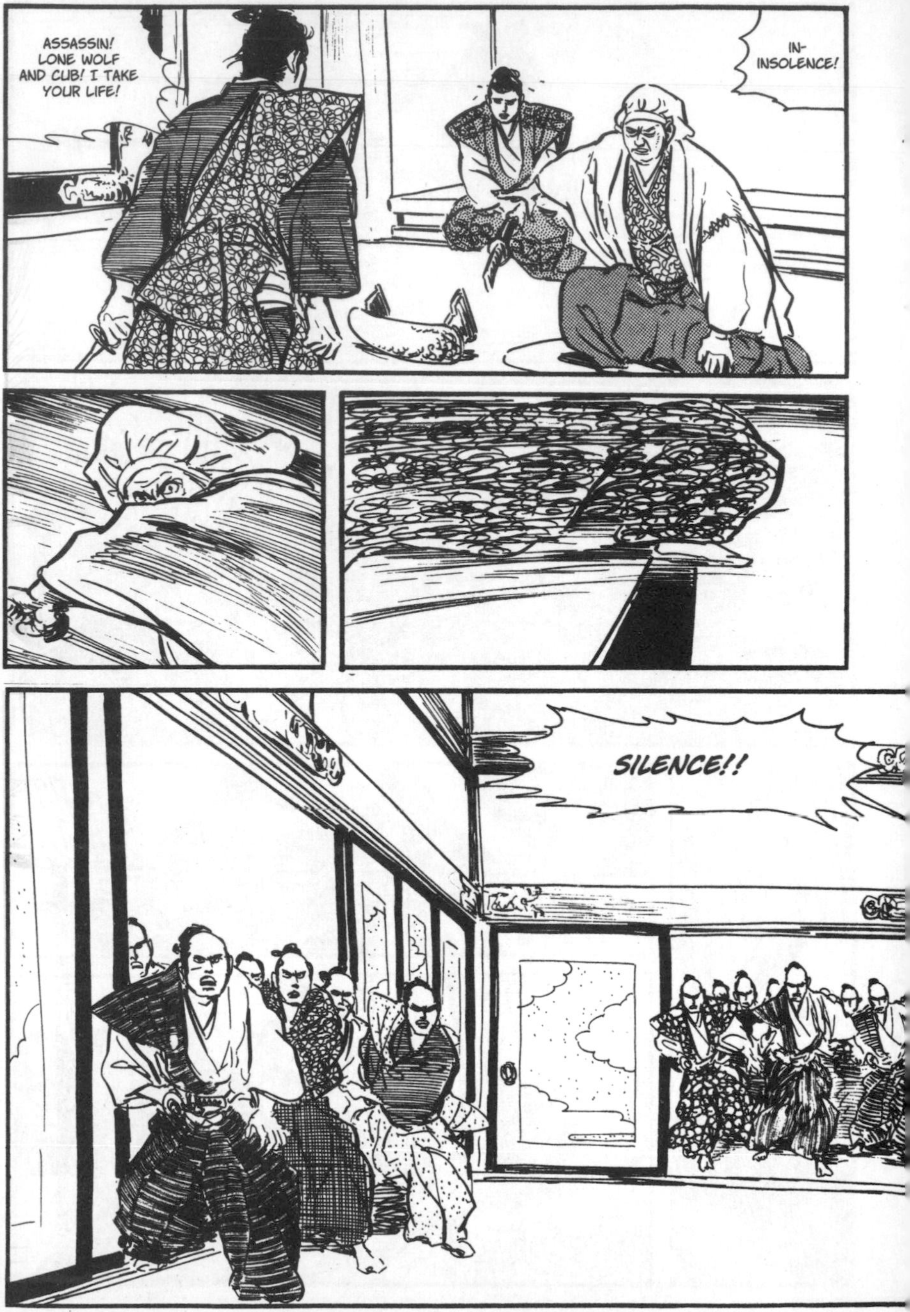
IN-
INSOLENCE!
ASSASSIN! LONE WOLF AND CUB! I TAKE YOUR LIFE!
SILENCE!!

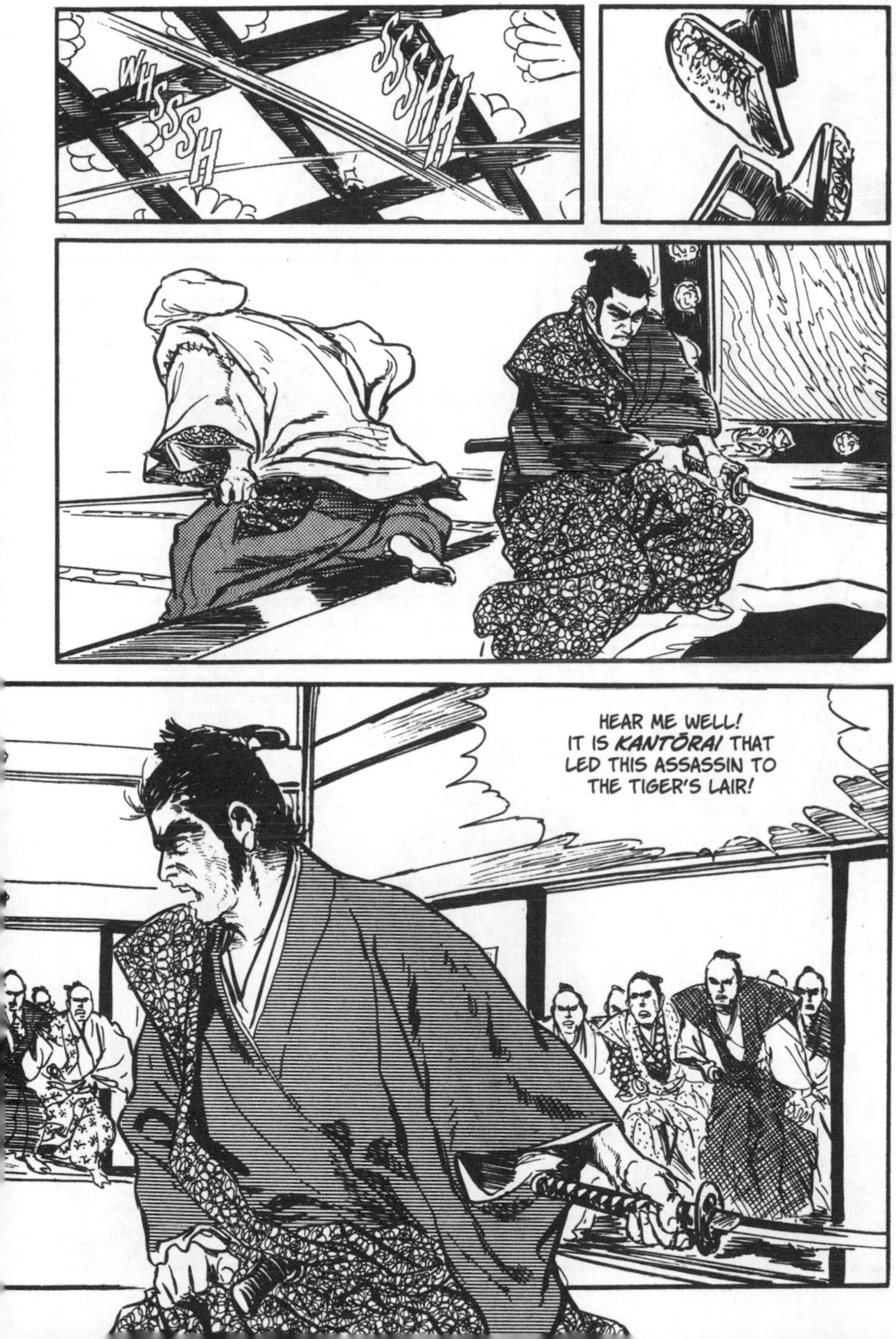
SSHH
WHSSH
HEAR ME WELL!
IT IS *KANTŌRAI* THAT
LED THIS ASSASSIN TO
THE TIGER'S LAIR!

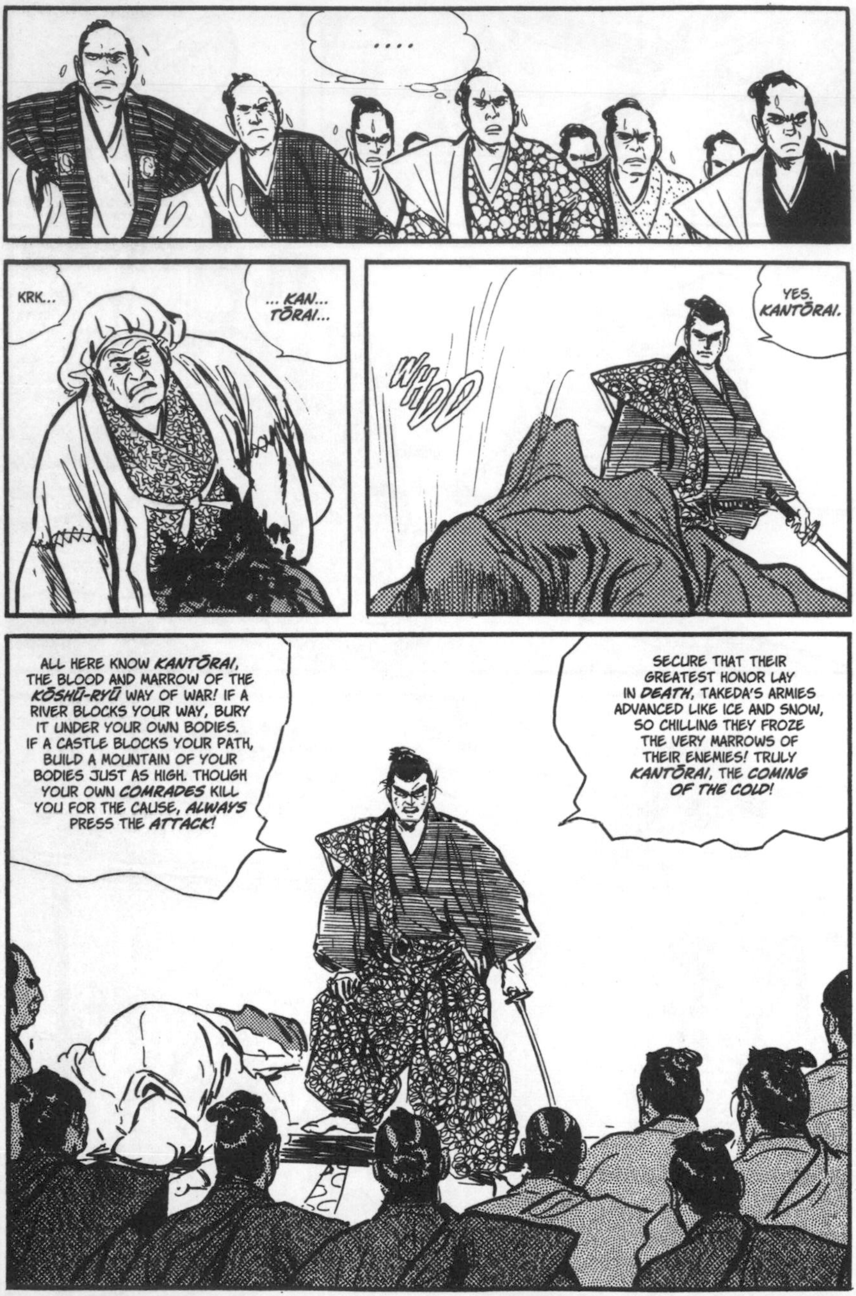
....
KRK...
...KAN... TŌRAI...
WHOO
YES. KANTŌRAI.
ALL HERE KNOW KANTŌRAI, THE BLOOD AND MARROW OF THE KŌSHŪ-RYŪ WAY OF WAR! IF A RIVER BLOCKS YOUR WAY, BURY IT UNDER YOUR OWN BODIES. IF A CASTLE BLOCKS YOUR PATH, BUILD A MOUNTAIN OF YOUR BODIES JUST AS HIGH. THOUGH YOUR OWN COMRADES KILL YOU FOR THE CAUSE, ALWAYS PRESS THE ATTACK!
SECURE THAT THEIR GREATEST HONOR LAY IN DEATH, TAKEDA'S ARMIES ADVANCED LIKE ICE AND SNOW, SO CHILLING THEY FROZE THE VERY MARROWS OF THEIR ENEMIES! TRULY KANTŌRAI, THE COMING OF THE COLD!

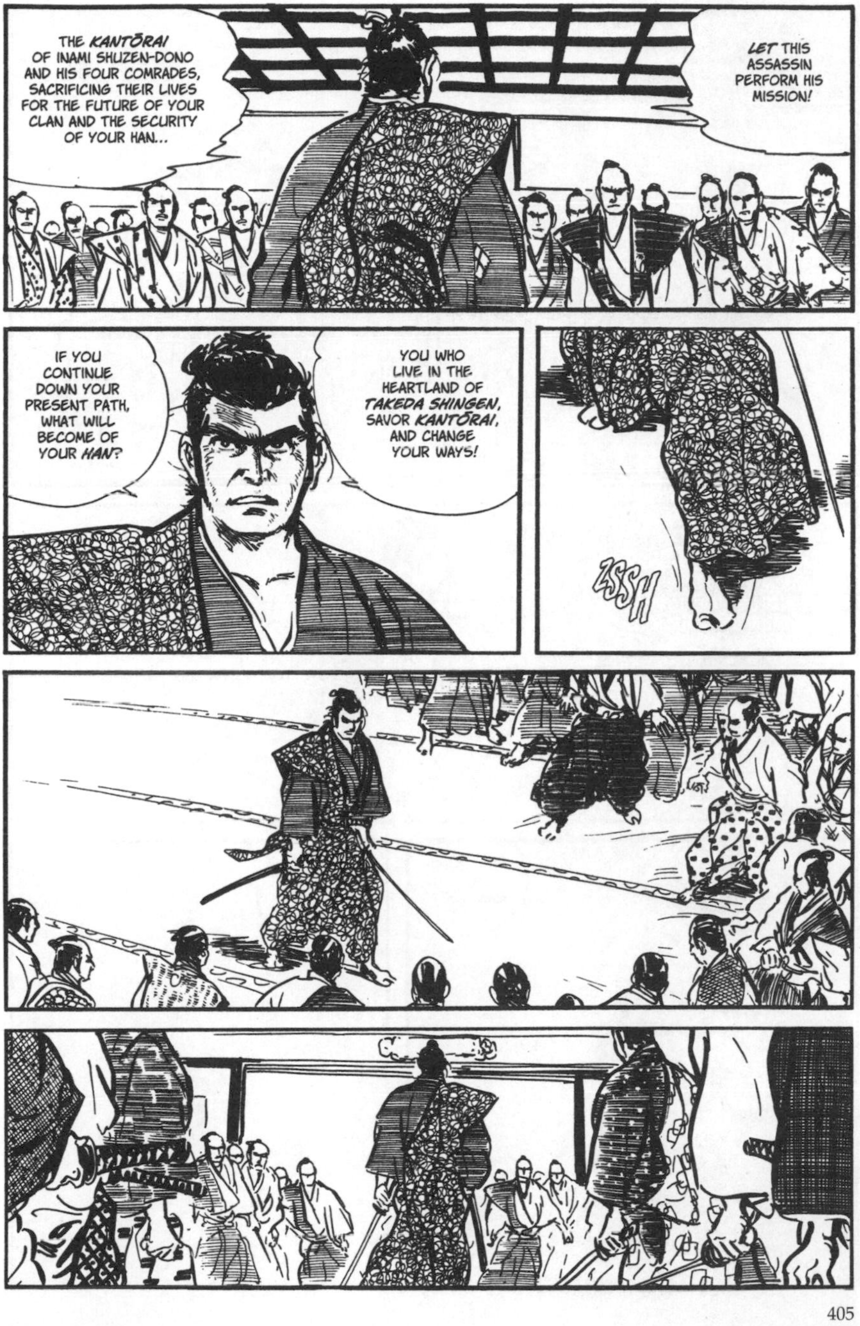
THE *KANTŌRAI* OF INAMI SHUZEN-DONO AND HIS FOUR COMRADES, SACRIFICING THEIR LIVES FOR THE FUTURE OF YOUR CLAN AND THE SECURITY OF YOUR HAN...
LET THIS ASSASSIN PERFORM HIS MISSION!
IF YOU CONTINUE DOWN YOUR PRESENT PATH, WHAT WILL BECOME OF YOUR *HAN*?
YOU WHO LIVE IN THE HEARTLAND OF *TAKEDA SHINGEN*, SAVOR *KANTŌRAI*, AND CHANGE YOUR WAYS!
ZSSH

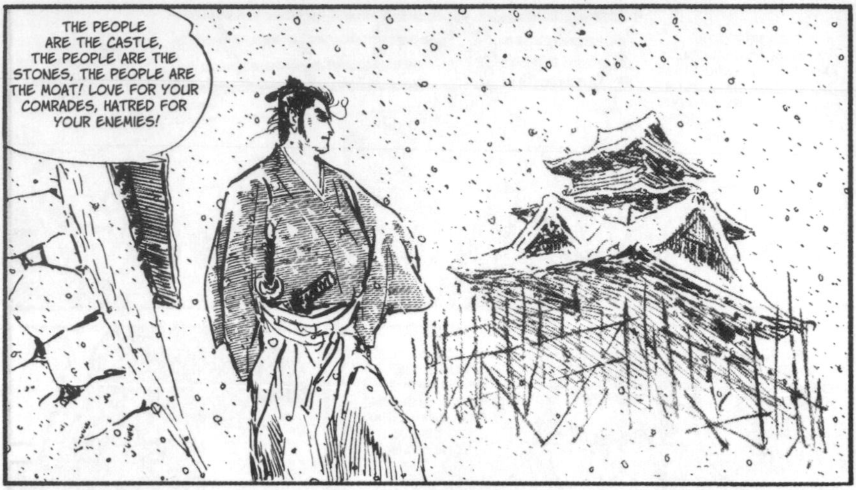
THE PEOPLE ARE THE CASTLE, THE PEOPLE ARE THE STONES, THE PEOPLE ARE THE MOAT! LOVE FOR YOUR COMRADES, HATRED FOR YOUR ENEMIES!

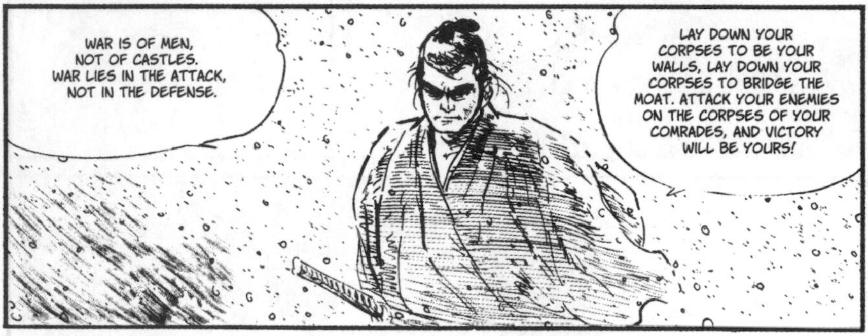
WAR IS OF MEN, NOT OF CASTLES. WAR LIES IN THE ATTACK, NOT IN THE DEFENSE.
LAY DOWN YOUR CORPSES TO BE YOUR WALLS, LAY DOWN YOUR CORPSES TO BRIDGE THE MOAT. ATTACK YOUR ENEMIES ON THE CORPSES OF YOUR COMRADES, AND VICTORY WILL BE YOURS!

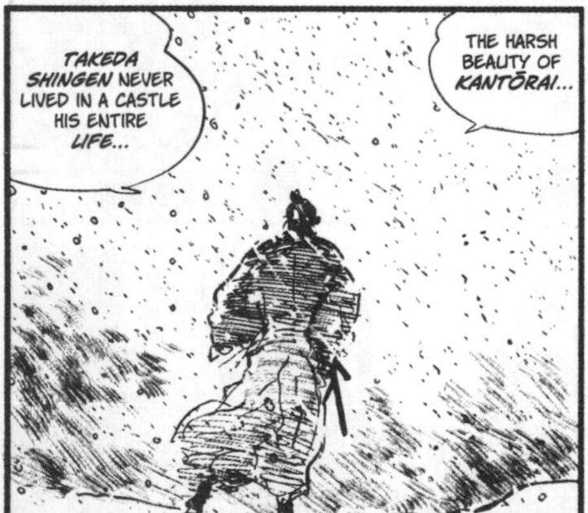
TAKEDA SHINGEN NEVER LIVED IN A CASTLE HIS ENTIRE *LIFE*...
THE HARSH BEAUTY OF *KANTŌRAI*...

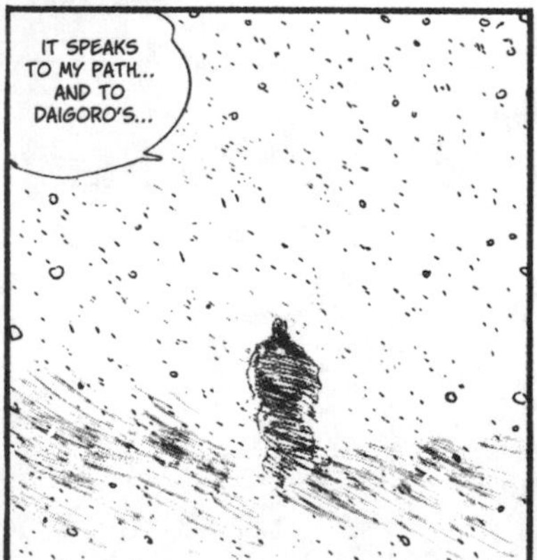
IT SPEAKS TO MY PATH... AND TO DAIGORO'S...

PERHAPS ŌGAMI'S PRAYERS TO *MEIFUMADŌ* HAD BEEN HEARD... FOR FIVE DAYS AND NIGHTS, IT SNOWED WITHOUT PAUSE.

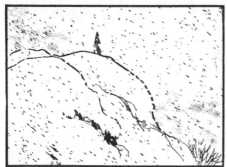

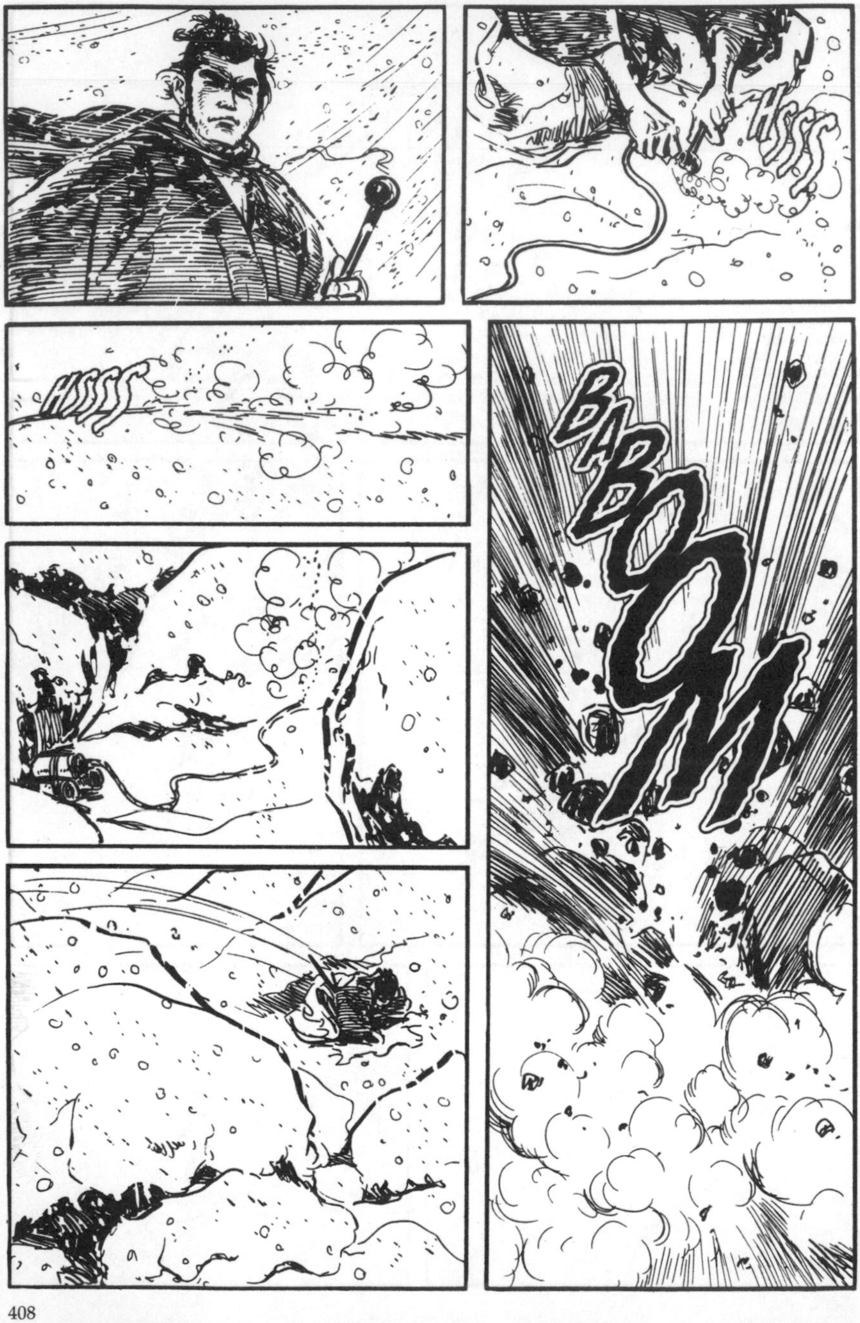
HSSS
HSSS
BABOOM

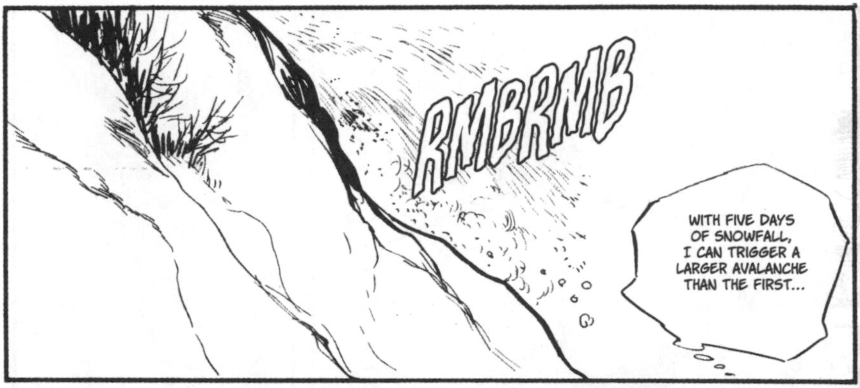
RMBRMB
WITH FIVE DAYS OF SNOWFALL, I CAN TRIGGER A LARGER AVALANCHE THAN THE FIRST...

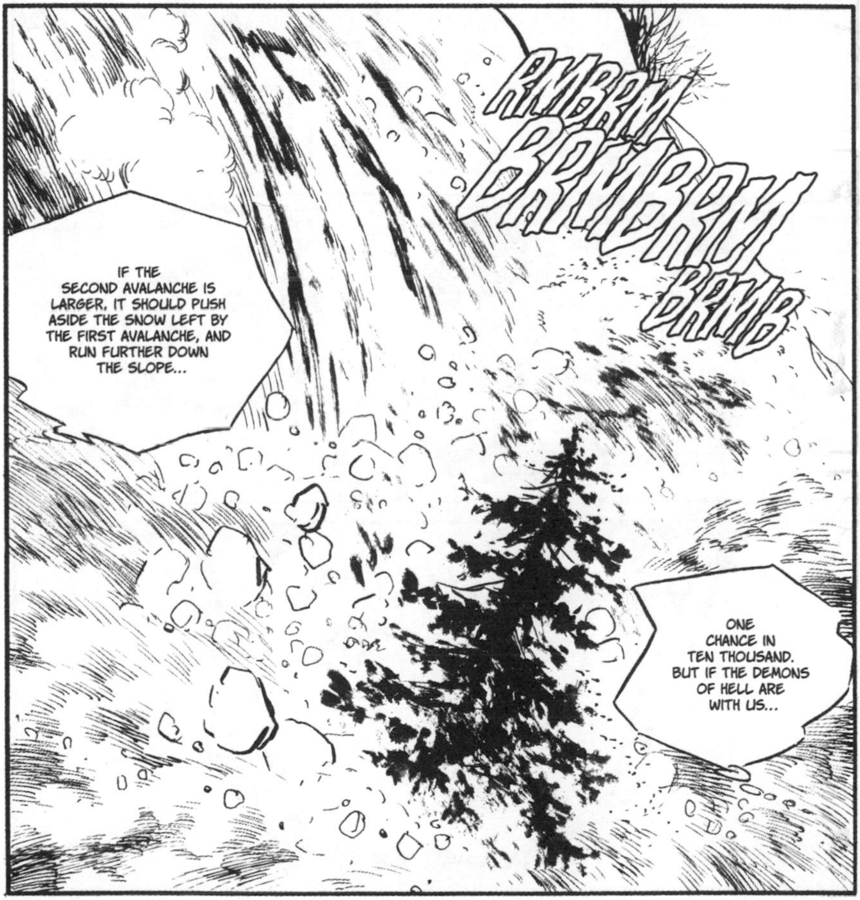
RMBRM
BRMBRM
BRMB
IF THE SECOND AVALANCHE IS LARGER, IT SHOULD PUSH ASIDE THE SNOW LEFT BY THE FIRST AVALANCHE, AND RUN FURTHER DOWN THE SLOPE...
ONE CHANCE IN TEN THOUSAND. BUT IF THE DEMONS OF HELL ARE WITH US...

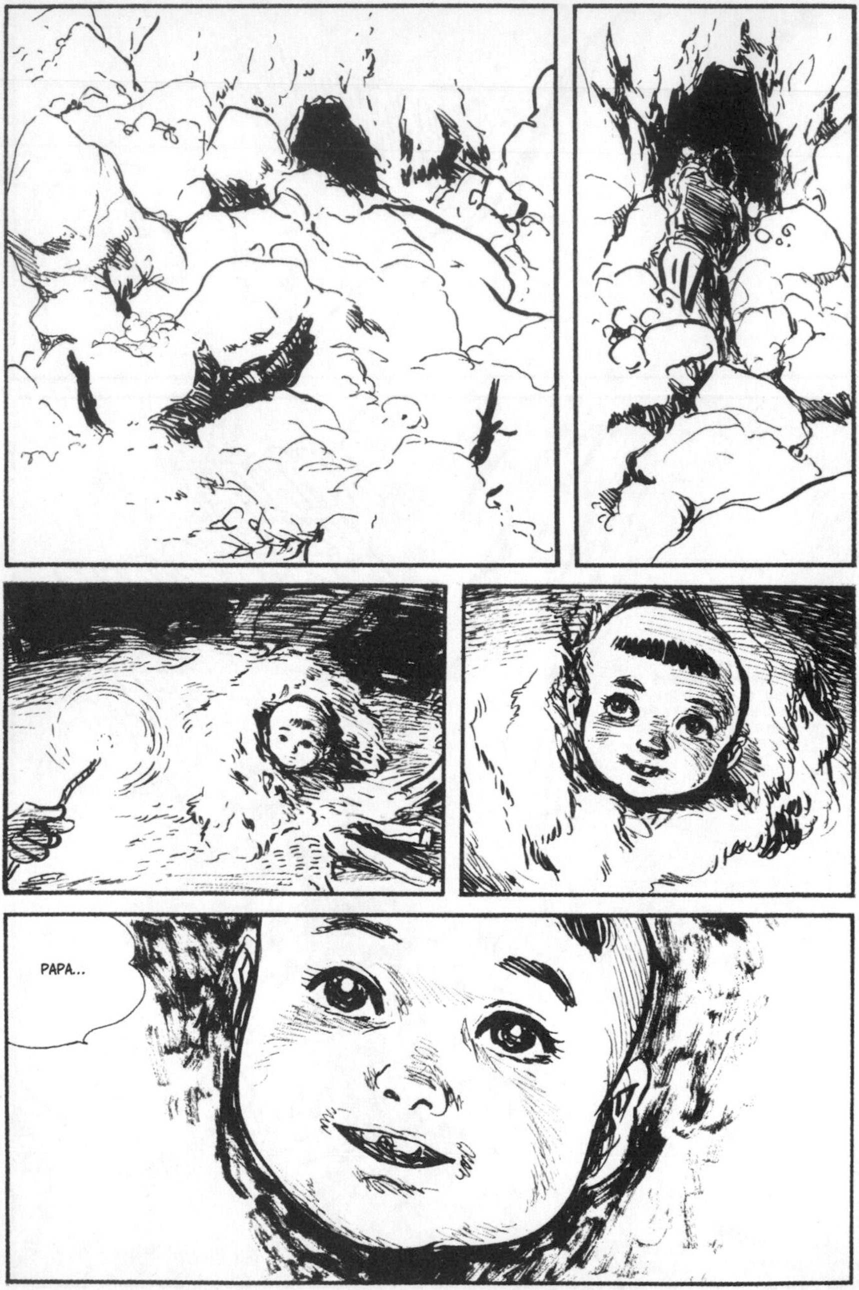
PAPA...

子連れ狼

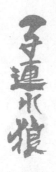

Tragic O-sue

12

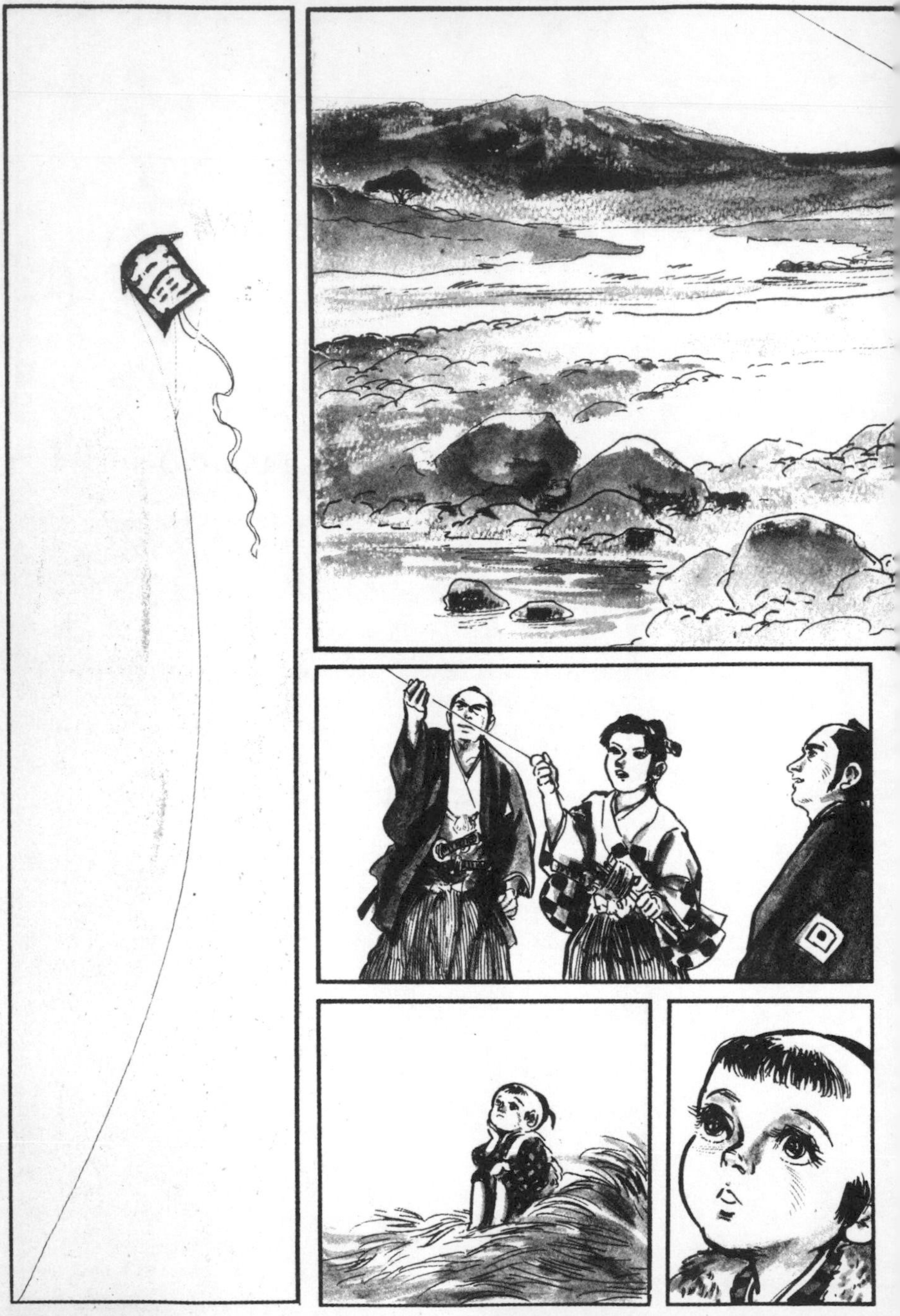

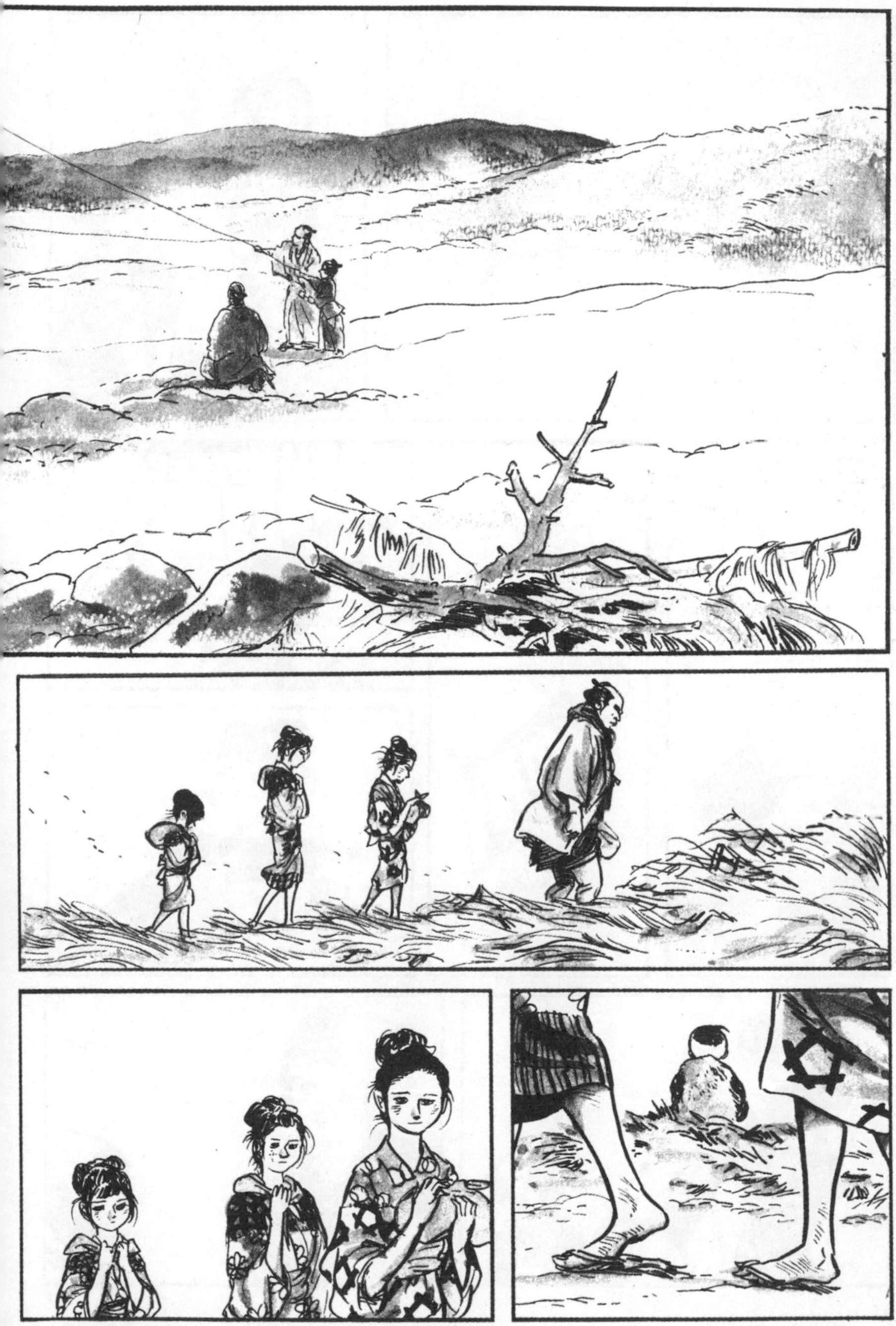

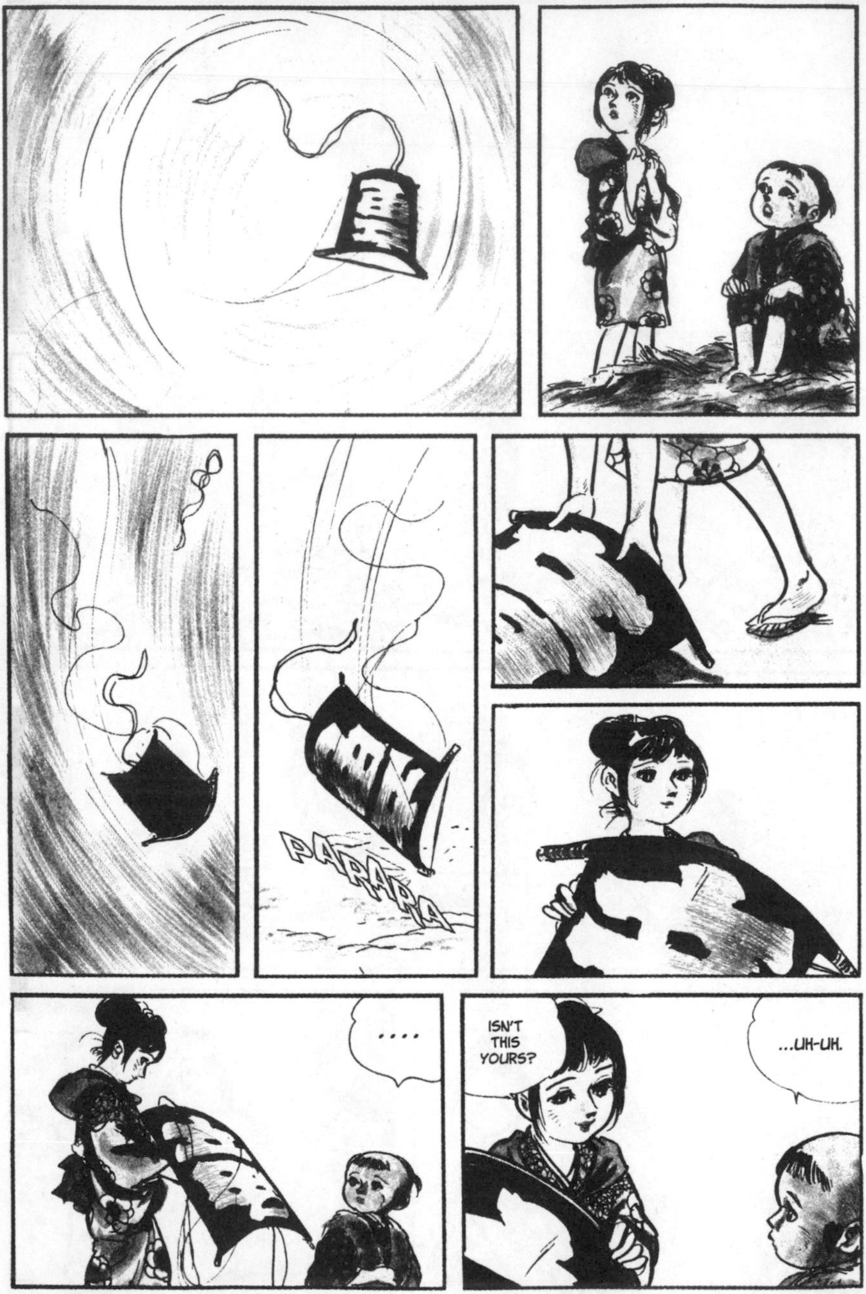
PAPARA
ISN'T THIS YOURS?
...UH-UH.
....

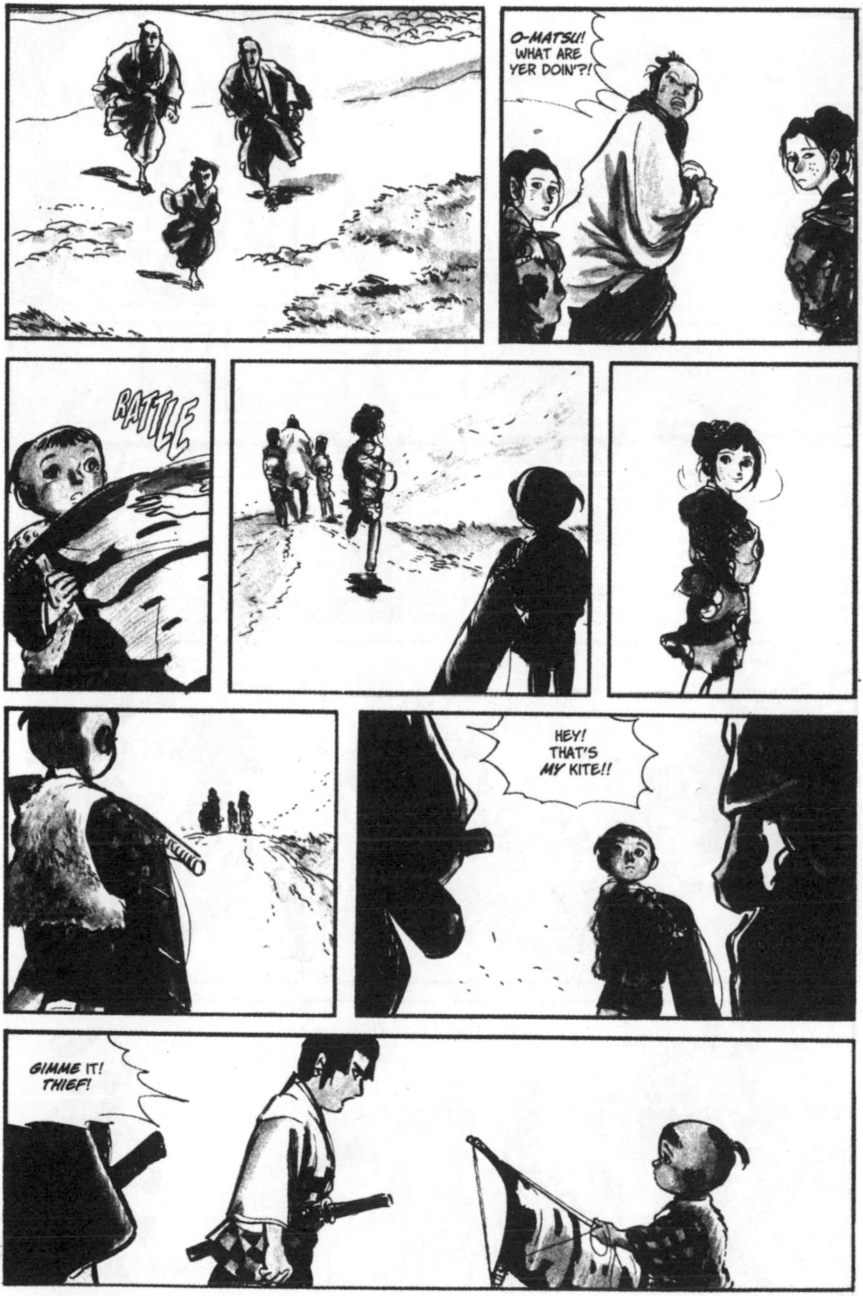
O-MATSU! WHAT ARE YER DOIN'?!
RATTLE
HEY! THAT'S MY KITE!!
GIMME IT! THIEF!

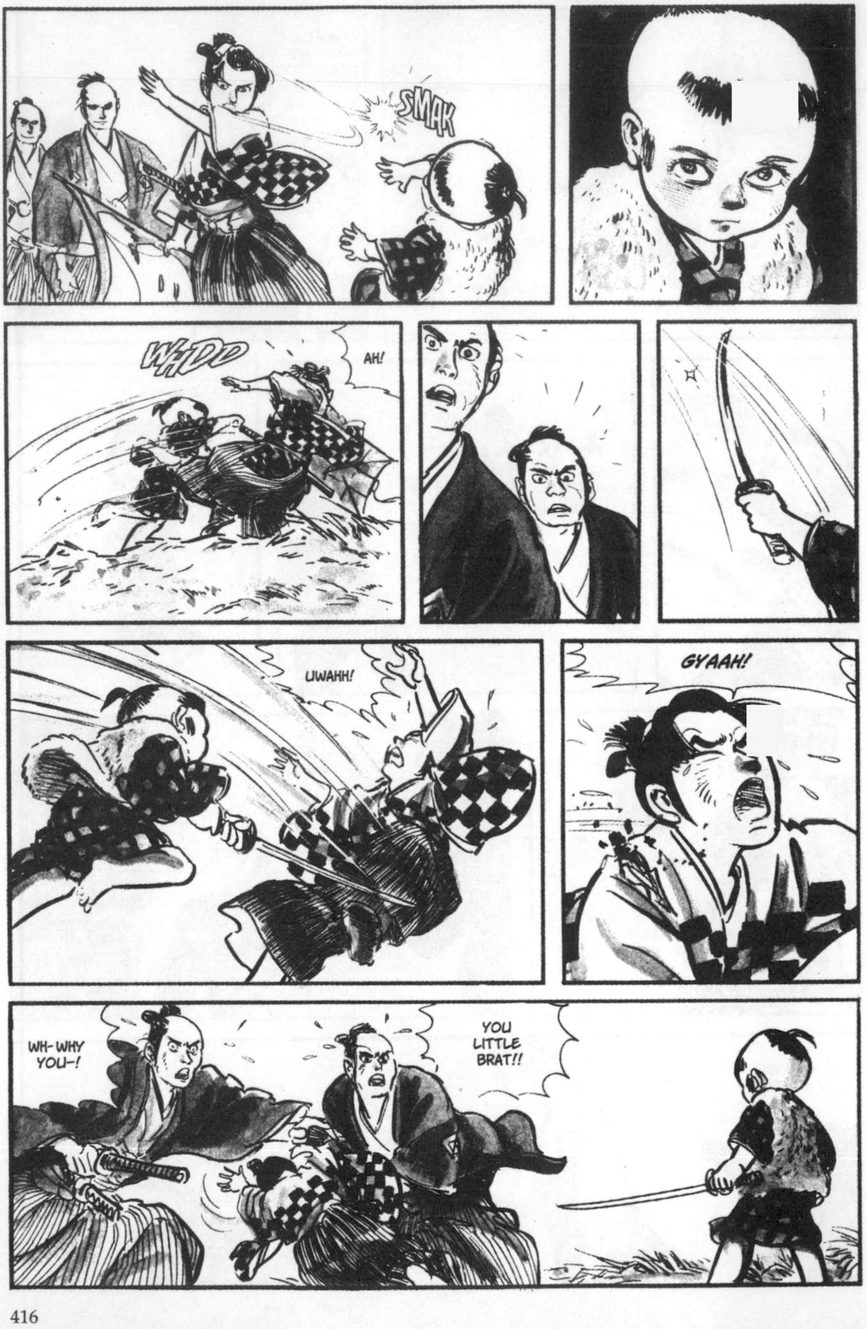
SMAK
WHDD
AH!
UWAHH!
GYAAH!
WH-WHY YOU-!
YOU LITTLE BRAT!!

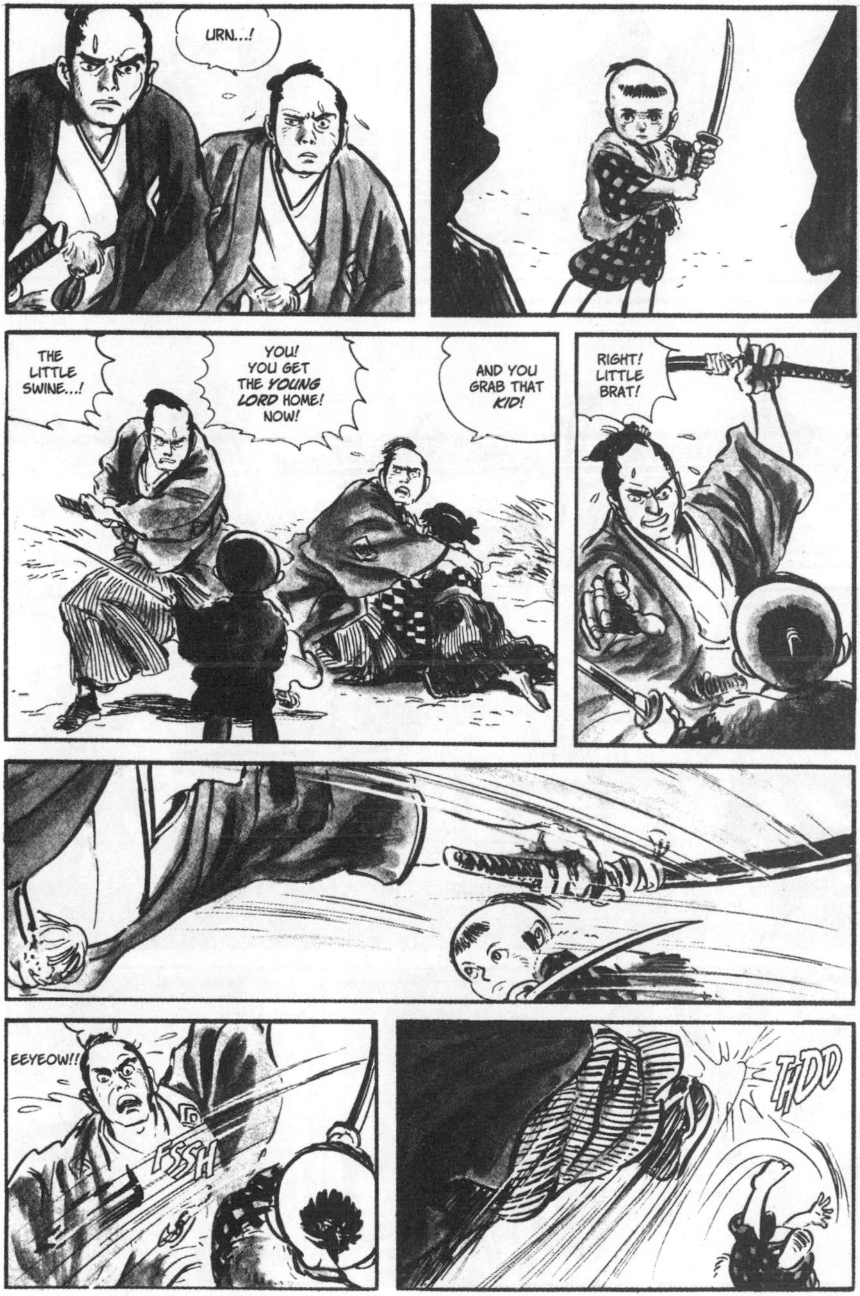
URN...!
THE LITTLE SWINE...!
YOU! YOU GET THE *YOUNG LORD* HOME! NOW!
AND YOU GRAB THAT *KID!*
RIGHT! LITTLE BRAT!
EEYEOW!!
FSSH
THDD

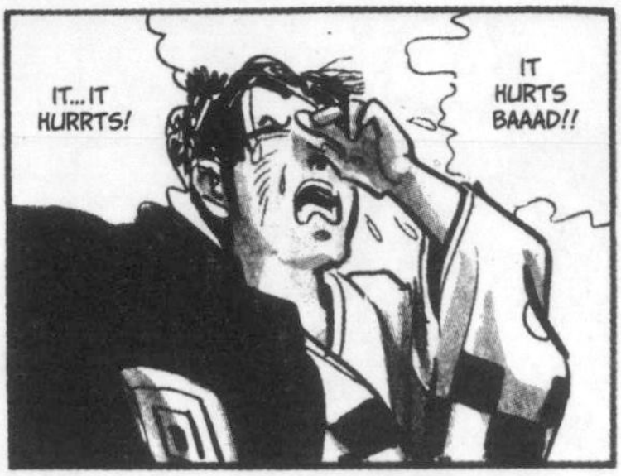
IT HURTS BAAAD!!
IT...IT HURRTS!
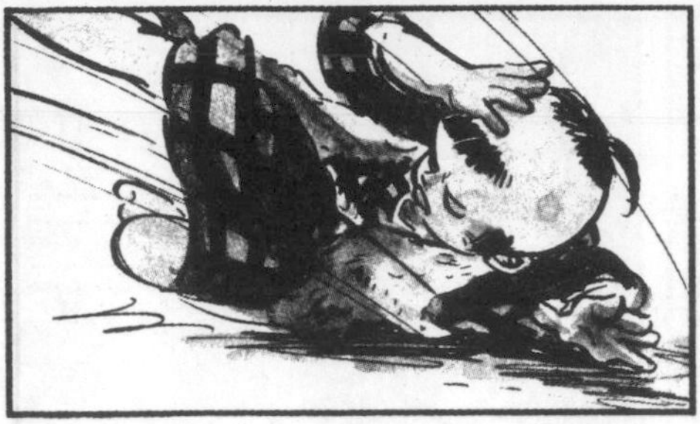
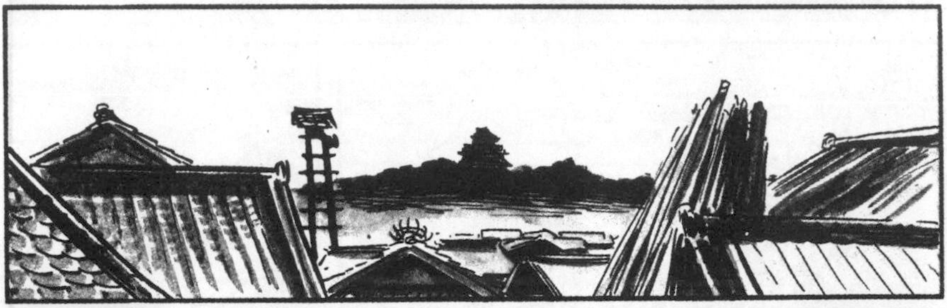
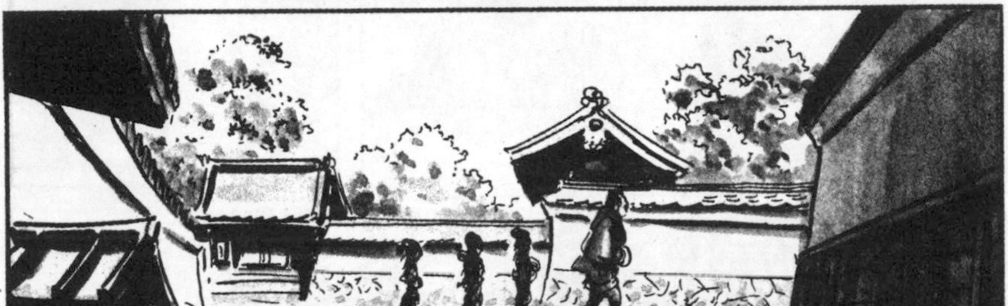
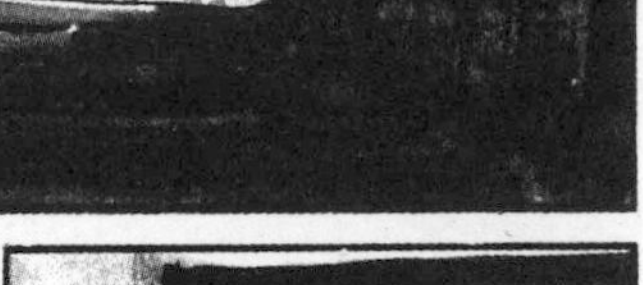
滝澤家通用門
*TAKIZAWA HOUSEHOLD SERVANTS ENTRANCE
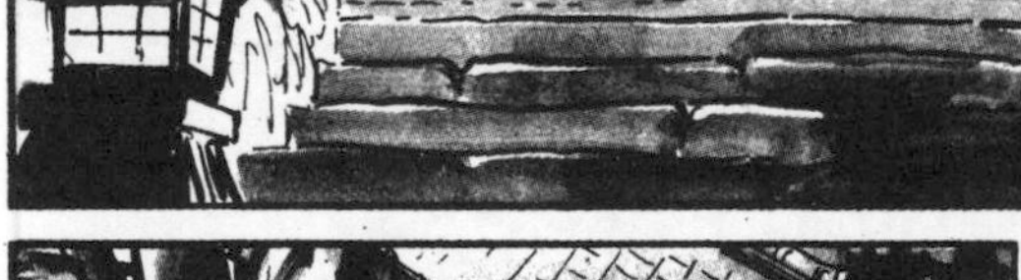

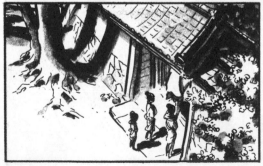

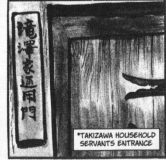

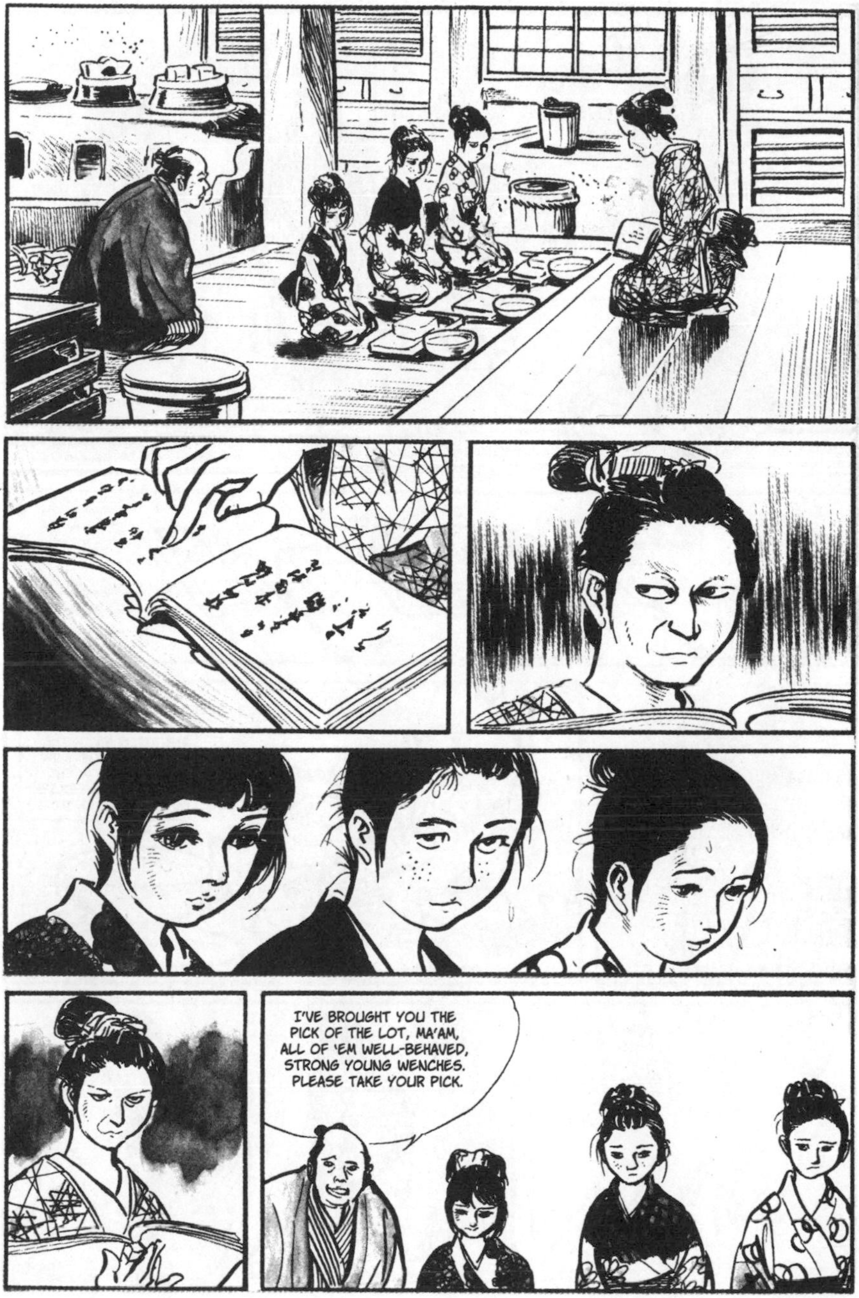
I'VE BROUGHT YOU THE PICK OF THE LOT, MA'AM, ALL OF 'EM WELL-BEHAVED, STRONG YOUNG WENCHES. PLEASE TAKE YOUR PICK.

RIGHT, THEN. BEGIN!

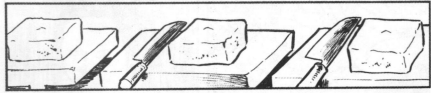

O-SUE. LITERALLY, "THE LAST." SUCH WAS THE TITLE GIVEN THE LOWEST OF THE LOW AMONG MAIDS IN THE SAMURAI HOUSEHOLDS OF EDO PERIOD JAPAN.

WHEN HIRING AN O-SUE, ALL THE GIRLS WERE GIVEN A TEST...

A TEST OF *SKILL*.

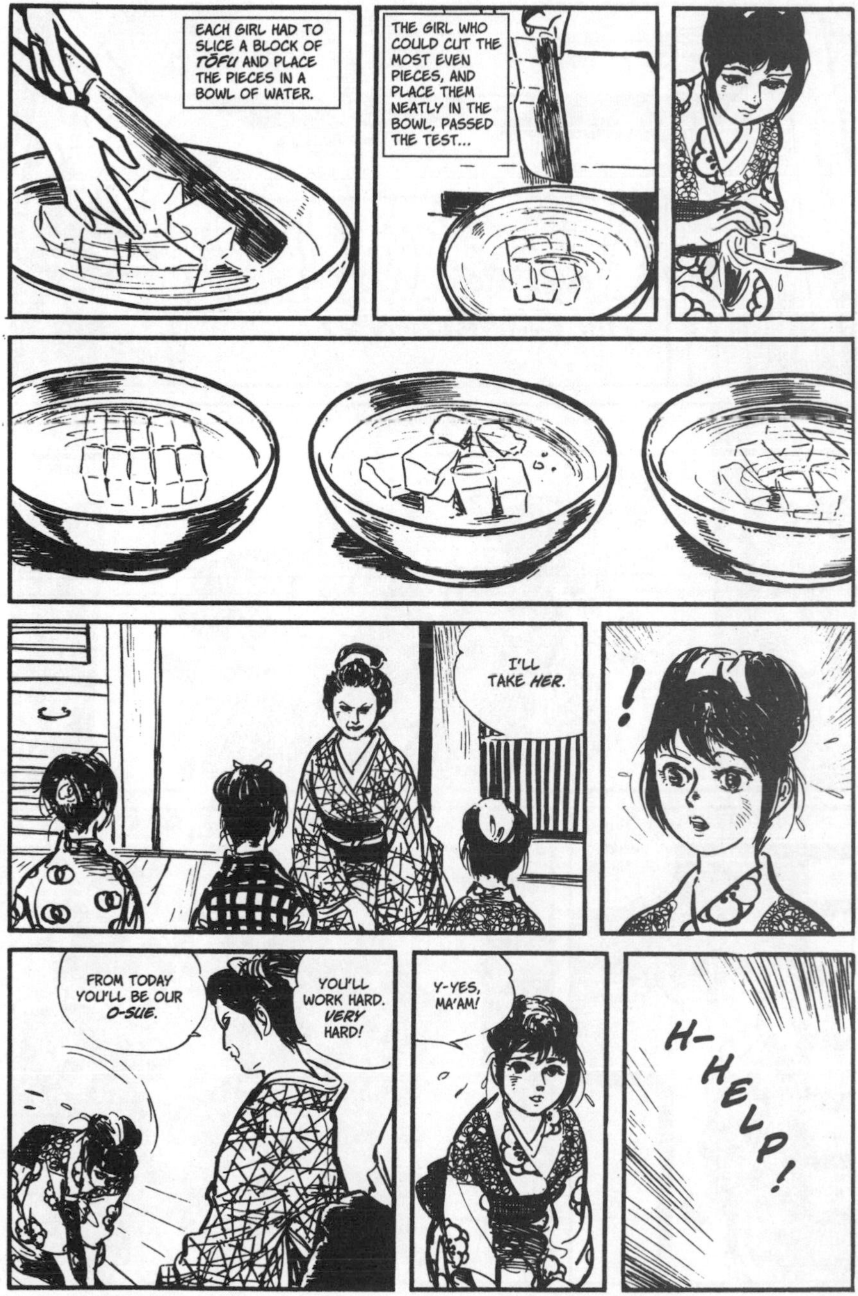
EACH GIRL HAD TO SLICE A BLOCK OF *TŌFU* AND PLACE THE PIECES IN A BOWL OF WATER.
THE GIRL WHO COULD CUT THE MOST EVEN PIECES, AND PLACE THEM NEATLY IN THE BOWL, PASSED THE TEST...
I'LL TAKE *HER*.
!
FROM TODAY YOU'LL BE OUR *O-SUE*.
YOU'LL WORK HARD. *VERY* HARD!
Y-YES, MA'AM!
H-HELP!

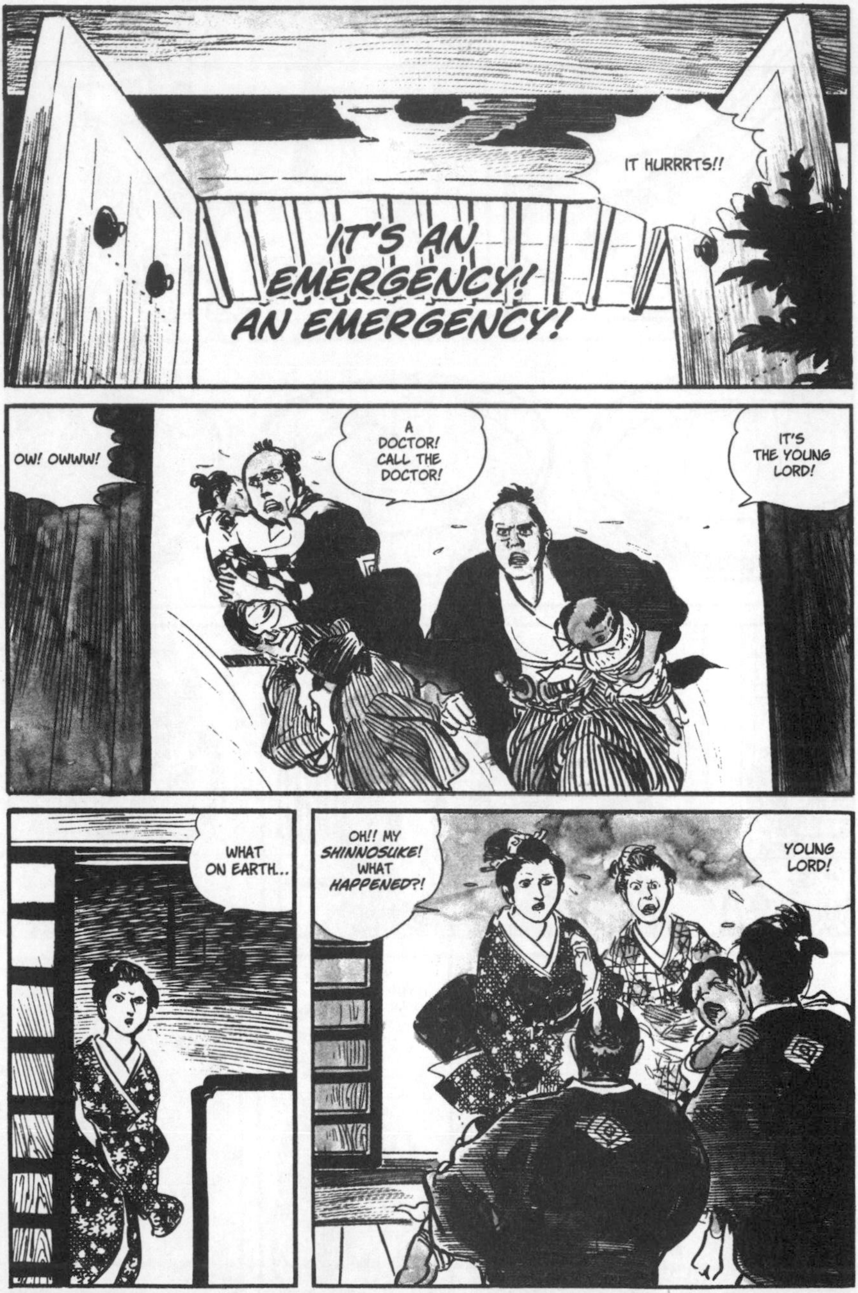
IT HURRRTS!!
IT'S AN EMERGENCY! AN EMERGENCY!
IT'S THE YOUNG LORD!
A DOCTOR! CALL THE DOCTOR!
OW! OWWW!
YOUNG LORD!
OH!! MY *SHINNOSUKE!* WHAT *HAPPENED?!*
WHAT ON EARTH...

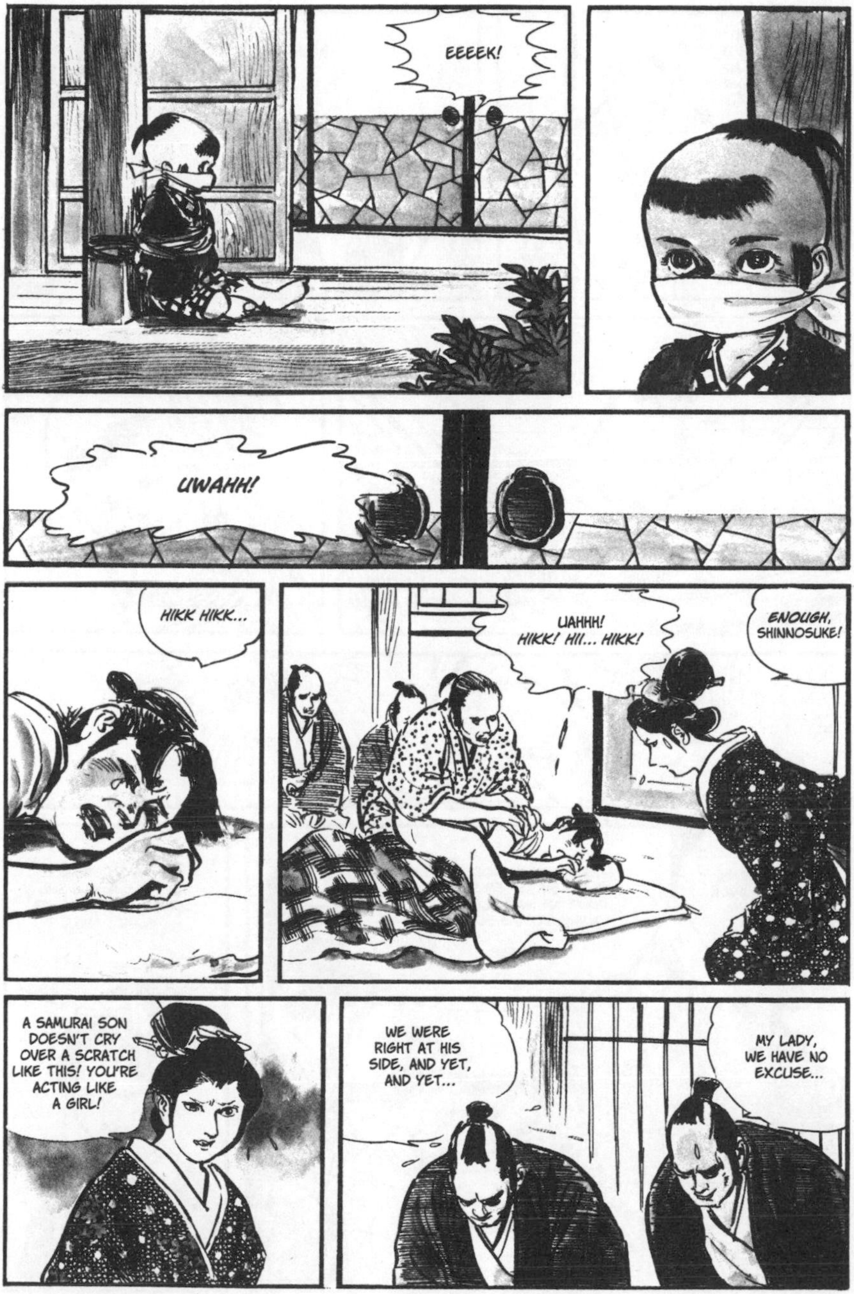
EEEEK!
UWAHH!
ENOUGH, SHINNOSUKE!
UAHHH! HIKK! HII... HIKK!
HIKK HIKK...
MY LADY, WE HAVE NO EXCUSE...
WE WERE RIGHT AT HIS SIDE, AND YET, AND YET...
A SAMURAI SON DOESN'T CRY OVER A SCRATCH LIKE THIS! YOU'RE ACTING LIKE A GIRL!

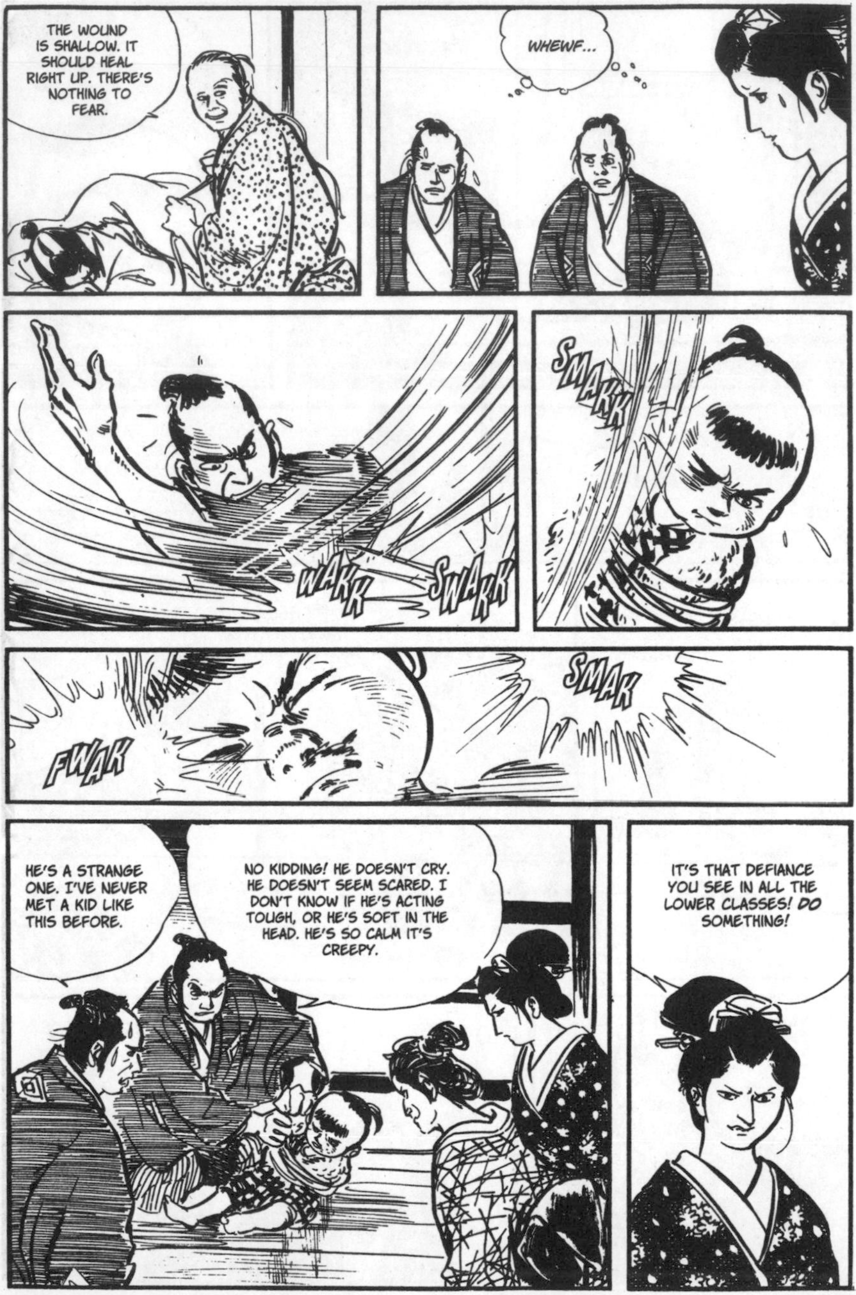
THE WOUND IS SHALLOW. IT SHOULD HEAL RIGHT UP. THERE'S NOTHING TO FEAR.
WHEWF...
WAKK
SWAKK
SMAKK
FWAK
SMAK
HE'S A STRANGE ONE. I'VE NEVER MET A KID LIKE THIS BEFORE.
NO KIDDING! HE DOESN'T CRY. HE DOESN'T SEEM SCARED. I DON'T KNOW IF HE'S ACTING TOUGH, OR HE'S SOFT IN THE HEAD. HE'S SO CALM IT'S CREEPY.
IT'S THAT DEFIANCE YOU SEE IN ALL THE LOWER CLASSES! *DO* SOMETHING!

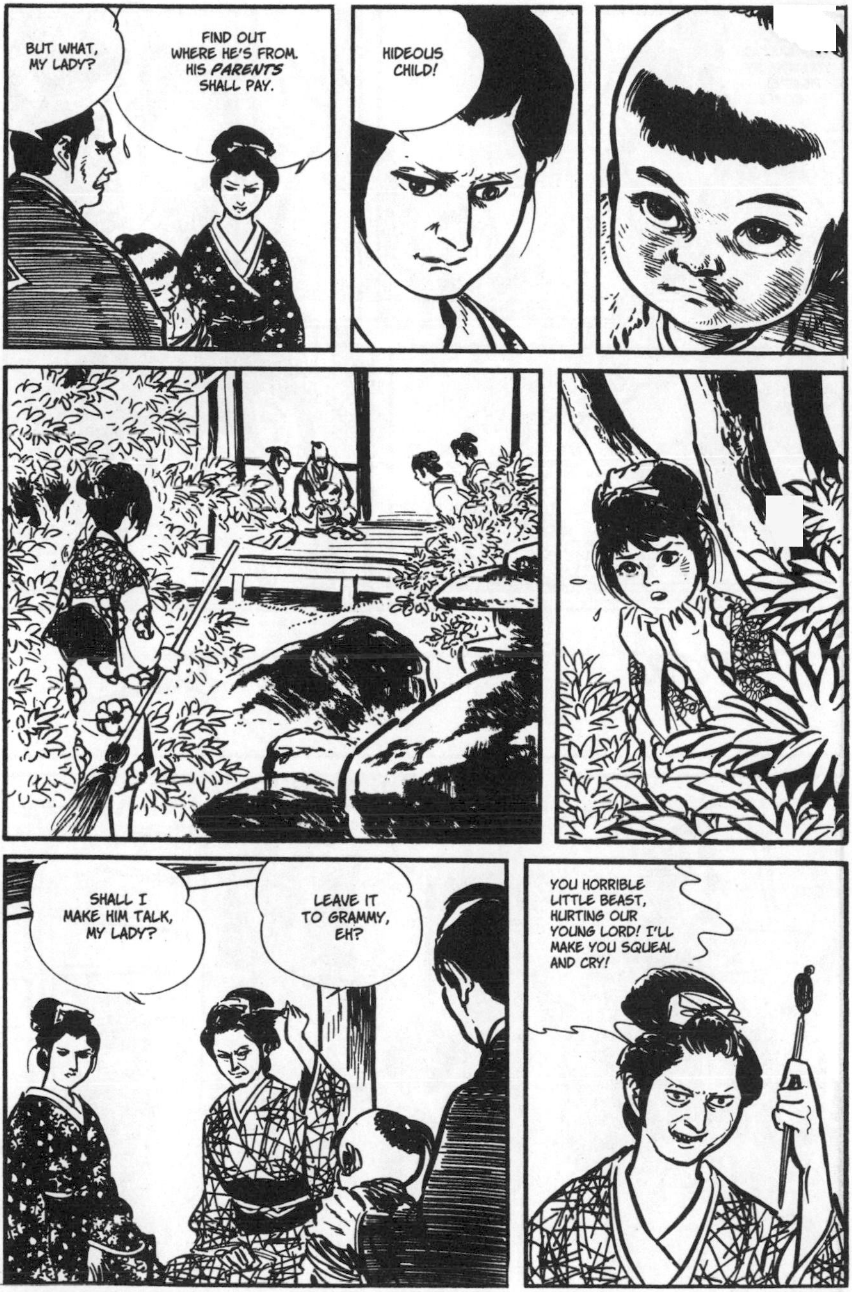
BUT WHAT, MY LADY?
FIND OUT WHERE HE'S FROM. HIS *PARENTS* SHALL PAY.
HIDEOUS CHILD!
SHALL I MAKE HIM TALK, MY LADY?
LEAVE IT TO GRAMMY, EH?
YOU HORRIBLE LITTLE BEAST, HURTING OUR YOUNG LORD! I'LL MAKE YOU SQUEAL AND CRY!

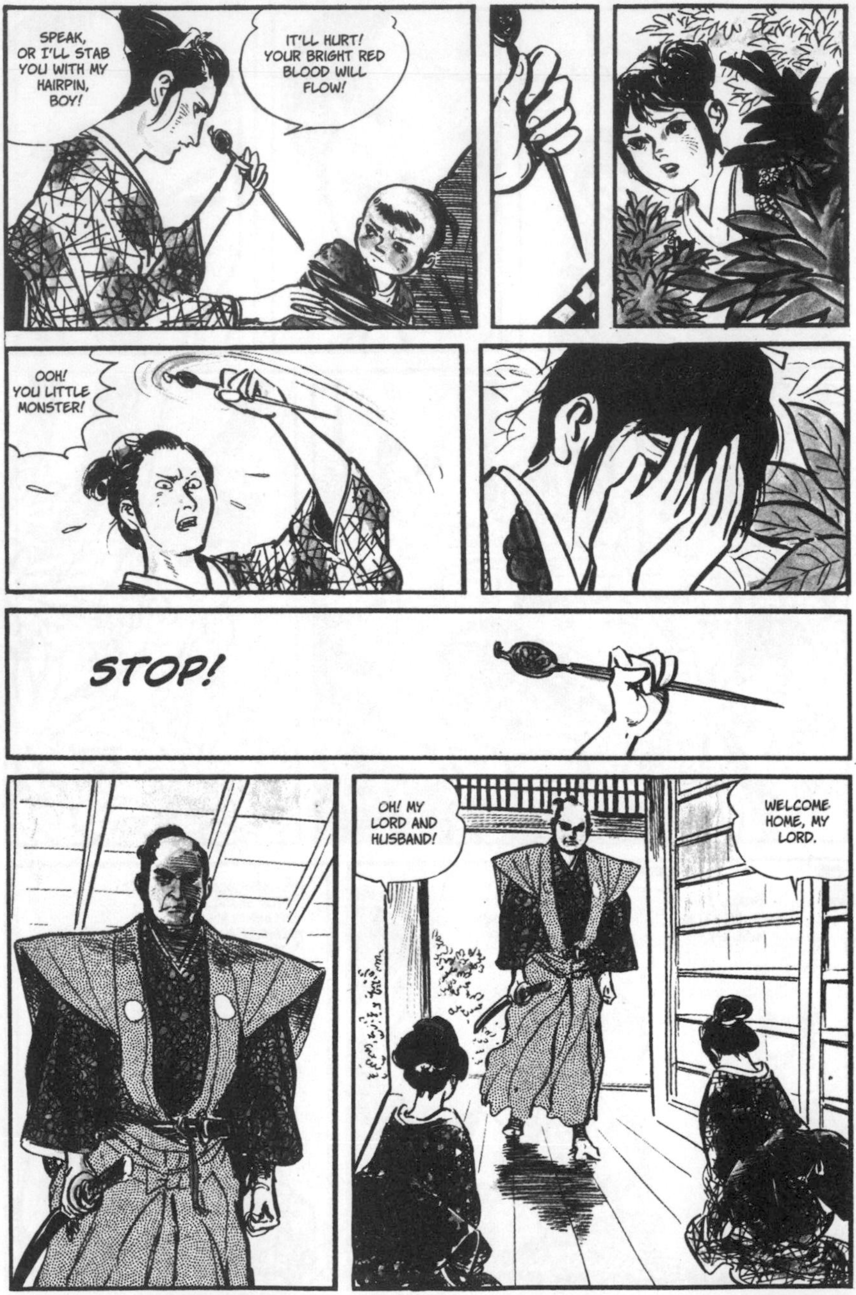
SPEAK, OR I'LL STAB YOU WITH MY HAIRPIN, BOY!
IT'LL HURT! YOUR BRIGHT RED BLOOD WILL FLOW!
OOH! YOU LITTLE MONSTER!
STOP!
OH! MY LORD AND HUSBAND!
WELCOME HOME, MY LORD.

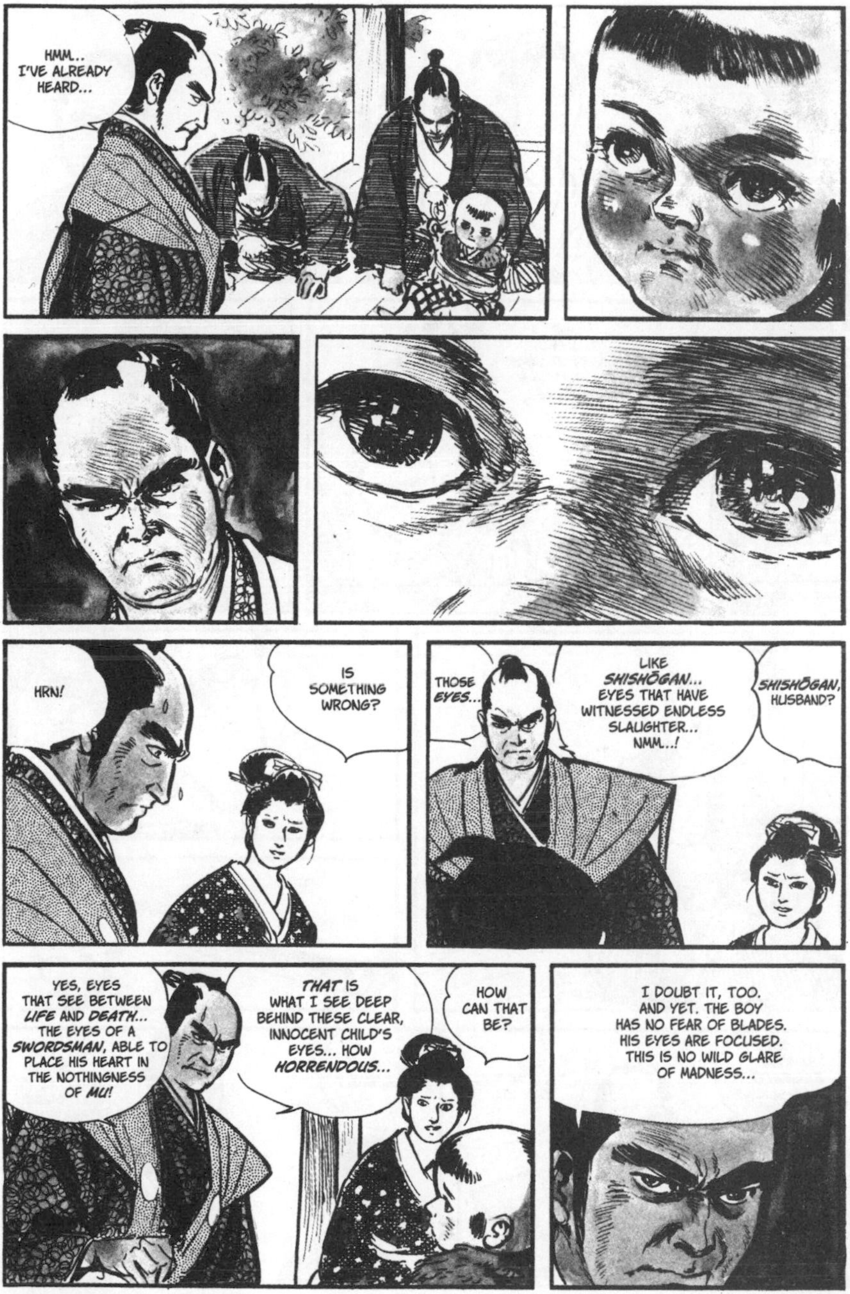
HMM.. I'VE ALREADY HEARD...
HRN!
IS SOMETHING WRONG?
THOSE *EYES*...
LIKE *SHISHŌGAN*... EYES THAT HAVE WITNESSED ENDLESS SLAUGHTER... NMM...!
SHISHŌGAN, HUSBAND?
YES, EYES THAT SEE BETWEEN *LIFE* AND *DEATH*... THE EYES OF A *SWORDSMAN*, ABLE TO PLACE HIS HEART IN THE NOTHINGNESS OF *MU*!
THAT IS WHAT I SEE DEEP BEHIND THESE CLEAR, INNOCENT CHILD'S EYES... HOW *HORRENDOUS*...
HOW CAN THAT BE?
I DOUBT IT, TOO. AND YET. THE BOY HAS NO FEAR OF BLADES. HIS EYES ARE FOCUSED. THIS IS NO WILD GLARE OF MADNESS...

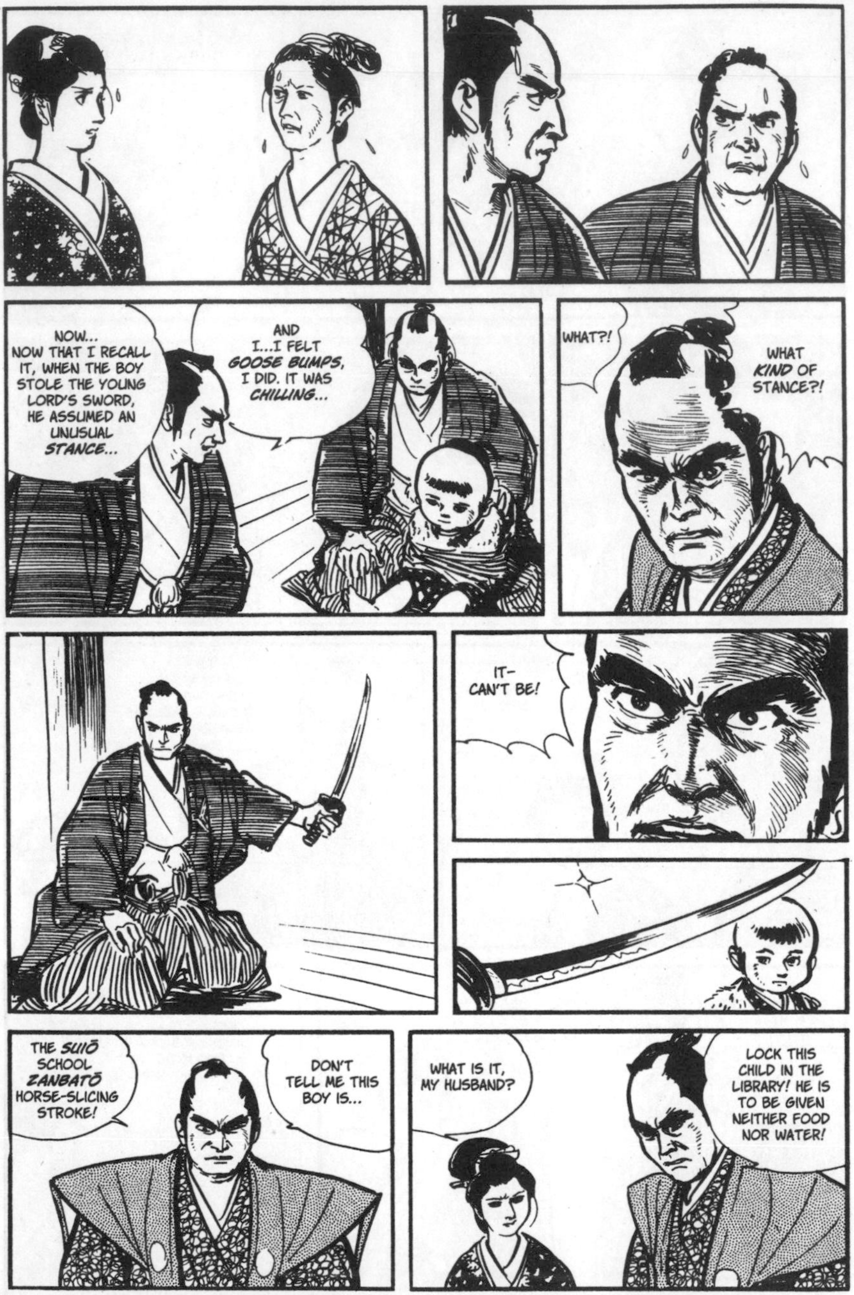

NOW... NOW THAT I RECALL IT, WHEN THE BOY STOLE THE YOUNG LORD'S SWORD, HE ASSUMED AN UNUSUAL STANCE...
AND I...I FELT GOOSE BUMPS, I DID. IT WAS CHILLING...
WHAT?!
WHAT KIND OF STANCE?!
IT- CAN'T BE!
THE SUIŌ SCHOOL ZANBATŌ HORSE-SLICING STROKE!
DON'T TELL ME THIS BOY IS...
WHAT IS IT, MY HUSBAND?
LOCK THIS CHILD IN THE LIBRARY! HE IS TO BE GIVEN NEITHER FOOD NOR WATER!

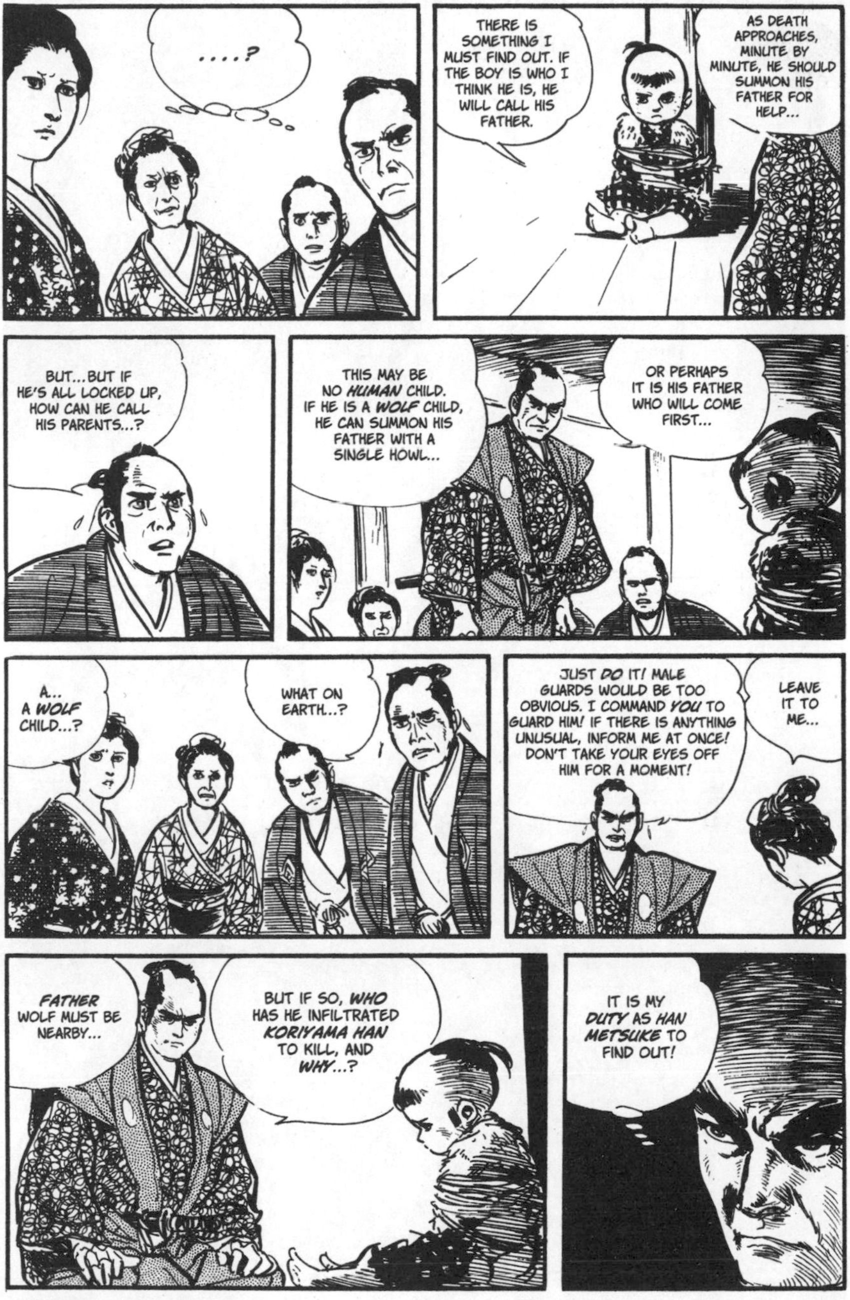
....?
THERE IS SOMETHING I MUST FIND OUT. IF THE BOY IS WHO I THINK HE IS, HE WILL CALL HIS FATHER.
AS DEATH APPROACHES, MINUTE BY MINUTE, HE SHOULD SUMMON HIS FATHER FOR HELP...
BUT...BUT IF HE'S ALL LOCKED UP, HOW CAN HE CALL HIS PARENTS...?
THIS MAY BE NO *HUMAN* CHILD. IF HE IS A *WOLF* CHILD, HE CAN SUMMON HIS FATHER WITH A SINGLE HOWL...
OR PERHAPS IT IS HIS FATHER WHO WILL COME FIRST...
A... A *WOLF* CHILD...?
WHAT ON EARTH...?
JUST *DO* IT! MALE GUARDS WOULD BE TOO OBVIOUS. I COMMAND *YOU* TO GUARD HIM! IF THERE IS ANYTHING UNUSUAL, INFORM ME AT ONCE! DON'T TAKE YOUR EYES OFF HIM FOR A MOMENT!
LEAVE IT TO ME...
FATHER WOLF MUST BE NEARBY...
BUT IF SO, *WHO* HAS HE INFILTRATED *KORIYAMA HAN* TO KILL, AND *WHY*...?
IT IS MY *DUTY* AS *HAN METSUKE* TO FIND OUT!

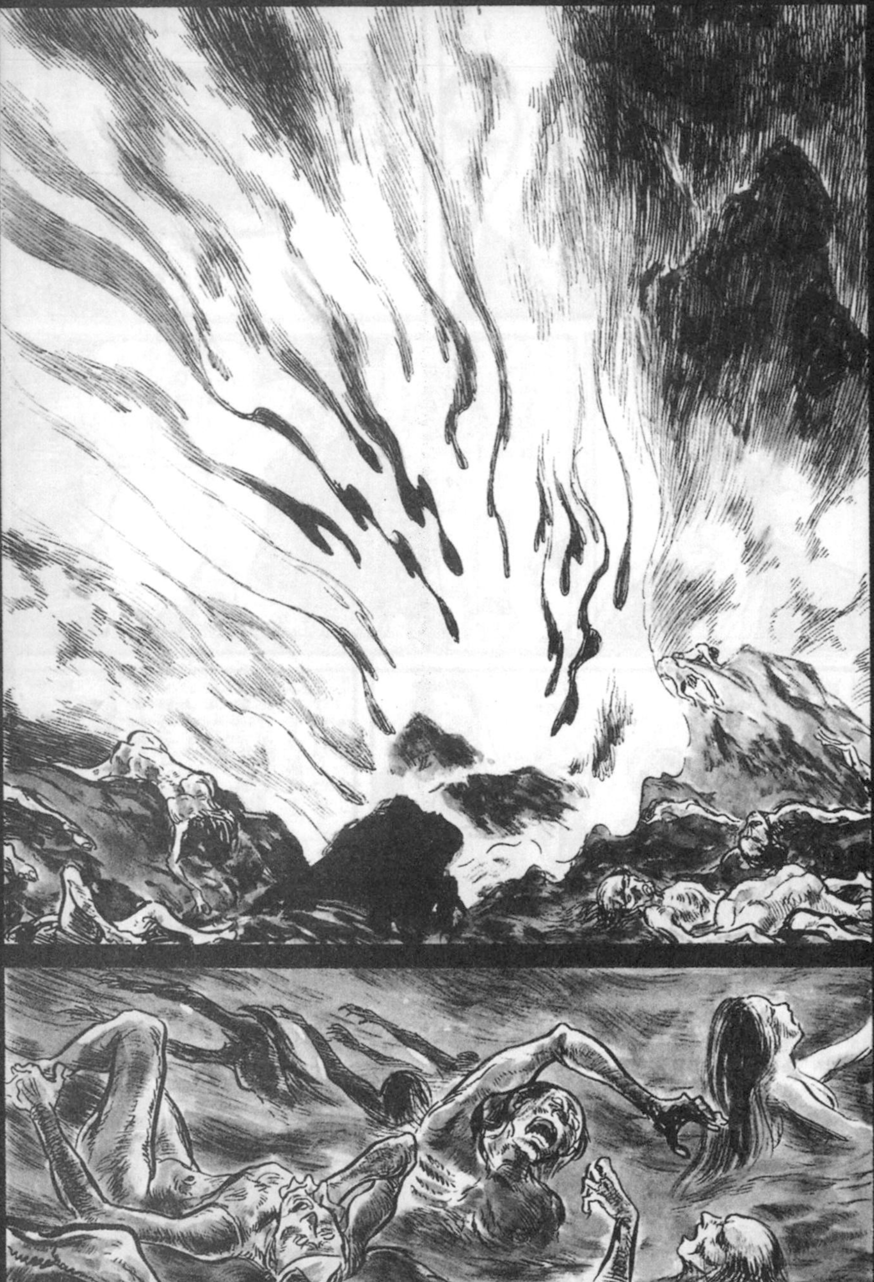

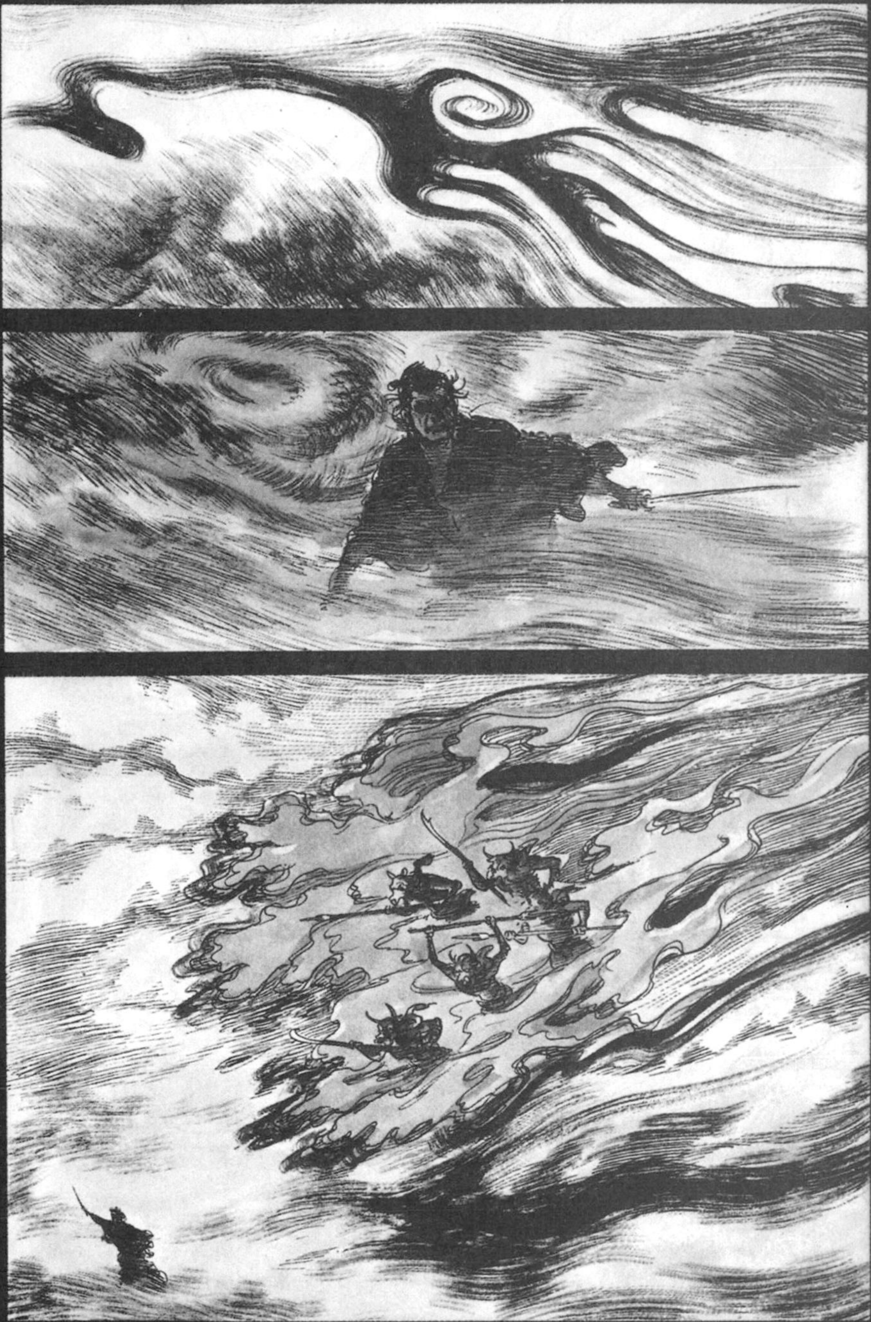

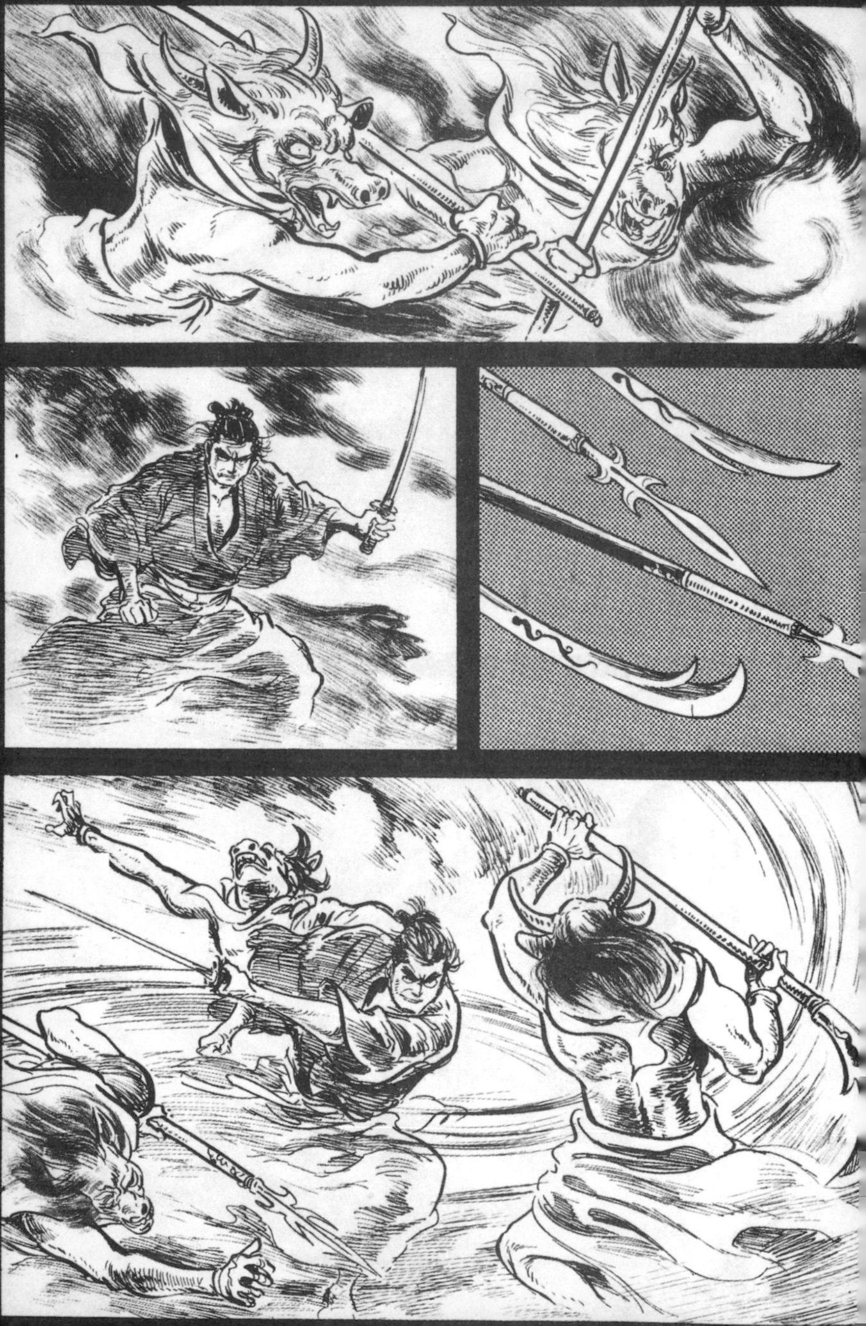

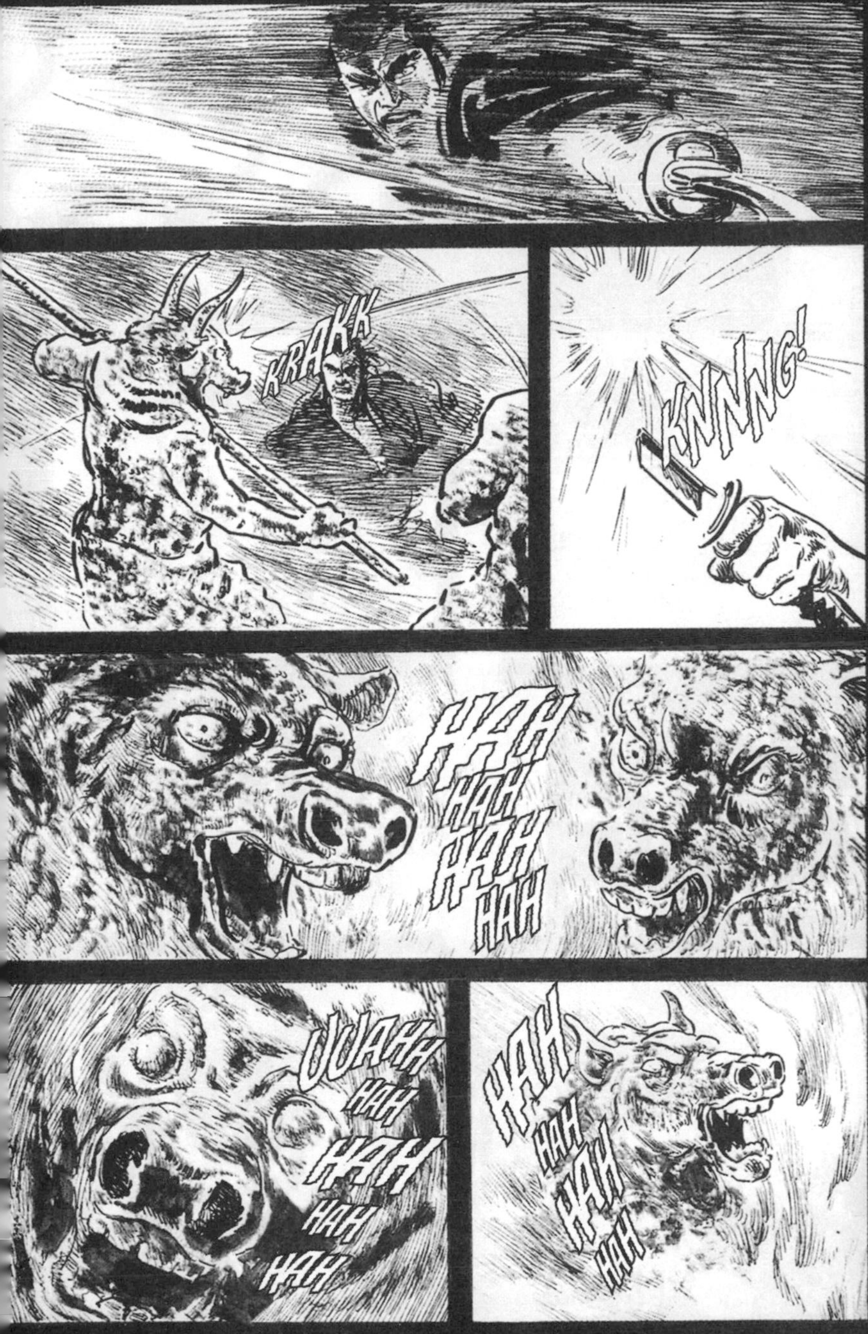
KNNNG!
KRAKK
HAH
HAH
HAH
HAH
HAH
HAH
HAH
HAH
UUAHH
HAH
HAH
HAH
HAH

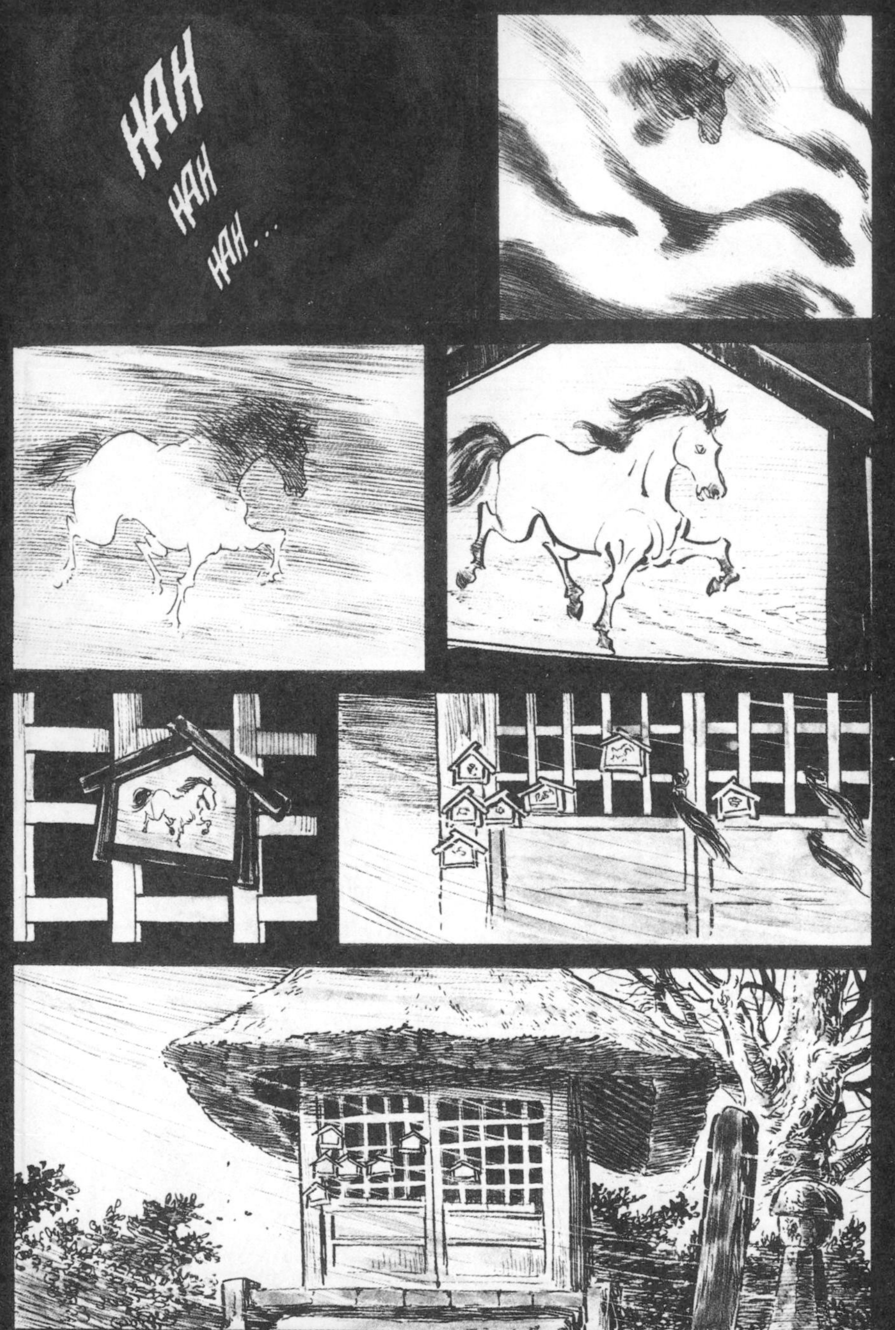
HAH
HAH
HAH...

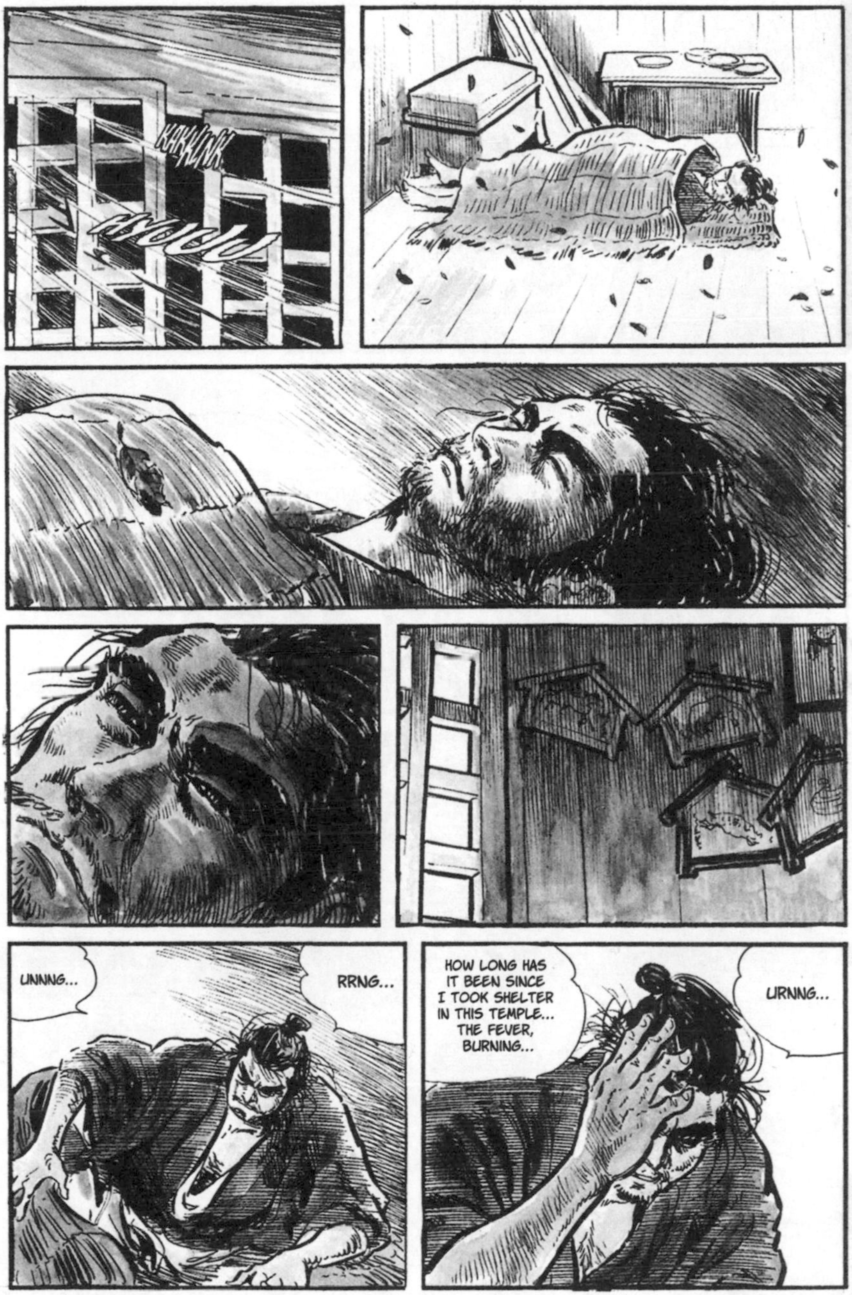
KAKLINK
HYOOOO
UNNNG...
RRNG...
HOW LONG HAS IT BEEN SINCE I TOOK SHELTER IN THIS TEMPLE... THE FEVER, BURNING...
URNNG...

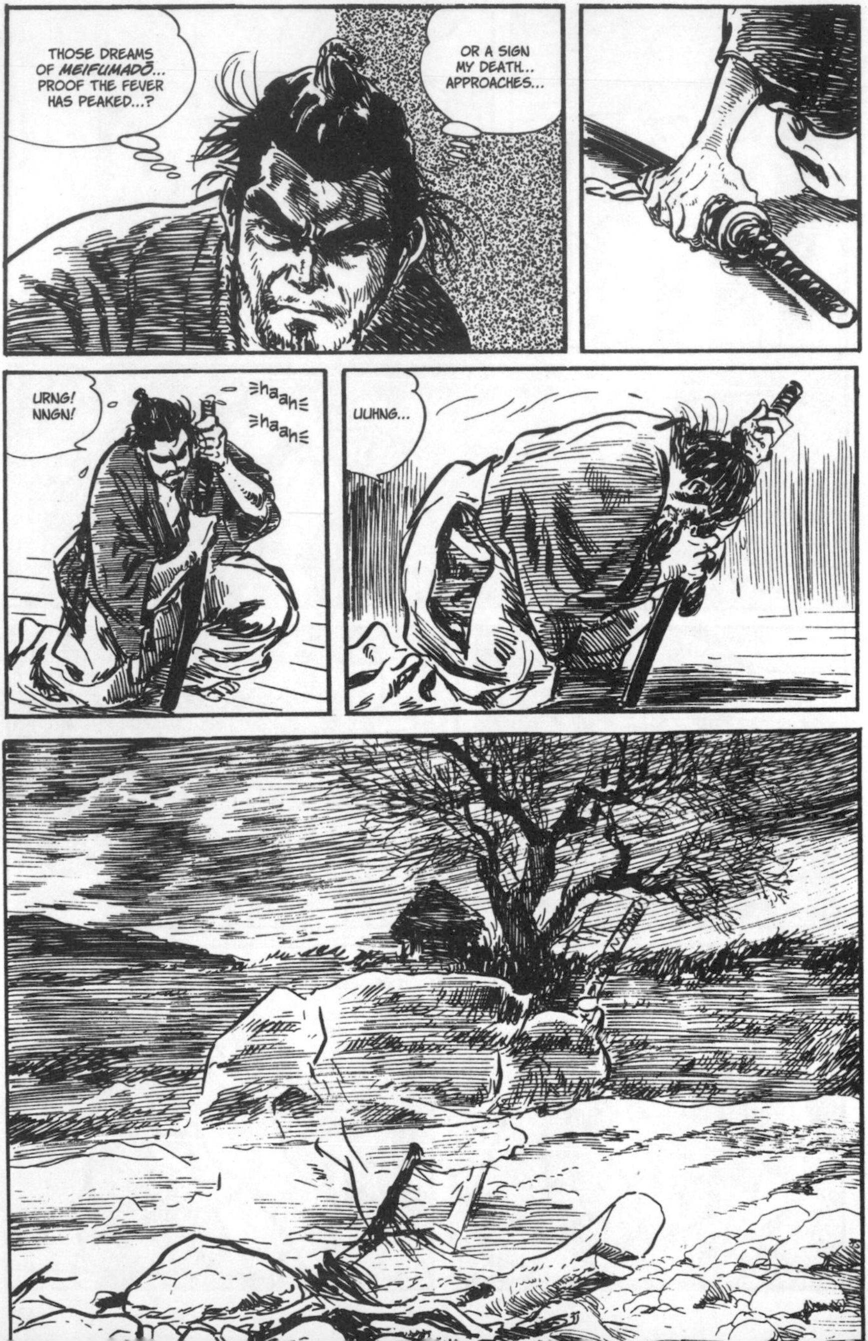
THOSE DREAMS OF *MEIFUMADŌ*... PROOF THE FEVER HAS PEAKED...?
OR A SIGN MY DEATH... APPROACHES...
URNG! NNGN!
haah
haah
UUHNG...

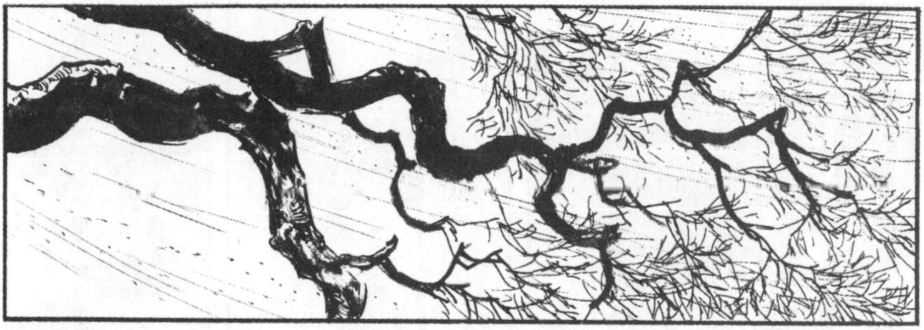
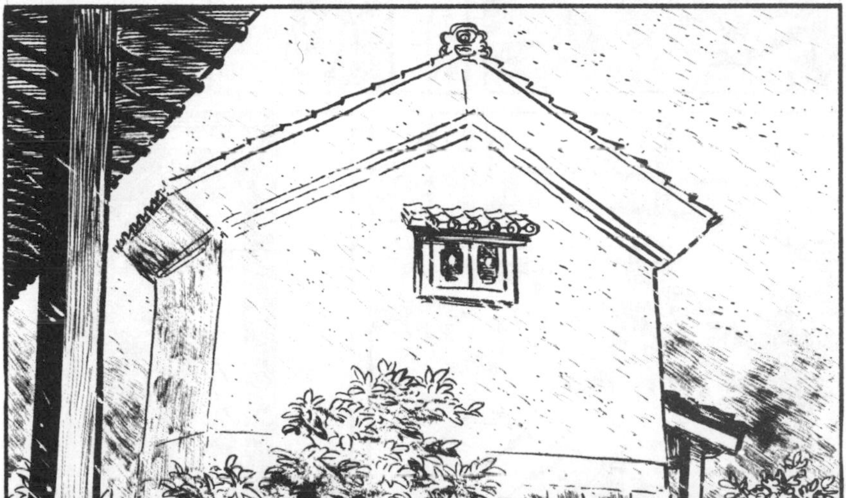
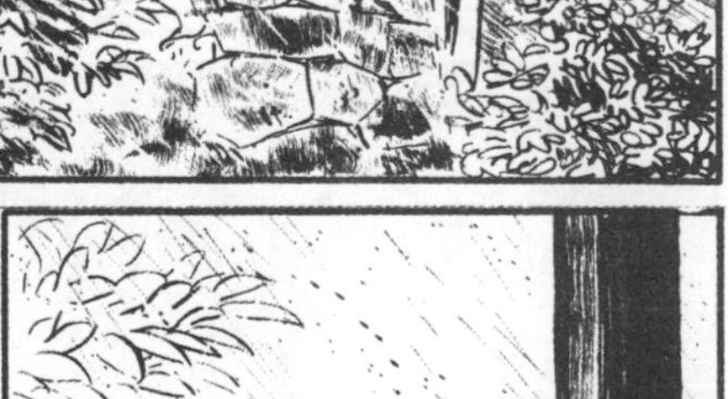
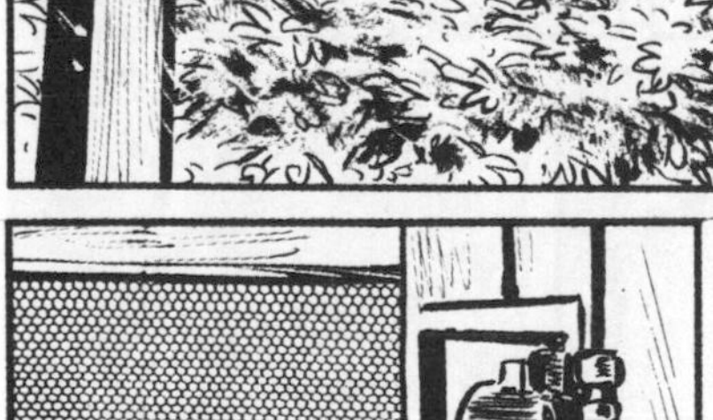

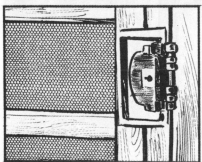

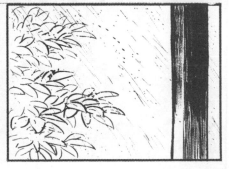

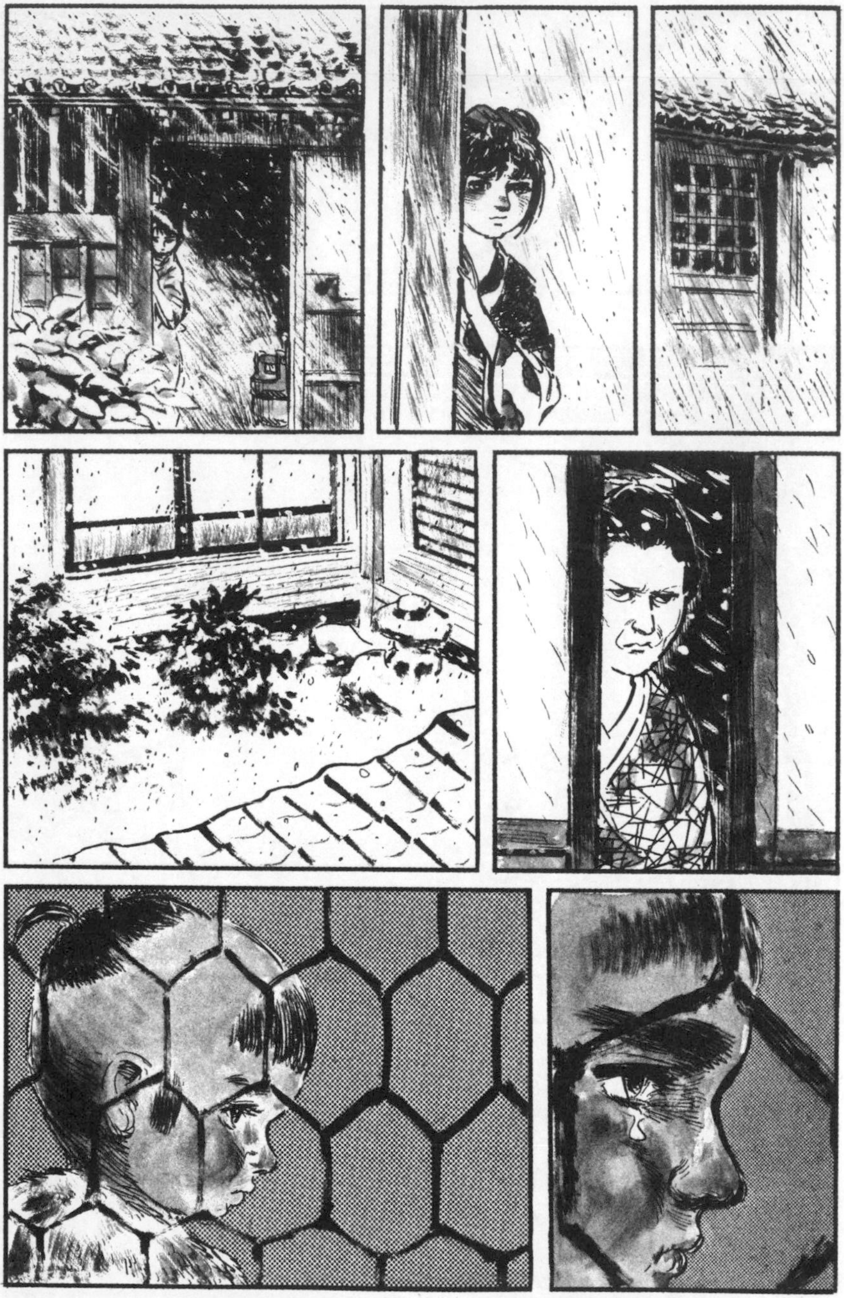

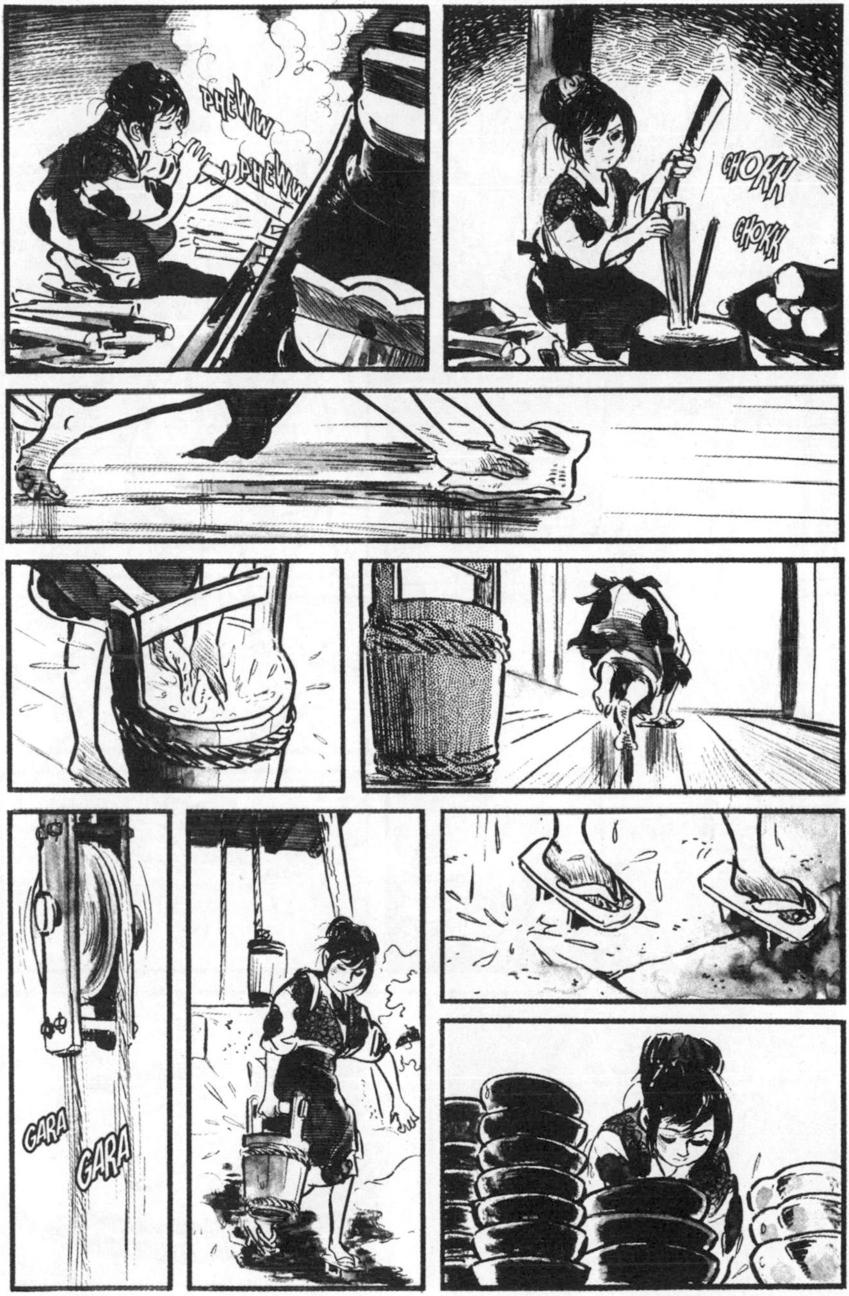
CHOKK
CHOKK
PHEWW
PHEWW
GARA
GARA

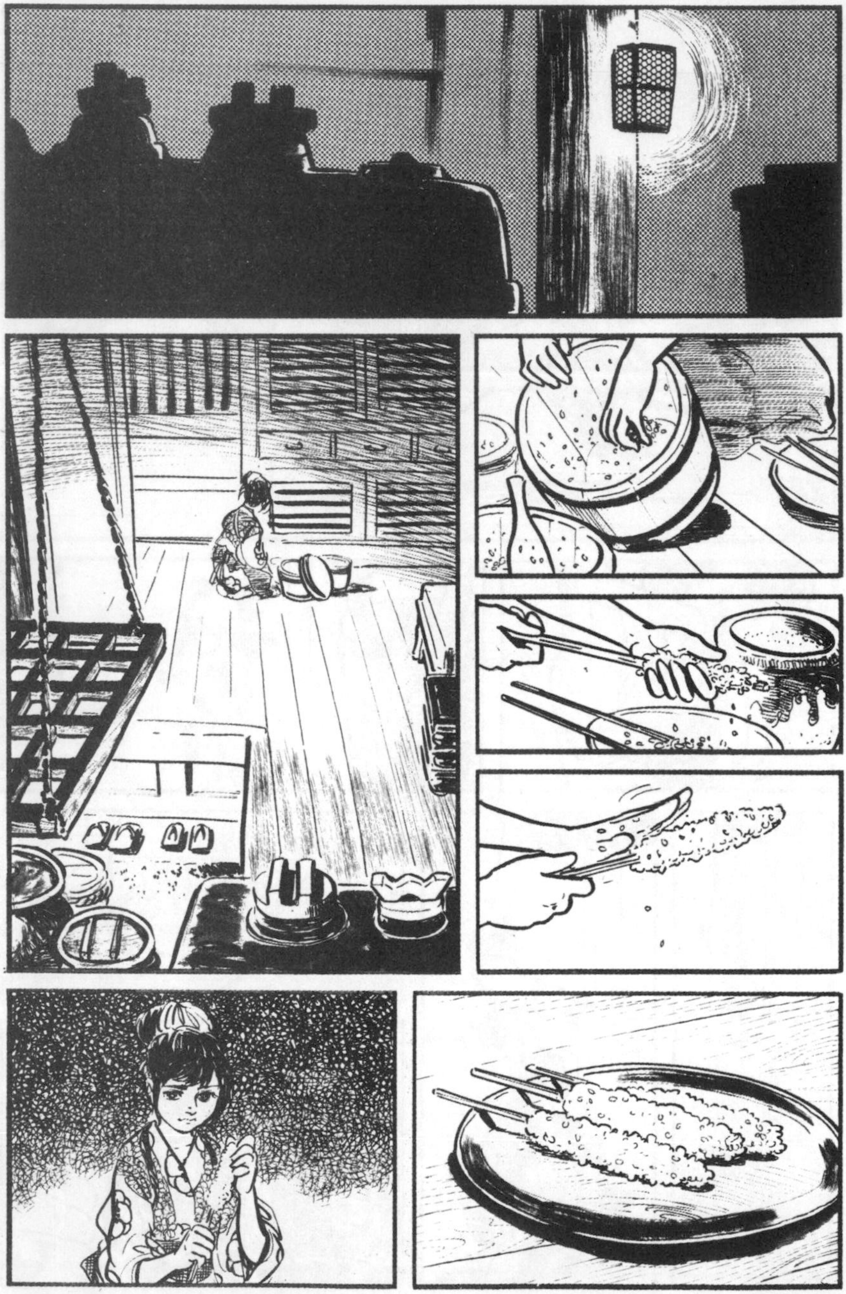

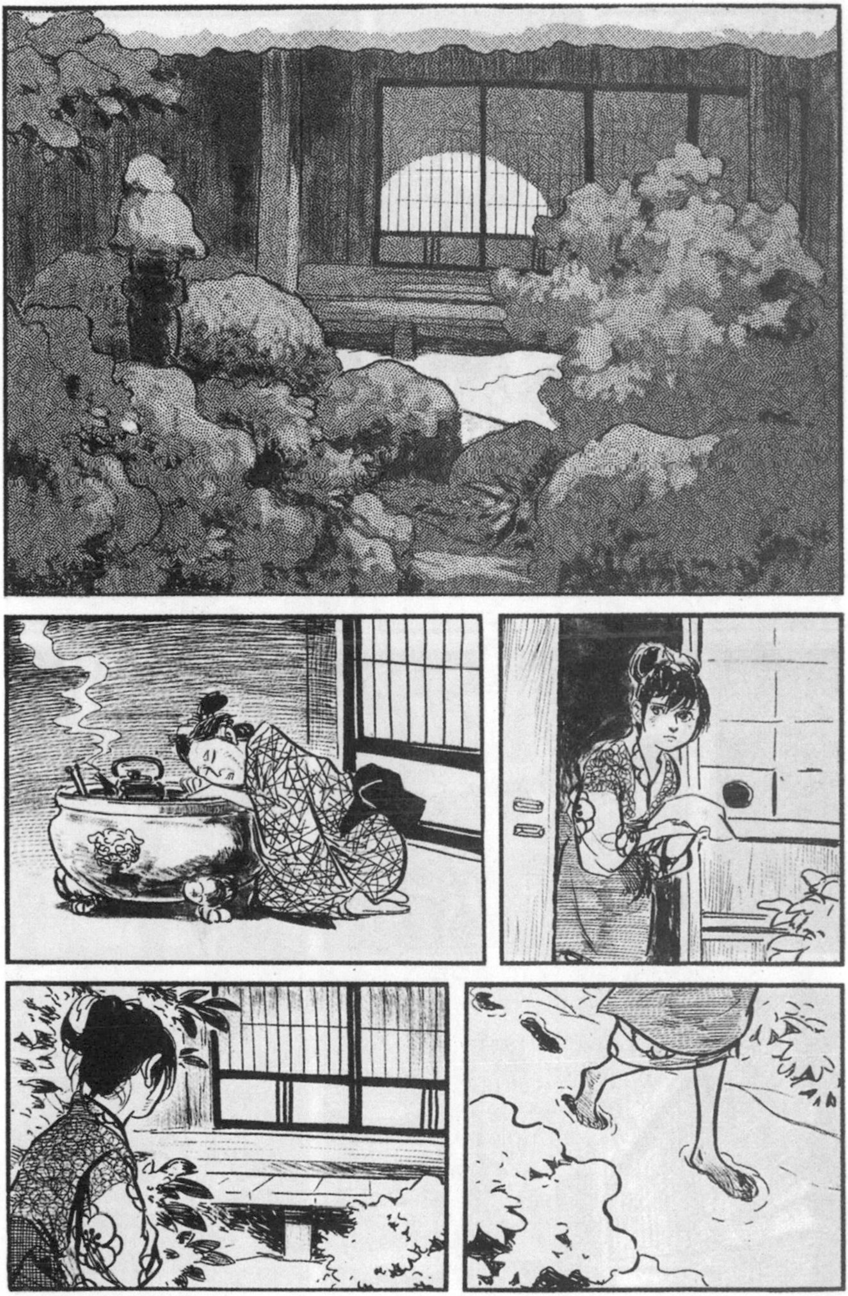

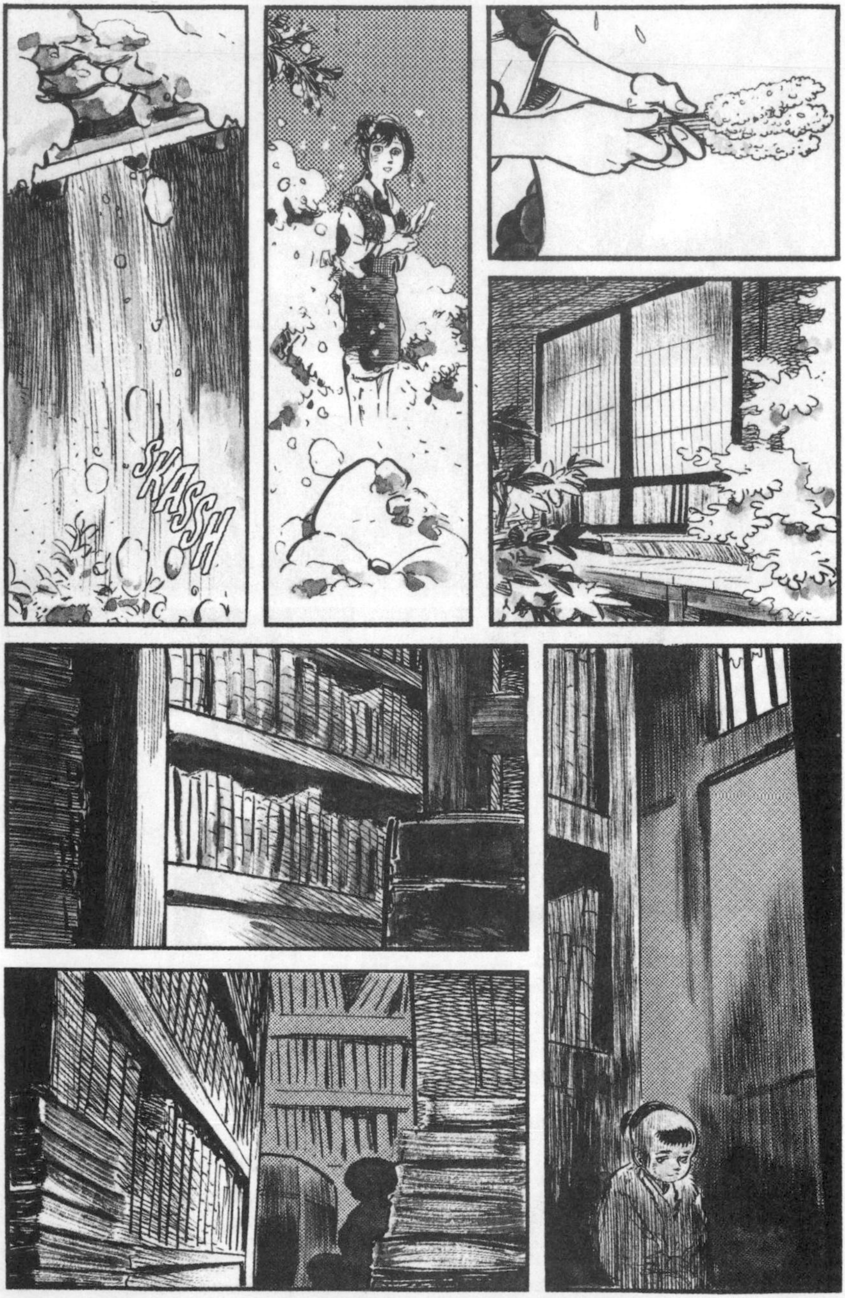
SKASSH

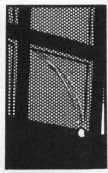

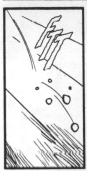

IT'S AWFUL WHAT THEY'RE DOING! TO A LITTLE CHILD LIKE YOU!

....

YOU MUST BE SO SCARED...

I PUT SALT ON IT TO MAKE IT YUMMY. WAIT... THERE'S MORE.

IF YOUR THROAT'S DRY, HERE'S SOME SNOW...

SIS. THANK YOU, SIS.

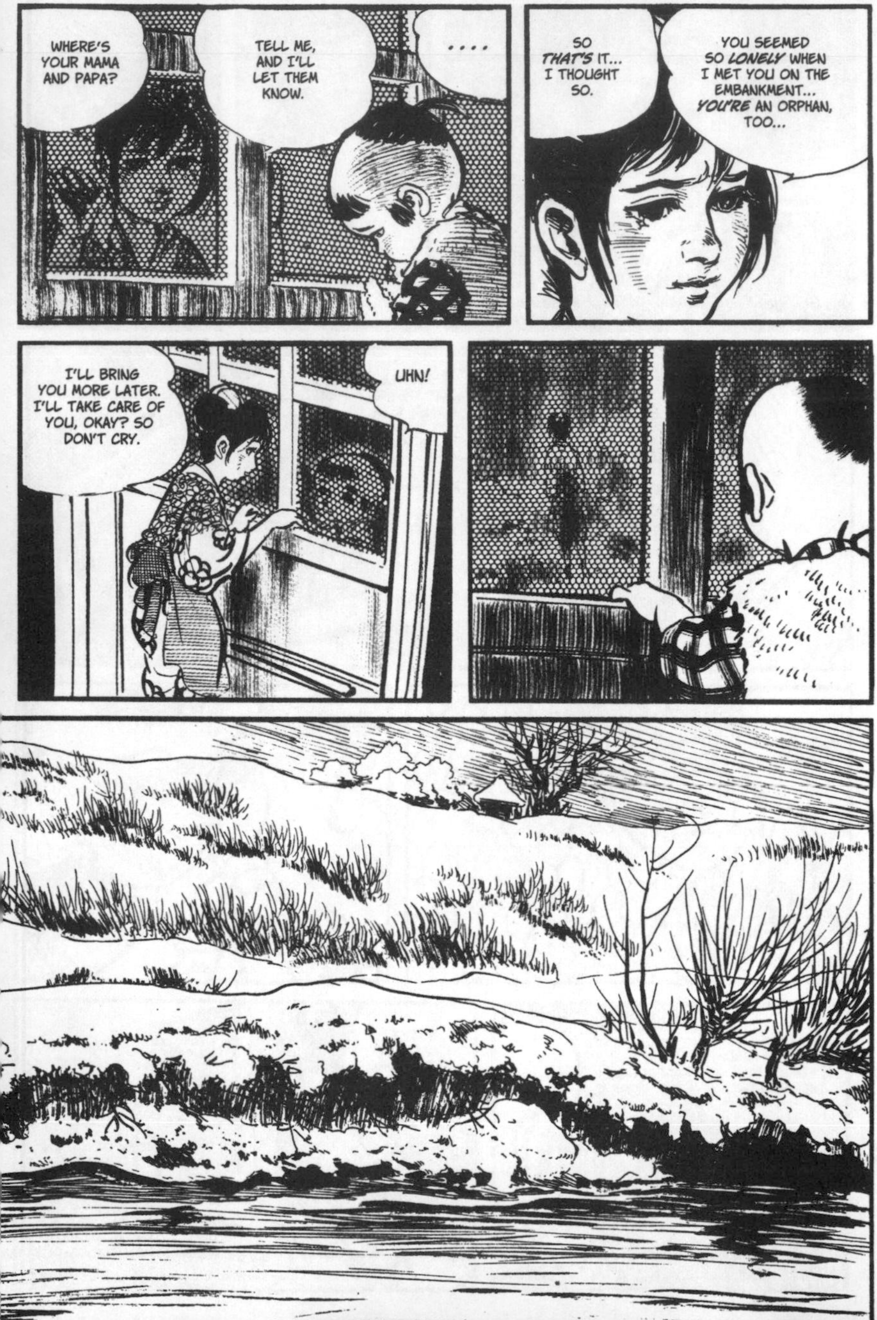
WHERE'S YOUR MAMA AND PAPA?
TELL ME, AND I'LL LET THEM KNOW.
....
SO *THAT'S* IT... I THOUGHT SO.
YOU SEEMED SO *LONELY* WHEN I MET YOU ON THE EMBANKMENT... *YOU'RE* AN ORPHAN, TOO...
I'LL BRING YOU MORE LATER. I'LL TAKE CARE OF YOU, OKAY? SO DON'T CRY.
UHN!

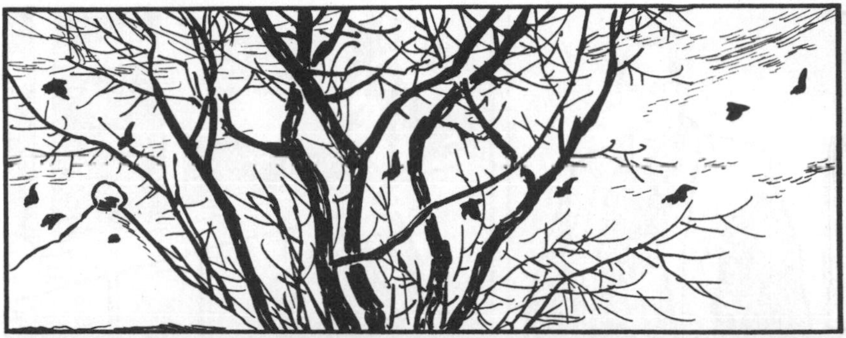
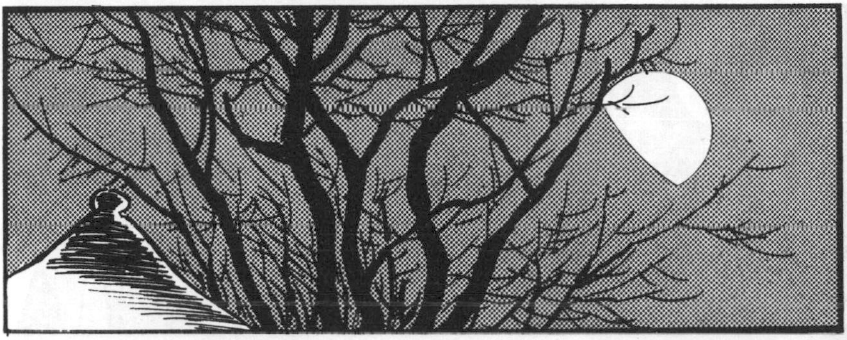
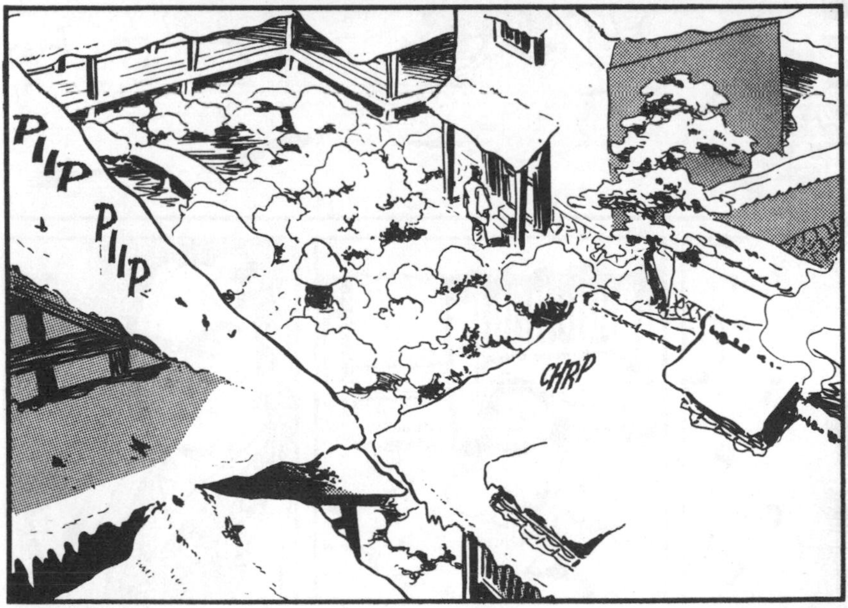
PIIP
PIIP
CHRP

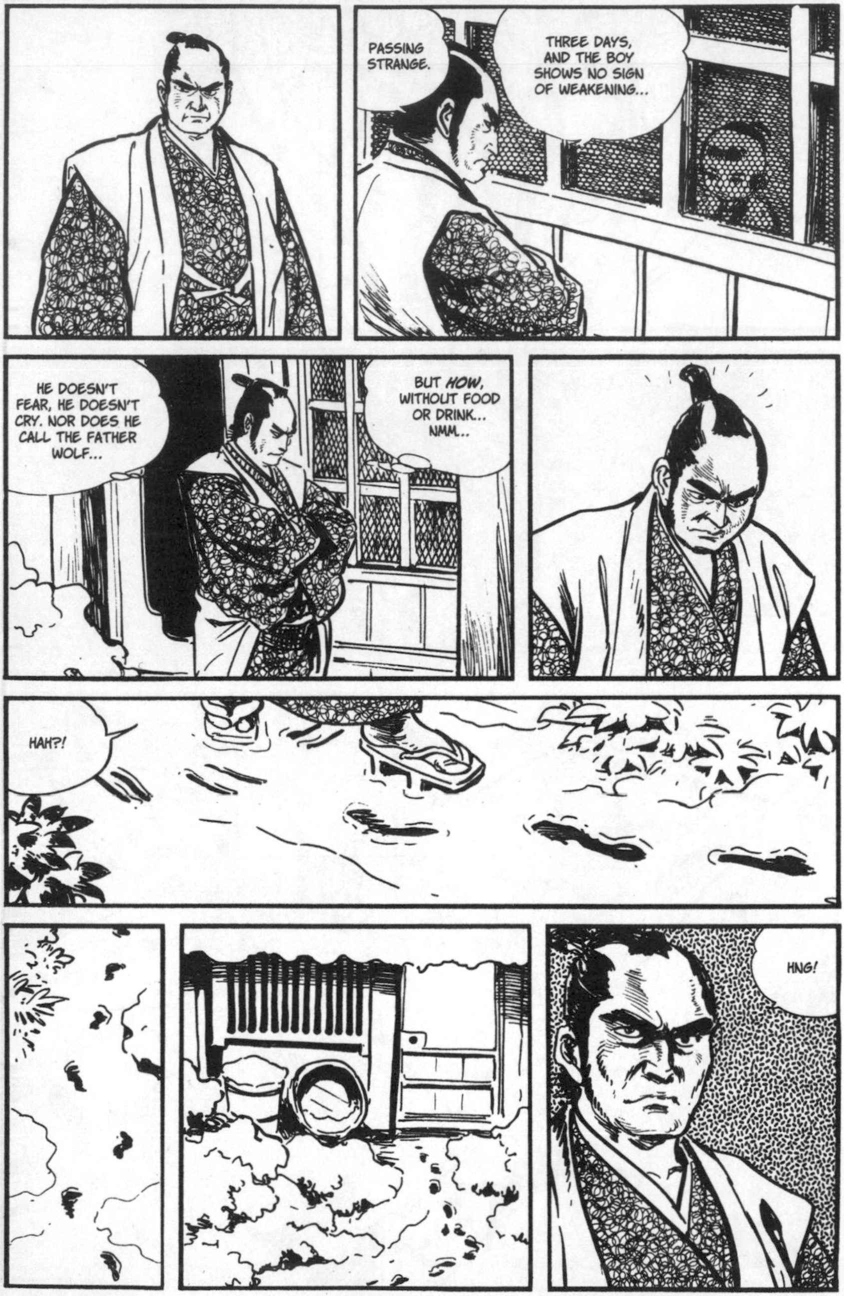
PASSING STRANGE.
THREE DAYS, AND THE BOY SHOWS NO SIGN OF WEAKENING...
HE DOESN'T FEAR, HE DOESN'T CRY. NOR DOES HE CALL THE FATHER WOLF...
BUT *HOW*, WITHOUT FOOD OR DRINK... NMM...
HAH?!
HNG!

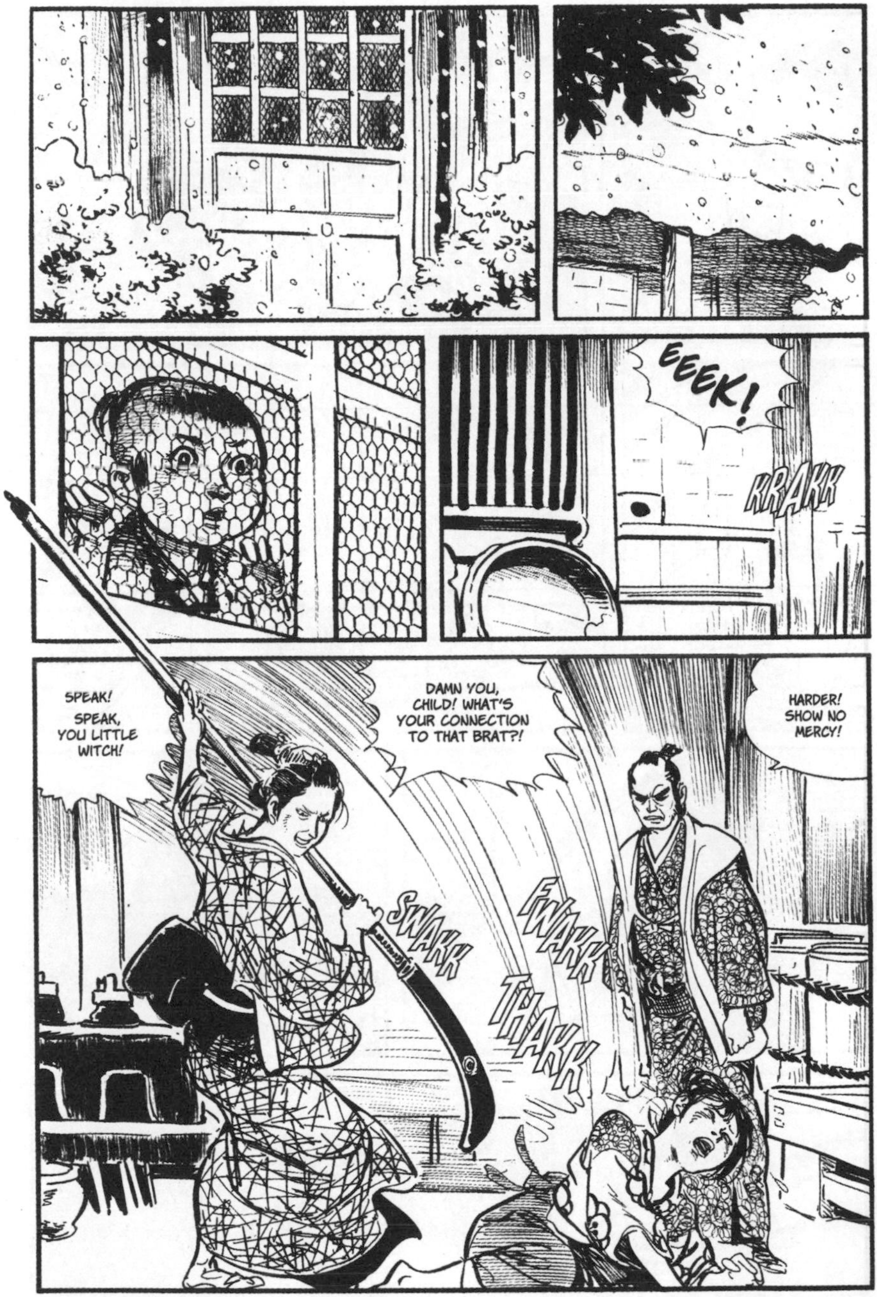
EEEK!
KRAKK
HARDER! SHOW NO MERCY!
DAMN YOU, CHILD! WHAT'S YOUR CONNECTION TO THAT BRAT?!
SPEAK!
SPEAK, YOU LITTLE WITCH!
FWAKK
THAKK
SWAKK

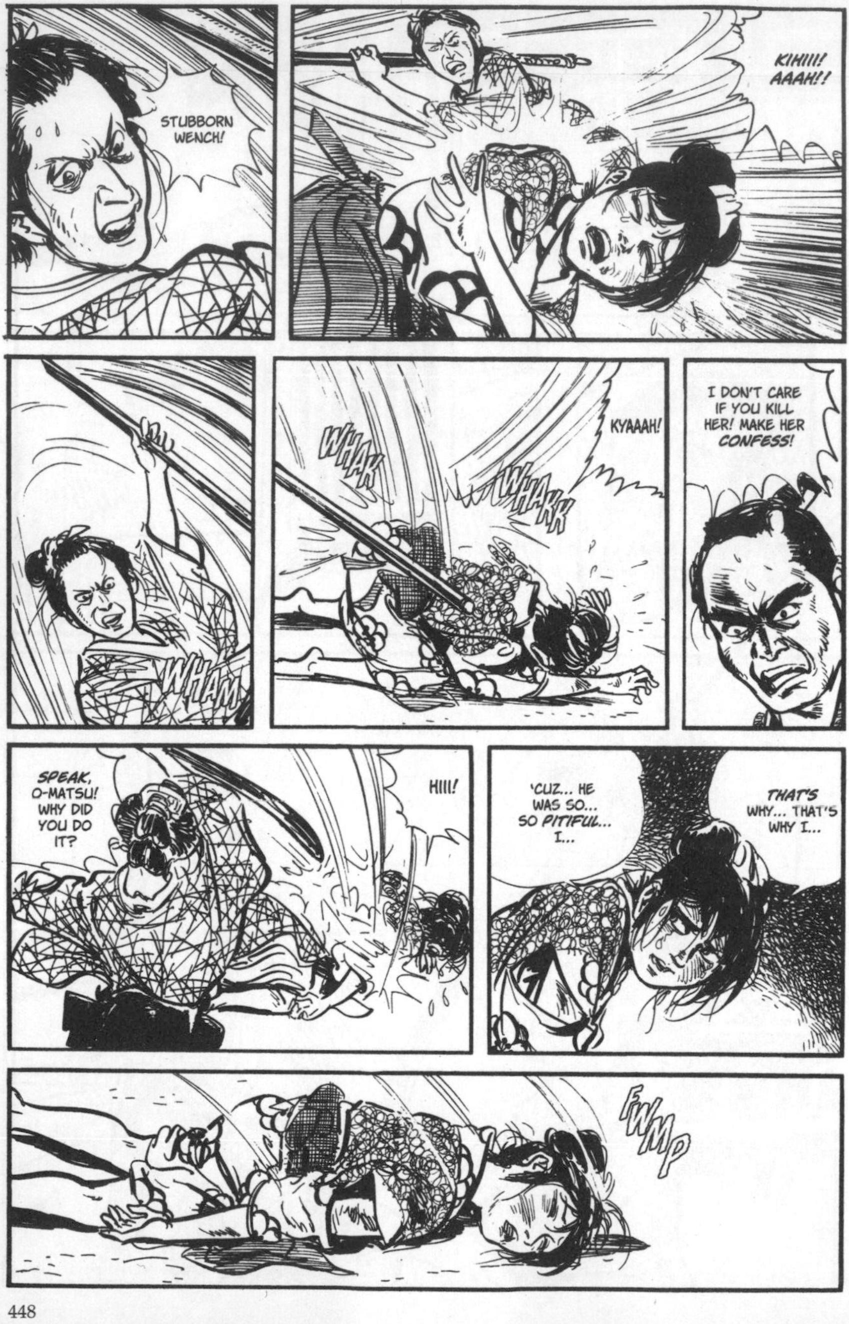
STUBBORN WENCH!
KIHIII! AAAH!!
WHAM
WHAK
WHAKK
KYAAAH!
I DON'T CARE IF YOU KILL HER! MAKE HER CONFESS!
SPEAK, O-MATSU! WHY DID YOU DO IT?
HIII!
'CUZ... HE WAS SO... SO PITIFUL... I...
THAT'S WHY... THAT'S WHY I...
FWMP

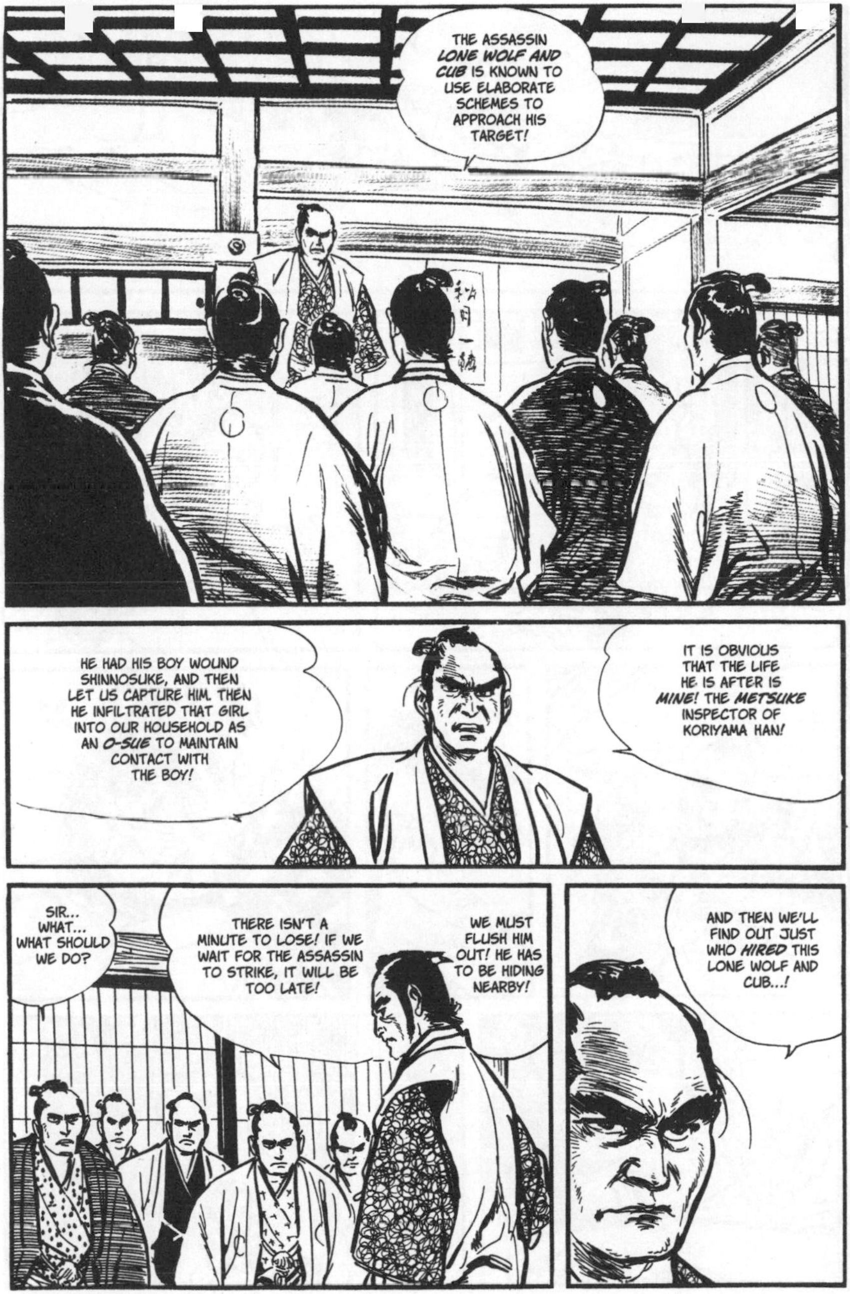
THE ASSASSIN *LONE WOLF AND CUB* IS KNOWN TO USE ELABORATE SCHEMES TO APPROACH HIS TARGET!
HE HAD HIS BOY WOUND SHINNOSUKE, AND THEN LET US CAPTURE HIM. THEN HE INFILTRATED THAT GIRL INTO OUR HOUSEHOLD AS AN *O-SUE* TO MAINTAIN CONTACT WITH THE BOY!
IT IS OBVIOUS THAT THE LIFE HE IS AFTER IS *MINE*! THE *METSUKE* INSPECTOR OF KORIYAMA HAN!
SIR... WHAT... WHAT SHOULD WE DO?
THERE ISN'T A MINUTE TO LOSE! IF WE WAIT FOR THE ASSASSIN TO STRIKE, IT WILL BE TOO LATE!
WE MUST FLUSH HIM OUT! HE HAS TO BE HIDING NEARBY!
AND THEN WE'LL FIND OUT JUST WHO *HIRED* THIS LONE WOLF AND CUB...!

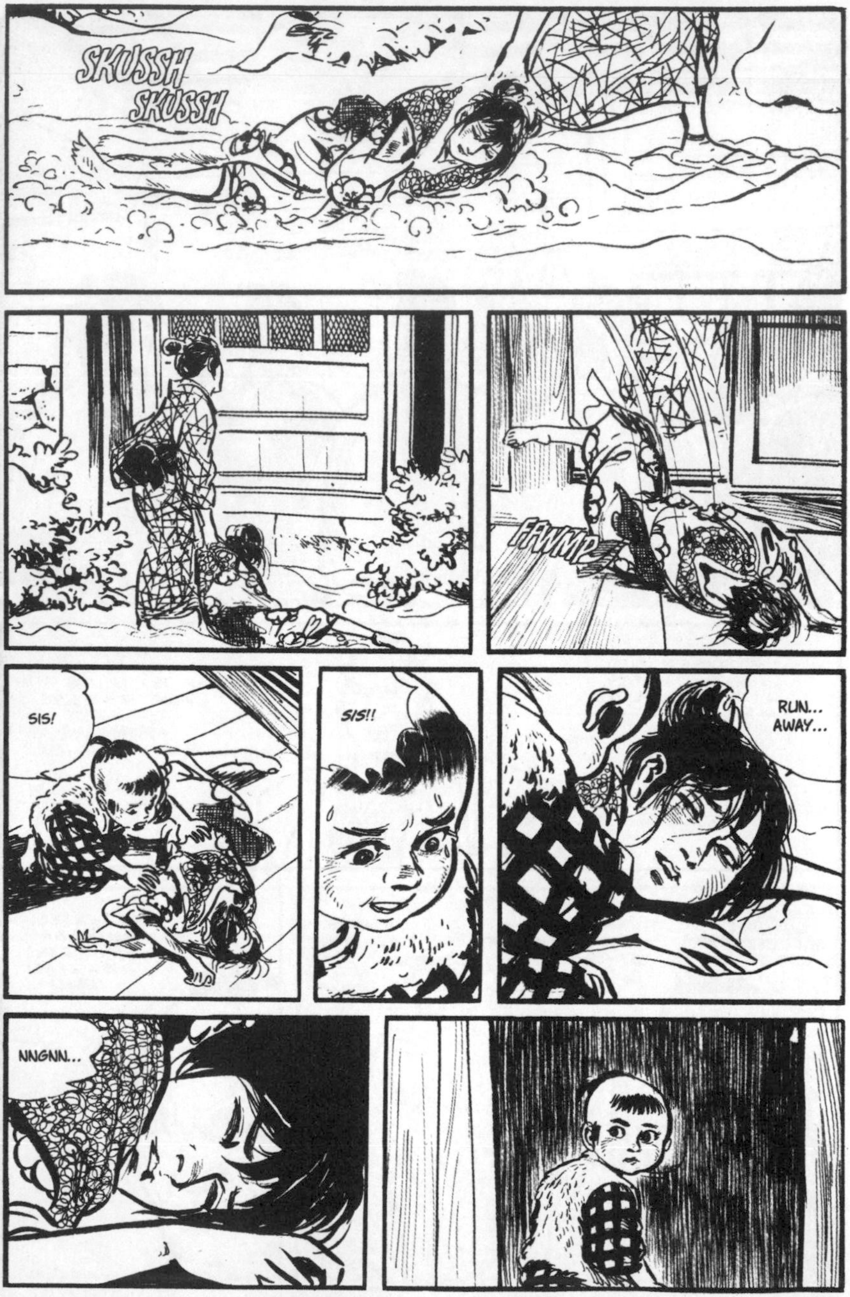
SKUSSH
SKUSSH
FFWMP
SIS!
SIS!!
RUN... AWAY...
NNGNN...

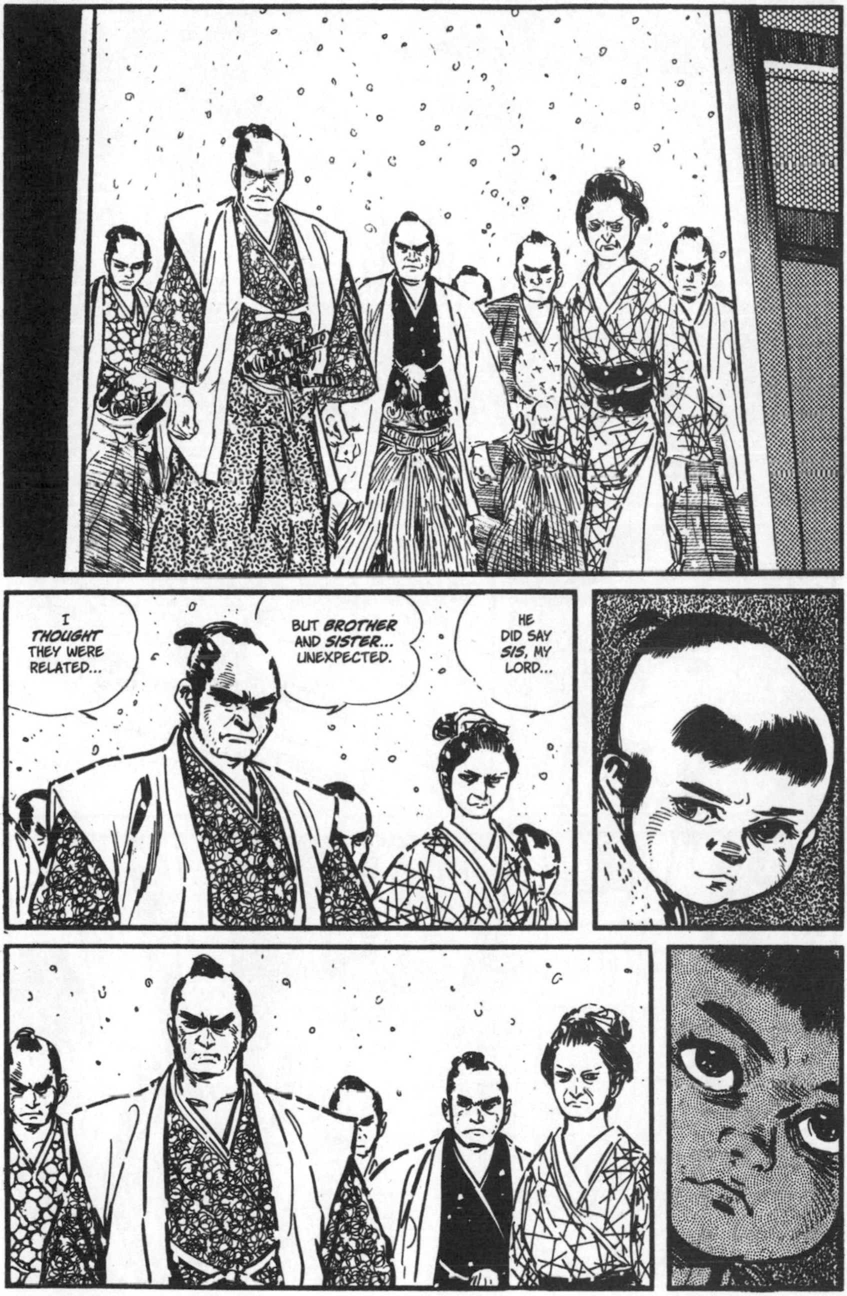
I *THOUGHT* THEY WERE RELATED...
BUT *BROTHER* AND *SISTER*... UNEXPECTED.
HE DID SAY *SIS*, MY LORD...

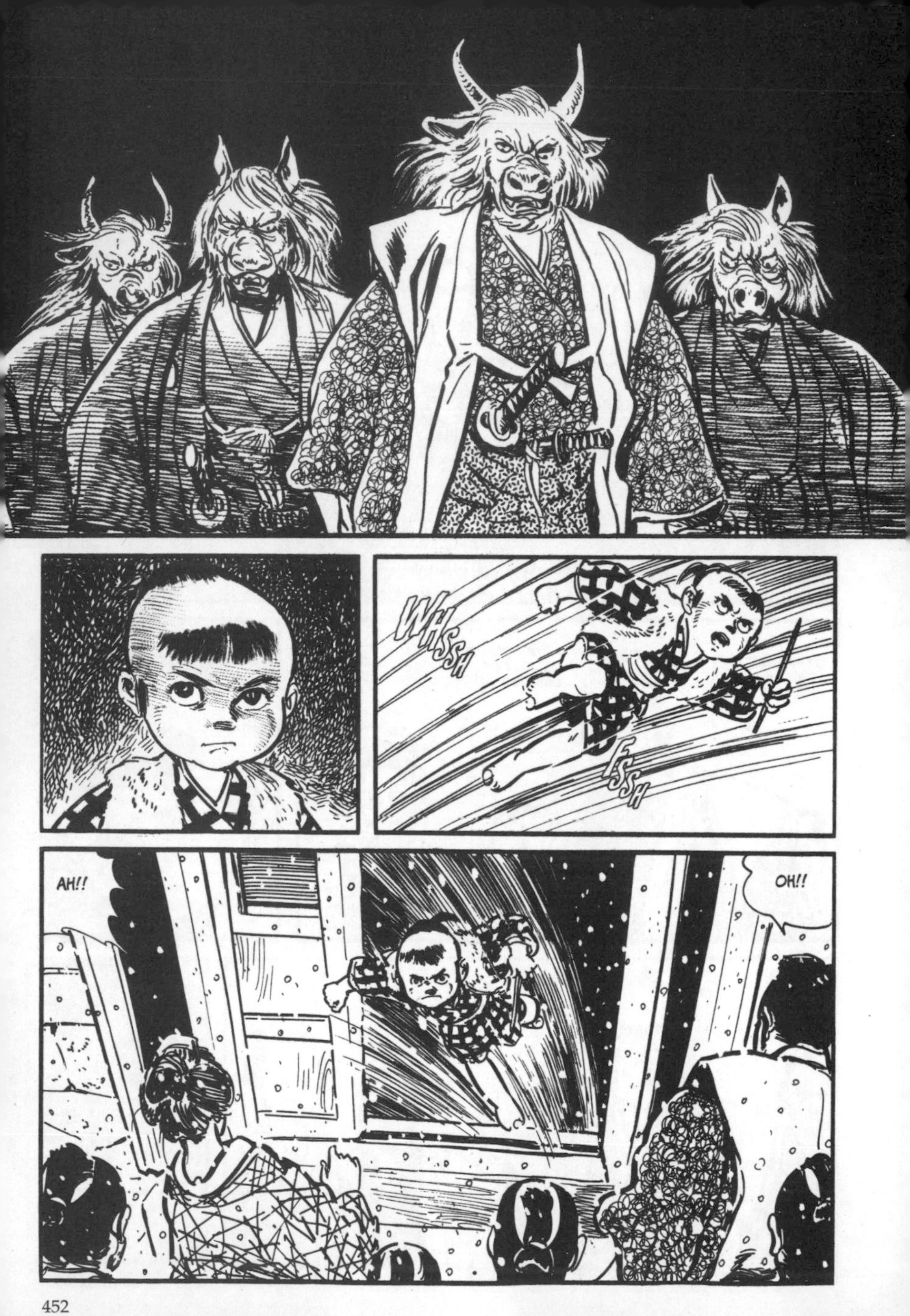
WHSSH
FSSH
OH!!
AH!!

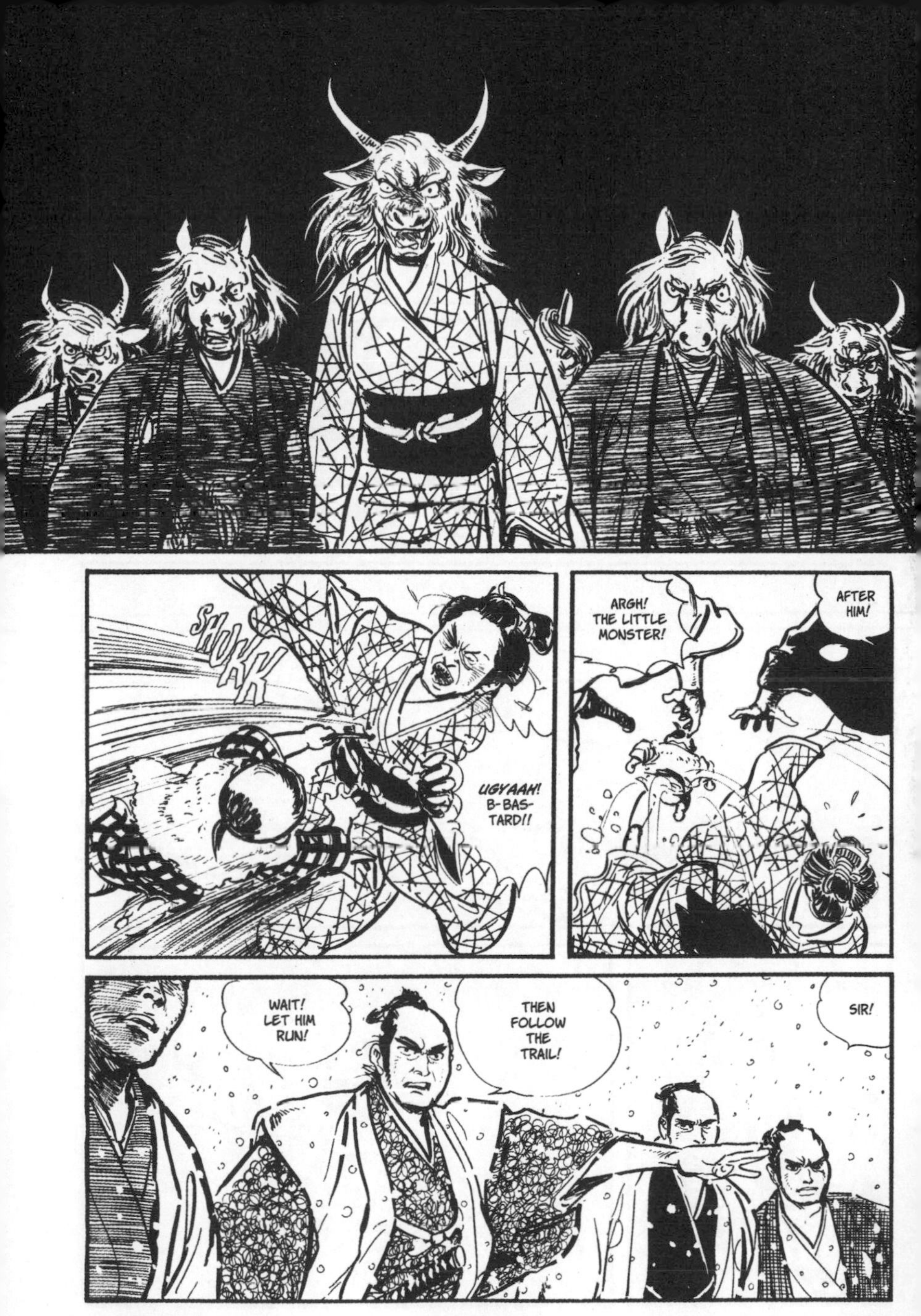
SHUKK
UGYAAH! B-BASTARD!!
ARGH! THE LITTLE MONSTER!
AFTER HIM!
WAIT! LET HIM RUN!
THEN FOLLOW THE TRAIL!
SIR!

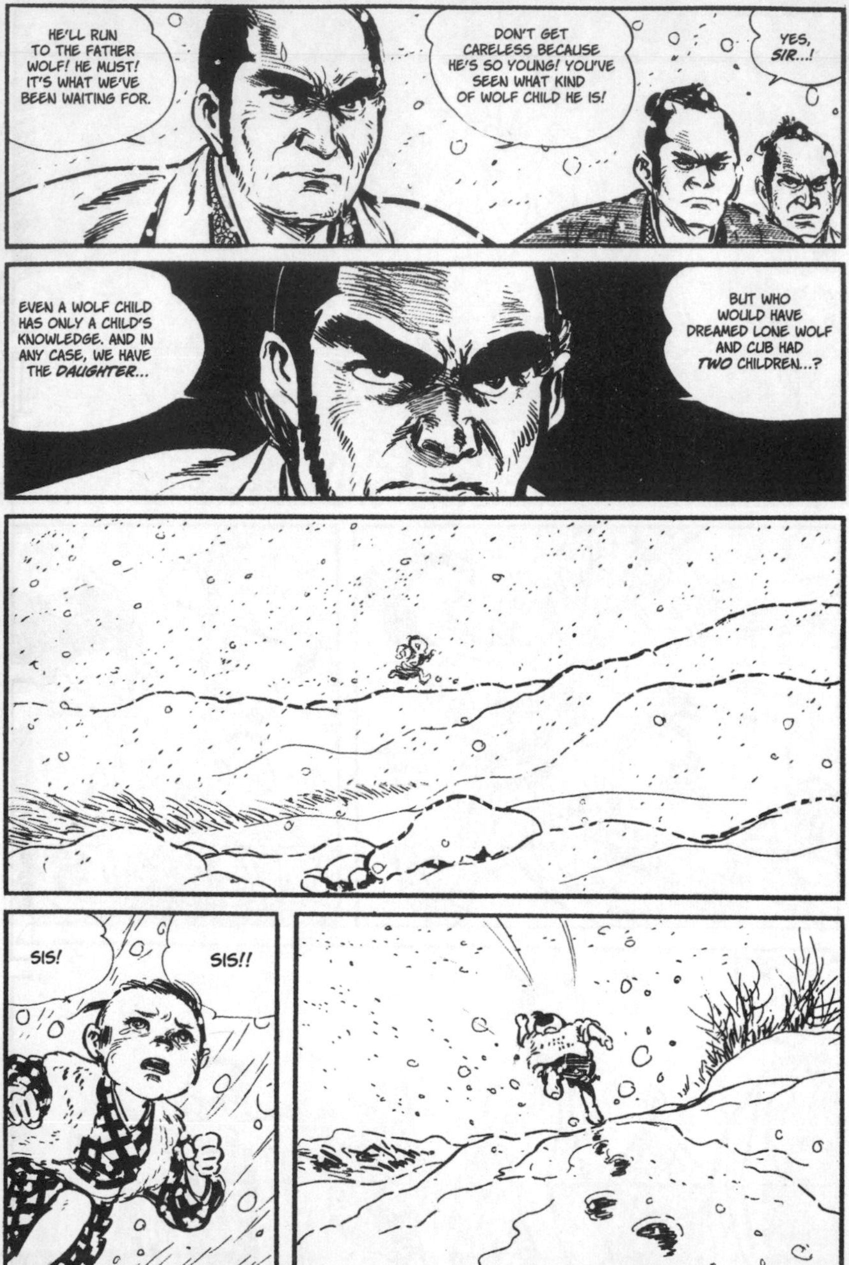
HE'LL RUN TO THE FATHER WOLF! HE MUST! IT'S WHAT WE'VE BEEN WAITING FOR.
DON'T GET CARELESS BECAUSE HE'S SO YOUNG! YOU'VE SEEN WHAT KIND OF WOLF CHILD HE IS!
YES, *SIR*...!
EVEN A WOLF CHILD HAS ONLY A CHILD'S KNOWLEDGE. AND IN ANY CASE, WE HAVE THE *DAUGHTER*...
BUT WHO WOULD HAVE DREAMED LONE WOLF AND CUB HAD *TWO* CHILDREN...?
SIS!
SIS!!

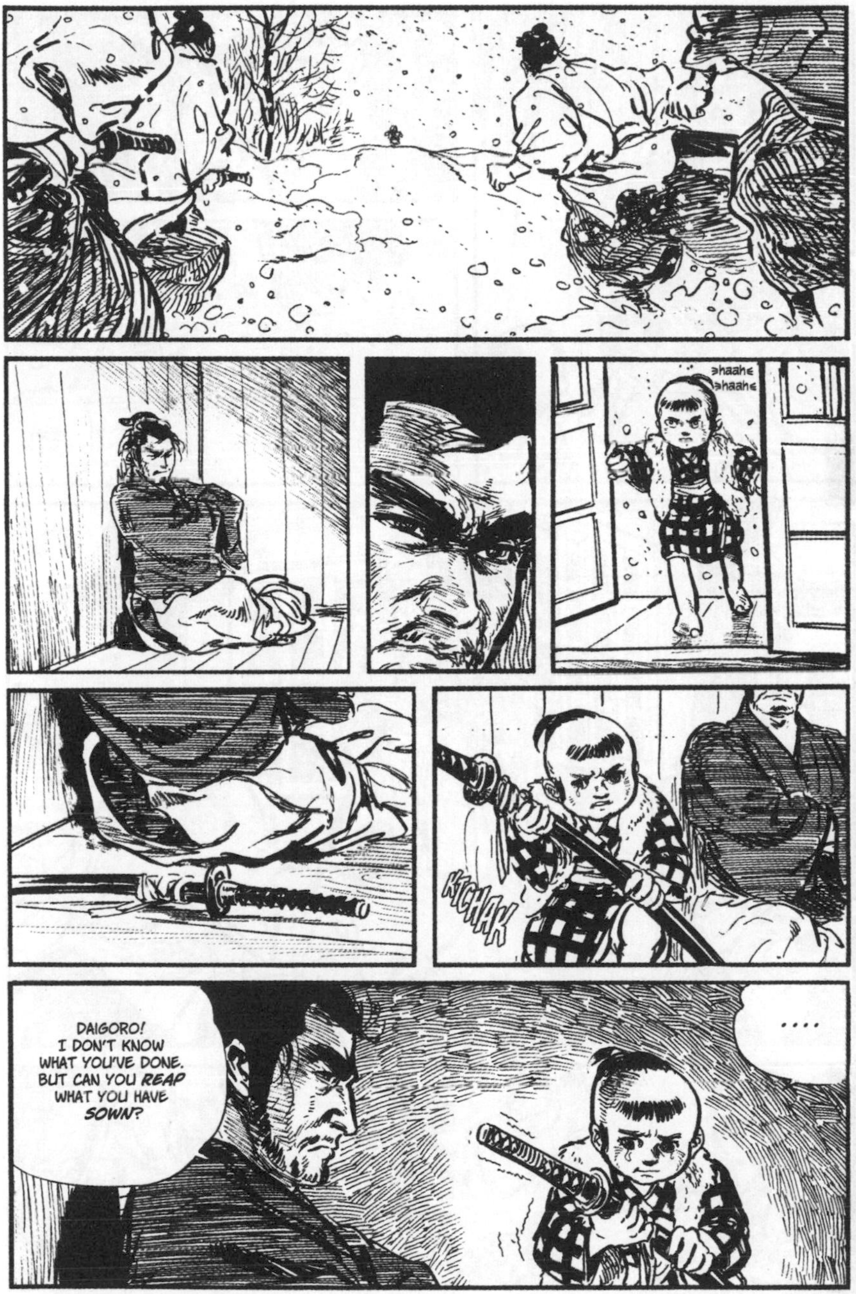
haah
haah
KITCHAK
....
DAIGORO! I DON'T KNOW WHAT YOU'VE DONE. BUT CAN YOU *REAP* WHAT YOU HAVE *SOWN*?

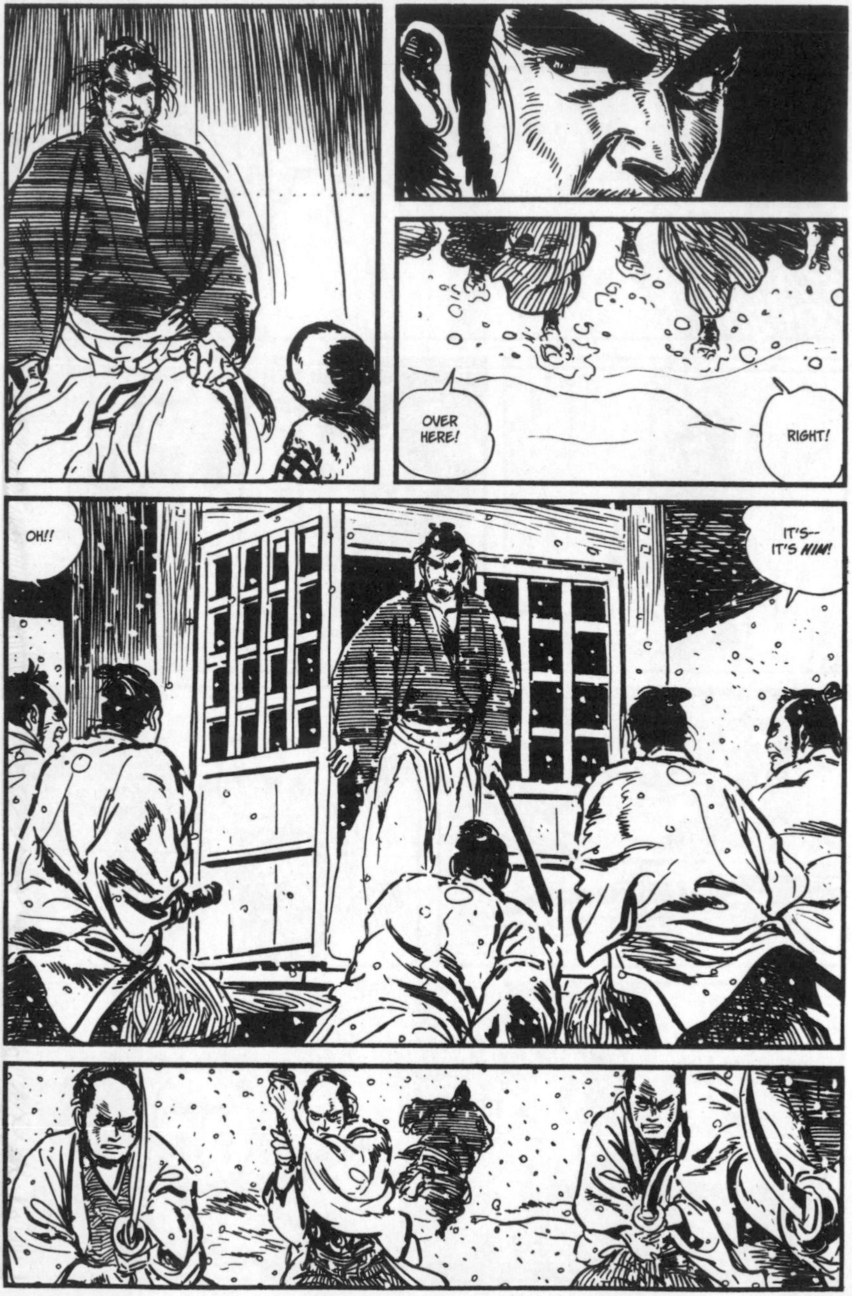
OVER HERE!
RIGHT!
OH!!
IT'S-- IT'S *HIM!*

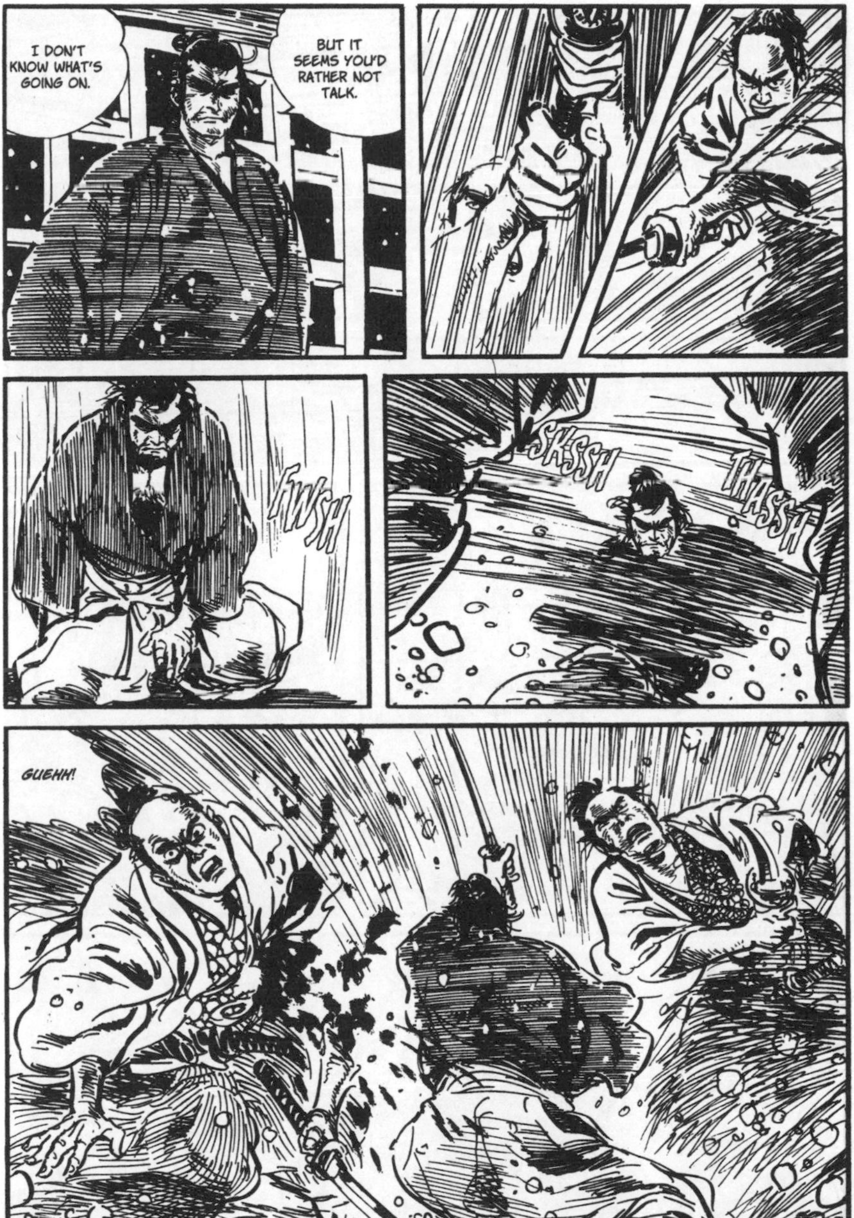
I DON'T KNOW WHAT'S GOING ON.
BUT IT SEEMS YOU'D RATHER NOT TALK.
FWSH
SKSSH
THASSH
GUEHH!

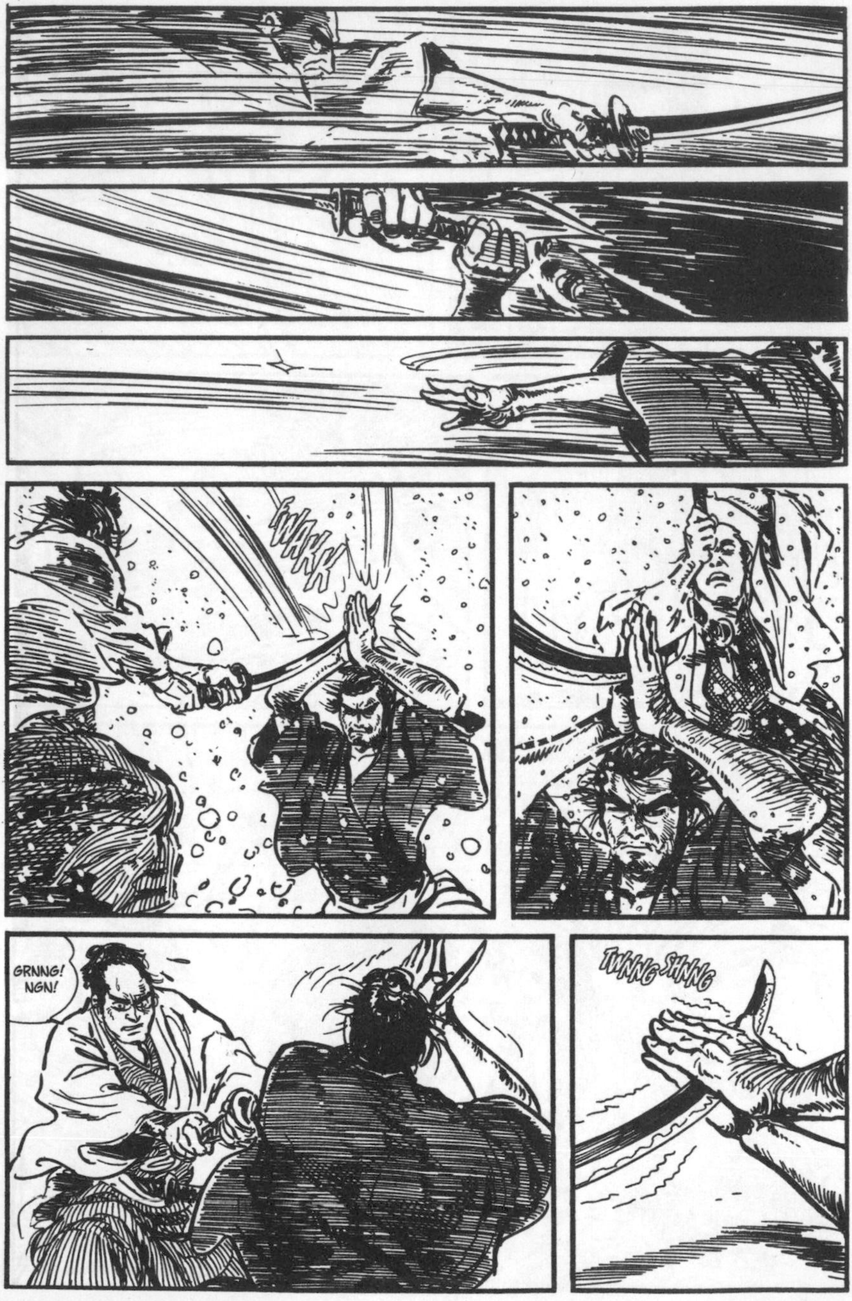
FWAKK
TWNNG SHNNG
GRNNG! NGN!

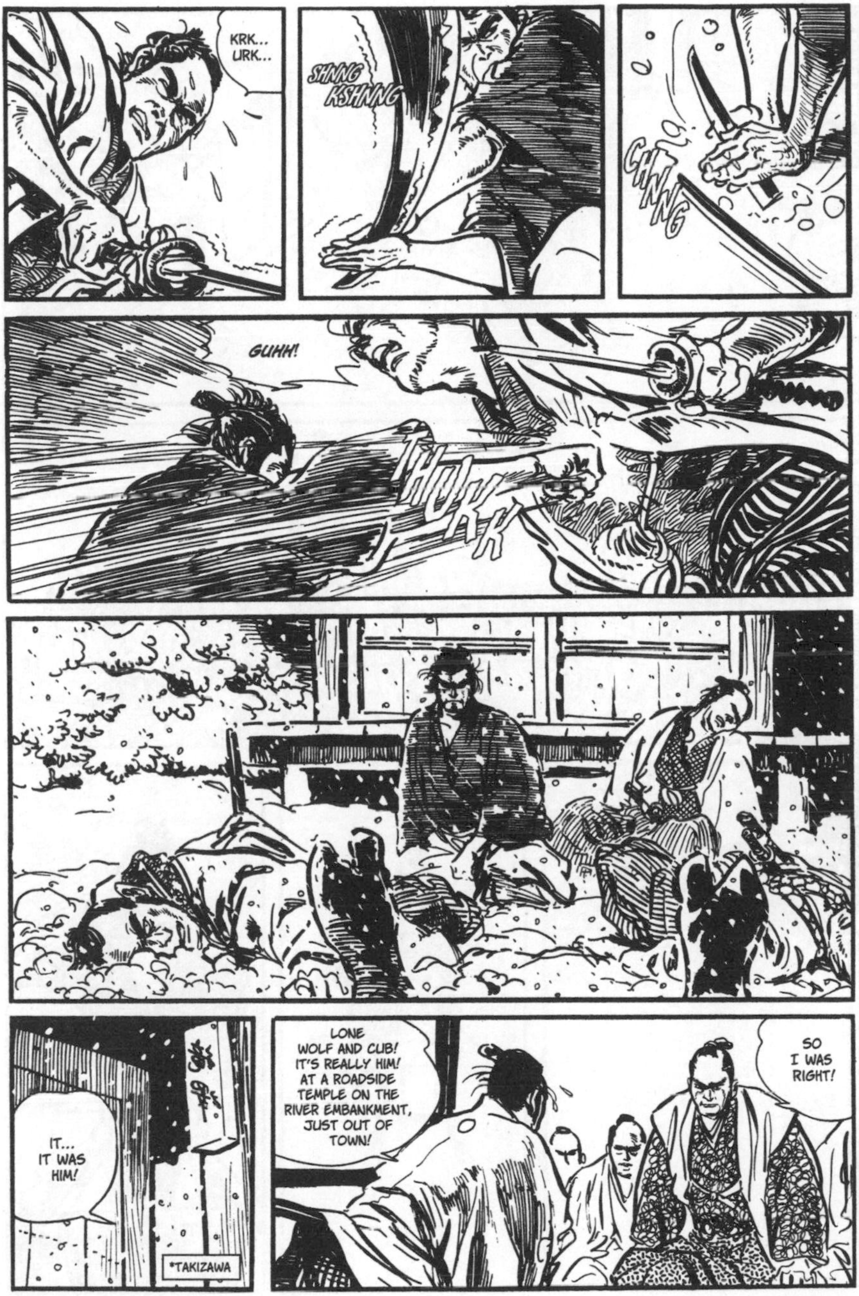
KRK... URK...
SHNNG KSHNNG
CHNNG
GUHH!
THUKK
IT... IT WAS HIM!
*TAKIZAWA
LONE WOLF AND CUB! IT'S REALLY HIM! AT A ROADSIDE TEMPLE ON THE RIVER EMBANKMENT, JUST OUT OF TOWN!
SO I WAS RIGHT!

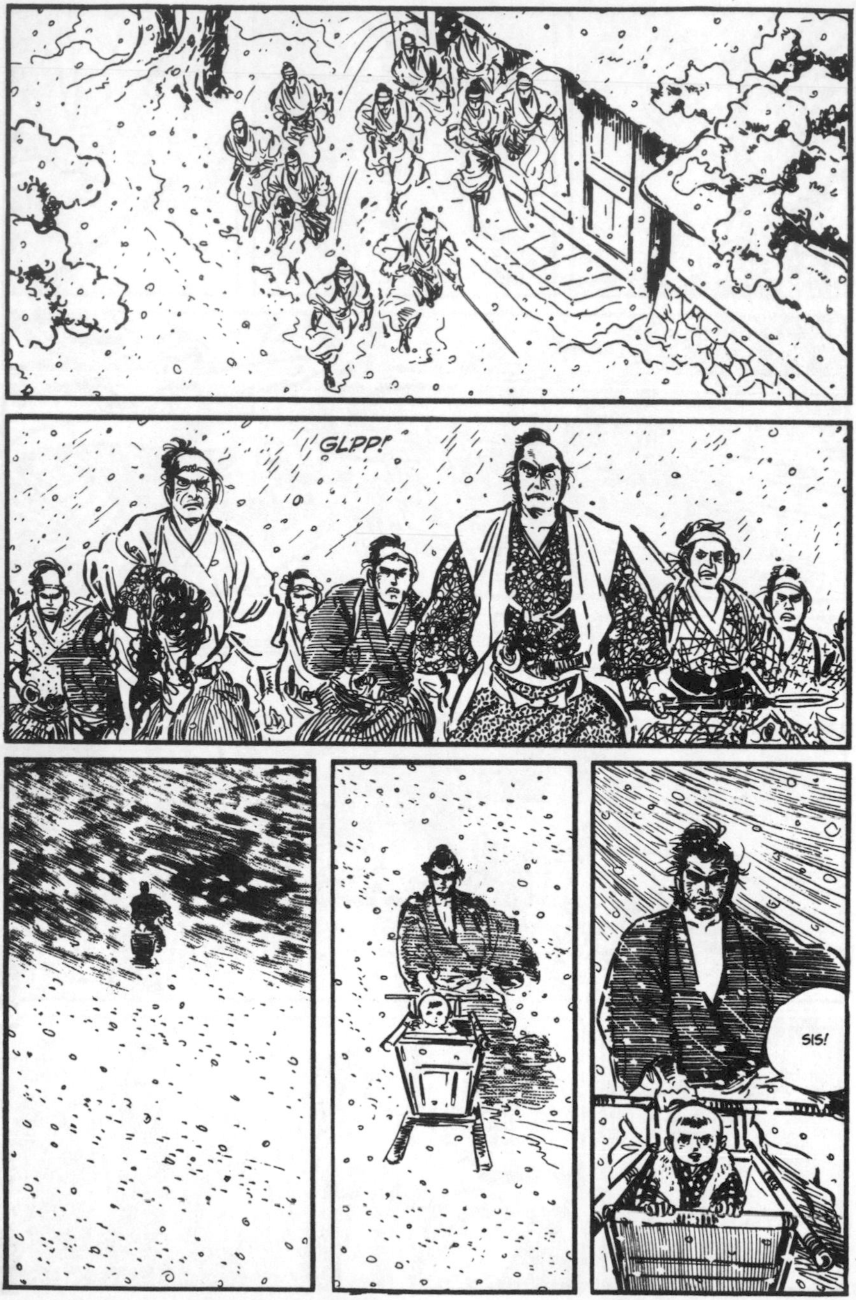
GLPP!
SIS!

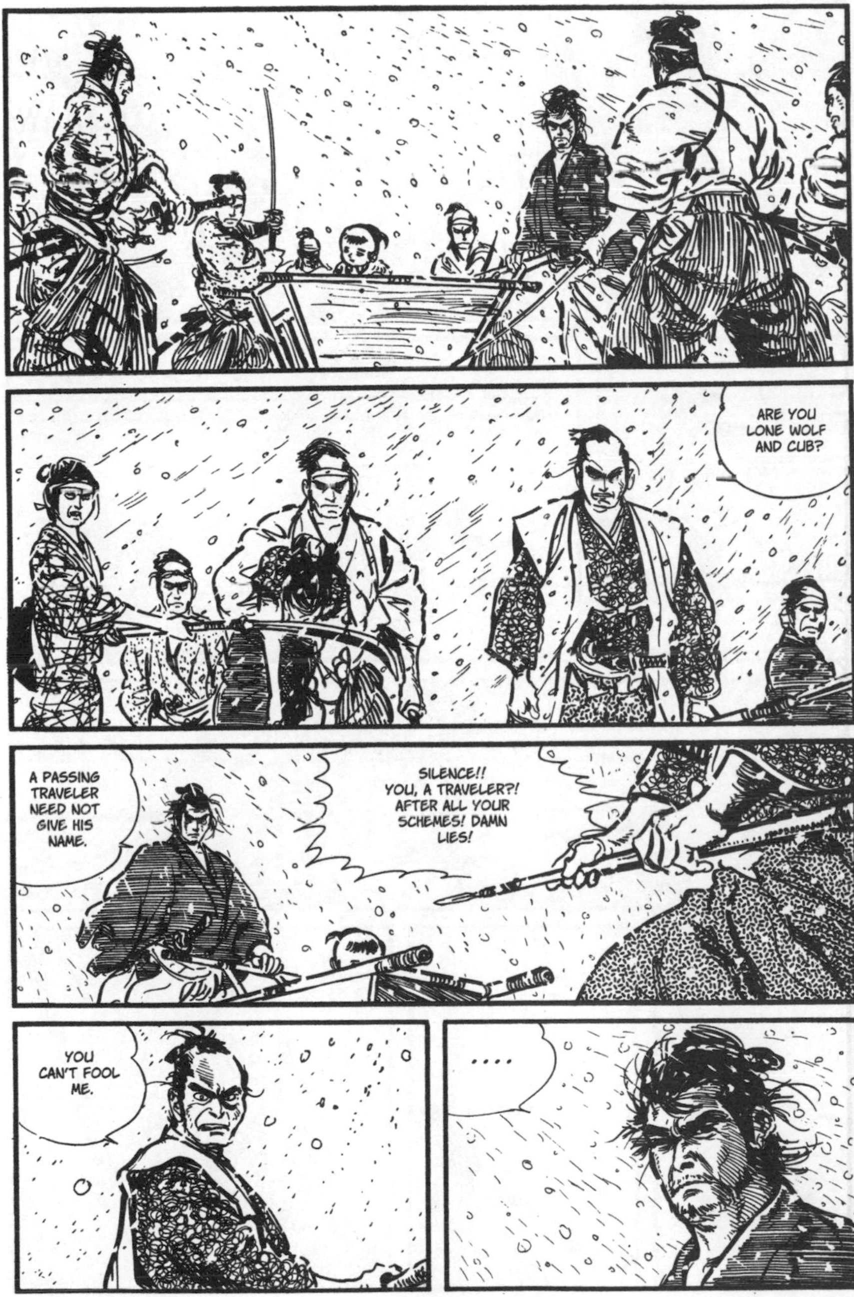
ARE YOU LONE WOLF AND CUB?
A PASSING TRAVELER NEED NOT GIVE HIS NAME.
SILENCE!! YOU, A TRAVELER?! AFTER ALL YOUR SCHEMES! DAMN LIES!
YOU CAN'T FOOL ME.
....

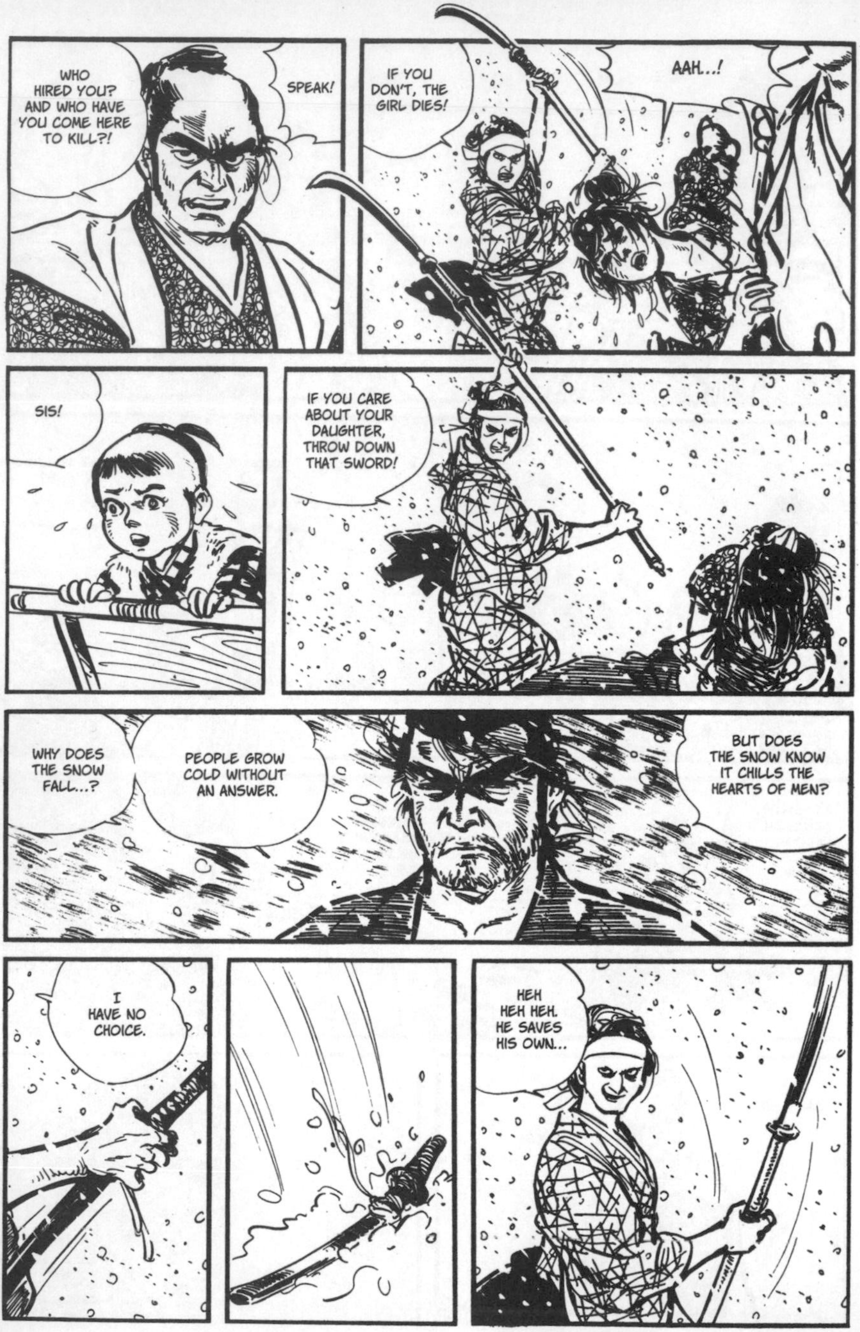
WHO HIRED YOU? AND WHO HAVE YOU COME HERE TO KILL?!
SPEAK!
IF YOU DON'T, THE GIRL DIES!
AAH...!
SIS!
IF YOU CARE ABOUT YOUR DAUGHTER, THROW DOWN THAT SWORD!
WHY DOES THE SNOW FALL...?
PEOPLE GROW COLD WITHOUT AN ANSWER.
BUT DOES THE SNOW KNOW IT CHILLS THE HEARTS OF MEN?
I HAVE NO CHOICE.
HEH HEH HEH. HE SAVES HIS OWN...

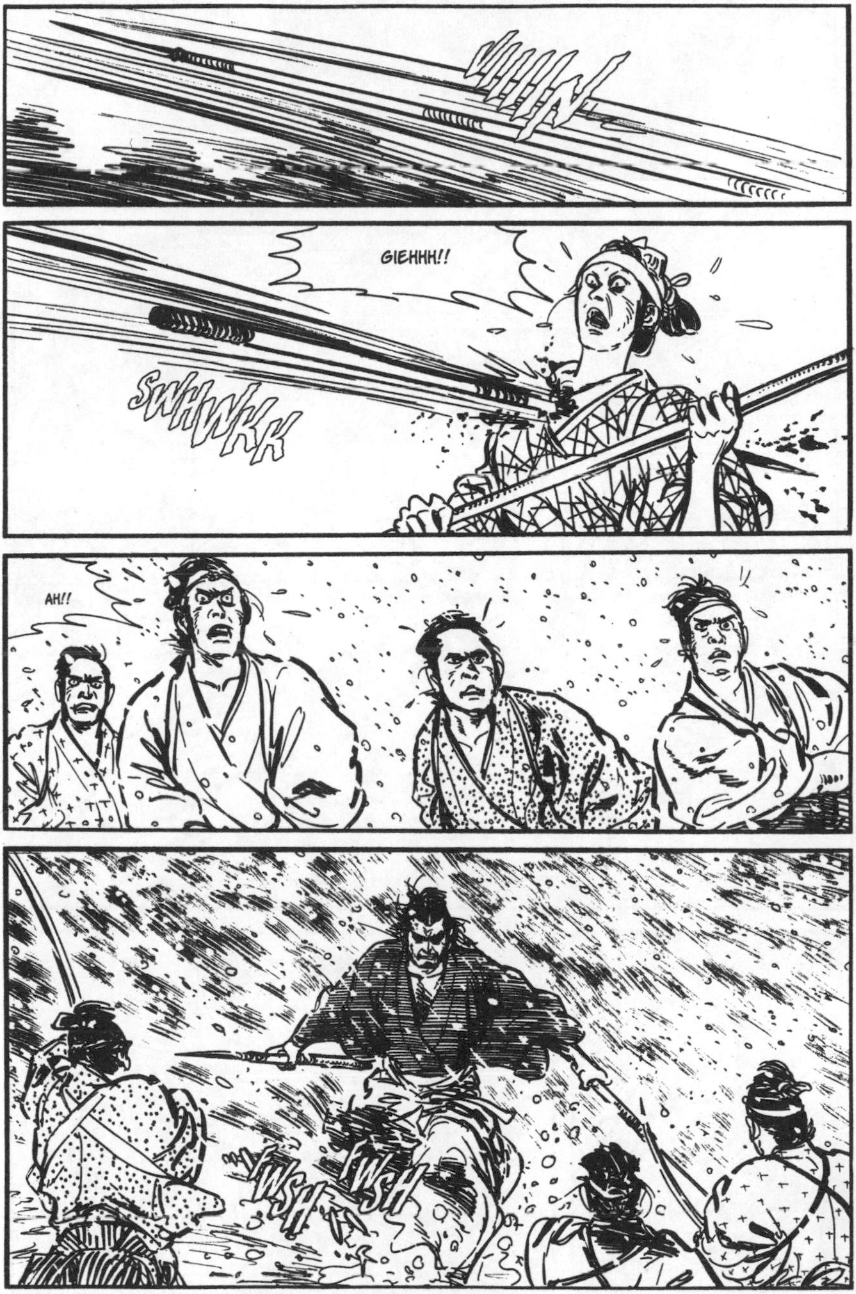
VHHN
GIEHHH!!
SWHNKK
AH!!
FWSH
FWSH

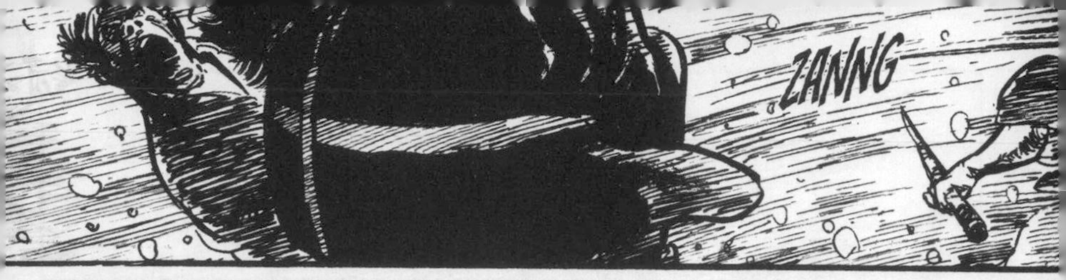
ZANNG

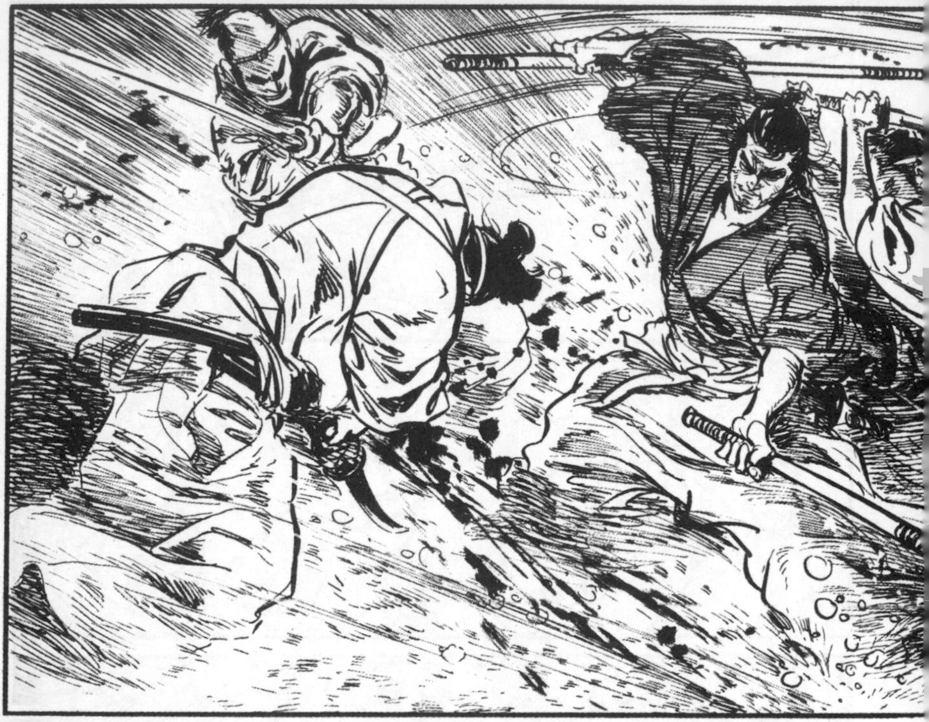

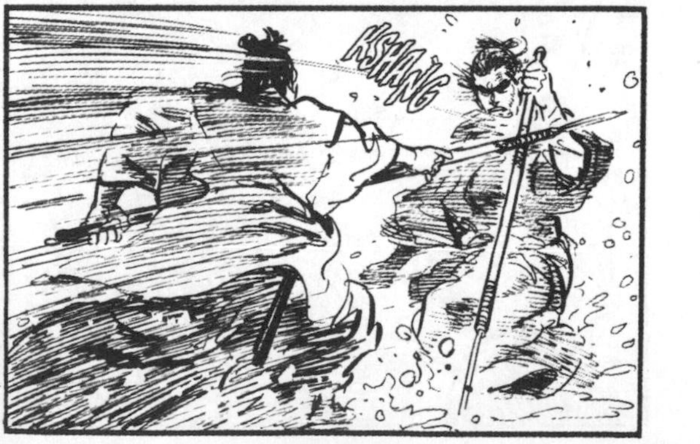
KSHANG

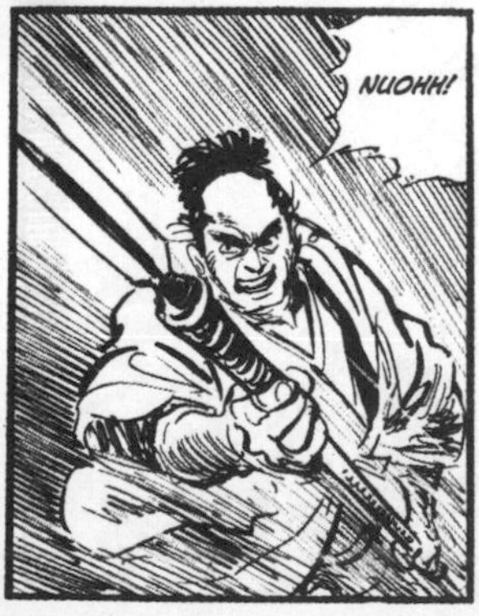
NUOHH!

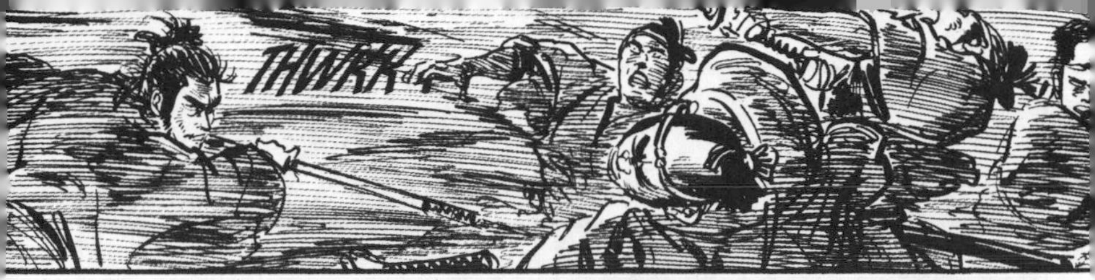
THWRR
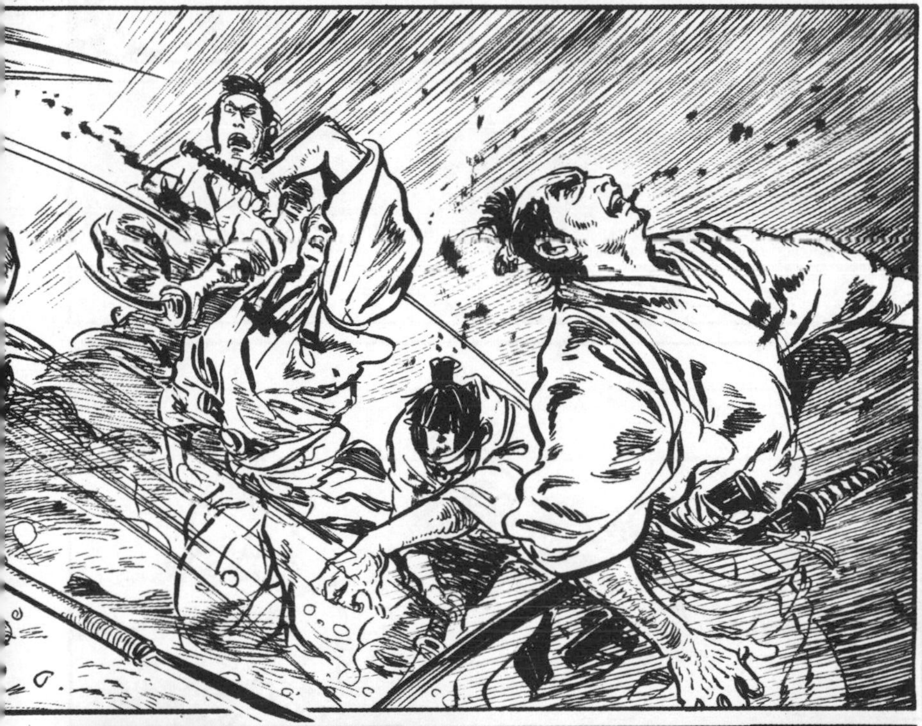
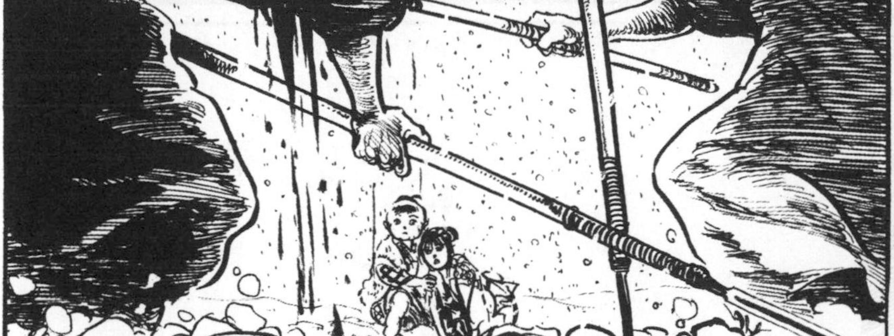

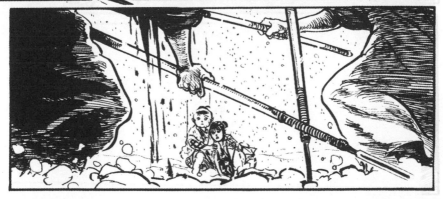

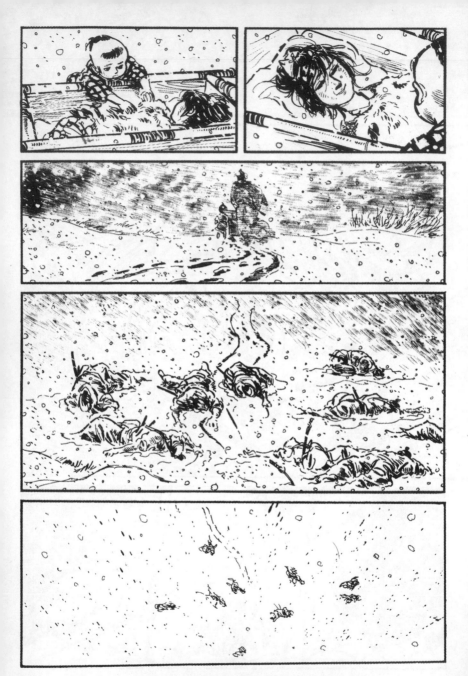

子連れ狼

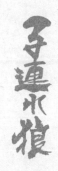

The Gateless Barrier

13

ON THE GREAT WAY
THERE IS NO GATE
BUT A THOUSAND PATHS
TO CHOOSE FROM.
FIND THE GATE
AND YOU MAY WALK ALONE
BETWEEN HEAVEN AND EARTH

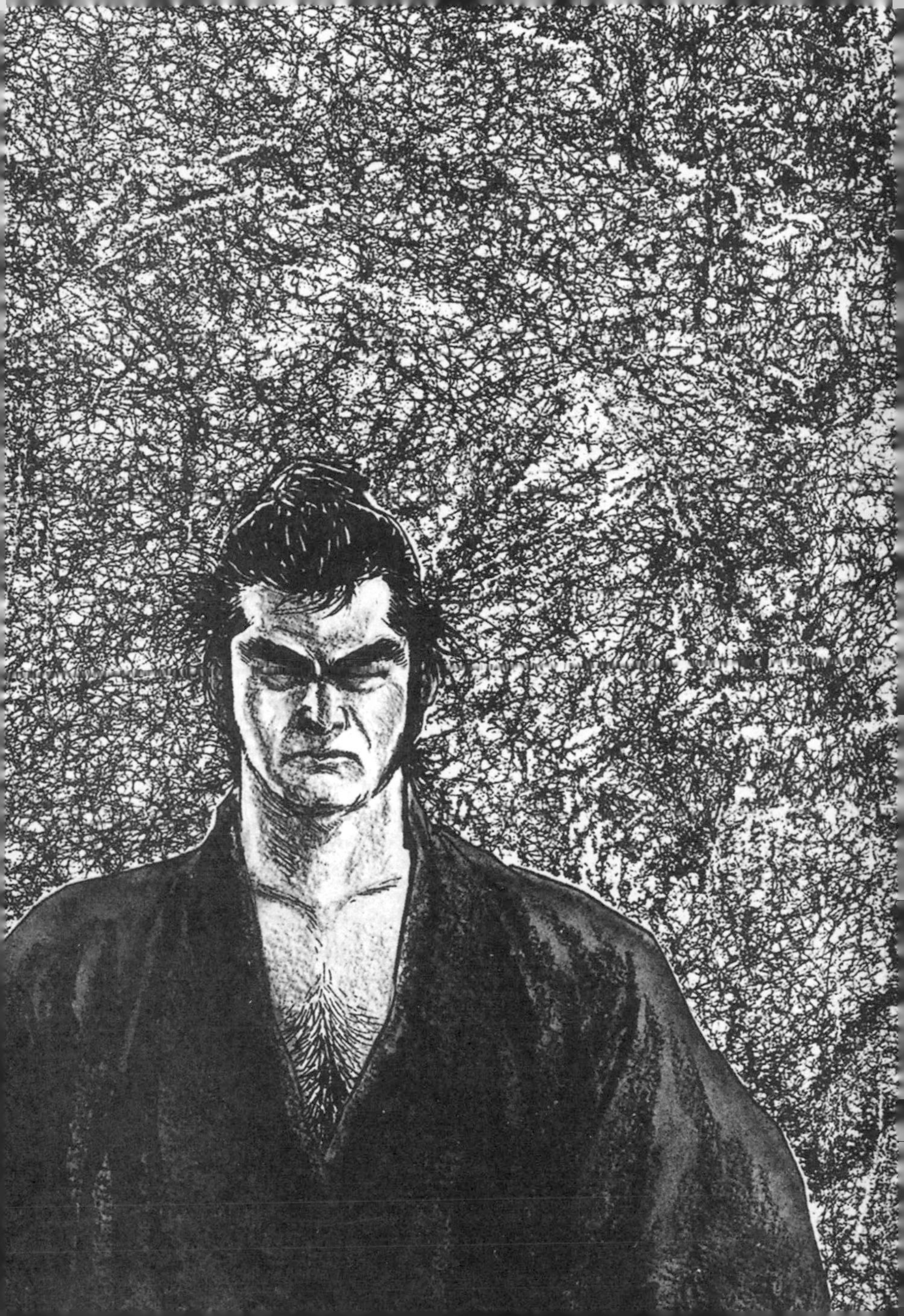

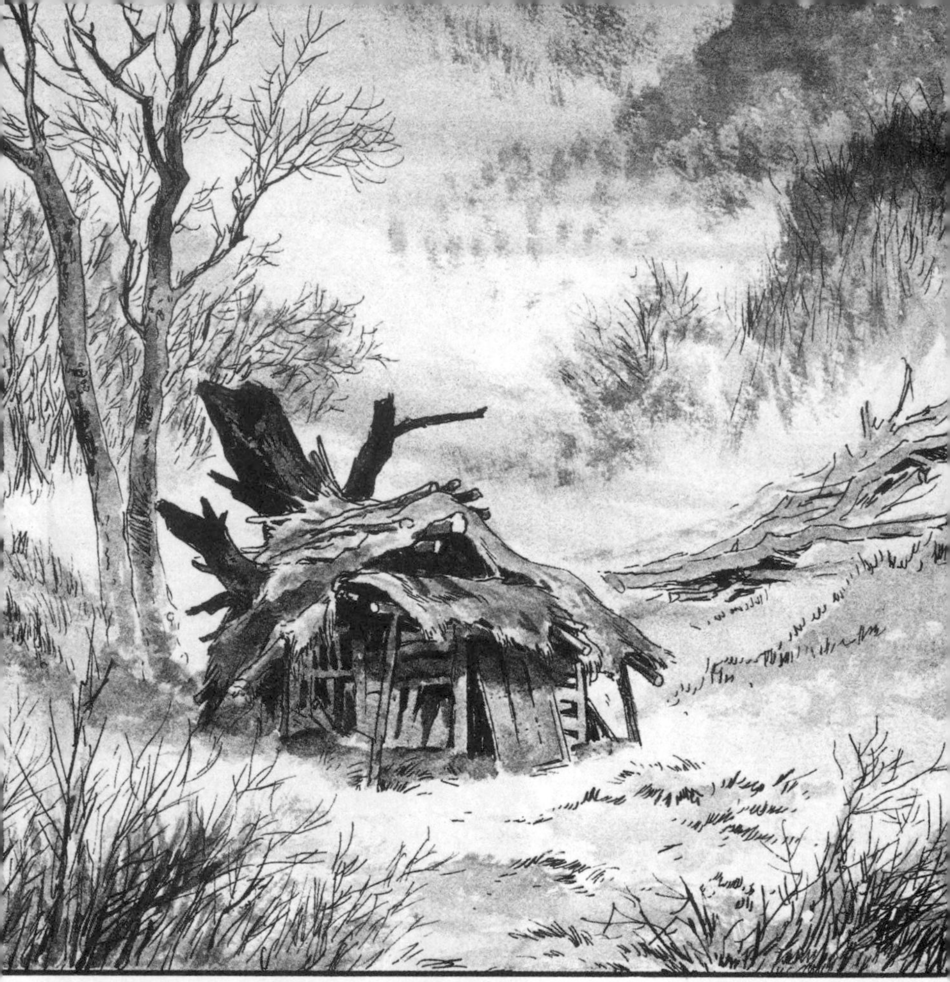

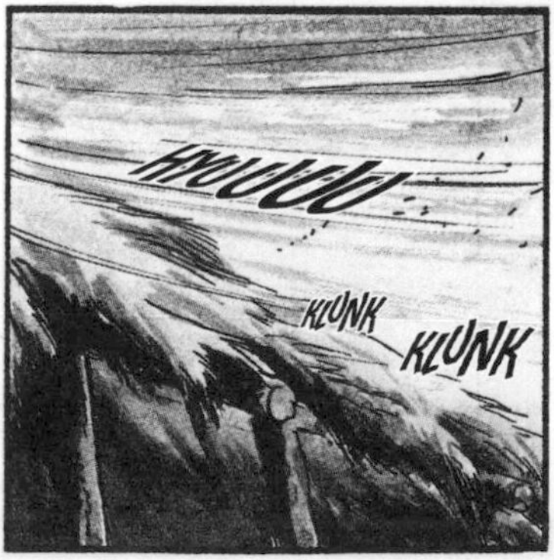
HYUUUU
KLUNK
KLUNK

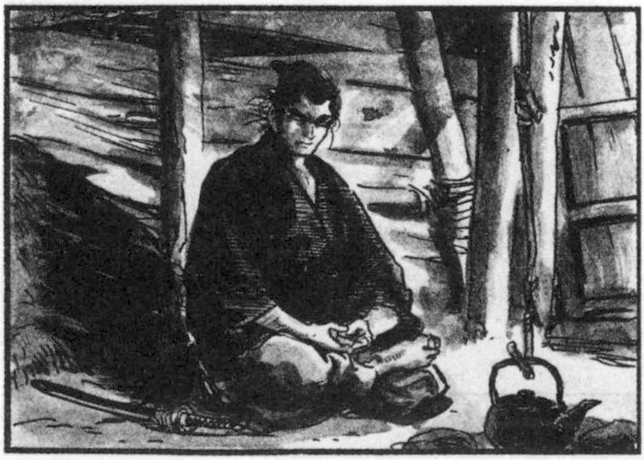

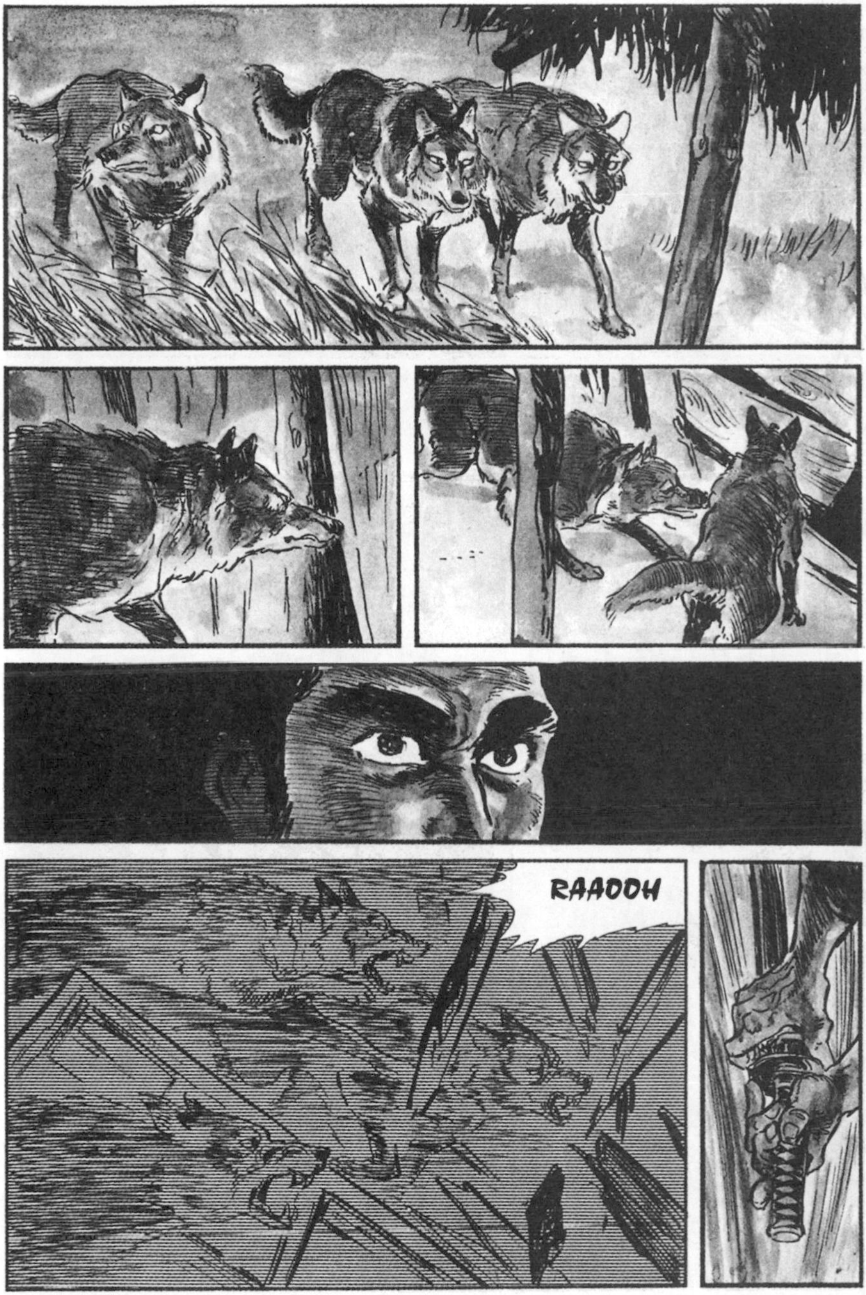
RAAOOH

SKRASSH FSSH

GROAN

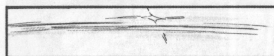

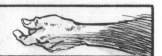

KRSSH
KRSSH
SHLRK
SHLKK

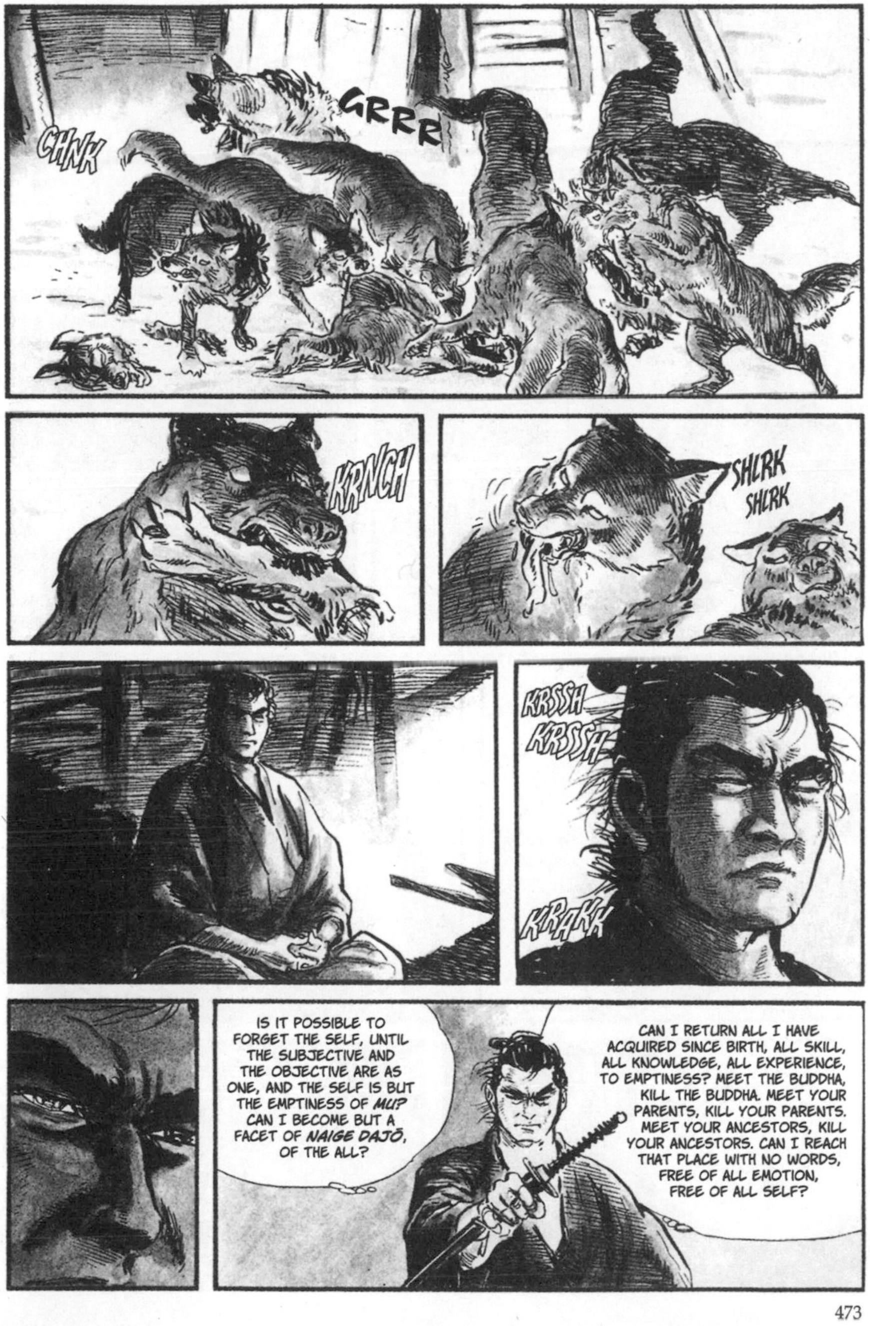
CHNK
GRRR
KRNCH
SHLRK
SHLRK
KRSSH
KRSSH
KRAKK
IS IT POSSIBLE TO FORGET THE SELF, UNTIL THE SUBJECTIVE AND THE OBJECTIVE ARE AS ONE, AND THE SELF IS BUT THE EMPTINESS OF *MU*? CAN I BECOME BUT A FACET OF *NAIGE DAJŌ*, OF THE ALL?
CAN I RETURN ALL I HAVE ACQUIRED SINCE BIRTH, ALL SKILL, ALL KNOWLEDGE, ALL EXPERIENCE, TO EMPTINESS? MEET THE BUDDHA, KILL THE BUDDHA. MEET YOUR PARENTS, KILL YOUR PARENTS. MEET YOUR ANCESTORS, KILL YOUR ANCESTORS. CAN I REACH THAT PLACE WITH NO WORDS, FREE OF ALL EMOTION, FREE OF ALL SELF?

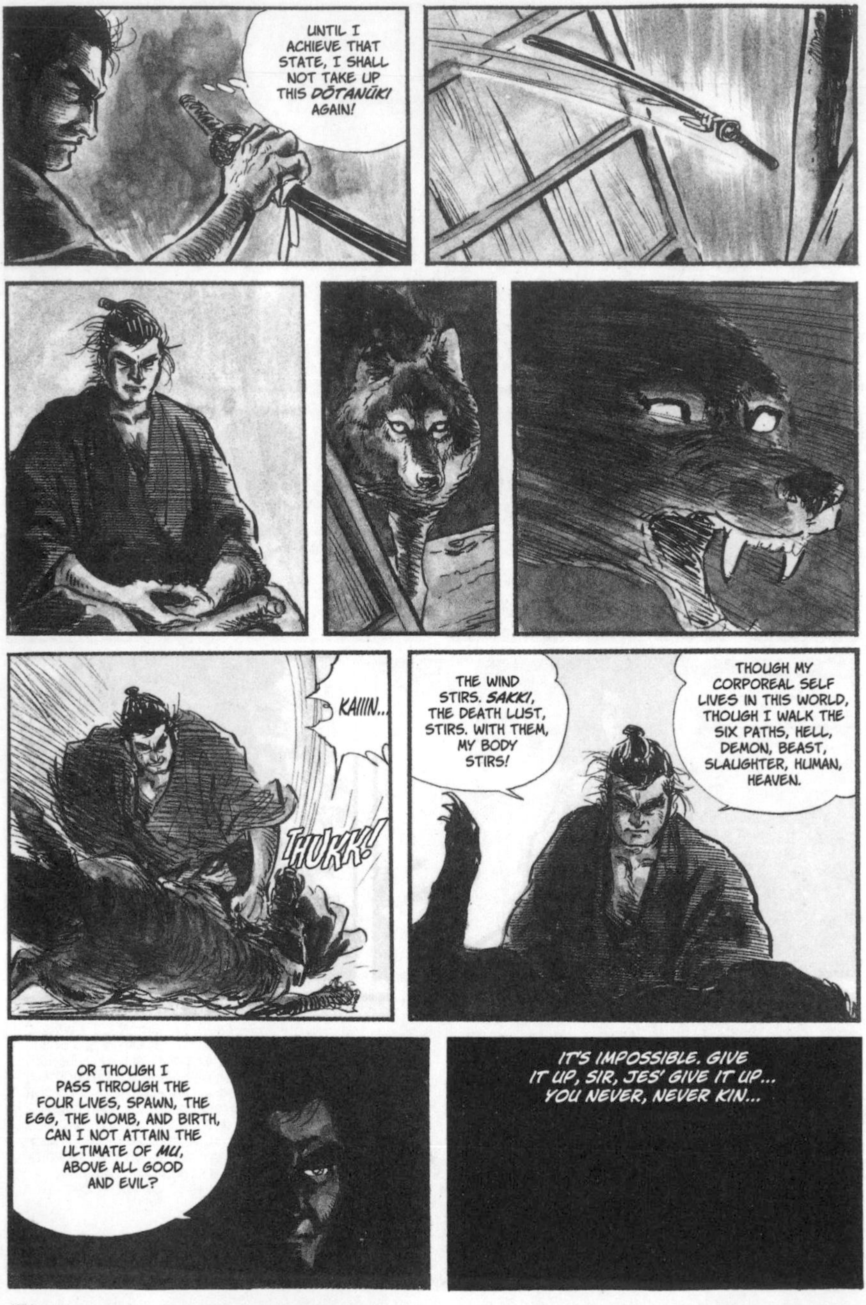
UNTIL I ACHIEVE THAT STATE, I SHALL NOT TAKE UP THIS *DŌTANŪKI* AGAIN!
KAIIIN...
THUKK!
THE WIND STIRS. *SAKKI*, THE DEATH LUST, STIRS. WITH THEM, MY BODY STIRS!
THOUGH MY CORPOREAL SELF LIVES IN THIS WORLD, THOUGH I WALK THE SIX PATHS, HELL, DEMON, BEAST, SLAUGHTER, HUMAN, HEAVEN.
OR THOUGH I PASS THROUGH THE FOUR LIVES, SPAWN, THE EGG, THE WOMB, AND BIRTH, CAN I NOT ATTAIN THE ULTIMATE OF *MU*, ABOVE ALL GOOD AND EVIL?
IT'S IMPOSSIBLE. GIVE IT UP, SIR, JES' GIVE IT UP... YOU NEVER, NEVER KIN...

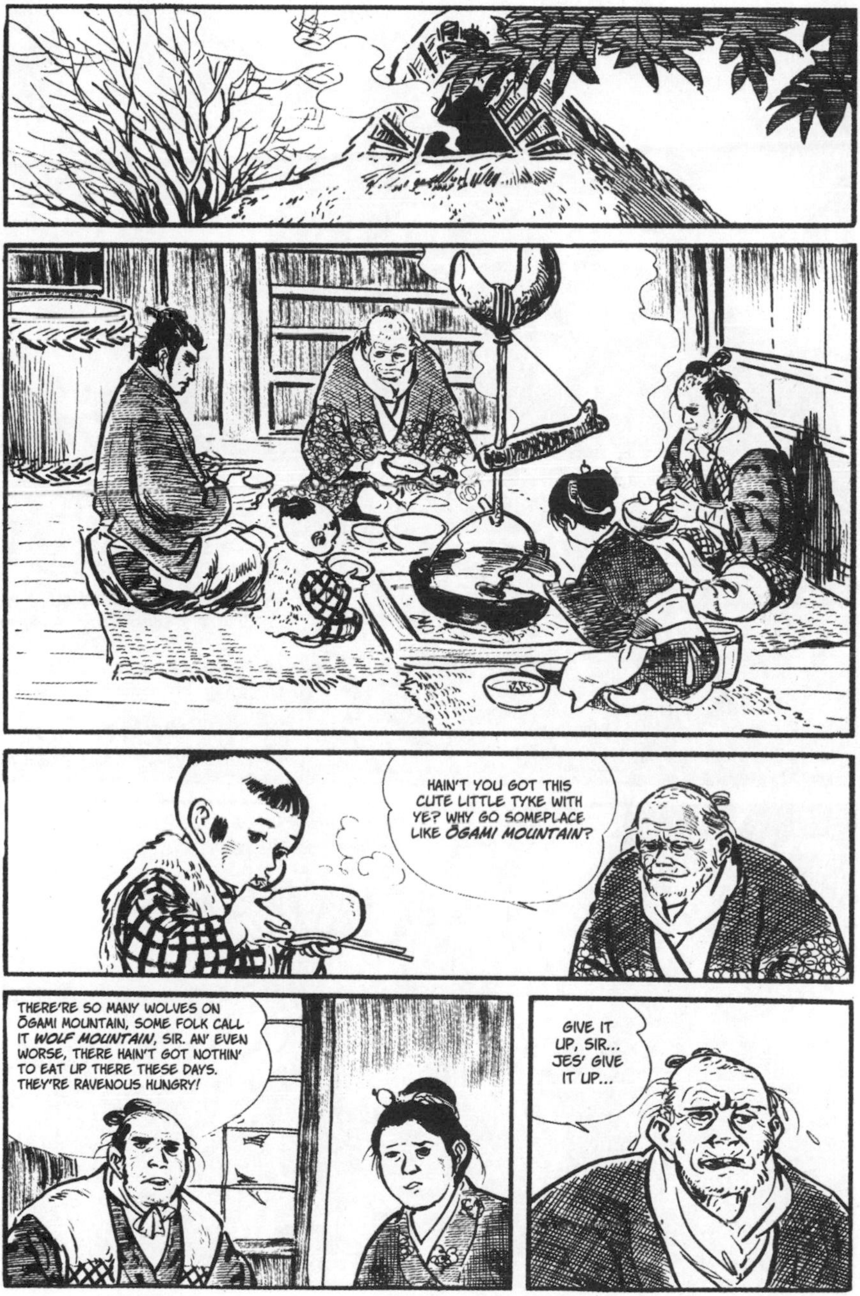
HAIN'T YOU GOT THIS CUTE LITTLE TYKE WITH YE? WHY GO SOMEPLACE LIKE ŌGAMI MOUNTAIN?
THERE'RE SO MANY WOLVES ON ŌGAMI MOUNTAIN, SOME FOLK CALL IT WOLF MOUNTAIN, SIR. AN' EVEN WORSE, THERE HAIN'T GOT NOTHIN' TO EAT UP THERE THESE DAYS. THEY'RE RAVENOUS HUNGRY!
GIVE IT UP, SIR... JES' GIVE IT UP...

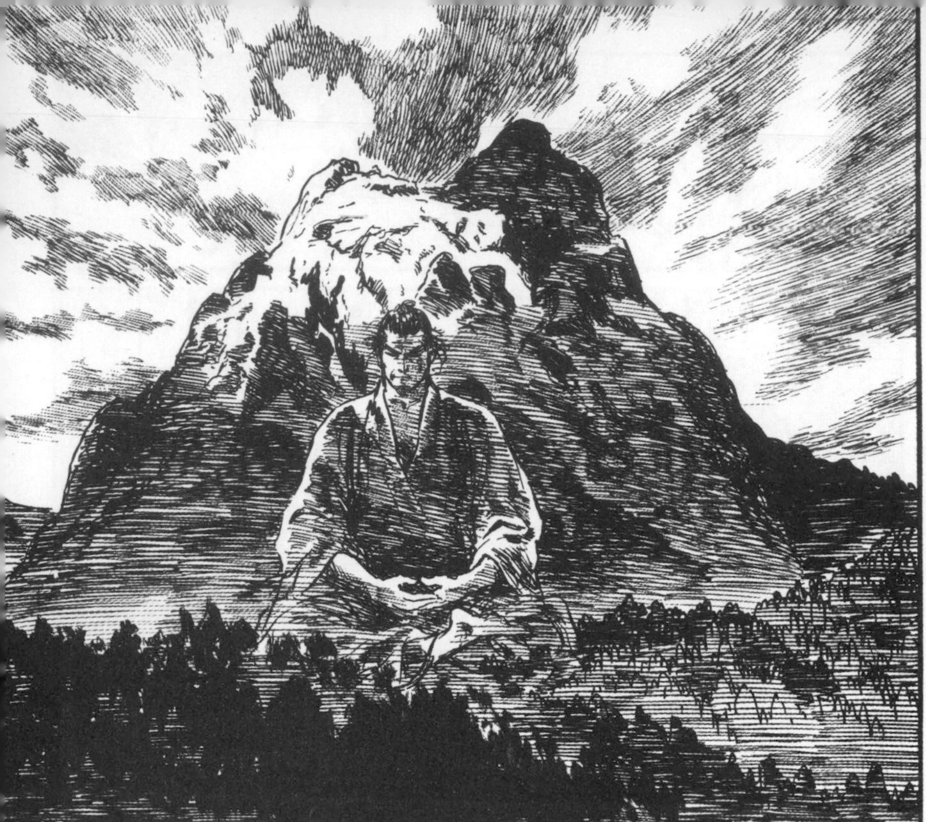
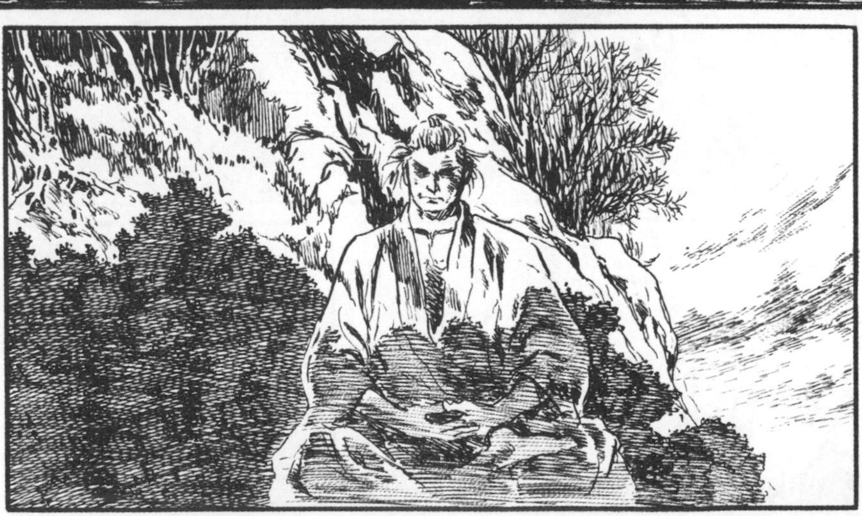

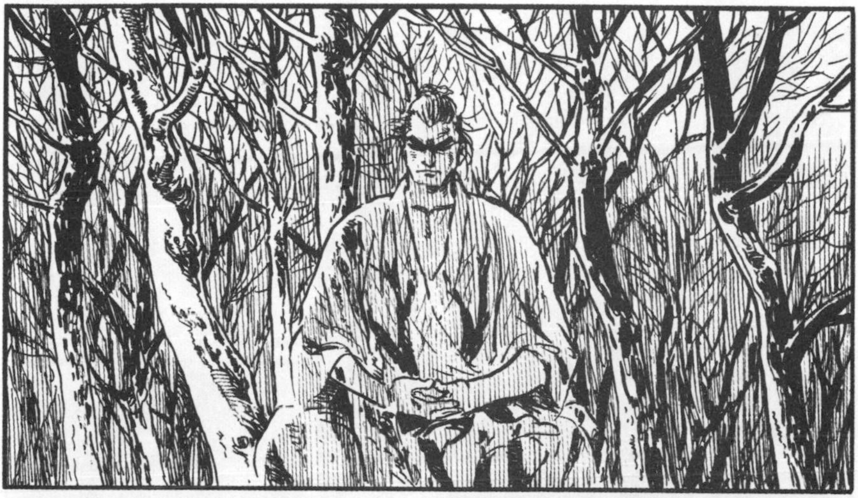
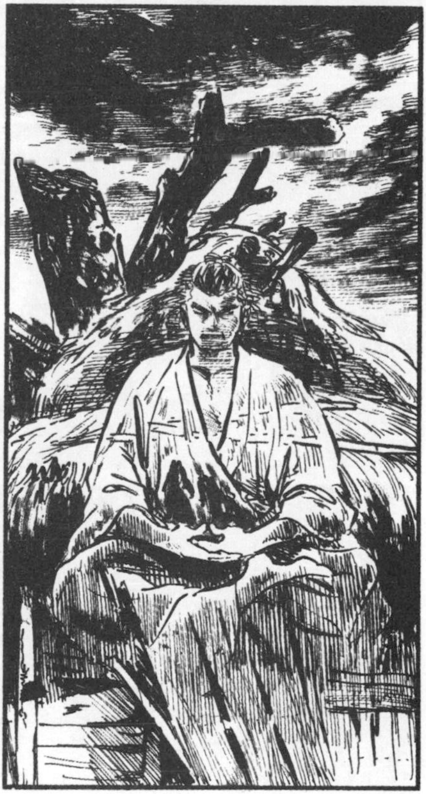
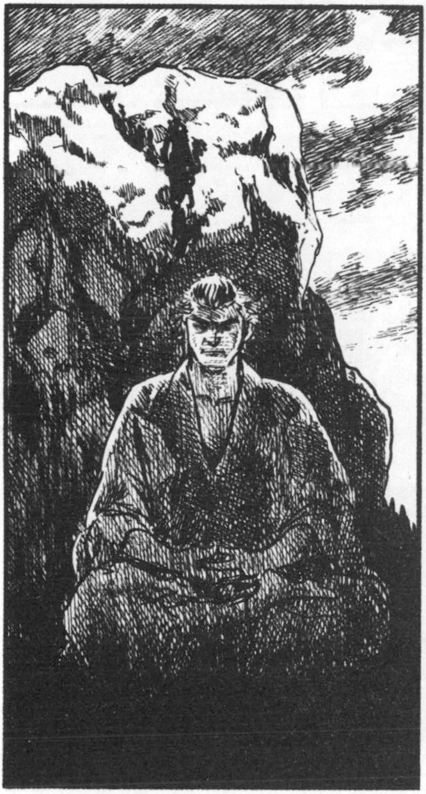

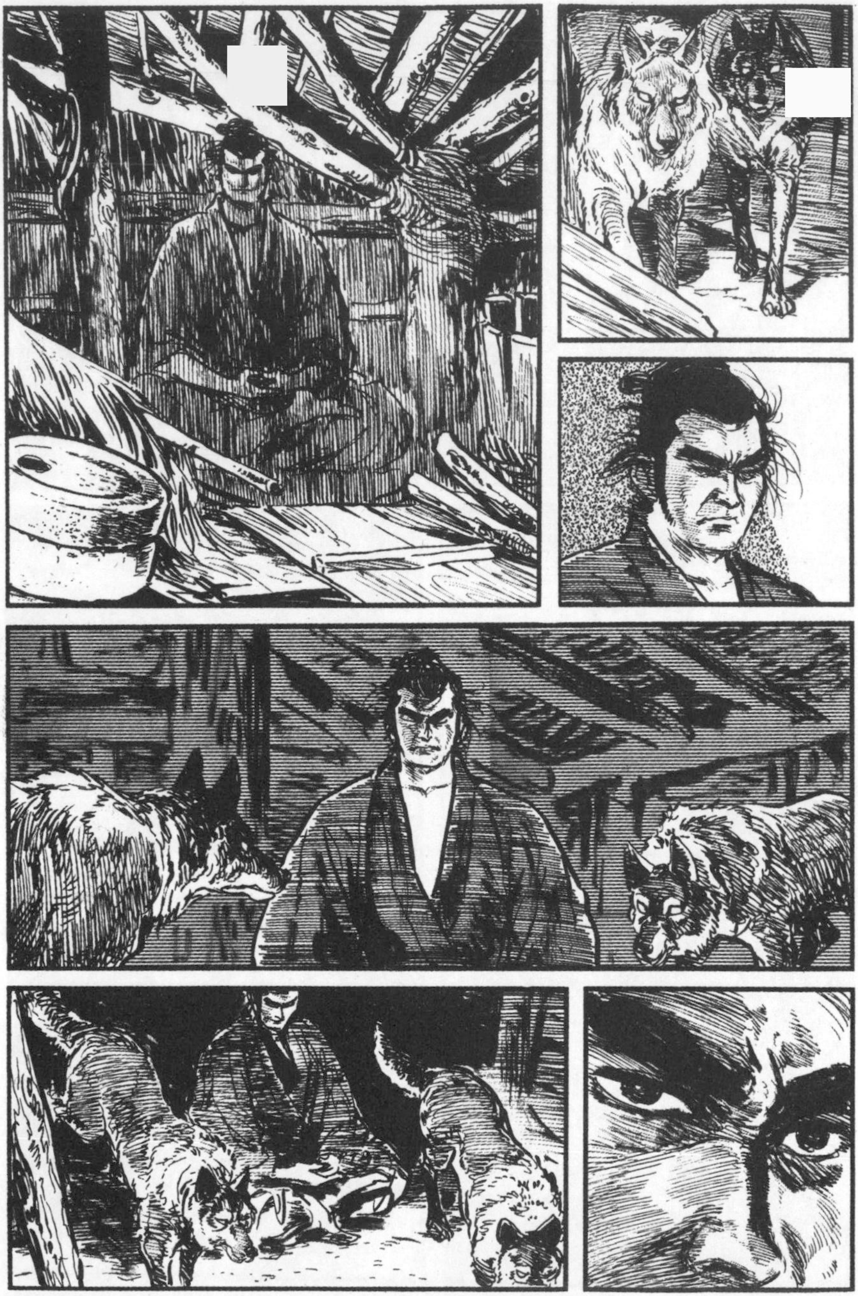

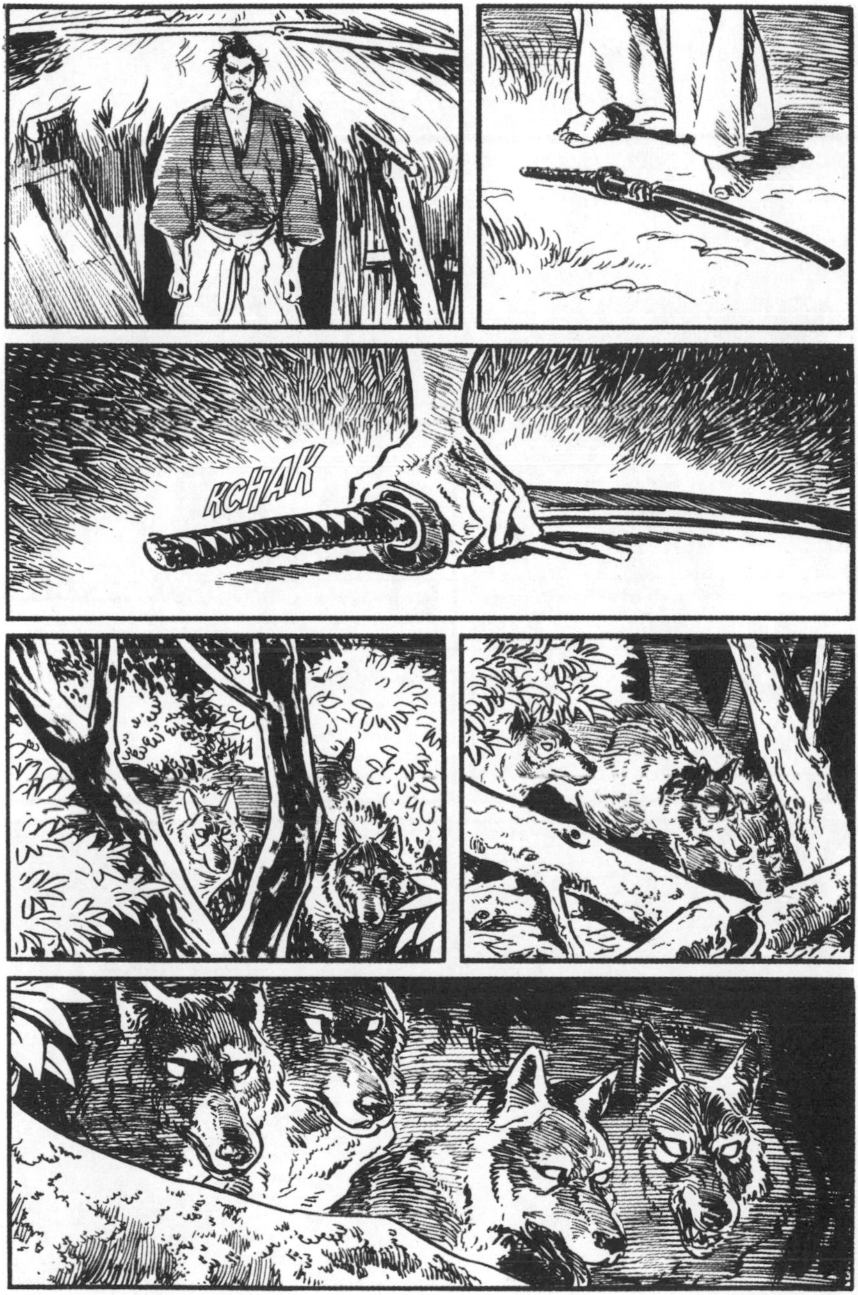
KCHAK

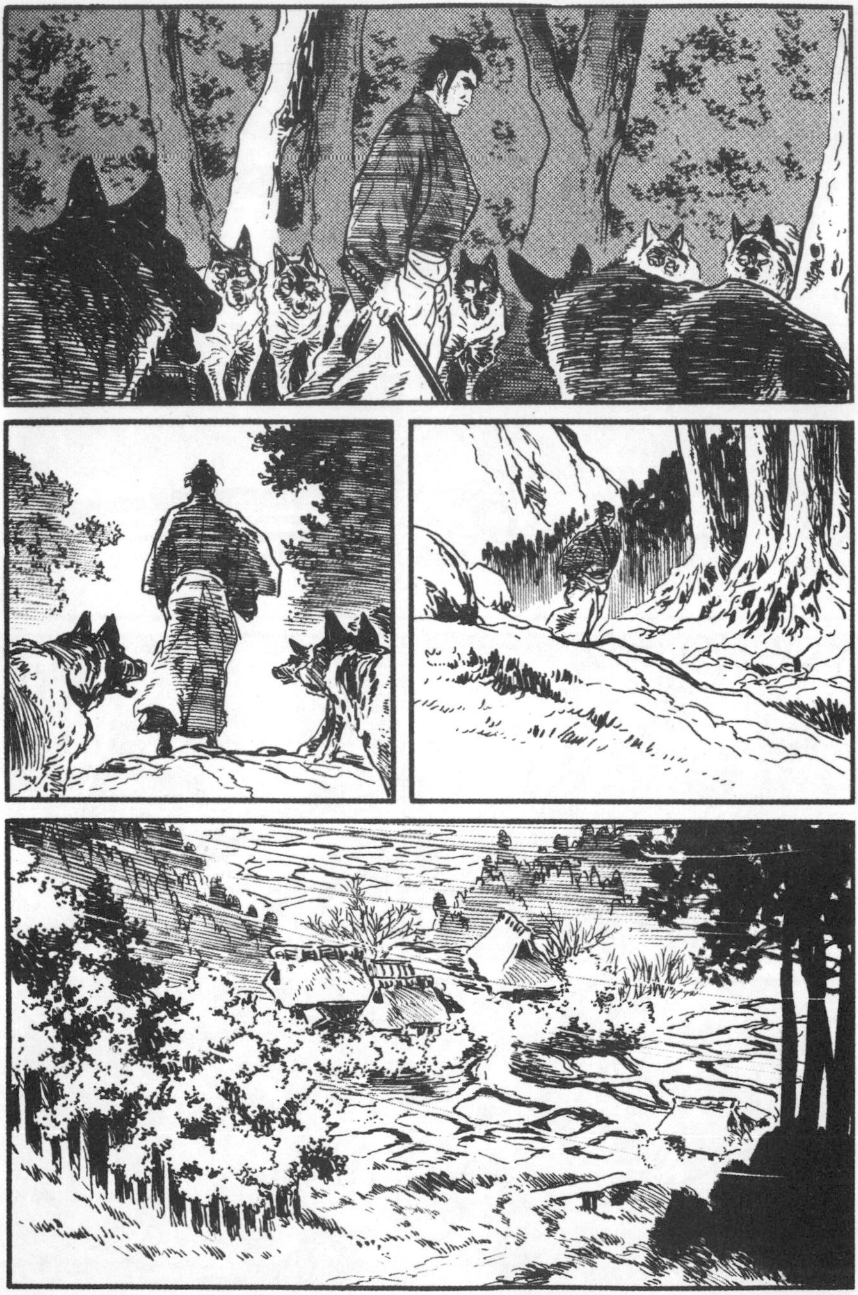

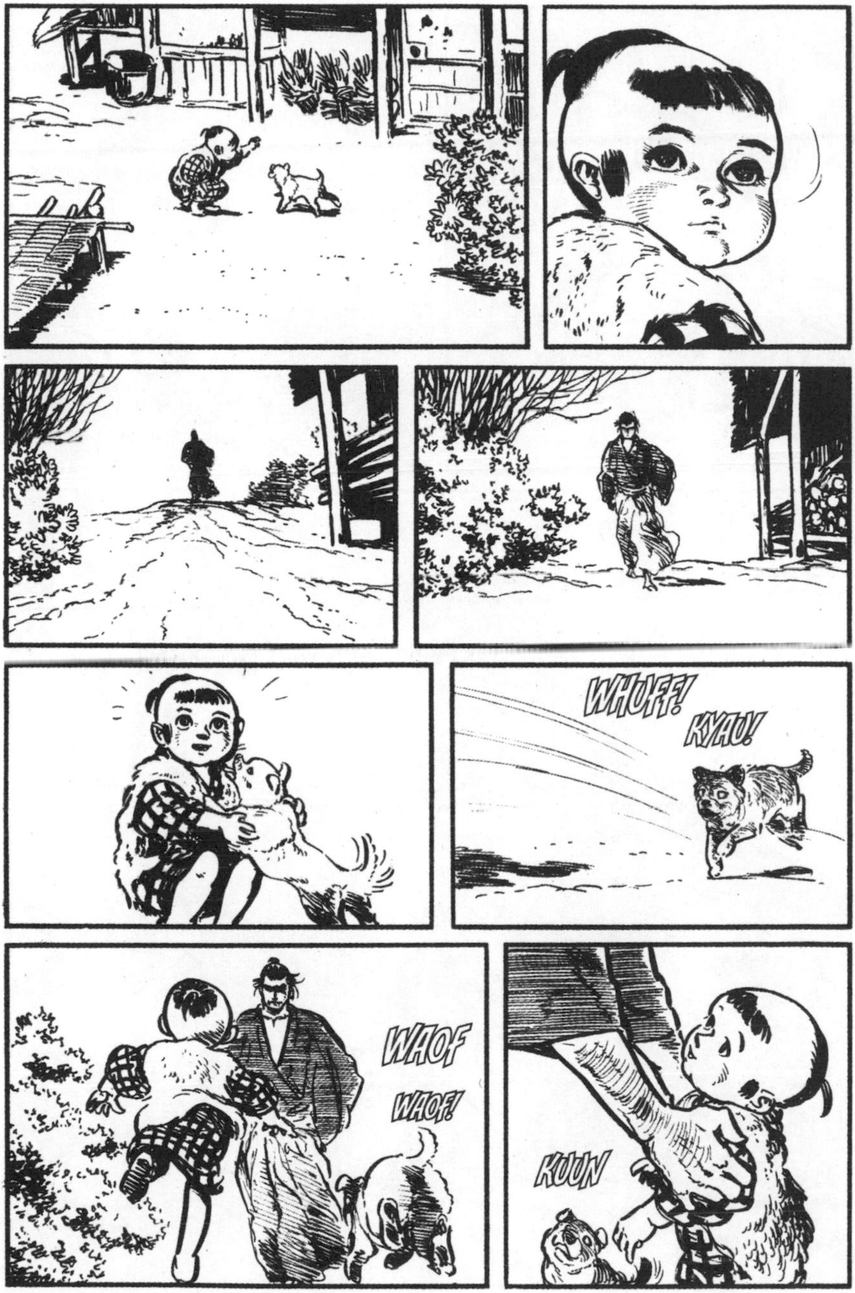
WHUFF!
KYAU!
KUUN
WAOF
WAOF!

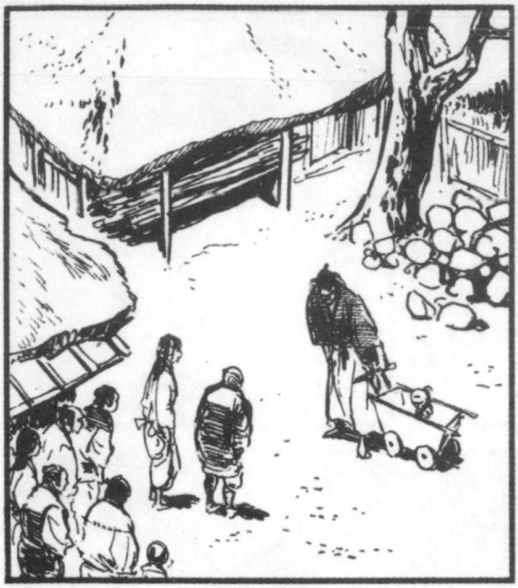

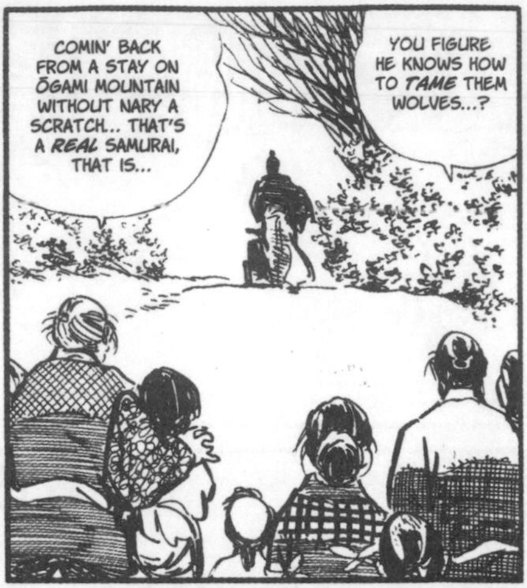
COMIN' BACK FROM A STAY ON ŌGAMI MOUNTAIN WITHOUT NARY A SCRATCH... THAT'S A *REAL* SAMURAI, THAT IS...
YOU FIGURE HE KNOWS HOW TO *TAME* THEM WOLVES...?

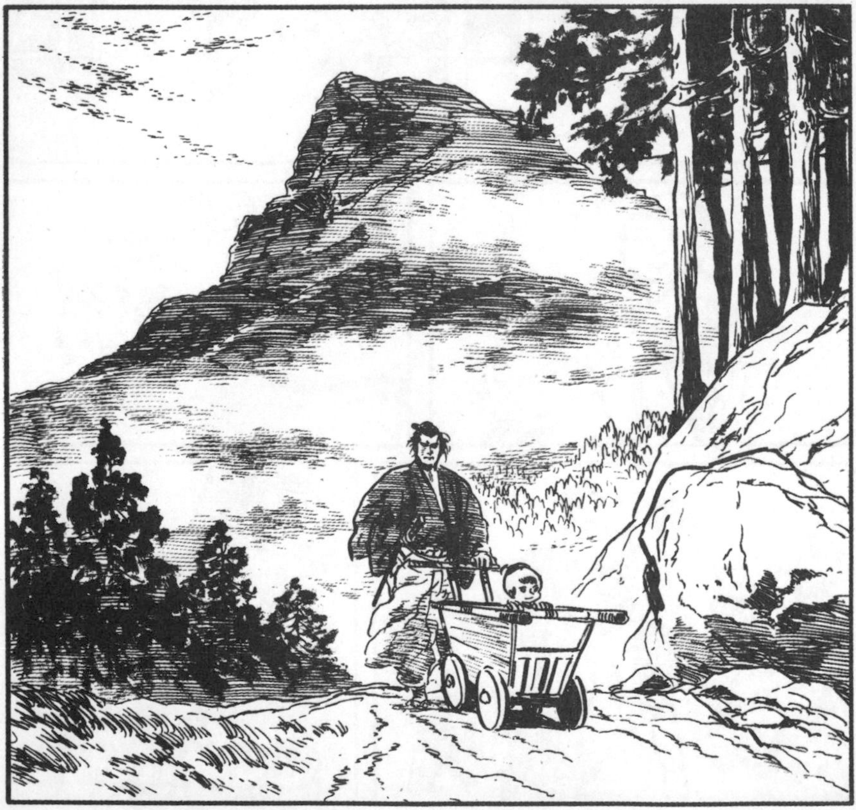

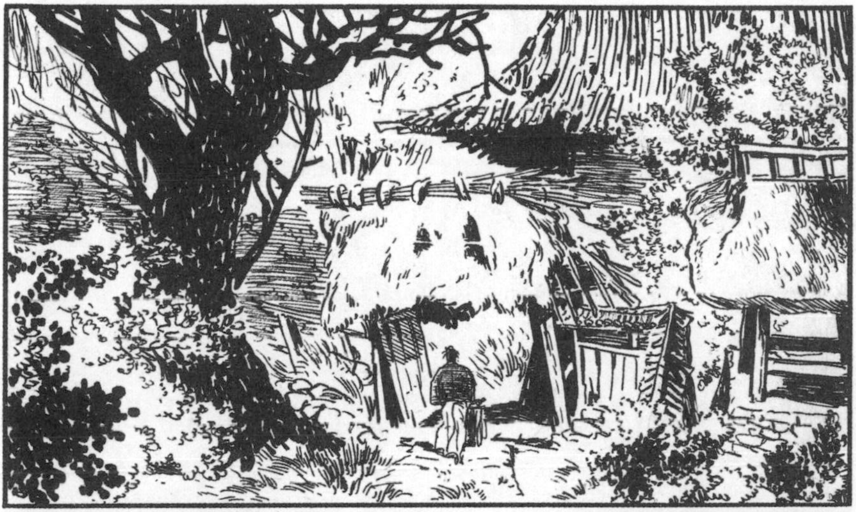
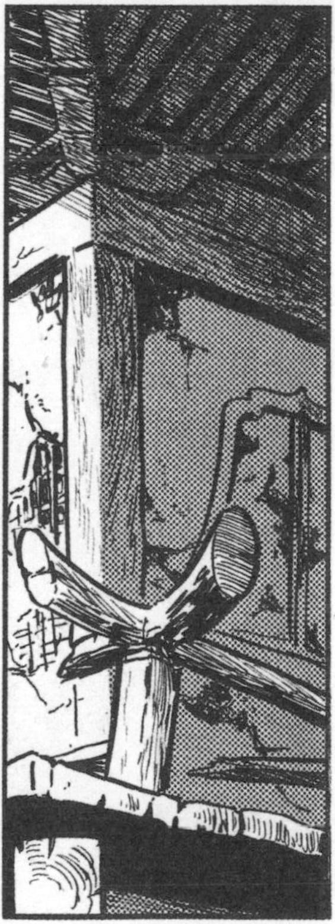
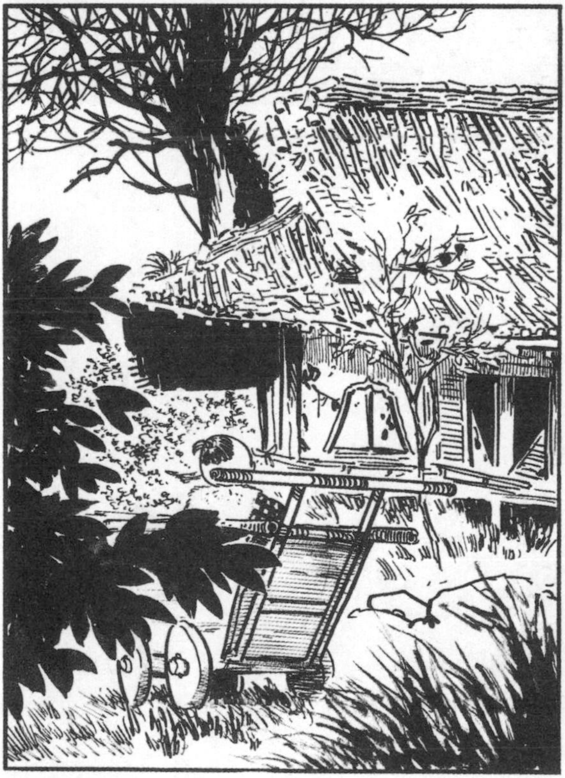

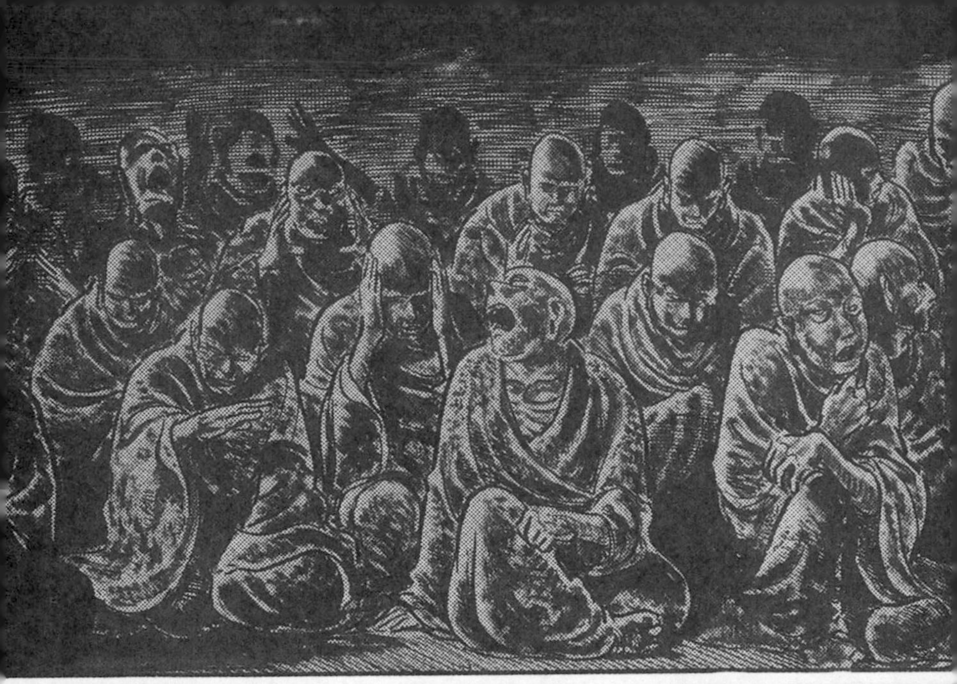
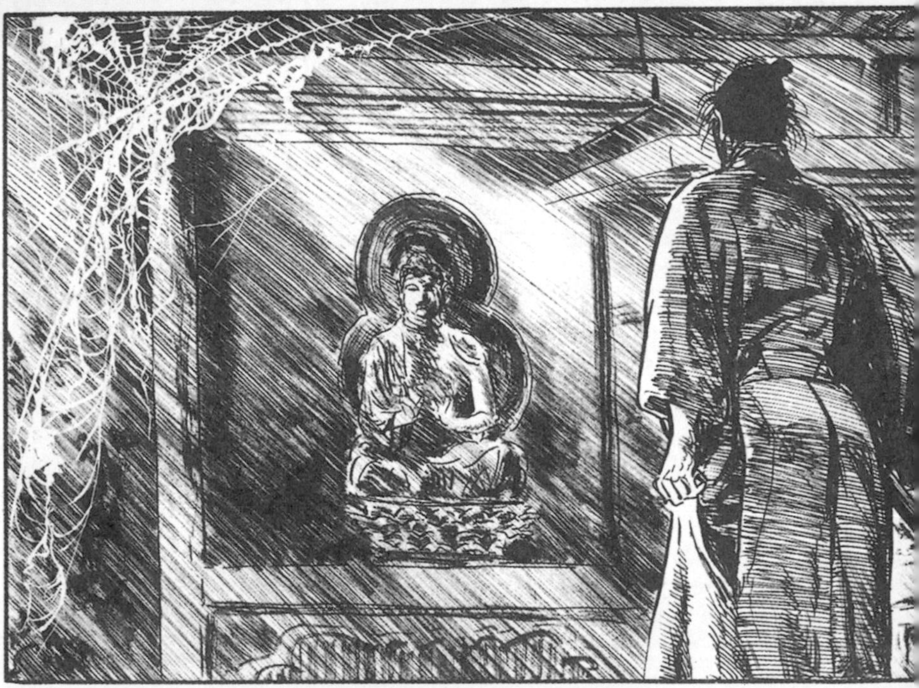

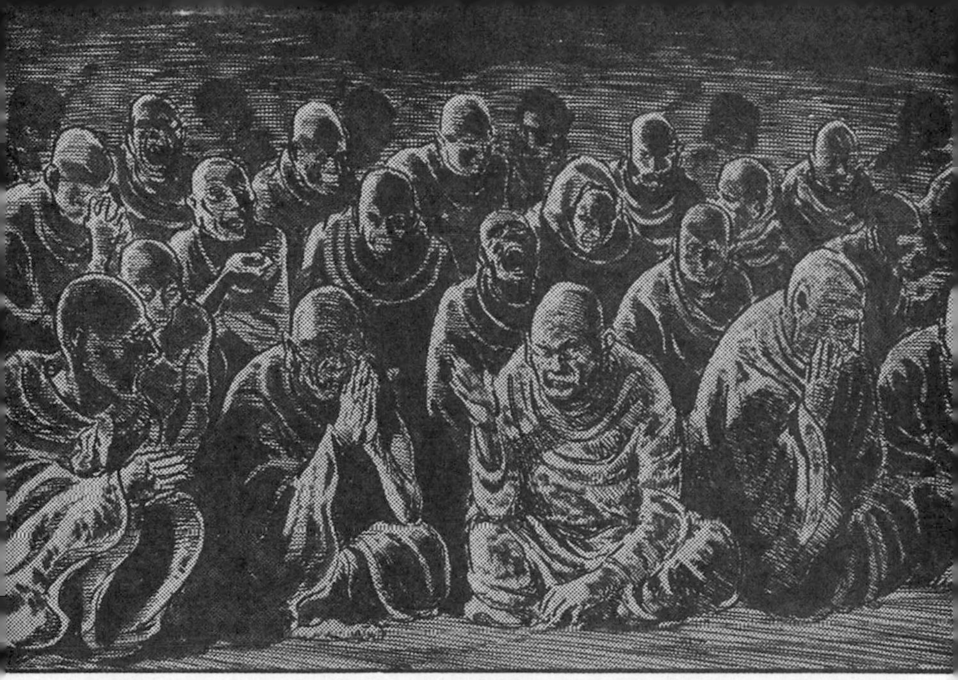
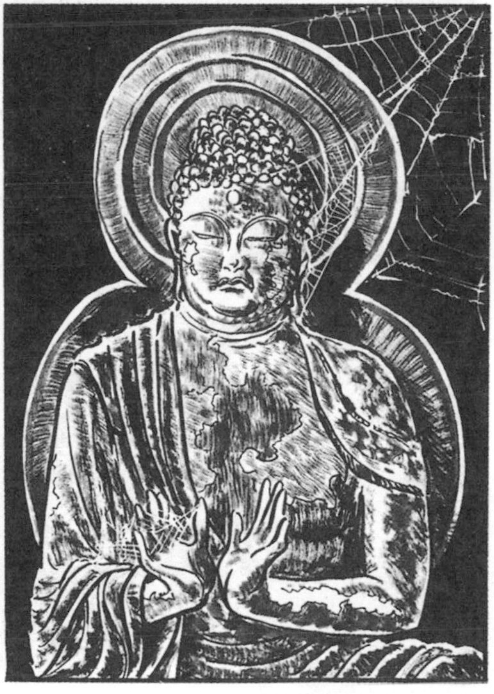
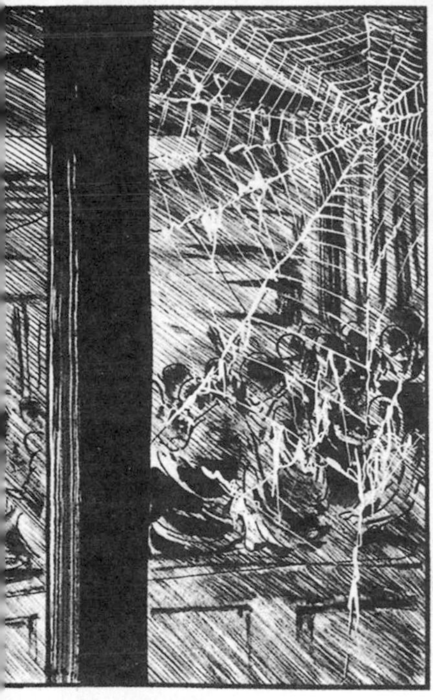

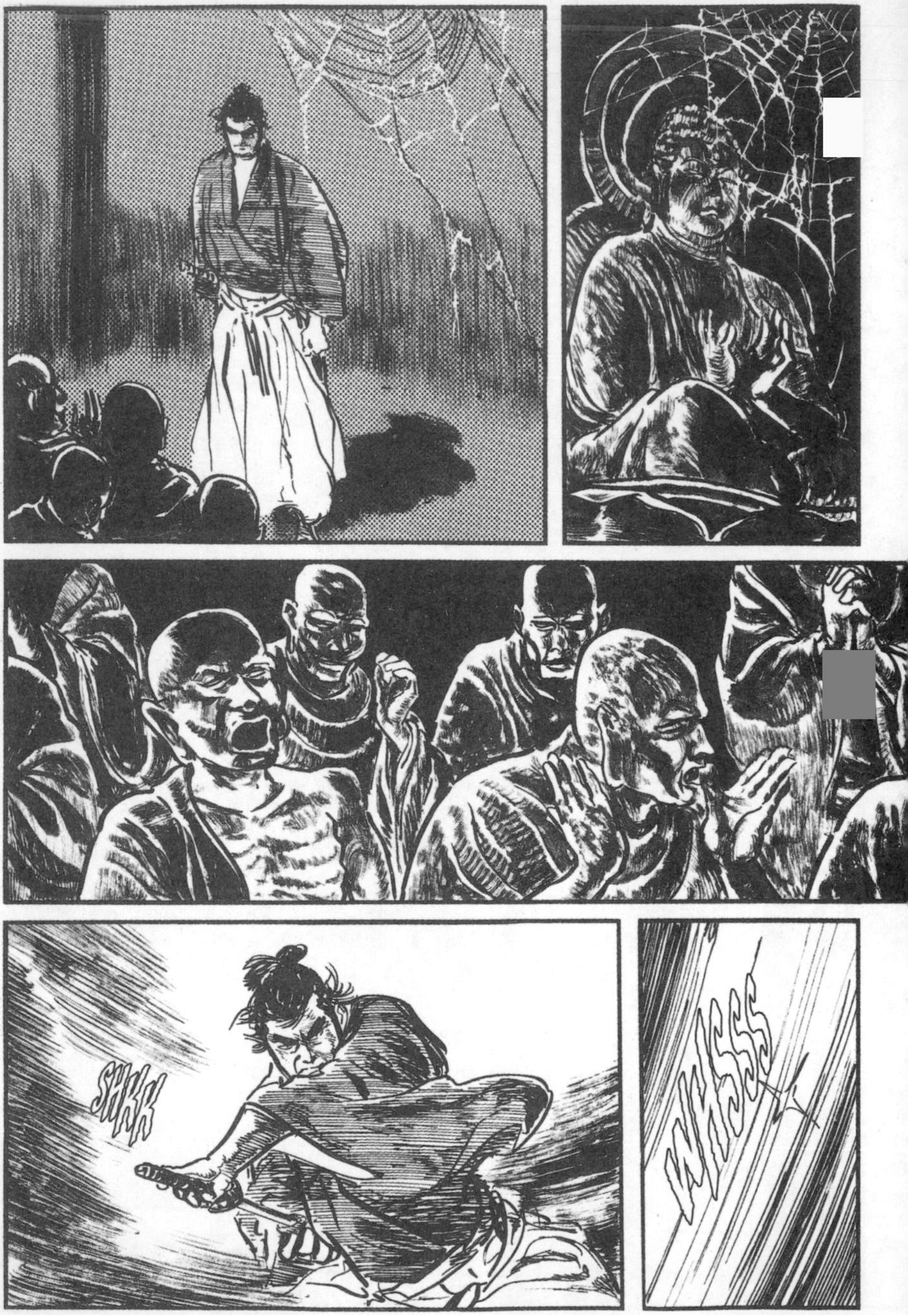
WHISSS
SHKK

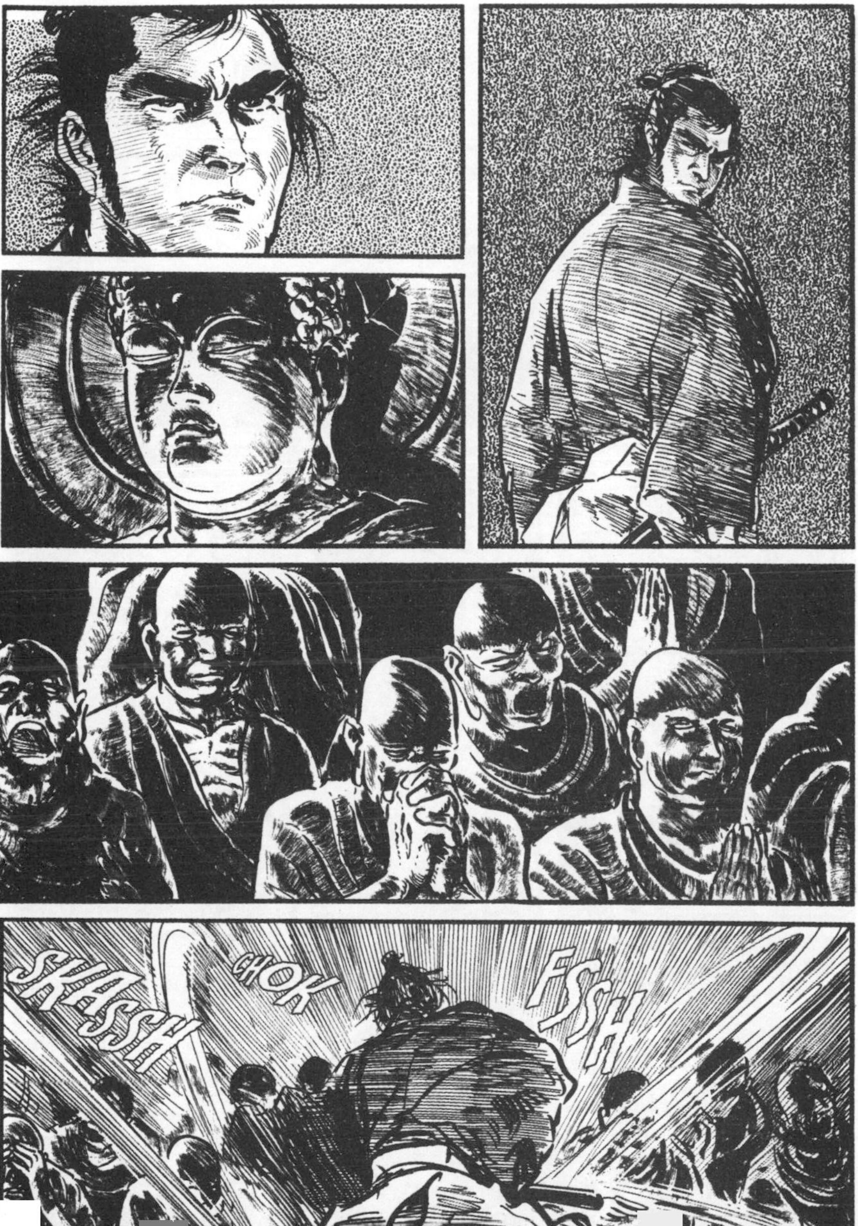
FSSH
CHOK
SKASSH

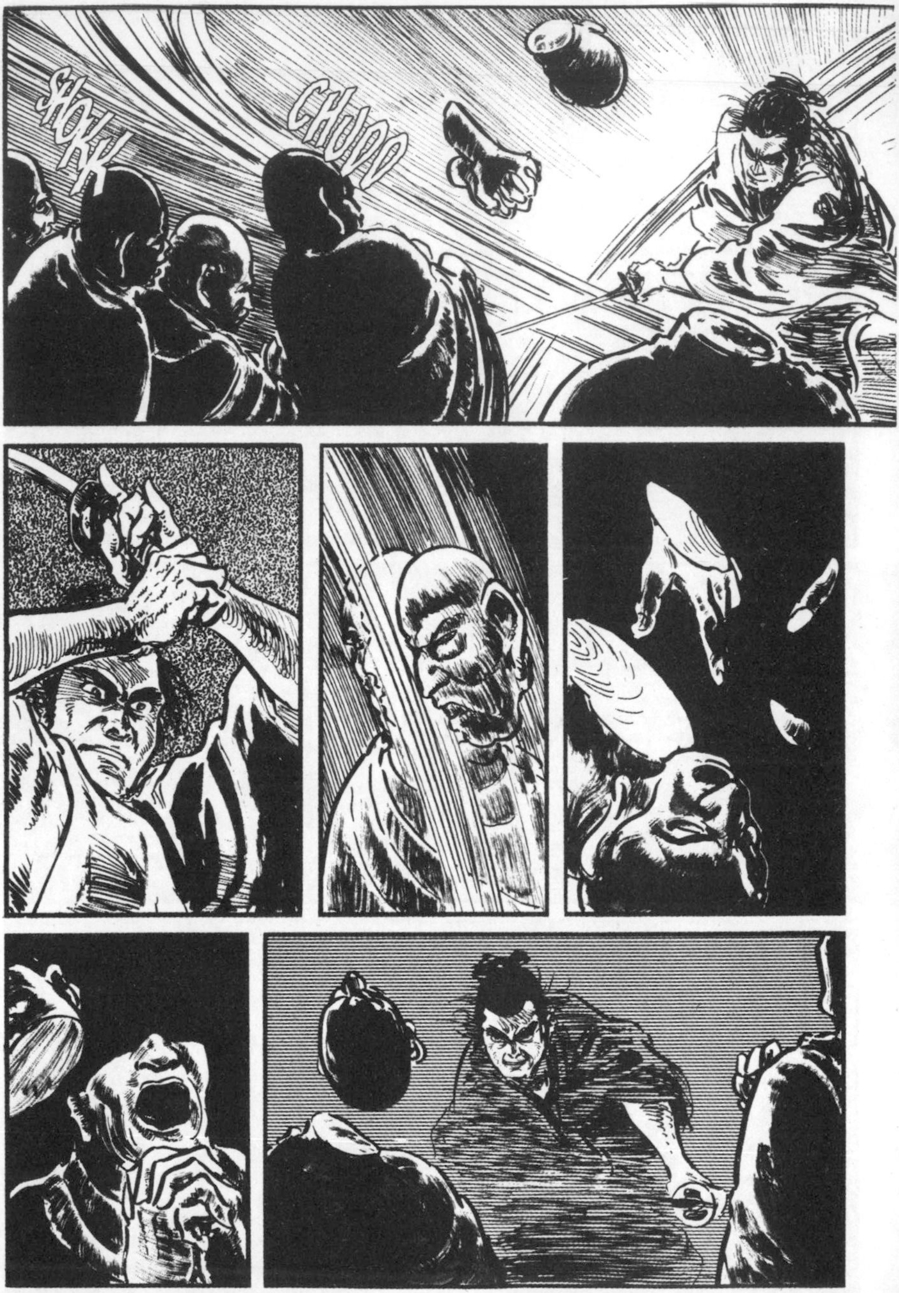
CHUNN
SHOKK

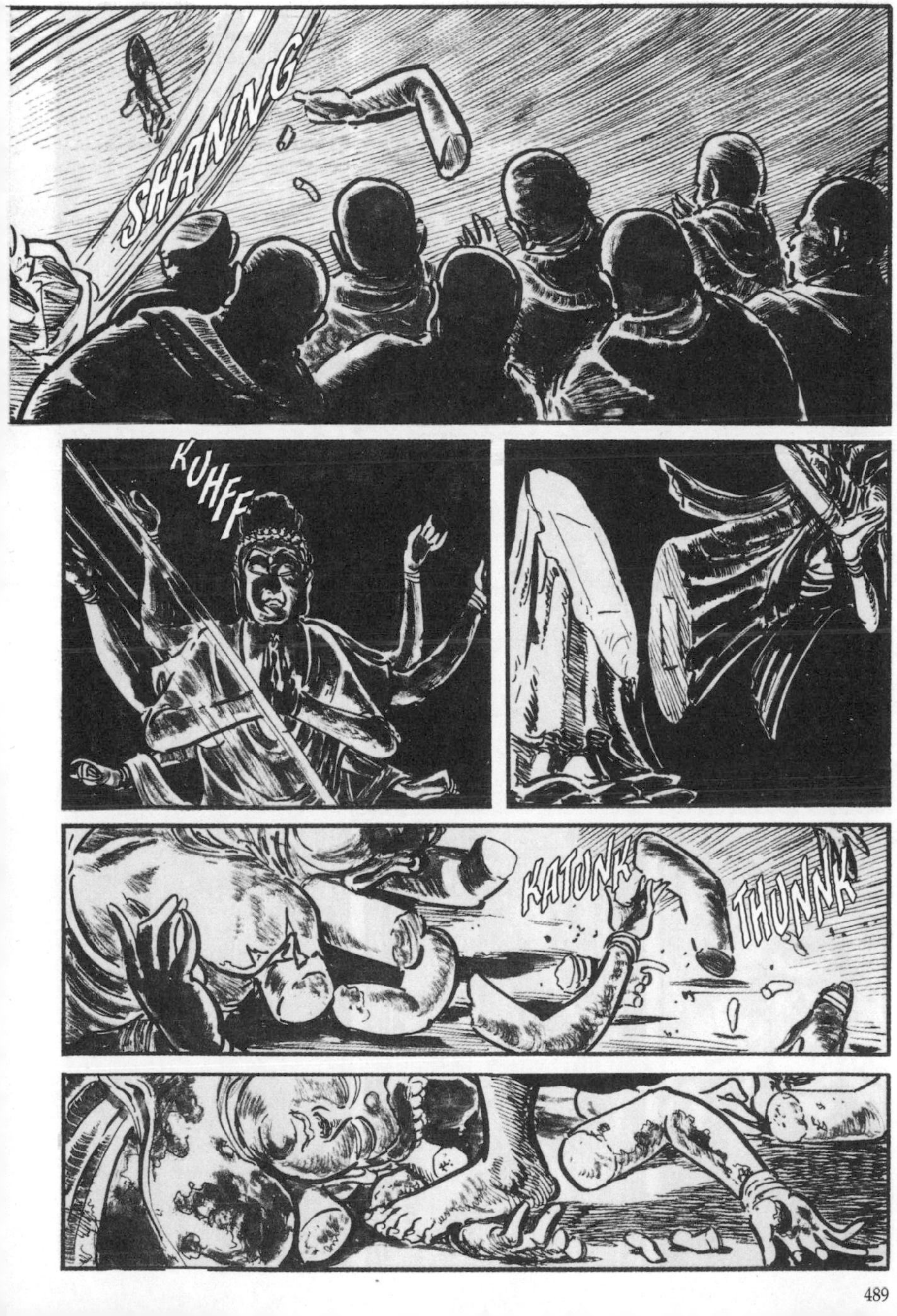
SHANING
KUHFF
THUNNK
KATUNK

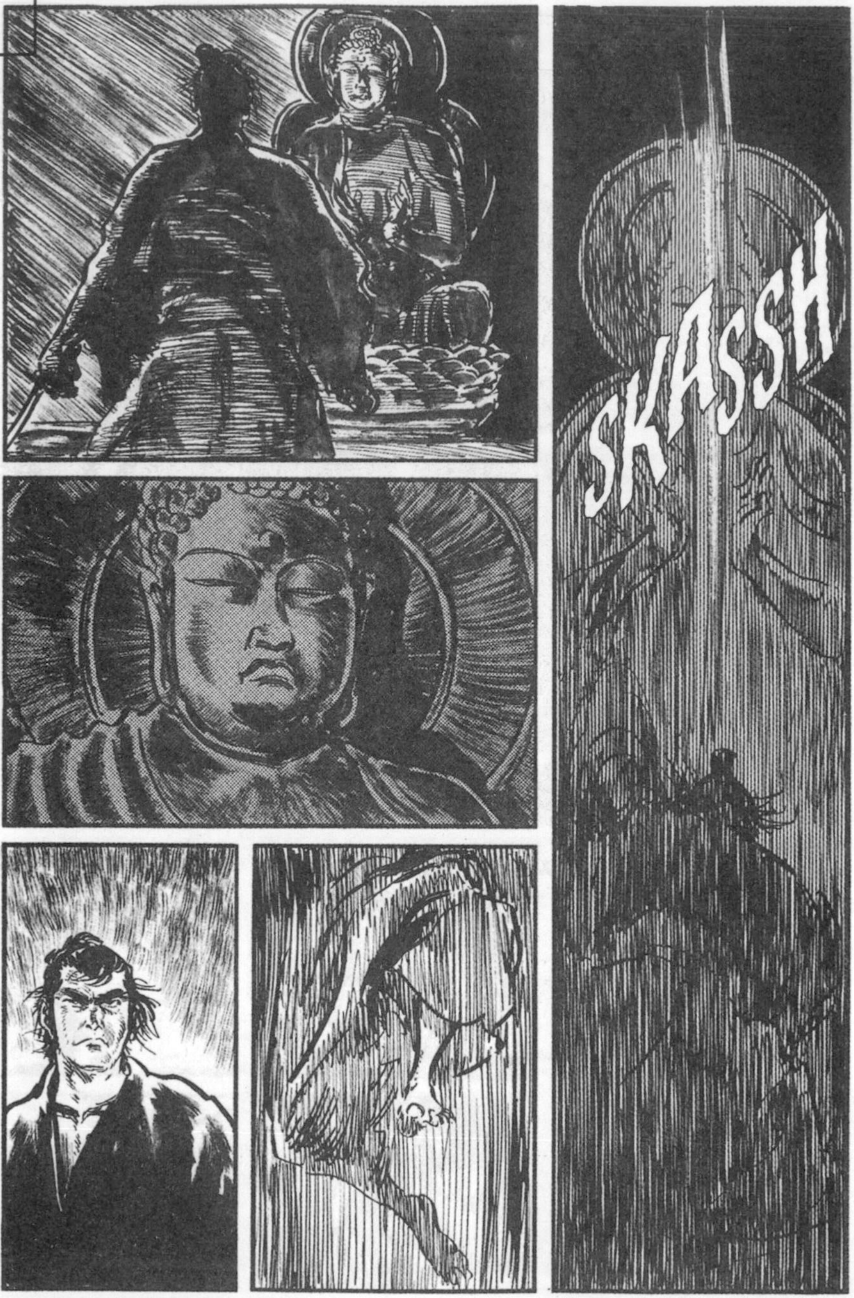
SKASSH

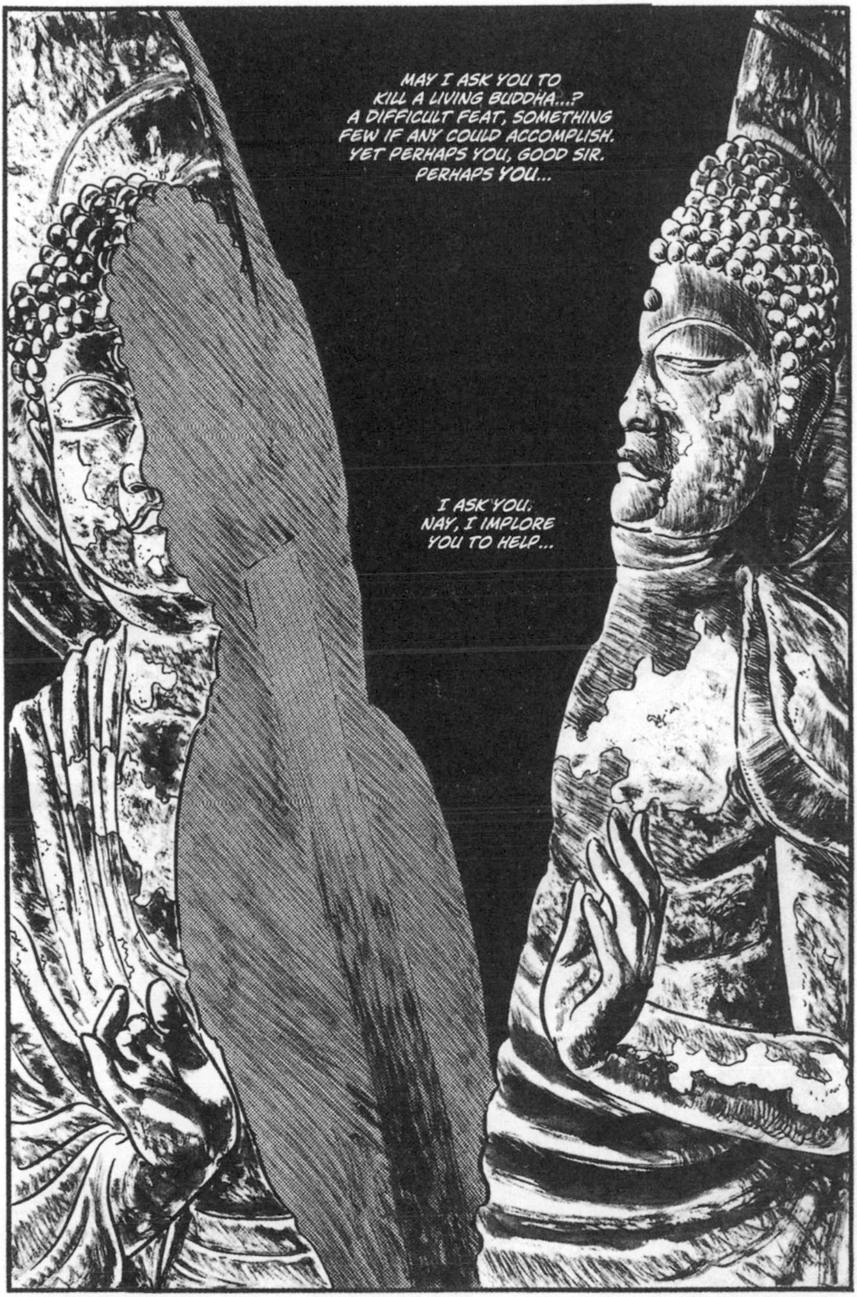
MAY I ASK YOU TO
KILL A LIVING BUDDHA...?
A DIFFICULT FEAT, SOMETHING
FEW IF ANY COULD ACCOMPLISH.
YET PERHAPS YOU, GOOD SIR.
PERHAPS YOU...
I ASK YOU.
NAY, I IMPLORE
YOU TO HELP...

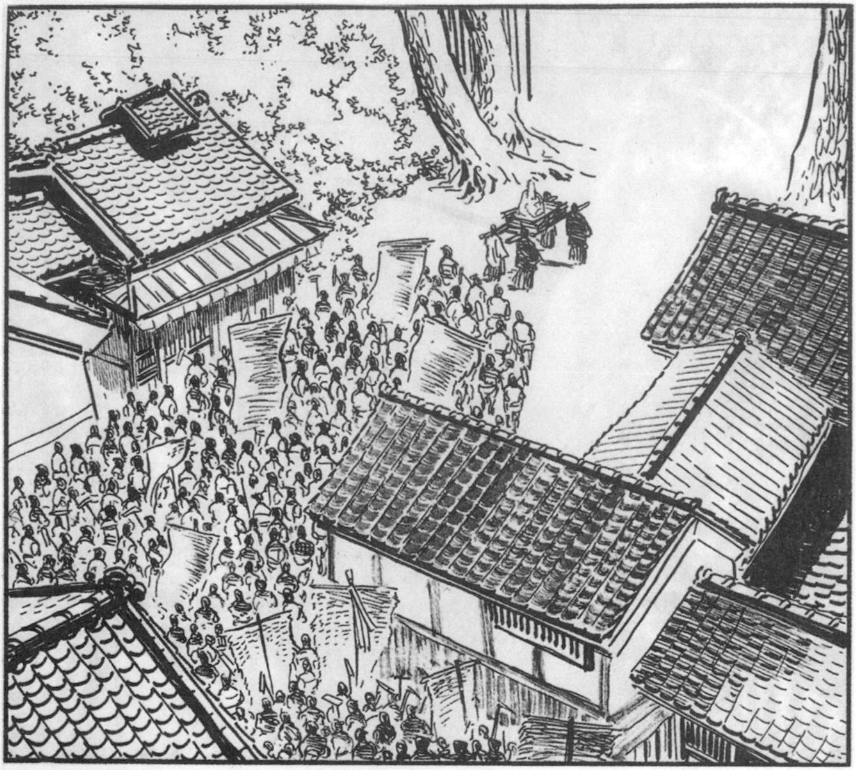
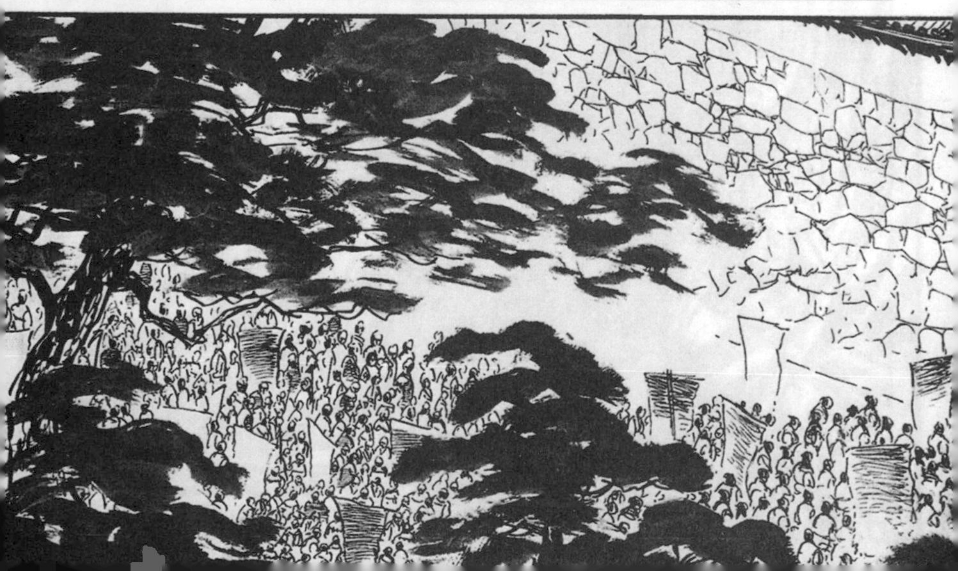

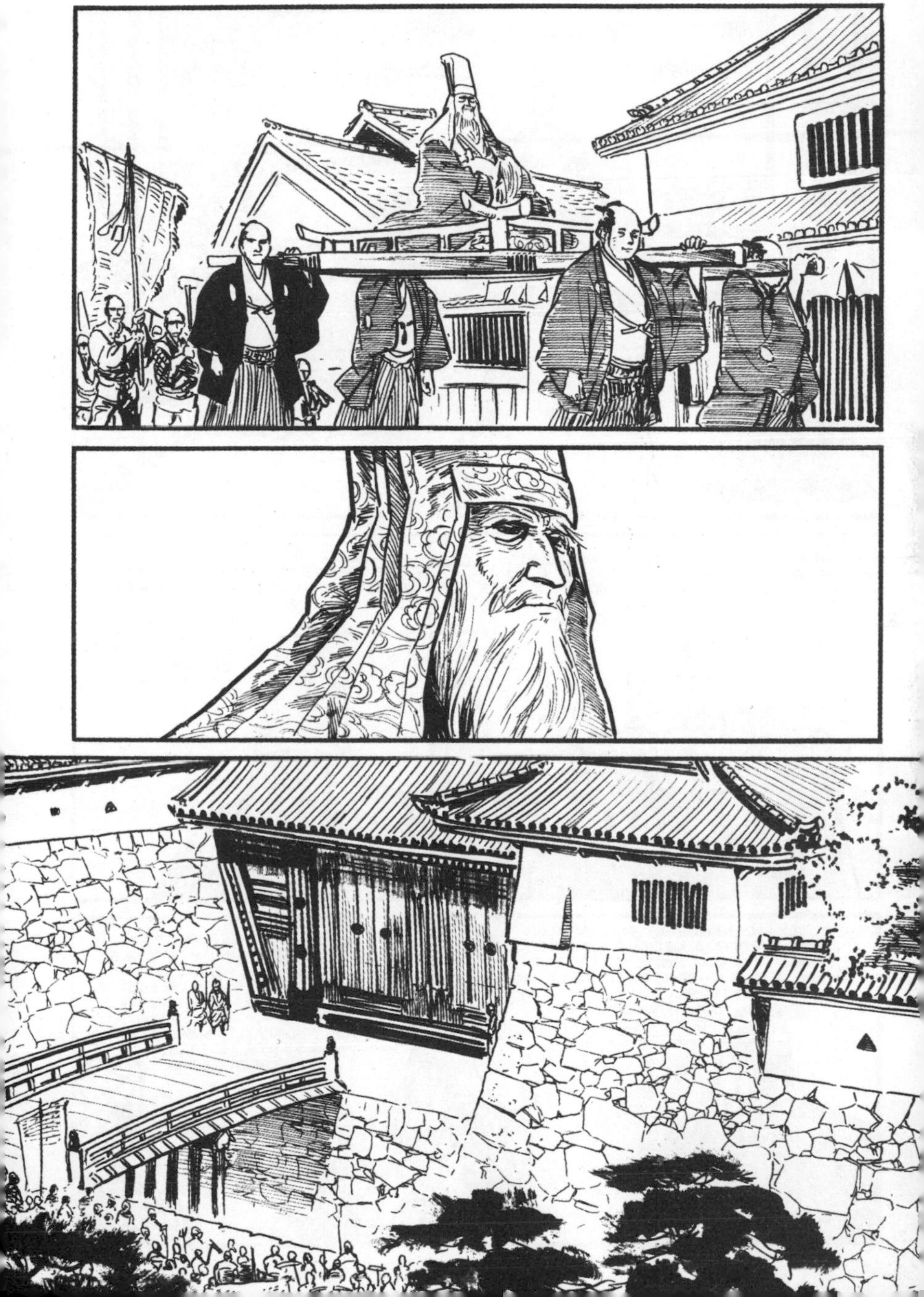

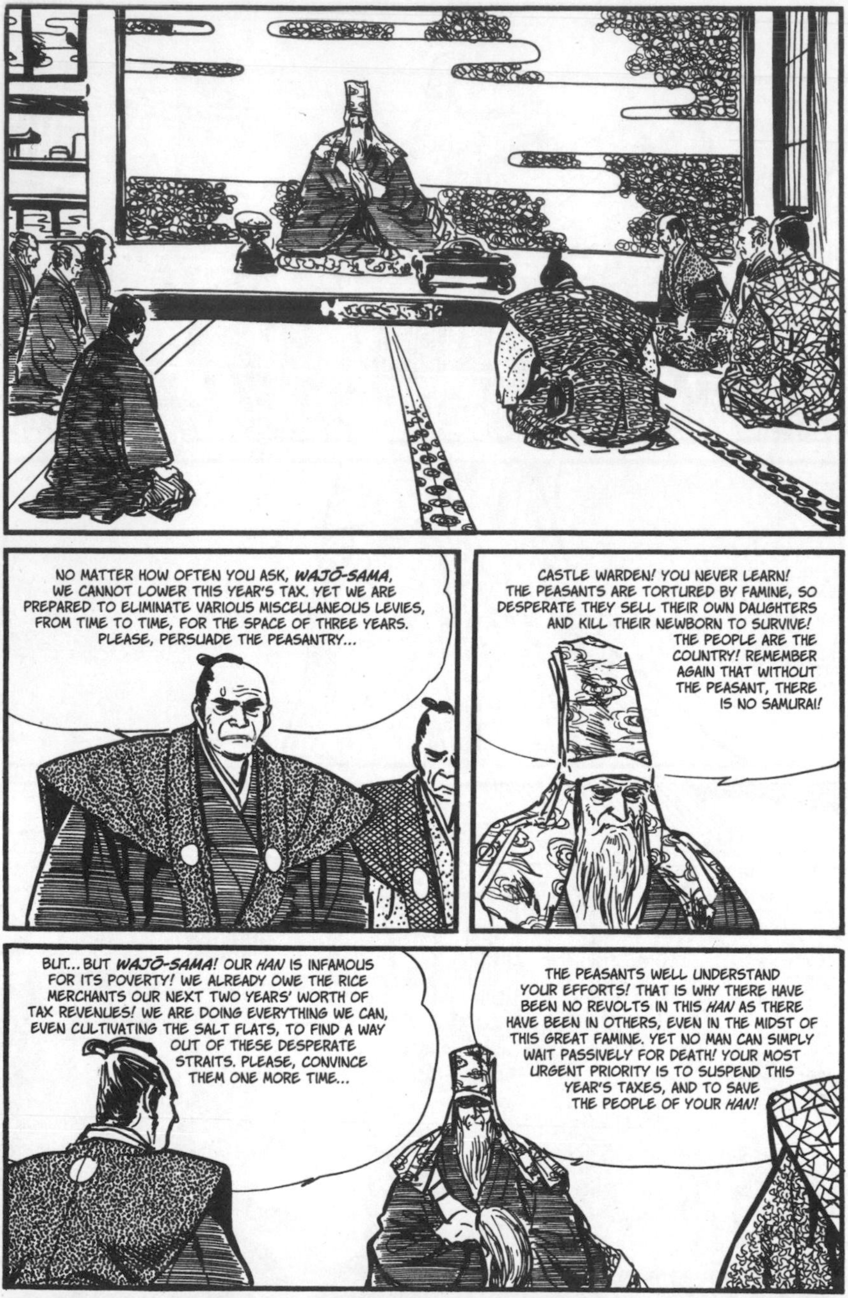
NO MATTER HOW OFTEN YOU ASK, *WAJŌ-SAMA*, WE CANNOT LOWER THIS YEAR'S TAX. YET WE ARE PREPARED TO ELIMINATE VARIOUS MISCELLANEOUS LEVIES, FROM TIME TO TIME, FOR THE SPACE OF THREE YEARS. PLEASE, PERSUADE THE PEASANTRY...
CASTLE WARDEN! YOU NEVER LEARN! THE PEASANTS ARE TORTURED BY FAMINE, SO DESPERATE THEY SELL THEIR OWN DAUGHTERS AND KILL THEIR NEWBORN TO SURVIVE! THE PEOPLE ARE THE COUNTRY! REMEMBER AGAIN THAT WITHOUT THE PEASANT, THERE IS NO SAMURAI!
BUT... BUT *WAJŌ-SAMA*! OUR *HAN* IS INFAMOUS FOR ITS POVERTY! WE ALREADY OWE THE RICE MERCHANTS OUR NEXT TWO YEARS' WORTH OF TAX REVENUES! WE ARE DOING EVERYTHING WE CAN, EVEN CULTIVATING THE SALT FLATS, TO FIND A WAY OUT OF THESE DESPERATE STRAITS. PLEASE, CONVINCE THEM ONE MORE TIME...
THE PEASANTS WELL UNDERSTAND YOUR EFFORTS! THAT IS WHY THERE HAVE BEEN NO REVOLTS IN THIS *HAN* AS THERE HAVE BEEN IN OTHERS, EVEN IN THE MIDST OF THIS GREAT FAMINE. YET NO MAN CAN SIMPLY WAIT PASSIVELY FOR DEATH! YOUR MOST URGENT PRIORITY IS TO SUSPEND THIS YEAR'S TAXES, AND TO SAVE THE PEOPLE OF YOUR *HAN*!

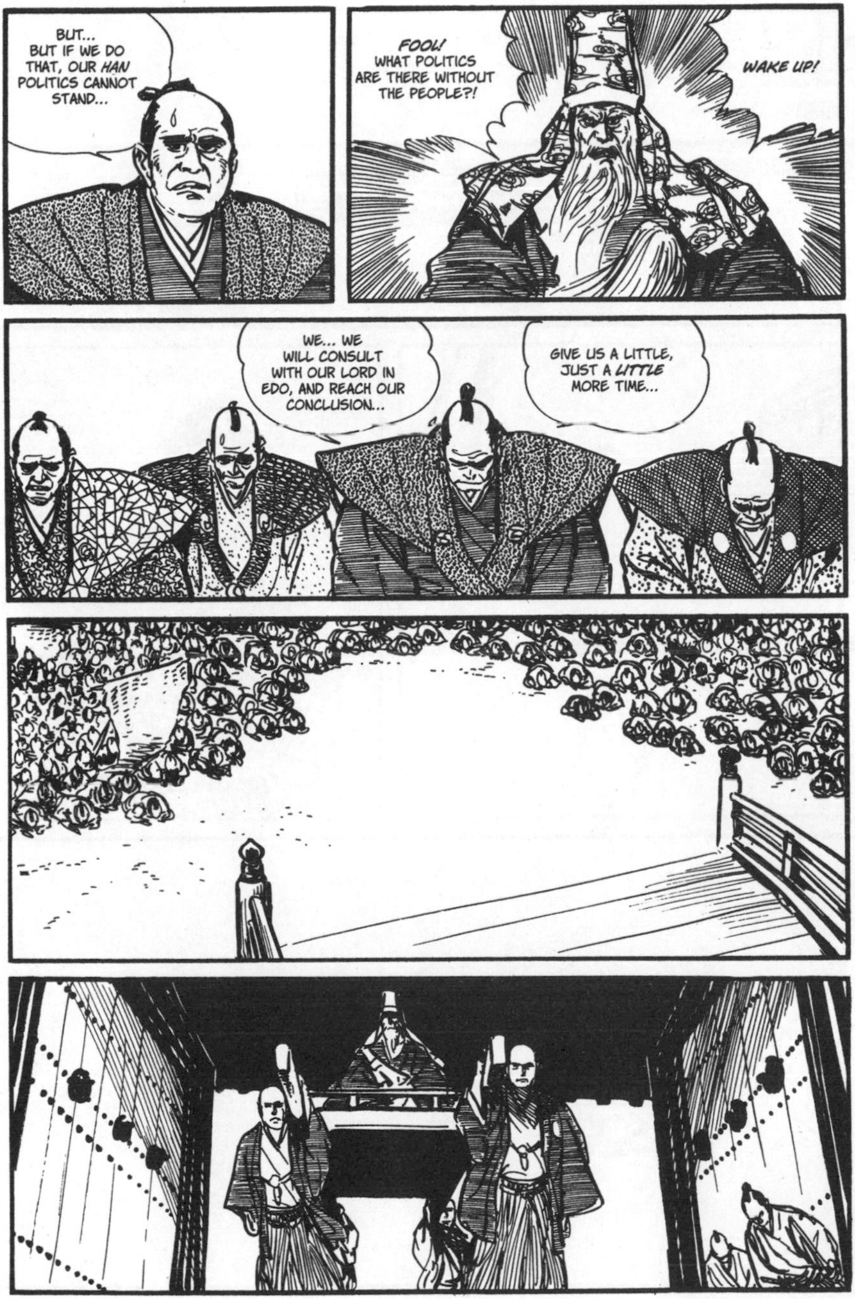
BUT... BUT IF WE DO THAT, OUR *HAN* POLITICS CANNOT STAND...
FOOL! WHAT POLITICS ARE THERE WITHOUT THE PEOPLE?!
WAKE UP!
WE... WE WILL CONSULT WITH OUR LORD IN EDO, AND REACH OUR CONCLUSION...
GIVE US A LITTLE, JUST A *LITTLE* MORE TIME...

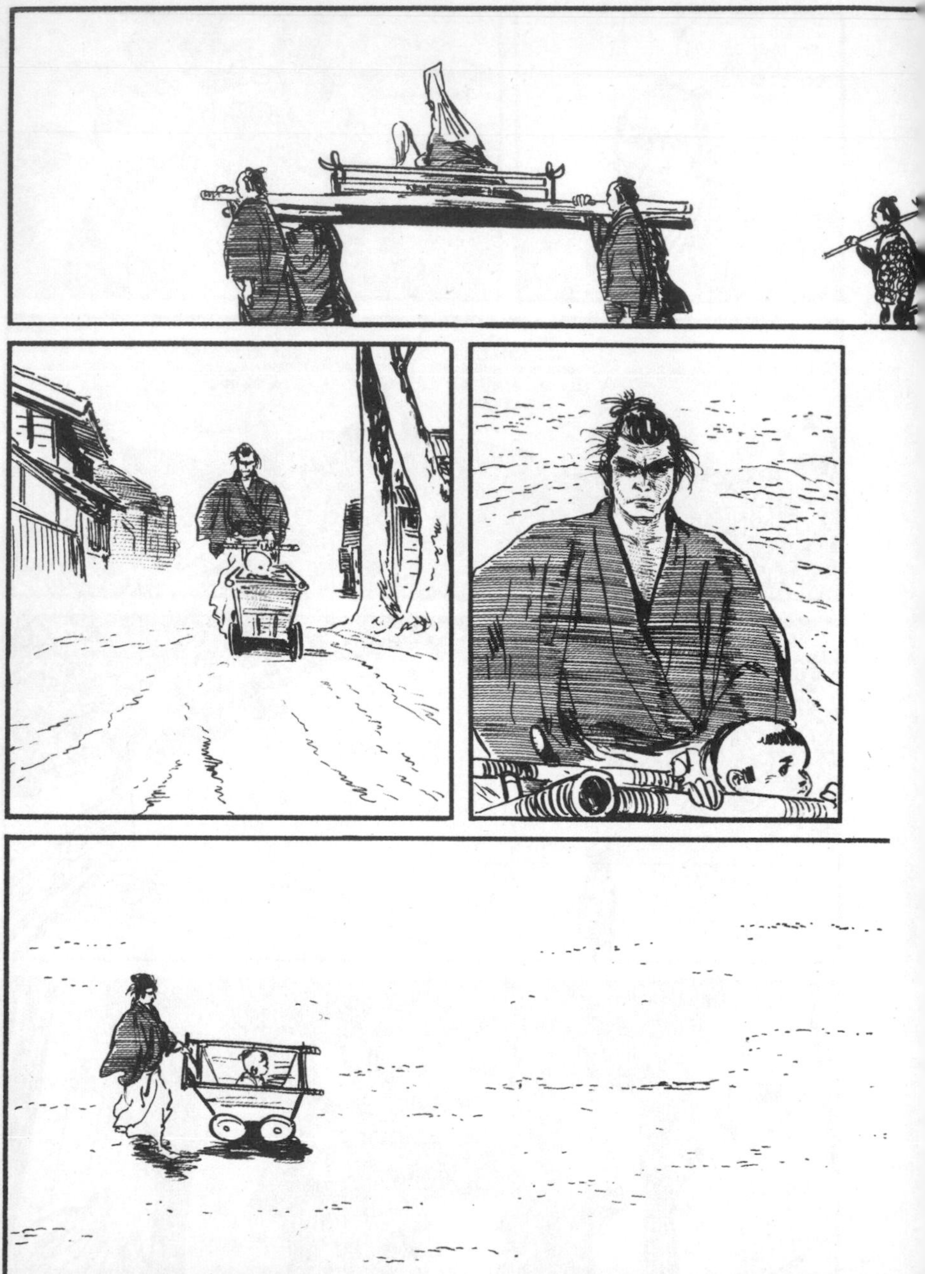

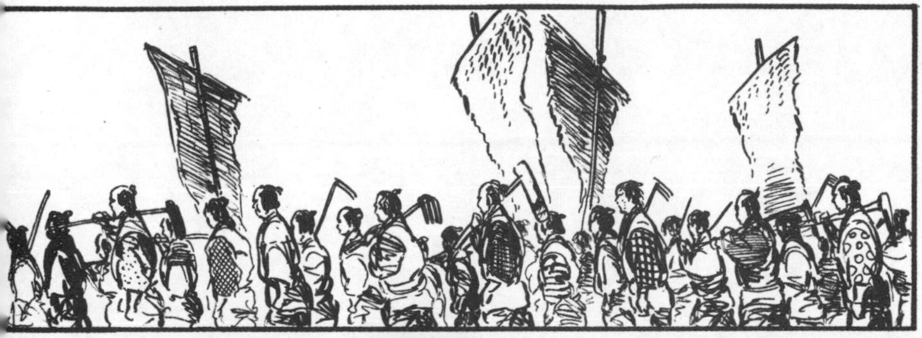
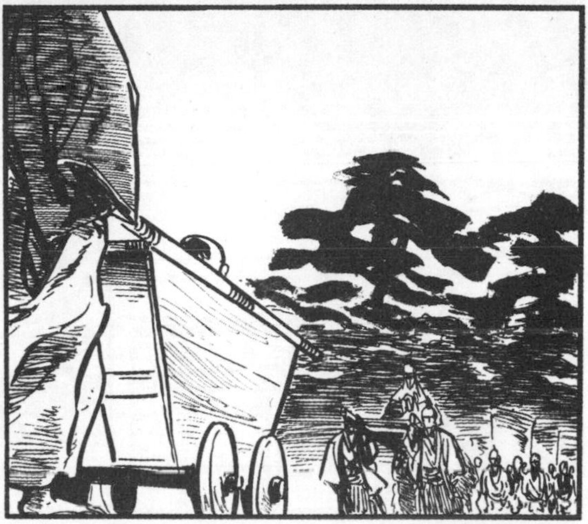
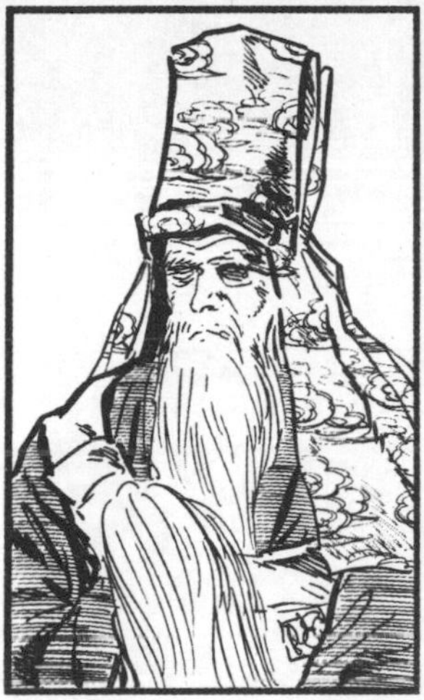
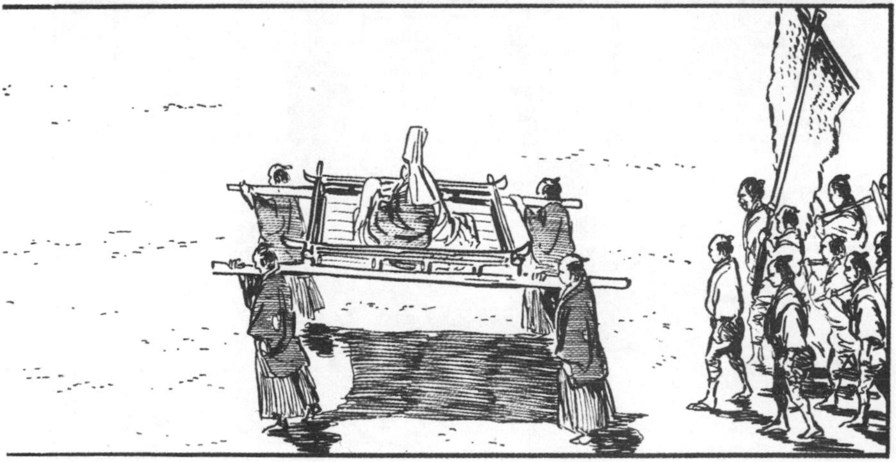

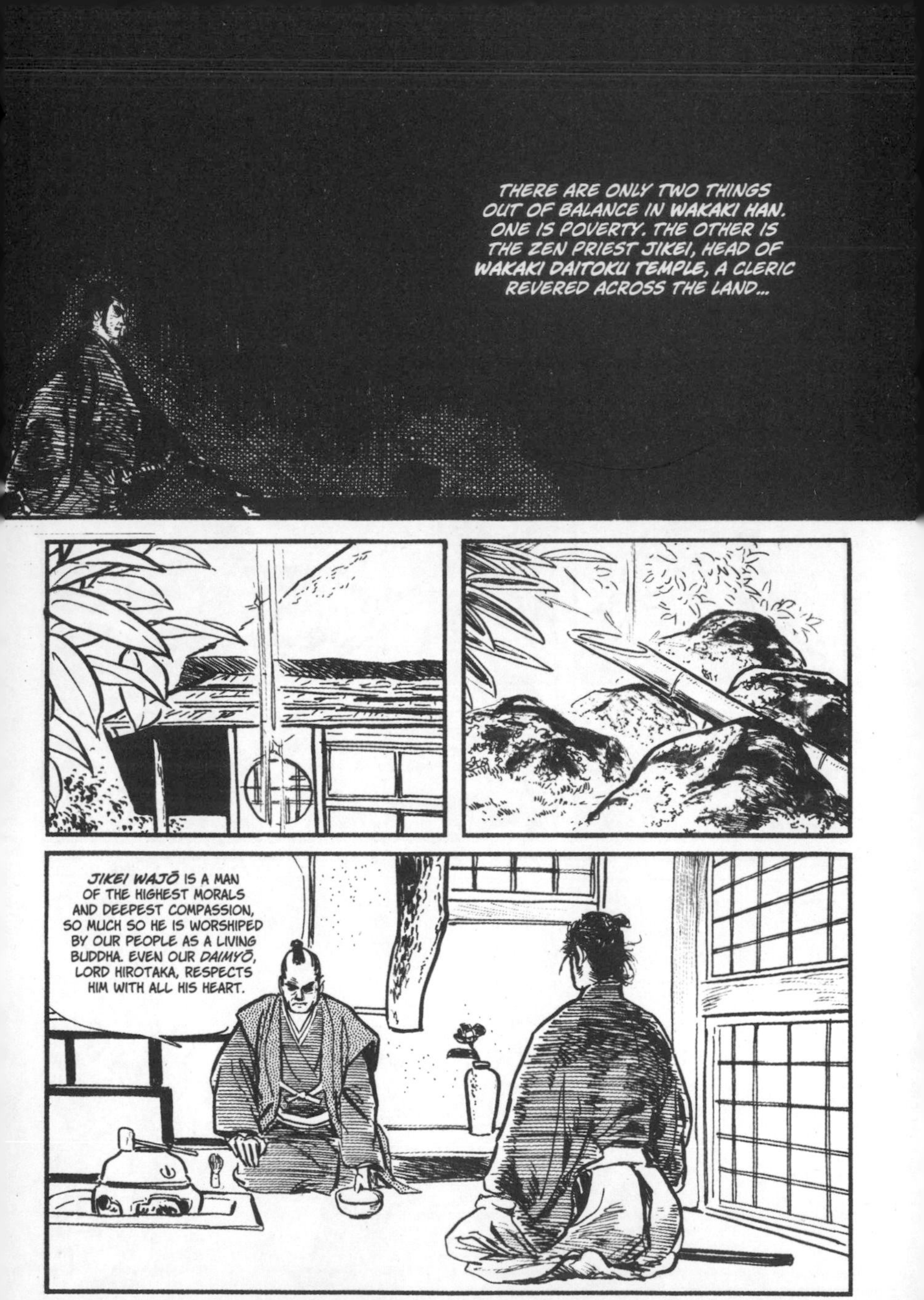
THERE ARE ONLY TWO THINGS OUT OF BALANCE IN WAKAKI HAN. ONE IS POVERTY. THE OTHER IS THE ZEN PRIEST JIKEI, HEAD OF WAKAKI DAITOKU TEMPLE, A CLERIC REVERED ACROSS THE LAND...
JIKEI WAJŌ IS A MAN OF THE HIGHEST MORALS AND DEEPEST COMPASSION, SO MUCH SO HE IS WORSHIPED BY OUR PEOPLE AS A LIVING BUDDHA. EVEN OUR DAIMYŌ, LORD HIROTAKA, RESPECTS HIM WITH ALL HIS HEART.

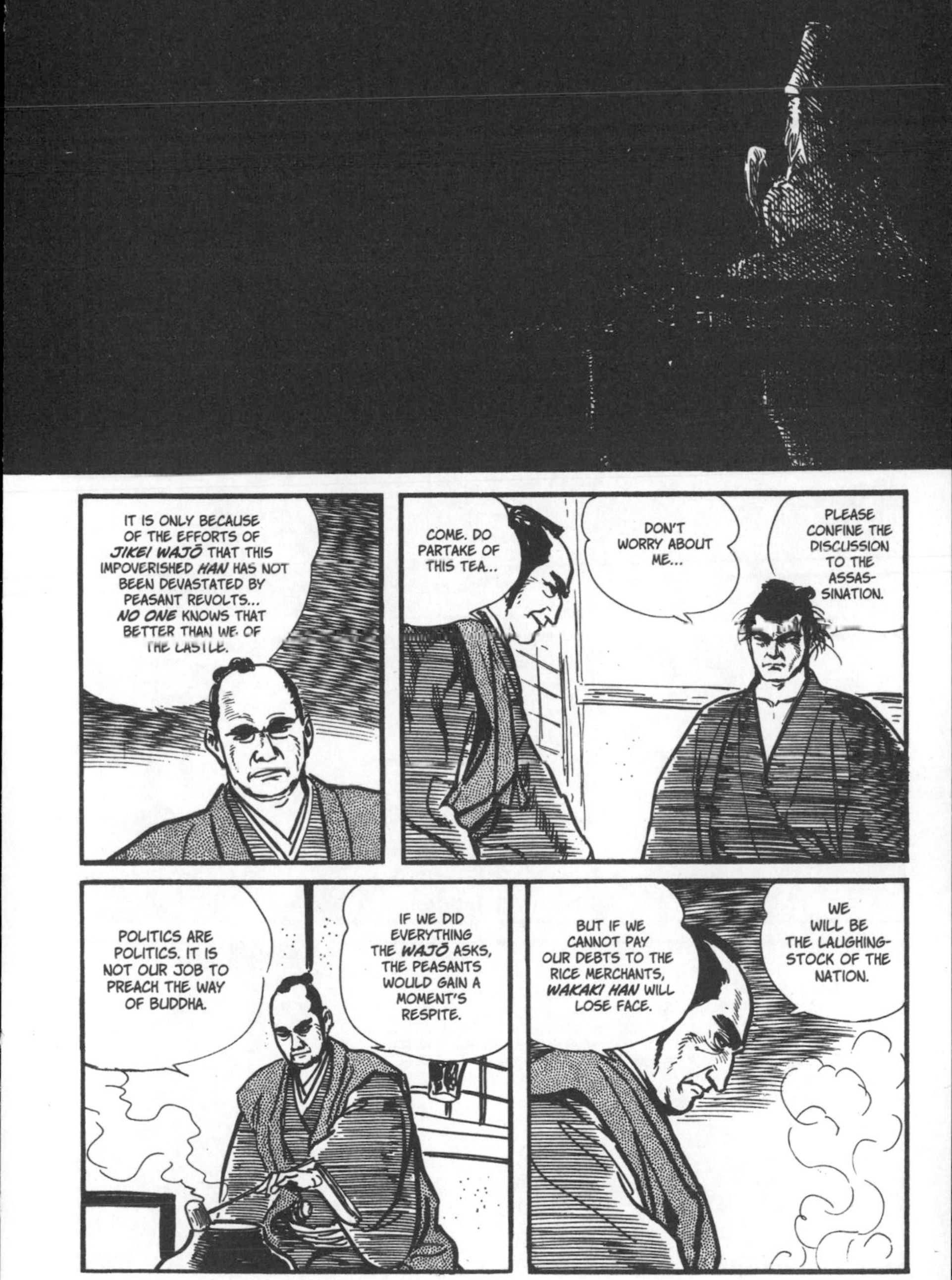

IT IS ONLY BECAUSE OF THE EFFORTS OF JIKEI WAJŌ THAT THIS IMPOVERISHED HAN HAS NOT BEEN DEVASTATED BY PEASANT REVOLTS... NO ONE KNOWS THAT BETTER THAN WE OF THE CASTLE.
COME. DO PARTAKE OF THIS TEA...
DON'T WORRY ABOUT ME...
PLEASE CONFINE THE DISCUSSION TO THE ASSAS-SINATION.
POLITICS ARE POLITICS. IT IS NOT OUR JOB TO PREACH THE WAY OF BUDDHA.
IF WE DID EVERYTHING THE WAJŌ ASKS, THE PEASANTS WOULD GAIN A MOMENT'S RESPITE.
BUT IF WE CANNOT PAY OUR DEBTS TO THE RICE MERCHANTS, WAKAKI HAN WILL LOSE FACE.
WE WILL BE THE LAUGHING-STOCK OF THE NATION.

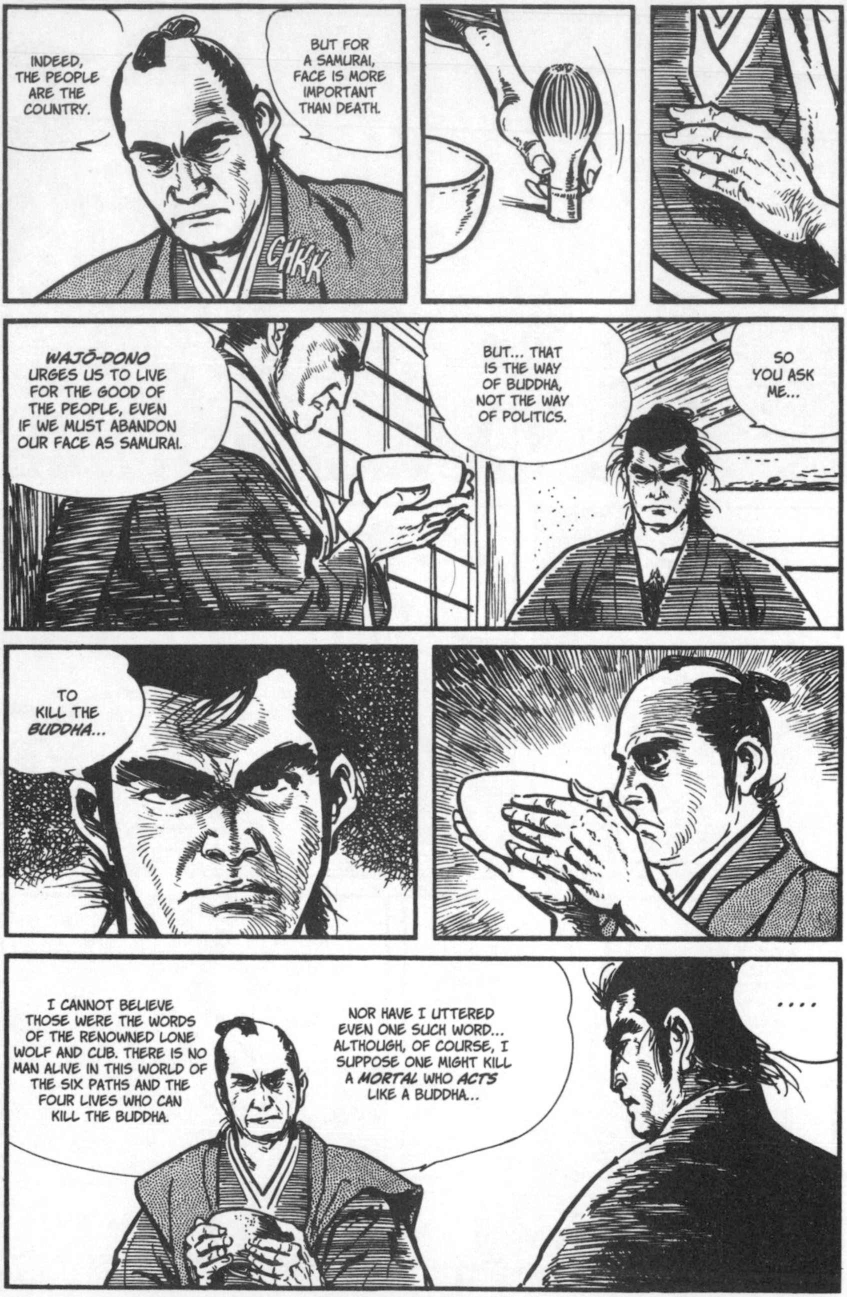
INDEED, THE PEOPLE ARE THE COUNTRY.
BUT FOR A SAMURAI, FACE IS MORE IMPORTANT THAN DEATH.
CHKK
WAJŌ-DONO URGES US TO LIVE FOR THE GOOD OF THE PEOPLE, EVEN IF WE MUST ABANDON OUR FACE AS SAMURAI.
BUT... THAT IS THE WAY OF BUDDHA, NOT THE WAY OF POLITICS.
SO YOU ASK ME...
TO KILL THE BUDDHA...
I CANNOT BELIEVE THOSE WERE THE WORDS OF THE RENOWNED LONE WOLF AND CUB. THERE IS NO MAN ALIVE IN THIS WORLD OF THE SIX PATHS AND THE FOUR LIVES WHO CAN KILL THE BUDDHA.
NOR HAVE I UTTERED EVEN ONE SUCH WORD... ALTHOUGH, OF COURSE, I SUPPOSE ONE MIGHT KILL A MORTAL WHO ACTS LIKE A BUDDHA...
....

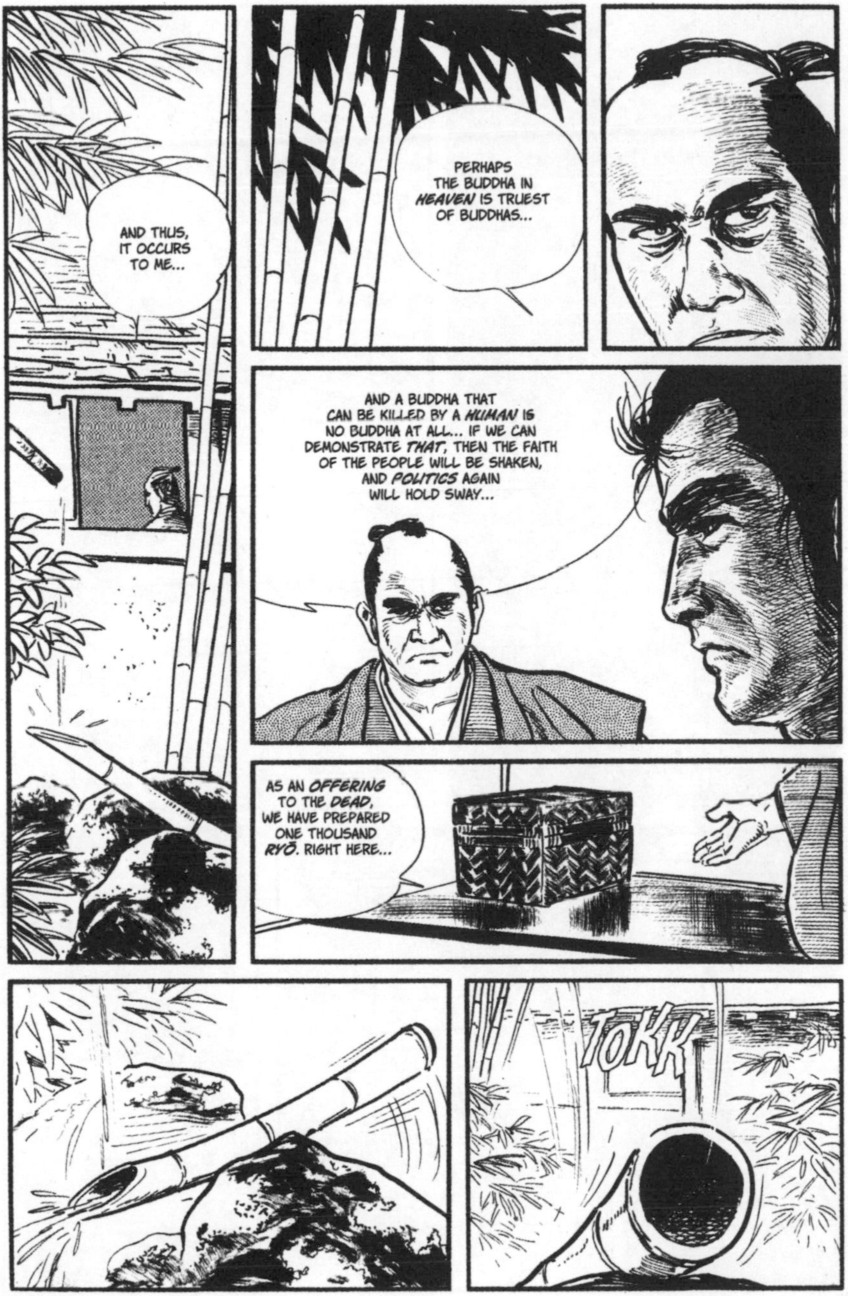
AND THUS, IT OCCURS TO ME...
PERHAPS THE BUDDHA IN *HEAVEN* IS TRUEST OF BUDDHAS...
AND A BUDDHA THAT CAN BE KILLED BY A *HUMAN* IS NO BUDDHA AT ALL... IF WE CAN DEMONSTRATE *THAT*, THEN THE FAITH OF THE PEOPLE WILL BE SHAKEN, AND *POLITICS* AGAIN WILL HOLD SWAY...
AS AN *OFFERING* TO THE *DEAD*, WE HAVE PREPARED ONE THOUSAND *RYŌ*. RIGHT HERE...
TOKK

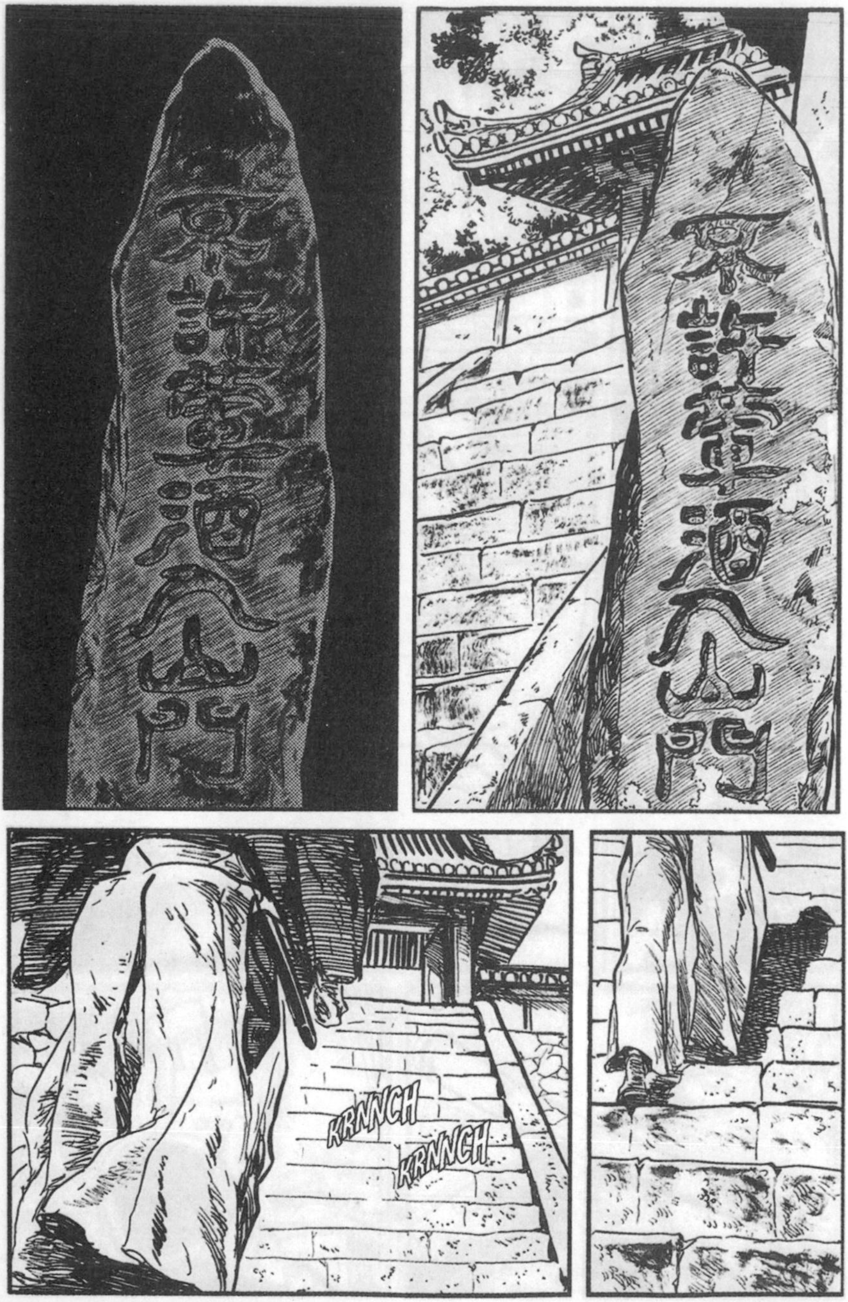
許葷酒入山門
許葷酒入山門
KRNNCH
KRNNCH

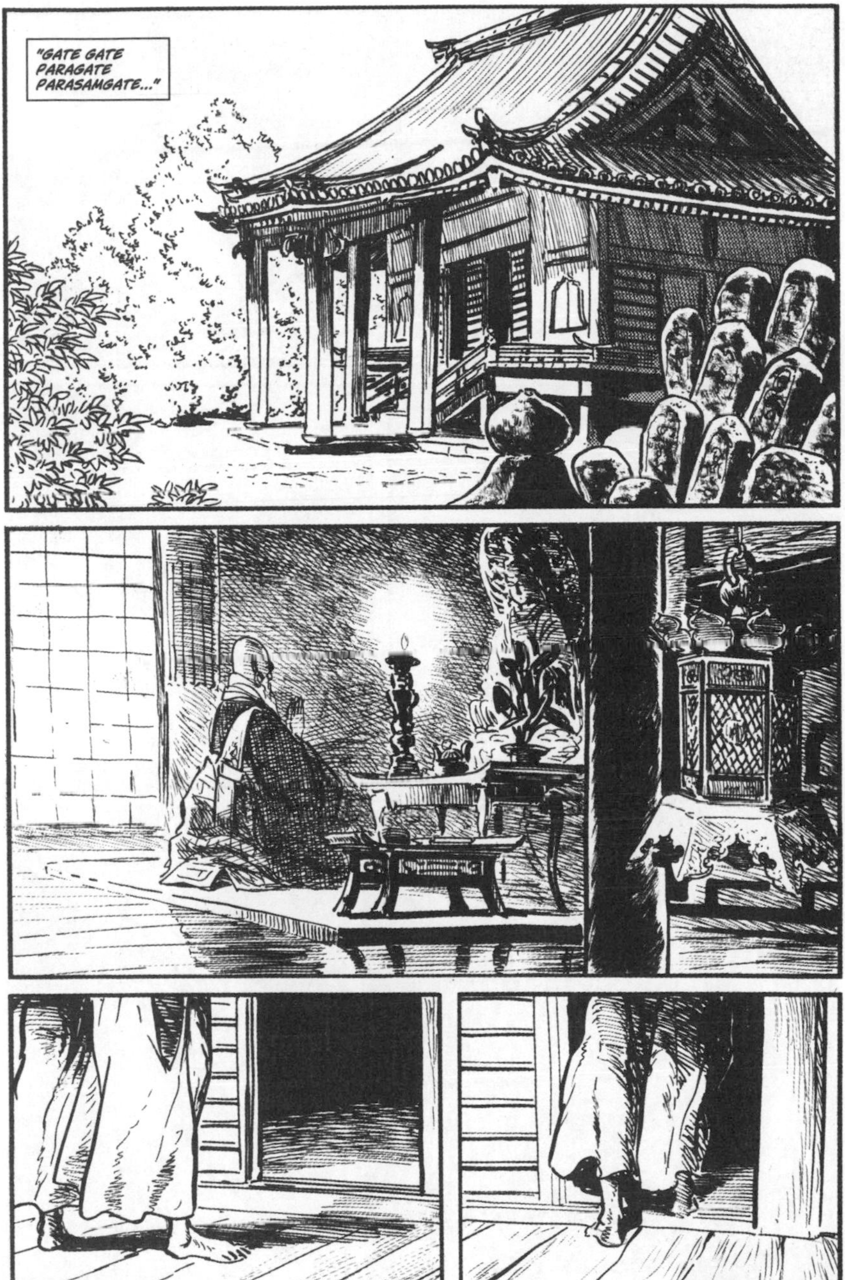
"GATE GATE PARAGATE PARASAMGATE..."

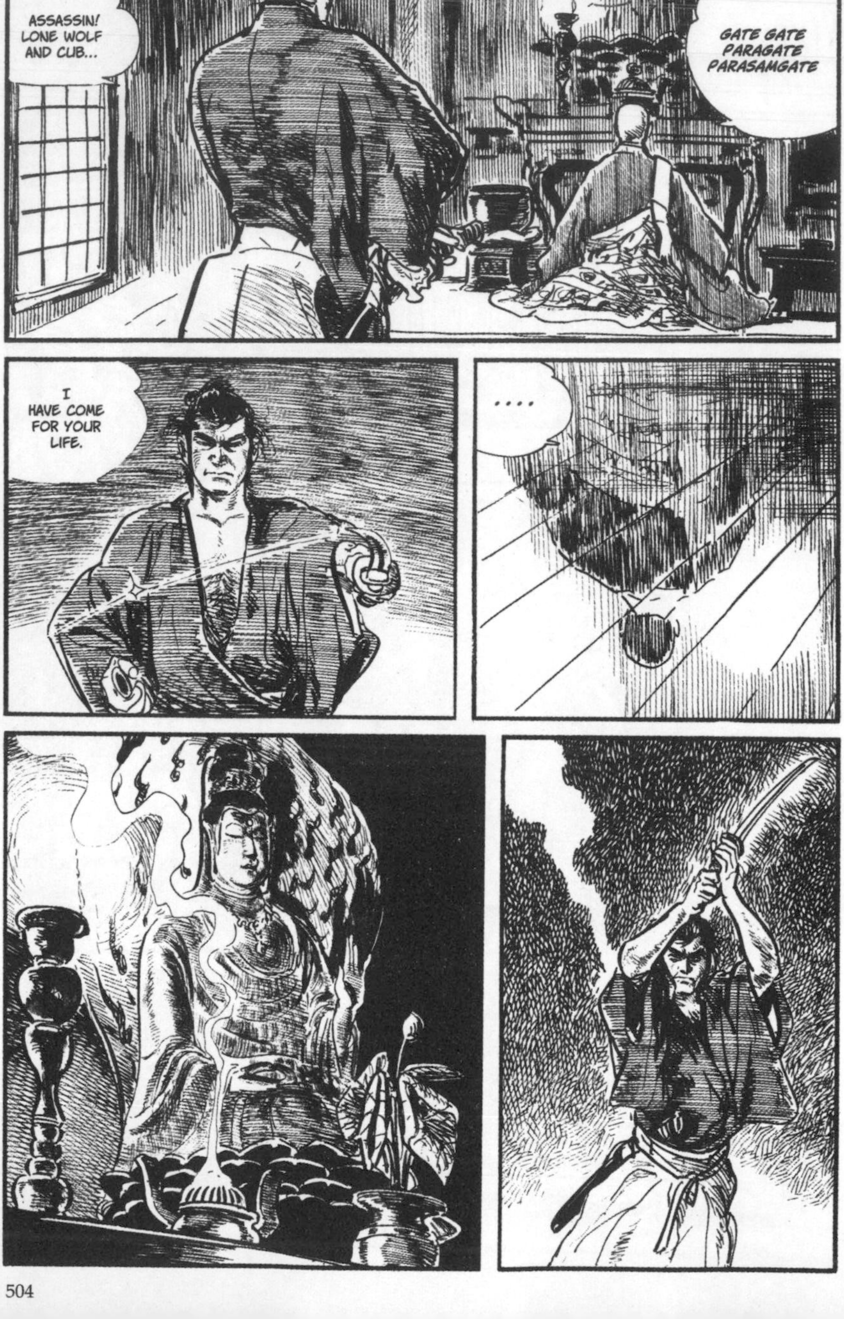
GATE GATE PARAGATE PARASAMGATE
ASSASSIN! LONE WOLF AND CUB...
....
I HAVE COME FOR YOUR LIFE.

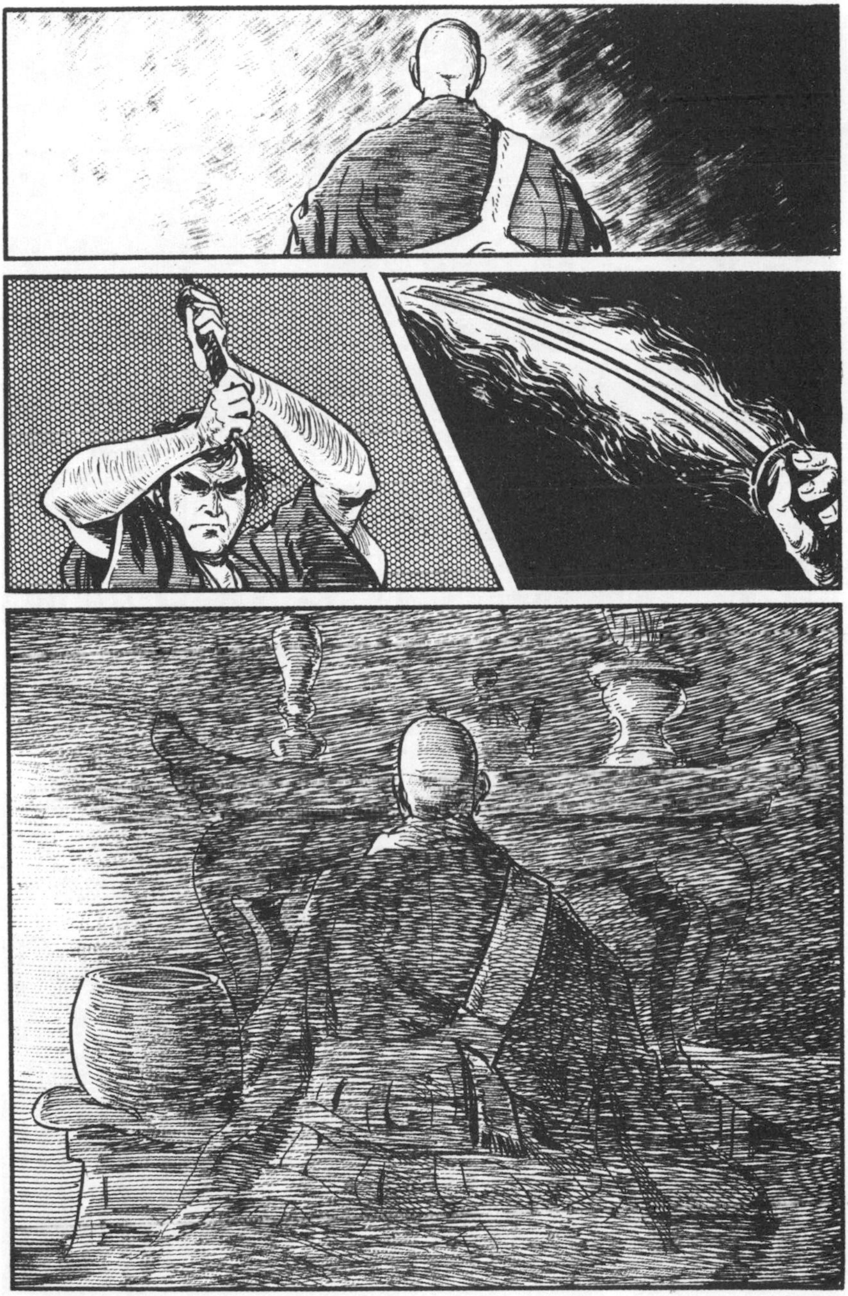

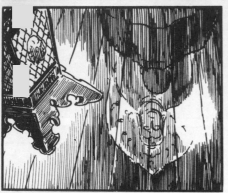

YOU CANNOT KILL THAT WHICH DOES NOT EXIST...

YOU CANNOT KILL ONE THAT HAS FORGOTTEN SELF AND MERGED WITH THE EMPTINESS OF *MU*, ONE FOR WHOM THE SUBJECTIVE AND THE OBJECTIVE ARE AS ONE, AND IS BUT A FACET OF THE TOTALITY OF *NAIGE DAJŌ*...

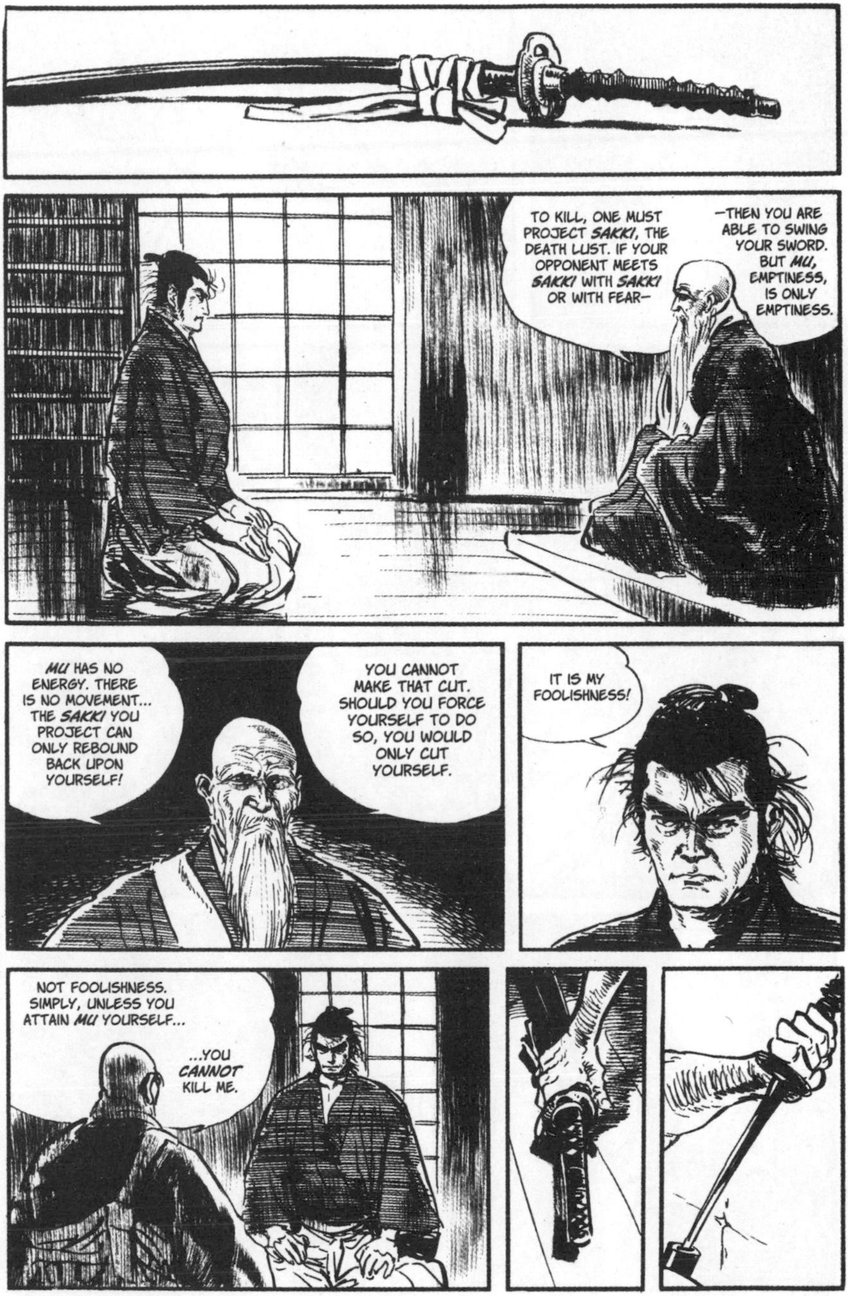
TO KILL, ONE MUST PROJECT *SAKKI*, THE DEATH LUST. IF YOUR OPPONENT MEETS *SAKKI* WITH *SAKKI* OR WITH FEAR—
—THEN YOU ARE ABLE TO SWING YOUR SWORD. BUT *MU*, EMPTINESS, IS ONLY EMPTINESS.
MU HAS NO ENERGY. THERE IS NO MOVEMENT... THE *SAKKI* YOU PROJECT CAN ONLY REBOUND BACK UPON YOURSELF!
YOU CANNOT MAKE THAT CUT. SHOULD YOU FORCE YOURSELF TO DO SO, YOU WOULD ONLY CUT YOURSELF.
IT IS MY FOOLISHNESS!
NOT FOOLISHNESS. SIMPLY, UNLESS YOU ATTAIN *MU* YOURSELF...
...YOU *CANNOT* KILL ME.

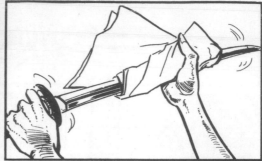

ONE WHO LIVES IN *MEIFUMADŌ* CAN CUT OPEN HIS STOMACH, EVEN BEFORE BUDDHA HIMSELF.

IF I CANNOT ASSASSINATE YOU, THEN I HAVE NO RIGHT TO WALK THE ASSASSIN'S ROAD... FORGIVE ME!

THEN *ABANDON* THAT ASSASSIN'S ROAD!

THAT I CANNOT DO. SO LONG AS I HAVE LIFE, MY QUEST WILL NOT PERMIT IT.

IF YOU TRULY CANNOT ABANDON THE ASSASSIN'S ROAD, THEN YOU MUST PERFECT *MUMON-SEKI,* THE GATELESS BARRIER.

...MUMON-SEKI...?!

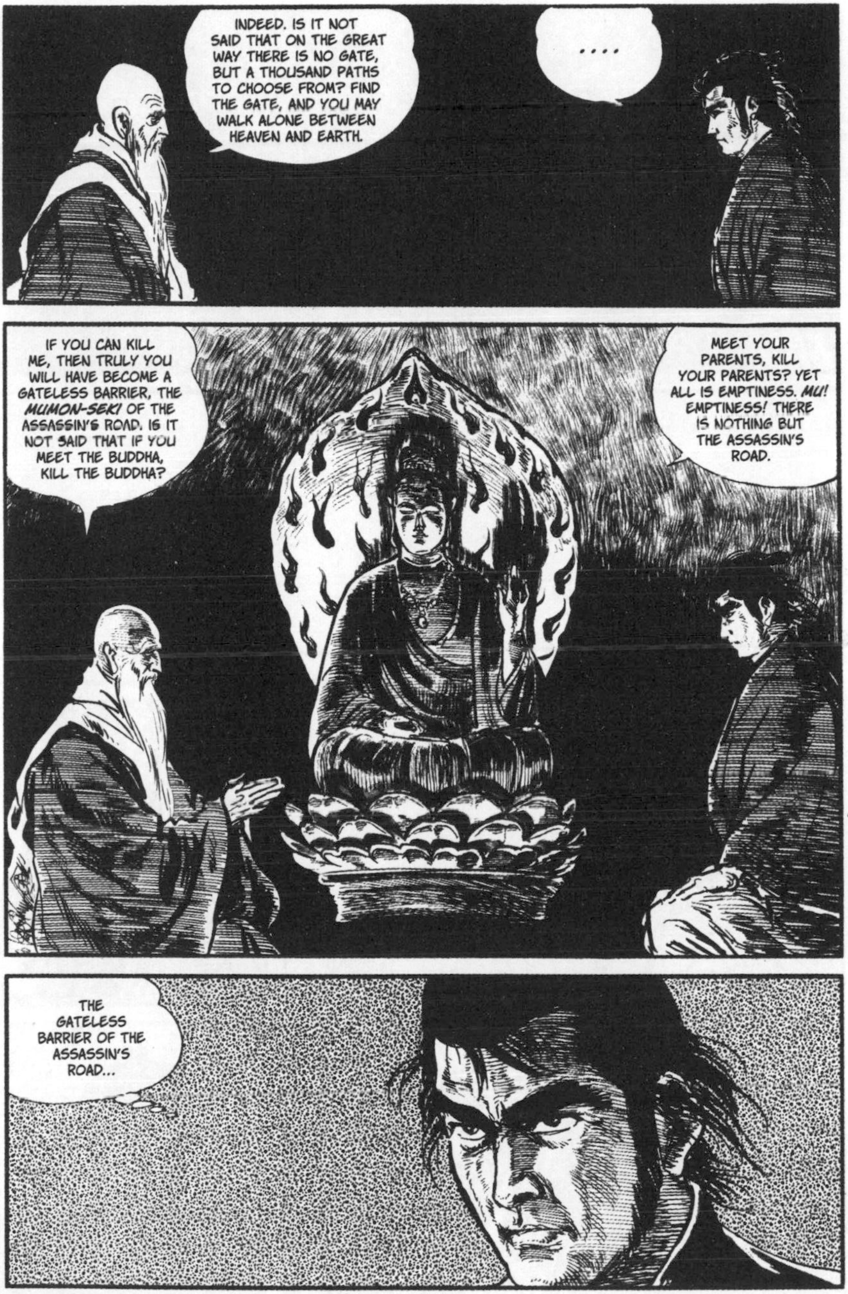
INDEED. IS IT NOT SAID THAT ON THE GREAT WAY THERE IS NO GATE, BUT A THOUSAND PATHS TO CHOOSE FROM? FIND THE GATE, AND YOU MAY WALK ALONE BETWEEN HEAVEN AND EARTH.
....
IF YOU CAN KILL ME, THEN TRULY YOU WILL HAVE BECOME A GATELESS BARRIER, THE *MUMON-SEKI* OF THE ASSASSIN'S ROAD. IS IT NOT SAID THAT IF YOU MEET THE BUDDHA, KILL THE BUDDHA?
MEET YOUR PARENTS, KILL YOUR PARENTS? YET ALL IS EMPTINESS. *MU!* EMPTINESS! THERE IS NOTHING BUT THE ASSASSIN'S ROAD.
THE GATELESS BARRIER OF THE ASSASSIN'S ROAD...

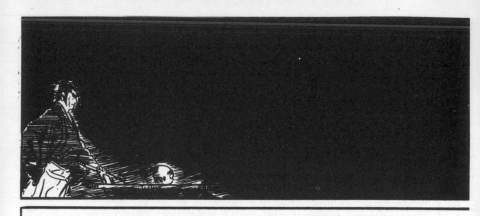

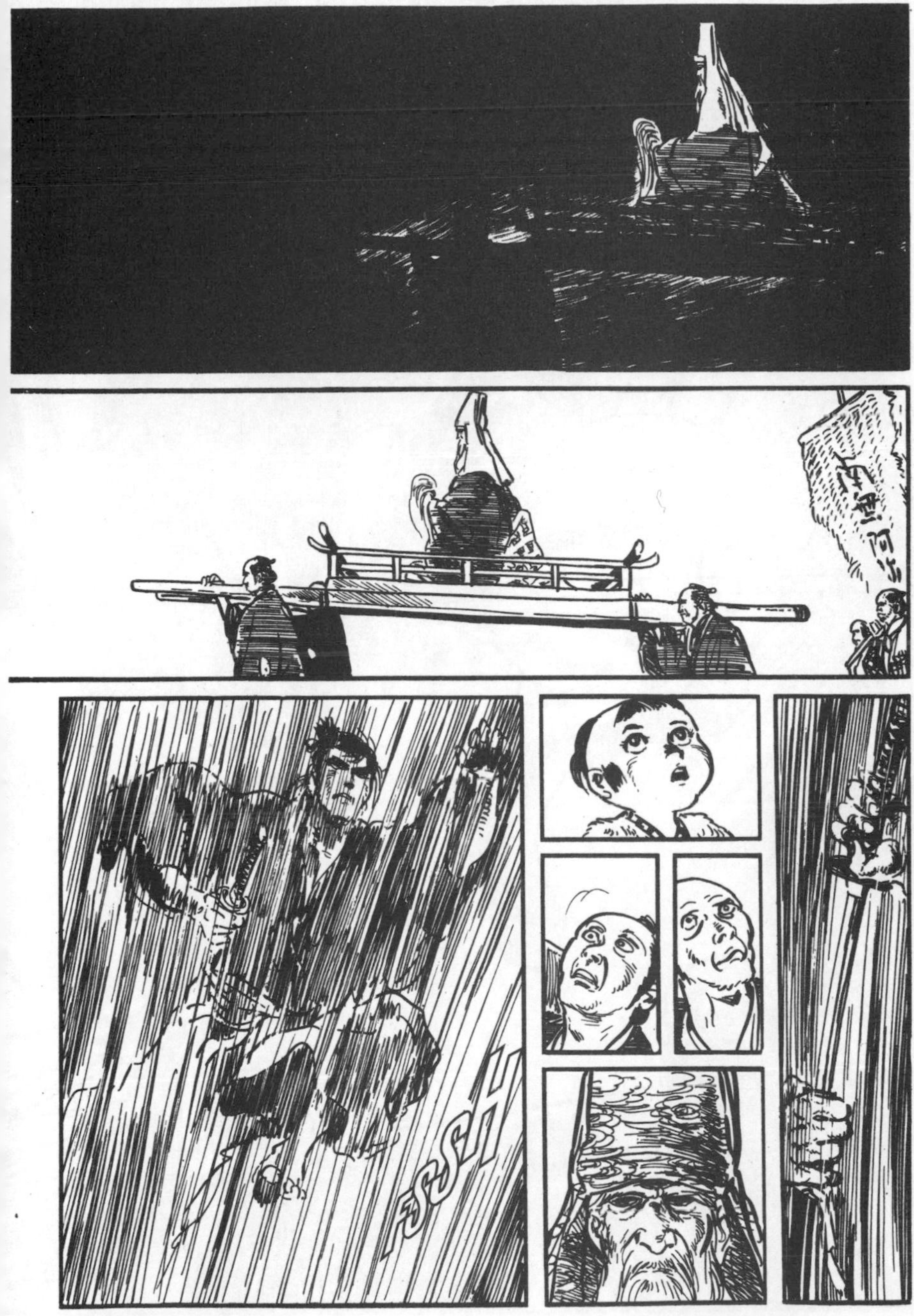
FSSH

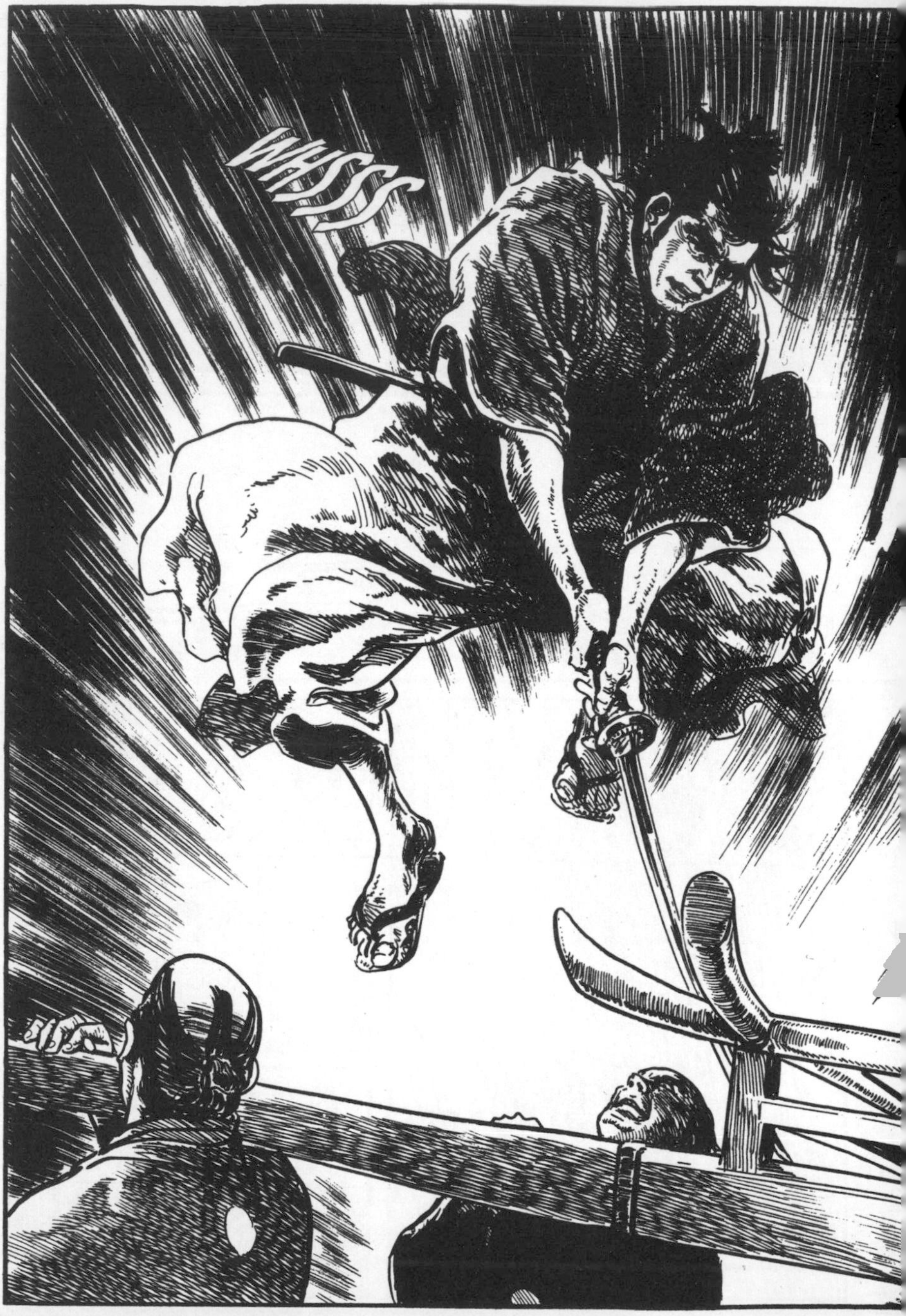
WHSSS

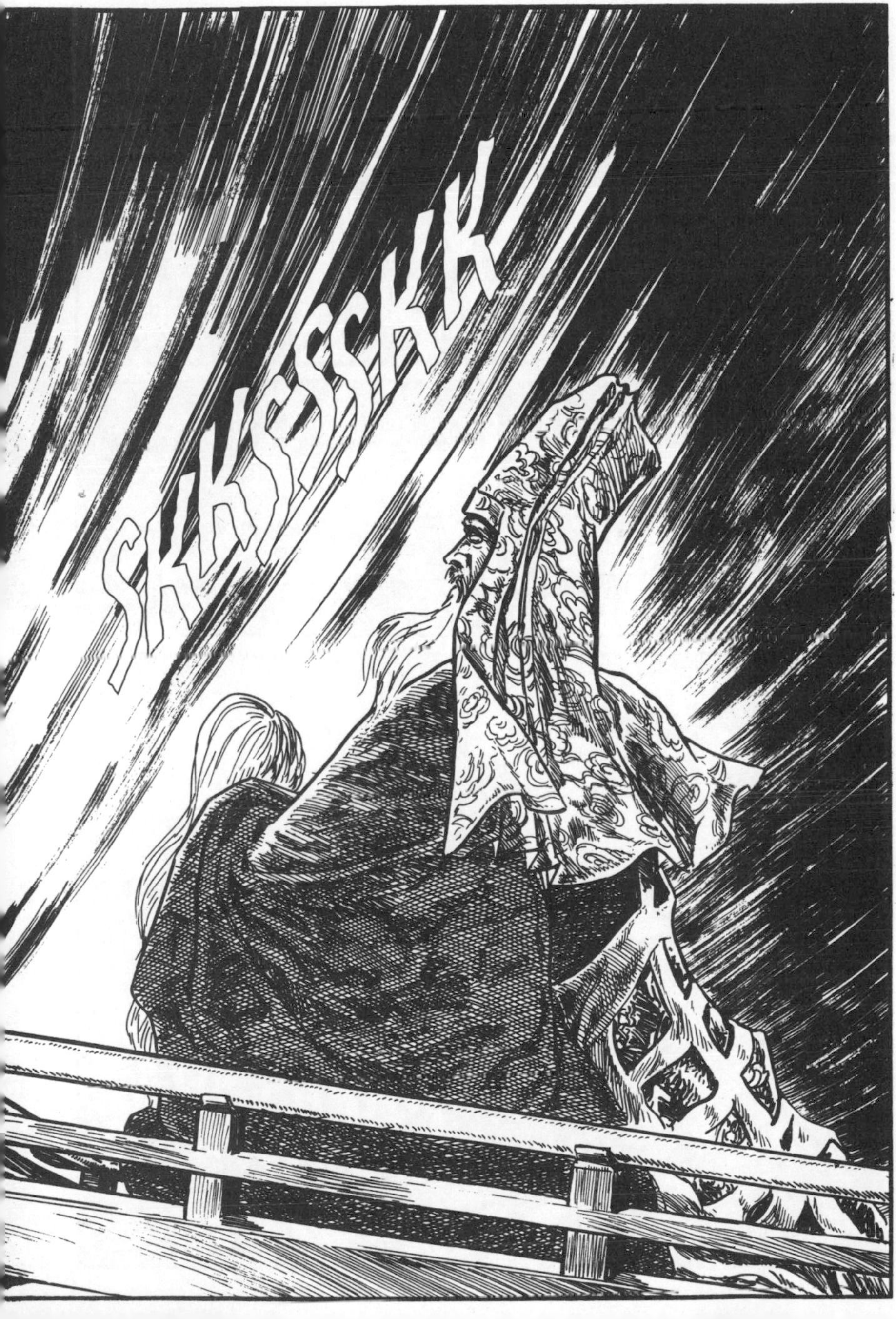
SKKSSSKK

IS THIS NOT GOOD? HE WHO PERFECTS HIS PATH?

IS THIS NOT GOOD? THE GATELESS BARRIER?

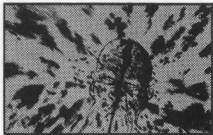

WAOHHH!

SPLLSSSH

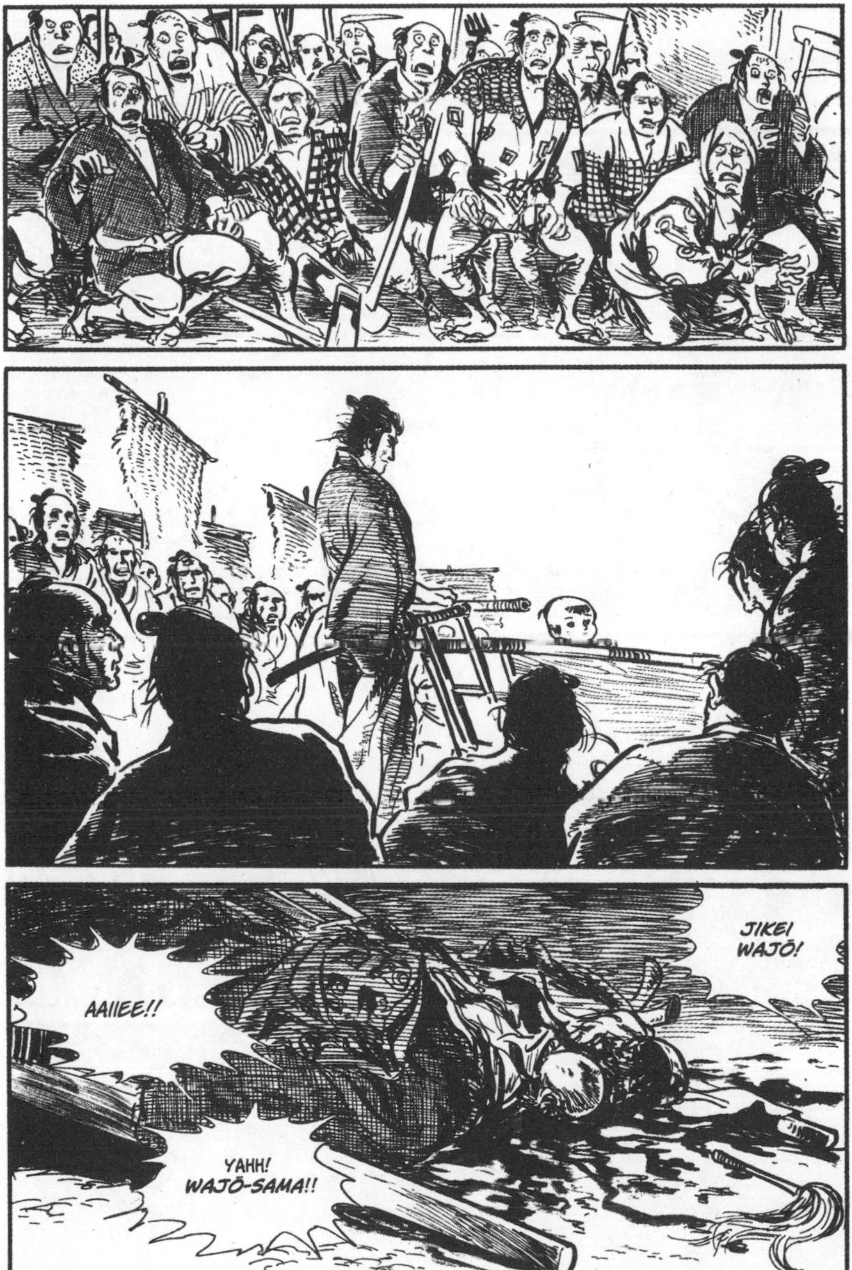
JIKEI WAJŌ!
AAIIEE!!
YAHH! WAJŌ-SAMA!!

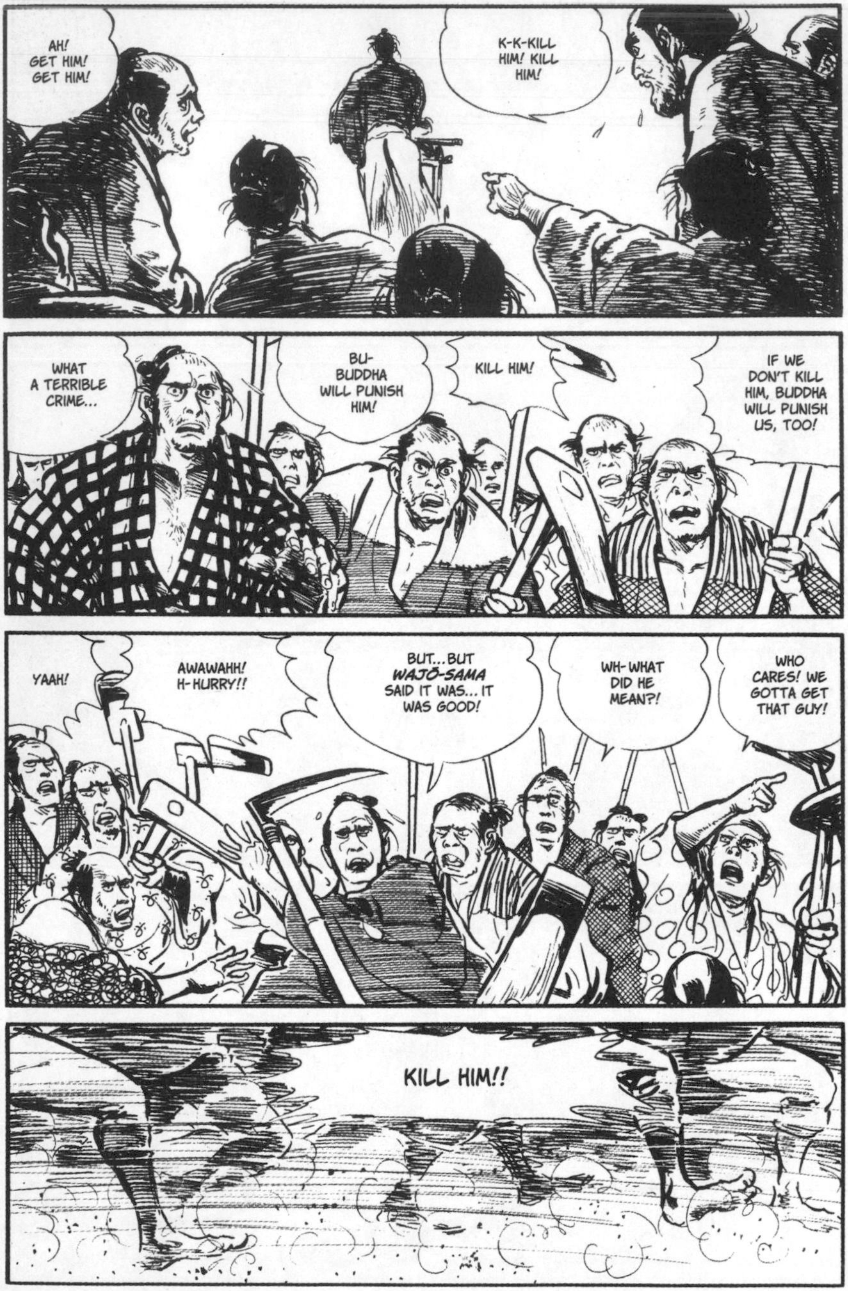
K-K-KILL HIM! KILL HIM!
AH! GET HIM! GET HIM!
IF WE DON'T KILL HIM, BUDDHA WILL PUNISH US, TOO!
KILL HIM!
BU-BUDDHA WILL PUNISH HIM!
WHAT A TERRIBLE CRIME...
WHO CARES! WE GOTTA GET THAT GUY!
WH-WHAT DID HE MEAN?!
BUT...BUT *WAJŌ-SAMA* SAID IT WAS... IT WAS GOOD!
AWAWAHH! H-HURRY!!
YAAH!
KILL HIM!!

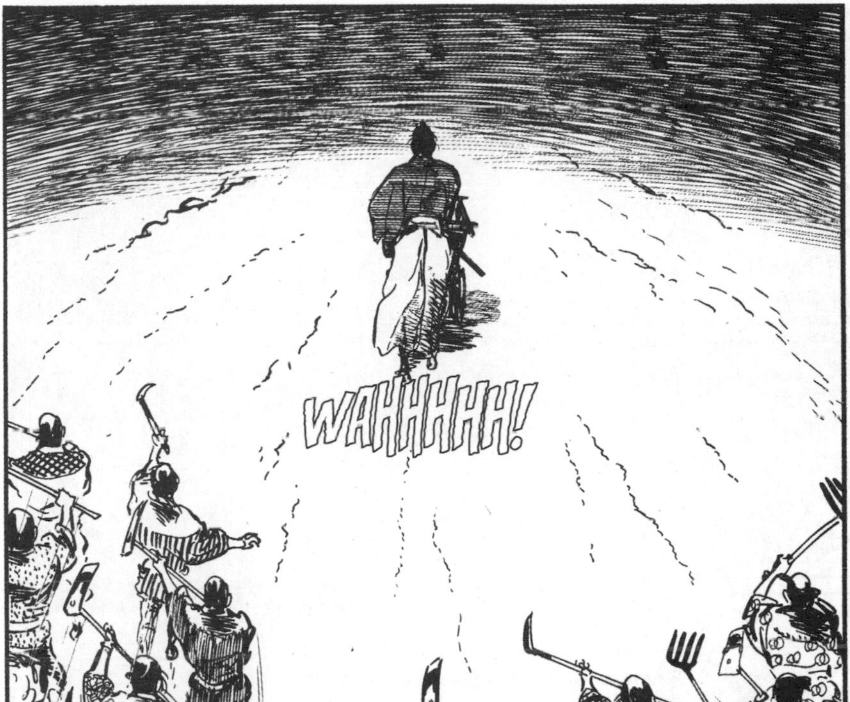
WAHHHHH!

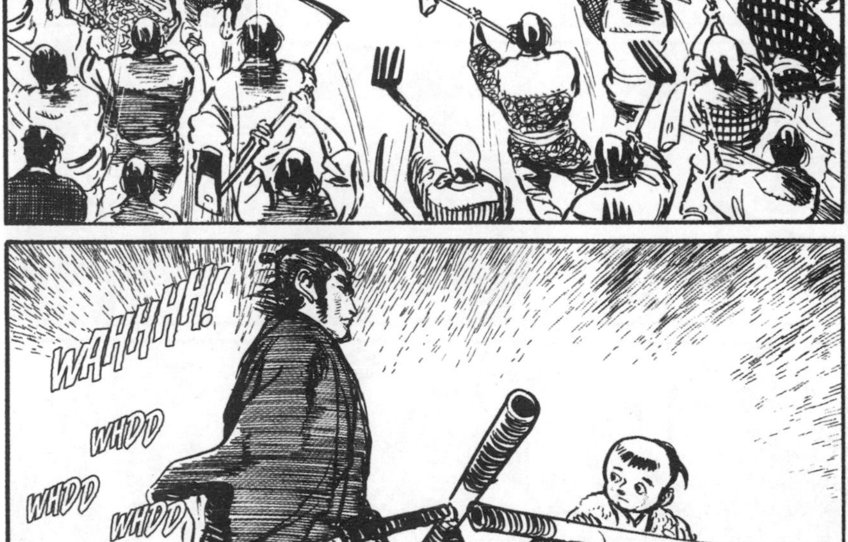
WAHHHH!
WHDD
WHDD
WHDD

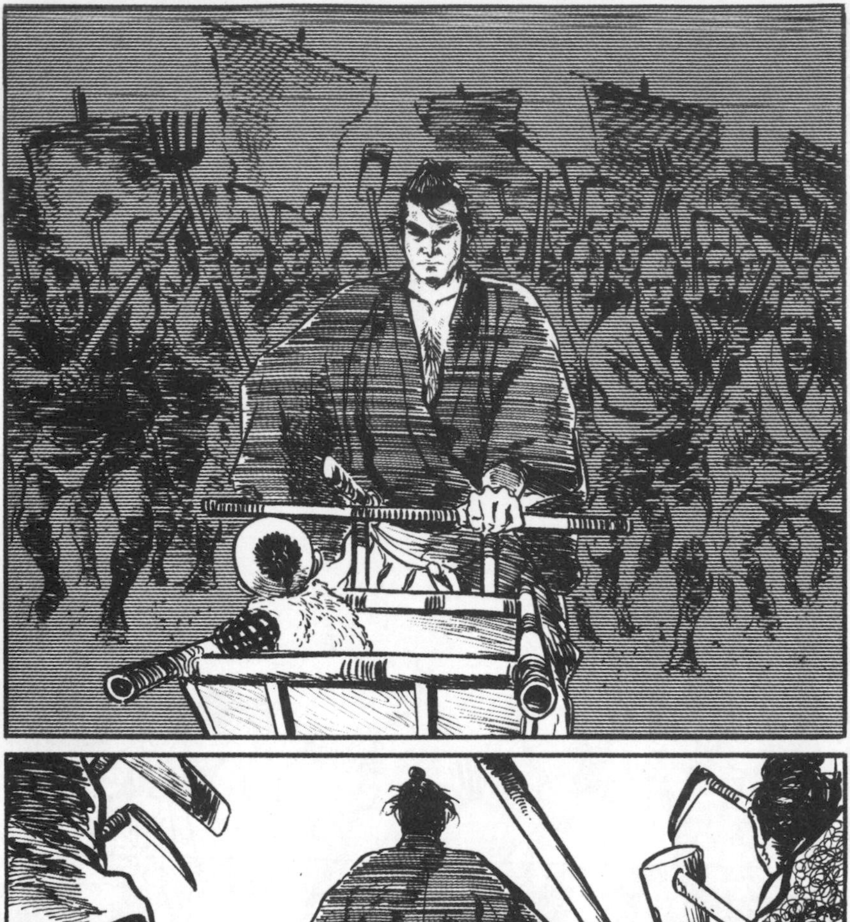

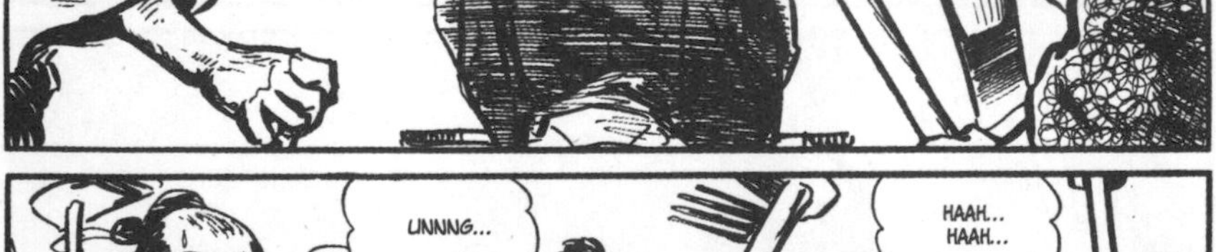

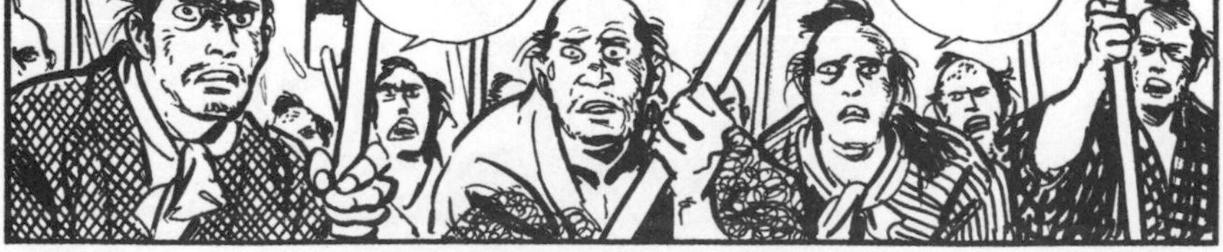
HAAH... HAAH...
UNNNG...

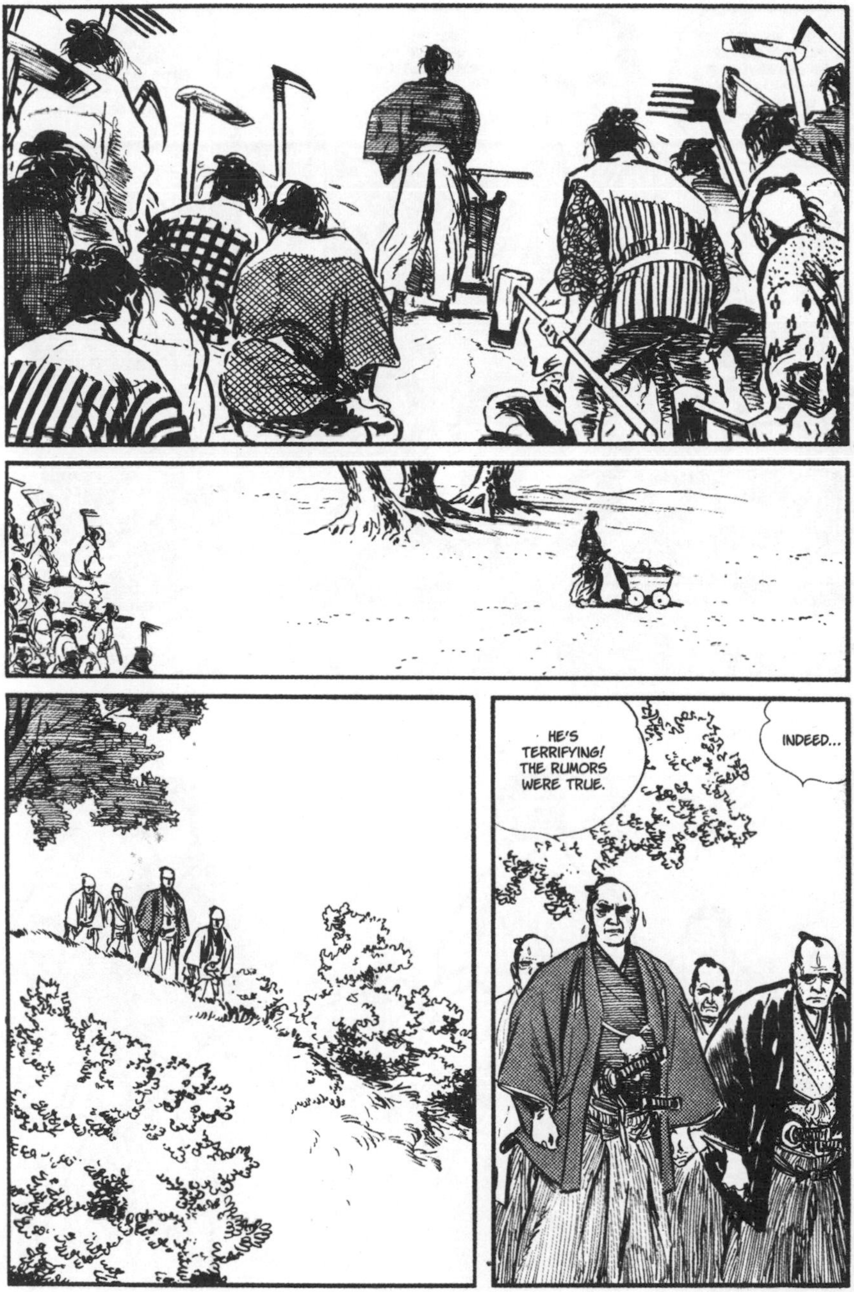
HE'S TERRIFYING! THE RUMORS WERE TRUE.
INDEED...

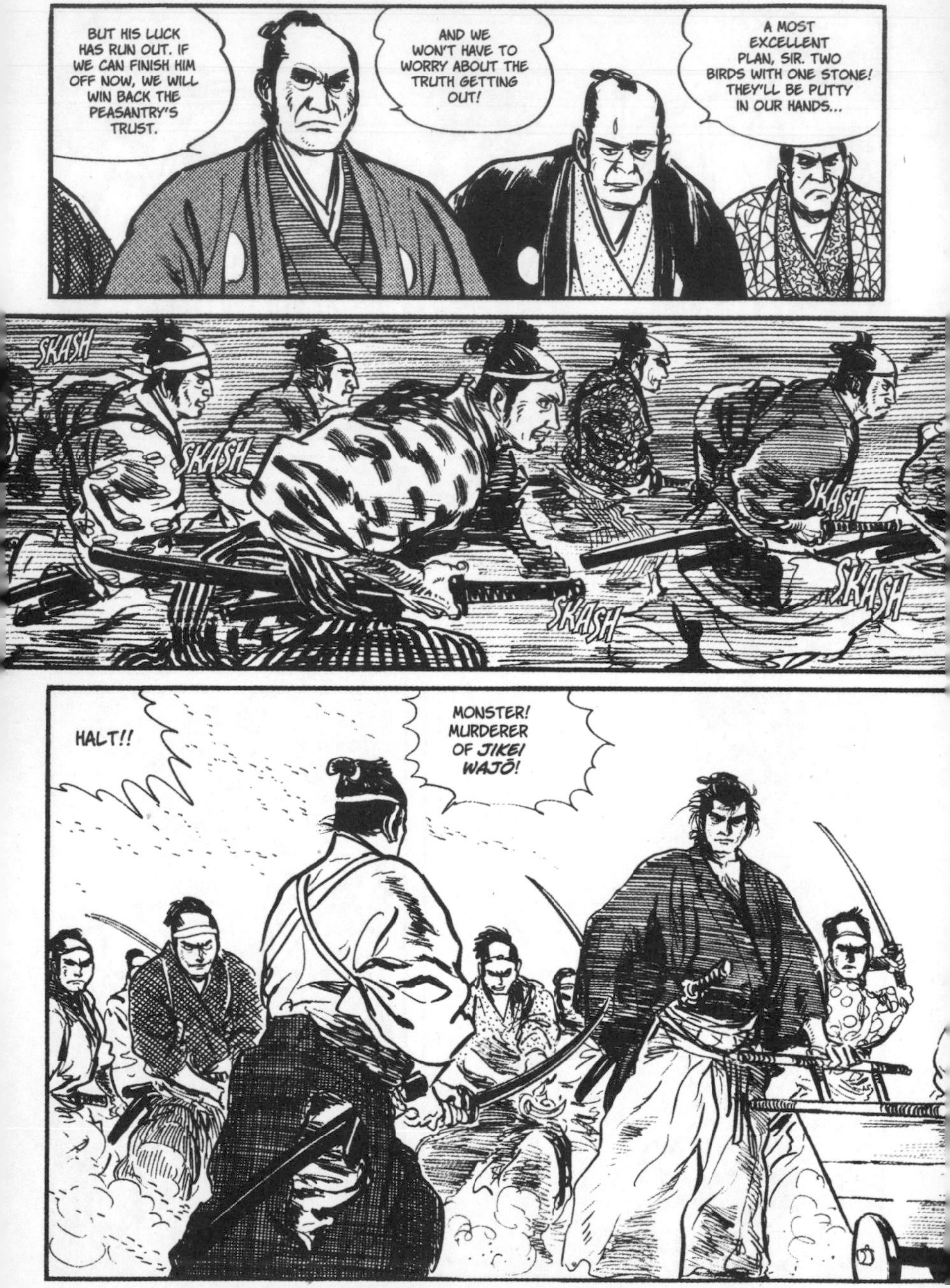
BUT HIS LUCK HAS RUN OUT. IF WE CAN FINISH HIM OFF NOW, WE WILL WIN BACK THE PEASANTRY'S TRUST.
AND WE WON'T HAVE TO WORRY ABOUT THE TRUTH GETTING OUT!
A MOST EXCELLENT PLAN, SIR. TWO BIRDS WITH ONE STONE! THEY'LL BE PUTTY IN OUR HANDS...
SKASH
SKASH
SKASH
SKASH
SKASH
HALT!!
MONSTER! MURDERER OF JIKEI WAJŌ!

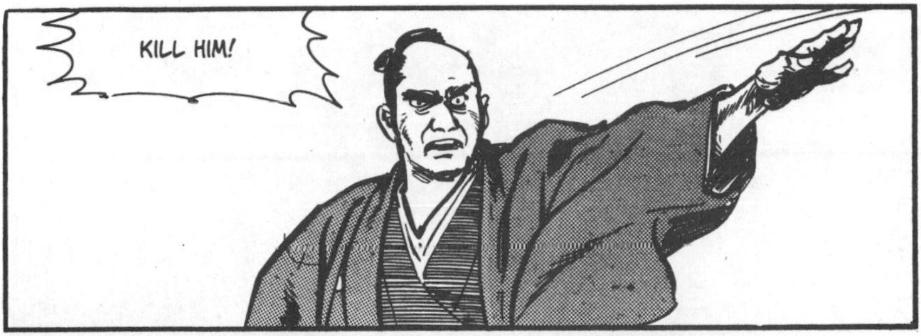
KILL HIM!

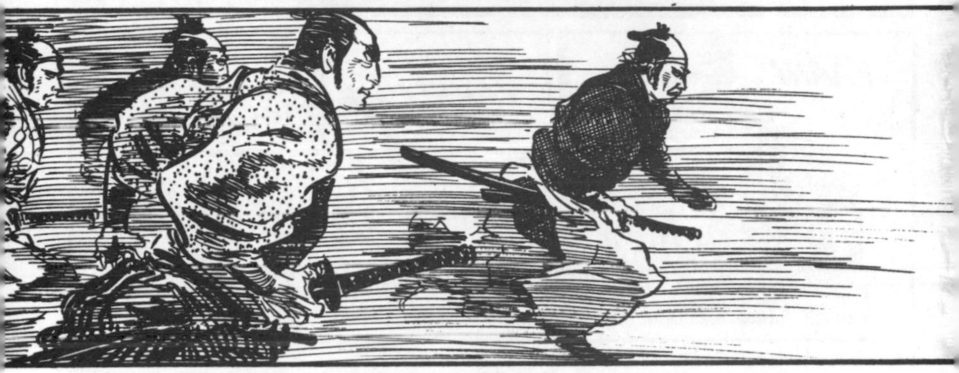

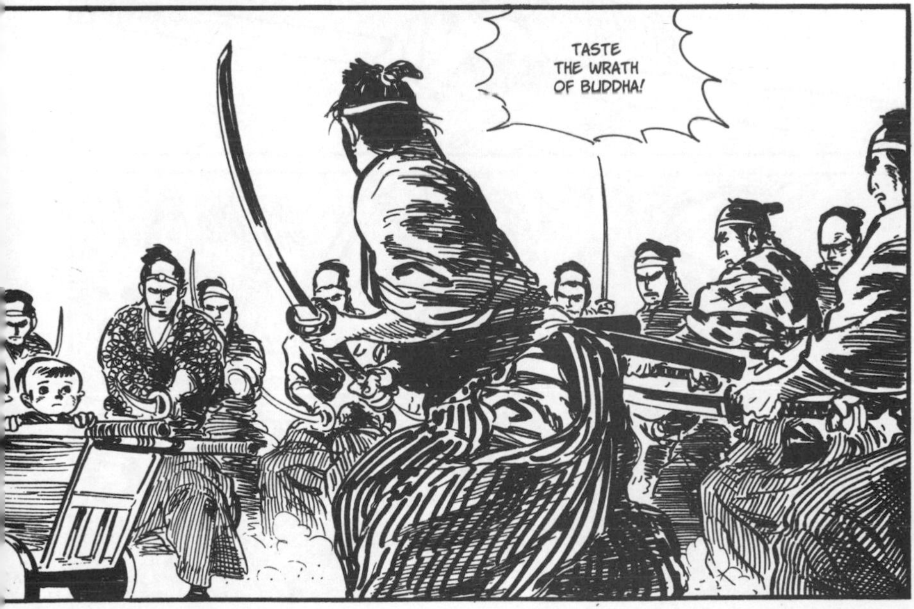
TASTE THE WRATH OF BUDDHA!

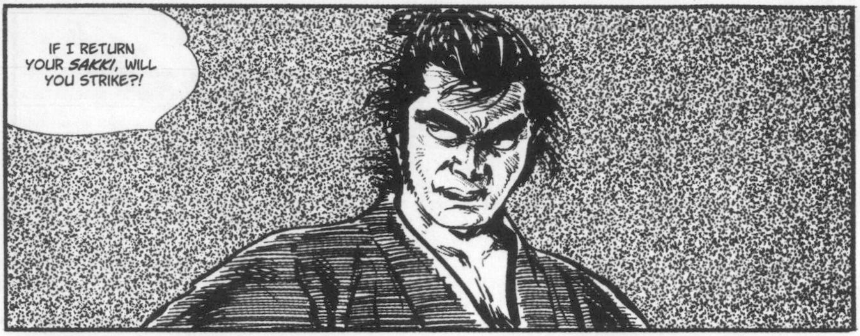
IF I RETURN YOUR *SAKKI*, WILL YOU STRIKE?!
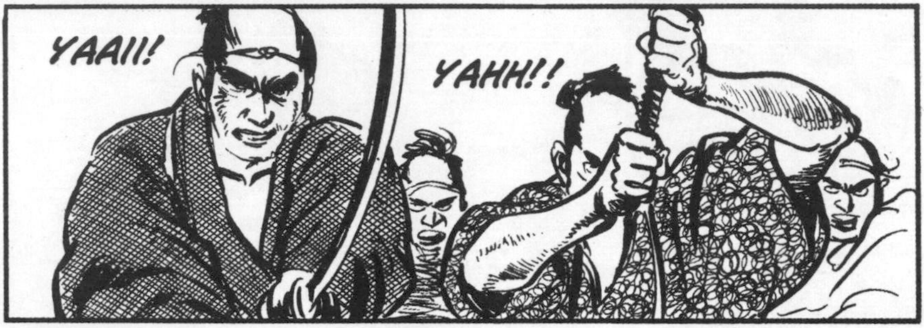
YAHH!!
YAAII!
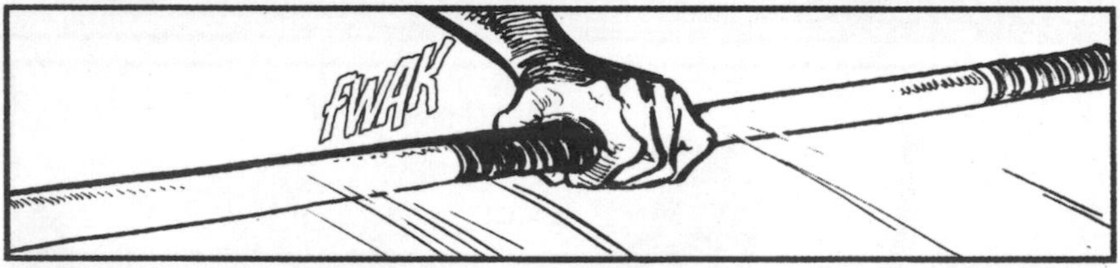
FWAK
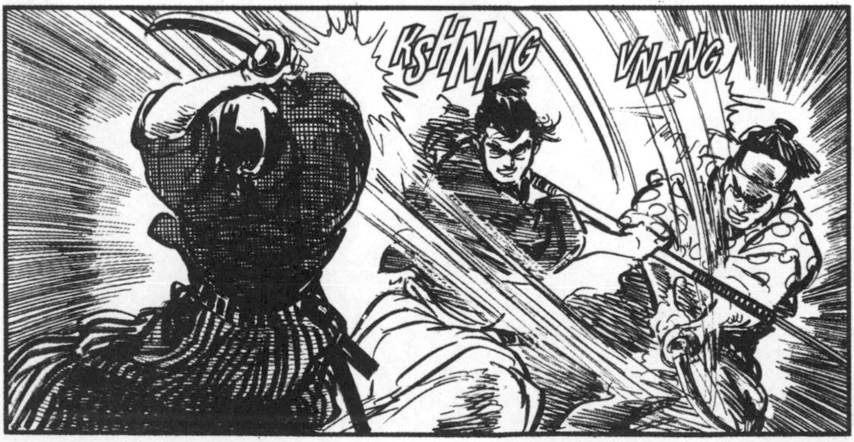
VNNNG
KSHNNG

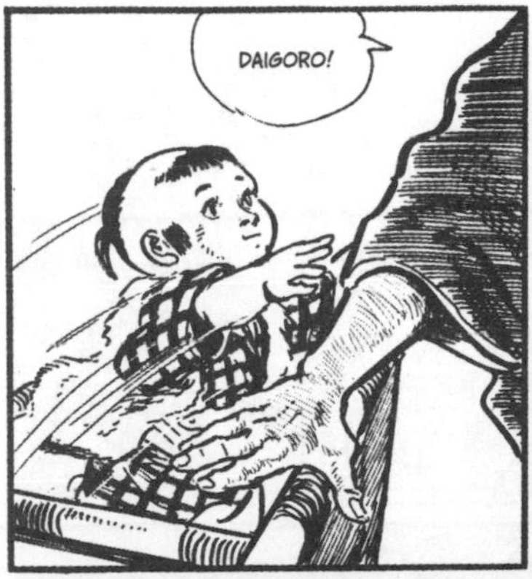
DAIGORO!
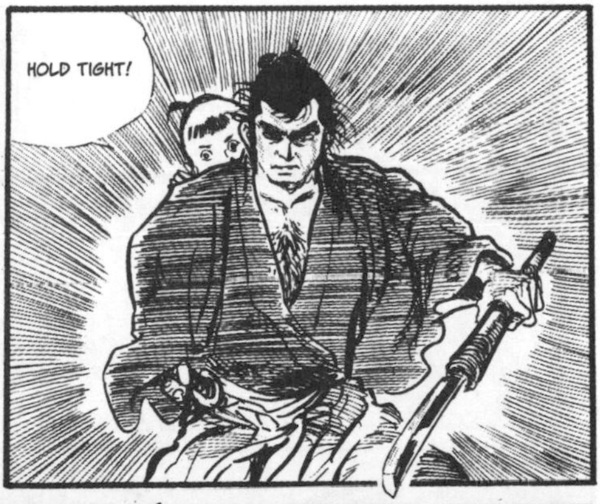
HOLD TIGHT!
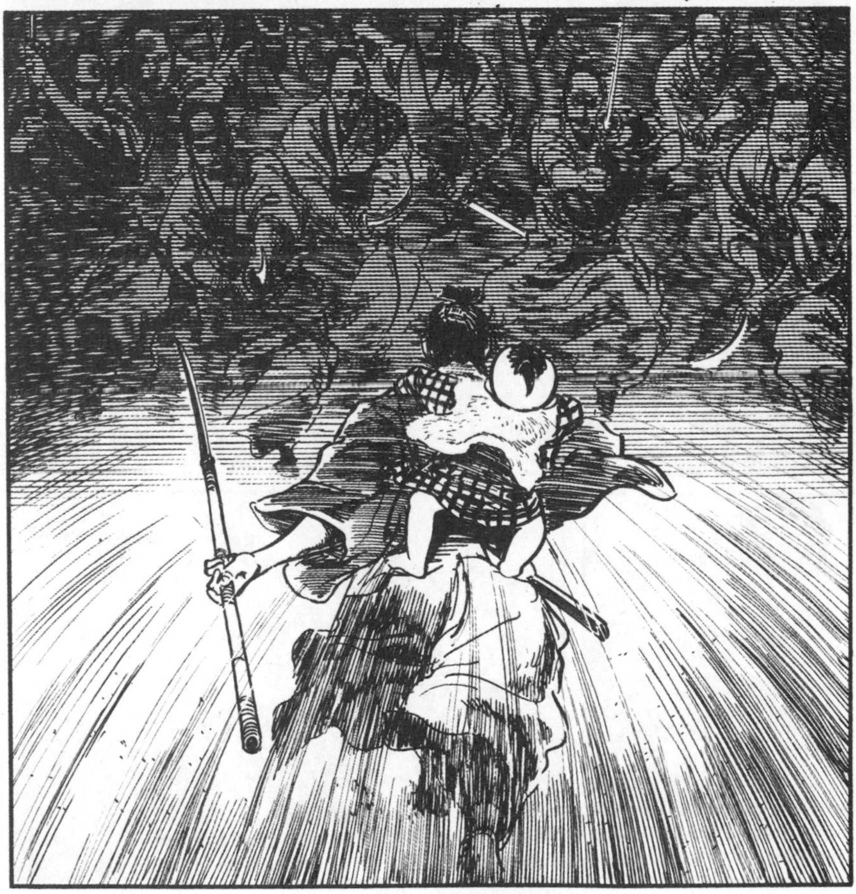

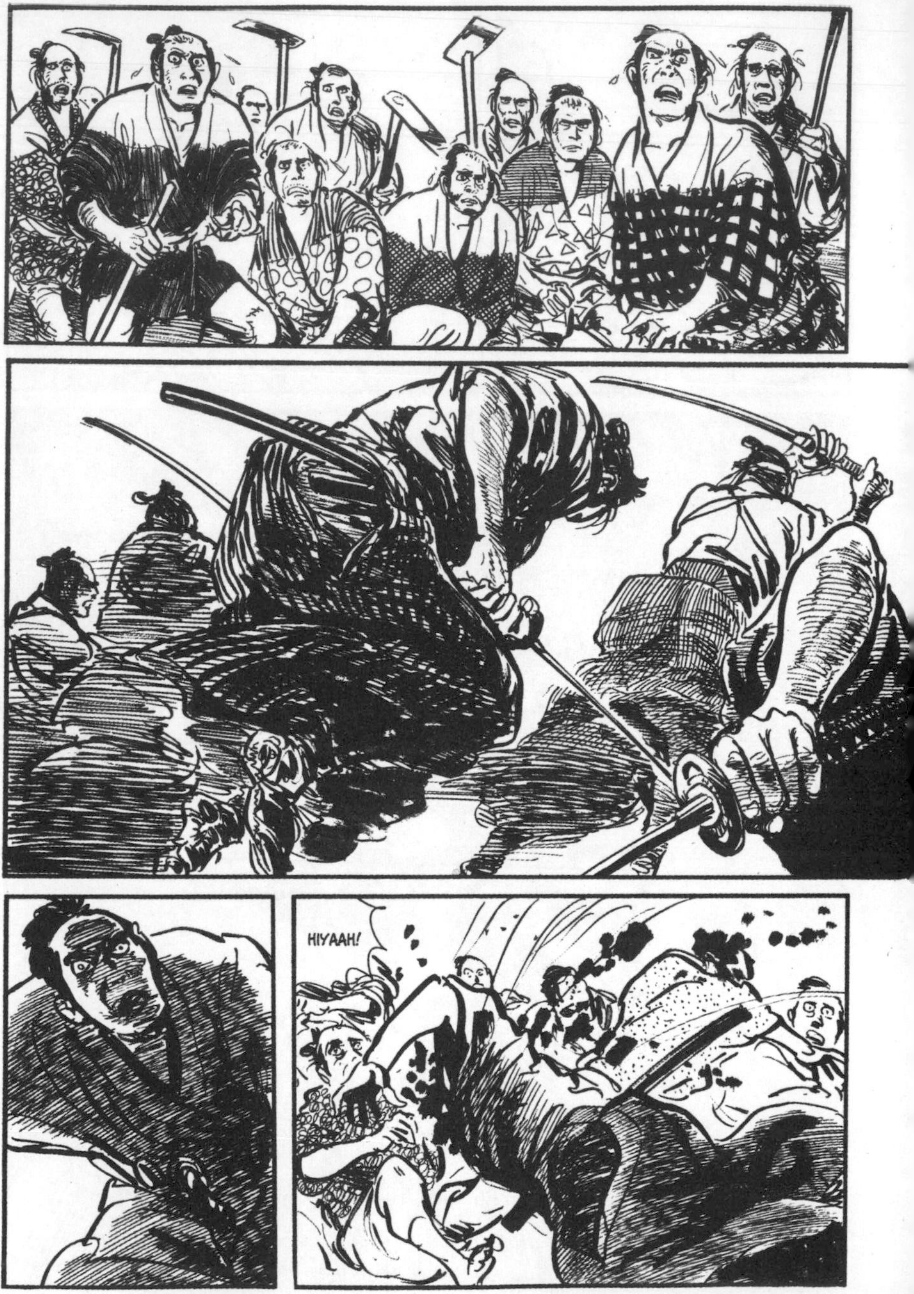
HIYAAH!

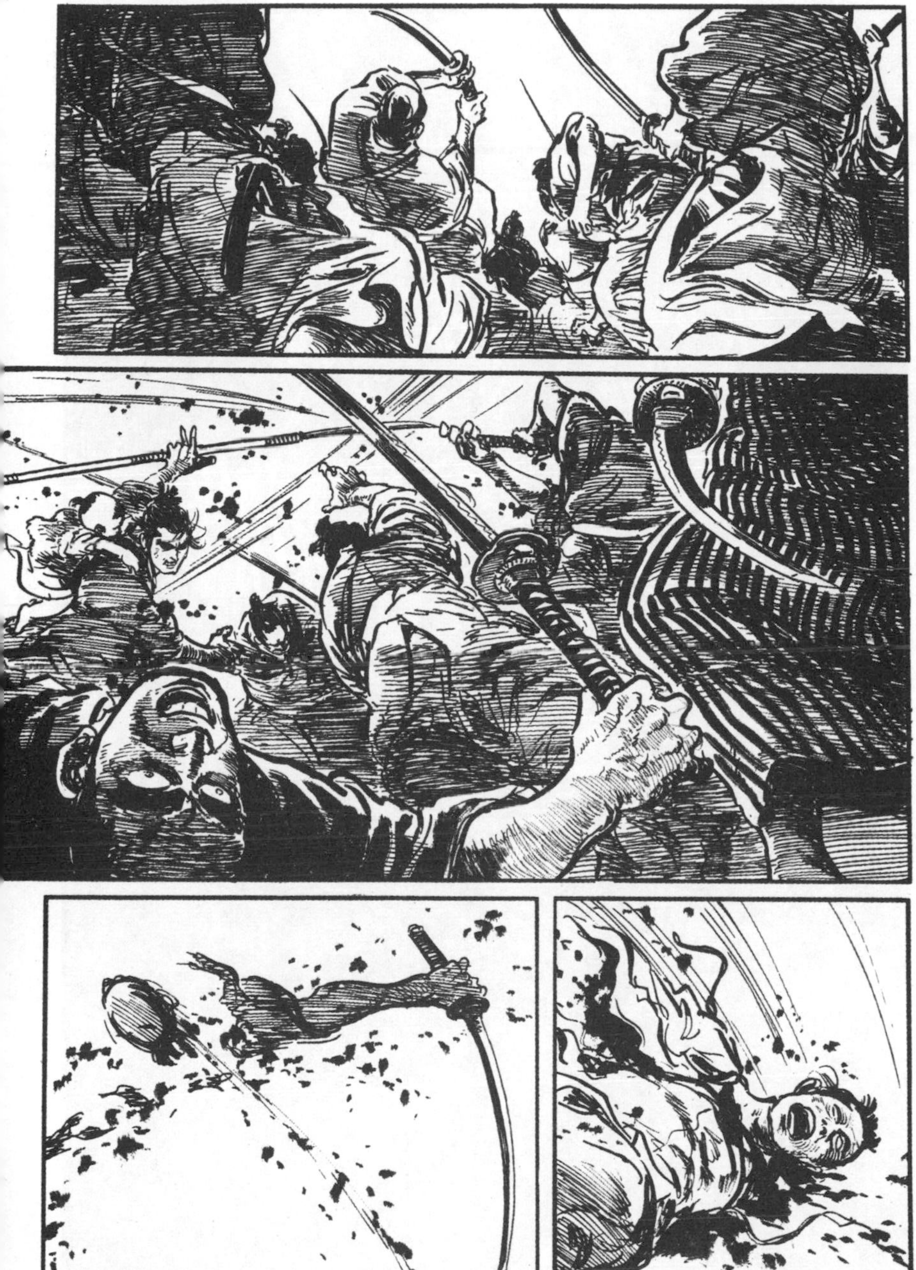

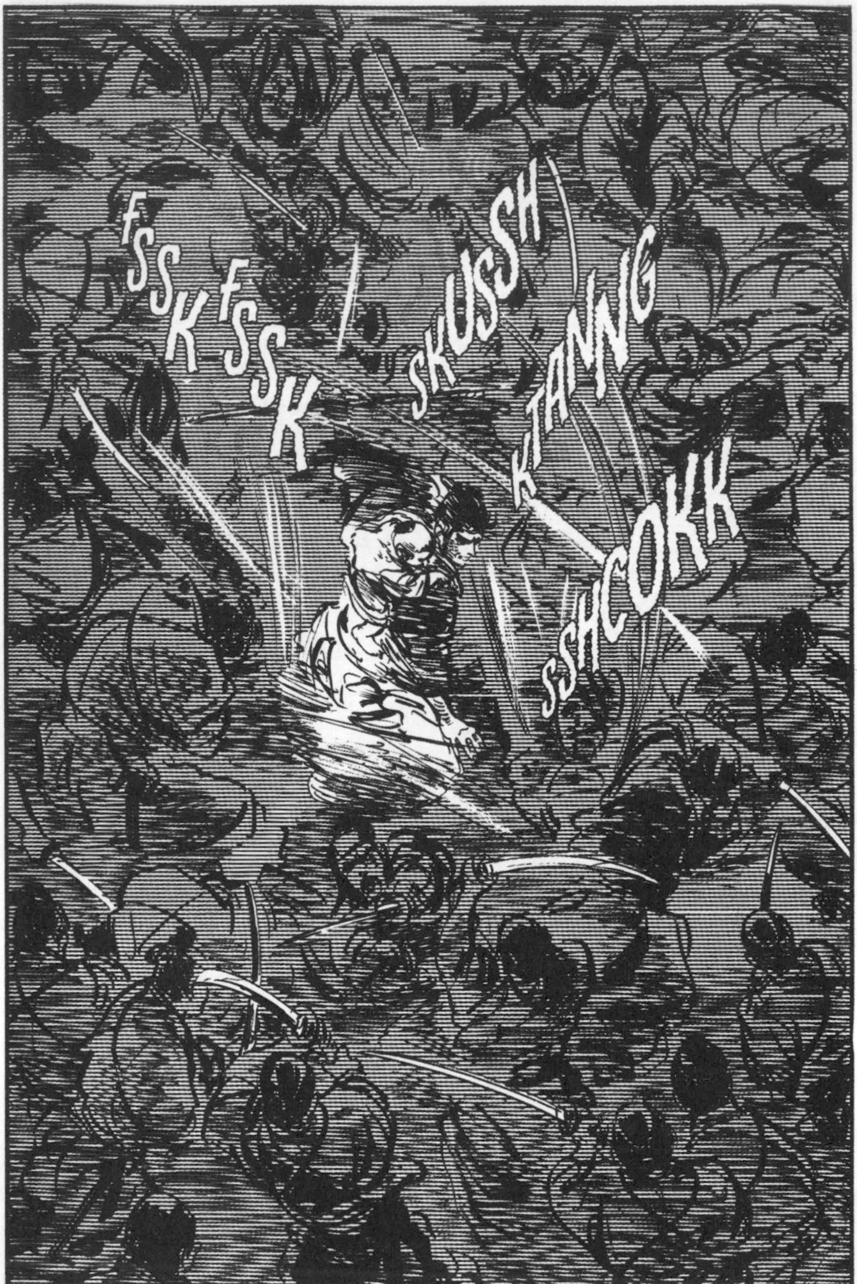
FSSK FSSK
SKUSSH
KTANNG
SSHCOKK

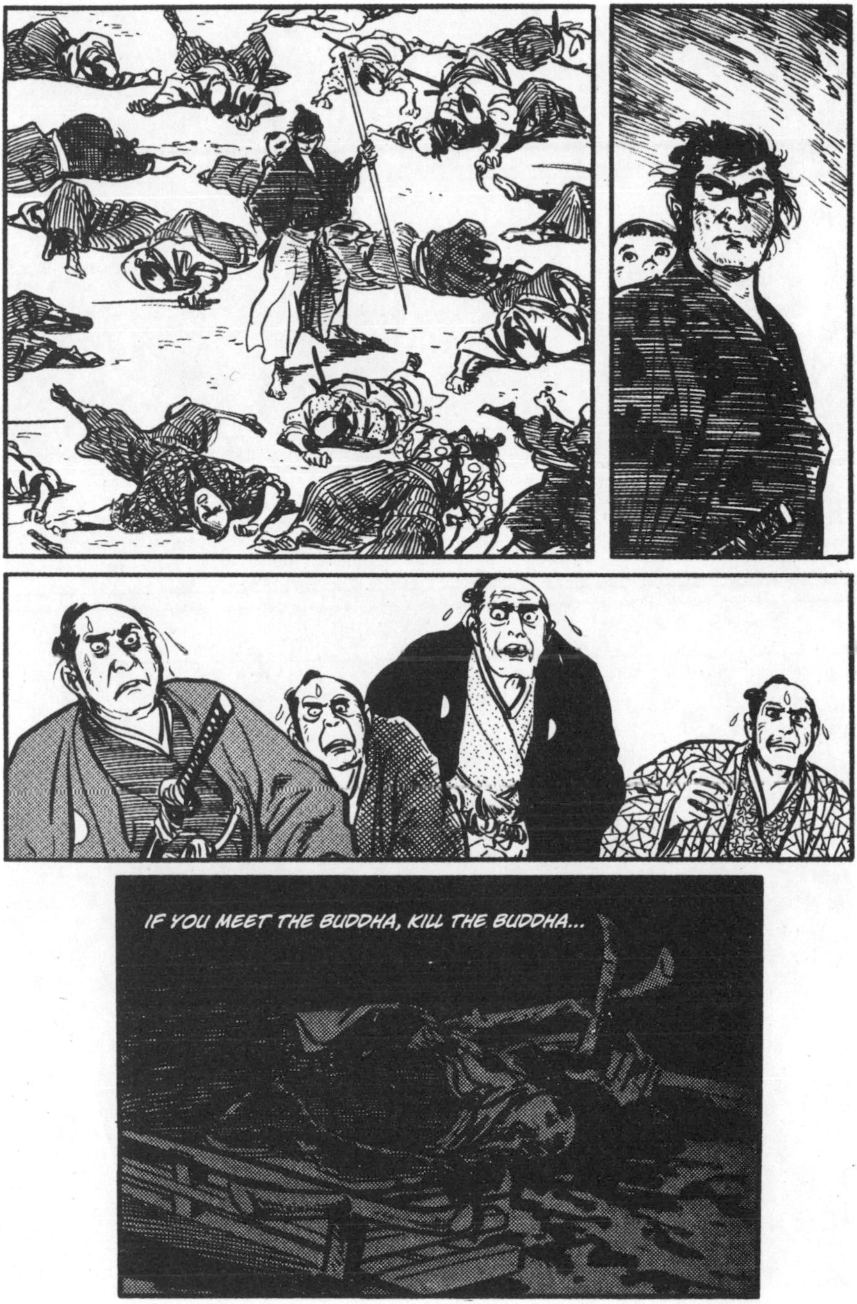
IF YOU MEET THE BUDDHA, KILL THE BUDDHA...

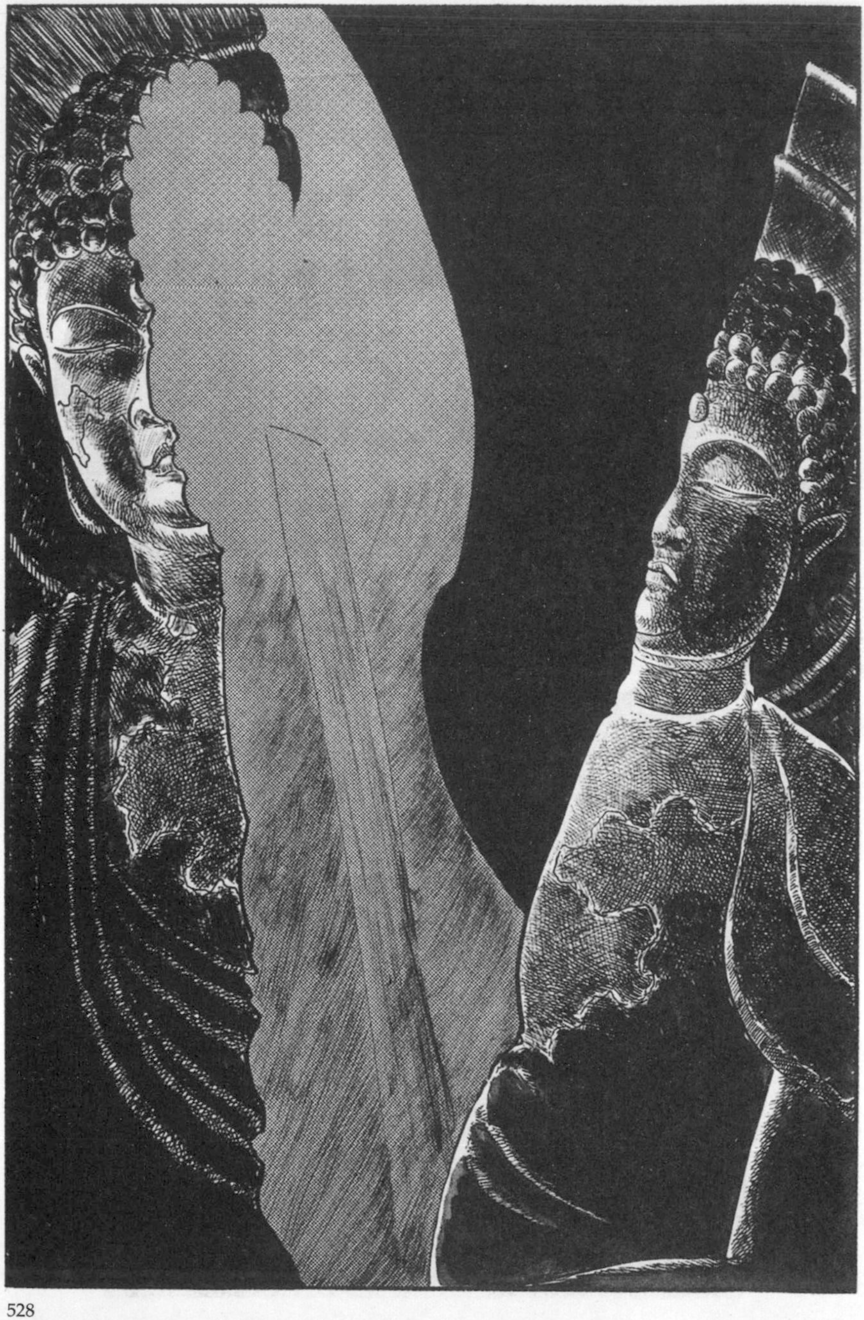

子連れ狼

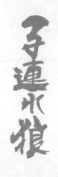

Winter Flower

14

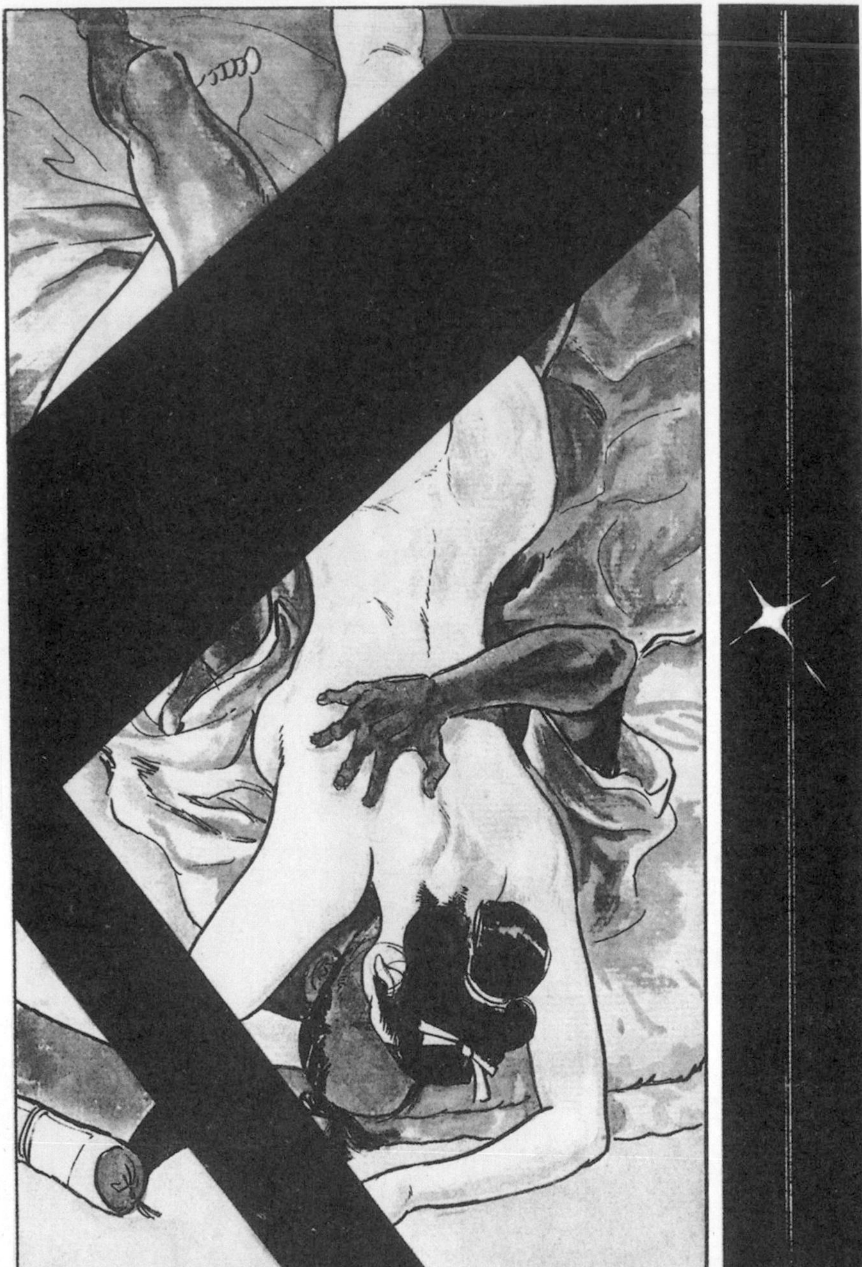

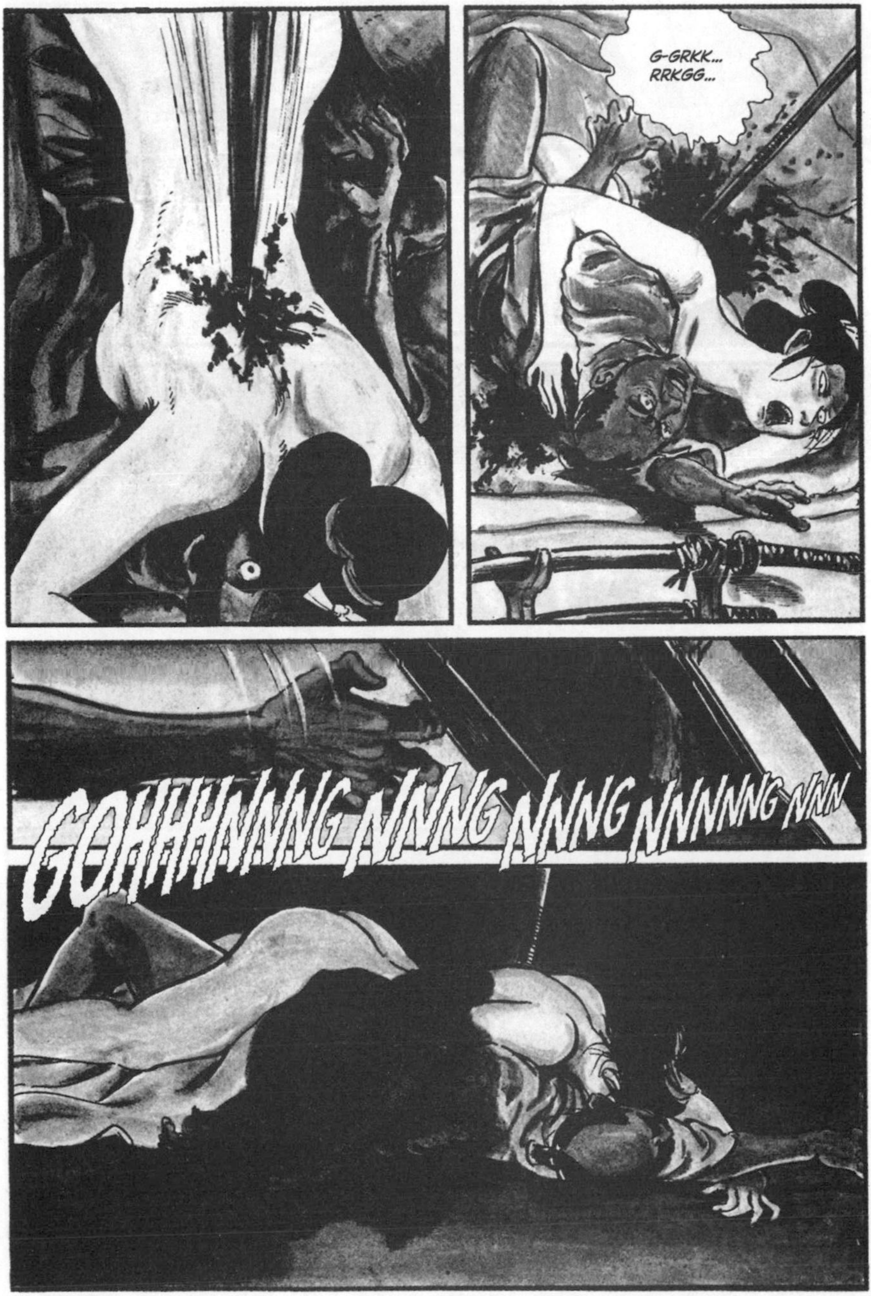
G-GRKK... RRKGG...
GOHHHNNNG NNNG NNNG NNNNNG NNN

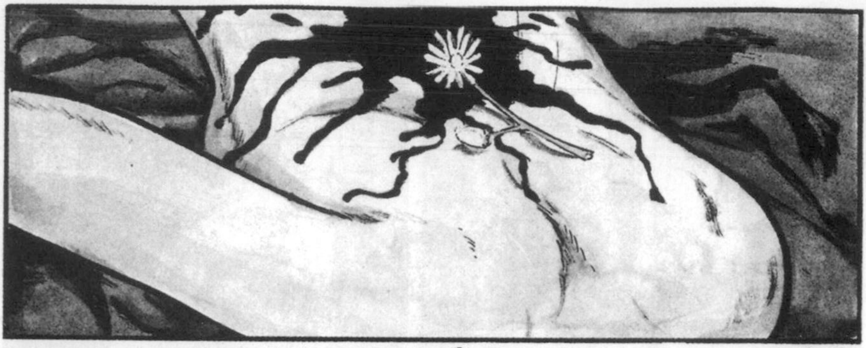

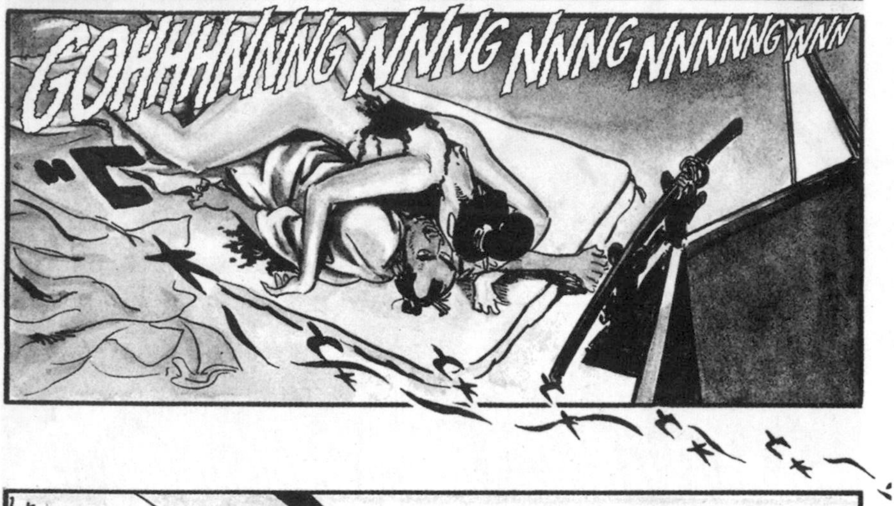
GOHHHNNNG NNNG NNNG NNNNNG NNN

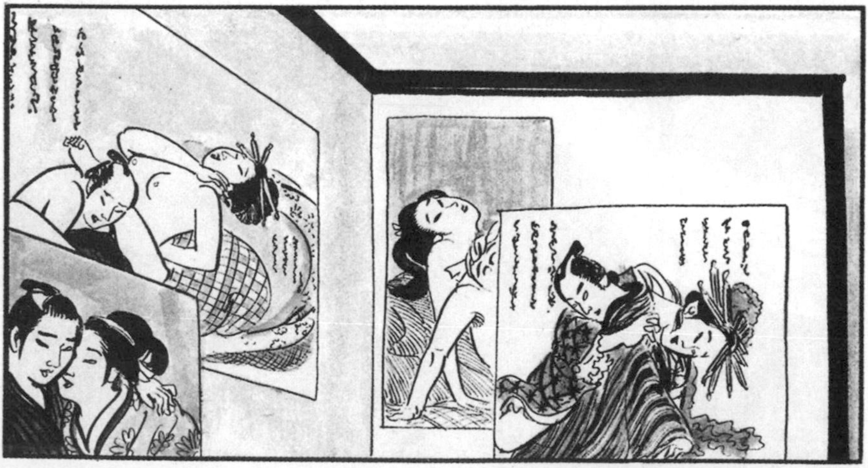

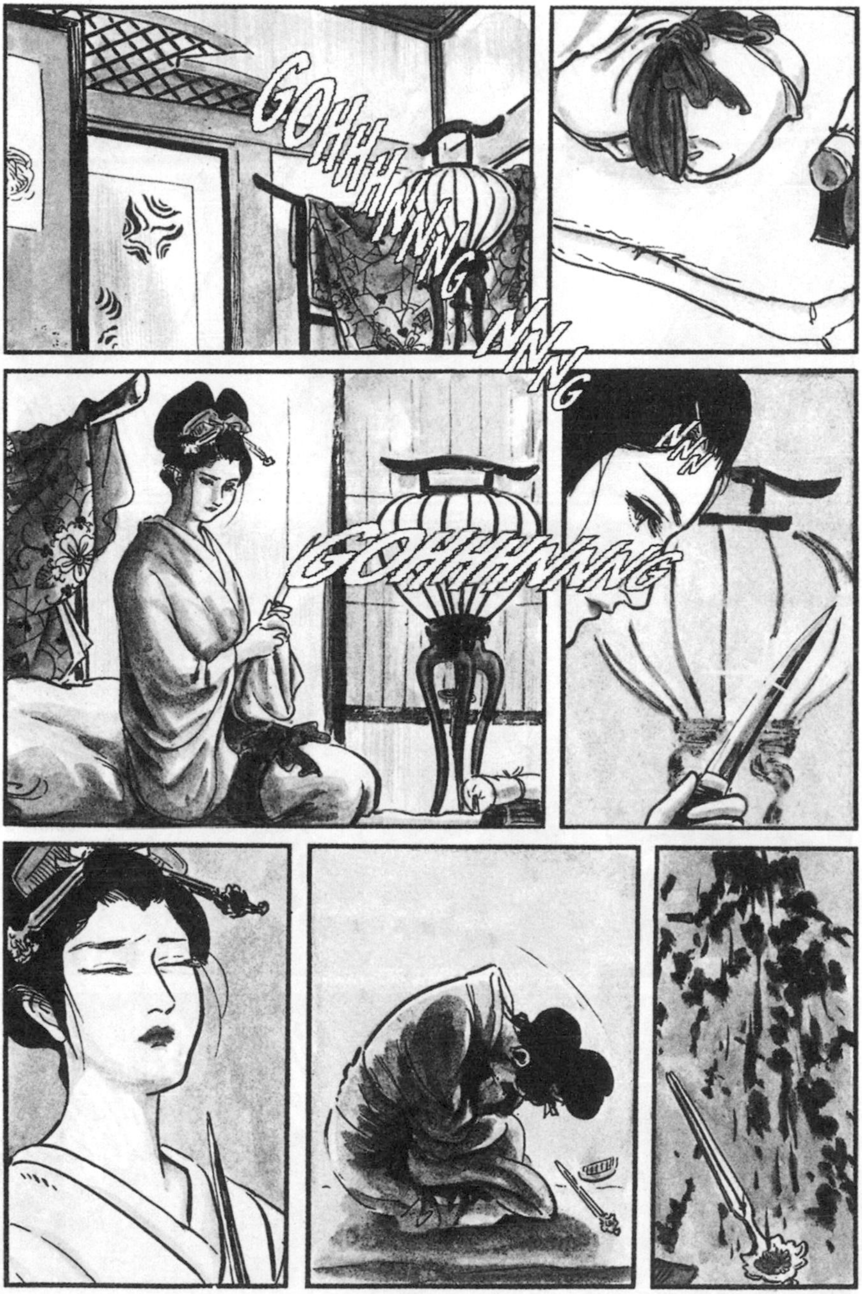
GOHHHNNNG
NNNG
NNN
GOHHHNNNG

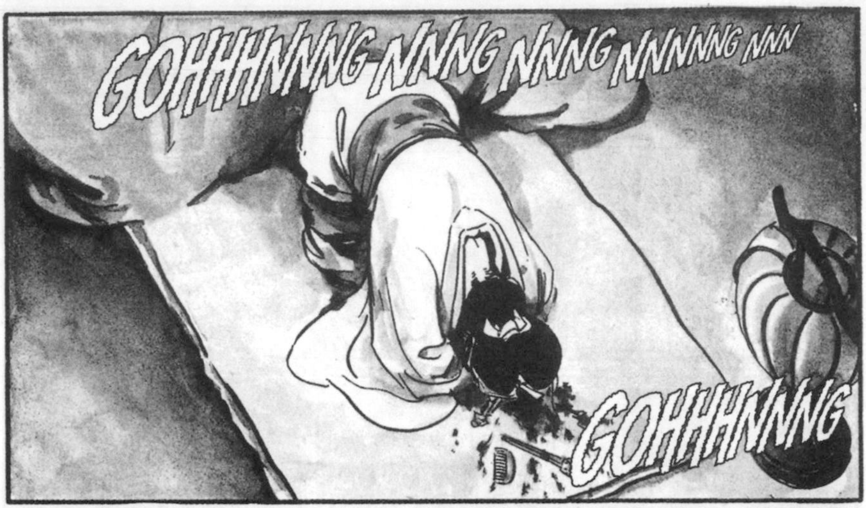
GOHHHNNNG NNNG NNNG NNNNNG NNN
GOHHHNNNG
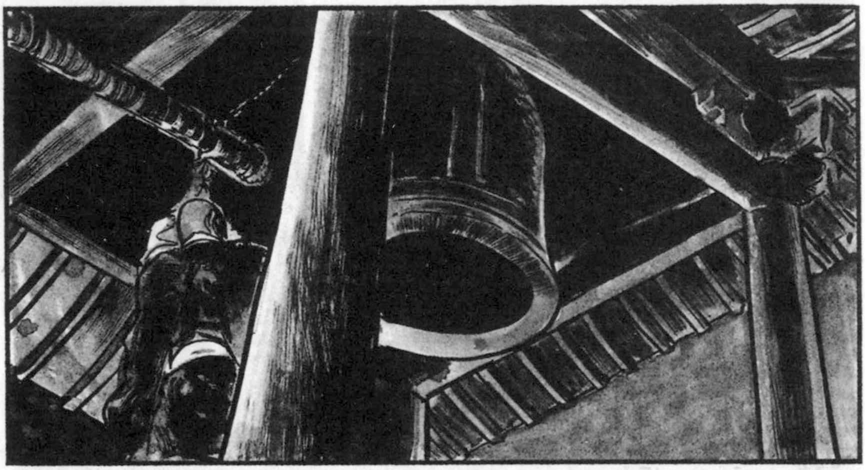
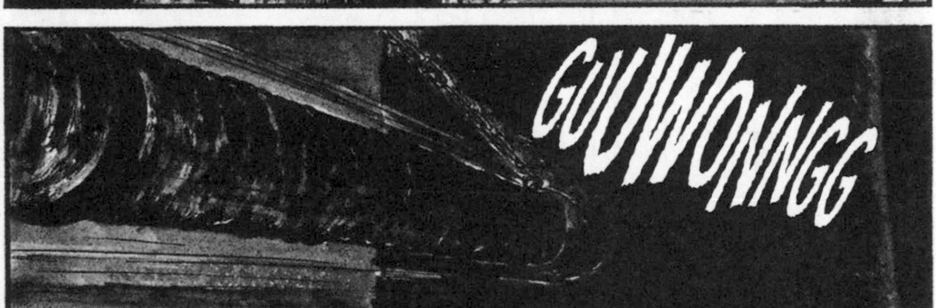
GUWONNGG

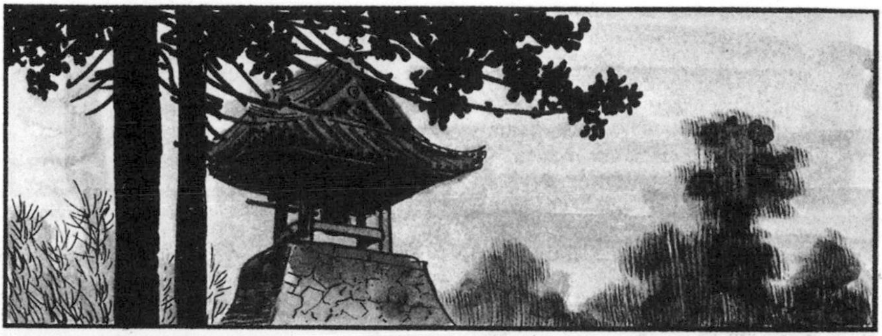
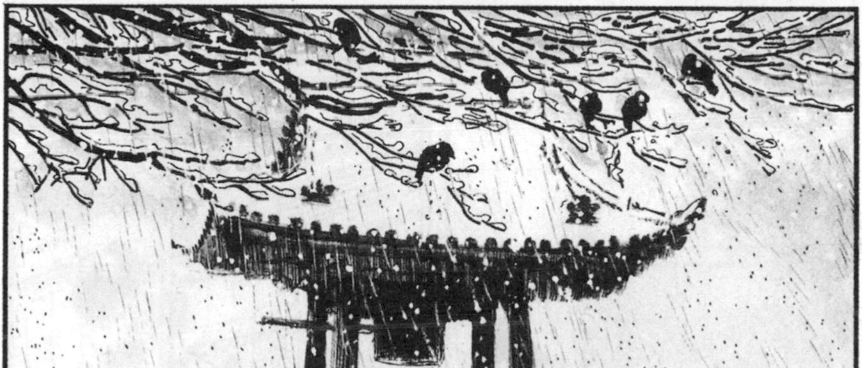
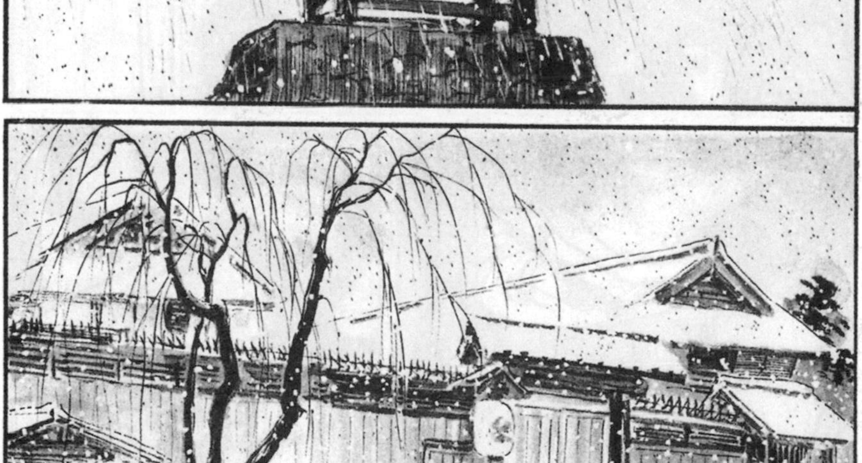

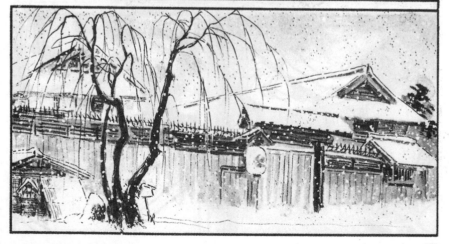

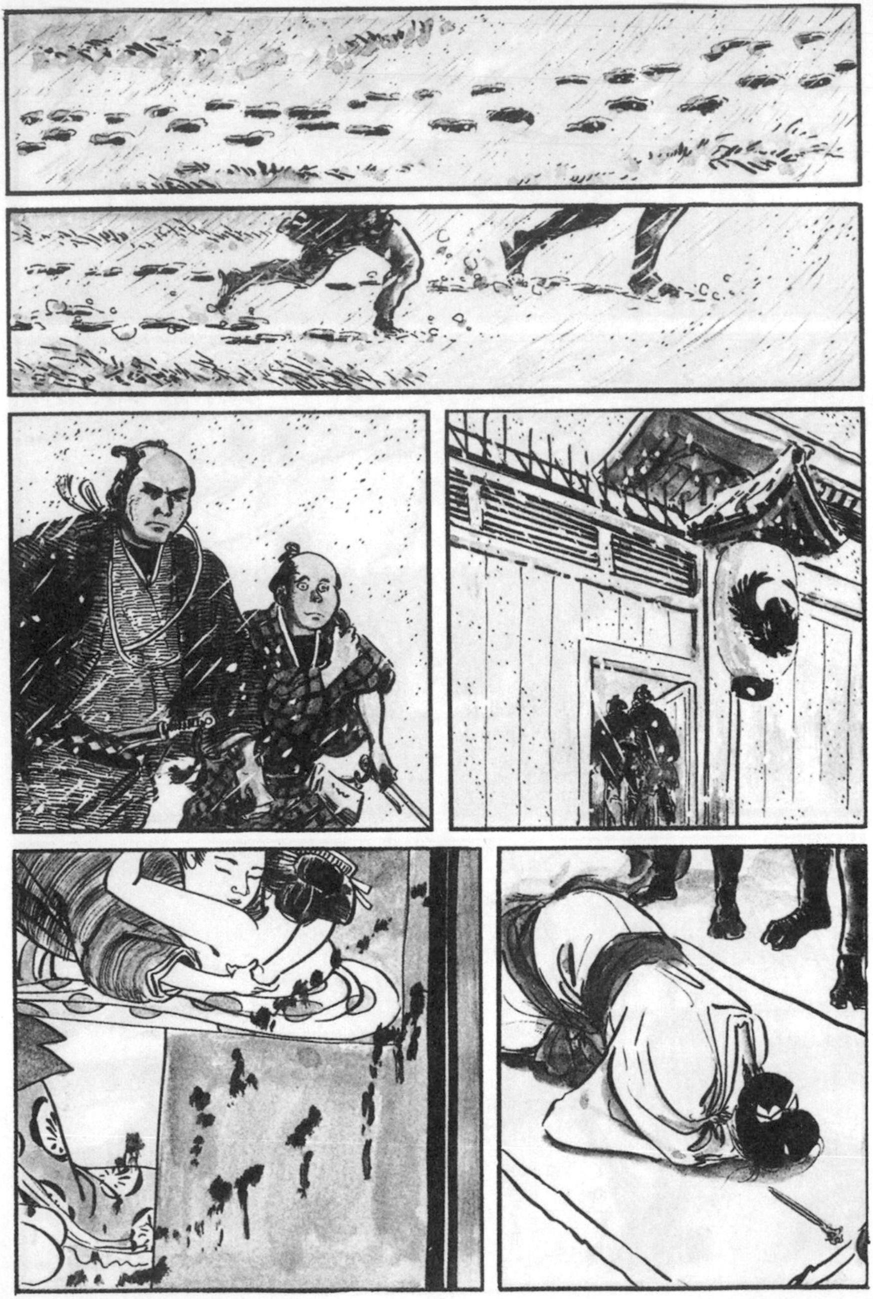

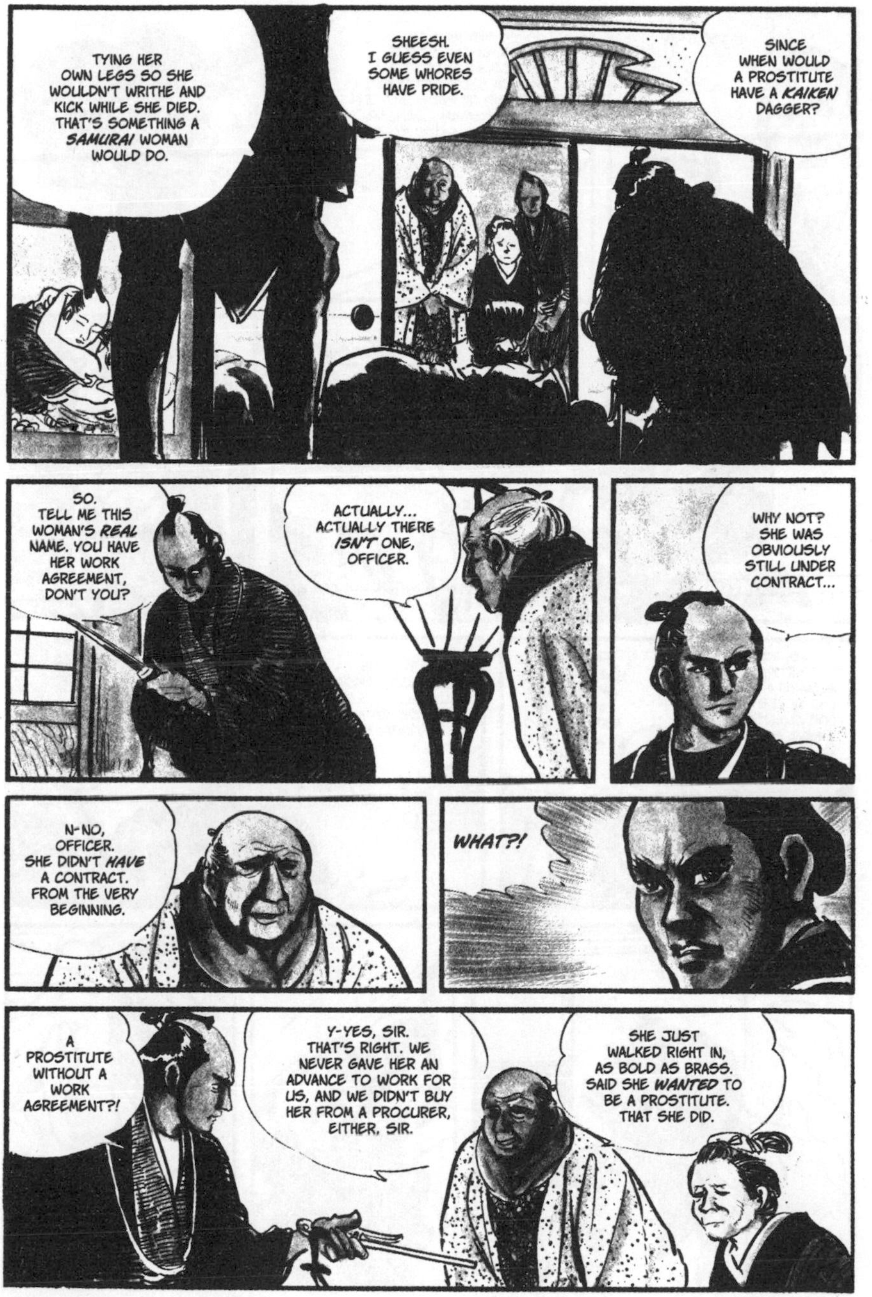

TYING HER OWN LEGS SO SHE WOULDN'T WRITHE AND KICK WHILE SHE DIED. THAT'S SOMETHING A *SAMURAI* WOMAN WOULD DO.
SHEESH. I GUESS EVEN SOME WHORES HAVE PRIDE.
SINCE WHEN WOULD A PROSTITUTE HAVE A *KAIKEN* DAGGER?
SO. TELL ME THIS WOMAN'S *REAL* NAME. YOU HAVE HER WORK AGREEMENT, DON'T YOU?
ACTUALLY... ACTUALLY THERE *ISN'T* ONE, OFFICER.
WHY NOT? SHE WAS OBVIOUSLY STILL UNDER CONTRACT...
N-NO, OFFICER. SHE DIDN'T *HAVE* A CONTRACT. FROM THE VERY BEGINNING.
WHAT?!
A PROSTITUTE WITHOUT A WORK AGREEMENT?!
Y-YES, SIR. THAT'S RIGHT. WE NEVER GAVE HER AN ADVANCE TO WORK FOR US, AND WE DIDN'T BUY HER FROM A PROCURER, EITHER, SIR.
SHE JUST WALKED RIGHT IN, AS BOLD AS BRASS. SAID SHE *WANTED* TO BE A PROSTITUTE. THAT SHE DID.

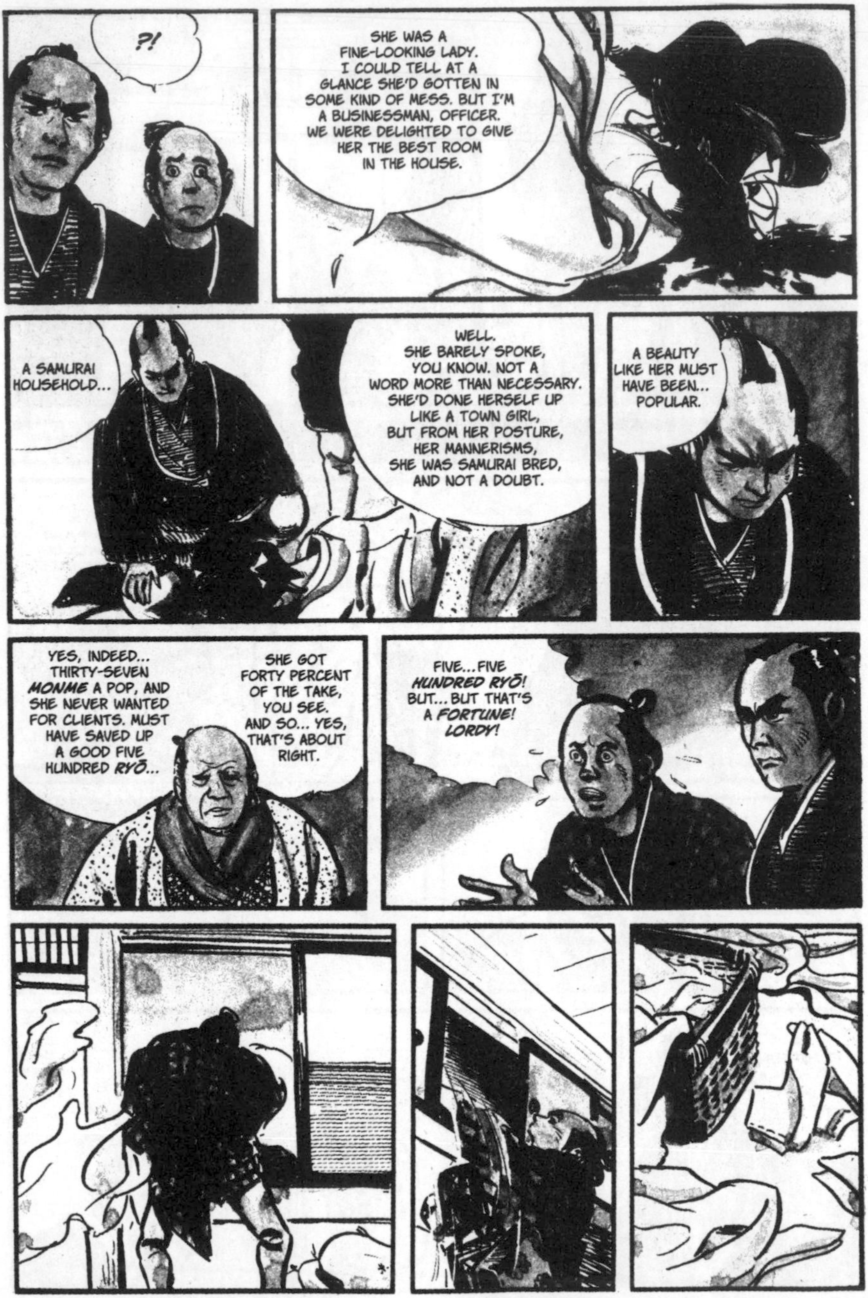
?!
SHE WAS A FINE-LOOKING LADY. I COULD TELL AT A GLANCE SHE'D GOTTEN IN SOME KIND OF MESS. BUT I'M A BUSINESSMAN, OFFICER. WE WERE DELIGHTED TO GIVE HER THE BEST ROOM IN THE HOUSE.
A SAMURAI HOUSEHOLD...
WELL. SHE BARELY SPOKE, YOU KNOW. NOT A WORD MORE THAN NECESSARY. SHE'D DONE HERSELF UP LIKE A TOWN GIRL, BUT FROM HER POSTURE, HER MANNERISMS, SHE WAS SAMURAI BRED, AND NOT A DOUBT.
A BEAUTY LIKE HER MUST HAVE BEEN... POPULAR.
YES, INDEED... THIRTY-SEVEN *MONME* A POP, AND SHE NEVER WANTED FOR CLIENTS. MUST HAVE SAVED UP A GOOD FIVE HUNDRED *RYŌ*...
SHE GOT FORTY PERCENT OF THE TAKE, YOU SEE. AND SO... YES, THAT'S ABOUT RIGHT.
FIVE...FIVE *HUNDRED RYŌ*! BUT... BUT THAT'S A *FORTUNE*! *LORDY*!

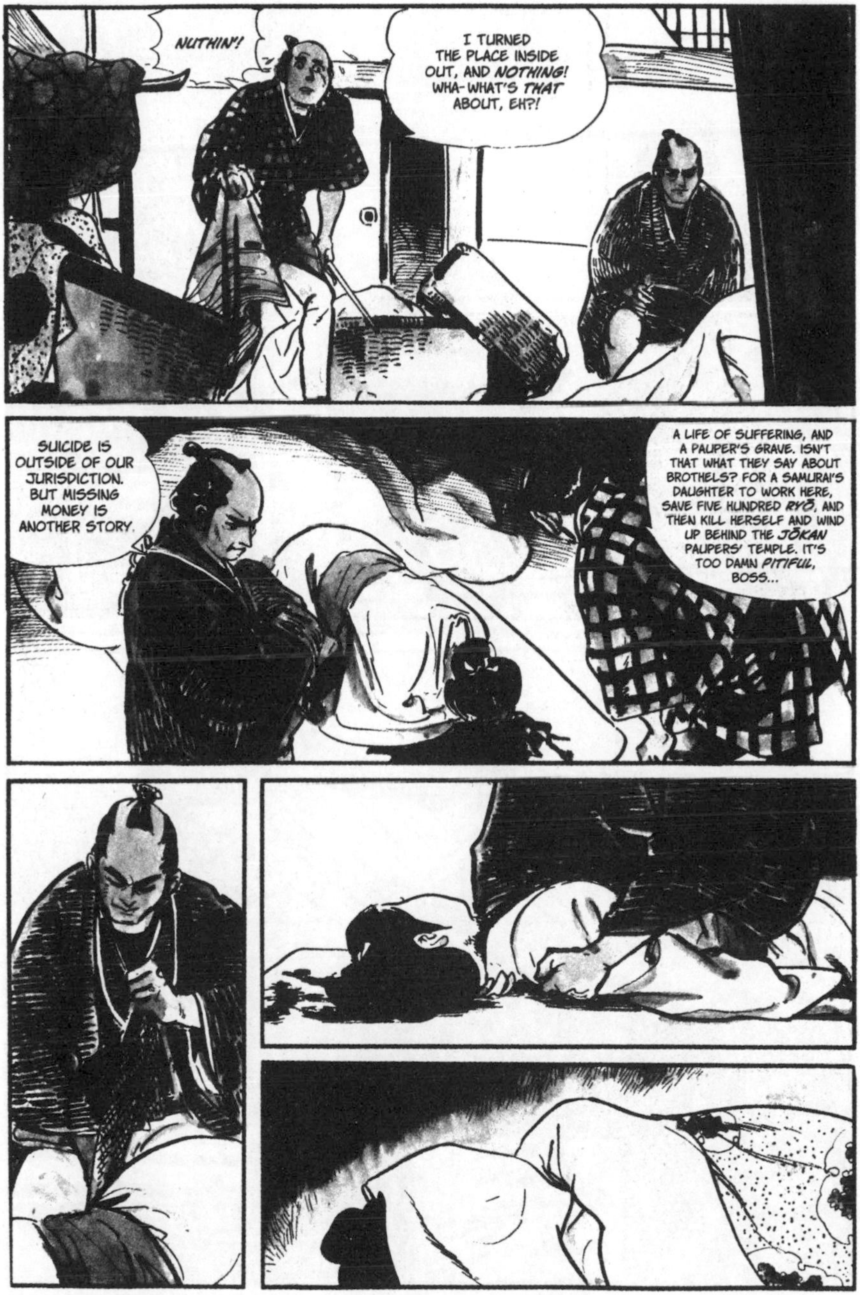
I TURNED THE PLACE INSIDE OUT, AND NOTHING! WHA-WHAT'S THAT ABOUT, EH?!
NUTHIN'!
A LIFE OF SUFFERING, AND A PAUPER'S GRAVE. ISN'T THAT WHAT THEY SAY ABOUT BROTHELS? FOR A SAMURAI'S DAUGHTER TO WORK HERE, SAVE FIVE HUNDRED RYŌ, AND THEN KILL HERSELF AND WIND UP BEHIND THE JŌKAN PAUPERS' TEMPLE. IT'S TOO DAMN PITIFUL, BOSS...
SUICIDE IS OUTSIDE OF OUR JURISDICTION. BUT MISSING MONEY IS ANOTHER STORY.

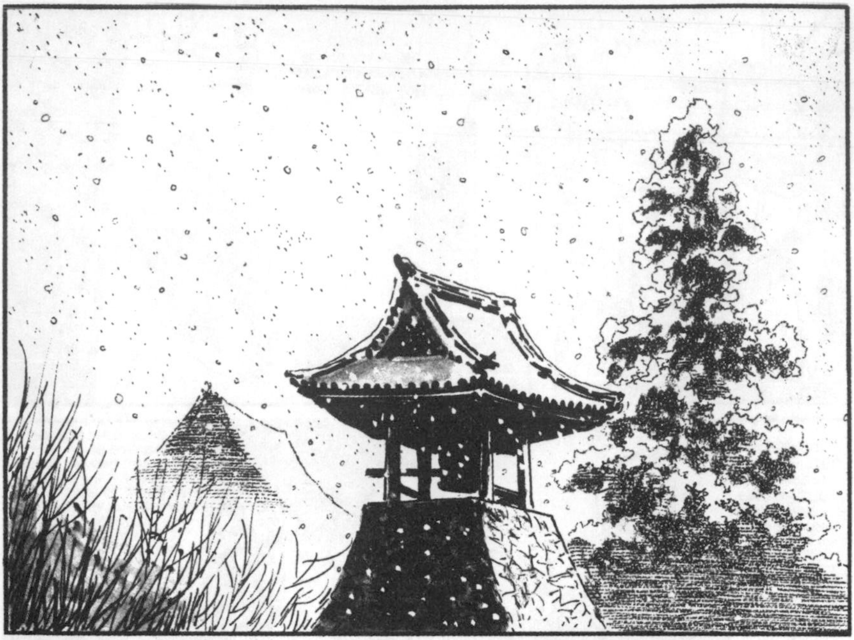
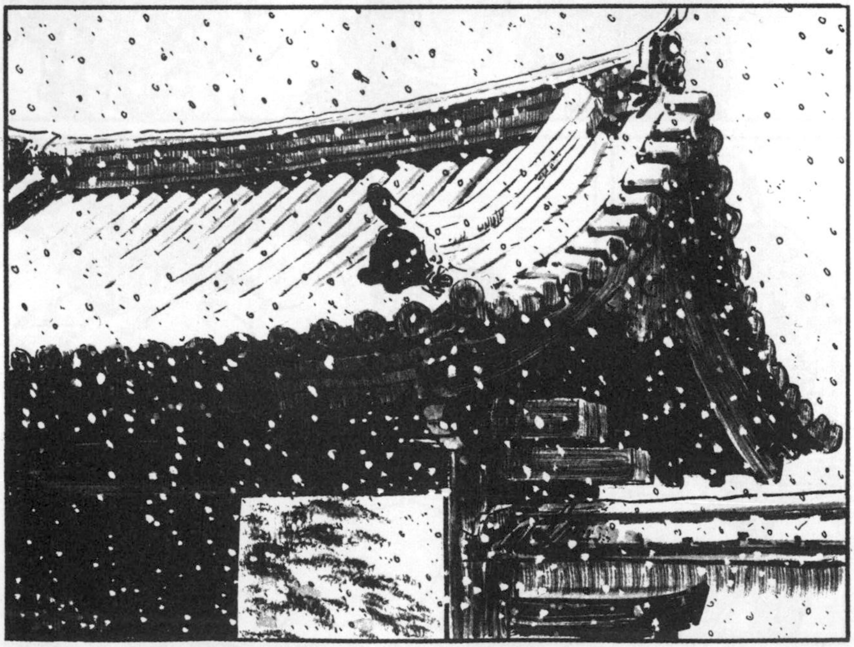

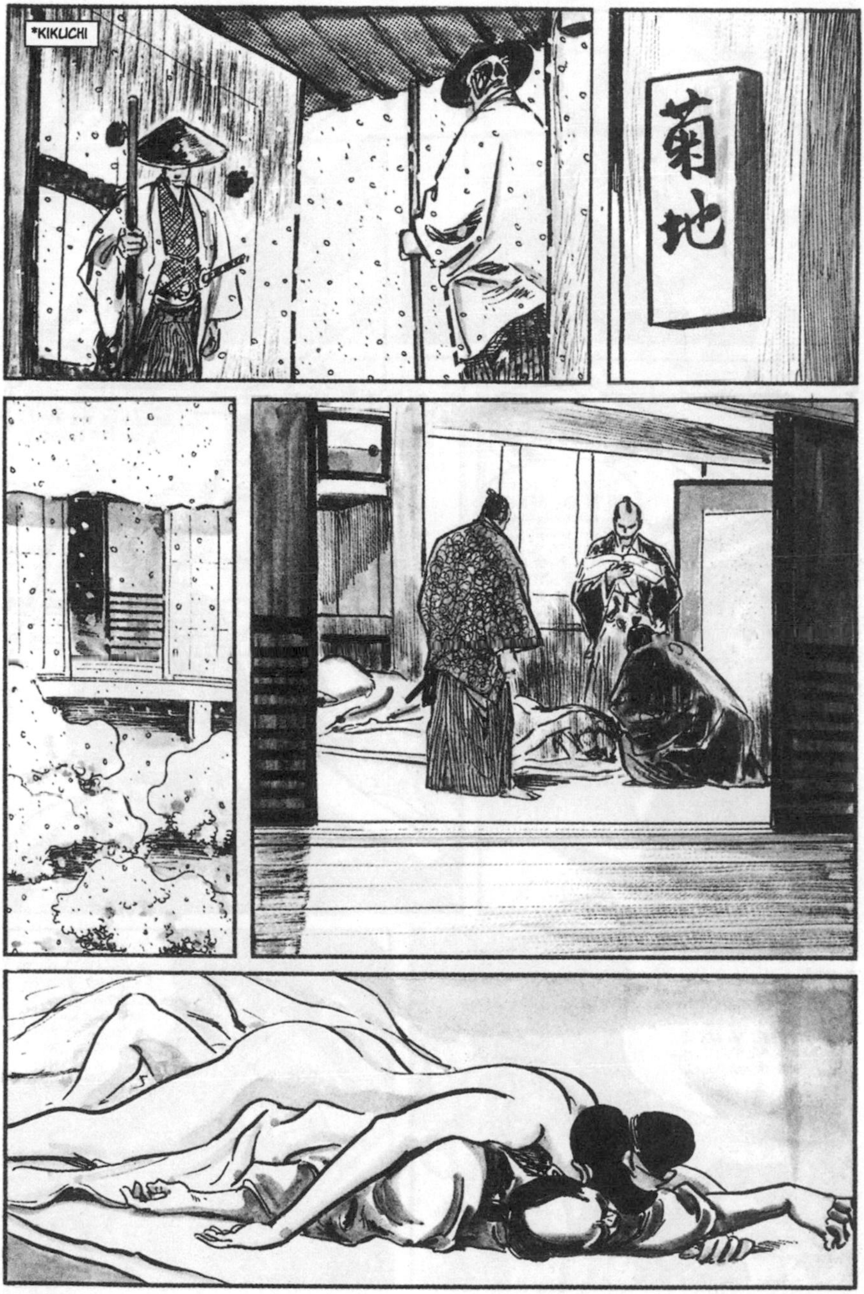
菊地
*KIKUCHI

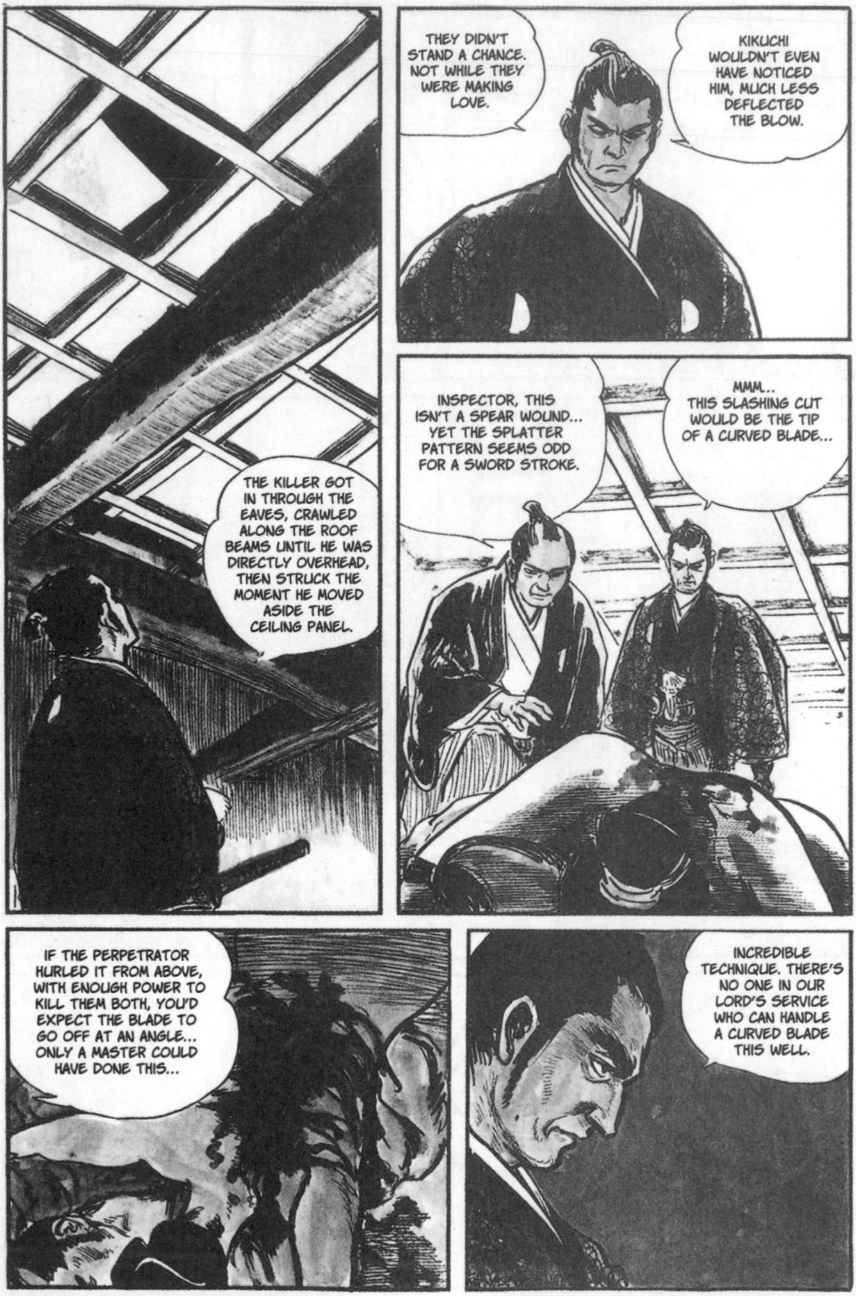
THE KILLER GOT IN THROUGH THE EAVES, CRAWLED ALONG THE ROOF BEAMS UNTIL HE WAS DIRECTLY OVERHEAD, THEN STRUCK THE MOMENT HE MOVED ASIDE THE CEILING PANEL.
THEY DIDN'T STAND A CHANCE. NOT WHILE THEY WERE MAKING LOVE.
KIKUCHI WOULDN'T EVEN HAVE NOTICED HIM, MUCH LESS DEFLECTED THE BLOW.
INSPECTOR, THIS ISN'T A SPEAR WOUND... YET THE SPLATTER PATTERN SEEMS ODD FOR A SWORD STROKE.
MMM.. THIS SLASHING CUT WOULD BE THE TIP OF A CURVED BLADE...
IF THE PERPETRATOR HURLED IT FROM ABOVE, WITH ENOUGH POWER TO KILL THEM BOTH, YOU'D EXPECT THE BLADE TO GO OFF AT AN ANGLE... ONLY A MASTER COULD HAVE DONE THIS...
INCREDIBLE TECHNIQUE. THERE'S NO ONE IN OUR LORD'S SERVICE WHO CAN HANDLE A CURVED BLADE THIS WELL.

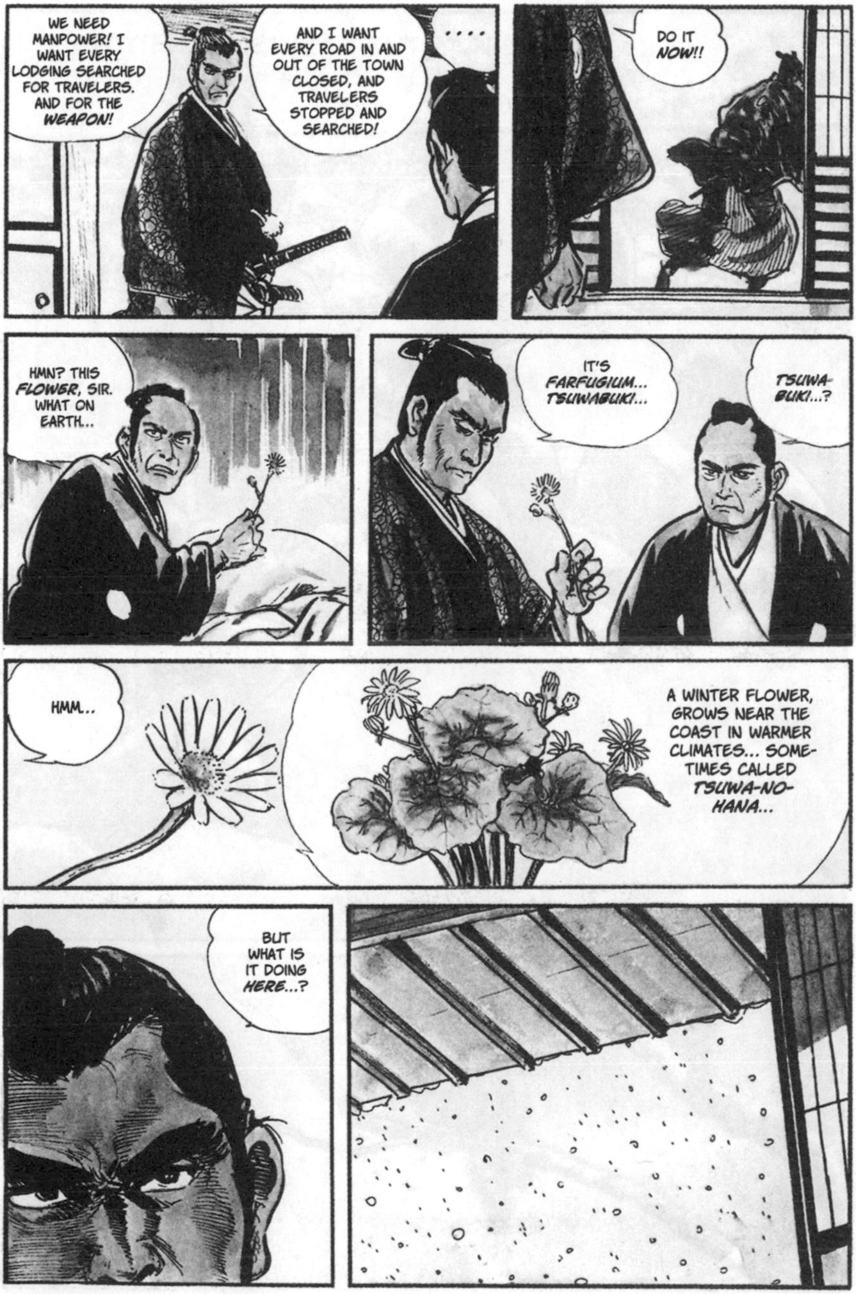
WE NEED MANPOWER! I WANT EVERY LODGING SEARCHED FOR TRAVELERS. AND FOR THE *WEAPON!*
AND I WANT EVERY ROAD IN AND OUT OF THE TOWN CLOSED, AND TRAVELERS STOPPED AND SEARCHED!
....
DO IT *NOW!!*
HMN? THIS *FLOWER*, SIR. WHAT ON EARTH...
IT'S *FARFUGIUM... TSUWABUKI...*
TSUWA-BUKI...?
HMM..
A WINTER FLOWER, GROWS NEAR THE COAST IN WARMER CLIMATES... SOME-TIMES CALLED *TSUWA-NO-HANA...*
BUT WHAT IS IT DOING *HERE...?*

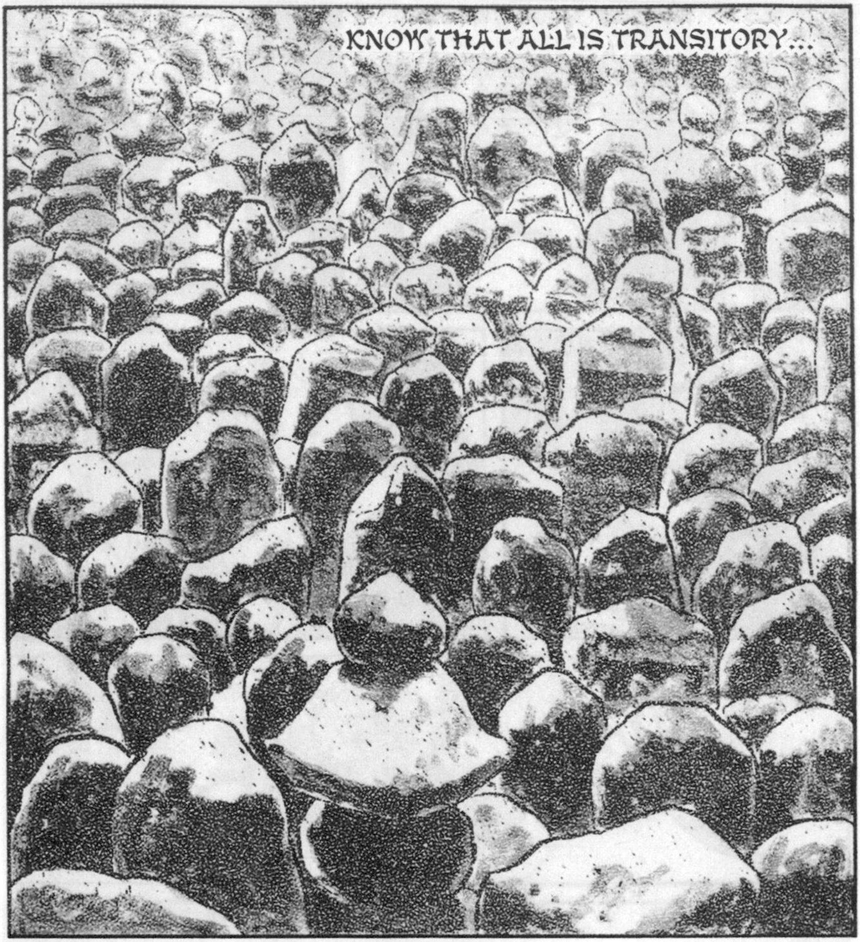
KNOW THAT ALL IS TRANSITORY...
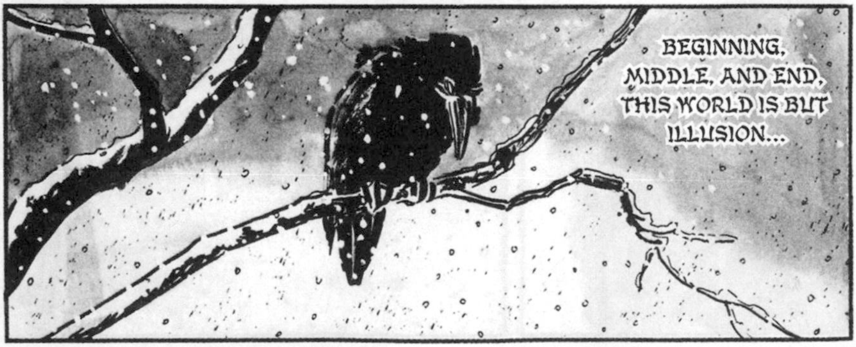
BEGINNING, MIDDLE, AND END, THIS WORLD IS BUT ILLUSION...

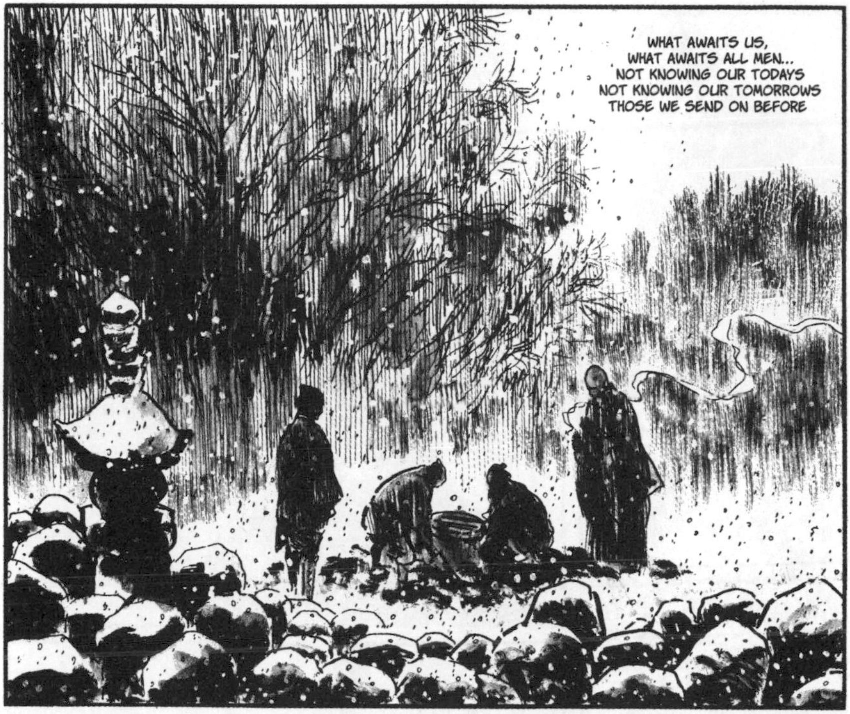
WHAT AWAITS US, WHAT AWAITS ALL MEN... NOT KNOWING OUR TODAYS NOT KNOWING OUR TOMORROWS THOSE WE SEND ON BEFORE
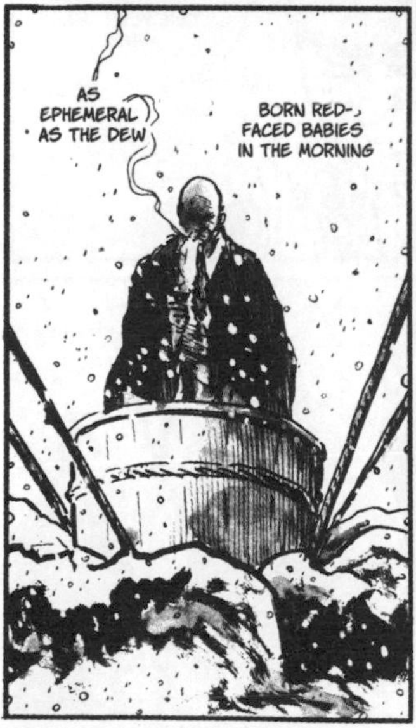
AS EPHEMERAL AS THE DEW
BORN RED-FACED BABIES IN THE MORNING
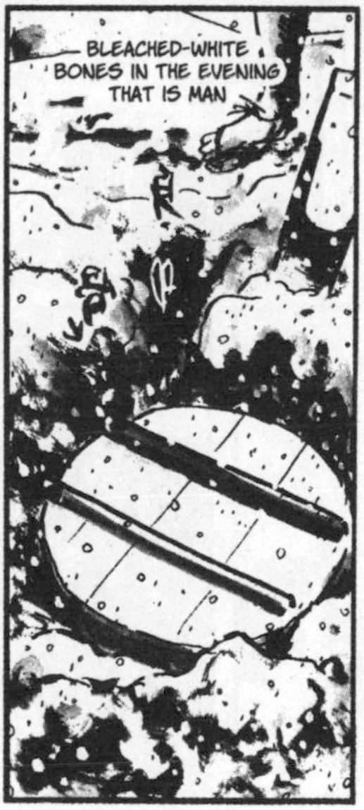
BLEACHED-WHITE BONES IN THE EVENING THAT IS MAN
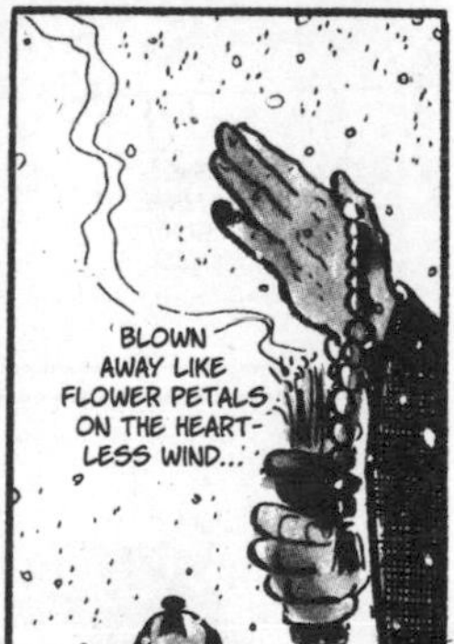
BLOWN AWAY LIKE FLOWER PETALS ON THE HEART-LESS WIND...

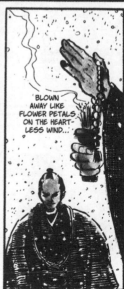

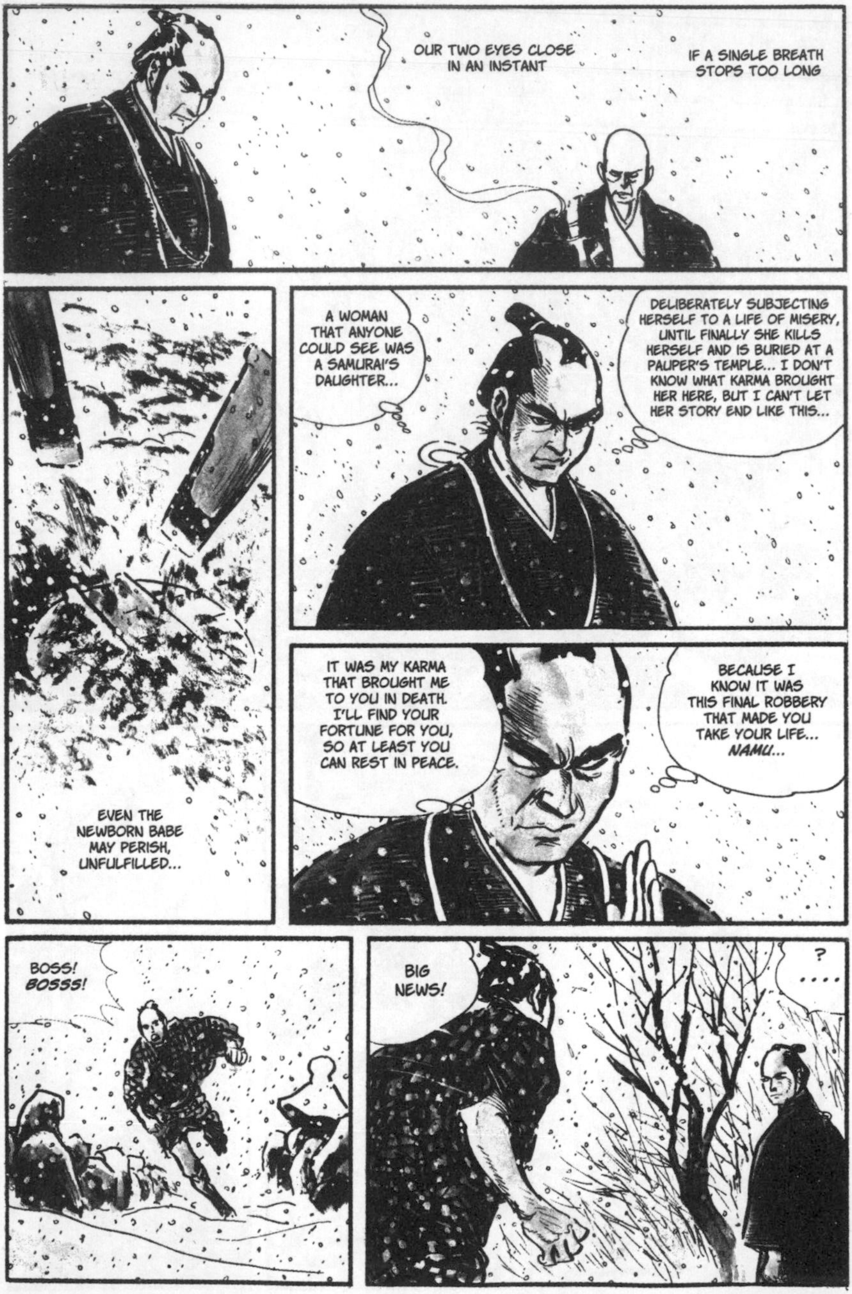
OUR TWO EYES CLOSE
IN AN INSTANT
IF A SINGLE BREATH
STOPS TOO LONG
EVEN THE NEWBORN BABE MAY PERISH, UNFULFILLED...
A WOMAN THAT ANYONE COULD SEE WAS A SAMURAI'S DAUGHTER...
DELIBERATELY SUBJECTING HERSELF TO A LIFE OF MISERY, UNTIL FINALLY SHE KILLS HERSELF AND IS BURIED AT A PAUPER'S TEMPLE... I DON'T KNOW WHAT KARMA BROUGHT HER HERE, BUT I CAN'T LET HER STORY END LIKE THIS...
IT WAS MY KARMA THAT BROUGHT ME TO YOU IN DEATH. I'LL FIND YOUR FORTUNE FOR YOU, SO AT LEAST YOU CAN REST IN PEACE.
BECAUSE I KNOW IT WAS THIS FINAL ROBBERY THAT MADE YOU TAKE YOUR LIFE... *NAMU*...
BOSS! *BOSSS!*
BIG NEWS!
?
....

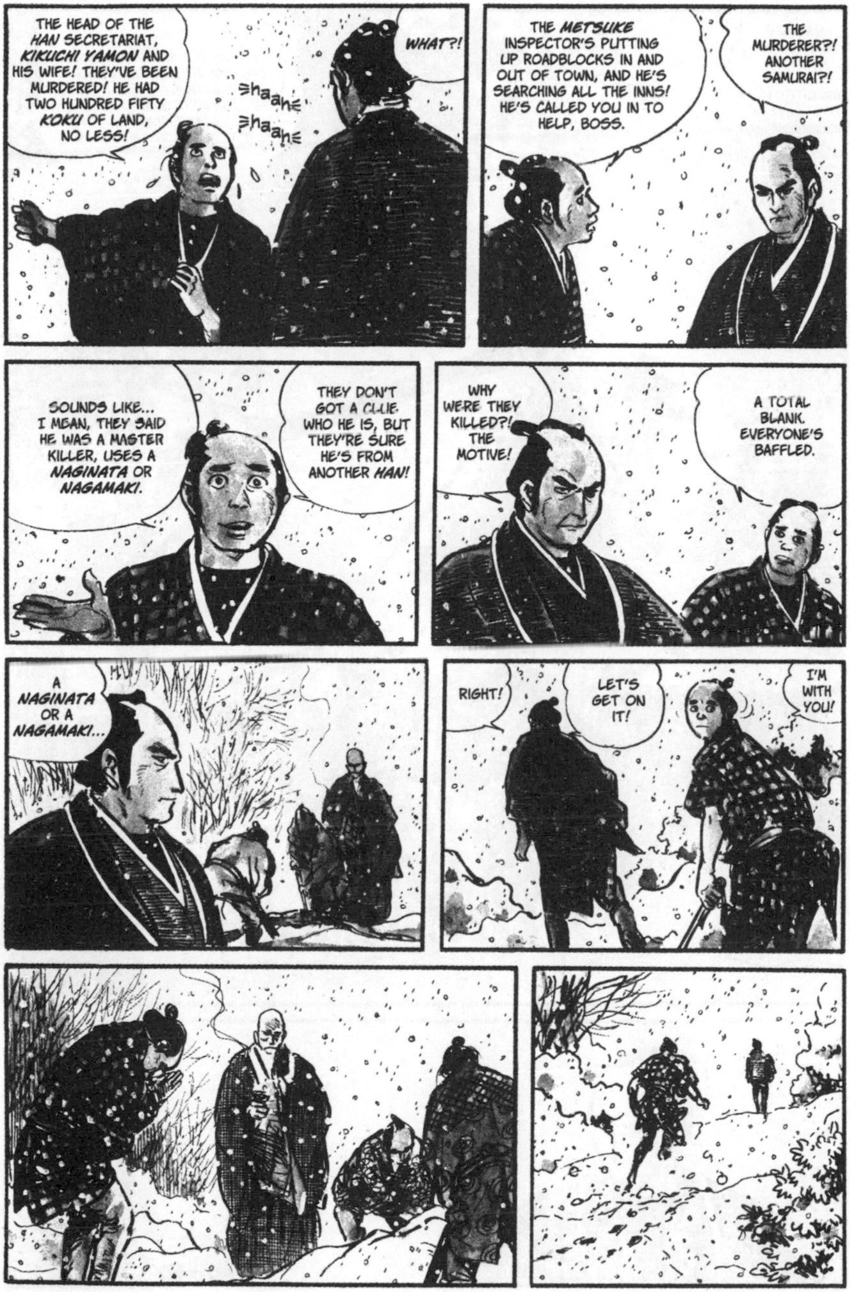
THE HEAD OF THE *HAN* SECRETARIAT, *KIKUCHI YAMON* AND HIS WIFE! THEY'VE BEEN MURDERED! HE HAD TWO HUNDRED FIFTY *KOKU* OF LAND, NO LESS!
haah
haah
WHAT?!
THE *METSUKE* INSPECTOR'S PUTTING UP ROADBLOCKS IN AND OUT OF TOWN, AND HE'S SEARCHING ALL THE INNS! HE'S CALLED YOU IN TO HELP, BOSS.
THE MURDERER?! ANOTHER SAMURAI?!
SOUNDS LIKE... I MEAN, THEY SAID HE WAS A MASTER KILLER, USES A *NAGINATA* OR *NAGAMAKI*.
THEY DON'T GOT A CLUE WHO HE IS, BUT THEY'RE SURE HE'S FROM ANOTHER *HAN*!
WHY WERE THEY KILLED?! THE MOTIVE!
A TOTAL BLANK. EVERYONE'S BAFFLED.
A *NAGINATA* OR A *NAGAMAKI*...
RIGHT!
LET'S GET ON IT!
I'M WITH YOU!

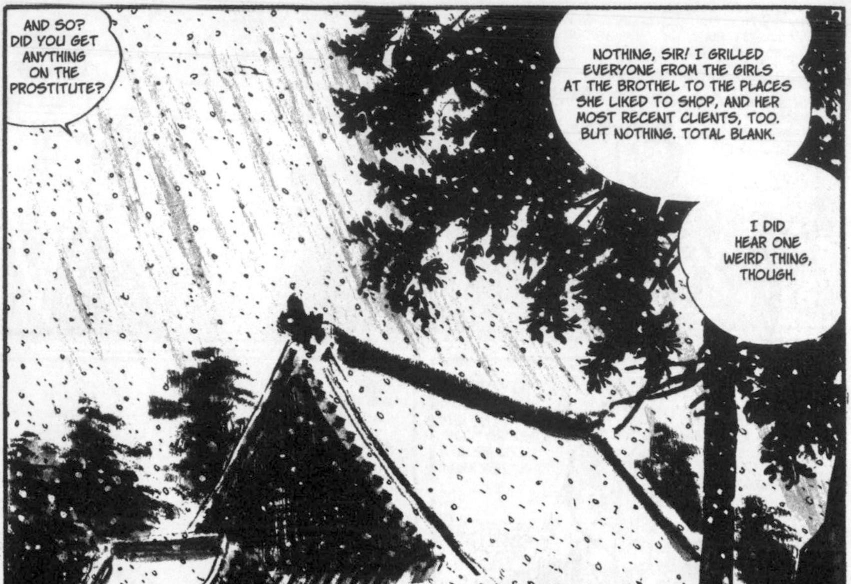
AND SO? DID YOU GET ANYTHING ON THE PROSTITUTE?
NOTHING, SIR! I GRILLED EVERYONE FROM THE GIRLS AT THE BROTHEL TO THE PLACES SHE LIKED TO SHOP, AND HER MOST RECENT CLIENTS, TOO. BUT NOTHING. TOTAL BLANK.
I DID HEAR ONE WEIRD THING, THOUGH.

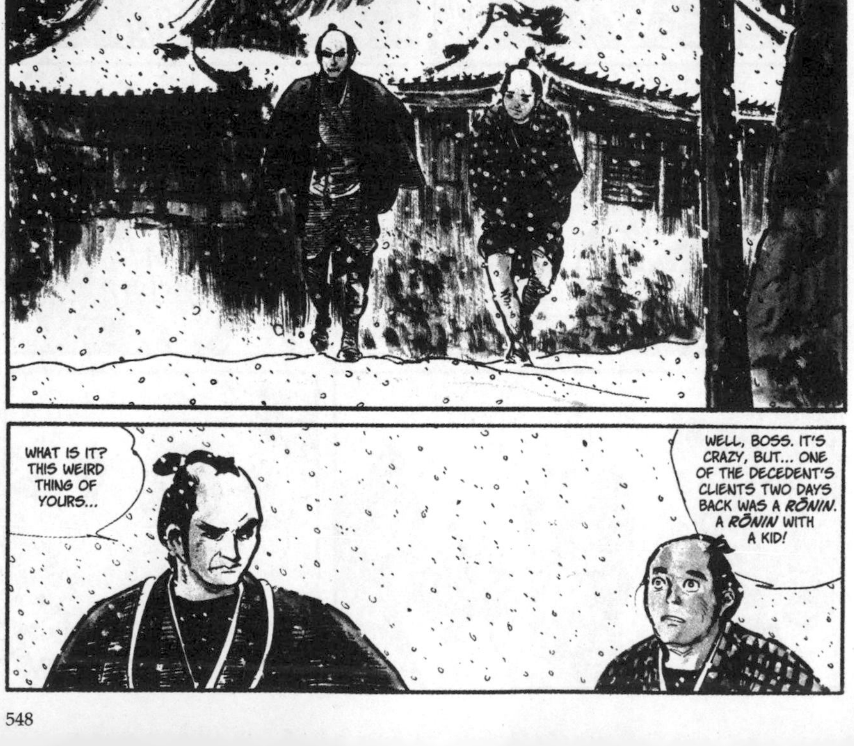
WHAT IS IT? THIS WEIRD THING OF YOURS...
WELL, BOSS. IT'S CRAZY, BUT... ONE OF THE DECEDENT'S CLIENTS TWO DAYS BACK WAS A *RŌNIN*. A *RŌNIN* WITH A KID!

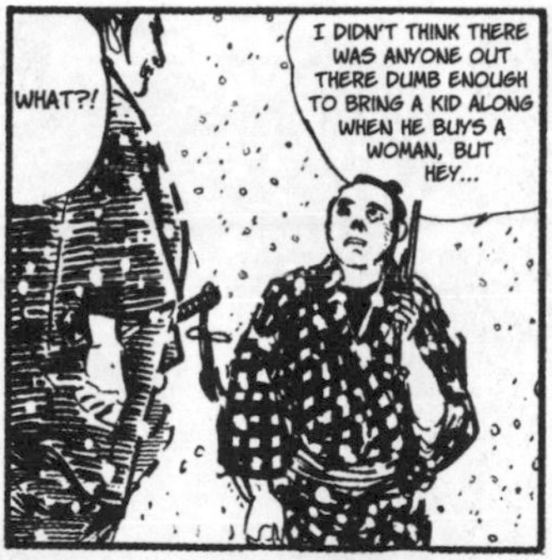
WHAT?!
I DIDN'T THINK THERE WAS ANYONE OUT THERE DUMB ENOUGH TO BRING A KID ALONG WHEN HE BUYS A WOMAN, BUT HEY...
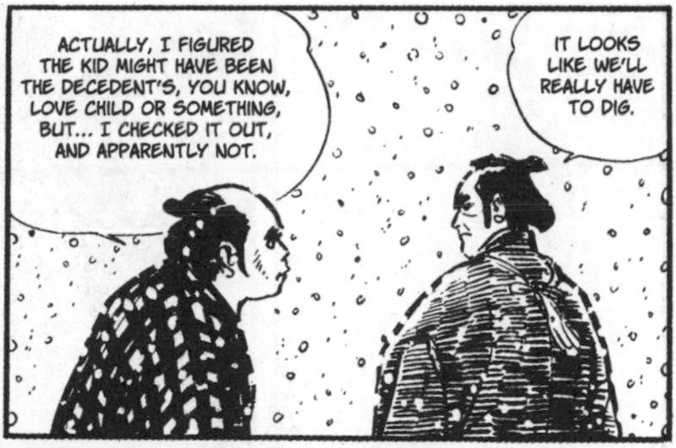
ACTUALLY, I FIGURED THE KID MIGHT HAVE BEEN THE DECEDENT'S, YOU KNOW, LOVE CHILD OR SOMETHING, BUT... I CHECKED IT OUT, AND APPARENTLY NOT.
IT LOOKS LIKE WE'LL REALLY HAVE TO DIG.
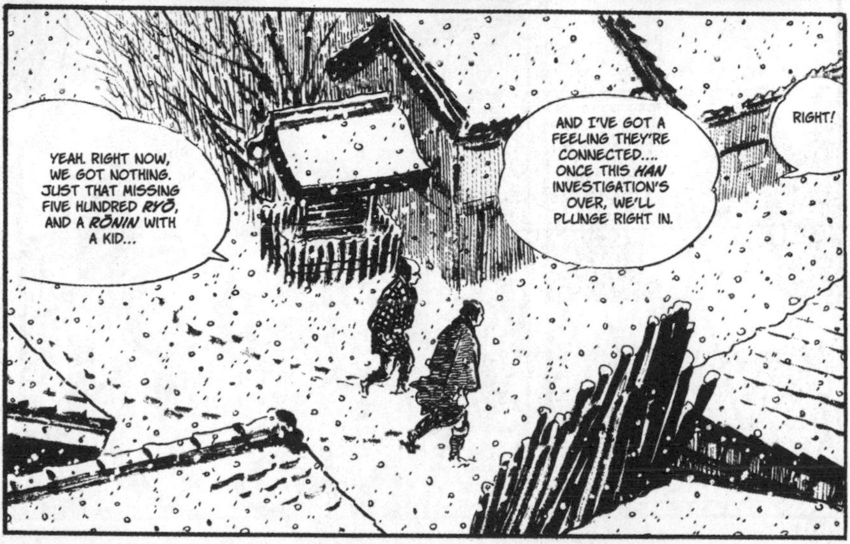
YEAH. RIGHT NOW, WE GOT NOTHING. JUST THAT MISSING FIVE HUNDRED *RYŌ*, AND A *RŌNIN* WITH A KID...
AND I'VE GOT A FEELING THEY'RE CONNECTED.... ONCE THIS *HAN* INVESTIGATION'S OVER, WE'LL PLUNGE RIGHT IN.
RIGHT!
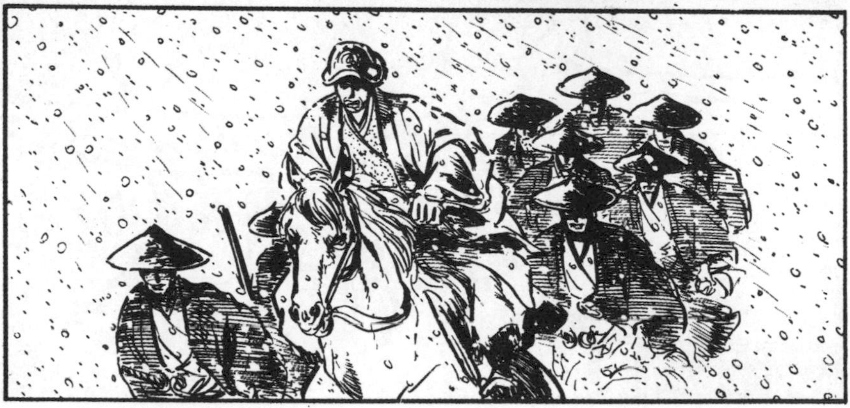

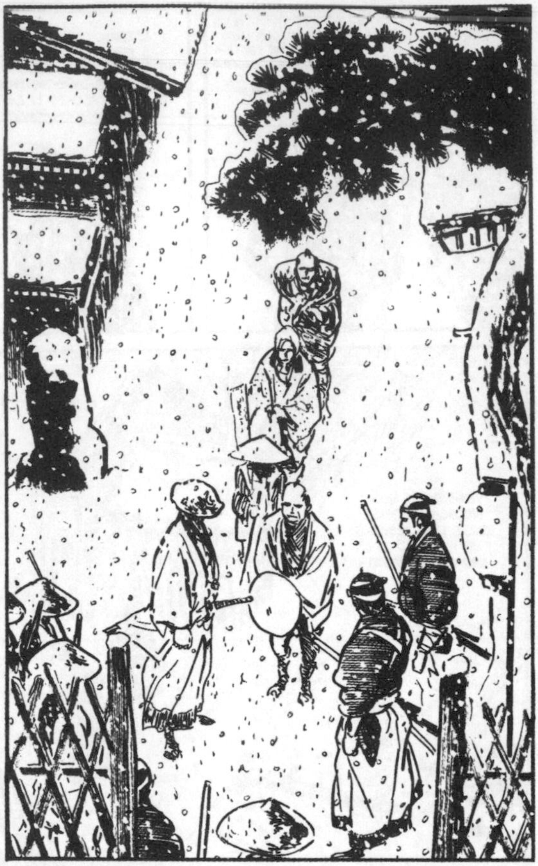

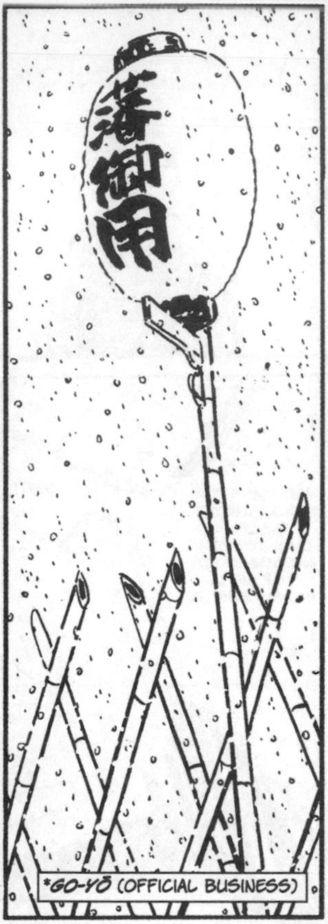
藩御用
*GO-YŌ (OFFICIAL BUSINESS)

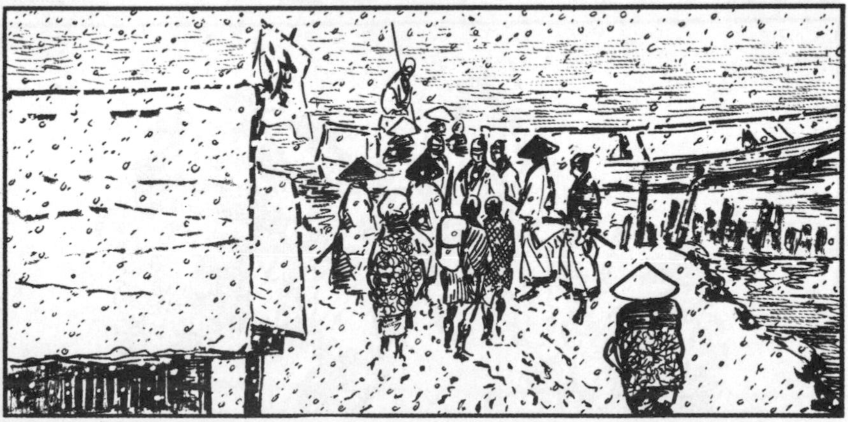

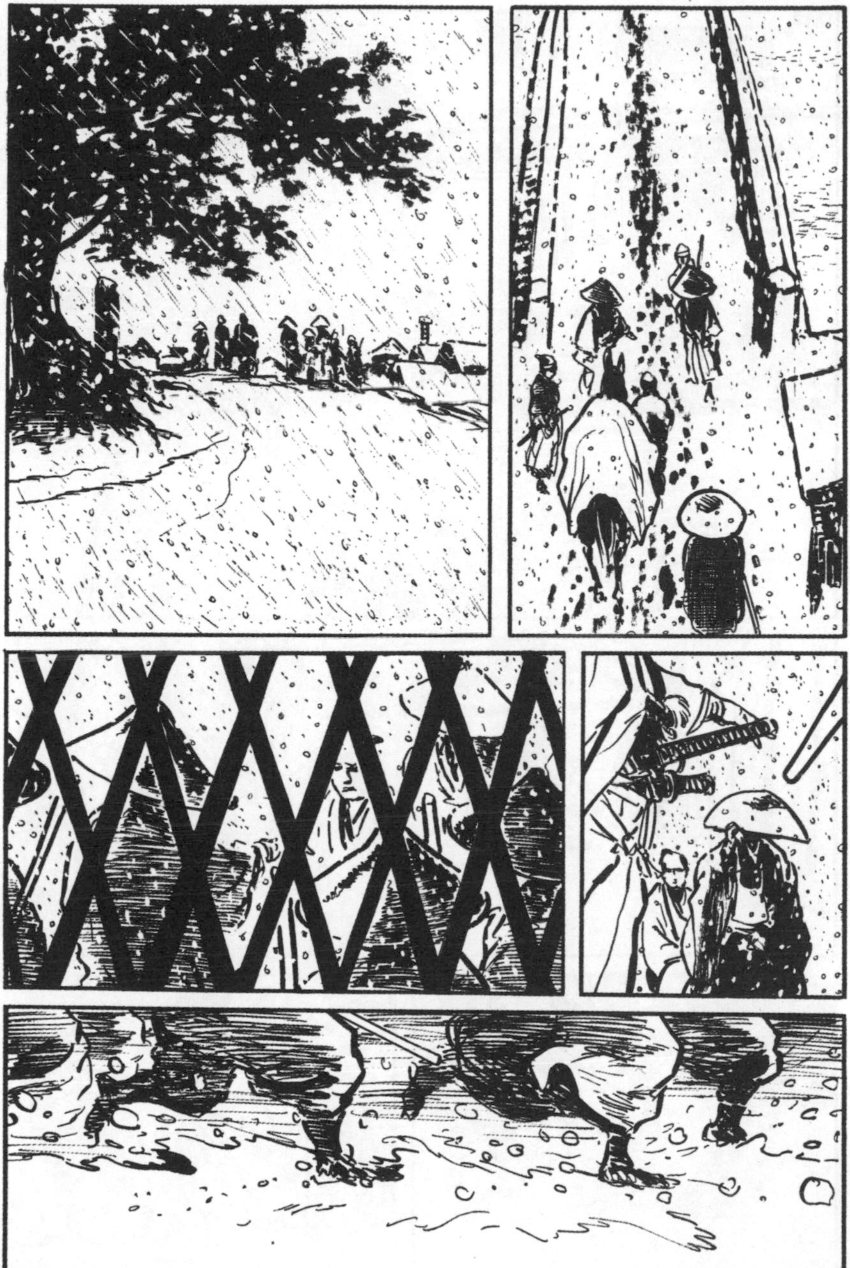

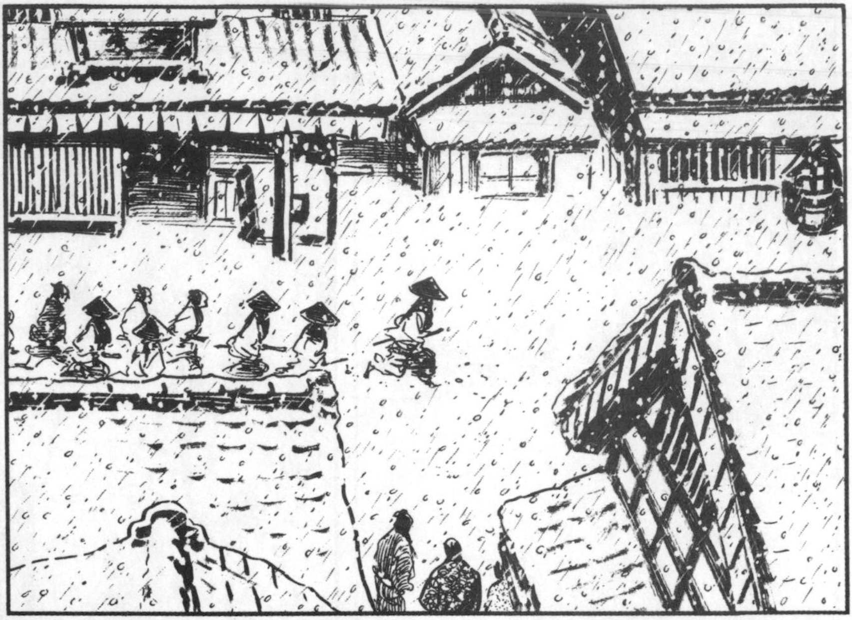
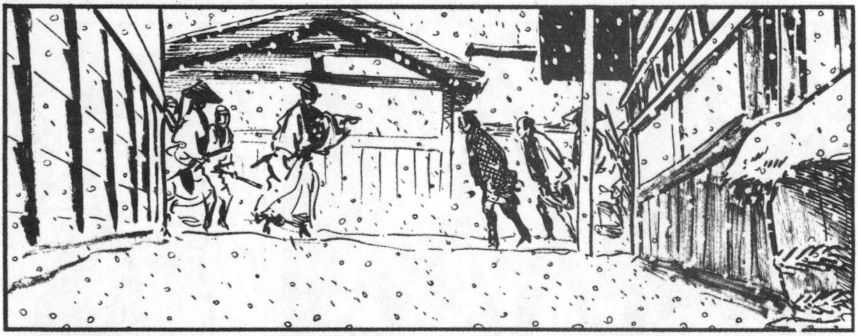
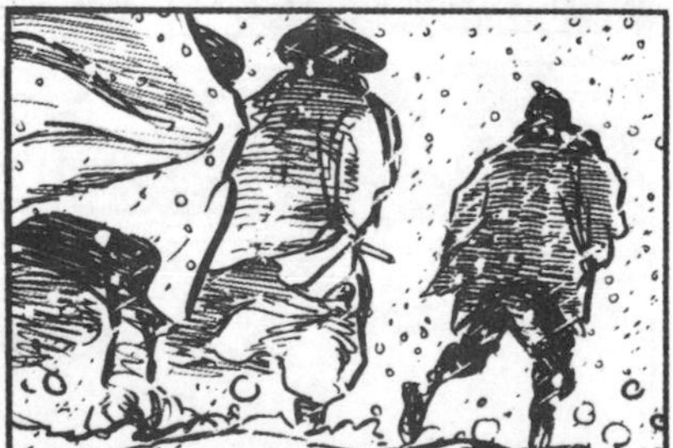
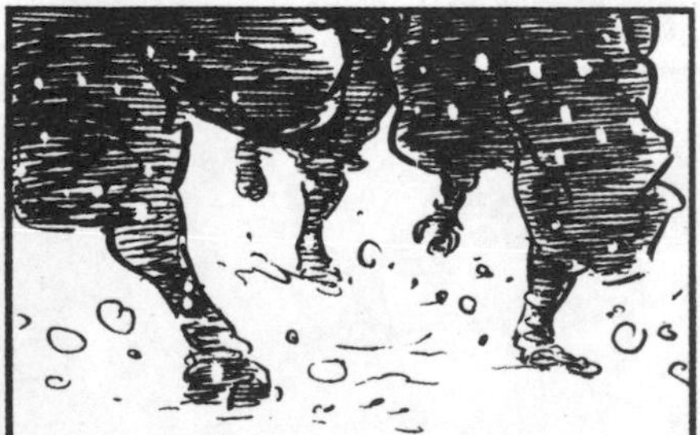

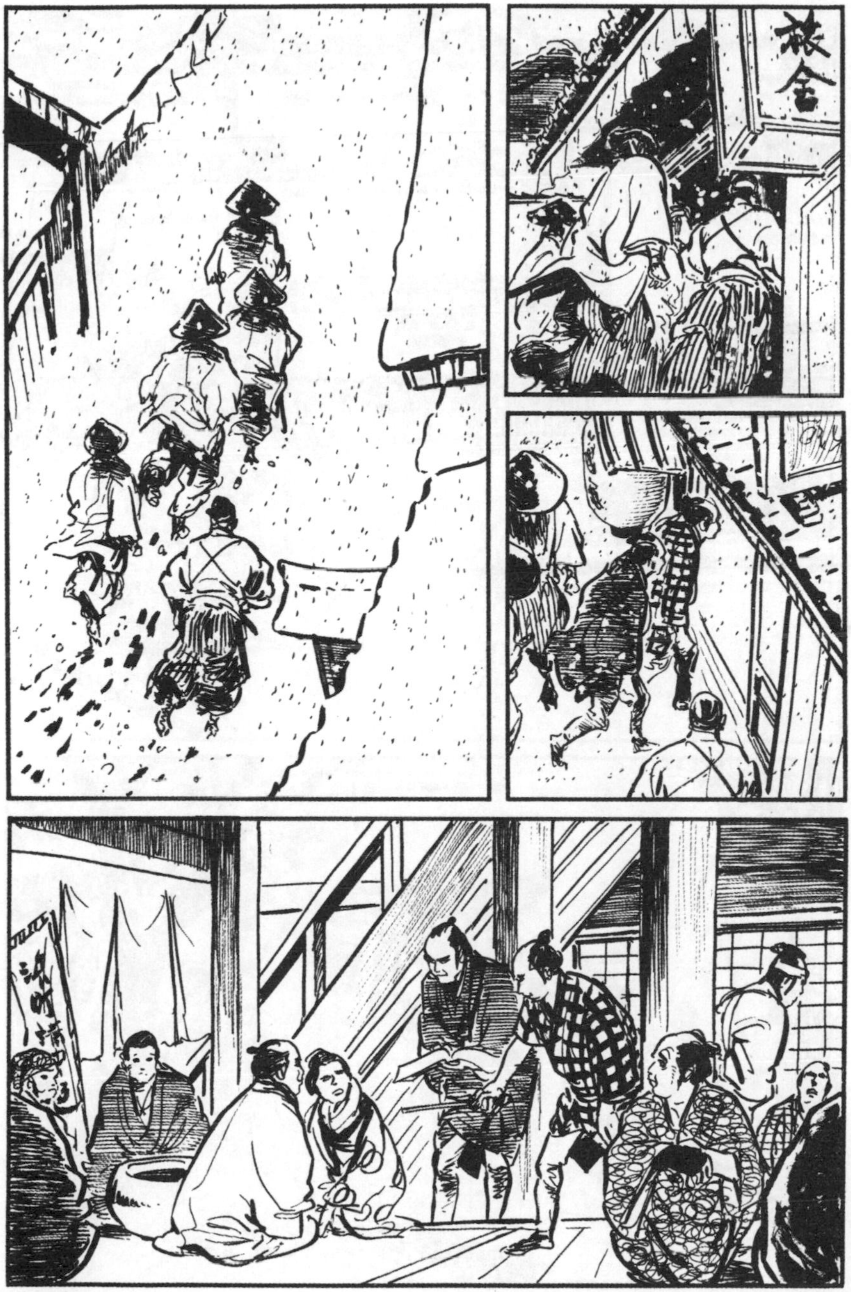
旅舍

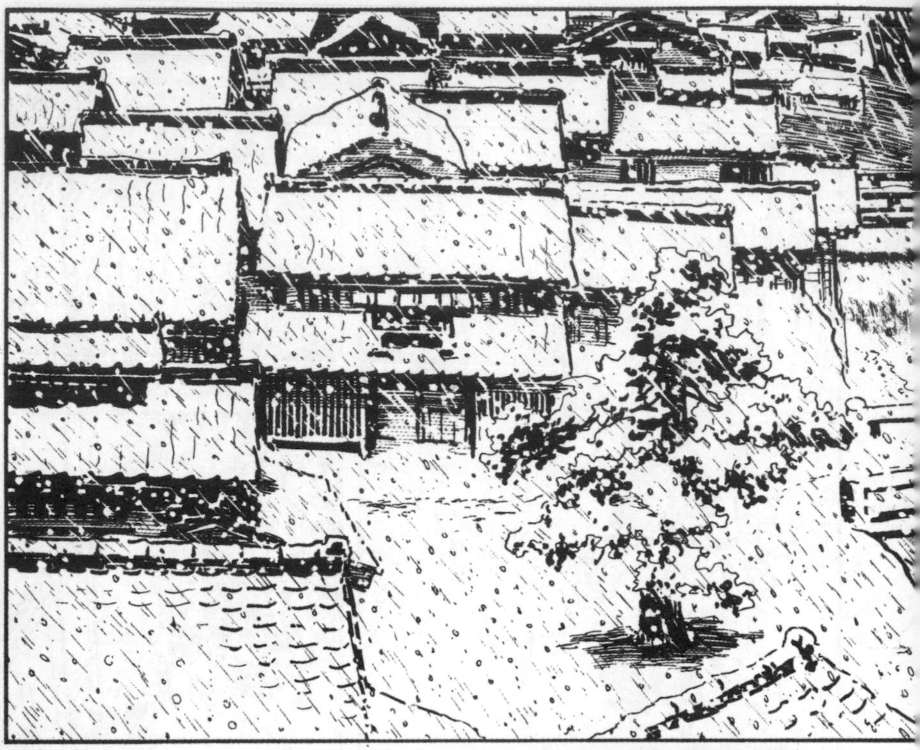
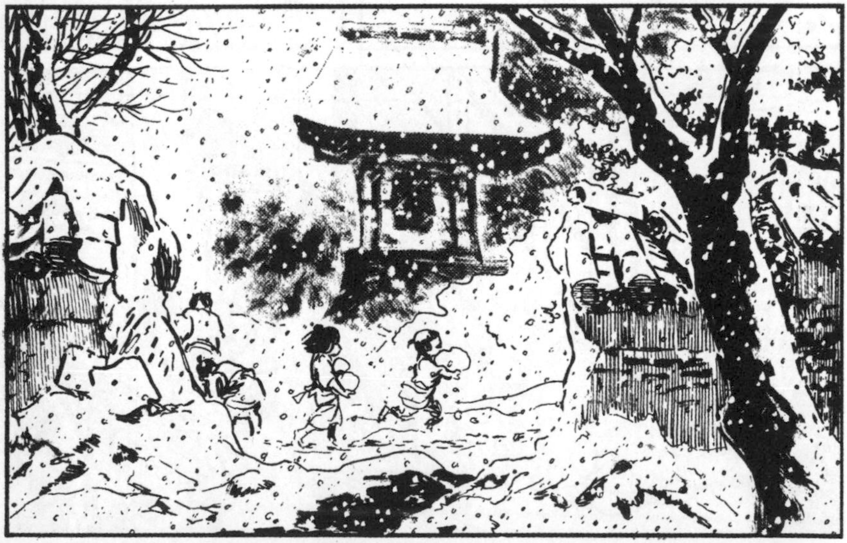

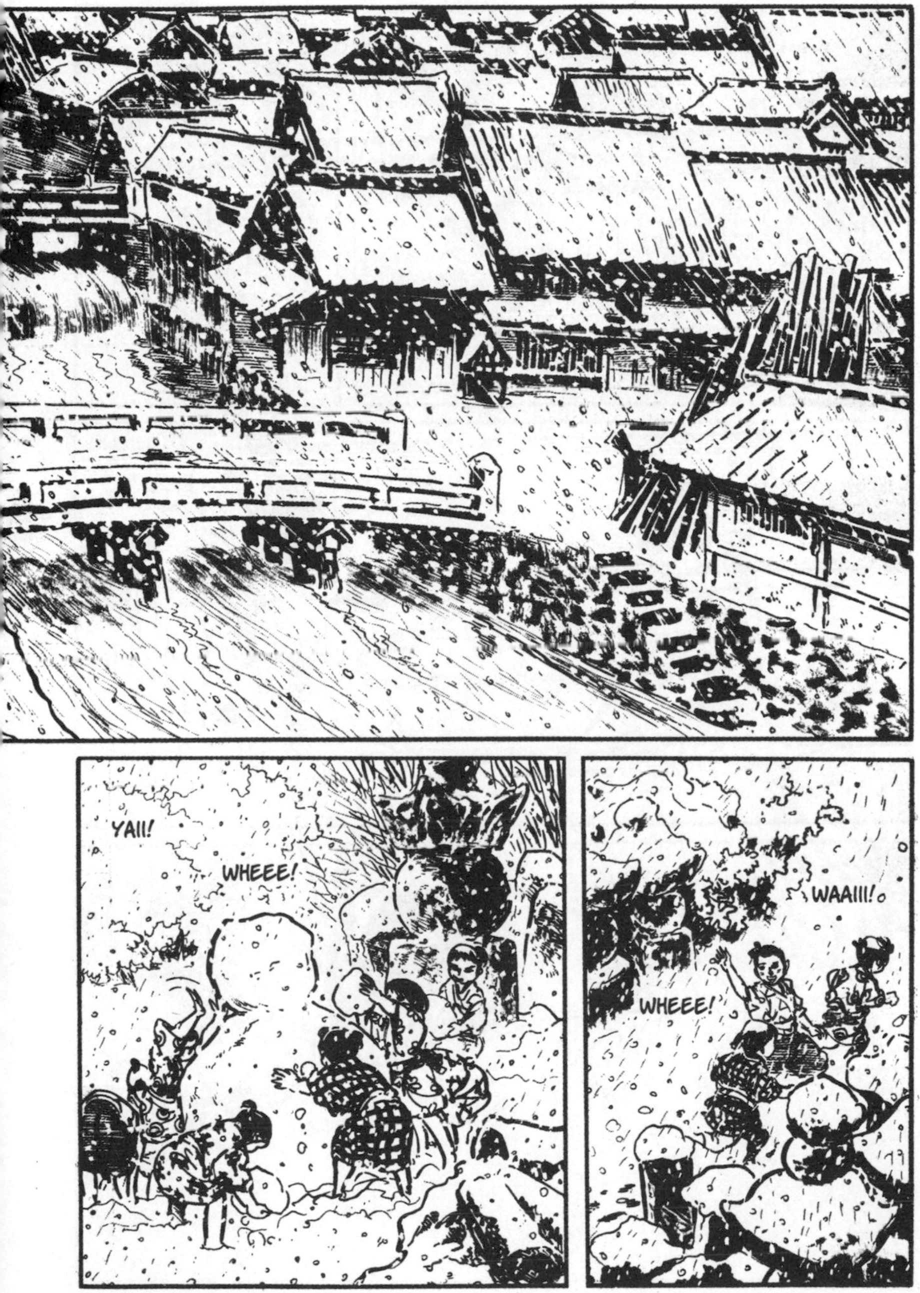
WAAIII!
WHEEE!
YAII!
WHEEE!

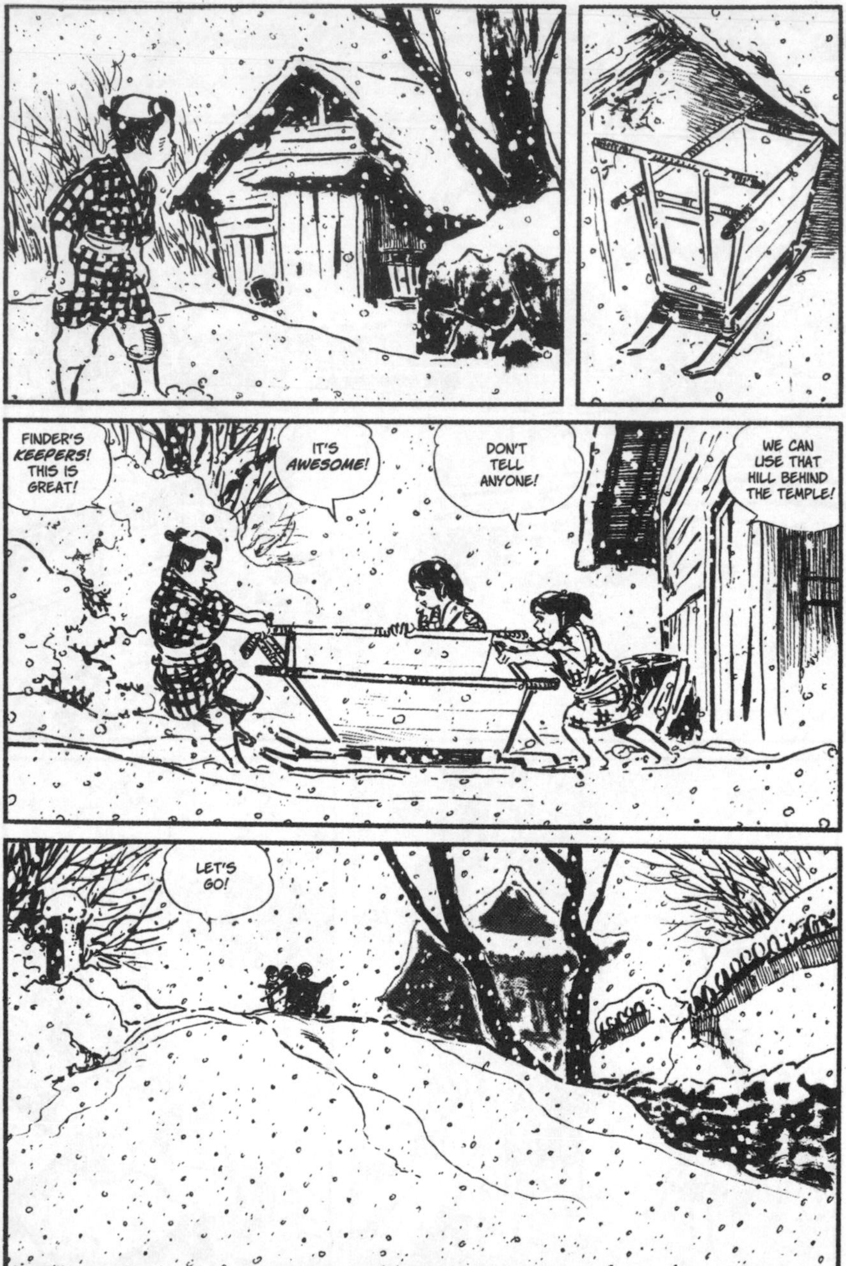
FINDER'S *KEEPERS!* THIS IS GREAT!
IT'S *AWESOME!*
DON'T TELL ANYONE!
WE CAN USE THAT HILL BEHIND THE TEMPLE!
LET'S GO!

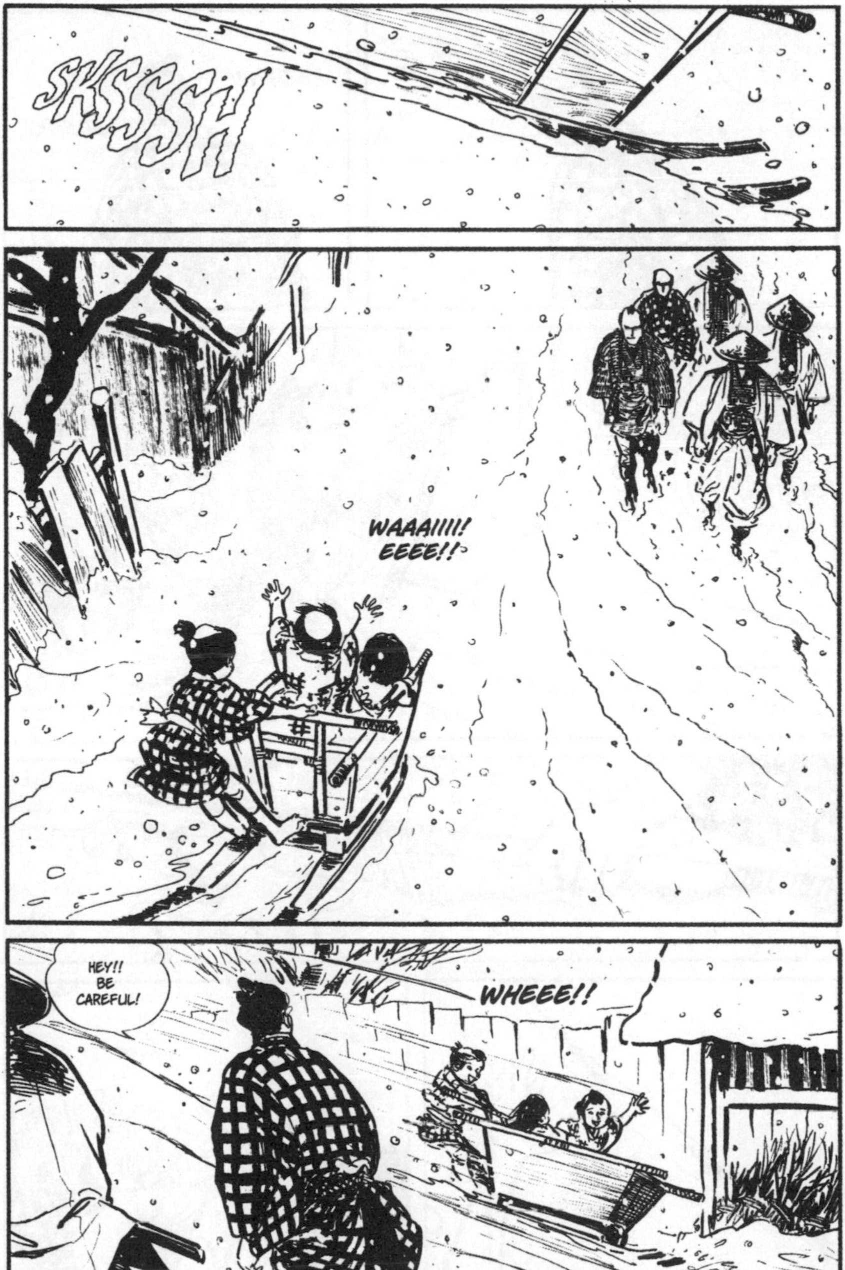
SKSSSH
WAAAIIII! EEEE!!
WHEEE!!
HEY!! BE CAREFUL!

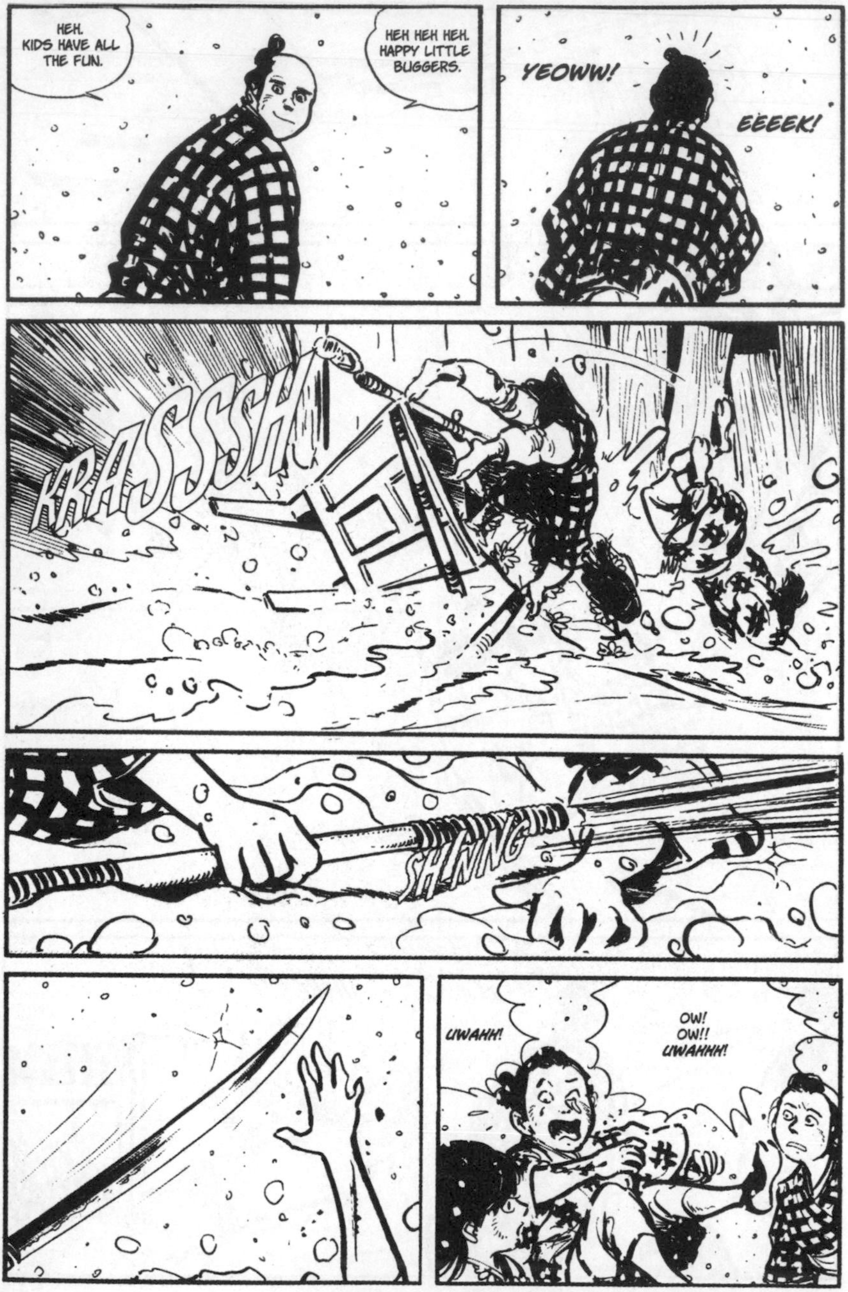
HEH. KIDS HAVE ALL THE FUN.
HEH HEH HEH. HAPPY LITTLE BUGGERS.
YEOWW!
EEEEK!
KRASSSH
SHING
UWAHH!
OW! OW!! UWAHHH!

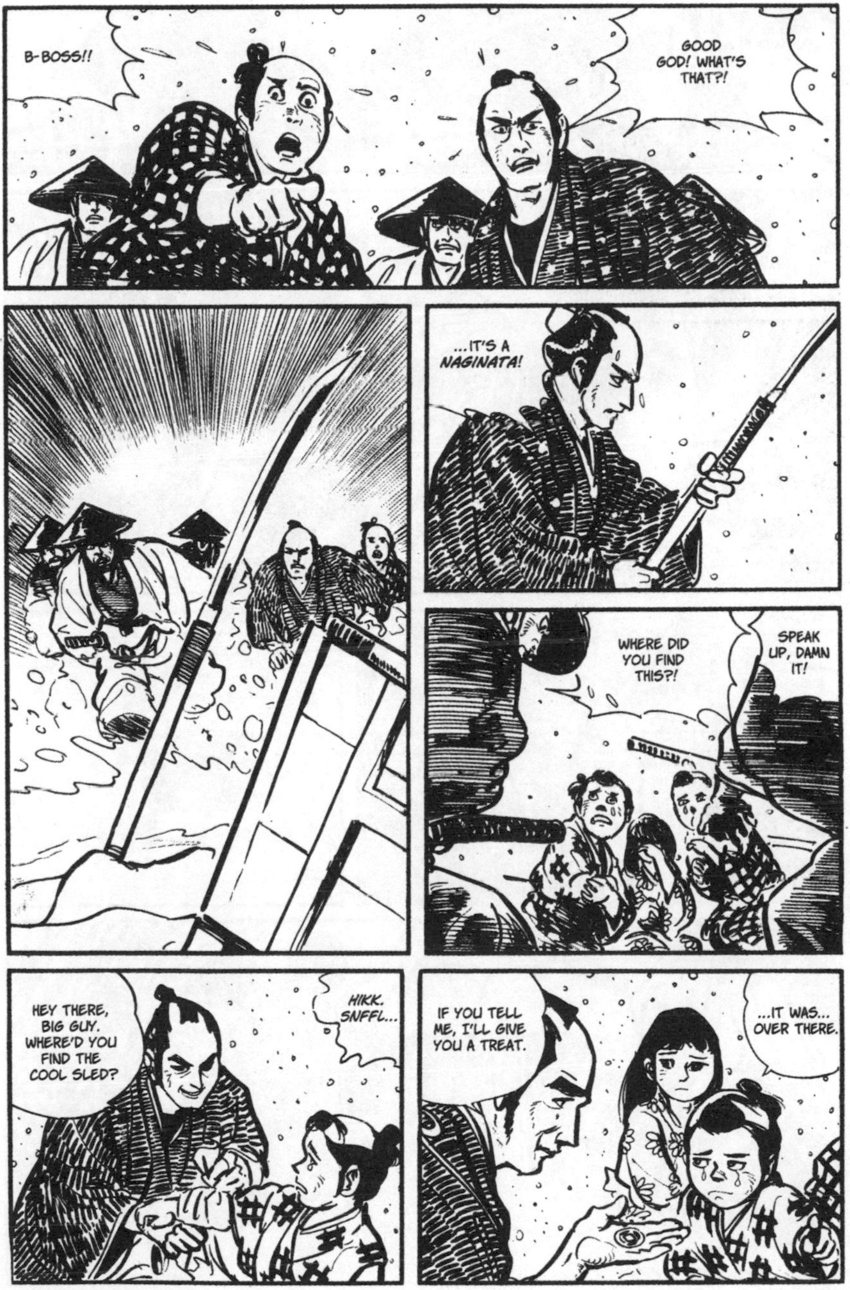
B-BOSS!!
GOOD GOD! WHAT'S THAT?!
...IT'S A NAGINATA!
WHERE DID YOU FIND THIS?!
SPEAK UP, DAMN IT!
HEY THERE, BIG GUY. WHERE'D YOU FIND THE COOL SLED?
HIKK. SNFFL...
IF YOU TELL ME, I'LL GIVE YOU A TREAT.
...IT WAS... OVER THERE.

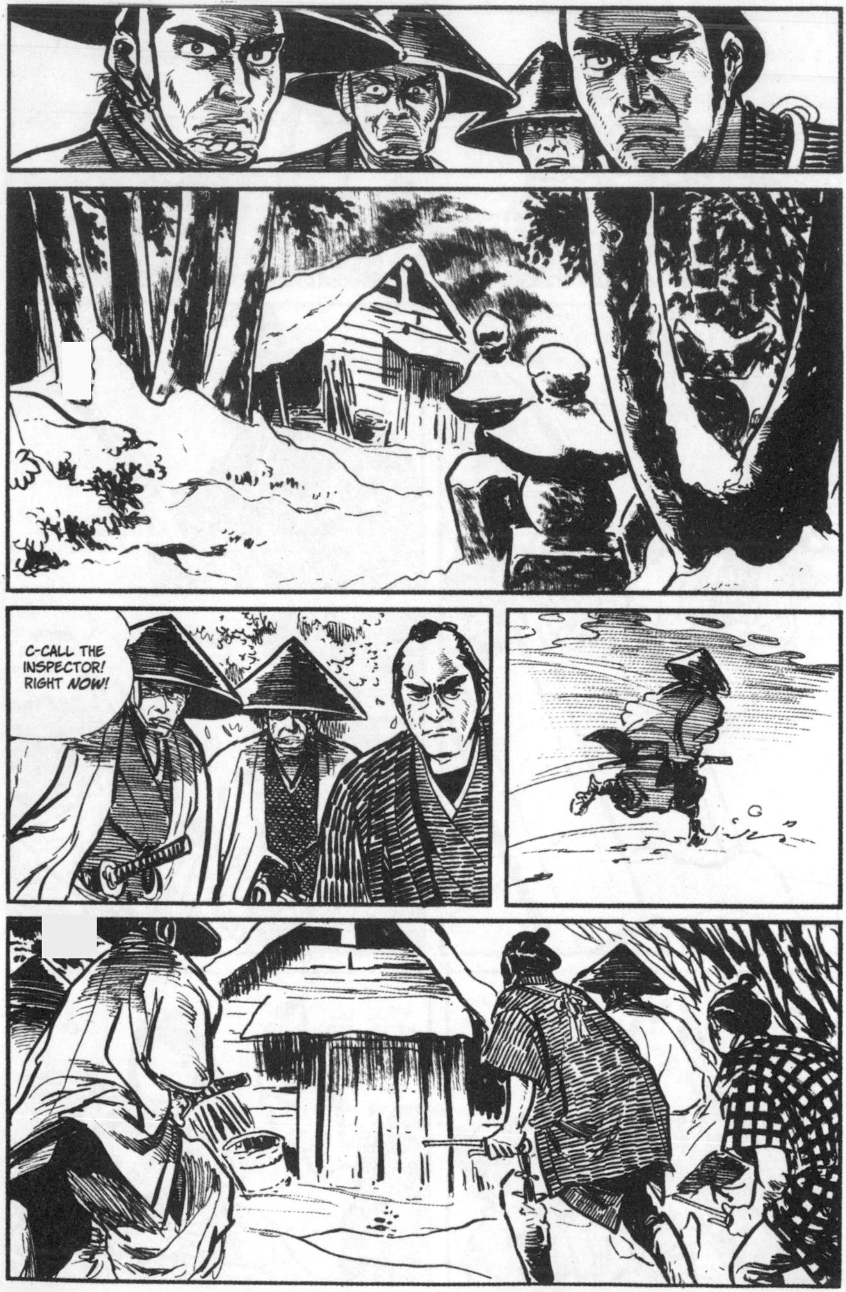
C-CALL THE INSPECTOR! RIGHT NOW!

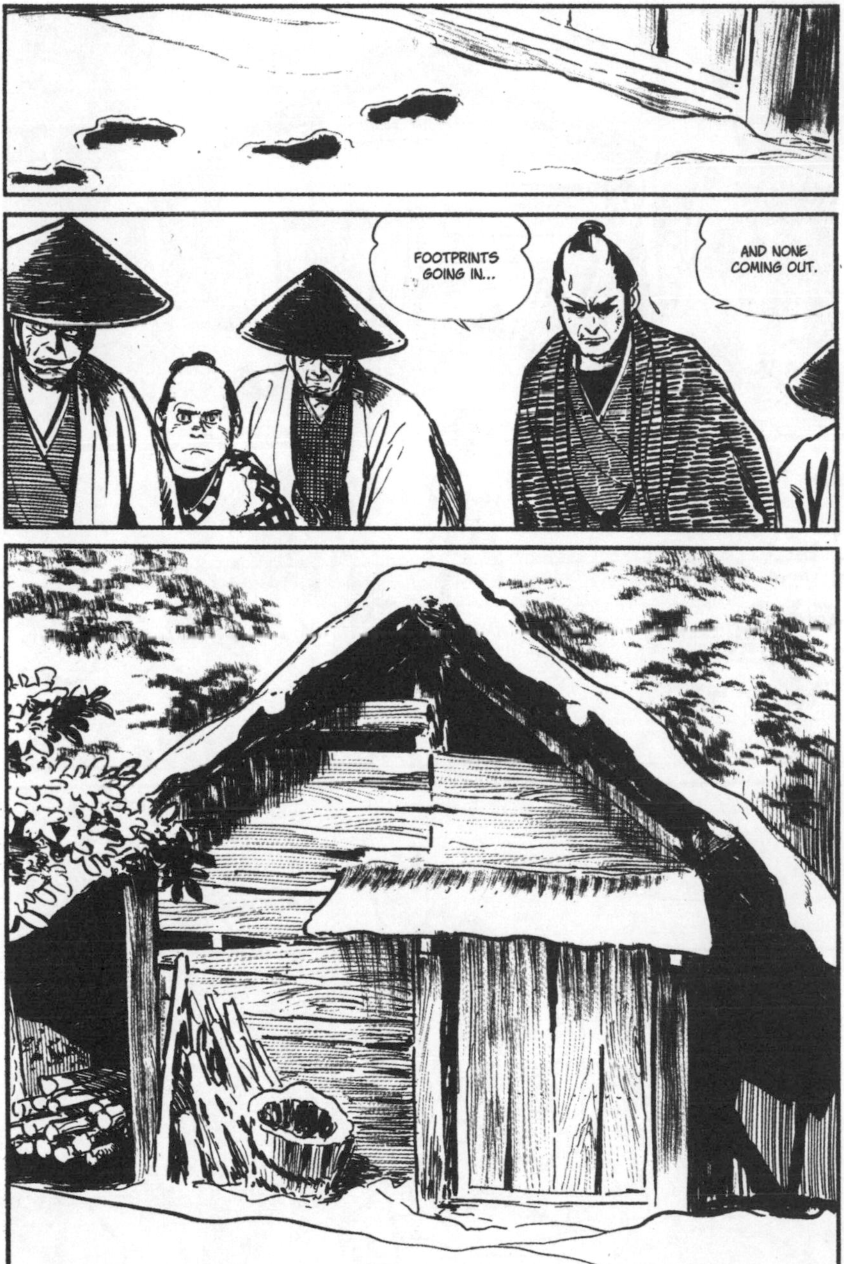
FOOTPRINTS GOING IN...
AND NONE COMING OUT.

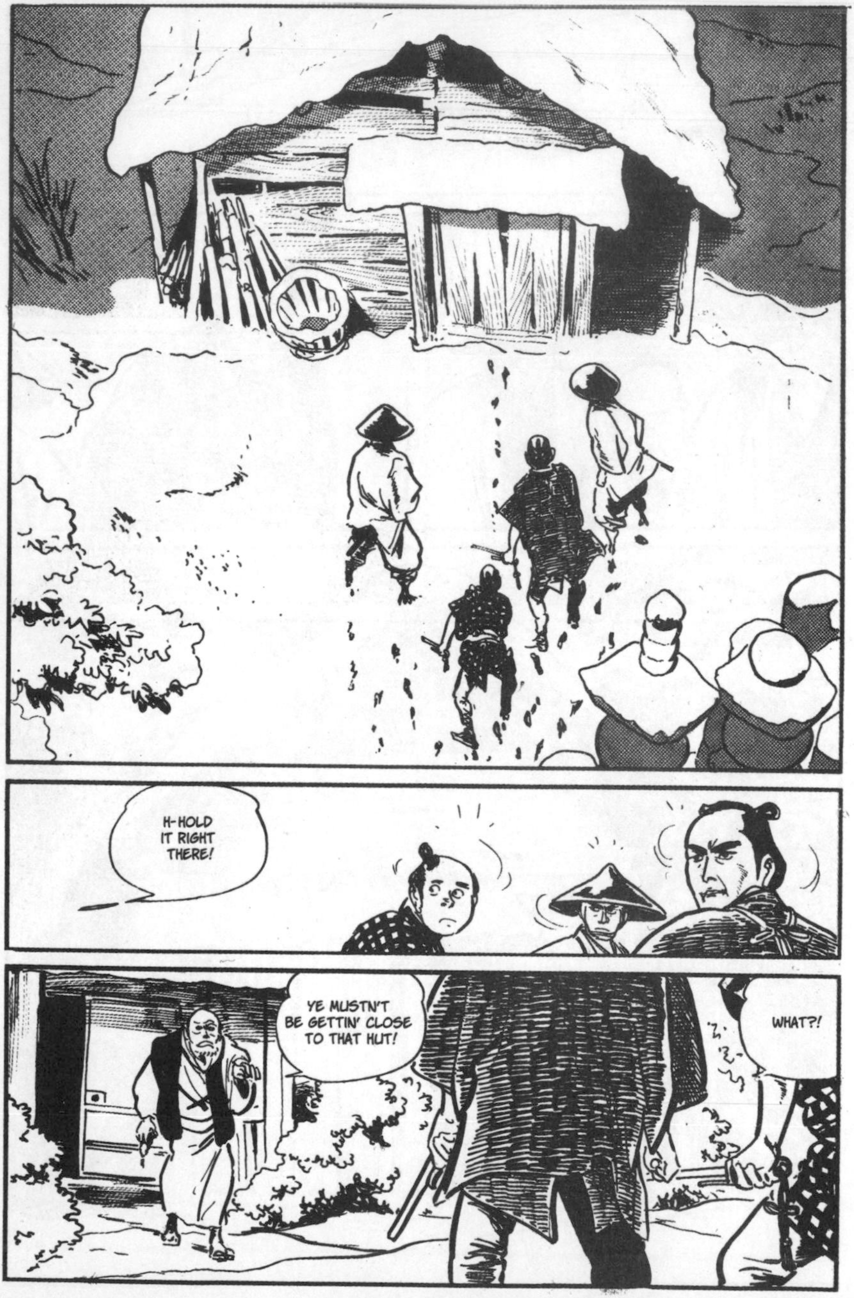
H-HOLD IT RIGHT THERE!
WHAT?!
YE MUSTN'T BE GETTIN' CLOSE TO THAT HUT!

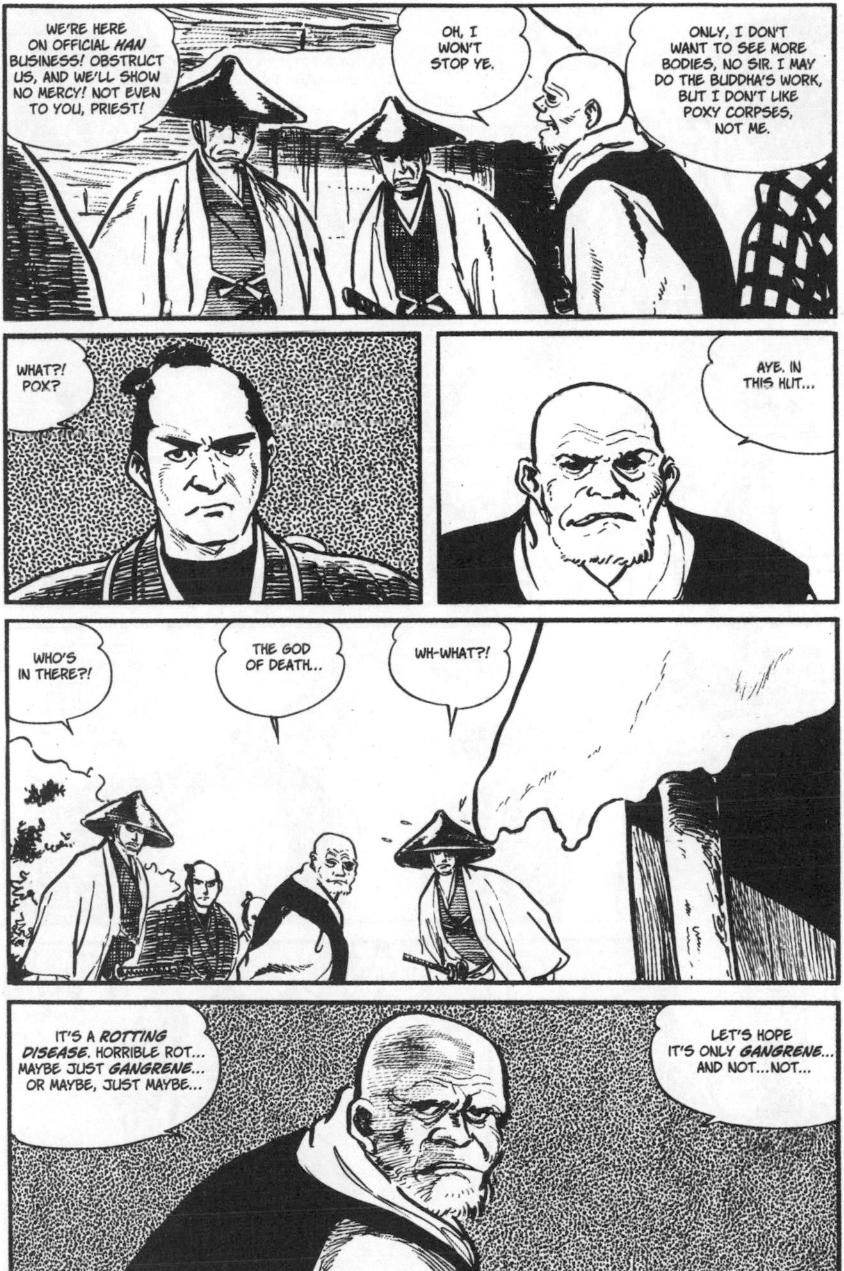
WE'RE HERE ON OFFICIAL *HAN* BUSINESS! OBSTRUCT US, AND WE'LL SHOW NO MERCY! NOT EVEN TO YOU, PRIEST!
OH, I WON'T STOP YE.
ONLY, I DON'T WANT TO SEE MORE BODIES, NO SIR. I MAY DO THE BUDDHA'S WORK, BUT I DON'T LIKE POXY CORPSES, NOT ME.
WHAT?! POX?
AYE. IN THIS HUT...
WHO'S IN THERE?!
THE GOD OF DEATH...
WH-WHAT?!
IT'S A *ROTTING DISEASE*. HORRIBLE ROT... MAYBE JUST *GANGRENE*... OR MAYBE, JUST MAYBE...
LET'S HOPE IT'S ONLY *GANGRENE*... AND NOT...NOT...

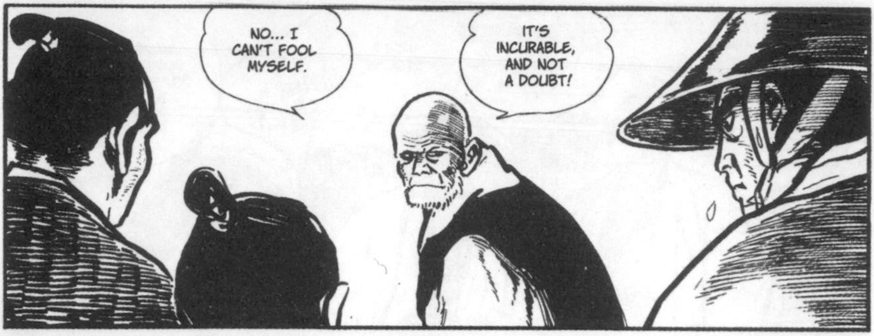
NO... I CAN'T FOOL MYSELF.
IT'S INCURABLE, AND NOT A DOUBT!
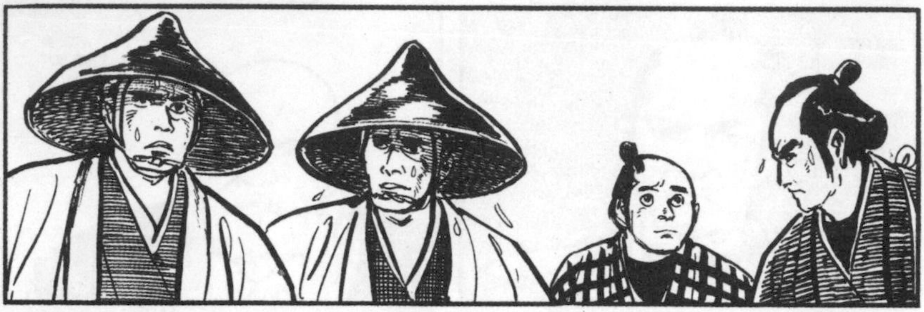
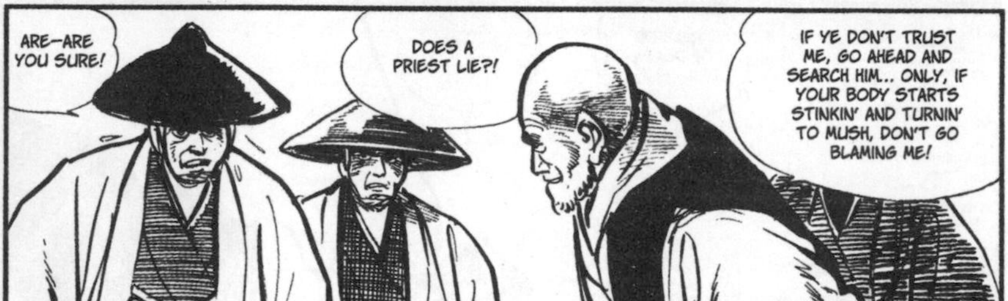
ARE-ARE YOU SURE!
DOES A PRIEST LIE?!
IF YE DON'T TRUST ME, GO AHEAD AND SEARCH HIM.. ONLY, IF YOUR BODY STARTS STINKIN' AND TURNIN' TO MUSH, DON'T GO BLAMING ME!
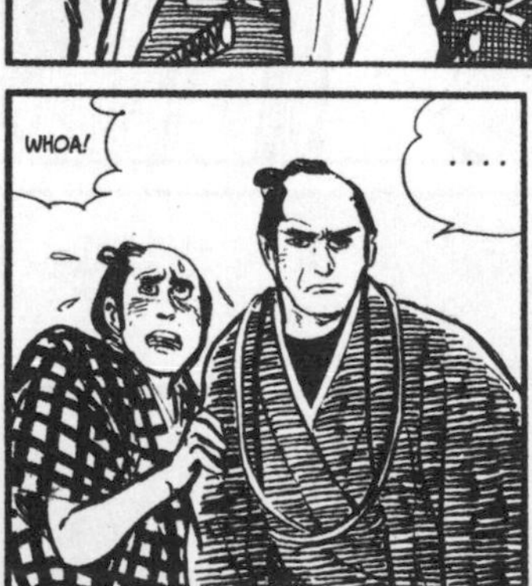
WHOA!
....
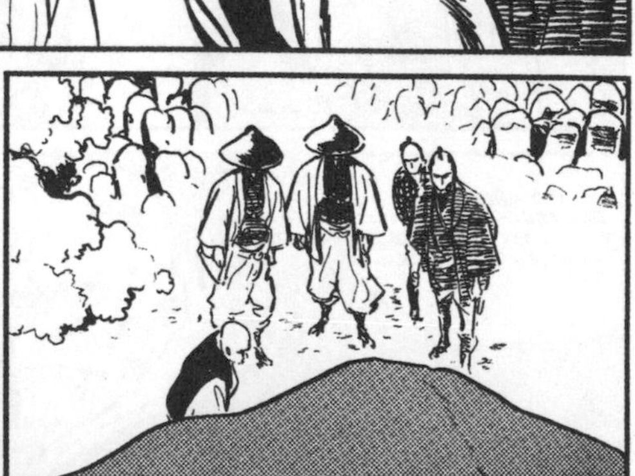

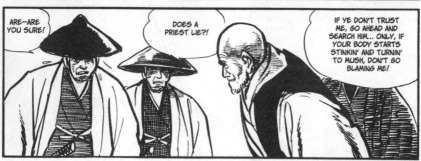

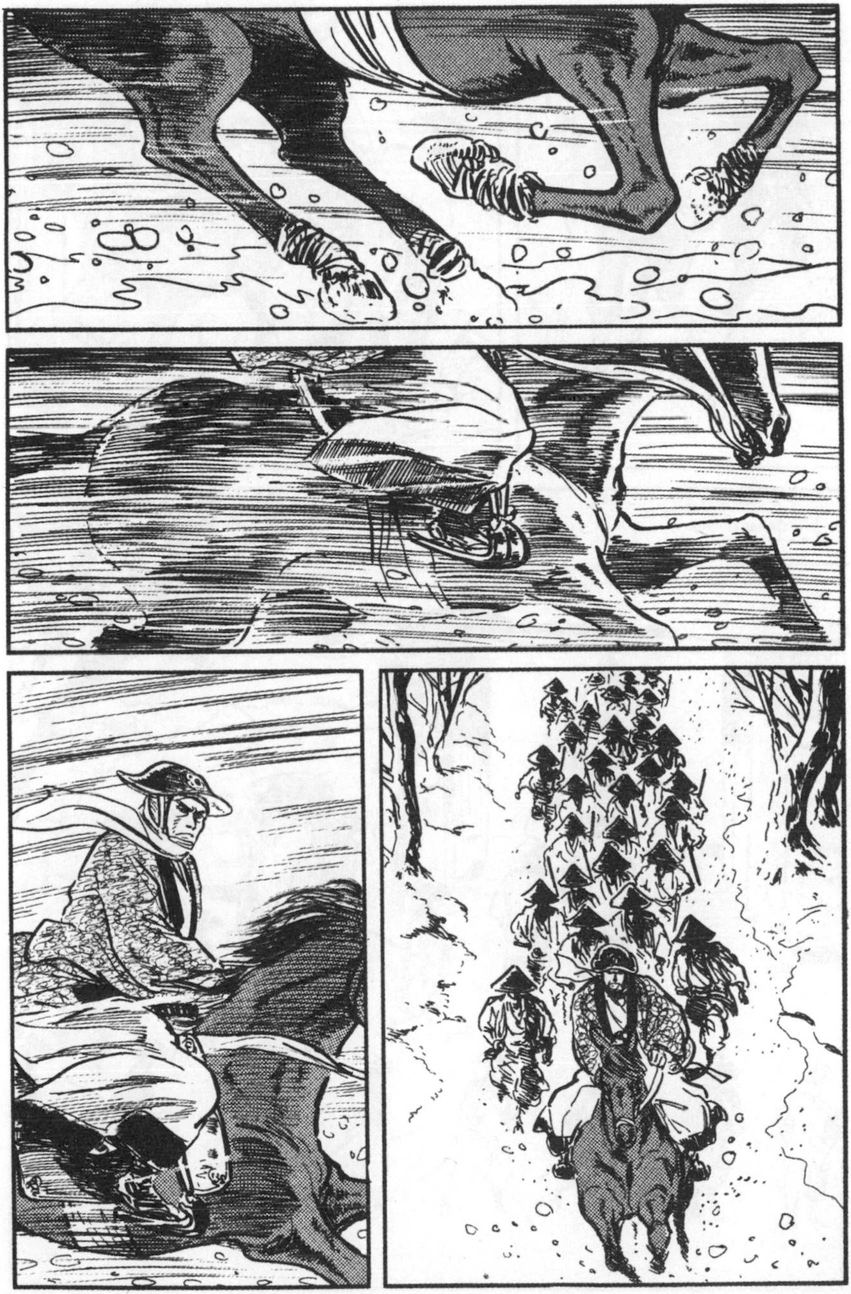

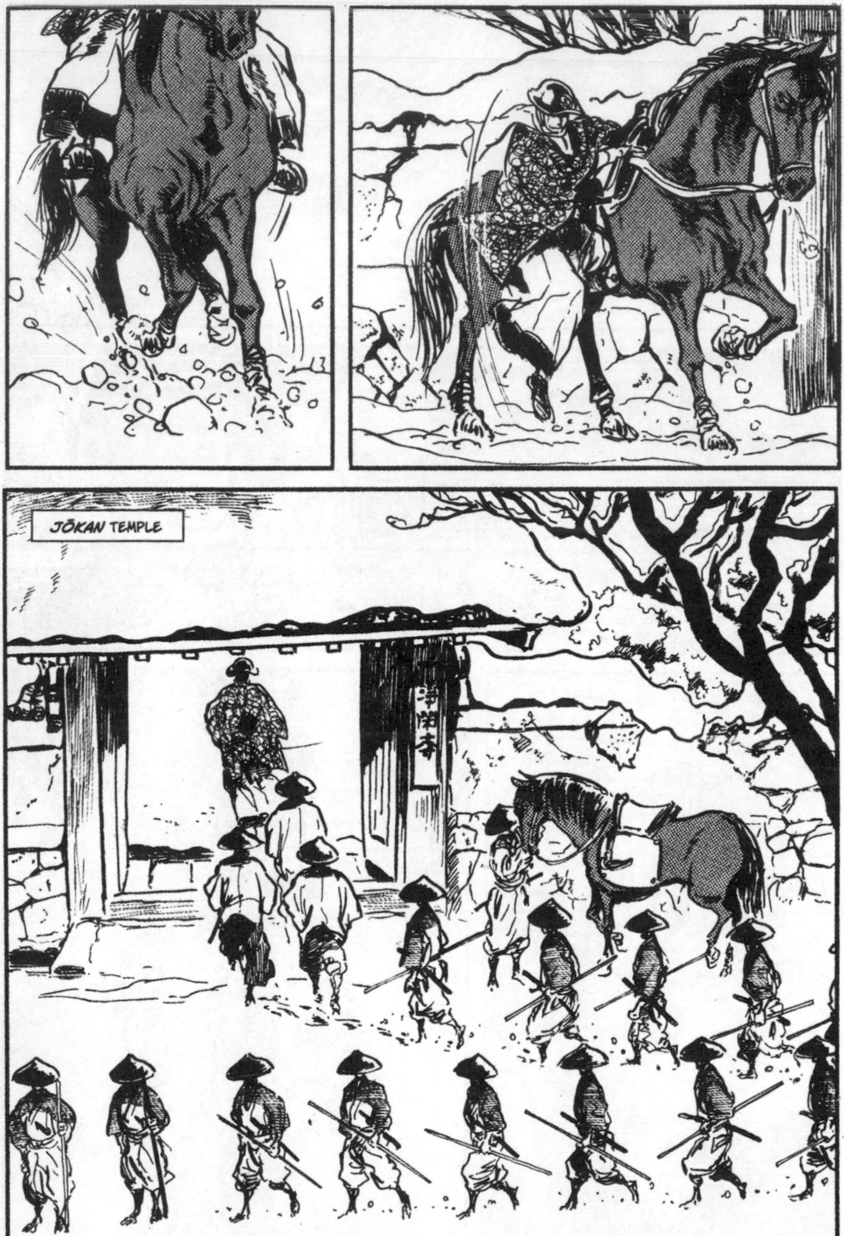
JŌKAN TEMPLE

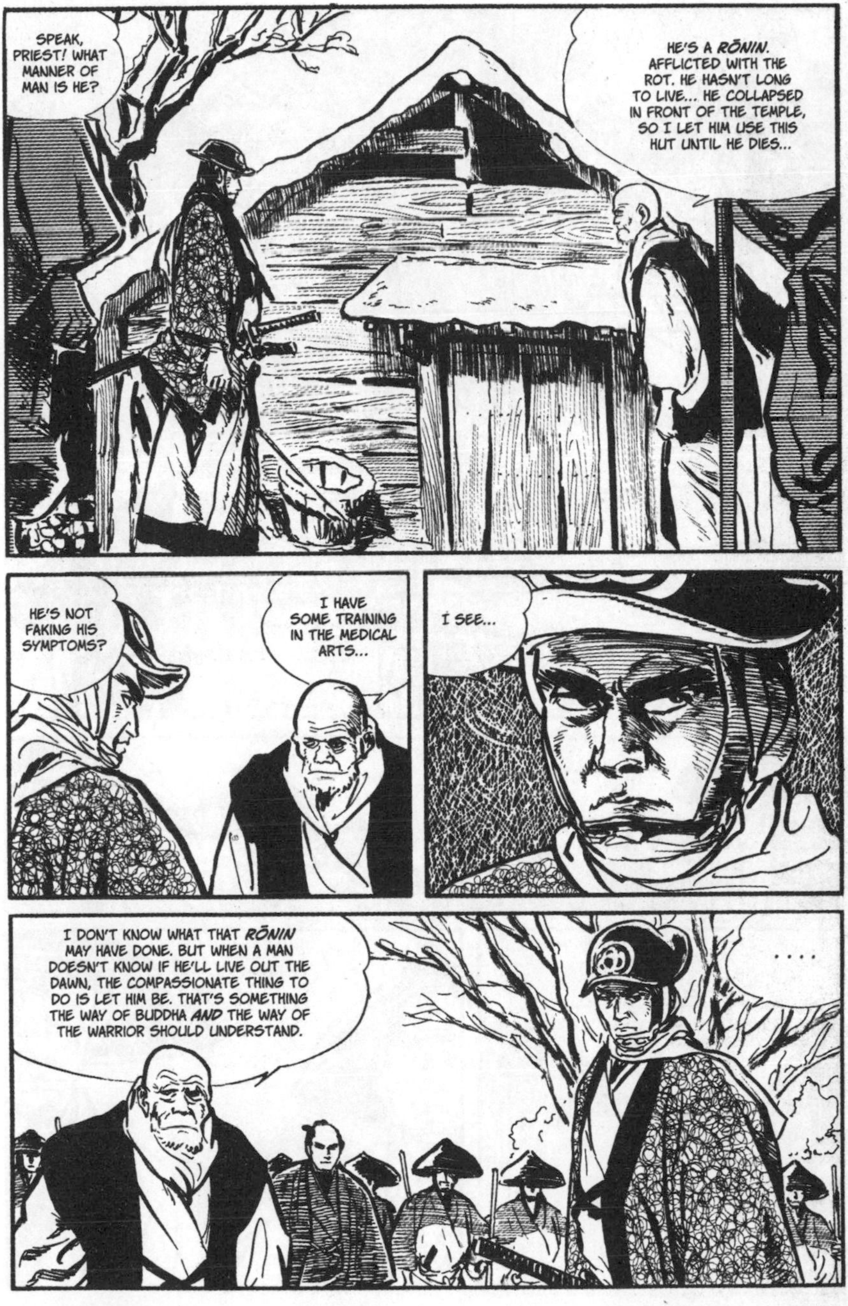
SPEAK, PRIEST! WHAT MANNER OF MAN IS HE?
HE'S A *RŌNIN*. AFFLICTED WITH THE ROT. HE HASN'T LONG TO LIVE... HE COLLAPSED IN FRONT OF THE TEMPLE, SO I LET HIM USE THIS HUT UNTIL HE DIES...
HE'S NOT FAKING HIS SYMPTOMS?
I HAVE SOME TRAINING IN THE MEDICAL ARTS...
I SEE...
I DON'T KNOW WHAT THAT *RŌNIN* MAY HAVE DONE. BUT WHEN A MAN DOESN'T KNOW IF HE'LL LIVE OUT THE DAWN, THE COMPASSIONATE THING TO DO IS LET HIM BE. THAT'S SOMETHING THE WAY OF BUDDHA *AND* THE WAY OF THE WARRIOR SHOULD UNDERSTAND.
....

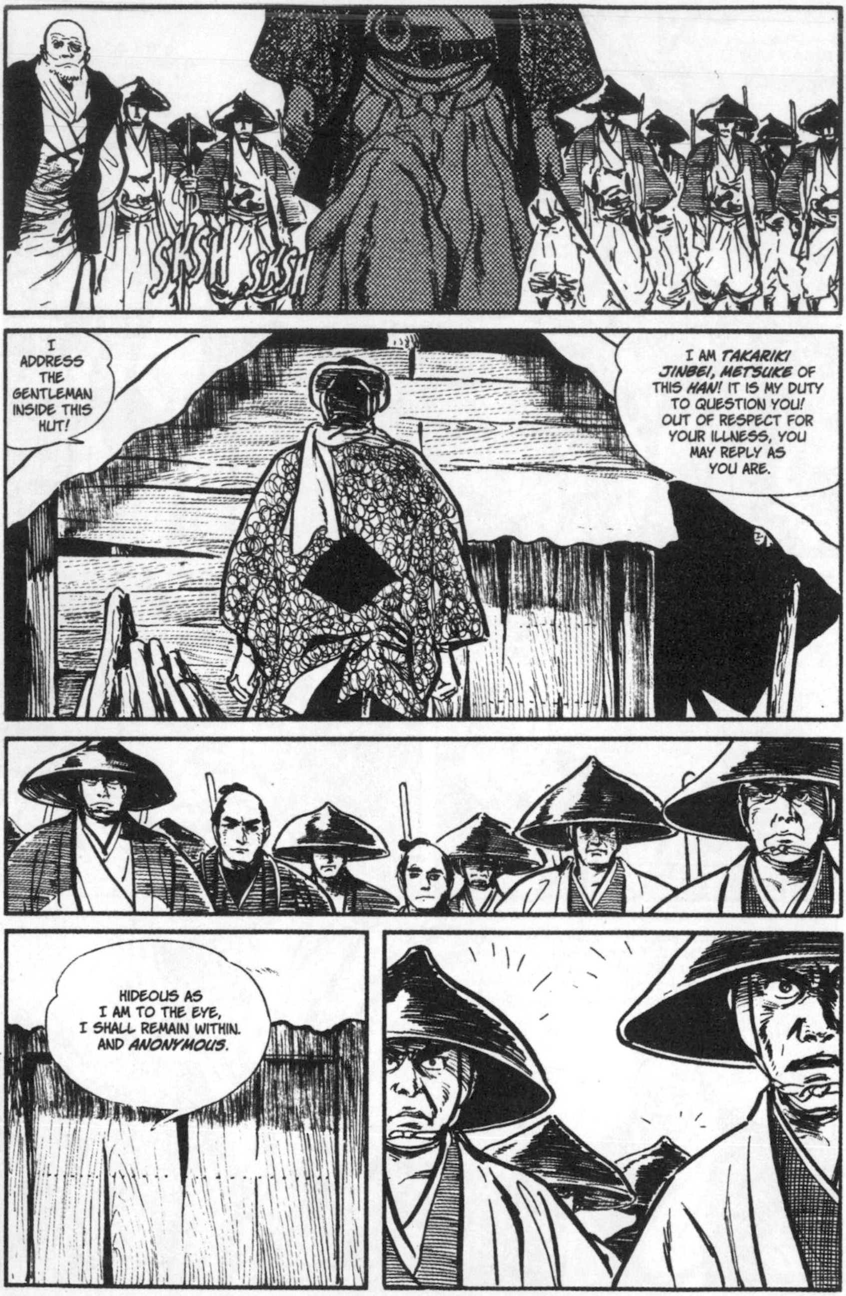
SKSH SKSH
I ADDRESS THE GENTLEMAN INSIDE THIS HUT!
I AM TAKARIKI JINBEI, METSUKE OF THIS HAN! IT IS MY DUTY TO QUESTION YOU! OUT OF RESPECT FOR YOUR ILLNESS, YOU MAY REPLY AS YOU ARE.
HIDEOUS AS I AM TO THE EYE, I SHALL REMAIN WITHIN. AND ANONYMOUS.

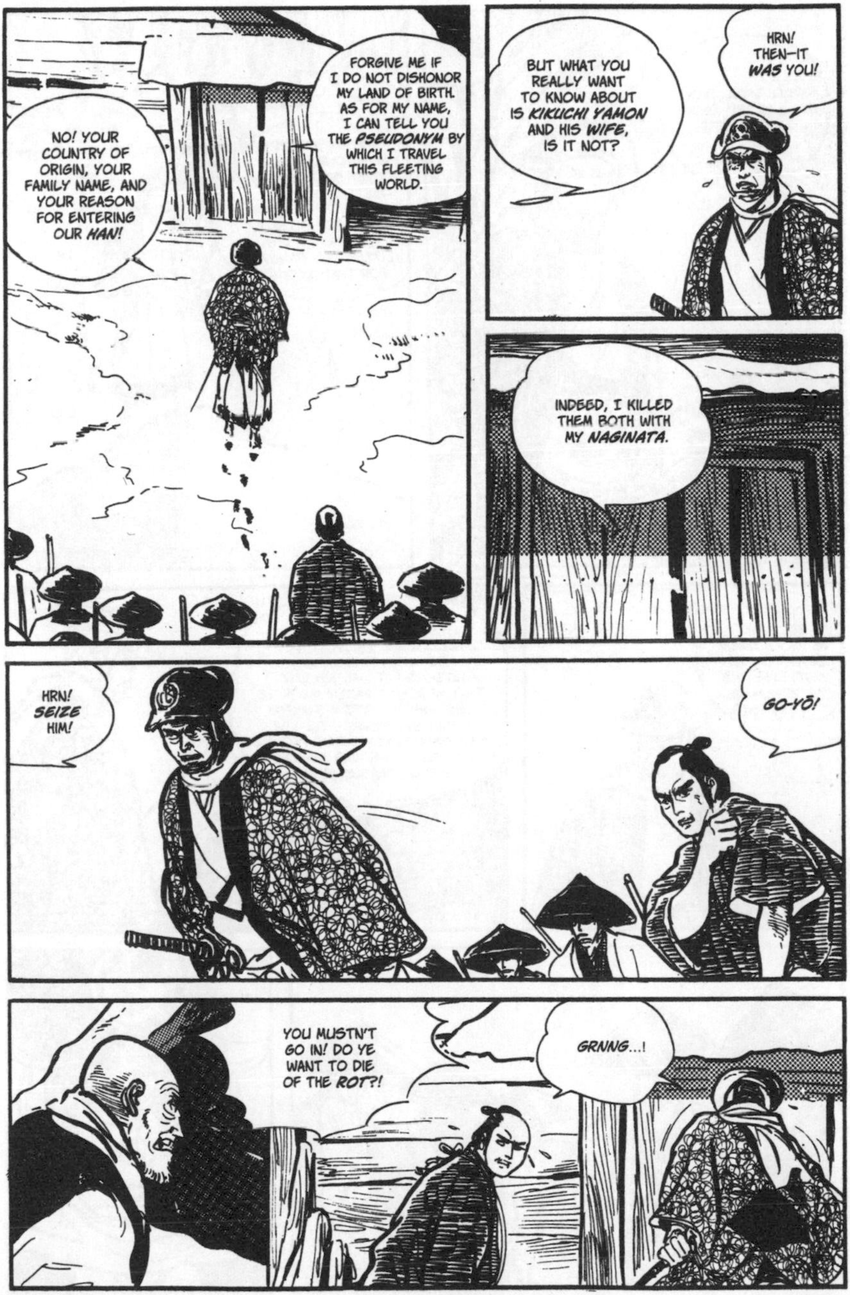
NO! YOUR COUNTRY OF ORIGIN, YOUR FAMILY NAME, AND YOUR REASON FOR ENTERING OUR *HAN*!
FORGIVE ME IF I DO NOT DISHONOR MY LAND OF BIRTH. AS FOR MY NAME, I CAN TELL YOU THE *PSEUDONYM* BY WHICH I TRAVEL THIS FLEETING WORLD.
BUT WHAT YOU REALLY WANT TO KNOW ABOUT IS *KIKUCHI YAMON* AND HIS *WIFE*, IS IT NOT?
HRN! THEN—IT *WAS* YOU!
INDEED, I KILLED THEM BOTH WITH MY *NAGINATA*.
HRN! *SEIZE* HIM!
GO-YŌ!
YOU MUSTN'T GO IN! DO YE WANT TO DIE OF THE *ROT*?!
GRNNG...!

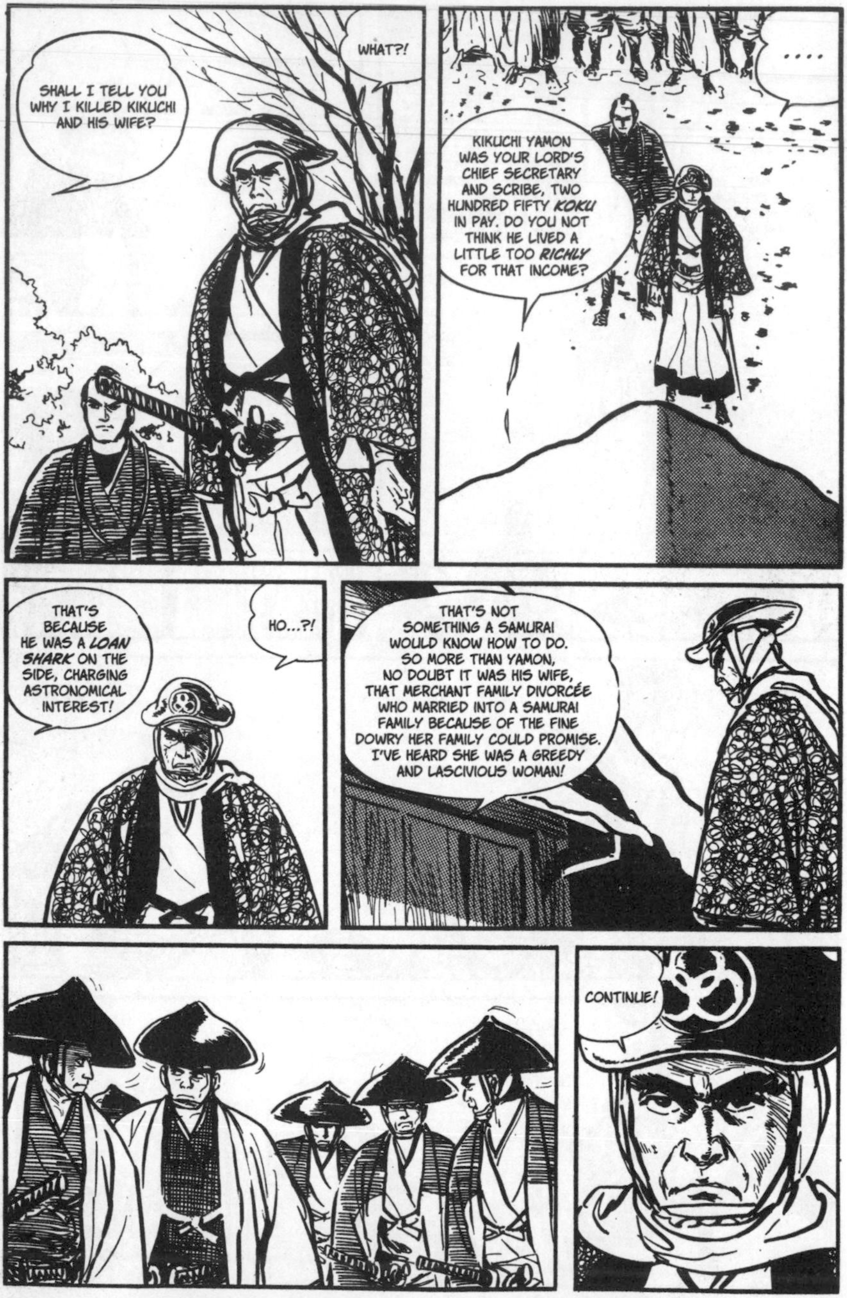
SHALL I TELL YOU WHY I KILLED KIKUCHI AND HIS WIFE?
WHAT?!
KIKUCHI YAMON WAS YOUR LORD'S CHIEF SECRETARY AND SCRIBE, TWO HUNDRED FIFTY *KOKU* IN PAY. DO YOU NOT THINK HE LIVED A LITTLE TOO *RICHLY* FOR THAT INCOME?
....
THAT'S BECAUSE HE WAS A *LOAN SHARK* ON THE SIDE, CHARGING ASTRONOMICAL INTEREST!
HO...?!
THAT'S NOT SOMETHING A SAMURAI WOULD KNOW HOW TO DO. SO MORE THAN YAMON, NO DOUBT IT WAS HIS WIFE, THAT MERCHANT FAMILY DIVORCÉE WHO MARRIED INTO A SAMURAI FAMILY BECAUSE OF THE FINE DOWRY HER FAMILY COULD PROMISE. I'VE HEARD SHE WAS A GREEDY AND LASCIVIOUS WOMAN!
CONTINUE!

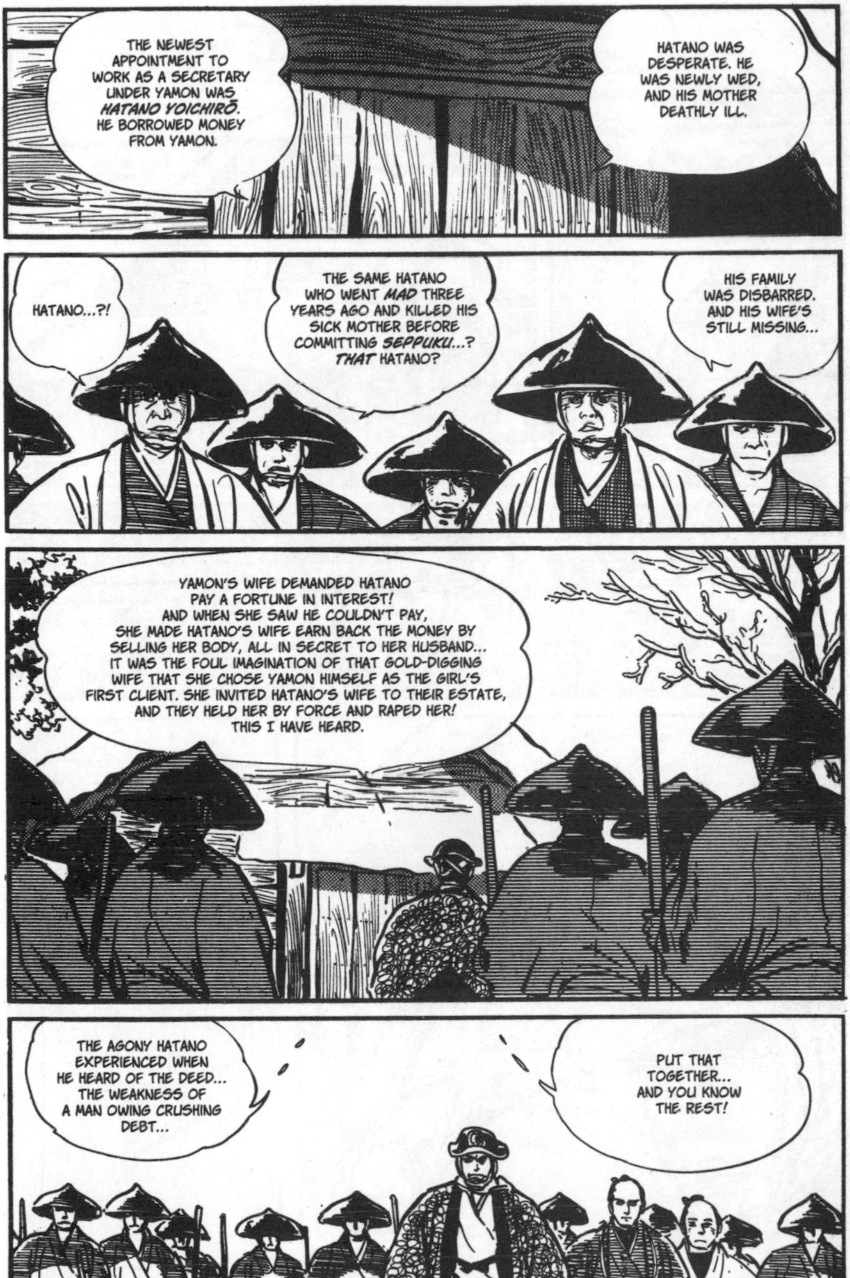
THE NEWEST APPOINTMENT TO WORK AS A SECRETARY UNDER YAMON WAS *HATANO YOICHIRŌ*. HE BORROWED MONEY FROM YAMON.
HATANO WAS DESPERATE. HE WAS NEWLY WED, AND HIS MOTHER DEATHLY ILL.
HATANO...?!
THE SAME HATANO WHO WENT *MAD* THREE YEARS AGO AND KILLED HIS SICK MOTHER BEFORE COMMITTING *SEPPUKU*...? *THAT* HATANO?
HIS FAMILY WAS DISBARRED. AND HIS WIFE'S STILL MISSING...
YAMON'S WIFE DEMANDED HATANO PAY A FORTUNE IN INTEREST! AND WHEN SHE SAW HE COULDN'T PAY, SHE MADE HATANO'S WIFE EARN BACK THE MONEY BY SELLING HER BODY, ALL IN SECRET TO HER HUSBAND... IT WAS THE FOUL IMAGINATION OF THAT GOLD-DIGGING WIFE THAT SHE CHOSE YAMON HIMSELF AS THE GIRL'S FIRST CLIENT. SHE INVITED HATANO'S WIFE TO THEIR ESTATE, AND THEY HELD HER BY FORCE AND RAPED HER! THIS I HAVE HEARD.
THE AGONY HATANO EXPERIENCED WHEN HE HEARD OF THE DEED... THE WEAKNESS OF A MAN OWING CRUSHING DEBT...
PUT THAT TOGETHER... AND YOU KNOW THE REST!

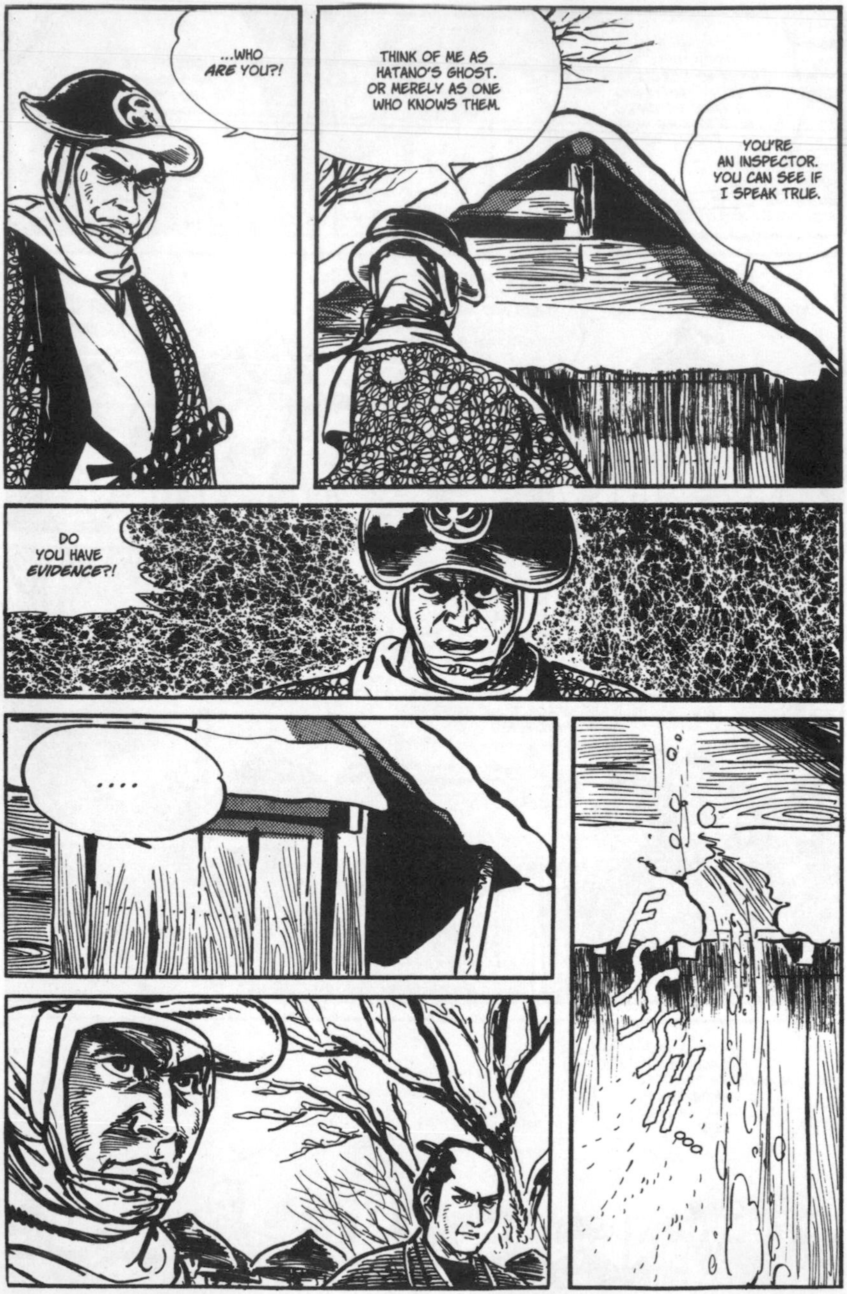
...WHO *ARE* YOU?!
THINK OF ME AS HATANO'S GHOST. OR MERELY AS ONE WHO KNOWS THEM.
YOU'RE AN INSPECTOR. YOU CAN SEE IF I SPEAK TRUE.
DO YOU HAVE *EVIDENCE*?!
....
FSSH

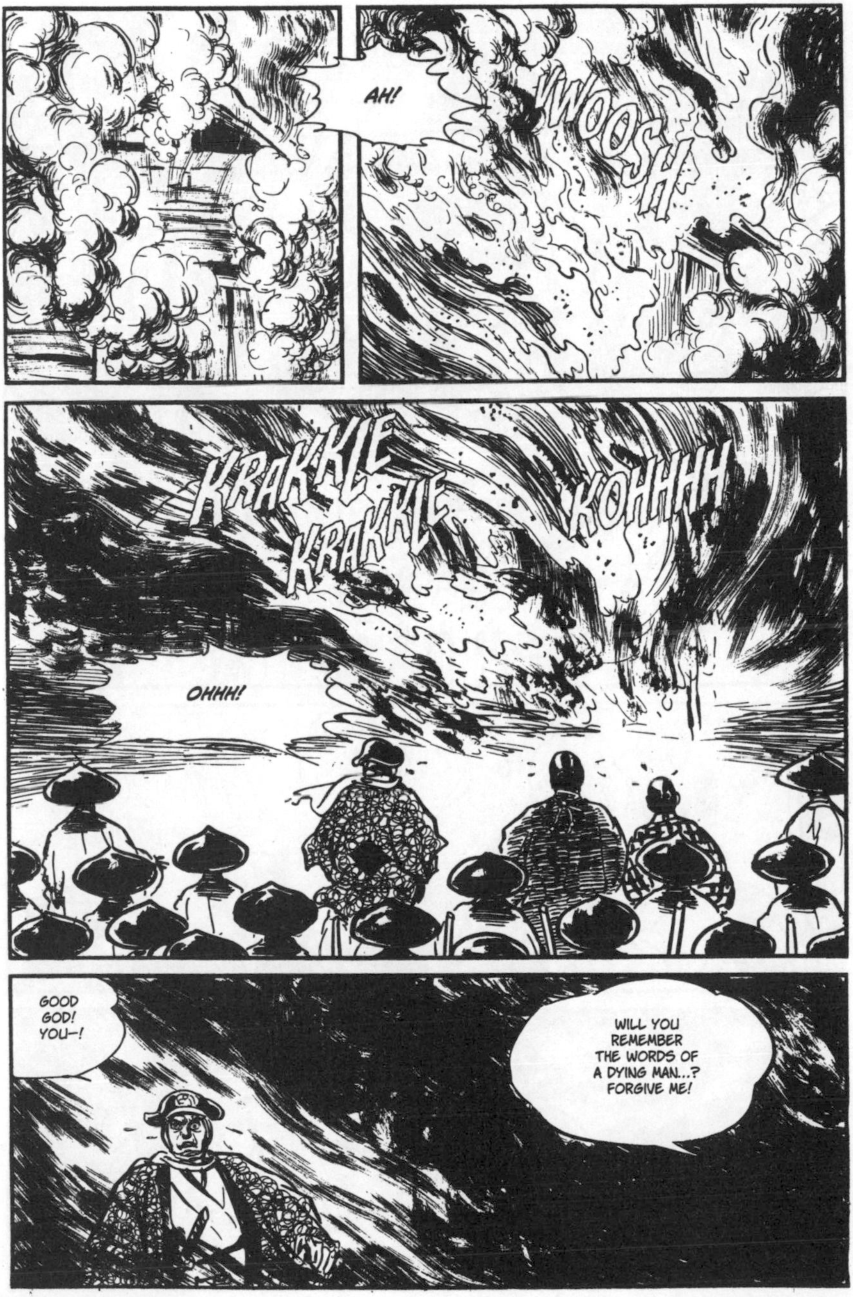
WOOSH
AH!
KOHHHH
KRAKKLE
KRAKKLE
OHHH!
WILL YOU REMEMBER THE WORDS OF A DYING MAN...? FORGIVE ME!
GOOD GOD! YOU–!

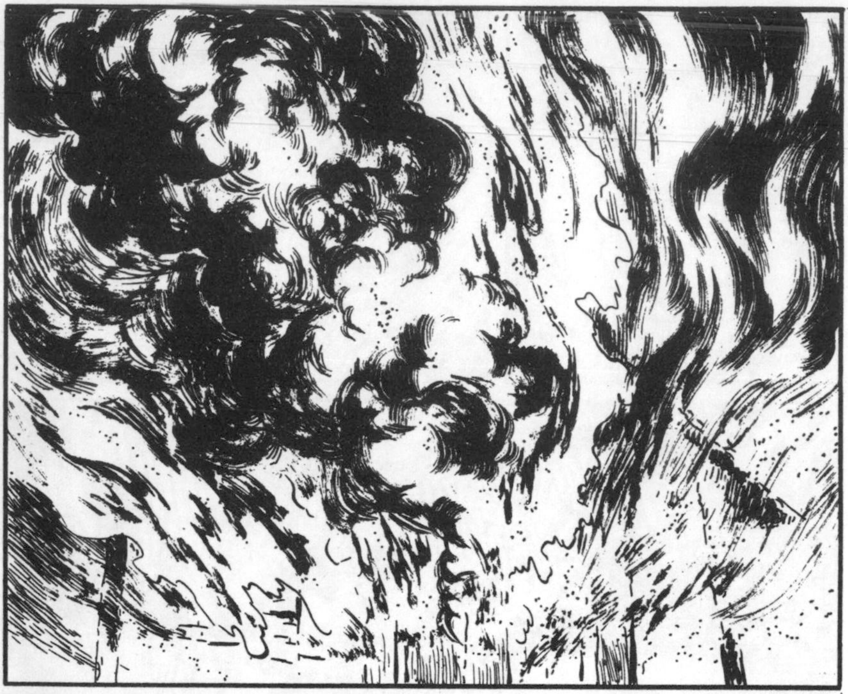

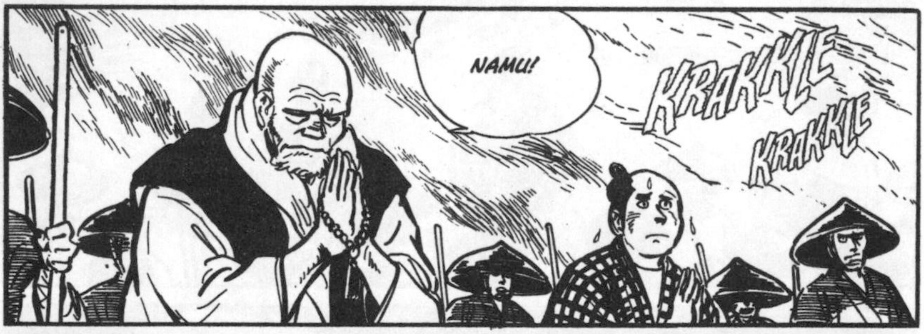
NAMU!
KRAKKLE
KRAKKLE

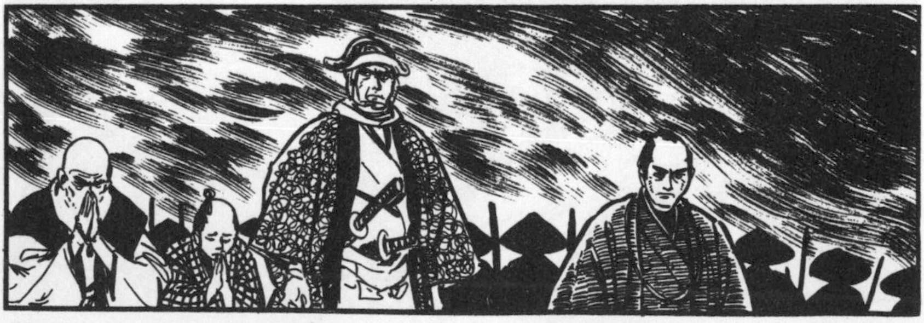

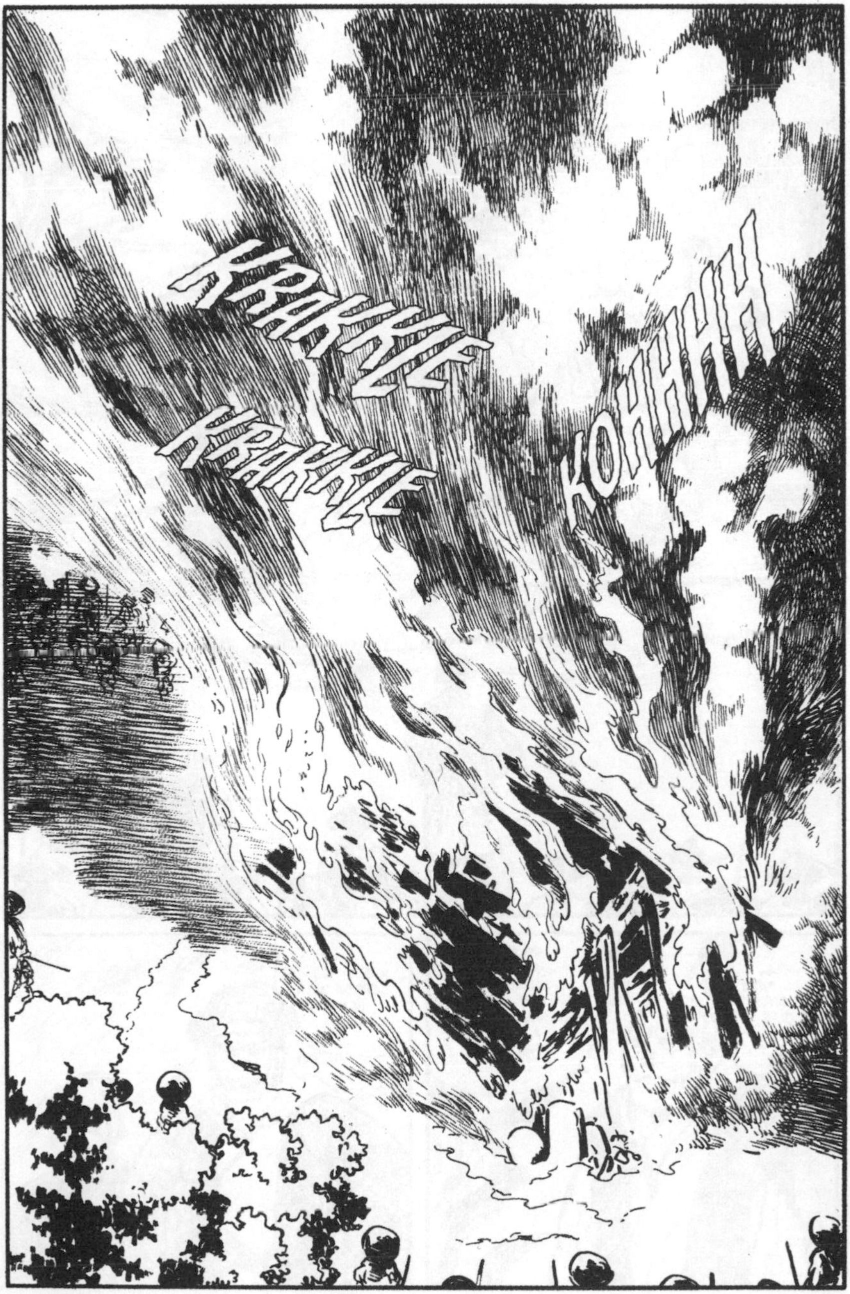
KRAKKLE
KRAKKLE
KOHHHH

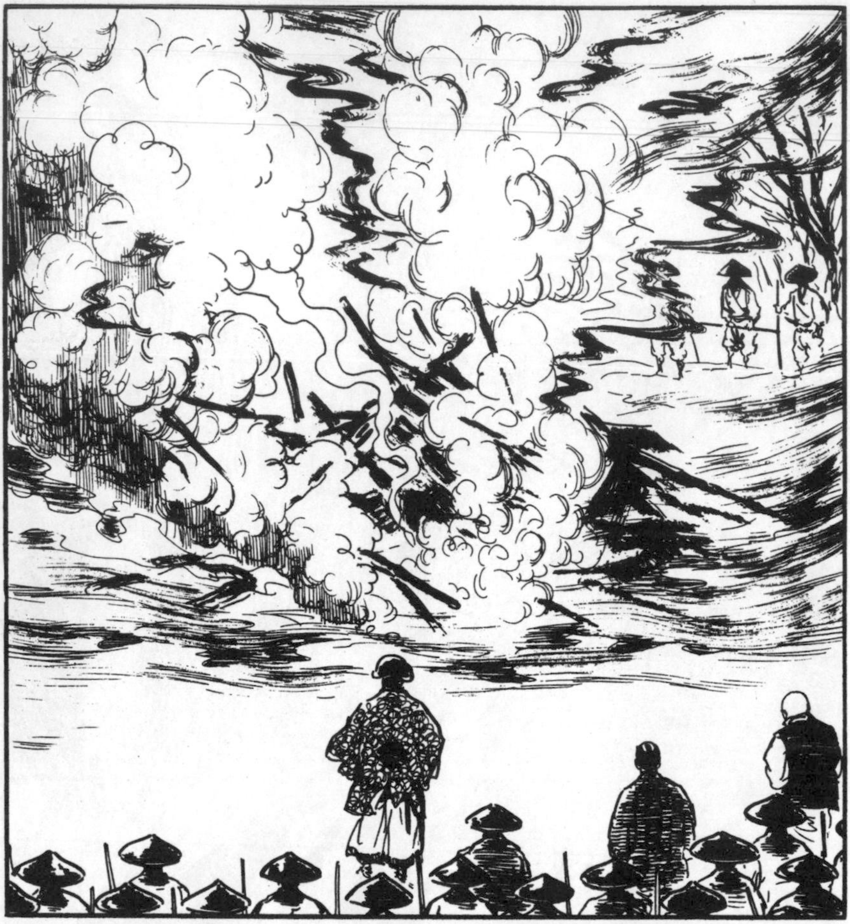

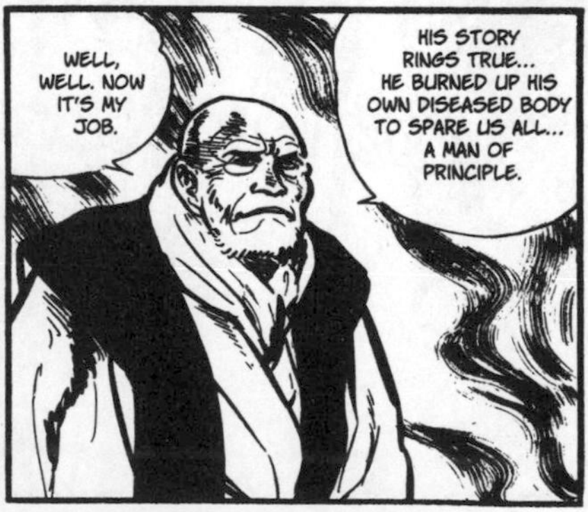
WELL, WELL. NOW IT'S MY JOB.
HIS STORY RINGS TRUE... HE BURNED UP HIS OWN DISEASED BODY TO SPARE US ALL... A MAN OF PRINCIPLE.

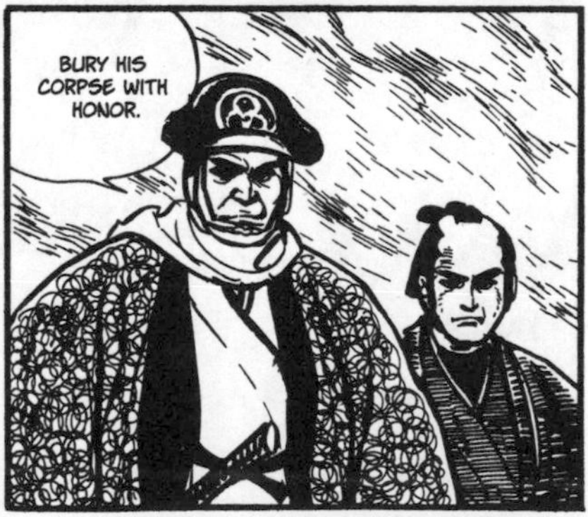
BURY HIS CORPSE WITH HONOR.

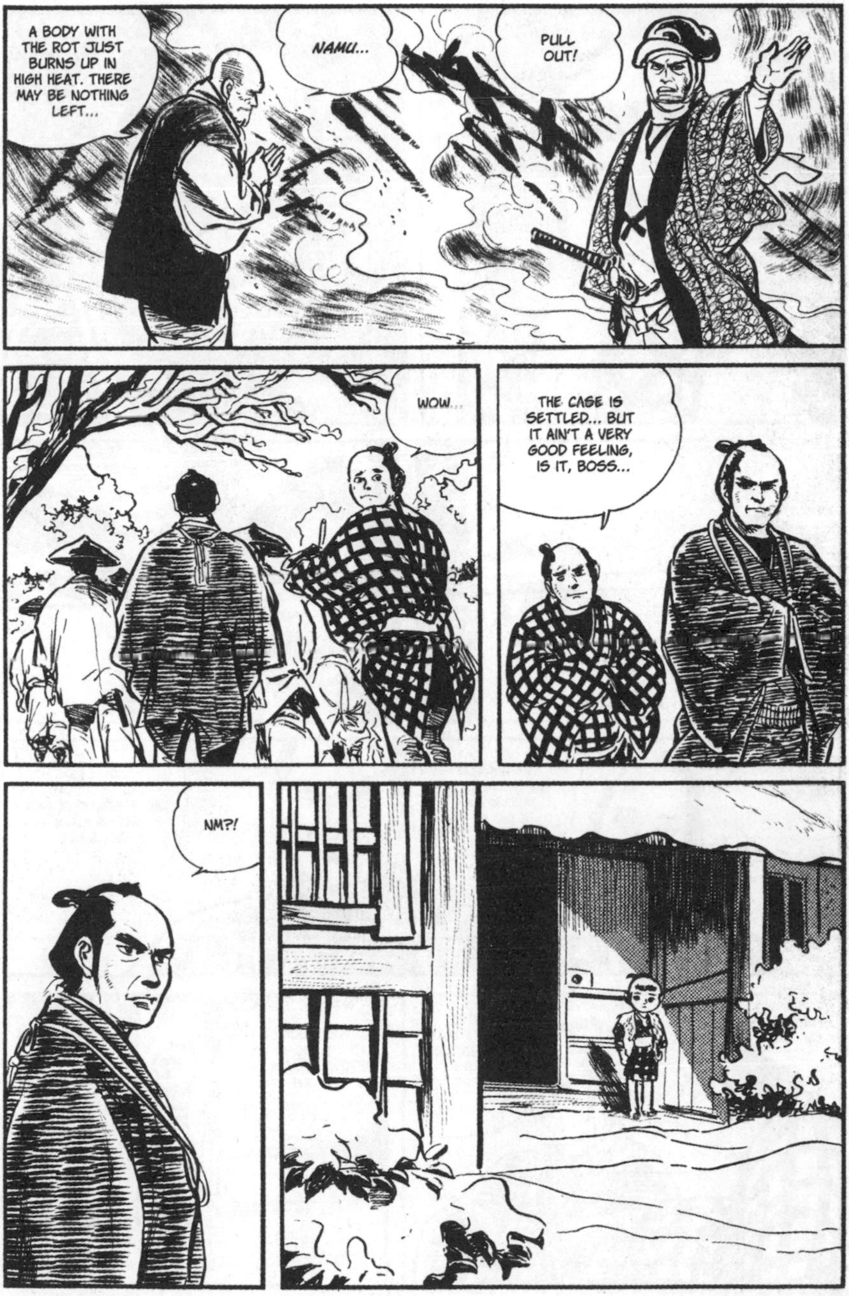
PULL OUT!
NAMU...
A BODY WITH THE ROT JUST BURNS UP IN HIGH HEAT. THERE MAY BE NOTHING LEFT...
THE CASE IS SETTLED... BUT IT AIN'T A VERY GOOD FEELING, IS IT, BOSS...
WOW...
NM?!

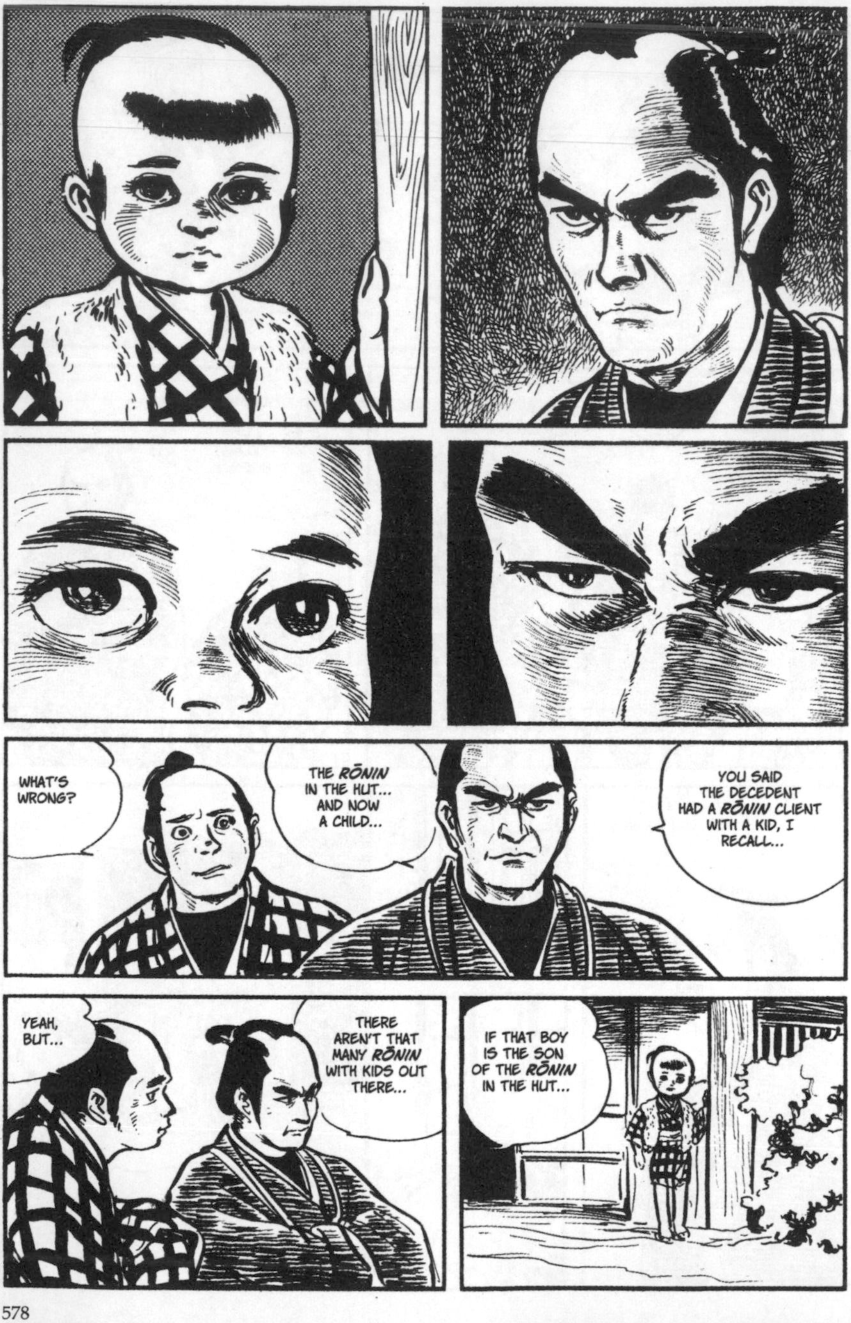
WHAT'S WRONG?
THE *RŌNIN* IN THE HUT... AND NOW A CHILD...
YOU SAID THE DECEDENT HAD A *RŌNIN* CLIENT WITH A KID, I RECALL...
YEAH, BUT...
THERE AREN'T THAT MANY *RŌNIN* WITH KIDS OUT THERE...
IF THAT BOY IS THE SON OF THE *RŌNIN* IN THE HUT...

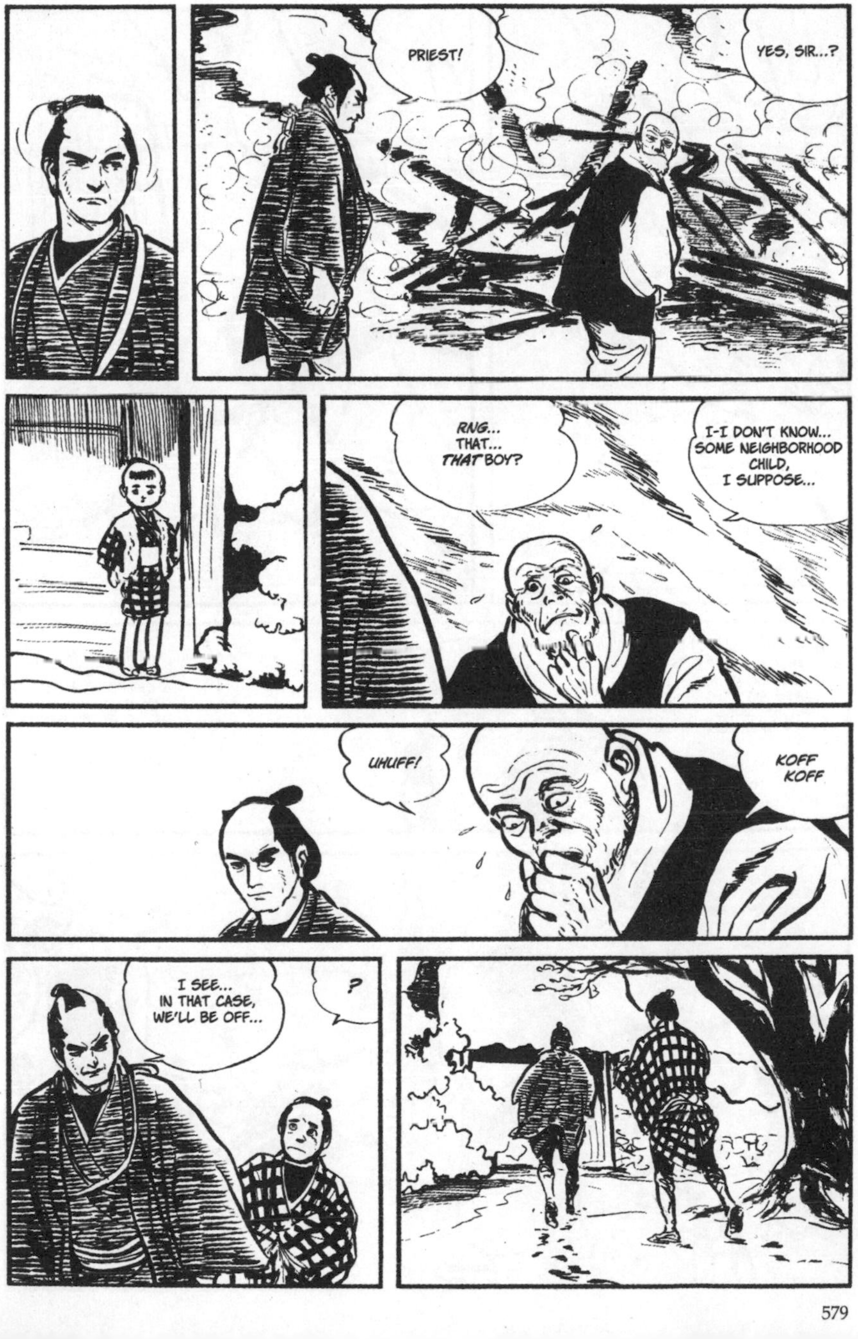
PRIEST!
YES, SIR...?
RNG... THAT... THAT BOY?
I-I DON'T KNOW... SOME NEIGHBORHOOD CHILD, I SUPPOSE...
UHUFF!
KOFF KOFF
I SEE... IN THAT CASE, WE'LL BE OFF...
?

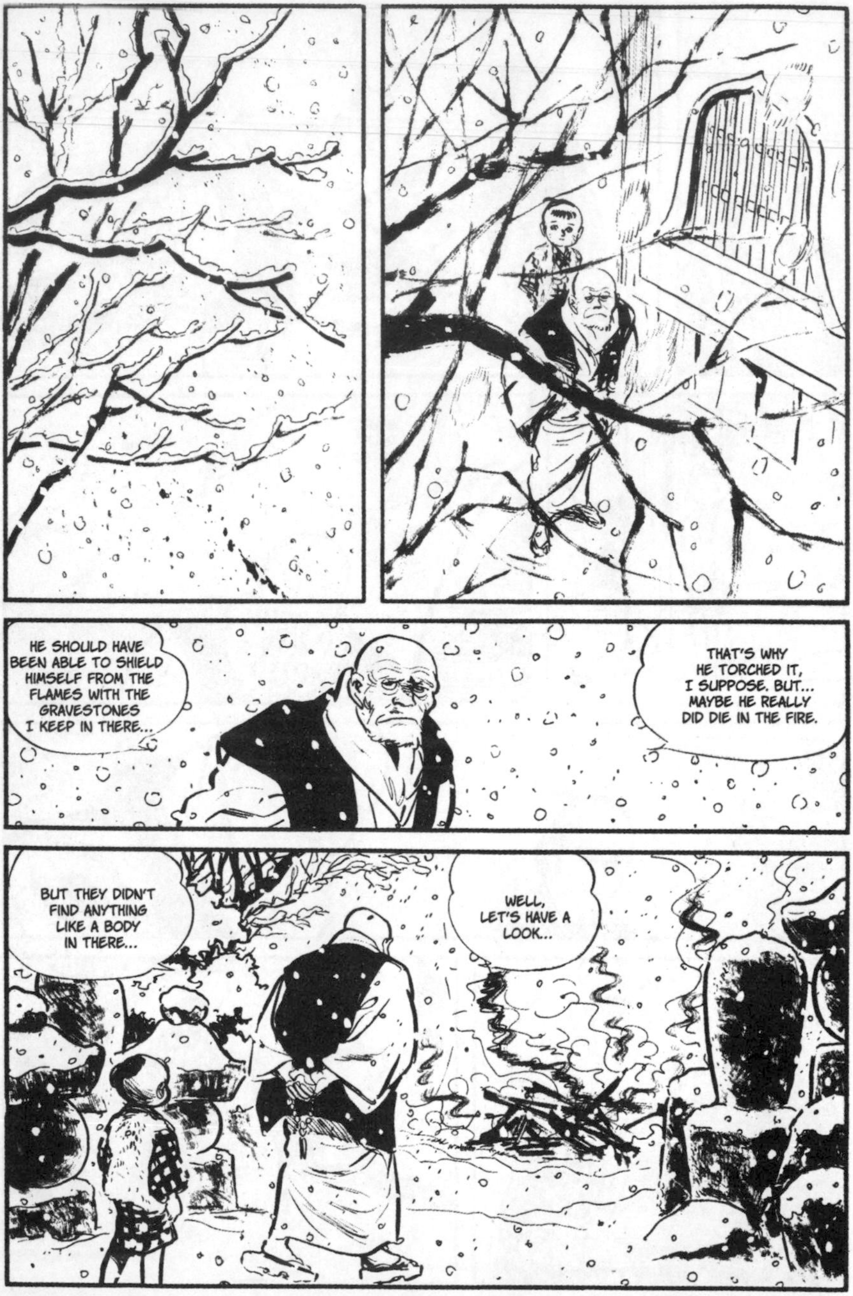
HE SHOULD HAVE BEEN ABLE TO SHIELD HIMSELF FROM THE FLAMES WITH THE GRAVESTONES I KEEP IN THERE...
THAT'S WHY HE TORCHED IT, I SUPPOSE. BUT... MAYBE HE REALLY DID DIE IN THE FIRE.
BUT THEY DIDN'T FIND ANYTHING LIKE A BODY IN THERE...
WELL, LET'S HAVE A LOOK...

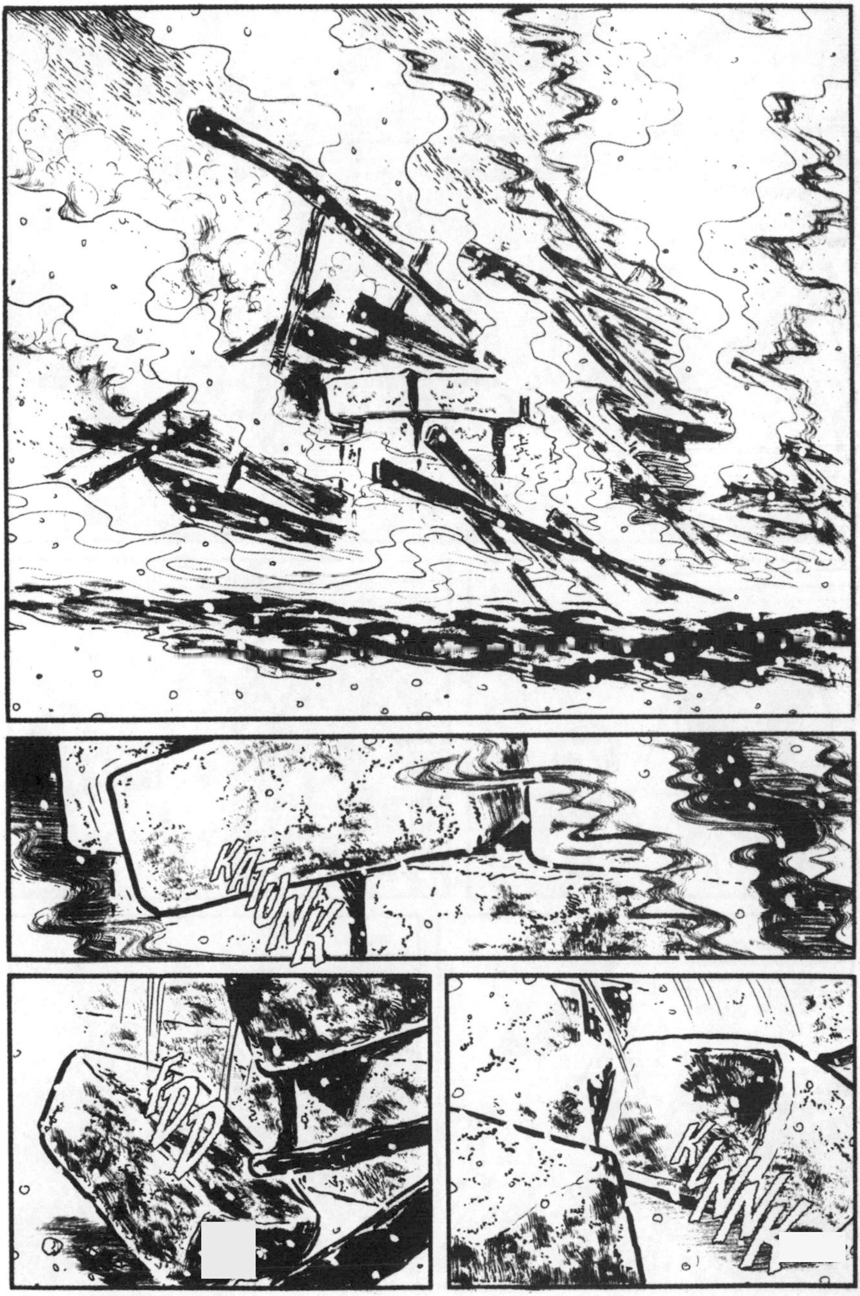
KATUNK
KLNNK
KOD

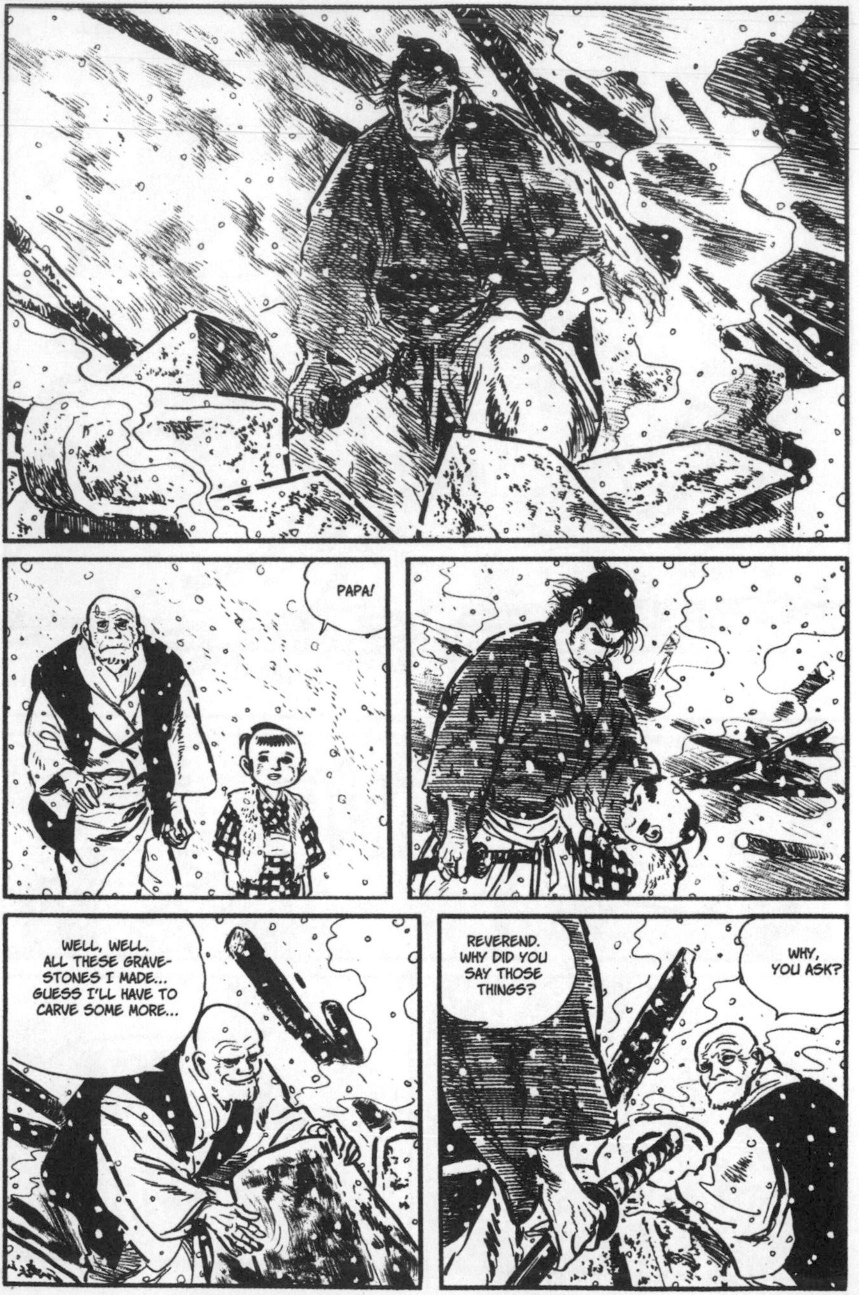
PAPA!
WELL, WELL. ALL THESE GRAVE-STONES I MADE... GUESS I'LL HAVE TO CARVE SOME MORE...
REVEREND. WHY DID YOU SAY THOSE THINGS?
WHY, YOU ASK?

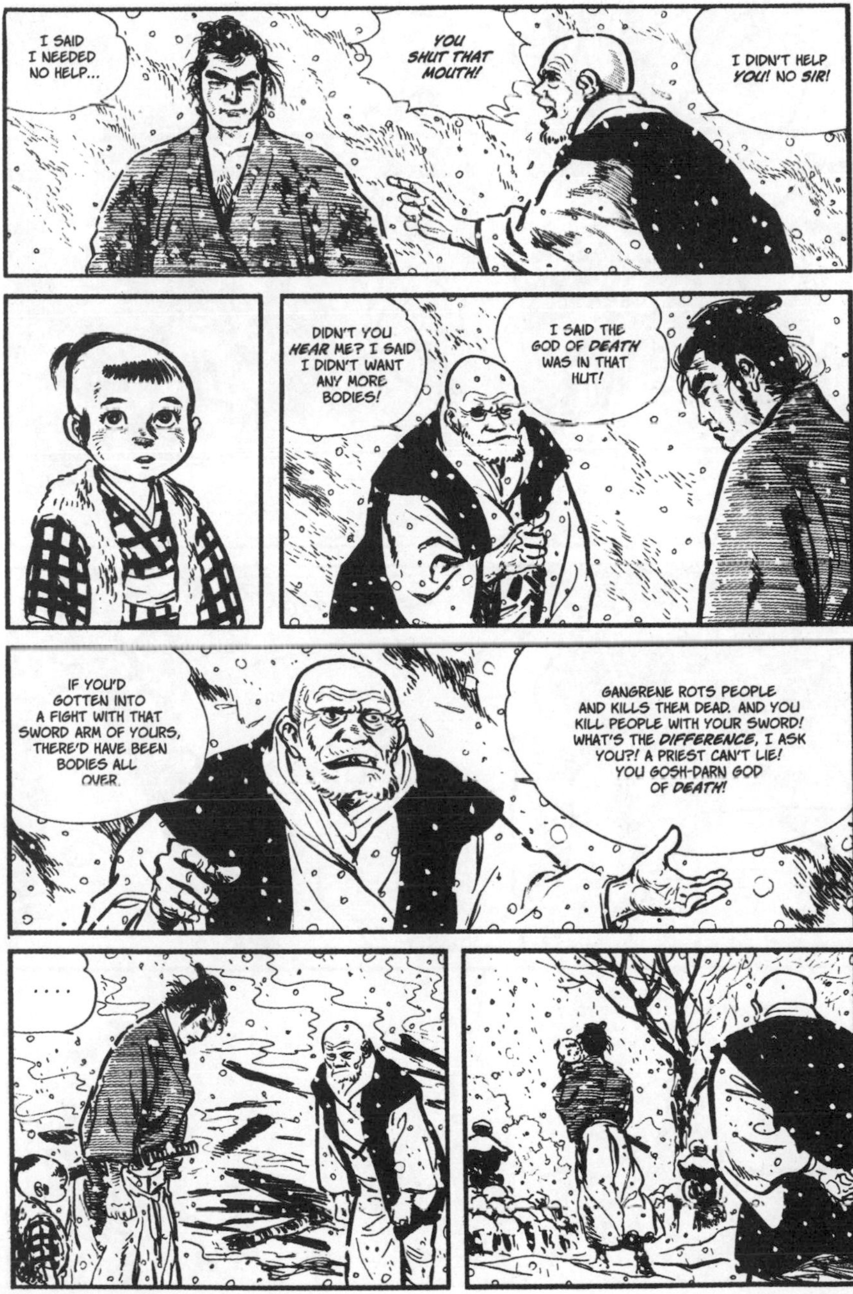
I SAID I NEEDED NO HELP...
YOU SHUT THAT MOUTH!
I DIDN'T HELP YOU! NO SIR!
DIDN'T YOU HEAR ME? I SAID I DIDN'T WANT ANY MORE BODIES!
I SAID THE GOD OF DEATH WAS IN THAT HUT!
IF YOU'D GOTTEN INTO A FIGHT WITH THAT SWORD ARM OF YOURS, THERE'D HAVE BEEN BODIES ALL OVER.
GANGRENE ROTS PEOPLE AND KILLS THEM DEAD. AND YOU KILL PEOPLE WITH YOUR SWORD! WHAT'S THE DIFFERENCE, I ASK YOU?! A PRIEST CAN'T LIE! YOU GOSH-DARN GOD OF DEATH!
....

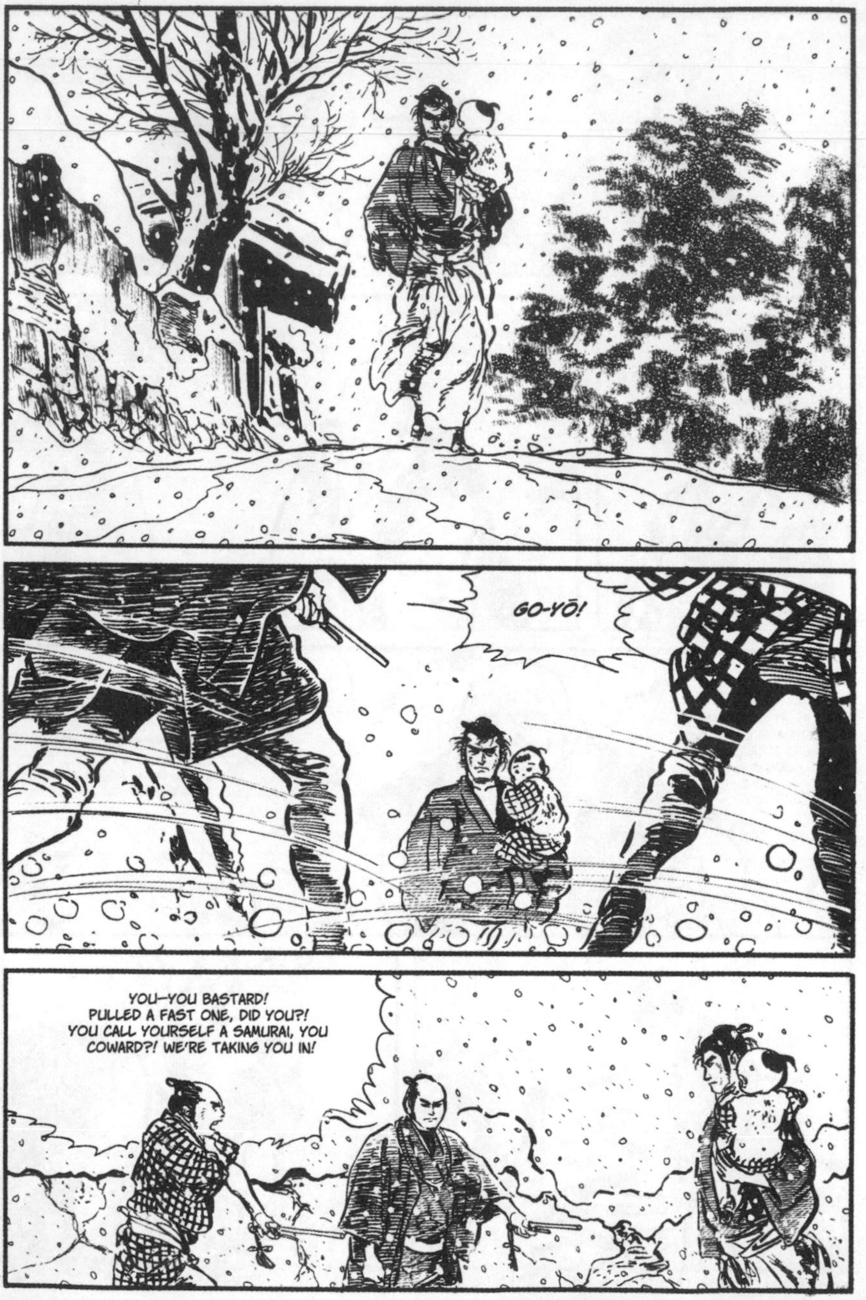
GO-YŌ!
YOU—YOU BASTARD! PULLED A FAST ONE, DID YOU?! YOU CALL YOURSELF A SAMURAI, YOU COWARD?! WE'RE TAKING YOU IN!

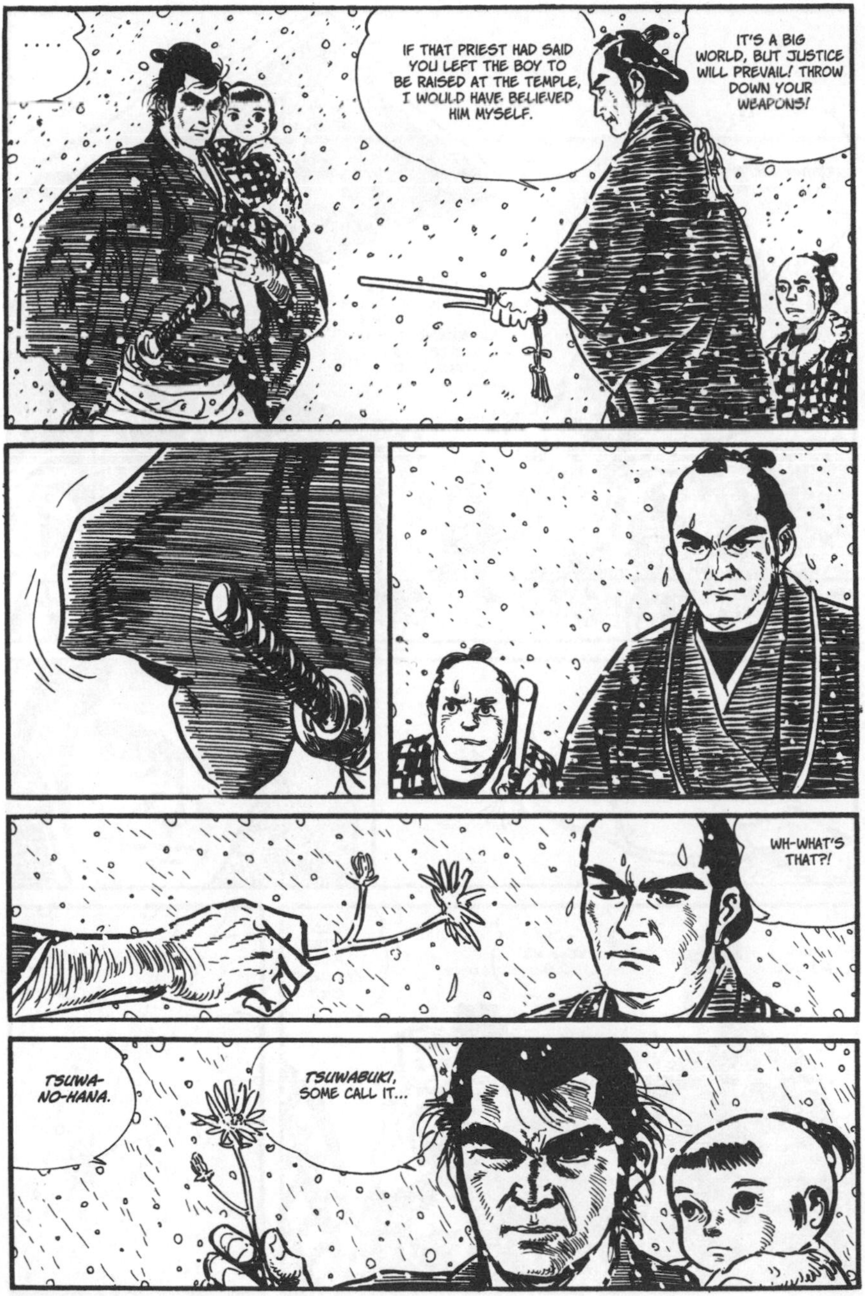
....
IF THAT PRIEST HAD SAID YOU LEFT THE BOY TO BE RAISED AT THE TEMPLE, I WOULD HAVE BELIEVED HIM MYSELF.
IT'S A BIG WORLD, BUT JUSTICE WILL PREVAIL! THROW DOWN YOUR WEAPONS!
WH-WHAT'S THAT?!
TSUWA-NO-HANA.
TSUWABUKI, SOME CALL IT...

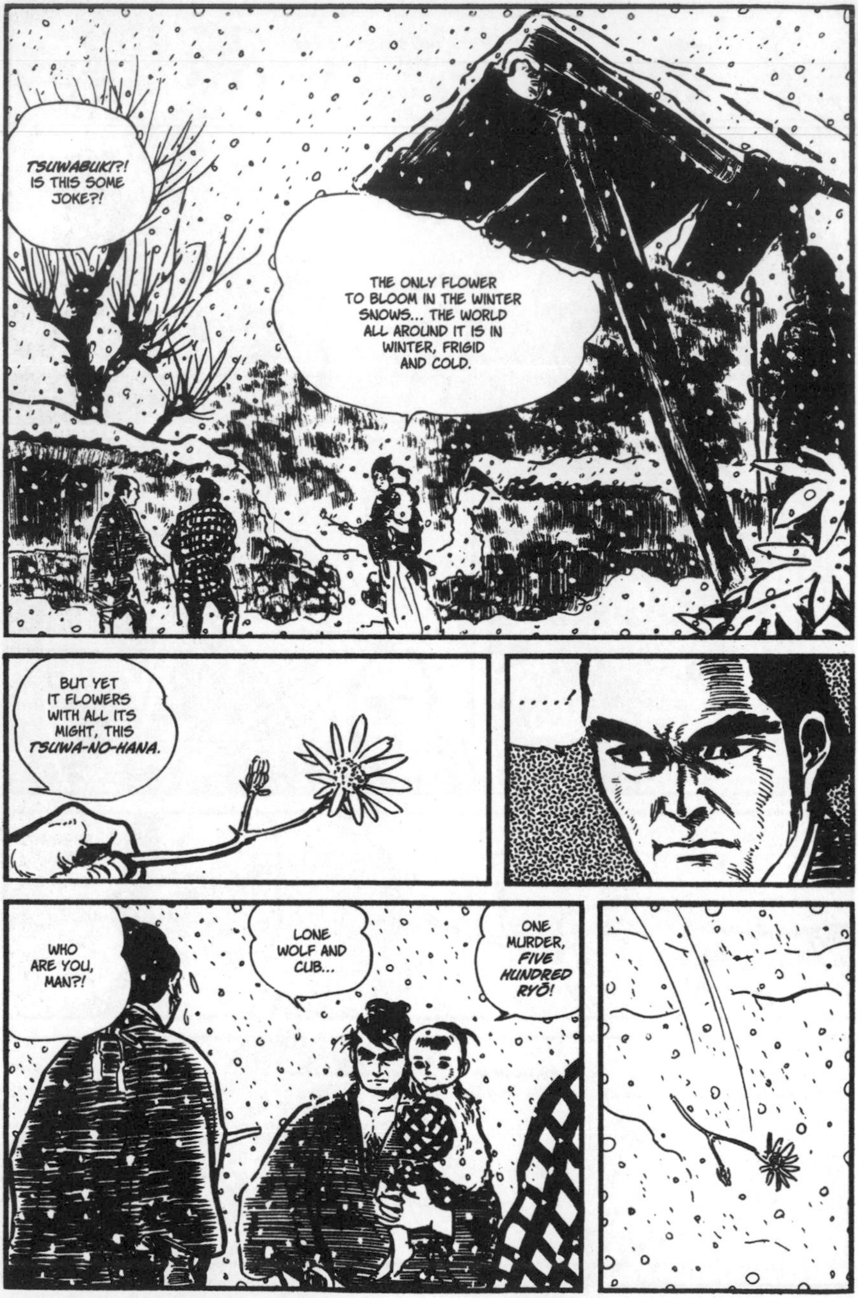
TSUWABUKI?! IS THIS SOME JOKE?!
THE ONLY FLOWER TO BLOOM IN THE WINTER SNOWS... THE WORLD ALL AROUND IT IS IN WINTER, FRIGID AND COLD.
BUT YET IT FLOWERS WITH ALL ITS MIGHT, THIS TSUWA-NO-HANA.
....!
WHO ARE YOU, MAN?!
LONE WOLF AND CUB...
ONE MURDER, FIVE HUNDRED RYŌ!

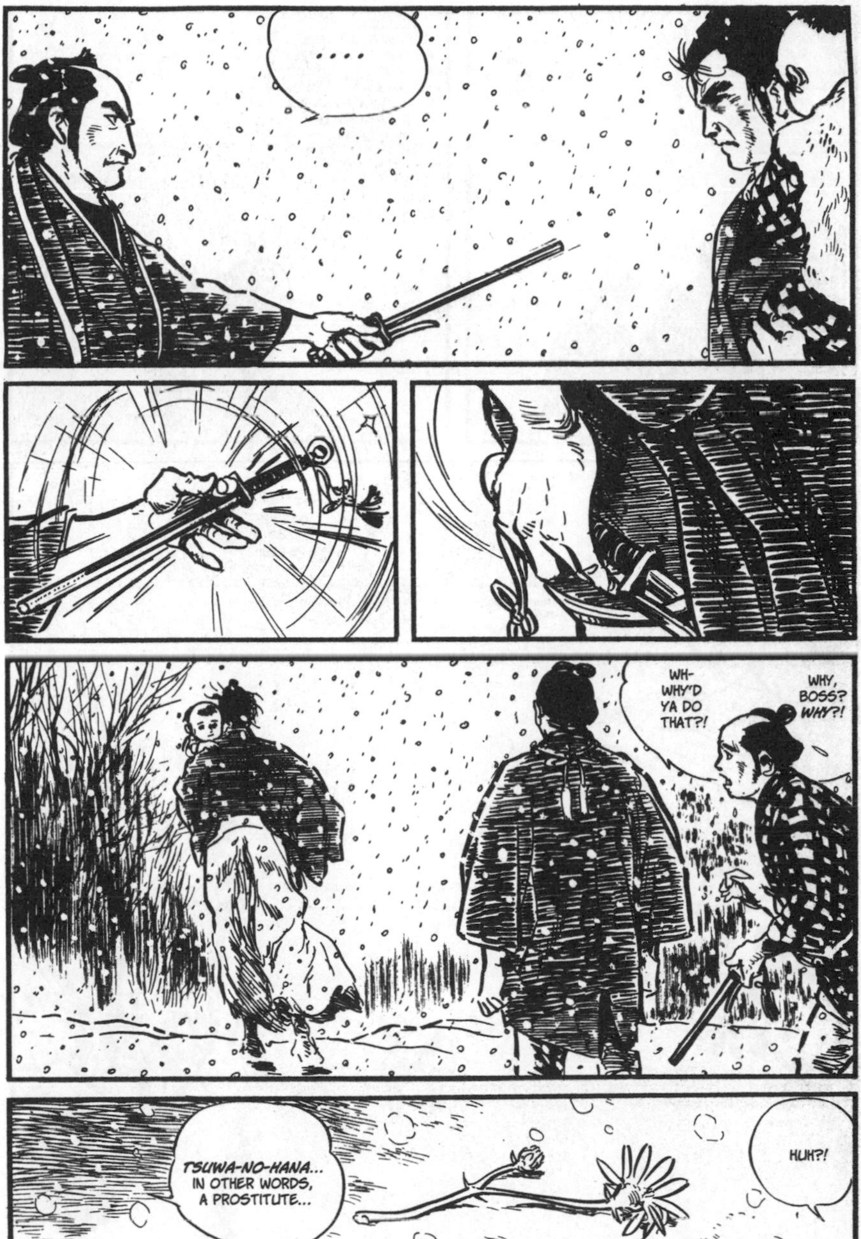
....
WHY, BOSS? WHY?!
WH- WHY'D YA DO THAT?!
HUH?!
TSUWA-NO-HANA... IN OTHER WORDS, A PROSTITUTE...

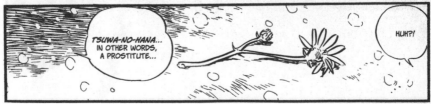

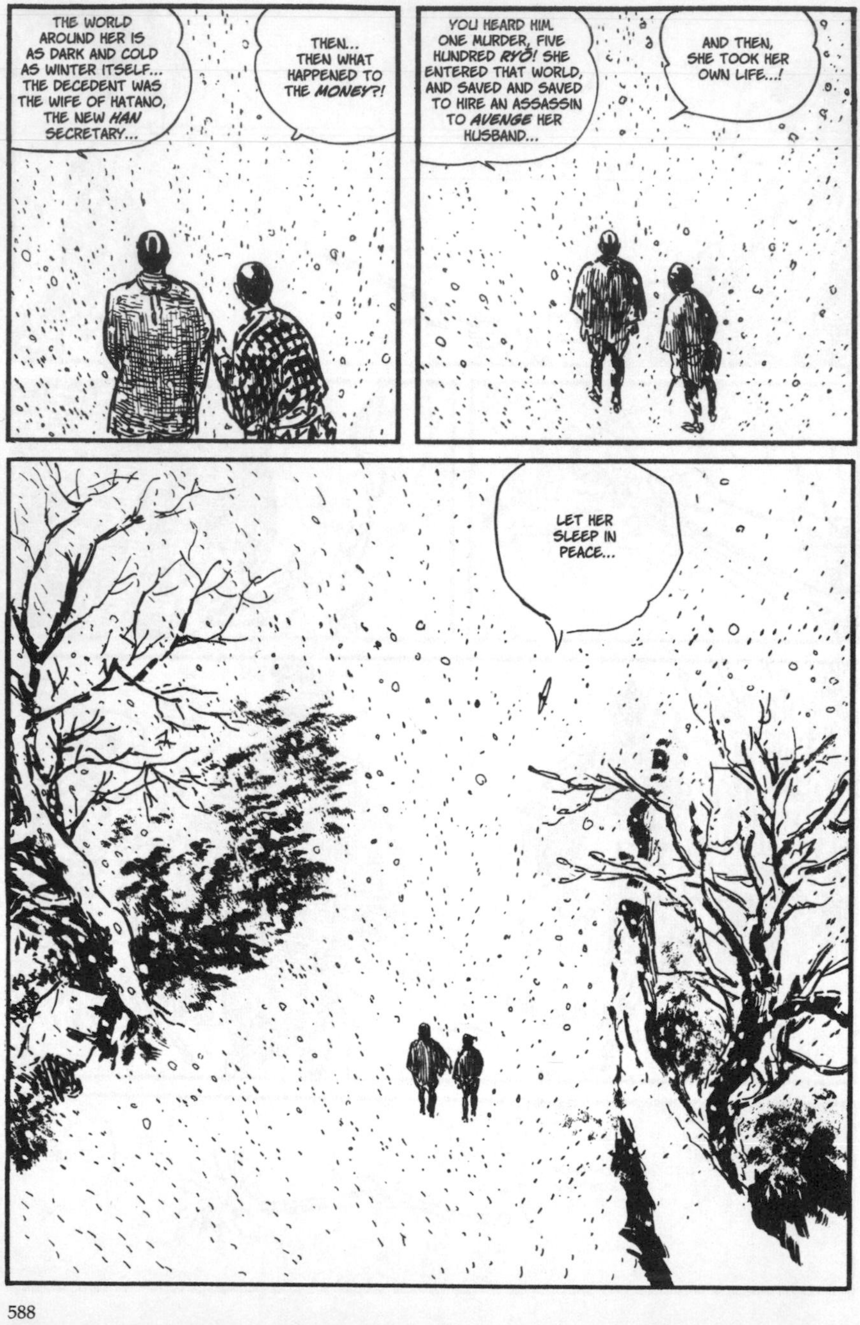
THE WORLD AROUND HER IS AS DARK AND COLD AS WINTER ITSELF... THE DECEDENT WAS THE WIFE OF HATANO, THE NEW *HAN* SECRETARY...
THEN... THEN WHAT HAPPENED TO THE *MONEY*?!
YOU HEARD HIM. ONE MURDER, FIVE HUNDRED *RYŌ*! SHE ENTERED THAT WORLD, AND SAVED AND SAVED TO HIRE AN ASSASSIN TO *AVENGE* HER HUSBAND...
AND THEN, SHE TOOK HER OWN LIFE...!
LET HER SLEEP IN PEACE...

THE FLUTE OF THE
FALLEN TIGER

15

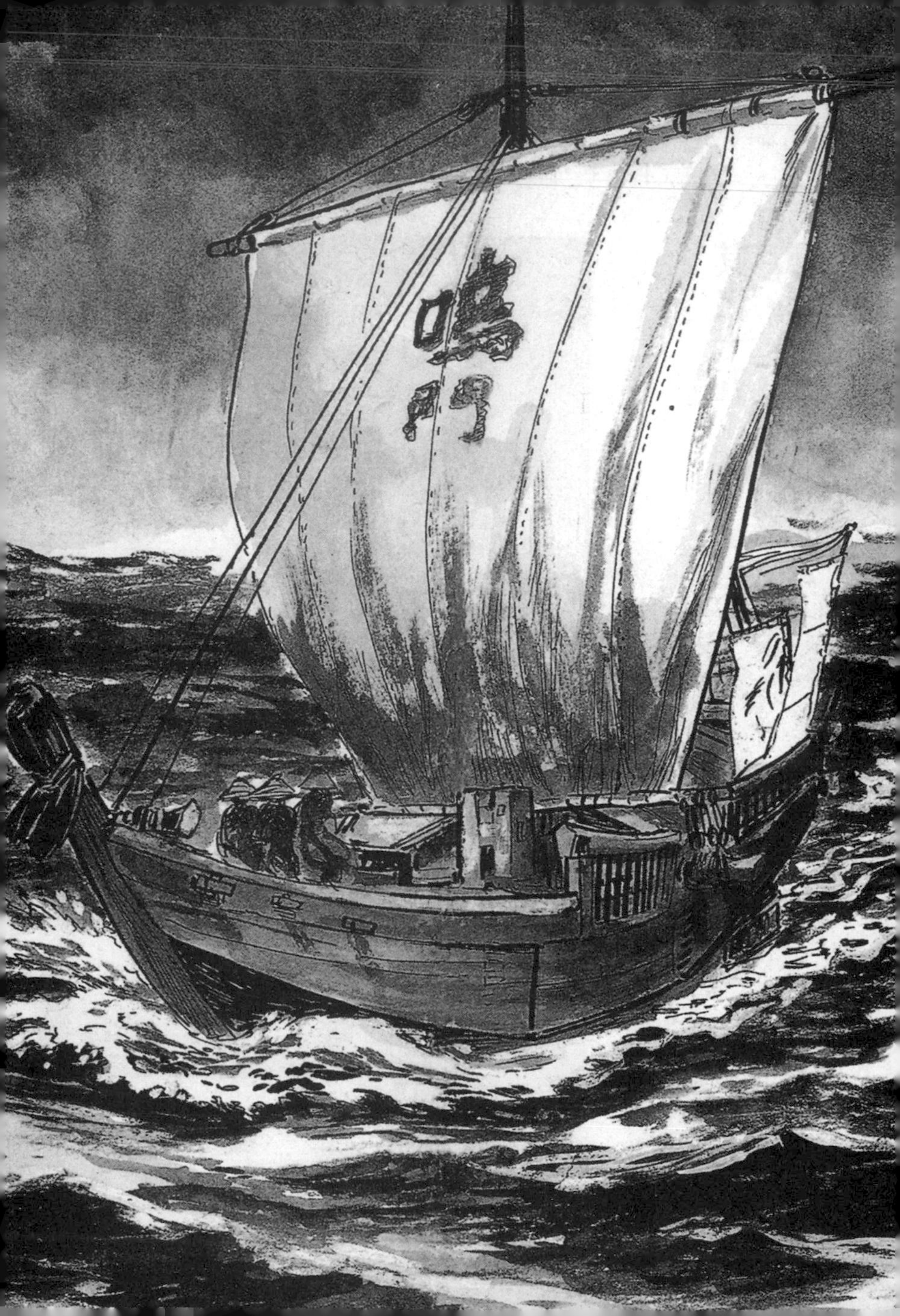
鳴門

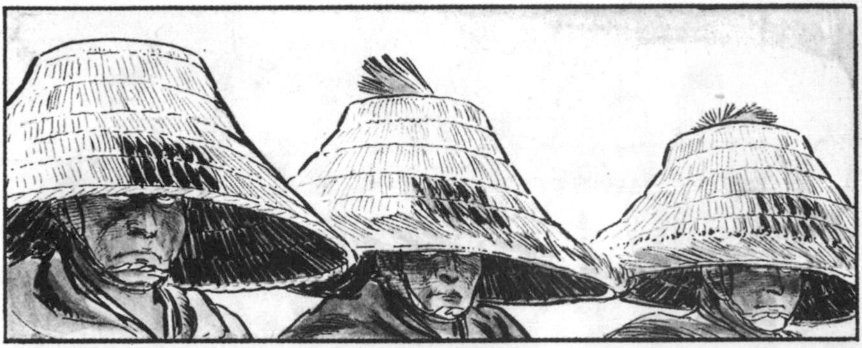
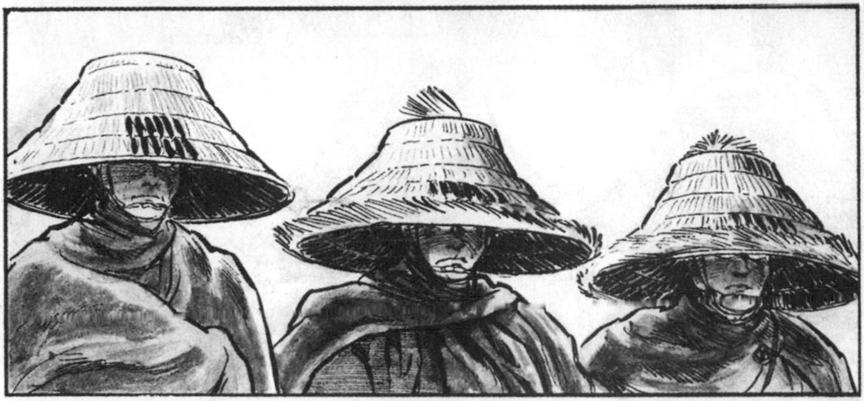
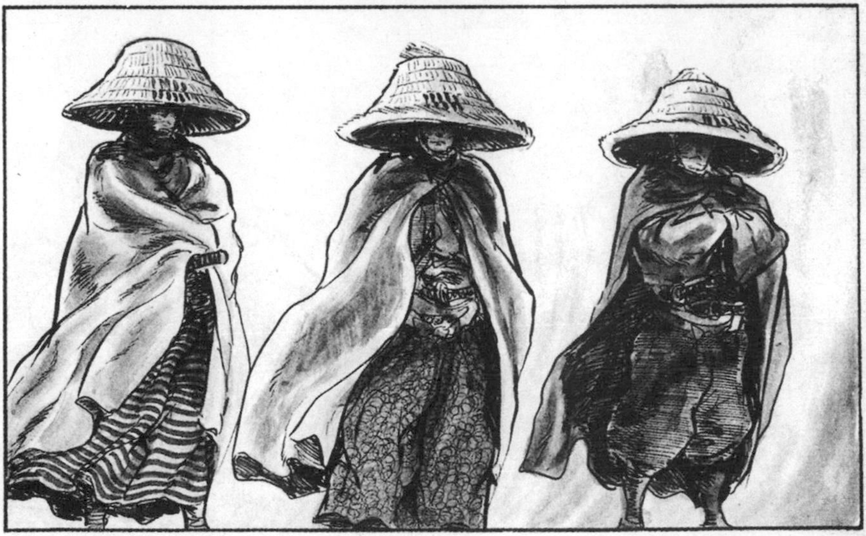

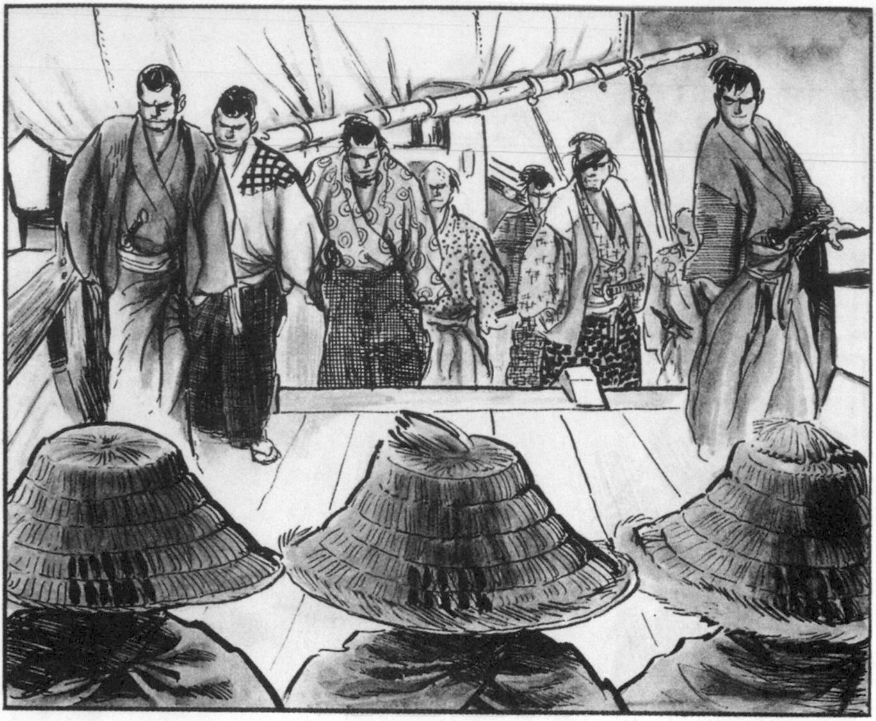

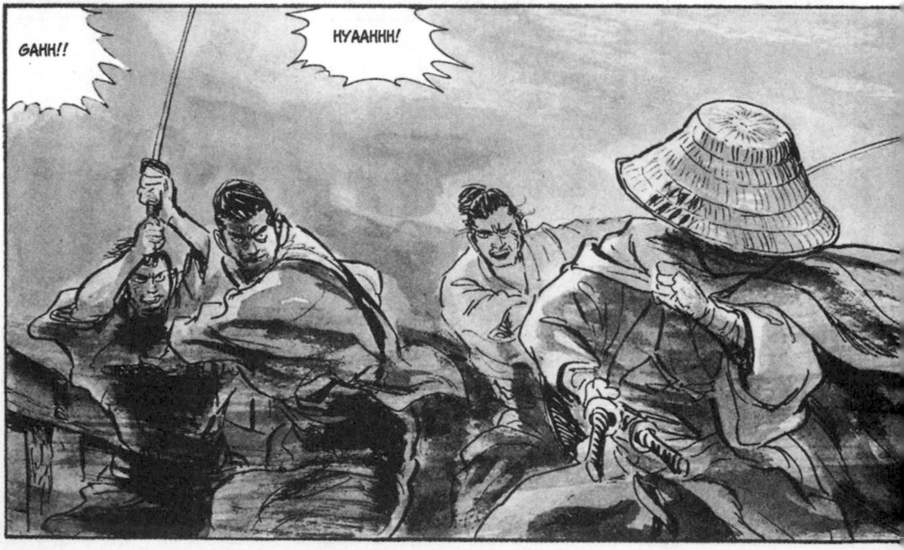
HYAAHHH!
GAHH!!

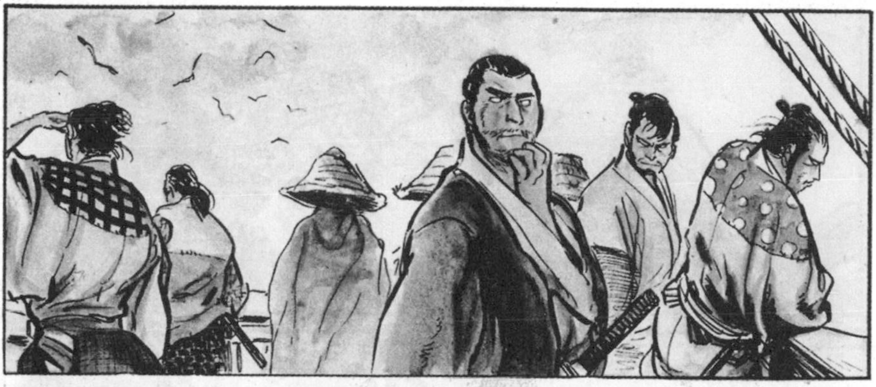

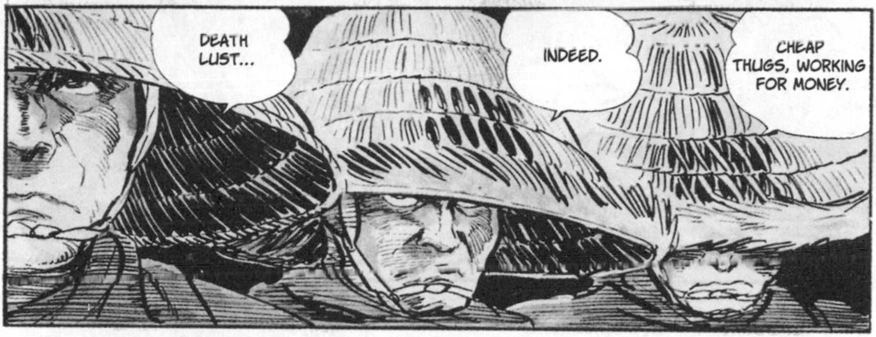
CHEAP THUGS, WORKING FOR MONEY.
INDEED.
DEATH LUST...

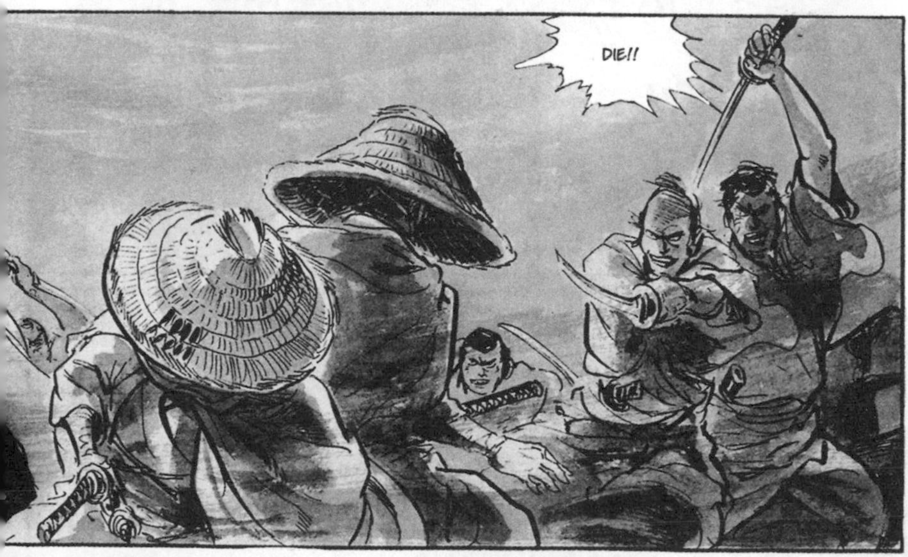
DIE!!

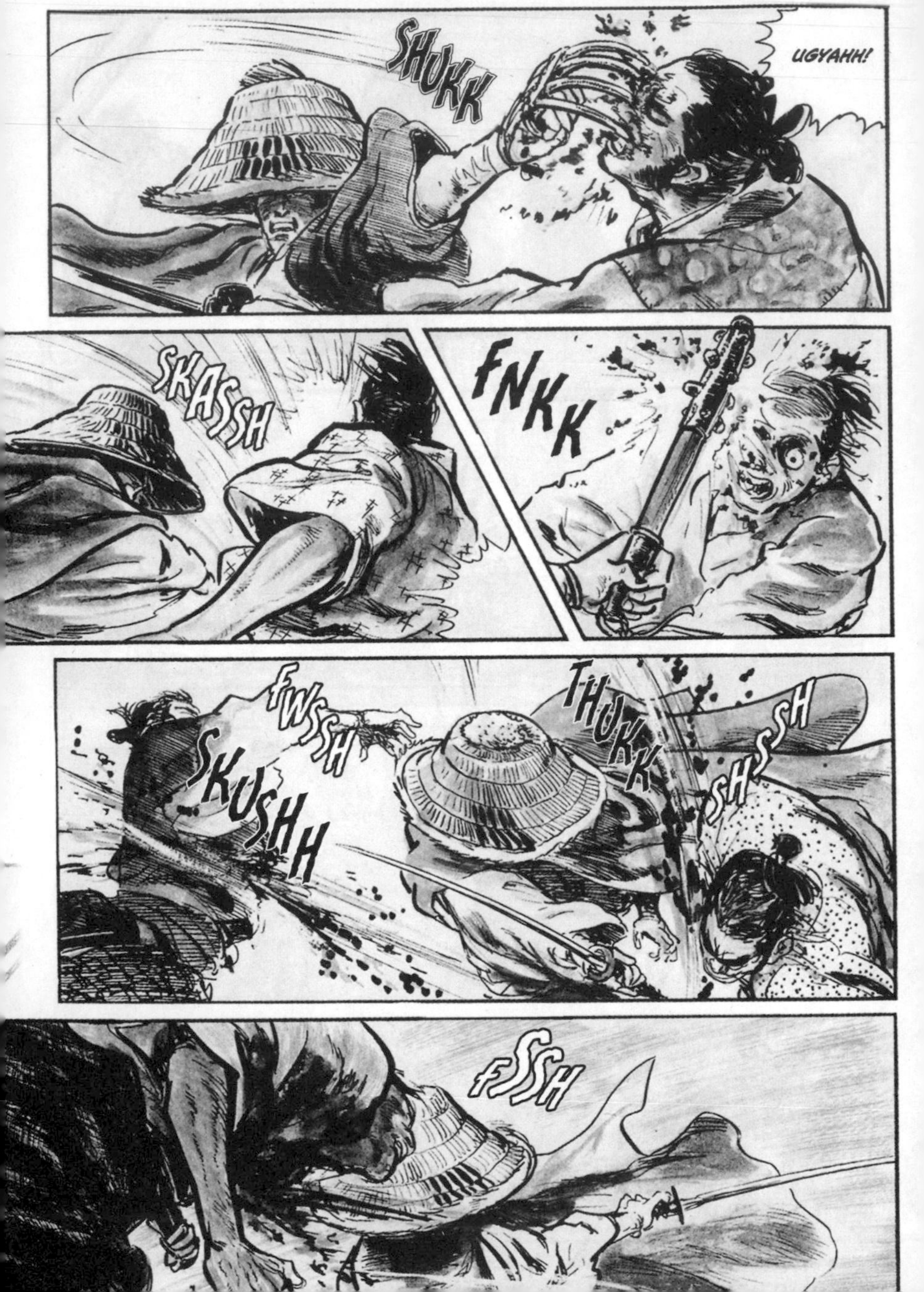
UGYAHH!
SHUKK
FNKK
SKASSH
THUKK
SHSSH
FWSSH
SKUSHH
FSSH

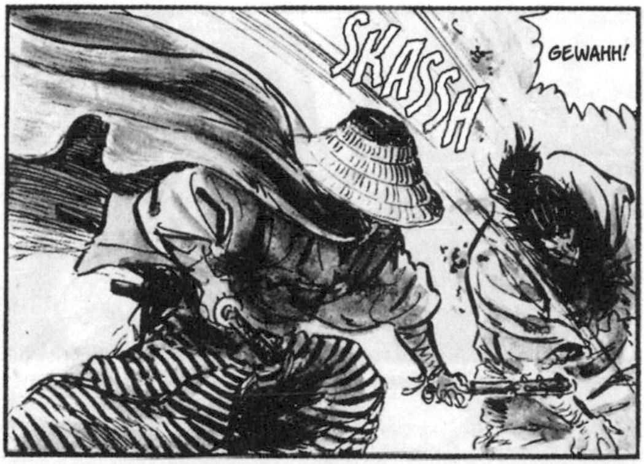
SKASSH
GEWAHH!
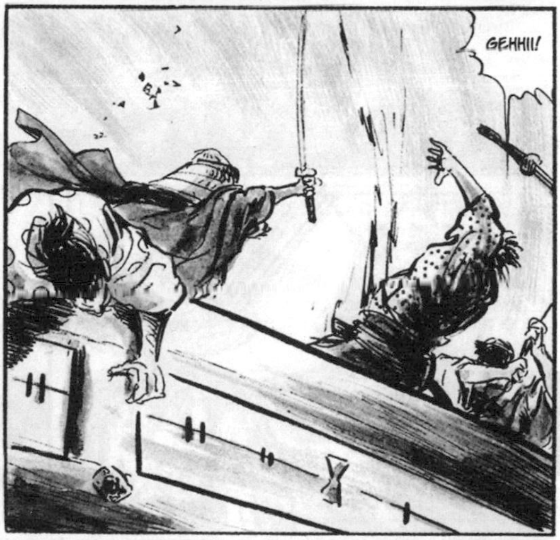
GEHHII!
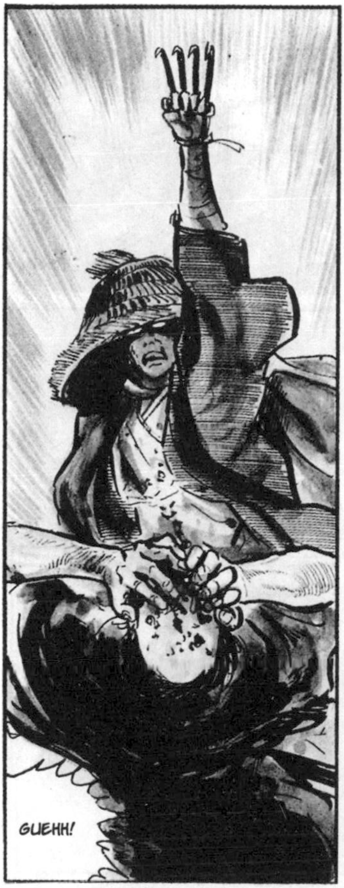
GUEHH!
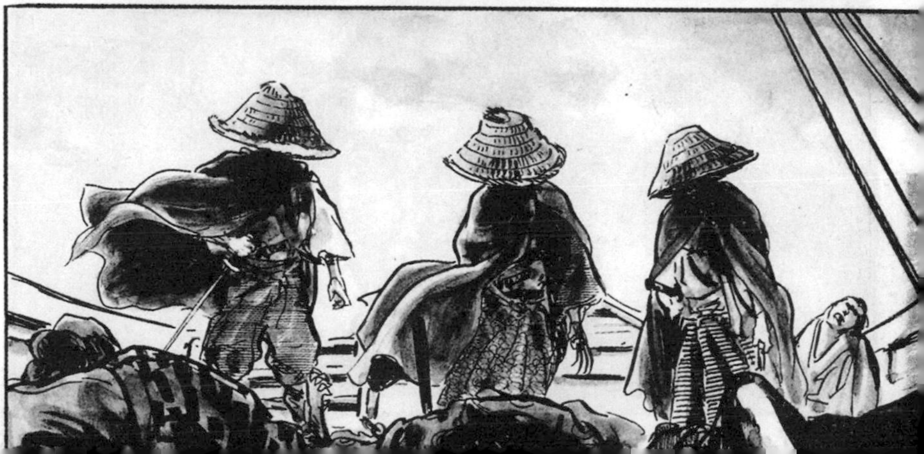

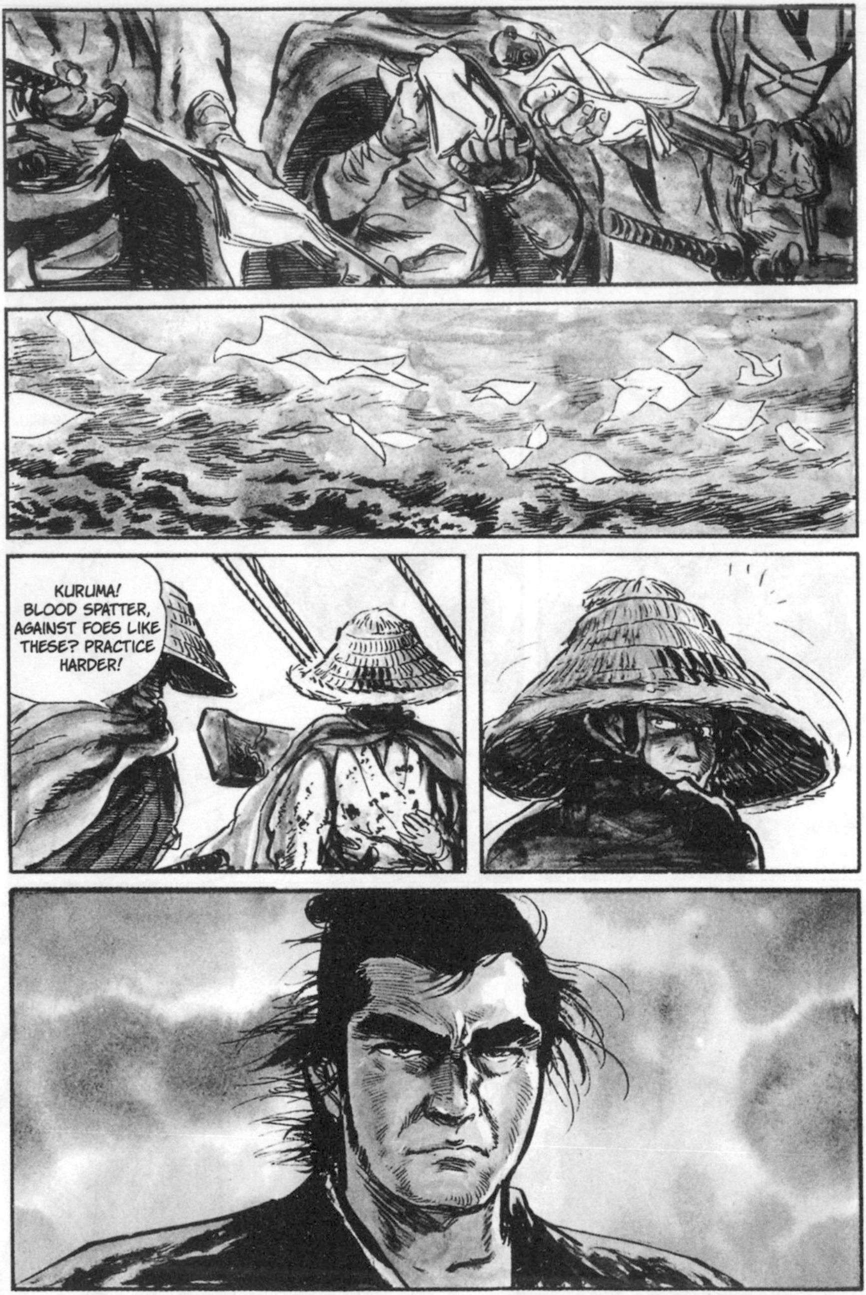
KURUMA! BLOOD SPATTER, AGAINST FOES LIKE THESE? PRACTICE HARDER!

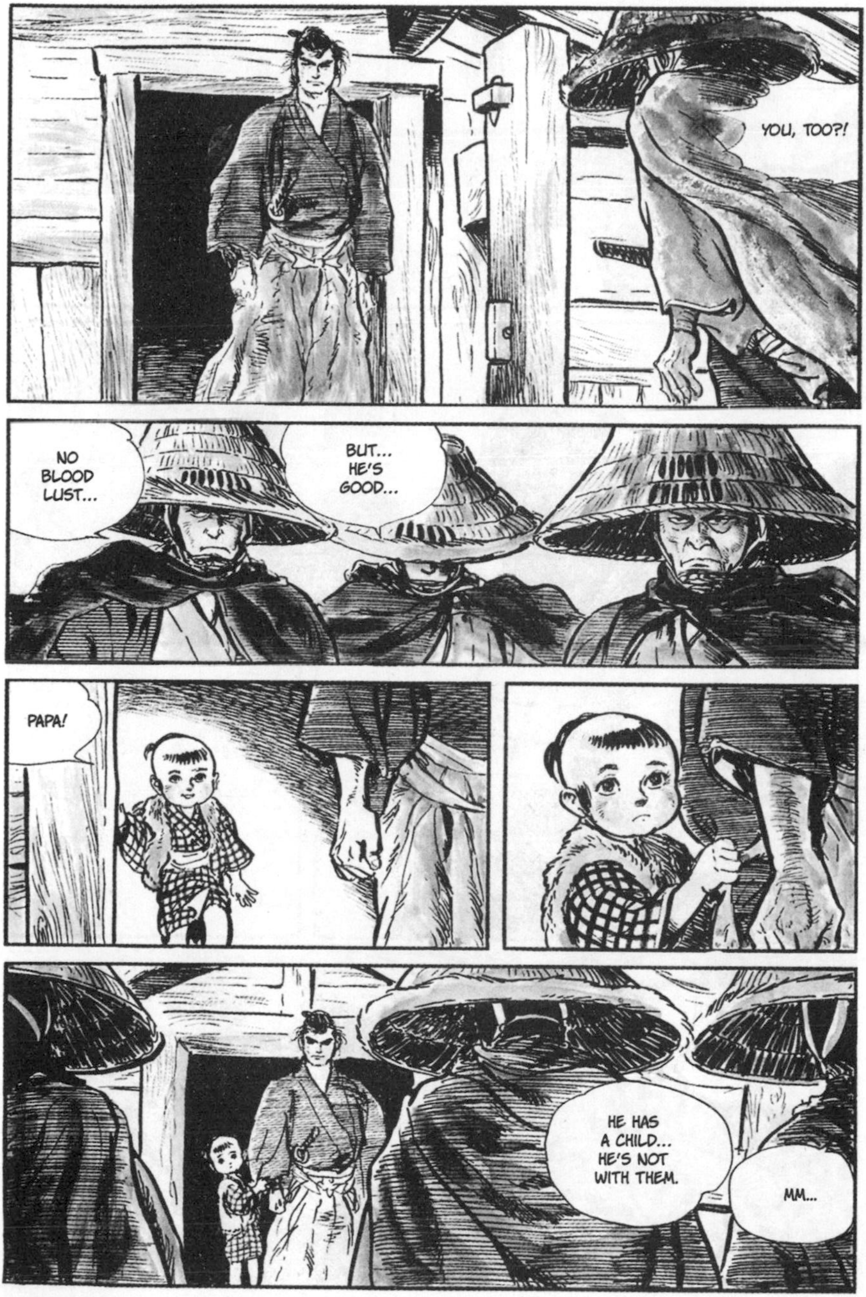
YOU, TOO?!
NO BLOOD LUST...
BUT... HE'S GOOD...
PAPA!
HE HAS A CHILD... HE'S NOT WITH THEM.
MM...

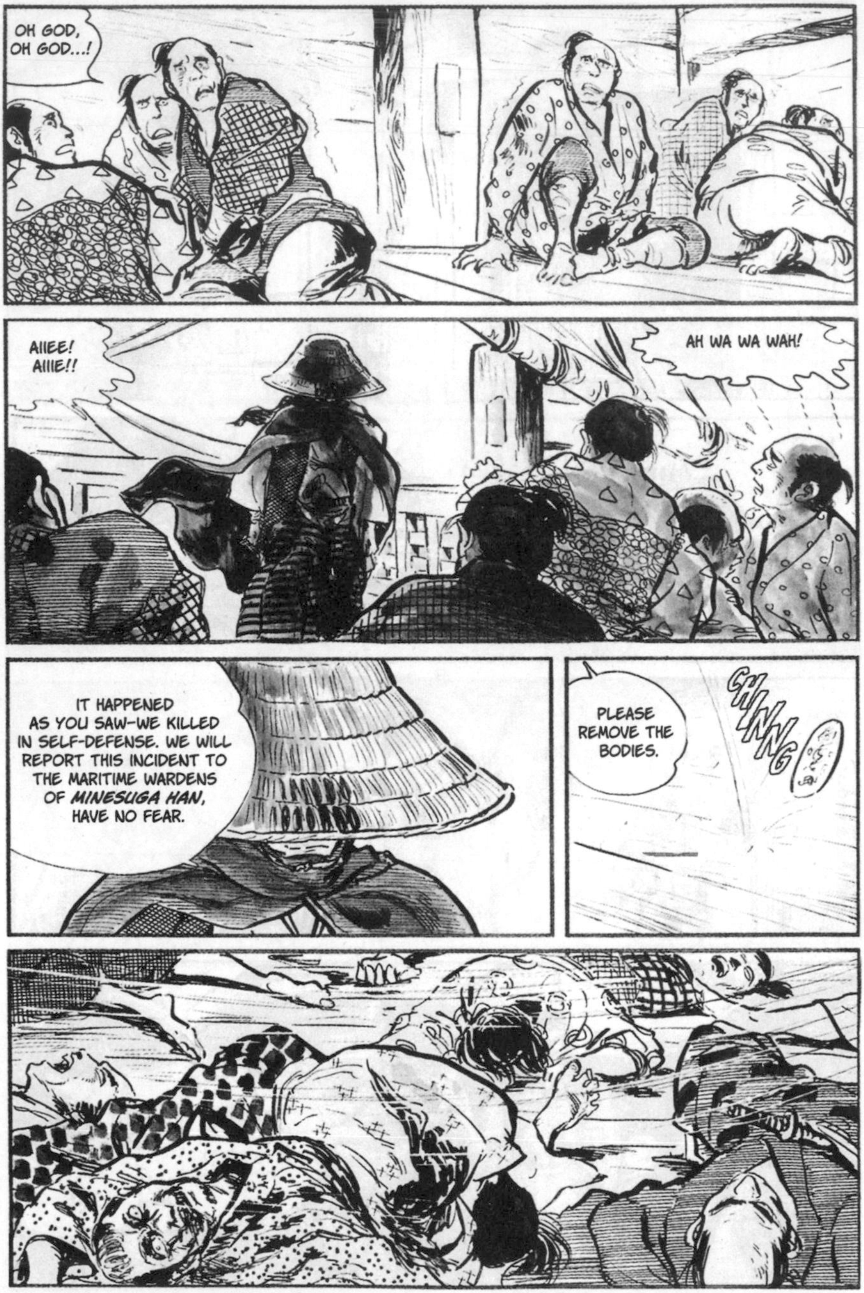
OH GOD, OH GOD...!
AIIEE! AIIIE!!
AH WA WA WAH!
IT HAPPENED AS YOU SAW–WE KILLED IN SELF-DEFENSE. WE WILL REPORT THIS INCIDENT TO THE MARITIME WARDENS OF *MINESUGA HAN*, HAVE NO FEAR.
PLEASE REMOVE THE BODIES.
CHINNG

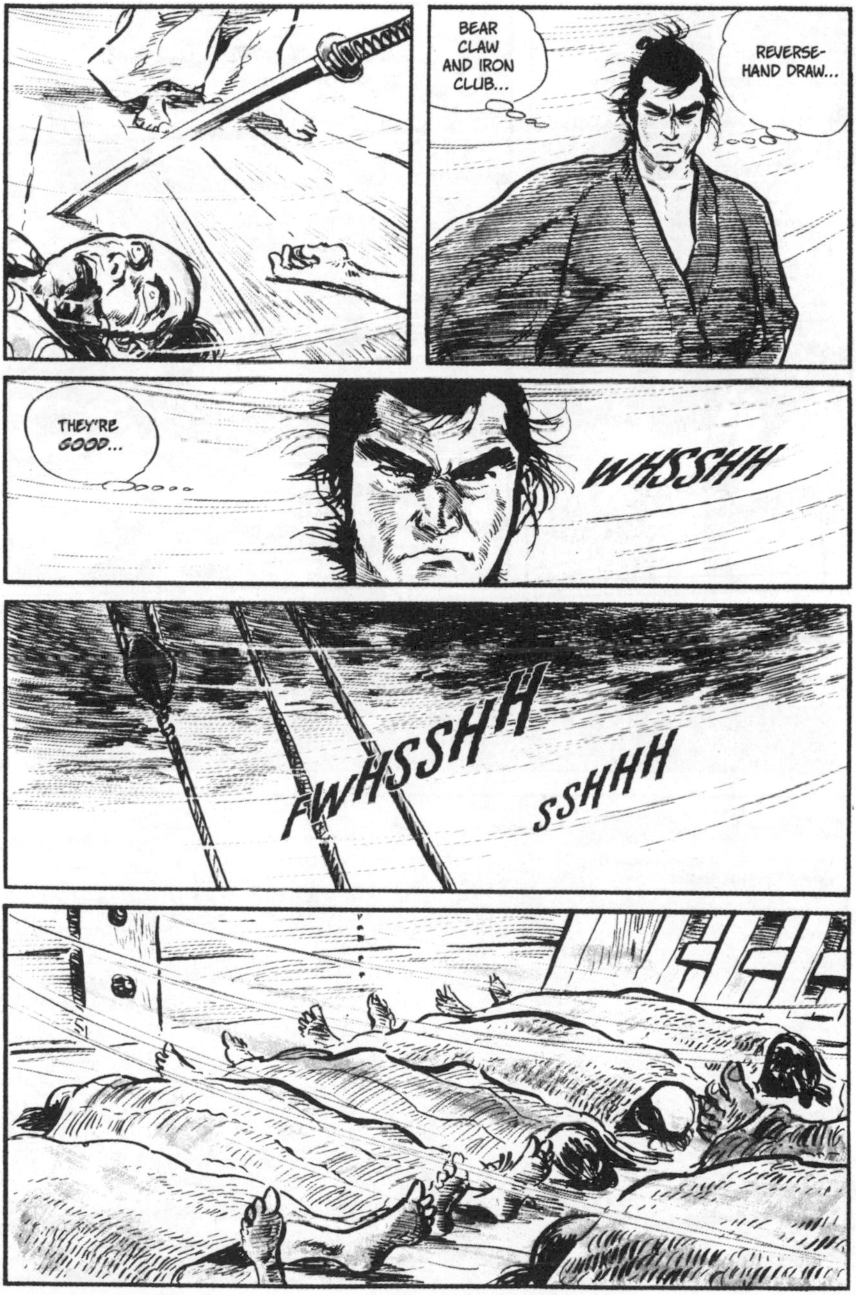
REVERSE-HAND DRAW...
BEAR CLAW AND IRON CLUB...
THEY'RE GOOD...
WHSSHH
FWHSSHH
SSHHH

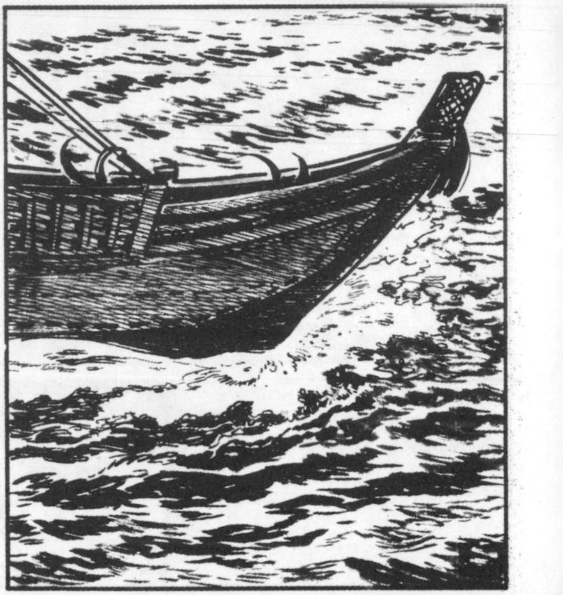
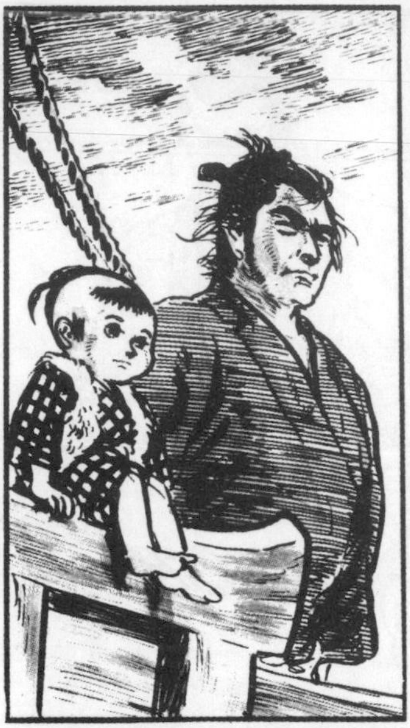
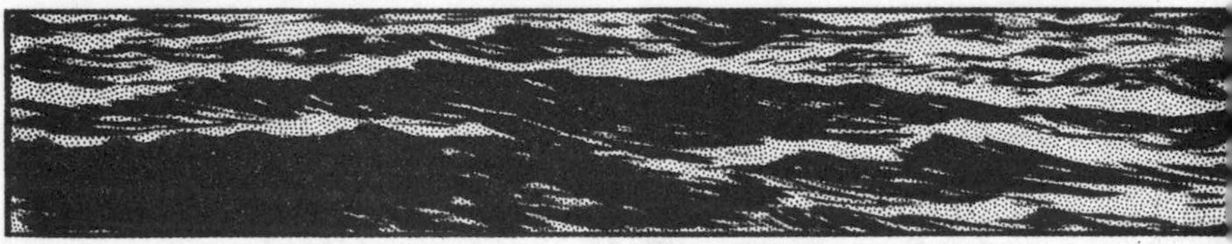
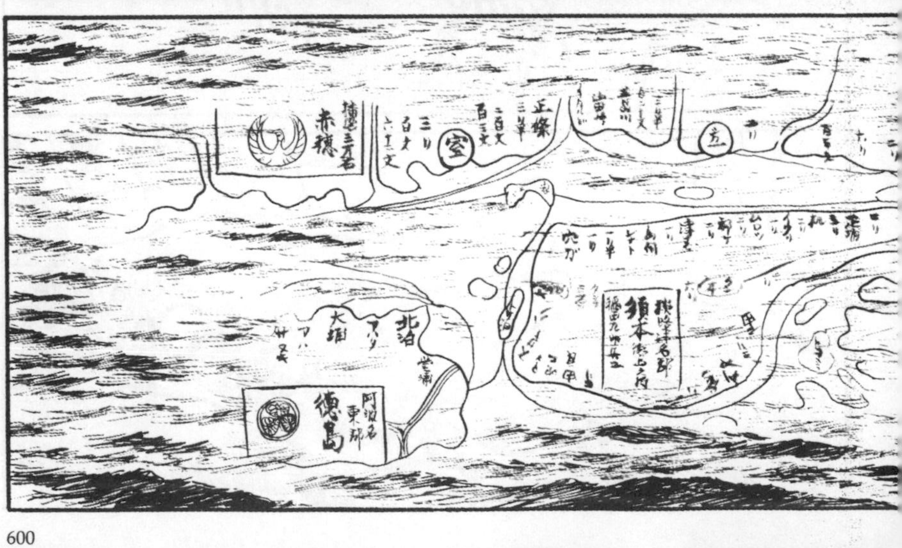
赤穂
室
正條
北泊
大堀
須本
阿波
徳島

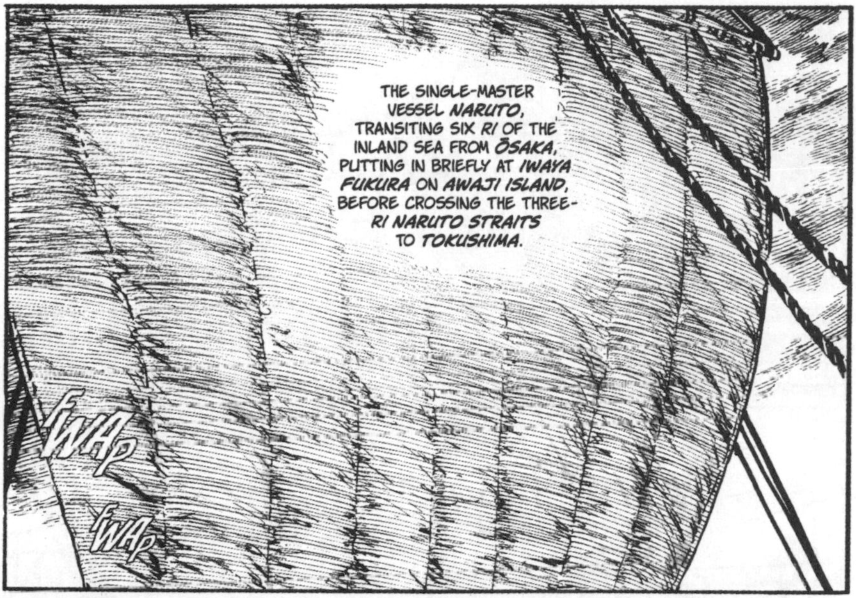
THE SINGLE-MASTER VESSEL NARUTO, TRANSITING SIX RI OF THE INLAND SEA FROM ŌSAKA, PUTTING IN BRIEFLY AT IWAYA FUKURA ON AWAJI ISLAND, BEFORE CROSSING THE THREE-RI NARUTO STRAITS TO TOKUSHIMA.
FWAP
FWAP
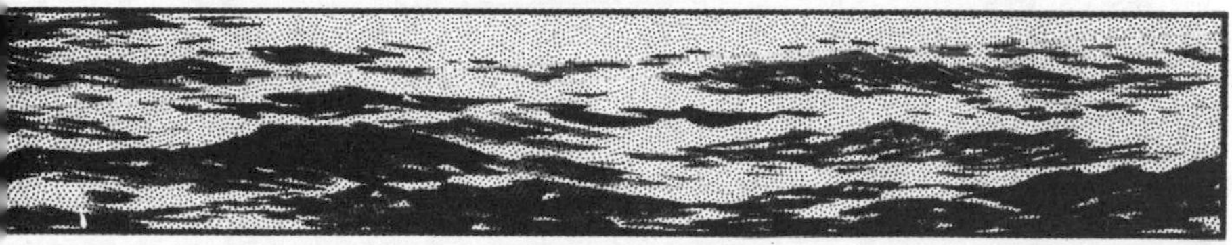
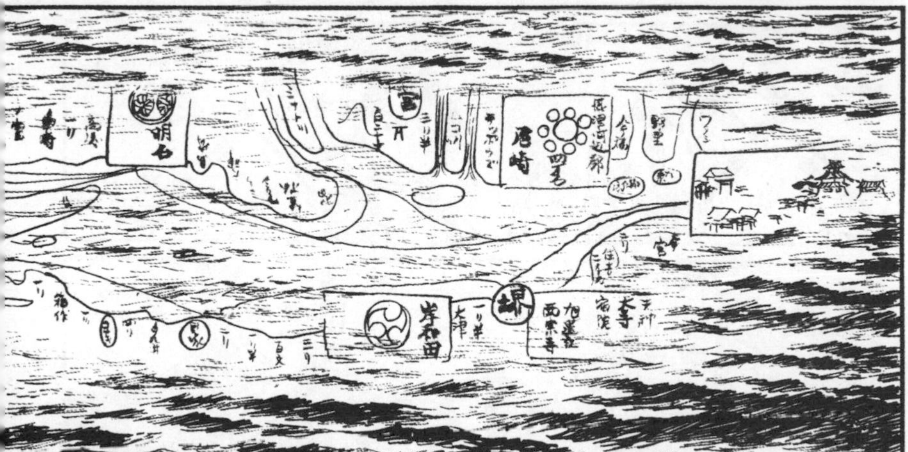
明石
岸和田

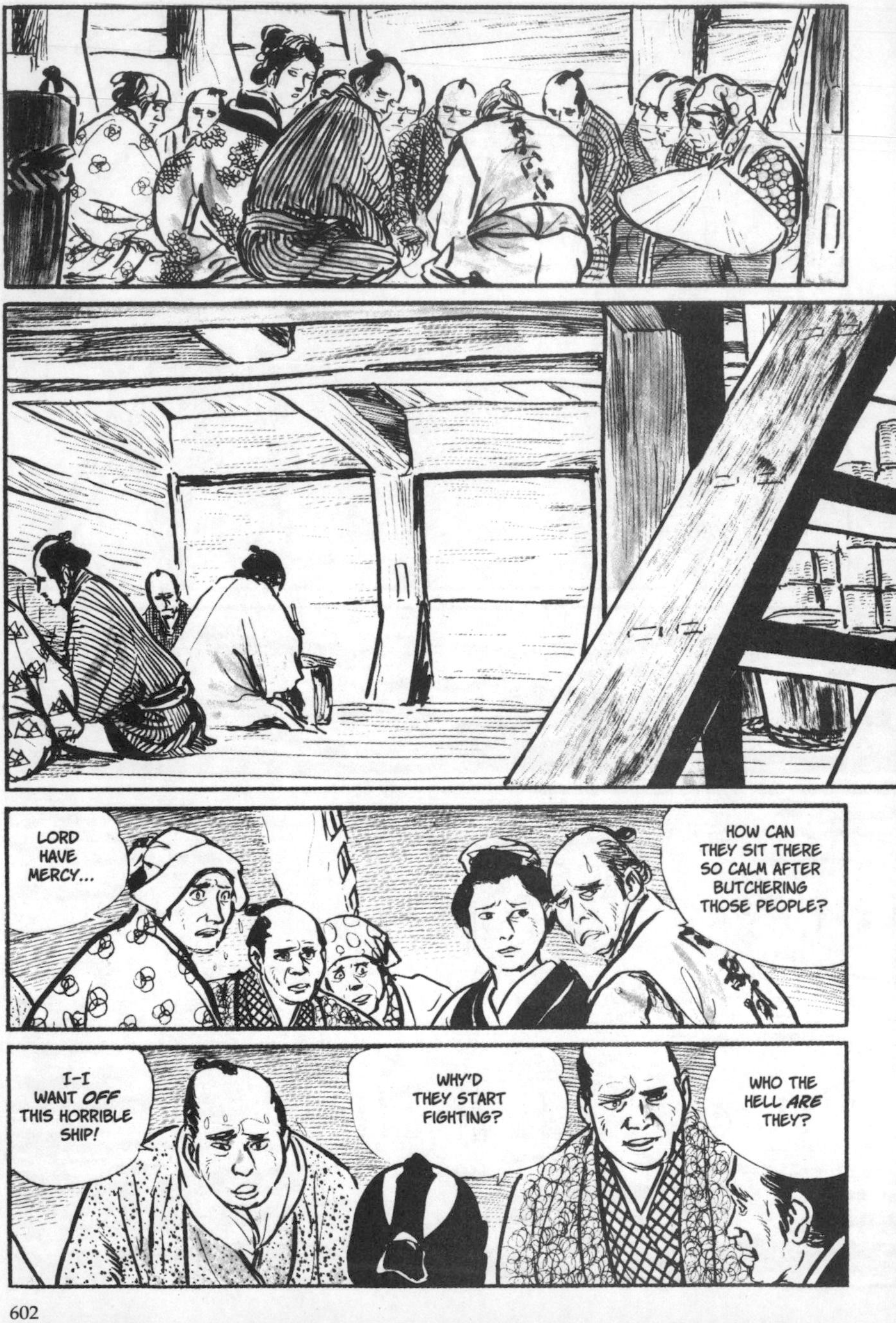
HOW CAN THEY SIT THERE SO CALM AFTER BUTCHERING THOSE PEOPLE?
LORD HAVE MERCY...
WHO THE HELL *ARE* THEY?
WHY'D THEY START FIGHTING?
I-I WANT *OFF* THIS HORRIBLE SHIP!

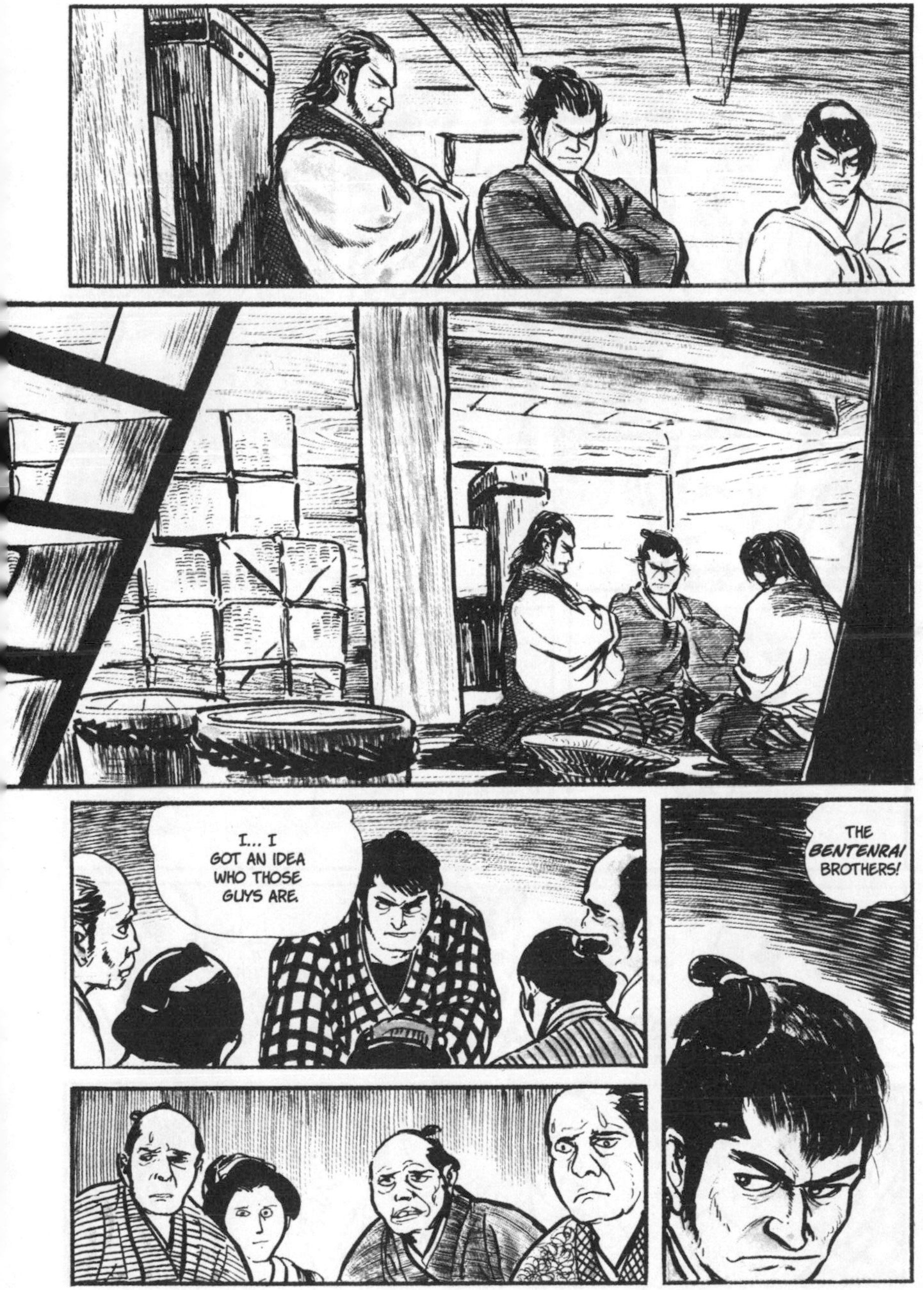
I... I GOT AN IDEA WHO THOSE GUYS ARE.
THE BENTENRAI BROTHERS!

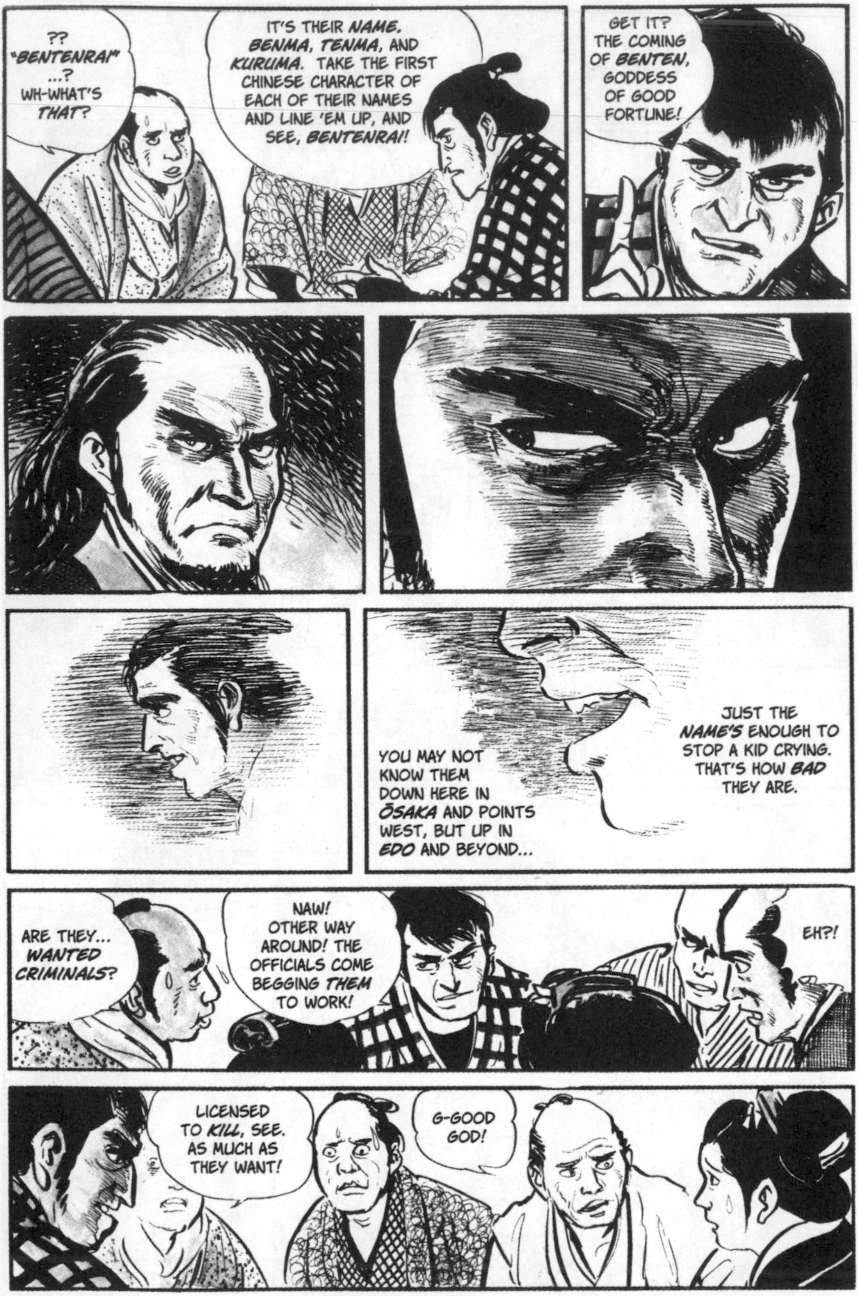

?? "BENTENRAI" ...? WH-WHAT'S THAT?
IT'S THEIR NAME. BENMA, TENMA, AND KURUMA. TAKE THE FIRST CHINESE CHARACTER OF EACH OF THEIR NAMES AND LINE 'EM UP, AND SEE, BENTENRAI!
GET IT? THE COMING OF BENTEN, GODDESS OF GOOD FORTUNE!
YOU MAY NOT KNOW THEM DOWN HERE IN ŌSAKA AND POINTS WEST, BUT UP IN EDO AND BEYOND...
JUST THE NAME'S ENOUGH TO STOP A KID CRYING. THAT'S HOW BAD THEY ARE.
ARE THEY... WANTED CRIMINALS?
NAW! OTHER WAY AROUND! THE OFFICIALS COME BEGGING THEM TO WORK!
EH?!
LICENSED TO KILL, SEE. AS MUCH AS THEY WANT!
G-GOOD GOD!

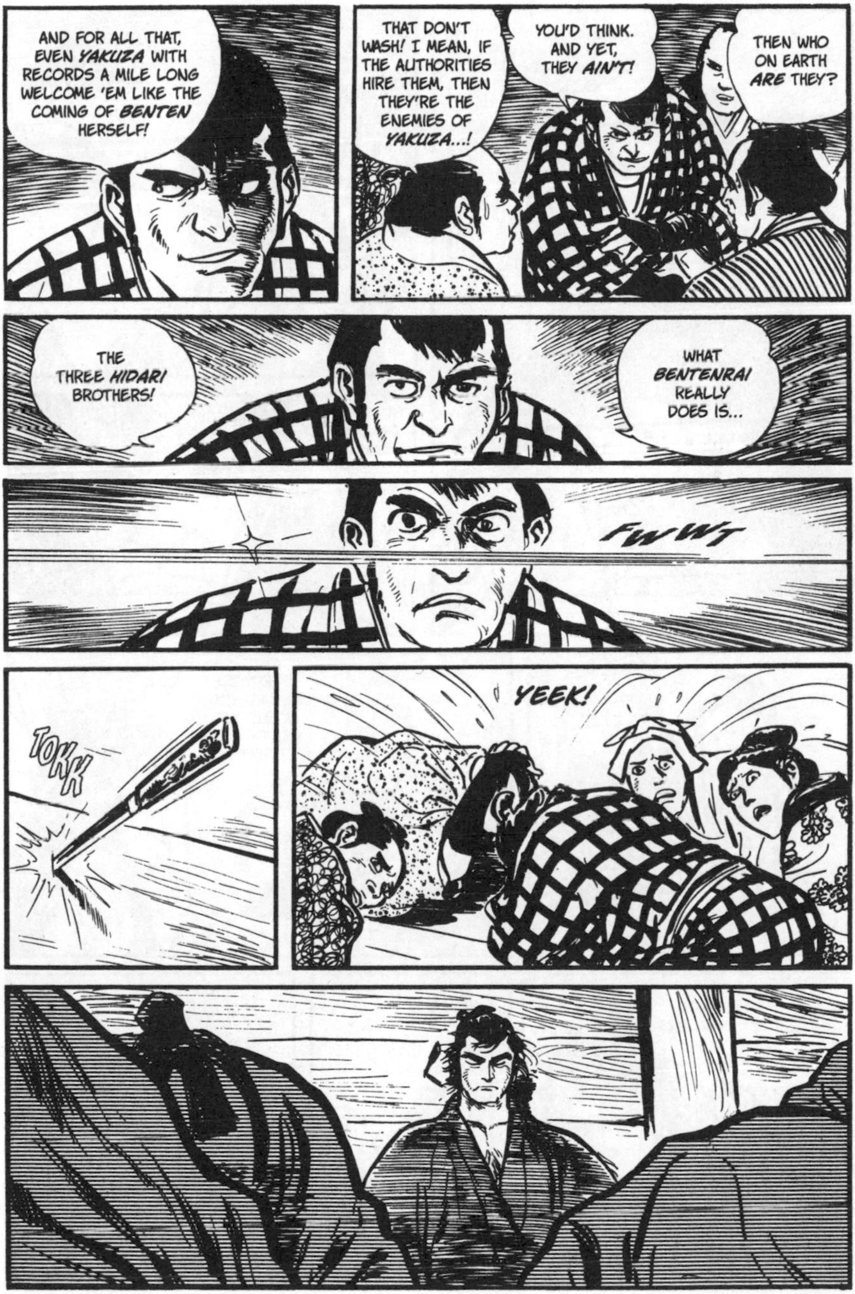
AND FOR ALL THAT, EVEN YAKUZA WITH RECORDS A MILE LONG WELCOME 'EM LIKE THE COMING OF BENTEN HERSELF!
THAT DON'T WASH! I MEAN, IF THE AUTHORITIES HIRE THEM, THEN THEY'RE THE ENEMIES OF YAKUZA...!
YOU'D THINK. AND YET, THEY AIN'T!
THEN WHO ON EARTH ARE THEY?
THE THREE HIDARI BROTHERS!
WHAT BENTENRAI REALLY DOES IS...
FWWT
TOKK
YEEK!

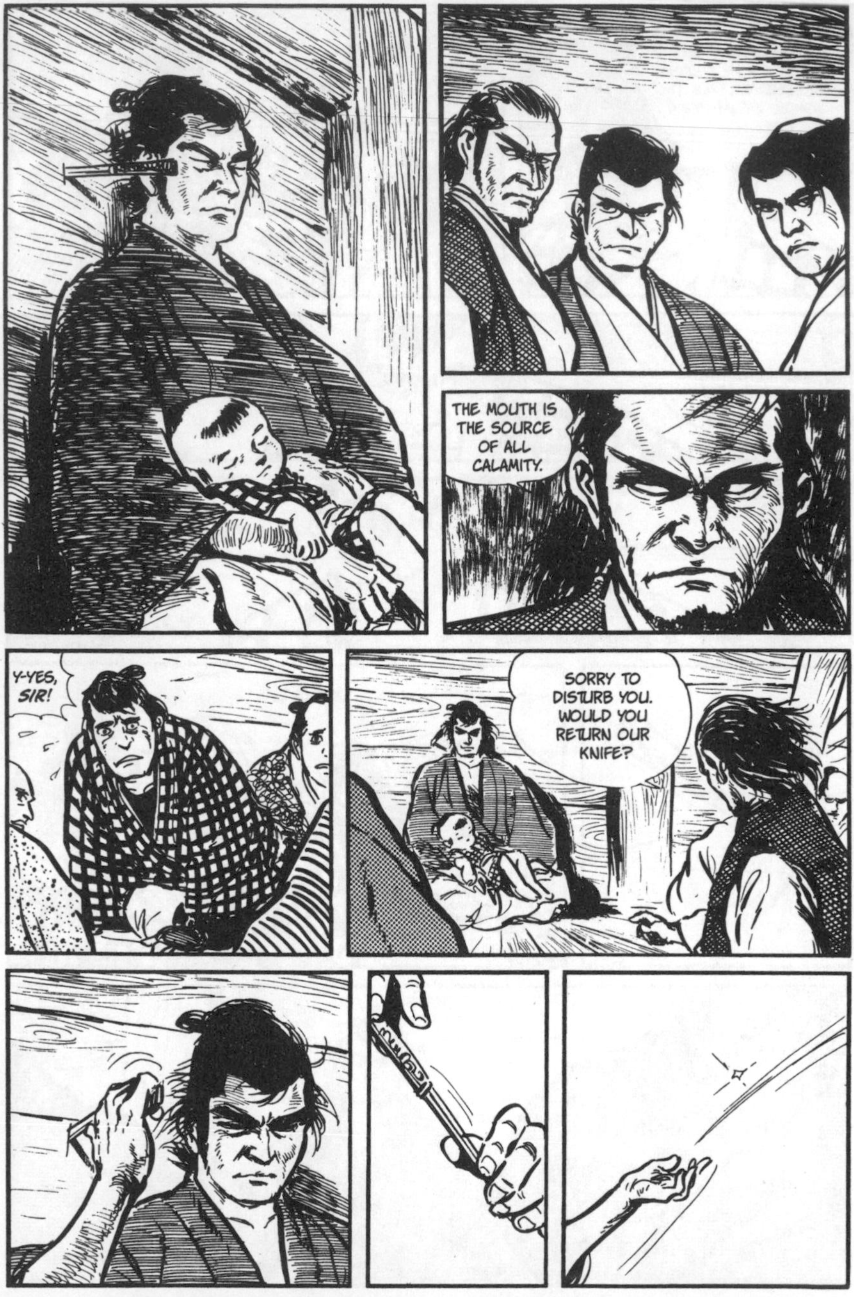
THE MOUTH IS THE SOURCE OF ALL CALAMITY.
Y-YES, SIR!
SORRY TO DISTURB YOU. WOULD YOU RETURN OUR KNIFE?

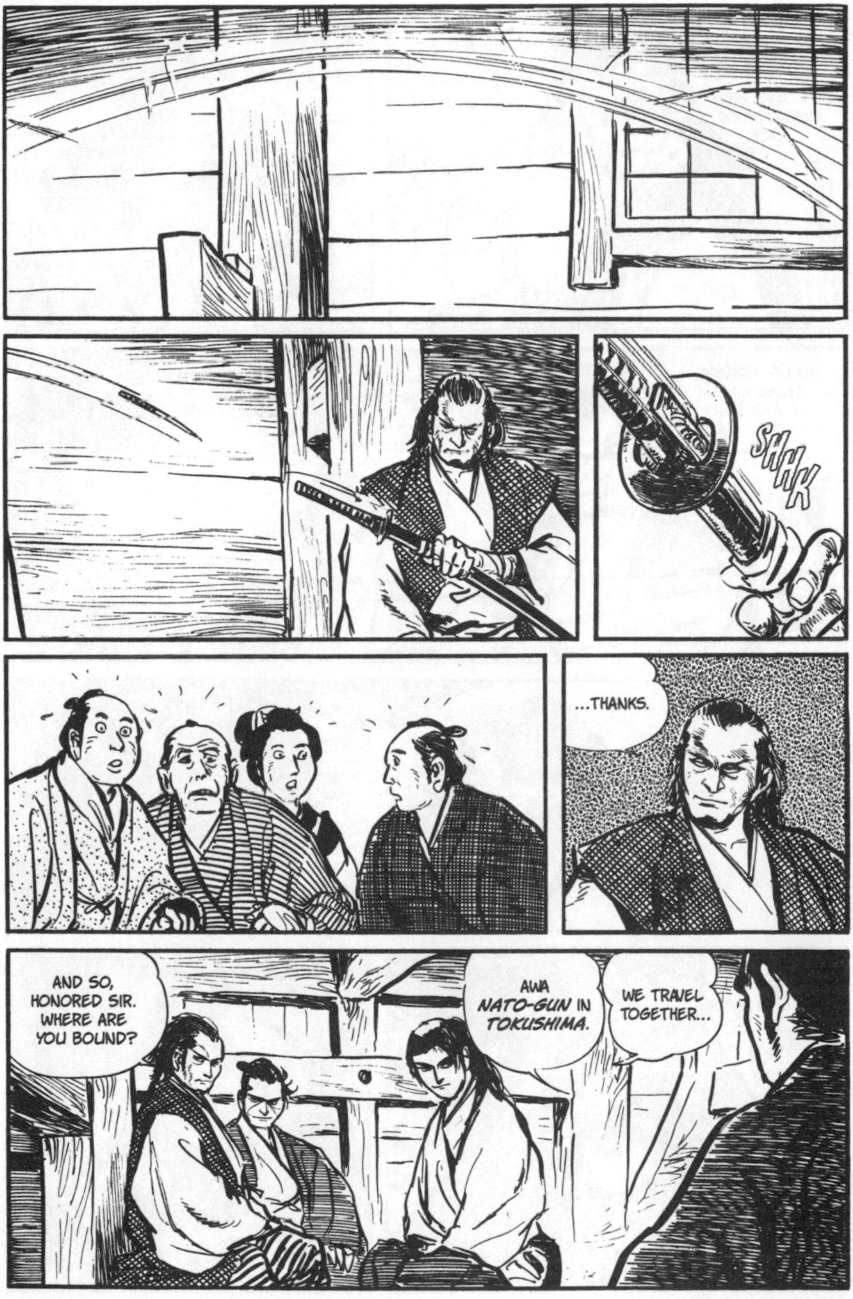

SHHK
...THANKS.
AND SO, HONORED SIR. WHERE ARE YOU BOUND?
AWA NATO-GUN IN TOKUSHIMA.
WE TRAVEL TOGETHER...

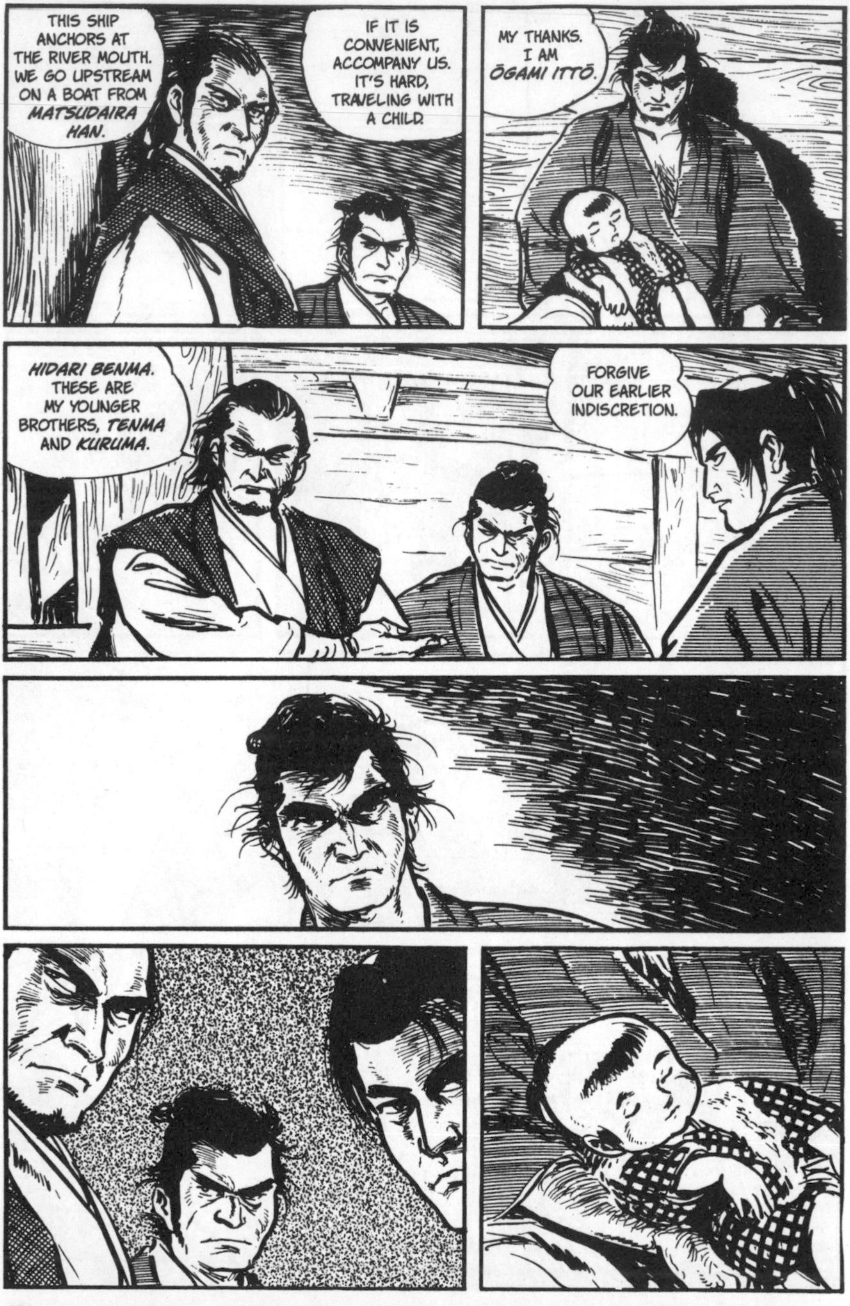
THIS SHIP ANCHORS AT THE RIVER MOUTH. WE GO UPSTREAM ON A BOAT FROM MATSUDAIRA HAN.
IF IT IS CONVENIENT, ACCOMPANY US. IT'S HARD, TRAVELING WITH A CHILD.
MY THANKS. I AM ŌGAMI ITTŌ.
HIDARI BENMA. THESE ARE MY YOUNGER BROTHERS, TENMA AND KURUMA.
FORGIVE OUR EARLIER INDISCRETION.

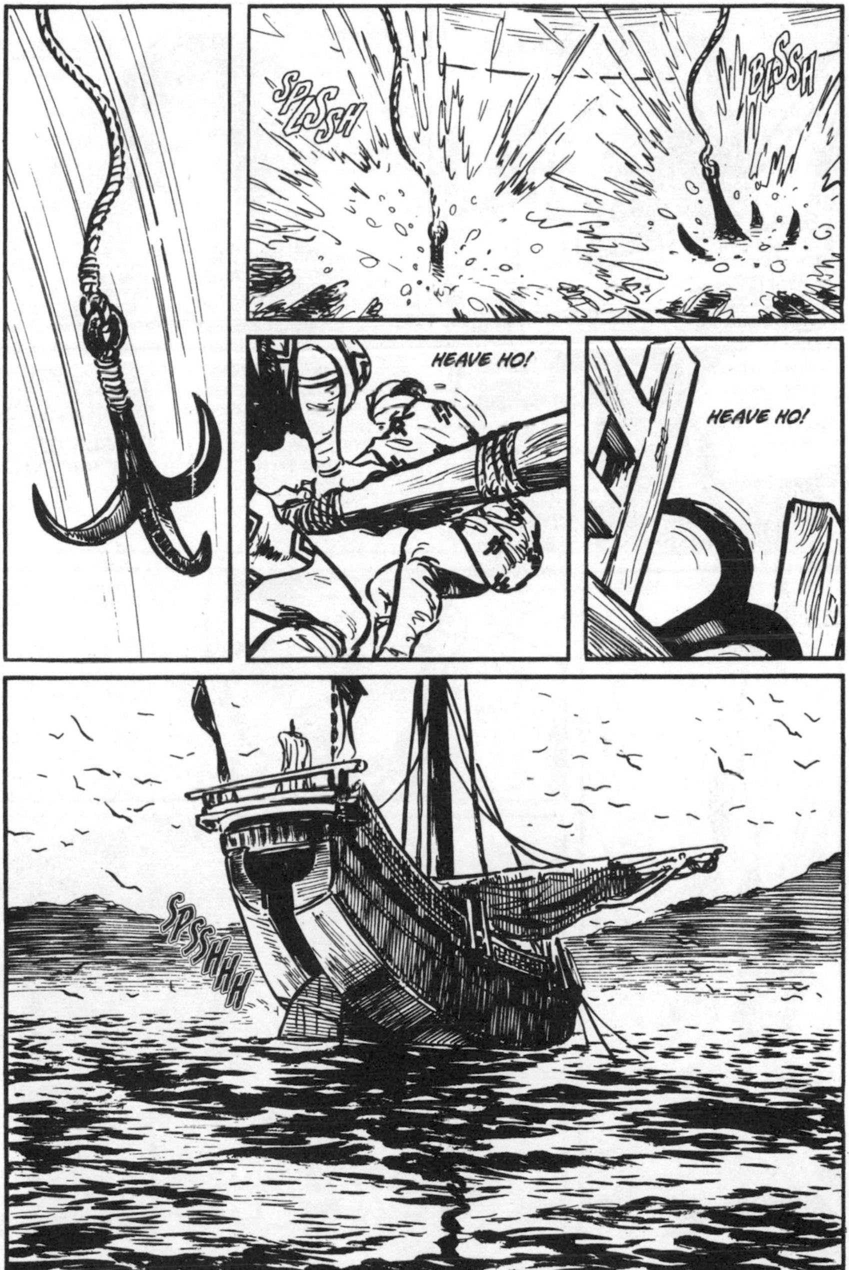
BLSSH
SPLSSH
HEAVE HO!
HEAVE HO!
SPSSHHH

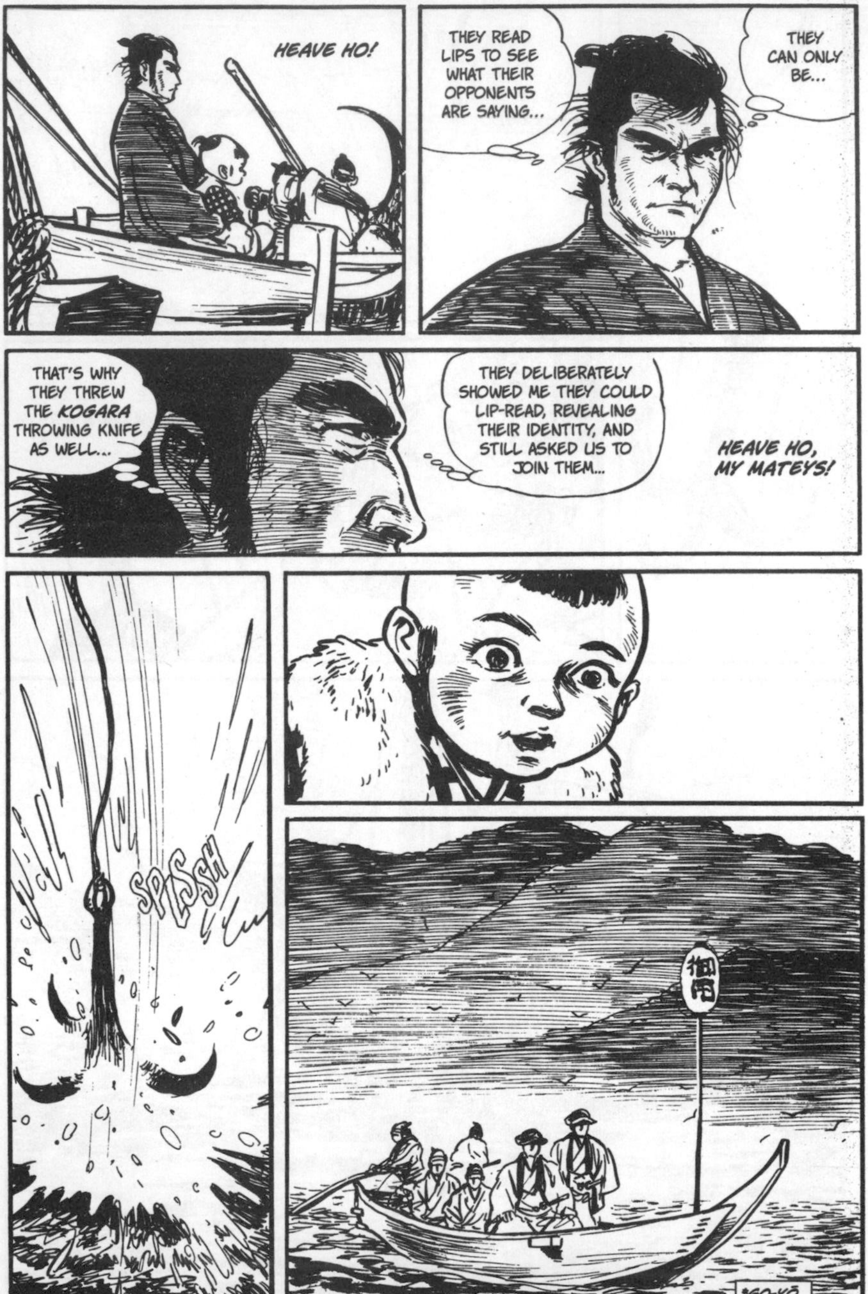
HEAVE HO!
THEY READ LIPS TO SEE WHAT THEIR OPPONENTS ARE SAYING...
THEY CAN ONLY BE...
THAT'S WHY THEY THREW THE *KOGARA* THROWING KNIFE AS WELL...
THEY DELIBERATELY SHOWED ME THEY COULD LIP-READ, REVEALING THEIR IDENTITY, AND STILL ASKED US TO JOIN THEM...
HEAVE HO, MY MATEYS!
SPLSSH
御用
*GO-YŌ

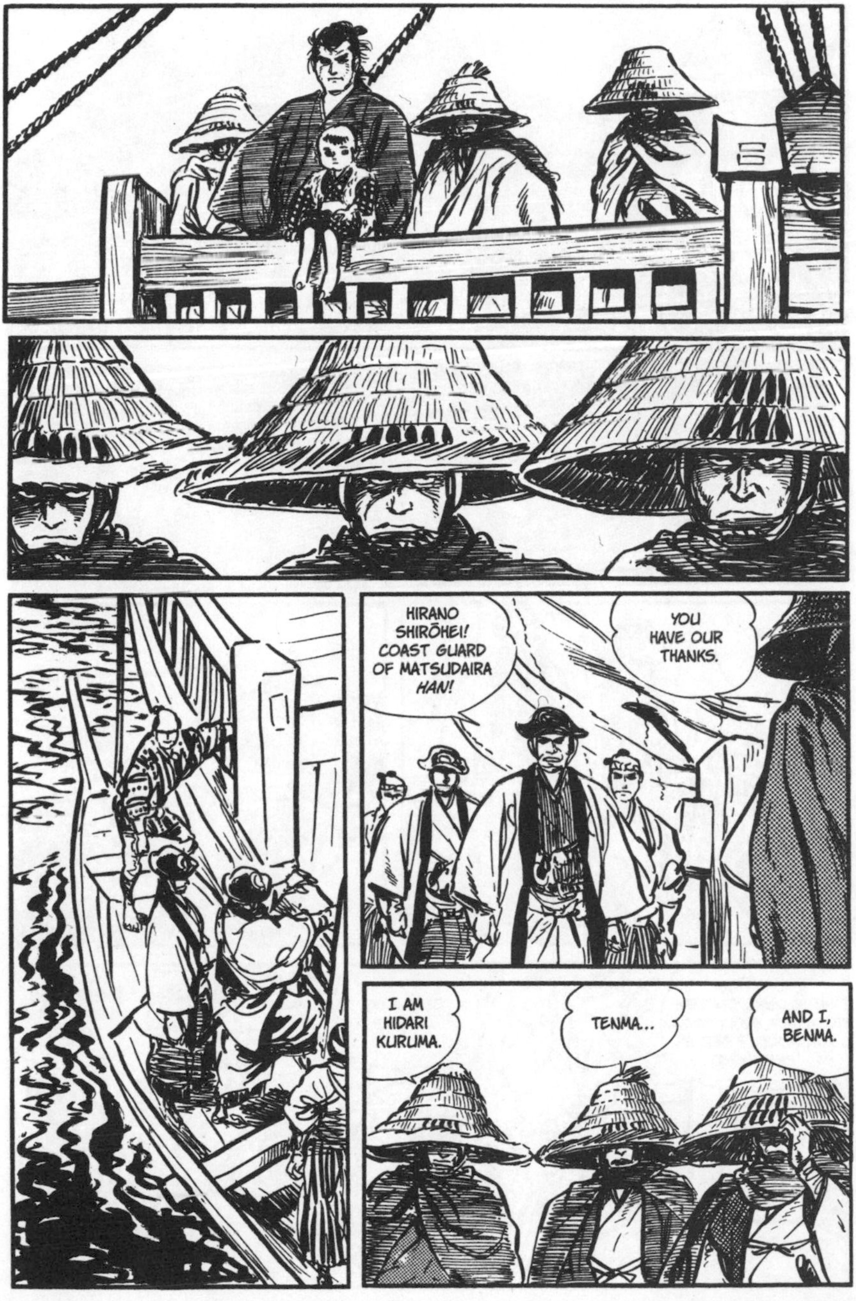
HIRANO SHIRŌHEI! COAST GUARD OF MATSUDAIRA *HAN!*
YOU HAVE OUR THANKS.
I AM HIDARI KURUMA.
TENMA...
AND I, BENMA.

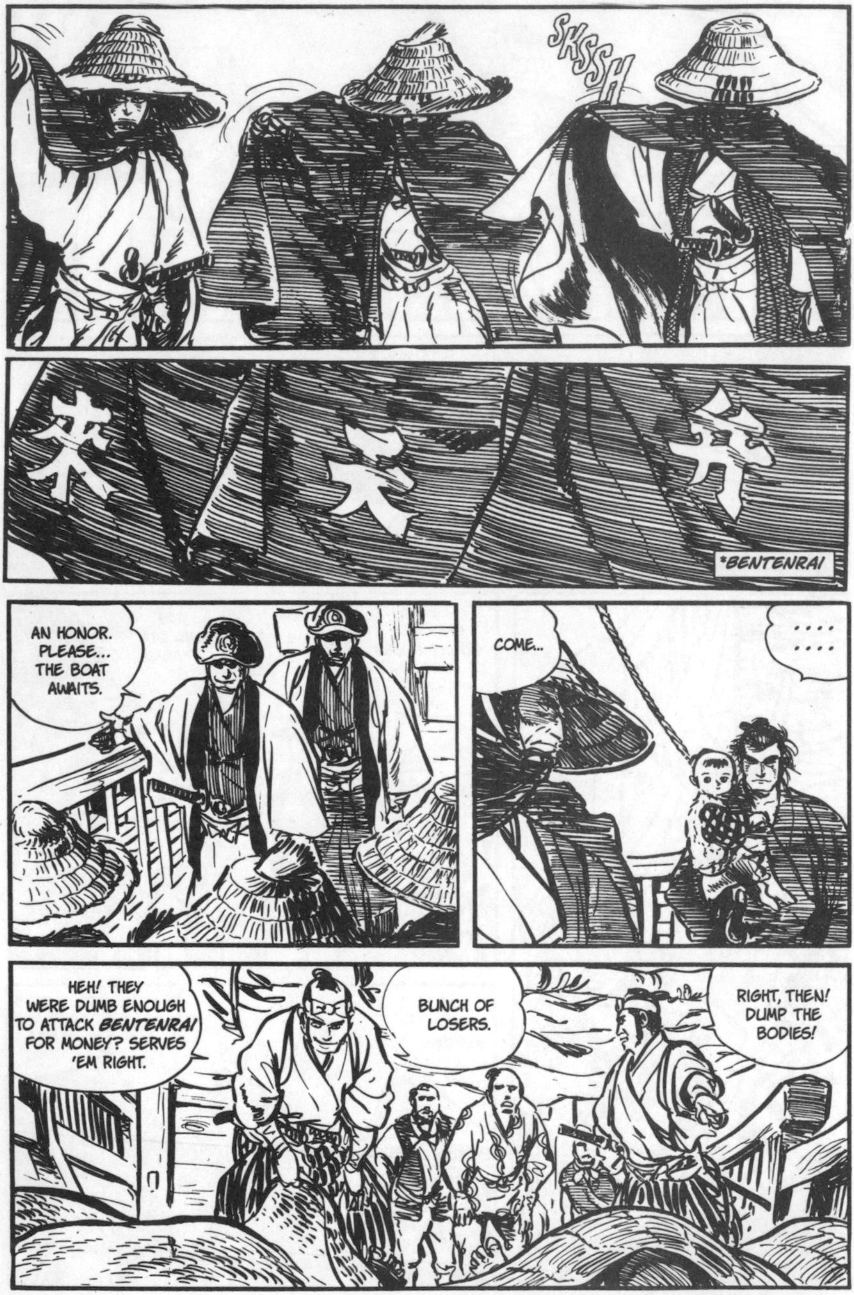
SKSSH
*BENTENRAI
....
....
COME...
AN HONOR. PLEASE... THE BOAT AWAITS.
RIGHT, THEN! DUMP THE BODIES!
BUNCH OF LOSERS.
HEH! THEY WERE DUMB ENOUGH TO ATTACK *BENTENRAI* FOR MONEY? SERVES 'EM RIGHT.

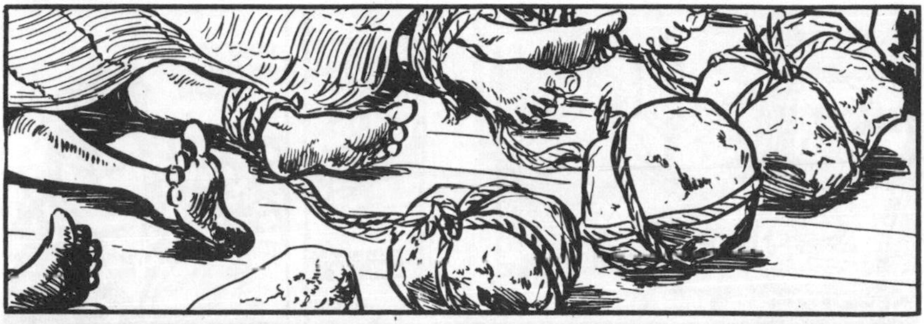
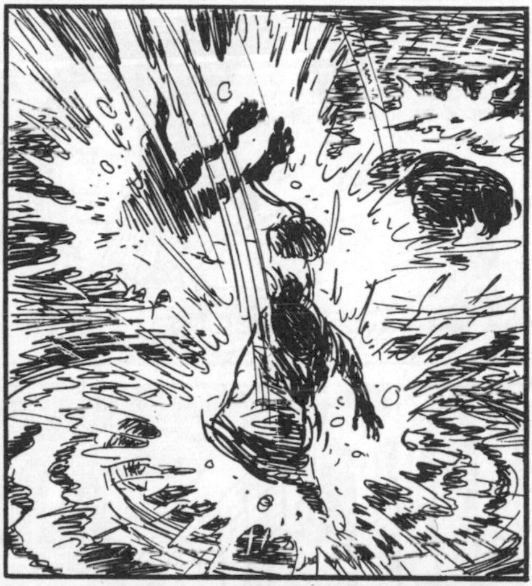
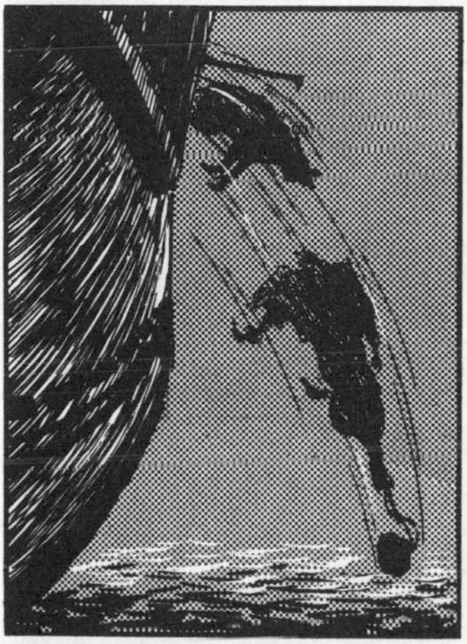
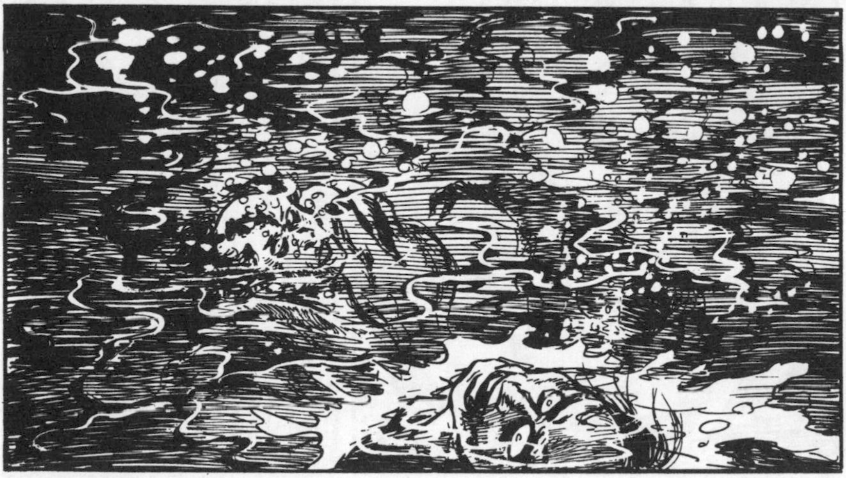

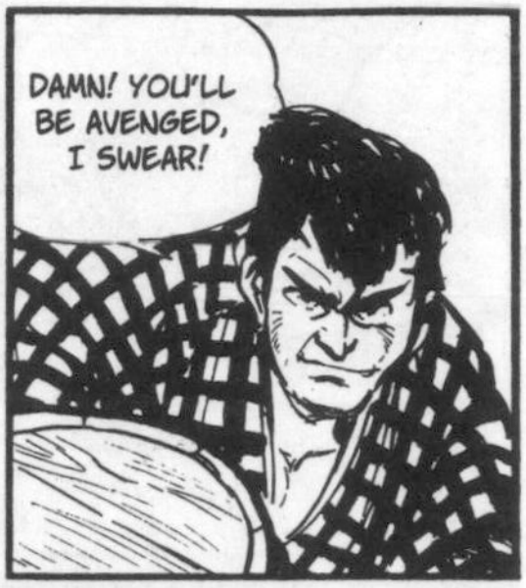
DAMN! YOU'LL BE AVENGED, I SWEAR!

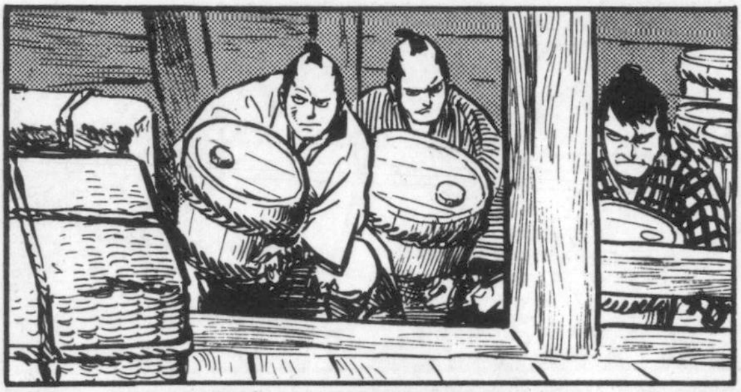

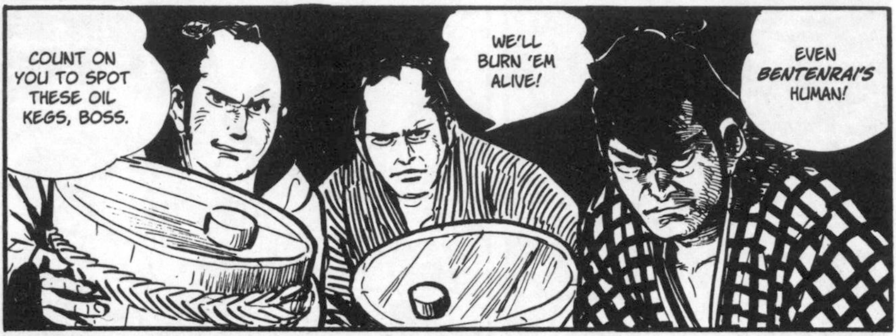
EVEN *BENTENRAI'S* HUMAN!
WE'LL BURN 'EM ALIVE!
COUNT ON YOU TO SPOT THESE OIL KEGS, BOSS.

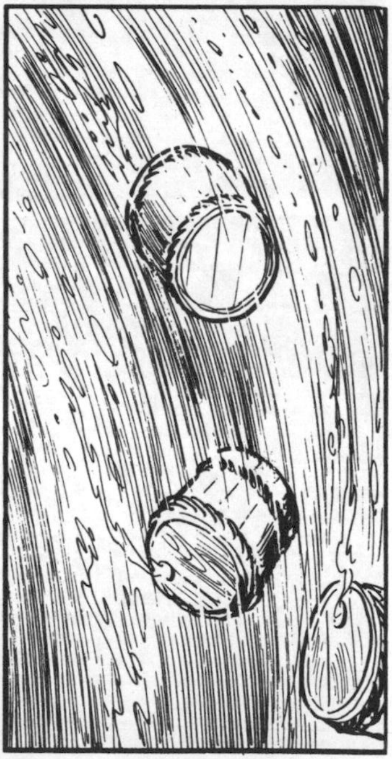

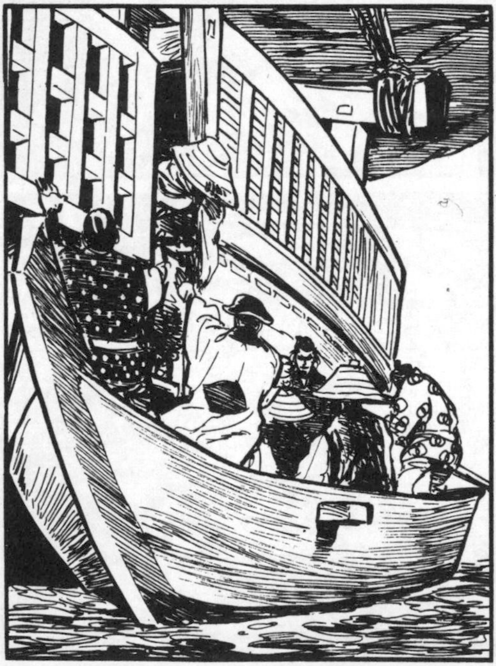

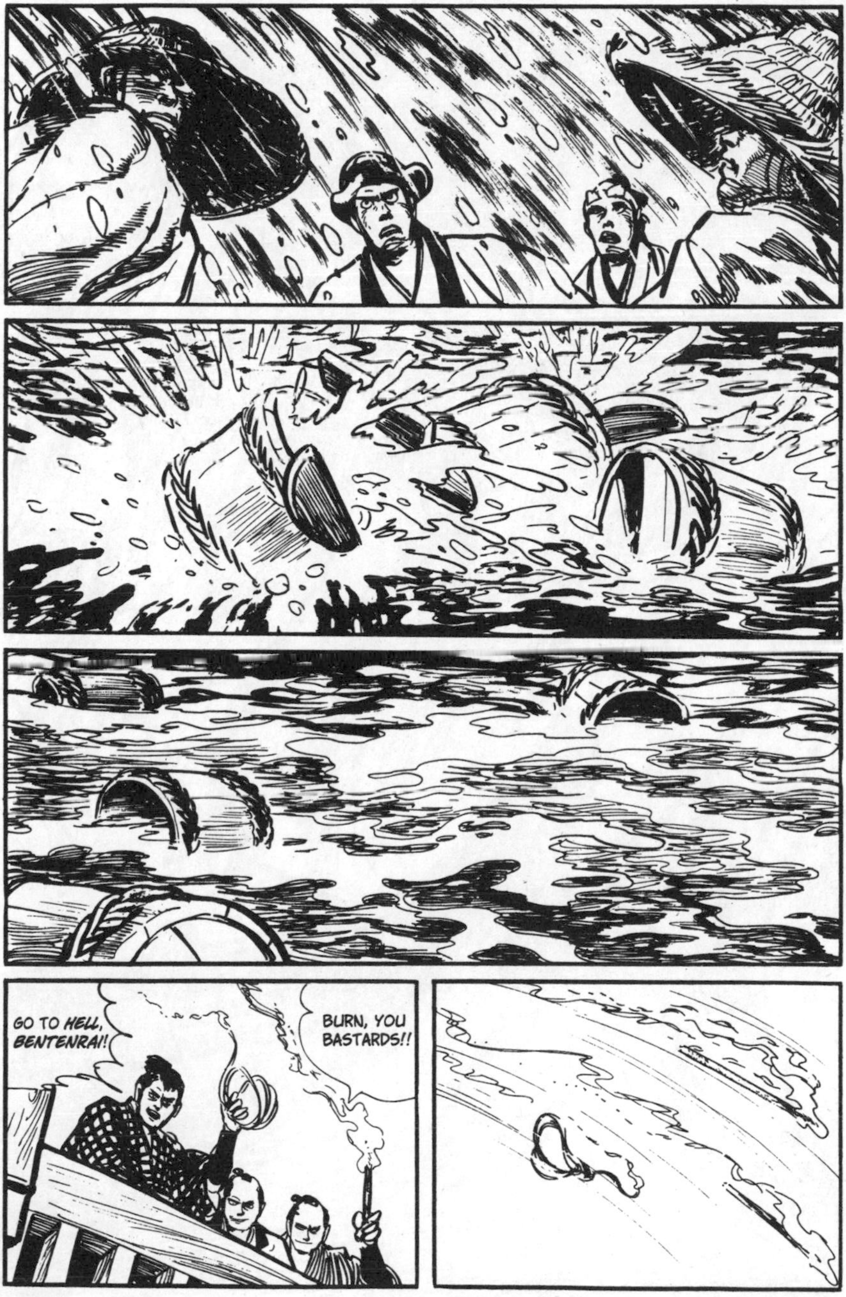
BURN, YOU BASTARDS!!
GO TO HELL, BENTENRAI!

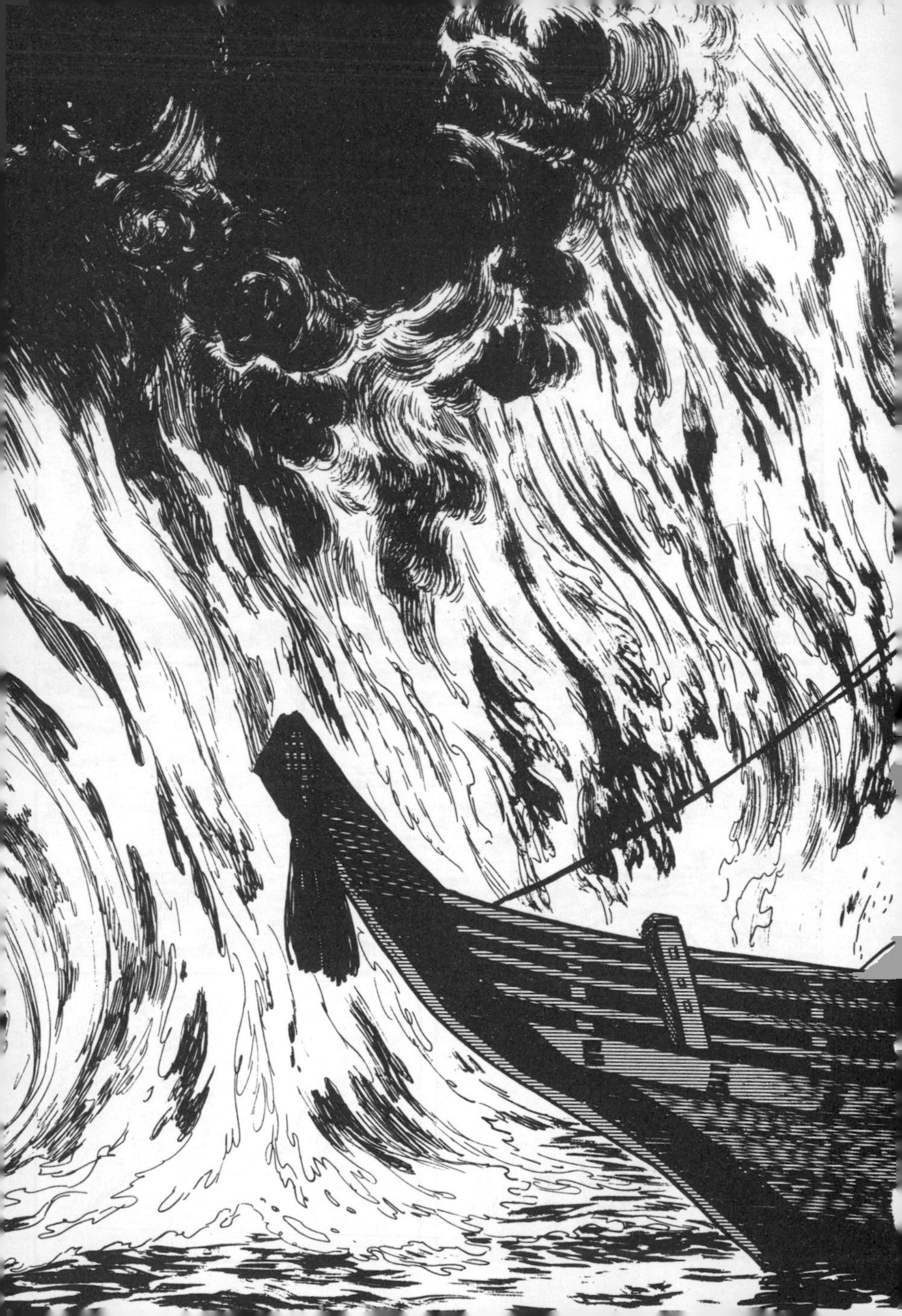

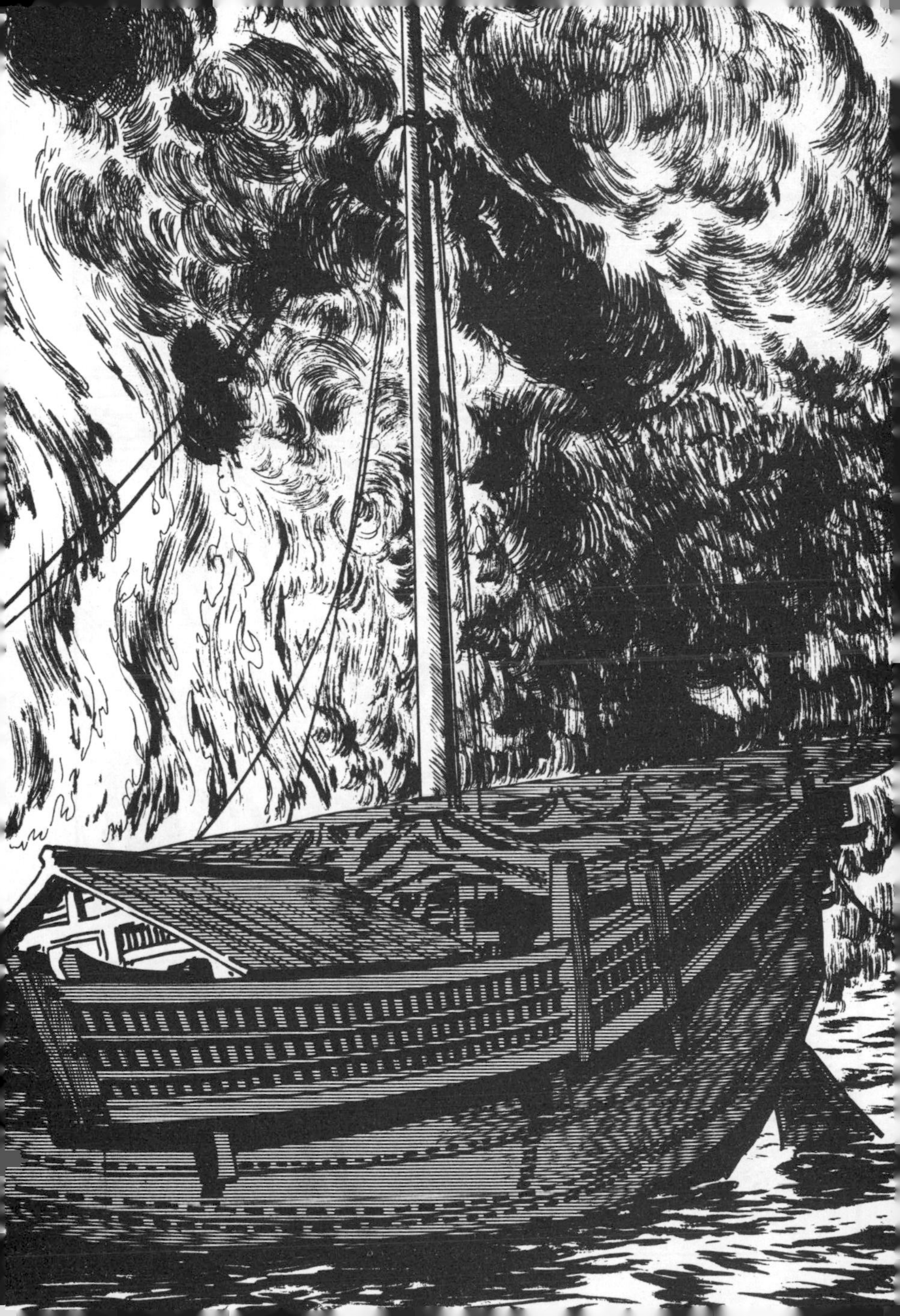

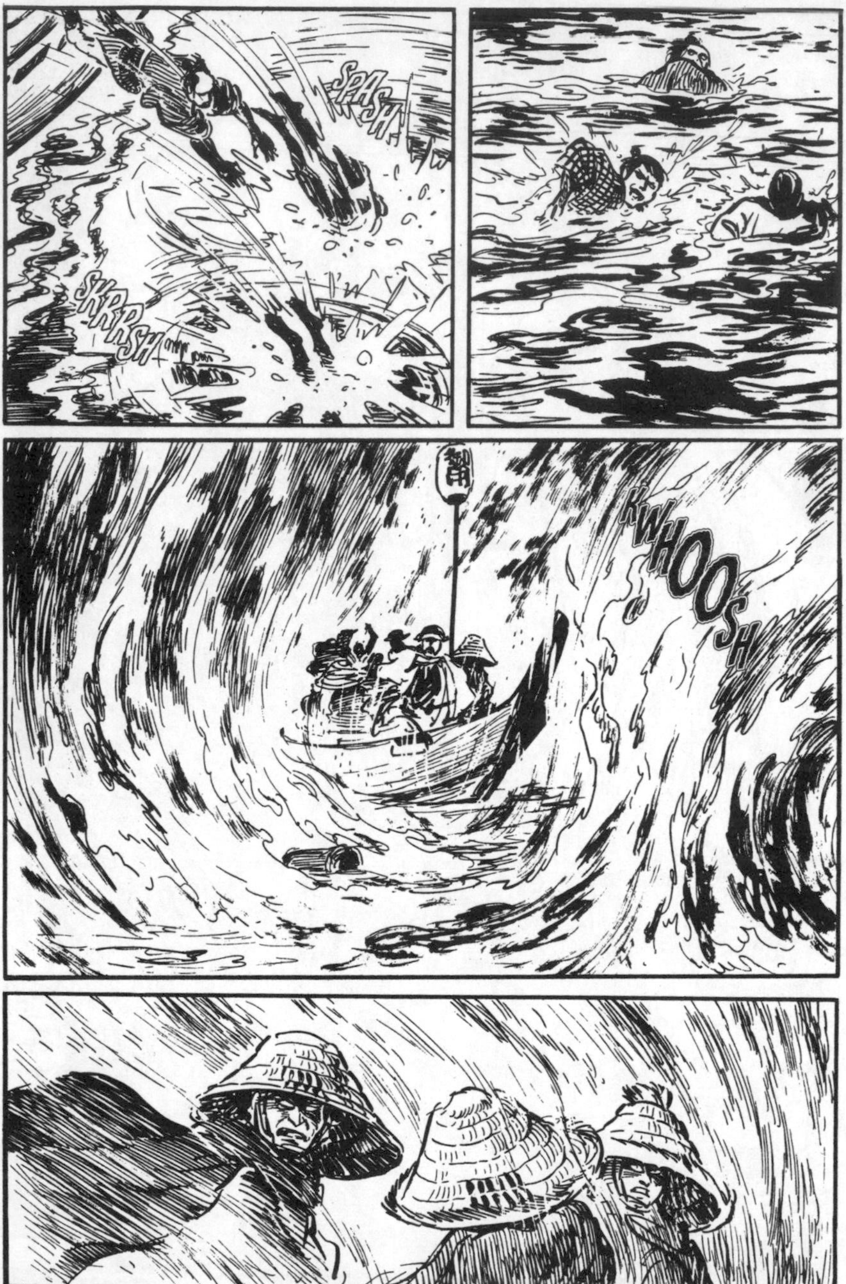
SPASH
SKRRSH
KWHOOSH

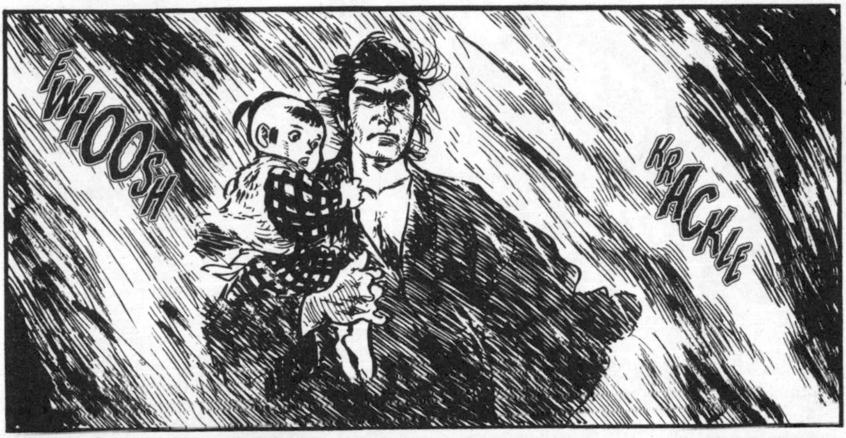
FWHOOSH
KRACKLE
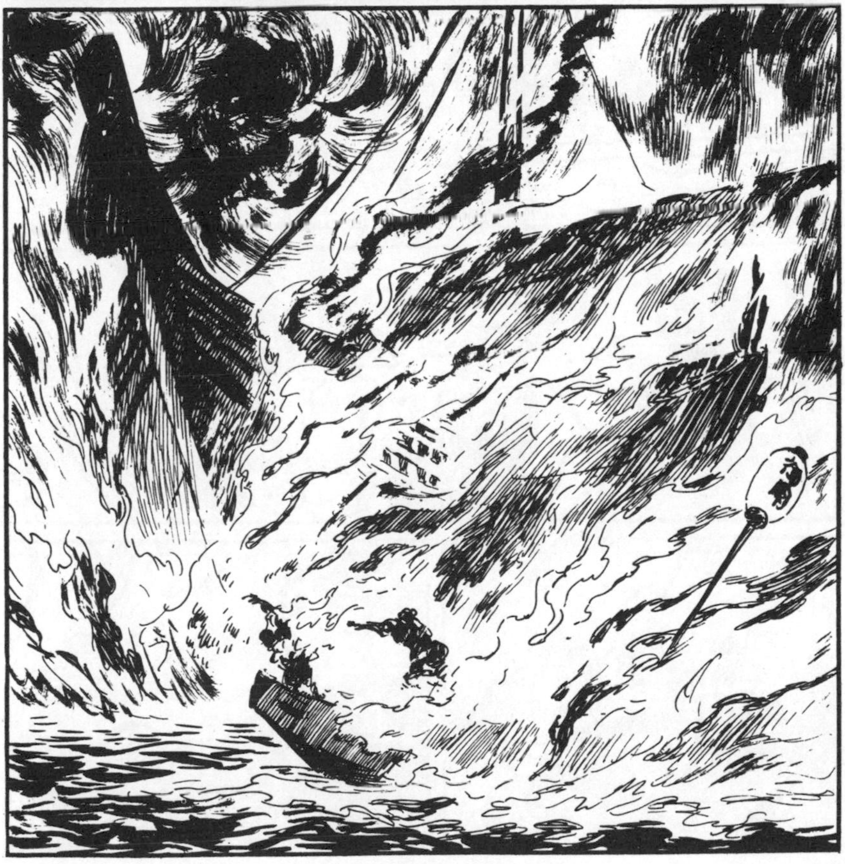

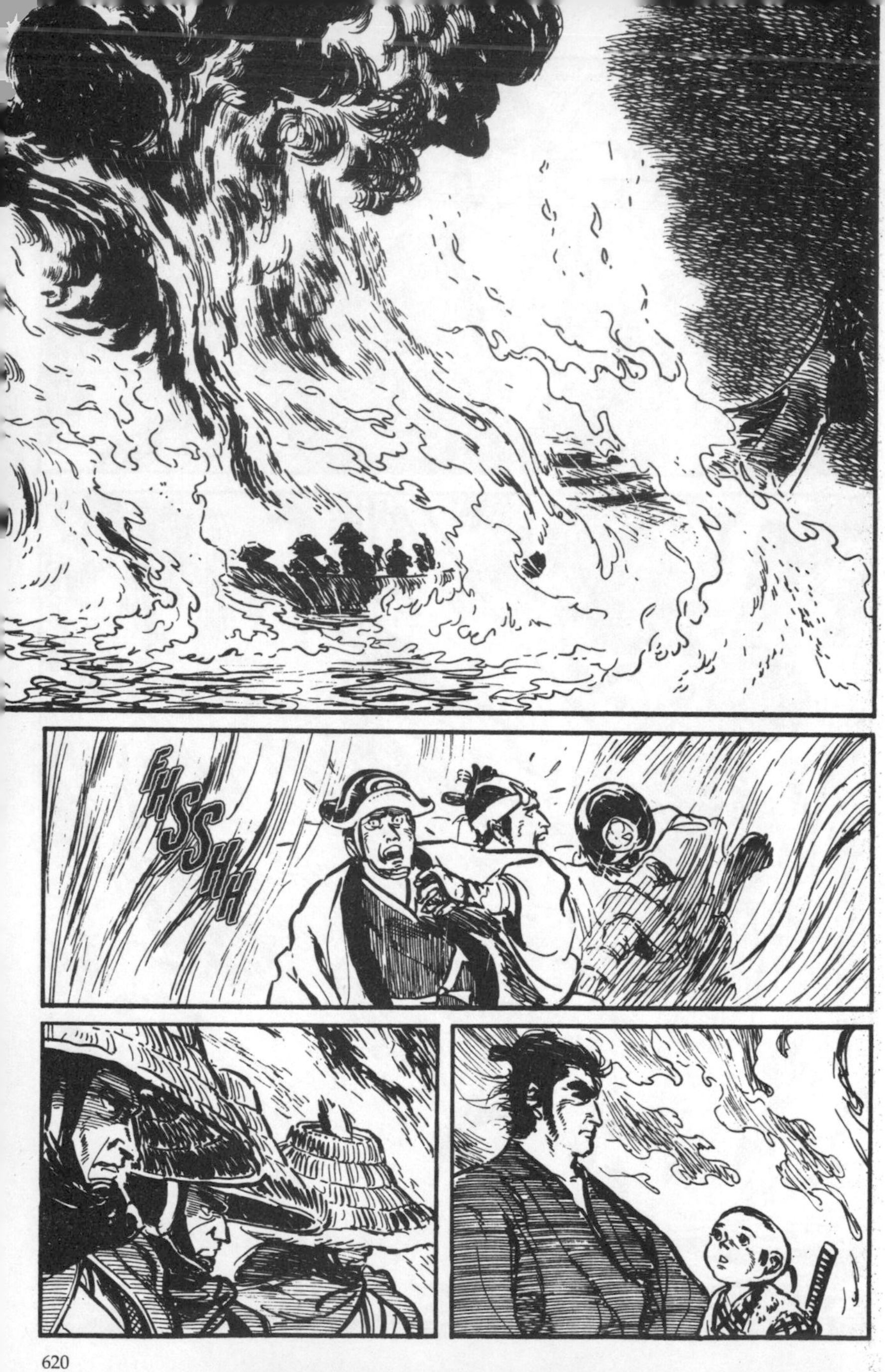
FHSSSHH

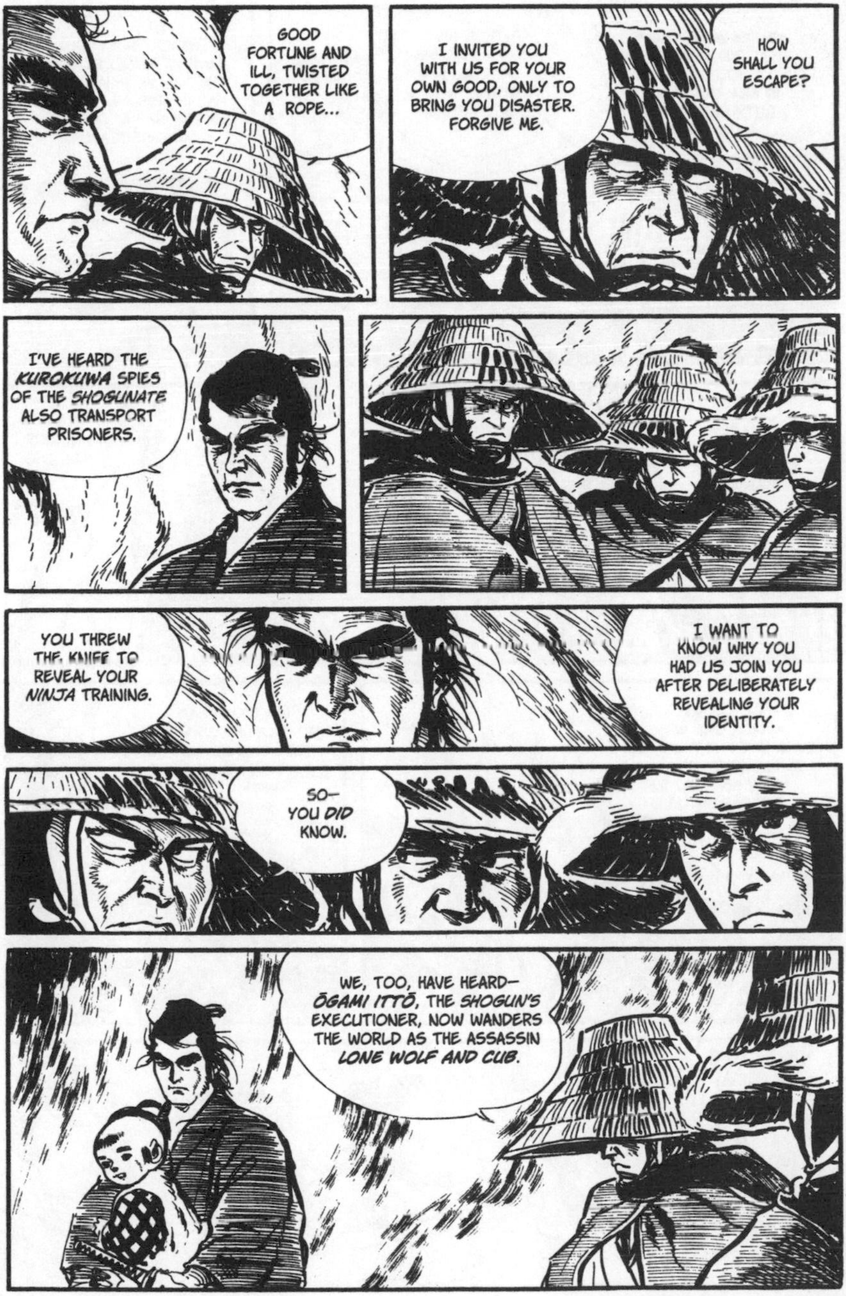
GOOD FORTUNE AND ILL, TWISTED TOGETHER LIKE A ROPE...
I INVITED YOU WITH US FOR YOUR OWN GOOD, ONLY TO BRING YOU DISASTER. FORGIVE ME.
HOW SHALL YOU ESCAPE?
I'VE HEARD THE *KUROKUWA* SPIES OF THE *SHOGUNATE* ALSO TRANSPORT PRISONERS.
YOU THREW THE KNIFE TO REVEAL YOUR *NINJA* TRAINING.
I WANT TO KNOW WHY YOU HAD US JOIN YOU AFTER DELIBERATELY REVEALING YOUR IDENTITY.
SO— YOU *DID* KNOW.
WE, TOO, HAVE HEARD— *ŌGAMI ITTŌ*, THE *SHOGUN'S* EXECUTIONER, NOW WANDERS THE WORLD AS THE ASSASSIN *LONE WOLF AND CUB*.

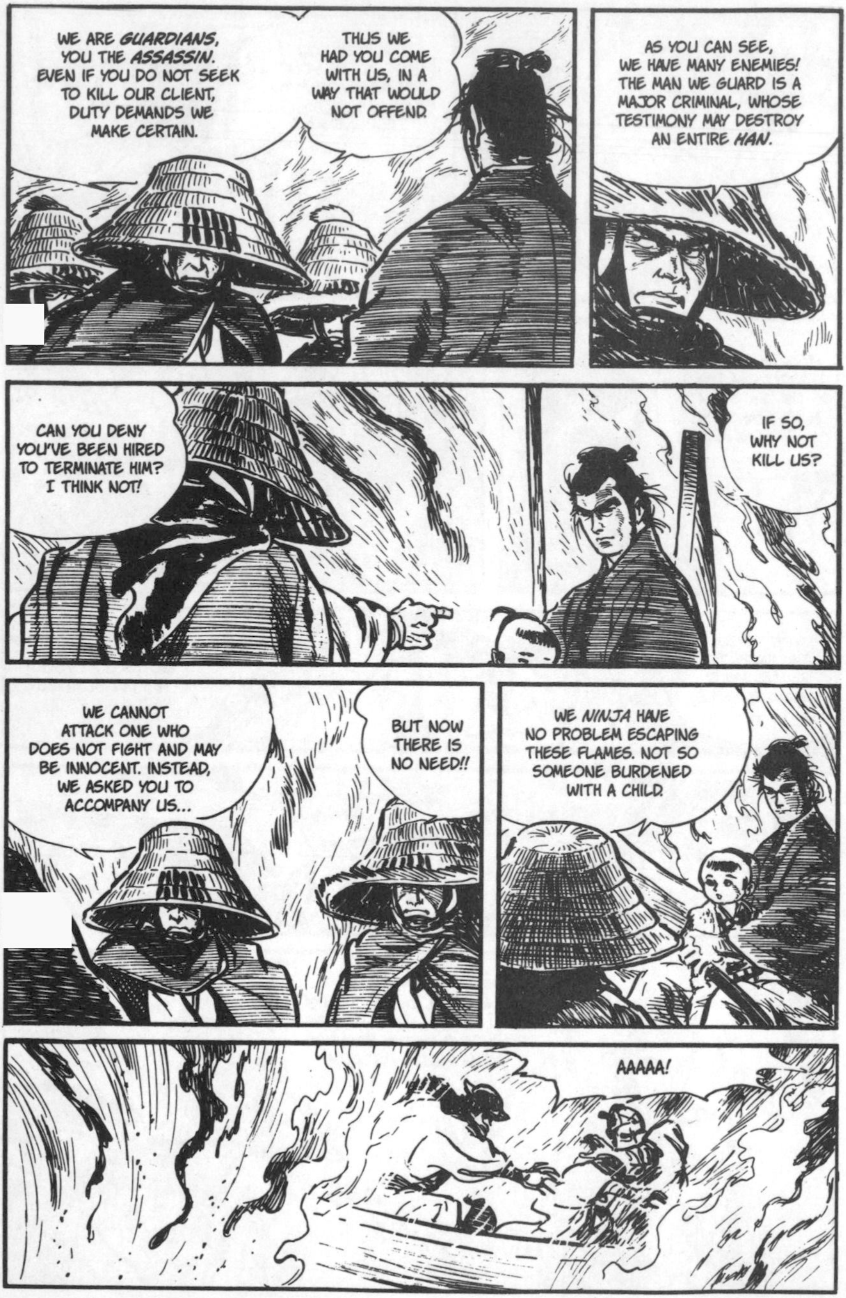
WE ARE *GUARDIANS*, YOU THE *ASSASSIN*. EVEN IF YOU DO NOT SEEK TO KILL OUR CLIENT, DUTY DEMANDS WE MAKE CERTAIN.
THUS WE HAD YOU COME WITH US, IN A WAY THAT WOULD NOT OFFEND.
AS YOU CAN SEE, WE HAVE MANY ENEMIES! THE MAN WE GUARD IS A MAJOR CRIMINAL, WHOSE TESTIMONY MAY DESTROY AN ENTIRE *HAN*.
CAN YOU DENY YOU'VE BEEN HIRED TO TERMINATE HIM? I THINK NOT!
IF SO, WHY NOT KILL US?
WE CANNOT ATTACK ONE WHO DOES NOT FIGHT AND MAY BE INNOCENT. INSTEAD, WE ASKED YOU TO ACCOMPANY US...
BUT NOW THERE IS NO NEED!!
WE *NINJA* HAVE NO PROBLEM ESCAPING THESE FLAMES. NOT SO SOMEONE BURDENED WITH A CHILD.
AAAAA!

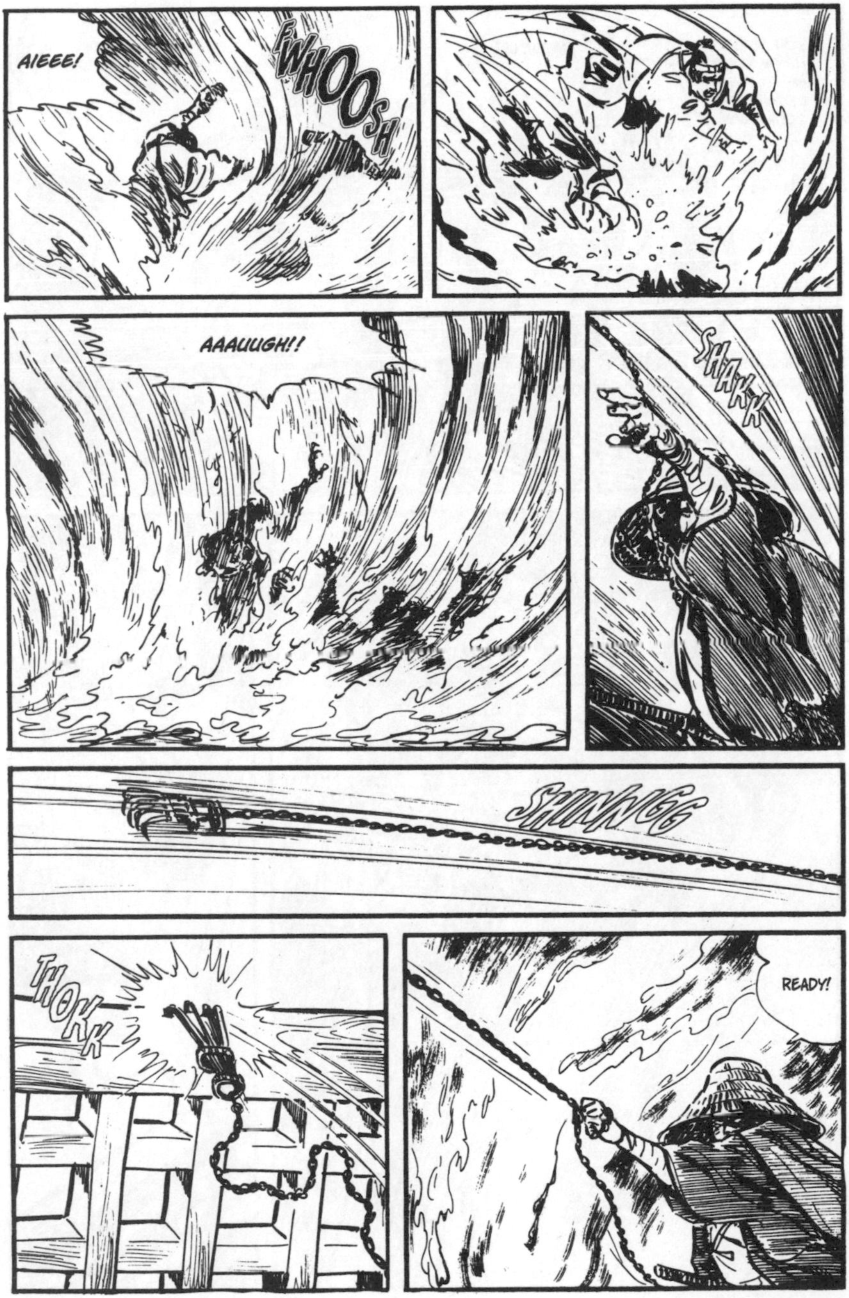
FWHOOSH
AIEEE!
SHAKK
AAAUUGH!!
SHINGG
READY!
THOKK

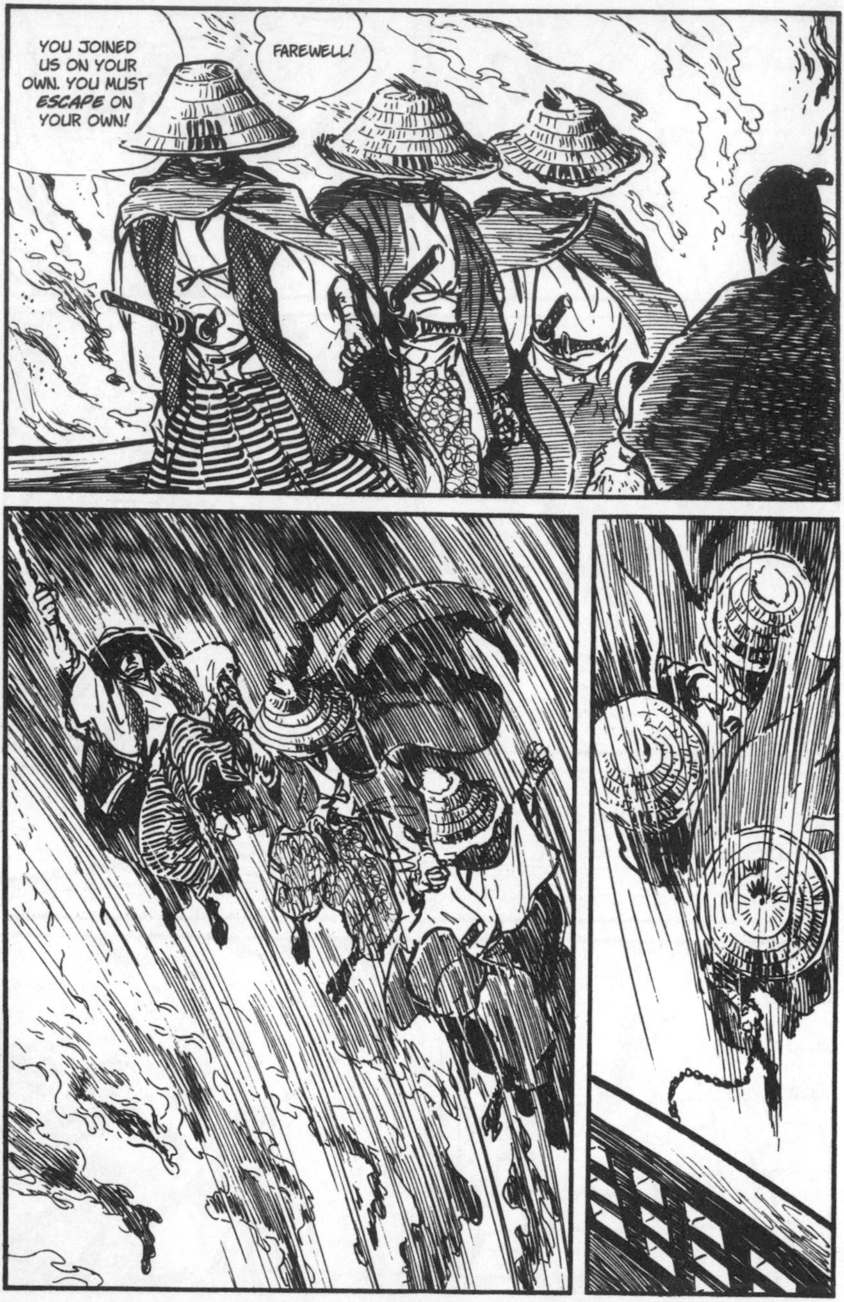
YOU JOINED US ON YOUR OWN. YOU MUST *ESCAPE* ON YOUR OWN!
FAREWELL!

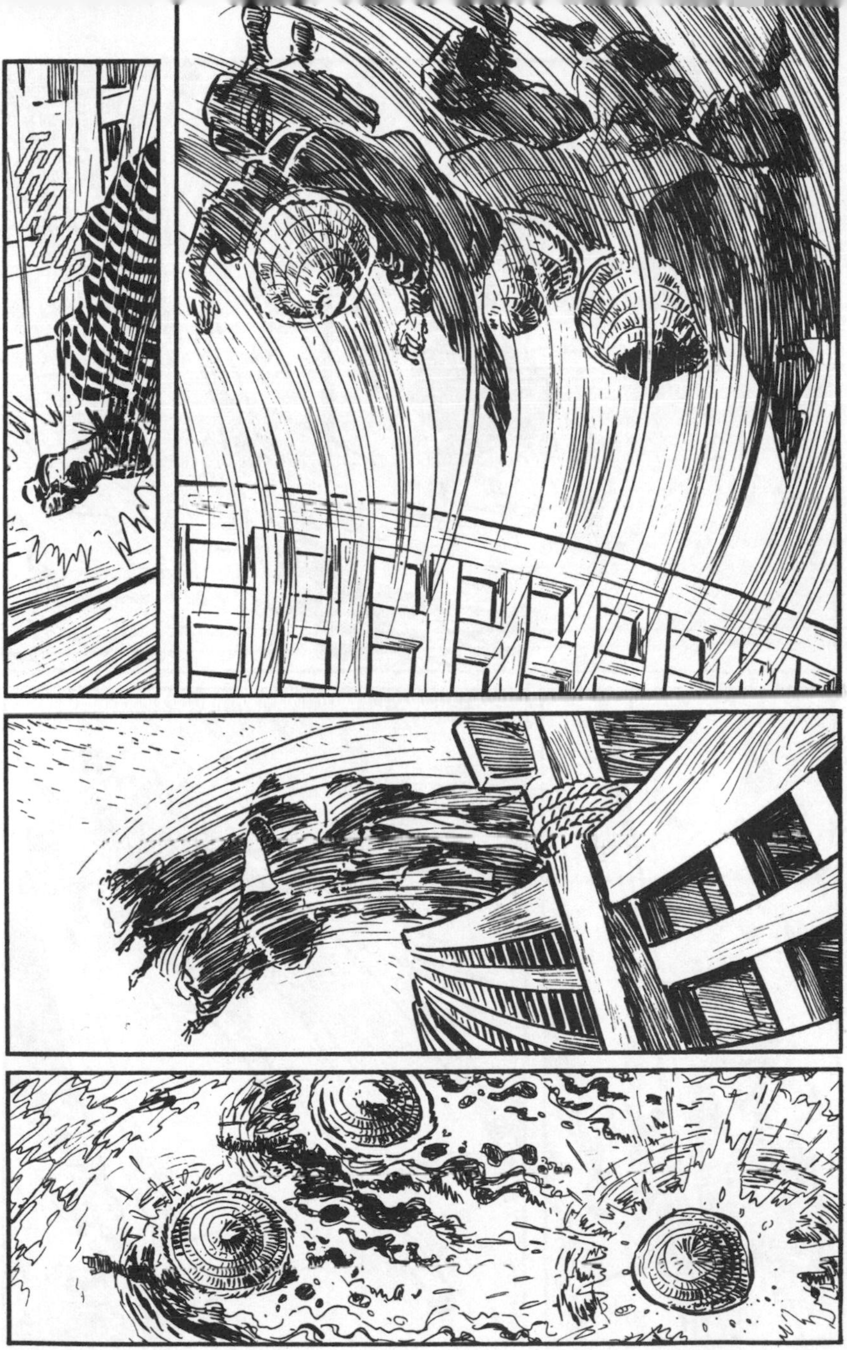
THAMP

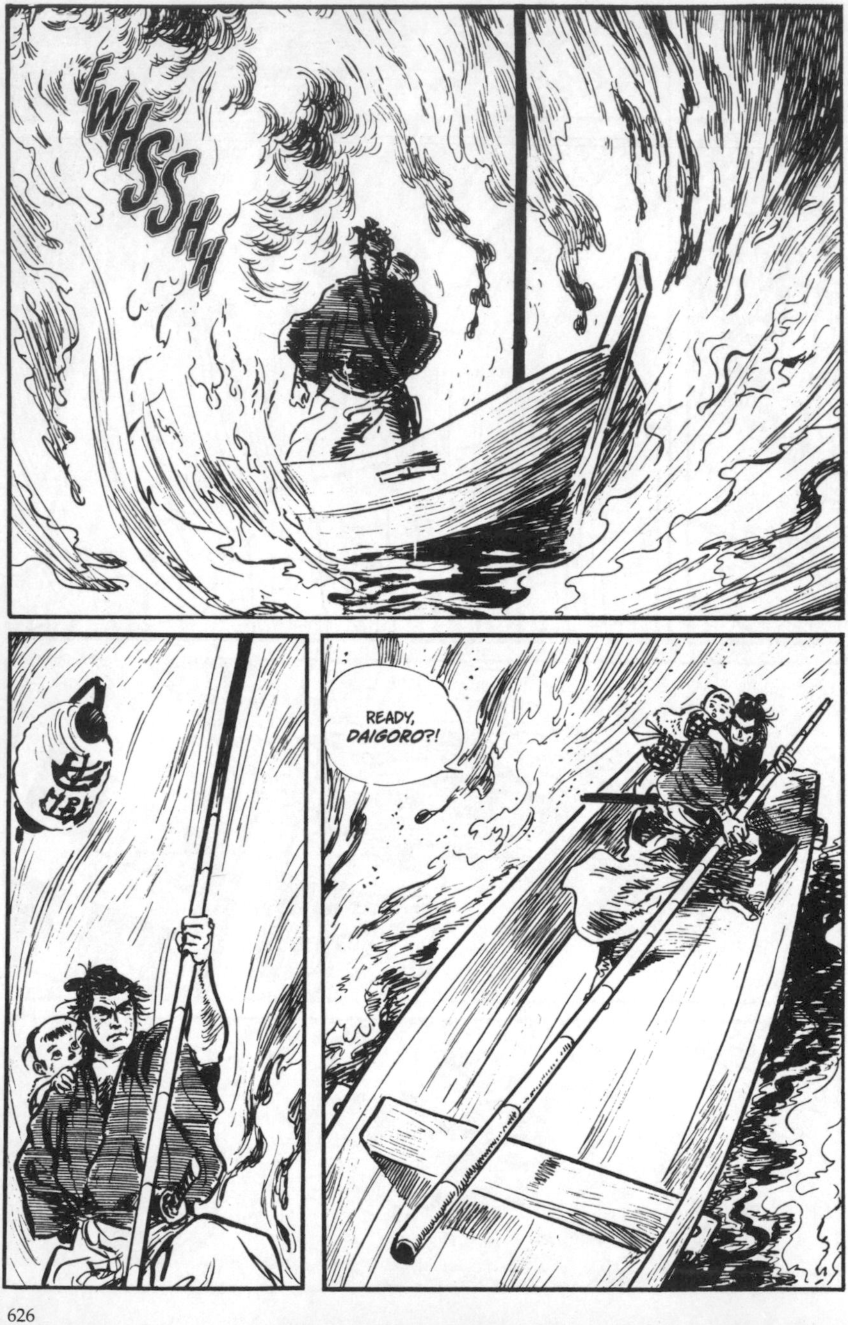
FWHSSHH
READY, DAIGORO?!

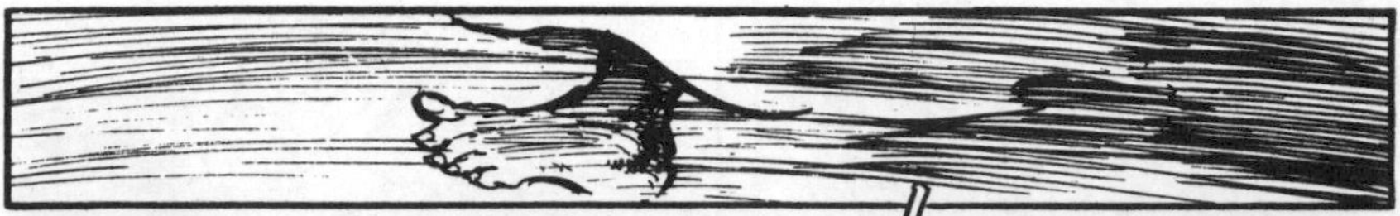

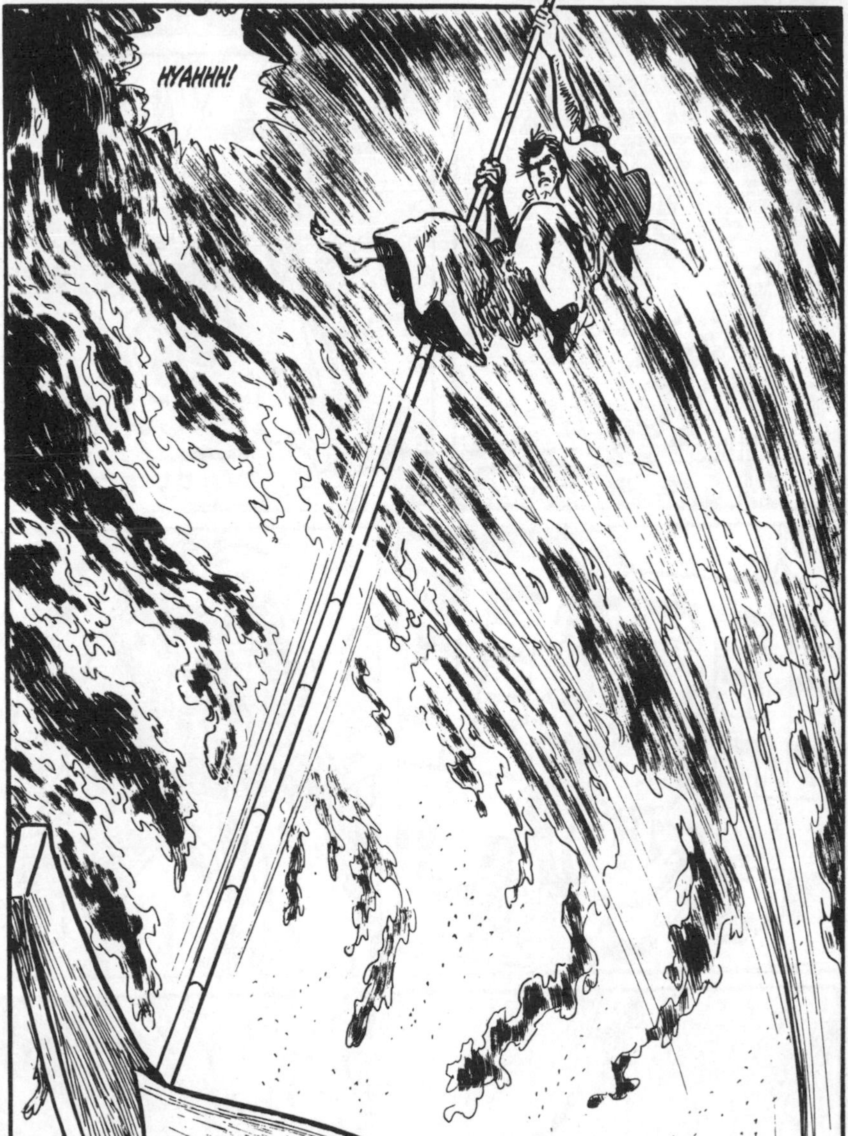
HYAHHH!

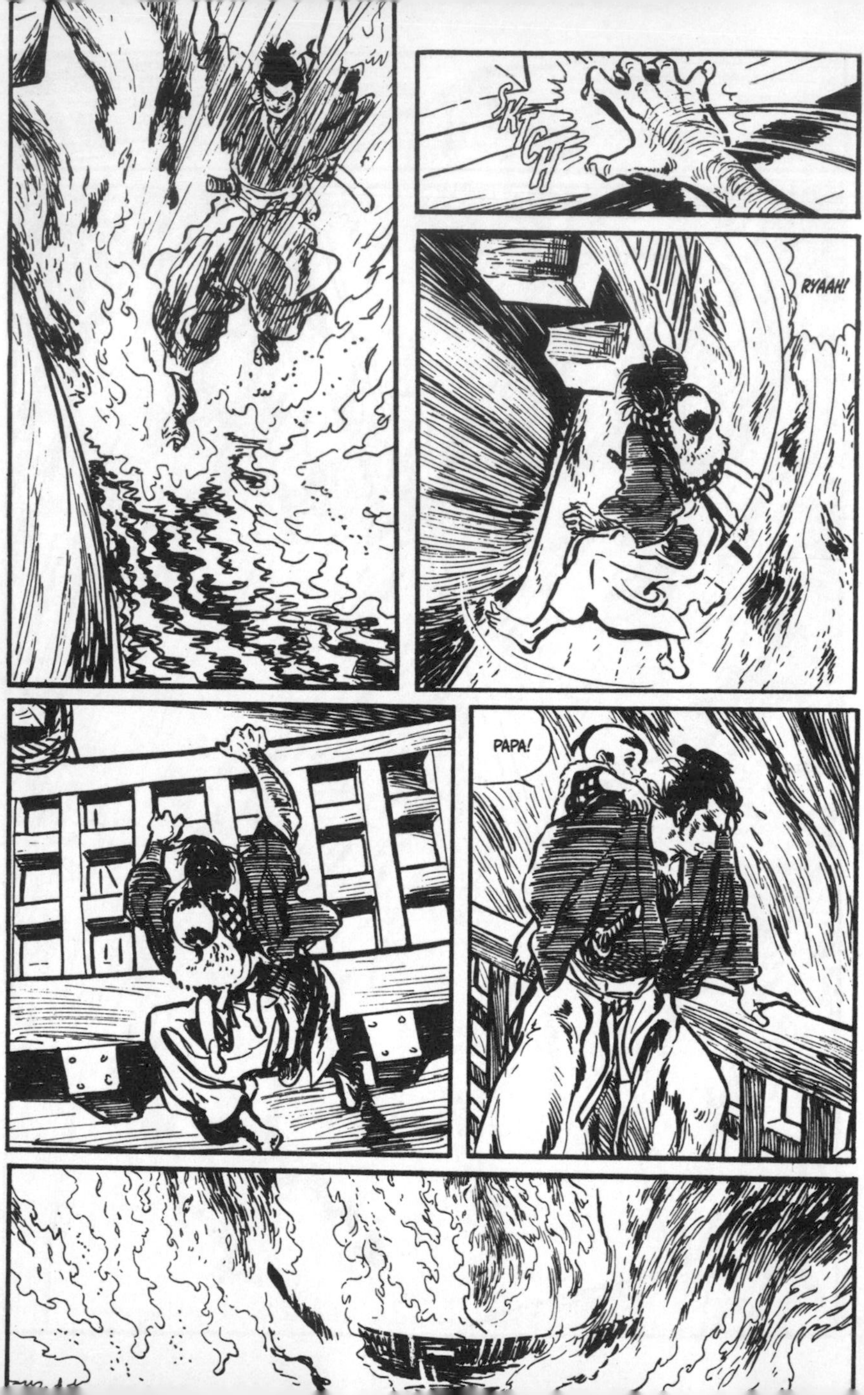
SKTCH
RYAAH!
PAPA!

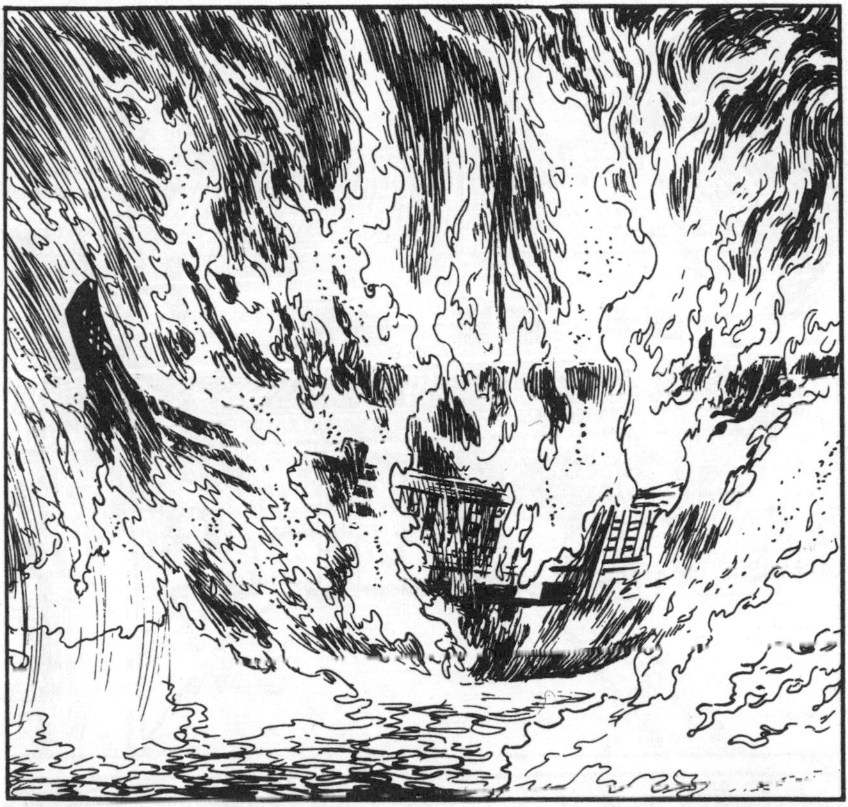

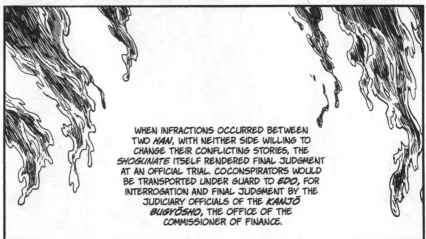

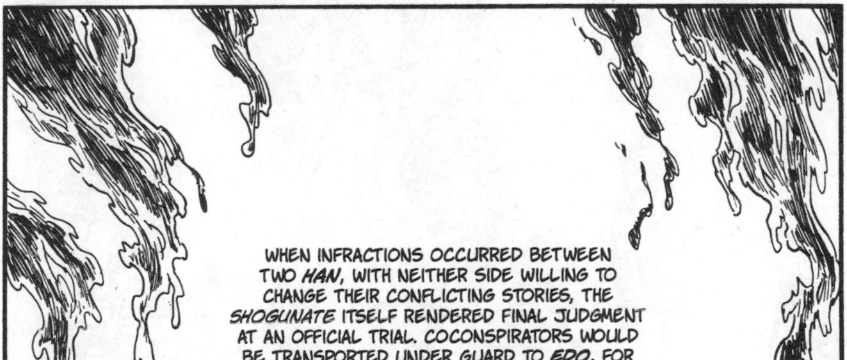
WHEN INFRACTIONS OCCURRED BETWEEN TWO *HAN*, WITH NEITHER SIDE WILLING TO CHANGE THEIR CONFLICTING STORIES, THE *SHOGUNATE* ITSELF RENDERED FINAL JUDGMENT AT AN OFFICIAL TRIAL. COCONSPIRATORS WOULD BE TRANSPORTED UNDER GUARD TO *EDO*, FOR INTERROGATION AND FINAL JUDGMENT BY THE JUDICIARY OFFICIALS OF THE *KANJŌ BUGYŌSHO*, THE OFFICE OF THE COMMISSIONER OF FINANCE.

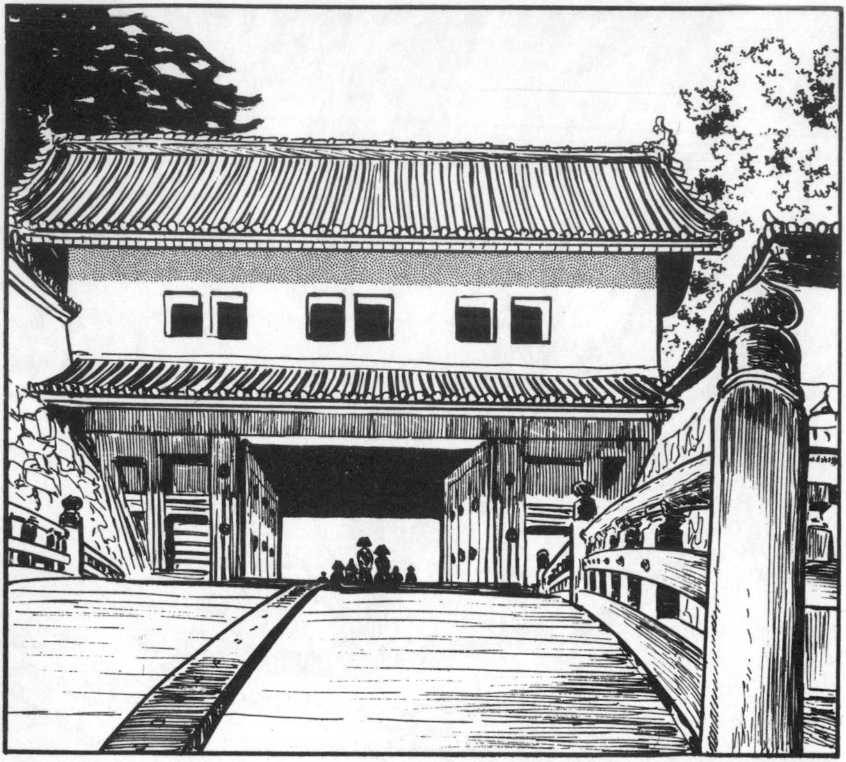
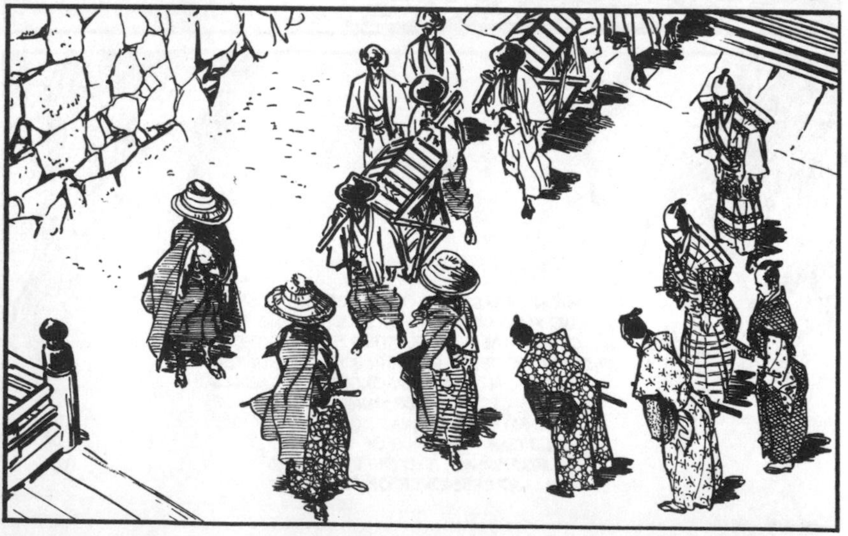

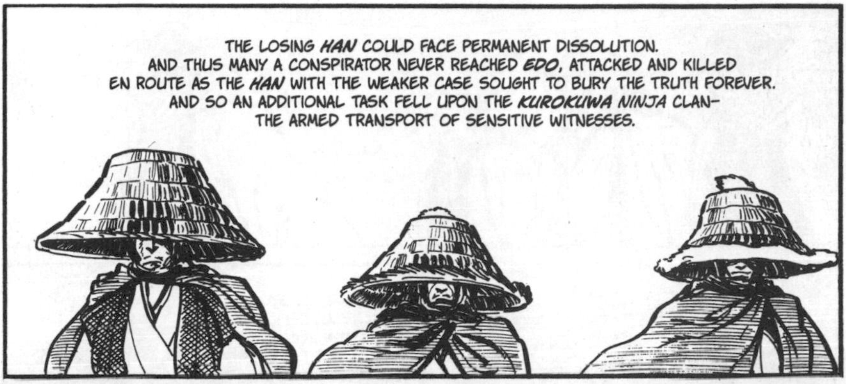
THE LOSING *HAN* COULD FACE PERMANENT DISSOLUTION.
AND THUS MANY A CONSPIRATOR NEVER REACHED *EDO*, ATTACKED AND KILLED EN ROUTE AS THE *HAN* WITH THE WEAKER CASE SOUGHT TO BURY THE TRUTH FOREVER.
AND SO AN ADDITIONAL TASK FELL UPON THE *KUROKUWA NINJA* CLAN— THE ARMED TRANSPORT OF SENSITIVE WITNESSES.
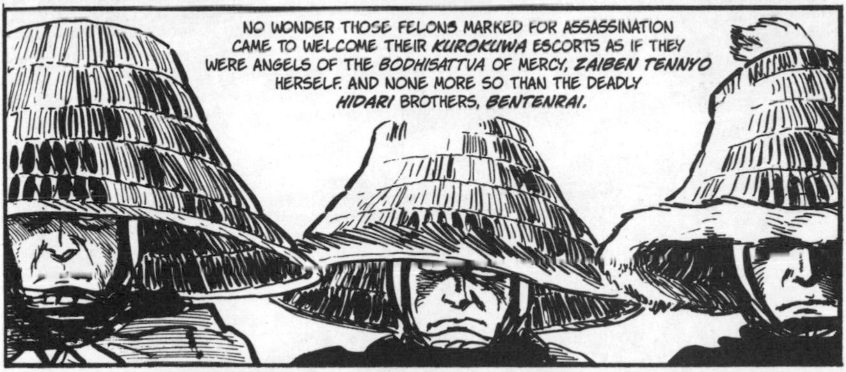
NO WONDER THOSE FELONS MARKED FOR ASSASSINATION CAME TO WELCOME THEIR *KUROKUWA* ESCORTS AS IF THEY WERE ANGELS OF THE *BODHISATTVA* OF MERCY, *ZAIBEN TENNYO* HERSELF. AND NONE MORE SO THAN THE DEADLY *HIDARI* BROTHERS, *BENTENRAI*.
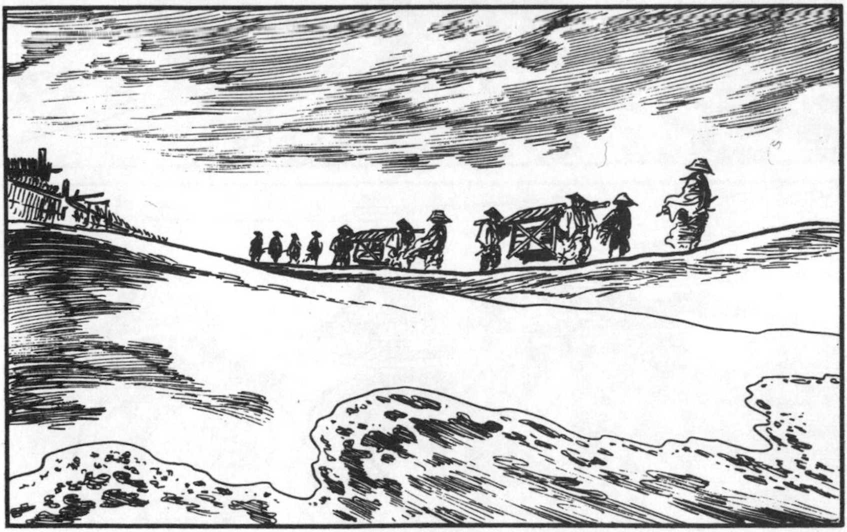

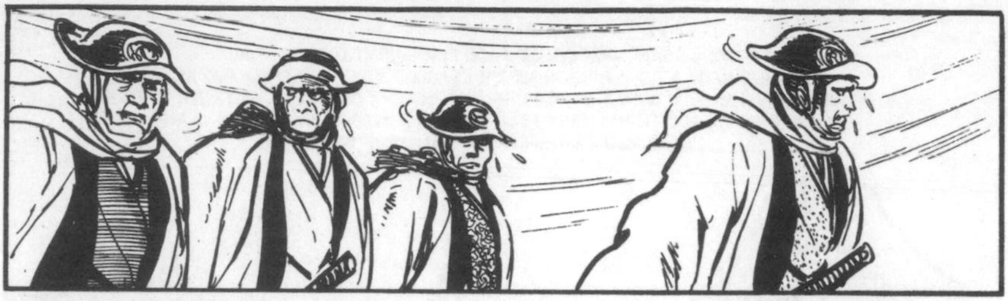

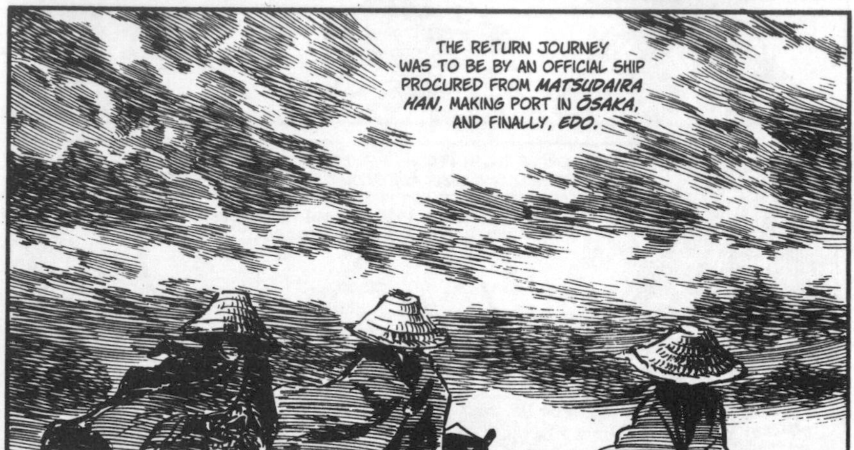
THE RETURN JOURNEY WAS TO BE BY AN OFFICIAL SHIP PROCURED FROM *MATSUDAIRA HAN*, MAKING PORT IN *ŌSAKA*, AND FINALLY, *EDO*.

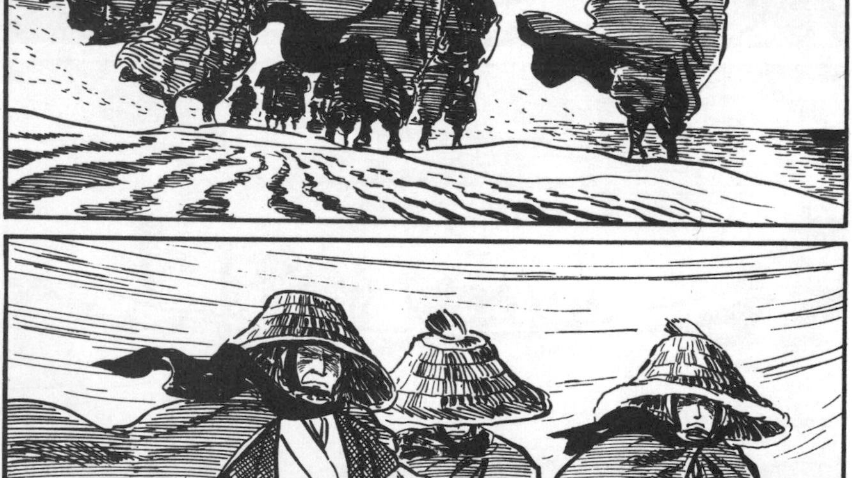

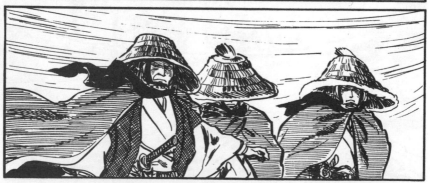

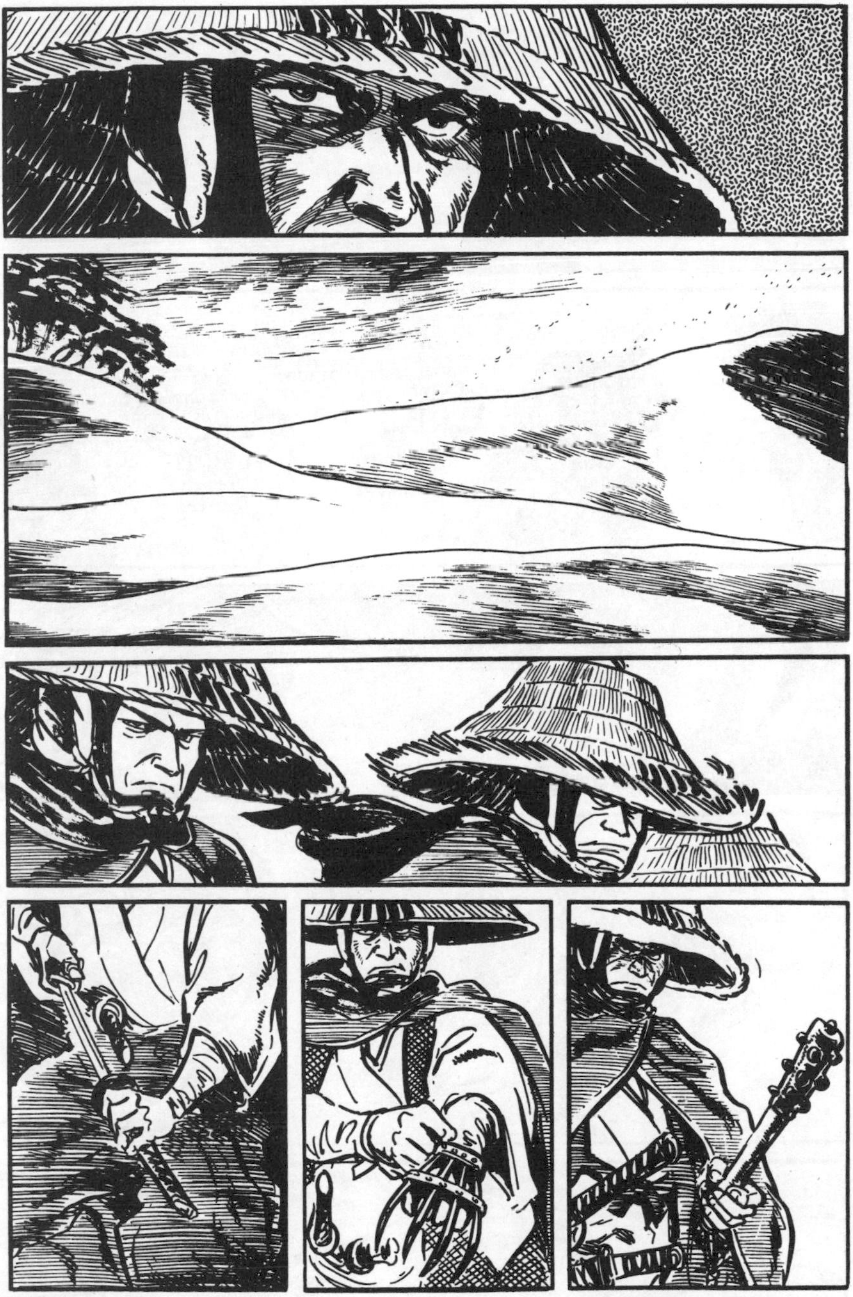

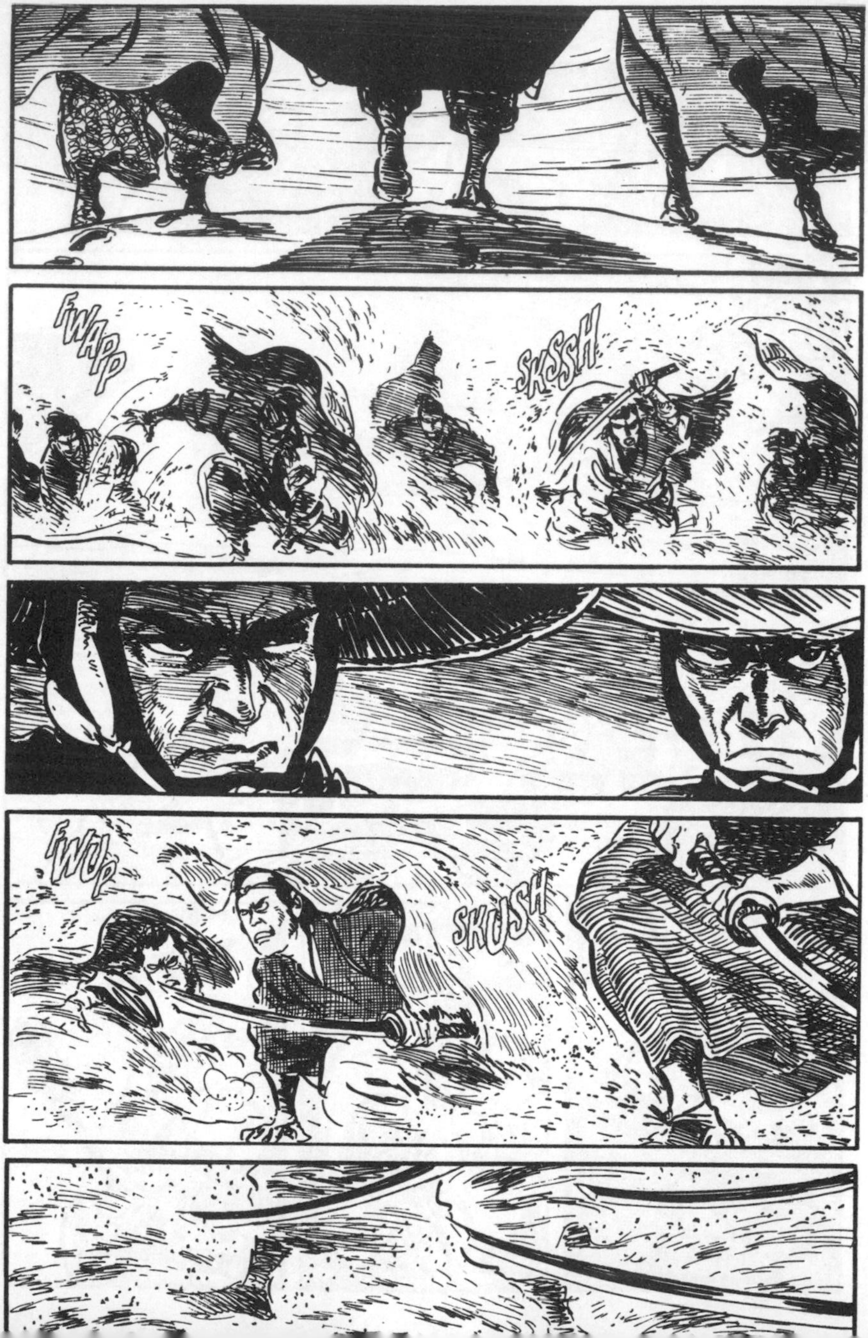
SKSSH
FWAPP
SKUSH
FWUP

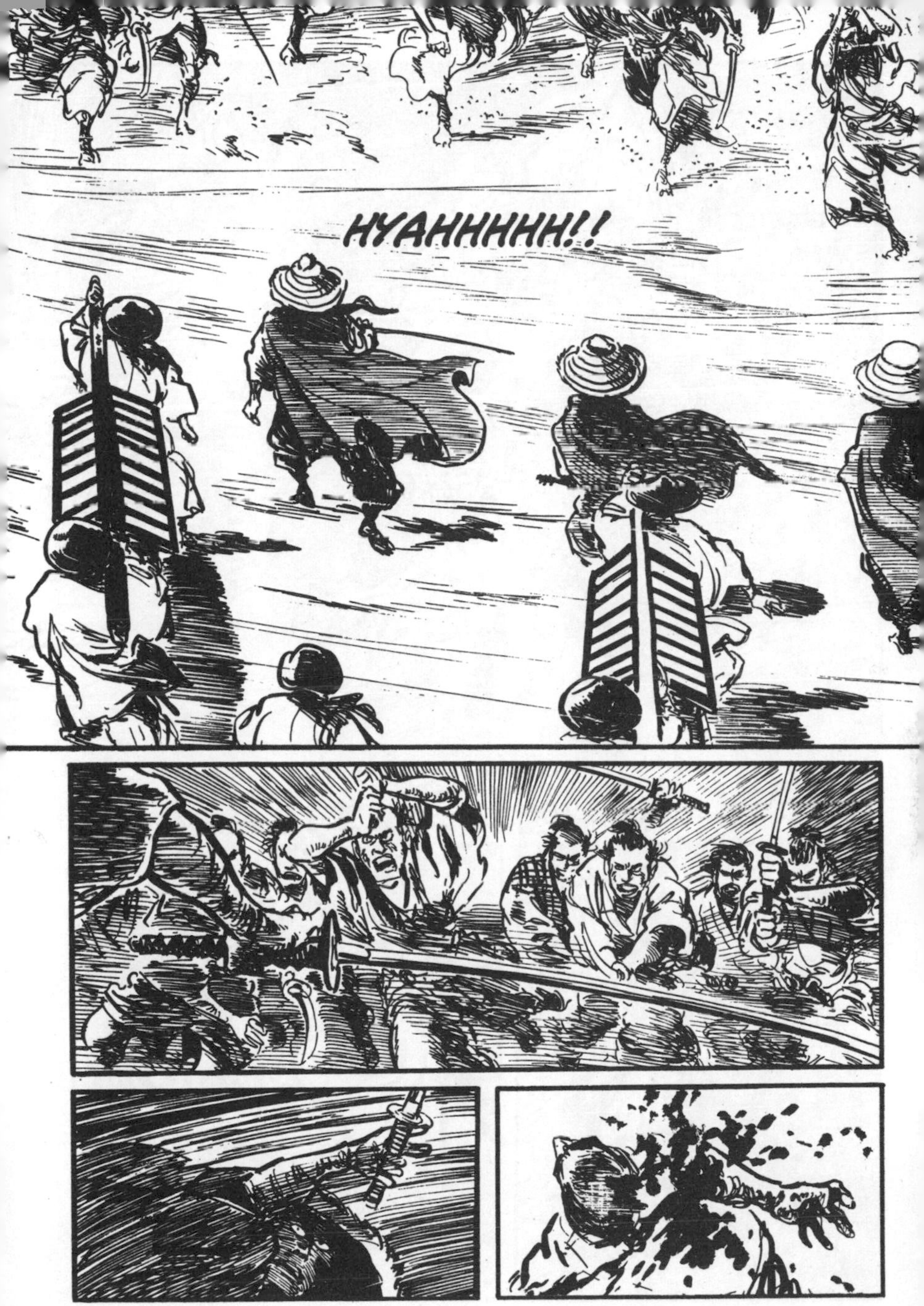
HYAHHHHH!!

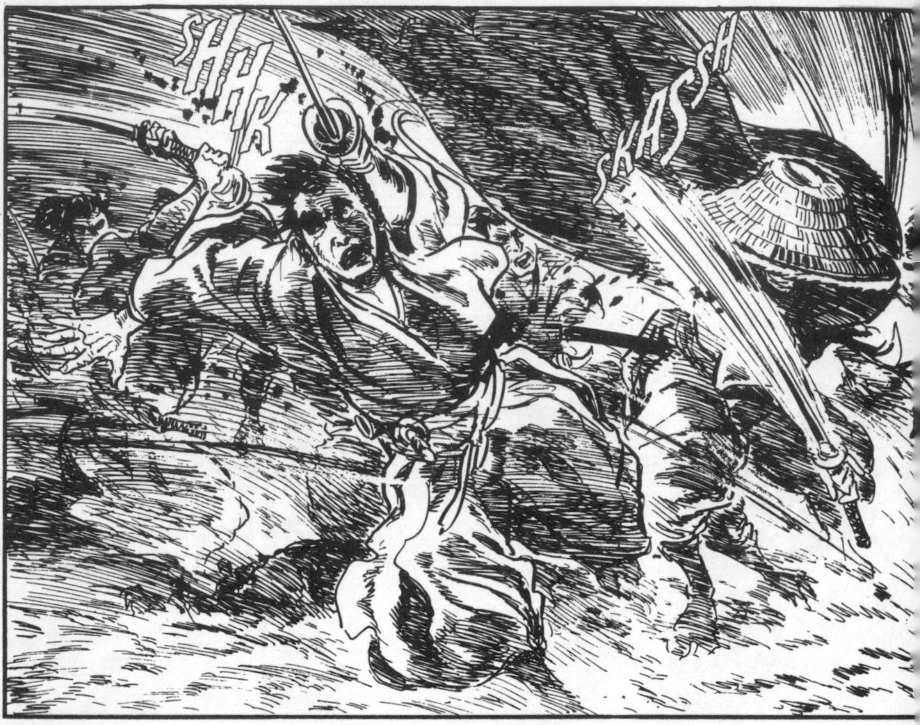
SHHK
SKASSH
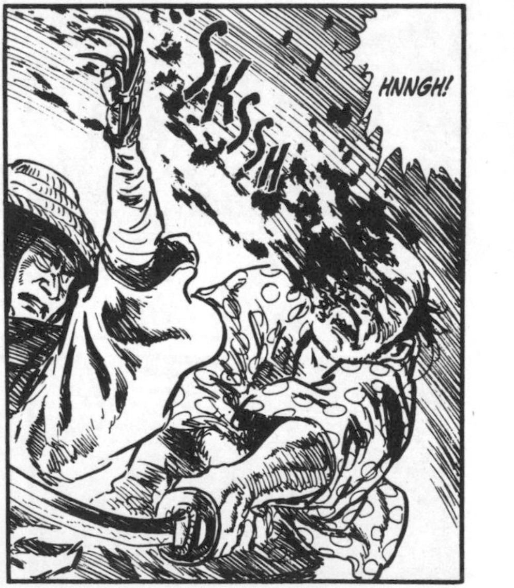
SKSSH
HNNGH!
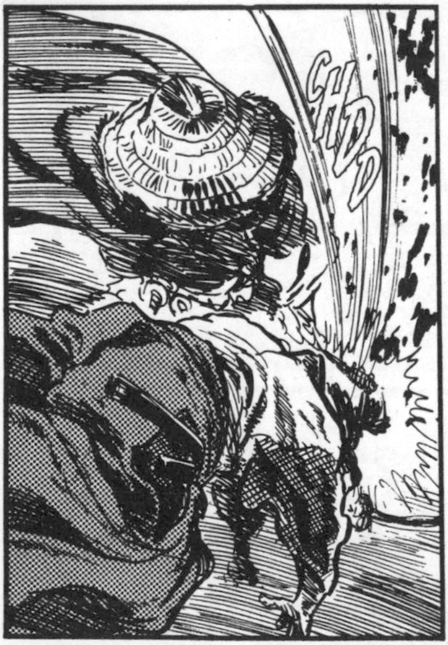
CHDD

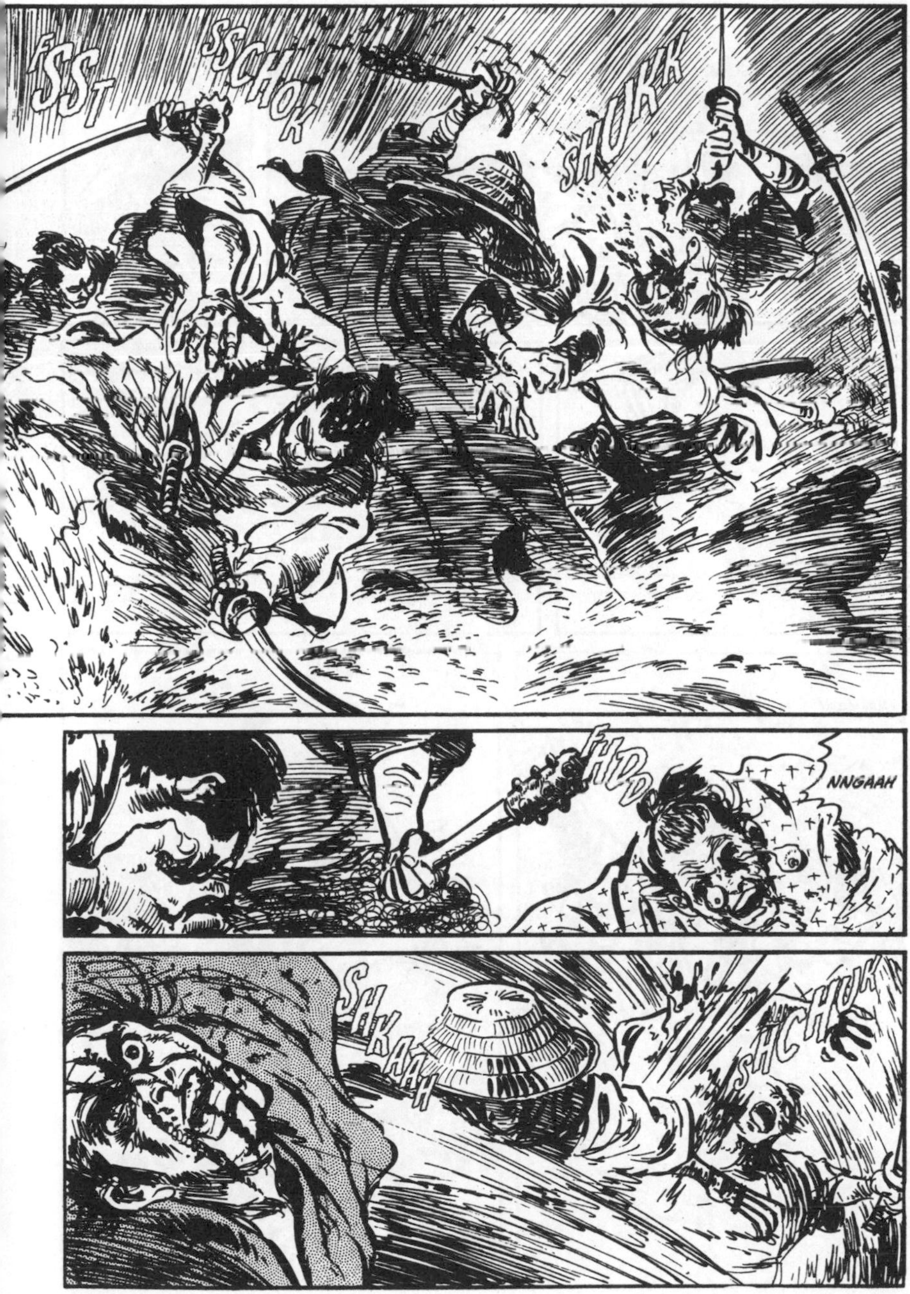
SHUKK
SSCHOK
FSST
NNGAAH
FHDD
SHCHUK
SHKAAH

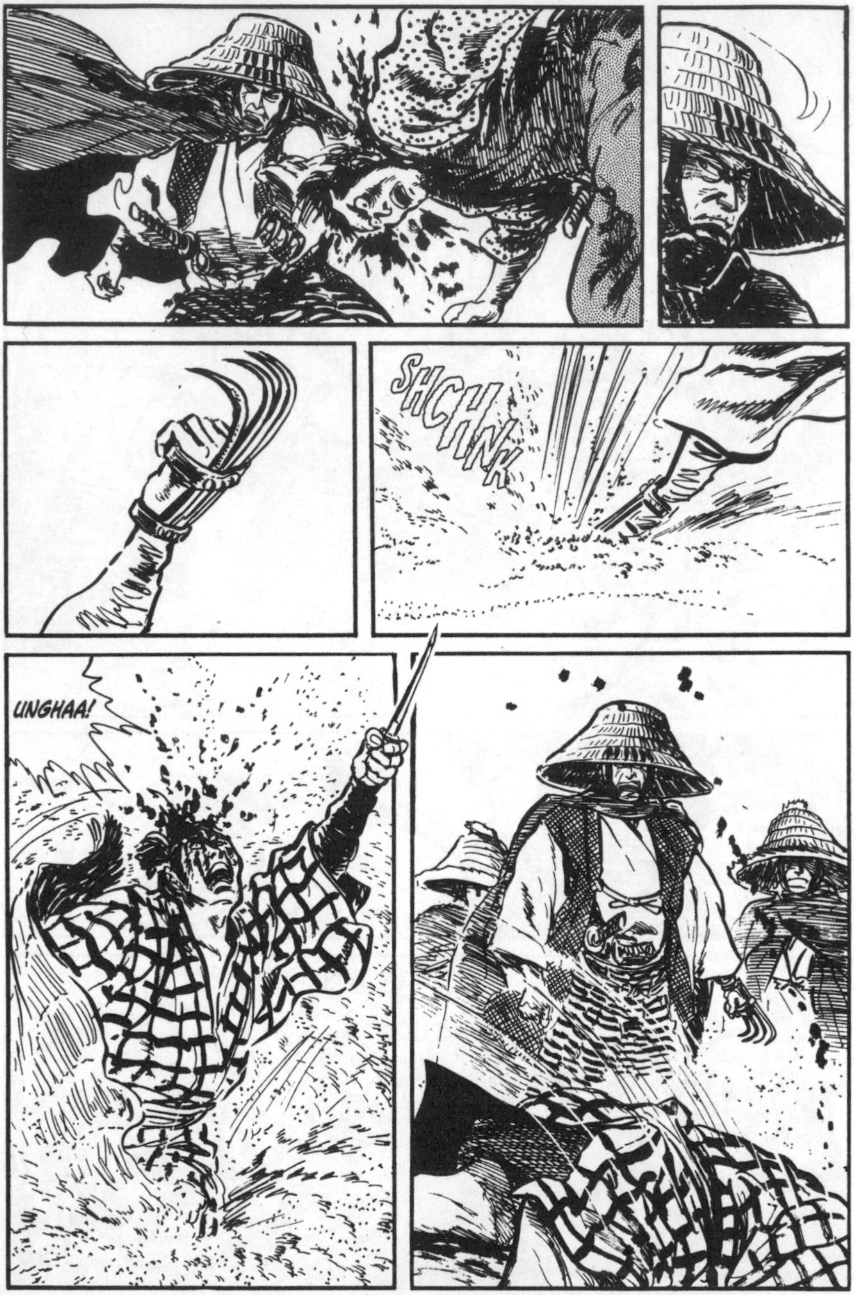
SHCHINK
UNGHAA!

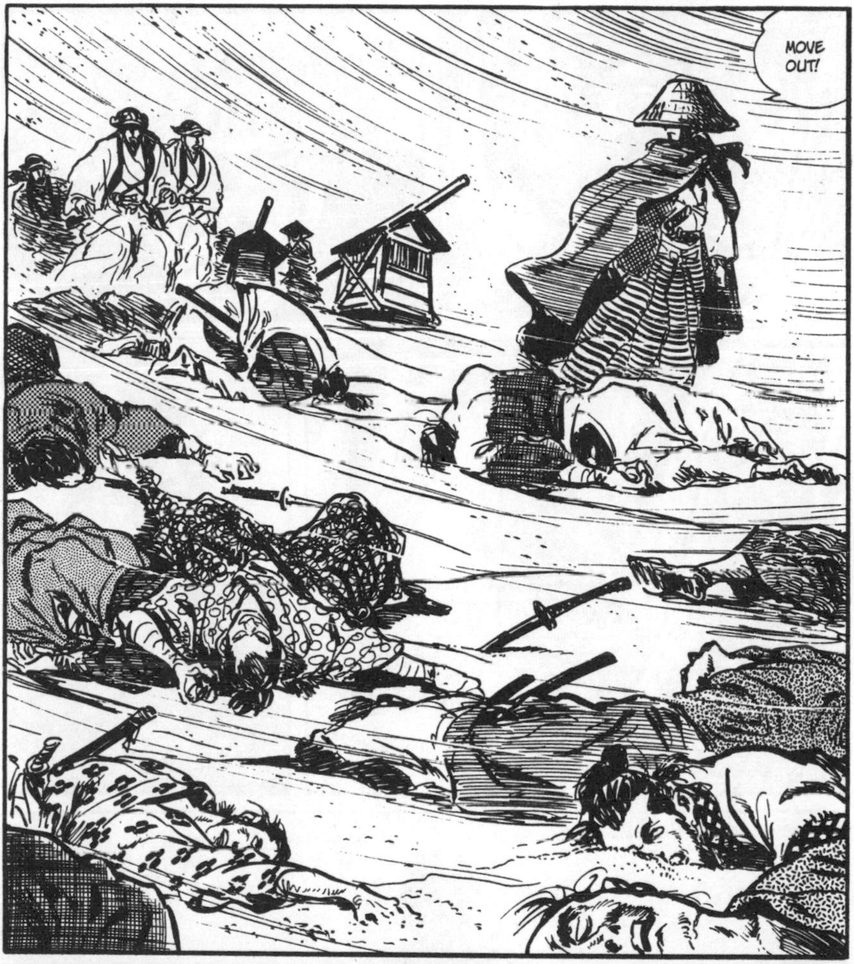
MOVE OUT!

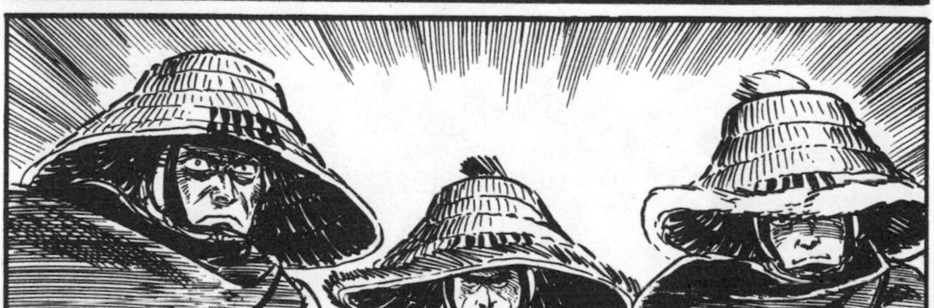

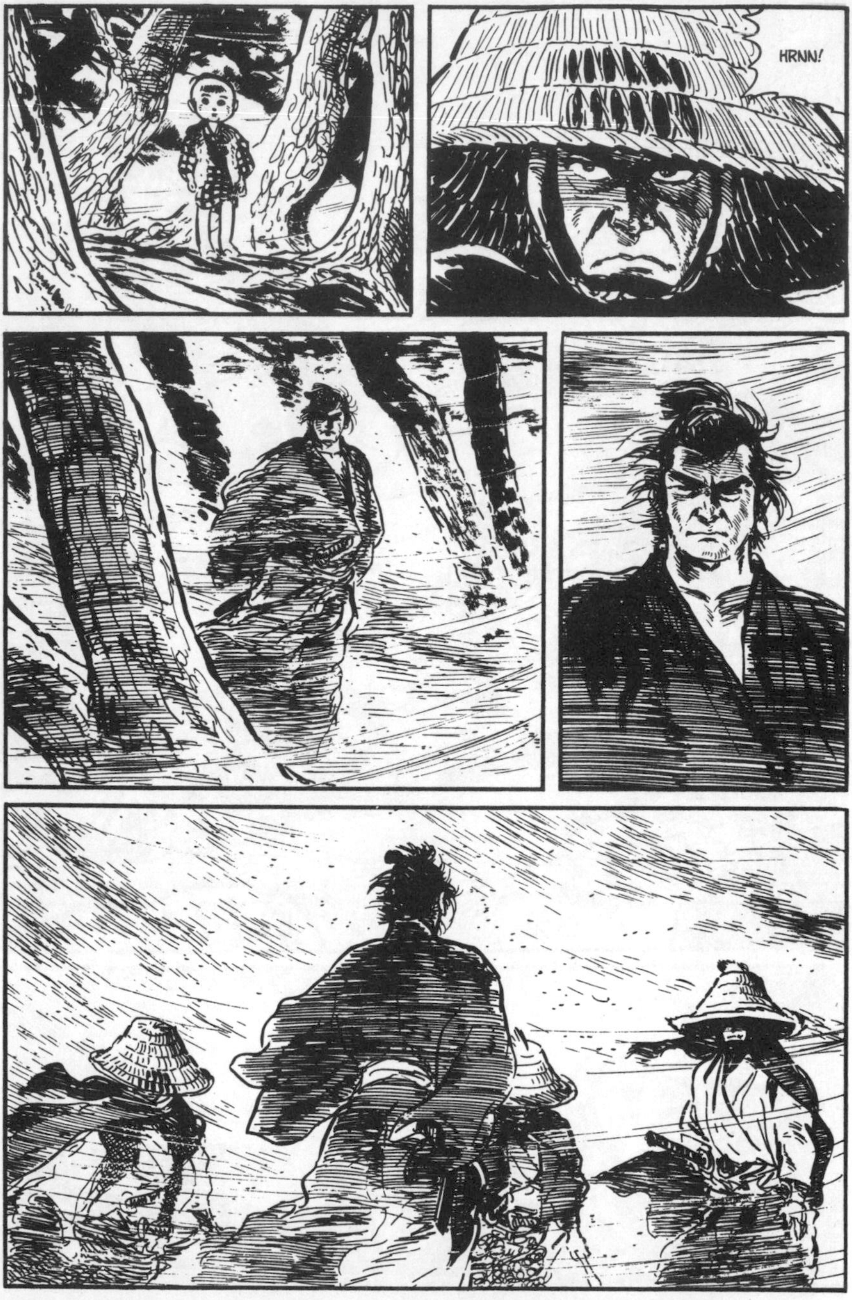
HRNN!

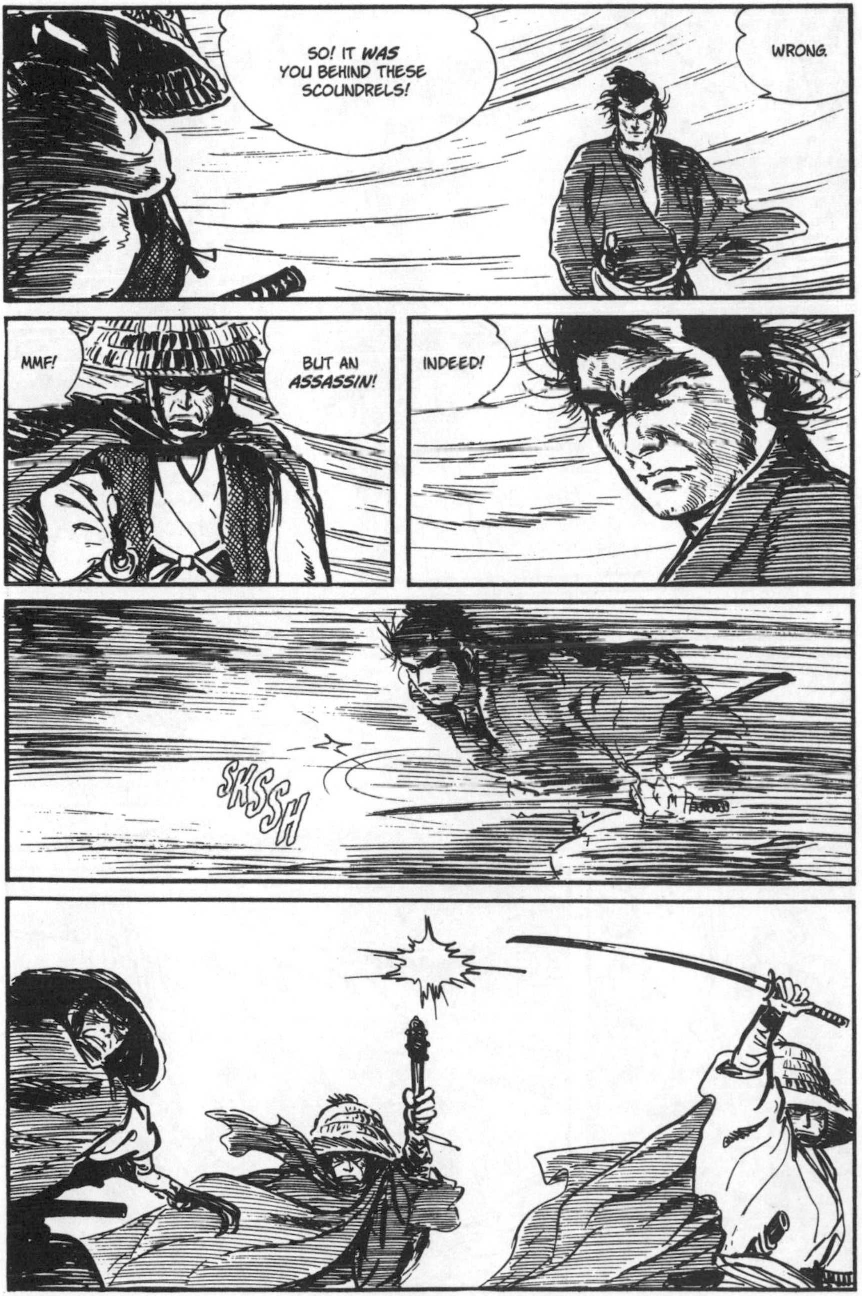
SO! IT WAS YOU BEHIND THESE SCOUNDRELS!
WRONG.
MMF!
BUT AN ASSASSIN!
INDEED!
SKSSH

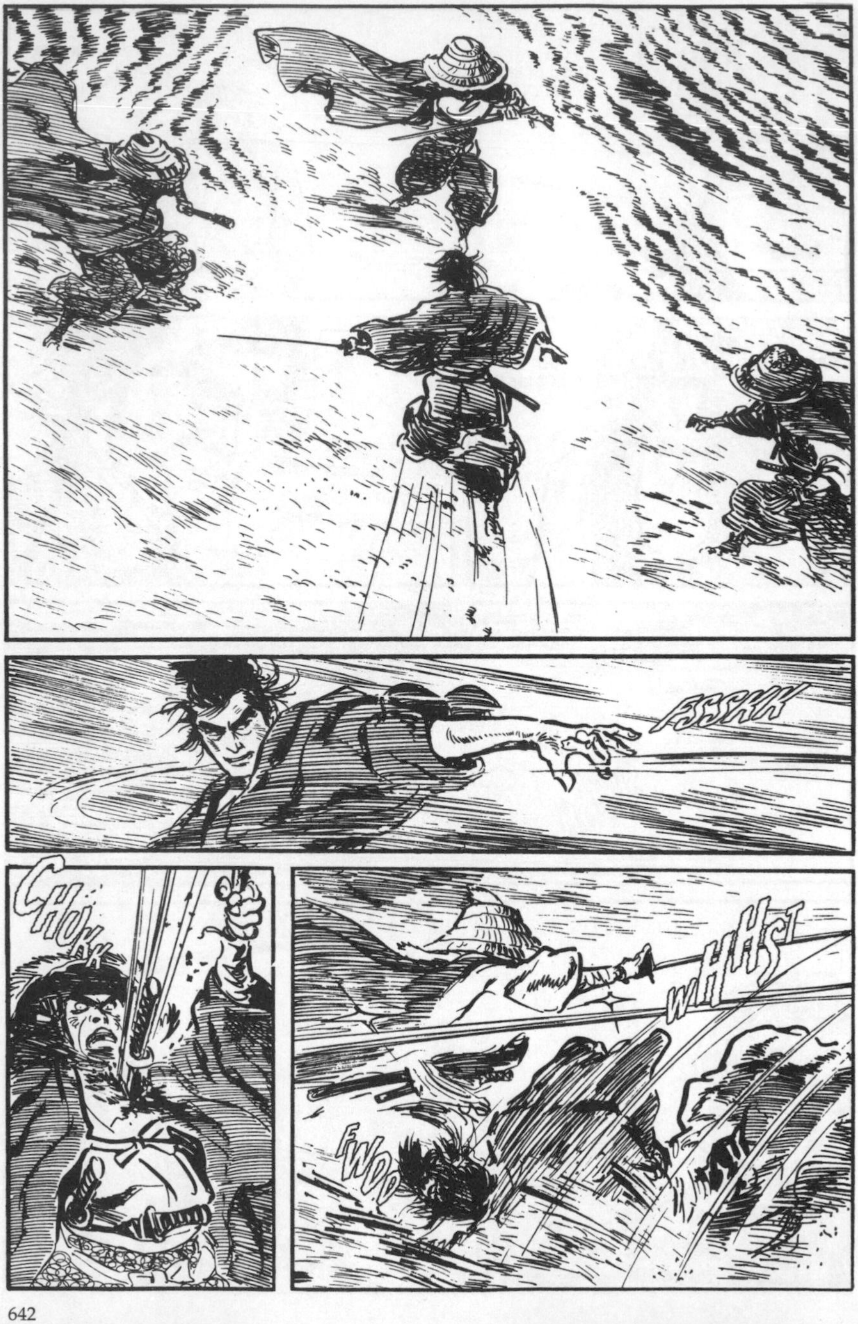
FSSKK
WHHST
FWOO
CHOKK

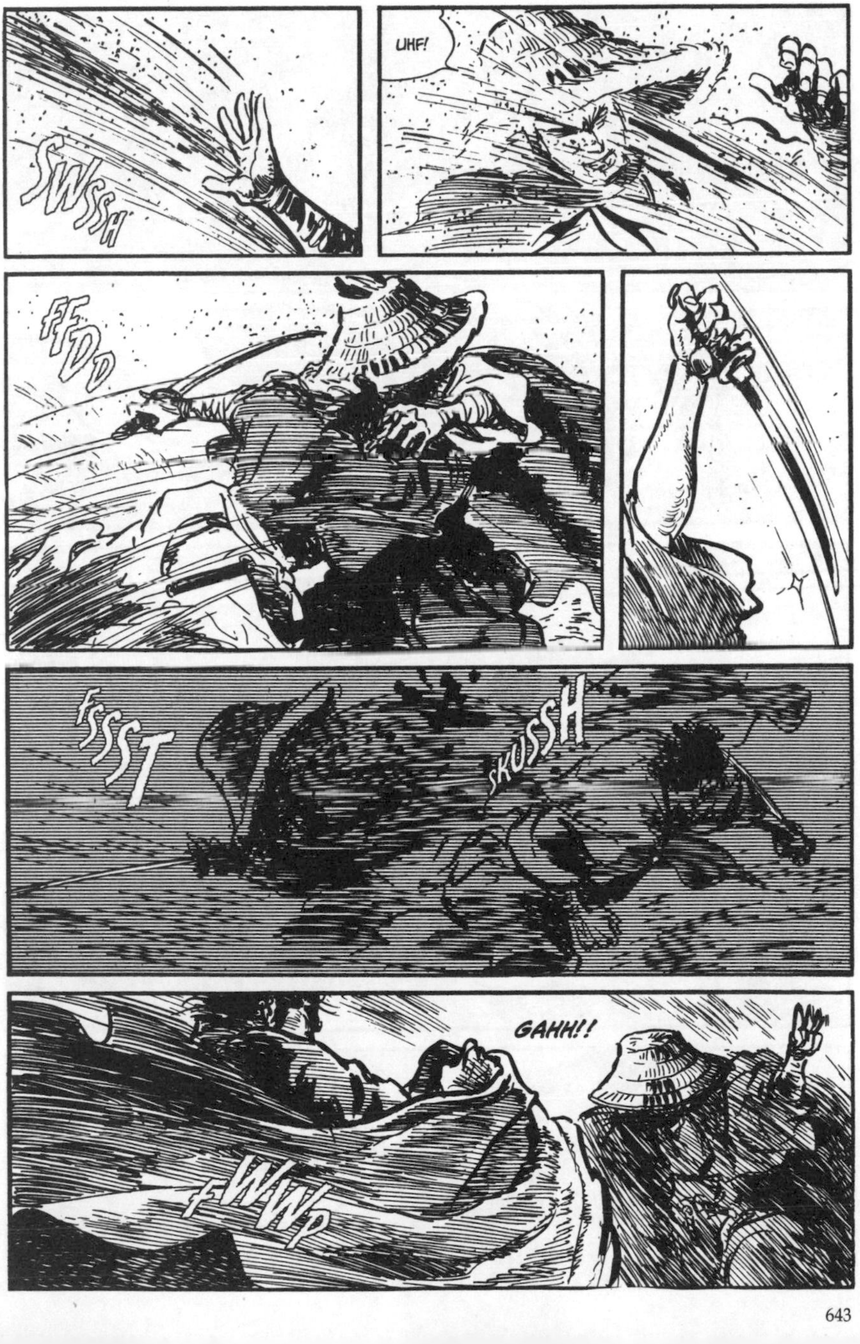
UHF!
SWSSH
FFDD
SKUSSH
FSSST
GAHH!!
FWWP

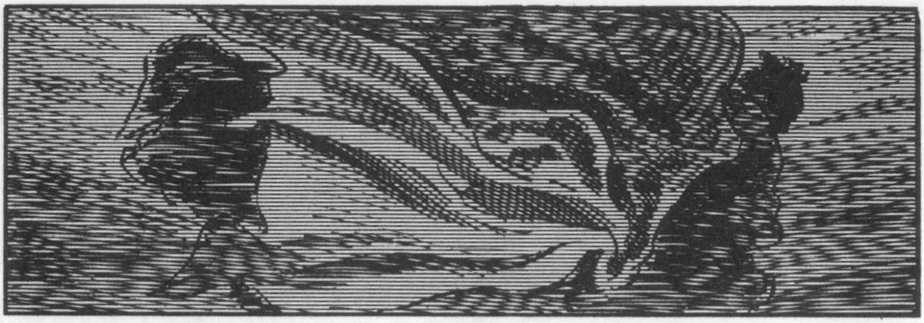

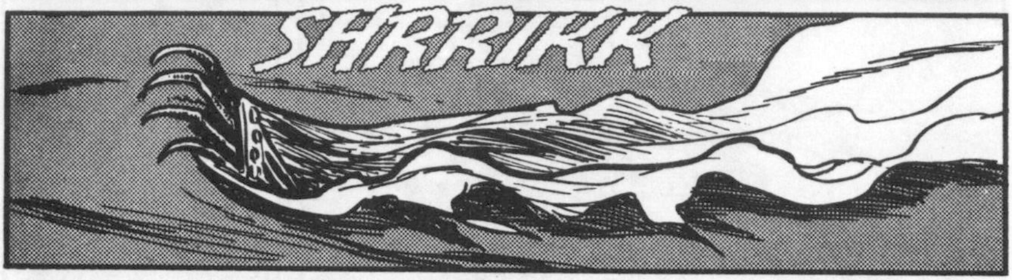
SHRRIKK

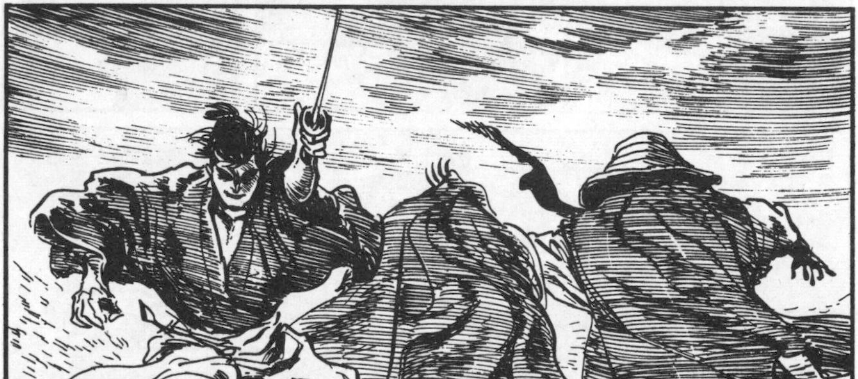

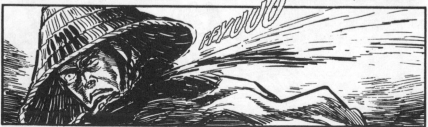

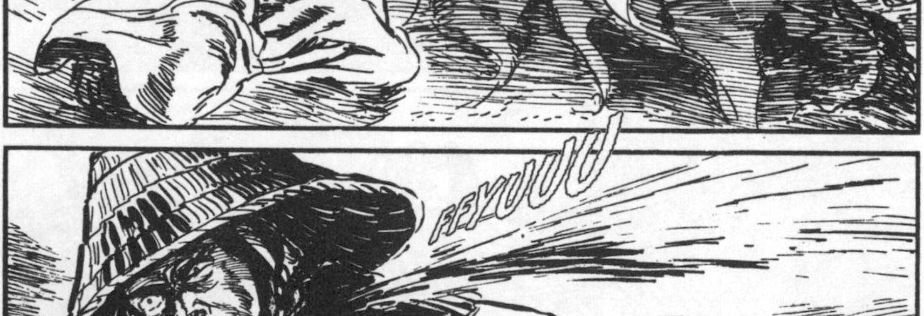
FFYUUU

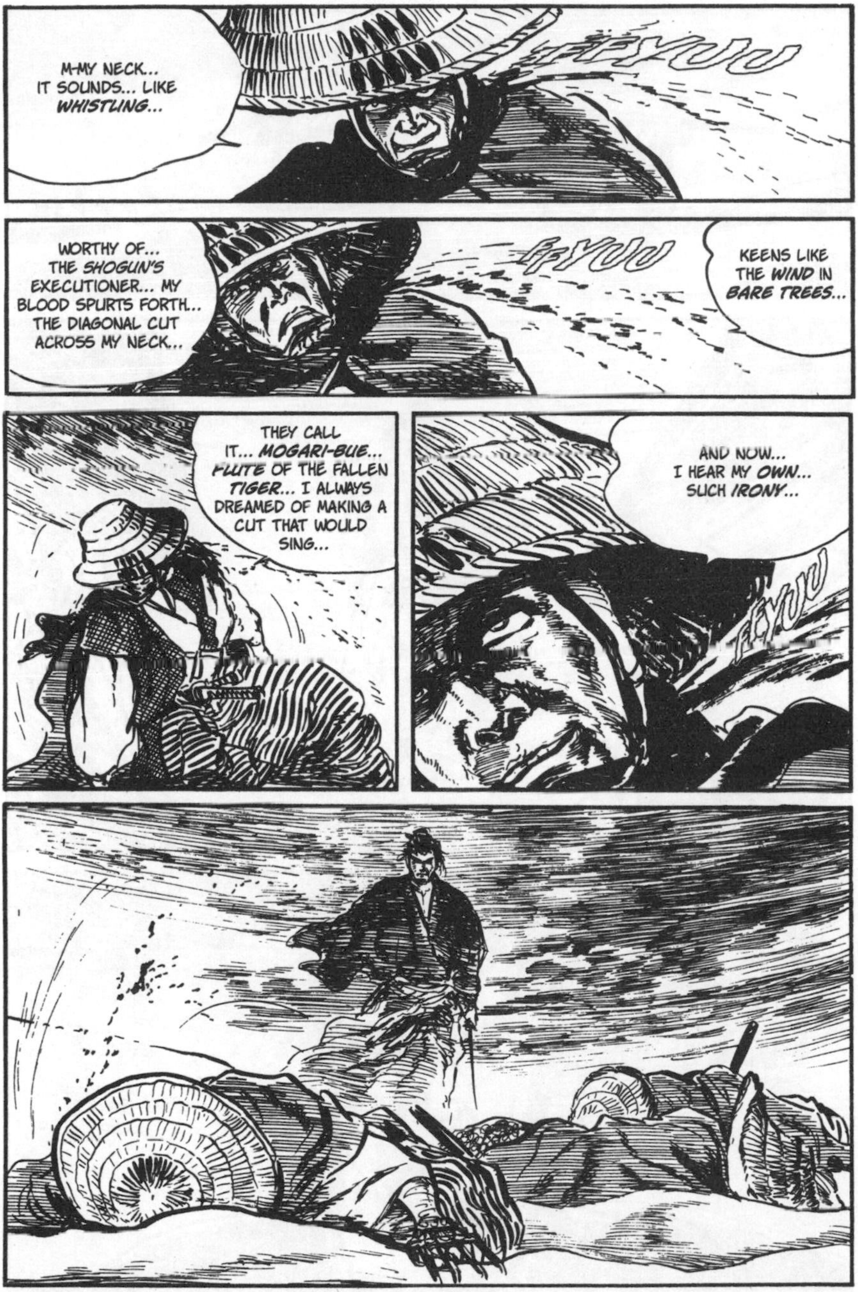
M-MY NECK... IT SOUNDS... LIKE *WHISTLING*...
FFYUU
WORTHY OF... THE *SHOGUN'S* EXECUTIONER... MY BLOOD SPURTS FORTH... THE DIAGONAL CUT ACROSS MY NECK...
FFYUU
KEENS LIKE THE *WIND* IN *BARE TREES*...
THEY CALL IT... *MOGARI-BUE*... *FLUTE* OF THE FALLEN *TIGER*... I ALWAYS DREAMED OF MAKING A CUT THAT WOULD SING...
AND NOW... I HEAR MY *OWN*... SUCH *IRONY*...
FFYUU

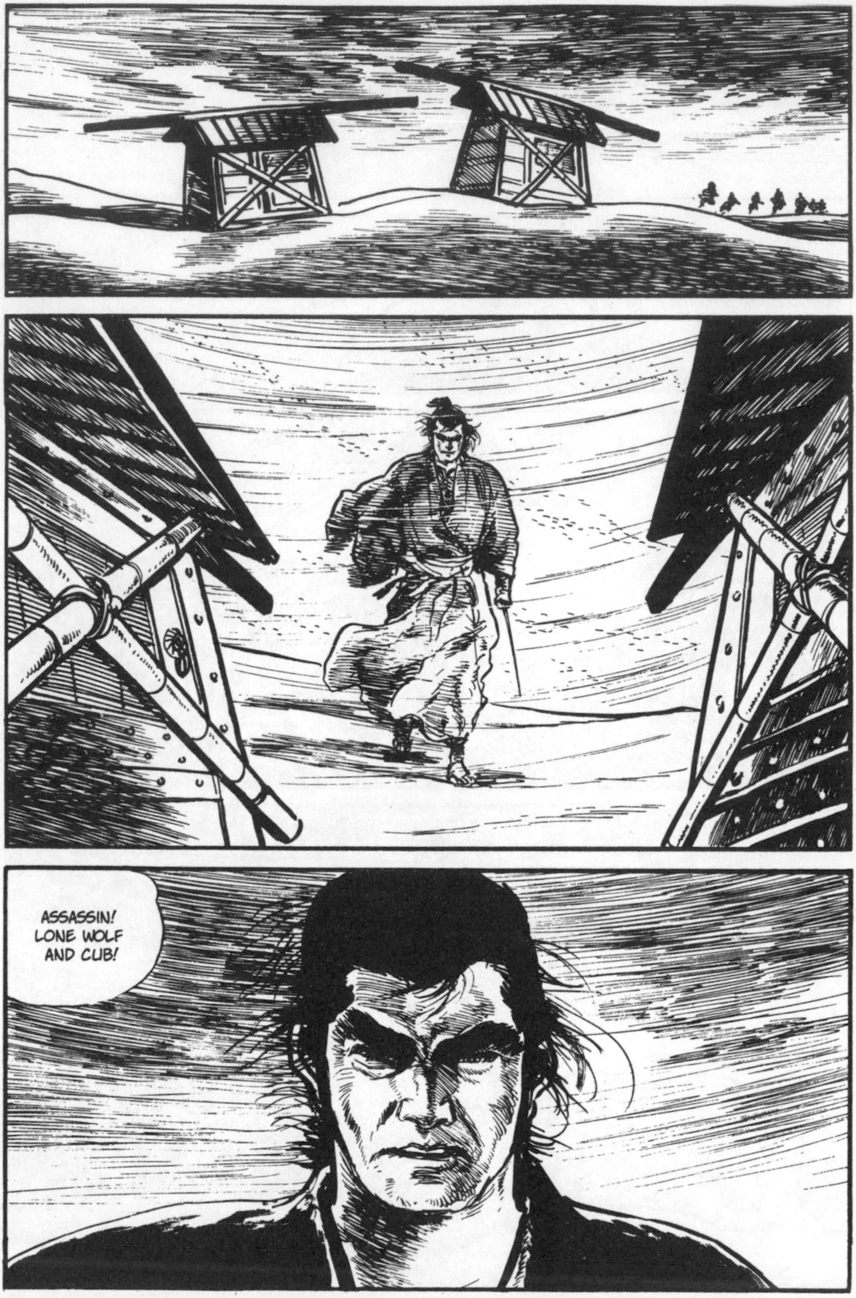
ASSASSIN! LONE WOLF AND CUB!

Half Mat, One Mat,
a Fistful of Rice

16

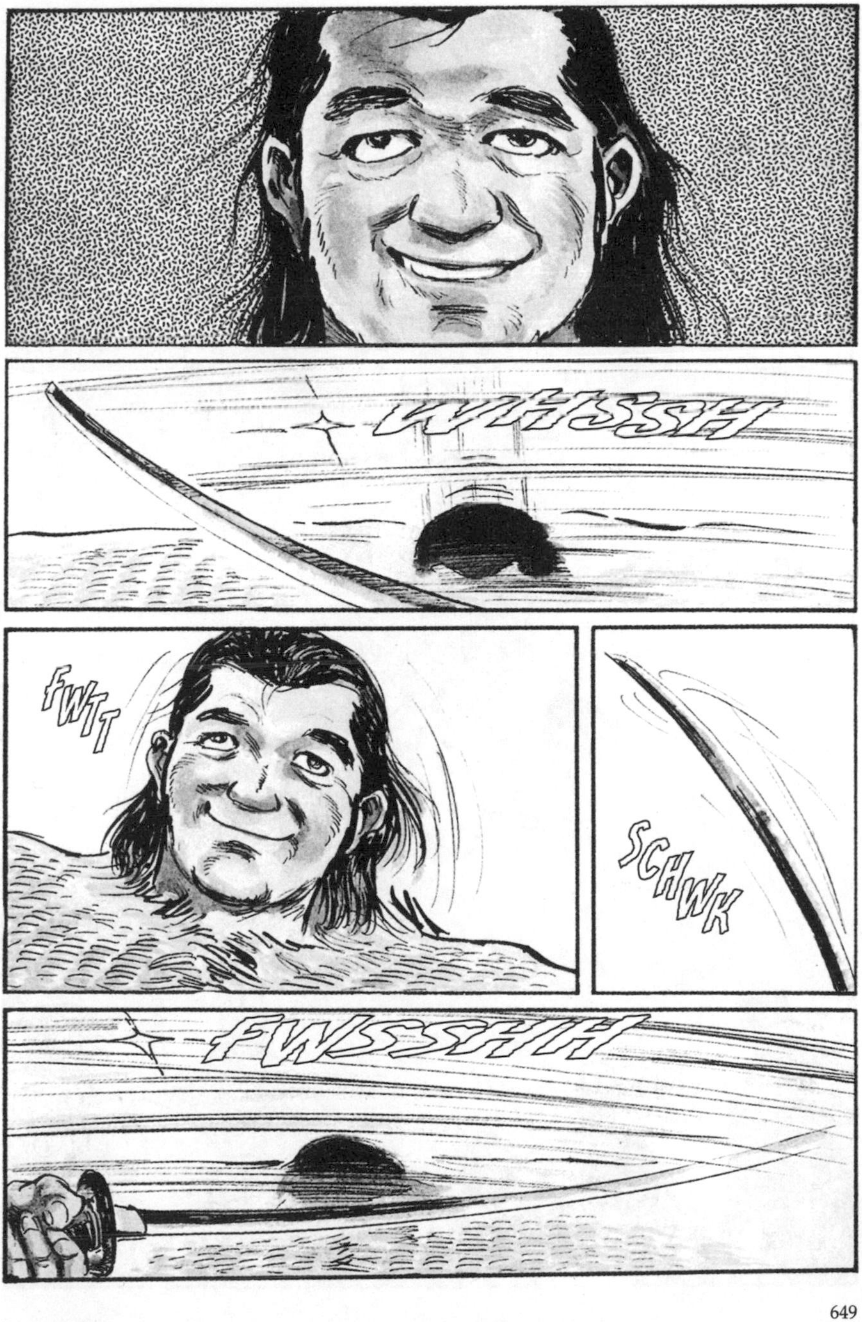
WHSSSH
SCHWK
FWTT
FWSSHH

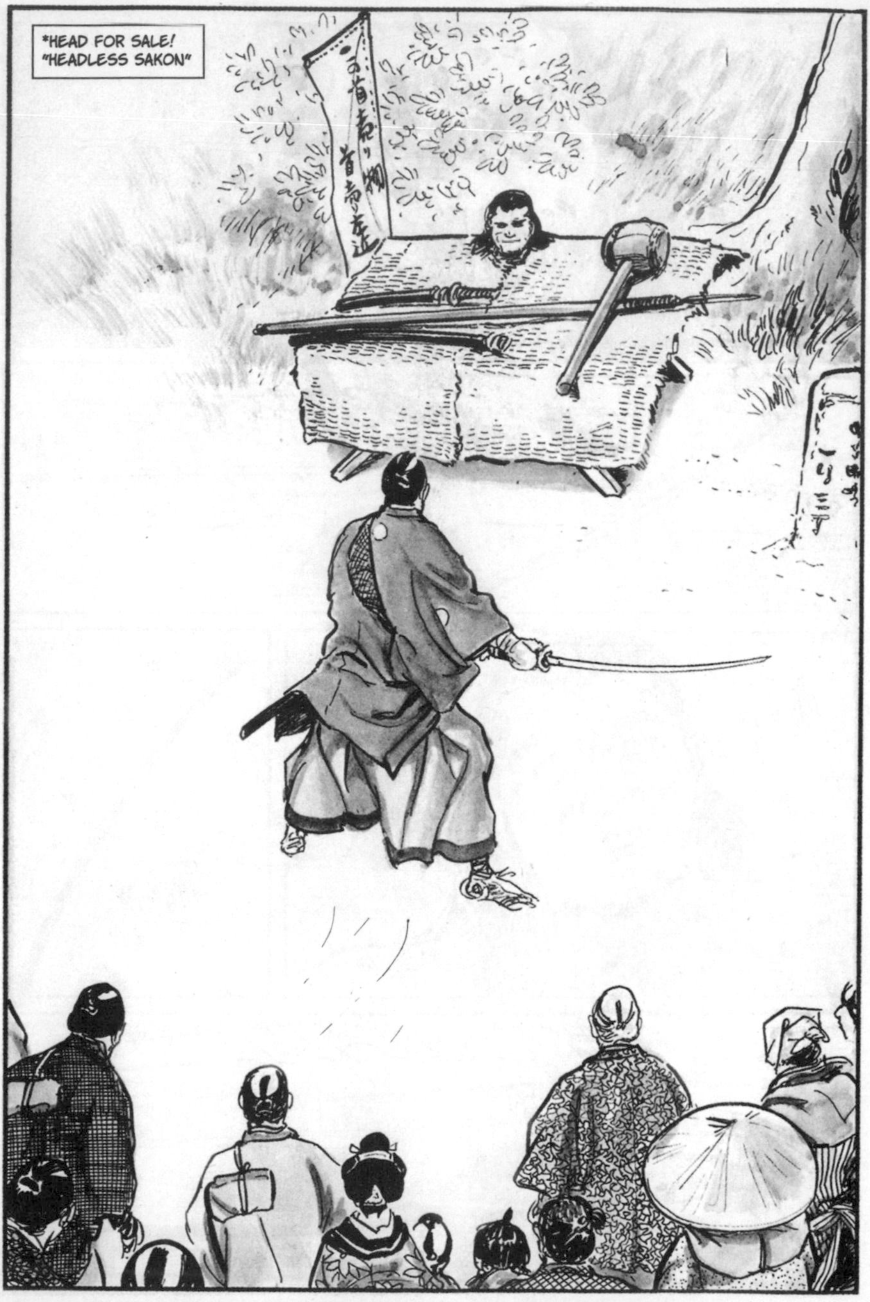
*HEAD FOR SALE!
"HEADLESS SAKON"

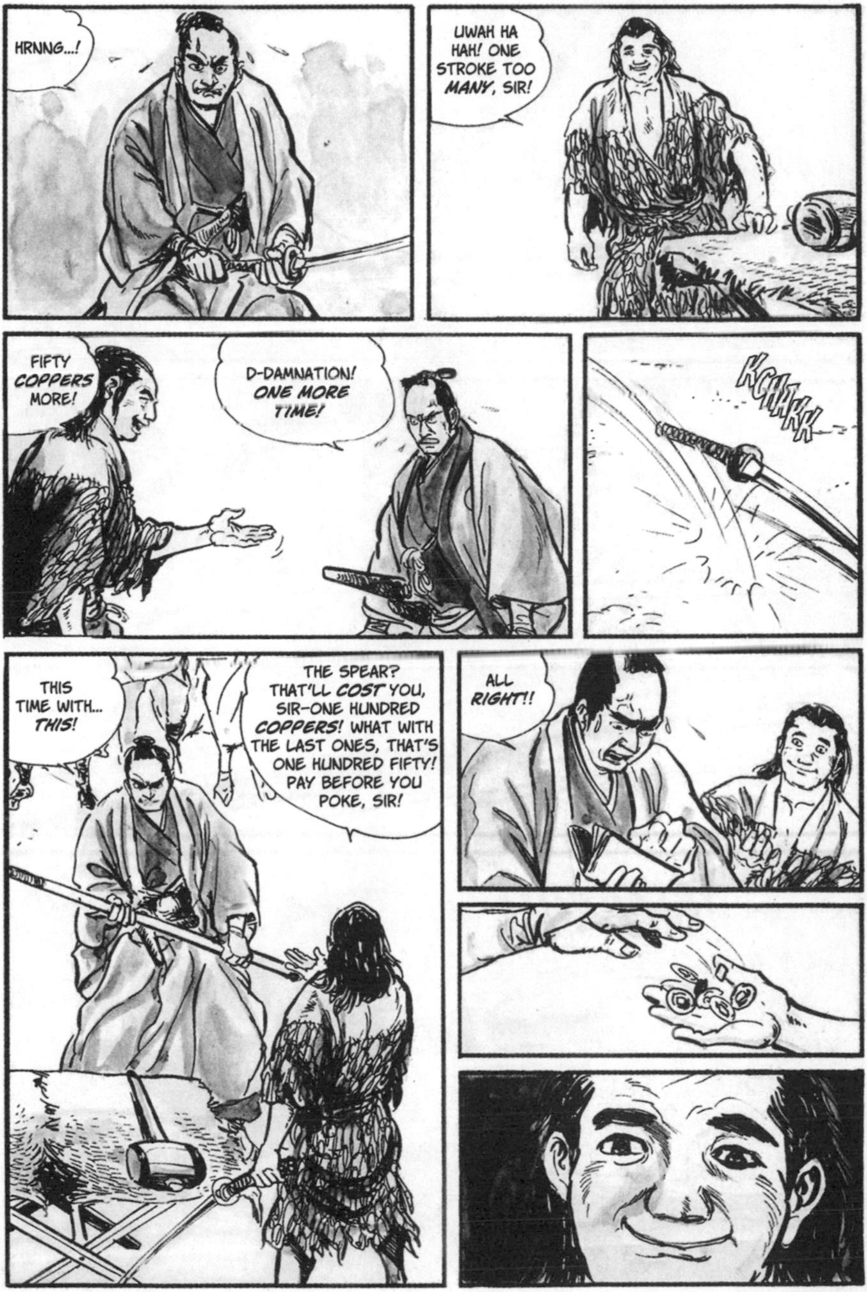
HRNNG...!
UWAH HA HAH! ONE STROKE TOO MANY, SIR!
FIFTY COPPERS MORE!
D-DAMNATION! ONE MORE TIME!
KCHHKK
THIS TIME WITH... THIS!
THE SPEAR? THAT'LL COST YOU, SIR–ONE HUNDRED COPPERS! WHAT WITH THE LAST ONES, THAT'S ONE HUNDRED FIFTY! PAY BEFORE YOU POKE, SIR!
ALL RIGHT!!

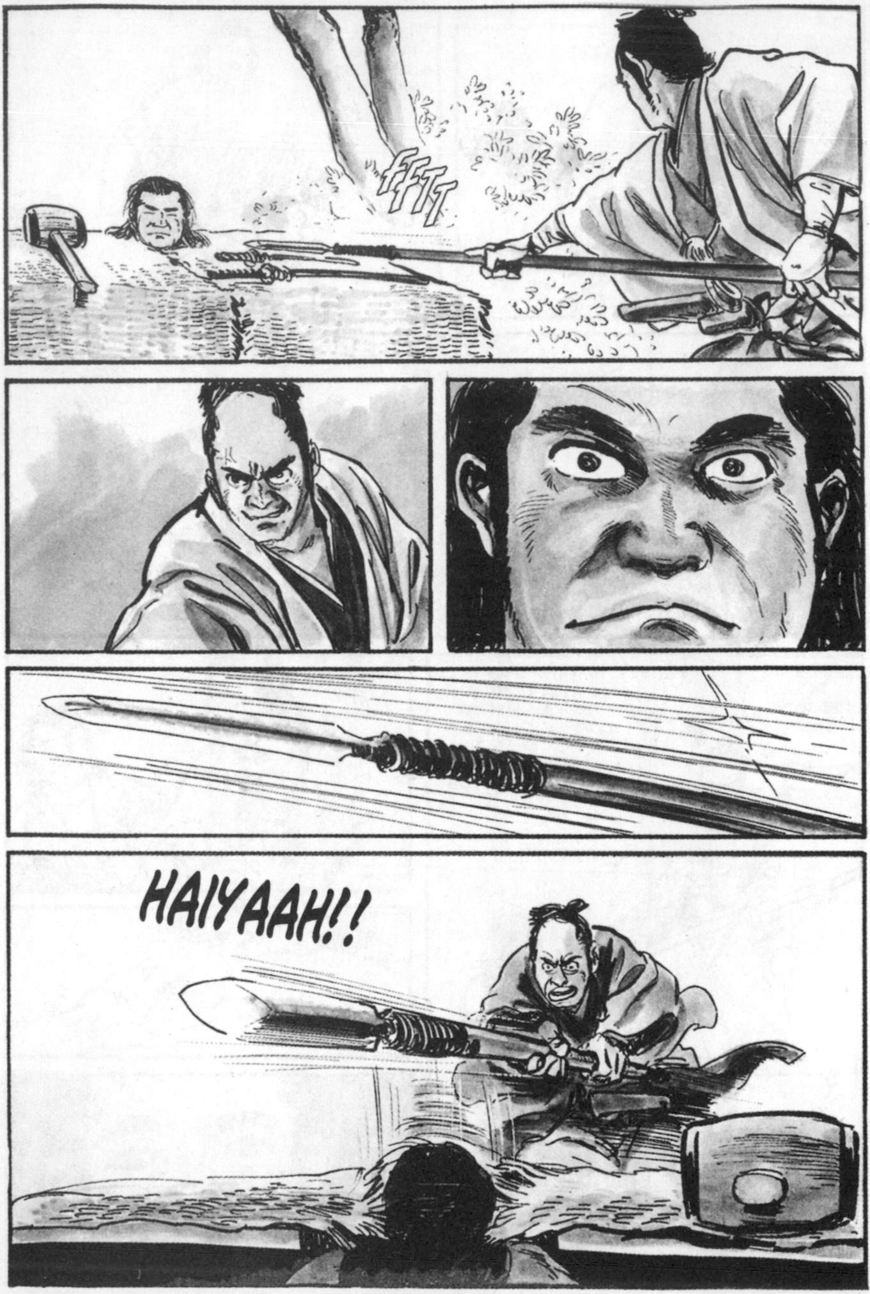
FFTT
HAIYAAH!!

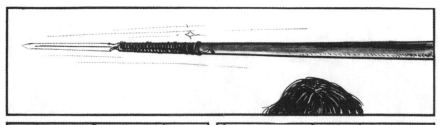

LORDY!

NEVER SEEN NUTHIN' LIKE IT!

LAND! GET COLD SWEATS JUST WATCHING.

SCARES THE WILLIES OUTTA *ME*!

KTHKK

WAH HAH HAH! *PRACTICE,* GREENHORN!

HAH HAH HAH HAH!

STEP RIGHT UP! *STEP* RIGHT UP! NO ONE LEFT TO TAKE A WHACK?! CHOP IT, SQUASH IT, FIFTY COPPERS! A LIVE HUMAN HEAD FOR FIFTY COPPERS!

PICK A *SWORD*! PICK A *MALLET*! ANYTHING GOES! I PRAY TO *BUDDHA, YOU* SWING LIKE HELL! I PROMISE I WON'T BE BACK TO HAUNT YOU!

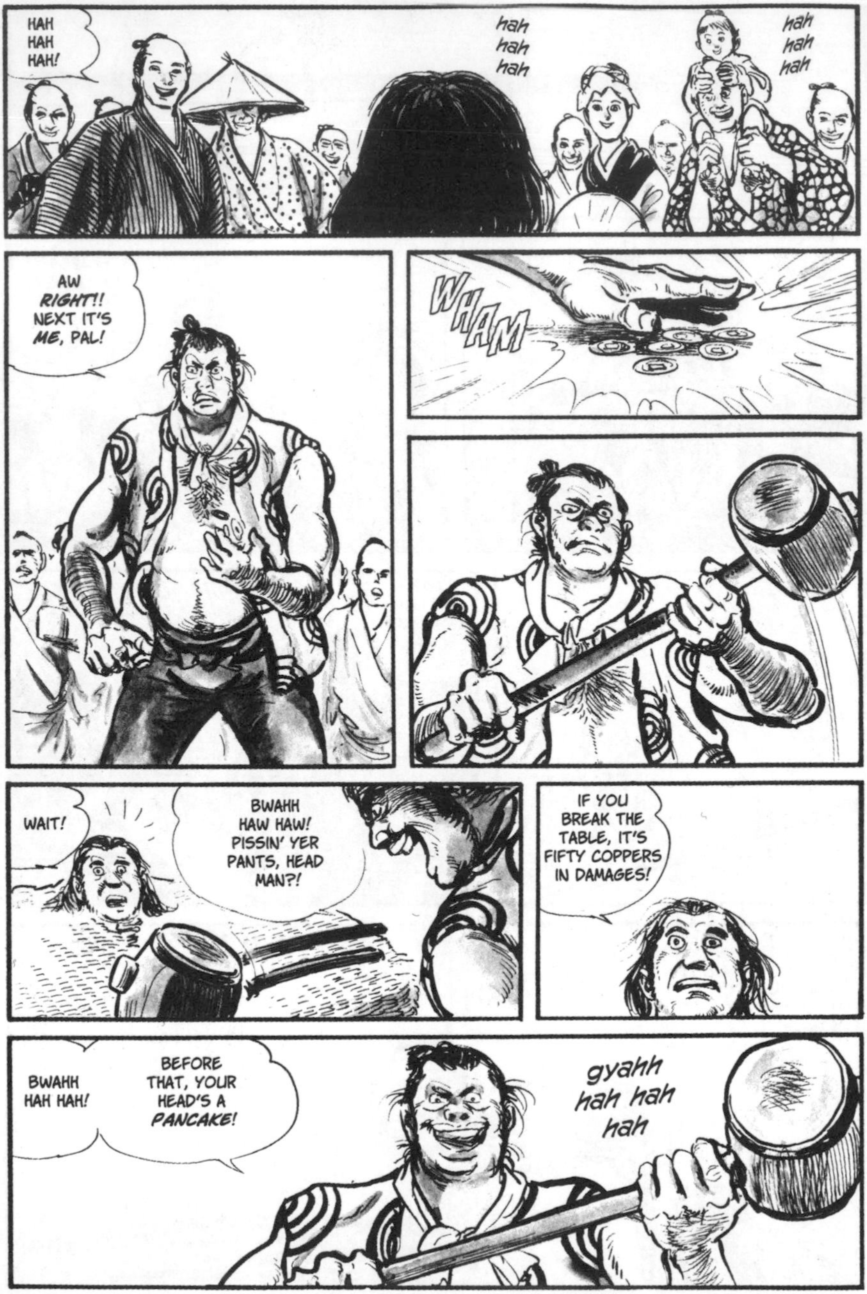
HAH HAH HAH!
hah hah hah
hah hah hah
AW RIGHT!! NEXT IT'S ME, PAL!
WHAM
WAIT!
BWAHH HAW HAW! PISSIN' YER PANTS, HEAD MAN?!
IF YOU BREAK THE TABLE, IT'S FIFTY COPPERS IN DAMAGES!
BWAHH HAH HAH!
BEFORE THAT, YOUR HEAD'S A PANCAKE!
gyahh hah hah hah

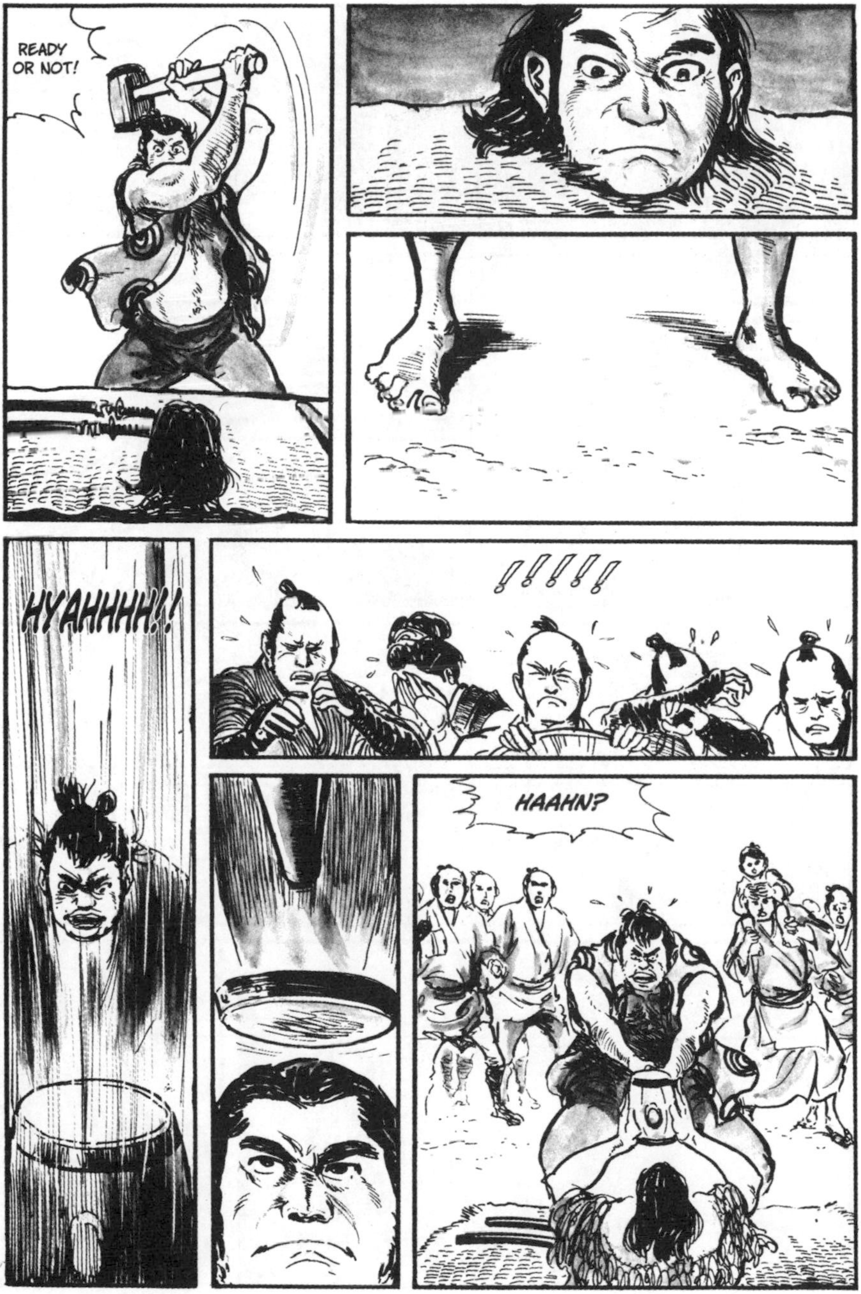
READY OR NOT!
!!!!!
HYAHHHH!!
HAAHN?

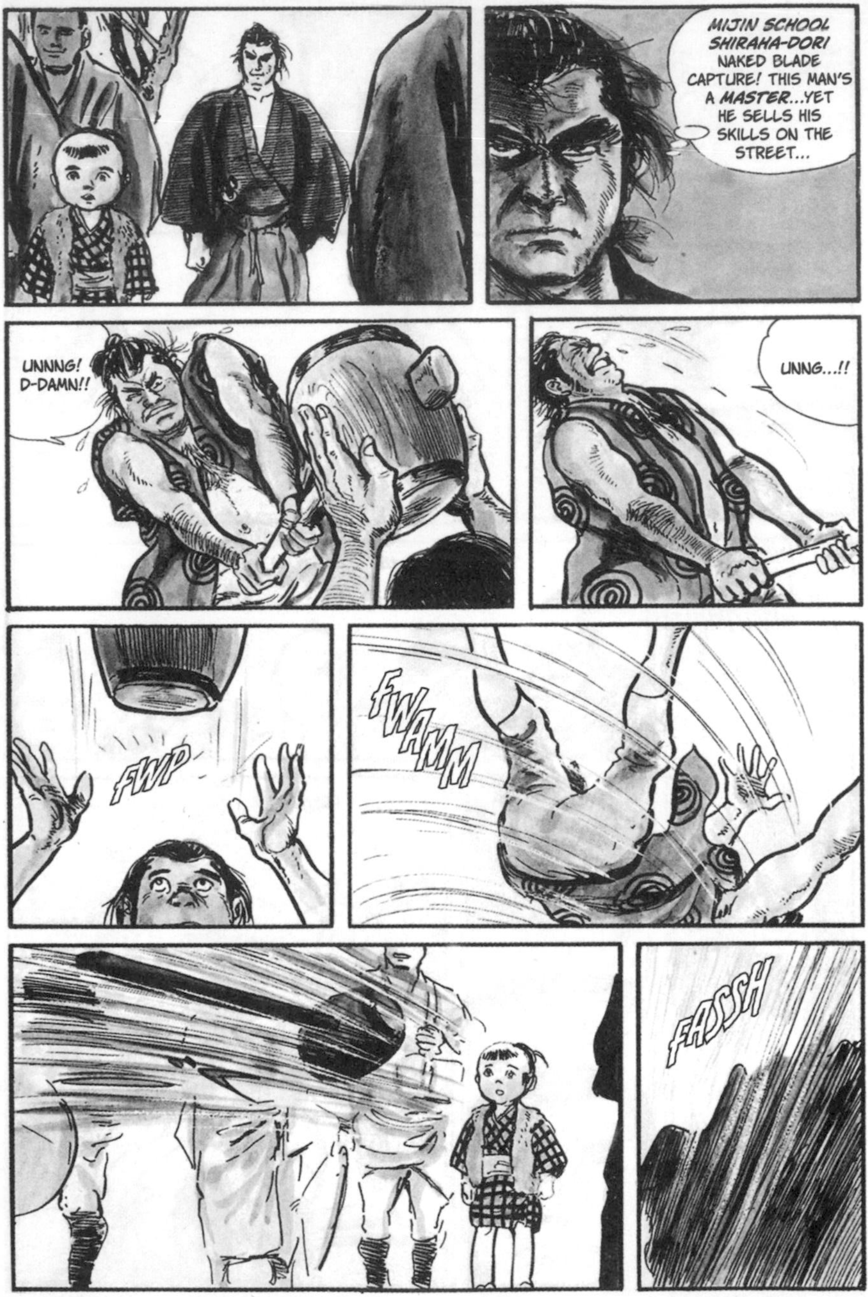
MIJIN SCHOOL SHIRAHA-DORI NAKED BLADE CAPTURE! THIS MAN'S A MASTER...YET HE SELLS HIS SKILLS ON THE STREET...
UNNNG! D-DAMN!!
UNNG...!!
FWP
FWAMM
FASSH

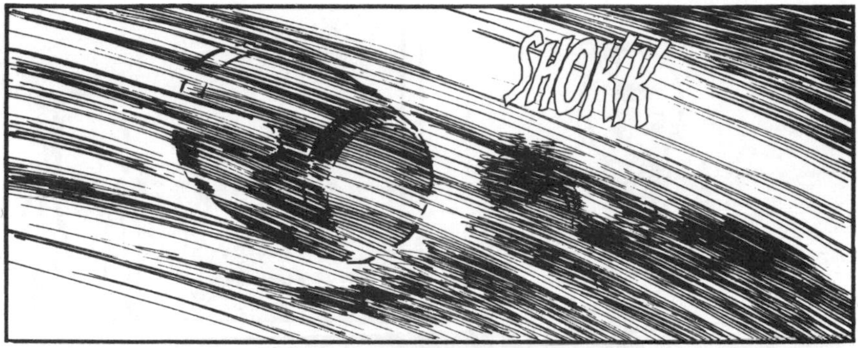
SHOKK
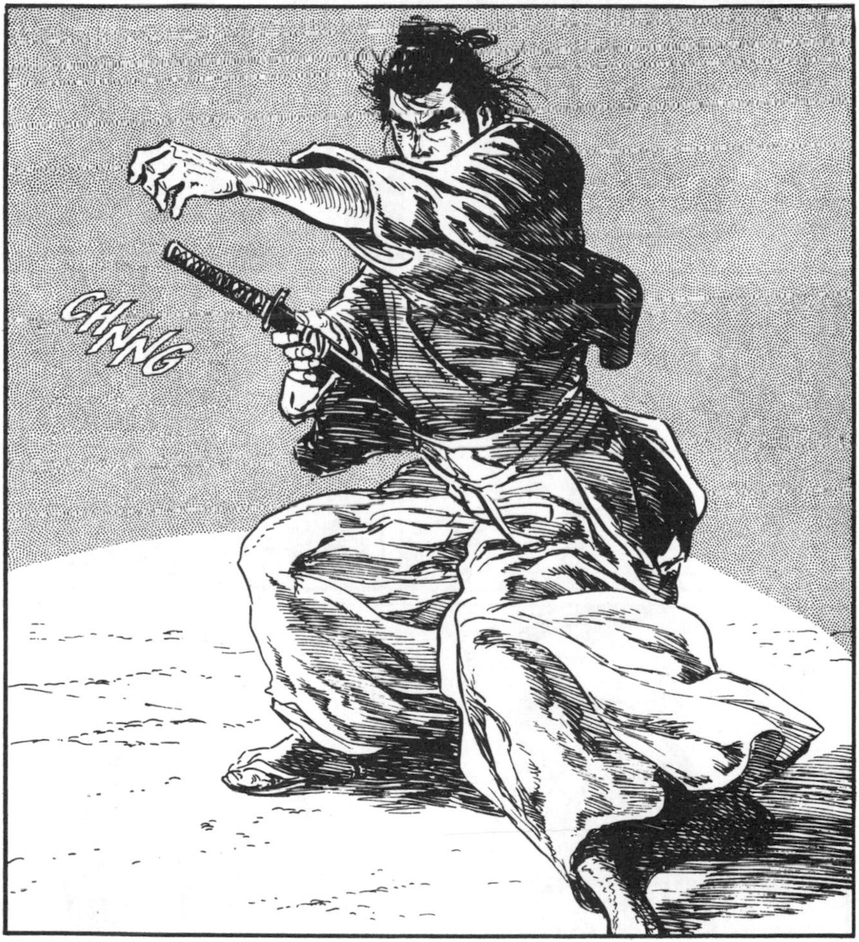
CHNNG

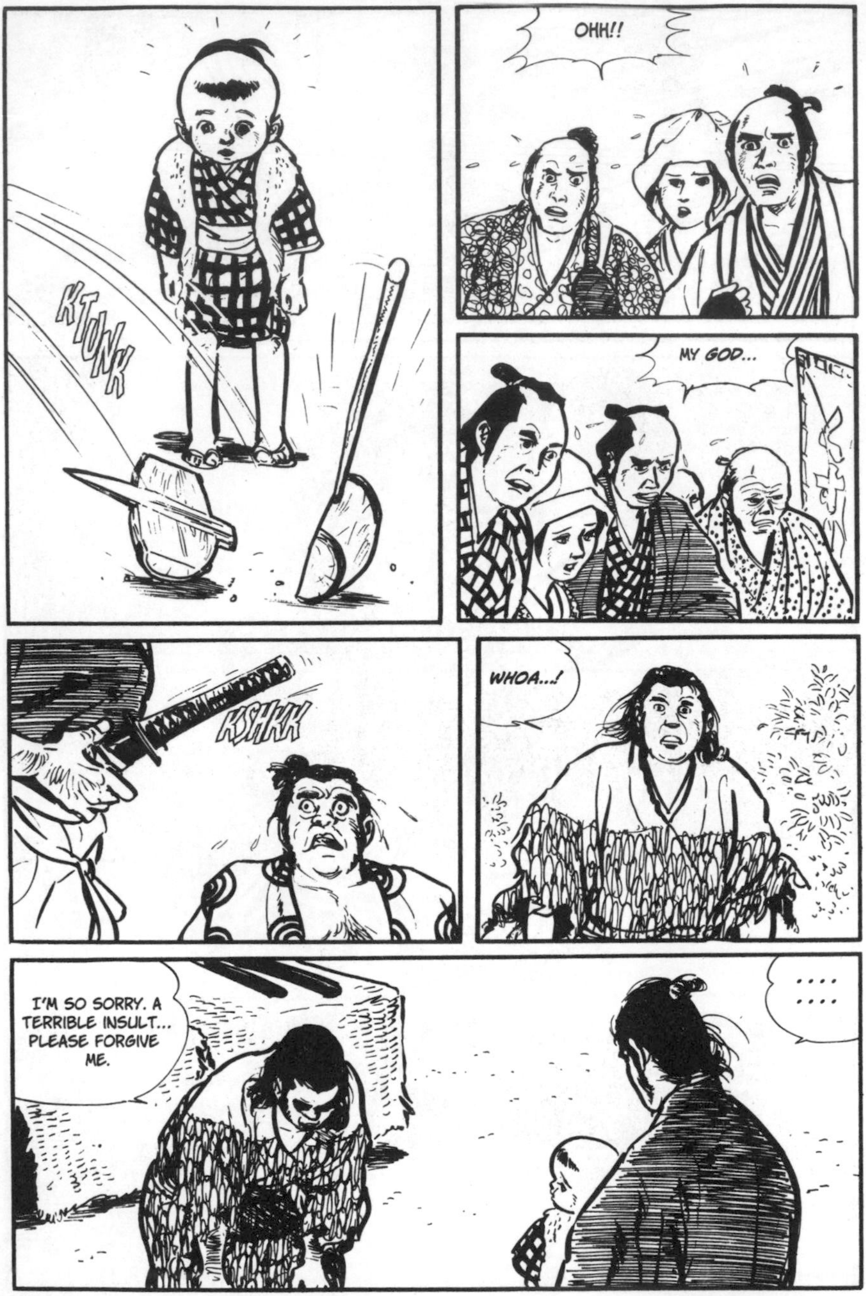
OHH!!
MY GOD...
KTUNK
WHOA...!
KSHKK
I'M SO SORRY. A TERRIBLE INSULT... PLEASE FORGIVE ME.
....
....

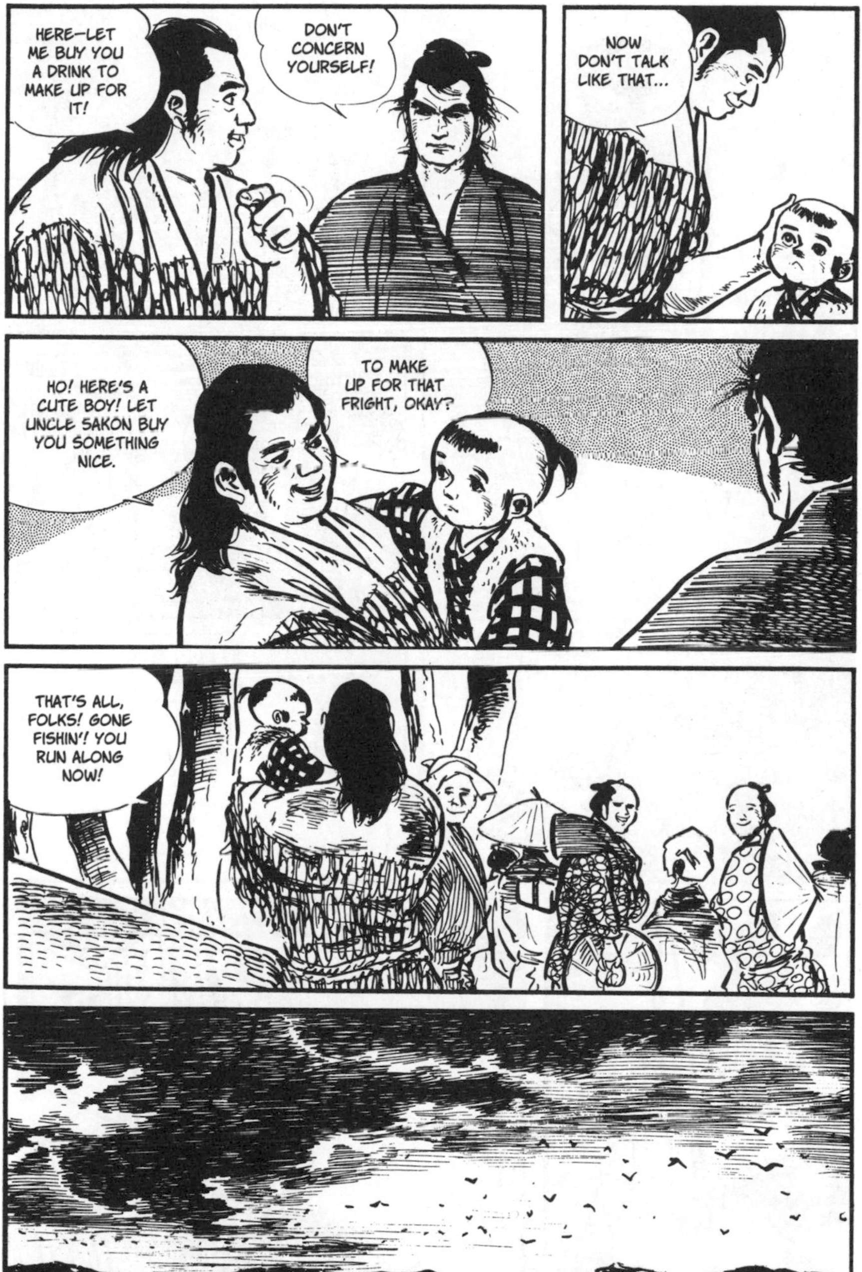
HERE—LET ME BUY YOU A DRINK TO MAKE UP FOR IT!
DON'T CONCERN YOURSELF!
NOW DON'T TALK LIKE THAT...
HO! HERE'S A CUTE BOY! LET UNCLE SAKON BUY YOU SOMETHING NICE.
TO MAKE UP FOR THAT FRIGHT, OKAY?
THAT'S ALL, FOLKS! GONE FISHIN'! YOU RUN ALONG NOW!

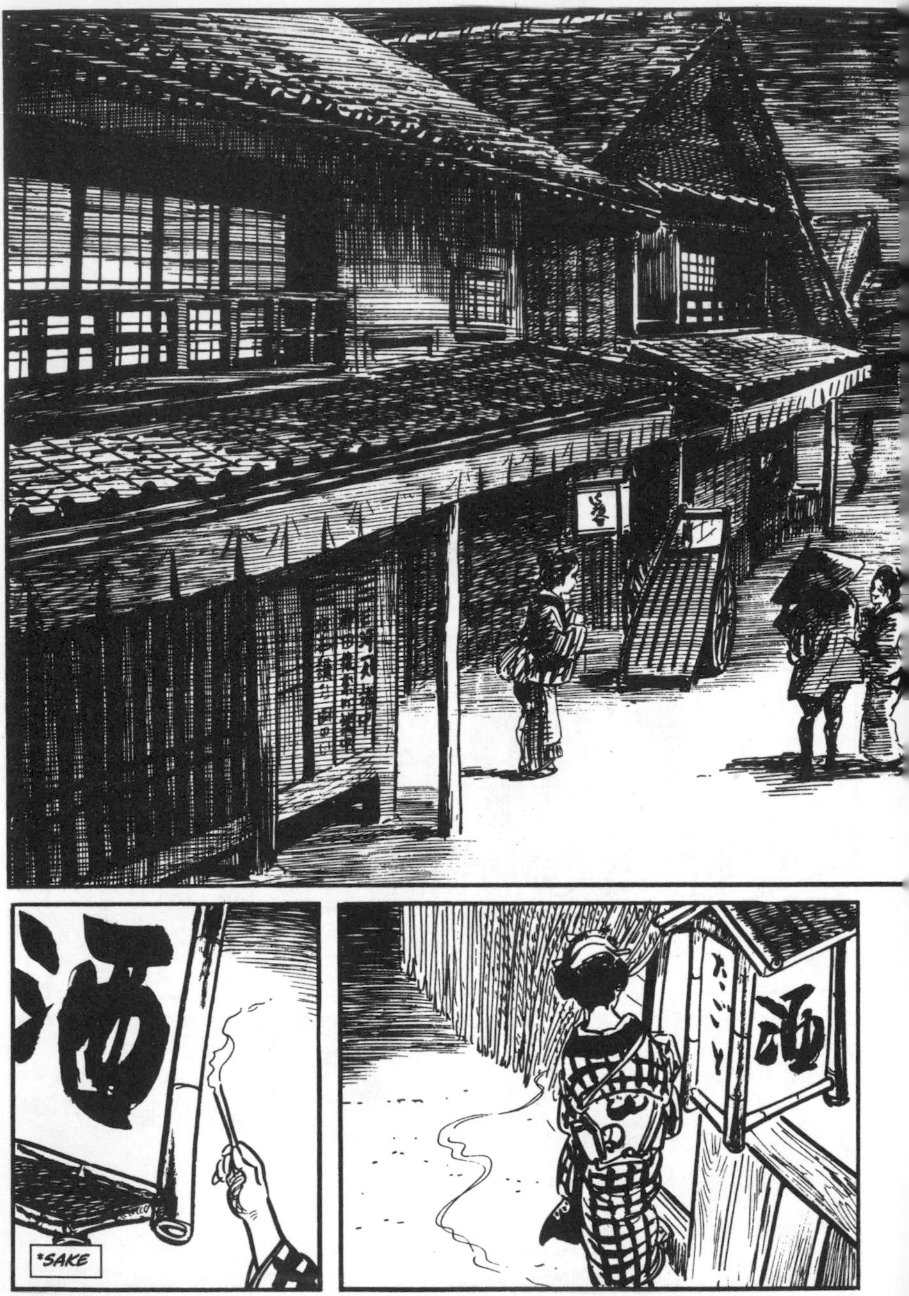
酒
*SAKE

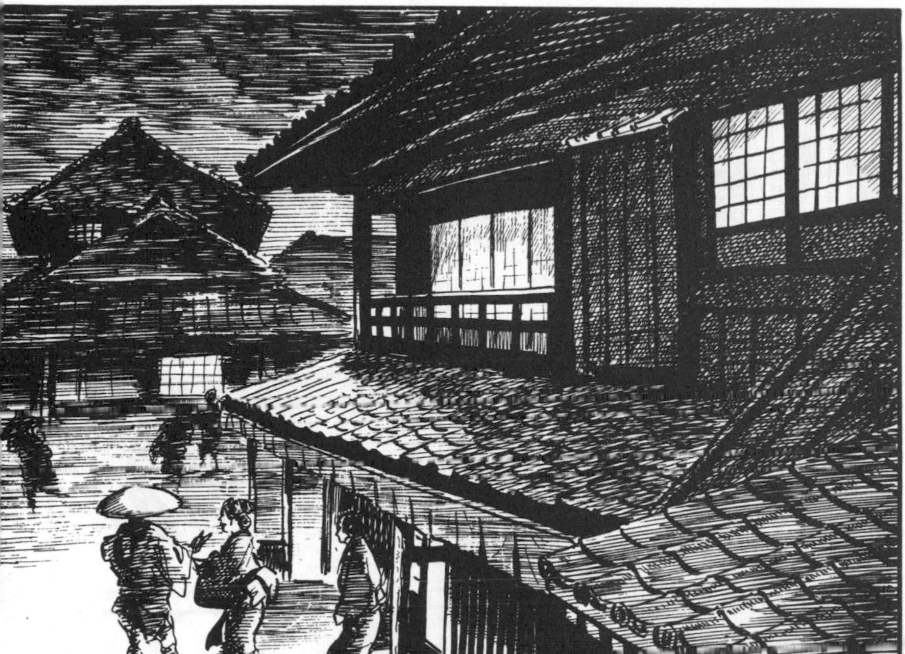

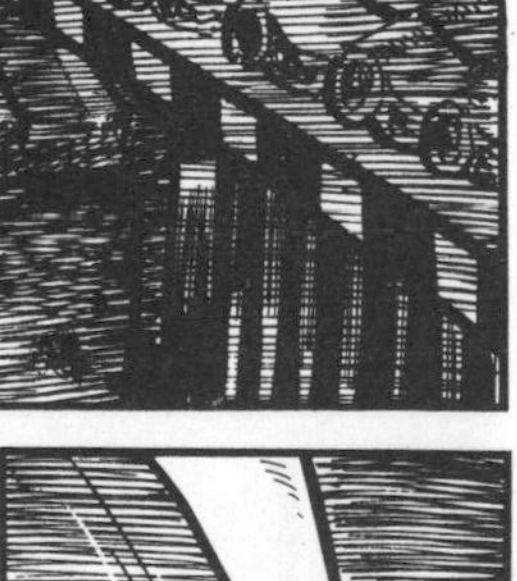

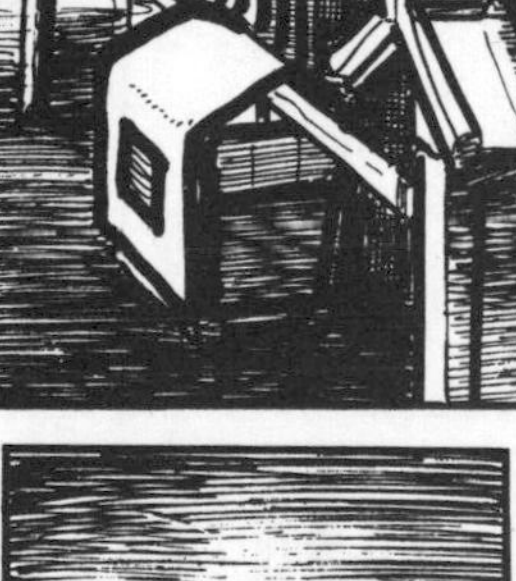

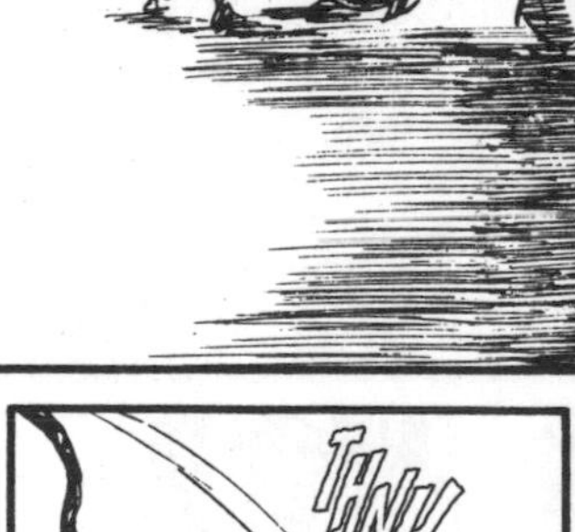

THNK

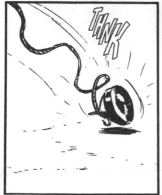

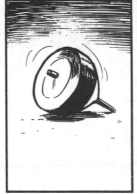

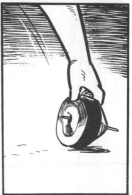

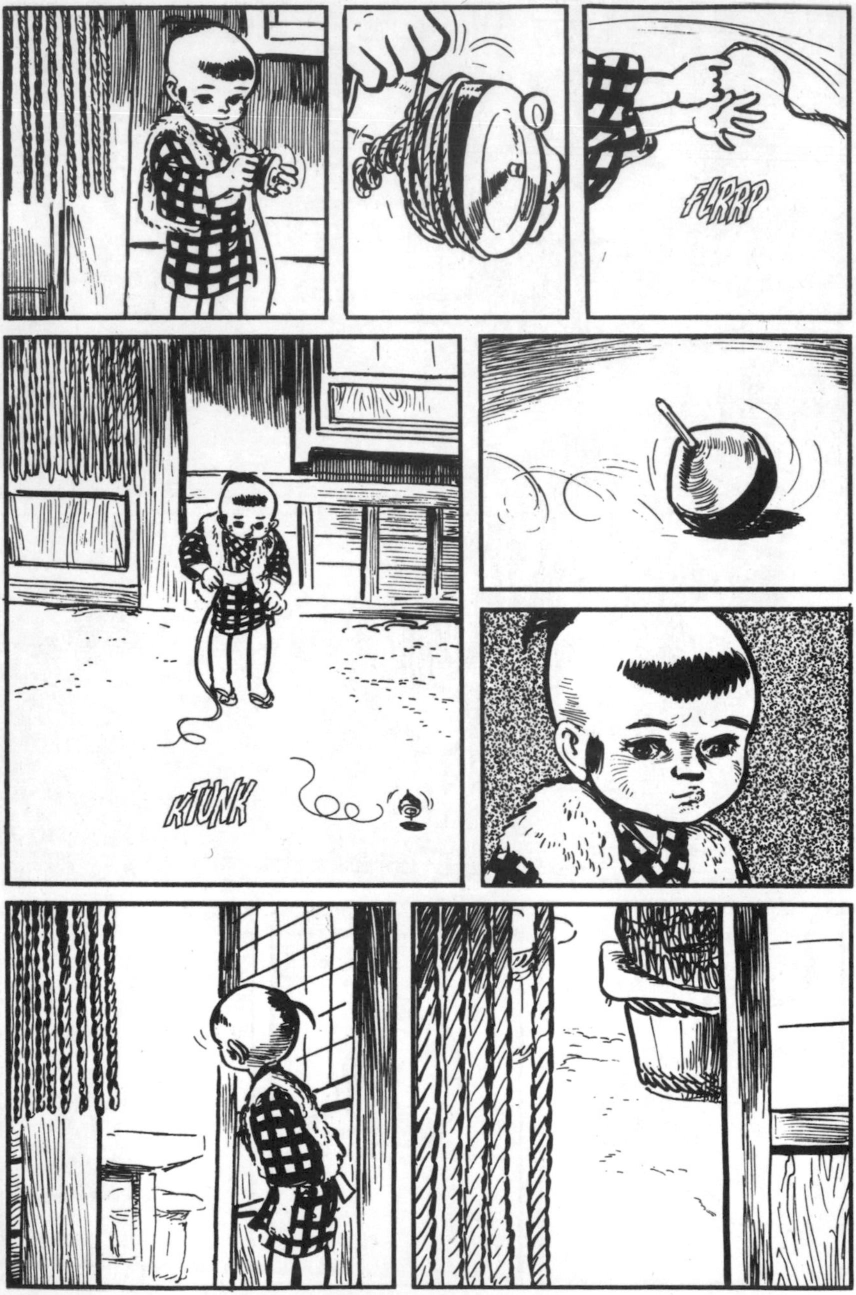
FLRRP
KTUNK

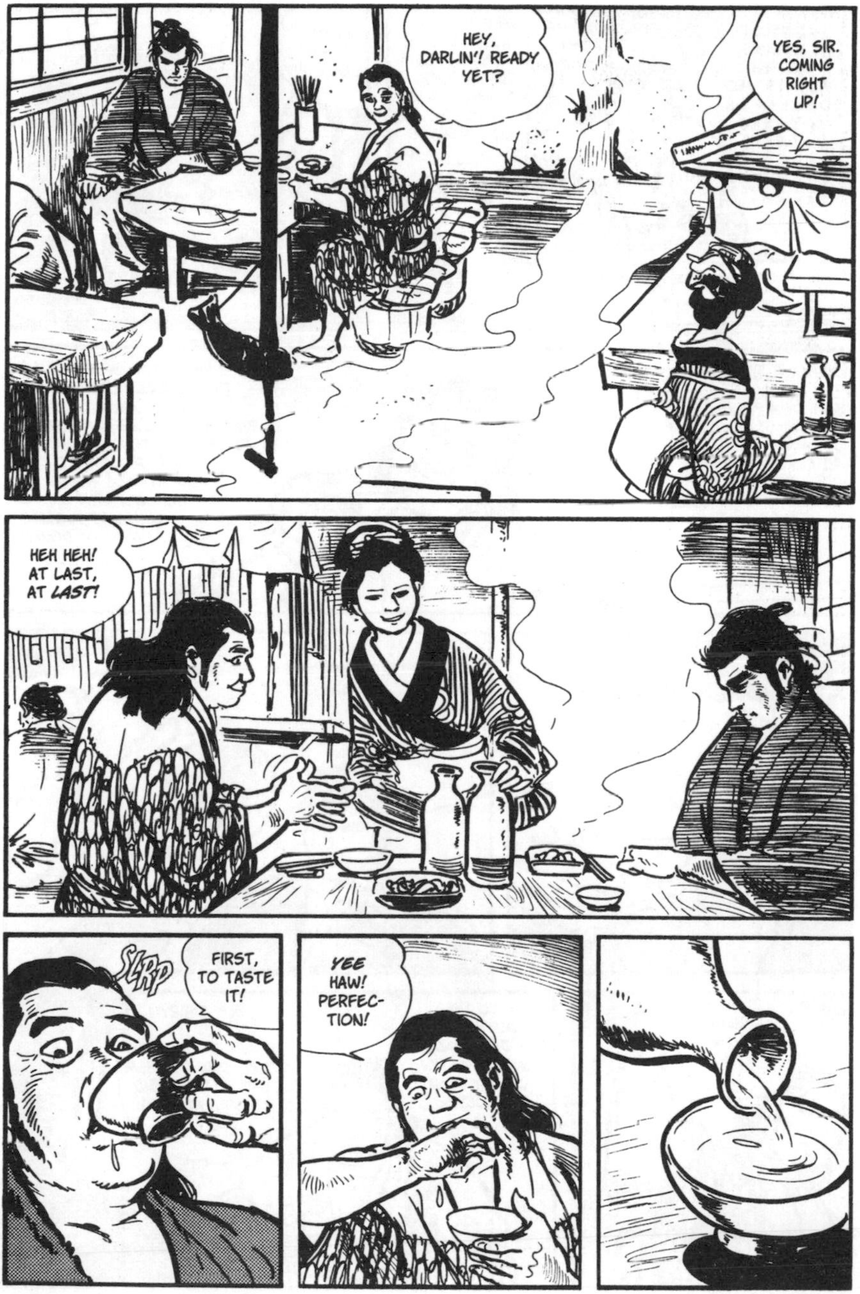
HEY, DARLIN'! READY YET?
YES, SIR. COMING RIGHT UP!
HEH HEH! AT LAST, AT *LAST*!
SLRP
FIRST, TO TASTE IT!
YEE HAW! PERFECTION!

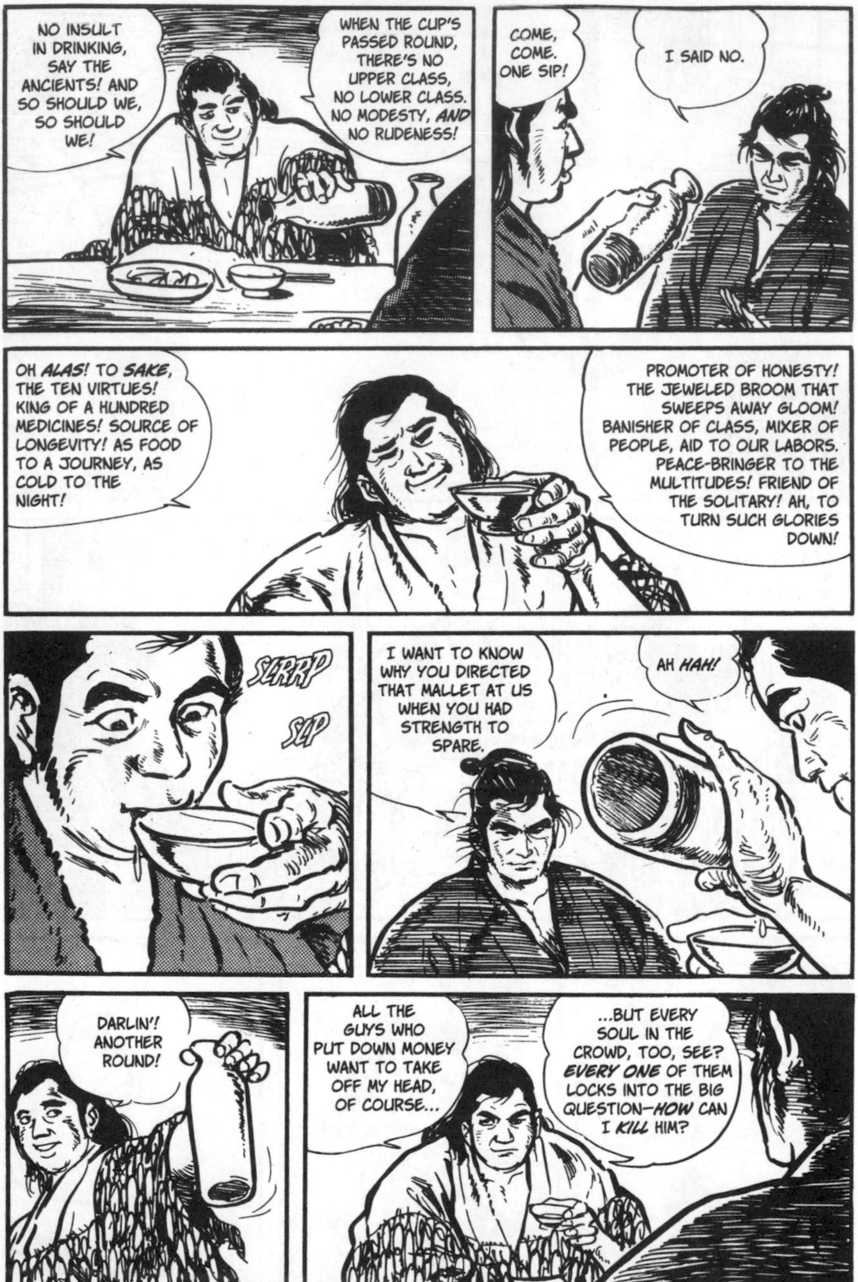
NO INSULT IN DRINKING, SAY THE ANCIENTS! AND SO SHOULD WE, SO SHOULD WE!
WHEN THE CUP'S PASSED ROUND, THERE'S NO UPPER CLASS, NO LOWER CLASS. NO MODESTY, *AND* NO RUDENESS!
COME, COME. ONE SIP!
I SAID NO.
OH *ALAS!* TO *SAKE*, THE TEN VIRTUES! KING OF A HUNDRED MEDICINES! SOURCE OF LONGEVITY! AS FOOD TO A JOURNEY, AS COLD TO THE NIGHT!
PROMOTER OF HONESTY! THE JEWELED BROOM THAT SWEEPS AWAY GLOOM! BANISHER OF CLASS, MIXER OF PEOPLE, AID TO OUR LABORS. PEACE-BRINGER TO THE MULTITUDES! FRIEND OF THE SOLITARY! AH, TO TURN SUCH GLORIES DOWN!
SLRRP
SLIP
I WANT TO KNOW WHY YOU DIRECTED THAT MALLET AT US WHEN YOU HAD STRENGTH TO SPARE.
AH *HAH!*
DARLIN'! ANOTHER ROUND!
ALL THE GUYS WHO PUT DOWN MONEY WANT TO TAKE OFF MY HEAD, OF COURSE...
...BUT EVERY SOUL IN THE CROWD, TOO, SEE? *EVERY ONE* OF THEM LOCKS INTO THE BIG QUESTION—*HOW* CAN I *KILL* HIM?

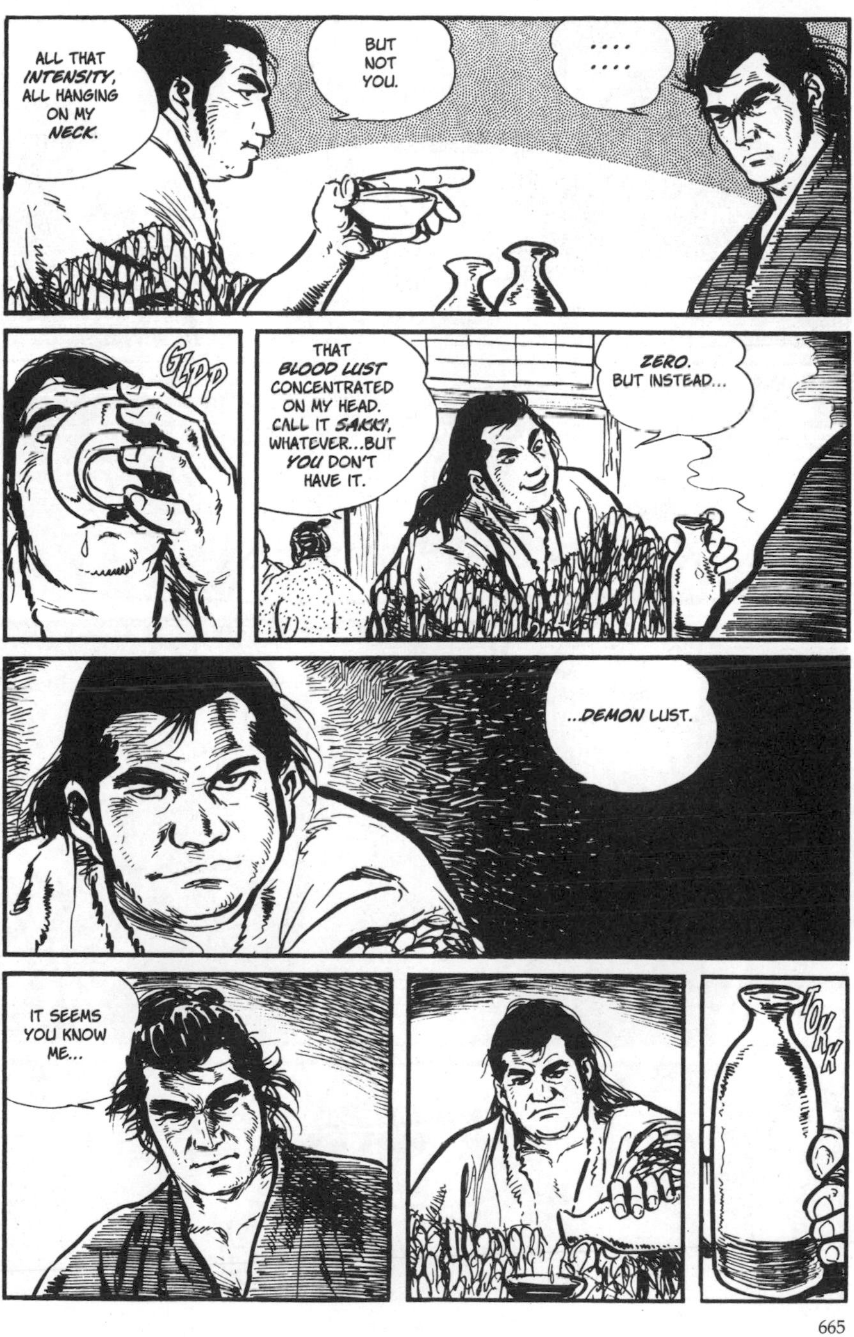
ALL THAT *INTENSITY*, ALL HANGING ON MY *NECK*.
BUT NOT YOU.
....
GLPP
THAT *BLOOD LUST* CONCENTRATED ON MY HEAD. CALL IT *SAKKI*, WHATEVER...BUT *YOU* DON'T HAVE IT.
ZERO. BUT INSTEAD...
...*DEMON* LUST.
IT SEEMS YOU KNOW ME...
TOKK

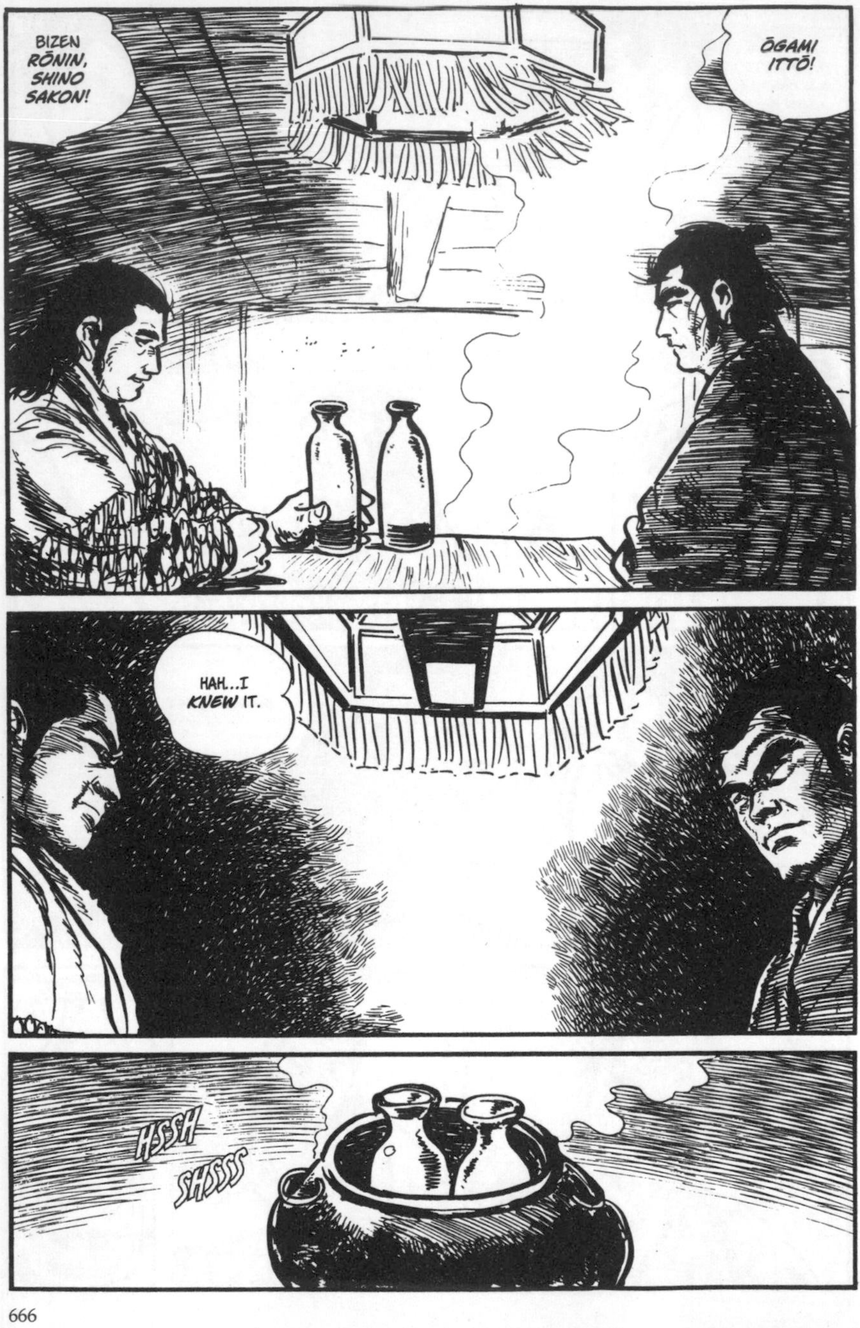
ŌGAMI ITTŌ!
BIZEN RŌNIN, SHINO SAKON!
HAH...I *KNEW* IT.
HSSH
SHSSS

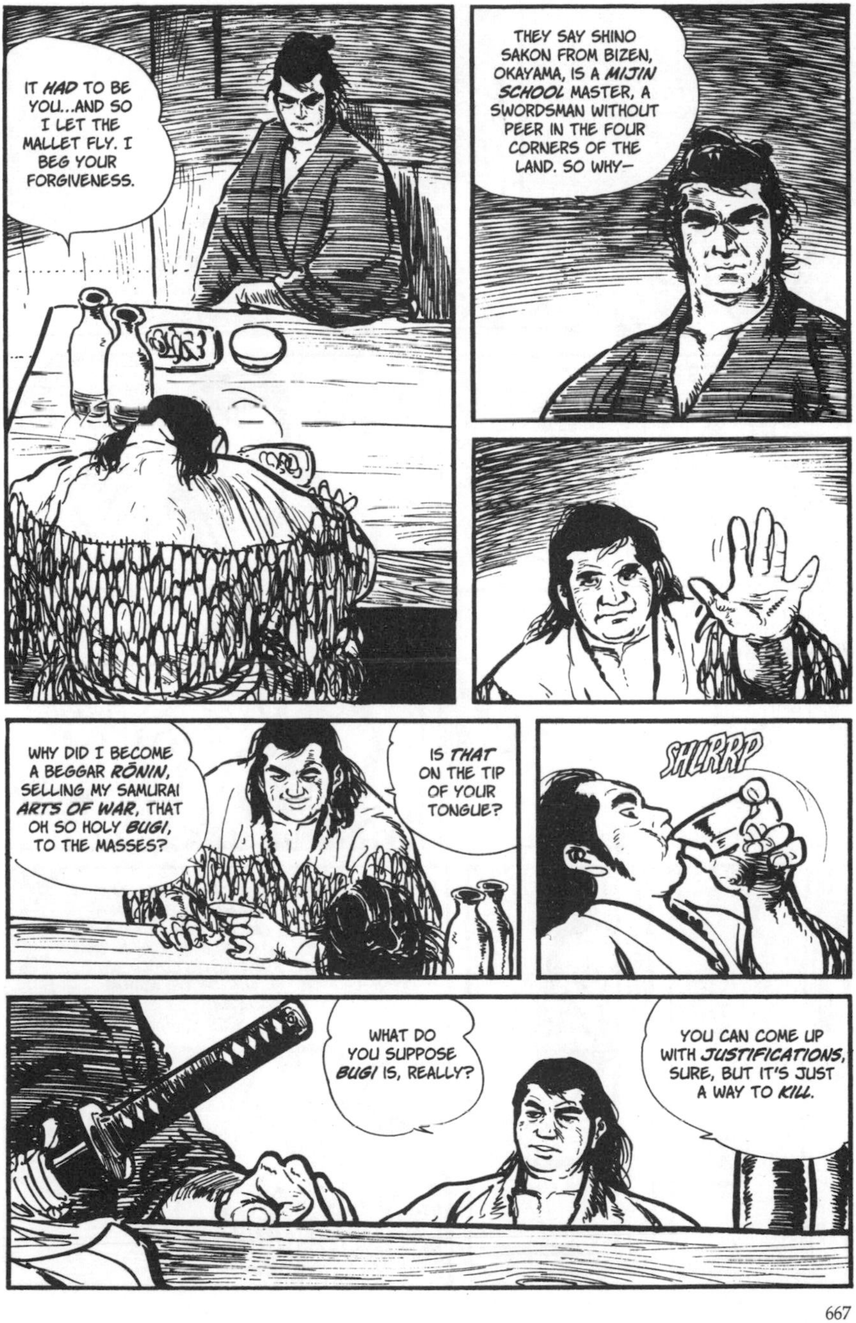
IT *HAD* TO BE YOU...AND SO I LET THE MALLET FLY. I BEG YOUR FORGIVENESS.
THEY SAY SHINO SAKON FROM BIZEN, OKAYAMA, IS A *MIJIN SCHOOL* MASTER, A SWORDSMAN WITHOUT PEER IN THE FOUR CORNERS OF THE LAND. SO WHY—
WHY DID I BECOME A BEGGAR *RŌNIN*, SELLING MY SAMURAI *ARTS OF WAR*, THAT OH SO HOLY *BUGI*, TO THE MASSES?
IS *THAT* ON THE TIP OF YOUR TONGUE?
SHLRRP
WHAT DO YOU SUPPOSE *BUGI* IS, REALLY?
YOU CAN COME UP WITH *JUSTIFICATIONS*, SURE, BUT IT'S JUST A WAY TO *KILL*.

I LOOKED LONG AND HARD FOR ANOTHER USE FOR IT, BUT IT WAS NO GOOD...

SAMURAI AND PEASANT, WE'RE ALL PEOPLE. WE EAT THE SAME RICE, DUMP THE SAME SHIT. BUT THE SAMURAI GETS *SEISATSU YODATSU*, THE RIGHT TO BUTCHER THE PEASANT.

AND WELL, SOMEHOW BEING SAMURAI GOT TO FEELING PRETTY *POINTLESS*. AND SO I FOUND THE ONLY OTHER WAY I COULD USE MY ART.

AND HERE I AM...GETTING BY.

SLRP

SLPP

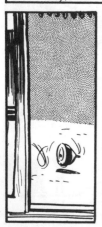

I'D HEARD FROM ONE OF THE *YAGYŪ'S* MEN THAT LORD *ŌGAMI*, THE SHOGUN'S OWN EXECUTIONER, HAD BECOME AN ASSASSIN CALLED *LONE WOLF AND CUB*. IF YOU'VE TAKEN THE *ASSASSIN'S WAY*, YOU COULD SAY I'VE CHOSEN THE WAY OF THE *HUMAN BEGGAR*.

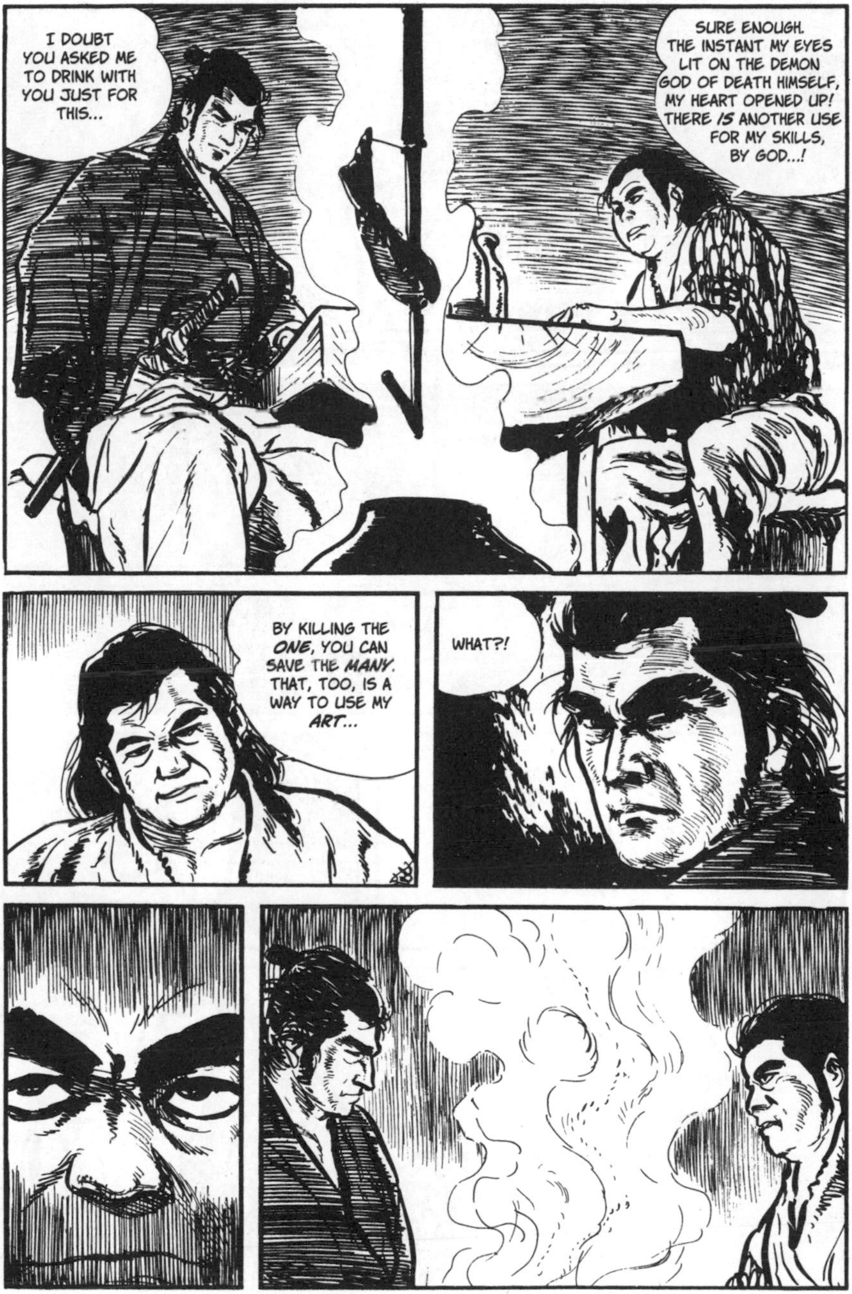
I DOUBT YOU ASKED ME TO DRINK WITH YOU JUST FOR THIS...
SURE ENOUGH. THE INSTANT MY EYES LIT ON THE DEMON GOD OF DEATH HIMSELF, MY HEART OPENED UP! THERE *IS* ANOTHER USE FOR MY SKILLS, BY GOD...!
BY KILLING THE *ONE*, YOU CAN SAVE THE *MANY*. THAT, TOO, IS A WAY TO USE MY *ART*...
WHAT?!

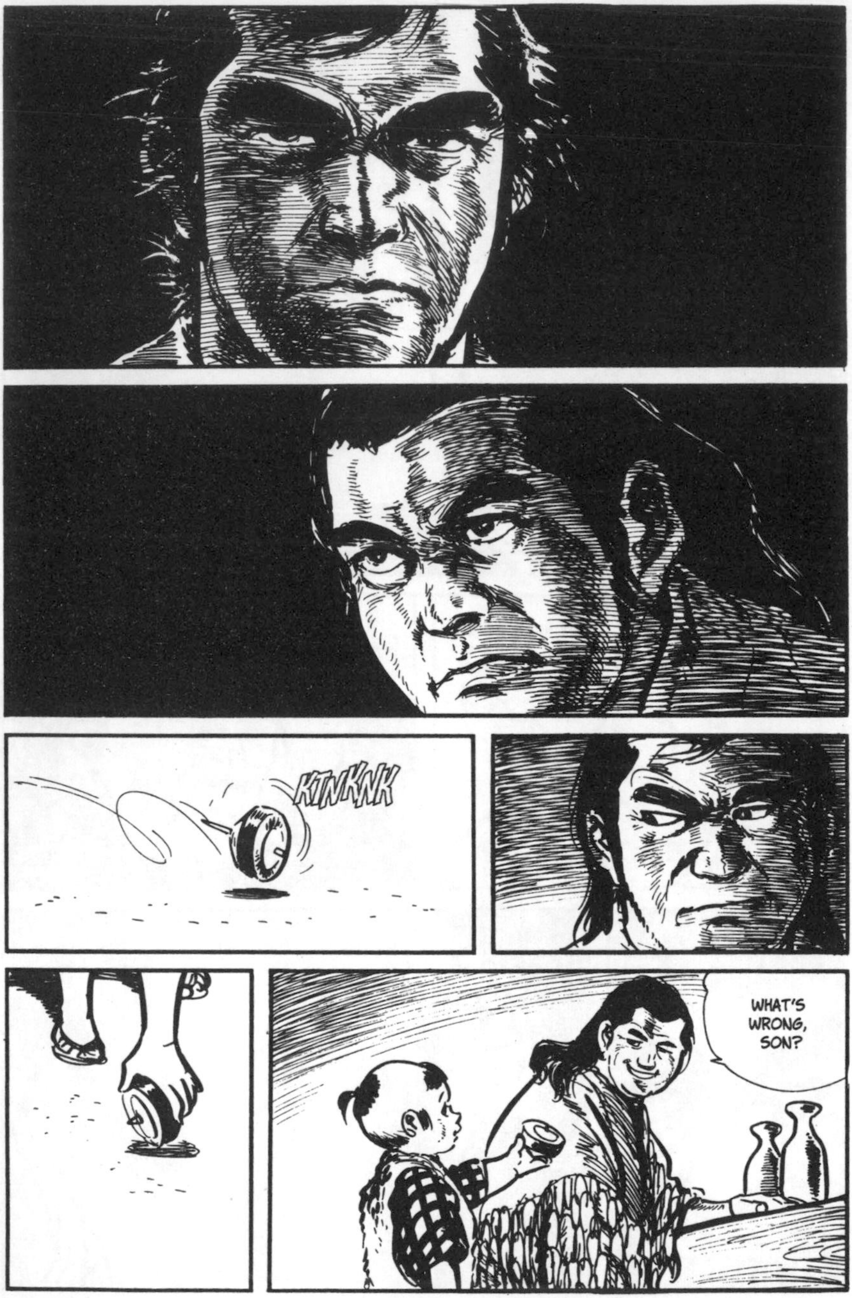
KTNKNK
WHAT'S WRONG, SON?

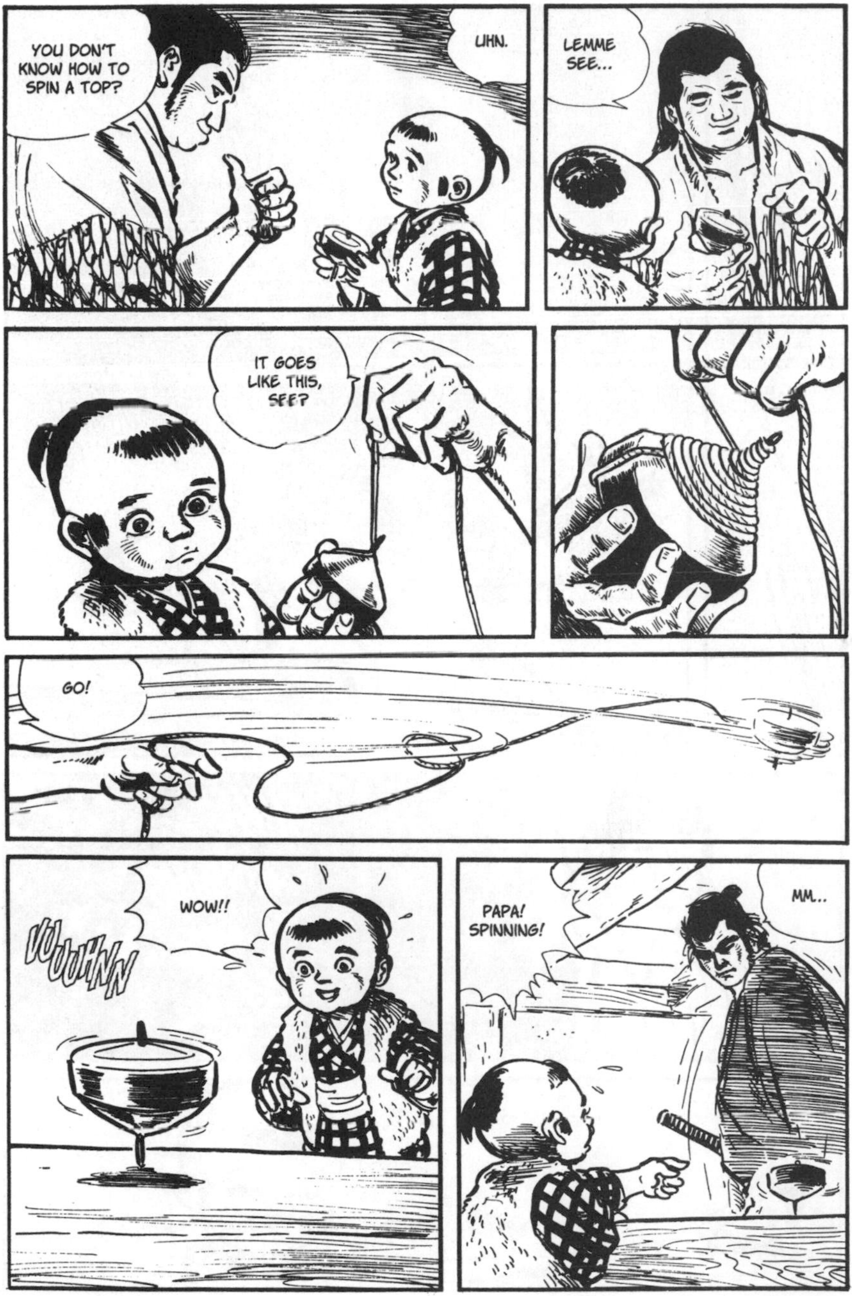
YOU DON'T KNOW HOW TO SPIN A TOP?
UHN.
LEMME SEE...
IT GOES LIKE THIS, SEE?
GO!
VUUUHNN
WOW!!
PAPA! SPINNING!
MM...

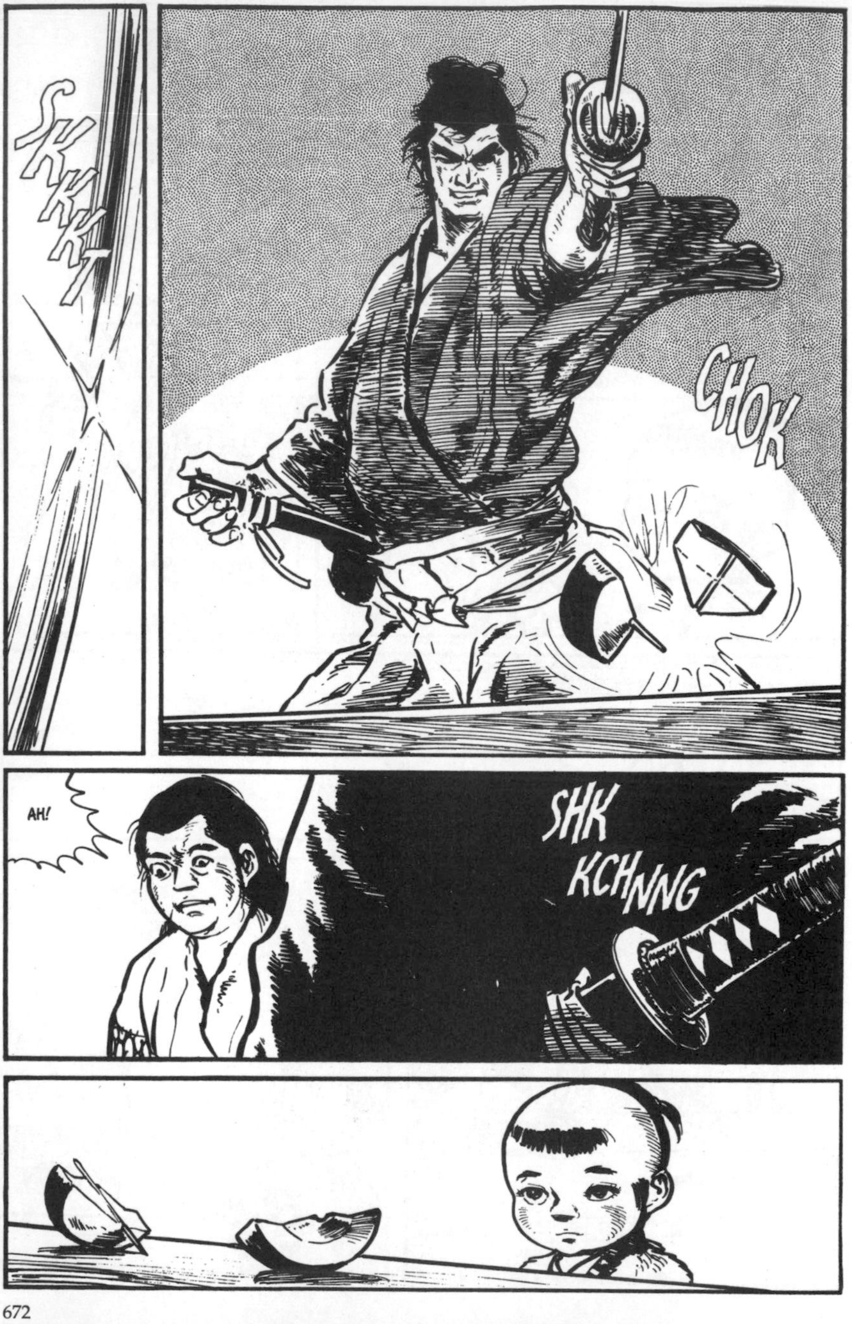
CHOK
SKKKT
SHK
KCHNNG
AH!

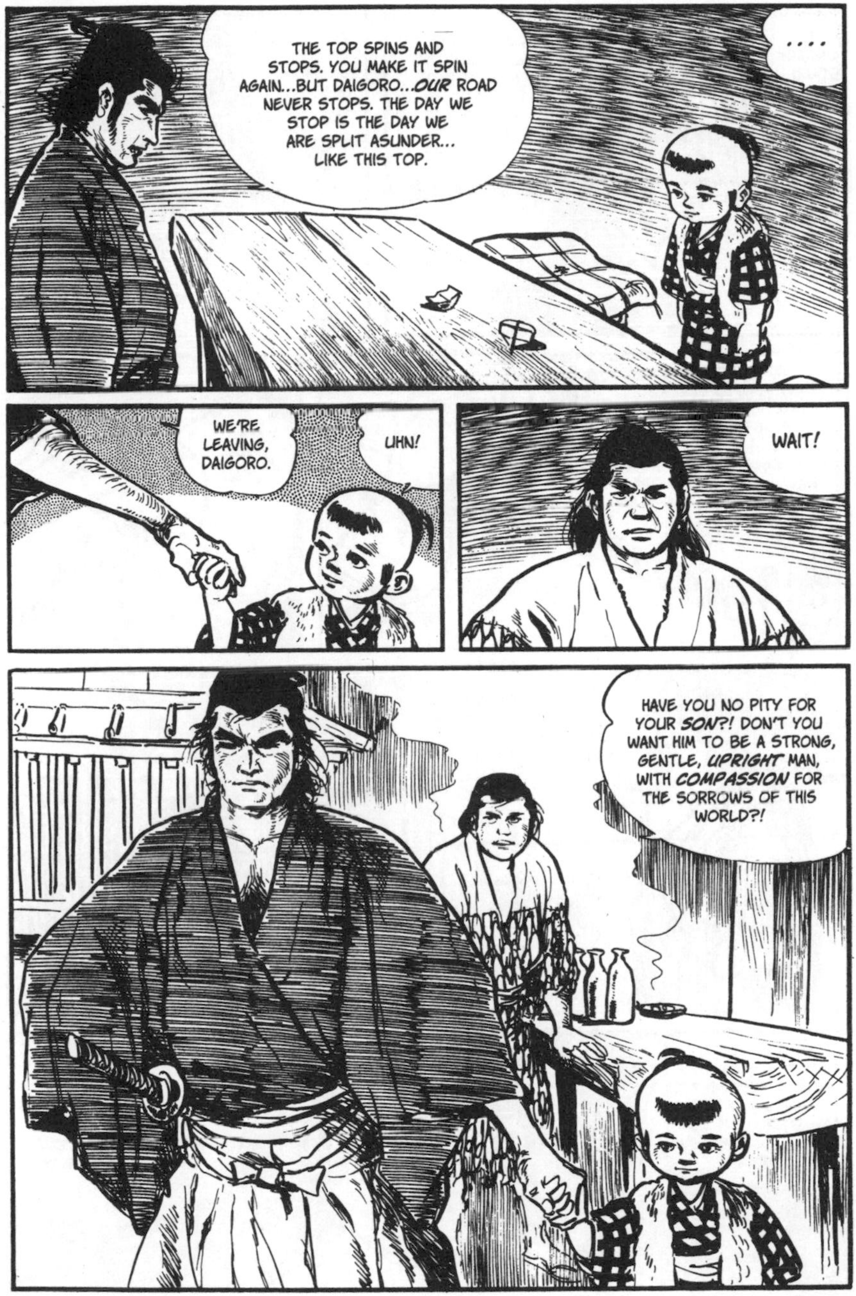
THE TOP SPINS AND STOPS. YOU MAKE IT SPIN AGAIN...BUT DAIGORO...OUR ROAD NEVER STOPS. THE DAY WE STOP IS THE DAY WE ARE SPLIT ASUNDER... LIKE THIS TOP.
....
WE'RE LEAVING, DAIGORO.
UHN!
WAIT!
HAVE YOU NO PITY FOR YOUR SON?! DON'T YOU WANT HIM TO BE A STRONG, GENTLE, UPRIGHT MAN, WITH COMPASSION FOR THE SORROWS OF THIS WORLD?!

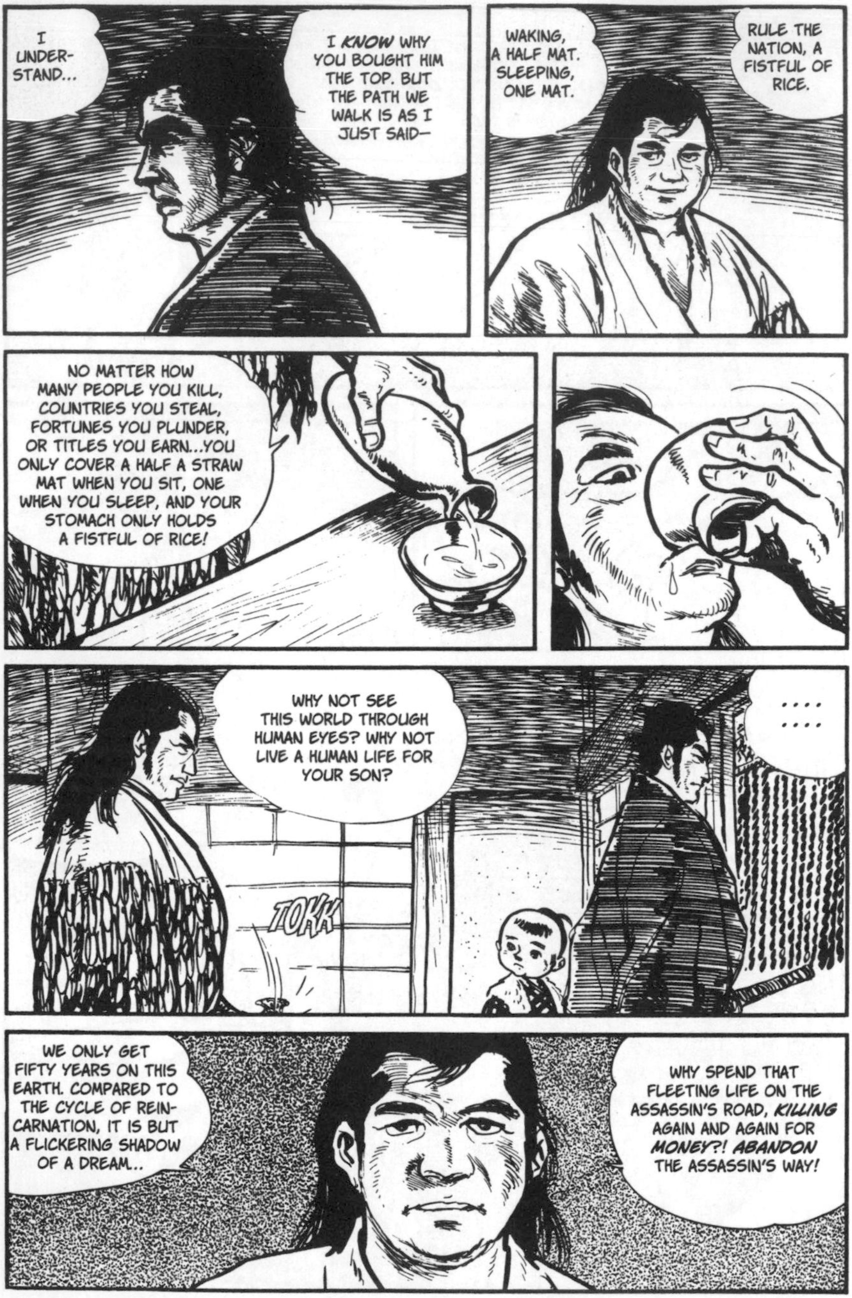
I UNDER-STAND...
I *KNOW* WHY YOU BOUGHT HIM THE TOP. BUT THE PATH WE WALK IS AS I JUST SAID—
WAKING, A HALF MAT. SLEEPING, ONE MAT.
RULE THE NATION, A FISTFUL OF RICE.
NO MATTER HOW MANY PEOPLE YOU KILL, COUNTRIES YOU STEAL, FORTUNES YOU PLUNDER, OR TITLES YOU EARN...YOU ONLY COVER A HALF A STRAW MAT WHEN YOU SIT, ONE WHEN YOU SLEEP, AND YOUR STOMACH ONLY HOLDS A FISTFUL OF RICE!
WHY NOT SEE THIS WORLD THROUGH HUMAN EYES? WHY NOT LIVE A HUMAN LIFE FOR YOUR SON?
TOKK
....
....
WE ONLY GET FIFTY YEARS ON THIS EARTH. COMPARED TO THE CYCLE OF REIN-CARNATION, IT IS BUT A FLICKERING SHADOW OF A DREAM...
WHY SPEND THAT FLEETING LIFE ON THE ASSASSIN'S ROAD, *KILLING* AGAIN AND AGAIN FOR *MONEY*?! *ABANDON* THE ASSASSIN'S WAY!

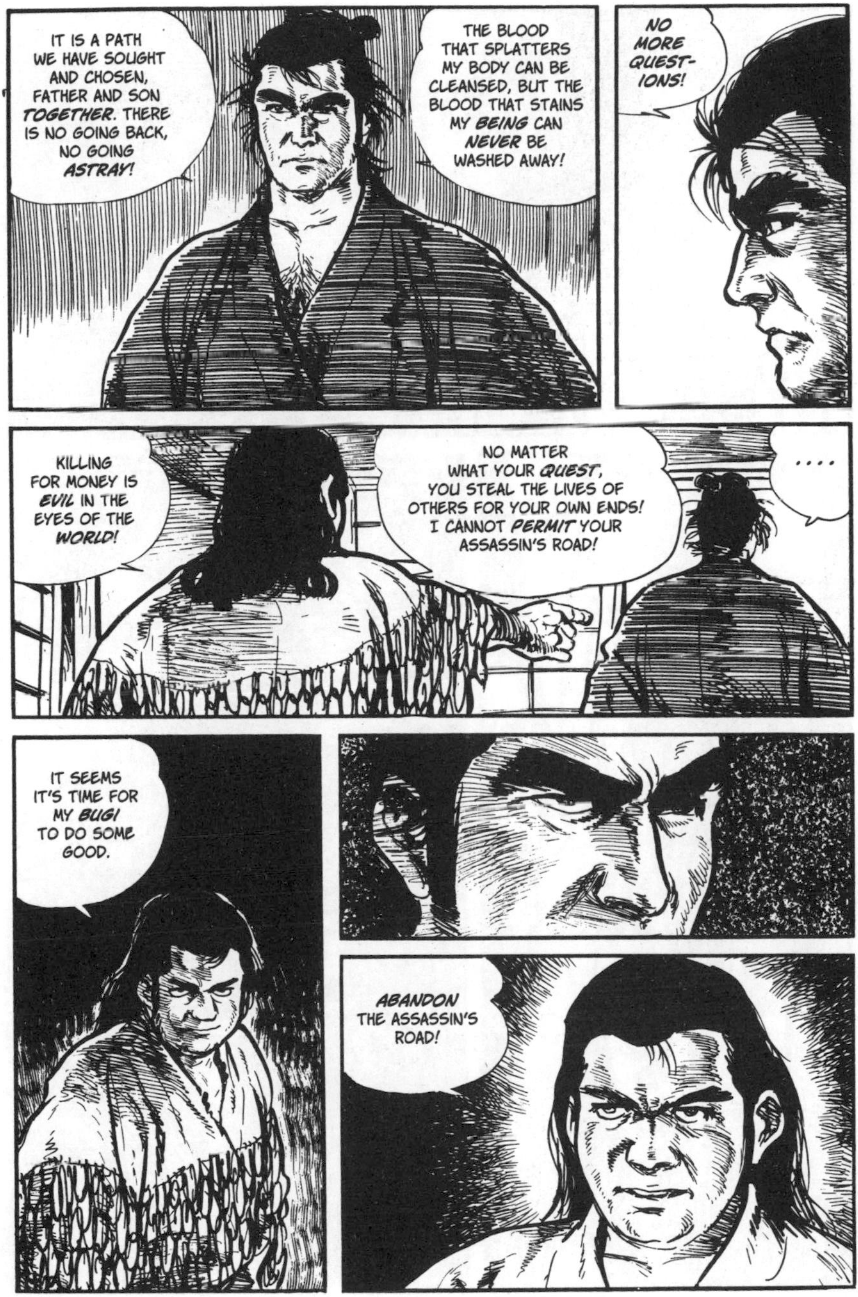
IT IS A PATH WE HAVE SOUGHT AND CHOSEN, FATHER AND SON TOGETHER. THERE IS NO GOING BACK, NO GOING ASTRAY!
THE BLOOD THAT SPLATTERS MY BODY CAN BE CLEANSED, BUT THE BLOOD THAT STAINS MY BEING CAN NEVER BE WASHED AWAY!
NO MORE QUEST-IONS!
KILLING FOR MONEY IS EVIL IN THE EYES OF THE WORLD!
NO MATTER WHAT YOUR QUEST, YOU STEAL THE LIVES OF OTHERS FOR YOUR OWN ENDS! I CANNOT PERMIT YOUR ASSASSIN'S ROAD!
....
IT SEEMS IT'S TIME FOR MY BUGI TO DO SOME GOOD.
ABANDON THE ASSASSIN'S ROAD!

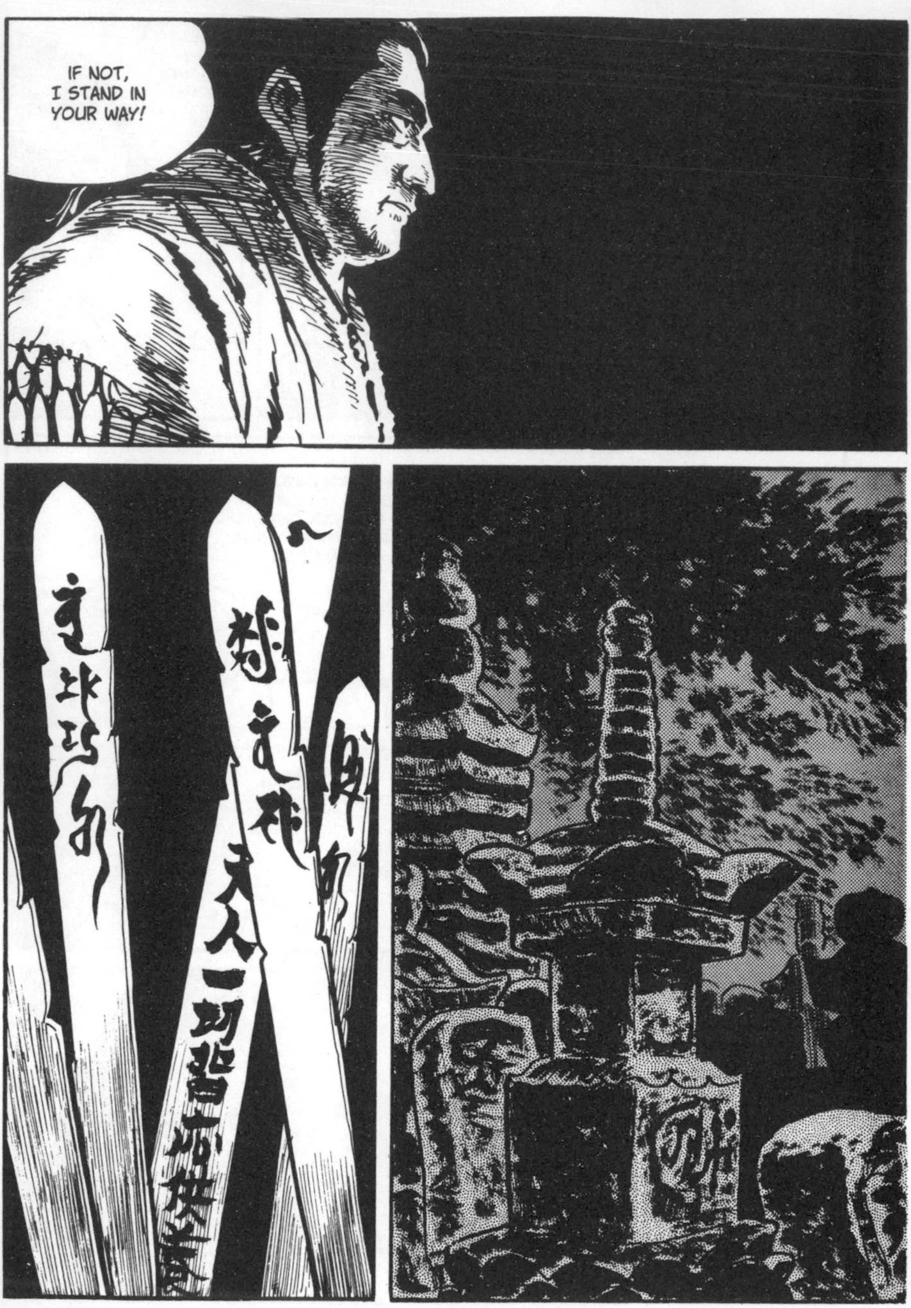
IF NOT, I STAND IN YOUR WAY!

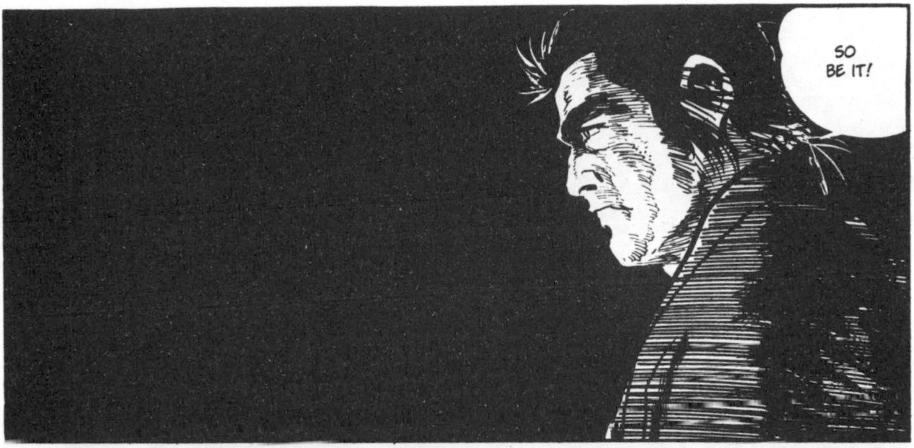
SO BE IT!
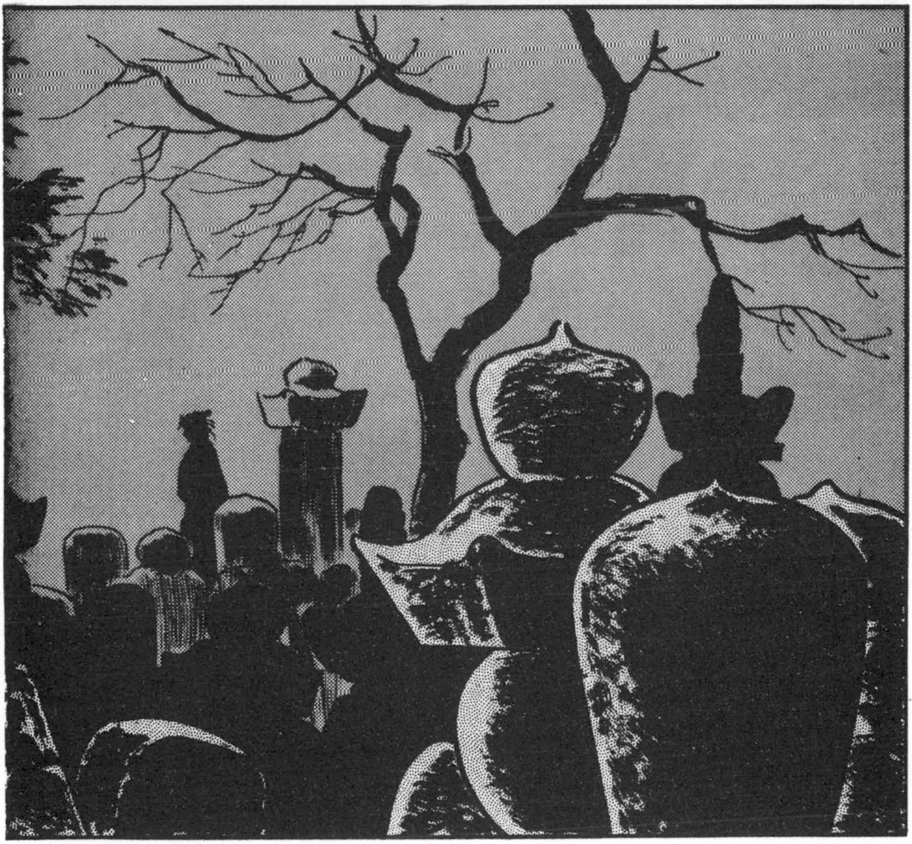

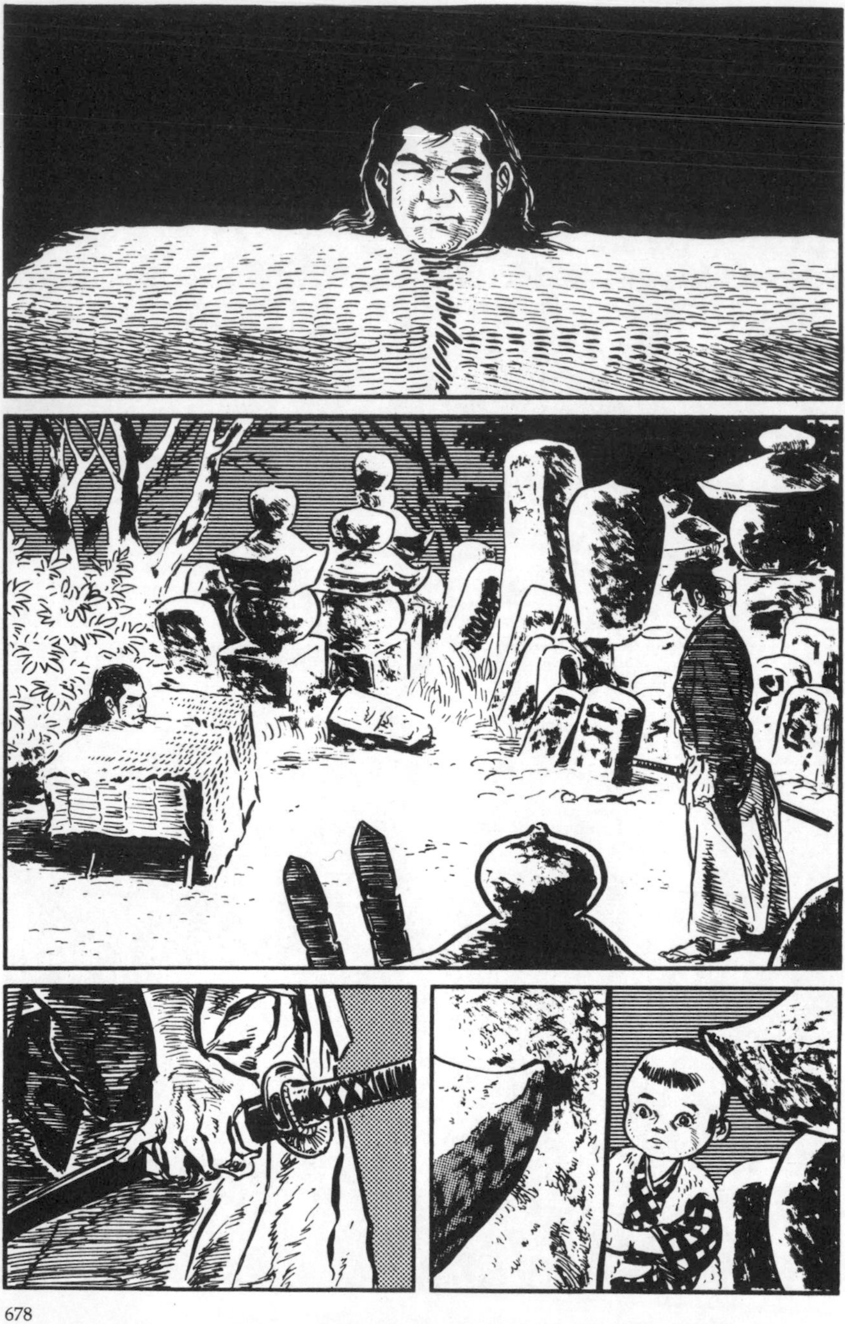

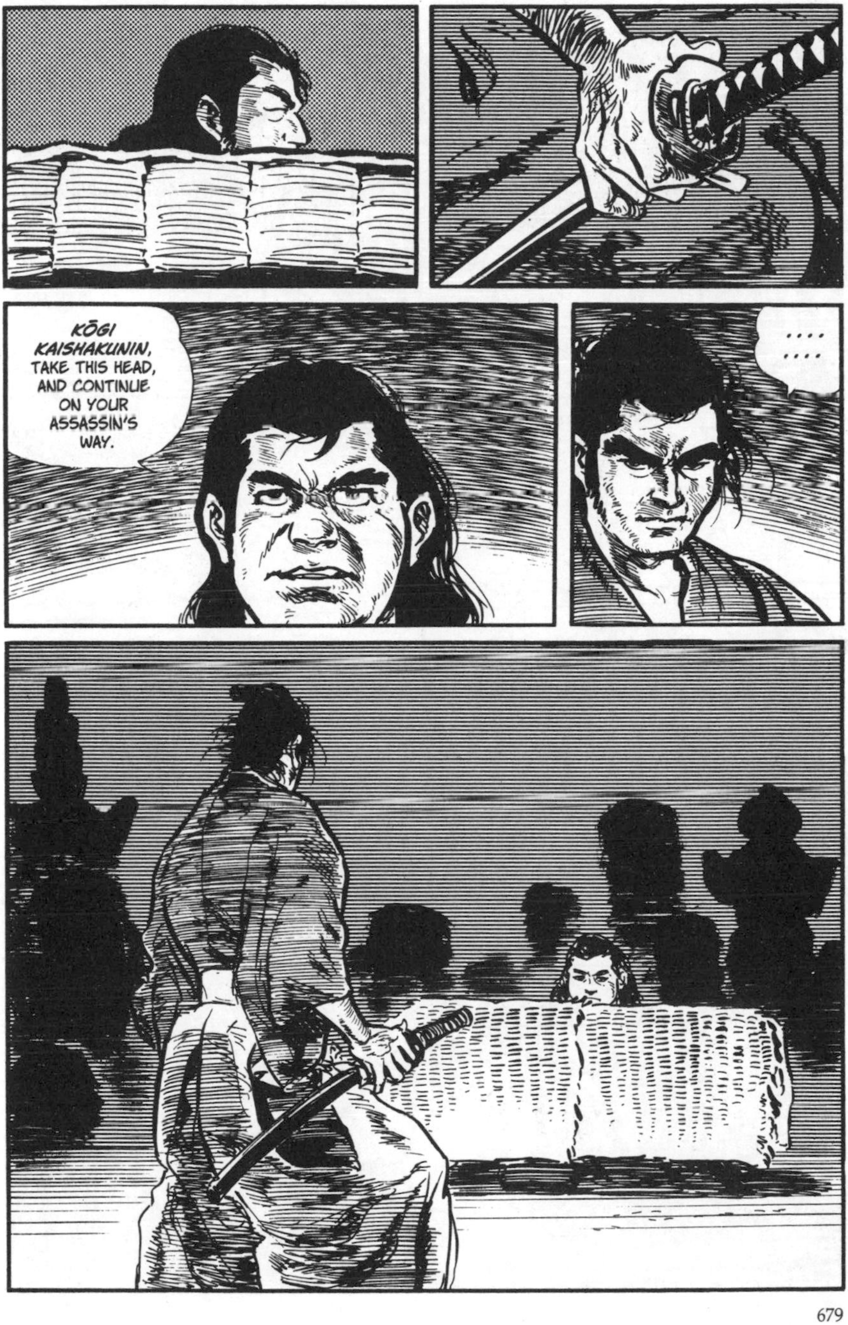
....
KŌGI KAISHAKUNIN, TAKE THIS HEAD, AND CONTINUE ON YOUR ASSASSIN'S WAY.

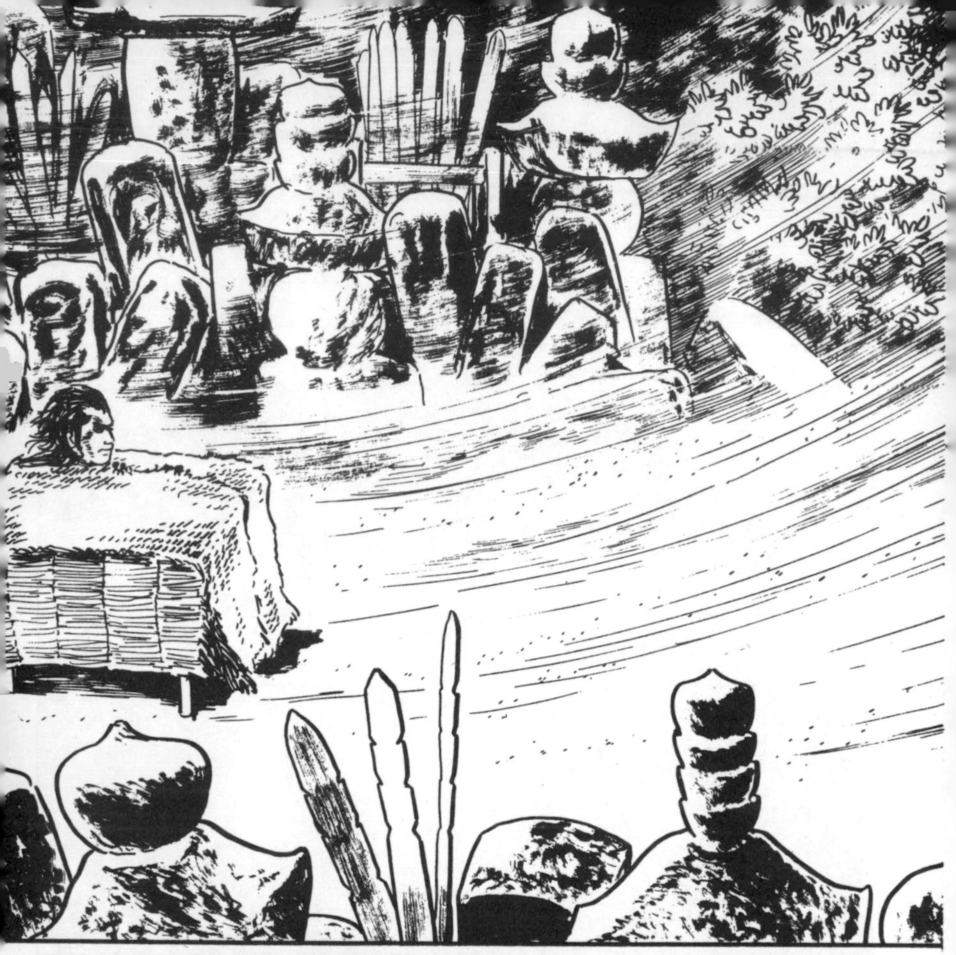

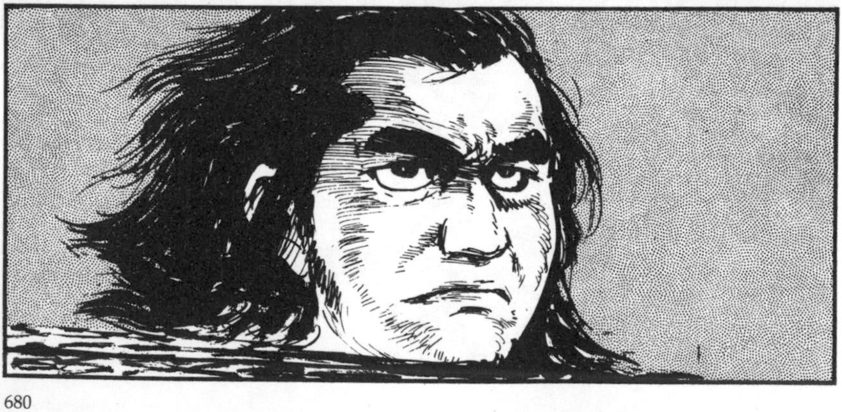

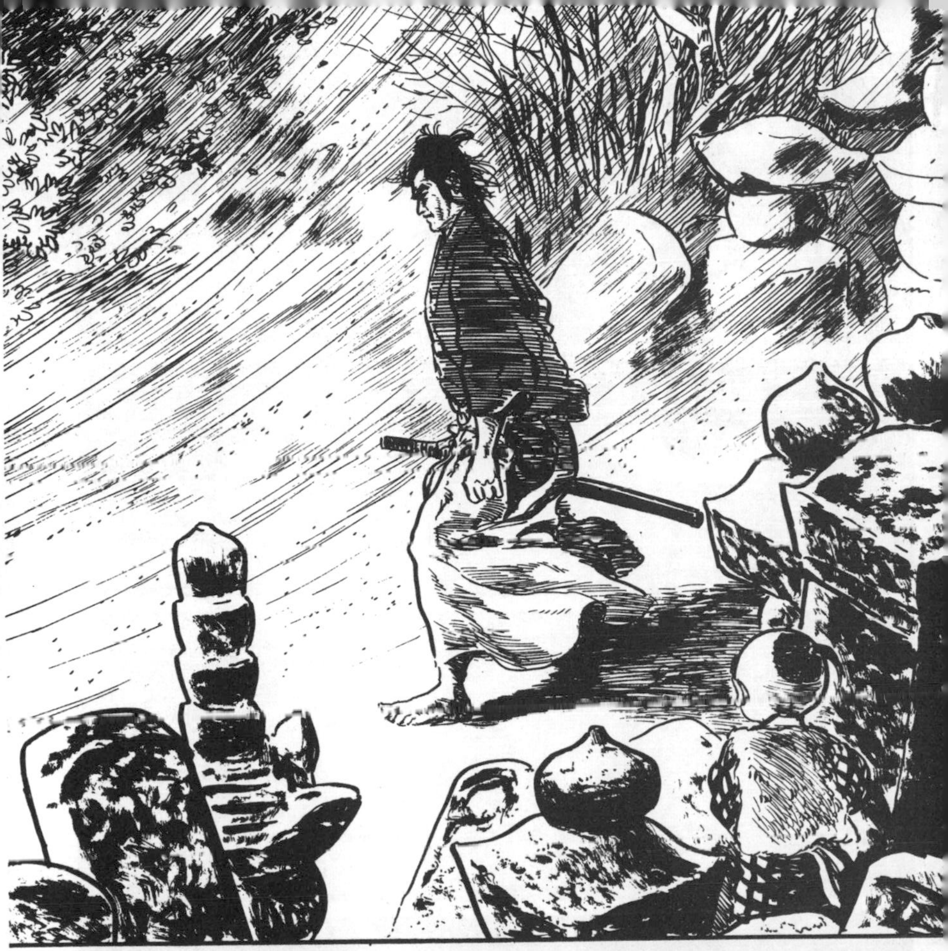
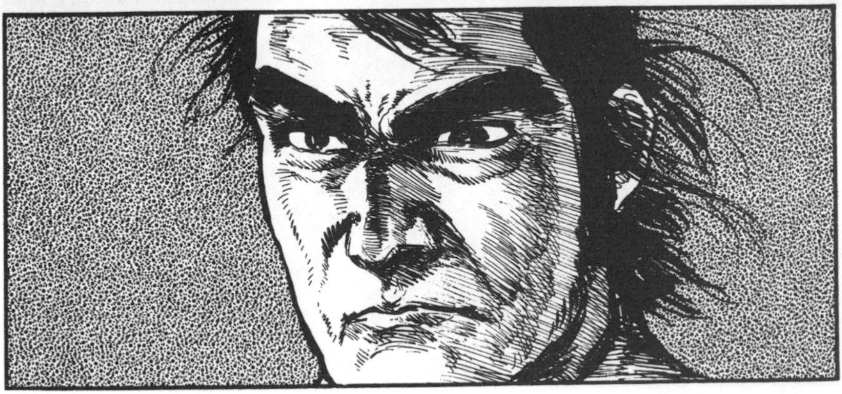

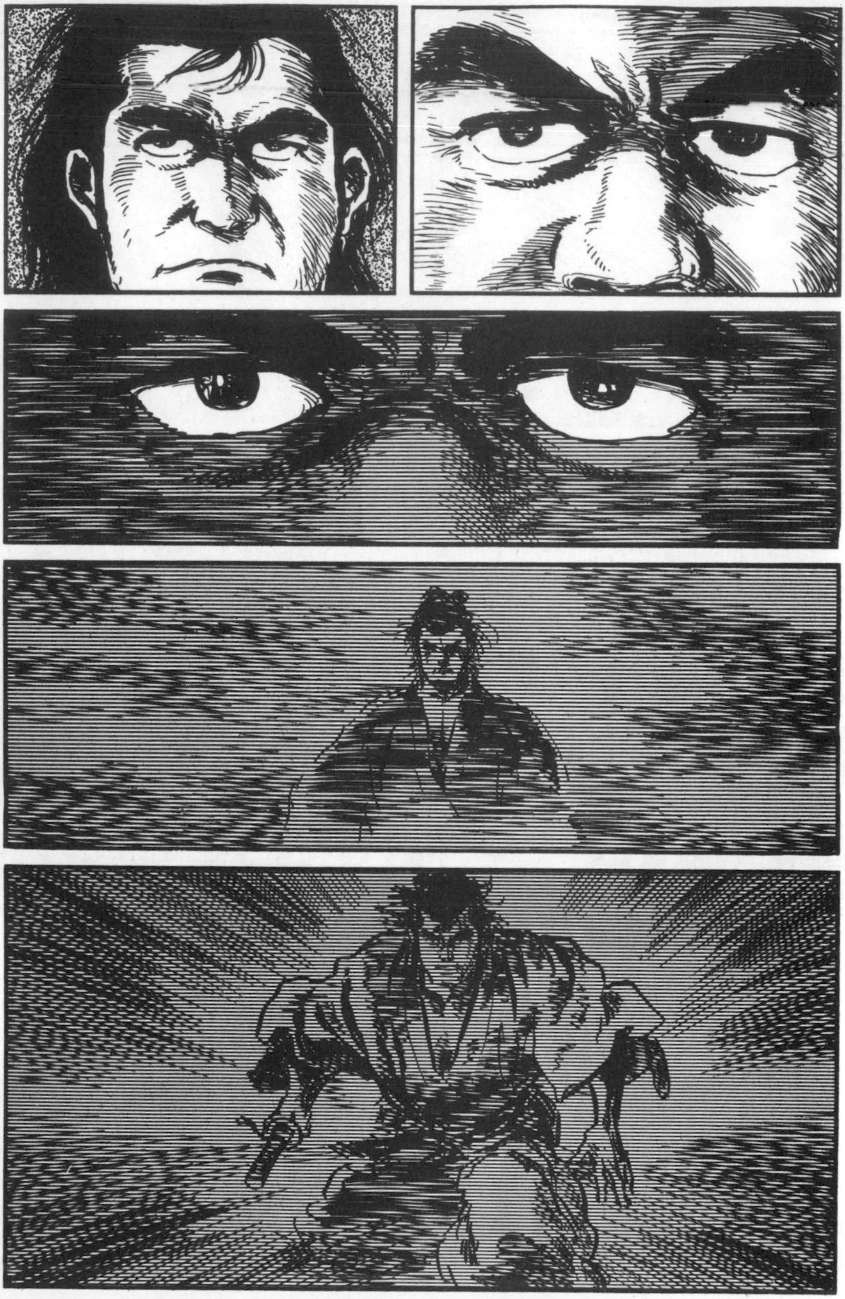

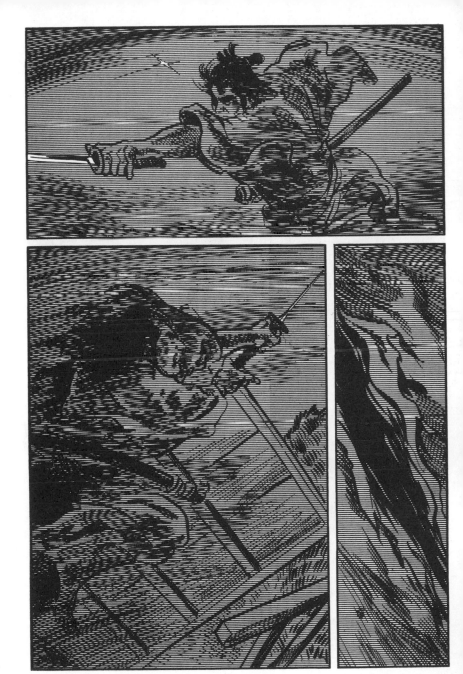

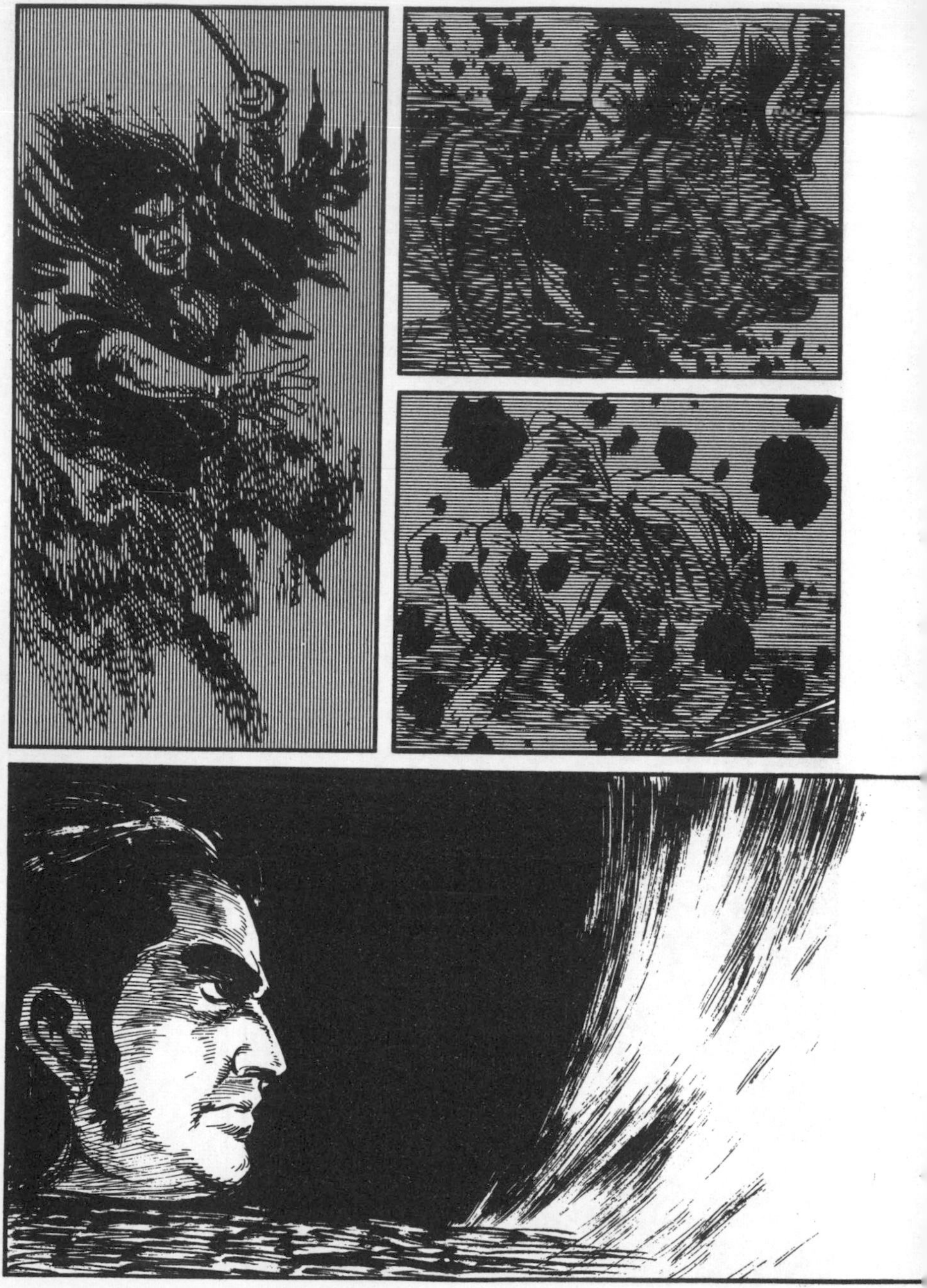

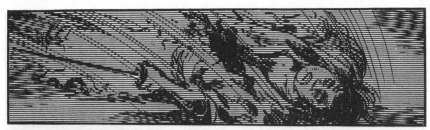

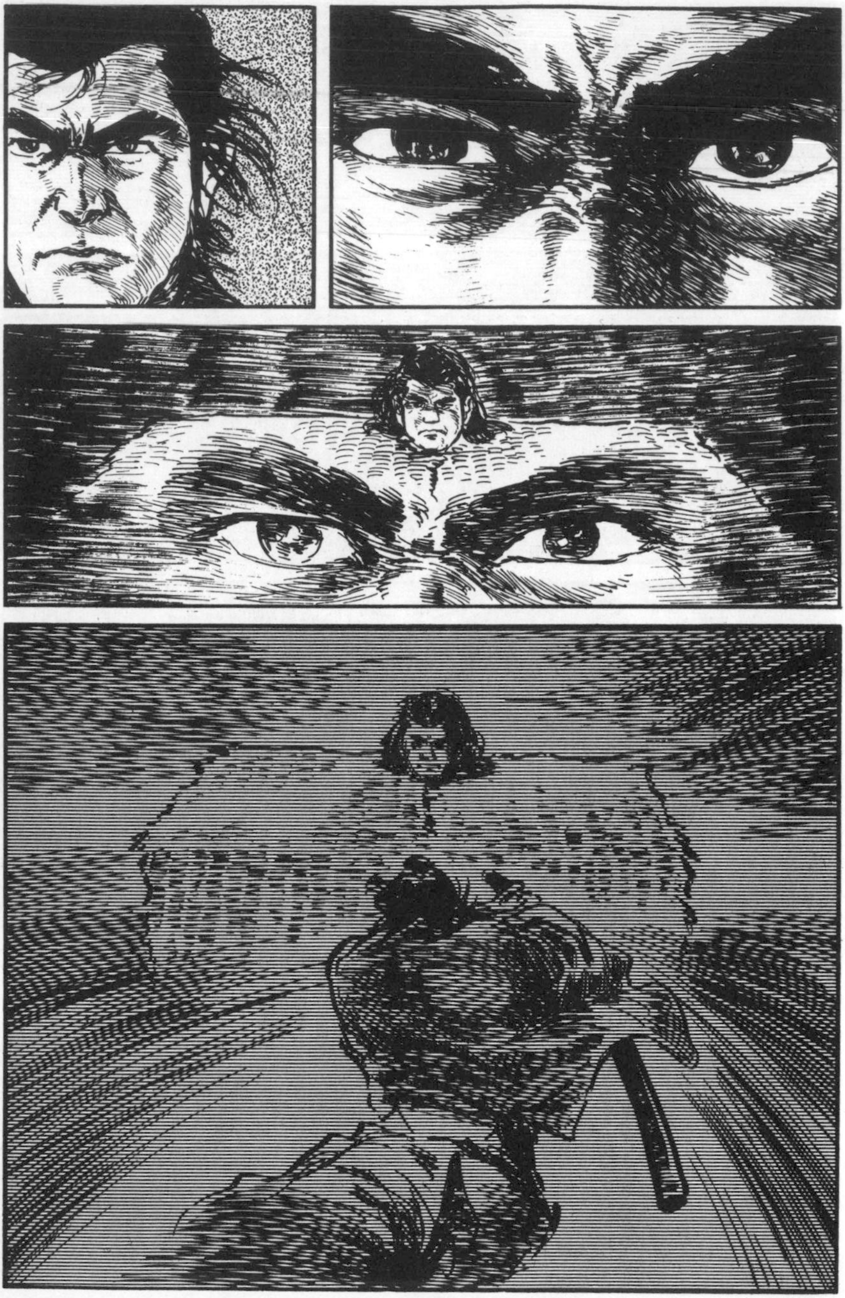

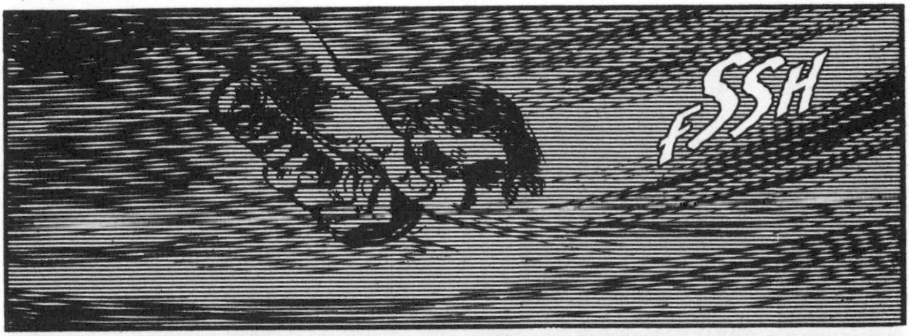
FSSH
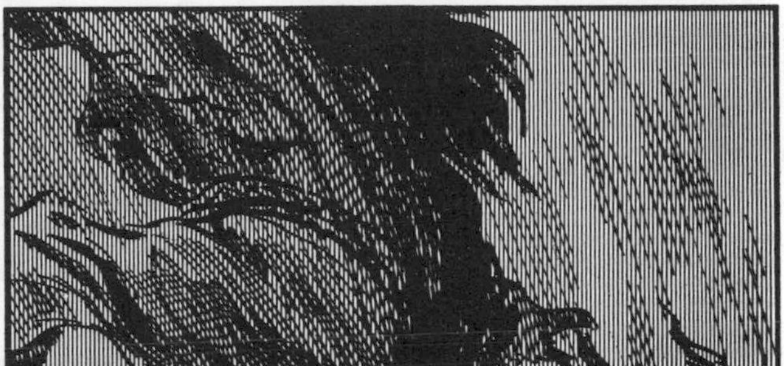
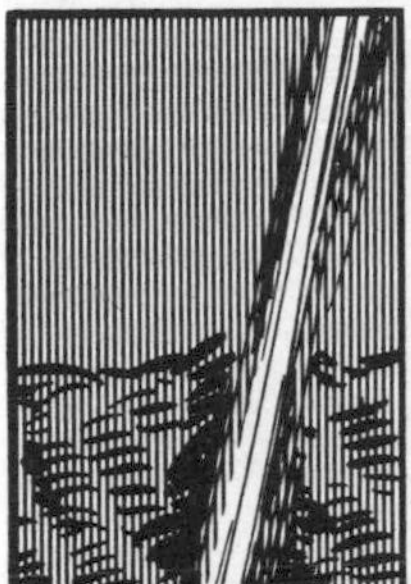
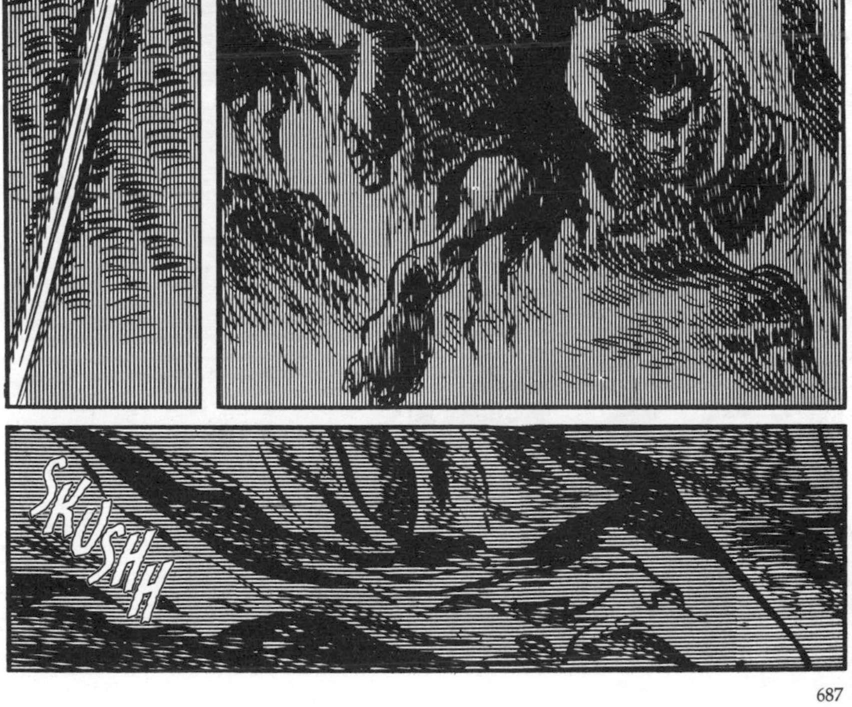
SKUSHH

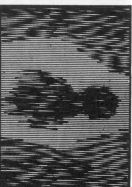

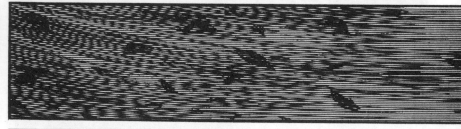

THPP

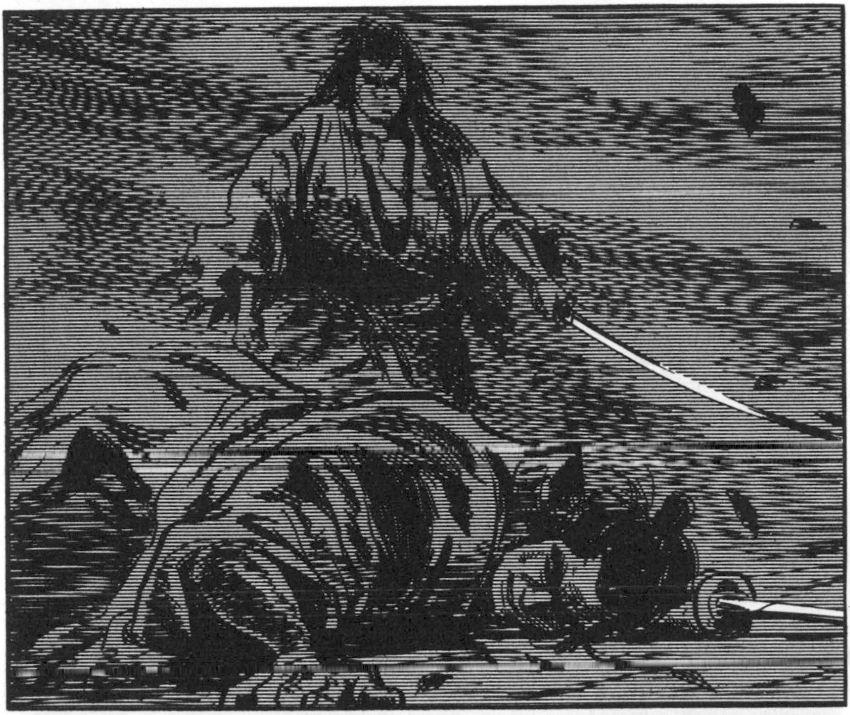

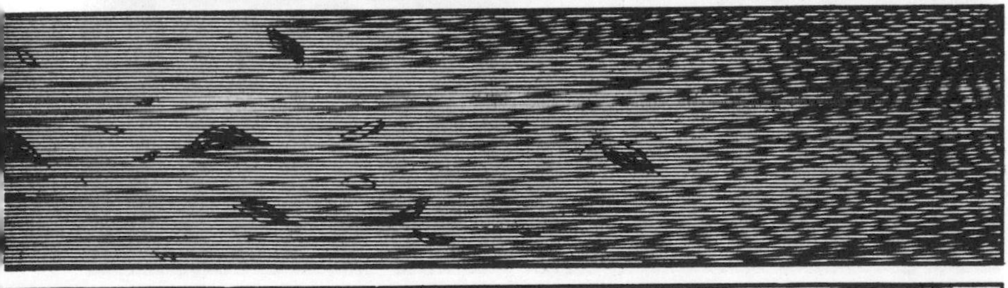

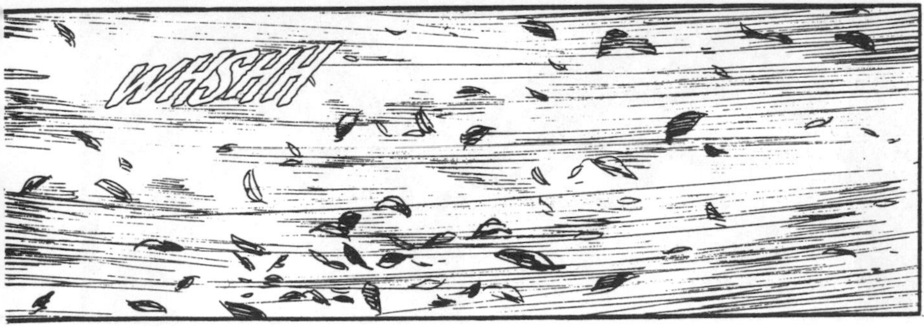
WHSHH

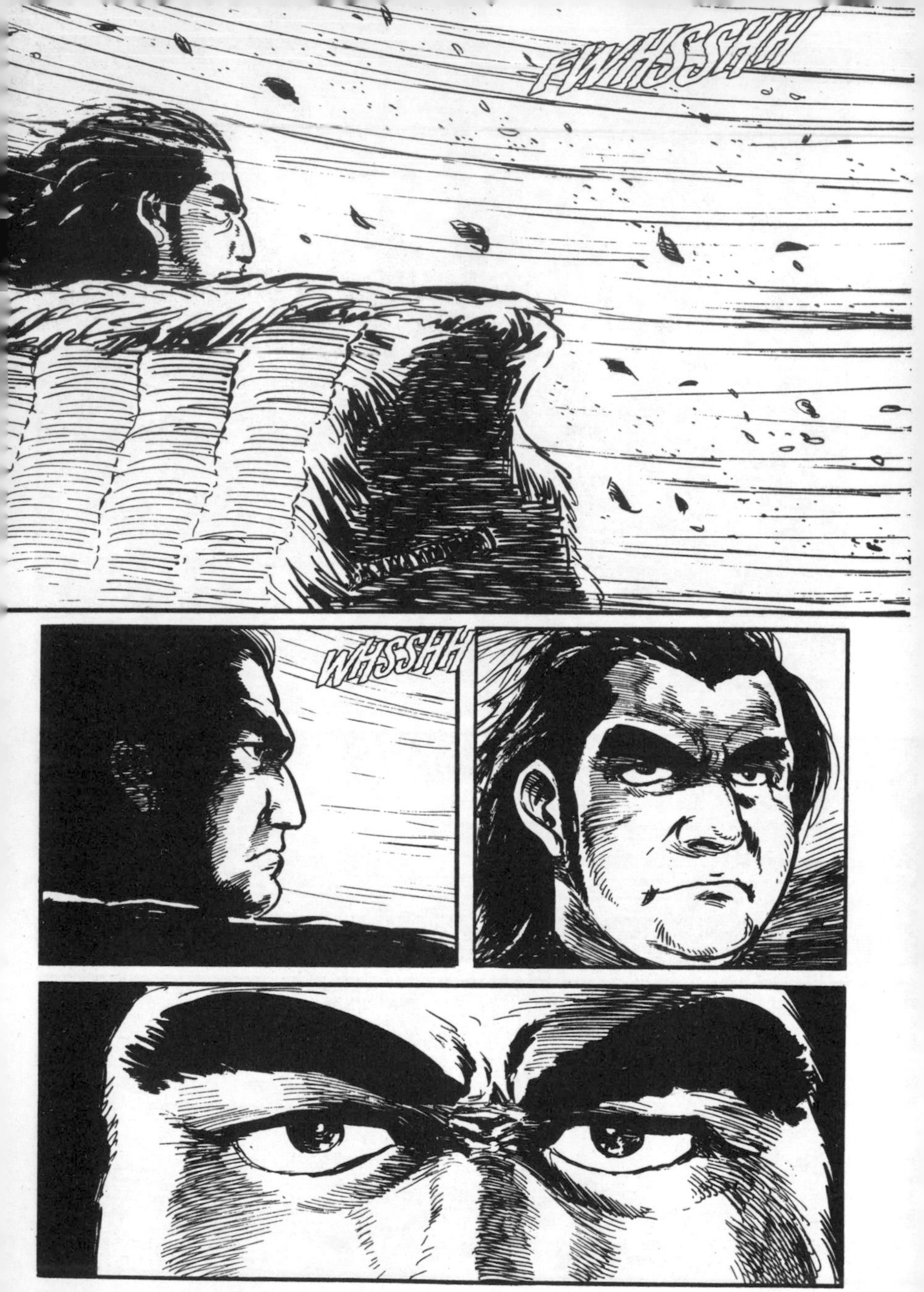
FWHSSHH
WHSSHH

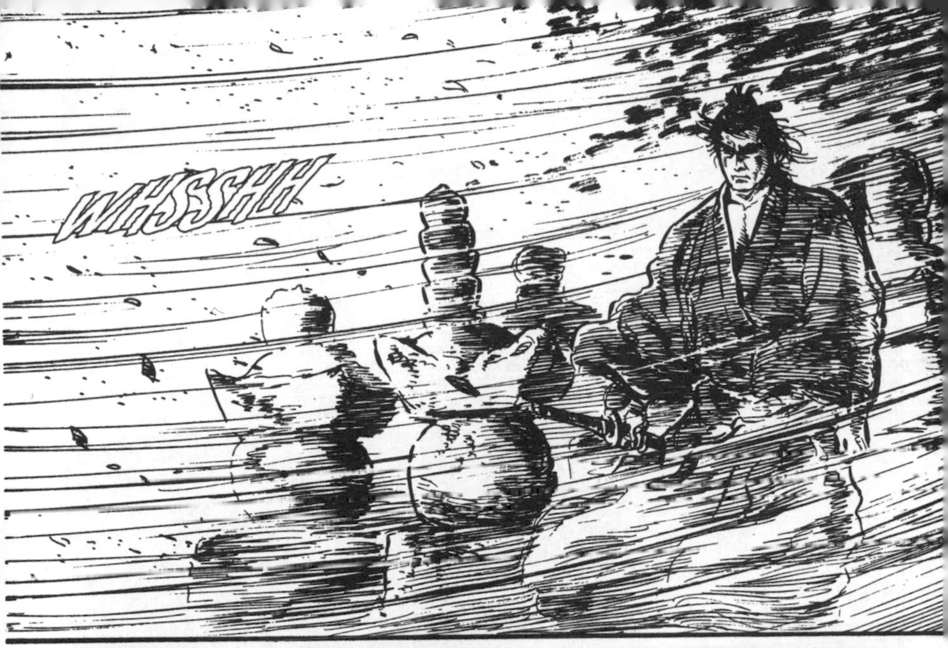
WHSSHH
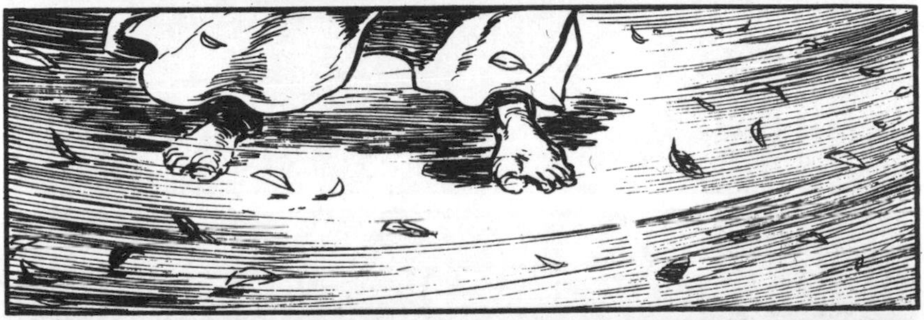
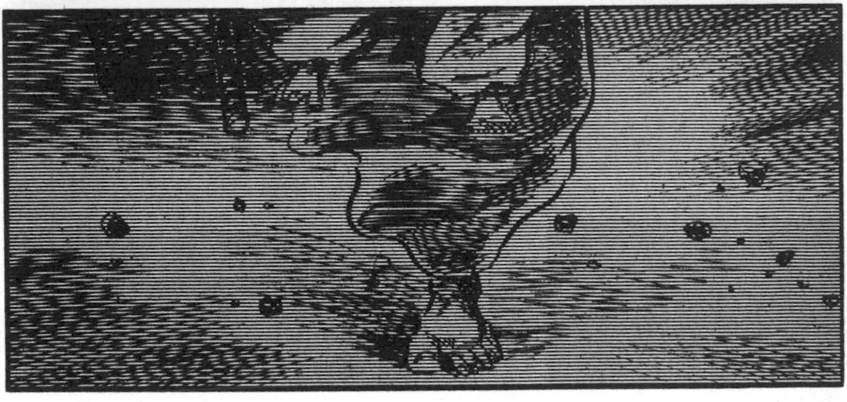

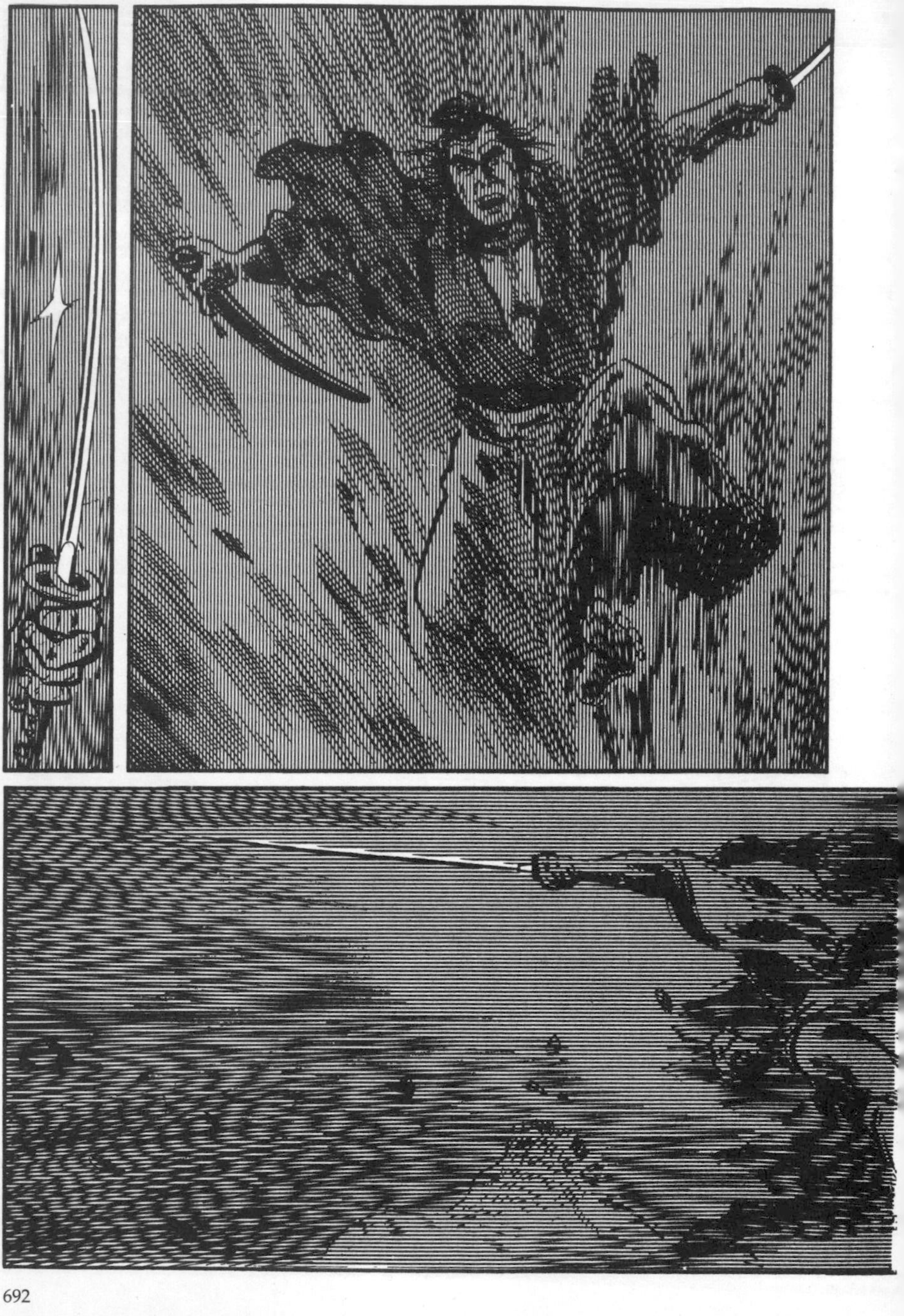

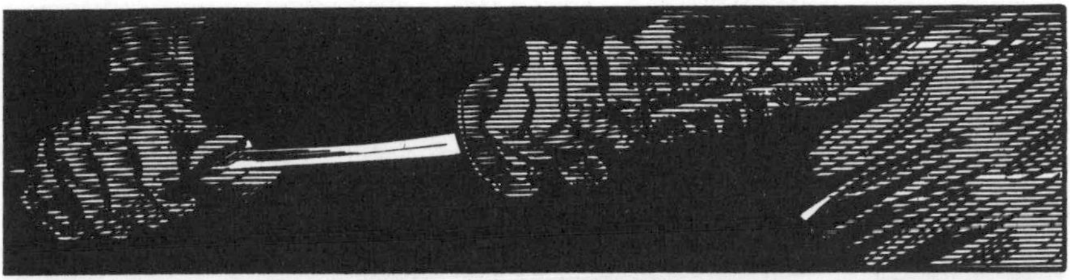
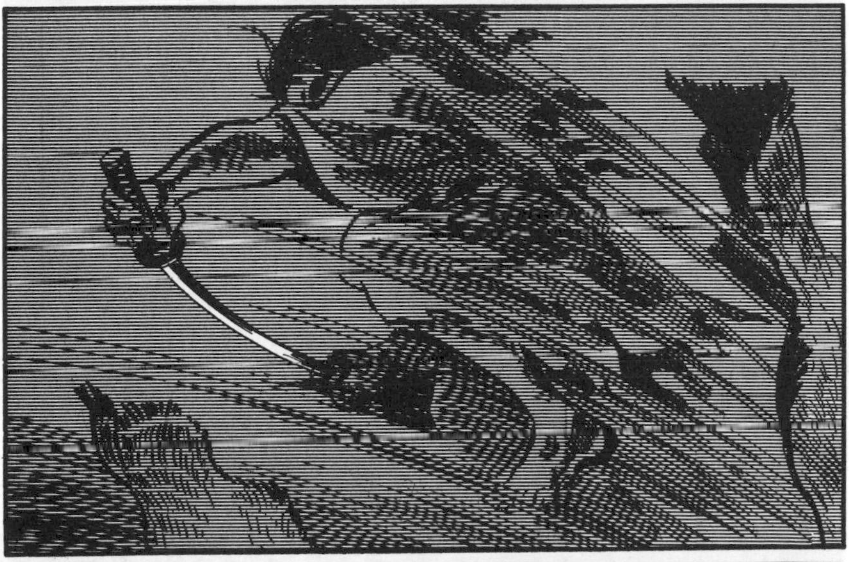
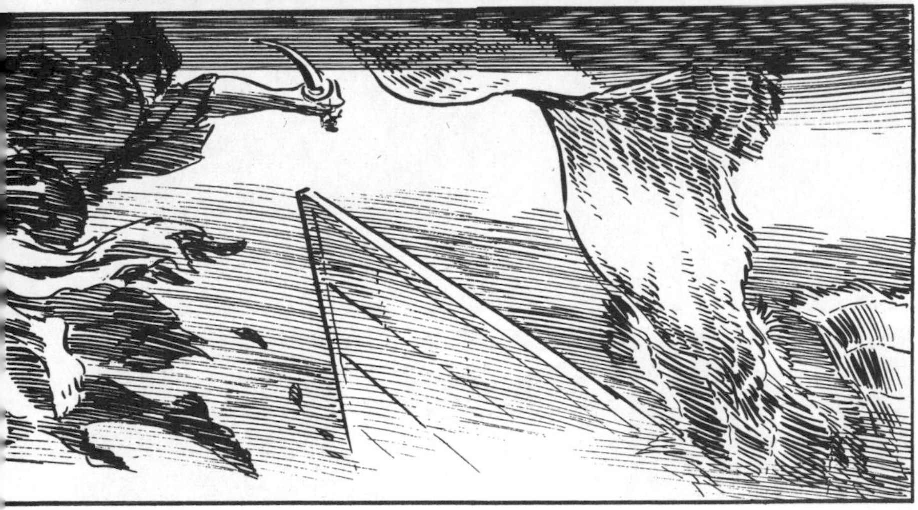

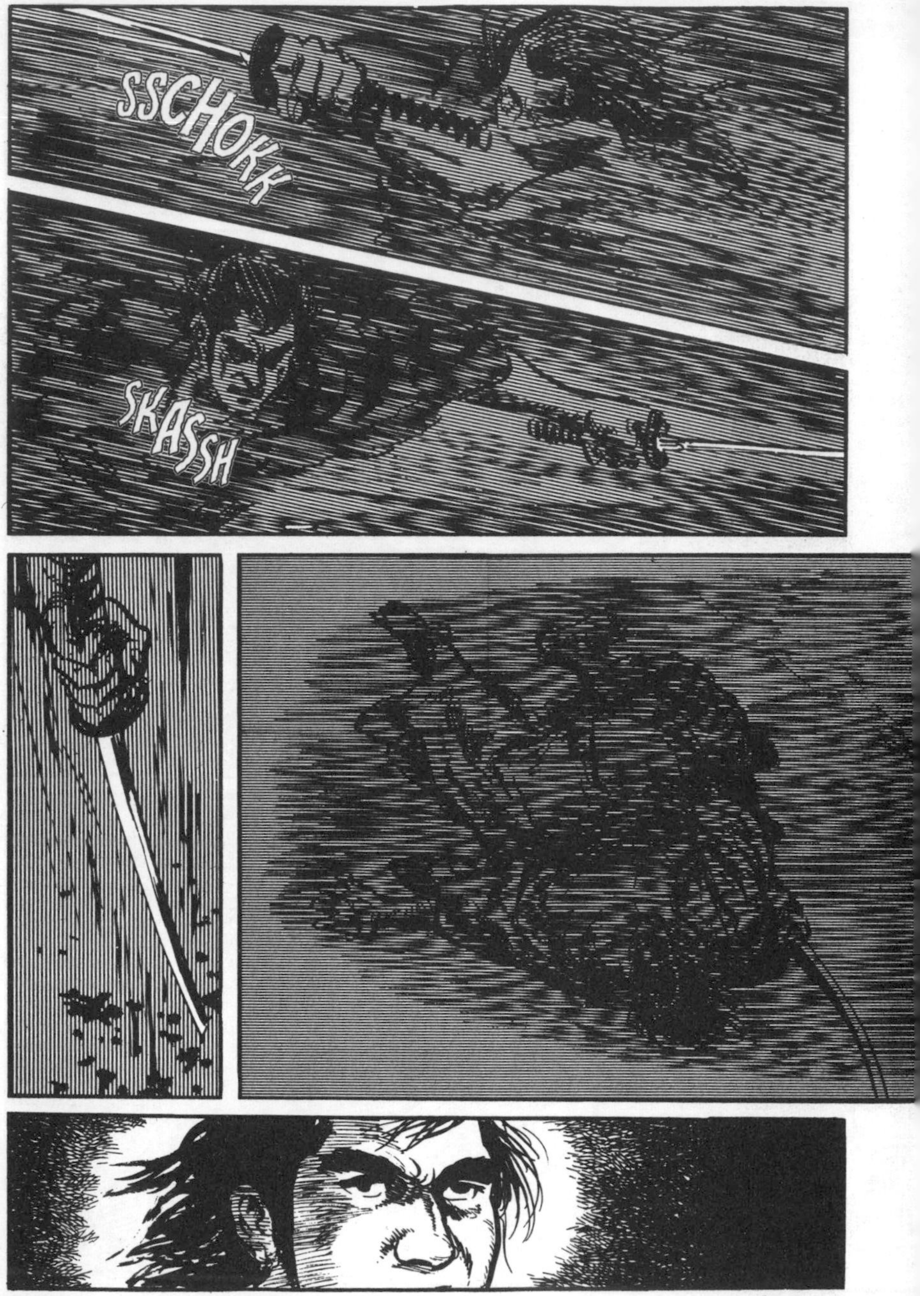
SSCHOKK
SKASSH

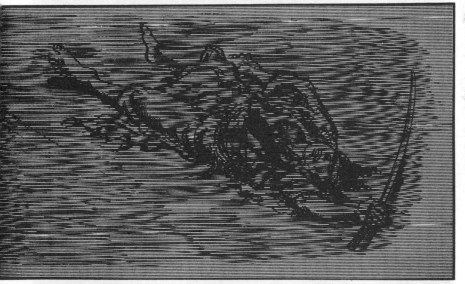

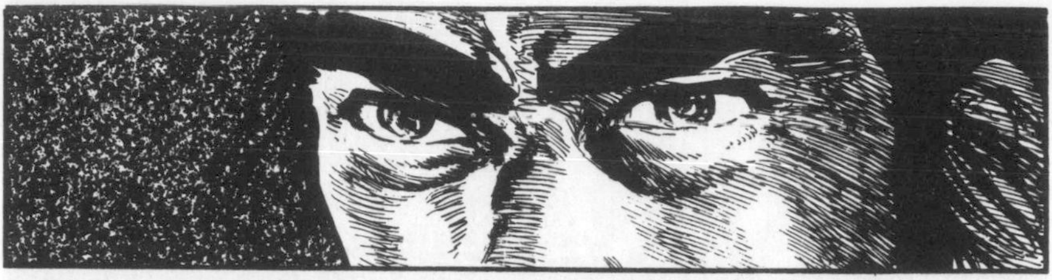
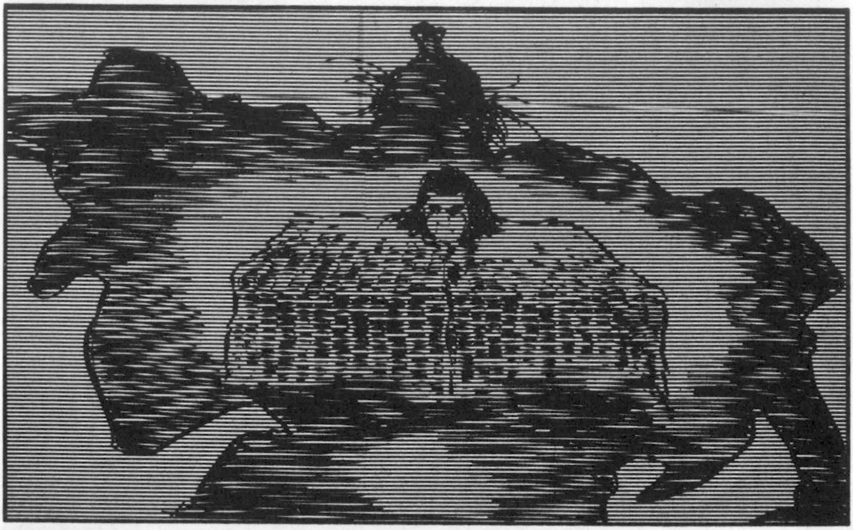
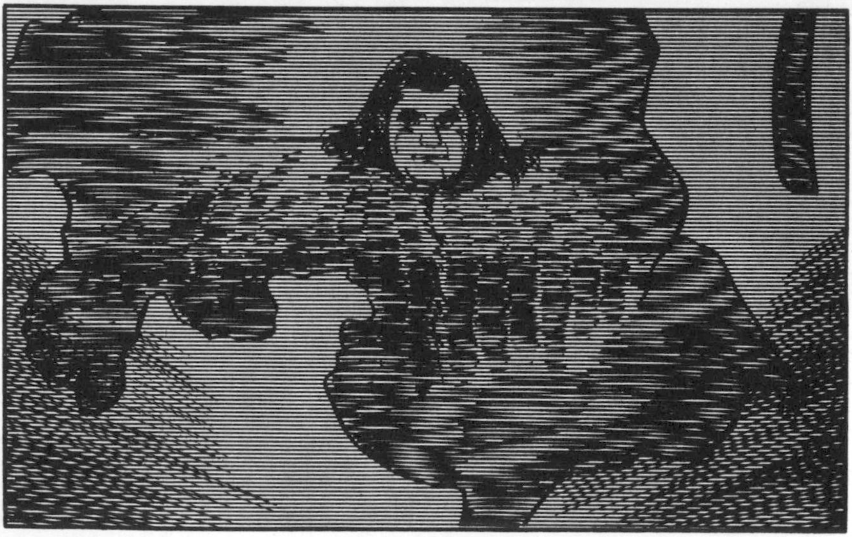

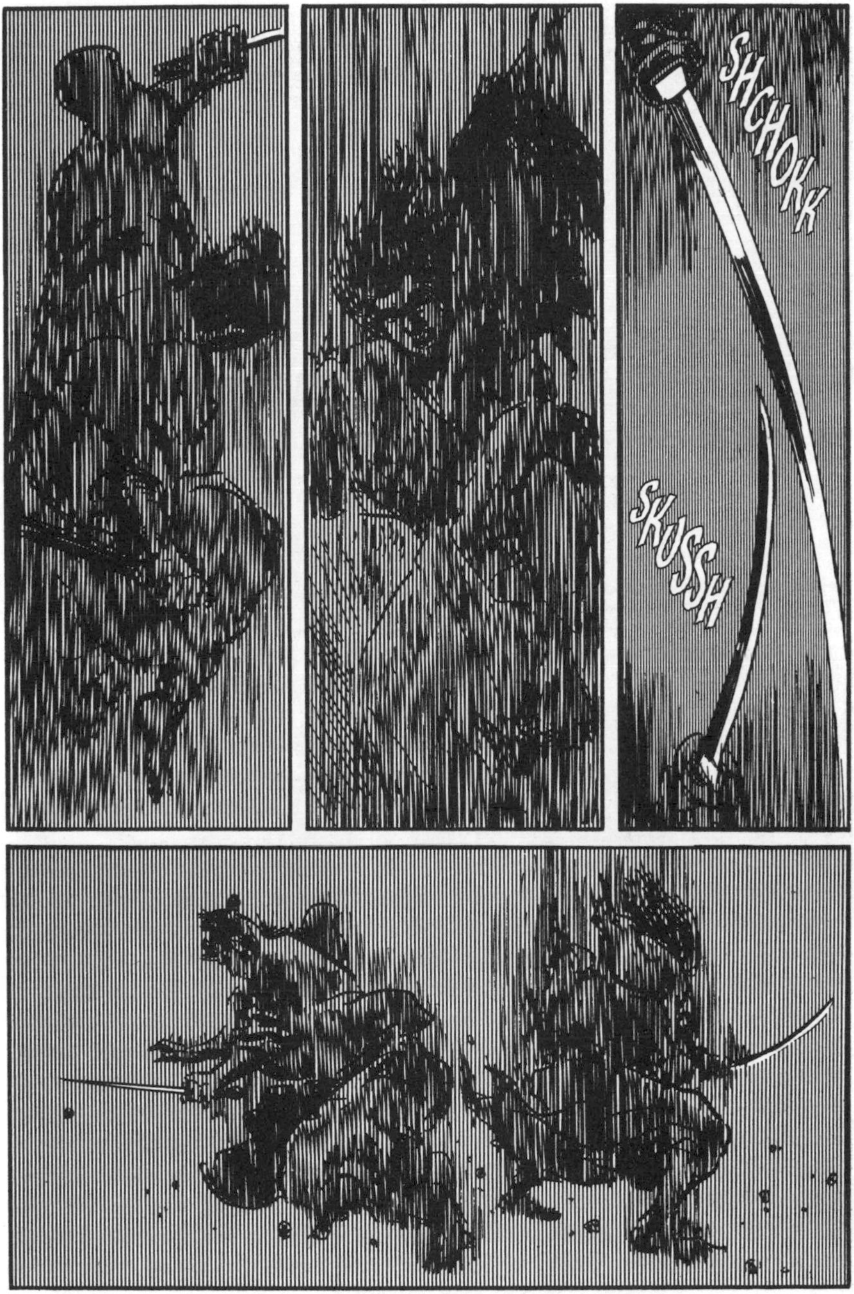
SHCHOKK
SKUSSH

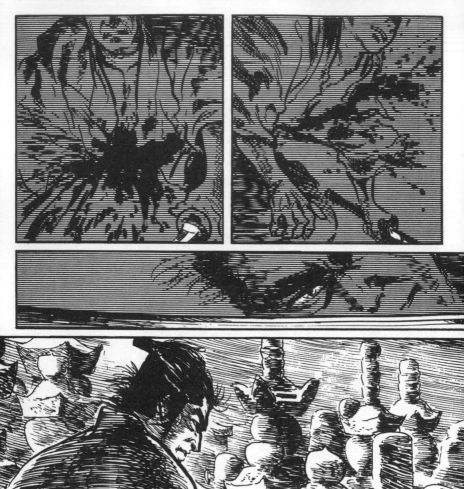

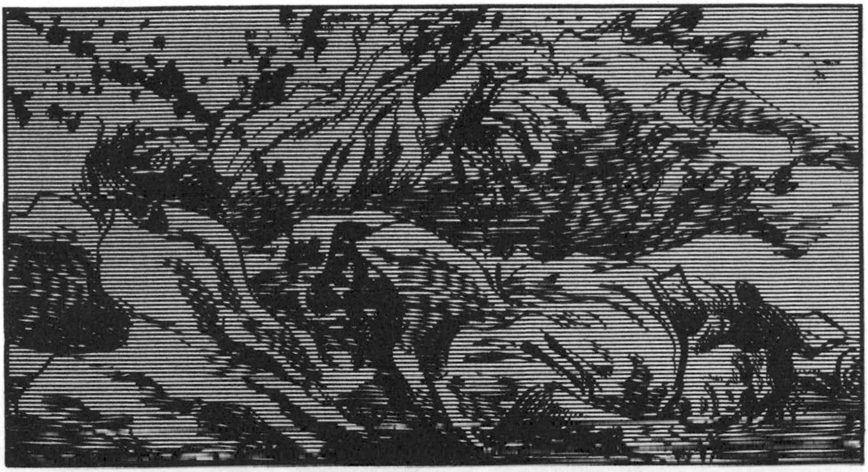
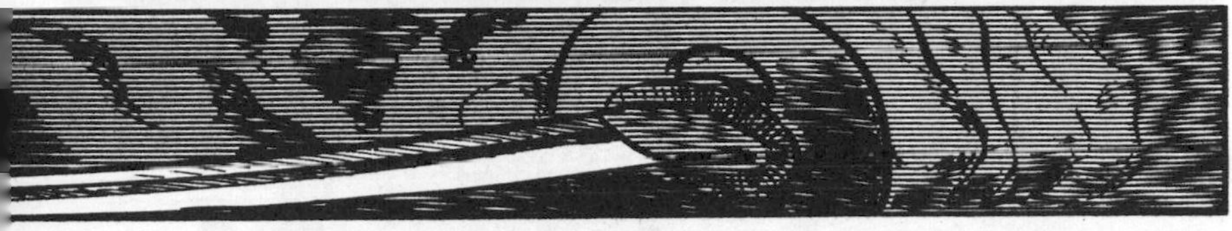
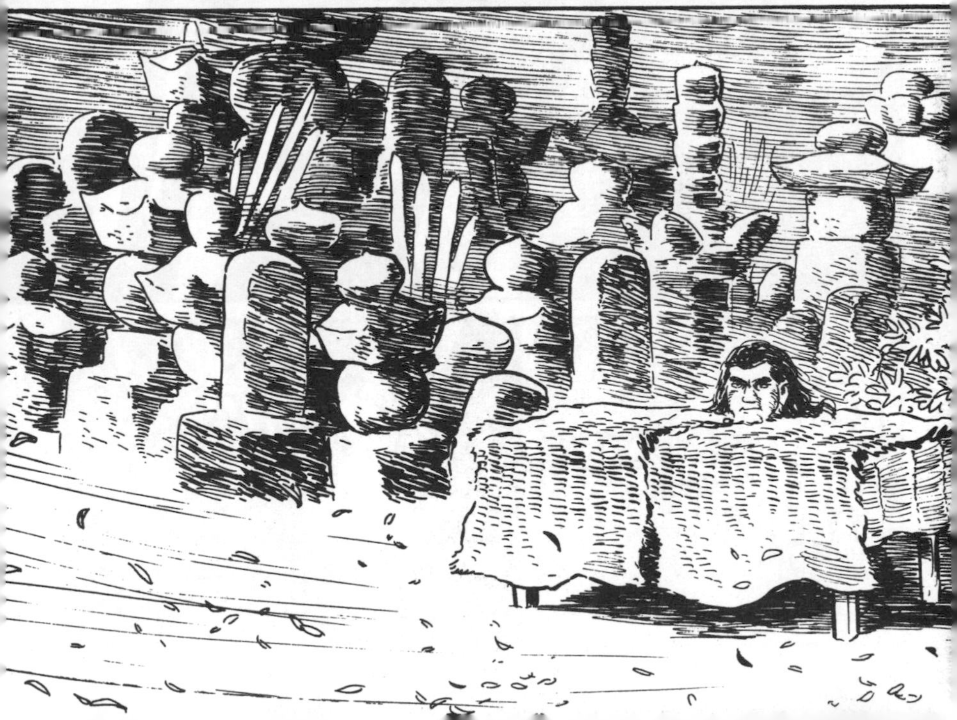

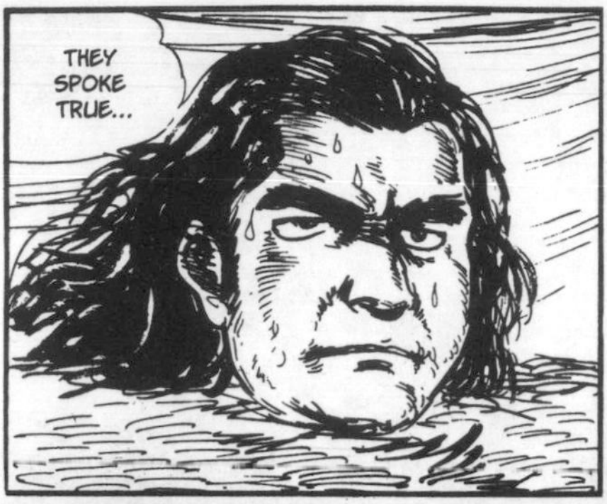
THEY SPOKE TRUE...
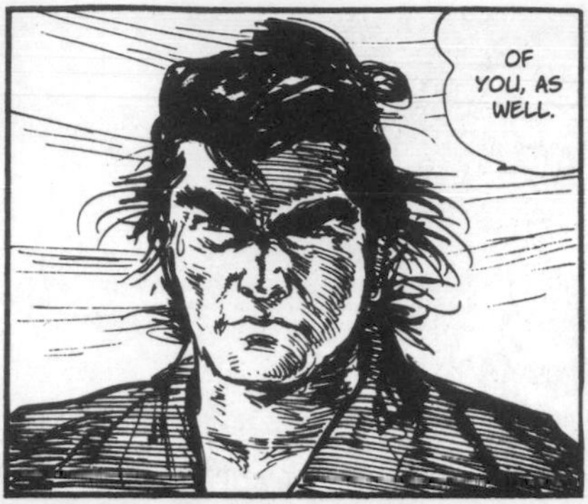
OF YOU, AS WELL.
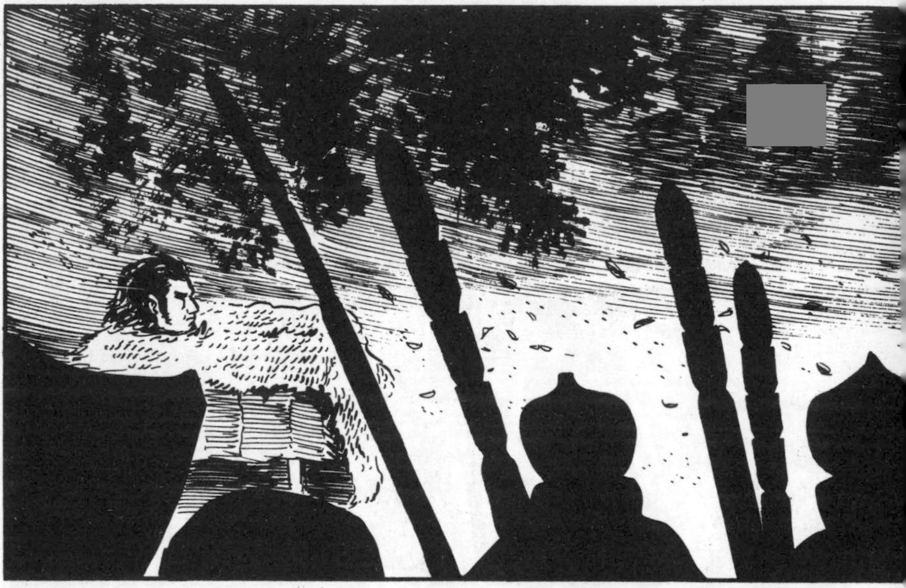
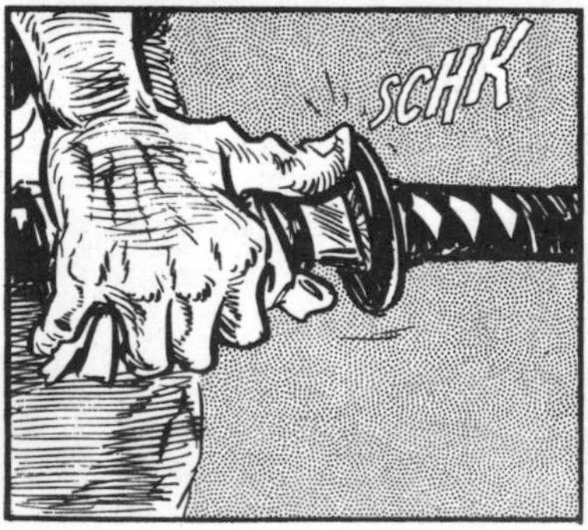
SCHK
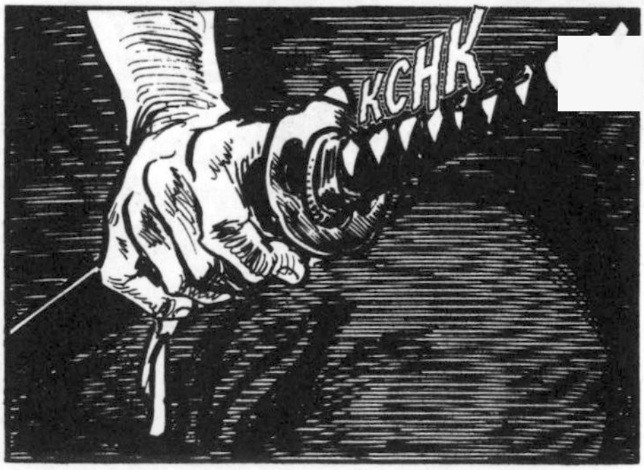
KCHK

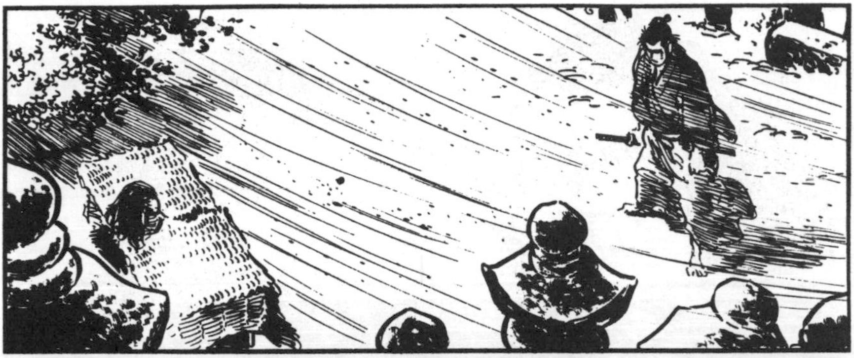
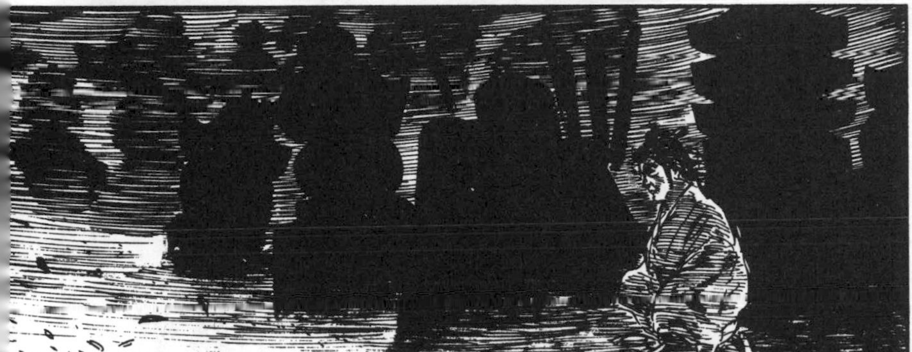
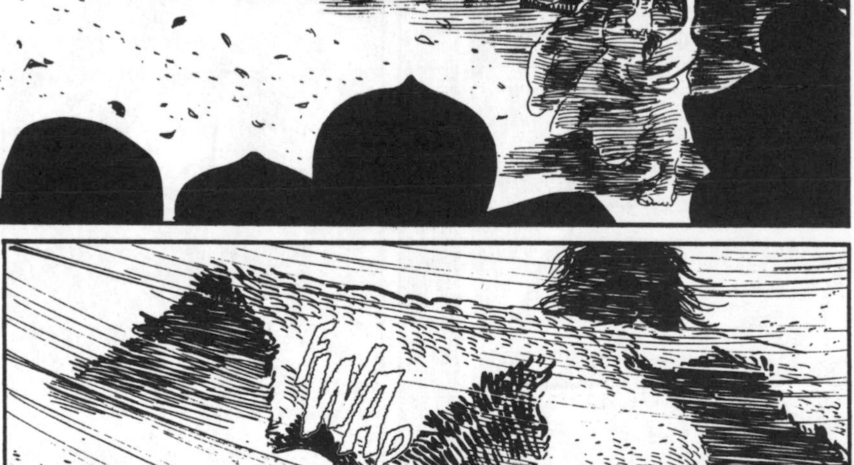
FWAP

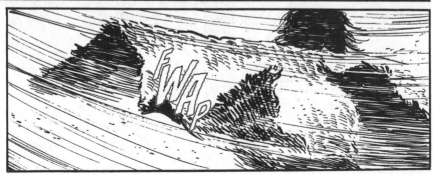

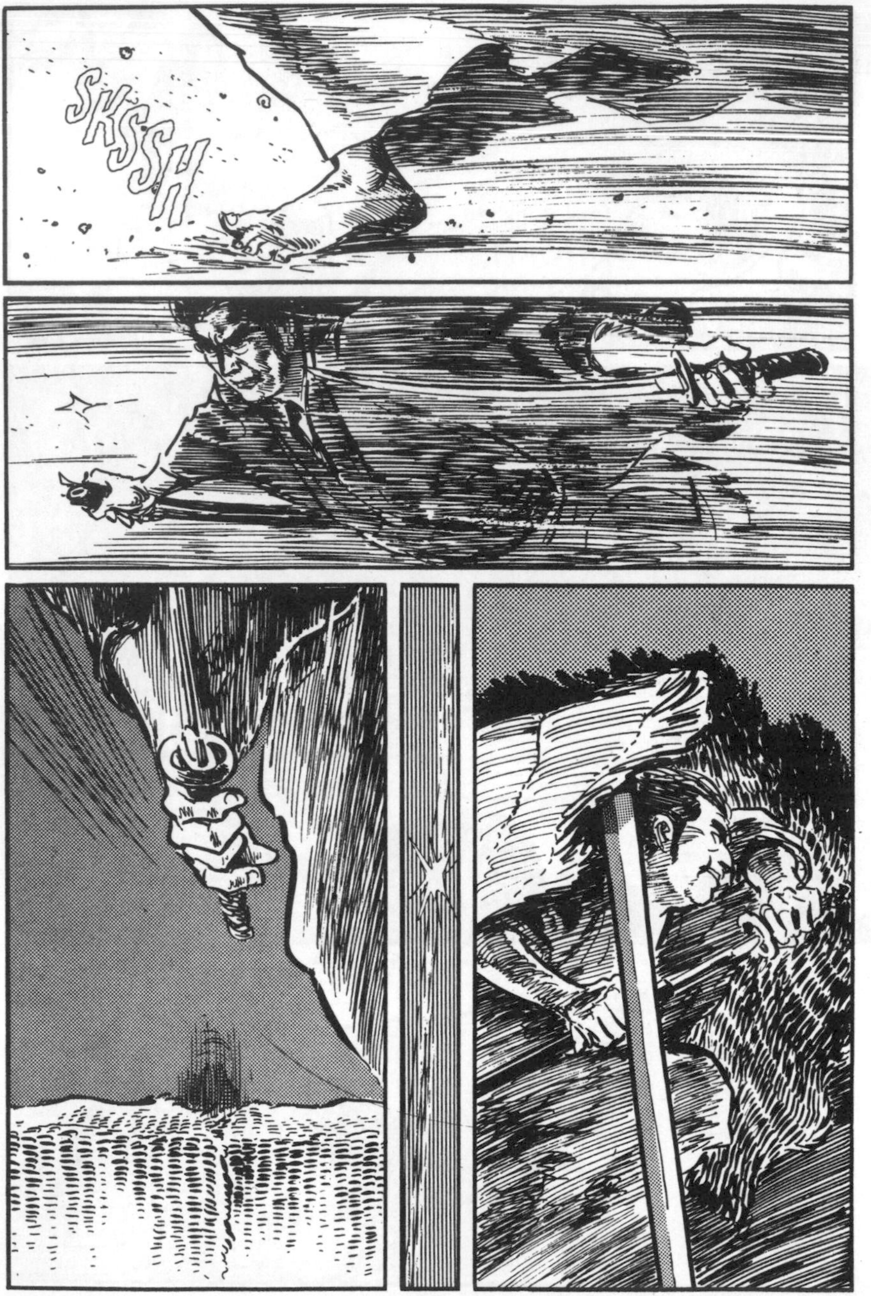
SKSSH

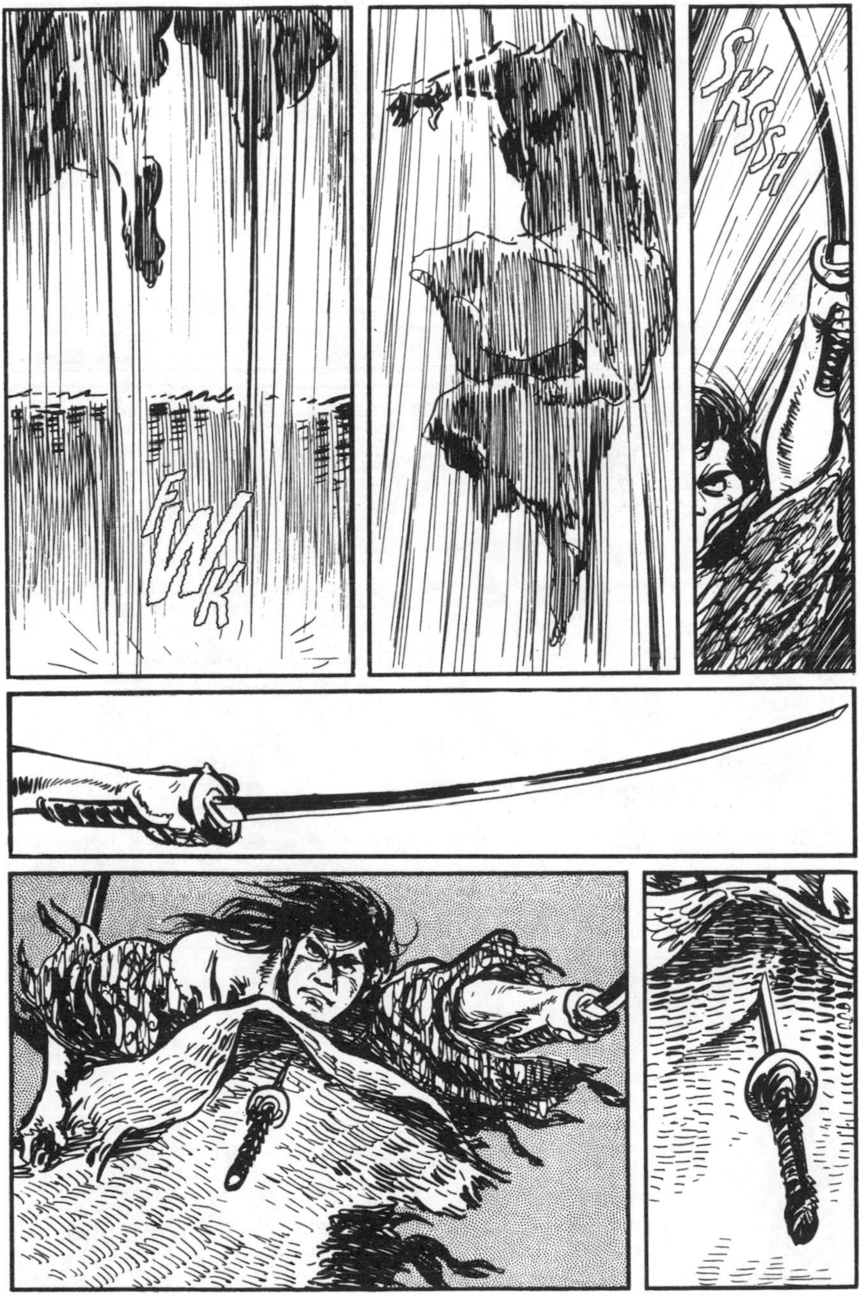
SKSSH
FWK

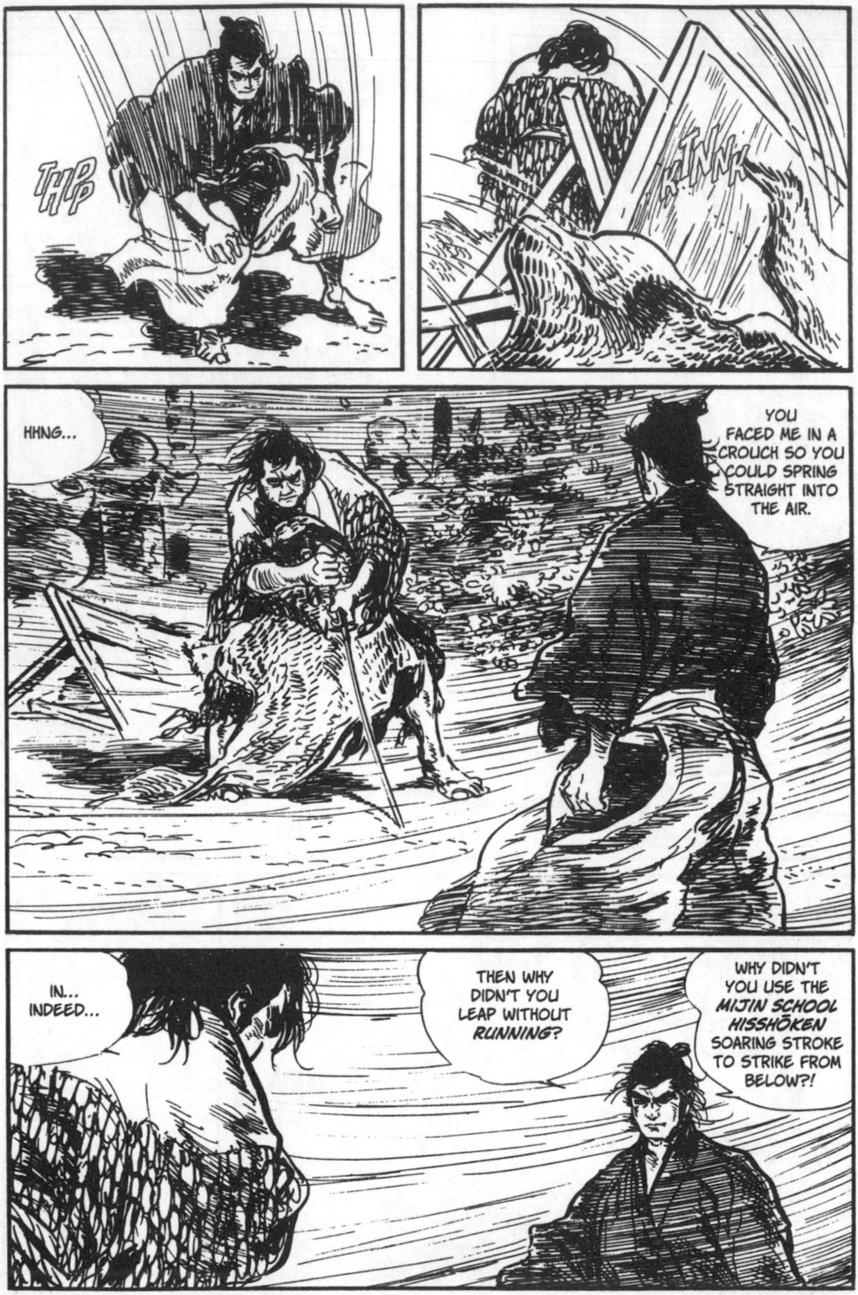
KINNK
THPP
YOU FACED ME IN A CROUCH SO YOU COULD SPRING STRAIGHT INTO THE AIR.
HHNG...
WHY DIDN'T YOU USE THE *MIJIN SCHOOL HISSHŌKEN* SOARING STROKE TO STRIKE FROM BELOW?!
THEN WHY DIDN'T YOU LEAP WITHOUT *RUNNING*?
IN... INDEED...

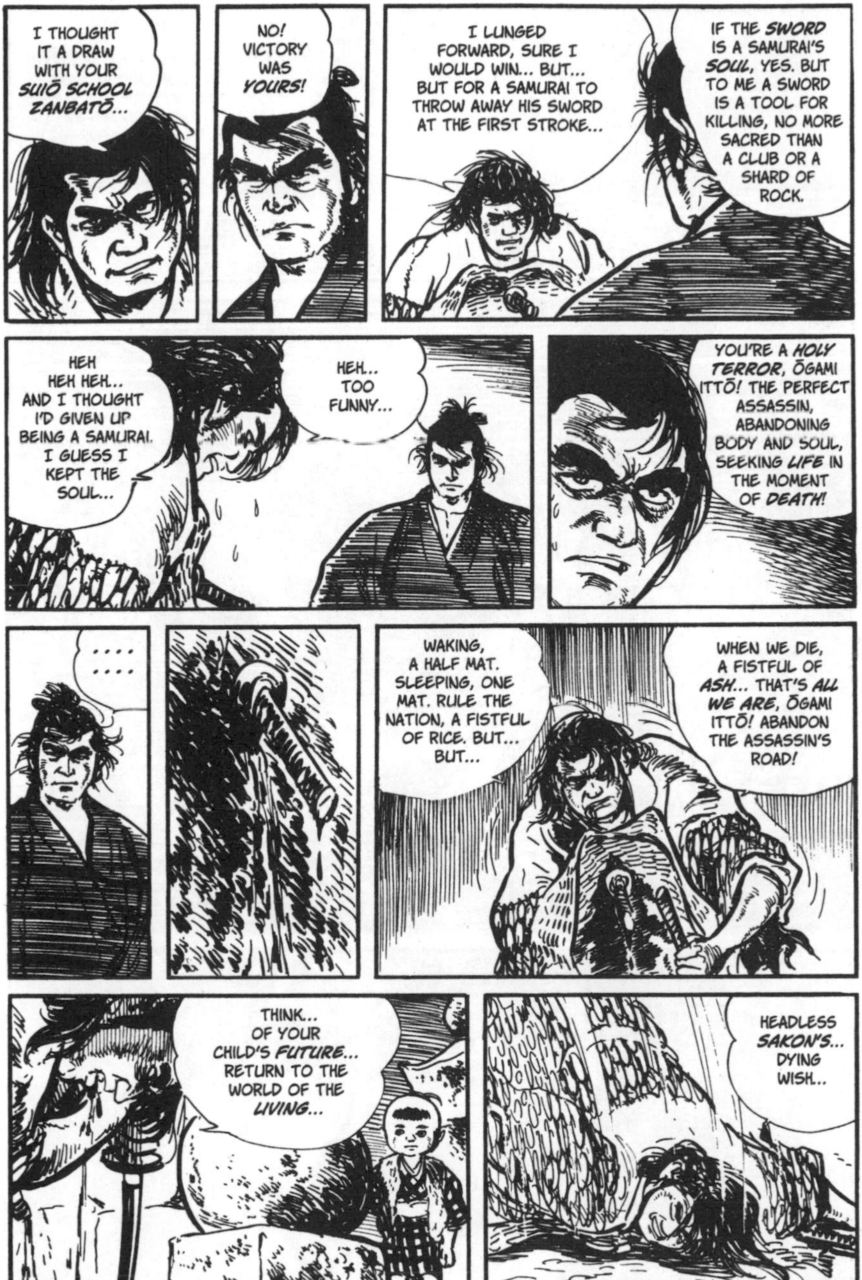

I THOUGHT IT A DRAW WITH YOUR SUIŌ SCHOOL ZANBATŌ...
NO! VICTORY WAS YOURS!
I LUNGED FORWARD, SURE I WOULD WIN... BUT... BUT FOR A SAMURAI TO THROW AWAY HIS SWORD AT THE FIRST STROKE...
IF THE SWORD IS A SAMURAI'S SOUL, YES. BUT TO ME A SWORD IS A TOOL FOR KILLING, NO MORE SACRED THAN A CLUB OR A SHARD OF ROCK.
HEH HEH HEH... AND I THOUGHT I'D GIVEN UP BEING A SAMURAI. I GUESS I KEPT THE SOUL...
HEH... TOO FUNNY...
YOU'RE A HOLY TERROR, ŌGAMI ITTŌ! THE PERFECT ASSASSIN, ABANDONING BODY AND SOUL, SEEKING LIFE IN THE MOMENT OF DEATH!
....
WAKING, A HALF MAT. SLEEPING, ONE MAT. RULE THE NATION, A FISTFUL OF RICE. BUT... BUT...
WHEN WE DIE, A FISTFUL OF ASH... THAT'S ALL WE ARE, ŌGAMI ITTŌ! ABANDON THE ASSASSIN'S ROAD!
THINK... OF YOUR CHILD'S FUTURE... RETURN TO THE WORLD OF THE LIVING...
HEADLESS SAKON'S... DYING WISH...

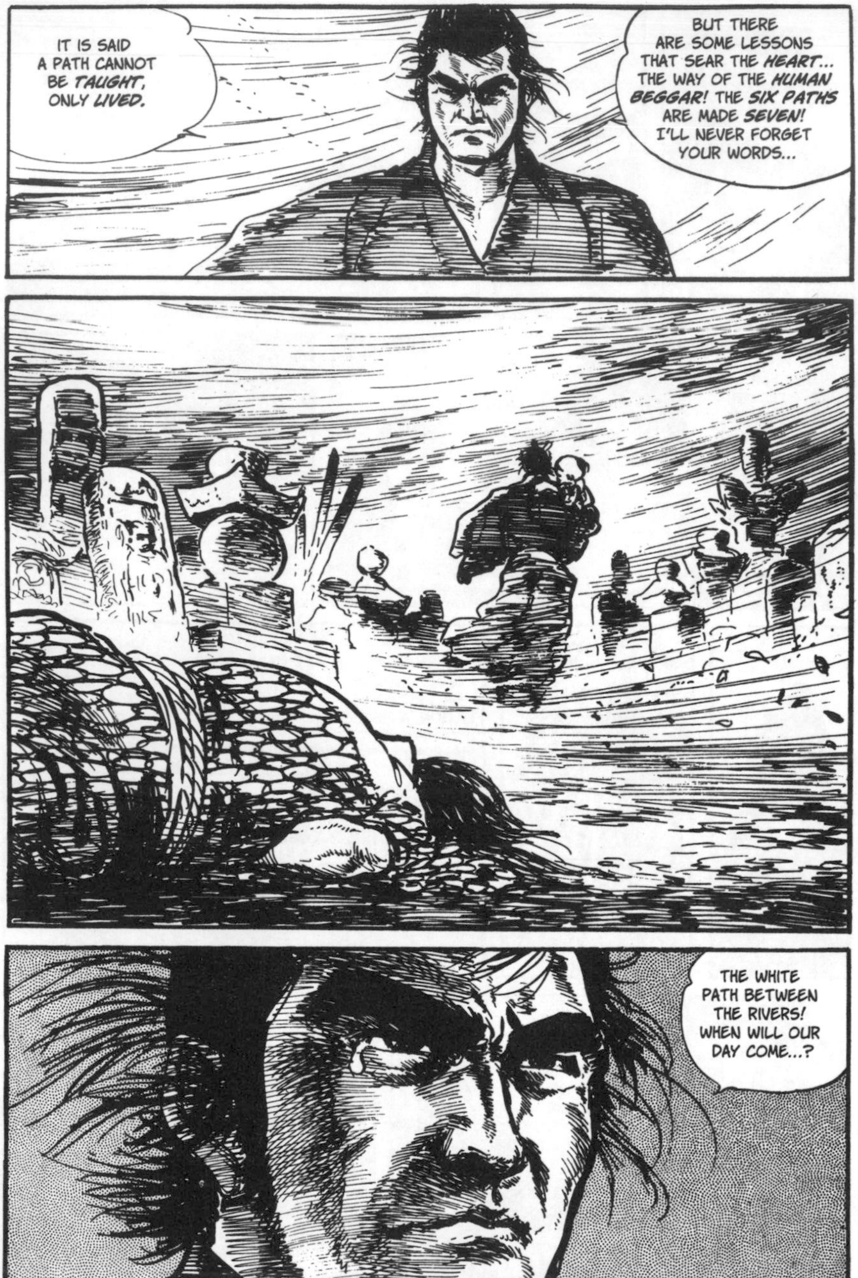
IT IS SAID A PATH CANNOT BE *TAUGHT*, ONLY *LIVED*.
BUT THERE ARE SOME LESSONS THAT SEAR THE *HEART*... THE WAY OF THE *HUMAN BEGGAR*! THE *SIX PATHS* ARE MADE *SEVEN*! I'LL NEVER FORGET YOUR WORDS...
THE WHITE PATH BETWEEN THE RIVERS! WHEN WILL OUR DAY COME...?

GLOSSARY

annya A working prostitute. There was a thriving sex industry in Edo-period Japan and scores of different words to describe the different varieties of sex workers.

ashigaru A foot soldier in the employ of *daimyō*. Lowest of the warrior ranks.

bangashira Commander of the guard. Each *han* had a standing guard—the *han*—of samurai to protect the lord and castle. The *ō-bangashira* was the supreme commander of the guard, the general of the *han* army.

Benten One of the seven gods and goddesses of good fortune popular among the common people, a folk version of the Buddhist *bodhisattva*, a manifestation of one aspect of the Buddha's nature. In this case, a *bodhisattva* of mercy and compassion, usually depicted as a female.

bōhachi, kutsuwa The Japanese yakuza specialize in different underworld activities, from gambling and protection scams to prostitution. *Bōhachi* and *kutsuwa* were Edo-period terms for yakuza dealing in organized prostitution.

bugi The martial arts, the arts of war. Restricted to the samurai class under the Tokugawa shogunate's strict social controls.

bushi A samurai. A member of the warrior class.

cho Old unit of measurement, approximately 109 meters (119 yards).

daikan The primary local representative of the shogunate in territories outside the capital of Edo. The *daikan* and his staff collected taxes owed to Edo and oversaw public works, agriculture, and other projects administered by the central government.

daikansho The office of the *daikan.*

daimyō A feudal lord.

danzai The samurai's right to put to death anyone who insults his honor.

deiri A fight between rival yakuza gangs. From their clothes, speech, and greetings, it is clear that the house of *Jizō* are yakuza, Japan's criminal syndicate.

dono A term of respect for a higher-ranking official or aristocrat. A more common term of respect among civilians is *sama*, indicating more respect than the most common, *san*.

dōtanūki A battle sword; literally, "sword that cuts through torsos."

Edo The capital of medieval Japan and the seat of the shogunate. The site of modern day Tokyo.

fudasashi Merchant houses specializing in rice. They loaned gold to *han* governments, loans secured by the *han*'s projected rice revenues.

gate gate paragate parasamgate The closing mantra of *Prajnaparamita Hridaya* (The Heart of the Perfect Wisdom Sutra), one of the central texts of Zen Buddhism. The sutra is in Sanskrit, and is chanted today in Zen temples around the world.

gomen "Forgive me."

go-yō Literally, "official business." Police and posses carried *go-yō* lanterns when searching for criminals, identifying themselves as law enforcers. A shouted "*Go-yō!*" could be the Edo equivalent of "Halt! Police!" for a *metsuke* or "Make way!" for an official procession.

han A feudal domain.

hanshi Samurai in the service of a *han*.

haori Half coats.

hina Elaborate dolls, traditionally displayed in the spring for the Girls' Day festival.

hollyhock crest Each samurai family had a family crest considered synonymous with the clan itself. The Tokugawa clan crest was a three-leafed hollyhock. To point one's sword toward the shogun's crest was to point your sword toward the shogun himself, an unforgivable act of treason.

honmaru The large, central keep of a Japanese castle.

honorifics Japan is a class and status society, and proper forms of address are critical. Common markers of respect are the prefixes *o* and *go*, and a wide range of suffixes. Some of the suffixes you will encounter in *Lone Wolf and Cub*:

   chan—for children, young women, and close friends

   dono—archaic; used for higher-ranked or highly respected figures

   sama—used for superiors

   san—the most common, used among equals or near equals

   sensei—used for teachers, masters, respected entertainers, and politicians

Iga-yashiki There were two main ninja clans in Japan, from the Iga and Kōga regions respectively. The Iga ninja served the shogunate. The *Iga-yashiki* (residence) was their base in Edo.

ihai A Buddhist mortuary tablet. The death name of the deceased, given after they have passed away, is written on the tablet, which is kept at the family temple or altar. *No-ihai* were placed on the grave; *uchi-ihai* on household altars.

jigoku-tabi Literally, "a journey to Hell." When yakuza would go ask allies to help them in a fight.

jōdai Castle warden. The ranking *han* official in charge of a *daimyō's* castle when the *daimyō* was spending his obligatory years in Edo.

juku Way station. The major byways through Japan during the Edo period had way stations a day's walk apart with inns, teahouses, and facilities for the traveler. The names of these old way stations still remain in many Japanese cities.

kaiken A dagger kept inside the *kimono* for self-defense. Common among the wives and daughters of samuari.

kaishaku A second. In the rite of *seppuku*, a samurai was allowed death with honor by cutting up his own abdomen. After the incision was complete, the second would perform *kaishaku*, severing the samurai's head for a quick death. The second was known as a *kaishakunin*.

kannenbutsu Literally, "cold prayers." There were many kinds of itinerant monks in Edo-period Japan, traveling the land as part of their religious discipline and relying on the handouts of the faithful. It was also a useful disguise for those with more than religion on their mind. *Kannenbutsu* were known for their penance in the chill of the coldest nights.

Kannon Buddhist goddess of mercy.

karō Elder, usually the senior advisor to the *daimyō*, the lord of a *han*. Since the *daimyō* was required to alternate each year between life in his castle in the *han* and his residence in Edo, the capital and seat of the Tokugawa shogunate, there was usually an *Edo-karō* (Edo elder) and a *kuni-karō* (*han* elder), who would administer affairs in Edo or in the *han* when their lord was away.

ken Old unit of measure. Approximately five feet.

kenshiyaku The shogunate official present at an execution to confirm the death of the person to be killed.

kimeban Boards on which prison rules were written

kōgi kaishakunin The shogun's official executioner and *kaishakunin* (see *kaishaku*).

koku (1) A bale of rice. The traditional measure of a *han*'s wealth, a measure of its agricultural land and productivity. (2) Standard time unit in the Edo period. Approximately two hours long, further subdivided into three equal parts.

kōmori A bat.

Kongming A famous general and tactician (181–234 AD) who lived during the Warring States period in ancient China.

kuramoto Merchant houses. Under the Confucian social order imposed by the Tokugawa shogunate, merchants ranked a lowly fourth in Japan's four-strata caste society. But, in fact, by the middle Edo period the merchant class had gained tremendous wealth and power by managing the assets of the *han* and selling *han* rice and other products. Many *han* fell deeply into debt to the big merchant houses.

kutsuwa See *bōhachi*.

makura-sagashi Literally, "pillow searcher." A wandering thief who preyed on other travelers, stealing their valuables from under their pillows while they slept.

meido The afterlife. The land after death, believed to be a place of darkness. Only a few Buddhist sects described a division between heaven and hell.

meifumadō The Buddhist hell, the way of demons and damnation.

metsuke Chief inspector, a post combining the functions of chief of police and chief intelligence officer.

monme Unit of currency. Worth 1/60th of a *ryo* gold piece.

mu Nothingness. A crucial concept in Zen Buddhism, and a goal of all the martial arts. Clearing the mind of all extraneous thoughts and connections, to exist wholly in the moment, freed of all attachment to life and the world around you.

naginata A two-handed weapon taller than a man, with a long, curved blade. The less common *nagamaki* was similar, with a shorter shaft and longer blade.

namu From the Sanskrit *namas*: "Take refuge in Buddha." A common prayer for the dead.

namu amida butsu One of the most common of all Buddhist chants, calling for mercy in the world to come.

o-bangashira The supreme commander of a *han's* standing guard (or *ban*) of samurai, charged to protect the lord and castle.

Ōgami Mountain "Mountain of the great gods." The Chinese characters are different from those in Ōgami Itto's own name ("to pray, to perceive, to see") but have a similar pronunciation. It is also a play on *okami*, or "wolf."

ogamu To pray.

o-niwaban A ninja. Literally, "one in the garden." The secret agent of the shogunate, heard but never seen.

ri Old unit of measurement. Approximately 4 kilometers (2.5 miles).

rōnin A masterless samurai. Literally, "one adrift on the waves." Members of the samurai caste who lost their masters through the dissolution of their *han*, expulsion for misbehavior, or other reasons. Prohibited from working as farmers or merchants under the strict Confucian caste system imposed by the Tokugawa shogunate, many impoverished *rōnin* became "hired guns" for whom the code of the samurai was nothing but empty words.

ryō A gold piece.

ryū Often translated as "school." The many variations of swordsmanship and other martial arts were passed down through generations to the offspring of the originator of the technique or set of techniques, and to any students that sought to learn from the master. The largest

schools had their own *dōjō* training centers, and scores of students. An effective swordsman had to study the different techniques of the different schools to know how to block them in combat. Many *ryū* also had a set of special, secret techniques that were only taught to school initiates.

sakki The palpable desire to kill, directed at another person. Sometimes called blood lust. Based on the concept of *ki*, or energy, found in spiritual practices and Japanese martial arts like aikido. These body energies can be felt beyond the physical self by the trained and self-aware.

Sakushū A town in what is today Okayama prefecture.

Sanzu-no-kawa The river Sanzu, the Japanese equivalent of the river Styx. On their way to the afterlife, the dead must take boats across the river Sanzu.

satoiri ninja Ninja in the *sato* (homeland). In addition to the ninja based in Edo, the shogunate placed ninja undercover in the various *han* of rival lords. These moles would monitor dissident *han* and gather evidence that could be used to blackmail or dissolve a *han* when it stepped out of line.

seisatsu yodatsu Under the four-caste social system imposed by the Tokugawa shogunate, the samurai class had the unquestioned right to kill those in lower castes, often for the smallest of insults and infractions.

seppuku The right to kill oneself with honor to atone for failure, or to follow one's master into death. Only the samurai class was allowed this glorious but excruciating death. The abdomen was cut horizontally, followed by an upward cut to spill out the intestines. When possible, a *kaishakunin* performed a beheading to shorten the agony after the cut was made.

shaba Yakuza divided the world between *shaba*, the normal world, and *shima* ("island"), the world of the yakuza.

shima Literally, "island." The world of the yakuza, the zone of death. See also *shaba*.

shinobi Ninja. The *yama-metsuke* work undercover, unlike the *dai-metsuke* in Edo.

sō-metsuke Another name for "*ō-metsuke*." The senior law-enforcement officer of the shogunate, reporting directly to the *rōjū* senior councilors who advised the shogun.

Sun Tzu The great Chinese military strategist (544–496 BC), author of the classic *Sun Tzu Bingfa* (*The Art of War*).

Takeda shidō A form of *Bushidō*, the way of the warrior. Takeda Shingen was one of the most feared warlords of the Sengoku period of warring states that ended with the ascendancy of the Tokugawa. If Takeda had not been felled by illness, he, not the Tokugawa, might have unified Japan.

Tōkaidō The most important of the Edo-era travel routes, connecting Edo with the Kamigata region of Kyoto and Ōsaka. It is now traversed by freeways and high-speed "bullet" trains.

Tokugawa The warlord clan that unified Japan following its victory at the Battle of Sekigahara in 1600 and ruled until 1867 from its castle in the city of Edo. This period is commonly known as the Edo period. The shogun was both the head of the Tokugawa clan and the head of the Tokugawa *bakufu*—the shogunate

government—that ran national policy and kept the often unruly *han* at heel.

tono Lord, *daimyō*. Sometimes used as a form of address, as in *tono-sama*.

toseinin Literally, "rootless one." One who travels the world. A euphemism for a wandering yakuza.

wajo A term of respect for a high priest or the head of a temple.

yakuza Japan's criminal syndicates. In the Edo period, yakuza were a common part of the landscape, running houses of gambling and prostitution. As long as they did not overstep their bounds, they were tolerated by the authorities, a tradition little changed in modern Japan.

zankanjō A confession. Vendettas were an accepted form of vigilante justice in the Edo period. While the killers knew the penalty for their act was death, they could exonerate their reputations after death with a *zankanjō* explaining their actions.

zegen Procurer. Prostitution was legal in the Edo period, and the procurer was an essential link in the chain. Impoverished rural families would sell their daughters to *zegen*, who sold them in turn to urban brothels.

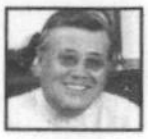

KAZUO KOIKE

Though widely respected as a powerful writer of graphic fiction, Kazuo Koike has spent a lifetime reaching beyond the bounds of the comics medium. Aside from cocreating and writing the successful *Lone Wolf and Cub* and *Crying Freeman* manga, Koike has hosted television programs; founded a golf magazine; produced movies; written popular fiction, poetry, and screenplays; and mentored some of Japan's top manga talent.

Lone Wolf and Cub was first serialized in Japan in 1970 (under the title *Kozure Okami*) in *Weekly Manga Action* magazine and continued its hugely popular run for many years, being collected as the stories were published, and reprinted worldwide. Koike collected numerous awards for his work on the series throughout the next decade. Starting in 1972, Koike adapted the popular manga into a series of six films, the *Baby Cart Assassin* saga, garnering widespread commercial success and critical acclaim for his screenwriting.

This wasn't Koike's only foray into film and video. In 1996, a movie version of *Crying Freeman*, the manga Koike created with artist Ryoichi Ikegami, was released to commercial success in Europe.

And to give something back to the medium that gave him so much, Koike started Gekiga Sonjuku, a college course aimed at helping talented writers and artists—such as *Ranma 1/2* creator Rumiko Takahashi—break into the comics field.

The driving focus of Koike's narrative is character development, and his commitment to character is clear: "Comics are carried by the characters. If a character is well created, the comic becomes a hit." Kazuo Koike's continued success in comics and literature has proven this philosophy true.

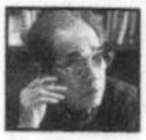

GOSEKI KOJIMA

Goseki Kojima was born on November 3, 1928, the very same day as the godfather of Japanese comics, Osamu Tezuka. While just out of junior high school, to pay his bills the self-taught Kojima began painting advertising posters for movie theaters.

In 1950, Kojima moved to Tokyo, where the postwar devastation had given rise to special manga forms for audiences too poor to buy the new manga magazines. Kojima created art for *kami-shibai* ("paper-play") narrators, who would use manga story sheets to present narrated street plays. Kojima moved on to creating works for the *kashi-hon* market, bookstores that rented out books, magazines, and manga to mostly low-income readers. He soon became highly popular among *kashi-hon* readers.

In 1967, Kojima broke into the magazine market with his series *Dojinki*. As the manga-magazine market grew and diversified, he turned out a steady stream of popular series.

In 1970, in collaboration with Kazuo Koike, Kojima began the work that would seal his reputation, *Kozure Okami* (*Lone Wolf and Cub*). Before long the story had become a gigantic hit, eventually spinning off a television series, six motion pictures, and even theme-song records. Koike and Kojima were soon dubbed the "golden duo" and produced success after success on their way to the pinnacle of the manga world.

When *Manga Japan* magazine was launched in 1994, Kojima was asked to serve as consultant, and he helped train the next generation of manga artists.

In his final years, Kojima turned to creating original graphic novels based on the movies of his favorite director, Akira Kurosawa. Kojima passed away on January 5, 2000, at the age of 71.